KU-574-786

Dana Facaros

# GREEK ISLANDS

'Some immortal hand or eye has framed
these islands to fit nearly everyone's idea of a
holiday paradise, with their picture-postcard
sandy beaches, cooling summer breezes,
thick pine forests and lush greenery.'

**CADOGAN**guides

# Contents

**Cadogan Guides**
Network House, 1 Ariel Way, London W12 7SL
cadoganguides@morrispub.co.uk
www.cadoganguides.com

**The Globe Pequot Press**
246 Goose Lane, PO Box 480, Guilford,
Connecticut 06437–0480

Copyright © Dana Facaros 1979, 1981, 1986, 1988,
   1993, 1995, 1998, 2002
Updated by Brian Walsh 2002

Cover and photo essay design by Kicca Tommasi
Book design by Andrew Barker
Cover photographs: Peter Phipp
Maps © Cadogan Guides,
   drawn by Map Creation Ltd
Editorial Director: Vicki Ingle
Editor: Philippa Reynolds
Art direction: Sarah Rianhard-Gardner/Jodi Louw
Proofreading: Alison Mills
Indexing: Isobel McLean
Production: Book Production Services

Printed in Italy by Legoprint
A catalogue record for this book is available
   from the British Library
ISBN 1-86011-855-0

The author and publishers have made every effort
to ensure the accuracy of the information in this
book at the time of going to press. However, they
cannot accept any responsibility for any loss, injury
or inconvenience resulting from the use of information contained in this guide.

Please help us to keep this guide up to date. We
have done our best to ensure that the information
in this guide is correct at the time of going to press.
But places and facilities are constantly changing,
and standards and prices in hotels and restaurants
fluctuate. We would be delighted to receive any
comments concerning existing entries or omis-
sions. Authors of the best letters will receive a copy
of the Cadogan Guide of their choice.

All rights reserved. No part of this publication may
be reproduced, stored in a retrieval system, or trans-
mitted, in any form or by any means, electronic or
mechanical, including photocopying and recording,
or by any information storage and retrieval system
except as may be expressly permitted by the UK
1988 Copyright Design & Patents Act and the USA
1976 Copyright Act or in writing from the publisher.
Requests for permission should be addressed to
Cadogan Guides, Network House, 1 Ariel Way,
London W12 7SL, in the UK, or The Globe Pequot
Press, 246 Goose Lane, PO Box 480, Guilford,
Connecticut 06437–0480, in the USA.

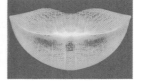

# Start with the spoken word...

**take off in...**

...*the easiest way
to learn a
language today*

Available from all good bookshops or to order
please call the 24-hour credit hotline on **+44 (0)1536 454534** or visit our website **www.oup.com**

# Greek Islands
# a photo essay

by Peter Phipp

01

*Temple of Aphaia,*
*Aegina*

*Melissáni Cave,*
*Kefaloniá*

*pyramid at*
*Exógi, Ithaca*

*kafeneíon culture, Crete*

*shops, Póros*

*Acropolis, with*
*amphitheatre*
*detail, Athens*

*colourful Fiskárdo*
*restaurant, Kefaloniá*

*bougainvillaea, Ithaca*

*Byzantine church*
*in Stavrós, Ithaca*

*evening dining*
*in Réthymnon, Crete*

*Santorini sunset*

*cruise liners*
*docking, Santorini*

*blue-topped*
*dome, Íos*

*Mýrtos Beach,*
*Kefaloniá*

*Paleokastrítsa*

*bays, Corfu*

*Exógi church,*
*Ithaca*

*lush coastline,*
*Ithaca*

*whitewashed villa*

*dolphin mural*

*church bells*

*dusk in Mýkonos*

*parliament*
*guards, Athens*

*Frikés Bay,*
*Ithaca*

*Basil's caique*

*Lindos, Rhodes*

### About the photographer
After life as a BBC cameraman, Peter Phipp now works from his own photographic studio in London. Specializing in travel, he shoots advertising for hotels, tour companies and editorial features. He has also established his own specialist photo library, 'Travel Pictures', on the internet.
all pictures © Peter Phipp

We exercise strict
Bench Marks
when considering
a property

## Greek Islands

Corfu, Paxos, Ithaca, Spetses, Skopelos, Alonissos, Crete

*CV Travel, specialists in exceptionally good villa & hotel holidays for 30 years.
We remain an independent company, whose philosophy is to provide holidays that are distinctly
unpackaged, for individuals who appreciate high levels of personal service, quality and product
knowledge.*

*Our other brochures:*

**Italian World** - Tuscany, Monte Argentario, Umbria, Lazio, Campania, Amalfi Coast, Sicily,
Sardinia, Ponza, Venice

**Mediterranean World** - Portugal, Morocco, Spain, The Balearics, France

 **CV TRAVEL** 43 Cadogan Street, Chelsea, London SW3 2PR
Tel (24 hrs) brochureline 0870 6039018  Fax: 020 7591 2802

Since 1972

# Introduction

*What weighs the bosom of Abraham and the immaterial spectres of Christian*
*paradise against this Greek eternity made of water, rock and cooling winds?*

Níkós Kazantzákis

There's nothing like the Greek islands to make the rest of the world seem blurred, hesitant and grey. Their frontiers are clearly defined by a sea that varies from emerald and turquoise to indigo blue, with none of the sloppiness of a changing tide; the clear sky and dry air cut their mountainous contours into sharp outline; the whiteness and simplicity of their architecture is both abstract and organic. Even the smells, be they fragrant (wild thyme, grilling fish) or stinks (donkey flops, caique diesel engines) are pure and unforgettable. In such an environment, the islanders themselves have developed strong quirky characters; they have bright eyes and are quick to laugh or cry or scream in fury, or shamelessly enquire into the intimate details of your personal life ('Just how much do you weigh?') or offer unsolicited lectures on politics, how to brush your teeth or find a good husband. 'Greece,' as the country's perennial president, Karamanlís once said, 'reminds me of an enormous madhouse.'

Since the 1970s this clarity and bright madness have been magnets to the grey world beyond. After shipping, tourism is Greece's most important source of income, to the extent that swallows from the north have become a regular fixture in the seasonal calendar: first comes Lent and Greek Easter, then the tourists, followed by the grape harvest, and, in December, the olives. From June to September, ferries and flights are packed with holidaymakers. Popular sites and beaches are crowded by day, and often by night, by people unable to find a room – they've been booked months in advance. Yet, as each island has its own strong character, each has responded to the tourism cash cow in a different way. On some islands, resort hotels have toadstooled up willy-nilly in search of the fast package-tour buck, sacrificing beauty, environmental health and sanity itself in their desire to please all-comers. And then there are other islands, more self-reliant, clinging stubbornly to their traditions and doing all they can to keep outside interests from exploiting their coasts. Others still, including some of the most visited islands, are enjoying a renaissance of traditional arts and customs, often led by the young who are pained to see their heritage eroding into Euro-blandness. A few islands have developed co-operatives to offer visitors a taste of rural life; others have gone swanky, with tennis courts and yacht marinas.

Gentle reader, may this book help you find the island you seek, whether you want all the mod-cons of home, sports facilities and dancing until dawn, or an island rich in ancient sites, Byzantine frescoes, landscapes and beautiful villages, or just an escape to a secluded shore, where there's the luxury of doing nothing at all. Or perhaps you want a bit of each. For, in spite of the rush to join the 21st century, the Greek islands have retained the enchantment that inspired Homer and Byron – the 'wine-dark sea', the scent of jasmine at twilight and nights alive with shooting stars. The ancient Greeks dedicated the islands to the gods, and they have yet to surrender them entirely to us mortals. They have kept something pure, true and alive. Or, as the poet Palamás wrote, 'Here reigns nakedness. Here shadow is a dream.'

## A Note on Pronunciation

There is no general agreement within Greece on a standard method of transliterating the Greek alphabet into Roman letters. This means that you will constantly come across many variations in the spellings of place names and words, on maps, in books and on road signs. To help you, this book includes island names and those of major towns in the Greek alphabet. When transcribing, we have used D for the Greek *delta* (Δ), which you may see elsewhere as DH or TH, CH for *chi* (Χ), which is pronounced like the 'ch' in 'loch' and which you may see written as H, e.g. in Chaniá or Chóra; F for *fi* (Φ), which you may see elsewhere as PH; and G for the Greek *gamma* (Γ), which sounds more like a guttural GH verging on a Y, e.g. with *agios* (saint), pronounced more like 'ayios'. Exceptions to this are made where there is a very common ancient name or modern English spelling such as Phaistos or Rhodes.

Stressing the right syllable is vital to the correct pronunciation of Greek; in this book the stressed letter of each word or name is accented with an acute (´) accent. **See** also **Language** pp.643–7.

# The Islands at a Glance

The 3,000 islands of Greece (of which a mere 170 or so are inhabited) are divided into seven major groupings: the Cyclades in the Aegean, surrounding the holy island of Délos; the Dodecanese, lying off the southwest coast of Asia Minor; the Northeastern Aegean islands, stretching from Thássos to Ikaría; the Ionian islands, sprinkled in the Ionian Sea, between Greece and Italy; the Saronic islands, in the Argo-Saronic Gulf; the Sporades, spread off the coast of Thessaly and Évia; and Crete, the largest island in Greece. Picking an island is as personal as choosing a flavour in an ice-cream parlour. You may want to start with a lively cosmopolitan place, followed by a few days of peace and quiet to recover. The following thumbnail sketches may give you an idea of what to expect, starting with the most popular.

**Mýkonos**, as jet-setty as you can get, still retains an air of class, despite the hordes that it attracts. It has great beaches, and the best nightlife (both gay and straight) is only a short boat ride from holy Délos, now an outdoor archaeology museum. Cosmopolitan **Skiáthos**, lusher, greener, has some of the best beaches in the Med. In **Íos** you'll feel old at 25; the emphasis here is on pubbing and beachlife. The lovely islands of **Kos** and **Zákynthos** have lost their original character under the strain of mass package tourism, but there's plenty going on to keep you amused, as in **Páros**, which paradoxically has retained its island charm, despite being one of the top destinations for backpackers and the jet set. Volcanic, dramatically beautiful **Santoríni** is the number one spot for visiting cruise ships and honeymooners. The two queens of Greek tourism, **Corfu** and **Rhodes**, are both large enough to absorb huge numbers of tourists, but suffer from pockets of unattractive mass package tourism. Both have stunning capitals and charming mountain villages. Small dry islands with beautiful Neoclassical towns are in fashion: **Hýdra**, Greece's St-Tropez, and now **Sými**. Other trendy, upmarket islands include **Pátmos**, with its famous medieval monastery;

olive-covered **Paxí**, with its sheltered bays and harbours, a haven for sailors; green **Spétses**, with its naval traditions and little **Koufoníssi**, a Cycladic gem behind Náxos.

**Crete**, 'the Big Island', has everything for everyone: the glories of Minoan civilization, the riviera around Ag. Nikólaos, the mighty mountain ranges, the Gorge of Samariá, the Venetian charms of Chaniá and Réthymnon, traditional villages, trendy Ag. Galíni, palm groves, superb beaches and a strong sense of island identity.

Arguably the best type of island holiday can be found on islands where there are enough tourists to ensure more than basic facilities – watersports, decent tavernas, a bar or two for an evening drink and a place to sit out and watch life idle by. **Sífnos**, **Kálymnos**, **Lefkáda**, **Mílos**, **Náxos**, **Límnos**, **Skópelos**, **Alónissos**, **Skýros**, **Ándros**, **Kefaloniá**, **Léros** and **Sýros** fall into this category; all have a mixture of rugged island scenery, typical villages, good restaurants and swimming. There are special cases like **Tínos** of the white dovecotes, mecca for pilgrims and popular with Greek families; **Kárpathos**, with dramatic scenery and strong folklore tradition; **Kéa**, close to Athens but very Greek; while, closer to Athens, **Aegina**, with its superb Temple of Aphaía, and green, friendly **Póros**, are easy targets for daytrippers and weekend crowds. In the Northeastern Aegean, the large, lush and lovely islands of **Sámos**, **Chíos**, and **Lésbos** (all with airports and growing package trade) and **Thássos** provide everything required for the perfect island holiday, as well as plenty of places to explore. Greek tourists have always preferred them to the barren Cyclades.

There remain islands that come under the heading of 'almost away from it all' – not quite desert islands but not a lot to do after two or three days unless you're resourceful – **Folégandros**, **Antíparos**, **Sérifos**, **Astypálaia**, **Amorgós**, **Samothráki**, **Ikaría**, **Kýthnos**, **Níssyros**, **Anáfi**, **Chálki**, **Kastellórizo**, **Kýthera**, **Tílos**, **Lipsí**, **Ithaca**, **Schinoússa** and **Heráklia** fall more or less into this category, each with its own individual charms. If, however, you genuinely want to get away from it all and don't mind eating in the same taverna every night, then head for **Antikýthera**, **Kássos**, **Donoússa**, **Psará**, **Inoússes**, **Kímolos**, **Foúrni**, **Síkinos**, **Ag. Efstrátios**, **Agathónissi**, **Arkí**, **Meganísi**, **Gávdos**, **Othoní**, **Eríkousa** or **Mathráki**. On these islands you can treat yourself to some serious introspection, read big fat novels and brush up on your modern Greek with the locals.

Last but not least, **Évia** and **Salamína** hardly feel like islands at all, but this can be part of their charm. The former has stunning scenery and an endless number of beaches, with a high percentage of Greek tourists to ensure you are experiencing the Real Thing. Salamína is little more than an Athenian suburb – unglamorous but very Greek, from its nondescript houses to its excellent cheap tavernas.

Timing is important. From mid-July to 20 August the footloose independent traveller can expect nothing but frustration trying to find an unbooked room on the more popular islands or on the smaller ones with a limited number of beds. Also, don't assume that the more isolated the island, the cheaper the rooms. You could well pay more in Folégandros than in Corfu Town, where accommodation is far more plentiful. Out of season you can pick and choose; islands with a high percentage of Greek tourists (Kýthnos and Évia) tend to be especially good value, although expect to see fewer signs in English. The majority of hotels and restaurants close in mid-October and reopen in April; Rhodes and Crete open the earliest and are the last to shut.

# Modern History, Art and Architecture

# Modern Greece: An Outline of Recent History

*Greece has been undergoing a political crisis for the past 3,000 years.*
                                      Politician during a recent election campaign

Aristotle declared man to be a political animal, and to this day no animal is as political as a Greek. If there are two *kafeneíons* in a village, one will be for the rightist
sympathizers, the other for the left. Over 50 parties crowd the typical ballot,
including five different flavours of Communists and exotica like the Self-respect
party and the popular Fatalist party. If you visit during an election, all transport to the
islands will be swamped with Athenians returning to their villages to vote. To begin
to understand current Greek attitudes, a bit of recent history is essential; ancient and
Byzantine history is dealt with under Athens and the individual islands.

## The Spirit of Independence

Since the 8th century BC, Greeks have lived beyond the boundaries of their mother-
land. Being Greek had nothing to do with geography, but everything to do with
language and religion. This has been both a source of strength and woe. To this day
Greeks consider the new Rome founded by Constantine, Constantinople, to be their
spiritual capital; Athens by the Middle Ages was a backwater. The Greeks retained
their identity during the Venetian occupation and the 400-year Turkish occupation –
the invaders let them be Greek as long as they paid their taxes. The revolutionary fires
that swept through Europe at the end of the 18th century found plenty of kindling
among Greeks. The War of Independence began in the Peloponnese in 1821, and
continued for over six years. In the end the Great Powers (Britain, Russia and France)
assisted the Greek cause, and, in the decisive Battle of Navarino (20 October 1827),
gave the new Greek state the Peloponnese and the mainland peninsula. They also
bestowed a king: Otho, son of Ludwig I of Bavaria, who immediately offended local
sensibilities by giving Bavarians all the official posts.

## The Birth of the Great Idea, and the Great Debacle

The fledgling Greek state was born with a mission: the *Megáli Idéa* (Great Idea) of
uniting all the Greeks into a kind of Byzantium Revisited, despite lacking the necessary military might. Otho's arrogant inadequacies led to revolts and dethronement in
1862, but the Great Powers found a replacement in William George, son of the King of
Denmark. In 1864, the National Assembly made Greece a constitutional monarchy, a
system that worked practically under Prime Minister Trikoúpis in 1875. In the long
reign of George I, Greece began to develop with shipping as its economic base.

In 1910, Elefthérios Venizélos became Prime Minister of Greece. He used the two
Balkan Wars of 1912–13 to further the Great Idea, annexing his native Crete, the North
Aegean islands, Macedonia and southern Epirus. During the First World War, the new
king Constantine I (married to Kaiser Wilhelm's sister) supported the Central Powers
while remaining officially neutral. Meanwhile, Venizélos set up a government with
volunteers, supporting the Allies in northern Greece. The Allies recognized Venizélos

and blockaded southern Greece supporting Constantine, and ordered the king to leave; Venizélos then sent troops to the Macedonian front to fight against Bulgaria.

After the war, Venizélos hoped to reap the rewards of his loyalty by claiming Smyrna (Izmir), which had a huge majority Greek population. Turkey was prostrate, and Britain, France and America agreed to a Greek occupation subject to a local plebiscite. Tragically, the Greek landings were accompanied by atrocities against the Turks, who began to rally around national hero Mustafa Kemal (later Atatürk). Venizélos, mean-while, was defeated in elections, partly from disgust with the foreign meddling in Greek affairs; Constantine and the Royalist party were elected on promises of a 'small but honourable Greece.' But Smyrna was too tempting a prize to give up. Encouraged by rhetoric from British Prime Minister Lloyd George, the Greek army marched on Ankara in March 1921, but in August 1922, Kemal's armies routed them at Smyrna. Constantine abdicated and Colonel Nikólas Plastíras took over. Turkish and Greek rela-tions had reached such an impasse that a massive population exchange was the only solution. Greece, then with a population of 4,800,000, had to find housing and work for 1,100,000 refugees, while 380,000 Muslims were sent to Turkey. There were enough refugees to change the politics of Greece, and most supported Venizélos. The monarchy was abolished in 1924, and after a brief interlude of military dictatorship under General Pangalos, Venizélos was elected Prime Minister in 1928. Trade unions and the Greek Communist party (KKE) gained strength. Venizélos made peace with Greece's neighbours and set the present borders of Greece, except for the Dodecanese Islands, which Italy still 'temporarily occupied'. His term also saw the start of another headache: the first uprising by Greek Cypriots, four-fifths of the population of what was then a British Crown Colony, who desired union with Greece.

## The Second World War and the Greek Civil War

What Venizélos couldn't heal was the increased polarization of Greek political life, especially as the Great Depression resulted in violent labour unrest. Martial law was declared, coups were attempted and in 1935, in a faked plebiscite, King George II returned to Greece, with General Ioánnis Metaxás as his Prime Minister. Metaxás assumed dictatorial control, exiled the opposition, instituted rigorous censorship and crushed the trade unions. Although he imitated the Fascists, Metaxás had sufficient foreboding to prepare the Greek army against occupation, and on 28 October 1940, responded with a laconic '*Óchi!*' (No!) to Mussolini's ultimatum that his troops on the Albanian border be allowed passage through Greece.

But by May 1941, after the Battle of Crete, all of Greece was in the hands of the Nazis. The miseries of the Occupation (more civilians died in Greece than in any other occupied country; *c.* 500,000 people starved to death the first winter) politicized the Greeks. The National Liberation Front (EAM), and its army (ELAS), led the resistance and had vast popular support, but its politics were unpalatable to Churchill, who was keen to restore the monarchy. Churchill made a secret deal with Stalin to keep Greece in the British sphere of influence in the famous 'percentages agreement'. Stalin, however, failed to tell the Greek Communists that he had abandoned them. The Greek Civil War – the first campaign of the Cold War – broke out three months after liberation. As Britain's containment policy was taken over by the Truman Doctrine, American money and advisors poured into Greece. The Civil War dragged on until 1949; leftists who were not shot or imprisoned went into exile.

## Recovery and Cyprus

The Greeks call the next two decades the 'Years of Stone.' Recovery was slow and the Greek diaspora that began in the early 1900s accelerated so fast that island villages became ghost towns. In 1951, Greece and Turkey became full members of NATO, an uncomfortable arrangement due to the unresolved issue of Cyprus. General Papágos of the American-backed Greek Rally party won the 1952 elections. He died in 1955, and Konstantínos Karamanlís replaced him as Prime Minister, inaugurating eight years of relative stability when agriculture and tourism grew rapidly. However, the opposition criticized his pro-Western policy and inability to resolve the worsening situation in Cyprus. Because one-fifth of Cypriots were Turkish, Turkey refused to let Cyprus join Greece. In 1960, a British-brokered compromise was reached: Cyprus became an independent republic with a complicated power-sharing constitution and elected Archbishop Makários President. Britain retained sovereignty over its military bases.

To add to the unhappiness, Greece was rocked with record unemployment. The royal family was unpopular; there were strikes and powerful anti-American feelings. In 1963 left-wing Deputy Lambrákis was assassinated, for which police officers were convicted. Karamanlís resigned and lost the next elections in 1965 to centre left warhorse George Papandréou, who gave a portfolio to his son Andréas, an economics professor, whose mildly inflationary policies horrifed the right. When King Paul died, he was succeeded by his young son, the conservative Constantine II. The combination did not bode well; a quarrel with the King over reforming the military led to Papandréou's resignation in 1966. Massive discontent forced Constantine to call for elections in May, but on 21 April 1967, a coup by an obscure group of colonels caught everyone by surprise. The Colonels, mostly of rural peasant stock and resentful of Athenian politicians, established a military dictatorship and imprisoned the Papandréous, charging Andréas with treason. Colonel George Papadópoulos made himself Prime Minister, while Constantine fled to Rome.

## A Vicious 'Moral Cleansing'

The proclaimed aim of the Colonels was a 'moral cleansing of Orthodox Christian Greece'. Human rights were suppressed, censorship imposed, and the secret police tortured dissidents. While condemned abroad, Greece's position in the volatile eastern Mediterranean and in NATO were reason enough for America, obsessed by the Cold War, to prop up the regime. The internal situation went from bad to worse, and on 17 November 1973 Athenian students went on strike. Tanks were brought in and many were killed. Popular feeling rose to such a pitch that Papadópoulos was arrested and replaced by the brutal head of the military police, Dimítrios Ioannídes. Relations with Turkey deteriorated when Ankara claimed the right to drill for oil in the eastern Aegean, and relations with Cyprus' President Makários collapsed due to Ioannídes' bullying. Ioannídes tried to launch a coup in Cyprus, to assassinate

Makários and replace him with a president who would declare the union of Cyprus with Greece. It was a fiasco. Makários fled, and the Turkish army invaded Cyprus. The Greek military rebelled, the dictatorship resigned and Karamanlís returned to form a new government, order a ceasefire in Cyprus and legalize the Communist party.

## A New Greek Alphabet: ND, EC, PASOK

Karamanlís and his conservative Néa Demokratía (ND) won the November 1974 elections. The monarchy did less well in the subsequent plebiscite, and Greece became a republic. That same year the country was anchored to the European Community (EC), of which Greece became a full member in 1981. Karamanlís brought stability but neglected badly needed economic and social reforms. These, along with a desire for national integrity, secured populist Andréas Papandréou's victory in 1981. His party, the Pan-Hellenic Socialist Movement (PASOK), promised much under the slogan 'Greece belongs to the Greeks', including withdrawal from NATO and the EC, and the removal of US air bases. Reconciliation with ethnically Greek resistance fighters from the war topped the agenda, and women were given more rights, as liberalization swept the land. PASOK won again in the 1985 elections, despite Papandréou's failure to deliver Greece from the snares of NATO, the US or the EC, or keep any of his economic promises. Inflation soared, and Greece was bailed out by a huge EC loan accompanied by an unpopular belt-tightening regime. In the end, scandal brought Papandréou down, including corruption at the Bank of Crete. In 1990, ND leader Konstantínos Mitsotákis took a slim majority in the elections. His austerity measures proved more unpopular than Papandréou's scandals – privatization of state-run companies and increased charges for public services, sparking off strikes in 1991 and 1992. By late 1992 Mitsotákis had also had his share of political scandals, and in October 1993 his party fell in the general election, returning Papandréou to office.

Third time proved lucky in 1994 when it came to closing down the US bases in Greece. Otherwise Papandréou kept Greece in his thrall as Yugoslavia disintegrated, pushing Balkan nationalist buttons over Macedonia and siding with the Serbs in Bosnia as Orthodox brethren oppressed by Muslim hordes. The once-reviled 'capitalist club', the EU, poured huge funds into Greece, resulting in new roads, schools, and agricultural subsidies. The once low prices that fuelled the Greek tourist boom of the 1970s and 80s inched up to match the rest of Europe, but after 1994, the strong drachma brought a decline. In late 1995 Papandréou, seriously ill, refused to resign, but was thwarted by a party revolt led by Kósta Simítis, a respected but 'bland' technocrat who completed Papandréou's term as Prime Minister. Simítis was severely tested when a dispute with Turkey erupted over a Dodecanese rock pile, nearly resulting in war; nationalists blamed Simítis for agreeing to an American-brokered mutual withdrawal, but the feeling after all the rhetoric was relief.

Non-dogmatic and untainted by scandal, Simítis has proved to be a hard worker for pragmatic common sense. With Papandréou's son George as Foreign Minister, he has made Greece a regional leader and prime investor in the Balkans, encouraged talks over Cyprus as it prepares to join the EU, and Greek-Turkish relations have improved, especially after helping each other following the 1999 earthquakes. Simítis' Greece is

trying to better itself: improving infrastructure, providing a climate for capital invest-
ments, building new ties with Eastern Europe and Russia, and joining the euro zone.
The biggest news, and the national deadline for every long-deferred project, is now
the 2004 Olympics, when Greece wants to shine in the international spotlight. Even
the smallest archaeology museums plan to re-open in 2004, and restoration of major
sights like the Parthenon is underway, so you may see a fair amount of scaffolding. For
Greeks this is a temporary glitch: 94 per cent support 'bringing the games home'.

# A Brief Outline of Greek Art and Architecture

Art begins on the Greek islands in the 7th millennium BC with their oldest settlements – Knossós and Phaistós on **Crete**, Phylokopí on **Mílos**, Paleóchni on **Límnos** and
Ag. Iríni on **Kéa**. Their art is typical of the age: dark burnished pottery, decorated with
spirals and wavy lines and statuettes of the fertility goddess in stone or terracotta.

## Bronze Age: Cycladic and Minoan Styles (3000–1100 BC)

Early contacts with Anatolia and the Near East put Crete and the Cyclades on the
cutting edge of European civilization. By 2600 BC Cycladic dead were being buried
with flat, abstract marble statues (*see* collections in Náxos and Athens). At this time
the Cretan people, dubbed the Minoans by Sir Arthur Evans, were demonstrating a
talent in polychrome pottery and gold jewellery. Over the next period (Middle
Minoan, 2000–1700 BC), when Crete's fleet ruled the seas, the Minoans felt sufficiently secure to build themselves unfortified palaces, centred around a rectangular
courtyard. They installed a complex system of canals, and kept accounts of the oil,
wine and grain stored in huge *pithoi*. Crete's civilization reached its apogee between
1700 and 1450 BC when Minoan colonies stretched across the Aegean. Minoan palaces
at **Knossós**, **Phaistós**, **Zákros**, **Mália** and at their outpost of **Akrotíri** on Santoríni and
**Phylokopí** on Mílos were adorned with elegant frescoes now in the archaeology
museums of **Heráklion** and **Athens**. Built of wood and unbaked brick, the palaces
collapsed in the earthquakes that marked the end of Minoan civilization. The
Mycenaeans, in the Peloponnese, filled the power vacuum, taking over the Minoan
colonies and artistic traditions. Little of this reached the islands, although many have
vestiges of Mycenaean stone walls, known as **cyclopean** after their gigantic blocks.
They failed to prevent the collapse of their civilization after the Trojan War.

## Geometric (1000–700 BC) and Archaic (700–500 BC)

The splintering of the Mycenaean world ushered in a Dark Age. The discovery in 1981
of the huge Proto-geometric sanctuary at **Lefkándi** on Évia, from *c*. 950 BC, has made it
less dark. It shows a complete break from Mycenaean styles. In Athens, *c*. 900 BC, a
new style of pottery appears known as Geometric for the simple, abstract designs.
The most complete Geometric town discovered so far is Zagorá on **Ándros**. The 8th
century was marked by the evolution of the *pólis*, or city-state, the egg from which the
Greek miracle would hatch. The first stone Temple of Hera on **Sámos** was up by 718 BC

and surrounded with a peristyle. **Corfu**'s Doric Temple of Artemis (580 BC) was a more advanced prototype with its columns and pediments decorated with a formidable 12ft relief of Medusa. The beautiful Doric Temple of Aphaia on **Aegina** was begun in the same period and decorated with a magnificent pediment sculpted with scenes from the Trojan War. The excavations at Embório, on **Chíos**, are among the best records of an Archaic town; the 6th-century Efplinion tunnel at Pythagório on **Sámos** was the engineering feat of the age. The Archaic era also saw the beginning of life-size figure sculpture, inspired by the Egyptians. The male version is a *kouros* (*see* the giants of **Sámos** and **Náxos**); the female is a *kore*. As they evolved their formal poses relaxed and reveal an interest in anatomy. The 7th century witnessed the development of regional schools of pottery, influenced by the black-figured techniques of Corinth: **Rhodes** and the Cyclades produced some of the best.

## Classical (500–380 BC)

Dominating the Aegean, Athens sucked up the artistic talent in Greece, culminating with the mathematical perfection of the Parthenon, the greatest of all Doric temples, built without a single straight line. Nothing on the islands comes close, but there are a few Classical sites to visit: Liménas on **Thássos** and Erétria on **Évia**, Líndos, Kámiros and Ialysós on **Rhodes**. In ceramics there was a change to more naturalistic red-figured black vases around 500 BC (*see* the National Archaeology Museum, **Athens**).

## Hellenistic (380–30 BC)

This era brought stylistic influences from the eastern lands conquered by Alexander the Great and his Successors. Compared to aloof Classical perfection, Hellenistic sculpture adopts a more emotional, Baroque approach, all windswept drapery, violence and passion, such as the Louvre's *Victory of Samothrace* from **Samothráki**'s Sanctuary of the Great Gods. Powerful Rhodes produced its long-gone Colossus and the writhing *Laocoön* (in the Vatican museum) and Aphrodites (including Durrell's *Marine Venus*) in the **Rhodes** museum. Houses became plush, many decorated with mosaics and frescoes as in the commercial town of **Délos** and in the suburbs of **Kos**.

## Roman (30 BC–AD 529)

The Pax Romana ended the rivalries between the Greek city-states and dried up their sources of inspiration, although sculptors and architects found a ready market in Rome, cranking out copies of Classic and Hellenistic masterpieces. The Romans built little in Greece: the stoa and theatre of Herodes Atticus (AD 160) were the last large monuments erected in ancient Athens. On the islands, the most important site is Górtyna, on **Crete**, the Roman capital of the island and Libya.

## Byzantine (527–1460)

The Byzantines revealed their stylistic distinction under the reign of Justinian (527–565),while the post-Justinian period saw a golden age in the splendour of Ag. Sofia in Istanbul and the churches of Ravenna, Italy. On the islands you'll find only the remains of simple three-naved basilicas – with two exceptions: the 6th-century

Ekatontapylianí of **Páros** and 7th-century Ag. Títos at Górtyna, **Crete**. After the austere, puritanical Iconoclasm (726–843) the Macedonian painting style infiltrated the Greek provinces. The Roman basilica plan was replaced with a central Greek cross crowned by a dome, elongated in front by a vestibule (narthex) and outer porch (exonarthex) and at the back by a choir and three apses. Two of these churches, **Dafní** near Athens and Néa Moní on **Chíos**, are decorated with superb mosaics from the second golden age of Byzantine art, under the dynasty of the Comnenes (12th–14th centuries). This period marked a renewed interest in antique models: the stiff figures are given more naturalistic proportions in graceful compositions. It also produced fine paintings: the 12th-century frescoes and manuscripts at the Monastery of St John on **Pátmos**, culminating in the early 13th-century church of Kerá Panagía at Kritsá, near Ag. Nikólaos, **Crete**. Crete's occupation by Venice after 1204 heralded an artistic cross-fertilization that developed into the Cretan school that in the 16th century produced El Greco.

What never changed was the symbolic intent of Byzantine art. Choreographed to a strict iconography, a Byzantine Christ and the Virgin *Panagía* reside on a purely spiritual and intellectual plane, miles away from Western art invented in the Renaissance 'based on horror, physical charm, infant-worship and easy weeping' as Patrick Leigh Fermor put it. Byzantine art never asks the viewer to relive the passion of Christ or coo over Baby Jesus; the *Panagía* has none of the fashionable beauty of the Madonna. They never stray from their remote otherworldliness. And yet, in the last gasp of Byzantine art under the Paleologos emperors (14th–early 15th centuries), humanist and naturalistic influences produced the Byzantine equivalent of the late Gothic/early Renaissance painting in Italy, in Mistrás in the Peloponnese. After the Turkish conquest, painters fled to Mount Áthos, **Zákynthos** and **Corfu**, but none of their work radiates the same charm or confidence in the temporal world.

## Turkish Occupation to the Present

The Turks left few important monuments in Greece. **Rhodes** town, followed by **Kos**, has the best surviving mosques and hammams. **Crete** and **Corfu** remained Venetian longer than most places, recalled by impressive fortifications and public buildings. Islands that had their own fleets, especially **Hýdra**, **Spétses**, and **Sými**, have impressive mansions built by ship owners, while other islands continued traditional architectural styles, such as the whitewashed asymmetry of the Cyclades. Folk art thrived in this period and the collections in the island museums (especially Skýros) are worth a look.

In the 19th century, Athens and Ermoúpoli, **Sýros** (briefly Greece's chief port) were built in Neoclassical style; elegant buildings are finally being restored to their former grandeur. Many grandiose Neo-Byzantine churches have appeared, while older ones were tarted up. The 1930s palazzi built by Mussolini in the Dodecanese are stylish, which is more than can be said of the modern beach hotels. The islands did produce one painter of note: the delightful artist Theóphilos Hadzimichális (1873–1934) of Mytilíni, which has a museum of his works, that he exchanged for food and lodging. Recent prosperity has enhanced interest in local architecture and historic preservation: programmes are saving some of Greece's most beautiful villages. New laws on many islands insist that further building conforms to traditional architectural styles.

# Topics

# The Bull in the Calendar

*...there too is Knossós, a mighty city, where Minos was king for nine years.*
Homer, *The Odyssey,* book XIX

The so-called 'Toreador Fresco', found in the palace at Knossós, is a compelling icon of the lost world of ancient Crete. The sensual bare-breasted maidens who seem to be controlling the action are painted in white, the moon's colour, as in all Cretan frescoes, while the athlete vaulting through the bull's horns appears like all males in red, the colour of the sun. Mythology and archaeology begin to agree, and the roots of the story of Theseus, Ariadne and the Minotaur seem tantalizingly close at hand. When you see this fresco in Heráklion's Archaeology Museum, study the decorative border – four striped bands and a row of multicoloured lunettes. Neither Arthur Evans nor any archaeologist since noticed anything unusual about it. It was Charles F. Herberger, a professor in Maine (*The Thread of Ariadne*, Philosophical Library, New York, 1972), who discovered that this border is a complex ritual calendar, including the key to the myth of Theseus in the Labyrinth. The pairs of stripes on the tracks, alternately dark and light, for day and night, count on average 29 through each cycle of the five-coloured lunettes, representing the phases of the moon – this is the number of days in a lunar month. By counting all the stripes on the four tracks, Herberger found that each track gives roughly the number of days in a year; the whole, when doubled, totals exactly the number of days in an eight-year cycle of 99 lunar months, a period in which the solar and lunar years coincide – the marriage of the sun and moon.

To decipher the calendar, you can't simply count in circuits around the border; there are regular diagonal jumps to each new row, giving the course of the eight-year cycle the form of a rectangle with an 'x' in it. The box with the 'x' is intriguing, a motif in the art of the Cretans and other ancient peoples as far afield as the Urartians of eastern Anatolia. A Cretan seal shows a bull apparently diving into a crossed rectangle of this sort, while a human figure vaults through his horns. Similar in form is the most common and enigmatic of all Cretan symbols, the double axe or *labrys*. The form is echoed in a number of Cretan signet-rings that show the x-shaped cross between the horns of a bull, or between what appear to be a pair of crescent moons.

The home of the *labrys*, the axe that cuts two ways, is the labyrinth. Arthur Evans believed the enormous palace of Knossós itself to be the labyrinth, a pile so confusing that even a Greek hero would have needed Ariadne's golden thread to find his way through it. In the childhood of archaeology, men could read myths so literally as to think there was a tangible labyrinth, and perhaps even a Minotaur. Now, it seems more likely that the labyrinth was the calendar itself, the twisting path that a Minos (generic name for Cretan priest-kings, representing the sun) followed in his eight-year reign before his rendezvous with the great goddess. This meeting may originally have meant his death and replacement by another Theseus. Later it would have been simply a ceremony of remarriage to the priestess that stood in the transcendent goddess' place, celebrated by the bull-vaulting ritual. It has been claimed that the occasion was also accompanied by popular dancing, following the shape of the labyrinth, where the dancers proceeded in a line holding a cord – Ariadne's thread. Homer said 'nine years', and other sources give nine years as the period after which the Athenians had to send their captives to Crete to be devoured by the Minotaur – it's a common ancient confusion, really meaning 'until the ninth', in the way the French still call the interval of a week *huit jours*. Whatever this climax of the Cretan cycle was, it occurred with astronomical precision according to the calendar, and followed a rich, layered symbolism difficult for us scoffing moderns to comprehend.

That the Cretans had such a complex calendar should be no surprise – for these people managed modern plumbing and three-storey apartment blocks, while still finding time to rule the seas of the eastern Mediterranean. The real attraction lies not in the intricacies of the calendar (many other peoples had equally interesting calendars) but more particularly in the scene in the middle, where the diagonals cross and where the ancient science translates into celebration, into dance. No other art of antiquity displays such an irresistible grace and joy, qualities which must have come from a profound appreciation of the beauties and rhythms of nature – the rhythms captured and framed in the ancient calendar.

# Endangered Animals and Plain Old Pests

When Western Europe was busy discovering the beauties of nature in the Romantic era, Greece was fighting for survival; when the rest of the west was gaining its current environmental awareness in the 1960s, the Greeks were throwing up beach resorts, making Athens the citadel of sprawl it is today, merrily chucking plastic bags of garbage in the sea and killing off the monk seals because they ate too many fish. Ever so slowly, the average Greek is waking up to the fact that nature can only take so much before she turns on her persecutors. A small but dedicated band of ecologists has been sounding the alarm for decades, but most Greeks only saw their country as something to exploit: if the law forbids building on forested land, the Greek solution was – and sadly, still is – to burn the forest. Past excesses are now beginning to hurt.

Tourism has been responsible for much of the damage, but also for many of the sea-changes in attitude. The great influx of people is in part responsible for the severe depletion of fishing stocks. Laws limiting industrial fishing and dynamiting are constantly flouted – demand for fish has drained the Aegean's key resource by nearly 60 per cent in recent years, making what used to be the cheapest staple food in Greece the most expensive. There is talk of a fishing moratorium for a year or two to give the Mediterranean a break, but the economic consequences are simply too over-whelming for the idea to go past the talk stage. On the positive side, tourist concerns about clean beaches (and Greece now proudly claims the cleanest in Europe) have resulted in proper sewage systems on most islands. The Greeks may return their beer bottles but they recycle absolutely nothing, not glass, not paper, not plastic.

In the 1980s, efforts to save the Mediterranean green loggerhead turtle centred around its nesting grounds on the beaches of Zákynthos. Battling hoteliers and envi-ronmentalists eventually reached a compromise, and now the turtles are one of the island's selling points. Another bright spot is the designation of the crystalline seas around Alónissos as the country's first National Marine Park, encompassing untouched islets and a diversity of marine life, including the most endangered species in Europe, the monk seal. Biologists consider the seal to be our closest marine relative, and use the animal as a yardstick to measure the sea's health and habit-ability. It doesn't bode well; only 300 monk seals remain in Greek waters, and a mere 500 in the entire world. A research station and rehabilitation centre on Alónissos run by the Hellenic Society for the Study and Protection of Monk Seals (HSSPMS) has rehabilitated a handful of orphaned seals, slowly increasing the park's population of 30. Another endangered species in the park is Eleanora's falcon, a small migratory falcon which nests almost exclusively in the Sporades in spring and summer.

Many other birds use the islands as stepping stones on their migratory paths – swallows, storks, pelicans, herons, egrets and a wide variety of indigenous birds. Eagles and vultures float over the mountains, including the massive Griffon vulture and rare lammergeier. Greece's extraordinary variety of wildflowers (6,000 native species) draws a colourful array of butterflies. All suffer in the annual forest conflagrations, which are nearly all set by local arsonists (in spite of loud accusations directed at the CIA, Turks and other bogeys); in the summer of 1997, when the Minister of Agricultural Stefanos Tsoumakas suggested giving in and legalizing buildings erected on burned land since 1975, there was an encouraging outcry from voters.

As for creatures unfortunately *not* on the endangered list, the wily mosquito tops the list for pure incivility. For your best defence, pick up an inexpensive electric mosquito repellent. Greek mosquitoes don't spread malaria, but bites from their sand-fly cousins can occasionally cause a nasty parasite infection. Wasps will appear out of nowhere to nibble your honey-oozing baklava (especially on the lush Ionian islands). Pests also lurk in the sea: harmless pale brown jellyfish (*méduses*) drift every-where depending on winds and currents, but the oval transparent model (*tsoúchtres*) are stinging devils; pharmacies sell soothing ungents. Pincushiony sea urchins live by rocky beaches, and if you're too cool to wear rubber swimming shoes and step on one, it hurts like hell. The spines may break and embed themselves deeper if you try to force them out; the Greeks recommend olive oil, a big pin and a lot of patience. Less common but more dangerous, the *drákena*, dragon (or weever) fish, with a poisonous spine, hides in the sand. If you step on one, you'll feel a mix of pain and numbness and should go the doctor for an injection. Greece's shy scorpions hide in between the rocks in rural areas, but their sting is no more painful than a bee's. Avoid the back legs of mules, unless you've been properly introduced. The really lethal creatures are rare: several species of small viper live in the nooks and crannies of stone walls, but only come out occasionally to sun themselves. Vipers will flee if possible. Since the time of Homer, mountain sheepdogs have been a more immediate danger in outer rural areas; by stooping as if to pick up a stone to throw, you might keep a dog at bay.

# On *Kéfi*, Music and Dancing

In the homogenized European Union, the Spaniards and Greeks are among the very few peoples who still dance spontaneously. It's no coincidence that both have untranslatable words to describe the 'spirit' that separates going through the motions and true dancing. In Spain, the word is *duende*, which has an ecstatic quality; in Greek, the word is *kéfi*, which comes closer to 'soul'. For a Greek to give his all, he must have *kéfi*; to dance without it could be considered dishonest. The young men in black trousers and red sashes who dance for you at a 'Greek Night' taverna excursion don't have it; two craggy old fishermen in a smoky *kafenion* in Crete, who crank up an old gramophone and dance for their own pleasure, do. It has no age limit: teenagers at discos pounding out hits are really only waiting for 1am, when the clubs switch over to Greek music and the real dancing can start. And you can feel the *kéfi* at Easter when an entire village joins hands to dance an elegant *kalamatianó*.

Greek music has been influenced by Italy (most notably on the Ionian islands), Turkey, the Middle East and the Balkans, all of whom were once influenced by the Byzantines, who heard it from ancient Greeks, who heard it from the Phrygians – and so on. Traditional island songs, *nisiótika*, are played on bagpipes (*tsamboúna*), clarinet (*klaríno*), various stringed instruments – the *laoúto* (a large mandolin, used for backing, traditionally picked with an eagle's quill), the *lýra*, a three-string fiddle, held upright on the knee, played on Crete and the southern Dodecanese, the *violí* (violin), the *kítara* (guitar) and the double-stringed hammer dulcimer (*sandoúri*), once limited to Greek Anatolia and now heard most often on the eastern islands. The best time to hear *nisiótika* is during a summer saint's day feast (*panegýri*) or at a wedding.

Contemporary composers like Mikis Theodorákis often put modern poetry to music, providing splendid renderings of the lyrics of George Seferis, Odysseas Elytis and Yánnis Rítsos; sung by the deep-voiced Maria Farandouri, they are spine-tingling, even if you don't understand a word. Even current Greek pop has surprisingly poetic moments. It owes much of its origins to *rembétika*, the Greek equivalent of the blues, brought over and developed by the more 'sophisticated' Asia Minor Greeks in the 1920s' population exchange, who in their longing and homesickness haunted the hashish dens of Athens and Piraeus. *Rembétika* introduced the *bouzoúki*, the long-necked metallic string instrument that dominates Greek music today, to the extent that nightclubs are called *bouzoúkia* – rougher ones are known as *skilákia* – 'dog' shops, where popular singers croon throbbing, lovelorn, often wildly melodramatic music with a Middle Eastern syncopation that offers Greeks some of the catharsis that ancient tragedies gave their ancestors. Although expensive, a night out at one of these nightclubs is an experience not to be missed. Members of the audience may take over the microphone, or the singer may be covered with flowers, or even make the enthusiasts forget the law against *spásimo*, or plate-breaking. If enough *kéfi* is flowing, you may see middle-aged bank managers dance with wine glasses or bottles on their heads. When the matrons begin to belly-dance on the table, it's time to leave.

Summer festivals and village weddings are the places to see traditional dancing. Every island has its own dances, some preserved, some quickly being forgotten. Cretan dances are among the most ancient and vigorous, fuelled by massive intakes of *rakí*; the *pedektó* demands furious steps, which resound under tall Cretan boots. Novice Greek dancers would do better starting with a *syrtó*, with a slow shuffling pace throughout, or perhaps the *kalamatianó*, a 12-step *syrtó*, the national dance for many people; everyone joins in, holding hands at shoulder-level, while men and women take turns improvising steps. Nearly as common is the dignified *tsamikó*, where the leader and the next dancer in line hold the ends of a handkerchief. Women are the centre of attention in the *tsíphte téli*, a free-spirited, sensuous belly dance from Asia Minor for the loose-limbed and swivel-hipped, but just as often men steal the show.

Other dances are normally performed by men. The *zeybékiko* is a serious, deliberate, highly charged solo dance with outstretched arms, evoking the swooping flight of the eagle; a companion will go down on one knee to encourage the dancer, hiss like a snake and clap out the rhythm. An introspective dance from the soul, the performer will always keep his eyes lowered; because it's private, you must never applaud. Another intense dance, the *hasápiko*, or butchers' dance, is better known as the Zorba dance in the West. The *syrtáki* is more exuberant, traditionally performed by two or three men, often to the *rembétika* tune; the leader signals the steps and it requires some practice but is well worth learning – as Alan Bates discovered, when he finally began to fathom *kéfi* from Anthony Quinn at the end of the film *Zorba the Greek*.

# An Orthodox Life

Except for a few thousand Catholics in the Cyclades and Protestants in Athens, all Greeks belong to the Orthodox (Eastern) church; indeed, being Orthodox and speaking Greek are the criteria in defining a Greek, whether born in Athens, Alexandria or Australia. Orthodoxy is so fundamental that only the greatest sceptics can conceive of marrying outside the church, or neglecting to baptize their children, even though Papandréou's government legalized civil marriages in the 1980s.

One reason for this deep national feeling is that, unlike everything else in Greece, Orthodoxy has scarcely changed since the founding of the church by Emperor Constantine in the 4th century. As Constantinople took the place of Rome as the political and religious capital, the Greeks believe their church to be the only true successor to the original church of Rome. Therefore, a true Greek is called a *Romiós* or Roman, and the Greek language is sometimes called *Roméika*. The Orthodox church is considered perfect and eternal; if it weren't, its adherents could not expect to be saved. The Greeks have been spared the changes that have rocked the West, from Vatican II and discussions over female clergy and married priests to political questions of abortion and birth control. Much emphasis is put on ceremony and ritual, spiritual and aesthetic, and services can be powerfully moving, especially at Easter.

This determination to never change explains the violence of Iconoclasm, the one time someone tried to tinker with the rules. Back in the early 8th century, Byzantine Emperor Leo III, shamed by what his Muslim neighbours labelled idolatry, deemed the images of divine beings to be sacrilegious. The Iconoclasm opened up a first major rift with Rome, and it worsened in 800 when the patriarch of Rome (the Pope) crowned Charlemagne as emperor, usurping the position of the Emperor of Constantinople. Further divisions arose over the celibacy of the clergy (Orthodox priests may marry before they are ordained) and the use of the phrase *filioque* ('and the son'), in the Holy Creed. This phrase caused the final, fatal schism in 1054 when the Papal legate Cardinal Humbert excommunicated the Patriarch of Constantinople and the Patriarch excommunicated the Pope. Ever since then the Orthodox hierarchy has kept a patriarchal throne vacant, ready for the day when the Pope returns to his senses.

After the fall of the Byzantine Empire, the Turks tolerated the Orthodox church, and had the political astuteness to impart considerable powers to the Patriarch. The church preserved Greek tradition, education and identity through the dark age of Ottoman rule, but it also left Greece a deeply conservative country and often abused its power, especially on a local scale. According to an old saying, priests, headmen and Turks were the three curses of Greece and the poor amiable priests have not yet exonerated themselves from the list they now share with the king and the cuckold.

The fantastic quantity of churches on most islands has little to do with the priests, however. Nearly all were built by families or individuals, especially by sailors, seeking the protection of a patron saint or to keep a vow or to thank a saint for service rendered. All but the tiniest have an *iconóstasis*, or altar screen, made of wood or stone to separate the *heirón* or sanctuary, where only the ordained are allowed, from the rest of the church. Most of the chapels are locked up thanks to light-fingered tourists; if you track down the caretaker, leave a few hundred drachmae for upkeep.

Many chapels have only one service a year, on the patron saint's day. Name days are celebrated in Greece rather than birthdays ('Many years!' (*Chrónia pollá!*) is the proper way to greet someone). This annual celebration is called a *yiortí* or *panegýri*, and if it happens in the summer it's cause for feasts and dancing the night before or after the church service. Apart from Easter, the Assumption of the Virgin (15 August) is the largest *panegýri* in Greece. The faithful sail to Tínos, the Lourdes of Greece, and to centres connected with Mary, making mid-August a very uncomfortable time to island-hop, especially in the Cyclades – ships packed to the brim with Greek matrons, the most ardent pilgrims of all, who are also the worst sailors.

Orthodox weddings are a lovely if long-winded ritual. The bride and groom stand solemnly before the chanting priest, while family and friends seem to do everything but follow the proceedings. White crowns, bound together by a white ribbon, are placed on the heads of bride and groom, and the *koumbáros*, or best man, exchanges them back and forth. The newlyweds are led around the altar three times, while the guests bombard them with fertility-bringing rice and flower petals. After congratulating the couple, guests are given a *boboniéra* of candied almonds. This is followed by the marriage feast and dancing, which in the past could last up to five days.

Baptisms are cause for similar celebration. The priest completely immerses the baby in the Holy Water three times (unlike Achilles, there are no vulnerable spots on modern Greeks) and usually gives the little one the name of a grandparent. For extra protection from the forces of evil, babies wear a *filaktó*, or amulet, the omnipresent blue glass eye bead. If you visit a baby at home you may be sprinkled first with Holy Water, and chances are there's a bit of beneficial garlic squeezed under the cradle. Compliments should be kept to a minimum: the gods do get jealous; many babies are given pet names until they're christened, to fool supernatural ill-wishers.

Funerals in Greece, for reasons of climate, are carried out within 24 hours, and are announced by the tolling of church bells. The dead are buried for three to seven years after which time the bones are exhumed and placed in the family box to make room for the next resident. *Aforismós*, or Orthodox excommunication, is believed to prevent the body decaying after death – the main source of Greek vampire stories. Memorials take place three, nine and forty days after death, and on the first anniversary, when sweet buns, sugared wheat and raisin *koúliva* are given out. But for all the trappings of Christianity, the spirit of Charos, the ferryman of death and personification of inexorable nature, is never far away, as beautifully expressed in a famous dirge:

> *Why are the mountains dark and why so woe-begone?*
> *Is the wind at war there, or does the rain storm scourge them?*
> *It is not the wind at war there, it is not the rain that scourges,*
> *It is only Charos passing across them with the dead;*
> *He drives the youths before him, the old folk drag behind,*
> *And he bears the tender little ones in a line at his saddle-bow.*
> *The old men beg a grace, the young kneel to impore him,*
> *'Good Charos, halt in the village, or halt by some cool fountain,*
> *That the old men may drink water, the young men play at the stone-throwing,*
> *And that the little children may go and gather flowers.'*
> *'In never a village will I halt, nor yet by a cool fountain,*
> *The mothers would come for water, and recognize their children,*
> *The married folk would know each other, and I should never part them.'*

# The *Períptero* and the Plane Tree

In Greece you'll see it everywhere, the greatest of modern Greek inventions, the indispensable *períptero*. It is the best-equipped kiosk in the world, a substitute bar, selling everything from water to cold beer; an emergency pharmacy stocked with aspirin, mosquito killers and condoms; a convenient newsagent for publications, from *Ta Néa* to *Die Zeit*; a tourist shop offering maps, postcards and stamps; a toy shop and general store for shoelaces, cigarettes, batteries and film. In Athens they're at most traffic lights. On the islands they are a more common sight than a donkey. You'll wonder how you ever survived before *perípteros* and the treasures they contain.

The other great meeting centre of Greek life is the mighty plane tree, or *plátanos*, where politics and philosophy have been argued since time immemorial. The Greeks believe that plane shade is wholesome and beneficial: one of the most extraordinary sights in the islands is 'Hippocrates' plane tree' on Kos, propped up on scaffolding and protected as a national monument. In Greek the expression *'cheréte mou ton plátano'* loosely translates as 'go tell it to the marines', presumably because the tree has heard all that nonsense before. The *plátanos* represents the village's identity; the tree is a source of life, and only grows near abundant fresh water, its deep roots a symbol of stability and continuity – a huge majestic umbrella, as even the rain cannot penetrate its sturdy leaves. Sit under its spreading branches and sip coffee as the morning unfolds before you; the temptation to linger for the day is irresistible.

## Lamp Chops and Sweat Coffee

For a country cursed with a mindlessly pedantic system of public education, where rote memorization is the only key to academic success, the Greeks speak astonishingly good English. The Greek dislike of, and incompetence at, dubbing the likes of *Miami Vice* and *Santa Monica* may have something to do with it, as well as the efforts of thousands of *frontistérion* (private school) teachers.

This is enough to make the devoted observer of Greek ways suspect that the English mistakes on taverna menus are no accident, but rather part of a crafty plot to keep tourists out of the locals' secret haunts by making menus such compelling reading that by the time you've spotted the Lamp Chops, and Sandwitches you're laughing too hard to go anywhere else. Will you have the Rabeet Soupee, Stuffed Vine Lives, String Deans, or Beet Poots to start? For main course, the Harmbougger sounds distinctly threatening; perhaps it's best to stick with dishes you know the Greeks do well: Staffed Tomatoes, Souvlaki Privates, Grumps Salad, T-Buogne Rum Stake and Veal Gogglets, or vegetable dishes such as Zucchini Bulls, Cheek Pees, or perhaps Grass Hill (it turned out to be a small mound of boiled greens). On Skópelos, you can smack your lips over a Rude Sausage; on Páros, you can ponder where your parents went wrong over a Freud Juice; in Mytilíni, either sex can enjoy a delicious Fish in Lesbian Sauce; cannibals can find solace at a place on Kos where 'We Serve Hot Tasty Friendly Family!' Then it's off to the Snake Bar for a Sweat Coffee, Kaputsino, before driving off in your Fully Incurable Rent-a-Care from the Vague Travel Agency of Piraeus.

## A Traditional Greek Island Calendar

If the Greek islands were the cutting edge of European culture from 2000–500 BC, the past thousand years have shoved them into such obscurity that in recent times they've proved to be goldmines of ancient beliefs and traditions. Crete, Skýros, Lésbos (where they still sacrifice bulls), Límnos, Ándros, Kéa and Kárpathos are rich sources for ethnologists – though they may not be for much longer, in the face of rural depopulation, mass tourism and television. Nevertheless, if you were to spend a year in an island village, you would find that St. Basil, the Greek Santa Claus, still comes from Caesarea on **New Year's Eve** with gifts (rather than on Christmas Day) and lucky gold coins are still baked in pies called *vassilopíta*. Since ancient times **January** has also been closely associated with the Fates; everyone gambles, and readers of palms and tarot cards are in demand. In Crete, water is brought in from a spring where the Fates have bathed; everywhere pomegranates, symbols of abundance and fertility, are smashed on thresholds, and a stone is cast to give the household good health. On 6 January, **Epiphany** (Theofánia, or Ta Fóta, the feast of lights, Christ's baptism), houses are sprinkled with holy water, and ashes from the hearth, kept ablaze since Christmas to ward off goblins (the *kallikántzaroi*), are scattered for good luck; the priest will often toss a crucifix in the sea, and men dive after it, hoping to be the lucky finder.

**February** has a reputation for wetness; one of its names, Flevarius, suggests opening of veins (*fleva*) of water; a dry February means Greece is in for a drought. The first finches are a harbinger of spring. Olive groves are ploughed in **March**, a variable month with strange nicknames – the Five-Minded, the Grumbler, the Flayer and *Paloukokáftis*, 'the Burning Pale'. Bracelets called *Mertoátanos* are tied on children's wrists to protect them from the sun; on Kárpathos they say they tie up 'fatness, beauty, whims and the March sun.' The first swallows come back on Annunciation Day; in Chálki they are greeted with 2000-year-old Swallow Songs.

On Rhodes, **April** used to be called the Goggler; autumnal food supplies would run out, leaving everyone 'goggle-eyed' – hungry; in the Cyclades they call it 'the basket thrower' for the same reason. Conveniently, most people are fasting anyway, for Lent. Wildflowers are gathered to decorate each church's **Good Friday** *Epitáphios*, or bier of Christ; the flowers or candles used in the service are in great demand for their special power against the evil eye. Easter eggs are dyed red, doors are painted with blood from the Easter lamb, and just after midnight when the priest announces the Resurrection (*Christós Anésti! Christ has risen!*), general pandemonium breaks out as bells ring, fireworks explode and people embrace. On Corfu women smash old crockery, symbolizing the shattering of death; on Kálymnos and Sými men throw dynamite, sometimes blowing themselves up. Families return home with lighted candles, mark the sign of the cross on the doorpost, and tuck into a meal of *magirítsa*, a soup made of minced lamb's tripe that soothes the stomach after the long Lenten fast. On Easter Day everyone dresses up for the service of Divine Love, then feasts on spit-roast lamb, drinking, singing and dancing into the night; effigies of Judas are burned, and special Easter swings are raised for the girls on Anáfi and Lésbos.

**May** is the month of flowers, when dead souls live, according to popular belief, granted a brief return to earth between Easter and Whitsun. In ancient times temples and statues would be purified then, and to this day it's a month for mischief and sorcery. On 1 May it's important to get up early and eat garlic before the first donkey brays or first cuckoo sings to avoid being 'stuffed' – losing the appetite, or being made somehow asinine. Everyone, even the urbane Athenians, goes to the countryside to 'fetch the May' and make wreaths to bring spring's blessing to the house. On Ándros a pig's tongue is cooked to ward off backbiting, and it's bad luck to lend anything or be married. In **June** wheat and barley are harvested, cherries and apricots are picked and the first tomatoes and aubergines are ripe. Bonfires are lit for St John's Eve and the young people take turns leaping over the flames. As the year changes with the summer solstice, so does luck. A widespread custom is the *kledónas* 'prophecy': water is drawn by girls named Maria to fill an urn, where everyone deposits a personal item and makes a wish. The water is left open to the stars and on St John's Day, as the wishes are recited, a Maria pulls the items out; the owner of each item as it is drawn forth gets the wish being sung at the moment, usually leading to great hilarity.

Hot **July** is the month for threshing and gathering herbs; the first melons, figs and grapes are ripe. On 17 July, songs summon Ag. Marína to cure the bites and stings of snakes, scorpions and insects; on 20 July it's the turn of Prophet Elijah, the saint of mountaintop chapels who inherited Zeus' meteorological tasks, controlling the rain, winds and sun. Cretans say anyone who sees a headless shadow at noon will not survive the year. **August** is known as the Vintner, for the grape harvests begin, or the Fig-gatherer or the Table-bearer for the abundant fruits that are ripe. It is especially sacred to the Virgin, who has feast days on the 15, 23 and 31 (her birthday) and it's the best month to eat mackerel, fruit and vegetables. However, the first six days, the *Drymes*, are unlucky, associated with nymphs, who make hair fall out if it's washed or combed. The pious fast two weeks before the Assumption of the Virgin on 15 August, celebrated everywhere in Greece but especially on Tínos, at Agiássos, Lésbos, on Astypália, Sámos, and Markópoulo on Kefaloniá. **September** is the month of wine-making. In Byzantine times 1 September was New Year's Day (and still is in the Orthodox ecclesiastical calendar), the day when Archangel Michael gets out his book and notes all the souls he will take during the coming year. On Kos children make New Year's garlands of garlic, grapes, pomegranates and a leaf from Hippocrates' plane tree; on Crete some people put a walnut on their roof at midnight and judge their chances for survival for the next year by the wholeness of the kernel. Sowing begins after 14 September, but take care not to cross a woman en route to the fields.

**October** usually has the first rains but generally fine weather; Greek Indian summer is the 'little summer of Ag. Dimítros'. Cranes fly south to Africa, chrysanthemums adorn the tables, priests bless and open the first wine barrel. **November**, 'the showery', signals the beginning of the olive harvests. Flocks are brought down from the mountain pastures, and icons are placed around newly sown fields. Pancakes are made on 30 November for St Andrew, who is known as *Trypanoteganitís*, the 'frying pan piercer'; a good housewife will use all her frying pans that day to keep them from getting holes. **December** is called 'good morning, good evening' for its short days. Eating sweet things on 4 December, St Barbara's Day, was believed to ward off smallpox, and women hide their brooms and refrain from cooking beans. Her holiday generally elides with that of St Nikólaos on the 6th, the protector of sailors, when boats are decorated and icons paraded around the shore. Christmas Eve marks the beginning of the twelve-day holiday period when the demonic *kallikántzaroi* and werewolves are afoot but can be kept at bay by not letting the hearth fire go out, so everyone chooses the fattest 'Christ log' they can. Pigs are slaughtered, and in the villages pork is the traditional Christmas meal. Among the many cakes are sweets made with flaky filo pastry to represent Christ's swaddling clothes.

# A Quick Who's Who in Greek Mythology

Like all good polytheists, the ancient Greeks filled their pantheon with a colourful assortment of divinities, perhaps more anthropomorphic than most, full of contradictions, subtleties, and regional nuances. Every island has stories about their doings; some have become part of the baggage of western civilization, others read like strange collective dreams. But as classical Greek society grew more advanced and rational-minded, these gods were rounded up and made to live on the sanitized heights of Mount Olympos as idols of state religion, defined and ridiculed in Homer. The meatier matters of birth, sex, death and hopes for an afterlife – the real religion – went underground in the mysteries and chthonic cults, surviving in such places as Eleusis (Elefsína) near Athens, and at the Sanctuary of the Great Gods on Samothráki.

The big cheese on Olympos was **Zeus** (Jupiter, to the Romans), a native of Crete, the great Indo European sky god, lord of the thunderbolt with a libido to match, whose unenviable task was to keep the other gods in line. He was married to his sister **Hera** (Juno), the goddess of marriage, whose role in myth is that of the wronged, jealous wife, who periodically returned to her special island of Sámos to renew her virginity. Zeus' two younger brothers were given their own realms: **Poseidon** (Neptune) ruled the sea with his wife **Amphytron** (they had special sanctuaries on Póros and Tínos, and the famous 'Heliotrope' on Sýros), while **Hades** (Pluto) ruled the underworld and dead and rarely left his dismal realm. Their sister was **Demeter** (Ceres), goddess of corn and growing things, who was worshipped in the mysteries of Eleusis. **Aphrodite** (Venus), the goddess of love, is nearly as old as these gods, born when Zeus overthrew their father **Cronus** (Saturn) by castrating him and tossed the bloody member in the sea foam. She first landed at Kýthera but later preferred Cyprus.

The second generation of Olympians were the offspring of Zeus: **Athena**, the urbane virgin goddess of wisdom, born full grown straight out of Zeus' brain and always associated with Athens; **Ares** (Mars), the whining bully god of war, disliked by the Greeks and associated with barbarian Thrace; **Hermes** (Mercury), the messenger, occasional trickster, and god of commerce; **Hephaistos** (Vulcan), the god of fire and the forge and metal working, married to Aphrodite and worshipped on Límnos; **Apollo**, the god of light, music, reason, poetry, and prophesy, often identified with the sun, and his twin sister **Artemis** (Diana), the tomboy virgin moon goddess of the hunt, both born and worshipped on the island of Délos. Anáfi was also sacred to Apollo, Léros to Artemis. Their cross-dressing half-brother **Dionysos** (Bacchus), the god of wine, orgies and theatre, was the favourite on Náxos. In addition to the twelve Olympians, the Greeks had an array of other gods, nymphs, satyrs, and heroes, the greatest of which was **Herakles** (Hercules), the mighty hero who earned himself a place on Olympos, and gods such as **Helios** (Sol), the sun god, whose special island has always been Rhodes.

# Food and Drink

*Life's fundamental principle is the satisfaction of the needs and wants of the stomach. All important and trivial matters depend on this principle and cannot be differentiated from it.*

Epicurus, 3rd century BC

Epicurus may have lent his name to gourmets, but in reality his philosophy advocated maximizing simple pleasures: rather than continually seek novelty, Epicurus suggests making bread and olives taste sublime by fasting for a couple of days. In that way Greeks have long been epicureans: centuries of occupation and poverty taught them to relish food more than cuisine. What has changed, especially on the islands, is that cuisine has inescapably arrived. The influx of international tourists is partly responsible, but so is the rise of a well-travelled generation of Greeks. Fusion is the rage, with a broad Mediterranean slant: the popular islands now have Italian, Chinese, Mexican, Indian, Japanese and Turkish restaurants to prevent food fatigue.

Of course most restaurants and tavernas are still fundamentally Greek, serving fish from the seas, fresh herbs and honey from the mountains, wild young greens from the hills, olives, fruits and nuts from the groves. Cooking methods tend to be simple, with strong Turkish and Italian influences, that enhance natural flavours. What's on offer depends very much on the season: a good cook almost never resorts to canned or frozen ingredients, or even the microwave – one criticism levelled at Greek food is that it's served cold. It usually is, because Greeks believe tepid food is better for the digestion and recent studies show that eating like a Greek is very healthy (*see* p.121).

It's an unfortunate irony that the hardest foods to find are native island dishes, based on recipes handed down from mother to daughter, many of which make ingenious use of meagre resources. Some foods are tainted in Greek minds with poverty; also, the rush towards fusion in the kitchen has made these dishes seem irrelevant to all but a few inquisitive chefs (like restaurant owners, they tend to come from Athens or Thessaloníki anyway). As demographics change, and daughters move on to follow careers, these unique traditional dishes are becoming harder to find even in the homes, and on islands such as Rhodes are in danger of being lost altogether. There are exceptions, however, especially on islands where tourism isn't the only show in town (Crete notably, along with some of the North Aegean islands).

# Greek Dishes

Many Greek dishes need no introduction – *tarama*, moussaka, *gýros*, retsina, vine leaves, Greek salads with feta, Greek yoghurt, and baklava have achieved the universality of lasagne and chicken tikka. Although some of the food may be familiar, if you've not been to Greece before, you may find eating on the islands different from what you're used to, with a big emphasis on informality. Meals begin with bread (usually excellent – it's one thing they do better than their Italian cousins) and starters (*mezédes*) to be communally shared: olives, *tzatzíki* (cucumbers and yoghurt), prawns, *tirosalata* (feta cheese dip), *koponistá* (pungent smoked or salted fish), roasted sweet peppers, cheese or spinach pies, meatballs, or *saganáki* (fried cheese sprinkled with lemon). These are followed (often before you've finished the starters, unless you specify otherwise) by a shared salad and potatoes, and your own main course. This could be a gorgeously fresh omelette, or an oven dish or stew (called 'Ready dishes', as they're already prepared). Typically choices are moussaká, *pastítsio* (baked macaroni, layered with ground meat, cheese, cream and topped with béchamel), roast lamb or chicken, *makaroniá* (basically spaghetti bolognese, which has been sitting there and isn't bad), *yemistá* (stuffed tomatoes or peppers), *stifádo* (spiced beef stew with baby onions), *lagostifádo* (rabbit stew, is similar, but flavoured with orange), *kokinistó* (beef cooked with tomatoes and a hint of cinnamon), lamb or veal *youvétsi* (baked with tomatoes and with tear-drop pasta), *chirinó me sélino* (pork with wild celery, in egg lemon sauce), or *kréas stin stamna* (lamb or beef baked in a clay dish). Meats grilled to order come under the heading *tis óras* ('the On Times') – pork chops (*brizóles*), lamb cutlets (*paidákia*), kebabs (*souvláki*), minced steak (*biftéki*), meatballs (*keftédes* or *sousoukákia*), sausage (*lukániko*), or chicken (*koutópoulo skára*). Greeks eat little duck; if you see 'Quacker', it's probably oats.

Seafood is fresh and delicious, but ironically relatively expensive (blame overfishing, and the fact that much of the catch goes to mainland markets) but you can usually find cheapies like fresh whitebait (*marídes*), fresh sardines (*sardínas*) cuttlefish stew (*soupiá*), and squid rings (*kalamári*). Baked or fried *bakaliáros* (fresh Mediterranean cod) is always a treat and shouldn't break the bank. Some places serve soups – *psaró-soupa* (with potatoes and carrots) or spicy tomato-based *kakavia*, a meal in themselves with hunks of fresh bread and a bottle of wine. Prawns (*garídes*) are lightly fried or baked with garlic, tomatoes and feta as *garídes saganáki*, a popular dish invented in the 1960s; spaghetti with lobster (*astakomakaronáda*) is another delicious recent addition to many Greek menus. Note that each type of fish has its own price, and portions are priced by weight; often you'll be asked to pick out the one you want cooked and the owner puts it on the scale in front of you.

Desserts are rare, although many places offer complementary watermelon or sliced apples sprinkled with cinnamon or nutmeg; Greeks make lovely sweets, puddings, cakes, and ice creams but tend to eat them in the late afternoon after the siesta.

# Greek Eateries

Eating out in Greece has always been something of a movable feast, without any rush (though the service is improving). On the popular islands, there are plenty of places offering familiar breakfasts, lunches and dinners at familiar hours for visitors, but you may find getting into the Greek pace of life more enjoyable. This means a light breakfast (many bars sell yoghurt and honey), supplemented mid-morning with a hot cheese pie (*tirópita*). At 2 or 3pm, indulge in a long al fresco lunch with wine, followed by a siesta or *mesiméri* to avoid the scorching afternoon heat. Get up at 6 or 7pm for a swim and an ice cream. Around 8pm, it's time for the *vólta* , the see-and-be-seen evening stroll and a sunset drink while deciding where to go. Greeks rarely eat before 10pm and meals can go on into the small hours. Children are welcome (they

## Greek Vegetarian Dishes

Of all the people in the EU, the Greeks now eat the most meat per capita, but they also eat the most cheese, more than even the French, and follow only the Italians in eating pasta. Basically they eat a lot, which means there are plenty of dishes for vegetarians and vegans, especially if you go to a *mezedopoieíon*, where you can make a meal out of an array of little non-meat dishes ('vegetarian' is *chortofágos*). Because of historic poverty and the demands of Orthodox fasts (which forbid animal and dairy products), Greece has many traditional vegetarian dishes, and if you're a vegan, Lent is an ideal time to come, because restaurants go out of their way to prepare them (especially artichokes, *angináres*, which go out of season by June). Any time of the year you should find pulses, in starters such as *gigántes* (giant butter beans in tomato sauce) or *revíthia* (chick peas, baked or in soups or fritters), bean soups (*fasoláda*), and occasionally lentils (*fakés*). Other vegan stand-bys are ratatouille-like *ládera* (fresh vegetables cooked in olive oil), a host of salads, sometimes enlivened with a handful of *kápari* (pickled caper plant which tastes delicious), *patzária* (beetroot drizzled with olive oil and vinegar), *yemistá* (peppers or tomatoes stuffed with rice), *bríams* (potato and aubergine/courgette, baked with olive oil), *imams* (aubergine stuffed with tomato and onion), *keftédes* (vegetable fritters from carrot to courgette), *dolmádes* (rice and dill-filled vine leaves), *oftés patátes* (potatoes roasted in their jackets) and everywhere, endless supplies of chips. Although *skordaliá*, the classic garlic dip served with fried vegetables or beetroot, is traditionally made simply with puréed potatoes and olive oil, some places now do it with soft cheese.

If you're a vegetarian or used to buying pre-packed, sanitized meat, it's worth pointing out that in many parts of Greece, especially remote islands, food comes on the hoof, on the wing or in the net. It's not uncommon to see a sheep dispatched near a taverna by day and then turn up on the menu at night. Bunnies hopping round the village also hop into the pot and the family pig turns into sausages.

too nap in the afternoon) – toddlers crawl under the table, while the adults become increasingly boisterous, punctuating the meal with fiery discussions, and bursts of song or dance. The more people round the table the merrier, and the more likely the meal will turn into a spontaneous cabaret that no tour operator's organized 'Greek Night' can match. After dinner, have a brandy in a café or hit the tiles until dawn.

Because dining is an integral part of social life, Greeks eat out more than most Europeans, and have a choice of places to choose from. In the older *estiatória* (restaurants), you'll find all the Greek standards on the steam table to point at. Among the newer ones, look out for those that have made an effort to revive traditional Greek décor and recipes – always ask the waiter about the day's specials. Popular *tavernas* are more like family-run bistros and can range from beach shacks to barn-like affairs with live music in the evening. Waiters will reel off what's available and if there's a menu, homemade translations may leave you more baffled than ever (*see* **Topics**). Increasingly popular *mezedopoieíons* specialize in a host of little dishes, where you can build up an entire meal. If lucky, you may even find a *mageiria*, simple places with old-fashioned pots simmering on the stove, usually only open for lunch.

At the seaside you'll find the fish tavernas, *psarotavérnes*, specializing in all kinds of seafood from sea urchins and octopus stew to red mullet, swordfish, bream and sardines. Most carry one or two meat dishes for fish haters who may be dragged along. If you're a red-blooded meat eater then head for a *psistariá*, specializing in charcoal-grilled chicken, lamb, pork or *kokorétsi* (lamb's offal, braided around a skewer). In some places you can still find *hasapotavérna*, a grill room attached to a local butcher's shop, offering fresh kebabs, home-made sausages and sometimes delicious stews, usually served by the butcher's assistant in a bloodstained apron for added carnivorous effect.

Other eateries in Greece need no introduction: the pizzeria (often spelled *pitsaria*), American fast food (with local adaptations, such as non-meat meals on offer during Lent) and Goody's, the Greek chain (with lots more variety). Even the smallest islands have at least one *gýros* or *souvláki* stand for cheap greasy fills. Bakeries sell an array of sweet and savoury hot pies; a *bougatsaría* (μπουγατσαρια) specializes in them. For something sweet, just look at the lovely displays in any *zacharoplasteío* or pastry shop. Greece's favourite ice cream maker, Dodóni (Δωδωνη) has a chain of shops.

## Kafeneíons and Cafés

Every one-mule village will have a *kafeneíon*: a coffee house but more importantly a social institution where men (and increasingly women) gather to discuss the latest news, read the papers, nap or play cards and incidentally drink coffee. Some men seem to live in them. They are so essential to the Greek identity that on Skópelos, when real estate interests threatened the last old *kafeneíon* with extinction, the town hall opened a municipal *kafeneíon*. The bill of fare features Greek coffee (*café ellinikó*), which is the same muddy stuff as Turkish coffee, prepared in 40 different ways, although *glykó* (sweet), *métrio* (medium) and *skéto* (no sugar) are the basic orders. It is always served with a cold glass of water. Other coffees in Greece, unless you find a proper Italian espresso machine, won't make the earth move for you: '*nes*' (aka instant Nescafé) has become a Greek word, and comes either hot or whipped and iced as a *frappé*, which usually tastes better. Tea, soft drinks, brandy, beer and *ouzo* round out the old style *kafeneíon* fare. Newer cafés usually open earlier and close much later than *kafeneíons*. Many offer breakfast, from simple to complete English, with rashers, baked beans and eggs. They also serve mineral water, ice cream concoctions, milk-shakes, wonderful fresh fruit juices, cocktails, and thick Greek yoghurt and honey.

## Bars (*Barákia*) and *Ouzeries*

Even the most flyspeck island these days tends to have at least one music bar, usually playing the latest hit records (foreign or Greek). They come to life at cocktail hour and again at midnight; closing times vary but dawn isn't unusual in the summer. In general, bars are not cheap and are sometimes outrageously dear by Greek standards. It can be disconcerting to realize that you paid the same for your gin fizz as you paid for your entire meal earlier in the taverna next door. However, remember that the measures are triples by British standards. If in doubt stick to beer (invariably Amstel or Heineken, although Greece has its own brand, the slightly sweet

*Mýthos*, and has recently revived an old favourite, *Fix*), *ouzo*, *suma* (like *ouzo*, but sweeter – each island makes its own), wine and Metaxá (Metaxá and Coke, if you can stomach it, is generally about half the price of a rum and coke).

Just when it seemed time to write the obituary on a grand old Greek institution, the **ouzerie**, it has returned as part of a national movement to hold on to Greek tradition in the face of an invasion of foreign spirits – Scotch whisky is now the country's tipple of choice. Still, the national aperitif, *ouzo* (the *rakí* drunk by the Byzantines and Venetians, renamed *ouzo* in the 18th century from the Latin *usere*, 'usable') is holding on among older Greeks. Clear and anise-flavoured, it is served in tall glasses or a *karafáki* holding three or four doses which *habitués* dilute and cloud with water and sometimes ice. If you dislike aniseed, the Greeks also make an unflavoured grappa-like *tsikoúdia* or *rakí*; the best comes from Mytilíni. As Greeks look askance at drunkenness – as in ancient times, when they cut their wine with water and honey – *ouzo* is traditionally served with a little plate of *mezédes*; for an assortment, ask for a *pikilía*.

# Wine

Greece has 300 different indigenous vines, and there could well be something to the myths that wine was invented here. Despite this big head start, the average Greek wine has long been that – average, if not wretched. This is changing so fast it's hard to keep up: in the past two decades, better education, the introduction of foreign expertise and modern techniques have improved many Greek wines. They also tend to be highly regionalized, each island and village offering their own varieties; even that humblest of bottles, Deméstica has become acceptable and bears little resemblance to the rough stuff that earned it some unflattering nicknames. Big wineries like Achaia Clauss, Botari, Carras and Cambas dominate the market, but small independent vineyards are becoming very trendy: in 1999, they contributed greatly to the 164 new bottled wines put on the market – a 25 per cent increase. Besides the island wines (*see* box) don't miss some of the country's noble reds ('AO' is the equivalent of the French AOC) – Náoussa, Nemea, or Limnio – a variety mentioned by Aristotle, that even tastes ancient. If you're buying wines, seek out a *káva*, or wine shop.

In a taverna, the choice of wine will probably be limited. Many serve the country's best-known (or most notorious) tipple, **retsína**, with its distinctive pine resiny taste so admirably suited to Greek food – in fact once you acquire a taste for it, other wines may taste bland. The ancient Greeks stored their wine in clay *amphorae* sealed with resin; the disintegration of the resin helped prevent oxidation and lent the wine a flavour that caught on (and is now supplied by pieces of resin). Like *ouzo*, though, young Greeks are turning their backs on it, and draught retsína (*retsína varelísio*) – the best – can only be found on larger islands. Traditionally retsína comes in chilled copper-anodized cans, by the kilo (about a litre), or *misó kiló* (half) or *tetárto* (250ml) and is served in tumblers. Kourtaki is a reliable bottled variety and widely available.

On the islands, most **house wines** (*krasí chíma*) are unresinated and can be incredibly good, but there are still some stinkers around, so start with just a *tetárto* when

# Wines of the Greek Islands

Nearly all the islands have vineyards, although often they are pocket-sized and the wine is made by a family for their own consumption. Crete, Santoríni, Kefalonía, Rhodes, Páros and Sámos support important wine estates that are beginning to export abroad (and usually welcome visitors if you ring ahead). Some of the wines are quite unusual: one well-known Santoríni vineyard, Gaia, offers a wine called Thalassitis, inspired by an ancient Greek wine that was mixed with a dollop of sea water. The most common varieties on the islands are:

**Aidani**: Somewhat rarified white grape found on the Aegean islands, especially Santoríni and known for its flowery bouquet.

**Assyrtiko**: One of Greece's best white grapes, the base for AO Santoríni (*see* p.281). Because the grapes adopt the character of the soil, the wines come in a surprising variety of styles – fruity, crispy or even slightly smoky.

**Athiri**: An Aegean grape often blended with Assyrtiko; makes fragrant, lemony white wines, the base of AO Rhodes.

**Kotsifali**: Sweet and spicy red grape unique to Archánes and Péza on Crete; it's blended with the Mandelaria for colour.

**Liatiko**: Red grape grown on the Aegean islands and on Crete, where it yields AO Daphnes and Sitia. The name comes from 'July', when these grapes ripen.

**Malvazia**: Grown in small vineyards on Páros and Sýros, this white grape from Monemvasia in the Peloponnese was used to make the popular medieval sweet wine, malvasia or 'malmsey' imported by the Venetians to Europe. Modern wines have a peachy aromatic tone.

**Mandelaria**: Ancient almost black variety grown in the Aegean, used for blending with grapes low in tannins for the AO wines Páros, Archánes, and Péza. On Rhodes, where it's sometimes known as Amorgiano, it is used by itself for AO Rhodes.

**Mavrodaphne**: Named after the grape, Mavro, and a beautiful grape picker named Daphne, who died before the wine maker who employed her could tell her he loved her. Grown in Patrás and Kefaloniá, it yields delicious rich, velvet wines like port.

**Muscat**: Like Assyrtiko, a white grape produced in a vast range of styles from dry to dessert wines. Grown on Kefaloniá, Rhodes, and Sámos, for both a dry white and a lovely dessert wine with ripe apricot nuances named after the island.

**Robola**: A grape of extremely low yields, unique to the Ionian islands. Most robolas are grown on the mountain sides of Kefaloniá (*see* p.453) producing an excellent fragrant, bone dry white wine that is one of the most pricey in Greece.

**Savatiano**: The most common variety grown in Attica and Évia, yielding the light white wines made into retsína. It has been improved dramatically due to early picking and modern processes and is now drunk as a soft fruity white wine.

**Villana**: Indigenous to Péza on Crete; produces that area's crisp white AO wines.

you order. In summer, the reds often come as chilled as the whites. When eating with Greeks, you keep topping up your companions' glasses, while drinking constant toasts – *steen yámass*, good health to us, *steen yássou* or *yássas*, good health to you or, in Crete, *Avíva* or *Áspro Páto* – bottoms up.

# The Greek Menu (Katálogos)

| Ορεκτικά (Μεζέδες) | Orektiká (Mezéthes) | Appetisers |
|---|---|---|
| τζατζίκι | tzatziki | yoghurt and cucumbers |
| εληές | eliés | olives |
| κοπανιστί (τυροσαλάτα) | kopanistí (tirosaláta) | cheese purée, often spicy |
| ντολμάδες | dolmáthes | stuffed vine leaves |
| μελιτζανοσαλατα | melitzanosaláta | eggplant (aubergine) dip |
| σαγανάκη | saganáki | fried cheese with lemon |
| ποικιλία | pikilía | mixed hors d'œuvres |
| μπουρεκι | bouréki | cheese and vegetable pie |
| τυροπιττα | tirópitta | cheese pie |
| αχινοί | achíni | sea urchin roe (quite salty) |

| Σούπες | Soópes | Soups |
|---|---|---|
| αυγολέμονο | avgolémono | egg and lemon soup |
| χορτόσουπα | chortósoupa | vegetable soup |
| ψαρόσουπα | psarósoupa | fish soup |
| φασολάδα | fasoláda | bean soup |
| μαγειρίτσα | magirítsa | giblets in egg and lemon |
| πατσάς | patsás | tripe and pig's foot soup (for late nights and hangovers |

| Λαδερά | Latherá | Cooked in Oil |
|---|---|---|
| μπάμιες | bámies | okra, ladies' fingers |
| γίγαντες | yígantes | butter beans in tomato sauce |
| μπριαμ | briám | aubergines and mixed veg |
| φακηές | fakés | lentils |

| Ζυμαρικά | Zimariká | Pasta and Rice |
|---|---|---|
| πιλάφι / ρύζι | piláfi/rízi | pilaf/rice |
| σπαγκέτι | spagéti | spaghetti |
| μακαρόνια | macarónia | macaroni |
| πλιγγούρι | plingoúri | bulgar wheat |

| Ψάρια | Psária | Fish |
|---|---|---|
| αστακός | astakós | lobster |
| αθερίνα | atherína | smelt |
| γάυρος | gávros | mock anchovy |
| καλαμάρια | kalamaria | squid |
| κέφαλος | kefalos | grey mullet |
| χταπόδι | chtapóthi | octopus |
| χριστόψαρο | christópsaro | John Dory |
| μπαρμπούνι | barboúni | red mullet |
| γαρίδες | garíthes | prawns (shrimps) |
| γοπα | gópa | bogue (boops boops) |
| ξιφίας | ksifias | swordfish |
| μαρίδες | maríthes | whitebait |
| συναγρίδα | sinagrítha | sea bream |
| σουπιές | soupiés | cuttlefish |

| φαγγρι | fangri | bream |
| κιδόνια | kidónia | cherrystone clams |
| σαρδέλλα | sardélla | sardines |
| μπακαλιάρος (σκορδαλιά) | bakaliáros (skorthaliá) | fried hake (with garlic sauce) |
| σαργός | sargós | white bream |
| σκαθάρι | skathári | black bream |
| στρείδια | stríthia | oysters |
| λιθρίνια | lithrínia | bass |
| μίδια | mídia | mussels |

## Εντραδες — *Entrádes* — Main Courses

| κουνέλι | kounéli | rabbit |
| στιφάδο | stifádo | casserole with onions |
| γιουβέτσι | yiouvétsi | veal in a clay bowl |
| συκώτι | seekóti | liver |
| μοσχάρι | moschári | veal |
| αρνί | arní | lamb |
| κατσικι | katsíki | kid |
| κοτόπουλο | kotópoulo | (roast) chicken |
| χοιρινό | chirinó | pork |

## Κυμάδες — *Kymadhes* — Minced Meat

| παστίτσιο | pastítsio | mince and macaroni pie |
| μουσακά | moussaká | meat, aubergine with white sauce |
| | | |
| μακαρόνια με κυμά | makarónia me kymá | spaghetti Bolognese |
| μπιφτέκι | biftéki | hamburger, usually bunless |
| σουτζουκάκια | soutzoukákia | meat balls in sauce |
| μελιτζάνες γεμιστές | melitzánes yemistés | stuffed aubergines/eggplants |
| πιπεριές γεμιστές | piperíes yemistés | stuffed peppers |

## Της Ωρας — *Tis Oras* — Grills to Order

| μριζολα | brizóla | beefsteak with bone |
| μπριζόλες χοιρινές | brizólas chirinés | pork chops |
| σουβλάκι | souvláki | meat or fish kebabs on a skewer |
| | | |
| κοκορέτσι | kokorétsi | offal kebabs |
| κοτολέτες | kotolétes | veal chops |
| πάιδακια | paidakia | lamb chops |
| κεφτέδες | keftéthes (th as in 'th') | meat balls |

## Σαλάτες — *Salátes* — Salads and Vegetables

| ντομάτες | domátes | tomatoes |
| αγγούρι | angoúri | cucumber |
| ρώσσικη σαλάτα | róssiki saláta | Russian salad |
| σπανάκι | spanáki | spinach |
| χωριάτικη | choriátiki | salad with feta cheese and olives |
| | | |
| κολοκυθάκια | kolokithákia | courgettes/zucchini |
| πιπεριεσ | piperiés | peppers |
| κρεμιδι | kremídi | onions |

| πατάτες | patátes | potatoes |
| παντσάρια | pantsária | beetroot |
| μαρούλι | maroúli | lettuce |
| χόρτα | chórta | wild greens |
| αγκινάρες | angináres | artichokes |
| κουκιά | koukiá | fava beans |

| **Τυρια** | **Tiriáv** | **Cheeses** |
| φέτα | féta | goat's cheese |
| κασέρι | kasséri | hard buttery cheese |
| γραβιέρα | graviéra | Greek 'Gruyère' |
| μυζήθρα | mizithra | soft white cheese |
| πρόβιο | próvio | sheep's cheese |

| **Γλυκά** | **Glyká** | **Sweets** |
| παγωτό | pagotó | ice cream |
| κουραμπιέδες | kourabiéthes | sugared biscuits |
| λουκουμάδες | loukoumáthes | hot honey fritters |
| χαλβά | halvá | sesame seed sweet |
| μπακλαβά | baklavá | nuts and honey in filo pastry |
| γιαούρτι (με μελι) | yiaoúrti (me méli) | yoghurt (with honey) |
| καριδοπιτα | karidópita | walnut cake |
| μήλο | mílo | apple |
| μπουγάτσα | bougátsa | custard tart |

### Miscellaneous

| ψωμί | psomí | bread |
| βούτυρο | voútiro | butter |
| μέλι | méli | honey |
| μαρμελάδα | marmelátha | jam |
| λάδι | láthi | oil |
| πιάτο | piáto | plate |
| λογαριασμό | logariazmó | the bill/check |

### Drinks

| άσπρο κρασί | áspro krasí | wine, white |
| άσπρο/κόκκινο/κοκκινέλι | áspro/kókkino/kokkinéli | white/red/rosé |
| ρετσίνα | retsína | wine resinated |
| νερό (βραστο/μεταλικο) | neró (vrastó/metalikó) | water (boiled/mineral) |
| μπύρα | bíra | beer |
| χυμός πορτοκάλι | chimós portokáli | orange juice |
| γάλα | gála | milk |
| τσάι | tsái | tea |
| σοκολάτα | sokoláta | chocolate |
| καφέ | kafé | coffee |
| φραππέ | frappé | iced coffee |
| πάγος | págos | ice |
| ποτίρι | potíri | glass |
| μπουκάλι | boukáli | bottle |
| καράφα | karáfa | carafe |
| στήν γειά σας! | stín yásas (formal, pl) | to your health! Cheers! |
| στήν γειά σου! | stín yásou (sing) | |

# Travel

and address of the hotel, villa or campsite; you don't really have to stay there. Although a formality, every so often there is a crackdown. Because the Greeks subsidise airline landing fees they want to prevent charter flights being used as a cheap way to get to other countries, especially Turkey. Visitors to Greece using a charter flight may visit any neighbouring country for the day, but must not stay overnight, at the very real risk of forfeiting your return ticket home. Travellers with stamps from previous holidays in Turkey will not be barred entry, but if you have Turkish Cypriot stamps check with the Passport Office before you go. Make sure you confirm your return flight three days prior to departure.

### Student and Youth Discounts

If you're under 26 or a full-time student under 32 with an **International Student Identity Card** to prove it, you're eligible for **student/youth charters**; these are exempt from the voucher system and are often sold as one-way tickets, enabling you to stay in Greece longer than is possible with a regular charter flight. Students under 26 are sometimes eligible for discounts on scheduled flights as well, especially with Olympic who offer 25% discount to ISIC holders on all connecting flights from Athens to the islands. Young people of Greek origin (age 10–15) may be eligible for Gold Card discounts (contact your country's Greek National Tourist Office).

### Children and Pregnancy

Free child places on package holidays and discount air fares for tiny travellers vary from company to company. Get a good travel agent, trawl through the brochures and read all the small print. The big package operators geared to family holidays like **Thomson** offer child discounts and seasonal savers with in-resort kiddie clubs and baby-sitting, as well as deals for kids under 12 in hotels and teenagers up to 17 in self-catering accommodation. On some UK charter flights infants under two travel free on a full fare-paying adult's lap, while on others you may be charged £15–20 for the baby, or 10% of the adult fare. Children from two to 12 cost 25%–65%, and over 12 you'll have to fork out full fare. On international Olympic flights you'll pay 67% of the adult fare for children aged two to 12, 10% for

infants under two, while under-12s go for half-fare on all domestic flights. If your toddler has crossed the magic two-year-old age barrier by the return journey you'll have to pay for another seat. Many airlines won't let single mothers travel with two infants, but you may get through the restriction by having one on your lap and one in a car seat; explain your position when you book.

If you're pregnant, think before you fly. Although Greek hospitals have improved, make sure your insurance covers repatriation. Most airlines will carry women up to 34 weeks pregnant – Olympic even later – but you will have to provide a doctor's certificate after 28 weeks to prove you are well enough to fly.

# By Air from the USA and Canada

**Olympic** and **Delta** offer daily non-stop flights from New York to Athens in the summer; Olympic also flies direct to Athens from Boston, and from Toronto and Montreal in Canada. American economy fares (Apex and SuperApex/Eurosavers, booked at least three weeks in advance) range from $750 return New York–Athens in low season to $1,200 high season; Canadian economy fares to Athens from Toronto or Montreal range from $1,000 low season to $1,400–1,900 high season. When ringing around, take into consideration the hefty discount offered by travel agents on domestic flights within Greece for travellers on Olympic Airways. From many cities in the USA and Canada, European airlines such as **KLM** or **Czech Airlines** offer the best deals to Greece. Finally, if you have more time than money, get a cheap or stand-by flight to London and once there, hunt down a cheap ticket to an island (although this may be a headache in July or August).

# Getting to and from El. Venizélos Airport, Athens

### By Bus

Elefthérios Venizélos Airport, 25km northeast of the centre of Athens, consists of a main terminal building and a satellite terminal connected by an underground tunnel. It houses shops, restaurants, cafés, banks, car rentals, travel agencies and an EOT (National Tourist Organization) kiosk on **Level 0. Airport Information, t** 010 353 0000, operates 24 hours a day in English and Greek. Note that there is a charge for luggage trolleys, so bring some euro coins with you.

There are three bus routes to and from the airport, each connecting with an Athens metro station. Buses leave from directly outside the main terminal building as follows:

**E95,** linking central Sýntagma Square, every half hour, 24 hours a day;

**E94,** linking the *Ethniki Amyna* metro station (Line 3, the closest to the airport, on a direct line to Sýntagma), operating every 16mins from 7.30am until 8.30pm and every half hour from 8.30pm to 11:30pm.

**E96,** 24 hours a day, to and from Karaïskaki Square, in Piraeus' main harbour (stopping at the Peace and Friendship stadium, opposite the *Faliro* metro station, Line 1), 5am–7pm every 20mins, 7pm–8.30pm every 30mins and 8.30pm–5am every 40mins. At the time of writing tickets cost €3, and are valid for 24 hours on all other forms of Athens' public transport system as well. Validate your ticket by punching it into the machine on the bus.

### By Car

A new super highway, the *Attikí Odós*, only partially completed at the time of writing, will connect the airport to Elefsína, handy for those who are on their way to the Peloponnese or Ionian islands. It is a toll highway (€3 – make sure you don't leave the airport without some euros). Downtown Athens can theoretically be reached in ½ hour, by taking the Pallini Junction turn-off, although traffic usually makes this longer. **Taxis** to the centre cost €17–20, the rate doubling between midnight and 5am.

## By Train

The best and most efficient route by train from the UK to the Greek Islands is through Italy. Starting with Eurostar from London Waterloo, the journey to Brindisi in the south of Italy should take about 24 hours. From Brindisi, take the ferry over to Corfu and Pátras. You can also travel by train to Venice and from there take a ship to Pátras. Hardy souls who deny themselves a cabin should bring plenty of provisions, including water, and some toilet paper.

For information on trains from the UK to Greece, and the various rail passes available, contact **Rail Europe, t** (08705) 848 848, *www.raileurope.co.uk*

## By Bus

Taking a coach from London through Europe to the Greek Islands is a possible alternative for those who decide that a train trip is too expensive or too easy a route to travel. It isn't usually much cheaper than a standby flight, and can take four days instead of four hours, but it's a chance to see Munich, Belgrade and other fine bus terminals en route. However, as with the trains, the most direct route to take is via Italy, where ferries to the islands can be picked up in Venice, Ancona and Brindisi.

**Busabout,** London Traveller's Centre, 258 Vauxhall Bridge Rd, London, SW1V 1BS, **t** (020) 7950 1661, **f** (020) 7950 1662, *www .busabout.com*. Hop-on, hop-off service for backpackers who want to take in various European capitals, using bus passes that cover travel from 2 weeks to 2 months.

**Eurolines,** 52 Grosvenor Gardens, Victoria, London SW1W 0AU, **t** 08705 143219, *www. gobycoach.com*. They no longer go direct to Athens, but again, they have a wide array of services that will transport you through various European cities to Athens or to Italy where you can catch a connecting ferry.

## By Sea

The most common sea route to Greece is from Italy, with daily ferry services from Ancona and Brindisi, and frequently from Bari and Venice. Brindisi ferries connect with the night train from Rome and arrive in Pátras the next morning. Passengers are usually allowed a free stopover in Corfu if that island is not their ultimate destination, before continuing to Igoumenítsa or Pátras, but make sure it is noted on your ticket. Prices vary, so shop

# Italy–Greece Ferry Services

| Ports | Seat Prices € | Company |
|---|---|---|
| Ancona (or Venice)–Corfu–Pátras and Brindisi–Corfu–Igoumenítsa | 53/76<br>30/50 | Strinzis Lines<br>26 Aktí Possidónos, ✉ 18531 Piraeus<br>t 010 422 5000, f 010 422 5265,<br>*sales@strintzis.gr* |
| Ancona–Pátras<br>Trieste–Corfu–Igoumenítsa–Pátras | 50/75<br>65/85 | ANEK Lines<br>54 Amalías, ✉ 10538 Athens<br>t 010 323 3481, f 010 323 4137,<br>*anek@anek.gr* |
| Ancona–Pátras | 75/100 | Superfast Ferries<br>30 Amalías ✉ 10538 Athens<br>t 010 331 3252,<br>*www.superfast.com* |
| Ancona–Igoumenítsa–Corfu–Pátras and Venice–Igoumenítsa–Corfu | 72/92<br>75/90 | Minoan Lines<br>2 Vass. Konstantinoú, ✉ 15125 Athens<br>t 010 751 2356, f 010 752 0540,<br>*info@minoan.gr* |
| Brindisi–Corfu–Igoumenítsa–Pátras and Brindisi–Kefaloniá–Páxi–Zákynthos–Pátras (summer only) | 22/55<br>price<br>on application | Hellenic Mediterranean Lines<br>PO Box 80057, ✉ 18531 Piraeus<br>t 010 422 5341, f 010 422 5317,<br>*hml@otenet.gr* |
| Bari–Igoumenítsa–Pátras | 35/55 | Ventouris Ferries<br>91 Pireós and 2 Kffithiron,<br>✉ 18541 Piraeus<br>t 010 482 8001, f 010 481 3701,<br>*info@ventouris.gr* |
| Brindisi–Corfu–Igoumenítsa | 22/42 | Fragline<br>5a Réthymnou, ✉ 10682 Athens<br>t 010 821 6004, f 010 823 7109,<br>*fragline@otenet.gr* |
| Brindisi–Corfu–Igoumenítsa–Pátras | 35/48 | Adriatica<br>85 Aktí Miaoúli, ✉ 18538 Piraeus<br>t 010 429 0487, f 010 429 0490 |
| Brindisi–Kefaloniá–Pátras | 38/54 | Med-Link Lines<br>15 Óthonos and Amalías,<br>Pátras, t 0610 623 011 |

around. In the summer, reserve in advance, especially if you bring a car (most travel agents can do this for you). Students, young people and pensioners can get a discount of up to 20%. Discounts of up to 30% on car prices are also offered when buying a return ticket. As a rule, the costlier the ferry, the faster it sails (Superfast, for instance, takes only 19 hours from Ancona to Pátras, 15½ hours from Bari to Pátras). There is also a high-season, high-speed catamaran from Brindisi to Corfu and Igoumenítsa in under four hours, run by Ventouris Ferries – *see* above.

## Italy–Greece Ferries

The fares listed in the table above are approximate 2002 prices in euros for an airline-type seat, one way, in low/high season; there are even cheaper deck class tickets, while cabins are considerably dearer. As a general rule, cars under 4.25m cost more than the low season seat prices listed opposite; double that for taking a car in high season.

# By Car

Driving from London to Athens (and taking the ferry from Italy to Greece) at a normal pace takes around 3½ days. Don't even consider driving down unless you are planning to spend a few weeks on one or two islands, and if that's the case the smaller the better, both for squeezing the car on to the ferry, and for negotiating the narrow village roads.

An **International Driving Licence** is not required from EU citizens. Other nationals (over 18) can obtain an international licence at home, or at one of the Automobile Club offices in Greece (ELPA), by presenting a national driving licence, passport and photo.

The **Motor Insurance Bureau**, 10 Xenofóntos, Athens, **t** 010 323 6733, can tell you which Greek insurance company represents your own, or provide additional cover for Greece.

The **Greek Automobile Club**, ELPA, in Athens at 395 Messogion Ave, Ag. Paraskevi 153 43, **t** 010 606 8800, **f** 010 606 898, operates a breakdown service within 60km (40 miles) of Athens, Thessaloníki, Laríssa and Pátras (**t** 104). Elpa also has a helpline for medical assistance (**t** 166). If you belong to an automobile club at home, breakdown service is free anywhere. Similar services are offered by Express Service (**t** 154), and Interamerican (**t** 1011).

**Customs** formalities for bringing in a car are easy and take little time. You're allowed six months' free use of a car in Greece before it must leave the country. If your visit is going to be longer, to avoid difficulties when you leave, make sure your car is stamped in your passport on arrival. This applies to all vehicles with foreign plates. (Only if you legally declare at an embassy in your home country that you intend to live in Greece, may you keep a car on foreign plates for two years.) If you leave Greece without your car, you must have it withdrawn from circulation by a customs authority. ELPA has a list of lawyers offering free legal advice. They also have a 24-hour information number for foreign motorists (**t** 174); Pátras Customs Office, **t** 02610 339 870.

# Entry Formalities

All **European Union** members can stay indefinitely. The only reason you would need special permission to stay would be for working or if complicated banking procedures were involved requiring proof of residence; contact the **Aliens Bureau**: 173 Leof. Alexándras, 11522 Athens, **t** 010 647 6000.

The formalities for **non-EU** tourists entering Greece are very simple. American, Australian and Canadian citizens can stay for up to 3 months in Greece on presentation of a valid passport. If you want to stay longer, take your passport, 20 days before your time in Greece expires, to the Aliens Bureau or your local police station, and be prepared to prove you can support yourself with bank statements and the like.

If you overstay your 3 months, be prepared to pay a fine that, at the moment is €150 for an overstay of three months, €300 if over six months.

# Getting Around

## By Air

Flights from Athens to the islands can be booked in advance through **Olympic, Aegean** and **Cronus**; as many planes are small, do this as far in advance as possible. Some only have 18 seats, and are good fun; they seem to just skim over the mountain tops (but note, they can't take off or land in high winds, and you could end up back where you started). Because planes are small, baggage allowances (15kg) tend to be enforced – unless you've bought your ticket abroad, when you're allowed 23kg.

Olympic Airways also offer island-to-island flights in season, which precludes the need to go to Athens. Although these have a habit of changing from year to year, flights between Crete and Santoríni/Mýkonos/Kárpathos/ Rhodes; Lésbos and Límnos/Chíos; Rhodes and Santoríni/ Mýkonos/Kastellórizo/Kárpathos; Kárpathos and Kássos; and Santoríni and Mýkonos are well-established. It's also possible to get a scheduled 'open-jaws' ticket to Athens and on to any permutation of islands, but you have to return home from Athens.

## Airlines in Athens

**Aegean and Cronus,** 572 Vouliagménis, Glyfáda, t 010 998 8300; airport t 010 353 4289, *www.aegeanair.com*

**Air Canada,** 8 Zirioi St, Maroussi, t 010 617 5321, f 010 610 8919.

**Air France,** 18 Vouliagménis, Glyfáda, t 010 960 1100, f 010 960 1457; airport t 010 353 0380.

**Alitalia,** 577 Vouliagménis, Argyroúpouli, t 010 998 8888, f 010 995 9214.

**American Airlines,** 15 Panepistimíou, t 010 331 1045, f 010 323 1205.

**British Airways,** 1 Themistokléos, Glyfada, t 010 890 6666, f 010 890 6510.

**Continental,** 25 Filellínon, t 010 324 9300.

**Cyprus Airways,** 25 Filellínon, t 010 322 6413, f 010 323 8472.

**Czech Airlines,** 65B Vouliagménis, Glyfada, t 010 969 4331, f 010 961 2712.

**Delta,** 4 Óthonos, t 010 331 1668, f 010 325 0451

**Iberia,** 8 Xenofóndos, t 010 323 4523, f 010 324 0655.

**KLM,** 41 Vouliagménis, Glyfada, t 010 960 5010, f 010 964 8868.

**Lufthansa,** 10 Zirioi, Maroússi, t 010 617 5200, f 010 610 8919.

**Malev,** 15 Panepistimíou, t 010 324 1116.

**Olympic,** 96 Syngroú, among many branches; reservations t 010 966 6666, f 010 966 6111.

**Singapore Airlines,** 9 Xenofóndos, t 010 324 4113, f 010 325 4326.

**Thai Airlines,** 32 El Venizélou, t 010 969 2020, f 010 960 2686.

**TWA,** 7 Syngroú, t 010 921 3400, f 010 921 3385.

**United Airlines,** 5 Syngroú, t 010 924 1389, f 010 924 1391.

**Virgin Atlantic,** 70 Panórmou, t 010 690 5300, f 010 699 5840.

## By Train

Domestic trains are very slow, with the exception of intercity trains, which by other European standards are still found wanting.

However, train fares are cheaper than buses by up to 40%. The Greek railways website is *www.ose.gr* and the national information number is t 010 529 7777.

In Athens, there are two stations. the railway station for northern Greece is *Lárissa* metro station, Deliyiánni St, t 010 529 7777. The station for the Peloponnese is behind it, across the tracks, reached by a handy pedestrian bridge, t 010 513 1601. In Piraeus, the station for the Peloponnese is near the Piraeus–Athens metro on Aktí Kalimassióti. The station for northern Greece lies further down the road on Aktí Kondyli.

## By Bus

The domestic bus service in Greece is efficient and regular, and still a bargain. Services start as early as 6 or 7am and run until early evening, depending on the route. In Greece, you'll find agencies selling bus tickets on the most obscure islands, as well as in Athens; **Filellínon Street** near Sýntagma Square is Athens' budget travellers' boulevard.

To get to the terminal at **100 Kifissoú St** (t 010 512 4910) take bus no.051 from Omónia Square (Zinonos and Menandroú Sts). For the terminal at **260 Liossíon Street** (t 010 831 7163) take bus no.024 from Leofóros Amalías, in Sýntagma Square (tell the driver you want the terminal; the bus doesn't go in it). Take tram 5 or 9 towards Areos Park on 28th Octovríou St for the **Mavromatéon** terminal.

**Note:** Because of the changes in Athens leading up to the Olympics, it does not hurt to call the tourist police (t 171) to get the latest update on where your bus begins its journey.

In August, reserve seats in advance on the long-distance buses. Two islands, Lefkáda and Évia, are joined to the mainland by bridge, which is good to remember if you need an island and the ferries aren't running due to strikes or bad weather.

### Train Routes for the Islands

| | | |
|---|---|---|
| Athens–Thessaloníki | for NE Aegean Is. | 10 a day |
| Thessaloníki–Alexandroúpolis | for Samothráki | 5 a day |
| Athens–Chalkída | Évia | 17 a day |
| Athens–Pátras | for Ionian Is. | 8 a day |
| Athens–Kalamáta | for Kýthera | 4 a day |
| Athens–Vólos | for Sporades | 2 a day |

## Domestic Buses

| Athens to | No. daily | Terminal | t (010–) | Duration |
| --- | --- | --- | --- | --- |
| Ag. Konstantínos (Sporades) | 13 | Lióssion | 831 7147 | 2.30hrs |
| Chalkída (Évia) | 33 | Lióssion | 831 7153 | 1.30hrs |
| Edipsoú (Évia) | 3–4 | Lióssion | 831 7153 | 3.15hrs |
| Gýthion (for Kýthera) | 4 | Kifissoú | 512 4913 | 4.30hrs |
| Kefaloniá | 4 | Kifissoú | 525 0785 | 8hrs |
| Kérkyra (Corfu) | 2 | Kifissoú | 512 9443 | 11hrs |
| Lefkáda | 4 | Kifissoú | 513 3583 | 5.30hrs |
| Lávrio (for Kéa) | 12 | Mavromatéon | 821 3203 | 2 hrs |
| Pátras (for Ionians, Italy) | 16 | Kifissoú | 514 7310 | 3hrs |
| Rafína (for Cyclades and Évia) | 18 | Mavromatéon | 821 0872 | 1.30hrs |
| Thessaloníki (for NE Aegean Is.) | 10 | Kifissoú | 514 8856 | 7.30hrs |
| Vólos (for Sporades) | 10 | Lióssion | 831 7186 | 5.15hrs |
| Zákynthos | 4 | Kifissoú | 512 9432 | 6hrs |

There never seem to be enough buses on the islands in the summer, nor is it customary to queue. However, you will not be left behind if it is humanly possible for you to squeeze on. If you can wake up in time, you will find that buses are rarely crowded early in the morning. Bear in mind also that different timetables apply at weekends.

# By Sea

Comfort on Greek ferries has improved by leaps and bounds in recent years, especially the long-haul ferries: shops, video rooms, air-conditioning, disco bars, slot machines and small swimming pools are added attractions to the old pleasures of lazily watching passing islands, feeling the sea breeze (or tempest, if the wind kicks up), looking out for dolphins during the day or shooting stars at night. Most island ferries have three classes: the first, or 'distinguished' class, with a plush lounge and private cabins (these often cost as much as flying); the second class, often with its own lounge as well, but smaller, porthole-less cabins, segregated by sex, not recommended for claustrophobes; and third or tourist class, which offers access to typically large rooms full of airline-type seats and the deck and snack bar area. As a rule the Greeks stay inside and the tourists stay out – on warm summer nights in particular this can be the most pleasant alternative, especially if you have a sleeping bag. Drinking water is never very good on the boats, but all sell bottled water, beer, coffee, and soft drinks (for about twice as much as on shore). Biscuits and cigarettes complete the fare on the smaller boats, while the larger ones offer sandwiches, self-service dining or full meals (usually adequate and fairly priced) served in a dining room.

Athens' port Piraeus is the busiest in Greece, the main launchpad for Crete, the Cyclades, the Dodecanese, Kýthera, the Saronic islands and most of the Northeastern Aegean Islands; see the map on p.111 for points of departure. Because Piraeus gets so busy (at peak times ferries circle about in holding patterns like planes waiting to land) there's a trend to use smaller mainland ports, especially Rafína (for Ándros, Tínos, Sýros, and Ilios hydrofoils to the Cyclades) and Lávrion (for Kéa); both ports are frequently linked by bus to Athens (see above), but most foreign tourists see them as a bother, which means that islands mainly served by these outlying ports tend be quieter and more 'Greek'. The main port for the Ionian islands is Pátras in western Greece, linked by train from Athens, while Évia, the Sporades, and the more northerly Aegean islands have their own mainland links that involve long chunks of overland travel; nearly all have airports, however.

The National Tourist Office publishes a free weekly list of ship departures, both abroad and to the islands; for serious island hoppers, ask for their free booklet, *Greek Travel Routes: Domestic Sea Schedules*. At the same time, be aware that any number of factors (weather, health emergencies and unforeseen repairs) can throw timetables out of the window, so if you have to catch a flight home allow for the eccentricities of the system and leave a day early to be safe. For the latest information on departures and arrivals, ring the relevant port authorities (*limenarchion*). Numbers are listed for each island. For mainland departures:

**Piraeus Port Authority**, t 010 422 6000 (for ferry schedules)

**Rafína Port Authority**, t 02940 28888

**Pátras Port Authority**, (for the Ionian Islands) t 02610 341 024

Before purchasing a ticket, check timetables in competing agencies – ticket prices will always be the same, but note that some ferries are faster than others, and others can take half a day stopping at tiny island ports. On smaller islands, agents moonlight as bartenders or grocers and may only have a handwritten sign next to the door advertising their ship's departures.

Always keep your ticket with you on a Greek ship, in case of a 'ticket control', necessary because the crew doesn't always check tickets when passengers board. Make sure that you have purchased a ticket before you get on, as in most cases tickets are not sold on board.

# Sea Travel Times and Prices

Below are some of the more popular mainland–island connections. Approximate 2002 fares and duration of each trip are given, but both are subject to change without notice. To roughly calculate the car prices on the ferries, multiply passenger fares by three to five.

**Piraeus to Crete, the Cyclades, Dodecanese and Northeastern Aegean Islands**

| | | |
|---|---|---|
| Heráklion (Crete) | €22 | 8–10hrs |
| Mýkonos/Páros | €16 | 6hrs |
| Sérifos | €12 | 4hrs |
| Sífnos | €15 | 5hrs |
| Folégandros | €17 | 10 hrs |
| Rhodes | €30 | 17hrs |
| Kos | €24 | 13hrs |
| Kálymnos | €22 | 10 hrs |
| Sými | €30 | 14–17hrs |
| Lésbos (Mytilíni) | €24 | 12–15hrs |
| Ikaría/Samos | €18–21 | 8–11hrs |

**Piraeus to the Saronic Islands and Kýthera (ferry/hydrofoil)**

| | | |
|---|---|---|
| Aegina | €5 | 1.30hrs (F) |
| | €10 | 30mins (H) |
| Hýdra | €7 | 4hrs (F) |
| | €16 | 1.30hrs (H) |
| Póros | €7 | 3hrs (F) |
| | €11 | 1hr (H) |
| Spétses | €21 | 2hrs (H) |
| Kýthera | €33 | 4hrs (H) |

**Sporades Line (ferry/hydrofoil)**
**Ag. Konstantínos to**

| | | |
|---|---|---|
| Alónissos | €14 | 5hrs (F) |
| | €29 | 3hrs (H) |
| Skiáthos | €12 | 3.15hrs (F) |
| | €21 | 1.30hrs (H) |
| Skópelos | €13 | 4hrs (F) |
| | €26 | 2hrs (H) |

**Kými (Évia) to**

| | | |
|---|---|---|
| Skýros | €8 | 2hrs (F) |

**Vólos to**

| | | |
|---|---|---|
| Alónissos | €12 | 4.30hrs (F) |
| | €25 | 2.30hrs (H) |
| Skiáthos | €10 | 2.30hrs (F) |
| | €18 | 1.15hrs (H) |
| Skópelos | €11 | 3.30hrs (F) |
| | €23 | 2hrs (H) |

**Rafína to Évia and Cyclades Line (ferry/cat)**

| | | |
|---|---|---|
| Amorgós | €31 | 6hrs (C) |
| Ándros | €8 | 2hrs (F) |
| | €16 | 1hr (C) |
| Kárystos (Évia) | €5 | 1hr (F) |
| Mýkonos | €14 | 4hrs (F) |
| | €27 | 2hrs (C) |
| Náxos | €28 | 3.30hrs (C) |
| Páros | €27 | 3hrs (C) |
| Tínos | €12 | 3hrs (F) |
| | €25 | 2hrs (C) |
| Psára | €16 | 6hrs (F) |

**Kéa–Kýthnos Line**
**Lávrion to**

| | | |
|---|---|---|
| Kéa | €6 | 1.30hrs |
| Kýthnos | €8 | 3hrs |

**Patrás and Killíni–Ionian Line (ferry/cat)**
**Patrás to**

| | | |
|---|---|---|
| Kefaloniá | €11 | 2.30hrs (F) |
| | €21 | 2hrs (C) |
| Corfu | €20 | 6.30hrs (F) |

**Killíni to**

| | | |
|---|---|---|
| Zákynthos | €5 | 1.30hrs (F) |

**Gýthio–Crete and Kýthera Line**
**Gýthio to**

| | | |
|---|---|---|
| Haniá | €16 | 7hrs |
| Kýthera | €5 | 2.30hrs |

Prices are still reasonable for passengers but rather dear for cars, between 3 and 5 times the passenger fare. All ships and hydrofoils are privately owned, and although the Greek Government controls prices, some will charge more for the same journey, depending on the facilities offered, speed, etc. In most cases kids under 4 travel free, and between 4 and 10 for half-fare. In the summer, especially in August, buy tickets well in advance if you have a car or want a cabin. If you miss your ship, you forfeit your ticket; if you cancel in advance, you will receive a 50% refund of the fare, or 100% in the case of major delays or cancellations, except those caused by *force majeure*. If you're greatly inconvenienced by a delay, you're entitled to compensation; contact the Ministry of the Merchant Marine (*www.yen.gr*), or the Piraeus or Rafina port police.

## Hydrofoils and Catamarans

There are several fleets of hydrofoils, several catamarans, and the occasional 'sea jet' thumping over the Greek seas, and new lines are added every year. Most services (especially to the Saronic Islands) run throughout the year but are less frequent between November and May. As a rule hydrofoils travel at least twice as fast as ferries and are twice as expensive. In the peak season they're often fully booked, so buy tickets early. In a choppy sea a trip may leave you saddle-sore, and beware, if the weather is very bad, they won't leave. The principal companies departing from the mainland are **Minoan** (from Zéa Marína in Piraeus for the Saronic Islands and Crete, and from Vólos, Ag. Konstantínos, and Thessaloníki for the Sporades, information **t** 010 408 0006 and 010 324 4600; and **Ellas Flying Dolphins**, with departures for the Cyclades and Sporades, information **t** 010 419 9200/419 9000.

## Tourist Excursion Boats

These are generally slick, numerous and more expensive than the regular ferries. But they often have schedules that allow visitors to make day trips to nearby islands, and are very convenient, having taken the place of the little caique operators, many of whom now specialize in excursions to remote beaches. Hydrofoils may allow for day trips to neighbouring islands too, but beware: all water transport is at the mercy of fickle Greek gales.

## Boats to Turkey

Whatever axes are currently being ground between Greece and Turkey, a kind of *pax tourista* has fallen over the mutually profitable exchange of visitors from the Greek islands to the Turkish mainland. Ferries run daily year-round between Rhodes and Marmaris (3½hrs); between Kos and Bodrum (1½hrs); from Chíos to Çeşme (1hr); from Sámos to Kuşadasi near Ephesus (1½hrs); and from Lésbos to Ayvalik (15 June–December only, 2hrs); in season excursion boats also sail over from most of the smaller Dodecanese. Prices, once outrageous, are more reasonable, although there is a mysterious array of taxes on both sides (sometimes less for a day excursion). Also, beware the charter restriction: if you spend a night in Turkey, the Greek authorities might invoke the law and refuse you passage home on your flight.

# By Car

There are countless rent-a-car firms on the islands; most are family-run, and fairly reliable (asking around will usually reveal who the stinkers are). If an island has a lot of unpaved roads and not a lot of competition, prices tend to be higher; at the time of writing, hiring a small car averages around €45–55 a day in the summer, and open-air Jeeps at least a third more. Most require that you be at least 21, some 25. Read the small print of your contract with care (look out for mileage limits, etc.), don't be surprised if you have to leave your driving licence as security. In the off season, negiotiate. Arriving at a car hire agent's with brochures from the competition has been known to strengthen one's bargaining position. Fuel at the time of writing is around 90¢ a litre; unleaded (*amólivdi*) a wee bit less.

While driving in the centre of Athens may be a hair-raising experience, the rest of Greece is fairly pleasant. There are few cars on most roads, even in summer, and most signs, when you're lucky enough to find one, have their Latin equivalents. Traffic regulations and signalling comply with standard practice on the European Continent (i.e. driving on the right). Crossroads, tipsy tourists, Greeks arguing and gesticulating while driving, and low visibility in the mountains are probably the greatest hazards. Where there are no right-of-way signs at a crossroads, give priority to traffic coming from the right, and always beep your horn on blind corners. If you're exploring, you may want to take a spare container of petrol along, as stations can be scarce (especially on the islands) and only open shop hours. There is a speed limit of 50km per hour (30mph) in inhabited areas.

## By Motorbike and Moped

Motorbikes and even more popular mopeds are ideal for the islands in the summer. It almost never rains, and what could be more pleasant than a gentle thyme-scented breeze freshening your journey? Scooters (the Greeks call them *papákia*, 'little ducks', supposedly for the noise they make) are more economical and practical than cars. They fit into almost any boat and travel paths where cars fear to tread. Rental rates vary (count on at least €15 a day), and include third party insurance coverage in most cases. You will need a valid driving licence (for Americans, this means an international one) For larger motorbikes (over 75cc) you may be asked to show a motorcycle driver's licence. The down-sides: many of the bikes are poorly maintained, many of the roads are poorly maintained, and everyone takes too many risks: hospital beds in Greece fill up each summer with foreign and Greek casualties (check your insurance to see if you're covered). Most islands have laws about operating motorbikes after midnight (the 'little ducks', often stripped of their mufflers, tend to howl like a flock of Daffys and Donalds on amphetamines) but they are as enforced as often as the compulsory helmet requirement. Actually, no: you do see Greeks wearing helmets, but only on their elbows, which, judging by the way they drive their machines, must be where they keep their brains. Literally hundreds of people, nearly all young, are killed every year in Greece. Be careful.

## By Bicycle

Cycling has not caught on in mountainous Greece, either as a sport or as a means of transport, though you can usually hire an old bike in most major resorts. Trains and planes carry bicycles for a small fee, and Greek boats generally take them along for nothing. Crete and Évia are the best islands for cycling, Crete being the more rugged by far. On both islands you will find fresh water, places to camp, and a warm and surprised welcome in the villages.

## Hitchhiking

Greek taxi drivers have recently convinced the government to pass a law forbidding other Greeks from picking up hitchhikers. As with the aforementioned helmet-wearing law, this is regarded as optional, but it is true that you may find hitching slow going; perhaps because of the law, motorized holidaymakers now seem to stop and offer more rides than the locals. The Greek double standard produces the following percentages for hopeful hitchhikers:

Single woman: 99% of cars will stop. You hardly have to stick out your thumb.
Two women: 75% of cars will find room for you.
Woman and man: 50%; more if the woman is pretty.
Single man: 25% if you are well dressed with little luggage; less otherwise.
Two men: start walking.

## Yachting, Sailing and Flotilla Holidays

*Are we sailing straight, or is the shore crooked?*
Old Greek proverb

One of the great thrills of sailing the Greek waters is the variety of places to visit in a relatively short time, with the bonus that nowhere in Greece is far from safe harbours with good facilities for yachtsmen. There is little shallow water, except close to the shoreline, few currents and no tides or fog. The 100,000 miles of coastline, and a collection of islands numbering 3,000, provide a virtually inexhaustible supply of secluded coves and empty beaches, even at the height of the tourist season. Equally, there are berthing facilities in the most popular of international hotspots – it's all there beneath the blue skies. The Greek National Tourist Organization has

# Specialist Tour Operators

A complete list is available from the
**National Tourist Organization of Greece**
(*see* p.86).

## In the UK

**Amathus Holidays**, 2 Leather Lane, London, EC1N 7RA, **t** (020) 7611 0901 *www .amathusholidays.co.uk*. Villas, apartments and hotels and cruise holidays.

**Argo Holidays**, 100 Wigmore St, London, W1 3RS, **t** 08700 677070, *www.argo-holidays .com*. Variety of holidays from painting and photography to watersports.

**British Museum Tours**, 46 Bloomsbury St, London WC1B 3QQ, **t** (020) 7436 7575, *www .britishmuseumtraveller.co.uk*. Different archaeological guided tours every year.

**Cox & Kings**, Gordon House, 10 Greencoat Lane, London SW1P 1PH, **t** (020) 7873 5027, *www.coxandkings.co.uk*. Botanic holidays to various islands (Lésbos and Sámos 2002).

**Explore Worldwide**, 1 Frederick St, Aldershot, Hants GUII ILQ, **t** (01252) 760101, *www .exploreworldwide.com*. Rambles in western Crete; caique cruises; Aegean Island hikes; Cyclades Island tour.

**Filoxenia**, Sourdock Hill, Barkisland, Halifax, West Yorkshire, HX4 0AG, **t** (01422) 375999, *www.filoxenia.co.uk*. Archaeological, walking, wine and cookery tours in Crete; cookery on Corfu and Léros; painting groups in Kýthera, and various holidays in Évia.

**Greco-File**, **t** (01422) 310330, *www.filoxenia .co.uk/greco.htm*. The dedicated Greek branch of Filoxenia. Expert advice on where to go, flights and '*couture*' holidays to unusual islands for the discerning traveller.

**Greek Islands Club**, 10–12 Upper Square, Old Isleworth, Middx, TW7 7BJ, **t** (020) 8232 9780, *www.sunvil.co.uk/sites/gic*. Helpful and friendly with choice villas and a range of activity holidays on the Ionian islands, Crete, Skiáthos and Skópelos, incl. sailing, water-sports and traditional Greek villages.

**Headwater Holidays**, 146 London Road, Northwich, Cheshire, CW9 5HH **t** (01606) 813333, *www.headwater-holidays.co.uk*. Walking holidays in Crete and Kefaloniá.

**Hidden Greece**, 47 Whitcomb St, London, WC2H 7DH, **t** (020) 7839 2553, **f** (020) 7839 4327. Organize language holidays in the Cyclades, Dodecanese, Crete and Rhodes.

**Island Holidays**, Drummond St, Comrie, PH6 2DS, **t** (01764) 670107, *www.24islandholidays.com*. Nature tours to Crete and Lésbos.

**Island Wandering**, 51A London Road, Hurst Green, Sussex TN19 7QP, **t** (01580) 860733, **f** (01580) 860282. Hotels and studios in the Cyclades, Ionians, Dodecanese, and NE Aegean, pre-booked or with a wandering voucher system.

**Laskarina Holidays**, St Mary's Gate, Wirksworth, Matlock, DE4 4DQ, **t** (01629) 822203, *www.laskarina.co.uk*. Painting holidays on the more remote Islands: Chálki, Sými, Tílos, Sámos, Ikaría, Kálymnos, Léros, Lipsí, Pátmos, Alónissos and Skópelos.

**Martin Randall**, 10 Barley Mow Passage, Chiswick, W4 4PH, **t** (020) 8742 3355. Cultural tours to Crete and Athens.

**Naturetrek**, Cheriton Mill, Cheriton, Alresford, Hampshire, SO24 0NG, **t** (01962) 733051, *www.naturetrek.co.uk*. Birdwatching and botanical trips to Crete and Lésbos.

**Peligoni Club**, PO Box 88, Chichester, W Sussex PO20 7DP **t** (01243) 511499, *www.peligoni .com*. A one-off, friendly, English-run water-sports club on the northeast coast of Zákynthos. They now also offer painting, sailing and relaxation holidays.

**Ramblers Holidays**, PO Box 43, Welwyn Garden City, Hertfordshire AL8 6PQ, **t** (01707) 331133, *www.ramblersholidays.co.uk*. Walking tours in Crete and Sámos.

**Simply Simon Holidays**, 1/45 Nevern Square London Sw5 9PF, **t** (020) 7373 1933, *www .simplysimon.co.uk*. Villas and hotels in the Cyclades, as well as naturist holidays.

**Skýros Holistic Holidays**, 92 Prince of Wales Rd, London NW5 3NE, **t** (020) 7284 3065, *www .skyros.com*. Creative writing courses, water-sports, spiritual development courses, artists' workshops, holistic bodywork work-shops in yoga, dance and massage.

**Solo's Holidays Ltd**, 54–8 High St, Edgware, Middx HA8 7EJ, **t** (020) 8951 2800, *www .solosholidays.co.uk*. Singles' group holidays in 4-star hotels in Aegina, Skópelos, Kos, Zákynthos, Rhodes, Corfu, Póros and Crete. For independent people in the 30–49 and 50–69 age brackets. Also spring and autumn rambling breaks in Évia.

**Sovereign**, Groundstar House, London Rd, Crawley, W Sussex, RH10 2TB, t 0870 366 1634, *www.sovereign.com*. Their 'Small World' holidays offer villa parties for single travellers in traditional houses on Sými and Kálymnos. Also 'Caique Cruising' for singles afloat. Like a villa party on the ocean waves with excellent food and drink and a chance to meet people and see the islands.

**Swan Hellenic Cruises**, 77 New Oxford St, London WC1A 1PP, t (020) 7800 2200, *www .swanhellenic.com*. Cultural, archaeological and art history tours and cruises.

**Travelux Holidays**, 40 High St, Tenterden, Kent, t 01580 765000, *www.travelux.co.uk*. Accommodation, fly-drive and special interest holidays; painting and photography, walking and trekking, sailing and yoga.

**Voyages of Discovery**, Lymen House, 1 Victoria Way, Burgess Hill BH15 9NF, t (01444) 462150, *www.voyagesofdiscovery.com*. Luxury cruises.

**Waymark Holidays**, 44 Windsor Rd, Slough SL1 2EJ, t (01753) 516477, *www .waymarkholidays.com*. Guided hiking groups on Milos, Crete and Sámos, spring and autumn breaks.

**Yoga Plus**, 177 Ditchling Road, Brighton, East Sussex, BN1 6JB, t (01273) 276175, *www.yogaplus.co.uk*. In Southern Crete, yoga and other holistic therapies.

## In the USA and Canada

**Aegean Workshops**, 148 Old Black Point Rd, Niantic, CT, 06357, t (941) 455 2623. Harry J. Danos, a university art teacher, offers water colour, drawing and design workshops of 15 to 21 days on Mýkonos, Pátmos, Sámos or Santoríni.

**Central Holiday Tours**, 120 Sylvan Avenue, Englewood Cliffs, NJ, USA 07632, t 800 935 5000, *www.centralh.com*. Tours in ancient history and archaeology, 'In the Steps of St. Paul', mythology and theatre.

**Classic Adventures**, PO Box 143, Hamlin, NY 14464, t (716) 964 8488, toll free t 800 777 8090, f 964 7297, *www.calssicadventures .com*. Bicycling and walking holidays in Crete.

**Cloud Tours**, Newtown Plaza, 31-09 Newtown Ave, 3rd Floor, L.I.C., N.Y. 11102, t (718) 721 3808, toll free 1 800 223 7880, f (718) 721 4019, *www.cloudtours.com*. Cruise and land tours, island-hopping and luxury hotels.

**Destination and Adventures International**, 8489 Crescent Drive, Los Angeles, CA 90046, t (323) 650 7267, 1 800 659 4599, f (323) 650 6902, *www.daitravel.co.uk*. Island cycling tours.

**FITS Equestrian**, 685 Lateen Rd, Solvang, CA, 93463, t (805) 688 9494, toll free 800 666 3487. Riding tours of Crete.

**Friends Travel**, P.O. Box 691309, West Hollywood, CA 90069, t (310) 652 9600, f (310) 652 5454. Gay and lesbian tours.

**IST Cultural Tours**, 225 West 34th St, Suite 913, New York, NY 10122, t (212) 563 1202, toll free 800 833 2111, f 594 6953, *www.ist-tours .com*. Customized tours including yacht cruises and lectures on archaeology.

**Meander Adventures**, 2029 Sidewinder Drive, P.O. Box 2730, Park City, UT 84060, t 800 367 3230 (toll Free in USA), 435 649 2495, f 435 649 1192, *www.greece-travel-turkey-travel.com*. Organized tours, boating and sailing holidays and also personalised itineraries.

**Metro Tours**, 484 Lowell Street, Peabody, MA 01960, USA, t 978 535 4000, toll free 800 221 2810, f 535 8830, *www.metrotours.com*. Specialize in honeymoons, yachting holidays and appropriate hotels.

## In Greece

**Candili**, Prokópi, 34004 Évia, Greece, t (00 30) 974 062100, *www.candili.co.uk*. Wide range of creative courses for all abilities from raku to ceramic sculpture on the idyllic Ahmetaga Estate of the Noel-Baker family in Western Évia. Ethnic accommodation, swimming pool, beach trips and good home cooking.

**Hellenic Culture Centre**, Ikaría, t (00 30) 275 061140 (00 30 2275061140 from October 2002), *www.hcc.gr*. Greek language courses pitched at all levels of ability.

**Hellenic Society for the Study and Protection of Dolphins and Whales**, 201 Thessalias St, 13231 Petroúpolis, Athens. Study cruises in the Ionian Sea, keeping tabs on the dolphin population.

**The Path of Avatar**, Corfu, t (00 30) 663 051845. Consciousness-raising (in English) with Nayana Gabriele Keller Jutta Weyck.

initiated a programme of rapid expansion in the face of mounting competition from Turkey and Spain; facilities are being improved and new marinas constructed everywhere.

Island group maps show main yacht supply stations and ports of entry and exit. Greek weather guarantees near-perfect sailing conditions. The only real problem you'll encounter are the strong winds in parts of the country at certain times of the year, notably April to October, when most yachtsmen are at sea. The Ionian Sea and the west coast of the Peloponnese are affected by the *maistros*, a light-to-moderate northwest wind which presents itself in the afternoon only. Less frequently there are westerly winds, from moderate to strong, to the west and south of the Peloponnese. To the south of Attica, and east of the Peloponnese, the sea is largely sheltered by land masses and it's not until summer that the menacing *meltémi* blows. The Aegean Sea is affected by a northwest wind in the south, and a northeasterly in the north, and when the *meltémi* blows in August and September, it can reach force eight. The Turkish coast has light, variable breezes, which are rudely interrupted by the forceful *meltémi*.

If you wish to skipper a yacht anywhere within the Greek seas, consult the *Compile Index Chart of Greek Seas (XEE)*, published by the Hellenic Navy Hydrographic Service. Basically it is a map of Greece divided into red squares, each with an index number, from which you can select the appropriate charts and order them accordingly. For non-Greeks, you can buy what is known as *XEE 64*, a booklet of abbreviations explaining the signs on the charts, with texts in English and Greek.

You also need one of the Pilot series books, which cover the following areas in great detail:

*Pilot A*: South Albania to Kýthera; Ionian Sea, Corinthian Gulf and North Peloponnese shores.

*Pilot B*: Southeastern Greek shores; Crete, Eastern Peloponnese, Saronic Gulf and Cyclades.

*Pilot C*: Northeastern Greek shores; Evoikos, Pagassitikos, Sporades, Thermaikos, Chalkidikí.

*Pilot D*: Northeastern Aegean shores; Eastern Macedonia, Thrace, Límnos, Lésbos, Chíos, Sámos, the Dodecanese and Asia Minor.

These describe geographical data, possible dangers, and the present state of transportation and communication. All ports and marinas are mentioned, including where to obtain fresh water and fuel, and there are descriptions of visible inland features. The Hydrographic Service constantly updates the books and sends additional booklets to authorized sellers and to port authorities, where you may consult them. The nautical charts are updated using the latest sophisticated methods, and follow standardized dimensions. They are on a 1:100,000 scale for bigger areas and 1:750,000 for ports. Heights and depths are given in metres with functional conversion tables for feet and fathoms.

Further information is provided in *Notes to Mariners*, published monthly and available for consultation at port authorities. These give information on any alterations to naval charts you have purchased for your voyage. Besides all this there is the Navtex service. A special department of the Hydrographic Service keeps you informed about the weather or any special warnings for the day, through telex or Navtex. The text is in Greek and English, and there are four re-transmission coastal stations covering the Greek seas. Weather forecasts for yachtsmen are broadcast at intervals throughout the day on VHF Channel 16 (in Greek and English); security warnings are also broadcast on this channel, e.g. dangerous wrecks, lights not in operation.

Yachts entering Greek waters must fly the code flag 'Q' until cleared by entry port authorities. Upon arrival the port authority (*Limenarchíon*) issues all yachts with a transit log, which entitles the yacht and crew to unlimited travel in Greek waters. It must be kept on board and produced when required, and returned to the customs authorities on leaving Greece at one of the exit ports. Permission is normally given for a stay of 6 months, but this can be extended. Small motor, sail or rowing boats do not require a '*carnet de passage*', and are allowed into Greece duty free for 4 months. They are entered in your passport and deleted on exit. For more information, apply to the **National Tourist Organization**, 4 Conduit St, London W1R 0DJ, **t** (020) 7734 5997, who produce a useful booklet, *Yachting*, which lists all official ports of entry or exit and every marina in

## Yacht Operators

**Anemos Yachting**, 39 Thoukididou, Alimos 174 55, t 010 985 0052, *www.anemos-yachting.gr*

**Cosmos Yachting**, 6 Rocks Lane, London SW13 0DB, t 0800 376 9070, *www.cosmosyachting .com*. Charters around the islands.

**Ghiolman Yachts**, 7 Filellínon St, Sýntagma, 10557, Athens, t 010 323 3696, *www .ghiolman.com*.

**Greek Island Cruise Centre**, 4321 Lakemoor Dr, Wilmington, 28405, USA, t 800 341 3030.

**Interpac Yachts**, 1050 Anchorage Lane, San Diego, CA, 92106 USA, toll free t 888 99 YACHT, *www.interpacyachts.com*.

**Just Boats**, Kontakáli 49100 Corfu, t (00 30) 661 90932, *just_boats@ker.forthnet.gr*. Crewed and bareboat yachts, flotillas.

**McCulloch Yacht Charter**, 32 Fairfield Rd, London E3 2QB, t (020) 8983 1487.

**The Moorings**, Bradstowe House, Middle Wall, Whitstable, CT5 1BF, England t (01227) 776677, *www.moorings.com*. Charters from Corfu, Skiáthos, Kos and Athens.

**Odysseus Yachting Holidays**, Temple Craft Yacht Charters, Middleham, Ringmer, Lewes, BN8 5EY t (01273) 812333, *www.odysseus .co.uk*. Flotillas around the Ionian Islands.

**Neilson Active Holidays**, Brighton Marina, Lock View, Brighton, BN2 5HA, t 0870 333335, *www.neilson.co.uk*. Flotilla holidays.

**Sunsail**, The Port House, Port Solent, Portsmouth PO6 4TH, t 0870 777 0313, *www.sunsail.com/uk*. Flotillas, tuitional sailing and watersports.

**Tenrag Yacht Charters**, Tenrag House, Freepost CU986, Preston, Kent CT3 1NB, t (01227) 721874, *www.tenrag.com*. Charters from Athens, Corfu, Rhodes and Mýkonos.

**Valef**, 7254 Fir Rd, PO Box 391, Ambler, Pa 19002, USA, t 800 223 3845, *valefyachts .com*. Reputable firm, 300 crewed yachts.

**Womanship, Learn to Sail Cruises For and By Women**, USA, t 800 324 9295, *www .womanship.com*. Women-only flotillas.

**Yacht Agency Rhodes**, 1 Byronos and Kanada St, P.O. Box 393, 85100 Rhodes, t (00 30) 241 22927, *www.yachtagency.com*

Greece, with a complete list of facilities offered, whether repair services, fuelling, telephones, showers or laundrettes. For more information in Greece, call the **National Tourist Organization**, Marine Division, 2 Amerikis, Athens, t 010 327 1672 or the Piraeus Port Authority, t 010 451 1311.

Anyone taking a yacht by road is advised to obtain boat registration documentation from the DVLA, Swansea SA99 1BX, t 0870 2400010. **The Royal Yachting Association**, R.Y.A. House, Romsey Road, Eastleigh, Hampshire SO5 9YA, t 023 8062 7400, *www.rya.org.uk*, is a useful source of yachting information.

### Yacht Charter

Chartering yachts is very popular and can be cheaper than staying in a hotel (if you have enough friends to share expenses). Between the various firms there are over 4,000 vessels available in all sizes, with or without a crew (without a crew – bareboat charter – both the charterer and another member of the party must show an official certificate as proof of seamanship). There are various options: motor yachts (without sails), motor sailors (primarily powered by motor, auxiliary sail power) and sailing yachts (with auxiliary motor power).

The National Tourist Organization has a list of Greek charter firms, or contact:

**The Hellenic Professional Yacht Owners Assoc.** Zéa Marína, Piraeus 18536, t 010 452 6335 and 010 428 0465, f 010 452 6335.

**Greek Yacht Brokers and Consultants Assoc.** P.O.Box 30393, 10033 Athens, t 010 985 0122.

**Yacht Charter Assoc.** Deacons Boatyard, Burseldon Bridge, Southampton SO31 8AZ, UK, t (023) 8040 7075, *www.yca.co.uk*. Supplies a list of recognized operators and advice on chartering overseas.

### Flotilla and Sailing Holidays

If you want to float among the islands, but don't own a yacht, or lack the experience to charter one, a flotilla holiday may be the answer. A growing number of companies offer 1–2-week sailing holidays, some instructing inexperienced sailors (beginning with a week on land). High season prices for a 2 week holiday are £600–1,000 p/p, on a 4-person yacht. The yachts have 4–8 berths (shared boats available for couples and singles) and sail in flotillas, usually 6–12 yachts, with experienced skipper, engineer and social hostess.

# Practical A–Z

07

# Children

Greeks love children, and children usually love Greece. Depending on their age, they go free or receive discounts on ships and buses. However, if they're babies, don't count on island pharmacies stocking your brand of milk powder or baby foods – it's safest to bring your own supply. Disposable nappies, especially Pampers, are widely available.

Travelling with a tot is like having a special passport. Greeks spoil them rotten, so don't be surprised if your infant is passed around like a parcel. Greek children usually have an afternoon nap (as do their parents) so it's quite normal for Greeks to eat *en famille* until the small hours. Finding a babysitter is rarely a problem: some of the larger hotels even offer special supervised kiddie campgrounds and activity areas for some real time off.

Superstitions are still given more credit than you might expect; you'll see babies with amulets pinned to their clothes or wearing blue beads to ward off the evil eye before their baptism. When commenting on a Greek child's beauty or intelligence, be prepared to offer a ritual dry spit sound, 'phtew, phtew, phtew', in the direction of the admired one. The 'spitting' admits the jealousy you may be feeling and thus wards off evil spirits. If you neglect this, don't be surprised if the old granny or even the trendy young mum, do the 'phtewing' for you, and add the sign of the cross and a small prayer to the Virgin to boot.

# Climate, Measurements and Time

Greece enjoys hot, dry, clear and bright Mediterranean summers, cooled by winds, of which the *meltémi* from the northeast is the most notorious and most likely to upset Aegean sailing schedules. Winters are mild, and in general the wet season begins at the end of October or beginning of November when it can rain 'tables and chairs' as the Greeks say. It begins to feel springlike in February, especially in Crete and Rhodes, when the first wild flowers appear.

Two uniquely Greek **measurements** you may come across are the *strémma*, a Greek land measurement (1 *strémma* = ¼ acre), and the *oká*, an old-fashioned weight standard, divided into 400 drams (1 *oká* = 3lb; 35 drams = ¼lb, 140 drams = 1lb).

'God gave watches to the Europeans and time to the Greeks,' they say, but if you need more precision, **Greek time** is Eastern European, two hours ahead of Greenwich Mean Time, seven hours ahead of Eastern Standard Time in North America.

# Disabled Travellers

Many of the Greek islands, with their ubiquitous steps and absence of suitable transport, would put severe constraints on visitors in chairs, and ferry and hydrofoil access is difficult. Major islands such as Corfu and Rhodes and many smaller ones that receive lots of visitors (such as Skiáthos, Zákynthos and Kos) have hotels with facilities – the Greek National Tourist Office has a list.

# Eating Out

A Greek menu (*katálogos*) often has two prices for each item – with and without tax. In most restaurants there's also a small cover charge. If you eat with the Greeks, there's no Western nit-picking over who's had what. You share the food, drink, company and the bill,

| Average Daily Temperatures in °C/°F | | | | | | | | |
|---|---|---|---|---|---|---|---|---|
| | Athens | Crete (Heráklion) | Cyclades (Mýkonos) | Dodecs (Rhodes) | Ionian (Corfu) | N.E. Aeg (Mytilíni) | Saronic (Hýdra) | Sporades (Skýros) |
| Jan | 11/48 | 12/54 | 12/54 | 12/54 | 10/50 | 10/50 | 12/53 | 10/51 |
| April | 16/60 | 17/62 | 17/60 | 17/60 | 15/60 | 16/60 | 16/61 | 15/58 |
| July | 28/82 | 26/78 | 25/76 | 27/78 | 27/78 | 27/80 | 28/82 | 25/77 |
| Aug | 28/82 | 26/78 | 25/76 | 27/79 | 27/78 | 27/80 | 28/82 | 25/77 |
| Sept | 25/76 | 25/76 | 23/74 | 25/78 | 23/74 | 23/74 | 25/76 | 22/71 |
| Nov | 15/58 | 18/64 | 17/62 | 17/66 | 15/ 58 | 15/58 | 17/62 | 15/58 |

# Organizations for Disabled Travellers

## Greece
The Panhellenic Association for the Blind, 31 Veranzérou St, Athens, 104 32, t 010 522 8333, f 010 522 2112.

## UK
**Thomsons**, and several other big package holiday companies, have some suitable tours. Otherwise, consult:

**Access Travel**, 6 The Hillock, Astley, Lancashire, M29 7GW, t (01942) 888 844, info@access-travel.co.uk, www.access-travel.co.uk. Travel agent for disabled people with a base in Rhodes: special airfares, car hire and suitable accommodation.

**Chalfont Line Holidays**, t (020) 8997 3799, f (020) 8991 2982, www.chalfont-line.co.uk. Escorted or individual holidays for disabled people.

**Greco-File's Opus 23**, t (01422) 310330, f (01422) 310340, www.filoxenia.co.uk/greco.htm. Offers special needs holidays and accommodation on the islands.

**Holiday Care Service**, Imperial Building, Victoria Rd, Horley, Surrey, RH6 7PZ, t (01293) 774535, f (01293) 784647, www.holidaycare.org.uk.

**RADAR** (Royal Association for Disability and Rehabilitation), 12 City Forum, 250 City Rd, London, EC1V 8AS, t (020) 7250 3222, www.radar.org.uk. Publishes *Holidays and Travel Abroad: A Guide for Disabled People*.

**Tripscope**, t (020) 8994 9294.

## USA
**Alternative Leisure Co**, 165 Middlesex Turnpike, Suite 206, Bedford, MA 01730, t (718) 275 0023, www.alctrips.com. Organizes vacations abroad for disabled people.

**Mobility International USA**, PO Box 10767, Eugene, OR 97440, USA, t/TTY (541) 343 1284, www.miusa.org. Information on international educational exchange programmes and volunteer service overseas for the disabled.

**SATH, (Society for Accessible Travel and Hospitality)**, 347 Fifth Avenue, Suite 610, New York, NY 10016, t (212) 557 0027, f (212) 725 8253, www.sath.org. Travel and access information.

## Other Useful Contacts
**The Able Informer**, www.sasquatch.com/able-info. International on-line magazine with tips for travelling abroad.

**Access Ability**, www.access-ability.co.uk. Information on travel agencies catering specifically for disabled people.

**Access Tourism**, www.accesstourism.com. Pan-European website with information on hotels, guesthouses, travel agencies catering for disabled people.

**Emerging Horizons**, www.emerginghorizons.com. International on-line travel newsletter for people with disabilities.

**Global Access**, www.geocities.com. On-line network for disabled travellers, with links, archives and information on travel guides for the disabled.

---

to *logariasmó*, although hosts will seldom let foreign guests part with a cent. The restaurants we recommend serve typical Greek food. In the fleshpot towns you'll find many fast-food chains and on the most touristy islands, a growing number of ethnic restaurants.

In the 'Eating Out' sections of this book, a price is only given when it exceeds the average and is per person with house wine. A typical meal at the huge majority of tavernas – if you don't order a major fish – usually runs at around €10–15 a head with generous carafes of house wine. Prices at sophisticated restaurants or blatantly touristy places with views can be much higher. Quite a few places

now offer set price meals with a glass of wine (often for under €10), some for two people, some better than others. In most places, waiters are paid a cut of the profits (which is why some obnoxiously tout for custom in busy resorts); tipping is discretionary but very much appreciated. By law, there's a little book by the door if you want to register a complaint. A law designed to catch tax evaders insists that you take a receipt (*apóthixi*) 150m from the door; the police make periodical checks. Recently, a boy on a beach was fined for not having a receipt for his ice cream, but his lawyer got him off as he had no pockets in his swimming trunks!

For further information about eating in the Greek Islands, including local specialities, wines and a menu decoder, see the **Food and Drink** chapter, p.53.

# Embassies and Consulates (in Athens)

**Australia**: 37 D. Soútsou, t 010 645 0404, f 010 646 6595.

**Canada**: 4 Ioan. Gennadíou, t 010 727 3400, f 010 725 3460.

**Ireland**: 7 Vass. Konstantínou, t 010 723 2771, f 010 729 3383. Also see Corfu.

**New Zealand**: 268 Kifissías, t 010 687 4701, f 010 687 4444.

**South Africa**: 60 Kifissías, t 010 610 6645, f 010 610 6636.

**UK**: 1 Ploutárchou St, t 010 727 2600, f 010 727 2720. Also see Corfu, Rhodes, and Heráklion (Crete).

**USA**: 91 Vassilías Sofías, t 010 721 2951, f 010 645 6282.

# Health and Emergencies

For **first aid**, go to the nearest Local Health Centre (ESY or 'kentro eEas') which are well equipped to deal with snake bite, jelly fish stings, grippe, etc., and treat foreigners for free. Where there are no ESY, the rural doctors (iatrós – there is at least one on every island with more than a couple of hundred people) do the same work, also for free.

For more **serious illnesses** or accidents, you'll need the hospital (nosokomio); the larger islands have them, and helicopters act as ambulances when necessary. EU citizens are entitled to free medical care; British travellers are often urged to carry a **Form E111**, available from DHSS offices (apply well in advance with a form available at all post offices), which will admit them to the most basic IKA (Greek NHS) hospitals for treatment; but this doesn't cover medicines or nursing care. In any case, the E111 is often looked on with total disregard outside Athens; expect to pay up front, and get receipts so you can be reimbursed back home. As private doctors and hospital stays can be very expensive, consider a **travel insurance** policy with adequate repatriation cover.

Non-Europeans should check their own health policies to see if they're covered while abroad.

Greek general practitioners' fees (office hours are 9–1 and 5–7) are usually reasonable. Most doctors pride themselves on their English, as do the **pharmacists** (found in the farmakeío), whose advice on minor ailments is good, although their medicine is not particularly cheap. If you forgot to bring your own condoms and are caught short, they are widely available from farmakeío, kiosks and supermarkets, with lusty brand names such as 'Squirrel' or 'Rabbit'. If you can't see them on display, the word kapótes (condom) gets results. You can also get the Pill (chápi anti-siliptikó), the morning-after Pill and HRT over the pharmacy counter without a prescription. Be sure to take your old packet to show them the brand you use.

For some reason Greeks buy more medicines than anyone else in Europe (is it hypochondria? the old hoarding instinct?), but you shouldn't have to. The strong sun is the most likely cause of grief, so be careful, hatted and sunscreened. If you find the olive oil too much, Coca Cola or retsina will help cut it. Fresh parsley is good for stomach upsets. See pp.43–5 for possibly unkind wildlife. If anything else goes wrong, do what the islanders have done for centuries: pee on it.

# Money and Banks

As of 1 January 2002, the official **currency** in Greece is the euro (evró), circulating in notes of 5, 10, 20, 50, 100, 200 and 500, with coins of €1 and €2, then 1¢, 2¢, 5¢, 10¢, 20¢, 50¢. Whilst on the one hand Greece (unlike some of its European partners) has embraced the euro – it means stability in an economy with a recent history of uncontrolled inflation – many mourn the demise of the old currency, the drachma, depicting heroes from mythology, history and the country's long struggle for independence and freedom, symbols still vital to the Greek psyche.

The word for **bank** in Greek is trápeza, derived from the word trapézi, or table, used back in the days of money-changers. On all the islands with more than goats and a few shepherds there is some sort of banking establishment, or increasingly, at least an automatic teller. If there's no bank, then travel agents, tourist offices or post offices will change cash and traveller's cheques. If you plan to spend time on a remote island, such as Schinoússa, it is safest to bring enough cash with you. Beware that small but popular islands often have only one bank, where exchanging money can take forever: beat the crowds by going at 8.20am, when the banks open (*normal banking hours are 8.20–2, 8.20– 1.30 on Fri*). The number of 24-hour **automatic cash-tellers** on the islands grows every year: some accept one kind of credit card and not another (VISA is perhaps the most widely accepted). You can also use these to withdraw cash at banks. Major hotels, luxury shops and resort restaurants take credit cards (look for the little signs), however, smaller hotels and tavernas certainly won't.

**Traveller's cheques** are always useful even though commission rates are less for cash. The major brands (Thomas Cook and American Express) are accepted in all banks and post offices; take your passport as ID, and shop around for commission rates.

**Running out?** Athens and Piraeus, with offices of many British and American banks, are the easiest places to have money sent by cash transfer from someone at home – though it may take a few days. **American Express** may be helpful here; their office in Athens is 2 Ermou St, right by Sýntagma Square, t 010 324 4975, and there are branches on Corfu, Mýkonos, Pátras, Rhodes, Santoríni, Skiáthos and Thessaloníki.

# National Holidays

Note that most businesses and shops close down for the afternoon before and the morning after a religious holiday. If a national holiday falls on a Sunday, the following Monday is often observed. The Orthodox Easter is generally a week or so after the Roman Easter.

In Greece, Easter is the equivalent in signifi- cance of Christmas and New Year in northern climes, the time when far-flung relatives return to see their families back home; it's a good time of year to visit for the atmosphere, feasts and fireworks. After Easter and 1 May, spring (*ánixi* – the opening) has officially

## National Holidays

**1 January** New Year's Day, *Protochroniá*; also Ag. *Vassílis* (Greek Father Christmas)
**6 January** Epiphany, *Ta Fóta/Theofánia*
**February–March** 'Clean Monday', *Katharí Deftéra* (precedes Shrove Tuesday, and follows a three-week carnival)
**25 March** Annunciation/Greek Independence Day, *Evangelismós*
**late March–April** Good Friday, *Megáli Paraskeví*, Easter Sunday, *Páscha* and Easter Monday, *Theftéra tou Páscha*
**1 May** Labour Day, *Protomayá*
**40 days after Easter** Pentecost (Whit Monday) *Pentikostí*
**15 August** Assumption of the Virgin, *Koímisis tis Theotókou*
**28 October** 'Ochí' Day (in celebration of Metaxás' 'no' to Mussolini)
**25 December** Christmas, *Christoúyena*
**26 December** Gathering of the Virgin, *Sináxi Theotókou*

come, and the tourist season begins. It's also worth remembering when planning your visit, that the main partying often happens the night *before* the saint's day.

# Opening Hours

The usual hours for **archaeological sites** and **museums** are Tuesday to Sunday, 8 or 9am to 2 or 3pm, closed Monday; major attractions such as Knóssos or Délos open daily and have much longer hours, although these are shorter in the winter. All close on 1 Jan, 25 Mar, Good Friday, Easter Sunday, 1 May, 25 May and 26 Dec. **Admission fees** are usually between €1.50 and €3; more expensive ones are listed as such in the text. Students with valid ID usually get a discount, and in state museums visitors under 18 or over 65 with ID get in cheaper or often free. Admission is free to all on Sundays from 1 Nov to 31 March and on 6 Mar, 18 April, 18 May, 5 June and last Saturday and Sunday in September.

Because of a surge in thefts, churches only open when there is someone around, often in the late afternoon (6–7pm); at other times you may have to hunt down the key (*kleethEE*). Monasteries tend to close for a couple of hours at midday. Note that visitors are expected to make a small contribution, or at least buy a candle and dress respectfully. The rule is long pants for men, knees covered for women, arms covered for men and women. Many (but not all) provide long skirts or robes for the scantily clad.

# Packing

Even in the height of summer, evenings can be chilly in Greece, especially when the *meltémi* wind is blowing. Always bring at least one warm sweater and a pair of long trousers, and sturdy and comfortable shoes if you mean to do any walking – trainers (sneakers) are usually good enough. Plastic swimming shoes are handy for rocky beaches, often the haunt of those little black pincushions, sea urchins; you can easily buy them near any beach if you don't want to carry them around with you. Greeks are inveterate night people: bring ear plugs if you don't want to hear them scootering home under your hotel window in the early hours.

Serious sleeping-baggers should bring a Karrimat or similar insulating layer to cushion them from the gravelly Greek ground. Torches come in very handy for moonless nights, caves and rural villages. Note that the **electric current** in Greece is mainly 220 volts, 50Hz; plugs are continental two-pin. Buy an adaptor in the UK before you leave, as they are rare in Greece; North Americans will need adaptors and transformers.

On the pharmaceutical side, bring extras of any prescription drug you need, just in case – other items, such as seasickness remedies, sunscreen, insect repellent, women's sanitary towels and sometimes Tampax, tablets for stomach upsets and aspirin are widely available in pharmacies and even kiosks, but on remote islands you'll need to seek out the *farmakeío*; if there's no pharmacy, you've had it. Soap, washing powder, a clothes line, a knife for picnics and especially a towel are essential budget traveller's gear. Let common sense and the maxim 'bring as little as possible and never more than you can carry' dictate your packing; work on the theory that however much money and clothing you think you need, halve the clothes and double the money.

# Photography

Greece lends herself freely to photography, but a fee is charged at archaeological sites and museums for any professional-looking camera. For a movie camera of any kind, including camcorders, you are encouraged to buy a ticket for the camera; with a tripod you pay per photograph at sites, but cameras (especially tripod-mounted ones) are not allowed in museums, for no particular reason other than the museum's maintaining a monopoly on its own (usually very dull) picture stock. 35mm film, both print and slide, can be found in many island shops, but it can be expensive and the range of film speeds limited. Disposable and underwater cameras are on sale in larger resorts. Large islands even have one-hour developing services.

If you have an expensive camera, it's best to insure it. Above all, never leave it alone. Although Greeks themselves rarely steal anything, other tourists are not so honest.

# Post Offices

Signs for post offices (*tachidromío*) as well as postboxes (*grammatokivótio*) are bright yellow and easy to find. Post offices (which are also useful for changing money) are open Monday–Friday 7.30am–2pm, although in large towns they may be open till 7.30–8pm and on Saturday morning as well. Stamps (*grammatósima*) can also be bought at kiosks and in some tourist shops, although they may charge a small commission. Postcards cost the same as letters and are given the same priority (they take about three days to the UK, unless posted from a remote island). If you're in a hurry, pay extra for an express service. To send a package, always go to an island's main post office. If you do not have an address, mail can be sent to you *poste restante* to any post office in Greece, and picked up with proof of identity (you'll find the postal codes for all the islands in the text, which will get your letters there faster). After one month all unretrieved letters are returned to sender. In small villages, particularly on the islands, mail is not delivered to the house but to the village centre, either a *kafeneíon* or bakery.

# Shopping

Official shopping hours in Greece are: Mon and Wed 9–3; Tues, Thurs and Fri 9–7, Sat 8.30–3.30 and Sun closed; in practice, tourist-orientated shops stay open as late as 1am in season. Leather goods, gold and jewellery, traditional handicrafts, embroideries, and weavings, onyx, ceramics, alabaster, herbs and spices and tacky knick-knacks are favourite purchases; also check the text for island specialities. Rhodes has some of the biggest bargains.

Non-EU citizens tempted by Greek jewellery, carpets, perfumes and other big ticket items can perhaps justify their indulgences by having the sales tax (VAT) reimbursed – this is 18% of the purchase price (or 13%, on Aegean islands). Make sure the shop has a TAX FREE FOR TOURISTS sticker in the window, and pick up a tax-free shopping cheque for your purchases. When you leave Greece, you must show your purchases and get the customs official to stamp your cheques (allow an extra hour for this, especially at the airport), and cash them in at the refund point as you leave. If you are flying out of another EU country, hold onto the cheques, get them stamped again by the other EU country's customs and use their refund point. You can also post your tax free cheques back to Greece for refund (10 Nikis, 10563 Athens, t 010 325 4995, f 010 322 4701), but they skim off 20% of the amount on commission.

# Sports

## Water Sports

Greece was made for water sports, and by law, all the beaches, no matter how private they might look, are public. All but a fraction meet European guidelines for water cleanliness, although a few could stand to have less litter on the sand. Beaches near built-up areas often have umbrellas and sunbed concessions and snack bars, and if there's a breeze you'll probably find a windsurfer to rent at affordable prices (favourite windy spots are Páros –

which holds world championships in August – Lefkáda, Rhodes, Lésbos, and Kárpathos). Bigger beaches have paragliding and jet skis, and waterskiing is available on most islands and large hotel complexes; on Kos you can bungee jump over the sea. The Ministry of Tourism has just allocated huge sums to build up marinas on the islands, which may improve chances of finding a small sail or motor boat to hire by the day; at the time of writing they are relatively few.

**Nudism** is forbidden by law in Greece, but tolerated in numerous designated or out-of-the-way areas. On the other hand, topless sunbathing is now legal on the majority of popular beaches as long as they're not smack in the middle of a village; exercise discretion. Even young Greek women are now shedding their tops, but nearly always on someone else's island.

**Scuba diving**, once strictly banned to keep divers from snatching antiquities and to protect Greece's much-harassed marine life, is permitted between dawn and sunset in specially defined coastal areas; local diving excursions will take you there. There are diving centres and schools on **Crete, Mýkonos, Kálymnos, Rhodes, Skiáthos, Corfu, Páxi** and **Zákynthos**. For information contact the Hellenic Federation of Underwater Activities, t 010 981 9961, or the Owners of Diving Centres, 67 Zeas, Piraeus, t 010 411 8909, f 010 411 9967.

## Land Sports

**Walking** is the favourite activity on every island, but especially on Crete, with its superb natural scenery, gorges, wild flowers and wide open spaces (see 'Specialist Holidays' in the **Travel** chapter, pp.75–6, for guided walking tours). Increasingly locals are arranging treks, and little, often locally produced maps and guides, are a big help for finding the most interesting country paths. Never set out without a hat and water; island shops have begun to sell handy water-bottle shoulder slings. If you like altitudes, Crete has a pair of mountain shelters, and there's one on Évia,

| Average Sea Temperatures in °C/°F | | | | | | | | |
|---|---|---|---|---|---|---|---|---|
| Jan | April | May | July | Aug | Sept | Oct | Nov | Dec |
| 15/59 | 16/61 | 18/64 | 24/75 | 25/77 | 24/75 | 22/72 | 18/64 | 17/63 |

all belonging to the **Greek Mountaineering Club** (5 Milioni St, Athens, **t** 010 364 5904).

Tennis is very popular in Athens with numerous clubs from Glyfáda to Kifissiá, and at all major resort hotels (many are lit up at night so you can beat the heat); often non-residents are allowed to play in the off season. Golf courses are rare and are found only on the islands of Crete, Rhodes and Corfu. Many small stables offer horse-riding on the islands. For precision, call the **Riding Club of Greece**, Parádissos, Athens, **t** 010 681 2506 and **Riding Club of Athens**, Gerákos, **t** 010 661 1088.

# Telephones

The new improved Organismós Tilefikinonía Elládos, or OTE, has replaced most of its old phone offices with new card phones, which work a treat, although many on the islands, for some reason, are set up for basketball players only. If you can reach the buttons, you can dial abroad direct (dial 00 before the country code). Cards (*télekartas*), sold in kiosks, come in denominations from €2.93 to €24.06. OTE also offers a Xronocarta €7.34, which is cheaper for long distance calls, but involves dialling more numbers. Some kiosks (*periptera*), *kafeneíons*, travel agents, hotels, and shops also have a telephone *me métriki* (with a meter), which are often more costly. **Telegrams** can be sent from one of the surviving OTE offices or from the post office. All Greek phone numbers are 10-digit; when **phoning Greece** from abroad, the county code is 30 and drop the first 'o'.

**Note:** In October 2002, the current first 0 of a Greek phone number will be changed to 2 for standard phones and to 6 for mobiles (which are designated as such in the text at the moment). After that, when phoning Greece from abroad, you'll dial the entire number after the 30 prefix.

# Tourist Information

## In Greece

The multilingual tourist information number in Athens, **t** 171 is good for all Greece (outside of Athens, **t** 010 171 or 210 171 after October 2002). As the tourist industry

## Greek Tourist Offices Abroad

If the National Tourist Organization of Greece (in Greek the initials are EOT) can't answer your questions about Greece, at least they can refer you to someone who can.
**Australia and New Zealand:** 51 Pitt Street, Sydney, NSW 2000, **t** 9241 1663/4; **f** 9235 2174.
**Canada:** 1300 Bay St, Toronto, Ontario, M5R3K8, **t** (416) 968 2220, **f** (416) 968 6533. 1233 De La Montagne, Suite 101, Montreal, Quebec, H3G1Z2 **t** (514) 871 1535, **f** (514) 871 1498.
**Netherlands:** Leidsestraat 13, NS 1017 Amsterdam **t** (206) 254 212, **f** (206) 207 031.
**UK and Ireland:** 4 Conduit Street, London W1R 0DJ, **t** (020) 7734 5997, **f** (020) 7287 1369.
**USA:** Head Office: Olympic Tower, 645 Fifth Avenue, 5th Floor, New York, NY 10022, **t** (212) 421 5777; **f** (212) 826 6940, *gnto@orama.com*. 168 N. Michigan Avenue, Chicago, Illinois. 60601, **t** (312) 782 1084; **f** (312) 782 1091. 611 West Sixth Street, Suite 2198, LA, Calif. 90017, **t** (213) 626 6696; **f** (213) 489 9744.

decentralizes in Greece, many islands have local tourist offices; if not, most have tourist police (usually located in an office in the regular police station, although often they're the only people on the island who don't speak any foreign language). If nothing else, they have lists of rooms. **Legal Assistance for Tourists** is available in Athens at 43–45 Valtetsiou St, **t** 010 330 0673, **f** 010 330 1137; in Vólos, 51 Hatziargiri St, **t/f** 04210 33 589; in Kavála: 3 Ydras St, **t/f** 0510 221 159; in Pátras, at 213B Korínthou St, **t** 0610 272 481.

# Where to Stay

## Hotels

All hotels in Greece are classed into six categories: Luxury, A, B, C, D and E. This grading system bears little relationship to the quality of service, charm, views, etc., but everything to do with how the building is constructed, size of bedrooms, lifts, and so on; i.e. if the hotel has a marble-clad bathroom it gets a higher rating. On the **Internet**, *www.greekhotel.com* lists, with musical accompaniment, 8,000 hotels and villas in Greece, with forms for more information about prices and availability and booking. Another useful website is *www.holidays-uncovered.co.uk*, which has reviews from clients of UK package holiday companies on many of the Greek Islands, so it's possible to get an inkling of what you're in for. Most large hotels have their own websites now, so if you have a name, just get a search engine to find it on the web.

**Prices** are set and strictly controlled by the tourist police. Off season (i.e. mid-September–mid July) you can generally get a discount, sometimes as much as 40%. Bear this in mind when looking at price categories given below and remember that walking in off the street and asking in the off season may get you a lower rate than the official one quoted on the phone. Charges include an 8% government tax, a 4.5% community bed tax, a 12% stamp tax, an optional 10% surcharge for stays of only one or two days, an air-conditioning surcharge, as well as a 20% surcharge for an extra bed. All these prices are listed on every room door and authorized and checked at regular intervals. If your hotelier fails to abide by the posted prices, or if you have any other reason to believe all is not on the level, take your complaint to the tourist police.

During the summer, hotels with restaurants may require guests to take their meals in the hotel, either **full pension or half pension**, and there is no refund for an uneaten dinner. Twelve noon is the official check-out time, although on the islands it is usually geared to the arrival of the next boat. Most Luxury and class A, if not B, hotels situated far from the town or port supply buses or cars to pick up guests. Hotels down to class B all have private en-suite bathrooms. In C most do, as do most Ds; E will have a shower down the hall. In these hotels don't always expect to find a towel or soap, although the bedding is clean.

Generally speaking, a hotel's category determines its price, i.e. a Luxury or A class hotel will charge the highest rates, whereas a B class falls into the expensive/moderate category, but this is not always the case. Sometimes a B class will be more expensive than an A class, and so on, as the lines between each category of hotel become more and more blurred with the improvement of services and facilities.

The importance of **reserving a room** in advance, especially during July and August, cannot be over-emphasized. Reservations can be made through the individual hotel, travel agents, the Hellenic Chamber of Hotels by writing, at least two months in advance, to XENEPEL, 24 Stadíou St, 10561 Athens, f 010 322 5449, or *grhotels@otenet.gr*, or in person in Athens, at the Hotels Desk in the National Bank of Greece building, 2 Karageórgi Servías, t 010 323 7193, open Mon–Thurs 8.30–2, Fri 8.30–1.30, and Sat 9–12.30.

## Rooms and Studios

These are for the most part cheaper than hotels and sometimes more pleasant. Although you can still find a few rooms (ΔOMATIA, *domátia*) in private houses, on the whole rooms to rent are found off a family's living quarters, sometimes upstairs or in a separate annexe; an increasing number have en suite baths. One advantage rooms hold over hotels is that nearly all will provide a place to handwash your clothes and a line to hang them on. Another is the widespread availability of basic kitchen facilities (sink, table and chairs, possibly a couple of gas rings, fridge, utensils and dishes) which may turn a room into a **studio**; these obviously cost a bit more, but out of season the difference is often negligible. Depending on facilities, a double room in high season will cost between €25 and €35 with bath, a studio from €35 up to €75. Until June and after August prices are always negotiable. Owners will nearly always drop the price per day the longer you stay, especially for a stay of three days or more.

Prices also depend on how much competition exists between owners on each island. On some it's good-natured dog eat dog (you can, for instance, get a very good deal on Santoríni, because the locals have overbuilt); when you step off the ferry you will be courted with all

---

### Hotel Price Ranges

Note: prices listed here and elsewhere in this book are approximate and for a **double room in high season**, so expect to pay a good deal less in May–June and late Sept–Oct.

*luxury* €90 to astronomical
*expensive* €50–90
*moderate* €35–50
*inexpensive* up to €35

# Self-catering Holiday Operators

On most islands it is possible to rent cottages or villas, generally for a week or more at a time. Villas can often be reserved from abroad: contact a travel agent or the National Tourist Organization (EOT) for names and addresses of rental agents, or see the list below. In the off season villas may be found on the spot with a little enquiry, which, depending on the facilities can work out quite reasonably per person. Generally, the longer you stay, the more economical it becomes. If you book from abroad, packages generally include flights, transfers by coach, ferry, hydrofoil or domestic planes.

## In the UK

**Catherine Secker** (Crete), 102A Burnt Ash Lane, Bromley, Kent BR1 4DD, **t** (020) 8460 8022, **f** (020) 8313 1431. Home-run business with the personal touch featuring luxury villas with swimming pools on the Akrotíri Peninsula near Chaniá. Catherine Secker offers all mod cons in quiet beachside villages with everything from hairdryers to high chairs and toyboxes. Removal of noisy dogs and cockerels guaranteed.

**CV Travel**, 43 Cadogan St, London SW3 2PR, **t** 0870 603 9018, **f** (020) 7591 2802, *www.cvtravel.com*. Upmarket villas at fair prices on Corfu and Páxos. The villas have a maid service; cooks provided on request. The friendly staff are very knowledgeable and really care about the islands; they support local charities and one employee also runs the Kérkyra Bird and Wildlife Sanctuary set up to treat injured birds.

**Direct Greece**, Granite House, 31–3 Stockwell St, Glasgow G1 4RY, **t** (0141) 559 7000, **f** (0141) 559 7272. Particularly good for Líndos on Rhodes with a wealth of traditional Lindian houses. Jenny May is uncrowned queen of Líndos. Also villas and flats on Crete, Corfu, Lésbos, Chálki, Lefkáda and Zákynthos plus

low season specials. Reps are extremely helpful and knowledgeable; most have lived in Greece for a long time.

**Elysian Holidays**, 16a High St, Tenterden, Kent TN30 6AP, **t** (01580) 766 599, **f** (01580) 765 416, *www.elysianholidays.co.uk*. Specialists in restored houses in Patmos, Chíos and other pretty spots.

**Filoxenia Ltd**, Sourdock Hill, Barkisland, Halifax, West Yorkshire HX4 0AG, **t** (01422) 375999, **f** (01422) 310340, *www.filoxenia.co.uk*. Haute couture holidays to Athens and a select range of islands from tiny Elafónissos and unknown Amoliani to arty Hýdra, Chíos and quiet parts of Corfu. Suzi Stembridge and family have scoured Greece for unusual holiday places and pass on their favourites to fellow Grecophiles. Houses, villas, tavernas, pensions, fly-drive. Also **Opus 23** for travellers with disabilities.

**Greek Chapters**, International Chapters, 47–51 St. John's Wood High St, London NW8 7NJ, **t** (020) 7722 0722, **f** (020) 7722 9140, *www.villa-rentals.com*. Particularly high quality villas, each with maid service and most with swimming pool. Located throughout the Greek islands.

**Greek Islands Club**, 10–12 Upper Square, Old Isleworth, Middx, TW7 7BJ, **t** (020) 8232 9780, **f** (020) 8568 8330, *info@vch.co.uk*, *www.sunvil.co.uk/sites/gic*. Well-run, established specialists of the Sporades and Ionian Islands, with helpful yet unobtrusive reps. They also offer an unusually wide choice of personalized activity holidays (*see* p.75). Their new Private Collection features hideaway hotels and exclusive villas on Santoríni, Mýkonos, Páros, Sýros, Hýdra, Spétses and Crete.

**Greek Sun Holidays**, 1 Bank St, Sevenoaks, Kent TN13 1UW, **t** (01732) 740317, **f** (01732) 460108, *www.greeksun.co.uk*. Helpful and family-run, offering Athens and a range of unusual islands like Síkinos, Ikaría, Mílos, Kárpathos, and Límnos. Tailor-made holidays and two-centre breaks.

kinds of interesting proposals, photos of the rooms and even guidebook reviews of their establishments. On others, room and hotel owners have co-operated to organize accommodation booths by the port to sort out

customers; if the room is not within walking distance, they'll collect you in a car or minivan. If you still can't find a room, most travel agencies will be able to dig one up (although these always cost more).

**Ilios Travel**, 18 Market Square, Horsham, West Sussex RH12 1EU, t (01403) 259788, *www.iliostravel.com*. Self-catering on the Ionians and Sporades, Páros and Náxos.

**Kosmar Villa Holidays Plc**, 358 Bowes Road, Arnos Grove, London N11 1AN, t 0870 7000 747, *www.kosmar.co.uk*. Self-catering villas, studios and apartments from Crete to Corfu, Rhodes, Sými, Kos and the Argo-Saronics. Two-centre holidays, flights from Glasgow and Newcastle and family savers.

**Laskarina Holidays**, St Mary's Gate, Wirksworth, Derbyshire, t (01629) 822203, f (01629) 822 205, *www.laskarina.co.uk*. Named after the heroine of Spétses, Laskarina has the largest independent programme in Greece, specializing in the Sporades, the lesser known islands of the Dodecanese and Spétses, sometimes featuring restored traditional accommodation selected by directors Kate and Ian Murdoch. The Murdochs were made citizens of Sými for services rendered and Kate Murdoch shares honorary citizenship of Chálki, the former UNESCO island of Peace and Friendship, with Lady Thatcher. Two-centre holidays, out of season long stays available.

**Manos Holidays**, Panorama House, Vale Road Portslade, East Sussex BN41 1HP, t (01273) 427333, f (01273) 439957, *www.manos.co.uk*. Good value holidays to the major resorts and lesser-known islands, island-hopping and two-centres. Ideal for children, particularly good low season specials and singles deals.

**Pure Crete**, 79 George Street, Croydon, Surrey CR0 1LD, t (020) 8760 0879, f (020) 8688 9951, *www.pure-crete.com*. Anglo-Cretan company with traditional village accommodation in Western Crete.

**Simply Simon Holidays Ltd**, 1/45 Nevern Square, London SW5 9PF, t (020) 7373 1933, f (020) 7370 1807, *www.simplysimon.co.uk*. Cyclades specialists, covering every island except Tínos and Ándros.

**Skiáthos Travel**, 4 Holmedale Road, Kew Gardens, Richmond, Surrey GU13 8AA, t (020) 8940 5157, f (020) 8948 7925. Packages to Skiáthos, Skópelos, Alónissos, Páros, Límnos, and Santoríni.

**Sunvil**, Sunvil House, Upper Square, Isleworth TW7 7BJ t (020) 8568 4499, f (020) 8568 8330, *www.sunvil.co.uk*. Very friendly, well run company offering good value self-catering and hotel accommodation on Límnos, Chíos and Crete, plus most of the Sporades, Cyclades and Ionian islands.

**Travel à la Carte**, 1st Floor, 32 High St, Thatcham, Berkshire, RG19 3JD, t (01635) 863030, f (01635) 867272, *www.travelalacarte.co.uk*. Select range of beach and rural cottages on Skiáthos, Corfu, Páxos, Chálki, Sými, Skópelos and Alónissos.

## In the USA and Canada

**Amphitrion Holidays**, 1506 21st St, NWm Suite 100A, Washington DC, 20036, t 800 424 2471, f (202) 872 9878. Houses, villas and apartments.

**Apollo Tours**, 1701 Lake St, Suite 260, Glenview, IL 60025, t 800 228 4367, f (847) 724 3277, *www.apollotours.com*. Upmarket villas and apartments.

**European Escapes**, 111 Ave. Del Mar, Suite 220D, San Clemente, CA 92672, t toll free 888 EUROLUX, *www.europeanescapes.com*. Luxury villas.

**Omega Tours**, 3220 West Broadway, Vancouver, British Columbia, t 800 663 2669, f (604) 738 7101, *www.oti.bc.ca*. A range of villas and apartments.

**Zeus Tours**, 120 Sylvan Avenue, Englewood Cliffs, NJ 07632, t 800 447 5667, *www.zeustours.com*.

## In Greece

**Women's Agricultural Co-operative of Pétra**, Mytilíni, t 02530 41 238, f 02530 34 1309 (*see* p.532). A women's agro-tourist co-operative on Lésbos that offers accommodation and a taste of Greek rural life.

## Youth Hostels

Some of these hostels are official and require a membership card from the Youth Hostels Association:

**UK**: Youth Hostels Association of England and Wales (YHA), Trevelyan House, Dimple Road, Matlock, Derbyshire, DE4 3YH, t 08708 708808, f (01629) 592702, *www.yha.org.uk*.

USA: American Youth Hostels Inc., 733 15th St,
NW, Suite 840, Washington DC, 20005,
**t** (202) 783 6161, **f** (202) 783 6171,
*www.hiayh.org*.
**Greece:** GYHA, 4 Dragatsaniou St, Athens, **t** 010
323 4107. Alternatively, they can supply an
International Membership Card (about €10).
Other youth hostels are more informal, don't
have as many irksome regulations, and will
admit almost anyone. Most of them charge
extra for a hot shower, and sometimes also for
sheets. Expect to pay around €6–12 per night,
depending on the quality of facilities and services offered. The official hostels have a curfew,
which in Greece means you miss out on all the
nightly fun.

## Camping

The climate of summertime Greece is
perfect for sleeping out of doors, especially
close to the sea, where breezes keep the worst
of the mosquitoes at bay. Unauthorized
camping is illegal (the law was enacted to
displace gypsy camps, and is still used for this
purpose) although each village on each island
enforces the ban as it sees fit. Some couldn't
care less if you put up a tent at the edge of
their beach; in others the police may pull up
your tent pegs and fine you. All you can do is
ask around to see what other tourists or
friendly locals advise. Naturally, the more
remote the beach, the less likely you are to be
disturbed. Most islands have at least one
privately operated camping ground, though
most have only minimal facilities. Islands with
no campsites at all usually have a beach
where freelance camping is tolerated. If the
police are in some places lackadaisical about
enforcing the camping regulations, they come
down hard on anyone lighting any kind of fire
in a forest, and may very well put you in jail for
two months; every year fires damage huge
swathes of land.

> **Camping Prices**
> These are not fixed by law but here are
> some approximate guidelines, per day:
>
> Adult €5
> Small/large tent €3/4
> Child (4–12) €3
> Car €3
> Caravan €5
> Sleeping bag €2

# Women Travellers

Greece is a choice destination for women
travellers but going it alone can be viewed as
an oddity. Be prepared for a fusillade of questions. Greeks tend to do everything in groups
or pairs and can't understand people who
want to go solo. The good news for women,
however, is the dying out of that old pest, the
*kamáki* (harpoon). These 'harpoons' – Romeos
in tight trousers and gold jewellery who used
to roar about on motorbikes, hang out in the
bars and cafés, strut about jangling their keys,
hunting in pairs or packs, would try to 'spear'
as many women as possible, notching up
points for different nationalities. A few professional *kamákia* still haunt piano bars in the
big resorts, gathering as many hearts, gold
chains and parting gifts as they can; they
winter all over the world with members of
their harem.

Thank young Greek women for the decline
in *kamáki* swagger. Watching the example set
by foreign tourists as well as the torrid soaps
and dross that dominate Greek TV, they have
decided they've had enough of 'traditional
values'. Gone are the days when families used
the evening promenade or *vólta* as a bridal
market for their carefully sheltered unmarried
daughters; now the girls hold jobs, go out
drinking with their friends, and move in with
their lovers. They laughed at the old *kamákia*
so much that ridicule, like bug spray, has killed
them dead.

# Athens and Piraeus

08

# Getting Around

## By Bus and Metro

For airport bus info, *see* pp.66–7.

The free **Athens Public Transport Pocket Map**, distributed by EOT (*see* below) marks the main metro bus and trolley routes. Purchase bus and trolley tickets (50¢) at the kiosks before boarding, and punch in the machine. For more info, call **t** 185 weekdays between 7am and 9pm; Sat–Sun 9–5.

The metro (tickets 75¢, sold in the stations) is an important means of getting across Athens, especially from Piraeus. Line 1 runs from Piraeus as far as Kifissiá, stopping at Thissío (near the Agora) Monastiráki (near Pláka), Omónia (10mins from the National Archaeology Museum) and Plateía Viktória (near Areos Park). Lines 2 and 3 run from Sýntagma Square to outlying residential districts. Line 2 goes to the Acropolis (15min walk). It's possible to buy a day ticket for €3, good for 24hrs on *all* city transport, even to the airport. Note that all city transportation with the exception of the airport buses and the Piraeus–Athens bus, stops at midnight.

## By Taxi

Compared to other Western cities, Athenian taxis are cheap. There are taxi stands in some squares, at the port, and bus and train stations, but most cabs cruise the streets. At the time of writing, the meter starts at 75¢ and adds 25¢ per kilometre. The minimum fare is €1.50. Rates double once you leave the city and its suburbs. There are small surcharges (airport, port and station trips, and baggage), and all prices double from midnight to 5am. On major holidays, such as Easter, the driver gets a mandatory 'present' of €1. A taxi between central Athens and the airport should be about €15–20 and from the Archaeology Museum to the Acropolis, €4.

**Sharing**: Because fares are so low and demand so great, Athenians often share cabs. Usually, the cabbie leaves his flag lit, even if he has passengers, to indicate that he is willing to take more people. Hailing a cab this way is not for the faint-hearted; the usual procedure is to stand by the street, flag down any passing cab, and if they slow down and cock an ear, shout out your general destination.

If the taxi is going that way, the driver will stop, if not, he won't. Check the meter when you board, and pay from there, adding €1.50 (min. fare), plus any baggage charges. If the cabbie asks for the full fare, start writing down his licence number and ask for a receipt. That usually settles the issue on the spot.

**Radio taxis** charge €1.50 to come from the moment you call, more if you book in advance. In many cases, especially the airport, it is well worth it. In Athens, try **Parthenon t** 010 581 4711 or 010 581 6141; **Enotita t** 010 645 9000, Ikaros **t** 010 525 2800; in Piraeus **t** 010 418 2333. Numbers are listed in the weekly English-language *Athens News*.

## By Car

Not much fun. Besides the traffic jams, the one-way system is confusing and parking is impossible. For assistance, call **ELPA**'s (Greek Automobile Club) tourist info service **t** 174.

# Tourist Information

**The tourist police** have a magic number: **t** 171. An English voice will answer your questions, incl. lost property queries.

**The National Tourist Organization** (EOT): 2 Amerikis St, between Stadíou and Panepistimíou, **t** 010 331 0561/331 0565, **f** 010 325 2895, *www.gnto.gr*; *open Mon–Fri 9–7, Sat 9–2, closed Sun*. They also have a booth at the airport. Pick up their free map with the city on one side, incl. bus routes, and Piraeus and Attica on the back. The weekly *Athens News* is a mine of info. It's published every Fri and on sale at most kiosks.

**Note**: Since Greece is in the throes of rapid change in preparation for the 2004 Olympics, it may be wise to get your hotel to ring ahead to museums and sites to check opening hours before setting out.

## Emergencies

**First aid (ambulance) t** 166
**Police t** 100
**Fire t** 199
**Emergency hospitals t** 106
**Pharmacies** on duty (Sun and hols) **t** 107
**European emergency call no.** (all cases) **t** 112
If a Greek speaker isn't there when you're calling, try **t** 171 and speak to the tourist police.

## Left Luggage

**Pacific Baggage Storage**, near Gate 1 on the Arrivals Level at the airport. Has a left luggage facility:

**Bellair Travel**, 40 Voulis St, **t** 010 323 9261; *open Mon–Fri 9–6, Sat 9–2*. When in central Athens, you can leave your luggage here.

**Pacific Limited**, 26 Níkis St, **t** 010 324 1007. Offers the same facility during business hours.

## Internet

There are many cybercafés in the city now – just look out for the signs.

**Internet Café**, 5 Stadíou St, **t** 010 324 8105, *sofos1@ath.forthnet.gr*. Charges around €4.5 an hour; *open Mon–Sat 10am–10pm, Sun 11am–7pm*.

## Books

**Eleftheroudákis**, 17 Panepistimíou St, **t** 010 331 4180. This is the megastore for books in central Athens, with 5 floors of books in Greek and English. There is also a smaller branch just behind Sýntagma at 20 Níkis St, **t** 010 322 9388, with a good selection of maps and tourist guides.

**Compendium**, 28 Níkis St. This bookshop is smaller, cozier and has only English books, magazines and guides. It also offers an eclectic selection of used paperbacks to buy or swap.

# Where to Stay

Athens is a big noisy city, especially so at night when you want to sleep – unless you do as the Greeks do and take a long afternoon siesta. If you cannot find a room, try the **Hotel Association**'s booking desk in Sýntagma Square, in the National Bank building; *open Mon–Thurs 8.30–2, Fri 8.30–1 and Sat 9–1*, **t** 010 323 7193.

## Luxury

**Grande Bretagne**, 1 Vass Georgíou St, on Sýntagma Square, **t** 010 333 0000, **f** 010 322 8034, *gbhotel@otenet.gr*. Beautiful hotel built in 1862 to house members of the Greek royal family who couldn't squeeze into the palace (the current Parliament building) up the square. It was used as a Nazis headquarters for a time, and by Winston Churchill, who had a lucky escape from a bomb planted in the hotel's complex sewer system while spending Christmas here in 1944. Totally modernized, with its vast marble lobby, elegant rooms and dining room, it offers grand style and service that the newer hotels may never achieve.

**Electra Palace,** 18 Nikodímou, **t** 010 337 0000, **f** 010 324 1875, *electrahotels@ath.forthnet.gr*. Close to Pláka, with views of the Acropolis and a wonderful rooftop swimming pool in a garden setting – a rare find in Athens. Rooms come with air-con and there's a garage adjacent to the hotel.

**Ledra Marriott**, 113–115 Syngroú, **t** 010 930 0000, **f** 010 935 8603, *marriott@otenet.gr*. One of a new luxury chain just outside the centre, featuring a Chinese-Japanese restaurant, and a hydrotherapy pool you can soak in with a view of the Acropolis.

**Pentelikon**, 66 Diligiánni St, Kefalári, in the northern suburb of Kifissiá, **t** 010 623 0650, **f** 010 801 0314. Ideal if you want to stay out of the centre. It also boasts a lovely garden and swimming pool.

**Philippos**, 3 Mitséon (Makriyiánni), **t** 010 922 3611, **f** 010 922 3615, *herodion@otenet.gr*. Quiet, well run, and recently renovated.

**Royal Olympic Hotel** at 28 Diákou, **t** 010 922 6411, **f** 010 923 3317, *royaloly@hol.gr*. Facing the Temple of Olympian Zeus and Mount Lykavitós, rooms are American in spirit, with some family suites. If you have the misfortune to get a room without a view, there's a wonderful panorama from the rooftop bar.

**St George Lycabettus**, 2 Kleoménous (Plateía Dexaménis, Kolonáki), **t** 010 729 0711, **f** 010 729 0439, *info@sglycabettus.gr*. Intimate, family-run atmosphere and wonderful views of the Parthenon or out to sea, and a pool too. The Grand Balcon dining room has views of most of Athens.

**Titania**, 52 Panepistimíou, **t** 010 330 0111, **f** 010 330 0700, *titania@titania.gr*. Practically on top of lively, traffic-clogged Omónia Square. They are pleasant rooms and there's a very fashionable rooftop terrace planted with old olive trees, and gorgeous views over the Acropolis and Lykavitós Hill. It also has parking for customers.

## Expensive

**Astor,** 16 Karagiórgi Servías (just off Sýntagma Square), t 010 335 1000, f 010 325 5115, *astor@astorhotel.gr.* Fully air-conditioned rooms (*lux* in high season) and a rooftop garden restaurant.

**Athenian Inn,** 22 Cháritos, t 010 723 8097, f 010 724 2268. In swanky Kolonáki, this was the favourite of Lawrence Durrell.

**Austria,** 7 Mousson-Filopappou, t 010 923 5151, f 010 922 0777, *austria@hol.gr.* A great location not far from the Acropolis entrance.

**Hera,** 9 Falírou (Makriyiánni), t 010 923 6682, f 010 924 7334, *hhera@hol.gr.* Modern but tasteful, with a roof garden.

**Hermes,** 19 Apóllonos (near Sýntagma), t 010 323 5514, f 010 323 2073. Comfortable and friendly, with a small bar and roof garden with Acropolis views.

**Parthenon,** 6 Makrí St (Makriyiánni, just south of the Acropolis), t 010 923 4594, f 010 923 5797, *airhotel@netplan.gr.* Great location and a pretty outdoor breakfast area.

## Moderate

**Acropolis House,** 6–8 Kódrou (off Kidathinéon St), t 010 322 3244, f 010 324 4143. Modernized rooms but in a traditional style, with antique furnishings, frescoes and a family welcome.

**Adam's,** 6 Herefóndos, t 010 322 5381, f 010 323 8553, *adams@otenet.gr.* Quiet location, 3mins from Hadrian's Arch; rooms are traditional, comfortable, but go up to the expensive rank when things are busy.

**Aphrodite,** 21 Apóllonos, t 010 323 4357, f 010 322 6047. In the Sýntagma-Pláka area. Basic rooms with air-con and free parking.

**Art Gallery,** 5 Eréchthiou and Veíkou Sts, t 010 923 8376, f 010 923 3025. Pleasant, quiet, well-run old-style hotel. Each room with its own bathroom, and the Pláka is a 15min walk away.

**Kouros,** 11 Kódrou (off Kidathinéou St), t 010 322 7431. Attractive old house near the Greek Folk Art Museum. The owner may be up for discussion if he's not full.

**Pension Adonis,** 3 Kódrou, t 010 323 1602. A gem, well run by the Greek who managed the Annapolis Hilton. All rooms have balconies, and there's a lovely breakfast roof garden (incl. breakfast) and bar.

## Inexpensive

**Dióskouros House,** 6 Pitákou (near Hadrian's Arch), t 010 324 8165, f 010 321 0907. This is a delightful hostelry with high-ceilinged rooms in an old Neoclassical building in a fairly quiet spot. It is old-fashioned, and the kind of place you are terrified will be replaced by an office building before your next visit.

**Dryades,** 105 Emm. Benáki and Anaxartissías, t 010 382 7362, f 010 330 5193. All the rooms have their own bath and the top 3 have lovely views.

**John's Place,** 5 Patróou (just behind the large Metrópolis church), t 010 322 9719. Simple and cheap option, with communal bathrooms down the hall.

**Marble House,** 35 A. Zínni, in Koukáki, t 010 923 4058, f 010 922 6461. Comfortable Greek-French-run hotel.

**Orion,** next door to the Dryades and run by the same manager. Communal facilities and a lovely roof garden with an equally great view.

**Pella Inn,** 104 Ermou (near Monastiráki metro), t 010 321 2229, f 010 325 0598, *pella@pella-inn.gr.* This is a simple hotel but with a welcoming atmosphere.

**Phaedra,** 16 Herefóndos, t 010 323 8461. Unreconstructed pre-war interior, with communal facilities and a great location near the Lysikrátes Monument. Free hot showers are promised.

**Student Inn,** 16 Kidathinéon, t 010 324 4808, f 010 321 0065. Organized along youth hostel lines and ideal for the younger crowd (1.30am curfew) who are travelling on a tight budget.

**Student's Hostel,** 75 Damaréos St, in Pangráti, t 751 9530, f 751 0616. Shared accommodation and kitchen facilities not far from the centre. Student cards are not required.

**Tembi,** 29 Eólou (near Monastiráki metro), t 010321 3175, f 010 325 4179. Nothing special, but it is central, cheap and has pleasant management.

**Camping Athens,** 198 Athinón (7km out on the main road to Corinth), t 010 581 4114, f 010 582 0353. *Open all year.*

**Camping N. Kifissiá,** near the National Road in Nea Kifissiá, t 010 807 9579, f 010 807 5579. *Open all year.*

# Eating Out

Athenians rarely dine out before 10pm, and they want to be entertained afterwards. If it's warm, chances are they'll drive out to the suburbs or the sea shore. Glyfáda and outer Piraeus (Kalípoli and Mikrolímano) are popular on a summer evening. The cool sea breeze can be a life-saver after the oppressive heat of the city centre. In Athens, prices are generally higher than elsewhere in this book, and can even hit London levels. Note that prices below are per person.

## Pláka

Pláka is the place to head for al fresco dining in the evening – the tinkling glasses, music, chatter and laughter ricochet in the narrow streets. Scores of places cater for the passing tourist trade (they aren't hard to spot) but it remains a perennial favourite with Greeks.

**Bakaliarakiá,** 41 Kydathinéon, t 010 322 5084. (€14). In a cellar supported by an ancient column; great snacks, fried cod, and barrel wine since the 1900s. *Eves only; closed Aug.*

**Byzantino,** 18 Kidathinéon, t 010 322 7368. Big portions (excellent fish soup and lamb *fricassée*) at tables under trees and one of few decent places open for Sun lunch.

**Daphne's,** 4 Lysikrátous (by the Lysikrátes Monument) t 010 322 7971 (€35). In a Neoclassical mansion with an elegant dining room with Pompeiian frescoes and beautiful garden courtyard – a rarity in Athens – serving generous, refined traditional Greek and international dishes.

**Eden,** 12 Lissíou and Mnissikléous, t 010 324 8858. Athens' oldest vegetarian restaurant, serving, amongst many things, mouthwatering quiches and soya moussakas. It is very popular, even with Athenian carnivores. *Open Wed–Mon.*

**Platanos,** 4 Diogénous, t 010 322 0666 (*around* €15). The oldest taverna in Pláka, near the Tower of the Four Winds, serves good wholesome food in the shade of an enormous plane tree. *Open Mon–Sat.*

## Psirrí/Monastiráki/Thíssio

**Taki 13,** 13 Táki, t 010 325 4707. Superb atmosphere: simple food but a great party bar, often featuring live music (jazz/blues Tues

and Wed, Greek at weekends) and sing songs till 1.30am.

**Zidoron,** 10 Táki and Ag. Anárgyro, t 010 321 5368. Good dishes if you arrive on the right day; try the *kolokithókéftedes* (courgette rissoles). Popular. *Closed Aug.*

**Psipsína,** 43 Ag. Avárgiro, t 010 331 2446 (€17–20). Modern chic décor and great fish.

## Koukáki and Makriyiánni

**Apanemiá,** 2 Erechthiou (at the corner of Drákou and Veíkou), t 010 922 8766. Good food in a lovely traditional setting with *bouzouki* and guitar music thrown in on Fri and Sat eves, and Sun midday.

**Fellos,** 3 Drákou, near Psitopoleío, t 010 924 8898. A cosy wine bar restaurant.

**Psitopoleío,** 16 Drákou, in Koukáki, t 010 922 5648. The best chicken in Athens, by the Syngrou-Fix metro.

**Strofi,** 125 Roberto Galli, (close to the Odeon), t 010 721 4130 (€17–20). This family-run restaurant has a rooftop terrace and Acropolis views from its second-floor windows. Famous for its *mezédes*. *Open every eve except Sun.*

**Symposio,** 46 Herodeio (close to the Odeon), t 010 922 5321 (€35–40). Upscale choice south of the Acropolis. Mediterranean cuisine, served in the garden in summer and in winter in a conservatory, attached to an old Neoclassical house.

## Kolonáki and Around

**Boschetto,** signposted in Evangelimós Park off Vass. Sofias, t 010 721 0893 (*around* €46–56). One of Athens' finest, a favourite of politicians and celebrities, serving Italian delicacies, outside in the summer or in a winter garden; great desserts and in-depth wine list. *Open Mon–Sat, eves only.*

**Gerofínikas,** 10 Pindárou, t 010 362 2719 (€40). Long Athens' most famous restaurant, with the ancient palm tree that gave it its name growing out of the middle; the food is renowned and the whole meal an experience. *Closed Sun and hols.*

**Vlássis,** 8 Pasteur St, t 010 646 3060 (*around* €20). Near the US embassy, a superb family-run taverna, the place to find true Greek cuisine and a rarity for its excellent wines and desserts, too. *Open Mon–Sat, book.*

## Around Omónia Square

**Andréas and Sons**, 18 Themistokléous St, t 010 382 1522. Tasty seafood at marble-topped tables in a cosy attractive setting; located in a quiet narrow street. *Open Mon–Sat.*

**Athinaikón**, 2 Themistokléous St, t 010 383 8485,(€15) Great place to fill up on tasty *mezédes* and swordfish or lamb kebabs while watching the passing crowds. *Open Mon–Sat.*

**Diporto**, Theatrou and Sofokléous (opposite the central market parking garage), t 010 321 1463. An Athens institution, serving delicious simple dishes and salads with barrelled retsina. *Open for lunch only.*

**Monastíri**, in the central meat market on Athinás, t 010 324 0773. Glassed-in restaurant that's been inside the main Athens meat market since 1924. The traditional Greek hangover cure, tripe soup (*patsás*) as well as other Hellenic soul food is dished up for trendy drunkards and hungry butchers. The food's great, but the setting is really not suitable for the squeamish. *Open Mon–Sat, lunch only.*

## Exárchia

**Ama Lachi**, 69 Kallidromiou, t 010 384 5978 (€15). Housed in an old school building; the food's good and the atmosphere is pleasant. *Open for lunch only.*

**Bárba Iánnis**, 94 Emm. Benáki St (corner of Derveníou, close to Exárchia Square), t 010 382 4138. This cheap, popular old standby has been serving wonderful Greek cooking (all on display) noon and evening, for years from an ungentrified Neoclassical house. *Closed Aug.*

**Oinomayeirémata**, 66 Themistokléous St, near Exárchia Square, t 010 383 1955. Spanking new eatery, painted yellow, with folk art; traditional food served noon and evening; lots of organic ingredients, and an eager young staff.

**To Stéki tou Xánthis**, 5 Irínis Athinéas (northeast side of Stréfi Hill), t 010 882 0780 (*around €20*). An historic house where Xánthis, the owner and a disciple of Theodorakis, leads the public in old Greek songs – a great night out. The food's good and plentiful. *Open eves only.*

# Entertainment and Nightlife

## Traditional Music and Dance

The summer is filled with festivals attracting international stars from around the world.

**Dora Stratou Theatre** on Philopáppos Hill, t 010 921 4650 or t 010 324 4395. Nightly folk dance performances. *Open May–Sept.*

**Greek National Opera House**, 59-61 Academías St, t 010 361 2461. Where Maria Callas got her start. Also home of the national ballet.

**Mégaron**, Vass. Sofías and Kokkáli, t 010 728 2333. Classical music fans can take in a performance at Athens' brand new acoustically wonderful concert hall.

**Rota**, 118 Ermoú, t 010 325 2517. A good venue for *rembétika*.

**Stoa Athanaton**, 19 Sophokleous, t 010 321 4362. *Rembétika*, the Greek blues, is in full revival in Athens. Here it's live and authentic.

**Diogenis**, 259 Syngroú, t 010 942 5754. Often has live *rembétika*. This is a useful street for finding *bouzouki* clubs (or a transvestite).

**Jazz in Jazz**, Deinokrátous St, t 010 725 8362. Good place for jazz.

**Half Note**, 17 Trivonianou, in Mets, t 010 923 3460. Greek and foreign jazz artists.

## Bars and Clubs

In summer, young fashion slaves and beautiful Athenians head out to Glyfáda:

**Club 22**, 22 Vougliamenis St, t 010 924 9814. For big Las Vegas style reviews, in winter.

**Romeo**, 1 Ellinikou, t 010 894 5345. A *skyládiko* club for a wild Greek night out.

**Splash**, **Lámda** and **Granázi**, along Lembéssi St, off Syngroú. Gay Athens gathers in Makriyiánni, south of the Acropolis. These are popular dancing bars with cover charges.

**Vareládiko**, 4 Alkondidon St, t 010 895 2403. The first 'hyper-club' in Greece, with the latest Greek hits.

## Cinema

In the summer, outdoor cinemas are a treat and all the films are in their original language: 2 of the nicest are in Kolonáki:

**Dexamení**, Dexamení Square, halfway up Lykavitós Hill, t 010 360 2363.

**Athinaía**, 50 Haritós St, t 010 721 5717.

*Love for Athens, a city once famous, wrote these words, a love that plays with shadows, that gives a little comfort to burning desire... Though I live in Athens I see Athens nowhere: only sad, empty, and blessed dust.*
                                    Michael Akominátos, 12th century

Travellers to the islands often find themselves in Athens, and, although it has perked up considerably since the days of Michael Akominátos, it's rarely love at first sight. Look closely, however, behind the ugly architecture and congestion and you may be won over by this urban crazy quilt – small oases of green parks hidden amidst the hustle and bustle; tiny family-run tavernas tucked away in the most unexpected places; the feverish pace of its nightlife and summer festivals; and best of all, the Athenians themselves, whose friendliness belies the reputation of most city dwellers. Another plus: Athens is the least expensive capital in the European Union – although the 2004 Olympics may change that.

## History: From Cradle to Grave and Back Again

Athens was inhabited by the end of the Neolithic Age (*c.* 3500 BC), but its debut on history's front stage began in the second millennium BC, when invaders, probably from Asia Minor, entered Attica and established small fortified enclaves. Their descendants would claim they were 'the children of Kekrops', a half-man, half-snake who united them into twelve villages, and founded Kecropia on the future Acropolis. Kekrops, whose sacred bird was the owl, gave them laws, taught them cultivation and uses of the olive, and instituted patriarchal marriage. The next step was the birth of **King Erechtheos** 'the earth-born'. Snake from the waist down, he was the official founding father of Athens, and through him and his mother the earth, Athenians claimed an inalienable right to Attica. According to myth, Erechtheos introduced the worship of **Athena**. The snake and the owl then become her symbols and, by extension, the city's.

Athens was a significant centre in the **Mycenaean** period and her hero **Theseus** dates from this era. Best known for killing the Minotaur in Crete, in the evolving civic mythology he won kudos for unifying Attica's villages and defeating rival Thebes. Politicians throughout Athenian history would scramble to be associated with his exploits; at the height of Athens' glory in 475 BC, Kimon brought his bones back from Skýros and gave them a hero's burial on the Acropolis. Athens escaped the Dorian invasions after 1200 BC, although her culture too declined during the Dark Ages. This escape was a point of pride with Athenians who considered themselves more legitimately Greek and refined than their Dorian counterparts. This created the amazing self-confidence that would produce the great Athenian city-state and democracy.

During the 8th century BC all the towns of Attica were united under the leadership of Athens. The city was ruled jointly by a king (who doubled as the chief priest), a *polemarch* (general), and an *archon* (civil ruler), positions that by the 6th century BC were annually elective. Conflict arose between the aristocracy and rising commercial classes and when **Solon**, an aristocrat, was elected Archon in 594 BC he was asked to break the impasse with a series of laws, which he wrote in exquisite poetry. Solon abolished slavery as a result of debt, forgave existing debt, and reformed the Athenian coinage to encourage trade. He had his laws written on slabs and displayed in the marketplace. This publishing of laws and notices would become a hallmark of Athenian democracy (and every citizen was expected to know them; there were no lawyers). Archaeologists would find over 7,500 such inscriptions in the Agora alone.

But Solon's good start didn't stop his relative Pisístratos from making himself a 'popular' dictator in 560 BC. He began the naval build-up that made Athens a threat to other Greek city-states. He enlarged the **Panathenaic Games** in an attempt to equate them with the Olympics, and instituted grandiose building projects, and encouraged the arts. Later, democratic Athens would vilify his name, but Pisístratos was undoubtedly a one-man chamber of commerce for the Archaic city. Pisístratos' son Hippias was deposed in 510 BC, when another democratic reformer, **Kleisthénes** made aristocratic takeovers harder by dividing the population into ten political tribes. Lots were drawn to choose 50 members of the people's assembly, from which a further lot was drawn to select ten *archons*, one from each tribe. The head *archon* gave his name to the Athenian year.

Meanwhile, as **Persian** strength grew in the east, Ionian intellectuals and artists took refuge in Athens, bringing with them philosophy, science and the roots of Attic tragedy. They prodded Athens to aid Ionia against the Persians, which landed the city in the soup when Darius, the Persian King of Kings, decided to subdue Greece and, in particular upstart Athens. In 490 BC Darius' army landed at **Marathon** to be defeated by a much smaller Athenian force under Miltiades. Although Sparta and the other Greek states realised the eastern threat, they continued to leave 'national' defence to the Athenian fleet, which grew mightier under **Themistocles**. In 480 BC the new Persian King of Kings, Xerxes, showed up with the greatest fleet and army the ancient world had ever seen. An oracle had told Themistocles that Athens would be saved by 'wooden walls', which he interpreted to mean the navy and he persuaded the army to abandon the Acropolis for the safety of Salamina where the fleet was anchored. Athens was razed by the Persians but their navy was outmanoeuvred by the Athenian fleet at Salamina. The Persian army was finally repelled by the Athenians and Spartans at the Battle of Plateía. With her superiority at sea, Athens set about creating a maritime empire, to increase her power and stabilize her combustible internal politics. She ruled the confederacy at Délos, demanding contributions from the islands in return for protection. Athenian democracy became truly imperialistic under **Pericles**, who brought the treasure of Délos to Athens to 'protect it' – and to skim off funds to beautify the city and build the **Parthenon**. It was the golden age of Athens, of Phidias, Herodotus, Sophocles, Aristophanes, and Socrates.

It couldn't last. The devastating **Peloponnesian War** (431–404 BC) began over Athenian expansion in the west. Back and forth the struggle went, Sparta with supe-riority on land, Athens on the seas, until both city-states were near exhaustion. Finally Lysander and the Spartans captured Athens and set up the brief rule of the Thirty Tyrants. Although democracy and imperialism made quick recoveries, the war had struck a blow from which ancient Athens would never totally recover. The population grew dissatisfied with public life, and refused to tolerate innovators and critics;

**Socrates** was put to death. Economically, Athens had trouble maintaining the trade she needed. Yet her intellectual and artistic tradition held true in the 4th century BC, bringing forth the likes of Demosthenes, Praxiteles, Menander, Plato and Aristotle.

**Philip II of Macedon** took advantage of the discontent to bully the city-states into joining the Macedonians against Persia. Athenian patriotism was kept alive by the orator Demosthenes until Philip subdued Greece (338 BC). Philip was assassinated shortly before the campaign, leaving his son Alexander to conquer the East. When Alexander died, Athens was a prize fought over by his generals, beginning with Dimitrios Poliorketes who captured the city in 294 BC. Alexandria, Rhodes and Pergamon became Athens' intellectual rivals, but they continued to honour Athens.

In 168 BC **Rome** captured Athens, and granted her many privileges. However, 80 years later, when Athens betrayed Roman favour by siding with Mithridates of Pontus, Sulla destroyed Piraeus, the Agora, and the walls of the city. But Rome always remembered her cultural debt; leading Romans attended Athens' academies, and endowed the city with monuments. **St Paul** started the Athenians on the road to Christianity in AD 44. In the 3rd century **Goths** and barbarians sacked Athens; in 529, Emperor **Justinian** closed the philosophy schools, and converted the Parthenon into a cathedral. It was a largely symbolic act; by then Athens had lost her place in the world.

Athens next enters history as the plaything of the **Franks** after they pillaged Constantinople in 1204. In 1456 the **Ottomans** converted the Parthenon into a mosque and the Erechtheion into a harem. The Venetians attempted to wrench it away; in Morosini's siege of 1687, a shell struck the Parthenon, where Turkish gunpowder was stored. In 1800 **Lord Elgin** began the removal of its marbles to Britain.

In 1834, after the **War of Independence**, Athens – population 200, in a clutch of war-scarred houses rotting under the Acropolis – was declared the **capital** of the new Greek state. Otto of Bavaria, first King of the Greeks, brought his own architects to lay out a new city, based on the lines of Stadíou and El. Venezélou Streets, which still boast many of Athens' Neoclassical public buildings. Much of the rest of the city was built on the quick and cheap in order to accommodate the flood of rural people and the Anatolian Greeks who arrived after the population exchange in 1922.

Today Athens resembles a dense domino game stacked over the hills of Attica. Greater Athens squeezes in four million lively, opinionated inhabitants – a third of the population of Greece – who, thanks to native ingenuity and EU-membership, are now more prosperous than they have been since the age of Pericles. Unfortunately this translates into a million cars, creating the worst smog problem east of Mexico City, although the metro system has begun to improve things. Modern Athens may never win any beauty prizes, but it's as alive as it is ugly – the opposite of its old master Venice, which is stunningly beautiful, and stunningly dead. Athens is undergoing a quiet renaissance under Mayor Dimitris Avramópoulos; Neoclassical buildings are being restored, trees planted, central car-less oases created, a modern airport at Spata, and new immigrants from Eastern Europe and the Balkans are giving the city a cosmopolitan buzz. Losing the centennial 1996 Olympics to Atlanta concentrated Athens' attention on its problems – hard work that's been rewarded by the selection of Athens to finally 'bring the Olympics home' in 2004.

## Orientation: Athens in a Nutshell

**Sýntagma** (ΣΥΝΤΑΓΜΑ) (or **Constitution**) **Square** is the city centre, site of the **Parliament Building** which backs on to the **National Gardens** and **Záppeion Park**, a haven of green shade to escape the summer heat. Traffic is slowly being syphoned away, so you can hear yourself think at the outdoor tables of the overpriced cafés. During construction of the metro, a 3rd-century AD Roman bath and villa, an 11th-century BC grave and a dog's tomb were found under the traffic jams; these archaeological finds are displayed in the metro's smart underground concourse.

From Sýntagma Square it's a short walk down Filellínon St to Kidathinéon St, the main artery into the **Pláka** (ΠΛΑΚΑ), the old town under the Acropolis, where many houses have been converted into intimate tavernas. This is a good area for mid-priced accommodation in quiet pedestrianized streets. At the top of the Pláka, tucked under the Acropolis, **Anafiótika** (ΑΝΑΦΙΟΤΙΚΑ) is a charming uncommercial enclave where the builders of Otto's palaces, from the island of Anáfi, tried to re-create their village. It's best reached from Tripódon and Epichármou Streets.

Athens' nearby flea market district, west of **Monastiráki** (ΜΟΝΑΣΤΙΡΑΚΙ) metro, contains shops selling everything from quality woollen goods to second-hand fridges. Several streets en route claim to be the flea market, but are merely fun and lively tourist-trap alleys. The area around Thissío, at the base of the Acropolis, is popular with young Athenians who want to see and be seen, and don't mind spending a hefty amount on coffee (*frappé*, of course) to be in the 'right' place.

The residential **Koukáki/Makriyiánni** area south of the Acropolis is central but just off the tourist trail; it's heart is along Veíkou and Drákou Streets, where all the locals gather to gossip at the cafés. This is the everyday Athens of the average citizen and can be reached on foot along Makriyiánni St (Acropolis metro stop).

North of Monastiráki metro, Miaoúli St leads to **Iróon Square**, the centre of **Psirrí**, a neighbourhood of winding little streets dating from Byron's time (he rented a room here) that has recently become one of the trendiest spots to eat and play in Athens.

A 10-minute walk east from Sýntagma, up Vass. Sofías to the Benáki Museum and then left, leads to Kolonáki Square, Athens' Knightsbridge in miniature, complete with fancy-pants shops, upmarket restaurants and well-heeled 'Kolonáki Greeks' – Athenian Sloane Rangers. Above the square rises **Lykavitós** (ΛΥΚΑΒΕΤΟΣ) **Hill**; there's a funicular every 10 minutes from the corner of Aristippoú and Ploutarhoú. The summit offers the best panoramic views of the city, smog permitting, the chapel

# Major Museums and Sites in Athens

## The Acropolis

*Site t 010 321 0219, museum t 010 321 4172; open 8–6.30 in summer, although on Mon the museum doesn't open until 10am, Mon–Fri 8–4.30, Sat and Sun 8.30–2.30 in winter (museum closes daily at 2.20pm in winter); adm.*

Acropolis in Greek means 'top of the town'. Many Greek cities have similar naturally fortified citadels crowned with temples, but Athens has *the* Acropolis, standing proud

of **St George**, a restaurant/bar, a lovely outdoor theatre and a cannon fired on national holidays.

Past the University (Panepistímiou) is a major node: **Omónia** (OMONIA) **Square**, a once funky 24-hour zone of which only a few traces linger after a big revamp; it has a useful metro stop, a huge music store and upmarket shopping centre and the noisiest daytime traffic Athens has to offer. The **National Archaeology Museum** is further north, about a 10-minute walk along Patissíon St (28 Octovríou) and behind it lies **Exárchia**, Athens' Latin Quarter, home of trendies, students and literati. Terra incognita for tourists, Exárchia Square is a lively centre after dark, with traditional *ouzeries* and *boîtes*, where you'll find hip-hop alongside bluesy, smoke-filled *rembétika* clubs.

A 20-minute walk from Sýntagma, along Vass. Sofías, leads to the Hilton Hotel. Behind it are the neighbourhoods of **Ilíssia** and **Pangráti**, good places to get a feel for everyday Athenian life. Lose yourself in their back streets littered with tavernas which are highly preferable to the central tourist haunts. Across Vass. Konstantínos Av from Záppeion Park, the landmark is the big white horseshoe of the **Ancient Stadium**, site of the 3rd-century BC original used during the Panathenaea festival, and rebuilt for the first modern Olympics in 1896. Behind this is **Mets**, an old-fashioned neighbourhood popular with artists, featuring some fine old houses and small pensions. Just outside the centre, it's a good place to stay with authentic tavernas and *kafeneions*.

From Záppeion Park buses run frequently down to the coastal suburbs of **Glyfáda**, **Voúla** and **Vouliagméni**. Pleasant green Glyfáda, site of the old airport, has grown into a busy resort and rival of fashionable Kolonáki. Smart city dwellers shop at the ritzy boutiques, and berth their gin palaces in the swish marina. At the other end of the scale it's the hub of British package holidays to the so-called Apollo Coast. Here and at Voúla are pay-beaches run by EOT, usually jammed with well-heeled Athenians. There are many facilities and the sea is cleaner at some than others – but nothing like the crystal waters of the islands. There's also good swimming in the rocky coves at Vouliagméni, a smart place for a fish lunch and haven for Greek yachties. **Kavoúri** has excellent fish restaurants, ideal for a romantic dinner overlooking the sea. Beyond Vouliagméni, the road continues to **Várkiza**, another beach playground, and winds to stunning **Cape Soúnion** and its **Temple of Poseidon** (440 BC), famous for its magnificent position and sunsets and where there's always at least one tourist searching for the column where Byron carved his name.

above the city. First inhabited in the late Neolithic Age, it had a Cyclopean wall and the palace of Athens' Mycenaean king. It was replaced by a Temple of Poseidon and Athena, after those two divinities competed to decide who would be patron of the city. Poseidon struck the spring Klepsydra out of the rock of the Acropolis, while Athena invented the olive tree, which was judged the better trick. In 480 BC the temple's statue of Athena was taken to Salamina, just before the Persians smashed the Acropolis. Renovations followed and the Acropolis as we see it today took shape, a showcase for the greater glory of the Athenian state.

Themistocles rebuilt the Panathenaic ramp leading to the **Propylaia**, the majestic entrance gate built in Pentelic marble by Pericles' architect Mnesikles in the 430s BC to complement the Parthenon. Take a close look at it; according to the ancients (and many modern architects), the Propylaia is the architectural equal of the Parthenon, ingeniously built over an uneven slope, leading to five gates large enough to admit horsemen and chariots. On either side of its entrance are wings; the one to the north held a picture gallery (*pinakothéke*) while the smaller one to the south appears to have the same dimensions as the *pinakothéke*, although in fact it is little more than a façade because the priests of Athena Nike refused to have a wing in their precinct.

To the right of the Propylaia, on a stone-filled bastion of the Mycenaean wall, stands the little Ionic **Temple of Athena Nike**, built by the architect Kallikrates in 478 BC of Pentelic marble. In 1687 the Turks demolished it to build a nearby wall, making it easy to rebuild in 1835. A cast replaces the frieze, now in the Acropolis Museum. From the temple platform, the whole Saronic Gulf can be seen on clear days, and it was here that King Aegeus watched for the return of his son Theseus from his adventure with the Minotaur. Theseus was to have signalled his victory with a white sail but forgot; at the sight of the black sail, Aegeus threw himself off the precipice in despair and, although he was miles from the sea at the time, gave his name to the Aegean.

## The Parthenon

The glorious Parthenon is a Doric temple constructed between 447 and 432 BC by Iktinos and Kallicrates under the direction of Phidias, the Michelangelo of the Periclean Age. Constructed of Pentelic marble, it held Phidias' chryselephantine (ivory and gold) statue of Athena, which stood over 36ft high. The Parthenon architects wrote the book on mathematical precision, grace and *entasis*, the art of curving a form to create the visual illusion of perfection. Look closely, and you'll see that there's not a straight line to be seen: the foundation is curved to prevent an illusion of drooping caused by straight horizontals. The columns bend inward, and those on the corners are wider to complete the illusion of perfect form. Above the 46 columns of the outer colonnade are the remnants of the Doric frieze: the east side portrayed the Battle of Giants and Gods, the south the Lapiths and Centaurs, the west the Greeks and the Amazons, and the north the Battle of Troy. Little remains of the pediment sculptures of the gods. Above the interior colonnade, 40ft up, is a unique feature: the exquisite 524ft continuous Ionic frieze designed by Phidias showed the quadrennial Panathenaic Procession in which the cult statue of Athena in the Erechtheion was brought a crown and a sacred garment, or *pelops*. After seeing it at eye level in the British Museum, it's startling to realize how hard it must have been to see in situ.

The Parthenon, used as a church and then a mosque, remained intact until 1687, when a Venetian bomb hit the Turks' powder stores and blew the roof off; the 1894 earthquake struck another blow. Entrance within is forbidden to save on wear and tear. The work of preserving the building from smog and undoing the damage of previous restorations has been ongoing since 1983. While discovering how to use hot, pressurized carbon dioxide to re-harden stone surfaces, Greek engineers have learned about ancient techniques and are reconstructing as much of the temple as possible.

## The Acropolis Museum

In ancient times the now bare rock of the Acropolis was thronged with exquisite Attic statues, many of which are now in this little museum tucked behind the Parthenon. The Archaic works are exceptional: painted pediments from the 6th-century BC Hecatompedon (or 'Old' Parthenon) and from the Temple of Athena Polias, with three impressive snake men; the smiling *Calf-Bearer* (Moschoforos) from 570 BC carrying his offering to the goddess; lovely Kore statues, votives to Athena, and each with her own personality; and the Rampin Horseman. There are several remarkable panels of the Parthenon frieze that Lord Elgin forgot, and the pollution-scarred Caryatids. At the time of writing, a new state-of-the-art museum is being built on Mitséon Street, with Acropolis views and space for the Elgin marbles, fingers crossed.

## The Erechtheion

The last great temple of the Acropolis, the Erechtheion, was completed only in 395 BC after the Peloponnesian War. This complex Ionic temple with three porches and none of the usual Classical colonnades owes its idiosyncrasies to the much older holies of holies it encompasses – the sanctuaries of Athena Polias, Poseidon, Erechtheus, Kekrops and the olive tree planted by the goddess – yet such is the genius of its structure that it appears harmonious. The southern porch facing the Parthenon is supported by six Caryatids (now casts), designed to complement the Parthenon opposite. Lord Elgin nicked one; the other girls, said to weep every night for their missing sister, rotted in the smog before they were rescued. Behind the east portico, with its six Ionic columns, the *cella* was divided up to serve both Athena Polias and Poseidon Erechtheos, and held the primitive cult statue of Athena Polias, who wore the *pelops* and had the biggest juju of all. Down the steps is the Erechtheion's best side: its north porch, defined by six tall and elegant Ionic columns. Part of the floor and roof were cut away to reveal the marks left by Poseidon's trident; when the Turks made the temple a harem, they used the sacred place as a toilet. This porch was the tomb of Erechtheos, some say Kekrops, and the traditional home of the Acropolis guardian snake. An olive tree replaces the original in the western court of the temple.

## Around the Acropolis

Below the Acropolis entrance, to the north towards the Agora, is the bald **Areópagos**, or hill of the war god Ares, once the seat of the High Council. It figured prominently in Aeschylus' play *The Eumenides* where mercy defeated vengeance for the first time in history during the trial of Orestes for matricide. Although Pericles removed much of the original power of the High Council, under the control of the ex-archons it continued to advise on the Athenian constitution for hundreds of years. Beyond it, across Apostolou Pávlou St, tucked in the side of Philopáppos Hill, is the **Pnyx**, where the General Assembly of Athens heard the speeches of Pericles and Demosthenes. On Assembly days it was sometimes necessary to round up citizens in order to fill the minimum attendance quota of 5,000. For important debates, 18,000 could squeeze in here. Later the Assembly was transferred to the Theatre of Diónysos. The Pnyx assemblies now consist of tourists watching the Sound and Light Show.

An attractive stone and marble lane leads via the lovely Byzantine church of **Ag. Dimítrios** up to the **Philopáppos Monument** (AD 114) built in honour of Caius Julius Antiochos Philopáppos, a Syrian Prince and friend of Athens. The surrounding park is a good spot for sunset views of the Acropolis, but very isolated at night. Nearby is the Dora Stratou Theatre, where Athens' folk dance troupe performs nightly in summer.

## The Theatre of Diónysos and Odeon of Herodes Atticus

Two theatres are tucked into the south flank of the Acropolis. The older, in fact the oldest in the world if you don't count the 'theatre' at Knossós, is the **Theatre of Diónysos** (*t 010 322 4625; open Tues–Sun 8.30–2.30; adm*). Built in the 6th century BC when Thespis created the first true drama, it was continually modified up to the time of Nero. Here, 17,000 could watch the annual Greater Dionysia, held in honour of Diónysos, the god of wine and patron divinity of the theatre; the dramatic competitions were awarded prizes, many of which went to the works of Aeschylus, Sophocles, Aristophanes and Euripides. The stage that remains is from the 4th century BC, while the area before the stage, the *proskenion*, is decorated with 1st century AD scenes based on the life of Diónysos. Further east in Pláka, the **Monument of Lysikrátes** was built by an 'angel' who funded the play that won top prize in 334 BC. It later passed into the hands of Capuchin friars, who hosted Lord Byron; another Lord, Elgin, wanted to take the monument to London but was thwarted this time by the friars.

Next to the Theatre of Diónysos, the **Odeon** (AD 161) was originally covered with a roof when built by the Rockefeller of his day, Herodes Atticus (like someone out of *Arabian Nights*: he inherited his great wealth from his father, who found a vast golden treasure outside Rome). The Odeon hosts the annual mid-May and September **Festival of Athens**, where modern European and ancient Greek cultures meet in theatre, ballet, and classical music concerts performed by international companies.

## The Heart of Ancient Athens: the Agora, Theseum and Stoa of Attalos

*t 010 321 0185; open Tues–Sun 8.30–3; adm.*

The Agora was not only the market but the centre of Athenian civic and social life. After the Persians destroyed all the buildings in 480 BC, the Agora was rebuilt in a much grander style; since then many landmarks have suffered, mostly from angry Romans or Athenians in need of cheap building stone. Only the foundations remain of the council house, or **Bouleuterion**, and the neighbouring Temple of the Mother of the Gods, the **Metroön**, built by the Athenians as reparation for the slaying of a priest from her cult. The round **Tholos**, or administration centre, is where the *prytanes* worked, and as some were on call day and night, kitchens and sleeping quarters were included. Nearby is the *horos*, or boundary stone still in situ; a path from here leads to foundations that have been tentatively identified as the prison where Socrates spent his last days and drank the fatal hemlock. Opposite the Metroön, a stone fence and statue bases mark the remains of the **Sanctuary of the Eponymous Heroes of Athens**, the ten who gave their names to Kleisthenes' ten tribes. The nearby **Altar of Zeus Agoraios** received the oaths of the new *archons*, a practice initiated by Solon.

The 4th-century **Temple of Apollo** was dedicated to the forebear of the Ionians, who believed themselves descended from Apollo's son Ion; the cult statue of Apollo it once held is now in the Agora Museum. Almost nothing remains of the **Stoa of Zeus Eleutherios**, the court of the annual *archon*, where trials concerning state security were held. By the Stoa of Zeus stood the **Altar of the Twelve Gods**, from which all distances in Attica were measured. Alongside it ran the sacred **Panathenaic Way** (566 BC) that ascended to the Acropolis, where devotees celebrated the union of Attica; signs of its Roman rebuilding can be seen by the Church of the Holy Apostles. South of the Altar of the Twelve Gods stood a Doric **Temple to Ares** (5th century BC). **The Three Giants** nearby were originally part of the **Odeon of Agrippa** (15 BC); parts of the orchestra remain intact after the roof collapsed in 190 AD. Both the site and giants were reused in the façade of a 5th-century AD gymnasium, that a century later became the University of Athens, until Justinian closed it down. Near the **Middle Stoa** (2nd century BC) are ruins of a **Roman temple** and ancient shops. On the other side of the Middle Stoa was the people's court, or **Heliaia**, organized by Solon in the 6th century BC to hear political questions; it remained active well into Roman times.

Between the South and East Stoas (2nd century BC) is the 11th-century Church of the Holy Apostles (Ag. Apóstoli), built on the site where St Paul addressed the Athenians; it was restored, along with its fine paintings, in 1952. Across the Panathenaic Way run the remains of Valerian's Wall thrown up in 257 AD against the Barbarians, its stone cannibalized from Agora buildings wrecked by the Romans. Between Valerian's Wall and the Stoa of Attalos are higgledy-piggledy ruins of the Library of Pantainos, built by Flavius Pantainos in AD 100 and destroyed 167 years later. Artefacts found in the Agora, which give a far better view of everyday life in Athens than the National Museum, are housed in the excellent **Agora Museum** in the Stoa of Attalos, the 2nd-century BC portico built by one of Athens' benefactors, King Attalos II of Pergamon, and reconstructed by a later benefactor, John D. Rockefeller of Cleveland, Ohio.

Adjacent to the Agora, the mid 5th-century BC **Theseum** is the best-preserved Greek temple in existence. Doric in order and dedicated to Hephaistos, the god of metals and smiths, it may have been designed by the architect of the temple at Sounion. It's constructed of Pentelic marble and decorated with *metopes* depicting the lives of Heracles and Theseus (for whom the temple was later misnamed). Converted into a church in the 5th century, it was the burial place for English Protestants until 1834.

## National Archaeology Museum

*Patissíon and Tossítsa Sts; t 010 821 7717; open Apr–mid-Oct Mon 12.30–7, Tues–Fri 8–7, Sat and Sun 8.30–3; winter Mon 11–5, Tues–Fri 8–5, Sat and Sun 8.30–3; adm.* **Note**: *museum is due to close for a year's renovations beginning autumn 2002.*

This is the big one, and deserves much more space than permitted here. It contains some of the most spectacular and beautiful works of the ancient Greek world – the Minoan frescoes from Santoríni, gold from Mycenae (including the famous 'mask of Agamemnon'), statues, reliefs, tomb *stelae*, and ceramics and vases from every period.

The Cycladic collection includes one of the first known musicians, the 4,000-year-old sculpture of the little harpist that has become the virtual symbol of the Cyclades. The star of the sculpture rooms is a virile bronze of Poseidon (5th century BC) about to launch his trident, found off the coast of Évia in 1928; around him are some outstanding archaic Kouros statues and the Stele of Hegeso, an Athenian beauty, enveloped by the delicate folds of her robe, seated on a throne. Don't miss the so-called Antikýthera Mechanism, the world's first computer, made on Rhodes c. 70 BC (see 'Antikýthera', pp.465–6).

# Other Museums and Sites in Athens

**Athens City Museum**: 7 Paparigópoulou St; t 010 324 6164; open Sun, Mon, Wed, Fri and Sat, 9–1.30; adm. This former residence of King Otto contains photos and water-colours of Athens as it was soon after becoming capital of modern Greece. Many show how built-up the Acropolis was before the archaeologists went to work.

**Benáki Museum**: Cnr of Vass. Sofías and Koumbári Sts; t 010 367 1000; www.benaki.gr; open Mon, Wed, Fri and Sat 9–5, Thurs 9–midnight, Sun 9–3; adm. One of the city's best museums, covering Greek civilization from the Stone Age to Odysseus Elytis. There are rare and beautiful items from all periods and among the icons, two painted by El Greco before he left Crete. The folk art section contains a superb collection of costumes and artefacts. There's a good lunch restaurant on top, but book.

**Byzantine Museum**: 22 Vass. Sofías St; t 010 721 1027; open Tues–Sun 8.30–3; adm. This impressive museum contains a monumental collection of religious treasures ranging from the Early Byzantine period to the 19th century – icons, marble sculptures, mosaics, woodcarvings, frescoes, manuscripts and ecclesiastical robes. There are three rooms on the ground floor arranged as chapels: one Early Christian, another Middle Byzantine, and the third post-Byzantine.

**Goulandrís Museum of Cycladic and Ancient Greek Art**: 4 Neofýtou Doúka St (off Vass. Sofías St); t 010 722 8321; open Mon and Wed–Fri 10–4, Sat 10–3; adm. This collection of Cycladic figurines going back to 3000 BC, as well as other ancient Greek art, is second only to the National Museum, but better documented and displayed. Don't miss the Cycladic toastmaster, or the 5th-century BC cat with a kitten in her mouth.

**Greek Folk Art Museum**: 17 Kidathinéon St, Pláka; t 010 322 9031; open Tues–Sun 10–2; adm. Exquisite embroideries, carvings, jewellery and paintings by Hatzimichail.

**Ilías Lalaoúnis Jewellery Museum**: 4a Karyátidon St, Acropolis; t 010 922 1044; open Mon 10.30–4.45, Tues–Sun 8.30–14.45; adm. Dedicated to the history of jewellery-making through the designs of the master jeweller, with a very pricey gift shop.

**Jewish Museum**: 29 Níkis St; t 010 322 5582; open Mon–Fri 9–2.30 and Sun 10–2. Jews lived in Greece since Hellenistic times, but the majority arrived from Spain after their expulsion in 1492; only a small minority of the 78,000 survived the Holocaust. Documents and artefacts go back to the 3rd century BC.

**Kanellópoulos Museum**: Cnr of Theorías and Panós Sts (near the Agora); t 010 321 2313; open Tues–Sun 8:30–3; adm. An eclectic private collection, including funeral vases and Tanagra figurines from Thebes, the forerunners of those Dresden figurines.

**Kerameikós and Museum**: *148 Ermoú St; t 010 346 3552; open Tues–Sun 8.30–3; adm.* This cemetery was used from the 12th century BC into Roman times, and is one of the most fascinating sites in Athens, carefully restored to look as it did in the 5th century BC – your best chance to get a feel for Periclean Athens. Stone vases mark the graves of the unmarried, while others are in the form of miniature temples and *stelae*. There's a small but excellent museum and booklet by the archaeologists.

**National Gallery**: *50 Vass. Konstantínos Av. (across from the Hilton); t 010 721 6560/723 5857; open daily exc Tues 9–3, Mon and Wed also 6–9pm, Sun and hols 10–2; adm.* Painting and sculpture, mostly Greek artists, including three El Grecos; works by the leading contemporary painter, Níkos Hadzikyriákos-Ghíkas, are on the first floor.

**National Historical Museum**: *13 Stadíou St; t 010 323 7617; open Tues–Sun 9–1.30; adm, free on Sun.* In the imposing Neoclassical Old Parliament of Greece are exhibits on Greek history, concentrating on the War of Independence. Highlights are the 25 small *naïf* paintings narrating Greek history from the fall of Constantinople, commissioned by General Makriyiánnis, who described the events to the painter Zographos (another set is in Windsor Castle library). Also see Byron's sword and helmet and his famous portrait dressed as a *klepht*, and a sumptuous collection of Greek folk costumes.

**Numismatic Museum**: *12 Panepistimíou St; t 010 364 3774; open Tues–Sun 8–2:30; adm.* This terrific museum featuring 600,000 coins is housed in Heinrich Schliemann's Neoclassical pile, designed by Ernst Ziller, that's worth a visit in itself.

**Popular Musical Instruments Museum**: *1–3 Diogénous St, Pláka; t 010 325 0198; open Tues, Thurs–Sun 10–2, Wed 12–7.* Great collection of old and new Greek instruments.

**Roman Forum**: *Pelopia and Eólou Sts (Pláka); t 010 324 5220; open Tues–Sun 8.30–3; adm.* At the end of the Hellenistic Age, feeling uncomfortable in the Greek Agora, especially after they laid waste to it (*see* below) the Romans built their own market-place. It has one of Athens' best loved monuments, the 1st century BC **Tower of the Winds**, or Clock of Andronikos Kyrrhestes, an all-marble tower, which was operated by a hydraulic mechanism, so the Athenians could know the time, day or night. Note the frieze of the eight winds that decorate its eight sides, although it has lost its original bronze Triton weathervane. The Turks made it a mini-mosque, with a niche indicating the direction of Mecca. At its west end, the forum contains the **Gate of Athena Archegetis**, built by Julius and Augustus Caesar; one of its posts, still in place, has the market-pricing rules imposed by Hadrian. There is also a court and ruined stoa, and the Fetchiyé Tzamí, the Victory or **Corn Market Mosque**, now used as a store-room. Opposite the Tower of the Winds, the **Medresse** (with Arabic script running over the door) was an Islamic seminary built in 1721 but later a prison.

**Temple of Olympian Zeus**: *Vass. Ólgas and Amalías Sts; t 010 922 6330; open Tues–Sun 8.30–3; adm.* Fifteen columns recall what Livy called 'the only temple on earth of a size adequate to the greatness of the god'. The foundations were laid by the tyrant Pisístratos, but work halted with the fall of his dynasty, only to be continued in 175 BC by a Roman architect, Cossutius. It was half finished when Cossutius' patron, Antiochos IV of Syria, kicked the bucket, leaving the Emperor Hadrian to complete it in 131 AD. At the far end stands **Hadrian's Arch**, erected by the Athenians to thank the emperor for his help. The complimentary inscription reads on the Acropolis side: 'This is Athens, the ancient city of Theseus', while the other side reads: 'This is the city of Hadrian, not of Theseus'. Athenians come here to celebrate Easter.

**War Museum of Greece**: *Vass. Sofías and Rizári Sts, t 010 723 9560; open Tues–Fri 9–2.* Weapons and battle relics past and present.

## Byzantine Churches and Monasteries

**Ag. Theódori**: *Klafthmónos Square (end of Dragatsaníou St)*. 11th-century church, notable for its beautiful door, bell tower and some more recent decorations inside.

**Kapnikaréa**: *Ermoú St*. This tiny late 11th-century chapel was built in the shape of a Greek cross. Its central cupola is supported by four columns with Roman capitals.

**Panagía Gorgoepíkoos** (also called **Ag. Elefthérios**): *Mitropóleos Square.* 'Our Lady who Grants Requests Quickly', the loveliest church in Athens, is known as the little cathedral and was built in the 12th century almost entirely of ancient marbles; note the ancient calendar of state festivals and signs of the zodiac. The adjacent 'big' **cathedral** (Metropolitan) was built in 1840–55 with the same collage technique, using pieces from 72 destroyed churches. The Glucksberg Kings of Greece were crowned here between 1863 and 1964, and it contains the tomb of the unofficial saint of the Greek revolution, the Patriarch of Constantinople Gregory V, hanged in 1821.

**Ag. Ioánnis**: *Evripídou St and Diplári St, off Athinás St in Psirrí*. A tiny church with a Corinthian column sticking out of its roof. People visited it to cure their fevers; the idea was to tie the fevers to the column with string or bits of wool. If you can find a custodian, ask to see those still dangling from the column behind the iconostasis.

**Moní Pendéli**: *Bus 450 from the National Gallery to Plateía Chalandri, and bus 426, 423 or 451 from there*. Founded in 1578, in a lovely wooded setting on the mountain of Pentelic marble, this huge monastery is a popular weekend refuge from the smog.

**Dafní Monastery**: *A16 bus from Plateía Koumoundoúrou. At the time of writing closed for repairs, following the 1999 earthquake; call t 171 for reopening date in 2004*. The name derives from the Temple of Apollo Dafneíos (of the laurel), built on the Sacred Way from Athens to Eleusis. Dafní existed as a walled monastery by the 6th century and, when a new church was built in 1080, it was decorated with some of the best Byzantine mosaics in southern Greece. If one were to pin down a setting for *A Midsummer's Night Dream*, Dafní's park is the most logical candidate. These days the moonstruck are confined to the psychiatric hospital across the road.

## Piraeus

The port of Athens, Piraeus (ΠΕΙΡΑΙΑΣ) – pronounced pi-ray-A – was the greatest port of the ancient world and remains one of the busiest in the Mediterranean. In a country that derives most of its livelihood from the sea, Piraeus is the true capital, while Athens is a sprawling suburb full of bureaucrats. Still, it's hard to find much charm in the tall buildings and dusty streets, although Zéa Marína and Mikrolímano with their yachts, brightly-lit tavernas and bars are a handsome sight.

## History

Themistocles founded the port of Piraeus in the 5th century BC when Pháliron, Athens' ancient port, could no longer meet the growing needs of the city. The Miletian geometrician Hippodamos laid it out in a straight grid of streets that have hardly changed. The centre of action was always the huge central *agora*, where the world's first commercial fairs and trade expositions were held. All religions were tolerated, and women were allowed, for the first time, to work outside the home.

As Piraeus was crucial to Athens' power, the conquering Spartans destroyed the Long Walls linking city and port in 404, at the end of the Peloponnesian War. After the 100-year Macedonian occupation and a period of peace, Sulla decimated the city to prevent any anti-Roman resistance, and for 1,900 years Piraeus dwindled away into an

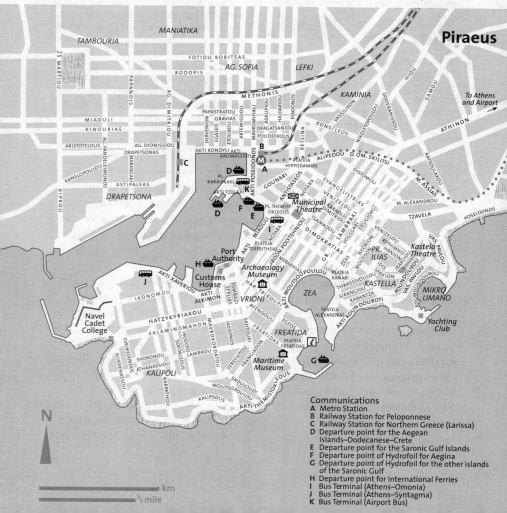

**Piraeus**

### Communications
A  Metro Station
B  Railway Station for Peloponnese
C  Railway Station for Northern Greece (Larissa)
D  Departure point for the Aegean
    Islands–Dodecanese–Crete
E  Departure point for the Saronic Gulf Islands
F  Departure point of Hydrofoil for Aegina
G  Departure point of Hydrofoil for the other islands
    of the Saronic Gulf
H  Departure point for International Ferries
I  Bus Terminal (Athens–Omonia)
J  Bus Terminal (Athens–Syntagma)
K  Bus Terminal (Airport Bus)

# Getting Around

The ticket agents are very competitive, but prices to the islands are fixed, so the only reason to shop around is to find an earlier or faster ship. For non-biased ferry schedules call the **Piraeus Port Authority t** 010 422 6000 or the tourist police, **t** 171. The **metro** is the quickest way into central Athens. To reach Zéa Marína (for **hydrofoils** to the Saronic Islands) catch bus no.904 from the main port.

# Tourist Information

**Zea Marina: t** 010 452 2586; *open 8–3.*
**Port police: t** 010 412 2501.
**Left-luggage:** facility in the metro station.

# Where to Stay

Unfortunately accommodation in Piraeus is geared towards businessmen, and less towards people who've arrived on a late ship.
**Cavo d'Oro,** 19 Vass. Pávlou (by Mikrolímano), **t** 010 411 3744, **f** 010 412 2210 (*lux*). The swishest choice, with a restaurant and disco.
**Kastella,** 75 Vass. Pávlou, **t** 010 411 4735, **f** 010 417 5716 (*lux*). Above the waterfront, with a roof patio.

**Triton,** 8 Tsamadou, **t** 010 417 3457, **f** 010 417 7888 (*exp*). One of the best of the many in the area, if you want to be near the docks. With a good restaurant.
**Ideal,** 142 Notára, **t** 010 429 4050, **f** 010 429 3890 (*mod*). Air-conditioned, but should be renamed the So-So.
**Lilia,** 131 Zéas, Passalimáni, **t** 010 417 9108, **f** 010 411 4311 (*mod*). Free transport to the port.
**Achillion,** 63 Notára, **t** 010 412 4029 (*inexp*). Some rooms have en suite baths.
**Glaros,** 4 Har. Trikoúpi (near the customs house), **t** 010 452 5421, **f** 010 453 7889 (*inexp*).

# Eating Out

**Jimmy the Fish,** 46 Akti Koumoundourou in Mikrolímano, **t** 010 412 4417 (*€24-29*). Great salads, spaghetti with lobster, or the fish of your choice, perfectly prepared.
**Nine Brothers** (Enneea Adélfi), 48 Sotiros St (behind Zea Marina) **t** 010 411 5273. Taverna with lots of locals, and a big choice.
**Varoúlko,** 14 Deligorgi St, **t** 010 411 2043 (*€35-44*). Serves some of the most imaginative seafood in Greece, but ring ahead for the venue, as it moves in the summer. *Open eves only; closed Sun.*

insignificant village with a population as low as 20, even losing its name to become Porto Leone. Since the selection of Athens as the capital of independent Greece, Piraeus has regained its former glory as the reigning port of a seagoing nation, but much of it dates from after 1941, when German bombers blew the port sky-high.

### The Sights

**Archaeology Museum:** *31 Har. Trikoúpi St; t 010 452 1598; open Tues–Sun 8–2.30; adm.* Excellent collection. Pride of place goes to five bronzes found in the port in 1959: archaic Kouros, two Artemises, Piraeus' Athena, a tragic mask and a 7th-century BC Protoattico amphora. The museum's newest display, the 24ft funerary Monument of Nikeratus (325 BC), is the largest ever found in Greece.

**Naval Museum of Greece:** *Akti Themistokléous, Freatída; t 010 451 6264; open Tues–Sun 9–2.* Plans of Greek naval battles, ship models (including the unique Onassis collection) and mementos from the War of Independence and the Second World War.

**The flea market** (*Dragatsaniou and Mavromicheli Sts*). Worth a look on Sunday mornings. Kastélla and Néo Fáliron are the closest **beaches**, but the sea isn't sparkling. Glyfáda and Vouliagméni offer more wholesome swimming, golf and EOT **marinas**.

# Crete

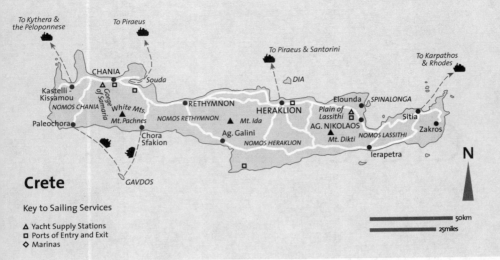

**Crete**

**Key to Sailing Services**

- △ Yacht Supply Stations
- ▢ Ports of Entry and Exit
- ◇ Marinas

*Column of the Levant,*
*My Crete, beautiful island,*
*Your soil is made of gold,*
*Your each stone a diamond.*
>            traditional Cretan *matináda*

On the map a horned, wasp-waisted creature scooting along the 35th parallel, Crete is Greece's largest island (260km by 50km), and its most extraordinary. Endowed with every earthly delight, Crete nurtured the first civilization on European soil, the Minoan, which, judging by its artistic and architectural talents was so graceful and inventive that Europe has yet to see the like. Crete is terribly old; the birthplace of Zeus, it gave Greece its first myths; in remote villages old customs retain their pull. Fifty years ago, guidebooks warned that a lingering glance at a Cretan girl might bring out a brother's shotgun; today you're more likely to be suffocated by the worst excesses of mass tourism. The lovely beaches along the north coast have been raped by toadstool strips of jerry-built hotels, shops, restaurants and discos, where bars advertise the latest football scores, baked beans and permanent happy hours. Crete's hot climate makes it a major package holiday destination from early spring until the end of October. Even once remote corners such as the Minoan palace of Zákros or the Diktean Cave are now besieged by coach parties. If you have fantasies of tripping alone through the labyrinth of Knossós, book your flight for winter; after the Acropolis, it's the most visited site in Greece.

Crete's popularity is a tribute to its extraordinary charms. Four mountain ranges lend the island a dramatic grandeur out of proportion to its size; the White Mountains in the west hold the Gorge of Samariá, the longest canyon in Europe. Some 1,500 kinds of wild flowers, including species unique to Crete, brighten the landscape in the spring with the intensity of 1950s Technicolor. No place in Greece can approach Crete's agricultural diversity: vineyards, olive and citrus groves cover the coastal plains and hillside terraces; cereals, potatoes, apples and walnuts come from the well-watered mountain plains, especially around Lassíthi; and acres of

## How Crete is Divided

Lofty mountain ranges neatly divide the island into four sections. These have become modern Crete's political divisions and are used for reference in this book. West of the White Mountains is the *nomós* (province) of Chaniá; between the White Mountains and Psilorítis (Mount Ida) is the *nomós* of Réthymnon; between Psilorítis and the Lassíthi Mountains lies the *nomós* of Heráklion; and east of the Lassíthi Mountains is the *nomós* of Lassíthi, of which Ag. Nikólaos is the capital. The description in the text covers Crete from west to east.

plastic greenhouses blanket the south coast, providing no advantage to the scenery but bushels of winter vegetables and fruit for the rest of Greece. Cretan art and architecture afford an equally rich feast: the fabled Minoan sites and artefacts in Heráklion's superb Archaeology Museum; Byzantine monasteries glowing with frescoes and icons by the Cretan School; the Venetian and Turkish quarters of Chaniá and Réthymnon; mountain villages that display the native sense of design. Crete, of all the islands, has the sharpest sense of a separate identity and a ferocious love of liberty, manifest in its own culture, dialect, music and dances, and in the works of its famous sons, El Greco, Elelocalithérios Venizélos, Níkos Kazantzákis and Míkis Theodorákis. Old men in the mountain villages cut a dash in their baggy breeches. On feast days, *matinádes* or *rizítika* ('songs from the roots') are sung with themes of Cretan patriotism. Such patriotism is far from dead. In the face of a creeping homogenized Europe, many young Cretans are helping to preserve their traditions, even moving back to their ancestral villages, where EU subsidies assure them a decent living. Paradoxes are rife, but the island can take some credit for making paradox an art form, when the Cretan sage Epimenides declared: 'All Cretans are liars.'

# Getting to Crete

## By Air

Heráklion, and to a lesser extent Chaniá, are linked by direct **charter flights** to London Gatwick, Stansted, Luton, Bristol, Exeter, Cardiff, Manchester, Birmingham, East Midlands, Glasgow, Newcastle, Dublin and Belfast. Major carriers **Olympic** and **Aegean** have frequent daily flights from Athens to Heráklion and Chaniá, and several times a week from Thessaloníki. Both airlines also operate flights several times a week from Heráklion to Rhodes and Santoríni. Olympic has 3 flights a week from Athens to Sitía.

## By Sea

Large comfortable **ferries** link Heráklion, Chaniá and Réthymnon to Piraeus daily, and sail frequently to Ag. Nikólaos and Sitía. The 10–12-hr night journey is fine with a cabin. There are daily ships in summer from Santoríni, and the other Cyclades: Mýkonos, Iós, Náxos, Páros, Tínos, Sýros and Mílos; others, sometimes calling at Ag. Nikólaos and Sitía, sail to the Dodecanese islands of Kárpathos, Kássos, Chálki, Rhodes; 5 times a week there are ferries from Thessaloníki and less frequently from Skýros and Skiáthos. Another line links Kastélli-Kíssimou on the west coast with Kýthera, Anitkýthera, and Gýthion and Kalamáta in the Peloponnese.

# When to Go

The ideal time to visit Crete is late April, when you'll avoid the worst crowds; the Libyan Sea is warm enough for bathing, the flowers are glorious and the higher mountains are still capped with snow. Note that the Gorge of Samariá rarely opens until early May, when its torrent recedes sufficiently for safe passage. October is another good month, with many perfect days and a lingering warm sea.

## Mythology

As Cronos (the Roman Saturn), the ruler of the world, had been warned that he would be usurped by his own child, he swallowed every baby his wife Rhea, daughter of the Earth, presented to him. After this had happened five times, Rhea determined on a different fate for her sixth child, Zeus. When he was born she smuggled him to Crete and gave Cronos a swaddled stone to swallow instead. Mother Earth hid the baby in the Diktean Cave and set Cretan warriors called Kouretes to guard him. As prophesied, Zeus grew up and dethroned his father by castrating him with a sickle.

When a Phoenician princess, Europa, caught Zeus' fancy, the god disguised himself as a beautiful bull and carried Europa off to Crete, where she bore him three sons: Minos, Rhadamanthys and Sarpedon, and gave her name to an entire continent. When Minos became the King of Crete at Knossós, he was asked to prove that his claim to the throne had divine sanction. Minos remembered the form his father had taken and asked Poseidon to send him a bull from the sea to sacrifice. However, the bull was so magnificent that Minos didn't kill it, but sent it to service his herds.

The kingdom of Minos prospered. But Poseidon, weary of waiting for the promised sacrifice, caused Minos' wife Pasiphaë to fall in love with the bull. The unfortunate Pasiphaë confided her problem to the inventor Daedalus, who constructed a hollow wooden cow covered with hide for her to enter and mate with the bull. This union resulted in the Minotaur, born with the head of a bull and the body of a man. Minos hid the monster in another invention of Daedalus, the Labyrinth (an impossible maze of corridors under his palace) and fed it with the blood of his enemies. Among these

## History

The first Cretans were Neolithic sailors, probably from Asia Minor, who arrived on the island *c.* 8000 BC. They built small houses in Knossós and other future Minoan sites, with small rooms clustered around a central open area, presaging the floor-plans of the famous palaces. They worshipped fertility goddesses, especially in caves on top of mountains – these evolved into the peak sanctuaries of the **Minoans**. Europe's first literate civilization was described by its first poet, Homer:

> One of the great islands of the world in midsea, in the winedark sea, is Krete: spacious and rich and populous, with ninety cities and a mingling of tongues. Akhaians there are found, along with Kretan hillmen of the old stock, and Kydonians, Dorians in three blood-lines, Pelasgians – and one among their ninety towns is Knossós. Here lived King Minos whom great Zeus received every ninth year in private council.
>
> (translated by Robert Fitzgerald)

Yet the Minoans only left the realm of myth in 1900, when Arthur Evans discovered a new Copper and Bronze Age civilization at Knossós that he called 'Minoan'. Since then, discoveries in Crete have continued apace, including remarkable finds that have altered Evans' vision of the Minoans as a non-violent society of artsy flower children. Their accomplishments may also go back further in time than Evans thought; the latest dating techniques add another few centuries to the timescale, i.e. Santoríni, the presumed culprit of their collapse, is now believed to have erupted around 1750 BC.

were seven maidens and seven youths from Athens, sent to Crete every nine years, the tribute extorted by Minos when his son was slain in an Athenian game.

Two tributes had been paid when Theseus, the son of Aegeus, King of Athens, demanded to be sent as one of the victims. He was so handsome that Minos' daughter Ariadne fell in love with him. She asked Daedalus to help her save his life, and the inventor gave her a ball of thread. Unwinding the thread as he went, Theseus made his way into the labyrinth, slew the Minotaur, retraced his way out with the ball of thread and escaped, taking Ariadne and the other Athenians with him.

Minos was furious when he discovered the part Daedalus had played in the escape, and threw the inventor and his young son Icarus into the Labyrinth. Although they found their way out, escape from Crete was impossible, as Minos controlled the seas. But Daedalus, never at a loss, fashioned wings of feathers and wax for himself and Icarus, and they flew towards Asia Minor. All went well until an exhilarated Icarus disobeyed his father's command not to fly too close to the sun. The wax in his wings melted, and he plunged and drowned off the island that took his name.

Minos heard of Daedalus' escape and pursued him all over the Mediterranean, hoping to trap the wily inventor by offering a reward to whoever could pass a thread through a nautilus shell. Finally, in Sicily, Minos met a king who took the shell away and brought it back threaded – it was Daedalus who had performed the task by tying the thread to an ant. Minos demanded that Daedalus be handed over. Instead, the king invited Minos to stay at his palace. While Minos was in his bath, Daedalus put a pipe through the ceiling and poured boiling water through it, scalding him to death.

Trade with Egypt, the Cyclades and the Middle East at the end of the Neolithic era introduced bronze to Crete and brought about the changes that distinguish the first Minoan period, the **Pre-Palatial** (2600–1900 BC), according to Níkos Pláton's widely accepted revision of Evans' chronology. Characteristic of the Pre-Palatial era are the first monumental *tholos* tombs (as at Archánes), the building of high sanctuaries and the beginning of a ruling priestly class, who dwelt in palaces with red-plastered walls. The Minoan taste for refinement shines through in exquisite work in gold, semi-precious stones and sealstones, some bearing the first signs of writing in ideograms.

Pláton's **Old Palace period** (Evans' Middle Minoan; 1900–1700 BC) saw a hitherto unheard of concentration of wealth in Crete. Power was concentrated in a few areas: in the 'palaces' of Knossós, Mália, Phaistós and Zákros, which were kitted out with the first-known plumbing and lavishly decorated with frescoes and stylized sacred 'horns of consecration'. Bulls played an important role in religion, which was dominated by the goddess, pictured in Minoan imagery in three aspects: as the mistress of the wild animals and earth; as the snake goddess, mistress of the underworld; and as the dove goddess, mistress of the sky. Towns and palaces were unfortified, suggesting political unity on the island and giving substance to the myth of Minos' thalassocracy, or sea reign: Crete's powerful fleet precluded the need for walls. Their ships, laden with olive oil, honey, wine, precious balsams and art, traded extensively with Cyprus, Egypt and the Greek islands; Minoan colonies have been found at Kéa, Mílos and Kýthera. The palaces/temples all had important stores, acting either as warehouses or distribution points. Writing was in ideograms, as on the Phaistós disc in the Heráklion Museum. Roads paved with flagstones linked settlements on the island, and the first large irrigation projects were begun. Art reached new heights, in gold and in ceramics, especially decorated Kamáres-ware. Then in 1700 BC a huge earthquake ripped across the Eastern Mediterranean and devastated the buildings.

Forced to start afresh, the Minoans built better than ever in the **New Palace period** (1700–1450 BC). The palace complexes were rebuilt in the same style: a warren of rooms illuminated by light wells, overlooking a central and western court, where religious ceremonies and the famous bull-leaping may have occurred. To make the new palaces more resistant to earthquakes, wooden beams and columns were combined with stone. Workshops and vast store-rooms were clustered around the palaces, their contents recorded on clay tablets in a writing system known as Linear A. Fancy villas were built outside the palaces, most famously at Ag. Triáda, and scattered throughout the countryside were centralized farms, with kilns, wine presses and looms. Densely populated towns existed at Gourniá, Móchlos, Palaíkastro, Zákros and Pseíra island. Burials became more elaborate; many were in painted clay sarcophagi, or *larnaxes*. Impressive port facilities were built and new trade centres established on Santoríni, Rhodes, Skópelos, and on the mainlands of Greece and Asia Minor. Shields, daggers, swords and helmets have been found, although land defences were still non-existent.

The Heráklion Museum is full of testimonials to the exuberant art of the period. The Minoans delighted in natural designs, especially floral and marine motifs. They portrayed themselves with wasp waists and long black curls, the men clad in codpieces and loincloths, the women with eyes blackened with kohl and lips painted red, clad in their famous bodices that exposed the breast, flounced skirts and exotic hats. All move with a natural, sensuous grace, completely unlike the stiffly stylized figures in Egyptian and Near Eastern art. The strong feminine quality of the art suggests that Minoan society was matriarchal, and that women were the equals of men, participating in the same sports and ceremonies. Vases and *rhytons* (libation vessels) made of basalt, marble and porphyry are unsurpassed in beauty and technique. Culturally Minoan influence spread north to mainland Greece, recently invaded by northerners known as Achaeans or Mycenaeans; the Minoans communicated with them in the lingua franca of the day, in the script Linear B – proto-ancient Greek.

But some time around 1450 BC disaster struck again. A tremendous volcanic eruption from Santoríni, and subsequent tidal waves and earthquakes, left Crete in ruins; in some places along the north coast a 20cm layer of *tefra* (volcanic ash) has been found – *under* structures belonging to the Late Minoan or **Post-Palace period** (1450–1100 BC). The old theory that mainland Mycenaeans invaded Crete, taking advantage of its disarray, has lost favour before the idea that their infiltration was much more gradual, and that for a long period the Mycenaeans co-existed peacefully with the Minoans. Of the great palaces, Knossós alone was rebuilt, only to burn down once and for all in *c.* 1380 BC; in other places, such as Ag. Triáda, typical Mycenaean palaces, (*megarons*) have been found. Linear B became the dominant script, and the natural, graceful motifs of the New Palace period became ever more conventional and stylized. Clay figurines of the goddess lose not only their sex appeal but any pretensions to realism; they resemble bells with upraised arms and primitive faces. The island maintained its great fleet and contributed 90 ships to the Trojan War.

## After the Minoans: The Dorians

By 1100 BC, Minoan-Mycenaean civilization had ground to a halt; trade disintegrated as the Dorians, armed with the latest technology – iron weapons – invaded Greece, and then Crete. Their coming brought confusion and a cultural dark age (the **Proto-Geometric period**, 1100–900 BC). The last Minoans took to the hills, especially south of Sitía, surviving in memory as the Eteocretans, or true Cretans, Homer's 'hillmen of the old stock'. Their art grew weird as they declined; in Praisós they left mysterious inscriptions in the Greek alphabet, still waiting to be translated. Other Cretans were treated according to the amount of resistance they had offered the Dorians; those who fought the most were enslaved.

By the **Geometric period** (900–650 BC) Crete was politically divided, like the mainland, into a hundred autonomous city-states. The Minoan goddess was adopted into the Greek pantheon – Atana became Athena, Britomartis became Artemis, her son and consort Welchanos became Zeus, father of the gods. Art from the period shows Eastern influences; works in bronze are especially fine. Towards the end, the first bronze statuettes attributed to 'Daedalos' (not to be confused with the mythical inventor) appear, with their characteristic wide eyes, thick hair and parted legs.

The style reached its peak in the **Archaic period** (650–550 BC), when Doric Crete was one of the art centres of Greece. Like the Spartans, the Cretans became austere, not caring to compete with the expanding Ionian commercial and cultural influence in the Mediterranean that created Greece's **Classical Age**. By the 2nd century BC Crete's coasts were little more than pirates' bases. When these pirates niggled Rome by kidnapping the families of nobles at Ostia, right under Rome's nose, the Senate sent Quintus Metellus Creticus to subdue the anarchic island once and for all (69–67 BC).

## Roman and Byzantine Crete

With the Romans, the centre of power on the island moved south to Górtyn, on the fertile Mesará plain, especially once it was made the capital of the Roman province of Crete and Cyrene (Libya) in West Africa. With peace, the population soared to some 300,000. Christianity came early when St Paul appointed his Greek disciple, Titus, to found the first church at Górtyn in AD 58. Richly decorated basilicas were constructed at Knossós, Chersónisos, Górtyn, Lissós, Sýia, Itanos and Kainoúrios.

In 823, the Saracens from North Africa conquered Crete, plunging much of it into misery and decimating Górtyn. One lasting feature of their stay was the building of the first castle at Heráklion, called Kandak ('deep moat'), or Candia, a name which grew to encompass all of Crete in the Middle Ages. In 961 the future Byzantine emperor Nikephóros Phokás reconquered Crete and sent the fabulous treasure of the Saracens back to Constantinople. The victorious Greek soldiers were among the first new colonists given tracts of land; Emperor Aléxis Comnénus later sent his son and other young Byzantine aristocrats, establishing a ruling class that would dominate Crete for centuries.

## Venetian and Ottoman Crete

With the conquest of Constantinople in the Fourth Crusade in 1204 and the division of the empire's spoils, Crete was awarded to Boniface of Montferrat. He sold Crete to the Venetians, who occupied it from 1210 to 1669. The first two centuries of rule by the Most Serene Republic were neither serene nor republican; the Venetians imposed an unpopular feudal system with a doge in Heráklion, and tried to replace the Orthodox hierarchy with a Catholic one. Uprisings occurred, often led by the *árchons*, or old Byzantine nobles. They won important concessions from the Venetians, until, by the 15th century, the Orthodox and Catholics (some 10,000) lived together harmoniously. Happiness was for the few, however – the majority of Cretans were compelled to build immense walls around the port cities, but were not allowed to live inside them.

Relations with Venice were cemented with the fall of Constantinople in 1453, when the Venetians were keen to keep the Cretans on their side against the Turks. In Greece's age-old tradition of absorbing the invader, many Venetians became Hellenized. As a refuge for scholars and painters from Constantinople and mainland Greece, Crete became the key point of contact between the East and the Italian Renaissance in the 15th and 16th centuries, producing, most famously, Doméniko Theotokópoulos, who moved to Venice and Spain and became known as El Greco. Cretan-Venetian academies, architecture, literature, song and romantic poetry blossomed, culminating in the dialect epic poem *Erotókritos* by Vicénzo Kornáros.

Although they had raided Crete periodically after the fall of Constantinople, the Ottomans finally caught the island by surprise. In 1645, Sultan Ibrahim declared war on the Knights of Malta and sent a huge fleet after them. They stopped in Kýthera for coffee and sugar, and the Venetian commander there sent word to his counterpart in Chaniá to allow the fleet safe passage; as the sultan's ships began to sail past, they turned their guns on the city. Chaniá and the rest of Crete soon fell but Heráklion resisted until 1669, after a 21-year siege. Crete proved to be a restive subject of the Ottoman Empire. The fertile lands were given to Turkish colonists, causing resentment and, although their religion was tolerated, many Orthodox Cretans publicly converted to Islam to avoid punishing taxes. Some emigrated to the Venetian-held Ionian islands; those who couldn't rose up against the Turks many times.

In 1898, Greece declared war on Turkey and asked the Great Powers for aid. Britain did little until the Turks made the fatal mistake of killing the British consul and 14 British soldiers in Heráklion. As British, French, Russian and Italian troops subdued sections of the island, Prince George was appointed High Commissioner of an independent Crete. His high-handed ways and imposition of a foreign administration led in 1905 to the Revolution of Therisso, led by Elefthérios Venizélos of Chaniá. In 1909 Venizélos was appointed Prime Minister of Greece, a position that enabled him to secure Crete's union with Greece after the Balkan War of 1913.

## The Battle of Crete

But Crete was to suffer one last invasion. As the Germans overran Greece, the government in Athens took refuge on Crete (23 April 1943), the last bit of Greek territory, defended by 30,000 British, New Zealand and Australian troops hastily

## Food and Wine: The Old/New Cretan Diet

In 1947, researchers for the Rockefeller Foundation noted with astonishment how healthy elderly Cretans were compared to their American counterparts. In spite of the privations of the war and their 'primitive' way of life, people in their 90s were still running up mountains and working in the fields. In 1956, the Foundation began a 15-year study in Japan, Finland, Yugoslavia, the USA, Holland, Italy, Corfu and Crete comparing diet, lifestyle and the incidence of cardiovascular disease and cancer. If health were a race, Crete lapped the competition several times; the difference in death rates, even compared with Corfu, was striking. And this in spite of the fact that Cretans consume as much fat as the Finns, who did the worst in coronary disease; in fact, the only Cretan who died of coronary failure during the study was a butcher.

Olive oil (the main source of fat), lots of legumes, greens and fresh vegetables, and little meat proved to be the secret and the basis of the Cretan diet that nutritionists, and now the Cretans, are beginning to promote. The island grows vegetables, nuts, olives and every kind of fruit from apples to bananas and citrus; market counters heave with herbs. Cretan honey and cheeses have had a high reputation since antiquity: the best is *myzíthra*, a white soft cheese similar to fresh ricotta, often served on rusks with tomatoes, as a starter (*dákos*); another is *stáka*, a rich white cheese, often baked in a cheese pie or served fried as a hot creamy dip. When Cretans do eat meat, they do delicious things to it, as in lamb *kriotópita* (baked in pastry with cheese), or kid stewed in fruit juice; and they eat more snails (*saligária*) than most Greeks.

No milk, but wine in moderation is definitely part of the diet. Crete itself produces two AO wines of distinction: fresh white Péza and spicy Archánes. *Tsikoudiá*, an *eau-de-vie* distilled in a hundred mountain stills, is Crete's firewater, its moonshine, its pure hot-blooded soul, its cure-all; for a change try it hot, with a spoonful of honey.

transferred from the mainland. Crete's own battalions were trapped near the Albanian frontier; the only Greek soldiers on the island were cadets. But then again, no-one suspected what Goering and General Student, his second-in-command of the Luftwaffe, had in store. After a week of bomb raids, Nazi paratroopers launched the world's first successful invasion by air on Crete (20 May 1941). The Allied and Greek forces, along with hundreds of poorly armed men, women and children, put up such resistance that the Germans were forced to expend the cream of their forces to subdue the island over the next 10 days – at the cost of 170 aircraft, 4,000 specially trained paratroopers, and their 7th airborne division. As Churchill wrote, 'In Crete Goering won a Pyrrhic victory, because with the forces he wasted there he could easily have conquered Cyprus, Syria, Iraq or even Persia...'

In spite of brutal German reprisals, resistance to the occupation, aided by British agents, was legendary, especially the daring abduction of German commander General Kreipe by Major Patrick Leigh Fermor and Captain Billy Moss in 1943. As a massive manhunt combed the island, the British and Cretan Resistance spirited Kreipe away to Egypt, earning a final, grudging compliment from the General: 'I am beginning to wonder who is occupying the island – us or the English.'

# Nomós Chaniá

Unless you have only a few days and want to concentrate on the high shrines of Minoan culture around Heráklion, consider easing yourself gently into this complex island by starting with its westernmost province. Nomós Chaniá has the fewest tourists but the most beautiful landscapes. This is the land of the White Mountains, which hit the sky at Mount Pachnés (8,041ft) and are sliced down the middle by one of Crete's five-star attractions, the Gorge of Samariá, the classic day-walk that emerges by the Libyan Sea. But it's only the most famous hiking path of many. Beaches in the province are mostly innocent of dense cacophonous strips of bars and fast food places. The best sands are on the far west coast, from Falassarná to the tropical lagoon of Elafonísi. In between the mountains and sea you'll find orange groves, olives, vineyards and cypresses, and landcapes more Tuscan than Greek. Another major attraction is the lovely city of Chaniá, capital of the province.

# Chaniá (XANIA)

Chaniá, Crete's second city (pop. 73,000), is the most elegant and seductive of the island's four provincial capitals, with the ghostly forms of the snow-capped White Mountains hovering over its palm trees. The old streets are lined with Venetian, Turkish and Neoclassical monuments. Unfortunately, many were lost in bombing raids during the Battle of Crete; fortunately, perhaps, the war-scarred ruins stood neglected for so many decades that they've now been incorporated into garden settings for bars and restaurants. The lovely inner and outer Venetian harbours are evening magnets, where dawdling over a drink can easily become addictive.

The ancient historian Diodoros Sikelus wrote that Chaniá was founded by Minos and was one of the three great cities of Crete. Buildings excavated in the Kastélli quarter go back to 2200 BC, and archaeologists are pretty sure that the Minoan palace and town, KY-DO-NI-JA, referred to on a Linear B tablet found at Knossós, lie hidden under the modern town. Kydonia was so important that for a time its name referred to all of Crete. In modern Greek, kydóni means quince, a fruit loved by the Minoans: the word (like 'hyacinth', 'labyrinth', and 'sandal') may well have come from the pre-Greek Minoan language. Quince Town survived the rest of Cretan history to get a mention in Homer, to know glory days in the Hellenistic and Roman periods, then to decline so far between the 10th and 13th centuries that it was better known as 'Rubbish City'. Revived under the Venetians, who called it La Canea, it was so splendid by the 1500s that it was renamed the 'Venice of the East'. Crete's capital from 1850–1971, Chaniá was the island's window on the outside world, with consulates and embassies, and it prospered as the fief of statesman Eleuthérios Venizélos.

## Into Old Chaniá

The vortex of daily life in Chaniá is its covered market, or *agora* (1911), standing at the entrance to the old town. The back stairs of the market and a left turn will take you to

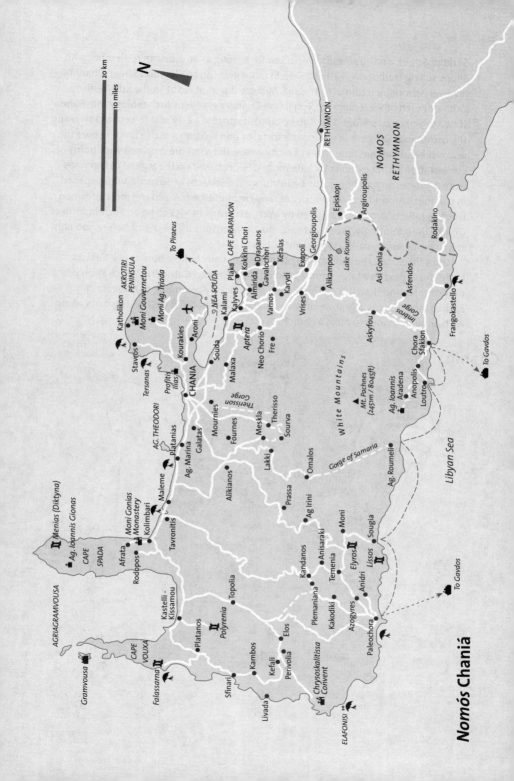

**Skrídlof** Street, a narrow lane jam-packed for as long as anyone can remember with shops selling traditional leathergoods. Skrídlof gives on to Chalídon Street, Chaniá's jewellery-shop-lined funnel to the sea. Midway down, at No.21, in the 14th-century Gothic church of San Francesco, you'll find Chaniá's excellent **Archaeology Museum** (t 082 109 0334; open Tues–Sun 8.30–3; adm). Its prize is a clay seal (c. 1450 BC) showing the commanding figure of a Minoan mortal or god holding a staff, standing over the sea as it breaks against the gates of a city where the roofs are crowned with horns of consecration. Other exhibits include mosaic floors based on the legend of Dionysos from a 3rd-century AD house, the beautiful gold necklaces of Sossima, who perished in childbirth around the 3rd century BC, and cases of Linear A and the more common Linear B tablets, proved on a hunch by Michael Ventris in 1952 to be an ancient form of Greek. Disappointingly, the tablets are mostly inventories: 'Five jars of honey, 300 pigs, 120 cows for As-as-wa' is a typical entry.

Across the street, the sad looking building with baby bubble domes is a Turkish bath. This is next to a large square holding the **Trimartyr Cathedral**, which should be more interesting than it is. In the 1850s a soap factory belonging to Mustafa Nily Pasha stood here; as a gesture of reconciliation he donated it to the Christians, along with enough money to build a church.

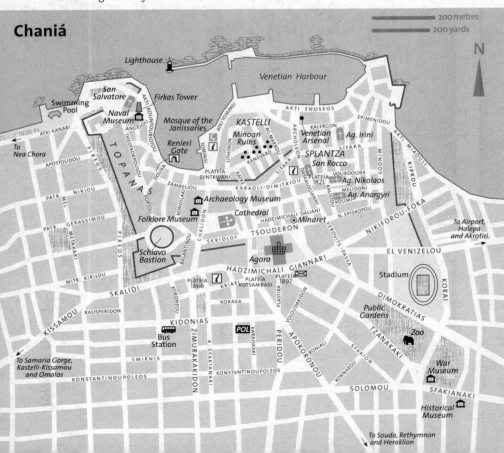

# Getting There and Around

## By Air

Chaniá **airport** is situated out on the Akrotíri Peninsula, **t** 082 106 3264; a taxi to the city centre costs around €15. The Olympic Airways office is located at 88 Stratigoú Tzanakáki, **t** 082 105 7700. Aegean/Cronus is at the airport, reservations **t** 080 120 000 and in town at 12 El. Venizélou, **t** 082 105 1100.

## By Sea

**Ferry** tickets from Soúda to Piraeus are available from ANEK (departs daily at 8pm), on Venizélou, in the market square **t** 082 102 7500, and from Minoan Lines (three times a week), also in the market square, **t** 082 104 5911. The nightly Piraeus–Chaniá ferry pulls in around 6am and is met by local buses. **Port authority: t** 082 104 3052.

## By Bus

**KTEL buses** travel from the station at Kidonías hourly to Heráklion and Réthymnon, at least hourly along the Stalos/Ag. Marina/ Platanías/Gerani route and almost as often to Kolimbári; the other larger villages of the *nomós* are serviced at least daily: for transport to the Gorge of Samariá, *see* p.136. For information call **t** 082 109 3052. Car rental can be organised at one of the many agencies lining Chalídon St.

# Tourist Information

**EOT:** 40 Kriári St, **t** 082 109 2943, **f** 082 109 2624 (*open Mon–Fri 8.30–2*).
**Tourist police:** 23 Iraklion St, **t** 082 105 3333.

# Internet

**E-Café**, 59 Theotokopoúlou. This is an impressive new venue with plenty of quiet cubicles where you can hook up and log on until 2am.
**Sante**, Aktí Koundouriótou, on the harbour, providing noisier services.
**Manos Internet Café**, Aktí Koundouriotoú.
**Ideon Andron**, 26 Chalídon, in a pleasant garden setting; there is also a restaurant on site.

# Festivals

**Mid–end May:** Chaniá Festival, commemorating the anniversary of the Battle of Crete.
**24 June:** St John's Day.
**15 Aug:** Chaniá hosts the lively Pan Cretan Festival.

# Shopping

Chaniá is one of the best places in Crete to spend some money.
**Neféli**, 20 Kondiláki. Sells jewellery based on traditional and ancient Greek designs.
**Eolos**, 7 Chalídon Street. Beautiful creations in lapis lazuli.
**Imeros**, 6 Zambéliou. Another jewellery shop.
**Apostolos Pachtikos**, No.14 Sífaka. Leather rules on Odós Skridlóf and there are several traditional knifemakers including this one, who also deals in mountain-goat horns and battered Nazi helmets.
**Top Hanas**, 3 Angélou in the Old Town. A red lair of traditional Cretan weavings and blankets.
**Plateía Sindrivani**, for the big international shop with the best choice of books or newspapers in English.
**Apogio**, 80 Hatzimicháli Giannári. For books new or old, tapes and CDs.
**Bizzarro**, 19 Zambéliou. Handmade dolls and puppets.

# Where to Stay

## Chaniá ✉ 73100

Chaniá's hotels have more character than any others in Crete, although be aware that some of the most picturesque places installed around the Venetian port can be very noisy at night.

### Luxury

**Villa Andromeda**, 150 El. Venizélou, **t** 082 102 8300, **f** 082 102 8303, *villandro@otenet.gr* (*B*). One of the fanciest hotels in Chaniá, out east in the Halepa quarter. This is the former German consulate, now divided into 8 air-conditioned suites; a lush garden, Turkish bath and swimming pool are some of the amenities.

Casa Delfino, 9 Theofánous, t 082 108 7400, f 082 109 6500, *www.casadel@cha.forthnet.gr (B)*. Classy conversion of a 17th-century town house; some suites feature data ports for fax/modem link-up as well as jacuzzis.

### Expensive

Contessa, 15 Theofánous, t 082 109 8566, f 082 109 8565 (A). Has the intimate air of an old-fashioned guesthouse, furnished in traditional style; book well in advance.

Doma, 124 El. Venizélou, t 082 105 1772, f 082 104 1578 (B). Comfortable rooms in a neoclassical mansion, decked out in antiques and Cretan rusticana. The owner has an unusual collection of hats (of all things) from all over the world.

El Greco, 49 Theotokopoúlou, t 082 109 0432, f 082 109 1829, *hotel@elgreco.gr (B)*. Modern rooms in an old building on Chaniá's prettiest street.

Halepa, 164 El. Venizélou, t 082 102 8440, f 082 102 8439, *hotel@halepa.com (B)*. This once housed Andromeda's British counterparts and, renovated in 1990, now offers 49 fully air-conditioned rooms in a quiet palm garden.

Nostos, 46 Zambelíou, t 082 109 4743, f 082 109 4740 (B). A small refurbished Venetian house on a busy lane; many rooms have views.

### Moderate

Palazzo, 54 Theotokopoulou, t 082 109 3227, f 082 109 3229 (A). For those seeking divine inspiration, this is the place, with each room named after a god.

Thereza, 8 Angélou, t/f 082 109 2798 (B). Charming rooms and studios oozing with character, and a tempting roof terrace in another restored Venetian house.

### Inexpensive

Chaniá's vast selection of inexpensive rooms are mostly located within a few blocks of the Venetian or inner harbour. The pick of the bunch are:

Konaki, 43 Kondiláki, t 082 108 6379. Eight rooms in a quirky house tastefully renovated – the two ground-floor ones have private bathrooms and open on to the banana palm garden.

Kydonia, 20 Chalídon, t 082 107 4650. Well-designed doubles, triples and quads in a quiet courtyard next to the archaeological museum.

Meltémi, 2 Angélou, t/f 082 109 2802. Above the mellow *Meltémi* café, with space to swing several cats in the bigger rooms, some of which have lovely views across the port to the White Mountains. *Open all year.*

Monastiri, 18 Ag. Markoú, t 082 105 4776 (E). Set in the ruined cloister of a Venetian church; some rooms with views.

Stella, 10 Angélou, t 082 1073 756. Airy, traditional rooms (cheaper at the back) that share a fridge, and perch above the eponymous boutique selling psychedelic hand-blown glass.

Camping Ag. Marína, t/f 082 106 8596. 8km west near the beaches, and open throughout the season (buses from the bus station).

Camping Chaniá, Ag. Apóstoli, t 082 103 1138, f 082 103 3371. 5km west of town (city bus from Platéia 1866). More basic. *Open March–Oct.*

## Eating Out

It's difficult not to find a good, authentic restaurant in Chaniá – the harbour area is one great crescent of traditional tavernas and pizzerias touting very enthusiastically for your custom.

To Pigadi tou Tourkou ('The Well of the Turk'), 1 Kalliníkou Sarpáki, t 082 105 4547 (€18–22). In the heart of the old Turkish quarter, this establishment has been delighting taste buds for years. The bias is, of course, middle eastern, with specialities from Egypt, Lebanon and Tunisia. Dishes include various Arabian pies (try the spinach pie with lemon, walnuts and raisins), humous and lamb with lemon.

Dino's, 3 Aktí Enóseos and Sarpidóna, t 082 104 1865 (€20–25). A long-time reliable favourite overlooking the inner harbour, specializing in fish, but also has a good selection of meat dishes too.

Aeriko, Aktí Miaoúli, t 082 105 9307. A good choice and considerably cheaper than the above, with some seafood on the menu and chicken on a spit.

**Tholos**, 36 Ag. Déka, t 082 104 6725 (*€18–20*). Serves excellent Greek specialities in the picturesque ruins of an old Venetian town house.

**Monastiri**, (*€20*) behind the Mosque of the Janissaries. Serves fresh fish, traditional Cretan dishes and barrelled wine and is well frequented by ex-prime ministers and the like.

**Ela**, 47 Kondiláki, t 082 107 4128 (*€12–15*). Good for Cretan specialities.

**Apovrado**, Isódon Street, t 082 105 8151 (*€10–12*). Serves a number of Chaniot specialities, including the local wine and country sausages.

**Mirovolos**, 19 Zambelíou, t 082 109 1960 (*€18–22*). In the lovely courtyard of a Venetian building dating from 1290, featuring ample well-prepared dishes and Cretan dancing, not to mention the live Greek music.

**Ekstra**, 8 Zambelíou, t 082 107 5725 (*€10*). Run by German ladies, who serve up a wide range of tasty vegetarian dishes. This is an unpressurised place ideal for the sole female traveller.

**Akrogiali**, Néa Chóra, t 082 107 3110 (*€12–15*). Grab a taxi for excellent seafood at excellent prices.

**Nikterida**, 7km east at Korakiés on the Akrotíri peninsula, t 082 106 4215. In the evening Chaniots like to head up here to one of the best tavernas in Crete, open since 1938, with lively music and traditional dancing on Saturday nights; book well in advance. *Closed Sun.*

# Entertainment and Nightlife

## Bars and Cafés

Chaniá is a delightful place after dark, for its many vibrant tavernas, bars and pubs, and just for strolling around the main squares and watching the passing pageant.

**Trilogy**, 16a Radamánthous, by the northeast bastion in the inner harbour. Have a look here at impressive Chaniot post-modern design.

**Synagogi**, an atmospheric bar housed in the old Jewish baths.

**Four Seasons**, by the port police. Very popular bar.

**Street**, around Salpidonos and the western end of the outer harbour. Another very popular music bar, playing a wide range of styles.

**Dhyo Lux.** This is a café to see and be seen in; there's a great atmosphere, oozing confidence.

**Tsikoudadiko**, 31 Zambelioú. A good choice for a more distinctly Cretan experience, try the particularly good *tsikoudi* and *mezédes* dishes.

**Fortetza**, by the lighthouse. This bar has its own shuttle boat to ferry about lively guests.

## Music and Clubs

Chaniá definitely loves its music. Plataniás, along the west coast, has built up a reputation for its trendy clubs and its popular summer cinema.

**Kriti**, 22 Kallergón. This hole-in-the-wall is something of a local institution, where from 9pm into the early hours of the morning, you can hear traditional Cretan music for the price of a drink or two. Certainly worth tracking down.

**Plateia**, in the old harbour. This club frequently offers blues nights, and other live music acts feature.

**Fedra**, 7 Isóderon, t 082 104 0789. Hosts very similar acts to Plateia, but also partial to a bit of jazz.

**Akti Miaouli**, in Koum Kapi area. Beautiful Chaniots decorate the cafés in this area. The Koum Kapi seafront venues are the place to be for a late night drink, and to watch the world pass by into the early hours of the morning.

**Owl** and **Nimfes**, in Akrotíri. These are also very popular night spots with the discerning locals.

**Vareladiko**, in Agia, 7km southwest of Chaniá. An alternative place to bop happily away. Worth the taxi ride out there.

**Privilege**, **Splendid** and **O Mylos.** These are just a few of the trendy clubs in Plataniás; also well worth the journey.

**Diogenis**, t 082 106 0360. A trendy venue with spectacular fountains and beautiful views to savour.

## Around the Venetian Harbour

Chalídon Street flows into the crescent of the **outer port**, lined with handsome Venetian buildings. The neighbourhood on the west side of the port, **Topanás**, has landmark status, although the interiors have nearly all been converted into bars, pensions and restaurants. The **Fírkas Tower** at the far west end of the port saw the first official raising of the Greek flag over Crete in November 1913, in the presence of King Constantine and Prime Minister Venizélos. Long used as a prison, the tower is now a **Naval Museum** (*t 082 109 1875; open Tues–Sun 10–4; adm*), containing photos, models of Venetian galleys and fortifications, and mock-ups of key Greek naval victories, all described in nationalistic, hysterical English translations. The first floor has an evocative collection of photos and memorabilia from the Battle of Crete.

Behind the tower, the simple little church of **San Salvatore** belonged to a Franciscan monastery and was converted by the Turks into a mosque. Near here begins picturesque **Theotokopoúlou Street**, lined with Venetian houses remodelled by the Turks. The **Byzantine Museum** (*78 Theotokopoúlou; open Tues–Sat 8.30–3; combined ticket with Archaeology Museum*) has a collection of Cretan icons, pottery coins and mosaics. On Theofánou Street (off Zambéliou) the **Renieri Gate** bears a Venetian coat-of-arms dated 1608. Further south stood the old Jewish ghetto, the Ovraiki, with a dilapidated synagogue on Kondiláki Street; the owner of Synagogi Bar next door can tell you its story. At the top of Kondiláki, along Portoú Lane, you can see the last bastion of the **Venetian walls**. In 1538, just after Barbarossa devastated Réthymnon, the Venetians hired their fortifications wizard, Michele Sammichele, to surround Chaniá with walls and a moat more than 147ft wide and 28ft deep. They weren't, however, up to the job; in 1645, the Ottomans captured Chaniá in two months.

The **east end** of the outer port has Chaniá's two most photographed landmarks: a graceful Venetian **lighthouse** in golden stone, restored by the Egyptians, and the **Mosque of the Janissaries** (1645), crowned with distinctive ostrich- and chicken-egg domes. Here the Christian-born slave troops of the Ottoman Empire worshipped, although it did little to improve their character; not only did they terrorize the Greeks, but in 1690 they murdered the Pasha of Chaniá and fed his body to the dogs. In 1812, even the Sublime Porte had had enough and sent Hadji Osman Pasha, 'the Throttler', into Crete to hang the lot of them; an act that so impressed the Greeks that rumours flew around that 'the Throttler' must be a crypto-Christian.

Behind the mosque lies the **Kastélli** quarter, spread across a low hill above the inner harbour. This was the acropolis of ancient Kydonia, and **excavations** along Kanéваro Street revealed a complex of Middle Minoan buildings, most with two storeys, flag-stoned floors and grand entrances onto narrow streets. The discovery of nearly 100 Linear B tablets and a large deposit of Linear A tablets unearthed in nearby **Katre Street** suggests the proximity of a palace. Kastélli took the brunt of the Luftwaffe bombs, but you can still pick out the odd Venetian architectural detail, especially along Kanéváro and Lithínon Streets. On the top of Ag. Markoú you can see the ruins of the Venetian cathedral, **S. Maria degli Miracoli**. Below, overlooking the inner harbour, rise seven of the original 17 vaulted shipyards of the **Venetian Arsenal** (1600).

East of Kastélli is **Splántza**, the Turkish quarter. Interesting churches are concentrated here, such as the underground **Ag. Iríni** from the 15th century, in Roúgia Square. South in Vourdouba Street, the early 14th-century Dominican church of **Ag. Nikólaos** was converted by the Turks into an imperial mosque to shelter a magical healing sword which the Imam held up while leading the Friday prayers. Note the *tugra*, or Sultan's stylized thumbprint, on the entrance and the minaret. The little **Mosque of Ahmet Aga** still stands in Hadzimichali Daliáni Street, while to the east 16th-century **Ag. Anargyri**, in Koumi Street, was for centuries the only church in Chaniá allowed to hold Orthodox services during the Venetian and Turkish occupations.

### Chaniá's Newer Quarters and Beaches

From the Agora, Tzanakáki Street leads to the shady **Public Gardens**, with a small zoo, café and outdoor cinema, often showing films in English. On the corner of Tzanakáki and Sfakianáki, the **War Museum** (*open Tues–Sat 9–1*) chronicles Crete's remarkable battle history, while a villa just south, at 20 Sfakianáki Street, houses the **Historical Archives of Crete** (*open Mon–Fri 9–1*). Greece's second largest archive (mostly in Greek) dates from the Venetian occupation to the liberation of Crete in 1944. In Plateía Venizélos to the east stands the house of Venizélos, the government palace built for Prince George (now the court-house), and a Russian Orthodox church. Further east, by the sea, is the fancy **Halepa** residential quarter, dotted with 19th-century Neoclassical mansions and ex-consulates from Crete's years of autonomy.

The town beach, **Néa Chorá**, is a 15-minute walk west, beyond the Fírkas tower. Although sandy and safe for children, it's not attractive. The beaches improve further west; city buses from Plateía 1866 go as far as lovely sandy **Oasis beach** and **Kalamáki**. The strip is well developed, with good swimming, windsurfing and tavernas. There are other, less crowded beaches along the way, but be prepared for a long walk.

# South of Chaniá: Venizélos and Citrus Villages

South of Chaniá, the rugged 18km **Thérisson Gorge** is famous in Cretan history for the Revolution of Therisso in 1905, led by Venizélos in response to the reactionary policies of Prince George. Venizélos was born near the gorge entrance, in sleepy **Mourniés**, and served as Greek Prime Minister between 1910 and 1932. Before he was born, his mother dreamed that he would liberate Crete and named him Elefthérios ('Freedom').

The best oranges in Crete grow in the lush Keríti Valley south of Chaniá. During the Battle of Crete, however, it was known as Prison Valley after the big calaboose near **Alikianós**, just off the main Chaniá–Omalós road. A memorial honours the Cretans who kept on fighting here, unaware that the Allies elsewhere were in retreat; their ignorance enabled the majority of British and ANZAC troops to be evacuated from the Libyan coast. During the Occupation, prisoners were executed near the crossroads. The wedding massacre of Kantanoléo's Cretans (*see* p.131) took place at Alikianós' ruined Venetian tower; next to the tower, the church of Ag. Geórgios (1243) has exceptional frescoes, painted in 1430 by Pávlos Provatás.

# Chaniá to Cape Spáda

Not a single hotel along this sandy stretch of coast existed when a rain of white parachutes fell on 20 May 1941. 'Out of the sky the winged devils of Hitler were falling everywhere,' wrote George Psychoundákis in *The Cretan Runner*. Few signs of the battle remain, although 2km west of Chaniá stands the German memorial to the 2nd Parachute Regiment – a diving eagle, known locally as the **Kakó Poulí**, or 'Bad Bird'.

Just beyond the reach of Chaniá's city bus lines, the beach strip of **Káto Stálos** merges with **Ag. Marína**, an old town with Venetian and Turkish houses and a vast tourist sprawl. It looks out over the islet of **Ag. Theódori**, a refuge for the rare Cretan ibex, the *kri-kri*. The gaping mouth of its cave once belonged to a sea monster which bore down on Ag. Marína with a huge appetite when Zeus spotted the threat to his birthplace and petrified the monster with a thunderbolt. Just west, **Plataniás** has two faces: an old village above and a resort annex by the sandy beach and cane forest, planted to protect the orange groves from the wind. The Battle of Crete began further west at **Máleme**; there's a moving German war cemetery as a grim reminder.

## Getting Around

There's a **bus** at least every half hour from Chaniá bus station (**t** 082 109 3052) to all the resorts as far as the Louis Creta Princess Hotel; roughly every hour they continue to Kastélli-Kíssamou. There are three morning buses and one afternoon bus to the Gorge of Samariá.

## Where to Stay and Eat

### Ag. Marína ✉ 73100

**Santa Marina**, on the beach, **t** 082 106 8460, **f** 082 106 8571, *Santamarina@grecian.net.gr* (*B; exp*). Somewhat bland but set in a garden with a pool, and often comes up with a room when the season is in full swing.

**Alector's Rooms**, east in Káto Stalós, **t** 082 106 8755 (*mod–inexp*). Immaculately run by Cretan-Californian Helen Zachariou. The Stavrodromi Restaurant, **t** 082 106 8104, nearby serves delicious fried squid.

**Alexia Beach**, near the beach at the Plataniás end of town, **t** 082 106 8110 (*C; inexp*). Small and attractive, with a pool, and fridges in every room.

**Angelika**, **t** 082 106 8642 (*inexp*). Rooms with kitchen.

**Villa Thodorou**, **t** 082 106 0665, **f** 082 106 8342 (*inexp*). Rooms with fridges and balconies facing the sea.

### Plataniás ✉ 73014

**Geraniotis Beach**, **t** 082 106 8681, **f** 082 106 8683 (*B; exp*). One of the more attractive of Plataniás' many hotels, set in lush green lawns on the edge of town. *Open April–Oct.*

**Kronos Apartments**, **t** 082 106 8630, **f** 082 106 8574 (*C; exp*). Well-kept, complex of 53 units, with a pool near the sea. *Open April–Oct.*

**Taverna Mylos**, on the west end of Plataniás, **t** 082 106 8578 (*€20–25*). Converted 15th-century water mill; a lovely place with Cretan and Greek spit-roasted meats.

**Haroupia**, up in Áno Plataniás, **t** 082 106 8603 (*€15*). Enjoys lovely sunset views from its creeper-covered terrace and has delicious Cretan food.

### Máleme ✉ 73014

**Louis Creta Princess**, **t** 082 106 2221, **f** 082 106 2406, *maleme-beach@cha.forthnet.gr* (*A; lux*). Shaped like a giant trident to give each of its 414 rooms a sea view. Family-orientated. *Open April–Oct.*

**Creta Paradise Beach**, in nearby Geráni, **t** 082 106 1315, **f** 082 106 1134, *cretpar@sail.vacation.forthnet.gr* (*A; lux*). All the trimmings and more for adults and children.

**Máleme Mare**, **t** 082 106 2121, **f** 082 109 4644 (*C; exp*). Modest but uninspiring apartments by the beach with pool. Nearby, the tables of the Maleme Taverna are set on the grass by the beach.

At the foot of rugged Cape Spáda, just before the road to Kastélli splits into old and new, **Kolimbári** (ΚΟΛΥΜΒΑΡΙ) has a beach of large smooth pebbles and, a short walk north, the most important monastery in western Crete. **Moní Gonías**, or Odigítrias (*open Sun–Fri 8–12.30 and 4–8, Sat 4–8*), was founded in 1618 by monks and hermits, who built a monastery fortress high over a sandy cove (or *gonías*, in Greek). The patriotic monks were often besieged by the Turks; a cannon ball fired in 1866 is still embedded in the seaward wall. The church contains a fine gilt iconostasis carved with dragons, a venerable *Last Judgement* painted on wood and a beautifully drawn St Nicholas, although the juju seems to be concentrated in an icon of the Virgin, covered with votive *tamata*, jewellery and a digital watch.

Beyond Moní Gonías, the road veers dizzyingly up the coast of Cape Spáda to **Afráta**, the last village accessible by car; from here you can follow the unpaved, treeless track north on foot or with a four-wheel-drive to **Diktyna**, in ancient times the most holy shrine in western Crete. Its little port, **Meniás**, is rocky, but the sea is transparent and caves offer shade. Diktyna's unexcavated shrine to Artemis dates back to the Minoans; enough remains to make it worth the scramble.

# Kastélli-Kíssamou and the West Coast

West of Cape Spáda, the coastal plain and knobbly hills are densely planted with olives and vineyards: the difference between its lush greenery and the arid hills of Crete's far east couldn't be more striking. The often wild and unruly west coast offers some of Crete's loveliest and most deserted beaches. The capital is Kastélli-Kíssamou, a working wine town charmingly devoid of any tourist attraction whatsoever.

### Kastélli-Kíssamou (ΚΑΣΤΕΛΛΙ ΚΙΣΣΑΜΟΥ)

Set at the bottom of a deep, rectangular gulf, Kastélli's long beach attracts visitors eager to shun the fleshpots. Its double-barrelled name recalls its predecessor Kissamos, the port of Dorian Polyrenia. Excavations behind the health centre have unearthed a lovely mosaic floor from the 2nd century AD; an **Archaeology Museum** is currently being arranged in the Venetian commandery. Ancient Kissamos' temple and theatre were dismantled by the Venetians in 1550 and refashioned as a castle – hence Kastélli. This castle has a melodramatic history: when the Cretan Kaptános Kantanoléo captured it, the Venetians pretended to recognize Kantanoléo's authority and offered a highborn Venetian girl as his son's bride. At the wedding the Cretans were given drugged wine, and the Venetians slit their throats and took Kastélli back.

A scenic 8km south of Kastélli, old-fashioned **Polyrénia** (ΠΟΛΥΡΡΗΝΙΑ) is set on a natural balcony. Polyrénia is older than it looks, even older than the Roman tower (itself a collage of older pieces) that stands at the village entrance. Founded in the 8th century BC by Dorian colonists from the Peloponnese, Polyrénia survived the Romans with the attitude that if you can't lick them, join them, but fell to the Saracens in the 9th century. Up on the acropolis, note the massive base of a 4th-century temple and altar of dressed stone, now supporting the church of the 99 Holy Fathers.

# Getting Around

Kastélli's **port** (2km from the centre – take a taxi) is linked by ANEN **ferries** to Gýthion (for Kýthera and Antikýthera), **t** 082 102 4148, **f** 082 102 8200, *www.anen.gr*; tickets from Xyroukákis Travel Agency in Kastélli, **t** 082 202 2655, **f** 082 102 4364 or Omalós Tours, Plateía 1866, Chaniá, **t** 082 109 7119. There are **buses** from Kastélli 3 times a week (Mon, Wed, Fri) to Polyrénia, 3 a day to Falassarná, 5 to Chóra Sfakíon, 6 to Paleochóra, 3 to Omalós and one morning bus to Chrysoskalítissa and Elafonísi. The Elafonísi Boat, **t** 082 304 1755, connects Elafonísi to Paleochóra every afternoon in summer. A daily direct bus to Elafonísi leaves Chaniá at 7.30am.

# Festivals

**Early Aug**: Kastélli wine festival.
**14–15 Aug**: a huge festival at Monastery Chrysoskalítissa in Elafonísi.
**First Sun after 20 Oct**: a Chestnut festival in Élos.

# Where to Stay and Eat

## Kastélli ☒ 73400
**Galini Beach**, at the far end of the beach, **t** 082 202 3288, *www.galinibeach.com* (*inexp*). Quiet rooms.

**Nopigia Camping**, **t** 082 203 1111, **f** 082 203 1700. Large swimming pool. *Open April–Oct.*
**Stimadóris**, at the west end of town, **t** 082 202 2057. Fresh fish caught by the owners and a tasty pickled red seaweed salad. *Open eves and lunch in summer.*
**Papadakis**, on the main seafront. Serves up the day's catch.
**Alatopiperi** ('Salt and Pepper'). Cooking as uncomplicated as its name.
**Agrimi**, centre of town. Reliable Cretan dishes.

## Falassarná ☒ 73400
New buildings with flats or rooms have sprouted up higgledy piggledy like toadstools.
**SunSet Rooms and Studios**, right on the beach, **t** 082 204 1204. Popular fish taverna.
**Romantica**, **t** 082 204 1740, *romantica@kissamos.net* (*mod*). Small apartments for 4–5 people, verandas with sea views and kitchenettes.
**Aqua Marine**, **t** 082 204 1414, *aquamarine@kissamos.net* (*mod–inexp*). New and spotless, all rooms with *en suite* baths.

## Vlátos Kissámou (near Elos)
**Mília**, **t/f** 082 205 1569 (*mod*). Experience the rural Crete of centuries past. Ecologically sound, traditional rooms in restored stone dwellings in a chestnut forest hamlet. Rooms furnished with antiques, heated by wood stoves and lit by candles. One house serves as a refectory, with delicious organic food, mostly produced on site. *Open all year.*

## Way Out West

Crete's west coast is dramatic, starkly outlined by mountains plunging straight into the sea. They give way to a coastal plain coated in plastic tomato tunnels and beautiful sandy beaches at **Falassarná** (ΦΑΛΑΣΑΡΝΑ), 15km from Kastélli, where more tavernas and pensions spring up every year. North of the beach at Koutrí stood **ancient Falassarná**, Polyrénia's bitter rival. You can measure how much western Crete has risen – Falassarná's port is now 200m from the sea. Bits of the ancient city lie scattered while, further up, archaeologists found a bathhouse. Most curious of all is a Hellenistic **stone throne**; possibly dedicated to Poseidon.

From Kastélli you can hire a caique to sail around the top of wild, uninhabited **Cape Voúxa** (with a gorgeous sandy beach) to the harbour of the triangular islet of **Ágria**, better known by the name of its Venetian fortress, **Gramvoúsa**. Like Néa Soúda and Spinalonga to the east, the fort held out against the Turks until the 18th century, when the Venetians gave up hope of ever reconquering Crete. The Renaissance church is fairly intact and the reservoirs, unused for over a century, are full to the brim.

## Down to Elafonísi

South of Falassarná, the partially paved but easy coastal road takes in spectacular scenery; try to travel in the morning to avoid the sea glare. In sprawling **Plátanos** a Proto-geometric tomb was unearthed during the road construction, while down in **Sfinári** there's a pebble beach and tavernas. The road then rides a corniche high over the sea to **Kámbos**, where a 3km track leads down to the wild sandy beach of **Livádia**. The main road becomes increasingly rough as it winds south to the Libyan Sea and the sheer rock pedestal of the bleached **Convent of Chrysoskalítissa**, 'Our Lady of the Golden Stair' (*open 7am–8pm*). The story goes that only persons without sin, or non-liars, can see which of the 90 steps is made of gold; a more prosaic version claims the Patriarch in Constantinople ordered the convent to sell off the golden step in the 15th century to pay off his debts. Tour buses from Chaniá besiege the last nun and monk.

The prime attraction in this corner of Crete, however, lies another 5km southwest, the islet of **Elafonísi** (ΕΛΑΦΟΝΗΣΙ). It's a magnificent place to while away a day, set in a shallow, almost tropical lagoon that comes in a spectrum of turquoise, blue and violet, rimmed by pink sand; the water is only 2ft deep so you can wade to Elafonísi and beyond to other beaches. Children love it. A little less virgin every year, it has so far managed to hold off the advances of the big resort hotel ventures.

## Inland: Chestnut Villages

Rather than backtrack, consider returning north via Crete's chestnut country, where the lush mountains are reminiscent of Corsica. Its nine villages, the *Enneachoria*, host some of the best weddings in Crete in July. On the road up from Elafonísi, **Kefáli** has magnificent sea views and fine frescoes in its church, **Metamórphosis tou Sotírou** (1320); note the English graffiti from 1553. Nearby **Perivólia** is a charming green oasis, home of a private **Ethnographic Museum**. **Élos**, the largest of the villages, is set in plane and chestnut trees, and has rooms to stay the night – a perfect antidote to the sunbaked sands. Six km beyond, the road forks for Paleochóra (*see* below).

# The Southwest: Paleochóra and the Sélino

The White Mountains only permit a few north–south roads to breach their rocky fastness. Those to the southwest run into the Eparchy of Sélino, where the attractive resort town of Paleochóra is the main attraction, along with a score of medieval churches that have escaped the ravages of time, especially around Kándanos. Most are locked, but asking in the nearest *kafeneíon* may produce an Open Sesame.

## Along the Road from Tavronítis to Paleochóra

Of the three roads from the north that wriggle down to the Sélino, the main one from Tavronítis gets the most takers. En route lies lush **Kándanos** with the highest rainfall in Crete, known as 'the city of victory'. Although inhabited since Roman times, nothing is over 50 years old; in the Battle of Crete the townspeople resisted the Nazi advance with such stubborn ferocity that the Germans were forced to retreat. They returned with reinforcements the next day, shooting everyone and burning the town to the ground. Among the memorials is the original sign erected by Germans: 'Here stood Kándanos, destroyed in retribution for the murder of 25 German soldiers.'

From Kándanos, take the left turn on the Soúgia road for **Anisaráki**. There are five Byzantine churches within the next few kilometres. **Taxiárchos Michaíl**, near Koufalotó, was frescoed in 1327 by one of the best artists working in Western Crete, Ioánnis Pagoménos. Anisaráki itself has three 14th-century frescoed churches: the paintings in a fourth church, **Ag. Anna**, date from the 1460s; among the pictures is a fine one of St Anne nursing the baby Virgin and St George on horseback. South of Kándanos, in **Plemanianá**, **Ag. Geórgios** has frescoes of the *Last Judgement* from 1410. In **Kakodíki** to the southwest, springs with soft mineral waters relieve kidney stones and two other churches have frescoes, near the modern Ag. Triáda.

## Paleochóra

If no longer nuptially fresh, **Paleochóra** (ΠΑΛΑΙΟΧΩΡΑ), the Old Town, still attracts many suitors, a mixture of charter flight tourists and hippies. It has the advantage of straddling two beaches – one stony, the other sandy, with superb windsurfing.

## Getting Around

Paleochóra is served by 5 **buses** a day from Chaniá; a 6.30am bus goes to Omalós for the Gorge of Samariá. 2 buses run daily between Chaniá and Soúgia. Small **boats** leave Paleochóra 3 times a week for Gávdos (*see* p.144); car ferry sails daily to Soúgia, Ag. Roúmeli, Chóra Sfakíon, Loutró and Elafónisi. Passenger boats daily to Elafónisi. **Port authority: t** 082 304 1214. Soúgia is linked daily by boat to Ag. Roúmeli when the Gorge of Samariá is open.

## Tourist Information

Paleochóra: town tourist office, El. Venizélos, t 082 304 1507; *open Wed–Mon 10–1 and 6–9*. Has an extensive list of rooms in the €18–25 range.

## Internet

PC–Corner, t 082 304 2422, *pc-corner@cha .forthnet.gr*

## Festivals

**1–10 Aug**: Paleochóra Musical.

## Where to Stay and Eat

**Paleochóra** ✉ 73001
**Efthisis Sfinarolákis, t** 082 304 1594 or 082 304 1596 (*exp*). Classy studios and apartments.
**Elman**, on the beach, t/f 082 304 1412 (*B; exp*). Big, modern apartments. *Open all year.*
**Aris**, near the beach, **t** 082 304 1502. *Arishotel @cha.forthnet.gr* (*B; mod*). A good bet.
**Polydoros**, on the main street between the beaches, **t** 082 304 1150, **f** 082 304 1578 (*C; mod*). Old favourite with self-catering suites.
**Ostria**, in the middle of the sandy beach, **t** 082 304 1055 (*inexp*). Rooms and a taverna with Greek dancing on Sat nights.
**Campsite**, by the pebble beach, **t** 082 304 1120.
**Pizzeria Niki**, in the centre makes good, fresh and cheap pies with some seating outside.
**The Third Eye**, near the beach, **t** 082 304 1055. Spicy Asian and Mexican specialities.

**Soúgia** ✉ 73011
**Santa Irene, t** 082 305 1181, **f** 082 305 1182 (*mod*). A small and friendly complex of apartments and rooms, with a breakfast bar. There's a fair choice of cheap rooms to rent:
**Lissos, t** 082 305 1244.
**Koumakakis, t** 082 305 1298.
**Maria Marináki, t** 082 305 1338.
**Liviko**. Popular, typical taverna treats.

On the tip of the peninsula, the Venetians built Paleochóra's **Castello Selino** in 1279, more to police the ornery Greeks than protect their new territory. When tested in 1539 by Barbarossa, the castle was easily destroyed. There are quieter beaches to the west, although the nearby greenhouses keep them off the postcards. But the water around pebbly **Ag. Kyriáki** at the end of the track is exceptionally crystal-clear.

## Inland from Paleochóra: Ánidri and Azogyrés

If you're spending time in Paleochóra, delve into the interior and its unspoiled mountain villages. Pretty **Ánidri** to the northeast is home to Ag. Geórgios Church, frescoed by Ioánnis Pagoménos in 1323. On the winding road through cypress forests towards Soúgia (*see* below), **Azogyrés** offers the pleasures of its deep green surroundings and gurgling stream, a fascinating one-room **historical museum** (*open Sat and Sun 9–2*) and one of Crete's rare **evergreen plane trees**, an enormous specimen growing next to the 19th-century cliff-side chapel of Ag. Páteres. The museum guardian has the key to the chapel with its charming iconostasis. Two km above Azogyrés, the **Cave of Souré** is said to have been the temporary home for the 99 Agii Páteres, or Holy Fathers, who came out of Egypt after the Byzantine reconquest of Crete. An iron stair leads steeply down to the little chapel, now home to 99 pigeons.

## Along the Road from Chaniá to Soúgia

It's an hour's caique ride from Paleochóra to Soúgia, but if you're coming from Chaniá, the new road branching off at Alikianós (*see* p.129) is quicker. It ascends the west edge of the Omalós plateau to **Ag. Iríni**, a pleasant village at the top of a beautiful walkable 8km gorge; the path continues down to Soúgia (Chaniá tourist office has a map). Also south of Ag. Iríni stood its predecessor, ancient **Elyros**, a pugnacious Dorian settlement that had risen to the level of a bishopric when the Saracens destroyed it in the 9th century. Walls and the acropolis lie unexcavated. The church of the Panagía was planted on top of an ancient temple, re-using its pretty 6th-century mosaic floor. Four km west, muscat-producing **Teménia** has a photogenic old stone church, the Sotír, and the double cyclopean walls of ancient **Irtakína**, which once minted coins with bees, deer, dolphins and eight pointed stars. Further along, **Moní**'s church, Ag. Nikólaos, was finely frescoed by the indefatigable Ioánnis Pagómeno.

The paved road ends at **Soúgia** (ΣΟΥΓΙΑ), a higgledy-piggledy wannabe resort with a long pebbly beach. The port of Elyros, its ancient name was Syia or 'pig town' for the porkers it raised; the nude beach is still known unflatteringly as the 'Bay of Pigs'. The ruins that stand are a modest blast from Syia's Roman past. Another church, **Ag. Antónios** (1382) has frescoes, and a nearby cave, **Spyliara**, is one of a multitude in the Mediterranean that claims to have belonged to the Cyclops Polyphemos.

From Soúgia you can sail in 20 minutes or take a pretty hour-and-a-half walk to **Lissós**. In ancient times renowned for its medicinal springs, it attracted enough trade at its Doric Asklepeion, or healing sanctuary (3rd century BC) to afford to mint gold coins. The sanctuary has a fine pebble mosaic floor and a (now empty) pit for sacred snakes. The population of Lissós is exactly one: the caretaker, who watches over the theatre, baths, and two old Christian basilicas with mosaic floors, rebuilt in the 1200s.

# The Gorge of Samariá (ΦΑΡΑΓΓΙ ΣΑΜΑΡΙΑΣ)

The single most spectacular stretch of Crete is squeezed into the 18km Gorge of Samariá, the longest in Europe and the last refuge of much of the island's unique fauna and flora, especially rare chasm-loving plants known as *chasmophytes*. Once a rather adventurous excursion, the walk is now offered by every tour operator; the gorge has been spruced up as a National Park and, in short, forget any private communion with Mother Nature. The walk takes most people between five and eight hours going down from Omalós south to Ag. Roúmeli on the Libyan Sea, and twice as long if they're Arnold Schwarzenegger, or just plain crazy, and walk up.

Not a few people return from the Gorge of Samariá having only seen their own feet and the back of the person in front of them. Staying in Ag. Roúmeli may be the answer; it will allow you more leisure to enjoy the beauty of the gorge and the rare flowers and herbs that infuse Samariá. Although the gorge is a refuge of the *kri-kri*, no-one ever seems to see them any more; the few that survived the 1993 epidemic of killer ticks, or *korpromantakes*, are shy of the hordes. Birds of prey (rare griffon vultures, very rare lammergeiers, buzzards and eagles) are bolder, and will often circle high overhead.

## Walking Down the Gorge

Just getting there is part of the fun. If you're on one of the early buses, dawn usually breaks in time for you to look over the most vertiginous section of the road, as it climbs 1,200m to the pass before descending to the Omalós Plateau, 25 sq km and itself no shorty at 1,080m. In winter, snows from the fairy circle of White Mountain peaks flood this uncanny plateau so often that the one village, **Omalós** (ΟΜΑΛΟΣ), is uninhabitable. The gorge **Tourist Pavilion** is a few kilometres south of Omalós. Some of the most spectacular views are from the pavilion, hanging over the edge of the chasm, overlooking the sheer limestone face of mighty 2,083m Mount Gýnglios, a favourite resort of Zeus when the shenanigans at Mount Olympos got on his nerves. If you come prepared and have mountain experience, you can go up from here rather than down: there is a 90-minute trail from the pavilion that leads up to the Greek Mountain Club's **Kallergi Shelter** (*t 082 107 4560; book in high season*), which can accommodate 45 people.

Just after dawn, the first people of the day begin to trickle down the **Xylóskalo**, a zigzag stone path with a wooden railing and lookouts along the way. The name Samariá derives from Ossa Maria, a chapel (1379) and abandoned village halfway down the gorge, now used as the guardians' station and picnic ground. There are several other abandoned chapels along the way, traditional stone *mitáto* huts (used by shepherds for cheese-making) and, near the end, the famous **Sideróportes** ('iron gates'), the oft-photographed section of the gorge where the sheer walls rise almost 1,000ft on either side of a passage only 9ft wide.

At the southern end of the gorge stands **old Ag. Roúmeli** (ΑΓ. ΡΟΥΜΕΛΙ), abandoned after a torrent swept through in 1954. Recently, some of the empty houses have been recycled as stalls selling Greece's most expensive cold drinks. When tourists

# Getting Around

**Buses** leave Chaniá for Omalós at 6.15, 7.30 and 8.30am and at 4.30pm; from Kastélli-Kíssamou at 5, 6 and 7 in the morning and Réthymnon at 6.15 and 7 in the morning. Others leave early from Plataniás, Ag. Marína, Tavronítis, Chandrís and Kolimbári. Organized **tour buses** leave almost as early (you can, however, get a slight jump on the crowds or at least more sleep by staying overnight at Omalós).

Once through the gorge to Ag. Roúmeli, **boats** run all afternoon to Chóra Sfakíon, Soúgia and Paleochóra, where you can pick up a late-afternoon bus back to the north coast (5.30, 6 and 7pm for Réthymnon). Consider paying the bit extra for a tour bus, especially in the summer, to make sure you have a seat on the return journey.

# Practicalities

The gorge is open when weather permits, usually around the beginning of May to 31 Oct, from 6am to 4pm, during which time the water is low enough to ensure safe fording of the streams. Staff of the National Forest Service patrol the area. Although last admission to the gorge is at 3pm, almost everyone starts much earlier, to avoid the midday heat and to make the excursion a single day's round-trip outing. It is **absolutely essential** to wear good walking shoes and socks; a hat and a bite to eat are only slightly less vital, and binoculars are a decided bonus for flower and bird observations. Dressing appropriately is difficult: it's usually chilly at Omalós and sizzling at Ag. Roúmeli. It's a good idea to remove rings in case your hands swell. The fresh streams along the gorge provide good drinking water at regular intervals. Mules and a helicopter landing pad are on hand for emergency exits; tickets are date-stamped and must be turned in at the lower gate, to make sure no-one is lost. If you haven't the energy to make the whole trek, you can at least sample Samariá by descending a mile or so into the gorge down the big wooden stair (the rub is you have to walk back up again). A less strenuous (and less rewarding) alternative, proposed by tourist agencies as 'the lazy way', is walking an hour or so up from Ag. Roúmeli to the Sideróportes. For up-to-date gorge information and walking conditions, **t** 082 106 7179.

# Where to Stay and Eat

**Omalós** ✉ 73005
**Neos Omalós, t** 082 106 7590, **f** 082 106 7190 (*C; inexp*). Recently built, with centrally heated rooms, bar and restaurant. *Open year-round.*
**To Exari, t** 082 106 7180, **f** 082 106 7124 (*C; inexp*). A bit larger and almost as nice.
**Drakoulaki, t** 082 106 7269. Simple and inexpensive rooms.

**Ag. Roúmeli** ✉ 73011
Ag. Roúmeli has plenty of rooms, but prices are over the odds. There are several restaurants with rooms. Try:
**Aghia Roúmeli, t** 082 509 1241 (*C; inexp*). *Open Mar–Oct.*
**Tara, t** 082 509 1231.
**Lefka Ori, t** 082 509 1219.

began to appear in the 1960s, a **new Ag. Roúmeli** obligingly rose out of the cement mixer like a phoenix (toadstool is more apt), another blistering 2km away, on the coast – which makes it as enticing as a desert oasis to the weary and foot sore. This new Ag. Roúmeli is built over ancient Tarra, where Apollo hid from the wrath of Zeus after slaying Python at Delphi. Here he fell so in love with a nymph that he forgot to make the sun rise and got into an even bigger jam with his dad. A sanctuary of Tarranean Apollo marked the spot, and on top of its foundations the Venetians built a church, **Panagías**. From Ag. Roúmeli, caiques sail to Paleochóra, Chóra Sfakíon (*see* p.142) and Soúgia. But if you linger, the beach to aim for is **Ag. Pávlos**, a 90-minute walk away, with fresh springs and a lyrical 10th-century stone church.

# East of Chaniá: Akrotíri (ΑΚΡΩΤΗΡΙ)

Akrotíri, the most bulbous and busiest of the three headlands that thrust out of Crete's northwest coast, wraps around to shelter the island's safest port, Soúda, from northerly winds. Its strategic position has assured it plenty of history, and now that Crete is safe from imminent invasion, the steep access road (Eleftheríou Venizélou) from Chaniá's Halepa quarter is often chock-a-block with locals heading out to Akrotíri's beaches, nightclubs and seaside villas. Outside these suburban tentacles, Akrotíri is a moody place, dusty and junky with military zones towards the airport, lonely and wild around its famous monasteries.

First stop should be little **Profítis Ilías** church (4.5km from Chaniá), Crete's chief **memorial to Venizélos**, its favourite statesman. Elefthérios Venizélos (1864–1936) and his son Sophoklís (1896–1964) asked to be buried here to posthumously enjoy superb views over Chaniá, but they had patriotic reasons as well: in the rebellion of 1897, Profítis Ilías was briefly the Revolutionary Military Camp of Akrotíri, located just within the Great Powers' 6km exclusion zone around Chaniá. To rout out the Greeks, the British, French, Italian and Russian navies bombarded it. In response, the Cretans raised the Greek flag. The admirals were so impressed as they stood there, holding up the flag with their bare hands even after it was shot off its pole, that they stopped bombing and applauded. Afterwards a Russian destroyed the monastery, but the Prophet Elijah (Ilías) got his revenge when the Russian ship was blown up the next day. When the news reached Europe that the Great Powers had bombed brave Christian Greeks, it caused such a stir that it led the Allies to offer Crete its autonomy.

Akrotíri's first sandy seaside playgrounds are **Kalathás** (ΚΑΛΑΘΑΣ) and its quieter beach of **Tersanás**. **Stavrós** (ΣΤΑΥΡΟΣ), further north, is the end of the trail for buses from Chaniá and owes its growing popularity to a lovely circular bay with shallow water; it was used for the beach scenes in the film *Zorba the Greek*. Above Stavrós sprawls the petrified body of one of Zeus' lovers, immortalised in stone by Hera, lying head-first in the deep blue sea. East of Stavrós, roads across the headland converge on **Moní Ag. Triáda**, or Tzagaróliou (*open officially 6–2 and 5–7; adm*). The cruciform church has a colonnaded Venetian façade, and in the narthex an inscription in Greek and Latin tells how Ag. Triáda was refounded in 1634 by Jeremiah Zangarola, a Venetian who became an Orthodox monk. A museum contains a 17th-century *Last Judgement*, among later icons and manuscripts.

## Where to Stay and Eat

### Stavrós ⌂ 73100

**Rea**, back from the sea, t 082 103 9001, f 082 103 9541 (*B; exp*). An air-conditioned complex offering everything from basketball and tennis to babysitting. *Open April–Oct.*

**Zorba's Studio Flats**, by the beach, t 082 103 9011 (winter t 082 105 2525), f 082 104 2616 (*mod*). Good for families, with a pool, tennis, garden, seaside taverna and a playground.

**Blue Beach**, adjacent to Zorba's, t 082 103 9404, f 082 103 9406, vepe@cha.forthnet.gr (*mod*). Villa and apartment complex and oh so blue, with a pool, restaurant, bar and sea sports. *Open April–Oct.*

**Kavos Beach**, t 082 103 9155 (*inexp*). Some of the nicest rooms to rent, with a nice pool and bar.

**Taverna Thanasis**, between Zorba's and Blue Beach. Varied food and wine selection; free sunbeds to taverna customers.

An even older monastery, fortified **Moní Gouvernétou** (*open 7–2 and 4–8; adm*), stands on a remote plateau, 5km above Ag. Triáda along a narrow road that just squeezes through the wild rocky terrain. Gouvernétou played a major role in reconciling the Cretans and Venetians at the end of the 16th century; the grotesque sandstone heads on the portal are curious Venetian fancies far from home. Gouvernétou supplanted two older holy places – a path from the car park leads in 10 minutes to the ruins of a hermitage by the cave named **Arkoudiótissa** ('Bear') after its bear-shaped stalagmite, worshipped since pre-Minoan times in the cult of Artemis, the Mistress of the Wild Animals. The stone bear leans over a cistern of water; the low ceiling is blackened with several thousand years of candle-smoke. A corner in the cave contains a small 16th-century chapel dedicated to Panagía Arkoudiótissa, 'Our Lady of the Bear', who shares the same feast day as Artemis: 2 February (Candlemas).

The path continues down, a rough and steep 20 minutes or so, past hermits' huts and a sea rock shaped like a boat (a pirate ship petrified by the Panagía). The path ends at the dark, complex **Cave of St John the Hermit** (or Stranger), who sailed from Egypt to Crete, founded a score of monasteries and retired here, becoming so stooped from his poor diet of roots and vegetables that a hunter shot him, mistaking him for an animal (7 October 1042 – the anniversary still brings crowds of pilgrims here). In this wild ravine, St John founded the **Katholikón**, a church gouged into the living rock of the precipice, straddled by a stone bridge. A path descends to a rocky but delightful swimming nook, especially enjoyable when you contemplate the killer walk back.

## Soúda and Ancient Aptera

Greater Chaniá trickles scrubbily along the road to **Soúda** (ΣΟΥΔΑ), the main port for western Crete, tucked into the magnificent sheltered bay. However, Soúda will never win a beauty contest; its most prominent features include a Greek naval base and a recently abandoned NATO base. The Venetians fortified the bay's islet, **Néa Soúda**, and took refuge there against the Turks. They finally surrendered in 1715, after frequent attacks and a gruesome pyramid of 5,000 Christian heads piled around the walls by the Turks. Signs in Soúda lead to the immaculate lawns of the seaside **Commonwealth War Cemetery**, where lie 1,497 British and ANZAC troops who perished in the Battle of Crete, the majority of them too young to vote. Two km west of Soúda towards Chaniá, a road forks south for the 16th-century **Moní Chryssopigí** (*open 3.30–6*); the church and museum house an exceptional collection of icons from the 15th century on, and a cross decorated with gold filigree and precious stones.

The Turks had an excellent, if frustrating, view of defiant Néa Soúda from **Idzeddin** fortress, east of Soúda on Cape Kalámi. Now Chaniá's prison, Idzeddin was built of stone from the ancient **Aptera**, which was high on a plateau 8.5km east of Soúda, above **Megála Choráfia**. Aptera (*open Tues–Sun 8.30–3*) was founded in the 11th century BC and was one of western Crete's chief cities until shattered by an earthquake in AD 700. Its mighty 4km walls have been compared to the great polygonal defences of Mycenaean Tiryns, and through the weeds you can see classical temple foundations, a theatre and the skeleton of a Roman basilica. The city's name (*aptera*, or 'featherless') came from a singing contest between the Muses and the Sirens. The Sirens were sore losers, and tore out their feathers and plunged into the sea, where they turned into the islets in Soúda Bay. Aptera is also the site of Maria Orfanoudaki's Laboratory of Peace, where she paints and promotes world peace.

## Cape Drápanon

East of Aptera, the highway dives inland to avoid rugged Cape Drápanon, missing lovely vineyards, olive groves and cypresses draped on rolling hills. A pair of resort towns dot the exposed north coast of Drápanon: **Kalýves**, with a long beach under the Apokoróna fortress, built by the Genoese when they tried to pinch Crete from the Venetians, and **Almirída**, smaller and more attractive, with a sandy beach and good windsurfing. From here, it's 4km to **Gavalochóri**, where exhibits of old village life in its **Folklore Museum** (*t* 082 502 3222; *open Mon–Sat 9–7, Sun 10–1.30 and 5–8; adm*) inspired a women's agrotourism co-operative to renew the local silk industry. East of Almirída, the road swings in from the rocky coast and continues up to picturesque **Pláka** and straggly **Kókkini Chório**, the latter used for most of the village scenes in *Zorba the Greek*. The best thing to do is circle around the cape, through **Drápanos** and **Kefalás**, sleepy villages reeking of past grandeur. The largest village, **Vámos** (ΒΑΜΟΣ), seems quite urban in comparison. Many stone houses have been restored; in August a local co-operative puts on exhibitions and concerts. In **Karýdi**, 4km south of Vámos, the **Metóchi Ag. Georgíou** (*open 7–3 and 4–7, Wed 3-7, Sun 4–7*) is both a working monastery and an impressive Venetian complex, including a huge olive press, in picturesque ruin. If you're heading for Georgioúpolis, stop in **Exópoli**, where the tavernas enjoy breathtaking sea views.

## Where to Stay and Eat

### Near Aptera ✉ 73003
**Taverna Aptera**, Megála Choráfia. This blue and white taverna just under the archaeological site, is a good bet.
**To Fangarifor**, in the centre of Stílos, provides more shade.

### Kalýves/Almirída
**Dimitra Hotel**, t 082 503 1956, f 082 503 1995 (*A; exp*). Stylish, with pool bar and tennis.
**Kalives Beach**, in Kalýves, t 082 503 1285, f 082 503 1134 (*B; exp*). By the sea, the pick of the hotels here.
**Almyrida**, on the sea, t 082 503 2128, f 082 503 2139, *Almyrida_beach@internet.gr* (*B, exp–mod*). With an indoor pool.

**The Enchanted Owl**, t 082 503 2494. The English owners serve dishes (Mexican, Indian or Italian) not offered by their Greek neighbours and even English roast dinners every Sun.

### Vámos
**Vámos S.A. Pensions**, t/f 082 502 3100 (*exp*). Local co-operative that's converted old stone olive presses and stables into traditional-style accommodation with a kitchen and living room. They organize walks to caves and monasteries nearby, and offer lessons in Greek dancing, cooking, language, ceramic making and icon painting. *Open all year*.
**I Sterna tou Bloumosofi** (around €20–25). Taverna run by the above, serving Cretan specialities baked in the wood oven and wine from its own barrels in the cellar.

# Vrises, Georgioúpolis, Lake Kournás and Around

South of the highway from Vámos, **Vrises** (ΒΡΥΣΕΣ) is an important crossroads in western Crete; a pleasant place, with lofty plane trees, and café terraces all along the torrential Almirós river, dotted with busts of heroic, moustachioed Cretans. The road follows the Amirós as it flows down to the genteel resort of **Georgioúpolis** (ΓΕΩΡ-ΓΙΟΥΠΟΛΗ), tucked in the crook of Cape Drápanon and a minute's walk from the coastal highway. Named in honour of Prince George, the High Commissioner of autonomous Crete, it has a long, sandy (if sometimes rough and windy) beach, part of the intermittent strand that extends to Réthymnon.

Inland from Georgioúpolis, the old Chaniá–Réthymnon road heads into the barren hills. They form a striking amphitheatre around Crete's only lake, **Kournás**, deep and eerie and full of eels. A place on the shore hires out boats and pedalos for a closer look; there is a story of a lost city dedicated to Athena in its environs, but not a trace has been ever been found.

From Kournás a lovely detour south (turn at Episkopí) will take you to the hill town of **Argiroúpolis**, overlooking the sea. This was Doric Lappa, destroyed by the Romans in 67 BC. In the later war between Octavian and Mark Antony, Lappa supported Octavian, who gave it the money to rebuild when he became Emperor Augustus. To the southeast of the village are ruins of the baths and aqueduct; a canopy protects a geometric mosaic in the upper part of town.

Just down the Asi Goniá road you'll find the **Mýli** or Watermills, where Réthymnon's drinking water comes spilling through the little troglodyte chapel of Ag. Dínami and down a stepped waterfall. A grove of plane trees and outdoor tavernas make this a favourite stop for Greeks. From here the road rises through a narrow gorge to a famous nest of Cretan dare-devilry, **Asi Goniá**, an old village and a slightly introspective one now that there isn't an enemy for its brave *pallikári* to fight.

## Georgioúpolis ✉ 73007

Come prepared: it's not unusual to see hotels in Georgioúpolis advertising their mosquito nets.

**Mare Monte**, t 082 506 1390, f 082 506 1274 (*A; lux*). One of the west's luxurious hotels.

**Pilot Beach**, t 082 506 1002, f 082 506 1397, *resv@pilot-beach.gr* (*A; exp*). Stylish complex with a pool, good for families but spread out in a number of different buildings.

**Mina**, at Kourvrá, next beach east, t 082 506 1257 (*C; mod*). Pleasant, medium-sized hotel.

**Almyros**, 100m from the sea, t 082 506 1349 (*E; inexp*).

**Villa Mouria**, t 082 506 1342. A cheaper option.

**Voula**, t 082 506 1259. Another budget choice.

Georgioúpolis has many *ouzeries*:

**Apolithos**, just up from the beach. Wide choice of Greek and international dishes.

**Georgis**, as you enter the resort from the main road. Best charcoal-grilled meats in town.

**Omorphi Limni**, on Lake Kournás, t 082 509 6221. Rooms on the lake; serves delicious *gýros*.

**Poseidon**, back off the hurly-burly in a narrow lane off the main road. Good for fish.

## Argiroúpolis/Mýli

There are 2 simple 'rooms' places here, both enjoying wide views over the mountains:

**Lappa Apartments**, t 083 108 1204.

**Zografáki**, near folk museum, t 083 108 1269.

**Paleo Mýli**, down the steep lane on the Asi Goniá road in an old mill. The best place to dine around Mýli, serving good Cretan specialities and local trout.

**Athivoles**, t 083 108 1011. Another reliable taverna, serving good fresh trout lunches.

# South to Sfakiá and Chóra Sfakíon

Sfakiá, long isolated under the White Mountains in the southeast corner of *Nomós* Chaniá, was the cradle of the island's most daring moustachioed desperados, who clobbered each other in blood feuds but in times of need became Crete's bravest freedom fighters. Now connected to civilization by a good (and beautiful) road, the Sfakiots have put their daggers away, and prey no more than any other Cretans on invading foreigners. Although most tourists see the chief town, Chóra Sfakíon, only as the place where they catch the bus after the boat ride after the Gorge of Samariá, you may want to linger on this sun-bleached coast, dotted with beaches, other gorges and places to explore. It's also a congenial spot for being incredibly lazy.

## South from Vrises to Chóra Sfakíon

From Vrises (*see* above) the road ascends the Krapí valley (prettier than it sounds) to the **Langos tou Katre**, the 2km ravine nicknamed the Thermopylae of Sfakiá. This was a favourite spot for a Cretan ambush, one that spelt doom to 400 Turkish soldiers after the capture of Frangokástello (*see* below), and again in 1866 to an army of Turks fleeing south after the explosion of Arkádi. The road joins the striking mountain plateau of **Askýfou**, where the ruins of the fortress of Koulés drape a long shadow over the fields. Further south, the Libyan sea sparkles into view, as the road noodles through the steep, wooded **Ímbros Gorge** before zigzagging down to Chóra Sfakíon.

## Chóra Sfakíon (ΧΩΡΑ ΣΦΑΚΙΩΝ) and Around

Legendary viper's nest of feuds and hot-blooded revolutionaries, Chóra Sfakíon is now, like any Cretan coastal village given over to the needs of tourists. At one time, however, it was the capital of its own province, one that, with few resources of its own, took everyone else's: smuggling, sheep-rustling and piracy brought home the bacon for centuries. To police the locals, the Venetians constructed the fortress at Frangokástello just to the east in 1317, then, after the revolt of 1570, they added the castle on the hill over Chóra. The tradition of resistance continued in the Battle of Crete, when locals helped ANZAC soldiers flee to North Africa; a monument by the sea commemorates the mass evacuation, while a memorial above town honours the locals executed by the Germans for their role. The big war, however, was only an intermission in a deadly private war between two Sfakiot families known as the 'Omalós feud' or the 'Vendetta of the Century', which took 90 lives in vendettas until 1960.

Buses leave at 11am and 6pm for **Anópolis** (ΑΝΩΠΟΛΗ), a pleasant, rustic village on a plateau offering a few rooms and places to eat. A statue honours Daskaloyánnis, the native son who organized the first revolt against the Turks in 1770. It went all wrong; promised aid from Russia never arrived, and in March 1771, Daskaloyánnis gave himself up, hoping to spare Sfakiá from reprisals; the pasha ordered him to be flayed alive. From Anópolis, it's 4km west to the new bridge that spans the dizzying gorge, making the once arduous journey up and down the steep rockface to **Arádena** a snap. Ironically, the bridge arrived too late for Arádena, now a near-ghost town after a particularly bloody feud. Arádena has a famous Byzantine church, the **Astratigos**,

## Getting Around

### By Bus

Chóra Sfakíon is linked by **bus** to Chaniá three/four times a day, and four times a day to Omalós, Georgioúpolis, Réthymnon, twice a day to Plakiás, and two/three times a day from Chaniá to Anópolis, Frangokástello and Skalotí. There is a **boat** service four times a day between Chóra Sfakíon and Ag. Roúmeli, at the mouth of the Gorge of Samariá, and three/four times a day to Soúgia and Paleochóra. Morning **excursion boats** link Chóra Sfakíon to Sweetwater Beach; four ferries a week (most at weekends) sail to the island of Gávdos. Check with the **Port authority: t** 082 509 1292.

## Where to Stay and Eat

### Chóra Sfakíon ✉ 73011

**Livikon**, on the quay next to the Samaria Hotel, **t** 082 509 1211 (*C; mod*). New, stylish and comfortable, with a harbour-side taverna. There are also plenty of rooms.

**Limani**, by the port. Fish fry or mixed grill and salad. Bakery has Sfakiá's famous *myzithrópittes* (*myzíthra* cheese pies).

**Porto Loutró 1 & 2**, Loutró, **t** 082 509 1433 or 082 509 1444, **f** 082 509 1091 (*B; exp*), Two hotels, same owners, English Alison and Greek Stavros. Newish, comfortable, with water sports facilities. *Open April–Oct.*

**Blue House, t** 082 509 1127, **f** 082 509 1035 (*mod–inexp*). Good rooms and restaurant.

dedicated to Archangel Michael, sporting a dome that looks like a tiled toupée. Of all the saints, Michael, weigher of souls, is the most remorseless; a Sfakiot suspected of sheep-rustling would be brought here to be questioned before the stern-eyed saint.

## Loutró (ΛΟΥΤΡΟ)

Linked to the rest of the world only by boat (several sail daily from Chóra Sfakíon), **Loutró** may be that quiet get-away-from-it-all spot you've been looking for. Although Loutró's bay is sheltered and perfectly transparent, it doesn't have much of a beach, but there are a number of coves nearby. Besides the regular boat trips to Mármara Beach, others go to Glykó Neró, or **Sweetwater Beach**, under sheer cliffs. True to its name, springs provide fresh water, and there's a taverna for more substantial needs. Other boat services to Sweetwater run out of Chóra Sfakíon: it can get busy.

## The Ghosts of Frangokástello (ΦΡΑΓΚΟΚΑΣΤΕΛΛΟ)

The Venetians built it, but as medieval Greeks called all Westerners Franks, the austere, crenellated 14th-century fortress of Ag. Nikítas is known as Frangokástello. Once splendidly isolated on its sandy beach 14km east of Chóra Sfakíon, it now has a straggle of pensions and tavernas for company. It was the scene of a famous event in 1828, during the Greek War of Independence, when an Epirot insurgent, Hatzimichális Daliánis, captured Frangokástello with 650 Cretans. Soon 8,000 Turkish troops arrived and killed all the Greeks. But bands of Cretans who'd remained outside captured the mountain passes and wreaked a terrible revenge on the Turks when they marched north. The Massacre of Frangokástello has given rise to one of the most authenticated of all Greek ghost stories. At the end of May, the anniversary of the massacre, phantoms of the Cretan dead, the *Drosoulités* (the 'dew shades') rise up at dawn from Ag. Charalámbos cemetery, mounted and fully armed, and proceed silently towards the shell of the fortress, before disappearing into the sea. Thousands have seen them, but many more haven't; the morning must be perfectly clear. Meteorologists pooh-pooh the ghosts – mere heat mirages from the Libyan desert, they say.

# Europe at its Southernmost: Gávdos

If you suffer from *mal de civilization*, catch one of the small ferries from Chóra Sfakíon that sail 24 nautical miles over rough seas to the triangular maquis-matted islet of **Gávdos**, at 35°10' the southernmost point in Europe. The current population is around 55 – down from 8,000 in its heyday in the 1200s. Gávdos (ΓΑΥΔΟΣ), ancient Clauda, puts in a fairly limp claim as the isle of Calypso, although its limited tourist amenities can be seductive for anyone seeking the Greek island of yore. Beware that although cedars provide some shade, it can get hot, and that the unpredictable sea can easily make your stay longer than you intended. Out of season ferries are so irregular that you'll have to stick around Chóra Sfakíon and wait for one to appear. Although minibuses meet the ferry, renting a moped to take with you isn't a bad idea; none are available on Gávdos. There are beaches, especially sandy **Sarakiníkos** with a few rooms and tavernas (a 40min walk north of the port), and **Kórfos**, reached by one of Gávdos' few roads to the south, with a taverna and rooms. A pierced rock, **Tripití** or 'Three Holes', marks the south end of Europe.

# *Nomós* Réthymnon

Crete's smallest province, the *nomós* of Réthymnon, is also the most mountainous, wedged in between the White Mountains to the west and Zeus' Mount Ida, or Psilorítis (2,452m), to the east. Over the past 10 years its north coast, fringed by a 12km sandy beach on either side of the provincial capital Réthymnon, has become a popular base for exploring Crete; the Minoan sites to the east and beaches to the west are all within reasonable striking distance. On the south coast there's Ag. Galíni, one of Crete's most picturesque resorts and Moní Préveli in a lush and beautiful setting. The fortress-monastery Arkádi is a popular day trip from Réthymnon, or you can venture into the haunting and lovely Amári valley to find Crete at its most traditional. A string of old mountain villages en route to Heráklion also provide a good day's exploration, with fine views, ancient sites and caves.

# Réthymnon (ΡΕΘΥΜΝΟ)

Delightful Réthymnon, Crete's third city (pop. 26,000), has for centuries paid a price for its beach with the lack of a proper harbour. The Venetians dug a cute round one, but it keeps silting up. Not having a harbour may have proved a blessing, inhibiting the economy enough to spare Réthymnon much of what passes for progress. Like Chaniá, its Venetian and Turkish buildings are under a historical preservation order; but unlike Chaniá, Réthymnon escaped the Luftwaffe's attentions. The fortress and its minarets lend the skyline an exotic touch; wooden balconies from the Turkish occupation project overhead, darkening the lanes. Its relative isolation attracted scholars who fled Constantinople, giving Réthymnon the reputation of the brain of Crete, confirmed by the recent construction of the University of Crete's arts faculty here.

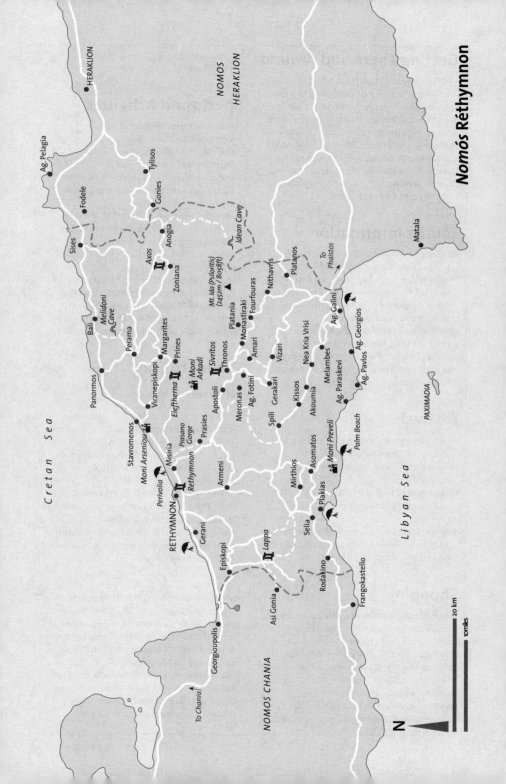

*Nomós Réthymnon*

## Getting There and Around

ANEK **ferries** sail to Piraeus daily (ANEK Lines, 250 Arkadíou, t 083 102 9874, f 083 105 5519, *www.anek.gr*.) **Port authority**: t 083 102 2276. The new **bus** station is by the sea in the west end, between Igoum Gavríl and the Periferiakos, t 083 102 2212; those labelled 'El Greco/Skaleta' depart every 20mins for the stretch of hotels along the eastern beaches. **Olympic Airways** is at 5 Koumoundoúrou, t 083 102 2257, f 083 102 7352.

## Tourist Information

**EOT**: along the town beach at E. Venizélou, t 083 102 9148; *open Mon–Fri 8–2.30.*

**Tourist police**: next door, t 083 102 8156. Look for the free English-language Cretasummer paper, published monthly and full of things to do in and around town.

**Ellotia Tours**, at 161 Arkadíou, t 083 102 4533, f 083 105 1062, *elotia@ret.forthnet.gr*. A particularly helpful and friendly agency, able to organize tickets, excursions, accommodation and car/bike rental.

## Festivals

**Thurs**: Réthymnon hosts a big weekly market and fair off Odós Kanzantzáki.

**Midsummer's Day**: Carnival, when there are bonfires.

**Last 10 days of July**: The Cretan Wine Festival and Handicrafts Exhibition, in the Public Gardens.

**Aug** and **Sept**: Renaissance Festival, performances in the Venetian fortress: call t 083 105 0800, f 083 102 9879 for events list.

## Shopping

**Soúliou Street**. Réthymnon's narrow tourist bazaar is crammed with desirable arty stuff and crafts to take home.

**Arkadíou Street**. Gold and jewellery shops.

**Talisman** and **The Olive Tree**, amongst other little shops along Theodóros Arabatzóglou. Ceramics or handmade jewellery.

**International Press**, 81 El. Venizélou. Stocks a range of English-language papers, as well as a vast selection of guides and literature about Crete.

## Sports and Activities

**Hellas Bike Travel**, 118 Machis Kritis, t 083 105 3328, *www.hellasbike.com*. For those who'd love to cycle down Mt Ida or the White Mountains but not up.

**The Happy Walker**, 56 Tombázi St, t 083 105 2920. Organized treks in the most scenic areas of western Crete.

**Portobello**, in Arkadio and Petáki. The local scuba diving centre, offering lessons.

**Atlantis** Diving Centre, t 083 107 1002, operates from the Grecotel Rithymna Beach Hotel.

The cornball **Pirate Ship** and its sister **Popeye** make daily excursions from the Venetian harbour to Maráthi (a fishing village in eastern Akrotíri) and to Balí, t 083 105 1643; nearby there are mini motorboats for hire.

## Where to Stay

### Réthymnon ✉ 74100

**Luxury**

**Grecotel Creta Palace**, 4km east, t 083 105 5181, f 083 105 4085 (*lux*). The most lavish, with an indoor heated pool and two outdoor ones, tennis courts and lots of sports. *Open Mar–Nov.*

**Rithymna Beach**, in Ádele (7km), t 083 107 1002, f 083 107 1668, *Grecotel@grecian.net.gr* (*L*). Grecotel also owns this plush place on a lovely beach and with similar facilities, especially for children, who even have their own campsite. Book early.

**Expensive**

**Mythos Suites Hotel**, 12 Plateía Karaóli, t 083 105 3917, f 083 105 1036 (*B*). 10 desirable suites sleeping 2–5 people and furnished in a traditional style, in a 16th-century manor house; all are air-conditioned and there's a pool in the central patio.

**Palazzo Rimondi**, 19 Xanthoudidou, t 083 105 1289, f 083 105 1013, *Rimondi@otenet.gr* (*A*). 25 suites in a renovated mansion, built around a courtyard with a small pool.

**Fortezza**, 16 Melissínou, **t** 083 105 5551, **f** 083 105 4073, *milodak@ret.forthnet.gr* (*B*). Just under the castle walls but a more modest affair; all rooms have balconies, and there's a garden courtyard and pool.

## Moderate

**Brascos**, at Ch. Daskaláki and Th. Moátsou, **t** 083 102 3721, **f** 083 102 3725, *brascos@ aias.gr* (*B*). Slick and clean. *Open all year.*

**Ideon**, Plateía Plastíra, **t** 083 102 8667, **f** 083 102 8670, *ideon@otenet.gr* (*B*). Enjoys a fine spot overlooking the dock and has a small pool; advisable to reserve.

**Leon**, 2 Váfe, **t** 083 102 6197 (*C*). A centrally located charmer, done up in traditional Cretan style. *Open all year.*

## Inexpensive

**Katerina**, next door to Ralia Rooms, **t** 083 102 8834. 3 attractive studios in another traditional house, up a somewhat vertiginous spiral staircase.

**Ralia Rooms**, at Salamnós and Athan. Niákou, **t/f** 083 105 0163. More atmospheric than most, with lots of wood.

**Sea Front**, 161 Arkadíou, **t** 083 105 1062. Run by friendly Ellotia Tours next door; nice pine-clad rooms; the one at the top benefits from a terrace.

**Zania**, Pávlou Vlasátou (a block from the sea), **t** 083 102 8169. A handful of pleasant rooms in a traditional house.

**Zorbas Beach** at the east end of the town beach, **t** 083 102 8540, **f** 083 105 1044 (*C*). This is a good choice for peace and quiet and it's reasonably priced.

**Youth hostel**, 41 Tombázi, **t** 083 102 2848, *www.rethymno.com* (*reception hrs 8–12pm and 5–9pm*). Friendly, clean and central; breakfast and cooking facilities available.

**Elizabeth campsite**, a few kilometres east of Réthymnon at Misíria, **t/f** 083 102 8694, *www.sunshine-campings.gr.*

# Eating Out

With its tiny fish restaurants, the **Venetian harbour** is the obvious place to dine in the evening, but expect to pay at least €25–30 for the privilege. Scan the menus – some places offer lobster lunches for two for €35–55. Other popular places are along the **Periferiakós**, the road under the fortress and near the fountain, in **Plateía Petiháki**.

**Alana**, Salamínas, just the other side of the fountain (*€25 for two*). Set in a pretty courtyard, and a nice enough place to bring your parents; offers a good fish-based menu.

**Antonias Zoumas**, by the bus station next to the small church. Doesn't look like much but on Sun afternoons it's packed with locals jawing through a 4-hr lunch.

**Avli**, 22 Xanthoúdou, **t** 083 102 4356. Set up on different levels in a garden; one of the prettiest places to eat but can get busy.

**Kyria Maria**, E. Fotáki (off Salamínas St), **t** 083 105 0208. Traditional and well worth a meal, accompanied by the chirping songbirds.

**Samaria**, **t** 083 102 4681. An exception to the mediocre restaurants along the beach and El. Venizélou this, despite plastic pictures and '*ordeure*' on the menu, has the tastiest Greek cooking, with good *giovétsi* and lamb *kléftiko.*

**Taverna Castelvecchio George**, 29 Himáras (just under the Fortezza), **t** 083 105 0886. A good Cretan atmosphere and plenty of fish dishes; rooms are also available.

**Veneto**, 4 Epiméndou, **t** 083 105 6634 (*€30–35*). The city's most beautiful restaurant, in the cellar of a 13th-century Venetian building, serving high class Greek and Cretan specialities, for a big night out.

# Entertainment and Nightlife

**T. N. Gounaki**, 6 Koronaíou St (near the church of the Mikrí Panagías). Simple but fun place summed up by its own sign: 'Every day folk Cretan music with Gounakis Sons and their father gratis/free/for nothing and Cretan meal/dish/food/dinner thank you'.

**Dimman Music Bar**, upstairs from 220 Arkadíou, on the corner of Paleológlou and Kátsoni. Attracts a young crowd.

**Baja**, on Salamínas. Popular hang-out, with a Greek and international music mix.

**Kastro**, on Salamínas. Greek music played every night.

**Fortezza Disco**, near the water. Attracts serious groovers.

## The Old Town

Although Réthymnon has been inhabited since Minoan times (the name, *Rithymna*, is pre-Greek), the oldest monuments in town are Venetian, beginning with the **Guóra Gate**, just below the Square of the Four Martyrs. Built in 1566 by the Venetian governor, the gate is the sole survivor of the walls erected after the sackings by Barbarossa in 1538, and by Uluch Ali in 1562 and 1571. Outside the gate, note the 17th-century Porta Grande or **Valide Sultana mosque** which was dedicated to the Sultan's mother; the Sultana's cemetery was converted after 1923 into the **Municipal Garden**. During the wine festival, it overflows with imbibers reviving ancient Dionysian rites.

From the Guóra Gate, Ethnikís Antistáseos leads past **San Francesco**, the friary where Crete's contribution to the papacy, Alexander V, began his career; when elected pontiff, he paid for its elaborate Corinthian portal. Further down the street is the quaint lion-headed **Rimondi Fountain** (1629) built by another Venetian governor at the junction of several streets, now packed with bars. The Rimondi Fountain marks the heart of town, and all the finest buildings are close by. The **Nerandzes Mosque** on Manoúli Vernárdou retains a monumental portal from its days as the Venetian church of Santa Maria. On its conversion into a mosque in 1657, it was capped with three domes; today it's used as a concert hall. Its graceful rocket of a minaret was added in 1890. The handsome Venetian **Loggia** (1550s), nearby on Arkadíou, was a club where the nobility would meet and gamble; it now does duty as an exhibition hall and museum replica shop. Northeast of here is Réthymnon's bijou **Venetian harbour**, lined with seafood restaurants and patrolled by black and white swans.

## The Fortezza and Archaeology Museum

In ancient times, when Cretans were bitten by rabid dogs they would resort to the temple of Artemis Roccaéa on Réthymnon's acropolis, and take a cure of dog's liver or seahorse innards. All traces of this interesting cult were obliterated in the late 16th century, when the Venetians forced local peasants to build the **Fortezza** over the temple (*open daily 9–4; adm*). It is one of the best-preserved and largest Venetian castles in Greece, with room for the entire population of Réthymnon and its environs; yet in 1645, after a bitter two-month siege, the defending garrison was forced to surrender it to the Turks. The church, converted into a mosque, is fairly well preserved, but the rest has been left in dishevelled abandon.

Near the entrance to the Fortezza, the **Archaeology Museum**, in the former Turkish prison (*t 083 105 4668; open Tues–Sun 8.30–3; adm*), is beautifully arranged and air-conditioned. The most dazzling pieces hail from the Late Minoan cemetery at Arméni: a boar-tooth helmet, bronze double axes, lovely delicate vases, fragile remains of a loop-decorated basket from 1200 BC, and *larnaxes* (sarcophagi), including one painted with a wild goat and bull chase and a hunter holding a dog on a leash. A coin collection covers most of the ancient cities of Crete. On Vernadoú St, the **Historical and Folk Art Museum** (*t 083 102 9572; open Mon–Sat 9.30–2; adm*) offers a delicious collection of costumes, photos, farm tools and pottery from ancient times to 40 years ago. Nearby, on Chimáras, the **Municipal Centre of Contemporary Art** (*t 083 102 1847; open Tues–Sun 10–2 and 5–8*) features exhibitions of Greek art from the last 200 years.

## Moní Arkádi

Four buses a day (three at weekends) go to **Moní Arkádi** (*t 083 108 3076; open daily 8am–pm; adm*), Crete's holy shrine of freedom. Founded in the 11th century on the lonesome flanks of Psilorítis, the monastery was mostly rebuilt in the 17th century, although the lovely sun-ripened façade of the church, Crete's finest essay in Venetian Mannerism, dates from 1587. During this time Arkádi was a repository for ancient Greek manuscripts, spirited out of Constantinople, and the monks performed important work in copying the texts and disseminating them in Europe. Arkádi resembles a small fort, which is one reason why Koronéos, head of the Revolutionary Committee of 1866, chose it for a base and a store for his powder magazine. When the Turks demanded that the abbot hand over the rebels, he refused; in response, a Turkish expeditionary force attacked on 7 November 1866. After a 2-day siege they breached the monastery walls. Rather than surrender, Abbot Gabriel set fire to the powder magazines, blowing up 829 Turks and Greeks. The suicidal explosion caused a furore in Europe, as Swinburne and Victor Hugo took up the cause of Cretan independence. The Gunpowder Room, where the blast left a gaping hole in the roof, may be visited, and there's the **Historical Museum** (*adm*), containing the holey, holy banner and portraits of the heroes of 1866, monkish embroideries and icons. An old windmill was made into an ossuary, displaying a stack of skulls blasted with holes.

## The Prasanó Gorge

Just east of Réthymnon is one of Crete's prettiest gorges, the **Prasanó**, formed by the Plataniás River, which courteously dries up between mid-June and mid-October so you can walk down the gorge (allow four to five hours, wear sturdy shoes and bring water). Take the early Amári bus as far as the first bend in the road after Prasiés, where the track begins; walk past the sheepfold and bear to the left. Lined with plane trees, dates, olives, cypresses and rhododendrons, the gorge has three sets of narrow 'gates' where the walls climb up to 480ft. The track ends near Misiriá, where you can swim and catch a bus back the last 5km to Réthymnon.

# From Réthymnon South to the Libyan Coast

The *nómos* of Réthymnon encompasses the narrow 'neck' of Crete, and there's a good road that cuts between the mountains for the south, where Plakiás and Ag. Galíni are major resorts, with Moní Préveli as the favourite day trip in between.

## Arméni to Plakiás

Directly south of Réthymnon, the village of **Arméni** was named after the Armenian soldiers granted land here by Nikephóros Phokás, following his reconquest of Crete from the Saracens in 961. They weren't the first to settle here: an unusually large **Late Minoan III cemetery** (signposted from the main road; *t 083 102 9975; open Mon–Fri 8.30–3*) was discovered near the crossroads with Somatás. Some 200 chamber tombs from 1350–1200 BC fill seven acres, including elaborate underground chambers;

the grave goods are in the Réthymnon and Heráklion museums. South of Arméni, the road cuts through the **Kourtaliótis Gorge** and emerges at **Asómatos**, the crossroads for Préveli and Plakiás, with magnificent sea views. **Plakiás** (ΠΛΑΚΙΑ) is a fine centre for rambles and swimming, from its own exposed grey sands, or on the sandy coves

## Getting Around

Plakiás has **7 buses** a day to Réthymnon, and two a day west along the south coast as far as Chóra Sfakíon, by way of Frangokástello, and two buses a day to Préveli. Ag. Galíni has 5 buses a day from Réthymnon, as well as connections to Heráklion, Phaistós, and Mátala by way of Míres.

## Where to Stay and Eat

### Plakiás ✉ 74060

**Damnoni Bay**, t 083 203 1373, f 083 203 1002 (*C; exp*). Cream-coloured complex with studio apartments, pool, water sports, and a seafood restaurant. Has the advantage of having a view that doesn't include the Damnoni Bay Hotel.

**Alianthos**, t 083 203 1196, f 083 203 1197 (*C; mod*). A popular Neo-Minoan family hotel, with green lawns and a pool near the beach.

**Lamon**, t 083 203 1425, f 083 203 1424 (*B; mod*). Pretty blue and white, a good bet at the bottom of the moderate price range.

**Youth hostel**, Plakiás, t 083 203 2118, *www.yhplakias.com*. Set in an olive grove.

**Apollonia Camping**, t 083 203 1318, f 083 203 1607. Has a pool, laundry and mini-market. *Open April–Oct*.

**Ariadni**, Oniroú, t 083 203 1640 (*€20*). A small, simple place that has rare Greek and Cretan specialities such as *monastiráko* (pork with mushrooms, peas and prunes) and *erofilí* (lamb with artichokes and potatoes).

**Christos**, by the little port, t 083 203 1472. Under the tamarisks, this place does a roaring trade with the locals and has a few rooms to rent upstairs.

**Sophia B**, on the waterfront next to the Livikon Hotel (*€15*). Tables set on tiers where you can feast on a choice of 32 different starters, a selection of pasta and meat or fish, all dishes irrigated with a long Cretan wine list.

### Spíli ✉ 74200

**Green Hotel**, t 083 202 2225 (*C; mod*). Bedecked with flowers, a delightful refuge when the coasts are unbearably hot and crowded; book early in the summer.

**Costas Inn**, on the main road near the fountains. Serves tasty Cretan mountain food and also has rooms for rent.

### Ag. Galíni ✉ 74056

Although stacked with all sorts of accommodation, don't arrive in Ag. Galíni without a reservation in the summer. Places generally not booked solid by package companies are:

**Galíni Mare**, t/f 083 209 1358 (*C; mod*). Good views and facilities.

**Aktaeon**, Kountouriótou, t 083 209 1208 (*E; inexp*). Private baths and good views over the town; good value.

**Argiro's Studios and Rooms**, t 083 209 1470 (*D; inexp*).

**Manos**, t 083 209 1394 (*D; inexp*). Near the bus station.

Some of Crete's best cooks work in the restaurants of Ag. Galíni.

**Madame Ordanz**, up on the second floor (*€20*). Looming over the waterfront. Lined with photographs of old Ag. Galíni, serves well-prepared French and Greek dishes with a glamorous touch.

**Ariston**, (*€12*). Very good *stifádo, moussaka*, and an excellent aubergine salad.

**El Greco**, next door. Just as good.

**Onar**. One of Ag. Galíni's favourites, with excellent Cretan food cooked by mama.

**La Strada**, in the centre. Has a real pizza oven, and serves it up to jazz music.

## Nightlife and Entertainment

**Legend** or **Zorbas** clubs, in Ag. Galíni. For working off the calories after midnight.

**Jazz n Jazz Bar**, Ag. Galíni. If you're a jazz fan, you'll love this excellent bar.

east of the headland at **Damnóni**; the concrete pillboxes offer a reminder from the war when this coast was an important escape route to Egypt. Half an hour's walk west of Plakiás, **Soúda** beach has a lovely taverna in a palm grove. Late in the day, head for **Mírthios**, where the tavernas offer sunset sea views.

From Plakiás or Damnóni, the Posidonia Fast Boat makes daily excursions to Préveli; there's also one bus a day to Préveli, two to Ag. Galíni, and one to Chóra Sfakíon. The latter passes via **Sélia**, with beautiful views from its church, and **Rodákino** ('peach'), a village hanging over a ravine with a grey beach. It was from here that Patrick Leigh Fermor and the Resistance spirited General Kreipe off Crete to Egypt in a submarine.

## Moní Préveli

Moní Préveli, 7km east of Lefkógia, is the beauty spot on the central Libyan coast. On the way, the road passes palm groves along the Megálo Pótamos River, just before a bridge and the abandoned lower half of the monastery, known as **Káto Préveli**. In the early 19th century, a few decades after Daskaloyánnis' aborted revolt in Sfakía (*see* p.142), Abbot Melchisedek Tsouderos began to collect arms for a new revolt. The Turks got wind of it, and in 1821, shortly before the War of Independence on the mainland, they came to destroy the monastery. Rather than resist, Abbot Melchisedek welcomed the Turks and got them so drunk they fell asleep, so the monks were able to flee before the Turks woke up and pillaged the monastery.

The 'Back' monastery, **Píso Préveli**, is 3km down, high on the coast overlooking exotic vegetation (*t 083 203 1246; open 8–1 and 3–7; adm*). The original Byzantine church was demolished by the monks in the 1830s, after the Turks kept refusing them permission to make repairs. They did, however, preserve the furnishings: the intricate gilt iconostasis, with 17th-century icons, and a miraculous piece of the True Cross. Note the famous Byzantine palindrome NIΨONANOMHMATA MHMONANOΨIN ('Cleanse your sins, not only your face') on the fountain. Throughout Crete's revolts in the 19th century, Píso Préveli took in refugees until boats could ferry them to independent Greece. In 1941, the monks sheltered hundreds of Allied troops until they could be picked up by submarine; in gratitude the British gave Préveli two silver candlesticks and a marble plaque, now cared for by the last monk. From the monastery it's a dangerous scramble down to **Palm Beach**, the lovely sands lined with groves of date palms at the mouth of the Kourtaliótis Gorge. Although today's invaders, mostly on boat excursions from Plakiás or Ag. Galíni, are more peaceful, there are far too many of them for the sparse facilities.

## Spíli and Ag. Galíni

The main road south towards Ag. Galíni continues past the Plakiás turn-off, passing by way of **Spíli** (ΣΠΗΛΙ), a charming farming village immersed in greenery. The village centrepiece is a long fountain, where water splashes from a row of 17 Venetian lion-heads. Further along are turn-offs for beaches: at Akoúmia a rough road leads down in 10km to pristine **Ag. Paraskeví**, while further east at Néa Kría Vrísi you can turn south for lovely **Ag. Pávlos**, a sheltered sandy beach, with a new yoga holiday centre and a few places to stay (*see* 'Specialist Holidays', p.76).

The roads end up at **Ag. Galíni** (ΑΓΙΑ ΓΑΛΗΝΗ), an old fishing village under a backdrop of mountains, easily the most photogenic resort on Crete's south coast. The beach is puny for the number of bodies that try to squeeze on it, but boat excursions sail in search of others, at Moní Préveli, Mátala, **Ag. Geórgios** (shingly with three tavernas) and Ag. Pávlos (50 minutes) and to the pebble-beached islets of **Paximádia**.

## Amári: The Western Slopes of Mount Ida

Wedged under Mount Ida, the ancient province of Amári consists of two valleys, well known for their spirited resistance in the last war, and also for their lush charms, cherry orchards, olive groves and frescoed Byzantine churches. Both are prime walking and touring territory. The main road leads south into the valleys by way of Prasiés and Apóstoli, with grand views and a frescoed church, Ag. Nikólaos, from the 1300s; Ag. Fotiní just beyond marks the crossroads of the east and west valleys. Many west valley villages were torched by the retreating Germans, but they have been rebuilt pretty much as they were. Méronas is worth a stop for its church of the **Panagía** with a Venetian Gothic doorway, crowned with the arms of the prominent Byzantine Kallergis family. Inside (the key's across the road) are early 14th-century frescoes showing the more naturalistic artistic trends from Constantinople. Gerakári, famous for cherries, is the starting point for a stunning drive over the Kédros Mountains to Spíli (*see* above). If you have to choose one route, the east valley is lovelier. From Ag. Fotiní, turn left for Thrónos, the heir of ancient Sybrito, a city destroyed by the Saracens in 824. The setting, especially Sybrito's acropolis, is superb, and in the centre of Thrónos, the mosaic carpet of a large basilica overflows from under the simple little church of the Panagía, containing exceptional frescoes.

Back on the main route, the University of Crete is excavating a Minoan Proto-Palatial villa near **Monastiráki**. After Chaniá and Réthymnon, Monastiráki is the most important site yet discovered in western Crete (and still off limits to visitors): it had abundant storage rooms, where the *pithoi* still contained grape pips. The villa burned in 1700 BC, the same time as Knossós. **Amári**, one-time capital of the province, is a lovely village, surrounded by enchanting views, especially from the Venetian tower. **Ag. Ánna**, outside the village, has the oldest dated frescoes in Crete (1225).

## Réthymnon to Heráklion: The Coastal Route

Between Réthymnon and Heráklion you can choose between the coast-skirting highway, or the old roads winding over the northern slopes of Mount Ida. The highway passes Réthymnon's beach sprawl before arriving at **Pánormos** (ΠΑΝΟΡΜΟΣ), a pretty place with a ruined 5th-century basilica and small beach, guarded by a Genoese fortress of 1206. Pánormos made its fortune in the 19th century as a port for carob beans – once an essential ingredient in the manufacture of film.

A popular excursion from Pánormos is up to the **Melidóni Cave**. Its small mouth belies the size: the ceiling, ragged with stalactites, rises 990ft overhead. The Minoans

# Where to Stay and Eat

## Pánormos ✉ 74057

**Villa Kynthia, t** 083 405 1148, winter **f** 081 022 2970 (*B; exp*). Intimate luxury in a 1898 mansion, lovely air-conditioned rooms with antiques and a pool. *Open Mar–Oct*.

**Panorma Beach, t** 083 405 1321, **f** 083 405 1403 (*C; mod*). A typical beach hotel.

**Lucy's, t** 083 405 1212. Pleasant, cheap rooms.

**To Steki**. One of the best places to eat.

## Balí ✉ 74057

Most of these places are only worth trying in the off-season, but Balí's much nicer then anyway.

**Bali Village, t** 083 409 4210, **f** 083 409 4252, *Balibeach@her.forthnet.gr* (*B; exp*). One of the first hotels here and still the nicest.

**Sophia, t** 083 409 4202 (*mod-inexp*). Good value for money, clean apartments, with pool and family-run taverna.

## Ag. Pelagía ✉ 71500

**Capsis Beach and Sofitel Palace, t** 081 081 1212, **f** 081 081 1076, *root@capsis-crete@her.forthnet.gr* (*A; lux*). Large hotel/bungalow complex on the peninsula, it has just about every luxury, including 3 beaches, several pools, a waterfall, zoo, horse-riding, and a water sports school.

**Peninsula, t** 081 081 1313, **f** 081 081 1291, *Peninsula@her.forthnet.gr* (*A; lux*). Perched on the rocks, with a lovely terrace overlooking the beach, has a long list of leisure activities, including a 'do-it-yourself hairdressing salon'.

**Alexander House, t** 081 081 1303, **f** 081 081 1381, *Alexhh@iraklio.hellasnet.gr* (*A; exp–mod*). Comfortable air-conditioned rooms with satellite TV, mini bars and balconies, and a good Chinese restaurant.

**Panorama, t** 081 081 1002, **f** 081 081 1273 (*B; mod*). Friendly, large hotel with a pool, water sports and tennis.

Eating out in Ag. Pelagía isn't cheap, but it's very good:

**Muragio**, by the sea. Delicious fish.

**Valentino**. Similar to above, and pizzas from a real Italian *forno*.

**Le Gourmet**. A pleasant waterfront taverna with a very good wine list.

worshipped in this gloomy place, and near the entrance is a 3rd-century BC inscription to Hermes Talaios, who shared offerings here with Zeus Talaios and Talos, the giant bronze robot that patrolled the Crete coasts until Medea pulled the pin out of his heel and drained away his life-giving *ichor*. In 1824, when the Turks were doing their best to cut short Crete's participation in the Greek War of Independence, 324 women and children and 30 revolutionaries took refuge in the cave. When the Turks found them, the Greeks refused to surrender; the Turks built a fire and asphyxiated them all. With its crumbling altar and broken ossuary the cave still seems haunted.

Further east, **Balí** (ΜΠΑΛΙ), in part thanks to its exotic name, has been transformed from a quiet steep-stepped fishing village overlooking a trio of sandy coves to a jam-packed resort. The lovely 17th-century **Monastery of Balí** is being restored; the Renaissance façade of the church and fountain are especially worth a look.

The **Old Road** between Pérama and Heráklion is pure rural Crete. Sleepy **Fódele** (ΦΟΔΕΛΕ), set in orange groves between the Old and New Roads, was, according to tradition, the birthplace in 1541 of Doménikos Theotokópoulos (El Greco); a plaque was put up by Spain's University of Toledo in 1934 and recently a '**House of El Greco**' (*open Tues–Sun, 9–5*) has been set up. Although El Greco never returned after leaving in 1567 for Venice (where he studied with Titian and Tintoretto), Rome and Spain, he signed his paintings in Greek. East of Fódele, the highway continues to the junction for the upmarket resort of **Ag. Pelagía** (ΑΓ. ΠΕΛΑΓΙΑ), strewn over the headland and protected sandy beach that marks the outer gate of the Bay of Heráklion.

# Réthymnon to Heráklion: Ancient Cities along the Inland Route

A choice of roads skirts the northern flanks of Psilorítis, and to see everything there is to see will involve backtracking. From Réthymnon, follow the coast as far as Stavroménos, where you can pick up the road for **Viranepiskopí**, with a 10th-century basilica near a sanctuary of Artemis, and a 16th-century Venetian church. Higher up, colourful **Margarítes** is home to a thriving pottery industry (they even make huge *pithoi*) and 14th-century **Ag. Demétrius** and 12th-century **Ag. Ioánnis**.

Another 4km south, **Eléftherna** (ΕΛΕΥΘΕΡΝΑ) is just below the ancient city of the same name, founded by the Dorians in the 8th century BC. The setting, above two tributaries of the Milopótamos River, is spectacular; mighty walls and a formidable tower, rebuilt in Hellenistic times, kept out most foes. Historian Dio Cassius wrote that the Romans under Metellus Creticus were only able to capture Eléftherna after the tower was soaked in vinegar (!). Near here is a section of the aqueduct carved into the stone, which leads to two massive Roman cisterns capable of holding 10,000 cubic metres of water. At the bottom of the glade there's a well-preserved bridge, with Mycenaean-style corbelled stone arches.

Even higher and more precipitous, **Axós**, 30km east along the mountain road, was founded around 1100 BC by Minoans seeking refuge from the Dorians. Axós was the only town on Crete to have a king of its own into the 7th century BC, and it continued to thrive well into the Byzantine period, when it counted 46 churches; today 11 survive, of which Ag. Iríni, with frescoes, is the most important. The scattered remains of ancient Axós reveal a huge town. The acropolis is scattered on terraces above its 8th-century BC walls; arrange to go with Antonia Koutantou (*t 083 406 1311*) who runs one of the shops and has the key to the churches.

On the road to the east of Axós, a splendid panorama of all the hill towns of the Milopótamo opens up. Just below the first one, **Zoniá**, the **Sendóni Cave** (*open 8 to sunset, closed hols; adm*) contains one of Crete's most striking collections of stalactites, cave draperies and petrified waves.

## Anógia and the Idean Cave

The next village east is **Anógia** (ΑΝΩΓΕΙΑ), where the inhabitants of Axós moved in the Middle Ages. A stalwart resistance centre, it was burned by both the Turks and the Germans, the latter in reprisal for hiding the kidnapped General Kreipe, when all the men in the village were rounded up and shot. Today rebuilt in an upper, modern town and lower, more traditional-looking town, Anógia is not without charm, and lives off its weavings; brace yourself for a mugging by little old ladies (including a few surviving widows of the martyrs).

Just east of Anógia begins the paved, 26km road south to the 5,052ft **Idean Cave** (ΙΔΑΙΟ ΑΝΔΡΟΝ; *closed at the time of writing*). In Archaic times, the Idean Cave took over the Diktean Cave's thunder, so to speak, in claiming to be the birthplace of Zeus. Ancient even to the ancients, the Idean cult preserved remnants of Minoan religion into classical times, presided over by Idean Dactyls, or 'finger men'. According to his 5th-century BC biographer, Pythagoras was initiated by the Dactyls into the Orphic mysteries of midnight Zagreus (i.e. Zeus fused with the mystic role of Dionysos), a cult that may have been behind his mystical theories on numbers and vegetarianism. Since 1982 Ioánnis and Éfi Sakellarákis' excavations have produced roomfuls of votive offerings from 3000 BC to the 5th century AD. A ski resort has opened nearby, and there's a marked track from the cave to the summit of **Psilorítis**, Crete's highest peak at 8,057ft, about 7 hours' round trip if you're experienced and equipped. The Greek Mountaineering Federation operates a pair of shelters: at 3,609ft Prinos (*t 081 022 7609*), and at 4,921ft Toumbotos Prinos (*t 083 102 3666*).

From Anógia, the road continues east to **Goniés**, a village set in an amphitheatre at the entrance to the Malevízi, which produced Malmsey, a favourite sweet wine in medieval Venice and England. Nearby, at **Sklavokámbos**, a Minoan villa went up in flames so intense that its limestone walls were baked; its ruins are next to the road.

### The Minoan Villas of Týlisos

Much more remains to be seen further east at **Týlisos** (ΤΥΛΙΣΟΣ), surrounded by mountains and swathed in olives and vineyards, where three large Minoan villas (*t 081 022 6092; open daily, 8.30–3; adm*) were unearthed between 1902 and 1913. Built in the prosperous New Palace period and destroyed *c.* 1450 BC, the villas stood two or even three storeys high and contained small apartments and extensive storage facilities; palatial elements such as light-wells, lustral basins, colonnaded courts and cult shrines are produced here in miniature.

The Minoan love of twisting little corridors is further complicated here by the fact that the Dorians founded a town re-using many of the walls. Rectangular Villa B, nearest the entrance, is the oldest and least intact; Villas A and C are extremely well built of finely dressed stone: door jambs, stairs, pillars and the drainage system survive. The presence of these elaborate villas in Týlisos and Sklavokámbos suggests that the Minoan nobility liked to take a few weeks off in the country, but the fact that they stand along the Knossós–Idean Cave road may be the true key to their purpose.

## *Nomós* Heráklion

This province, the cradle between the Psilorítis range and the Diktean Mountain was the core of Minoan Crete: not only Knossós, but Mália, Phaistós, Archánes and Ag. Triáda, along with countless smaller sites are here. The magnificent works of art they yielded, now in the Heráklion Museum, are one of the glories of Greece. Besides the finest Cretan art and culture, the province also contains much of the dark side of what the last 40 years have wrought – the hedonistic beach resorts along the lovely north coast, thrown up in the first flush of mass tourism in the 1960s, about which you often hear people say that what the Venetians, Turks and Germans couldn't conquer, money has undone without a fight. Big, busy Heráklion is both the capital of the province and of Crete.

# Nomós Heráklion

NOMOS LASSITHI

HERAKLION

DIA

To Ag. Nikolaos

To Ierapetra

To Rethymnon

Ammoudara

Chersonisou
Liménas Chersonísou
Stalida
Malia
Mochos
Kras̆
Tzermiadon
Ano Simi
Kato Vigla
Moni Arvi
Amiras
Ano Viannos
Chondros
Kastri
Afendis (2141m)
Embaros
Martha
Panagia
Kastelliana
Priansos
Philippi
Tsoutsouros
Pyrgos
Charakas
Moni Koudoma
Lebena
Lendas
Kali Limenes
Matala
Kommos
Pitsidia
Kalamaki
Ag. Triada
Phaistos
Tymbaki
Vori
Kamilario
Kamares
Votizia
Moni Vrondisi
Kamares Cave
Zaros
Ag. Deka
Gortyn
Platanos
Mires
Ag. Varvara
Prinias
Venerato
Krousonas
Ag. Myronas
Rafkos
Sklavokambos
Tylisos
Gonies
Anogia
Fodele
Rogdia
Skavidaras
Ag. Galini
Mt. Ida (Psiloritis) (2452m / 8058ft)
Anemospilia
Archanes
Profitis Ilias
Vathypetro
Ag. Vasilios
Voni
Myrtia
Thapsano
Arkalochori
Poros
Xidas
Kastelli
Lyttos
Avdou
Knossos
Ammisos
Karteros
Kokini Chani
Gouves
Gournes
Ammisos

20 km
10 miles

N

# Heráklion (ΗΡΑΚΛΕΙΟ)

Hustling, bustling Heráklion is Crete's capital and Greece's fourth city (pop. 127,000) – the kind of place that most people go on holiday to escape. But Heráklion boasts two unmissable attractions: a museum containing the world's greatest collection of Minoan art, and the grand palace of Knossós in its suburbs.

Heráklion has gone through several name changes. It began modestly as Katsamba, the smaller of Knossós' two ports, and took on its current name in the classical period. In the 800s the Saracens saw the potential of the site and built their chief town here, naming it Kandak ('the moats') after the trench they dug around its walls. By the time it was reconquered by Nikephóros Phokás, Kandak was the leading slave market in the Mediterranean. The Venetians made Kandak into Candia and kept it as the capital of Crete; the mighty walls they built around it so impressed the Cretans that they called it Megálo Kástro, the 'Big Castle'. The Turks kept it their seat of government until 1850, when they transferred it to Chaniá. When Crete became autonomous, the classical name, Heráklion, was revived and it reclaimed its capital role in 1971.

## Venetian Heráklion

When Crete won its autonomy in 1898, Arthur Evans, already a local hero for his news reports in Britain on Turkish atrocities, was instrumental in persuading the Cretans to safeguard their Venetian heritage, and it's a good thing he did because otherwise Heráklion would be a mess. The **Venetian Harbour**, west of the modern ferry docks, still offers the best introduction to the city, guarded by the restored 16th-century fortress **Rocco al Mare** (*t 081 028 9935; open Tues–Sat 8.30–3, Sun 10–3; adm*) still wearing its lion of St Mark. There are splendid views of the city from here. The **Arsenali**, or shipyards, recall Venetian seamanship and superior facilities at sea that supplied Heráklion during the great 21-year siege.

The main street up from the Venetian Harbour, **25 Avgoustou**, has always been lined with the sort of businesses it supports today: shipping agents, car rental outlets and banks. Halfway up, the church of **Ag. Títos** owes its cubic form to the Turks, who used it as a mosque and rebuilt it after several earthquakes. The chapel to the left of the narthex houses the island's most precious relic, the head of St Titus, a disciple of St Paul and the apostle of Crete. When forced to give up Crete, the Venetians made off with Titus' skull and only returned it when Pope Paul IV forced them to, in 1966.

It takes imagination to reconstruct, but the Venetians designed what is now **Plateía Venizélou**, at the top of 25 Avgoustou, as a miniature Piazza San Marco. Heráklion's City Hall occupies the **Venetian Loggia** (1628), built as a meeting place for the Venetian and Cretan nobility, and completely reconstructed after being hit in the Battle of Crete. **San Marco** (Ag. Márkos), the first Venetian church on Crete (1239), was twice rebuilt after earthquakes and converted into a mosque by the Turks. Water dribbles from the mouths of the lions of the **Morosini Fountain**, commissioned in 1626 by governor Francesco Morosini, who brought water in from Mount Júktas to replace the old wells. Although the fountain is minus its figure of Neptune, the remaining sea nymphs, dolphins and bulls are some of the finest Venetian works left on Crete.

Cretaphone, 6–10 Odós 1821. A wide choice of Cretan music.

Aerákis, 34 Daedálou. Cretan music and honey and herbs too.

Planet International, at the corner of Kydonias and Chándakos Sts. A wide choice of books in English.

Lexis, Evans St. Also a very good bookshop for English speakers.

Astrakianákis, Platéia Venizélou. Yet more books in English.

# Where to Stay

## Heráklion ✉ 71202

Book in the summer. If you haven't, try the Hotel Managers' Union, 19 Giannitóson, t 081 028 1492, or the Room Renters' Union, 1 Gamaláki, t 081 022 4260.

## Luxury

Atlantis, 2 Ighías (near the Archaeology Museum), t 081 022 9103, f 081 022 6265, Reserv_atl@atl.grecotel.gr (A). Luxurious air-conditioned rooms (some with disabled access), a swimming pool, satellite TV and roof garden.

Astoria Capsis Hotel, Platía Eleftherías, t 081 034 3080, f 081 022 9078, astoria@her .forthnet.gr (A). Similarly priced and just as smart, with rooftop pool and bar.

Candia Maris, west in Ammoudára, t 081 031 4632, f 081 025 0669, Candia@maris.gr (L). Plush rooms and bungalows give all-inclusive comfort at a price (€310 a head); there is even a thalassotherapy centre.

Grecotel Agapi Beach, Ammoudára, t 081 031 1084, f 081 025 8731, agap@ab.grecotel.gr (A). Offers all the fancy beach accessories you could desire.

## Expensive

Galaxy, 67 Demokratías (just outside the walls to the southeast), t 081 023 8812, f 081 021 1211, Galaxyir@otenet.gr (A). Contemporary serenity and full air-conditioning in the rooms; ask for one overlooking the swimming pool.

Lato Hotel, 15 Epimenídou, t 081 022 8103, f 081 024 0350, lato@her.forthnet.gr, (A). Well-kitted-out, modern rooms with lovely sea views from the balconies.

Minoa Palace, one of the many resort hotels on the beaches: east in Amnisós, t 081 038 0404, f 081 038 0422, minoapalace@akashotels.com (A). A big, fancy beachside complex with a pool, floodlit tennis court, and activities and sports for all ages.

Dolphin Bay, in Ammoudára, t 081 082 1276, f 081 082 1312 (A). Similar facilities to the Minoa Palace.

## Moderate

Many of these are conveniently located near the port and bus stations; among the best are:

Ilaira, 1 Ariádnis, t 081 022 7103 (C). Traditionally decorated rooms with balcony, and a cafeteria roof terrace.

Kris, 2 Doúkos Bófor, t 081 022 3211 (C). Friendly, with cheerful blue-and-red colour scheme and well-positioned rooms with fridge/sink.

Daedalos, 15 Daedálou, t 081 024 4812, f 081 022 4391 (C). Plain and modern, convenient for the Archaeology Museum and centre, on a pedestrian-only street.

## Inexpensive

Lena, 10 Lahaná, t 081 022 3280, f 081 024 2826 (E). Clean, simple rooms on a quiet street west of 25 Avgoustou.

Rea, 1 Kalimeráki, t 081 022 3638, f 081 024 2189 (D). A good, quiet choice near the sea.

## The Archaeology Museum

*t 081 022 6092; open 8–7, Mon noon–7; adm. If you get overwhelmed (or hungry) you can go out and return with your date-stamped ticket.*

A few blocks east of Platéia Venizélou, on the north side of **Platéia Eleftherías**, is the **Archaeology Museum**, an ungainly coffer that holds the Minoan masterpieces. Thanks to local archaeologist Joseph Hadzidákis, a law was passed in the early days of Crete's autonomy stating that every important antiquity found on the island belongs to the museum. The result is dazzling, delightful and too much to digest in one visit.

**Atlas**, 6 Kandanoléontos, **t** 081 028 8989 (*E*). A touch of streamlined Art Deco on a noisy pedestrian-only street near the centre, although the rooms don't all live up to the promise of the exterior. *Open April–Oct.*

**Youth hostel**, 5 Víronos, **t** 081 028 6281. Well run and convenient, with usually a dorm bed to spare.

**Camping Creta**, at Kókkini Hani, near Gournés, **t** 081 041 400, and at Goúves, **t** 089 704 1400.

# Eating Out

The fashionable set has created a car-free haven in the narrow streets between **Daedálou** and **Ag. Títou**; buildings have been restored and charming little restaurants and bars appeared on cue to fill them up; this is the young and hip place to be seen.

**Loukoulous**, 5 Korái, **t** 081 022 4435 (€25–30). An elegant Italian restaurant in a beautifully restored mansion.

**Giovanni**, just opposite, **t** 081 034 6338 (€20–25). A choice of fixed-price menus for two: fish, Italian, Greek and vegetarian dishes; extensive wine list.

**Ippokampos** on the Sófokli Venizélou waterfront (€20). Has the best seafood, to go with its exquisite *mezédes*.

The restaurants around the Morosini fountain tend to be rip-offs, but the tavernas jammed along the narrow **Fotíou** ('Dirty') **Lane**, between the market and **Evans Street**, all offer the Greek essentials and grills at moderate prices;

**Ionia**, Evans St. Claims to be the oldest taverna in town, serving some unusual mountain dishes, such as goat with chestnuts and liver with rosemary.

**Kyriakos**, Leof. Demokratías, **t** 081 022 4649. A Heráklion institution, popular with locals. *Open all day, closed Sun.*

**Ta Psaria**, at the foot of 25 Avgoustou, with a view over the Rocco and the port. The day's catch is enticingly hooked up by your table.

**Toumbrouk**, in Karterós, east of Amnisós. An excellent fish taverna.

**Chryssomenos**, Ag. Iríni, just after Knossós. A good place for lunch after doing the site. Typical Cretan fare can be had at the tavernas up in the village of **Rogdiá**, between Ammoudára and Ag. Pelagía.

# Entertainment and Nightlife

When the Heráklioniots want to spend a night on the town, they often leave it in summer, when the clubs move out;

**Chersónisos** and **Ammoudára**. Nightspots that are especially popular. Among the clubs, **Granazi** and **Edem** often have live music.

**Doúkos Beaufort (aka Bófor) Street**, in town, above the main bus station, has a whole strip of clubs, including:

**Diamonds and Pearls**. A lap-dancing bar.

**Kastro**. Cretan music played nightly after 10pm by the island's best lýra maestros.

**I Palia Aigli**, at the end of Theríssou, **t** 081 025 2600. Live *rembétika* music.

**Café Veneto**, on Epimenídou. This elegant nightspot has an alluring roof terrace overlooking the port.

**Idomeneos Street**. Contains a clutch of popular bars. Try **Blue Iguana** or **Xitzaz**.

**DNA** or **Fougaro**, both on Ikarou, in town. For those who are still full of beans late at night.

**Ideion Andron**. For quiet backgammon and drinks.

The collection is arranged in chronological order. In **Room I**, containing Neolithic (from 5000 BC) and Pre-Palatial periods (2600–2000 BC), the craftsmanship that would characterize Minoan civilization proper is already apparent in the delicate golden leaf pendants, the polished stone ritual vessels, the bold, irregularly fired red and black Vasilikí pottery and carved sealstones. Early Cycladic idols and Egyptian seals from the tombs of Mesara point to a precocious trade network. **Rooms II** and **III** are devoted to the Old Palace period (2000–1700 BC), when the Minoans made their first polychromatic Kamares-ware vases, marrying form and decoration with stylized motifs from the natural world. The virtuosity of Minoan potters 3,500 years ago can be measured by their 'eggshell-ware' cups. One case displays the Knossós Town Mosaic: faïence plaques of miniature Minoan houses. The mysterious clay **Phaistós Disc** (*c.*1700 BC) is the world's first example of moveable type: 45 different symbols, believed to be phonetic ideograms, are stamped on both sides in a spiral.

Items from the Minoans' Golden Age, the New Palace period (1700–1450 BC), are divided geographically in **Rooms IV–IX**. Potters turned to even freer, more naturalistic designs. Stone carving became ever more rarefied as the Minoans used porphyrys and semi-precious stones, cutting and polishing them to bring out their swirling grains. **Room IV** contains many of their masterpieces: a naturalistic bull's head rhyton carved in black steatite found in the Little Palace at Knossós, the leopard axe from Mália, and bare-breasted snake goddess statuettes from Knossós; the draughtsboard in ivory, rock crystal and blue glass paste; and the ivory bull leaper, the first known statue of a freely moving human figure, the muscles and tendons exquisitely carved. **Room V** contains finds from Knossós that just pre-date its destruction in 1450 BC, including a model of a Minoan palace *c.*1600 BC. Artefacts from cemeteries fill **Room VI**, where miniature sculptures offer hints about funerary practices, banquets and dances; an ivory *pyxis* shows a band of men hunting a bull. Goldwork reached its height in this period; see the Isopata ring, showing four ladies ecstatically dancing. The Mycenaeans are made to answer for the weapons – the boar-tusk helmets and 'gold-nailed swords' as described by Homer.

Items found in central Crete are displayed in **Room VII**. The show-stoppers here are the gold jewellery, particularly the exquisite pendant of two bees depositing a drop of honey in a comb from Mália, and the three superb steatite vessels from Ag. Triáda, decorated in low reliefs: the Harvesters' Vase shows a band of men with winnowing rods; on the 'Cup of the Chieftain', a young warrior reports to a long-haired chieftain; a rhyton has four zones of athletic scenes: boxing, wrestling and bull sports. The contents of **Room VIII** come from Zákros, the only large palace that escaped the ancient plunderers. The stone vases are superb, most notably a rock crystal amphora (it was in over 300 pieces when found) and a rhyton showing a Minoan peak sanctuary, with goats springing all around and birds appearing as an epiphany of the goddess. **Room IX** has items found in ordinary Minoan houses. The seal engravers achieved an astounding technique; suspicions that they had to use lenses to execute such tiny detail was confirmed when one made of rock crystal was found in Knossós.

After the Golden Age, the Post-Palace period artefacts in **Room X** (1450–1100 BC) show a coarsening and heavier Mycenaean influence. Figures lose their *joie de vivre*; the goddesses are stiff, their flouncy skirts reduced to smooth bells, their arms invariably lifted, supplicating the fickle heavens. One goddess wears an opium poppy hat; Minoan use of opium and alcohol may possibly explain a lack of aggression typical of other 'cradles of civilization'.

The Dorians heralded the artistic decline apparent in **Room XI** (1100–900 BC); the quality of the work is poor all round, whether made by pockets of unconquered Minoans or by the invaders. The pieces in **Room XII** show an improvement in the Mature Geometric and Orientalizing periods (900–650 BC), as familiar gods make an appearance: Zeus holding an eagle and thunderbolts on a pot lid, Hermes with sheep and goats on a bronze plaque. Orientalizing pottery shows the Eastern influences that dominated Greek civilization in the 8th–7th centuries. Griffons, sphinxes and lions are favourite motifs; one vase shows a pair of lovers, naturally presumed to be Theseus and Ariadne. At the foot of the stairs, **Room XIII** contains Minoan *larnaxes*, or terracotta sarcophagi. Minoans were laid out in a foetal position, so they are quite small. In the Old Palace days they were made of wood; the changeover to clay suggests the Minoans were over-exploiting their forests.

## The Frescoes and Ag. Triáda Sarcophagus

Yet another art the Minoans excelled at was fresco, displayed upstairs in **Rooms XIV–XVI**. Almost as fascinating as the paintings themselves is the work that went into their reconstruction (sometimes based on only a fraction of the original) by the Swiss father-and-son team hired by Evans. Cretan artists followed Egyptian conventions in colour: women are white, men are red, monkeys are blue, a revelation that led to the re-restoration of *The Saffron Gatherers*, one of the oldest frescoes, originally restored as a boy and now reconstructed as a monkey picking crocuses after a similar subject was found on Santoríni. The first room contains the larger frescoes from the palace of Knossós, such as the nearly intact *Cup-Bearer* from the *Procession* fresco, which originally is estimated to have had 350 figures. Here, too, are *The Dolphins*, *The Prince of the Lilies*, *The Shields*, and also the charming *Partridges* found in the 'Caravanserai', near Knossós. The 'miniature frescoes' in the other two rooms include the celebrated *Parisienne*, as she was dubbed by her discoverers in 1903, with her eye-paint, lipstick and 'sacral knot' jauntily tied at the back. Take a good look at the most famous fresco, *The Bull Leapers*, which doubled as a calendar (*see* **Topics** pp.42–3).

Occupying pride of place in the centre of the upper floor, the Ag. Triáda sarcophagus is the only one in stone ever found on Crete, but what really sets it apart is its elaborately painted layer of plaster. The subject is a Minoan ritual: a bull is sacrificed while a woman makes an offering on an altar next to a sacred tree with a bird in its branches, the epiphany of the goddess. On the other long side, two women bear buckets, perhaps of bull's blood, accompanied by a man in female dress, playing a lyre. On the right, three men are bearing animals and a model boat, which they offer to either a dead man, wrapped up like a mummy, or an idol (*xoanan*), as worshipped at Archánes. Near the sarcophagus is a wooden model of Knossós, and the entrance to the Giamalakis collection (**Room XVII**), containing unique items from all periods.

Downstairs, products of ancient Crete's last breath of artistic inspiration, the bold, severe and powerfully moulded 'Daedalic style' from the Archaic period (700–650 BC), are contained in **Rooms XVIII** and **XIX**. There is a striking frieze of warriors from a temple at Rizenia (modern Priniás) and lavish bronze shields and cymbals from the Idean Cave. The bronze figures of Apollo, Artemis and Leto from Dreros are key works: the goddesses are reduced to anthropomorphic pillars, their arms glued to their sides, their hats, jewellery and flounced skirts as plain as a nun's habit. They could be a salt-and-pepper set. Yet the real anticlimax is reserved for **Room XX**, the classical Greek and Graeco-Roman periods (5th century BC–4th century AD), when Crete was reduced to an insignificant backwater.

## Other Museums in Heráklion

**Battle of Crete and Resistance Museum** (*corner of Doukós Bófor and Hatzidáki Sts, just behind the Archaeology Museum; t 081 034 6554; open Mon–Fri 8–3*). This new museum houses a collection of weapons, photos and uniforms.

**Historical Museum of Crete** (*across town, on Lisimáhou Kalokairinoú; t 081 022 8708; open Mon–Fri 9–5, Sat 9–2, closed hols; adm*). Picks up where the Archaeology Museum leaves off, with fascinating artefacts from Early Christian times. The basement contains delightful 18th-century Turkish frescoes of imaginary towns and a Venetian wall fountain made of tiny jutting ships' prows. On the ground floor are portraits of Cretan revolutionaries and their 'Freedom or Death' flag and 14th-century murals in a chapel setting, from Kardoulianó Pediádos. Next door, hangs the *Imaginary View of Mount Sinai and the Monastery of St Catherine* (*c.* 1576) by Doménikos Theotokópoulos (El Greco), his only known painting on Crete and one of his few landscapes. The first floor has pictures of mustachioed and swaggering Cretan *kapetános* and the recon-structed libraries of Níkos Kazantzákis and Emmanuél Tsouderós, once Prime Minister of Greece. Other rooms contain a sumptuous array of traditional arts, in particular intricate red embroideries; a noteworthy artistic achievement by Ottoman Cretans.

**Natural History Musem of Crete** (*outside the city walls, southwest of town at 157 Knossós; t 081 032 4711; open daily 9–7; adm*). A newly opened venture run by the University of Crete that takes a serious look at the flora and fauna of the island, with a botanical garden devoted to plants endemic to Crete.

## The Cathedral and Byzantine Museum

West of Plateía Venizélou, and south of Kalokairinoú, the overblown cathedral dedi-cated to Heráklion's patron **Ag. Miná** (1895) dwarfs its predecessor. The interior is illuminated by an insanely over-decorated chandelier, the vaults frescoed with stern saints and a ferocious Pantocrator. Old Ag. Miná has a beautiful iconostasis and fine icons; that of Ag. Minas on his white horse has long been the protector of Heráklion (martyrologies claim that Minas was a 3rd-century Egyptian soldier, but maybe his cult has something to do with the memory of Minos in this ancient port of Knossós).

Nearby, the sun-bleached **Ag. Ekateiína** (1555) was an important school linked to the Monastery of St Catherine in the Sinai. Icon-painting was taught (El Greco studied here before leaving for Venice) and today the church holds a **Museum of Byzantine Icons** (*t 081 028 8825; open Mon–Sat 9.30–2.30, also Tues, Thurs and Fri 4.30–6.30; adm*). The highlight is six icons by Mikális Damaskinós, a contemporary of El Greco who also went to Venice but returned to Crete; the use of a gold background and Greek letters are the only Byzantine elements in his *Adoration of the Magi*; in his *Last Supper*, Damaskinós placed a Byzantine Jesus in a setting from an Italian engraving – a bizarre effect heightened by the fact that Christ seems to be holding a hamburger.

## The Venetian Walls and the Tomb of Kazantzákis

Michele Sammicheli, the greatest military architect of the 16th century, designed Candia's walls so well that it took the Turks from 1648 to 1667 to breach them. The Venetians tried to rally Europe to the cause of defending Candia as the last Christian outpost in the East, but only received ineffectual aid from the French. Stalemate characterized the first 18 years of the siege; the sultan found it so frustrating that he banned the mention of Candia in his presence. In 1667 both sides sent in their most brilliant generals, the Venetian Francesco Morosini (uncle of the Morosini who blew the top off the Parthenon) and the Turk Köprülü. The arrival of Köprülü outside the walls with 40,000 troops finally nudged the Europeans and the Holy Roman Emperor to action, but their troops and supplies were too little, too late. Morosini negotiated the city's surrender with Köprülü, and with 20 days of safe conduct, sailed away with most of the Christian inhabitants and the city's archives – an outcome that had cost the lives of 30,000 Christians and 137,000 Turks.

Brilliantly restored, Sammicheli's massive walls are nearly as vexing to get on top of today as they were for the besieging Turks – 4km long, in places 44ft thick, punctuated with 12 fort-like bastions. Tunnels have been punched through the old gates, although the **Pórta Chaniá** (Chaniá Gate) at the end of Kalokairinoú preserves much of its original appearance. From Plastirá Street, a side street leads up to the Martinengo Bastion and the simple **tomb of Níkos Kazantzákis**, who died in 1957 and chose his own epitaph: 'I believe in nothing, I hope for nothing, I am free.' In the distance you can see the profile of Zeus in Mount Ioúchtas (*see* p.170).

## Beaches Around Heráklion

Heráklion is surrounded by sand, and you have a choice of backdrops for your beach idyll: a power plant and cement works at **Ammoudára** (ΑΜΜΟΥΔΑΡΑ), just west, linked by bus no.6 from Hotel Astoria in Plateía Elefthería; and to the east, the airport – from the same Hotel Astoria, bus no.7 crawls through the suburbs to the not exceptionally attractive city beach of **Karterós** (7km) and beyond to **Amnisós** (ΑΜΝΙΣΟΣ). It overlooks the islet of Día, once sacred to Zeus and now a sanctuary for Crete's endangered ibexes, or *kri-kri*, who somehow have learned to cope with the charter flights.

Amnisós has been a busy place since Neolithic times. A port of Knossós, it was from here that Idomeneus and his 90 ships sailed for Troy; here the ship of Odysseus was prevented from sailing by the north wind. The Minoans must have often encountered the same problem, and got around it by loading at a south-facing port on Día islet. Minoan Amnisós had two harbours, on either side of a hill, now topped by the ruins of a Venetian village. The east end is the fenced-off villa of 1600 BC that yielded the *Fresco of the Lilies* in the Heráklion Museum; on the northwest side is an Archaic sanctuary of Zeus Thenatas. In the 1930s, while excavating Amnisós' Minoan 'Harbour Master's Office', Spyridon Marinátos discovered a layer of pumice, the evidence he needed to support his theory that Minoan civilization had been devastated in its prime by ash flung from Santoríni's explosion (*see* pp.274–5).

One km from Amnisós is the **Cave of Eileithyia**, goddess of fertility and childbirth, daughter of Zeus and Hera (ask at the Archaeology Museum in Heráklion if you wish to visit). Few divinities enjoyed Eileithyia's staying power; her cave, which was also mentioned by Homer, attracted women from the Neolithic era to the 5th century AD. Stalagmites resembling a mother and her children were the main focus; pregnant women would rub their bellies against a third one, resembling a pregnant belly.

# Knossós (ΚΝΩΣΟΣ)

*Every 10mins a city bus (no.2) departs from Heráklion's main bus station for Knossós, with a stop in Plateía Venizélou. The site, t 081 023 1940, is open daily 8–7, except for important hols; adm. To avoid the crowds, arrive as the gate opens, or come late in the day.*

The weird dream image has come down through the ages: Knossós, the House of the Double Axe, the Labyrinth of Minos. The bull dances, mysteries and archetypes evoke a mythopœic resonance that few places can equal. Thanks to Arthur Evans' imaginative reconstructions, rising up against the hill-girded plain, Knossós is now the most visited place in Greece after the Acropolis, with a million admissions a year. Evans' reconstructions are now themselves historical monuments, and the work you'll see on the site is reconstructions of reconstructions.

## History

The first Neolithic houses on the hill by the River Kairatos date from the 7th millennium BC, or earlier; few Neolithic sites in Europe lie so deeply embedded in the earth. In the 3rd millennium, a Minoan Pre-Palace settlement was built over the houses, and *c.* 1950 BC the first palace on Crete was erected on top. It collapsed in the earthquake of 1700 BC. A new, even grander palace, the Labyrinth, was built on its ruins. 'Labyrinth' derives from *labrys*, or 'Double Axe', a potent symbol that suggests the killing of both the victim and slayer; you'll see them etched in the pillars and walls throughout Knossós. In 1450 BC (give or take a century or two) Knossós was again destroyed, this time by fire but, unlike the other Minoan palaces, it was repaired once more, probably by Mycenaeans, and survived until at least 1380 BC. After a final destruction, the site of the Labyrinth was never built on again; it was considered cursed. Evans noted that the guardians he hired to watch the site heard ghosts moaning in the night.

In the Geometric era, a community near Knossós adopted the venerable name. By the 3rd century BC this new Knossós became Crete's second city after Górtyn and survived until the early Byzantine period. Meanwhile, the ruined palace was slowly buried, but not forgotten; unlike Troy and Mycenae, the site was always known. Cretans would go there to gather sealstones, which they called *galopetres* – 'milk-stones' – prized by mothers as amulets to increase their milk.

The Labyrinth lay undisturbed until Schliemann's excavations of Troy and Mycenae electrified the world. In 1878, a Heráklion merchant, named Mínos Kalokairinós, dug the first trenches into the palace of his namesake, at once finding walls, enormous *pithoi* and the first Linear B tablet. Schliemann heard the news, and in 1887 negotiated the purchase of the Knossós site. However, the Turkish owners were impossible to deal with and the German archaeologist gave up in despair, dying in 1890.

The field thus cleared, Evans, then curator of the Ashmolean Museum in Oxford, arrived in Crete in 1894. A student of early forms of writing, he was fascinated by the sealstones and Linear B tablet shown him by Mínos Kalokairinós. With dogged persistence, he spent the next five years purchasing the property with the help of

Cretan archaeologist Joseph Hadzadákis, while supplying reports of Turkish oppression to British newspapers. The purchase of Knossós coincided happily with Cretan independence, and in March 1900 Evans received permission to begin excavations in concert with the British School at Athens. Of the workmen hired, Evans insisted that half be Greek and half Turk as a symbol of co-operation for the newly independent Crete. Within the first three weeks the throne room had been excavated, along with fresco fragments and the first Linear A tablets, apparently belonging to a civilization that predated the Mycenaeans, which Evans labelled 'Minoan' for ever after.

In 1908, Evans used his considerable inheritance to embark on a project he had dreamed of from the beginning, to 'reconstitute' part of Minos' palace. Scholars dispute the wisdom and accuracy of these reconstructions, sniffing at them as if they were an archaeological Disneyland; they disagree perhaps even more on the purposes Evans assigned to the rooms of the palace, along with his interpretation of the Minoans as peaceful, flower-loving sophisticates. Evans' queen's bathroom, for instance, is another man's basin where dead bodies were pickled before mummification. No single conjecture seems to cover all the physical evidence, all the myths; the true meaning and use of Knossós may only lie in an epiphany of the imagination. The Cretans of 4,000 years ago saw a different world through different eyes.

## The Site

Evans' reconstructions result from guesses as good as anyone else's and do succeed in his goal of making Knossós come alive for visitors, evoking the grandeur of a 1,500-room Minoan palace of *c.* 1700 BC that none of the unreconstructed sites can match; a visit here first will make Phaistós and Mália easier to understand. Tours go through so frequently that it's easy to overhear the explanations as you follow the maze.

Unlike their contemporaries in the Near East, the Minoans oriented their palaces to the west, not the east, and the modern entrance is still by way of the **West Court**. The three large pits were grain silos, originally protected by domes. A porch on the right from the West Court leads to the **Corridor of the Procession**, named after the fresco in the Heráklion Museum, and to the Propylon, or south entrance, with reproductions of original frescoes. A staircase from the **Propylon** leads to an upper floor, which Evans, inspired by Venetian palaces, called the '**Piano Nobile**'. Of all his reconstructions, this is considered the most fanciful. The **Tripartite Shrine**, with its three columns, is a typical feature of Minoan palaces, and may have been used to worship the Goddess in her three aspects as mistress of heaven, earth and the underworld.

A narrow staircase descends to the **Central Court**, measuring 190 by 95ft. Originally this was closed in by tall buildings, which may have provided safe seats to view the bull leaping, although like much in Knossós, this is problematic: how did they lead bulls in through the Labyrinth? How could they squeeze in all the action? Or was the Central Court really Homer's 'Ariadne's dancing floor'? The sacral horns on the cornices and altars are the most universal Minoan symbol, and may have had multiple levels of meaning; in one Minoan picture, there's a bull with a double axe between its horns. Knossós was littered with sacral horns of all sizes (one pair, in fragments, stood about 3ft high). From the Central Court, enter the lower levels of the

# Knossós

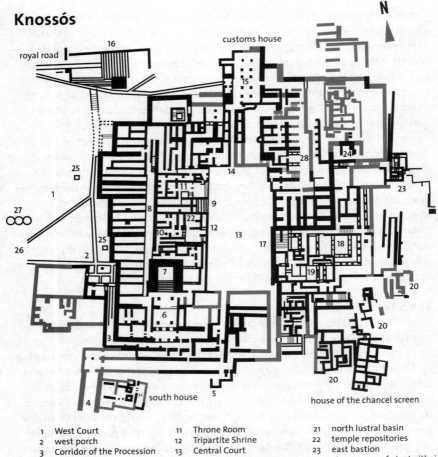

royal road

customs house

N

| | | |
|---|---|---|
| 1 | West Court | 11 Throne Room | 21 north lustral basin |
| 2 | west porch | 12 Tripartite Shrine | 22 temple repositories |
| 3 | Corridor of the Procession | 13 Central Court | 23 east bastion |
| 4 | stepped porch | 14 north entrance passage | 24 store rooms of giant pithoi |
| 5 | south entrance | 15 North Pillar Hall | 25 altar |
| 6 | south Propylon | 16 theatre | 26 bust of Arthur Evans |
| 7 | Grand Stair | 17 Grand Staircase | 27 storage silos |
| 8 | store room corridor | 18 Hall of the Double Axes | 28 Corridor of the |
| 9 | stair | 19 Queen's Megaron | Draughtboard |
| 10 | pillar crypts | 20 southeast house | |

West Wing, site of the tiny **Throne Room**, where Evans uncovered a scallop-edged
stone throne in the same place as it stood 3,800 years ago. Wear and tear has made it
necessary to block off the room, so that you can no longer sit where Minos supposedly sat (although if you're a judge of the Court of International Justice in The Hague
you may sit on a reproduction). On either side are gypsum benches and frescoes of
griffons, the heraldic escorts of the goddess. The **Lustral Basin** in the Throne Room, like
others throughout Knossós, may have held water used in rituals, or reflected light
from light wells, or perhaps both. Evans found evidence here of what appeared to be a
last-ditch effort to placate the gods as disaster swept through Knossós.

The stair south of the antechamber of the Throne Room ascends to an upper floor, used partly for storage, as in the **Room of the Tall** *Pithos* and the **Temple Repositories**, where the Snake Goddess statuette was found. The pillars thicken near the top, unique to Minoan architecture and similar to the trunk of the 'horizontal' cypress native to the Gorge of Samariá. Back in the Central Court, note the relief fresco copy of the '**Prince of the Lilies**' to the south, at the end of the Corridor of the Procession.

Evans, who grew up taking monarchies for granted, had no doubt that the more elaborate **East Wing** of the palace contained the **Royal Apartments**. Here the **Grand Staircase** and **Central Light Well** are a dazzling architectural *tour de force*; almost five flights of broad gypsum steps are preserved. However, descending to the two lower floors (which were found intact) it is hard to imagine that anyone of any social class would choose to live buried so deep, with little light and air; the proximity of the 'Royal Workshops' would have made them noisy as well. The rooms did have something that modern royals couldn't live without: plumbing. The excellent water and sewer system is visible under the floor in the **Queen's Megaron** and its bathroom, complete with a flush toilet – an amenity that Versailles could scarcely manage. The King's Megaron, also known as the **Hall of the Double Axes**, due to the many carvings on the walls, opens on to the **Hall of the Royal Guard**, decorated with a copy of the fresco of cowhide figure-of-eight shields.

North of the Royal Apartments, the **Corridor of the Draughtboard** is where the game-board in the Heráklion Museum was found; here you can see the clay pipes from the Mount Júktas aqueduct. The **Magazines of Giant** *Pithoi* bring to mind the strange old myth of Minos' young son Glaukos. While wandering in the Labyrinth, the boy climbed up into a *pithos* of honey to steal a taste, but fell in and drowned. The anxious father eventually located his body thanks to his prophet Polyidos. In grief, Minos locked Polyidos in a room with Glaukos' body and ordered him to bring the boy back to life. As Polyidos despaired, a snake came out of a hole in the wall. He killed it, and then watched in amazement as another snake appeared with a herb in its mouth, which it rubbed against its friend and brought it back to life. Polyidos tried the same on Glaukos and revived the boy, but Minos, rather than reward Polyidos, ordered him to teach Glaukos the art of prophecy. Polyidos obeyed, but as he sailed away from Crete, he told the boy to spit in his mouth, so that he forgot everything.

As you leave through the north, there's a relief copy of the bull fresco, and near this the so-called **Customs House**, supported by eight pillars, which may have been used for processing imports and exports. Below is the oldest paved road in Europe, the **Royal Road**, lined with various buildings and ending abruptly at the modern road; originally it continued to the Little Palace and beyond. The road ends at the so-called **Theatre** (it looks more like a large stairway), where 500 people could sit to view religious processions or dances, as pictured in the frescoes.

## Around Knossós

Other Minoan buildings have been excavated outside the palace. Nearest are the reconstructed three-storey **South House**, complete with a bathroom and latrine, the **Southeast House**, and the **House of the Chancel Screen**, both perhaps residences of

VIPs – the latter has a dais for a throne or altar. Other sites require special permission to visit, such as the **Royal Villa**, with its throne and beautifully preserved Pillar Crypt. The **Little Palace**, just across the modern road, had three pillar crypts and was used after the Minoans as a shrine; the magnificent bull's head rhyton was found here.

To the south, a sign on the main road points the way to the **Caravanserai**, as Evans named it, believing weary travellers would pause here to wash their feet in the stone trough. The walls have a copy of the lovely partridge fresco. Further south are four pillars from the Minoan aqueduct that carried water over a stream, and south of that the unique **Royal Temple Tomb**, where the natural rock ceiling was painted blue and a stair leads up to a temple. One controversial find was Peter Warren's 1980 unearthing of the **House of the Sacrificed Children**, named after a large cache of children's bones bearing the marks of knives, as if they'd been carved up for supper. The Minoans, having been found guilty of human sacrifice at Archánes (*see* below), now had canni-balism to answer for. But maybe the children had already died and their bones were stripped of flesh before re-burial – a Greek custom that survived into the 19th century.

## South of Knossós: Archánes

One of the ancient proofs of Epimenides' paradox 'All Cretans are liars' was the fact that immortal Zeus was born on Crete, but buried here as well; the profile of his bearded face is easily discerned in Mount Ioúchtas as you head south of Knossós. The road follows a Minoan highway, and has seen some modern history as well: at the T-junction turn-off for Archánes, Cretan Resistance fighters, led by Major Patrick Leigh Fermor and Captain W. Stanley Moss, kidnapped General Kreipe on 26 April 1944. His car was abandoned on Pánormos Beach with a note saying that it was the work of English commandos and that any civilian reprisals would be against international law (*see* Captain Moss's *Ill Met by Moonlight*). But the Germans were (rightly) convinced that the General was still on Crete and launched a massive search for him.

Well-watered Archánes (ARCANES) has often supplied the north; the Minoan and Venetian aqueducts to Knossós began here, ending in Morosini's fountain in Heráklion. Archánes also produces wine and table grapes called *rozáki*. The village recently received second prize in the EU's competiton for the best upgraded village for its restoration of 170 traditional buildings. Its church of the Panagía has exceptional 16th–19th-century icons (*open mornings*). The **Cretan Historical and Folklore Museum**, signposted 3km from Archánes (*t 081 075 1853; open Wed–Mon daily 9.30–2*), has a vast collection of memorabilia from the Battle of Crete, including personal belongings of General Kreipe, and displays of the daring abduction. South of town, the lovely church of the Asómatos is decorated with frescoes dated 1315: *The Battle of Jericho*, *The Sacrifice of Abraham* and *The Punishment of the Damned* are especially good.

### Where to Stay and Eat

**Orestes Rent Rooms, t 081 075 1619.** Simple and just out of the centre.

**Myriofyto**, in the main square. Offers light lunches under the trees.

**Lykastos**, also in the main square, **t 081 075 2433**. Has excellent Cretan food.

From the 15th century on, visitors would come up to Archánes, intrigued by the story of Zeus' tomb, but the first hint of something more than stories here had to wait until the early 1900s, when an alabaster ladle inscribed with Linear A was found. In 1922 Evans surmised the existence of a 'summer palace' in Archánes. Then, in 1964, Ioánnis and Éfi Sakellarákis began excavating what was to become, after Zákros, the biggest Minoan discovery since the war. The **palace**, unfortunately, is right in the centre of town, on a site inhabited continuously since 2000 BC (the largest visible section lies between Mákri Sokáki and Ierolóchiton streets). Dating from the New Palace period (*c.* 1700–1450 BC), the walls are very thick, to support one or more storeys; only in Knossós and Phaistós were similar coloured marbles, gypsum and other luxury materials used. It had elaborate frescoes, a drainage system and a large cistern built over a spring. A 'theatrical area', with raised walkways forming the usual triangle, a small *exedra*, horns of consecration and an archive of Linear A tablets were also found.

In Minoan times, a paved road from the palace led to the **necropolis of Phourní** (*t 081 075 1907; open daily 8–2, but ring ahead* ), set atop a rocky ridge 1.5km to the southwest (a very steep walk up from the road; by car, take the rural road up from Káto Archánes). This 5-acre site is a very important prehistoric Mediterranean cemetery, in use for 1,250 years (2500–1250 BC). Most spectacular of all are the three *tholos* tombs, especially Tholos A, which was used as a hiding place in the Second World War. Debris filled the bottom floor, while below, tucked in a side chamber behind a false wall, lay a priestess or royal lady from the 14th century BC, buried in a gold-trimmed garment and surrounded by her grave offerings: gold and ivory jewellery, a footstool decorated with ivory and the remains of a sacrificed horse and bull, carved into ritualistic bits. The bottom layer of the collective burials in Tholos C goes back to 2500 BC and yielded marble Cycladic figurines and jewellery in the same style as the Treasure of Priam that Schliemann found at Troy. The Mycenaean grave enclosure with seven shaft tombs and three *stelae* is unique on Crete. Its libation pit, or *bothros*, was so saturated with offerings to the dead from thousands of years ago that when the Sakellarákis team found it they were overwhelmed by 'the unbearable stench'.

Five kilometres southwest of Archánes, above the town dump, on the windswept promontory of **Anemospiliá** (*open daily 8–8*), the Sakellarákises discovered an isolated **tripartite shrine** in 1979 (*same hours*). Often depicted in Minoan art, this was the first and, so far, the only one ever found. The middle room contained a pair of clay feet from a *xoanon*, or idol made from wood and other perishable materials worshipped in Greece since Neolithic times; Pausanius wrote that the Greeks believed they were first made by Daedalos on Crete. The eastern room was apparently used for bloodless sacrifices. The western room, however, produced one of the most startling finds in nearly a century of Minoan archaeology: it contained bodies of people caught in the sanctuary as a massive earthquake struck *c.* 1700 BC. The skeleton of a 17-year-old boy was found bound on an altar, next to a dagger; examination by the University of Manchester showed that the blood had been drained from his upper body, and that he had probably had his throat cut. The other skeletons belonged to a man wearing an iron ring and a woman who carried sickle cell anaemia: people of fine breeding, according to Manchester. By a fourth skeleton, a precious Kamáres-ware vase was found; it may have been full of the boy's blood, perhaps an offering to appease their god, possibly Poseidon, the Earth-shaker.

The Anemospiliá findings came as a shock. Evans' Minoans seemed too sophisticated for such barbarities, despite hints of human sacrifice in myth – there's the tribute of youths to the Minotaur, and an account of the Cretan Epimenides who went to Athens to deliver the city from a curse, which he did through human sacrifices. But perhaps such extreme acts were resorted to only in extraordinary situations, where the sacrifice of one is made in the hope of saving many, in this case from violent earth tremors. Even then, the practice was so disagreeable that it was not done in public, but hidden behind the doors of the shrine.

Two kilometres south of Archánes, the villa complex of **Vathýpetro** (*open mornings only; check at the Iouktas Café*), is spectacularly set on a spur facing Mount Ioúchtas. In plan it resembles a baby Knossós: it has a small west court and larger central court, a tripartite shrine, and a three-columned portico with a courtyard, closed off by a unique, fancy recessed structure, supported by symmetrical square plinths. First built c. 1580 BC, the villa was shattered by an earthquake c. 1550 BC. It seems to have been rebuilt as a craft centre; loom weights and potters' wheels were found, along with the oldest wine press in Greece: 3,500 years old. To this day, the vintners in the area repeat a ritual that may be as old as Vathýpetro itself: every 6 August the first fruits of the harvest are ritually offered to the deity on the summit of **Mount Ioúchtas**. A road just before Vathýpetro leads up to the church where it all happens, the Christian replacement for the Minoan peak sanctuary of **Psilí Korfí** just to the north. This has yielded large quantities of votive gifts and bronze double axes. A young Poseidon was one of the gods worshipped here; the mountain was an important navigational landmark.

The road south of Vathýpetro continues to Ag. Vasílios and Moní Spiliótissa, a convent with a frescoed church built into a dim cave; the spring water bubbling out of its foundations was known for its curative properties and was piped into Heráklion by the pashas. It's a pretty, short walk to the church of **Ag. Ioánnis**, with frescoes dated 1291. Just south, a white road to the west allows you to circle back behind Mount Ioúchtas via Kanlí Kastélli, or the Bloody Fortress, built by Niképhoros Phókas in 961.

## Myrtiá and Níkos Kazantzákis

Alternatively, you could turn back east from Ag. Vasílios to Heráklion by way of Crete's most prestigious wine region, Pezá, and the village of **Myrtiá** (ΜΥΡΤΙΑ), set high on a ridge over a majestic sweeping landscape. If you're coming from Heráklion, the turn-off is just before the road to Archánes. Myrtiá is the home of the **Kazantzákis Museum** (*t 081 0741 689; open daily 9–1 and Mon, Wed, Sat and Sun 4–8, closed Thurs; adm*), in the house where Kazantzákis' father was born: photos, documents, dioramas and memorabilia evoke the life and travels of Crete's greatest novelist, the father of *Zorba the Greek*, who was inspired by a Macedonian miner and skirt-chaser named George Zorbas, with whom Kazantzákis operated a lignite mine in the Mani. Kazantzákis was 74 when he was nominated one last time for the Nobel Prize (the Church lobbied against him, and he lost by one vote to Albert Camus) and he died shortly after, in October 1957, from hepatitis contracted from a vaccination needle.

# Southwest of Heráklion

The main road southwest of Heráklion to Górtyn, Phaistós and Mátala passes through dense vineyards. **Veneráto** offers the principal reason to stop, with a 2km detour to the serene convent of **Palianí**, home to 50 nuns. Besides early Christian capitals and 13th-century frescoes, Palianí has the venerable Holy Myrtle; the nuns claim there's an icon of the Virgin in the heart of the tree and use a pair of ancient capitals for the consecration of bread offerings every 23 September. To the south, the large, straggling village of **Ag. Varvára** stands amid cherry orchards at approximately the geographical centre of the big island, and in June shop fronts are festooned with garlands of delicious cherries; a chapel dedicated to the Prophet Elijah sits atop a large rock known as the '*omphalos*', or navel, of Crete. The weather in this area can be dramatic: at Mégali Vríssi, to the east, Crete's first aeolian park harnesses the vigorous cross-island winds with V-39 Vesta windmills, the biggest and strongest windmills in Greece.

A lovely road west of Ag. Varvára skirts the groves and orchards on the southern flanks of Psilorítis. Nearly all the villages here began as Minoan farming communities, among them **Zarós** (ΖΑΡΟΣ), a famous local beauty spot and source of bottled mineral water. The Romans built an aqueduct from here to Górtyn so they wouldn't have to drink anything else. The **gorge of Zarós** is a good place to bring a picnic: the walk begins at the monastery of **Ag. Nikólaos**. Another monastery to the west, **Moní Vrondísi**, was burned by the Turks in 1821, but it still has a pretty gate and a charming 15th-century Venetian fountain, next to a massive plane tree. The tree's core, blasted hollow by a lightning bolt, houses the kitchen of the monastery's café. The 14th-century frescoes in the church are only a shadow of the treasures Vrondísi once had – in 1800, having had a premonition of its sacking, the abbot sent its finest works, by Michael Damáskinos, to Ag. Kateríni in Heráklion, where they remain. **Moní Valsamonérou**, 5km west, is reached by path from **Vorízia**, another village rebuilt after being obliterated in Nazi reprisals (the guardian lives here, although he's usually at the church on weekday mornings). Once an important monastery, Valsamonérou is now reduced to an enchanting assymetrical church dedicated to Ag. Fanoúrios, in charge of heaven's lost and found; the exceptional 14th-century frescoes are by Konstantínos Ríkos.

The road continues to **Kamáres** (with tavernas and rooms), the base for the 3–4-hour walk up Mount Ida to the **Kamáres Cave** (5,003ft), an important Minoan cave sanctuary. Its gaping mouth, 66ft high and 130ft wide, is visible from Phaistós; pilgrims brought their offerings in the colourful pottery first discovered here – hence the Minoan pottery styled 'Kamáres-ware' (*see* p.118).

## Where to Stay and Eat

**Zarós** ✉ 70002

**Idi Hotel, t** 089 403 1302, **f** 089 403 1511 (*C; mod*). One of the nicest mountain hotels on the island, with a verdant garden surrounding pools.

**Taverna Votomos, t** 089 403 1071 (€15). With lovely views of the valley. Fresh salmon and trout, served with delicious rice, hold pride of place on the menu.

## Human Rights, Dorian-style

The first block of engraved limestone, discovered in a mill stream in 1857, was purchased by the Louvre. It attracted a good deal of attention. At the time no-one had ever seen such an ancient inscription in Greek, and it wasn't until 1878 that this first bit, dealing with adoption, was translated, using the writing on ancient coins as a guide. No-one suspected there was more until 1884, when the archaeologist Halbherr noticed a submerged building – the Odeon – while cooling his feet in the same mill stream. The rest of the inscription, over 600 lines on 12 blocks, was found soon nearby ; only the tops of blocks X and XII and a piece of block IX are missing.

The code, written in *boustrophedon*, 'as the ox ploughs' – from left to right, then right to left – is in the Doric dialect of *c.* 500 BC. It is the longest such inscription to survive, and due to it, the civil laws of Archaic Crete are better known in their specific detail than Roman law. The code was made for public display, and significantly, in spite of the ancient Greek class system, which had a different set of rules for citizens, serfs (the native Minoans) and slaves, the Górtyn Code allows women property rights they've lacked in more recent laws. Slaves had recourse against cruel masters, and there was a presumption of innocence until proven guilty long before this became the core of Anglo-American law.

## The Mesará Plain and Górtyn (ΓΟΡΤΥΣ)

*t 089 203 1144; Górtyn is open daily 8–7; adm. If you're arriving by bus, get off at the Górtyn entrance and walk back towards the village of Ag. Déka.*

Tucked under the southern flanks of Mount Ida, the long Mesará Plain is the breadbasket of Crete and a densely populated area since Minoan times. After the Dorian invasion, **Górtyn** (or Gortys) gradually supplanted Phaistós and later Knossós as the ruling city of Crete. Hannibal's brief sojourn here in 189 BC after his defeat by Rome may have given the inhabitants some insight into the Big Noise from Italy, because they helped the Romans capture Crete. In reward, Rome made Górtyn the capital not only of Crete but of their province of Cyrenaica, which included much of North Africa. In AD 828 the Saracens wiped it off the map.

In its prime, Górtyn counted 300,000 souls. Its ruins are scattered through a mile of olive groves – only the basilica and Odeon are fenced in. The apse is all that survives of the 6th-century **Basilica of Ag. Títos**, once one of the most important in Greece but now a roosting place for birds. Titus, originally buried here, was one of Paul's favourite disciples and first bishop of Górtyn. Nearby, built into the walls of the elegant **Roman Odeon** (reconstructed by Trajan in AD 100), is Górtyn's prize, the **Law Code of Górtyn**, now covered by a shelter. Just behind the Law Code is the rare and famous Cretan evergreen **Plane Tree** of Górtyn, by the Lethaios River. The story goes that it has kept its leaves for modesty's sake ever since Zeus in bull disguise brought the Phoenician princess Europa into its shade and had his evil way with her, resulting in the birth of Minos, Rhadamanthys and Sarpedon.

If it's not too hot, consider climbing the **Acropolis**. Currently being excavated by the Italians, it has the remains of an 8th-century BC temple and sacrificial altar, Roman walls and a well-preserved defensive building, perhaps built at the expense of the **Theatre**, chewed away in the hillside below. A few minutes' walk down to **Mitrópolis** reveals an Early Byzantine church with a mosaic floor, cut in two by the modern road. The ground is littered with broken tiles and the half-hearted fences make the ruins especially evocative, as if you were intruding into an old painting. There's a small **Temple of Isis and Serapis**, the Egyptian gods popular in the late Empire, and the elaborate **Temple of Pythian Apollo**, the most important in Górtyn; the inscription is another segment of Górtyn's law code, written in an even older dialect. Most imposing of all is the 2nd-century AD **Praetorium**, seat of the Roman governor; the building continued in use as a monastery until Venetian times. Part of the complex includes the **Nymphaeum**, where the waters from the Zarós aqueduct flowed into the city. Further south are the ruins of the gate, amphitheatre, stadium and cemetery, while the main path leads to the village **Ag. Déka**, named after ten martyrs of *c.* AD 250. The block on which they were beheaded is kept in the church, and their tombs in the new chapel are the subject of much Cretan devotion.

**Mires** (ΜΟΙΡΕΣ), 9km to the west, is a lively agricultural town that has taken over Górtyn's role as the commercial centre of the Mesará. On Saturday it hosts a big market. If you're relying on buses, count on spending time here, waiting for changes for Phaistós, Mátala, Ag. Galíni, the Amári Valley or Réthymnon.

## Phaistós (ΦΑΙΣΤΟΣ)

*t 089 204 2315; open daily 8–7; adm. Arrive early or late afternoon to avoid the crowds. A pavilion on the site has a café and rooms, t 089 204 2360.*

Superbly overlooking the Mesará Plain and Psilorítis, Phaistós was one of Crete's oldest cities, the fief of Minos' brother Rhadamanthys and the birthplace of the sage Epimenides. The first palace was constructed in the Old Palace period, *c.* 2000 BC, and destroyed in an earthquake in 1700 BC; the second one was destroyed in turn in *c.* 1450 BC. Like Knossós but on a smaller scale, it was built of luxurious alabaster and gypsum, with an elaborate drainage system. Its workshops produced exquisite art, and yet no frescoes were found. Below the palace, 50,000 people lived and worked, and Minoan villages dependent on the palace were scattered across the Mesará. Into Hellenistic times Phaistós remained an independent city-state, warring with Górtyn, until the latter crushed it in the 3rd century BC. Excavations by the Italians, led by Halbherr, began in 1900, just after Evans began digging at Knossós.

Purists dismayed by Evans' reconstructions at Knossós will breathe a sigh of relief at Phaistós, where only your imagination will reconstruct the three-storey palace from the low, complicated walls and foundations; the fact that much of the second palace was built over the first means that, unless you have an especially good imagination, or opt for a guided tour, you may leave feeling singularly unenlightened. Visits begin in the northwest, in the paved **Upper Court** with its raised **Processional Way**. This continues down the steps into the **West Court**, originally part of the Old Palace – the only section the architects of the New Palace re-used after the earthquake, when the lines of the building were otherwise completely reorientated; the lower façade of the

Old Palace survives just before the Grand Stairway. The West Court has the eight straight tiers known as the **Theatre**, where people may have watched performances, and two circular granaries or silos, originally protected by domes.

The **Grand Stairway** was carved with special care, partly from stone and partly from the living rock; note how the steps are slightly convex, to allow rainwater to run off quickly. At the top, the **Great Propylon**, the main entrance to the West Wing, stands just before a light-well with three columns. Another stair descends to the **Antechamber of the Store Rooms**, where Halbherr found a huge cache of sealstones, while beyond are the **Store Rooms**; one, covered with a roof, still contains its giant *pithoi*, along with a stone stool for standing on to scoop out the contents, and a built-in vessel in the floor to collect wine or oil run-offs. An important corridor separated the storage areas from the main **Shrine**, lined with stone benches.

From the Antechamber of the Store Rooms opens the **Central Court**, its long sides originally sheltered by porticoes; buildings on all sides would have hidden the tremendous views it enjoys today. A stepped block in the northwest corner may have been the platform used by bull dancers as a springboard for 'diving leaps'. To the southwest is a series of rooms fenced off and mingled with bits of the Old Palace and the foundations of a classical-era temple. Landslides have swept away much of the **East Wing**, but the small chamber just to the north, a bathroom and a gypsum-paved lustral basin with steps earned it the name of 'Prince's Apartment'. A horseshoe-shaped **Forge**, built in the Old Palace era for smelting metals, is at the end of the corridor to the north, the earliest one yet discovered in Greece.

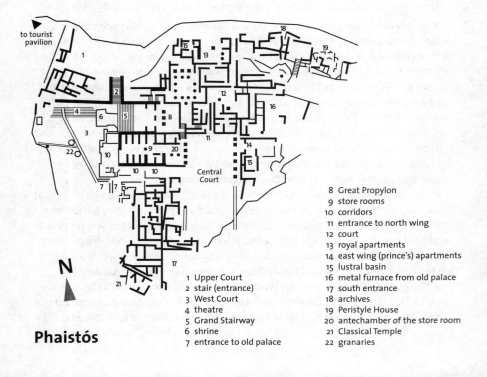

to tourist pavilion

Central Court

**Phaistós**

N

1 Upper Court
2 stair (entrance)
3 West Court
4 theatre
5 Grand Stairway
6 shrine
7 entrance to old palace
8 Great Propylon
9 store rooms
10 corridors
11 entrance to north wing
12 court
13 royal apartments
14 east wing (prince's) apartments
15 lustral basin
16 metal furnace from old palace
17 south entrance
18 archives
19 Peristyle House
20 antechamber of the store room
21 Classical Temple
22 granaries

North of the Central Court, a grand entrance with niches in the walls and another corridor leads to more **Royal Apartments**, paved with delicate alabaster and gypsum and now fenced off; you can barely make out the **Queen's Megaron**, furnished with alabaster benches. An open peristyle court tops the **King's Megaron**, which once must have offered a royal view to the Kamáres cave sanctuary (that dark patch between the twin summits). The famous Phaistós Disc was found east of here, with pottery from 1700 BC, in the 'archives', a series of mud-brick rooms from the Old Palace.

## The 'Summer Villa' of Ag. Triáda (ΑΓ. ΤΡΙΑΔΑ)

Just 3km west of Phaistós is the smaller Minoan palace of Ag. Triáda (*t 089 209 1360; open daily 8.30–3; adm*), named after a diminutive Venetian church on the site. No-one knows why such a lavish little estate was built so close to Phaistós. Guesses are that a wealthy Minoan fell in love with the splendid setting, or it may have been a summer palace; Phaistós can turn into a frying pan in the summer and Ag. Triáda usually has a sea breeze. In Minoan times, the sea came further in and the ramp under the villa may have led down to a port. It's certainly an old site; Neolithic *tholos* tombs and dwellings were discovered under the 'palace', built *c*.1600 BC. It burned in the widespread destruction of 1450 BC. The Minoans rebuilt it and the Mycenaeans added a *megaron* over the top and a village, dominated by a building that looks like a *stoa* – a row of shops under a porch – 1,000 years before they were invented. The site has yielded some of the Minoans' finest art, including frescoes, the Harvesters' Vase and the sarcophagus of Ag. Triáda, all now in the Heráklion museum.

The intimate scale and surroundings – and lack of tour groups – make Ag. Tríada the most charming of the major Minoan sites. The villa had two main wings, one orientated north–south, the other east–west. The north–south wing, overlooking the sea, was the most elaborate, with flagstone floors, and gypsum and alabaster walls and benches. One room had frescoes (the stalking cat), another had built-in closets. *Pithoi* still stand intact in the store rooms. At the entrance, **Ag. Geórgios Galatás** (1302) has good frescoes (*the guardian has the key*).

# Around the Southwest Coast

This corner offers more than the exquisite fossils of long-lost civilizations. North of Phaistós, the old village of **Vóri** (ΒΩΡΟΙ) on the road to Ag. Galíni (*see* p.151) boasts a superb **Museum of Cretan Ethnology** (*t 089 209 1394; open 10–6; adm*), the best place to learn about traditional Cretan life – a civilization not yet lost, if in danger of extinction – with excellent detailed descriptions in English. Charmless **Tymbáki**, 3km west, combines tomatoes under plastic and dogged tourism, thanks to its long ugly beach, **Kókkinos Pírgos**, the 'red tower', a name that predates its career as the Ketchup Coast. Elsewhere, this is a wild shore, which only here and there permits roads to descend to the sea. One south of Phaistós leads to **Mátala** (ΜΑΤΑΛΑ), the lovely and once notorious beach enclosed by sandstone cliffs. The cliffs are riddled with tombs from the 1st and 2nd centuries AD, which the locals enlarged into cosy little rooms. In the early

# Where to Stay and Eat

## Mátala ✉ 70200

Although Mátala closes shop at the end of October, by Easter it's nearly impossible to find a room as many Greeks come down for their first swim of the year.

**Valley Village**, on the edge of the village, t 089 204 5776 (B; mod). With a swimming pool, Greek dancing shows and barbecue nights.

**Zafira**, t 089 204 5112 (D; mod). Handy for town and beach, and reasonably priced, although completely booked by operators in season.

**Nikos**, t 089 204 5375 (E; inexp). A pleasant choice with a little garden

**Mátala Camping**, just behind the beach, t 089 204 5720. Offering plenty of shade and low prices.

**Syrtaki**. Has centre spot in the row of seaside tavernas and serves all the Greek favourites at reasonable prices.

**Zeus Beach Taverna**, right on the beach. Offering stuffed tomatoes and other traditional Greek dishes made by mama, and you can feed your extra bread to the ducks.

**Giorgio's Bar**, at the end. Serves cocktails to go with Mátala's famous sunsets.

**Kivotos**, up in Sivas, t 089 204 2744. Delicious oven-baked dishes and live music daily in the summer.

1960s, Americans bumming around found that the caves made a perfect place to crash in the winter, and before long they were joined by an international hippy colony. In the killjoy 1990s, the impecunious hippies were banished for the hard currency of package tourism. If you stay overnight, their spirit lingers in Mátala's laid-back atmosphere, otherwise grannies hawking rugs may be your strongest memory. If the town beach is a massive body jam, a 20-minute scramble over the rocks will take you to Mátala's excellent second beach, **Kókkinos Ámmos**, 'red sand', with caves; excursion boats sail south to other small beaches at Ag. Farago and Vathí. Avoid walking on the beaches on summer nights, when loggerhead turtles make their nests.

Mátala has been a midwife of tourism for **Pitsídia**, and more recently for **Kalamáki**, an embryonic resort down by the long beach north of Mátala. At the south end of this beach (easiest reached by a track from Pitsídia) is **Kómmo**, where since 1976 a Canadian and American team have uncovered substantial remains of the largest Minoan port discovered on the south coast. Although not officially open for visits, you can see a massive building of dressed stone, believed to have been a warehouse, dry docks with five slips and a paved road with worn ruts that led to Phaistós. Near the beach stood an important sanctuary, sacred long after the Minoans: the Dorians built a temple here in the 10th-century BC, as did the sea-trading Phoenicians, and the Classical and Hellenistic-era Greeks.

Phaistós' rival Górtyn had ports to the east, including **Kalí Liménes**, the 'Fair Havens', a steep winding drive by way of Sívas. This is where the ship carrying St Paul put in on its way to be wrecked off Malta. Unlike its neighbours, Kalí Liménes has kept pace with the times; instead of saints, the Fair Havens now host oil tankers. Ruins of another of Górtyn's harbours, **Levín** (or Lebena) lie near the ramshackle fishing village of **Léndas**. From Kalí Liménes, get there by way of the rough coastal road, or there's a new road south of Górtyn. The natural hot springs east of the village (now pumped elsewhere) led to the construction in the 4th century BC of an Asklepeion; there are mosaics, bits of a temple, and a pool where patients used to wallow in the waters. Nearly all the wallowing in Léndas these days happens 3km west at **Yerókambos**, a magnificent long beach where clothes are optional and a few tavernas rent rooms.

# Southeast of Heráklion:
# Villages under the Diktean Mountains

Some attractive Cretan villages in the western foothills of Mount Díkti are linked by a good road south of Chersónisos. **Káto** and **Páno Karouzaná** are 'traditional villages' offering Greek nights to coach parties; but, hidden away south just before Kastélli, signs for 'Paradise Tavern' point the way to lovely **Ag. Pandeleímonos**, under huge plane trees by a spring, built in AD 450 over a temple to Asklepeios (the taverna owners will summon the caretakers). The church is said to have had 101 doors, but after being ravaged by the Saracens it was rebuilt on a more modest scale *c.* 1100. The bell is made out of a German shell and, inside, the nave is supported by marble columns from ancient Lyttos, including one made of nothing but Corinthian capitals.

**Kastélli** is the largest village of the Pediáda region, named after its long-gone Venetian castle. A short detour west to **Sklaverochóri** has its reward in the 15th-century church **Eisódia tis Theotókou**, decorated with excellent frescoes, the forerunners of the Cretan school: a fairy-tale scene with St George and the princess, allegories of the river gods in the Baptism and, on the north wall, a benign Catholic intruder – St Francis holding a rosary. Four kilometres east of Kastélli, ancient **Lyttos** (modern Xidás) was a fierce rival of Knossós after the Doric invasion and remained sufficiently wealthy to mint its own coins until 220 BC, when Knossós, allied with Górtyn, demolished it. As the Minoans hog the funds on Crete, Lyttos is just beginning to be investigated, but you can see Hellenistic walls, a theatre and a frescoed church built over the early Christian basilica of Ag. Geórgios.

Potters in **Thrapsanó** (8km west) have made bowls and *pithoi* for centuries. The technique for making the great jars is the same as in Minoan times. **Arkalochóri**, just south, is the scene of a large Saturday produce and animal fair. In 1932, Marinátos and Pláton excavated the village's sacred cave and brought forth some exceptional Minoan ritual weapons: the longest prehistoric Greek bronze sword ever found and bronze axes, one engraved with Linear A, the other with symbols similar to those on the Phaistós Disc – which put paid to notions that the disc was a forgery.

The road rises for **Embaros**: when Aeneas was wounded in the Trojan war, Aphrodite rushed over to Mount Ida to gather dittany to heal him; *Origanum ditamnus*, as it's officially known, is Crete's miracle herb and aphrodisiac. Cretans have often risked their lives to pluck it from the cliffs, but in Embaros, dittany is now safely cultivated.

## Áno Viánnos and the Southeast Coast

Beyond Mártha (where you can pick up the road west to Górtyn, *see* above), **Áno Viánnos** (ΑΝΩ ΒΙΑΝΝΟΣ) hangs on the southwest flanks of Mount Díkti. Inhabited since early Minoan times, it founded a colony on the Rhône–Themain route to the tin mines of the British Isles. In more recent times the village was a citadel of resistance against the Turks and the Germans; the latter executed 820 people in the area. On the acropolis of Áno Viánnos are the ruins of a Venetian castle and Turkish tower;

in the Pláka area is 14th-century Ag. Geórgios, near the incredible plane tree (possibly the oldest in Greece after the granddaddy of them all, Hippocrates' Plane Tree on Kos).

Two km west, near Káto Viánnos, a good road to the coast descends by way of **Chóndros** to **Keratókambos**, an attractive fishing village that was especially well defended: this was the beachhead used by the Saracens to invade Crete in 823, and to make sure it wouldn't happen again the Venetians built a fort and another one to the east known as **Kastrí**. A rough-and-tumble road links Keratókambos to **Árvi** (APBH), although the road down from Amirás east of Áno Viánnos is much easier; at the Amirás crossroads there's a monument to the 600 Cretans killed by the Germans in September 1943. Set in the cliffs, Árvi is enclosed in its own little world, at the head of a valley of banana plantations. It has good pebble beaches and a monastery that originally supported a temple of Zeus.

Lastly, if you continue northeast, you'll come across tiny **Áno Sími**. From here a narrow track (best on foot) leads a few kilometres up the mountain, where three terraces and an altar of a temple dedicated to Aphrodite and Hermes remained open for business between 1600 BC and AD 300. Beyond, the road descends through porphyry-coloured badlands where nothing grows, towards the oasis of Myrtos.

# Heráklion's East Coast: Chersónisos and Mália

East of Heráklion and Amnisós (*see* p.165), Europa, once raped on the island by Zeus, gets her revenge on Crete. Even more depressing than the god-awfulness of the architecture of this coast are the rusting rods curling out of the flat roofs, promising more layers of the same. Yet there are a couple of reasons to put on the brakes. At Vathianó Kambó, by the Hotel Demetrato, there's a well-preserved Minoan villa **Nírou Cháni** or House of the High Priest (*t 089 707 6110; open Tues–Sun 8.30–3*), where a trove of 40 tripods and double axes was found. It has two paved courts with stone benches, perhaps used in ceremonies. At **Goúves**, signs point the way to Skotinó, and the

## Where to Stay and Eat

### Chersónisos (Liménas Chersonísou)
✉ 70014

Don't expect to find any cheap rooms here, or even a hotel in season, although the **tourist office on Giaboúdaki St** will do its best to help.

**Creta Maris, t** 089 702 2115, **f** 089 702 2130, *Creta@maris.gr* (*L; lux*). The most luxurious hotel here, with lots of sports, six bars, free kindergarten, open-air cinema and all the works.

**Knossós Royal Village, t** 089 702 3375, **f** 089 702 3150, *krv@aldemar.gr* (*L; lux*). New and glossy, with outdoor and indoor pools, water slide and floodlit tennis courts.

**Cretan Village, t** 089 702 3750, **f** 089 702 2300, *cretanvillage@hrs.forthnet.gr* (*A; lux*). Traditional village-style two-storey houses, catering mainly for young families.

**Silva Maris**, in quieter Stalída, east of Chersónisos, **t** 089 702 2850, **f** 089 702 1404, *silva@maris.gr* (*A; lux*). Another pseudo Cretan village, with an attractive pool, water sports and frequent buses to Heráklion. *Open April–Oct.*

**Katrin Hotel, t** 089 703 2137, **f** 089 703 2136, *katrin@hrs.forthnet.gr* (*B; mod*). The pick of this category, with three pools.

**Caravan Camping, t** 089 702 2025. Plenty of shade.

**Artemis, t** 089 703 2131, by the beach in Stalída. Serves Greek and Cretan specialities.

enormous **cave of Skotinó**; the path begins by a white chapel. The cave has a 180ft-high ballroom lit by sun pouring through the cave mouth, with a stalagmite mass in the centre. A huge amount of Minoan cult activity took place in the low-ceilinged chambers at the back, around natural altars and formations like the 'head of Zeus'.

Further east, past the turn-off at Lagadá for the Lassíthi Plateau (*see* p.184), **Chersónisos** (ΧΕΡΣΟΝΗΣΟΣ), or more properly Liménas Chersonísou, is a popular synthetic tourist ghetto, complete with a Cretan museum village, the **Lychnostatis Museum** (*t 089 702 3660; open Sun–Fri 9.30–2; multilingual guided tour; adm*). An $8 million 18-hole golf course and 'academy' are under development in the area, due for completion in March 2003. Chersónisos was the port of ancient Lyttos and had a famous temple to Britomartis Artemis. Little remains of its ancient glories: a reconstructed Roman fountain by the beach, a Roman aqueduct (inland at Xerokámares, on the road to Lassíthi) and, to the west, overlooking the harbour, the ruins of a 5th-century basilica, seat of one of Crete's first bishoprics.

# Mália (ΜΑΛΙΑ)

East of Chersónisos, in the centre of a wide sandy bay, Mália has taken over as the busiest, most party-driven tentacle of the holiday sprawl east of Heráklion. There is an older, wiser village inland, and the **Minoan Palace of Mália** (*t 089 703 159; open daily 8.30–3; adm*), 3km east (*buses to Ag. Nikólaos will drop you nearby*). The legendary fief of Minos' brother Sarpedon, Mália controlled the fertile coastal plain under the Lassíthi mountains. Its history follows that of Knossós: inhabited from the Neolithic era, the first palace was built on the site in 1900 BC. Devastated by the earthquake 200 years later, another palace was built on top, then ruined in the catastrophe traditionally dated 1450 BC. Compared to Knossós and Phaistós, Mália is 'provincial': built from local stone rather than alabaster, marble and gypsum, and without frescoes. However, the lack of later constructions makes it easy to understand.

Entrance is by way of the **West Court**, crossed by the usual raised flagstones of the Processional Way. Eight grain 'silos', originally covered with beehive domes (similar

**Kavouri**, Archéou Théatro, Chersónisos (€12). Better than usual Greek food.

**Ta Petrina**, Ano Chersónisos, in upper Chérsonisos, t 089 702 1976 (€15). Pleasant courtyard setting, with tasty meat and home-grown vegetarian dishes.

After dinner, everyone gathers in the bars and clubs around **El. Venizélou Street**.

## Mália ✉ 70007

**Grecotel Mália Park**, towards the Minoan palace, t 089 703 1461, f 089 703 1460 (*A; lux*). Plush, air-conditioned bungalows, watersports and a mountain-bike centre.

**Ikaros Village**, t 089 703 1267, f 089 703 1341, *Ikaros@hrs.forthnet.gr* (*A; exp*). Large hotel complex, designed as one of those tradi-tional Cretan villages, incl. pool, tennis and sea sports. *Open April–Oct*.

**Alexander Beach**, t 089 703 2134, f 089 703 1038 (*B; exp–mod*). A recently-built complex, a stone's throw from the beach, with a heated pool, tennis and other sports.

**Ermioni**, in Mália proper, t 089 703 1093 (*E; inexp*). A blessing for budget travellers.

**Ibiscus**, just along the main road, t 089 703 1313, f 089 703 2042 (*inexp*). Has a pool.

The best place to eat is in the **old village**, south of the main road, where traditional tavernas serve barrelled wine and good Greek food at reasonable prices: try **Yannis** and **Kalimera**, or any of the others around the **main square**, all far from the cacophony along the beach road.

ones have been found in Egypt), are at the south end. The **Central Court,** re-used from the Old Palace, had galleries at the north and east ends; in the middle are the supports of a hollow altar, or sacrificial pit. A Grand Stairway led up into the important **West Wing**, which may have had a ritual role: the raised **Loggia**, where ceremonies may have been performed, is near a mysterious round stone stuck in the ground. The **Treasury**, behind it, yielded a sword with a rock crystal pommel and a stone axe shaped like a pouncing panther. The **Pillar Crypt** has a variety of potent symbols (double axes, stars and tridents) carved in its square pillars. The four broad steps here may have been used as a theatre, while in the southwest corner is the unique limestone *kernos*, a round wheel of an altar with a deeper hollow in the centre and 34 smaller hollows around the circumference. Its similarity to the *kernos* used in classical times is striking, and it may have been the Minoans who originated the rite of *panspermia*, or offering of the first fruits to the deity.

A long portico of square stone pillars and round wooden columns ran along the east side of the Central Court. The narrow store rooms that take up most of the East Wing (now protected by a roof) are equipped with drainage channels from the first palace. North of the centre, the **Pillar Hall** is the largest room in the palace; the chamber directly above it, reached by the surviving stair, may have been for banquets. Behind it is another pillar room, and the **oblique room**, its different orientation suggesting some kind of astronomical observation. A suite of **Royal Apartments**, with a stepped, sunken lustral basin, are in the northwest corner. A number of Linear A tablets were found in the **Archive Room**. A paved road leads north to the **Hypostyle Crypt**, under a barrel-vaulted shelter; no-one has the foggiest idea what went on here.

If Málía seems somewhat poor next to Knossós and Phaistós, the Minoan estates found in the outskirts were sumptuous, especially those to the northeast, where the only fresco at Málía was found. In the seaside cemetery, the **Chrysolakkos tomb** may have been the family vault of Málía's rulers; although the 'gold pit' was looted, the French found the magnificent twin bee pendant inside. Stylistic similarities suggest that the Aegina Treasure in the British Museum was pillaged from here in antiquity.

# *Nomós* Lassíthi (ΛΑΣΙΘΙ)

The name of Crete's easternmost province comes from the Greek mispronunciation of the Venetian La Sitía, one of its chief towns. Lassíthi doesn't have the towering peaks that characterize the rest of Crete (although Mt Díkti, on its western fringes, isn't exactly a peewee at 7,027ft), but it manages to be the most varied province, framed in the west by a plateau hanging in the clouds, planted with apple orchards and wheat, and irrigated by white-sailed windmills, while its east coast ends at Vaï's palm-lined tropical beach. Ag. Nikólaos, set in the magnificent Gulf of Mirabélo, is the most cosmopolitan and touristy of Crete's four capitals, with most of the island's luxury hotels. But traditional Crete awaits only a few miles inland.

Lassíthi was densely populated in Minoan times: if the unplundered palace of Zákros is the most spectacular find, town sites such as Gourniá, Paleokástro, Vasilikí,

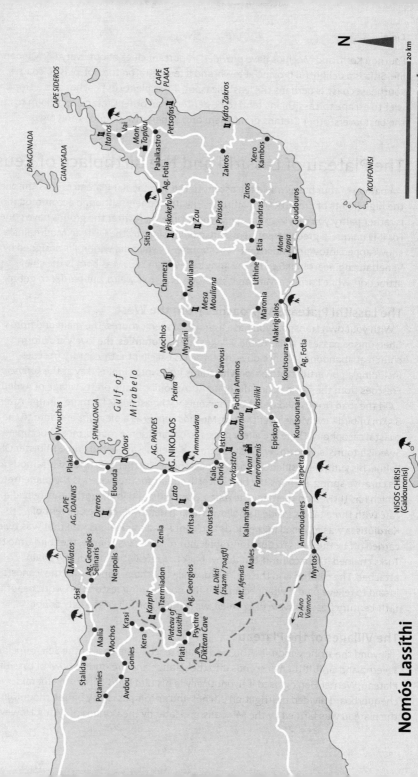

# Nomós Lassíthi

N

20 km
10 miles

DRAGONADA

GIANYSADA

CAPE SIDEROS

Itanos
Vai
Moni
Toplou
CAPE
PLAKA

Palaikastro
Ag. Fotia
Petsofas
Káto Zakros

Piskokefalo
Zou
Praisos
Zakros
Xero
Kambos

Sitia
Ziros
Handras
Goudouros

Chamezi
Mouliana
Etia
Lithine
Moni
Kapsa

Mesa
Mouliana
Maronia

Mochlos
Myrsini
Makrigialos

Kavousi
Koutsouras

Pachia Ammos
Ag. Fotia

Gulf
of
Mirabelo

Psera
Vasiliki
Koutsounari

Gournia
Episkopi

AG. PANDES
Ammoudara
Istro
Vrokastro
Moni
Faneromenis

Vrouchas
AG. NIKOLAOS

SPINALONGA
Olous
Kalo
Chorio

Plaka
Elounda
Kalamafka

CAPE
AG. IOANNIS
Lato
Ierapetra

Dreros
Kritsa
Kroustas
Males
Ammoudares

Milatos
Zenia
Ag. Georgios
Selinaris
Neapolis
Ano
Viannos
Myrtos

NISOS CHRISI
(Gaidouronisi)

Sisi
Ag. Georgios
Tzermiadon
Karphi
Plateau of
Lassithi

Stalida
Krasi
Plati
Mt. Dikti
(2142m / 7045ft)
Mt. Afendis

Malia
Kera
Psychro
Diktean Cave

Potamies
Mochos
Gonies
Avdou

KOUFONISI

Fournoú Korifí and Móchlos have provided important clues about everyday Minoan life. Sitía is a delightful provincial town, and if Ierápetra, on the hot, plastic-coated southeast coast, is perhaps the least pleasant, it has plenty of beaches and a tropical islet to escape to. Lassíthians tend to be gentler than other Cretans, and claim to be the best lovers; other Cretans grant them only superlative potatoes and pigs.

# The Plateau of Lassíthi and the Birthplace of Zeus

A parade of tour buses make the ascent to the spectacular Plateau of Lassíthi, one of the high points of Crete, both in altitude and atmosphere; although accommodation is rather paltry, you may want to spend more time there after the groups have gone. For it is unique: a green carpet hemmed in on all sides by the Díktean Mountains, snowcapped into April and irrigated in summer by splendid windmills designed by Venetian engineers in 1564. The uncanny cave where Zeus was born is the chief attraction, while Karphí, a Minoan last refuge, is just as weird, but harder to get to.

## The Lassíthi Plateau: Approaches from the West

With your own transport you have a choice of scenic routes. The main one from Chersónisos passes a series of old villages; above **Potamiés**, the lovely cruciform church at abandoned Moní Gouverniótissa has excellent 14th-century frescoes, including a powerful Pantocrator who stares holes into sinners (key at the *kafeneíon*). Frescoes from the same period decorate Ag. Antónios in the pretty village of **Avdoú**.

On the road from Stalída, east of Chersónisos, the ascent is far more abrupt. After 8.5km of bird's eye views over the sea, **Mochós** comes as a pleasant antidote to the coastal cacophony. There are a few places to eat and some rooms, mostly occupied by Swedish tourists, who know Mochós through their assassinated Prime Minister Olaf Palme; his summer residence is now a local shrine. Further south, **Krási** is famous for its curative spring. Perhaps the best advertisement for the waters is the plane tree, which has thrived on them for the past 2,000 years, and in the 19th century, had a café with three tables inside its hollow trunk. In nearby **Kerá**, the **Convent of Kardiótissa** was founded in the 1100s and contains a miraculous icon that was twice carried off by the Turks to Constantinople but made its way home; the third time the Turks chained it to a column, but it flew back to Crete with column and chain attached. The column is in the courtyard, while the chain, hanging on the iconostasis, is said to relieve pain if wrapped around the body. During restoration work, beautiful 14th-century frescoes were discovered, with a fine portrait of the lady donor.

## The Villages of the Plateau

Beyond the stone windmills, the road finally reaches the pass at the Seli Ampelou Taverna and Grill. It then descends into the strange and dream-like bowl of Lassíthi Plateau; Werner Herzog used it hypnotically in his film *Signs of Life*. An emerald chequerboard divided by irrigation ditches and encompassed by barren mountains, the plateau was farmed by the Minoans, and later by the Dorians of Lyttos. However,

# Getting There and Around

One or two daily **buses** from Heráklion, Mália and Ag. Nikólaos wind their way up to the plateau, taking in most of the villages and ending up at the Diktean Cave.

# Where to Stay and Eat

## Avdoú ✉ 75005

**Villa Avdoú**, t 089 705 1606, f 089 705 1374, *www.avdou.com* (*exp*). Well appointed studios and villas on an organic fruit'n'veg farm, on the road up to the plateau and 20 mins to the beach. Courses in organic farming, Cretan diet cookery, plus meals made from the produce. Has internet access.

## Tzermiádon/Ag. Geórgios ✉ 72052

**Kourites**, in Tzermiádon, t 084 402 2194 (*B; inexp*). The smartest place to stay on the plateau. *Open all year.*
**Lassithi**, t 084 402 2194 (*E; inexp*). Owned by the same family as the Kourites, and has a restaurant. *Open all year.*
**Rhea**, in Ag. Geórgios, t 084 403 1209 (*E; inexp*).

## Psychró

**Dikteon Andron**, t 084 403 1504 (*E; inexp*).
**Hotel Zeus**, t/f 084 403 1284 (*D; inexp*).

## Sísi ✉ 72400

**Kalimera Kriti**, on the east end of Sísi, t 084 107 1134, f 084 107 1598, *Kalimerakriti@kalimerakriti.gr* (*A; lux*). Vast and luxurious with 2 private beaches, outdoor and indoor pools, tennis courts and 27 hectares of gardens.
**Minos Imperial**, 5km east, t 081 024 2082, f 081 024 3757, *www.minosimperial,gr* (*L; lux*). Opened in June 2001, hotel and bungalow complex, with several pools, tennis, children's club, water sports, big food buffets.
**Hellenic Palace**, on the far west edge of Sísi, t 084 107 1502, f 084 107 1238 (*A; exp*). Stylish, modern and comfortable, near the local riding centre.
**Zygos Apts**, t 084 107 1279 (*C; mod*). Reasonable choice with kitchenettes.
**Angela Hotel**, t 084 107 1176, f 084 107 1121 (*C; mod*). With pool and bar.
**Elite Restaurant**. Run by George Sevadalis, has an excellent reputation.
**Mediterraneo**. Serves good fresh fish.

in 1293 it was such a nest of resistance that the Venetians demolished the villages, set up a guard around the passes and persecuted anyone who came near. Only in 1543 were Greek refugees from the Turkish-occupied Peloponnese permitted to resettle the plateau. To re-establish the orchards, the Venetians built 10,000 white-sailed irrigation windmills. In the 1970s they were still a remarkable sight, but, sadly, since then most have become derelict in favour of the more reliable petrol pump.

Eighteen villages dot the plateau's circumference. The largest, **Tzermiádon** (TZEP-MIAΔO; pop. 1,500), is near a sacred Minoan cave and peak sanctuary. The cave, **Trápeza**, was used from 5000 BC; long before the first temples, Cretans left ivory votive offerings in the mysterious penumbra behind its narrow opening; the Middle Minoans used it for burials. The loftiest of all Minoan peak sanctuaries (3,800ft) is an hour's walk up a strenuous path: **Karphí** (ΚΑΡΦΙ), the 'nail', an accurate description of its weird mountain. Excavated by John Pendlebury between 1937 and 1939 – his last project before he was killed in the Battle of Crete – Karphí was the refuge of some 3,000 Minoans, or Eteocretans ('True Cretans'), during the Dorian invasion in 1100 BC. For a century they tried to keep the fires of their civilization burning, before the harsh winters got to them. In this mighty setting, Pendlebury found 150 small houses, a temple, a chieftain's house, a tower and barracks, and a shrine that contained five of the very last Minoan clay idols of the goddess (*c.* 1050 BC, now in the Heráklion Museum), distorted and a metre tall, with a cylinder skirt, detachable feet and long neck, like Alice in Wonderland when she was mistaken for a serpent.

Clockwise from Tzermiádon, **Ag. Konstantínos** has the most souvenir shops on the plateau, while just above it the 13th-century **Moní Kristalénias** enjoys a lovely panoramic spot. In **Ag. Geórgios**, the next village, a 200-year-old farmhouse contains a **Folk Museum** (*open June–Aug 10–4*), including a wine-press that doubled as a bed; it also has a fascinating collection of photos of Níkos Kazantzákis.

## Psychró and the Díktean Cave

Psychró (ΨΥΧΡΟ), to the southwest, is the base for visiting the **Díktean Cave**, the birthplace of Zeus (*t 084 403 1316; open 10–5; adm*). From the car park it's a 1km ascent up a rocky path; sure-footed donkeys are available, while local guides at the entrance hire lanterns, although it's wise to set a price from the start. Rubber-soled shoes are important; the descent is slippery and a bit dangerous (tour leaders often fail to warn their elderly clients, creating massive single-file jams).

If you get there before or after the groups, the cave is a haunting, other-worldly place worthy of myth. Only rediscovered in the 1880s, it contained cult items from Middle Minoan up to Archaic times; its role as the birthplace and hiding place of Zeus from his cannibal father Cronos was confirmed by the discovery in Paleókastro of an inscription of the *Hymn of the Kouretes* (the young men who banged their shields to drown out the baby's cries). Down in the cave's damp, shadowy bowels the guides point out formations that, if you squint, resemble the baby god, his cradle and the place where the nanny goat Amaltheia nursed him; to help conceal the birth, Rhea, his mother, spurted her own breast milk into the heavens, creating the Milky Way. Tradition has it that Minos came up here to receive the Law of Zeus every nine years, and that Epimenides the Sage lived in the cave as a hermit, having strange visions.

# Between Mália and Ag. Nikólaos

After Mália, the New Road cuts inland, avoiding rugged Cape Ag. Ioánnis. This is good news for the last two resorts, Sísi and Milátos, which are free of the heavy traffic that bedevils the coast to the west. Laid-back **Sísi** (ΣΙΣΙ) is like a chunk of southern California, with its modern pastel architecture, sandy beaches and little port – a turquoise crique under the cliffs, lined with a palm garden and a cascade of tavernas.

To the east, **Paralía Milátou** (ΠΑΡΑΛΙΑ ΜΙΛΑΤΟΥ) is just the opposite: low-key and a bit dumpy. Yet ancient Milátos was one of the most important cities of Homeric Crete. In myth, Minos, Rhadamanthys and Sarpedon once competed for the favours of a beautiful boy. When the boy chose Sarpedon, his brothers were such poor sports that Sarpedon moved to Asia Minor, taking with him not only the boy but the inhabitants of Milátos, where they founded the great city of Miletus. The dusty old village still wears a forsaken air. It has a more recent reason to look forlorn. In 1823, during the War of Independence, the large stalactite **Cave of Milátos** (on the edge of a wild ravine, 6km drive from the beach then a 10-minute walk from the car park) served as a refuge for 3,600 people. The Turks forced the Greeks to surrender and, although promising them safe conduct, all the men and children were massacred and the women enslaved. Inside the cave is a chapel containing a glass reliquary full of bones.

## Neápolis (ΝΕΑΠΟΛΙΣ) and Ancient Dreros

Immersed in almond groves, **Neápolis** is the largest town on the Heráklion–Ag. Nikólaos road. In its former incarnation as Karés, it was the birthplace of Pétros Fílagros in 1340. Raised by Catholics, he became a professor of theology and was elected Pope Alexander V in 1409, one of several popes-for-a-year during the Great Schism. Karés predeceased him, when the Venetians destroyed it in 1347 after a revolt. The rebuilt village grew into the 'new town', Neápolis, the provincial capital before Ag. Nikólaos. It has a leafy central square and a small **museum** (*open Tues–Sun 10–1 and 6–9; adm*), housing traditional crafts and finds from **Dreros**, a wild place a few miles north (cross under the New Road and follow signs for Kouroúnes; from the parking area, a rough path leads up to a saddle between two peaks). There's an Archaic agora and a 7th-century BC Geometric Temple to Apollo Delphinios; the latter yielded the oldest hammered bronze statues ever found in Greece (now in the Heráklion Museum) and Eteocretan inscriptions – Minoan words in Greek letters.

# Ag. Nikólaos (ΑΓ. ΝΙΚΟΛΑΟΣ)

When Ag. Nikólaos was selected capital of *nomós* Lassíthi in 1905, only 95 people lived in the village, built in an amphitheatre overlooking a round lake and the breathtaking Gulf of Mirabélo. It didn't have a proper port; ships had to call at Pachiá Ámmos to the east. A new port in 1965 attracted the first yachties, and what has happened since is not exactly hard to guess: the resident population of Agnik, as the Brits call it, has multiplied by 100. A few years back it was the first place on Crete to cross over the courtesy threshold; in response, the mayor erected signs, pleading: 'Please respect our local mores and customs. Do not disrupt the town's tranquillity and keep the environment clean.' They must have worked – the rowdies and louts now hone in on Mália, leaving Agnik older, wiser and noticeably nicer.

### Around Town

Ag. Nikólaos stands on the ruins of Lato Pros Kamara, the port of ancient Lato, and the town still concentrates much of its mercenary soul around the port, overlooking the islet of **Ag. Pándes**. Its chapel draws pilgrims on 20 June, but at other times you need to go with a cruise party to visit the *kri-kri* goats, the only inhabitants, who will probably play hide-and-seek anyway. The other vortex is circular **Lake Voulisméni**, the 'bottomless' (although it has been measured at 210ft). It was often stagnant until 1867, when the local pasha connected it to the sea. Fish, some over 2ft long, call it home, fattened by bread from the restaurants, only to appear later on their menus. Behind the tourist office, there's a small but choice **Folk Art Museum** (*t 084 102 9573; open Sun–Fri 10–4; adm*), with icons, embroideries, instruments and stamps from independent Crete. Aktí S. Koundoúrou follows the waterfront past rocky places where you can swim. There is a beach at the end and the little stone church that gave the town its name, **Ag. Nikólaos**, with rare 9th-century Geometric frescoes from the Iconoclastic period (*key at the Minos Palace Hotel*).

# Getting Around

The **Olympic Airways** office is at Plastíra 20, **t** 084 102 2033. LANE, 5 K. Sfakianákis St, **t** 084 102 6764, **f** 084 102 7052 operates 2 **ferries** a week to Piraeus and Sitía, and 1 ferry a week to Kássos, Kárpathos, Mílos. **Port authority**: **t** 084 102 2312. The **bus station** (**t** 084 102 2234) is near the rocky beach of Ámmos at the end of Sof. Venizélou. Beaches within easy bus range are Eloúnda and Kaló Chorió (on the road to Sitía).

# Tourist Information

**Tourist office**: between the lake and the sea, 20 Aktí S. Koundoúrou, **t** 084 102 2357; *open daily 8.30am–9.30pm in season.*
**Tourist police** and **lost property**: 47 Erithoú Stavroú, **t** 084 102 6900.

# Festivals

**Easter**: festivities incl. burning of an effigy of Judas in the middle of the harbour.
**6 Dec**: Ag. Nikólaos.

# Shopping

Try not to confuse the three streets named after the Koundoúrou family. Mixed in with the many shops flogging embarrassing T-shirts, Ag. Nikólaos has some excellent boutiques:
**Maria Patsaki**, 2 K. Sfakianáki. Embroideries, clothes and antiques.
**Syllogi**, Aktí S. Koundoúrou. Old paintings, antiques, silver and other fine crafts.

**Natural Sea Sponge Workshop**, 15 R. Koundoúrou. Selection of sponges, herbs, spices, teas and oils.
**Kerazoza**, 42 R. Koundoúrou. Puppets, toys and postcards from the 1950s.
**Anna Karteri**, 5 R. Koundoúrou. Wide range of titles in English.
**Polihoro Peripou**, by the lake. Cybercafé that doubles as a lending library.

# Where to Stay

## Ag. Nikólaos ✉ 72100

**Luxury**
**Minos Beach**, on the secluded, garden-covered promontory of Ammoúdi, **t** 084 102 2345, **f** 084 102 2548, *Minosb@her.forthnet.gr* (*L*). 132 sumptuous bungalows, good restaurant, bars, private beach and diving school; although built practically in the Minoan era by Agnik standards (1962), it was renovated in 1990 and is still one of the best.
**St Nicholas Bay**, spread over a narrow peninsula 2km from Ag. Nikólaos, **t** 084 102 5041, **f** 084 102 4556, *stnicolas@otenet.gr* (*L*). A 130-bungalow complex which includes a private sandy beach, one indoor and four outdoor pools (not to mention the private pools accompanying some suites), a health club and an art gallery. *Open Mar–Nov.*

**Expensive**
**Coral Hotel**, on the waterfront along Aktí Koundoúrou, **t** 084 102 8363, **f** 084 102 8754, *ermis1@ath.forthnet.gr* (*B*). A smart town option, with rooftop pool and terrace.
**Melas**, 26 Koundoúrou, **t** 084 102 8734. Stylish apartments for 2–5 people.

The **Archaeology Museum**, (**t** *084 102 2382; open Tues–Sun 8.30–3; adm*), up the hill at 68 K. Paleológou, displays artefacts discovered in eastern Crete; among the highlights are a Neolithic phallus-shaped idol from Zákros, the peculiar Early Minoan pinhead chicken-like 'Goddess of Myrtos', lovely gold jewellery from Móchlos, a stone vase from Mália in the form of a triton shell, engraved with two demons making a libation, a Daedalic bust from the 7th century BC that looks like Christopher Columbus and a unique lamp from Olous with 70 nozzles. In the last room, a 1st-century AD skull still has a fine set of teeth, a gold burial wreath embedded in the bone of its brow, a silver coin from Polyrenia (to pay Charon, the ferryman of the Underworld), and a plate of knucklebones, perhaps used for divination.

**Ormos**, near the sea, t 084 102 4094, f 084 102 5394 (*B*). Family orientated, with air-conditioning, pool and playground; rates plummet off-season.

**Moderate**

**Panorama**, also on Aktí Koundoúrou, t 084 102 8890, f 084 102 7268 (*C*). Offers just that over the harbour, and all rooms come with their own bath.

**Inexpensive**

**Doxa**, 7 Idomeneos, t 084 102 4214, f 084 102 4614 (*C*). A good, year-round bet.

**Green House**, 15 Modátsou, t 084 102 2025 (*E*). A cheapie, with little rooms leading out to a small courtyard, overflowing with greenery, and patrolled by a small army of cats.

**Perla**, t 084 102 3379 (*E*). Pleasant, clean guesthouse in the centre.

**Rea**, on the corner of Marathónos and Milátou, t 084 102 8321, f 084 102 8324 (*B*). A good value hotel with character and excellent sea views.

**Aouas K. Paleológou**, halfway up to the Archaeology Museum. Small, inexpensive and good, serving Cretan dishes in a green shady courtyard far from the madding crowd.

**Trata**, on Akti Pangalou, near Kitroplateía Beach. Serving excellent fish soup and chicken *kleftíko* (with cream, cheese and ham), as well as a long list of casserole dishes.

**Ofai to Lo**, at the far end of Kitroplateía. Boiled kid, tigania pork with white sauce, roast lamb stuffed with garlic and various cheeses are among the specialities.

**Dolphin**, Ammoúdi Beach. Good food served by jovial twin waiters.

**Grigoris**, at Stavrós, 200m after the bridge to Almyrós. Exceptionally friendly and reasonable.

**Synantysi**, on the Old Road to Heráklion, t 084 102 5384. Another good choice popular with locals for its excellent array of *mezédes*, including mussels, mushrooms, scampi and squid. Good selection of wines and desserts.

# Eating Out

**Pelagos**, on Str. Kóraka, just in from Aktí Koundoúrou (€20). A trendy, if pricey, seafood restaurant, with a long list of tasty *mezédes* to start with.

**Pefko** (or 'The Pines'). Dining on the lake, popular with locals, with delicious, reasonably priced taverna food.

**Itanos**, next to the cathedral on Str. Kíprou, t 084 102 5340. Some of the finest traditional cooking in eastern Crete (the lamb and spinach in egg-lemon sauce is excellent), good barrelled wine.

# Entertainment and Nightlife

After-dark action is not hard to find, concentrated around the **lake** and **port**.

**Alexandros**, K. Paleológou. Its perennially popular roof terrace for background music.

**Lipstick**, overlooking the main port, one of the dancing disco bars churning out more pulsating sounds, or try one of the string along **25 Martíou**.

*Kri-Kri*, opposite the Minos Beach Hotel, has live Greek music and dancing.

Many tourists are surprised to discover that Agnik was asleep when God was handing out beaches: there's a little sand at shingly **Kitroplateía**, sheltered and safe for children, named after the cypress wood once exported from here. The pocket-sized sand beach of **Ammoudara** is at the end of Aktí S. Koundoúrou, while at the other end of town, near the bus station, sandy **Ámmos** is clean, but not terribly atmospheric. To the south, on the other side of the stadium, is the crowded but clean **municipal beach** (*fee for use of beach club facilities*); from here, a walking path leads past little, sandy **Gargardóros** Beach and beyond that to **Almyrós**, the best beach within a reasonable distance of Ag. Nikólaos.

# Eloúnda, Olous and Spinalónga

Tantalizing views across the Gulf of Mirabélo unfold along the 12km from Ag. Nikólaos north to Eloúnda; below, the rocky coastline is interspersed with tiny coves, draped with Crete's most glamorous hotels. **Eloúnda** (ΕΛΟΥΝΤΑ) attracts many Brits, who never seem to drift far from the bars in the central square. There's even a nine-hole golf course at the Porto Eloúnda Deluxe Resort Hotel.

South of Eloúnda, a bridge crosses an artificial channel dug by the French in 1897 to separate the promontory of Spinalónga from mainland Crete. Along this channel lies the sunken harbour of **Olous**, the port of ancient Dreros (see p.187) and goal of the 'sunken city' excursions from Ag. Nikólaos. The moon goddess Britomartis, inventor of the fishing net, was worshipped here, represented by a wooden cult statue (a *xoanon*) with a fishtail, made by Daedalos. Fish also figure in the mosaic floor of an Early Byzantine basilica near the Canal Bar.

The tiny island of **Spinalónga** (ΣΠΙΝΑΛΟΓΚΑ; *t 081 024 6211; adm*), not to be confused with the promontory, is a half-hour caique trip from Eloúnda, or an hour by excursion boat from Ag. Nikólaos. Venetian engineers detached it from the promontory in 1579 when they dug a channel to defend their fortress. It held out against the Turks until 1715, when the Venetians surrendered them by treaty. When the Turks left in 1904, Spinalónga became a leper colony, surviving until 1957. **Pláka**, opposite the islet, was its supply centre and now has a tiny laid-back colony of its own, dedicated to relaxation by the pebble beach and eating in its excellent fish tavernas.

# Above Ag. Nikólaos: Kéra Panagía and Kritsá

From Ag. Nikólaos, it's a short hop up to Kritsá and, 1km before the village, the church of **Kéra Panagía** (*t 084 105 1525; open Mon–Sat 9–3, Sun 9–2; adm*). It looks like

## Where to Stay and Eat

### Eloúnda ✉ 72053

**Eloúnda Mare, t** 084 104 1102, **f** 084 104 1307, *elmare@agn.forthnet.gr* (*L; lux*). Member of the prestigious Relais & Chateaux complex, renovated in 2000, incl. bungalows with private pools on the seafront, not to mention restaurants and watersports.

**Eloúnda Beach, t** 084 104 1412, **f** 084 104 1373, *elohotel@compulink.gr* (*L; lux*). Traditional Cretan architecture, a sandy beach, its own cinema, deep-sea-diving expeditions, fitness centre and heated pool. Royal Suites boast pools, butler, pianist and gym with trainer.

**Eloúnda Blue Bay, t** 084 104 1924, **f** 084 104 1816 (*B; exp*). A rather more modest complex offering a pool, playground and tennis.

**Akti Olous**, near the causeway **t** 084 104 1270, **f** 084 10 41 425 (*C; exp*). A popular place with a pool and roof garden.

**Korfos Beach, t** 084 104 1591, **f** 084 104 1034 (*C; inexp*). Within spitting distance of the strand, with watersports on offer.

Fine dining experiences can be had at the top hotels, but Eloúnda is also well endowed with restaurants, especially around the **port**.

**Vritomartis**, out on its little islet, **t** 084 104 1325 (*€22*). Well-prepared seafood and lobster.

**Kalidon, t** 084 104 1451 (*€15–20*). Romantically located out on a small pontoon, with a good selection of vegetarian dishes and *mezédes*.

**Marilena, t** 084 104 1322 (*€20–25*). Attractive garden, serving Cypriot and fish dishes.

**Taverna Despina**, on the Pláka road. Has a good name for fish.

no other church on the island: the three naves, coated with centuries of whitewash, trailing long triangular buttresses and crowned by a simple bell tower and a drum dome. Within, it's alive with the colours of Crete's best fresco cycle, that illustrates the evolution of Byzantine art before it ceased with the Turks. The central aisle, dedicated to the Virgin, dates from the 12th to mid-13th centuries: on the northwest pillar look for *St Francis*, with his Catholic tonsure. It's rare that a Western saint earns a place among the Orthodox, but Francis, introduced by the Venetians, made a great impression among the people. The two side aisles were later additions, painted in the more naturalistic style emanating from Constantinople in the early 14th century. The south aisle is devoted to St Anne, while the north aisle belongs to Christ Pantocrator and a *Last Judgement* covers most of the nearby vaults. Among the saints here, don't miss the donors with their small daughter, rare portraits of medieval Cretans.

In 1956, director Jules Dassin chose the lovely white village of **Kritsá** (ΚΡΙΤΣΑ) as the location for his film *He Who Must Die* starring Melina Mercouri, and ever since its role has been that of a film set – a traditional Cretan village swamped by Agnik tourists, who are in turn swamped by villagers selling them tablecloths, rugs and lace. Kritsá is famous for throwing real roll-out-the-barrel Cretan weddings and in August, weddings are re-enacted with food, drink and dancing for fee-paying 'guests'.

## Ancient Lato

A scenic 3km walk (the path begins near the crossroads) or drive north of Kritsá leads to the remains of Dorian **Lato** or, more properly, Lato Etera (*t 084 102 5115; open Tues–Sun 8.30–3*). Named after the Minoan goddess Leto (or Lato), the city was founded in the 7th century BC; it flourished and gave birth to Nearchus, Alexander the Great's admiral and explorer, before it was abandoned in favour of its port, Lato Kamara (Ag. Nikólaos). Lato displays unusual Minoan influences on Dorian design: the double gateway, the street of 80 steps lined with houses and workshops, and the architecture of its agora, with its columnless sanctuary and central cistern. The wide steps that continue up to a peristyle court and *Prytaneion*, where the sacred fire burned, date from the 7th century BC and may have been inspired by Minoan 'theatres'; spectators could sit and watch events in the agora below. Monumental towers stood on either side of a narrower stair leading up to the altar. On the second hill stands a beautiful, column-less temple, an isolated altar and a primitive theatre.

# East of Ag. Nikólaos: The Gulf of Mirabélo

The coastline that lends Ag. Nikólaos its panache owes its name to the Genoese fortress of Mirabélo, 'Beautiful View', demolished by the Turks. The land is immensely fertile, and has been populated for the past 5,000 years; fortunately archaeological zoning has kept more recent Agnikish development down. Frequent buses run the 12km out to the sandy beach of **Kaló Chório**; the road east continues past the up-and-coming resort of **Ístro** to the turn-off for the 12th-century **Moní Faneroménis**, possessing a stupendous view over the Mirabélo gulf. The monastery is built into the cliff, sheltering a frescoed cave church with a miraculous icon of the Virgin.

## Where to Stay and Eat

**Móchlos** ✉ 72057
Sofia, t 083 409 4554, f 083 409 4238 (*D; inexp*). Small, pleasant and well run.

Mochlos, t 083 409 4205 (*E; inexp*). Similarly priced and close to the beach. *Open all year.*
**Sta Limenaria**, far end of the beach. More rooms and good food, incl. vegetarian; most seaside tavernas specialize in fresh fish.

## Minoans along the Riviera: Gourniá, Vasilikí and Móchlos

East of Ístro, the road passes below the striking hillside site of Gourniá (*t 084 209 4604; open Tues–Sun 8.30–3; adm*), excavated between 1901 and 1904 by American Harriet Boyd, the first woman to lead a major dig. Gourniá reached its peak at around 1550 BC, and was never rebuilt after a fire in *c.* 1225 BC. At the highest point, a small 'palace' with store rooms surrounds a rectangular court; there's a mini theatrical area and Shrine of the Snake Goddess, with a shelf for long, tube-like snake vases.

From Gourniá, it's a short drive down to **Pachiá Ámmos**, a woebegone seaside village that corners most of the garbage in the Cretan sea. It stands at the beginning of the Ierápetra road (*see* p.197) bisecting the isthmus of Crete, a mere 12km of land separating the Aegean from the Libyan sea. The isthmus is undergoing a close survey; as Gourniá wasn't a palace, archaeologists suspect one must be nearby, especially as this was one of the first places settled by the Minoans. By 2600 BC, in the Pre-Palace era, they had built a settlement at **Vasilikí**, 5km south of Pachiá Ámmos. In 1906, it yielded specimens of what's since been known as 'Vasilikí ware', the Minoans' first distinctive pottery style, mottled in red and black, an effect produced by uneven firing.

Pachiá Ámmos is also the crossroads for Sitía, east down the Cretan riviera, on a corniche road that slithers along the precipitous coast. Midway is **Móchlos** (ΜΟΧΛΟΣ), a charming fishing village, set between barren cliffs and a small islet a stone's throw from the shore; originally attached to the mainland, it gave Minoan Móchlos two harbours. These Minoans specialized in pots with lid handles shaped like reclining dogs; some were found in the chamber tombs cut into the cliffs. One building is called 'the House of the Theran Refugees' for its similarities to the timbered houses at Akrotíri; on Santorini (*see* p.277) pot shards from Akrotíri littered the floor *on top of* a layer of volcanic ash. Life obviously went on after the Big Bang.

Another Minoan settlement existed from 3000 BC on **Pseíra**, 2km offshore, where the inhabitants used the pumice that floated ashore to build up the floor of their shrine. Judging by the rich finds, it was a prosperous little town, although now it's completely barren. Pseíra's House of the Pillar Partitions, with a bathroom equipped with a sunken tub, plughole and drains, is the most elegant in eastern Crete.

# Sitía (ΣHTEIA)

As an antidote to Ag. Nikólaos, sunny Sitía has kept its Greek soul, perhaps because it has a livelihood of its own, based on sultanas and wine. Set in an amphitheatre, it is a thoroughly pleasant place, endowed with a sandy blue flag beach. Its Byzantine, Genoese and Venetian walls fell to earthquakes and Barbarossa's bombardments, leaving only a restored Venetian fortress to close off the western end of the port.

## Around the Town

Sitía, filled with provincial bustle, the pranks of its pet pelicans and general schmoozing along the waterfront, is a paradise for lazy visitors. But *la dolce vita* is nothing new here; under the fortress are the ruins of a Roman fish tank, where denizens of the deep were kept alive and fresh for the table. The **Archaeology Museum** (*Ítanos Street; t 084 302 3917; open Tues–Sun 8.30–3; adm*) has a collection of Minoan *larnaxes*, a wine press and Linear A tablets from Zákros, and offerings from the 7th century in the Daedalic style. Some of the newest finds are from Pétras, just south of Sitía, where a large structure from the New Palace period is currently being explored: it may well be the Se-to-i-ja of the Minoan tablets. If the town beach is too crowded, try the sandy cove of **Ag. Fotía**, 5km to the east. In 1971 a large Pre-Palatial Minoan cemetery of 250 chamber tombs was discovered near the sea here. The hill above is the site of a large Old Temple building that was mysteriously but peacefully destroyed just after its construction and replaced with a round fortlike building – perhaps part of a coastal warning system.

## Getting There and Around

Sitía's little **airport**, 1km out of town (taxi costs €5), is linked to Athens 3 times a week. The **Olympic Airways** office is by the Tourist Information Office, **t** 084 302 2270. For airport information, call **t** 084 302 4666. **Ferries** run four times a week to Kárpathos and Kássos, Ag. Nikólaos and Piraeus. **Port authority: t** 084 302 2310. The **bus station** at the south end of the waterfront, **t** 084 302 2272, has connections 5 times a day to Ag. Nikólaos and Ierápetra, 4 to Vaï and 3 to Káto Zákro.

## Tourist Information

**Municipal Tourist Office**: on the marina, **t** 084 302 8300; *open Mon–Fri 9–2.30 and 5–8.30*. **Tourist police: t** 084 302 4200.

## Festivals

**24 June**: large local festival, Piskokéfalo.
**Mid July–mid Aug**: Kornaria cultural festival.
**Mid Aug**: 3-day wine and sultana festival, Sitía.

## Where to Stay

**Sitía** ✉ **72300**
**Itanos**, 4 Karamanli, **t** 084 302 2900, **f** 084 302 2915 (*C; mod*). Stylish hotel with roof garden and special rooms for the disabled.

**Archontikon**, 16 Kondiláki, **t** 084 302 8172 (*D; inexp*). Small, clean, quiet and friendly.
**Stars**, 37 M. Kalyváki, **t** 084 302 2917 (*D; inexp*). Offers peace and quiet.
**Nora**, 31 Rouseláki, near the new port, **t** 084 302 3017 (*D, inexp*).
**Youth hostel**, 4 Theríssou St, just east of town, **t** 084 302 2693. Pleasant and friendly, with kitchen use and camping in the garden.

## Eating Out

Sitía is a civilized place, where *mézedes* automatically come with your drink.
**Zorba's**, **t** 084 302 2689 (*€18*). Wonderful location on the waterfront; delicious seafood.
**Balcony**, just up Kazantzaki from the water, **t** 084 302 5084 (*€25*). Great seasonal menu, incl. delicious Asian dishes, pasta with seafood and roast meats with local veg.
**Mixos Taverna** *Ouzerie*, close to the port. Serves lamb baked or on the spit.
**Neromilos**, 4km east of Sitía in Ag. Fotia. Local favourite, in a former water mill; good view.

## Entertainment and Nightlife

There is a stylish clutch of bars near the pelican's house; for more of a sweat, head for:
**Hot Summer**. Disco with a pool to cool off in.
**Planitarion**, 1km beyond ferry port. Huge disco.

## South of Sitía: the Last True Cretans and a Venetian Villa

Along the main road south is ancient **Praisós**, the last stronghold of the Eteocretans – the 'true Cretans', or Minoans – who took refuge here during the Dorian invasion and survived into the 3rd century BC, running their shrine of Diktean Zeus at Palaíkastro and keeping other cults alive. When Praisós began to compete too openly with Dorian Ierapytna (Ierápetra) in 146 BC, it was decimated. Ironically, this last Minoan town was one of the first to be discovered, in 1884 by the Italian Halbherr, who was mystified by the inscriptions in Greek letters, now held to be in the native Minoan language of Linear A. The scenery is lovely, the ruins pretty sparse.

The slightly more substantial remains of another vanished civilization may be seen further south in pretty **Etiá**. In the Middle Ages, Etiá was the fief of the Di Mezzo family, who in the 15th century built themselves a beautiful fortified villa – three storeys high, with vaulted ceilings and intricate decorations. Destruction of it began when a band of Turkish administrators were besieged here by angry locals in 1828, and a fire and earthquake finished the job. Now partially restored, the entrance, ground floor and fountain house offer a hint of the villa's former grandeur.

## East of Sitía: the Monastery of Toploú

This, one of Crete's wealthiest monasteries, is formally called Panagía Akroteriani, but Toploú ('cannoned' in Turkish) more aptly evokes this fortress of the faith, isolated on a plateau 3.5km from the Sitía–Palaíkastro road. It started off with a chapel dating from Nikephóros Phokás' liberation of Crete (961), while the monastery itself (*open 9–1 and 2–6*) was founded in the 15th century by the Kornáros family and rebuilt after the earthquake of 1612. Square 30ft walls defend Toploú; the gate is directly under a hole named the *foniás* ('killer'), through which the besieged monks used to pour rocks and boiling oil on their attackers. Much of Toploú's building stone came from ancient Itanos: note the inscription from the 2nd century BC embedded in the façade.

Toploú has a venerable history as a place of refuge, revolution and resistance. At the beginning of the War of Independence in 1821, the Turks hanged 12 monks over the gate as a warning, although it only made the Cretans mad as hell, and by the end of the war Toploú was theirs again. During the Second World War, the abbot was shot by the Germans for operating a radio transmitter for the Resistance. Artefacts from Toploú's battles are on display in the museum (*adm*); the finest icon is one of the masterpieces of Cretan art: the *Great is the Lord* by Ioánnis Kornáros (1770).

# Palaíkastro, Vaï and Itanos

All roads on the east coast converge at **Palaíkastro** (ΠΑΛΑΙΚΑΣΤΡΟ), with a fine beach a kilometre below. The first edition of Palaíkastro was down here, at **Roussolakos**, a Late Minoan settlement similar to Gourniá. In summer, excavations continue apace. Later, the inhabitants moved up the hill to **Kastrí**, where, in the ruins of a 4th-century BC temple to Diktean Zeus, the *Hymn of the Kouretes* (*see p.186*) was found engraved on a stone; in fact the words are much older than the temple.

## Where to Stay and Eat

**Palaíkastro** ✉ 72300

**Marina Village**, 1 km out of town, 500m from the sea, t 084 306 1284, *Relakis@sit.forthnet.gr (C; exp)*. A little resort complex with its own snack bar, pool and tennis.

**Hellas**, near the central square, t 084 306 1240, *Hellas_h@otenet.gr (C; inexp)*. Good value and has a restaurant. *Open all year.*

**Thalia**, t 084 306 1217 *(D; inexp)*. Smothered in bougainvillaea. *Open all year.*

### Zákros

In summer there are a few rooms to let along the road to Káto Zákros, and about 50 beds (€30–35 a room) scattered in rent-rooms near the sea that are in great demand.

**Athena**, on the sea at the end of the beach road, t 084 309 3458 *(inexp)*.

**George**, Káto Zákros, t 084 309 3201 *(inexp)*. Clean, tasteful rooms and a terrace.

**Zákros**, in the upper village, t/f 084 309 3379 *(C; inexp)*. Small and a bit frayed at the edges. *Open all year.*

**Nikos Platanákis**, near the archaeological site, t 084 302 6887. The owner, a gourmet cook, serves delicious specialities incl. rabbit *stifádo*, meat casserole in tomato sauce and grilled fish.

**Maria's**. Another good choice, serving fresh fish under the tamarisks.

Nearby is the island's most stunningly beautiful beach at **Vaï** (ΒΑΪ). Its silver sands are lined with Europe's only wild palm trees, a species unique to Crete called *Phoenix theophrastii*. A banana plantation completes the Caribbean ambience. The only way to avoid sharing this tropical paradise with thousands of body-bakers is to arrive at the crack of dawn, come out of season or star in the next Bounty ad filmed there.

Small surrounding beaches act as crowd overflow tanks and free campsites. The three best lie north of Vaï, 1.5km up Cape Sideros near ancient **Itanos**. Inhabited from Early Minoan times, Itanos minted the first coins on Crete. After the razing of Praisós, the city was a fierce rival of Ierápetra for control of Palaíkastro's temple of Diktean Zeus, leading to the Arbitration of the Magnesians of 132 BC – a decision in Itanos' favour, as we know from the inscription embedded in the Toploú's wall. The Ptolemies of Egypt used Itanos as a naval station, but pirates forced its abandonment in the 8th century; best preserved of the remains are a basilica and fine cut Hellenistic wall.

# The Minoan Palace of Zákros

*t 084 309 3323; open daily 8–7 in season, otherwise 8–2.30; adm.*

From Palaíkastro, the road south cuts through olive groves and sleepy hamlets to **Zákros** (ΖΑΚΡΟΣ). A rich Minoan villa of the New Palace era, with wall paintings, sewers and wine presses, was found near the head of a dramatic gorge, the 'Valley of Death', named after the Minoan cliff tombs from 2600 BC. With sensible shoes it's a reasonable 8km walk down to **Káto Zákros**. The new road is plied by buses from Sitía.

For decades farmers dug up seals by the sea at Káto Zákros, and it was there that English archaeologist David Hogarth, who excavated the villa at upper Zákros in 1901, uncovered 12 houses before a torrential downpour forced him to abandon the site – literally a few feet from the prize. This, the **Palace of Zákros**, the fourth largest on Crete, waited patiently underground until 1961, when Níkos Pláton began digging where Hogarth left off. Built over an older site in the New Palace period (c. 1700 BC),

# Zákros

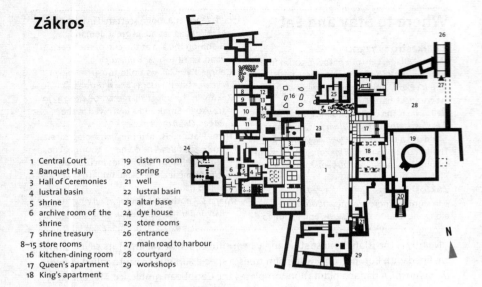

1 Central Court
2 Banquet Hall
3 Hall of Ceremonies
4 lustral basin
5 shrine
6 archive room of the shrine
7 shrine treasury
8–15 store rooms
16 kitchen-dining room
17 Queen's apartment
18 King's apartment
19 cistern room
20 spring
21 well
22 lustral basin
23 altar base
24 dye house
25 store rooms
26 entrance
27 main road to harbour
28 courtyard
29 workshops

N

the surrounding town was probably the Minoans' chief port for Egypt, the base of the 'Keftiu' (as the Egyptians called them, and as the Minoans may well have called themselves); the importance of trade for Zákros is highlighted by the fact that the valley could never have supplied such a large settlement with enough food. Pláton found large quantities of unworked ivory; sculpting it may have been a local speciality. The palace collapsed in the general catastrophe of 1450 BC and was never rebuilt, never plundered; the discovery of cult items suggests that disaster overwhelmed the residents. The slow subsidence of the east coast of Crete (or rise in Mediterranean sea-levels), has left the once important harbour now under the sea.

The palace entrance is by way of the original harbour road, leading into the northeast court; the covered area is a foundry predating the palace. A corridor leads into the long **Central Court**, which preserves the base of an altar. As usual, there are sanctuaries and ritual chambers in the West Wing, entered by way of a monolithic portal near the altar base. The large **Hall of Ceremonies** extends to the west, with a paved light-well in front and two windows; traces of frescoes were found here. A quantity of wine vessels found in the large room to the south led the archaeologists to dub it the **Banquet Hall**. Behind this are a **Shrine** and **Lustral Basin**, probably used for purification, and the **Shrine Treasury**, where Pláton found the precious rock-crystal libation vase now in Heráklion's Archaeology Museum. Boxes of Linear A tablets came out of the shrine's **Archive**; unfortunately the wet dissolved the bulk of them into a clay mass. In the southeast corner, a **Well** with worn steps was used for sacrificial offerings. At the bottom, Pláton found a bowl of perfectly preserved Minoan olives, which apparently tasted pretty good. The East Wing of the palace is tentatively identified as the **Royal Apartments**. Behind them, the so-called **Cistern Room,** with a balustrade and steps leading down to the paved floor, is even more of an enigma: guesses are that it was a swimming pool, a fish pond, or a basin to float a Egyptian-style sacred ship. Nearby, steps lead down to a '**well-fashioned spring**', as Pláton called it after Homer's description, which may have been a shrine connected to the spring that fed the cistern. At the north end is a large **kitchen** – the only one ever found in a palace.

As a protected archaeological zone, the fishing hamlet of **Káto Zákros** is idyllic, with no new buildings or big hotels. The pebbly beach is fine for swimming, but if it's remote soft white sands you have a yen for, make your way 10km south down the tortuous coastal road to **Xerókambos**, where the Liviko View Restaurant will feed you.

# Ierápetra (ΙΕΡΑΠΕΤΡΑ) and Around

As the southernmost town in Europe and main market for Crete's banana and winter veg crops, **Ierápetra** should be a fascinating place instead of irritatingly dull. The myths say it was founded by the mysterious, mist-making Telchines who named it Kamiros. The Dorians, in turn, renamed the town Ierapytna. Under Dorian tutelage the city boomed and bullied its way into ruling much of eastern Crete by Hellenistic times, and held out against the Romans after they'd conquered all the rest of Crete. Piqued, the Romans flattened it; then rebuilt it. The Byzantines made it a bishopric, but it was sacked by the Saracens and toppled by an earthquake in 1508.

Dominating Ierápetra's seafront is the 13th-century Venetian **Kastélli** in the ancient harbour, once Roman Crete's chief port for Africa. Nearby is a house where Napoleon supposedly spent the night of 26 June 1798, before sailing off to campaign in Egypt. The most beautiful things in Ierápetra are a Late Minoan *larnax* painted with scenes

## Getting There

The **bus station** is on Lasthénou, t 084 202 8237: there are frequent connections to Sitía (by way of Makrigialós), Gourniá and Ag. Nikólaos, Mýrtos, Koustounári, and Ferma.

## Festivals

**July** and **Aug**: Kyrvia cultural festival.

## Where to Stay

**Ierápetra** ✉ 72200
**Petra Mare**, close to town on the edge of the beach, t 084 202 3341, f 084 202 3350 (*A; exp*). Modern; water park and indoor pool.
**Astron**, 56 Kothrí, t 084 202 5114 (*B; exp–mod*). Pristine and pleasant. All rooms have air-con and sea-view balconies.
**Iris**, 36 Kothrí, t 084 202 3136 (*D; mod*). By the water, with 12 pleasant rooms.

**Coral**, 12 Emm. Nikikatsanváki, t 084 202 2846 (*D; inexp*). Quiet district. *Open all year.*

**Mýrtos** ✉ 72200
**Esperides**, 200m from the sea, t 084 205 1207, f 084 205 1298 (*C: mod*). New, large hotel.
**Mýrtos**, t 084 205 1226, f 084 205 1215 (*C: mod*). Has a good restaurant. *Open all year.*
**Mertiza**, t 084 205 1208 (*mod-inexp*). Furnished apartments.

## Eating Out

Tavernas line the *parália* along Samonil and Kougoumoutzáki, on either side of the fort.
**Napoleon**, on the waterfront (*€18 for fish*). Great favourite with authentic Greek and Cretan food. Fresh fish and snail varieties.
**Siciliana**, near town beach, t 084 202 4185. Real pizza oven and good honest pie.
**Lambrakis**, 1km east, t 084 202 3393. Meat and fish grills, and delicious *myzithropitákia* (Cretan cheese pies).

of a hunt, and a charming Roman Demeter, both residents of the **Archaeology Museum** (*Plateía Dimarchéiou*; *t 084 102 4943; open Tues–Sat 9–3; adm*).

All in all, the best thing to do in Ierápetra is leave – take an excursion boat to the golden sands of **Nisos Chrisí** (or Gaidouronísi – 'Donkey Island'; *3 boats leave town at 10.30, returning at 5*), an uninhabited islet where one of Crete's last natural cedar forests survives. The sea deposits seashells by the million on Chrisí's shores; there are sunbeds and in season one taverna by the beach wards off starvation. In summer you can also find excursion boats to **Koufonísi**, a remote island to the east, where the seashells were used to dye cloth royal purple. This resource made it a prize that Ierápetra and Itanos fought over endlessly; a theatre and settlement have been excavated, and the water is crystal-clear for snorkelling. Every year new developments sprout up **east of Ierápetra**. Old houses at the abandoned village of **Koutsounári** have been restored for rental, and **Ag. Fotiá** has an attractive beach and plenty of rooms. The best beach is further east, at **Makrigialós**, with fine sand and shallow waters.

## Along the Costa Plastica to Mýrtos

Spain has its Costas, so it seems only fair that Crete should take the public relations by the horns and flaunt the greatest assets of its southeastern coast: sand and plastic, the latter to force endless fields of tomatoes to redden before their time. West of Ierápetra, the Costa Plastica is almost metaphysically dull in its featureless anomie. In the coastal hills, however, pretty villages such as **Kalamáfka** have a sense of place; the hill just above it is apparently the only spot on Crete where you can see both the Libyan and Cretan seas.

West of Gra Lygiá there's a beach with a plastic hinterland at **Ammoudáres**. Things were no doubt prettier back in the days when the early Minoans lived further west, at Néa Mýrtos, a site better known as **Fournoú Korifí**. In 1968 the British School excavated this Minoan proto-town of close to 100 rooms, occupied in two periods between 2600 and 2100 BC, when it was destroyed by fire. Finds here proved vital in reconstructing life in the Pre-Palatial period. The small quantity of precious imported goods such as metal, obsidian from Mílos and stone vases from Mochlós suggest that such valuables were exchanged as dowries or gifts. Cereals, grape pips, olive stones and the bones of cattle, goats and sheep confirm that the essentials of the Cretan diet were already established; the oldest known potter's wheel in Greece was found here, from 2500 BC, with discs which were turned by the potter's hands, predating the later, spindle-turned wheels. By the find-places of the storage vessels and the cooking and dining areas, it is estimated that the population ranged between 25 and 30 people in five families, supporting the theory that the nuclear family may have been the essential social unit. The shrine is one of the oldest and yielded the Goddess of Mýrtos in the Ag. Nikólaos Museum. Further west, **Mýrtos** is the one place along this coast where you may want to linger: although burned by the Germans it was rebuilt with a good deal of charm and atmosphere – the way a Cretan fishing village is supposed to be. The beach is clean but shingly.

# The Cyclades

In myth, King Minos of Crete conquered the Aegean Islands in order to rid himself of his overly just brother Rhadamanthys, whom he sent to administer the new Cretan colonies. This corresponds to the Minoan influence that marks the prosperous Middle Cycladic period, when artists adopted a more natural style. The Late Cycladic period coincides with the fall of Crete and the rise of the Mycenaeans. When they in turn were overrun by the uncouth Dorians, the islands dropped out of history for hundreds of years. The luckier islands fell under the sway of the Ionians, and at the end of the 8th century BC, were part of the Ionian cultural rebirth in the Archaic period.

The rise of the Persians forced the Ionians to flee westwards to Attica, leaving the islands in Persian hands; several sided with the Persians at Marathon and Salamis, and were subsequently punished by Athens. To prevent future breakaways, Athens obliged the islands to enter into the new maritime league at Délos in 478 BC, replacing an older Ionian council, or Amphictyony. But what began as a league of allies gradually turned into vassals paying tribute to the Athenians, whose fleet was the only one capable of protecting the islands from the Persian menace. Cycladic resentment often flared into open revolt, and the Athenians had to work ever harder to extort the islands' annual contribution of money and ships.

During the Peloponnesian War the islands tended to side with the front-runner at any given time, and many jumped at the chance to support Sparta against their Athenian oppressors. But when Athens recovered from the war in 378 BC, it was only to form a second Delian League, again subjugating the Cyclades. Most of the islands turned to Philip of Macedon as a saviour from the Athenian bullies, only to be fought over a generation later by the generals of Alexander the Great. The 2nd-century BC Roman conquest finally brought the Cyclades peace, except for the islands given to Rhodes, a less kindly ruler than distant Rome. The fall of Rome spelt centuries of hardship; although the Cyclades remained part of the Byzantine Empire, Constantinople could not protect them from marauders, and the islanders were left to fend for themselves, building villages in the most inaccessible places possible.

When Constantinople fell in 1204, the Frankish conquerors allotted the Aegean to the Venetians, and the Archipelago, as the Byzantines called it, became the prey of grasping young noblemen and pirates (often one and the same). The Cyclades became the special territory of Marco Sanudo, nephew of Doge Enrico Dandolo. Sanudo declared himself Duke of Náxos and personally ruled that island and Páros, and gave his faithful thugs the smaller Cyclades as fiefs. The Sanudos gave way to the Crispi Dynasty in 1383, but, threatened by pirates and the growing Ottoman Empire, Venice herself stepped in to police the Cyclades at the end of the 15th century. There was little even Venice could do against the fierce renegade admiral Khair-ed-din-Barbarossa, who decimated the islands in the name of the Sultan. By the mid 16th century they were under Turkish domination.

Venetian priests had converted many of the Greeks on the Cyclades to Catholicism and despite the Ottoman occupation, both Orthodox and Catholic monasteries thrived. Turkish rule in the Archipelago was harsh only in economic terms and most of the islands were spared the cruelties inflicted on Crete. From 1771–74, one of the more outlandish episodes in Greek history brought a brief interlude from the Ottomans:

Russia and Turkey were fighting over Poland, so Catherine the Great opened a second front in the war by capitalizing on Greek discontent. Her fleet in the Aegean led an insurrection against the Sultan and occupied some of the Cyclades. By the time the Russians went home, they had made themselves unpopular with all concerned.

When the Greek War of Independence broke out, the Cyclades offered naval support and a safe harbour for refugees; the islands with large Catholic populations were brought under French protection and remained neutral. Nevertheless, the Cyclades were soon incorporated in the new Greek state, and Sýros became the country's leading port until Piraeus took over with the advent of the steamship. Today Sýros' capital, Ermoúpolis, is still the largest town and administrative centre of the Cyclades.

# Amorgós (ΑΜΟΡΓΟΣ)

*How very much I loved you only I know*
*I who once touched you with the eyes of the Pleiades,*
*Embraced you with the moon's mane, and we danced on the meadows of summer...*
        Nikos Gatsos, 'Amorgos VI' (trans. by Edmund Keeley and Philip Sherrard)

Easternmost of the Cyclades, Amorgós is also one of the most dramatically rugged islands, with a south coast of cliffs plunging vertically into the sea. It was for centuries virtually two islands, with the main port of Katápola almost a stranger to Aegiáli in the northeast, until a paved road in 1995 introduced them. After years as an island of political exile, Amorgós gradually became a destination for the adventurous, then

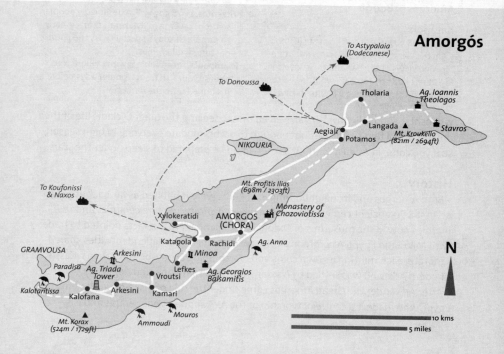

# Getting There and Around

**By sea**: daily **ferry** in summer from Náxos, via Heraklía, Schinoússa, Koufoníssi and Donoússa to Katápola, 4–5 times a week to Aegiáli. Infrequent **hydrofoils** in summer from Sýros, Páros, Íos and Santoríni call at Katápola. Check with the **Port authority**: Katápola, **t** 028 507 1259 and Aegiáli, **t** 028 507 3260.

**By road**: daily **bus service** from Katápola to Chóra (Amorgós Town) and Aegiáli; others via Chóra to the Chozioviótissa Monastery, Ag. Ánna, Paradísi and Kalotaritíssa beaches. For a **taxi** in Katápola, call **t** 028 507 2205; in Aegiáli, **t** 028 507 3570. Cars and motorbikes for rent in both towns.

# Tourist Information

**Regular police**: **t** 028 507 1210.
**Aegiális**: **t** 028 507 3394. Naomis is very helpful.
**Katápola**: Synodino Travel, **t** 028 507 1201, *synodinos@nax.forthnet.gr*.

# Where to Stay and Eat

## Amorgós ✉ 84008

### Katápola
**Eleni**, **t** 028 507 1628, **f** 028 507 1543 (*C; mod*). On the western edge of town, with unimpeded views of the bay and the sunset.
**Big Blue**, **t** 028 507 1094, (*C; mod*). In the centre of town. Large rooms, each with its own balcony and a common terrace for guests to gather and share the view.
**Minoa**, in the port square, **t** 028 507 1480, **f** 028 507 1003, *hotelmin@otenet.gr* (*C; mod*). More traditional, but might be noisy.
**St. George**, in Xylokeratídi, **t** 028 507 1228, **f** 028 507 1147 (*C; mod*). Modern and comfortable, sitting pretty on the hill.
**Villa Catapoliana**, one street back from the port, **t** 028 507 1064, *Katapol@otenet.gr* (*mod–inexp*). Courtyard setting around a small archaeological dig. Nice, quiet rooms with fridges and a roof garden with views.
**Voula Beach**, near the port police, **t** 028 507 4052 (*inexp*). Set around a shaded garden full of geraniums, all rooms are en suite.
**Anna**, set back from the waterfront, **t** 028 507 1218, **f** 028 507 1084 (*inexp*). Rooms and studios, incl. breakfast. Front rooms have views, and there's a garden.
**Katápola Camping**, by the beach at the base of the bay, **t** 028 507 1257/1802. Tends to open when the rooms start filling up.
**Minos**, at the quieter south end of the waterfront, with a glassed-in side garden for when it's windy. An old-fashioned place with good home-cooking; try the *patáto casserole* (a kid, lamb or pork island speciality), rabbit *stifádo* or, if you have deep pockets, lobster.
**Vitzentos**, **t** 028 507 1518. A deservedly popular seafront taverna in Xylokeratídi, arrive early to sample the day's speciality. Try the *patáto*, or stuffed aubergines.
**Psaropoula**. An amiable taverna where you choose your fish from wooden trays before it's hurled onto the barbecue.

whoosh! – suddenly travellers arrived en masse seeking the quiet Cycladic life of their dreams. You'll find rooms, but not enough to accommodate everyone in high season, so if you come in August without a reservation be prepared to sleep under the stars.

### History

Both Amorgós and its neighbouring islet Kéros were inhabited as far back as 3300 BC. In 1885 11 ancient cemeteries were uncovered, producing fine ceramics and marbles now in the museums of Oxford and Copenhagen; artefacts pointed to trade with Mílos and Egypt. A commonwealth of three ancient independent cities shared Amorgós, each minting its own coins and worshipping Dionysos and Athena: Kástri (modern Arkesíni) was settled by Naxians, Minoa by Samians, and Aegiáli by Milians.

After Alexander the Great, Amorgós came under the rule of his general, Ptolemy of Egypt, who made it a centre of worship of the Alexandrian gods Serapis and Isis.

## Chóra

**Pension Chora**, on the edge of the village, t 028 507 1110 (*mod*). Comfortable with a minibus pick-up service.

**Panorama**, at the beginning of the village, t 028 507 1606 (*inexp*). Small, but ask for one of its newer six large rooms.

**Yannakos** family, t 028 507 1367/1277. Seems to have the monopoly on rooms in the town.

**Kastanis**. Tiny, good, inexpensive and very Greek taverna.

**Liotrívi**, on the edge of town, t 028 507 1700. Has a roof garden, and elaborate dishes such as *kalogíros* (aubergine with veal, feta and tomatoes), *exohikó* (lamb and vegetables in a pastry) and baked vegetarian *briams*.

**Vegera Café**. Serves the likes of carrot cake and milkshakes to go with its views.

**Kallistó**. Coffee shop in a narrow alley by the whitewashed church; a popular spot to try the island speciality, *pastélli xerotígano* – fritters with honey, and *ráki psiméno* – schnapps tinged with cinnamon and cloves.

**Café Loza**. An authentic *ouzerie*.

## Aegiáli

**Lakki**, set back from the beach, t 028 507 3253, f 028 507 3244 (*B; mod*). Has a lovely garden with a tree house for kids. Cycladic-style, immaculate self-contained rooms, excellent food served outdoors from their taverna.

**Aegiális**, isolated, across the harbour, t 028 507 3393, f 028 507 3395, *aegialis@hotmail.com* (*B; mod*). A smart hotel complex, with pool, taverna and trendy nightclub, and a great sea view from the veranda. There's also a minibus service.

**Mike**, t 028 507 3208, f 028 507 3633, *hotelmik@otenet.gr* (*C; mod*). This was the port's first hotel, but has recently had a facelift.

**Akrogiali**, t 028 507 2208 (*mod–inexp*). Clean, comfortable rooms, all with en suite bathrooms.

**Camping Aegiáli**, in a field off the Tholaria road, t 028 507 3500. With decent facilities and a café.

**To Limani**, (known as **Katerina's**). A favourite grazing ground, packed out for its great food, wine from the barrel and mellow sounds.

**Korali**. Tasty fish and the best sunset views.

## Langáda

**Nikos**, t 028 507 3310 (*inexp*). Comfortable rooms and bougainvillaea cascading over the terrace; specializes in roast kid and baked aubergines.

**Pension Artemis**, t/f 028 507 3315 (*inexp*). Simple and pleasant.

**Taverna Loza**. As above, also run by the kind Dimitri Dendrinos.

## Tholária

**Vigla**, t 028 507 3288, f 028 507 3332 (*B; mod*). With views, bar and restaurant.

**Adelfi Vekri**, t 028 .507 3345/254 (*mod–inexp*). Rooms over the excellent fish taverna.

**Panorama**. Blessed with wonderful views, as its name promises.

The Romans were the first to use the island as a place of exile, beginning a downhill trend which continued as Goths, Vandals and Slavs ravaged it during the Byzantine period. One bright moment in this dark history came during the War of the Iconoclasts, when a miraculous icon sailed to Amorgós, set adrift, according to tradition, by a pious lady from Constantinople. Where the icon had landed, by the cliffs on Amorgós' south coast, Emperor Alexis Comnenus founded the Chozoviótissa Monastery in 1088. In 1209 the Duke of Náxos, Marco Sanudo, seized the island, and gave it to the Gizzi, who built the town castle. In spite of the Turkish occupation, Amorgós prospered in the 17th century, mostly from the export of exquisite embroideries, some of which are now in the Victoria and Albert Museum in London. Between the 17th and 19th centuries so many pieces were sold that War of Independence hero General Makriyiánnis threatened to declare war should the island send any more abroad. Rather than fight Makriyiánnis, the islanders just stopped making them.

Political prisoners were exiled on the island during the sixties under the colonels' junta. The filming here of Luc Besson's cult 1988 movie *The Big Blue* attracted trendy tourists, keen to see the wreck of the *Olympia* off the west coast. Present-day Amorgós is a wonderful choice for savouring the fast-disappearing Cycladic way of life, especially off season, when its 1,800 inhabitants far outnumber the visitors.

## Middle Amorgós: Katápola and Chóra

**Katápola** (ΚΑΤΑΠΟΛΑ) sits on a pretty, sheltered horseshoe bay looking out towards the islet of Keros. The harbour links two other villages – **Rachídi** on the hillside in the middle and **Xýlokeratídi**, the fishing port at the northern end. The entire bay can be easily walked in 25 minutes – a good thing, too, as the beach near Rachídi is grotty, leaving the one at Katápola and the two at Xýlokeratídi for decent swimming. It's a bustling, attractive, workaday port with smallholders selling produce from their trucks and villagers sending parcels via the bus to families in Chóra. From Katápola you can walk up the Mudulias Hill to the ancient city of **Minoa**, where bits of the acropolis, a gymnasium and a few remains of a Temple to Apollo can still be seen; the name suggests it may have begun as a colony of Crete. Amorgós has yielded up many treasures: the largest Cycladic figurine in the National Archaeology Museum in Athens was unearthed near Katápola. Beyond Minoa is the little village of Léfkes, from where you can visit **Ag. Geórgios Balsamítis**, with good frescoes, built on the site of an ancient 'aquatic' oracle where people came to have their fortunes told by signs on the surface of a sacred spring. There's an old Venetian towerhouse and watermill nearby.

The island capital, **Amorgós Town**, or **Chóra**, is a typical white Cycladic town, perched more than 1,300ft above sea level, with a neat spinal ridge of decapitated windmills – each family had its own – which once laboured with the winds that rose up the dizzying precipices from the sea. It has a perfect, eucalyptus-shaded *plateía*, lanes painted with big flowers and abstract patterns, and more churches than houses; especially note the ancient and Byzantine inscriptions and reliefs over the doors. One, with three vaulted aisles, melts like a meringue into the wall behind it; another, **Ag. Iríni**, only slightly larger than a phone box, is the smallest church in Greece. There's also a tiny **Archaeology Museum** (*t 028 507 1831; open Tues–Sun 9–1 and 6–8.30*). Steps lead up a huge rocky thumb rising out of the centre of town to **Apáno Kástro**, the well-preserved Venetian fortress built by Geremia Gizzi in 1290 (get the key from the town hall or the coffee shop, both in the square). From Chóra, it's an hour's walk down to Katápola; the views as you descend are especially dramatic around sunset.

### The Monastery of Chozoviótissa

*t 028 507 1294; open 8–1 and 5–7; donation; strict dress code (gowns available).*

To get to the island's astonishing **Monastery of Chozoviótissa**, you can either take a rubbly *kalderími* path from Chóra, zig-zagging down the magnificent natural amphitheatre, or the bus, leaving you with a 20-minute walk up, with superb views over the multi-coloured sea below. Built into sheer 600ft orange cliffs, the monastery is a stark white fort of the faith, embedded in the living rock, supported by two enormous buttresses. Within its eight storeys are some 50 rooms, two churches, and a library containing 98 precious manuscripts, but only the small museum and chapel with the icon are open to the public. Chozoviótissa was founded *c.* 800 by monks from Hozova in the Middle East, fleeing the Iconoclasm with their miraculous icon reputedly painted by St Luke; they were guided to the site by a mysterious nail stuck in the cliff (which finally rusted away and fell a few years back). Rebuilt in 1088, the monastery had 100 monks by the 17th century. It now gets by with just three, whose assistants provide visitors with a warm welcome in the form of brandy and/or water. Below, the bus continues down to the pebble beaches at **Ag. Ánna**. The series of coves lead to a larger bay, popular with nudists, a trifle sacrilegious given the neighbours.

## The South: Káto Meriá

The paved road and occasional buses continue south into the least visited and most traditional part of Amorgós: the fief of ancient Arkesini, better known these days as Káto Meriá. The landscape is dotted with curious old churches. Extensive tombs, walls, a subterranean aqueduct, and houses of ancient **Arkesíni** are near the mountain village of **Vroútsi**. The easiest way to get there is to get off the bus at **Kamári** and head north. A well-preserved 4th-century BC Hellenistic tower, the **Pírgos Ag**. **Triáda**, is near modern Arkesíni, another mountain village. Kalofana is the most remote of all, but near several quiet beaches: **Paradísa** and **Kalotaritissa** on the west coast are especially delightful; **Moúros** and **Ammoúdi** on the south coast are also popular.

# Aegiáli

Small, charming **Aegiáli** (ΑΙΓΙΑΛΗ), also known as **Ormós Aegiáli**, is Amorgós' northern port and main resort, thanks to the island's one genuine sandy beach, its striking views over the great granite lump, the islet **Nikouriá**, once a leper colony. Like Katápola, Aegiáli is hidden from view until you enter its horseshoe bay, and there it sits in splendour, a picture-perfect Cycladic town, complete with blue-domed church. You can follow the path over the headlands to a series of isolated sand or shingle coves (bathing costumes optional) or take a boat excursion to quieter beaches.

From Aegiáli you can take in the scant remains of ancient Aegiáli or take the bus to the pretty hill villages of **Tholária**, named for its vaulted *tholos* tombs from the Roman period, and **Langáda**, one of the island's prettiest villages, under a rocky thumb similar to Chóra. A circular walk along the herb-scented hill ridge links them and the port; the section from Langáda's church of the Panagía to Tholária poignantly passes through 'the valley of the old, useless, doomed donkeys' and takes about an hour and a half. From Langáda a path leads up to the decapitated windmills, by way of a frescoed cave church, **Yero Stavros**; another path leads out east in about an hour to frescoed **Ag. Ioannis Theológos**, an 8th-century monastery, recently restored; one window is a replica of Aghia Sophia in Istanbul. The path continues to another church, **Stávros**, and down to an abandoned bauxite mine.

# Between Amorgós and Náxos: the Back Islands

Between Amorgós and Náxos lie a bevy of tiny islands known as the Back Islands because they're in the back of beyond – Schinoússa, Koufoníssi, Donoússa and Heráklia (or Iráklia) are the four inhabited ones. Once a hide-out for pirates and wartime partisans, they are now firmly on the holiday map. All have post offices to change money and most have tourist agencies. They are quiet off season, with sandy beaches and wonderful walking country, but don't arrive in August without booking.

## Koufoníssi (ΚΟΥΦΟΝΗΣΙ)

Koufoníssi is tiny and flat – you can walk around it in three hours – and it has a thriving fishing fleet. It exerts such a compelling charm on its visitors that many can't stay away. Once the hideaway of intrepid independent travellers, it's now jammed in July and August with trendy Athenians and Italians into spear-fishing and perfecting their tans. The *meltémi* rages at exactly the same time, and has been known to launch tents into space from the free but unsheltered campsite by Fínikas Beach.

## Getting There

**By sea**: the islands are served daily in summer by the *Skopelitis*, which rolls its way between Náxos and Amorgós, and the occasional **ferry** from Piraeus. When it operates, the **hydrofoil** from Amorgós also calls in at the islands apart from Donoússa. Wherever you are coming from, and whatever your destination, if you get off at one of the back islands, you'll be spending the night there, unless you take a day trip from Náxos. **Port authority** (Náxos): **t** 028 502 2300.

## Tourist Information

**Koufoníssi**: The **Prassinos agency** next door to post office, **t** 028 507 1438. Changes money, sells ferry tickets on the quay and runs excursions. **Koufoníssi Tours, t/f** 028 507 4091 can help with accommodation.

**Schinoússa**: The **Grispos Tourist Center** in Chóra, **t** 028 507 1930, **f** 028 507 1176, at the top of the mule path from Myrsíni, is run from a mini-market, which arranges accommodation, ferry tickets and round-island trips. **Port Authority: t** 028 502 2300.

**Heráklia**: Most of the island's tourist infrastructure is at Livádi. **Gavalos Tours, t/f** 028 507 1561 may help you find a room.

## Where to Stay

**Koufoníssi** ✉ 84300

Small new hotels and studios are sprouting up like crazy, and most offer generous off-season discounts.

**Villa Ostria**, at Ag. Geórgiou, **t/f** 028 507 1671 (*exp*). Pretty veranda over the sea and comfortable rooms, with fridges.

**Keros Studios, t** 028 507 1600 (*exp in season*). Neo-Cycladic, with a garden and seaside bar.

**Christina's House, t** 028 507 1736 (*mod*). Similar but on a more modest scale.

**Petros Club, t** 028 507 1728 (*mod*). Near the sea, with a large garden and restaurant; mini-bars in each room. *Open July–Sept.*

**Finikas, t** 028 507 1368 (*C; mod*). Self-contained double rooms in a cluster of white buildings near Fínikas Beach; the owner meets ferries with his truck.

**Katerina**, just up the hill from the port, **t** 028 507 1455 (*mod*). Ebullient landlady.

**Hondros Kavos, t** 028 507 1707 (*mod*). Brand new.

**E. N. Simos, t** 028 507 1445 (*mod*). Also brand new.

**Camping Charakópou, t** 028 507 1683. With simple facilities. There's also a free campsite east of the port behind Finikas Beach, with two areas each fronted by tavernas.

The enchanting one and only village, on a hill above the quay, has its back to the sea. Life centres on the cobbled main street; in summer it turns into a big party, with fashionable island-hoppers carousing at the taverna tables. Koufoníssi has gorgeous beaches, some with shade, tucked under golden rocks eroded into bulging *mille feuille* pastries. The first, **Fínikas**, east of the village, is lined with sleeping bags in high season. Over a rocky spit there are two more lovely beaches, **Charakópou** and **Porí**. There are daily excursions in season on the caique *Prásinos* to **Káto Koufoníssi**, the island opposite, for skinny dipping and the occasional excursion to the beaches on the island of **Kéros**. This has the ruins of a Neolithic settlement at **Daskálio**, where the 'Treasure of Kéros' was unearthed in the 1950s and 60s, producing many fine Cycladic figurines (including the famous 'Harpist' in the Archaeology Museum in Athens). There's also an abandoned medieval settlement in the north.

## Schinoússa (ΣΧΟΙΝΟΥΣΣΑ)

**Schinoússa** is scenically less attractive than the other small islands, but it's still very Greek and charming. There are only 85 inhabitants in winter, increasing in summer to

### Schinoússa

**Anesi**, in Chóra, t 028 507 1180 (*mod*). On the main street with wonderful views.

**Provaloma**, just outside Chóra, t 028 507 1936 (*mod*). Offers more fine views, mini-bus service, rooms with bath, and a good taverna, with an old-fashioned stone oven.

**Panorama Taverna**. Rooms to let (*inexp*), basic home cooking and great views to Tsigoúra.

**Grispos Beach Villa**, in Tsigoúra, t 028 507 1930 (*inexp*). Run by the tourist agency.

### Heráklia

**Zografos**, 700m back from the sea in Livádi, t 028 507 1946 (*mod*). Rooms with verandas, baths, fridges and a communal barbecue.

**Mary**, in Livádi, t 028 507 1485 (*inexp*). Rooms and apartments. The owner meets ferries.

**Livadi**, on the beach. Rooms to let (*inexp*). Also serves good food and plays old *rembétika* songs. The owner Geórgios organizes boat trips to Alimniás Beach and meets ferries.

**Angelos**, t 028 507 1486. More inexpensive rooms in the village.

## Eating Out

### Koufoníssi

**Taverna Melissa**, on the main street. Best food on the island, serving Greek favourites.

**Lefteris**, on the waterfront. Popular for its food and setting.

*Ouzerie*, in the village. Serving octopus, kalamári and shrimps from an outside brazier. *Open eves only*.

**The Mill**. An old windmill atop the village converted into a bar; a great place to watch the sun set, and in the summer, nights in the bars are rarely dull.

### Schinoússa

**To Kentro**. General store-cum-*kafeneíon* where the locals play backgammon. Serves beer, snacks and pungent home-made cheese.

**Skhinoussa**. The usual Greek fare and pizzas.

**Taverna Myrsíni**, in Myrsíni, t 028 507 1154. Its spartan kitchen conjures up delicious seafood in the evenings and it doubles as a left-luggage store by day.

*Meltémi*. Good food and nice views.

### Heráklia

**Melissa**, in Ag. Geórgios t 028 507 1539/1561. Taverna with a good budget menu, *kafeneíon* and general store. Has basic rooms upstairs.

**Kordalou Taverna**, t 028 507 1488. Another decent taverna with cheap rooms above.

**Dimitris Gavalas**. The best eating place with Greek dishes, sometimes pizza, served beneath the pine tree.

around 200, most of them farmers trying to make ends meet. Ferries dock at the tiny port of **Myrsíni**, but the main settlement is **Chóra**, also known as **Panagía**, less than a mile up the hill, where village life goes on regardless of tourists. You can take the old cobbled mule track for a short-cut, but it's a hot hike in summer. From there a steep track runs down to the grey sand beach at **Tsigoúra**, with a rather expensive taverna and disco. There are about seventeen beaches on the island, many bleak and littered by the wind, but **Psilí Ámmos** is worth the 45-minute walk from Chóra across the island, via the ghost hamlet of **Messariá**. A rough track takes you to the duny sands with turquoise waters; in summer it's a favourite unofficial camping spot.

# Donoússa (ΔΟΝΟΥΣΑ)

**Donoússa**, due east of Náxos, and northernmost of the chain, is even more remote and has fewer ferry links. Larger and more mountainous, it's a good place for walkers and hermits; most of the tourists so far are German. **Donoússa** (or Stávros), the port and village, has rooms, tavernas and a shop; the sandy beach **Kédros** is a 15-minute walk. Resources are stretched with the influx of tourists in high season. There's a summer-only bakery, but food and water can get scarce. A Geometric-era settlement (900–700 BC) was excavated by Vathí Limenarí, but most visitors come for the fine beaches, at **Livádi** and **Fýkio**, reached in two hours on foot via the hamlets of **Charavgí** and **Mersíni** (or 20 minutes by caique); **Kalotarítissa** beach, is an hour's walk north.

# Heráklia (ΗΡΑΚΛΕΙΑ)

**Heraklía**, the most westerly and largest of the Back Islands, is only an hour's ferry hop from Náxos, but even in mid-August it remains quiet and inviting. Unusually for the Cyclades, it's a good time to visit and join in the Festival of the Panagía on 15 August, with three days of non-stop eating, drinking and dancing. The attractive port, **Ag. Geórgios**, is set in the hills, with a small beach and a little fishing fleet. From here it's a 20-minute walk to the large sandy beach at **Livádi**, popular with Greeks and campers. The old Chóra, **Panagía**, named after its main church, is about an hour's walk into the hills. It's pretty and sleepy, but primitive and unlikely to have rooms. There is, however, an excellent **bakery** – the baker picks wild sesame seeds for his bread on his journey from the port. From Panagía a path leads to sandy **Alimniás Beach**. Another excursion is the three-hour walk along the mule path, southwest from Ag. Geórgios to the large stalactite cave of **Ag. Ioánnis**, overlooking Vourkaria Bay, with two chambers over 240ft long; the chapel at the entrance sees a huge *panegýri* on 28 August.

# Anáfi (ΑΝΑΦΗ)

**Anáfi**, the most southerly of the Cyclades, looks like a tadpole, but with a tail swollen like the Rock of Gibraltar. It is a friendly and unpretentious island, the ideal place for peace and solitude. If the crowds and noise seem too thick elsewhere, Anáfi may be the antidote: the islanders go about their lives as they always have, with few conces-sions to tourism. But be warned, if the weather breaks, ferries may not dock and you could get marooned, so allow plenty of time to get back. Little contact with the outside world has meant that old customs have been preserved, and scholars have found in the Anáfiots' songs and festivals traces of the ancient worship of Apollo.

## History

In the 15th century BC, Anáfi gained a certain stature in the form of volcanic rock, 517ft thick in places, carried to the island by wind and tidal wave after the explosion of Santoríni. The twelfth Duke of Náxos, Giacomo Crispi, gave Anáfi to his brother who built a castle, but it had little effect when Barbarossa turned up in 1537 and enslaved the population. Anáfi remained deserted for a long time after that. When King Otho arrived in Athens, he asked for the best Greek builders to build him a place, and he was sent a contingent of Anáfiots, who built themselves the delightful neigh-bourhood Anafiótika at the foot of the Acropolis, taking advantage of the law that stated that if you could erect four walls and a roof by sunrise, the place was yours.

## Around the Island

The island's one village, quiet, laid back **Chóra** (pop. 260), an amphitheatre of white domed houses and windmills with views all around, is a short steep walk up from the landing, **Ag. Nikólaos**, although the new road and a bus makes life considerably easier. Guglielmo Crispi's half-ruined **Kástro** is to the north of the village; a path leads to its rocky height. There are attractive **beaches** along the coast around Ag. Nikólaos, from **Klisídi** east of the port, to a range of bays signposted from the Chóra road and littered with freelance campers. The only spring is at **Vagia**, on the west coast.

The favourite path on Anáfi runs east of Chóra to **Kastélli** (about two hours), site of the ancient town and the country chapel **Panagía tou Doráki**, decorated with a pair of Roman sarcophagi and the trunk of a statue. Another hour's walking from Kastélli,

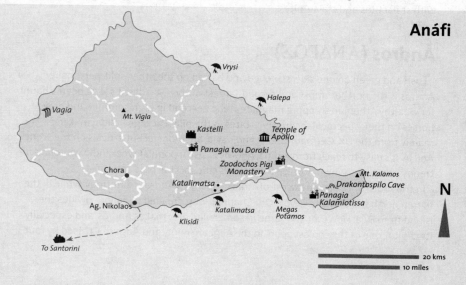

**Anáfi**

Vrysi

Halepa

Vagia

Mt. Vigla

Kastelli

Temple of Apollo

Panagia tou Doraki

Zoodochos Pigi Monastery

Mt. Kalamos

Drakontospilo Cave

Chora

Katalimatsa

Panagia Kalamiotissa

Ag. Nikolaos

Katalimatsa

Megas Potamos

Klisidi

To Santorini

N

20 kms

10 miles

## Getting There and Around

By sea: ferry connections 6 times a week connecting with Santoríni, 5 times a week with Íos, Náxos and Páros, 4 times a week with Piraeus, twice a week with Folégandros, Síkinos and Sýros. Weekly connection in high season with the Dodecanese Islands. **Port authority, t** 028 606 1216. **Buses** are few and there are no taxis. For **motorbike** rentals, call **t** 028 606 1292. In the busy season, caiques in Ag. Nikólaos do trips to all the local beaches.

## Tourist Information

**Zeyzed Travel**, in the port, **t** 028 606 1253, **f** 028 606 1352. The best help with accommodation, in the absence of an official booth.

## Festivals

**8 Sept**: Panagía at the monastery, known for its authentic folk-dances.

## Where to Stay

**Anáfi** ✉ **84009**

Room-owners travel down from Chóra by bus or car to meet ferries.

**Villa Apollon**, above Klisídi Beach, **t** 028 606 1348, out of season **t** 010 993 6150, **f** 028 606 1287 (*mod*). Classy, with garden, verandas and fridges in each room. *Open May–Oct.*

**Anatoli**, in Chóra, **t** 028 606 1279 (*mod–inexp*). Rooms with verandas.

**Ta Plagia**, up by Chóra, **t** 028 606 1308, out of season **t** 010 412 7113 (*inexp*). Similar, with a restaurant. *Open May–Sept.*

## Eating Out

Everything has to be imported, so prices are higher. Count on €15 for a meal, more for fish.

**To Steki** in Chóra. Cheap and cheerful.

**Alexandra**. More upmarket.

**Kyriakos**. Another good option for dinner.

**Roussos** in Ag. Nikólaos.

past the ruined hamlet of **Katalimátsa**, will bring you to the summit of the tremendous tadpole-tail, **Mount Kálamos**. Along the way, huge square blocks mark the temple of Apollo Aiglitos. Other blocks went into the construction of the nearby **Monastery of Zoodóchos Pigí**. On top of Kálamos, the pretty 16th-century **Monastery of Panagía Kalamiótissa** (1,476ft over the sea) is Anáfi's most important, built where an icon of the Virgin was found hanging on a cane; it enjoys tremendous views, especially sunrises. Nearby you can poke around in an old dragon's lair, the **Drakontóspilo**, with stalactites and stalagmites.

# Ándros (ΑΝΔΡΟΣ)

Lush and green on one side, scorched and barren on the other, split-personality Ándros is the northernmost and second-largest of the Cyclades. It's long been a haunt for wealthy Athenian shipping magnates who descend in high summer and breed horses on their spectacular country estates in the hills. Package holidaymakers, mainly from the UK, Germany and Scandinavia, are more recent arrivals on the scene. And as it's easy to reach from Rafína, Ándros is also a popular weekend playground for trendy Athenians who patronize the island's chic cocktail bars and cafés.

In the south only the narrowest of straits separates Ándros from Tínos, while in the barren north the blustery Cavo d'Oro Channel, long dreaded by sailors, divides the island from Évia. However, the same irksome wind also makes Ándros, and especially its capital, one of the coolest spots in the Aegean in July and August. Crossed by four parallel mountain ridges, it has green valleys; water gushes from the mossy springs of the villages; flowers and forests cover the south. Fields are divided by unique dry stone walls, *xerolithiés*. Ándros is a prosperous island, well-ordered and adorned with white dovecotes first built by the Venetians and famed for its captains.

## History

Originally known as Hydroussa ('watery'), the island is thought to derive its name from the Phoenician Arados, or from Andrea, the general sent by Rhadamanthys of Crete to govern it. In 1000 BC Ionians colonized Ándros, leading to its early cultural bloom in the Archaic period. Dionysos was the most popular god worshipped at the pantheon of Palaiopolis, the leading city at the time, and a temple of his had the amazing talent of turning spring water into wine during the festival of the Dionysia.

For most of the rest of its history, Ándros has been the square peg in a round archipelago. After the Athenian victory at Salamis, Themistocles fined Ándros for supporting Xerxes. The Andrians refused to pay and Themistocles besieged the island,

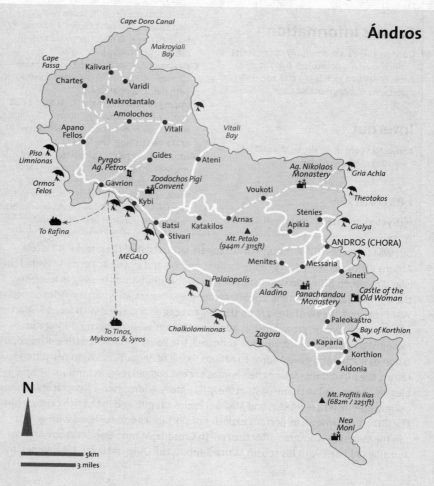

**Ándros**

Cape Doro Canal

Makroyiali Bay

Cape Fassa

Kalivari

Chartes

Varidi

Makrotantalo

Amolochos

Apano Fellos

Vitali

Vitali Bay

Piso Limnionas

Pyrgos Ag. Petros

Gides

Ateni

Ag. Nikolaos Monastery

Gria Achla

Ormos Felos

Gavrion

Zoodochos Pigi Convent

Voukoti

Theotokos

Kybi

Stenies

To Rafina

Batsi

Katakilos

Arnas

Apikia

Gialya

Stivari

Mt. Petalo (944m / 3115ft)

ANDROS (CHORA)

MEGALO

Menites

Messaria

Sineti

Palaiopolis

Aladino

Panachrandou Monastery

Castle of the Old Woman

To Tinos, Mykonos & Syros

Chalkolominonas

Zagora

Paleokastro

Bay of Korthion

Kaparia

Korthion

Aidonia

Mt. Profitis Ilias (682m / 2251ft)

N

Nea Moni

5km
3 miles

# Getting There and Around

**By sea:** several daily **ferry**, **catamaran**, and **hydrofoil** connections with Rafína, Tínos and Mýkonos, and daily via Mýkonos to Náxos, Páros, Íos, Santoríni and Sýros. Infrequently with Amorgós and Chíos. **Port authority** (Gávrion): t 028 207 1213.

**By road: buses** (t 028 202 2316) run from Chóra to Batsí, Gávrion, Apoíkia, Strapouriés, Steniés, and Kórthi; buses for Batsí, Chóra and Kórthi leave from near the dock at Gávrion, linking with the ferries. **Cars** and **bikes** are widely available for rent. In Gávrion try **Tassos Rent A Car**, t 028 207 1040, f 028 207 1165; in Batsí, **Hermes**, t 028 204 2070; in Chóra, **Riva Rent A Bike**, t 028 202 4412. **Taxis:** in Gávrion, t 028 207 1561. In Batsí: t 028 204 1081.

## Tourist Information

**Gávrion:** there's a sporadically open tourist office in an old dovecote, t 028 207 1785. **Batsí: Greek Sun Holidays**, t 028 204 1198. For accommodation, rentals and excursions.

## Internet

**AndrosNet Center**, Korthi, t 028 206 2148, *info@androsnetcenter.gr*.

## Festivals

**15 days before Easter:** Theoskepastí, Chóra.

**19 June** (date varies): Análipsis, Ándros Town.
**15 Aug:** Kórthinon.
**23 Aug:** Ménites.

## Where to Stay and Eat

Like Kéa, Ándros is an island where the tourism infrastructure is geared to long-term stays, and it may be difficult, especially in the capital, to find a place that will let you stay for only a few nights. Although attractive Batsí is the tourist centre, Andros Town is charming and a better bet for a genuine Greek experience. Also, most of its hotels are open all year.

### Gávrion ☒ 84501

**Ándros Holiday**, on the beach, t 028 207 1443, *androshol@otenet.gr* (*B; lux*). Smart, with half-board, pool, tennis, sauna and gym.

**Ostria Studios**, just out of town, t 028 207 1551, f 028 207 1554 (*C; exp*). Upmarket self-catering apartments .

**Galaxias**, on the waterfront, t 028 207 1228 (*D; mod–inexp*). Also has a good taverna, with house specialities.

**Camping Ándros**, along the Batsí road, t 028 207 1444. In an attractive site with a mini-market, swimming pool, excellent taverna and a van to meet the ferries.

**Karlos**, halfway to the campsite. Excellent restaurant hidden away, where the locals come for traditional dishes and low prices.

**Sunset**, en route to the Ándros Holiday Hotel. Try the Ándros speciality, *froutália*, omelette made with potatoes and local sausage.

---

but was unsuccessful. Although the islanders later assisted the Greeks at Plateía, Athens continued to hold a grudge against Ándros, and in 448 BC Pericles divided the island between Athenian colonists, who taxed the inhabitants heavily. In response, the Andrians abetted Athens' enemies whenever they could: when the Peloponnesian War broke out, they withdrew from the Delian League and sided with Sparta. Spartan oppression, however, proved just as awful and things were no better during the Hellenistic rulers. For resisting their conquest, the Romans banished the entire population to Boetia, and gave Ándros to Attalos I, King of Pergamon. When permitted to return, the inhabitants found their homes sacked and pillaged. Byzantium proved a blessing compared with the past: in the 5th century Ándros had a Neoplatonic philosophy academy, where Proclos and Michael Psellos taught, and in the 11th century (until the 18th) it became an important exporter of silk fabrics embroidered with gold.

In the Venetian land-grab after the Fourth Crusade, Marino Dandolo took Ándros and allied himself with his cousin Marco Sanudo, the Duke of Náxos. Later Venetian

Batsí ✉ 84503
**Skouna, t** 028 204 1240 (C; exp). Small but a good seafront bet.
**Aneroussa, t** 028 204 1044, **f** 028 204 1444 (exp–mod). Refined, shaded by banana groves, it tops the cliff at Apróvato like an iced cake and has its own private sands next to Delavóyos Beach, popular with nudists.
**Chryssi Akti, t** 028 204 1236, **f** 028 204 1628 (C; mod). Reasonable, and also on the beach. The wide range of eateries do justice to Ándros' old reputation as an island of chefs.
**Stamatis.** Good food and rooftop views over the harbour.
**Takis.** The town's hotspot for fish.

Ándros Town/Chóra ✉ 84500
**Paradise, t** 028 202 2187, **f** 028 202 2340 (B; exp). Graceful, Neoclassical confection, with a pool, tennis and air-conditioned rooms.
**Irene's Villas,** by the sea, **t** 028 202 3344 (exp–mod). Charming, set in flower gardens.
**Aegli, t** 028 202 2303, **f** 028 202 2159 (C; mod). Traditional place between the two squares, is also air-conditioned. Open all year.
**Elli,** in the seaside Plakoúra area, **t** 028 202 2213, **f** 028 202 4412 (studios lux, rooms mod–exp). Well-placed and friendly.
**Parea** on the main square. Cosy taverna, with excellent Greek menu.
**Archipelagos,** on the edge of town towards Giálya Beach. Where the locals head for great traditional food, service and prices.
**Palinorio,** at Embório. Also popular with locals, serving everything from beans to lobster.

**Onónas,** at Embório. Good place for ouzo and snacks before dining.

Apíkia ✉ 84500
**Pigi Sarisa, t** 028 202 3799, **f** 028 202 2476, pighi@athserve.otenet.gr (B; mod). Swish, almost on top of the famous mineral spring; a holiday complex with a pool and games facilities, restaurant and minibus for transfers. Open all year.
**Restaurant Tassos** at Ménites. Tables overlooking the stream and specialities like froutália and tomatoes stuffed with chicken.

Kórthion ✉ 84502
**Korthion,** right on the sea, **t** 028 206 1218, **f** 028 20 61118 (C; mod–inexp). Family run, spotless and with a restaurant.
**Villa Korthi,** in spitting distance of the sea, **t** 028 206 1122, **f** 028 206 2022 (mod). Another pleasant choice, all blue and white.

## Entertainment and Nightlife

Ándros, especially Batsí, is full of slick cocktail bars and discos which change names from season to season, or there are organized **Greek nights** at 3 tavernas in Katákilos above Batsí. Batsí also has an open-air **cinema**. In Chóra, nightlife is more Greek-orientated, centring round the bars and clubs. **Vegera, Soleil** and **Cavo del Mar** are all outdoors bars with chill-out music and sunset views.

rulers were nasty and incompetent and Barbarossa easily took the island in 1530. Apart from collecting taxes, the Turks left it to its own devices, and 10,000 Albanians, many from nearby Kárystos (Évia) settled on Ándros. In 1821 Ándros' famous son, the philosopher Theóphilos Kaíris, declared the revolution at the cathedral of Ándros, and the island contributed large sums of money and weapons to the struggle. In 1943 the Germans bombed the island for two days when the Italians refused to surrender.

# Gávrion and the West Coast

All ferries dock at the main port, **Gávrion** (ΓABPIO), on the northwest coast. From Gávrion, it's a 40-minute walk east up the **Pyrgós Ag. Pétros,** the best-preserved ancient monument on Ándros. Dating from the Hellenistic era, this mysterious tower stands 70ft high – the upper storeys were reached by ladder – and its inner hall is still crowned by a corbelled dome. The landscape around here squirms with stone walls, or *xerolithiés*, resembling huge caterpillars. There are good beaches to the north: **Ormos Felós** is the best but Athenians are developing the coastline with villas. **Amólochos**, on the road to the remote beach at Vitáli Bay, is a beautiful isolated mountain village.

**Kybí**, south of Gávrion, is another fine sandy beach, near the junction for the 14th-century Convent of **Zoodóchos Pigí**, 'Spring of Life', which has impressive icons. A handful of nuns run a weaving factory (*open until noon*). Further down the coast, **Batsí** (ΜΠΑΤΣΙ), built around a sweeping sandy bay, is Ándros' biggest resort, with a little fishing harbour and a cute, rather artificial charm oozing from its maze of narrow lanes. The BBC TV series *Greek Language and People* put it on the map, and it's been very popular with UK package companies ever since. The tree-fringed town beach gets busy with families, so head along the coastal track to **Delavóyas Beach** for an all-over tan. From Batsí a road ascends to shady **Arnás**, a garden village on the northern slopes of Ándros' highest peak, Mount Pétalo (3,115ft).

**Palaiópolis**, 9km down the coast, was the original capital of Ándros, founded by the Minoans and inhabited until *c.* 1000 AD when the people moved to Mesariá. An earthquake in the 4th century AD destroyed part of it, and over the years pirates mopped up the rest. The current edition of Palaiópolis is on top of a steep hill, from where 1,039 steps lead down to the ancient site, partly underwater. The road to Chóra continues through rolling countryside dotted with dovecotes and the ruined stone tower-houses of the Byzantine and Venetian ruling classes.

Further down the west coast, **Zagora** (ΖΑΓΟΡΑ) was inhabited until the 8th century BC, when it boasted a population of 4,000. It was solidly defended; sheer cliffs surrounded it on three sides and on the fourth a mighty wall was built. Within, inhabitants lived in flat-roofed houses (some remains still exist) and cultivated the fields outside. Excavated by Australians in the 1960s, finds are now in the island's museum.

# Ándros Town/Chóra

The capital, **Ándros** (ΑΝΔΡΟΣ) or **Chóra** (ΧΩΡΑ), sits on a narrow tongue of land, decorated with the grand Neoclassical mansions of ship-owning families; between the two world wars, the Andrians owned one out of five Greek merchant ships. One of their legacies is a rare sense of public spiritedness and tidiness. At the edge of town, a stone arch is all that survives of the bridge to the Venetian castle, **Mésa Kástro**, built by Marino Dandolo and damaged in the 1943 bombardment; the ruins are guarded by the statue of the **Unknown Sailor** by Michael Tómbros in **Plateía Ríva**. There's a small **museum** dedicated to Ándros' seafaring history (*ask around for the key*). **Káto Kástro**, the maze of streets that form the medieval city and the mansions of the Ríva district are wedged between **Parapórti** and **Embórios** bays, with steps down from the central square, **Plateía Kaíri**. These beaches are sandy but often windswept, and holiday bungalows and trendy restaurants are springing up at Embórios.

The pedestrianized main street, paved with marble slabs, is lined with old mansions converted into public offices; post and telephone offices and banks are in the centre of town, and the bus station and outdoor cinema just a few steps away. A small white church, **Ag. Thalassíni**, guards one end of Embórios harbour from a throne of rock. The cathedral, **Ag. Geórgios**, is built on the ruins of a 17th-century church. A legend is told about a third church, **Theoskepastí**, built in 1555. When the wood for its roof arrived in Ándros from Piraeus, the priest couldn't afford the price demanded by the ship's captain. Angrily, the captain set sail again, only to run into a fierce tempest. The sailors prayed to the Virgin Mary, promising to bring the wood back to Ándros should she save their lives. Instantly the sea grew calm again, and Theoskepastí, or 'Sheltered by God', was completed without further difficulty. It was dedicated to the Virgin Mary, who apparently is on a hotline to the miracle-working icon inside the church.

Just north of Plateía Kaíris are the museums endowed by Basil and Elise Goulándris of the ship-owning dynasty. The **Archaeology Museum** (*t 028 202 3664; open Tues–Sun 8.30–3; adm*) houses the outstanding *Hermes Psychopompos*, Conductor of the Dead, a 2nd-century BC copy of a Praxiteles original, discovered by farmers in Palaiópolis. Other exhibits include the *Matron of Herculaneum*, finds from the ancient cities of Zagora and Palaiópolis, architectural illustrations and pottery collections. The island's other gem, the **Museum of Modern Art**, in Plateía Kaíris (*t 028 202 2650; open Wed–Mon, 10–2 and 6–9*) occupies two buildings, with exhibitions of international modern artists, contemporary Greek artists, and sculptures by Michael Tómbros.

# Villages Along the East Coast

Lovely villages surround Chóra: **Steniés**, 6km north, is the island's most beautiful village, its pedestrianized lanes heavy with the scent of blossoms in spring. A few mulberries remain; in the old silk-making days the precious cocoons would be brought into the houses in the winter to keep them warm. The sandy beach, **Gialyá**, is close by, with a good and affordable fish taverna. The famous Sáriza mineral water flows in the hill village of **Apíkia**, above Steniés. The village owns the 16th-century **Ag. Nikólaos Monastery** to the north (*proper attire only*).

The main road west passes through farming villages of the fertile **Messariá Valley**. One old custom may still be heard: in the evening after a hard day's work, the patriarch will pipe the family home from the fields. **Messariá** itself has a Byzantine church, **Taxiárchis** built in 1158 by Emperor Emmanuel Comnenus. Another church, **Ag. Nikólaos**, has an icon made from an 18th-century faith-healing nun's hair. Further west, lush **Ménites** has springs gushing from marble fountains, and the church of **Panagías tis Kóumoulous**, the 'Virgin of the Plentiful', which may have been the site of Dionysos' miraculous water-to-wine temple. The village is known for its nightingales, spreading trees and the most important monastery on Ándros, **Panachrándou** – an hour's steep walk away. Now home to three monks, it was founded after Niképhoros Phokás' liberation of Crete in AD 961, and supposedly visited by the emperor himself. Southwest of Messariá, at **Aladinó**, you can visit a stalactite cave called Cháos.

The **Bay of Kórthion** (ΟΡΜΟΣ ΚΟΡΘΙ) is 30km southeast of Chóra, at the bottom of a lush valley with a beach and some modest tourist development. North of the bay, the ruined Venetian fort is known as the **Castle of the Old Woman**, after a gritty old lady who abhorred the Venetians. She tricked them into letting her inside the fort and then opened the door to the Turks. Appalled at the subsequent slaughter of the Venetians, she leapt from the castle and landed on a rock now known as '**Tis Grias to Pidema**' or 'Old Lady's Leap'. The inland villages of **Kapariá** and **Aidónia** have the island's prettiest dovecotes.

# Folégandros (ΦΟΛΕΓΑΝΔΡΟΣ)

Arid and mountainous, long an island of exile – Socialist Prime Minister George Papandréou, father of Andréas, was once an unwilling guest – Folégandros is now a great place to get away from it all by choice. With sheer cliffs and a breathtaking Chóra built to defy pirates, it's one of the most alluring of the Cyclades and the perfect base since 1984 for the Cycladic Centre of Art. With only 300 inhabitants (down from 4,000 in the 1940s) Folégandros is one of the smallest Greek islands with a permanent population, swollen in the summer with Danes, Italians and others

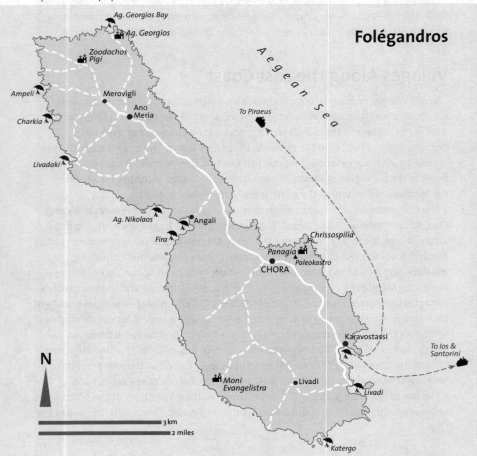

## Getting There and Around

**By sea:** 4–5 times a week to Piraeus, Íos and Santoríni; less frequently to Kímolos, Mílos, Sífnos, Sérifos, Kýthnos, Páros and Náxos. Excursions to Ag. Nikólaos, other beaches and Sikínos. **Port authority: t** 028 604 1249.

**By road:** the island **buses** link the port Karavostássi to Chóra and meets all ferries, even late ones; another bus goes from Chóra to Angáli and Áno Meriá. Caiques take passengers for trips around the island or to nearby beaches.

## Tourist Information

**Sottovento Agency,** in Chóra, near the Áno Meriá bus, **t** 028 604 1444, **f** 028 604 1430. Very helpful and speak English.

**Maraki Travel, t** 028 604 1273. Exchanges money (as of 2002 there are no banks) and has **Internet** access.

## Festivals

**Easter:** an icon is paraded and trips are made in boats around the island.
**27 July:** Ag. Panteleím, in Áno Meriá.
**15 Aug:** Panagía.

## Where to Stay and Eat

**Folégandros** ✉ **84011**

Folégandros has more accommodation every year, but there's never enough in the summer (even in the campsite) so be prepared to sleep out (beware the strong winds). However, the restaurants are better than average, thanks to a lack of package hotels and daytrippers.

### Karovostássi

**Aeolos, t** 028 604 1205, **f** 028 604 1336, book in Athens, **t** 010 922 3819 (*C; mod*). Immaculate rooms overlooking the beach; lovely garden.

**Vardia Bay Studios, t** 028 604 1277, book in Athens, **t** 010 684 2524, **f** 010 685 3456 (*mod*). Well kept.

**Vrachos,** on the sea, **t** 028 604 1450, **f** 028 604 1304 (*C; mod*). Airy rooms that come with verandas and mini-bars.

**Camping Livadi,** 1km beyond Karavostássi, **t** 028 604 1204. Taverna, bar and laundry.

**Kati Allo.** For traditional cuisine.

### Chóra

**Anemomílos Apartments, t** 028 604 1309, **f** 028 604 1407 (*B; exp*). Newly built in traditional style, with balconies over the sea. Also an apartment for disabled travellers.

seeking genuine island life or partied out by the fleshpots of Íos. In myth, Folégandros was a son of King Minos of Crete, and his legacy can be seen in the labyrinthine paths across the island, laid out to confound invaders. Linguists, however, say the name Folégandros comes from the Phoenician Phelekguduri, 'rock-built'; one ancient nickname was Aratos, 'the Iron-bound'. Many of the landscapes look as if they had been whipped to a froth by a furious god, then suddenly petrified, an effect curiously softened by a smattering of churches with breast-shaped domes.

### Around the Island

Boats land at **Karavostássi**, the tiny east coast harbour, with a tree-fringed pebbly beach. Shady **Livádi** Beach is a 15-minute walk from the port, while pretty **Katérgo** Beach is another 45 minutes. A path from the inland hamlet of Livádi takes an hour to remote **Evangelístra Monastery**, dominating the island's rocky southern shores.

An improved road leads up to **Chóra**, the capital, a stunning sight perched on the pirate-proof, 1,000ft-high cliffs; the tall houses turn their backs on the sea, fused along the ridge with a sheer drop below. Part of the charm is the lack of cars (confined to the periphery) and life revolves around four interlinking squares. The first, shaded by rowan trees, is the hub of nocturnal action; the second is quieter;

**Folégandros Apartments, t** 028 604 1239, *foleaps@ath.forthnet.gr* (C; *exp–mod*). Built in Cycladic style around a courtyard.

**Castro**, in the Kástro, **t/f** 028 604 1230, (*B; mod*). A gem – lovely 500-yr-old house owned by the same family for generations, with pebble mosaic floors. Rooms and roof terrace look down the sheer cliffs to the sea.

**Polikandia, t** 028 604 1322 (*C; mod*). Traditional-style place, rooms with minibars.

**Odysseus**, in Chóra, **t** 028 604 1276, **f** 028 604 1366 (*C; mod*). Pleasant, located on the cliffs.

**Fani-Vevis, t** 028 604 1237 (*C; mod*). A popular old mansion, now renovated.

**Pavlo's Rooms,** on the road to Chóra, **t** 028 604 1232 (*inexp*). Basic chalet-style rooms in converted stables, with a lovely garden.

**Maria, t** 028 604 1265 (*inexp*). A good bet.

**Spiridoula, t** 028 604 1078 (*inexp*).

**Nikos 'Turbo Service',** on the main square next to the Kástro. An institution, with the largest menu this side of a New York diner, washed down with Santoríni wine, all 'Turbo-served' by the wise-cracking Nikolas; live *syrtáki* music in summer and 2nd-hand books.

**To Sik**, on the second square. Good *mezédes*, dips and vegan main courses.

**Pounta**, at the bus stop at the entrance to Chóra. Charming courtyard, serving breakfast and unusual dishes, from spaghetti with Roquefort to rabbit casserole, and a choice of vegan dishes.

**O Kritikos**, on the third square. Delicious chicken on the spit; a very Greek hang-out.

**I Piatsa**. The place for backgammon as well as delicious food.

**Kellari**. A little wine bar with snacks that seems to be open all hours.

**Melissa**, between the two churches. Pleasant atmosphere. Try their speciality *strangistó*, soft Folégandros goat's cheese.

**Tavernas Iliovassilema** and **Mimis**, up in Áno Meriá, near the folk museum. Free range chicken and local specialities like *matzáta*, pasta with tomato, rooster or rabbit; the former has sunset views over Mílos.

# Entertainment and Nightlife

Chóra's bars turn into a village-wide party on summer nights.

**Avli**. Popular, smart disco.

**Pakentia**. Music bar with a lovely view, which gets jammed in high season.

**Patitiri**. Plays traditional music.

**Astarte**. Serves the local drink *rakómelo*, *rakí* with honey, still used medicinally in Greece; it won't cure a hangover, though.

the third has *kafeneía* full of locals and **Ag. Antónis** with a charming portal; the fourth houses the post office. Newer parts of town look distinctly Andalucian. The fortified **Kástro** quarter, built in the 13th century by Marco Sanudo, is a maze of dazzling alleys filled with geraniums and white houses sporting wooden balconies. There's a pretty 17th-century church, **Pantánassa**, and if you're interested in drawing classes (*May–Oct*) you can usually find the teacher, Fotis Papadopoulos up here somewhere.

From Chóra, a path climbs the hill of Paleokastro to the church of the **Panagía** (*get the key from the town hall*), set on a sheer cliff, illuminated at night. According to legend, pirates once stole an icon of the Virgin and kidnapped an islander. As they fled they capsized and drowned, all except the local who clung to the icon, floated to the foot of the cliff and built the church in gratitude, coincidentally on the site of an ancient temple to Artemis. Every year the icon goes on an island tour, to bless the fishermen's houses. The castle that stood here has gone, but beyond it, **Chríssospiliá** ('Golden Cave') has huge stalactites and legends that Barbarossa's treasure is buried in its depths. An exploration in 1988 produced no treasure, but some ancient tombs and Classical-era inscriptions. Access is difficult; ask in Chóra for a guide.

A bus, departing from the far side of town, serves the island's other settlement 5km west, **Áno Meriá** (ΑΝΩ ΜΕΡΙΑ), a string of farming hamlets surrounded by terraced fields. There is a new spiffy hotel (*the Kalistí*, **t** *028 604 1555*), some tavernas and rent rooms (*ask at the Papadópoulos Kafeneíon*) and wonderful sunsets; on a clear day you can see Crete. Áno Meriá also has an excellent **Folk Museum** (**t** *028 604 1387; open daily 5–8*) with exhibits on traditional peasant life. With decent shoes and water, you can walk to remote beaches at **Ampeli**, **Livadáki** and **Ag. Geórgios Bay**; the bus drops you at the appropriate track. Between Áno Meriá and Chóra a road descends to the main sandy beach **Angáli**, with a steep scramble down to the sands; there's a donkey-hire service at the top of the road. There are two tavernas, pine trees, rent rooms and free camping. Next door is quiet sandy **Ag. Nikólaos** Beach with a good taverna and free camping, and **Fíra**, both popular with nudists. Most of these beaches can be less strenuously reached by caique from Karavostássi.

# Íos (ΙΟΣ)

Although desperately trying to change its image from the Benidorm or Fort Lauderdale of the Aegean, Íos remains the mecca for throngs of young people who spend their days lounging on the best beach in the Cyclades and their evenings staggering from one watering hole to another. To discourage raucous parties and late-night revellers sleeping out on the beach, four lovely campsites have been provided, but rows of sleeping bags by night and naked bodies by day are still the norm. The seasonal Irish invasion is so great that the island's name has been re-interpreted as the acronym for 'Ireland Over Seas'. If you're a party animal then it's the place for you. Otherwise, despite the island's glorious sands and pretty Chóra with its blue-domed churches, you may feel disenchanted, unless you take refuge in one of the upmarket coastal resort hotels, far from the thumping discos. In early spring, when the locals reclaim it, you might find Íos as Lawrence Durrell did, full of 'silences, fractured only by some distant church bell or the braying of a mule'.

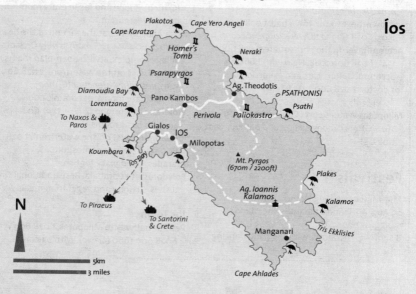

# Gialós and Íos Town

The island's name, also spelled Níos (the locals say Nío), comes from the Ionians who built cities on the sites of Gialós and Íos Town, when the island was famous for its oak forests. Over the centuries, the oaks became ships and Íos became an arid rockpile; after the earthquake of 1951, when all the water was sucked out of Íos Bay and rushed back to flood and damage Gialós, the island might have been abandoned had not the first tourists begun to trickle in.

## Getting There and Around

**By sea**: Íos is well connected. There are daily **ferries** and in summer **hydrofoil** connections with Piraeus, Santoríni, Páros, Náxos and Mýkonos, six times a week with Rafína and Sýros, four times a week with Folégandros and Síkinos, once a week with Heráklion, Crete; excursion boats to nearby islands. **Port authority**: t 028 609 1264.

**By road**: the **bus** service is the best on any island, calling at Koumbára, Gialós, Íos Town to Milapótas Beach every 10 mins all day and night; 3-day unlimited travel cards are available. Excursion buses daily to Manganári Bay. Less frequent buses to Ag. Theodotis Beach. For car rentals, **Íos Rent-a-car**, in Íos Town, t 028 609 2300, f 028 609 1088.

## Tourist Information

**Gialós port**: t 028 609 1028; *opens when ferries arrive for bookings.*
**Íos Town**: next to the town hall, t 028 609 1505, f 028 609 1228, *www.iosgreece.com.*
**Acteon Travel**: in the port square, t 028 609 1343, f 028 609 1088. Help with booking accommodation, cars and excursions.
**Íos doctor**: t 028 609 2227 (credit cards accepted!).
**Milopótas Water Sports Centre**: t 028 609 1622. Offers canoes, sailing and banana-boat rides.

## Festivals

**Mid-May**: week-long Homer festival.
**29 Aug**: Ag. Ioánnis Kálamos, the island's biggest *panegýri.*
**8 Sept**: Ag. Theodótis, with food and dancing.

## Where to Stay and Eat

**Íos** ✉ 84001

Íos, the paradise of the footloose and fancy-free, can be reasonable, though the unprepared have paid dearly for a cramped room in peak season; try the **Rooms Association**, t 028 609 1205. Generally, the young and wild head up for 'the Village', oldies and less riotous types stay down in Gialós. Most hotels operate May–Oct.

Before Guinness, Íos' speciality was *meyífra*, a hard white cheese, mixed with perfume and fermented in a goatskin – hard to find these days (all the better, some might add). Don't confuse it with *mezíthra*, the soft ricotta-like sheep's-milk cheese. But *meyífra* cheese is not the answer to Homer's riddle: what the fishermen caught was lice.

### Gialós (Ormos)

**Mare-Monte**, on the harbour, t/f 028 609 1585, (*C; mod*). Phone and fax in every room, and its own restaurant.
**Petra Apartments**, at the far end of the beach, t/f 028 609 1049 (*C; mod*). Lovely Cycladic village complex; stylish open-plan rooms.
**Poseidon**, just off the waterfront, t 028 609 1091, *poseidht@otenet.gr* (*C; mod*). Immaculate rooms; panoramic pool.
**Violetta**, t 028 609 1044 (*E; inexp*). Cheapest of all, with basic rooms.
**Íos Camping**, just off the waterfront, t 028 609 1329. Beware of mosquitoes.
**Psarades**. Good place for fish.
**Polydoros**, at Koumbára. Best traditional Greek dishes, seafood and vegetarian meals.

### Íos Town

**Petradi**, halfway to Milopótas, t 028 609 1510, f 028 609 1660 (*C; exp*). With balconies,

The port, **Gialós** (ΓΙΑΛΟΣ), or Ormós, has grov...
right. Under the Turks, its nickname was 'Little M...
loafing place for young pirates (some things nev...
note the pretty 17th-century chapel of **Ag. Iríni**, v...
altars. Gialós has a beach but it tends to be wind...
minutes or catching the bus to **Koumbára**, where...
rock that's fun for snorkelling; rooms and taverna...
desires. There are other quieter beaches sprinkled...

The Cyclades

**Íos Town**, 'the Village', is
houses, domed church
through the mist
selling rude T-
new theat
culture
rep

224

private baths and a terrace restaurant with great views over Síkinos.

**Sunrise**, on the hill, **t** 028 609 1074, **f** 028 609 1664 (*C; exp*). Stunning views over the town, with pool and bar.

**Hermes**, halfway to Milopótas, **t** 028 609 1471, **f** 028 609 1608 (*mod*). With pretty sea views and a snack bar.

**Homer's Inn** (there had to be one!), **t** 028 609 1365, **f** 028 609 1888 (*C; mod*). A good bet, with a pool.

**Afroditi**, **t/f** 028 609 1546 (*D; mod–inexp*). One of the best places for value.

**Íos Club**, on the footpath up from the harbour. Renowned for sunset views over Síkinos, good drinks, classical music and jazz.

**Pithari**, near the church. One of the best places on the island, serving excellent Greek food and barrelled wine. Just stroll into the kitchen and point out what you want.

**Pinocchio's**. Great pasta and pizza under lovely bougainvillaea.

**Vesuvius**. Another good choice for decent Italian fare, with roof garden and views.

**Lord Byron**, in the centre. An oasis of Greek tradition and sanity, specializing in an array of Anatolian *mezédes*, with *rembétiko* music.

## Milopótas Beach

**Íos Palace**, on the beach, **t** 028 609 1224, **f** 028 609 1082 (*B; lux–exp*). Designed and decorated in the old island style; two pools, tennis, billiards, jazz bar and good views.

**Dionyssos Hotel**, **t** 028 609 1630, *dionyssos@otenet.gr* (*B; exp*). Traditional style, with pool, tennis, air-con and transfer service.

**Far Out Hotel**, a few minutes from the beach, **t** 028 609 1446, *farout@otenet.gr* (*C; exp*). Named because of guests' reactions to the view; comfortable rooms in Cubist style clustered on the hillside; with a pool.

Mark...
**f** 02...
room...
The beach has 3 campsites:

**Camping Stars**, **t** 028 609 1302. With a pool and small bungalows.

**Milopótas**, **t** 028 609 1554.

**Far Out Camping**, **t** 028 609 1468, **f** 028 609 1560. Apparently just that, with a restaurant, minibus, pool, and sports facilities, incl. Íos Diving Centre – instruction, night diving, life-saving courses and bungee jumping.

## Manganári Bay

**Manganári Bungalows**, **t** 028 609 1200, **f** 010 363 1204 (*B; lux*). German-owned rooms and suites, with a restaurant and nightclub for those who like their entertainment sane and close to home. *Open June–Sept.*

**Christos**, **t** 028 609 2286. Beach taverna serving traditional Greek fare.

# Entertainment and Nightlife

'**The village**' is one long rave-up, all the bars offering different amusements from videos to rock bands and happy hours. Serious drinkers pack the main square bars after midnight and go on until dawn. Each bar/disco posts its nightly programme so you can choose. Among the classics are:

**Slammer**, in the main square.

**Jungles**. A Kiwi/Aussie bar.

**Sweet Irish Dream**. Open until the wee hours.

**Q Club**, on the way to Milopótas. Attracts late-night boppers.

**Scorpion**, down in Milopótas. Biggest disco in the Cyclades.

In more staid **Giálos**, bars tend to show videos outdoors at night, usually in English.

one of the finest in the Cyclades, a dream vision of white ... es and tall palms. It is increasingly hard to find at street level ... of overcharged hormones behind the bars, burger stands and shops ... hirts. However, Mayor Poussaios, a Homer enthusiast, has just built a ... e to host quality concerts in the hope of diluting some of the excess with ... Of the 18 original windmills behind the town, 12 remain in various states of ... ir. Traces of the ancient walls are preserved, and only bits more survive of the fortress built in 1400 by the Venetian Lord of Íos, Marco Crispi. Here **Panagía Gremiotissa**, 'Our Lady of the Cliffs', houses a miraculous icon that floated to Íos from Crete then refused to be put anywhere else, because it is the only spot on Íos from where Crete is (sometimes) visible. Amidst all the hubbub it's worth recalling a story from more innocent days. When Otho of Bavaria, the first King of Greece, paid a visit to Íos, he treated the villagers to a round of drinks in the *kafeneíon* and promised to pay to have the village cleaned up. The grateful Niots, scarcely knowing what majesty Otho pretended to, toasted him warmly: 'To the health of the King, Íos' new dustman!'

## Around the Island

Íos has 35 beaches, but only a handful of them have been developed. **Milopótas** (ΜΥΛΟΠΟΤΑΣ) is a superb sandy beach that starred in Luc Bresson's *Le Grand Bleu* and hosts every conceivable water sport, posh hotels, and campsites. Don't count on getting much shut-eye near the sands: Íos' all-night beach parties are infamous and have unfortunately ended in several deaths by overdose. For something less Babylonian, you can take a bus, hire a motorbike or catch one of the excursion boats which leave Gialós daily for the chic golden coves of **Manganári Bay**, where nudism rules and new hotels have sprouted; long, quiet **Kalamós Beach** is a 30-minute walk north on a track (do-able on a motorbike) beginning at the pretty church of **Ag. Ioánnis Kálamos**. For real isolation, walk over to **Plakés** Beach, which is often empty.

Once remote but now accessible by bus, **Ag. Theodótis** (ΑΓ. ΘΕΟΔΟΤΗΣ) has a fine beach looking out towards Heráklia island. The beach is overlooked by the ruined 15th-century Venetian fortress of **Paliokástro**, with a well-preserved Byzantine church inside. Once marauding pirates managed to bore a hole in the fortress gate, big enough to allow one man in at a time – only to be scalded to death in burning oil poured on them by the villagers; the door is on display in the church of Ag. Theodótis. The road continues to the coarse golden sands of **Psáthi**, where a church dedicated to the Virgin fell into the sea – a prophetic statement on raunchy Íos. Psáthi is a favourite for windsurfing and loggerhead turtle nests; it's now the haunt of wealthy Athenians. **Perivóla** in the middle of the island has Íos' fresh-water springs and trees. **Páno Kámbos**, once inhabited by a hundred families but today reduced to three or four, is another pretty place. Nearby in **Helliniká**, are monoliths of mysterious origin.

### Plakotós and Homer

Tradition has it that the mother of Homer came from Íos, and it was here that the great poet came at the end of his life. Some say it was a riddle told by the fishermen of Íos that killed Homer in a fit of perplexity, to wit: 'What we catch we throw away; what we don't catch, we keep' (not wanting any readers to succumb to a similar fate, the answer's in the earlier grey box). Homer's tomb is on the mountain at **Plakotós**, and although earthquakes have left only the rock on which it was built, the epitaph was copied out by ancient travellers: 'Here the earth covers the sacred head of the dean of heroes, the divine Homer.' Plakotós was an Ionian town that once had a temple to Apollo, but like the church at Psáthi it slid down the cliff. You can look down and see the ruined houses; only one tower, **Psarápyrgos**, remains intact.

## Kéa/Tzía (KEA/TZIA)

Closest of all the Cyclades to Athens, Kéa, with its fine beaches, has for many years been a favourite place for Athenians to build their summer villas – the island can be reached from the metropolis in less than four hours, and it's guaranteed to have no room on holiday weekends, when jeeps, dogs, boats and windsurfers pile off the ferries and the jet-set sails over to Vourkári from Glyfáda in a flotilla of gin palaces; if you want to make a short stay, time it for mid-week. Kéa feels very different from the other Cyclades, with lush valleys and terraces of fruit trees, fields grazed by dairy cattle and grubbing pigs; since antiquity it has been famed for its fertility, its red wines, lemons, honey and almonds. Its traditional architecture may lack the pristine white Cubism of its sister isles but there's almost a touch of Tuscany about Ioulís, with its red-pantiled houses and higgledy-piggledy lanes.

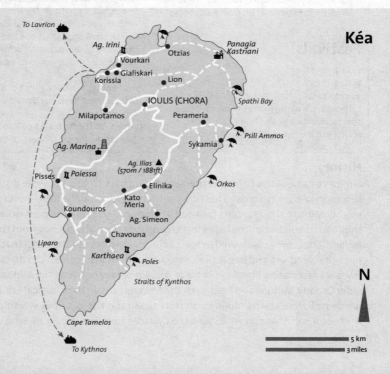

# Getting There and Around

**By sea**: at least 4 times daily **ferry** and **Flying Cat** (75 mins) connections with Lávrion (passing by sinister Makrónissos, a prison island and torture chamber used in the Civil War and by the Junta; poet Ioánnis Rítsos spent years there); 3–4 times a week to Kýthnos and once a week to Sýros. Daily hydrofoil service in summer with Kýthnos and Piraeus (Zéa). **Port authority: t** 028 802 1344.

**By road**: the **bus** runs 3–4 times daily from Ioulís to Vourkári, and is seldom seen anywhere else; the tourist police have the ever-changing schedule. **Taxis: t** 028 802 2444. For wheels, try **Adonis Moto Rental, t** 028 802 1097 (follow the signs from the port).

# Tourist Information

**Tourist police**, two blocks in from the Karthea Hotel in Korissía, **t** 028 802 1100.
**Town Hall** (*dimarchío*), near the port. Has a list of accommodation.
**To Stegadi**. This bookstore is run by the former mayor, Mr Lepouras, who will bend your ear about his beloved island (you may even be tempted to buy one of his own guidebooks).

# Festivals

**17 July**: Ag. Marína.
**15 Aug**: Chóra.
**7 Sept**: Otziás.
The island's *panegýria* are known for their spectacular dances and traditional instruments like the *tsamboúna*, *doubi* and lute.

# Where to Stay and Eat

## Kéa ✉ 84002

Most of Kéa's accommodation is furnished seaside apartments aimed at families. Simple rooms to rent are like gold dust at weekends or in high season, with prices to match. Foreign visitors have begun trickling in, but Kéa is still very Greek and the tavernas serve unadulterated Greek fare at reasonable prices. Look for *pastéli*, a delicious sticky bar made from local thyme honey and sesame seeds. Other specialities include pungent *kopanistí* cheese and *paspallá*, preserved fat pork, usually eaten at Christmas, *tiganía*, chopped pork in a white sauce, *lozá*, a local sausage and *xinó*, another local cheese.

## Korissía

**United Europe Furnished Flats**, close to the beach, **t** 028 802 1362, **f** 028 802 1122 (*A; exp–mod*). A smart self-catering option.
Other furnished apartments worth trying:
**To Korali, t** 028 802 1268 (*mod*).
**To Oneiro, t** 028 802 1118 (*mod*). *Open all year*.
**I Tzia Mas, t** 028 802 1305, **f** 028 802 1140 (*C; mod*). A modest motel fronting the town beach, but it's right on the main road, so isn't very peaceful. *Open Mar–Sept*.
**Korissia, t** 028 802 1484, **f** 028 802 1355 (*E; mod*). In a quiet backwater with a nice terrace, bar and large rooms or studios. *Open May–Oct*.
**Kyria Pantazi**, in a back alley, **t** 028 802 1452 (*mod–inexp*). Basic but quaint village rooms, but no view.
**Karthea**, off the harbour, **t** 028 802 1222, **f** 028 802 1417 (*C; inexp*). Gloomy, clean and quiet.

# History

Traces of a Neolithic fishing settlement dating back to 3000 BC were discovered at Kefala on Kéa's north coast. These first settlers were certainly no pushovers; when the mighty Minoan thalassocrats founded a colony *c.* 1650 BC on the peninsula of Ag. Iríni, they had to build defences to protect themselves from attacks, not from the sea but by land. The colony, discovered in 1960, coincides nicely with the myth that Minos himself visited Kéa and begat the Kéan race with a native named Dexithea; it also reveals a fascinating chronicle of trade and diplomacy between the Minoans and the older Cycladic culture, and later, with the Mycenaeans. In the Classical Era, Kéa was divided into four towns: Ioulís, Karthaea, Poiessa and Korissía. They worshipped Aristeos, a son of Apollo, who saved the Cyclades from the star Sirius, who wanted to

I **Apolavsi** ('The Enjoyment'), **t** 028 802 1068 (*inexp*). Comfortable, basic studios and a huge sun terrace overlooking the harbour.

**Akri**, past the supermarket. For a pleasant evening over grilled fish or moussaka.

**Apotheki**. In a whitewashed ruin, popular, with a large choice of dishes.

*Ouzerie* **Lagoudera**, on the harbour. Smart place in a refurbished Neoclassical house; great menu featuring tasty prawn *saganáki*.

**Ravaisi**. Run by Menelaos and his English wife. Popular eatery, especially with fishermen.

**To Mouragio**, on the harbour. Greek fare.

### Vourkári/Otziás

At Vourkári furnished apartments to let (*all exp–mod*) include:

**Nikitas**, **t** 028 802 2303, on the waterfront.

**Lefkes**, **t** 028 802 1443.

**Petrakos**, **t** 028 802 1197.

**Kastrianí Monastery**, on the north coast, an hour's walk east of Otziás, **t** 028 802 1348. The monks have cheap guest rooms if you get desperate.

**Aristos**. Vourkári is the best place for seafood at a price, where yachties moor a few feet from their tables. If there's been a good haul of fish, a delicious *kakavia* (Greek bouillabaisse) will be on the menu.

**Nikos**, next to the art gallery, **t** 028 802 1486. Cheaper and popular for lunch and dinner.

**Thalia** *Ouzerie*, nearby. A cheap favourite.

I **Strofi**. Otziás' favourite fish taverna, with a certain romantic touch.

### Ioúlis

**Ioúlis**, **t** 028 802 2177 (*C; mod*). One of the few choices here, full of character.

**Filoxenia**, **t** 028 802 2057 (*E; inexp*). Definitely a second choice, with shared bathrooms.

**Ioúlis**, on the Town Hall square. Good place to have a grilled lunch with sensational views.

**Katomerítiko**, in Káto Meriá. Locals go out of their way to come here for its Kéan specialities, including *tiganía* and *lozá*.

**O Kalofagás** ('The Good Eater'), in the square. Popular, with succulent meat dishes.

**Piatsa Restaurant**. In a lovely setting through the main archway.

### Písses/Koúndouros

**Galini**, in Písses, **t** 028 803 1316 (*mod*). If these furnished apartments are full, try the others run by the **Polítis family**, **t** 028 803 1343/1318.

**Kéa Camping**, **t** 028 803 1332. Pleasant and only site on Kéa. Owner also has rooms.

**Simitis**. Respected fish taverna

**Akroyiali**, **t** 028 803 1301. Another fish taverna, with rooms.

**Nikolas Demenegas**, in increasingly popular Koúndouros, **t** 028 803 1416 (*mod*). Tidy studios in a garden setting.

A stone windmill, contact **Nikolas Tsirikos** in Athens, **t** 010 897 4534. Sleeping 6–8, complete with a kitchen; can be fun.

## Entertainment and Nightlife

Ioúlis is now the 'in' place to spend the evening: **Kamini**, **To Palió Monopólio**, **Apano** and **Leon** are popular, and **Milos** has live *rembetiko*. In Vourkári at night, **Kouros** and **Prothikos** are popular music bars and **Vinilio** is good for a dance.

blast them with hot arrows; Sirius was known as an archer, and its current reputation as the Dog Star shows he's still a sizzler. The poet Simonides (557–467 BC), famous for his epigram after the Battle of Thermopylae, his lyrical nephew Bacchylides, the philosopher Ariston, and the physician Erasistratos were all sons of Kéa. Kéa was also famous for its retirement scheme called the *geroktonia*: citizens were required to take a glass of conium when they reached 70, although the Kéans say it only happened when the island was besieged by the Athenians and food was low.

## Korissía and the North Coast

Kéa's port **Korissía** (ΚΟΡΗΣΣΙΑ) has a few pretty Neoclassical buildings and a lovely church but otherwise it's a functional little place with a bust to the poet Simonides.

Anxious to become a resort like Kéa's other coastal villages, it boasts a few boutiques and an art gallery among the waterfront tavernas. At the time of writing, a folklore museum was in the works (*for information, call* **t** *028 802 1435*). Korissía recalls the ancient town that once stood on the site, but most locals still call it Livádi, as they continue to call their island Tzía instead of the official Kéa. The bay sweeps round to the sandy if not tidy town beach; a footpath over the headland leads past the old castle-like country house of the Maroúli family, then north to small, sandy **Gialiskári** Beach. A playground for rich Athenians, the area bristles with exclusive holiday villas.

A kilometre further north, on attractive Ag. Nikólaou Bay, **Vourkári**, the pretty fishing village, has metamorphosed into a smart little resort, with more pleasure-cruisers now than fishing boats. Around the bay, on the church-topped peninsula of **Ag. Iríni**, are the excavations of the **Minoan–Mycenaean settlement** (excellent local guidebook available). It's not difficult to make out the narrow temple, first constructed in the

## The Sinking of the Britannic

On 21 November 1916, the Britannic sank in the Kéa channel. One of the fabulous White Star Liners, a tenth larger (883ft) than her sister ship the Titanic, the Britannic was given added safety features after the Titanic went down. Originally called the Gigantic, she was patriotically renamed at the advent of the First World War and was requisitioned by the British Government before her maiden voyage to serve as a hospital ship and bring the wounded back from the slaughter of the Dardenelles. Under Captain Charles Bartlett, HMHS Britannic was on her sixth voyage, sailing from Naples to Moudros Bay on Límnos to pick up casualties. It was 8am, the sea was calm, when suddenly an explosion blasted in her bow compartment. Although she should have survived with little problem, the fatal sixth bulkhead failed to close properly; in addition, the nurses had opened all the port hole windows to air the wards, allowing water to pour in. Only two miles from Kéa, the Britannic went down in a mere 55 minutes. Fortunately, there were more than enough lifeboats available, and of the 1,134 people on board, only 30 died, and these mostly when their lifeboats were sucked under by the still-turning propeller as the stern started to rise.

What caused the explosion? Guesses have ranged from a German mine, to a torpedo, to an explosion caused by coal dust. There were rumours that the ship was being used to secretly transport munitions. Others have even suggested that the British blew it up, hoping to shock America into entering the war. Suspicions that the Admiralty had something to hide were fueled by its own maps, which widely mischarted the location of the wreck; when Jacques Cousteau went in search of it in 1975, he found the Britannic 6.75 nautical miles away from its charted position. In 1995, explorers returned, among them Dr Robert Ballard (one of the discoverers of the Titanic) who sent down video robots. They showed the wreck nearly completely intact, down to the whistles on the funnels. Divers in 1997 were able to do a complete survey: the ship's immense floor, doors, and storage rooms are in an excellent state of preservation. They found no sign of the rumoured munitions, nor any sign of torpedo damage or a mine anchor. The mystery continues. In the meantime, there is talk of making the wreck into the world's first underwater museum.

Bronze Age, a late Minoan *megaron*, Late Bronze Age houses, fortifications, and a spring chamber outside the walls. Inscriptions in the Minoan Linear A were among the finds now displayed in the Archaeology Museum in Ioulís. From here the coastal road continues to the delightful beach resort at **Otziás** (ΟΤΖΙΑΣ), its bay ringed with almond blossom in spring. From here you can walk up to wind-whipped **Panagía Kastriáni**, with panoramic views. The 18th-century monastery is noted for its miracle-working icon of the Virgin. There are two churches, the first built in 1708 after shepherds saw a strange glow on the mountain pinpointing the presence of the icon.

## Ioulís (Chóra) and Around

High above Korissía, the island's now trendy capital **Ioulís** (ΙΟΥΛΙΔΑ) is hidden inland, like so many Cycladic towns, from sea-going predators. As the bus climbs, the views down the terraced hillside to the sea are stunning. En route note the school, built in the Neoclassical style, one of the finest in Greece. Ioulís also boasts the largest collection of **windmills** in the Cyclades: 26 stand on the Mountain of the Mills.

The town is a pretty place to wander around with its flower-filled balconies and covered galleries known as *stegádia*, a maze of alleys, the white houses topped with red-tiled roofs. The fine Neoclassical Town Hall, topped with statues of Apollo and Athena, has a sculpture of a woman and child found at Karthaia and ancient reliefs set into niches. The **Kástro** quarter, reached through a dazzling white archway (note the coat of arms of the Pangalos family) occupies the site of the ancient acropolis and Temple of Apollo. In 1210, the Venetian Domenico Michelli cannibalized its marbles to build a castle; in the 1860s the Greek Government dismantled the castle to put the Classical bits in a museum. Bits remain, as well as a few Venetian mansions and Byzantine churches. The **Archaeology Museum** (*at the time of writing, closed for restoration, due to reopen in summer 2002; t 028 802 2079; open Tues–Sun 8.30–3*) contains Minoan finds from Ag. Iríni, and the tall Bronze Age terracotta female figures from the 14th-century BC temple – these are the oldest yet found in the Aegean. Made after the fall of Minoan Crete, the figures are in the style of the Cretan bare-breasted goddesses, and yet are unlike anything ever found on Crete, moulded over wooden skeletons, no two the same and all painted bright yellow, white and red. Other artefacts in the museum come from ancient Kéa's four cities, as well as a copy of the wonderful *Kouros of Kéa*, discovered in Korissía and now in the National Archaeology Museum in Athens.

A 10-minute walk east of Chóra leads to the island's watchdog – the 6th century BC **Lion of Kéa**, the 'Leonda', an ancient guardian 10ft high and 19ft long. Tales about the lion abound: one says he symbolizes the bravery of the Kéans, another recounts how evil nymphs were killing the wives of Ioulís and the men, fed up, were ready to abandon the city. The priest prayed to Zeus to send the nymphs away, and he delivered an enormous lion, which chased them across the water to Kárystos in Evía. The Kéans then carved the lion in stone, to keep the nymphs permanently at bay; others say this is the lion himself, as still as stone, ready to spring at the whiff of a bad fairy.

The countryside north of Ioulís, the **Peraméria** region, still has its oakwoods and traditional country houses. Above Peraméria Town the lush valley of Spathí ends at sandy **Spathí Bay**. Another road east from Ioulís branches for three fine beaches: **Sykamiá**, **Psíli Ammos** and **Orkós**.

## Southern Kéa

The main road south of Ioulís leads 5km through rolling green countryside to the ruined Monastery of **Ag. Marína**, built around a square, three-storey Hellenistic tower; one of the finest in Greece. From here the road cuts across to the west-coast resort of **Písses** (which perhaps should consider reviving its ancient name, Poiessa, of which a few traces remain). Backed by a lush valley full of orchards and olive groves, Písses has a sweeping sandy beach, one of Kéa's finest. The next bay along, **Koúndouros**, is just as lovely, and has several smaller coves, as well as a crop of bungalows for Athenian weekenders. Another gorgeous beach is further along the coast at **Liparó**. On the southeast shore at Póles Bay (with a great beach) stood **Karthaea**, once Kéa's most important city. Simonides had his school of poetry here; now you'll only find scant remains of the walls and Temple of Apollo. It's still possible to follow the course of the Hellenistic road from **Káto Meriá** or **Elliniká**, lovely places for woodland walks.

# Kímolos (ΚΙΜΩΛΟΣ)

Kímolos is Mílos' little sister, and until fairly recently they were Siamese twins, connected by an isthmus with a town on it, dating back to the Mycenaeans. But the isthmus sank, leaving a channel a kilometre wide. Once known as Echinousa, or sea urchin, which it proudly depicted on its coins, the island gave its modern name to *kimolía* ('chalk' in Greek), and to cimolite in English, a mineral similar to soft, chalk-like Fuller's Earth, an essential ingredient in cloth dying. Kímolos remains a top producer of cimolite, and you can see the workings as the boat pulls in.

Kímolos with its 720 souls is a quiet, untainted Greek island with plenty of beaches and freelance camping; a perfect place to relax and do absolutely nothing, with no

## Getting There

**By sea**: connections 5 times a week with Piraeus, Mílos, Kýthnos, Sérifos and Sífnos, three a week with Folégandros, Síkinos, Íos and Santoríni; **water taxi** 3 times a day to Apollonia on Mílos; caiques to the beaches. Day trips in high season to Mílos and Sífnos. **Port authority** (in Mílos – Kímolos is too small to have its own): t 028 702 2100. There's a ticket agency in Psáthi, t 028 705 1214.

## Tourist Information

**Police**: t 028 705 1205.

## Festivals

**21 Nov**: traditional music and dancing.

## Where to Stay and Eat

Most people come for the day. If you want to stay you'll have to ask around in the bars and tavernas to see who has a vacant room. Camping is usually 'no problem' as the Greeks say – try **Klíma** and **Alíki** beaches. Up in Chóra three tavernas all serve standard Greek fare at low prices: **Ramfos**, **Panorama** and **Boxoris**, which also has rooms. In Alíki, tavernas offer simple rooms. Try **Taverna Alíki**, t 028 705 1340.

cars and few tourists, even in August. Although rocky and barren ever since the Venetians set the olive groves ablaze in 1638, there are patches of green, including 140 species of rare plants on the southeast coast, and rare blue lizards. The island's largest building is a retirement home built by local philanthropist Geórgios Afendákis.

## Chóra and Around

From the pretty little port, **Psáthi** (ΨΑΘΗΣ), it's a 15-minute walk up to **Kímolos** or **Chóra**. On the way up you'll pass the Afendákis Foundation building and a small museum in the basement takes in whatever ancient bric-à-brac the locals happen to dig up. Blizzard-white, Chóra is a tangle of paved lanes with flowers at every turn. It's divided into two settlements: **Mésa Kástro** (or **Palío Choró**, the bit in the castle walls) and **Éxo Kástro**, or **Kainoúrio Choró**, on the outside. The houses of Mésa Kástro form the inside of the fortress with loophole windows and four gates. The outer village has a beautiful domed cathedral church, **Panagía Evangélistra**, built in 1614. Other impressive churches are the **Panagía Odygítria**, 1873; **Taxiárchis**, 1670 and **Chrisóstomos**, 1680, and the ruins of the Catholic church, the **Madonna of the Rosary**. One of the six windmills still grinds wheat – the last truly functioning one in the Cyclades.

From Chóra you can walk up to the ruined Venetian castle built by Marco Sanudo at Kímolos' highest point (1,165ft). Within its forbidding walls is the island's oldest church, **Christós**, dating from 1592. Another walk by way of **Alíki** ends at **Ag. Andréas** and the **Ellinikó necropolis** – all that survives of the city that sunk with the isthmus – and its graves from the Mycenaean period (2500 BC) to the early centuries AD. You can end with a swim at **Ellinikó** Beach (where loggerhead turtles nest) or **Kambána**. There are other beaches along the east coast. A path from Chóra descends to **Goúpa**, a hamlet with the most abundant fish in the Aegean these days, and where, supposedly, people used to scoop them out by the basketful. It's a pretty little place, with a good, unspoilt beach. There's another lovely beach at **Klíma** and 7km north at **Prássa** are radioactive thermal springs good for rheumatism. Goats are the only inhabitants of **Políegos**, the islet facing Psáthi, but the rare monk seal has been sighted as well.

# Kýthnos (ΚΥΘΝΟΣ)

Time your visit right and you can have this island to yourself, avoiding the Athenian summer invasion. Like its neighbour Kéa, Kýthnos attracts relatively few foreigners, and even the majority of Greek arrivals are not tourists, but folks full of aches and pains who come to soak in the thermal spa at Loutrá; the locals often call their island Thermia after the springs. Since the closure of Kýthnos' iron mines in 1940, the 1,500 islanders have got by as best they could by fishing, farming (mostly figs and vines), basket-weaving and making ceramics; the one thing that has stopped the population from dropping any further is the construction of a harbour mole in 1974, allowing ships to dock. Perhaps to make up for its slow start, Kýthnos became the first Greek island (1982) to get all of its electricity from renewable sources – wind in the winter and sun in the summer, inspiring similar projects on Mýkonos, Kárpathos, Samothráki

# Kýthnos

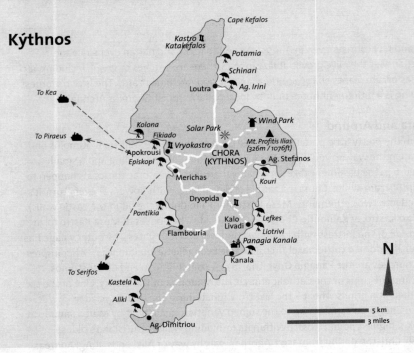

and Crete. Perhaps because of their frugal lives, Kythniots tend to celebrate *panegýria* with gusto, donning their traditional costumes; carnival is a big event here. There are quiet sandy beaches, a rugged interior great for walkers, and welcoming people. Best of all, it's the kind of island where the old men still offer to take you fishing.

## History

In Classical times the tale was told that Kýthnos was uninhabited because of its wild beasts and snakes, and Ofiohousa ('snaky') was one of the island's ancient names. Recently, however, archaeologists have uncovered a Mesolithic settlement (7500–6000 BC) north of Loutrá that spits in the eye of tradition and is currently the oldest settlement yet discovered in the Cyclades. Much later the Minoans held the island, followed by the Driopes, a semi-mythical tribe who were chased out of their home on the slopes of Mount Parnassós by Heracles and scattered to Évia, Cyprus and Kýthnos; their king Kýthnos gave his name to the island and their old capital is still called Drýopis. During the Hellenistic period Kýthnos was dominated by Rhodes. Two great painters came from the island, Kydian and Timatheus (416–376 BC); the latter was famous in antiquity for his portrait of Iphigenia. In 198 BC all Kýthnos was pillaged, except for Vyrókastro, which proved impregnable. Marco Sanudo took the island for Venice, and for 200 years it was under the rule of the Cozzadini family.

## Beaches, Chóra and Loutrá

**Mérichas** (ΜΕΡΙΧΑΣ) is a typical Greek fishing harbour, the ferry dock and yacht berths giving way to a tree-fringed bay backed by lively tavernas. It's a laid-back, cheerful place, kept tidy by the village elders who also tend the ducks that live on the sandy beach, and who posted the sign by the litter bins: 'The sea is the spring of life and joy.' In the morning fishermen sell the day's catch; forklifts buzz about delivering sacks of potatoes and cases of beer. Up the steps from the harbour and a short walk off the Chóra road is the much nicer little beach of **Martinákia**, popular with families. To the north are the unexcavated Hellenistic ruins of the once impregnable Vyrókastro, set on the headland above the lovely beaches at **Episkópi** and **Apókrousi**, although the prettiest sandy beach on the island, **Kolona**, is just beyond.

The 7½km bus trip north from Mérichas to the capital **Chóra** (or Kýthnos), winds through barren hillsides rippled with stone-wall terraces, deep wrinkles filled with oleanders, fruit trees and vines. Although as Cycladic towns go it's not that spectacular, it's a workaday town with a certain charm. The pavements are beautiful, painted with mermaids, fish and flowers. It has several pretty churches including **Ag. Sávvas**, founded in 1613 by the Cozzadini, who decorated it with their coat-of-arms. The oldest is **Ag. Triáda**, a domed, single-aisle basilica. Other churches in Chóra claim to have icons by the Cretan-Venetian master Skordílis, while the **Prodrómos** ('the Scout' or St John the Baptist) has a valuable 17th-century screen. Outside Chóra are the solar park and modern windmills, providing the island's power.

## Getting There and Around

**By sea**: daily with Piraeus, Sérifos, Sífnos and Mílos, 2–3 times a week with Lávrion, Kéa, Kímolos, Folégandros, Síkinos, Íos and Santoríni. Kýthnos has 2 ports; all ships put in at Mérichas on the west coast, but when the winds are strong they'll come in to Loútra in the northeast. **Hydrofoil**: daily to Kéa and Piraeus. **Port authority**: t 028 103 2290.

**By road**: the island's two **buses** run regularly to Chóra and Loutrá and to Drýopida and Panagía Kanála. **Taxis**: Kýthnos, t 028 103 1272; Drýopida t 028 103 1290.

## Tourist Information

**Tourist police**: Chóra, t 028 103 1201.
**GATS Travel**, Mérichas, t/f 028 103 2055. Agent for tickets, accommodation and excursions.
**Mílos Express Travel**, Mérichas, t 028 103 2104, f 028 103 2291. Has car and bike rentals.
**Cava Kýthnos off-licence**, Mérichas. Doubles as Bank of Greece and hydrofoil agency.

## Festivals

**Suns**: hear the island's music at Drýopida.
**15 Aug** and **8 Sept**: Kanála.
**2 Nov**: Mérichas.

## Where to Stay and Eat

**Kýthnos** ✉ 84006

### Mérichas

**O Finikas**, behind the supermarket, t 028 103 2323 (*exp*). Mérichas is the most convenient place to stay, and these upscale rooms in Cycladic style and garden setting, are the most comfortable.
**Kythnos**, slap on the waterfront, t 028 103 2092 (*mod–inexp*). Friendly but basic, above a *zacharoplasteío* that does breakfast and home-made rice-puddings and jellies.
**Panorama**, on the hill, t 028 103 2184/2182 (*mod–inexp*). Recently built, great sea views.
**Paradissos**, t 028 103 2206 (*mod–inexp*). Comfortable rooms with vine-shaded terraces and stunning views over the bay.
**Kaliopi**, t 028 103 2203. Rooms in the village with a nice garden.
**Chryssoula Laranzaki**, t 028 103 2051. Quiet rooms with views.
**Kissos**, t 028 103 2370. Family-run taverna, good for basic Greek favourites and fish.
**Martinakia**, on the beach of the same name, t 028 103 2414. With a friendly parrot in the garden, serving good *kalamária* and grills, rooms to let.
**Ostria**, close to where the ferry docks (*€20–25 for a lobster dinner*). A new grill restaurant,

The buses continue to **Loutrá** (ΛΟΥΤΡΑ), the most important spa in the Cyclades. Iron impregnates the water and since ancient times Loutra's two springs, **Kakávos** and **Ag. Anárgyri**, have been used for a cure for gout, rheumatism, eczema and 'women's problems'. There's a hydrotherapy centre (**t** *028 103 1277; open July and August 8–noon*) there today. Carved marble baths dating from ancient times are now inside the Xenia Hotel, from which steaming water bubbles down a gully and out to sea. Loutrá is a straggling, windswept resort with castle-like villas and a sandy beach. Over the headland are two more bays, pebbly **Ag. Iríni** and **Schinári**, exposed to the north winds. The aforementioned Mesolithic settlement was found on the promontory just to the north. A hard hour's walk from Loutrá towards the northernmost tip of Kýthnos will bring you to the medieval citadel **Kástro Katakéfalos**, with its derelict towers, houses and churches, all abandoned around the middle of the 17th century.

## Drýopida and Kanála

The other road and bus out of Mérichas heads up to **Drýopida** (ΔΡΥΟΠΙΔΑΣ) or Drýopis, the only other inland village and former capital, in part because of nearby **Katafíki Cave**, where the people hid during pirate raids. Huddled on the sides of a

serving everything from *tzatziki* to lobster. Has modest, but handy, rooms for rent.

**To Kantouni**, at the far end of the beach (towards the derelict hotel), t 028 103 2220. Tables at the water's edge where they specialize in grills and *sfougáta*, feather-light rissoles made from the local cheese, *thermiotikó*; also barrelled retsina and a romantic view across the bay.

**Yialos** (or Sailors), in Mérichas, t 028 103 2102. Has tables on the beach and does a fine *pikilía* of Greek starters and good specialities such as *kalogíros*, a casserole of meat, aubergines, tomatoes and feta; ask to try Kýthnos' wine.

### Chóra/Drýopida

**To Steki** and **To Kentro**. Chóra has these tavernas but no rooms.

**Taverna Pelegra**, in Drýopida, behind the butcher's shop. Basic, but at least the meat's fresh. Look out for local sausages drying on the balcony next door.

### Loutrá

**Kythnos Bay**, t 028 103 1218, f 028 103 1444 (*C; exp*). Very comfortable, geared towards long stays by spa customers.

**Porto Klaras apartments**, t 028 103 1276, f 028 103 1355 (*A; exp–mod*). Beautifully appointed

family suites or doubles. All have sea-view terraces.

**Meltémi**, t 028 103 1271, f 028 103 1302 (*C; mod*). Rather more modest flats.

**Xenia Anagenissis**, overlooking the beach, t 028 103 1217 (*C; mod–inexp*). Popular with old ladies taking the waters.

**Taverna Despina**. Good fresh fish soup and meat from Kýthnos.

**Taverna Katerina**, at Schinári Beach. With stunning views.

### Kanála

**Oneiro**, t 028 103 2515 (*inexp*). Pleasant rooms.

**Nikos Bouritis**, t 028 103 2350. Good value rooms.

**Yiannis Kallilas**, at Ag. Dimítrios, t 028 103 2208. Rooms and restaurant by the sea.

## Entertainment and Nightlife

**Byzantino**, in Mérichas. After midnight head for its ultra-violet lights.

**Akrotiri**, in Mérichas, on the far side of the port. Open-air night club.

**Kousaros** and **Apocalypse**, in Chóra/Drýopida. Night owls from around the island flock to these music bars.

small canyon, Drýopida could be in Spain, with its red-pantiled houses. There are two districts, **Péra Rouga**, by the river valley, where they grow crops, and **Galatás**, the upper village, a labyrinth of crazy-paved, neatly white-washed lanes. There are a few cafés and even fewer tourists. Once a great ceramics centre, only one pottery remains, belonging to the Milás family. Kýthnos was also a centre of icon-painting in the 17th century, led by the Skordílis family; much of their work can still be seen, including the iconostasis in **Ag. Mínas**, which also has an Easter bier with folk-art decorations. It takes an hour to walk to Chóra along the ancient cobbled way, or you can go down to the beaches at **Ag. Stéfanos**, a chapel-topped islet linked by a causeway, or **Léfkes**.

The bus terminates at **Kanála**, a popular summer resort. A village has sprung up around the church of **Panagía Kanála**, the island's patroness, housing a venerated icon, painted by St Luke himself (or more likely, by a member of the Skordílis clan). Chalets dot the peaceful grounds, pine trees shade picnic areas, and below, Greek families laze and splash in a string of sandy coves. There are wonderful views over to Sýros and Sérifos, and the water is so shallow that you feel you can almost walk across. A rough track leads to **Flamboúria** Beach on the west coast, but you need transport to get to **Ag. Dimitríou** way down at the southern tip.

# Mílos (ΜΗΛΟΣ)

Like Santoríni, **Mílos**, the most westerly of the Cyclades, is a volcanic island. But where the former is a glamorous beauty associated with misty tales of Atlantis, Mílos is a sturdy fellow who has made his fiery origins work for a living. Few places can boast such a catalogue of geological eccentricities: hot springs bubble in its low rolling hills, rocks startle with their Fauvist colours and the landscape is gashed with obsidian, sulphur, barium, alum and bensonite quarries begun in the Neolithic era. In a beach beauty contest Mílos would score over Santoríni hands-down with miles of pale golden sands, among the finest in Greece; long strands and weird fjord-like inlets all lapped by deep turquoise waters, some bubbling with geothermal springs. It seems an odd trick of Mother Nature to so endow such an out-of-the-way island with this mineral cornucopia. Yet in spite of all its strange and wonderful rocks, Mílos still mourns for the one it lost – the renowned Venus, now in the Louvre.

Walks through the gently undulating countryside will bring you down to tiny white-washed chapels at the water's edge, or unique little settlements that sit on the water, with brightly painted boat garages. Mílos is receiving more tourists every year (especially Italians and Germans), numbers that will only increase once the new jet runways are complete and the marina is in place in the island's magnificent harbour.

## History

But Mílos has long been a popular place. In the Neolithic era, as far back as 8000 BC people braved the Aegean in papyrus boats to mine Mílos' abundant veins of obsidian; the petroleum of its day, hard black volcanic glass prized for the manufacture of tools. Until the recent discovery of the Mesolithic settlement in Kýthnos, Mílos

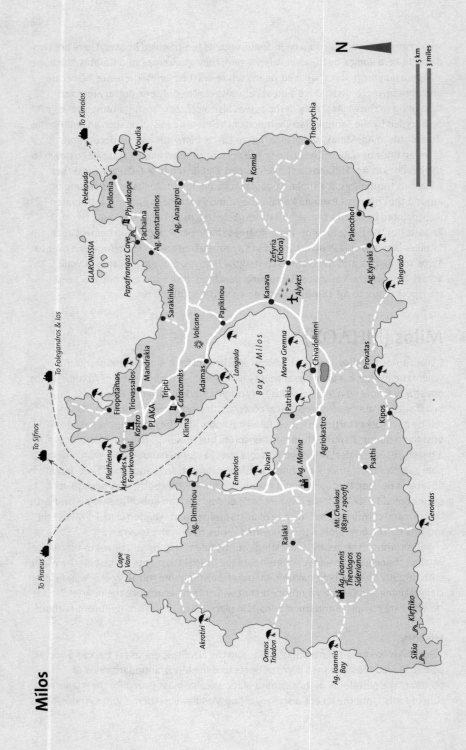

Milos

N

5 km
3 miles

To Kimolos

To Folegandros & Ios

To Sifnos

To Piraeus

Pelekouda
Pollonia
Voudia
Phylakope
Pachaina
Ag. Konstantinos
Papafrangas Cave
GLARONISSIA
Ag. Anargyroi
Komia
Theorychia
Sarakiniko
Zefyria (Chora)
Paleochori
Mandrakia
Papikinou
Kanava
Alykes
Ag. Kyriaki
Tsingrado
Firopotamos
Volcano
Triovassalos
Langada
Tripiti
Catacombs
Adamas
Bay of Milos
Mavra Gremna
Plathiena
Kastro
PLAKA
Klima
Chivadolimni
Provatas
Arkoudes
Fourkovouni
Patrikia
Kipos
Cape Vani
Rivari
Agriokastro
Psathi
Ag. Marina
Emborios
Ag. Dimitriou
Mt. Chalakas
(883m / 2900ft)
Ralaki
Gerontas
Akrotiri
Ag. Ioannis
Theologos
Siderianos
Ormos Triadon
Ag. Ioannis Bay
Sikia
Kleftiko

laid claim to the oldest town in the Cyclades, at Phylakope, settled by either Phoenicians or Cypriots; under Minoan and later Mycenaean rule the island became rich from trading obsidian all over the Mediterranean.

As later inhabitants of Mílos were predominately Dorian like the Spartans, they declared themselves neutral in the Peloponnesian War. In 415 BC, Athens sent envoys to change their minds. Their 'might makes right' discussion, known as 'the Milian Dialogue', in the fifth chapter of Thucydides, is one of the most moving passages in classical history. When Mílos still refused to co-operate, the Athenians besieged them and when the Milians unconditionally surrendered they massacred the men, enslaved the women and children and resettled Mílos with Athenian colonists. They were famous in antiquity for raising the toughest cock fighting roosters.

Christianity came early to Mílos in the 1st century, and the faithful built the only series of catacombs in Greece. Marco and his brother Angelo Sanudo captured Mílos and placed it under the Crispi Dynasty. The Turks laid claim to the island in 1580, even though Mílos was infested with pirates. One of them, John Kapsís, declared himself King of Mílos, a claim which Venice recognized for three years, until the Turks flattered Kapsís into coming to Istanbul and ended his pretensions with an axe. In 1680 a party from Mílos emigrated to London, where James, Duke of York, granted them land to build a Greek church – the origin of Greek Street in Soho. In 1836 Cretan war refugees from Sfakiá fled to Mílos and founded the village Adámas, the present port. During the Crimean War the French navy docked at the harbour of Mílos and left many monuments, as they did during the First World War; at Korfos are the bases of anti-aircraft batteries installed during the German occupation in the Second World War.

# Adámas and Beaches Around the Bay

If you arrive by sea, you can see a sample of Mílos' eccentric rocks before you disembark: a formation called the **Arkoúdes**, or bears, rises up from the sea on the left as you turn into the largest natural harbour in the Mediterranean – so large it feels like a vast lake. The port, bustling **Adámas** (ΑΔΑΜΑΣ), is also the main tourist centre. The Cretans who founded the town brought their holy icons, which are displayed in the churches of Ag. Tríada and **Ag. Charálambos**; in the latter, one ex-voto, dating from 1576, portrays a boat attacked by a raging fish; the captain prayed to the Virgin, who resolved the struggle by snipping off the fish's nose. There's also a new **Mining Museum** (*t 028 702 2481; open daily 9.30–1 and 5–8*), south along the waterfront, illustrating Milos' geological and mining history. West of town you can ease your aches and pains wallowing in the warm sulphurous mineral waters of the municipal **spa baths**, in an old cave divided into three bathrooms (*open daily 8–1; adm*). Beyond is small **Langáda Beach**, popular with families; a monument at Bombarda commemorates the French who died there during the Crimean War. Further along the track, gurgling hot mud pools mark the route to the '**Volcano**', a glorified steaming fissure.

The vast, sandy **Bay of Mílos** is fringed with a succession of beaches like **Papikinoú**, backed by hotels and apartments. There's a quieter beach at **Alýkes**, the salt marshes

# Getting There and Around

**By air**: at least 1 **flight** daily from Athens. Olympic Airways is just past the *plateía* in Adámas, **t** 028 702 2380; for airport information, call **t** 028 702 2381. A **taxi** from the airport to Adámas will cost about €8.

**By sea**: 2 or more **ferries** daily to and from Piraeus, with daily connections to Sífnos, Kýthnos and Sérifos; once a week with Folégandros and Santoríni; **taxi boat** 5 times a day from Pollónia to Kímolos in season; round-island excursion boats, or alternatively, hire the *Apollonía* for your own excursion from **Manolis Galanos, t** 028 705 1385. Port authority: **t** 028 702 2100.

**By road**: hourly **buses** from Adámas Square to Pláka, via Tripití; nine times a day to Pollónia by way of Filikopi and Pachera; seven times to Paleóchora via Zephyria and Provatás. For a **taxi**, call **t** 028 702 2219. Or rent your own wheels: ask at **Vichos Tours** (*see* below) or **STOP**, by the port, **t** 028 702 2440.

# Tourist Information

**Municipal booth**: on the Adámas quay, **t** 028 702 2445. Has accommodation lists. *Only open in season.*

**Vichos Tours**, on the waterfront, **t** 028 702 2286, **f** 028 702 2396. Very helpful for tickets, accommodation and car hire.

# Internet

**Cybercafé** in Adámas, by the Ecclesiastical Museum.

# Festivals

**Easter**: Triovassálos.
**50 days after Greek Easter**: Adámas.

**19 July**: Profítis Ilías on the mountain, and in Chalákas and Tripití.
**26 July**: Plakotá.
**5 Aug**: Paraskópou.
**15 Aug**: Adámas.
**7 Sept**: Psathádika.
**16 and 25 Sept**: Chalákas.

# Where to Stay and Eat

## Mílos ✉ 84800

Mílos fills to the brim from 15 July to 15 Sept, so be sure to book then. If you get stuck, call the **Rooms to Let Association, t** 028 702 3429.

## Adámas

**Seagull Apartments, t** 028 702 3183/3193 (*lux–exp*). Smart new complex.

**Kapetan Georgadas, t** 028 702 3215, **f** 028 702 3219 (*C; exp*). Re-vamped traditional style apartments, small but exclusive, with satellite TV, mini-bars, air-con and pool.

**Mílos**, on the seafront, **t** 028 702 2087, **f** 028 702 2306 (*C; exp*). White and quiet, doesn't look much but has an excellent restaurant popular with Greeks. *Open April–Oct.*

**Popi's**, by the water, **t** 028 702 2286, **f** 028 702 2396, in Athens **t** 010 361 3198 (*C; exp*). Comfortable, with helpful management.

**Santa Maria Village**, set back from the beach, **t** 028 702 1949, **f** 028 702 2880 (*C; exp*). A smart mix of rooms, studios and apartments; wheelchair access.

**Adámas**, perched above the harbour, **t** 028 702 2322, **f** 028 702 2580 (*C; mod*). Well-equipped rooms with air-con. *Open April–Oct.*

**Delfini, t** 028 702 2001, **f** 028 702 2688 (*D; mod*). Friendly family-run (same as Seagull Apts) hotel with a nice breakfast terrace.

**Portiani**, on the sea, **t** 028 702 2940, **f** 028 702 2766, *sirmalen@otenet.gr* (*C; mod*). Comfy choice with sumptuous buffet breakfast.

before the Mávra Gremná, or the black cliffs, with fantastical rock formations; at several places out in the bay the sea bubbles from the hot springs released below. The generous spring near the Kanava junction supposedly is a sure cure for sterility in women. Past the salt-beds and the airport clutter stretches the spectacular sandy beach at **Chivadólimni**, the island's longest, with a deep turquoise sea in front and a saltwater lake behind, named after the clams who live there; it also hosts the island's official campsite. Continuing along the coast, other pale golden beaches are **Patrikia**,

**Semiramis, t** 028 702 2118, **f** 028 702 2117 (*D; mod*). Excellent with a pretty vine-clad terrace – help yourself to grapes – bar, transfer minibus and rent-a-bike service.

**Kanaris,** a little inland, **t** 028 702 2184 (*inexp*). A good budget choice, and the owner will pick you up at the port.

Adámas has most of the island's restaurants; if you come in the right season, look for clams from Chivadólimni.

**Barko,** on the waterfront. The best bet for Greek home cooking, with good barrel wine.

**Flisvos.** Friendly place with the usual fish and oven-ready dishes.

**Kynigos.** Serves good, standard fare in unpretentious but pleasant surroundings.

**Ta Pitsounakia.** Spit-roasts of all kinds of meats and *kokorétsi*.

**Trapatseli's.** Fish come up to feed beneath the terrace here; there's an excellent menu, especially for fish dishes. The *spetsofái* fish stew and *soupiés*, cuttlefish *stifádo*, are good as well as the local *dópio* hard cheese.

**Navayio,** next door. Good value, also has fresh fish and local *mezédes*.

**Vedema,** above the ferry port. Serves tasty Greek and Middle Eastern dishes.

### Pláka/Tripití/Klíma

**Plakiotiki Gonia,** in Pláka. A sweet little taverna with local dishes like cheese pies and country bread with tomatoes.

**Kástro,** in Pláka's square. Popular, with views up to the castle.

**Popi's Windmill,** in Tripití, **t** 028 702 2287, **f** 028 702 2396 (*exp*). Has rooms that sleep 4–5 in 2 beautifully converted mills. *Open June–Sept.*

**Sophia Apartments, t** 028 702 2039, **f** 028 702 1980 (*mod*). Traditionally furnished and overflowing with arches. *Open all year.*

**Mayeriko,** in Tripití. The best of many tavernas, with superb views.

**Methismeni Politia,** in Tripití (€*15–20*). The 'Drunken State' is pricier, specializing in *mezédes*, wines and *ouzo* in a romantic garden setting with views across the gulf.

**Panorama,** in Klíma, **t** 028 702 1623, **f** 028 702 2112 (*C; mod*). Has rooms with private bath and dining terrace with great views; a good bet for lunch.

### Pollónia

**Kapetan Tassos,** 100m from the beach, **t** 028 704 1287, **f** 028 704 1322 (*A; exp*). Smart Cycladic-style apartments.

**Apollon Apartments and Studios, t** 028 704 1347 (*exp*). Views over Kímolos and home-cooking at the family taverna.

**Araxovoli** and **Kapetan Nikolas.** Two other local favourites.

### Paleochóri /Ag. Kyriakí

**Artemis,** in Paleochóri, near the beach, **t** 028 703 1221. A restaurant with bungalows.

**Pelagos.** Taverna with great food.

**Thirios Restaurant,** in Ag. Kyriakí, **t** 028 702 2779/2058. Has rooms.

## Entertainment and Nightlife

Mílos has quite a sophisticated nightlife with scores of dancing bars and discos; there's even a roller-skating rink in Adámas.

**Yanko's,** Adámas, near the bus stop. A local hang out.

**To** *Ouzerie*, Adámas, on the front.

**To** *Kafeneion*, Adámas. For cocktails and Greek music in a flower-filled courtyard.

**Fuego, Plori, La Note** and **Feggera.** Other Adámas hot spots in the open air.

**Milo Milo Disco,** at Langáda Beach.

**Viagra,** at the end of the sand. It doesn't stop.

**Puerto.** For Greek music.

**Rivári** (backed by a lagoon once used as a vivarium by the monks up at **Ag. Marína Monastery**) and **Emboriós**. Further north, **Ag. Dimitríou** is often battered by winds.

## A Geological Mystery Tour

From Adámas, excursion boats tour the island's fascinating rock formations from the sea. Highlights include the **Glaroníssia**, four cave-pocked basalt islets shaped like organ pipes, off the north coast; **Paleoréma** on the east coast with a disused sulphur mine which turns the water emerald-green; on the southwest corner, the sea caves of **Sikía** where the sun's rays slant through the roof to create dramatic colours in the water; and next door **Kléftiko**, the pirates' hideaway with another set of fantastic cream and white rocks rising from the sea. You can also sail near **Andímilos** to the northwest, a reserve for the rare Cretan chamois goat, or *kri-kri*.

# Pláka: Ancient Melos and its Catacombs

Buses leaves frequently for **Pláka** (ΠΛAKA), the labyrinthine sugar-cube capital, 4km uphill from Adámas, blending into the windmill-topped suburb of **Tripití** (TPΥΠHTH). Next to the bus stop is the **Archaeology Museum** (*t 028 702 1620; open Tues–Sun 8.30–3; adm*). Inside is a plaster copy of Venus, a consolation prize from Paris, but the real finds are from the Neolithic era: terracotta objects and lily-painted ceramics from Phylakope, including the famous *Lady of Phylakope*, a decorated Minoan-style goddess. There are Hellenistic artefacts from Kímolos and statues, but like Venus, the famous marble *Poseidon* and the *Kouros of Mílos* are not at home (this time all are in the National Archaeology Museum in Athens). The **Historical and Folklore Museum** (*t 028 702 1292; open Tues–Sat 10–1 and 6–8, and Sun 10–1; adm*), housed in a 19th-century mansion, include everything down to the kitchen sink.

Steps lead up to the Venetian **Kástro**, set high on a volcanic plug. Houses formed the outer walls of the fortress. Perched on top was an old church, Mésa Panagía, blown up by the Germans during the Second World War. After liberation, a new church was built lower down, but the old icon of the Virgin reappeared in a bush on top of the Kástro. Every time they moved the icon it returned to the bushes, so they gave in and built another church, **Panagía Skiniótissa**, 'Our Lady of the Bushes'. There are stunning views from here, and on the way up from **Panagía Thalassítras**, 'Our Lady of the Sea' (1228), where the lintel bears the arms of the Crispi family, who overthrew the Sanudi as dukes of Náxos. The church houses fine icons by Emmanuel Skordílis. **Panagía Rosaria** is the Roman Catholic church built by the French consul Louis Brest, and **Panagía Korfiátiss**, on the edge of a sheer cliff to the west of the village, has Byzantine and Cretan icons rescued from the ruined city of Zefyría.

**Pláka** itself is built over the acropolis of ancient **Melos**, the town destroyed by the Athenians and resettled by the Romans. In the 1890s the British school excavated the site at **Klíma**, a short walk below Pláka (*get off the bus at Tripití*), where you can visit a termitary of **Catacombs** (*t 028 702 1625; open Tues–Sun 8–2*), dating from the 1st century AD. One of the best-preserved Early Christian monuments in Greece, it has long corridors of arched niches carved in the rock. When first discovered, the tombs were still full of bones, but contact with the fresh air quickly turned them to dust. Some held five or six bodies; other cadavers were buried in the floor. On various tombs, inscriptions in red remain, as well as later black graffiti. The habit of building underground necropoli (there are catacombs in Rome, Naples, Sicily and Malta) coincides with the presence of soft volcanic tufa, more than with romantic notions of persecution and secret underground rites; interring the dead underground saved

## The Venus de Milo, or Unclear Disarmament

On 8 April 1820, farmer Geórgios Kentrotás was ploughing a field when he discovered a cave containing half of a statue of the goddess Aphrodite. A French officer, Olivier Voutier, who happened to be visiting Mílos, urged the farmer to look for the other half. He soon found it, along with a 6th-century BC statue of young Hermes and Hercules as an old man – an ancient art lover's secret cache, hidden from the Christians. Voutier sketched the Aphrodite for Louis Brest, the French vice consul for Mílos. Brest sent this on to the French consul in Constantinople, who decided to obtain Aphrodite for France, and sent an envoy over to complete the deal. But meanwhile Kentrotás, persuaded by the island's elders, had sold the statue to another man on behalf of the translator of the Turkish fleet, the Prince of Moldavia, Nichólas Mouroúzis. The statue was in a caique, ready to be placed aboard a ship for Romania, when the French ship sailed into Adámas. Eventually, after some brisk bargaining, the envoy and Brest managed to buy the Aphrodite as a gift for Louis XVIII (although some say the French sailors grabbed her by force). On 1 March 1821 she made her début in the Louvre. Somewhere along the line she lost her arms and pedestal with the inscription *Aphrodites Nikiforos*, 'Victory-bringing Aphrodite'. The French cadet's sketch showed the arms, one hand holding an apple. Why an apple? If you haven't conned up on your Greek, check the menu decoder, on p.62. And then there's the Adámas connection (Adam – right?) but that's in another, much longer book.

valuable land. (Curiously, the modern cemetery near Pláka resembles a row of catacombs above ground; the posh ones are even done out with carpets.) A path from the catacombs leads to where Venus was discovered – there's a marker by the fig tree.

The path continues past the ancient Cyclopean city walls to the well-preserved **Roman Theatre**, where spectators looked out over the sea, reconstructed to something approaching its former glory; a company from Athens sometimes performs in the theatre in August (*ask at the tourist office for details*). Remains of a **temple** are on the path back to the main road. From there you can take the road or an old *kalderími* pathway down to the picturesque fishing hamlet of **Klíma**, with its brightly painted boat garages, *syrmata*, carved into the soft volcanic tufa, with rickety balconies above and ducks waddling on the beach below. A museum-style reconstruction shows how the fishing families once lived around their caiques.

# Around the Island

## Around Pláka and the North Coast

Near Pláka, the market village **Triovassálos** merges into **Péra Triovassálos**. The churches in Triovassálos contain icons from the island's original capital Zefyría. The great rivalry between the two villages expresses itself on Easter Sunday, when after burning an effigy of Judas, the young bloods hold a dynamite-throwing contest on the dividing line between the villages; the most ear-splitting performance wins. Tracks lead down to a selection of beaches, some adorned with wonderfully coloured rocks. One of the best beaches is **Pláthíena** near the Arkoúdes, with dazzling orange and white rock formations; it's also the best place to watch the sun set. The old path from Pláka leads past **Fourkovoúni** with picturesque *syrmata* hewn into the cliffs. **Mandrákia**, under Triovassálos, is one of the island's outstanding beauty spots, a stunning little cove studded with garages and topped by a white chapel. Further north, **Firopótamos** is a pretty fishing hamlet.

## Phylakope and Pollónia

The road from Adámas or Pláka to Pollónia offers a pair of very tempting stops along the north coast. A side road descends into the bleached moonscape of **Sarakíniko**, of huge rounded rocks and pointed peaks whipped by the winds into giant white petrified drifts, with a tiny beach and inlet. To the east the fishing hamlets of **Pachaina** and **Ag. Konstantínos** have more *syrmata*; from the latter it's a short walk to **Papafrángas Cave**, actually three sea caves, where the brilliant turquoise water is enclosed by the white cliffs of a mini fjord, once used by trading boats as a hiding place from pirates.

On the other side of Papafrángas, **Phylakope** (ΦΥΛΑΚΩΠΗ) is easy to miss but was one of the great centres of Cycladic civilization, excavated by the British in the 1890s. The dig yielded three successive levels of habitation: early Cycladic (3500 BC), Middle Cycladic (to *c.* 1600 BC) and Late Cycladic/Mycenaean. Even in Early Cycladic days Mílos traded in obsidian far and wide – pottery found in the lowest levels showed an Early Minoan influence. Grand urban improvements characterize the Middle Cycladic period: a wall was built around the more spacious and elegant houses, some with delightful frescoes of flying fish (now in Athens, too). A Minoan-style palace contained fine ceramics imported from Knossós, and there was trade with the coasts of Asia Minor. In this period Mílos, like the rest of the Cyclades, may have come under the direct rule of the Minoans; a tablet found on the site is written in a script similar to Linear A. During the Late Cycladic age, the Mycenaeans built their own shrine, added a wall around the palace, and left behind figurines and ceramics. Phylakope declined when metals replaced the need for obsidian. For all its history the actual remains at the site are overgrown and inexplicable.

The bus ends up at Apollo's old town, **Pollónia** (ΠΟΛΛΩΝΙΑ) on the east coast, a popular resort with a tree-fringed beach, fishing boats, and tavernas. There's quite a bit of new holiday development on the **Pelekóuda** Cape, popular as it is with windsurfers. **Voúdia** Beach to the south has a unique view of the island's mining activities.

## Central Mílos: Zefýria, Paleochóri and Around

Buses cross the island to **Zefýria** or Chóra, the capital of Mílos from 800 to 1793. **Panagía Portianí** was the principal church; its priest was accused of fornication by the inhabitants, and although he denied it, the villagers refused to believe him. With that the priest angrily cursed the people, a plague fell on the town, and everyone moved down to Pláka. Today Zefýria is a very quiet village of crumbling houses, surrounded by olive trees. A paved road continues to popular sandy **Paleochóri Beach** and quieter **Ag. Kyriakí** to the west. **Kómia**, east of Zefýria, has ruined Byzantine churches and nearby at **Demenayáki** are some of Mílos' obsidian mines.

## South and West Mílos

If eastern Mílos is fairly low and green, the south and west are mountainous and dry. Just south of Chivadólimni, **Provatás** has another sandy beauty and hot springs, **Loutrá Provatá**, where you can examine remains of Roman mosaics, followed by a natural sauna to ease your rheumatism, recommended by no less than Hippocrates himself. **Kípos**, further along the coast, has two churches: one, the 5th-century **Panagía tou Kipou**, is the oldest in Mílos. To the west, in the wild **Chalákas** region, where small woods of rare snake root and cedars survive in little canyons, the old monastery at **Ag. Marína** is worth a trip; from here you can climb to the top of **Profítis Ilías**, with a gods' eye view over Mílos and neighbouring islands.

Down in the southwest, at the famous monastery of **Ag. Ioánnis Theológos Siderianós**, St John is nicknamed the Iron Saint – once during his festival, revellers were attacked by pirates and took refuge in the church. In response to their prayers, the saint saved them by turning the church door to iron (you can still see a scrap of a dress caught in the door as the last woman entered). The pirates couldn't break in, and when one tried to shoot through a hole in the church dome, Ag. Ioánnis made his hand wither and fall off. Another miraculous story from April 1945 tells of a shell from an English warship embedding itself in the church wall without exploding.

# Mýkonos (ΜΥΚΟΝΟΣ)

This dry, barren island plagued by high winds, but graced with excellent beaches and a beautiful, colourful, cosmopolitan town, has the most exciting and sophisticated nightlife in Greece. If the surge in tourism in recent years caught the other islands unawares, Mýkonos didn't bat a mascaraed eyelid, having made the transformation long ago from a traditional economy to one dedicated to every whim of the international set. If you seek the simple, the unadorned, the distinctly Greek – avoid Mýkonos like the plague. But the party will go on without you; Mýkonos' streets are jammed with some of the zaniest, wildest, raunchiest and 'Most Beautiful People' in Greece. It also has the distinction of being one of the most expensive islands, and the first officially to sanction nudism on some of its beaches, as well as being the Mediterranean's leading gay resort and setting for the film *Shirley Valentine*.

## History

The Ionians built three cities on Mýkonos: one on the isthmus south of Chóra, the second at Dimastos, dating back to 2000 BC and the third at Panórmos near Paliókastro. During the war between the Romans and Mithridates of Pontus, all three were destroyed. Chóra was rebuilt during the Byzantine period, and the Venetians surrounded it with a wall that no longer exists; however, at Paliókastro a fort built by the Gizzi rulers still remains. In 1537 Mýkonos fell to Barbarossa, and came into its own with pirate families who ran a profitable plunder market. Even so, it was on the front line in the War of Independence, its fleet of 22 ships led by Mantó Mavrogenous, the local heroine, who donated all of her considerable fortune to the cause.

# Mýkonos

N

5km
3 miles

TRAGONISI

Meralias Bay

Profitis Ilias
(392m / 1294ft)

Tigani

Kalafatis

Ag. Anna

Dimastos

Kalo
Livadi

Cape
Mavros

Poliokastro

Ano Mera

Elia

Agrari

Super
Paradise

Ag. Sostis

Panormos
Bay

Ftelia

Marathi

Linos

Paradise

Paraga

Proftis
Ilias
(372 m)

Ag. Stefanos

Tourlos

Tagoo

CHORA
(MYKONOS)

Platis
Gialos

Psarou

Fanari

Tourlos Bay

Korfos Bay

Megali
Ammos

Vrissi

Ornos

Korfos

To Ikaria & Samos

Ag. Ioannis

PRASONISI

To Tinos

KOUNELONISI

MEGALO
REMATIARIS

DELOS

To Naxos, Paros
& Santorini

To Syros

RHENEIA

# Getting There and Around

**By air**: several connections daily with Athens, several a week with Thessaloníki, Santoríni, Rhodes and Heráklion (Crete). The **Olympic Airways** office is at the end of Ag. Efthimiou St, **t** 028 902 2490. Airport: **t** 028 902 2327. Buses stop by the airport.

**By sea**: several **ferry** and **hydrofoil** connections daily with Piraeus, Rafína, Ándros, Tínos, Sýros, Náxos, Páros, Íos and Santoríni; at least 3 times a week with Heráklion (Crete), Amorgós and Sífnos; less frequently with Mílos, the Back Islands, Thessaloníki and Skiáthos; there are **excursion boats** to Délos daily 8.30–1, returning noon–3, except Mon; also to Paradise, Super Paradise, Agrari and Eliá from both Chóra and Platís Gialós, **Port authority**: **t** 028 902 2218.

**By road**: there are 2 **bus** stations and buses run frequently. The one on the north side of the quay by the Archaeology Museum, serves Ag. Stéfanos, Tourlos, Áno Merá, Eliá, Kalafátis and Kaló Livádi. The one by Olympic Airways is for Ornós, Ag. Ioánnis, Platís Gialós, Paradise Beach, Psaroú, Kalamopódi and the airport. For information, **t** 028 902 3360. **Taxis: t** 028 902 3700 or **t** 028 902 2400. Car and bike rental places abound around the 2 bus stations, but any one of the travel agencies in town will rent wheels; just don't expect to pick up a bargain there.

# Tourist Information

**Tourist police**: on the quay, **t** 028 902 2482.
**Post office**: one is near Ag. Anna and 'taxi square'; the other is on Koutsi Street, near Olympic Airways.

# Internet

**Angelos Internet Café**, between the bus station and the windmills, **t** 028 902 4106.
**Mykonos Cyber Café**, M. Axioti 26, **t** 028 902 7684, *info@mykonos-cyber-cafe.com*

# Festivals

**15 Aug**: Panagía Tourliani. But then every day's a party on Mýkonos.

# Where to Stay and Eat

## Mýkonos ✉ 84600

There's certainly no lack of places to stay on Mýkonos, although prices tend to be the highest in Greece and you should book from June on. Sleek new Cycladic-style hotels occupy every feasible spot on the coast, especially along the road to Platís Gialós. Most are open April–Oct, and provide free transfer to and from the airport. Alternatively, when you step off the ferry you'll be inundated with people offering rooms, but beware that many are up the hill above Chóra, in an isolated and ugly area of holiday apartments. You'll probably do better using the internet (*www. mykonos.forthnet.gr/skaphp1.htm*) or the accommodation desks in the quay complex:
**Hotel Reservations Office**, **t** 028 902 4540.
**Association of Rooms and Flats**, **t** 028 902 4860; *open 10–6*.
**Camping Information Office**, **t** 028 902 2852.
**Mýkonos Accommodation Centre**, 10 Enoplon Dynameon, in the old town, **t** 028 902 3160, *mac@mac.myk.forthnet.gr*. This Belgian-run agency is very helpful and able to arrange accommodation by email.
**Sea and Sky Travel Agency**, on the waterfront near 'taxi square', **t** 028 902 2853, *sea-sky@ myk.forthnet.gr*. Also friendly and helpful.

### Chóra (Mýkonos Town)

**Leto**, **t** 028 902 2207, **f** 028 902 4365, *leto@ leto.myk.forthnet.gr* (*A; lux*). Has a wonderful view over the harbour and town, and was for many years the classiest place to stay on the island.
**Elysium**, overlooking town, **t** 028 902 3952, **f** 028 902 3747, *www.elysiumhotel.com* (*C; exp*). Exclusively gay and adds a fitness centre, Jacuzzi and pretty pool to the views from its bungalows.
**Lefteris**, **t** 028 902 3128, **f** 028 902 7117, *lefter-ishot@yahoo.com* (*E; exp*). Great roof terrace and the wonderfully laid-back Costas.
**Veranda**, above town, **t** 028 902 3670, **f** 028 902 5133 (*exp*). Panoramic views and pool.
**Manto**, 1 Evangelístrias, **t** 028 902 2330, **f** 028 902 6664 (*C; exp–mod*). Convenient for connoisseurs of the night scene.
**Rania**, above taxi square, **t** 028 902 2315, **f** 028 902 2370, *rania-ap@otenet.gr* (*mod*).

Tasteful, quiet rooms and studios; the owners are very helpful.

**Philippi**, in the heart of Chóra at 32 Kalogéra St, **t** 028 902 2294, **f** 028 902 4680, *chriko@otenet.gr* (*D; mod*). Delightful hotel, with rooms scented by the lovely garden.

**Chóra** has food for every pocket and appetite – you just need deeper pockets.

**Philippi**, *see* above; **t** 028 902 2295/3470 to book (*€30*). Spot the celebrity in this town landmark. Has a good reputation for Greek and international cuisine, served in the garden.

**Edem**, **t** 028 902 2855 (*€25*). Offers a varied international menu around a courtyard pool by Panachrandou church.

**Chez Maria's**, Kalogéra St, **t** 028 902 7565 (*€30–35*). Elegant, romantic dining in a bougainvillaea garden. Seafood pasta a speciality, but lots more unusual dishes.

**Katrin's**, **t** 028 902 7391 (*€25*). Again, centrally placed but not much lighter on the wallet; has many good French specialities; reservations recommended.

**Yves Klein Blue**, **t** 028 902 7391 (*€25–30*). Offers pricey but good Italian dishes, and is extremely popular.

**Niko's Taverna**, behind the town hall, **t** 028 902 4320 (*€12*). If you need to be reminded that you're in Greece, head here for good dinners.

**Spilia**. Nearby, a little hole in the wall with friendly staff serving good traditional Greek fare at low prices.

**Antonini's**, slap in the middle of the activity on taxi square. A notable exception to the rule that the back streets hide the best, secret tavernas. Here you'll find genuine Greek food at fair prices: varied and excellent *mezédes*, shrimp salad and very tasty veal or lamb casserole.

**Kounelas**, at the end of the waterfront (*€15–20*). The owner, a colourful character, promises consistently fresh seafood.

**Sesame Kitchen**, near the Naval Museum, **t** 028 902 4710. English-run establishment and a vegetarian's haven, with unusual rice dishes at good prices.

**Appaloosa's**, Mavrogenous St, **t** 028 902 7086 (*€15–20*). Mexican fare and good salads.

**Hard Rock Café** (*€25*). Take the free shuttle bus out of Chóra for the real thing (or almost), where you can eat expensive fast food and lounge by a pool.

## North of Chóra: Tagoo

**Cavo Tagoo**, on the beach, within walking distance of Chóra, **t** 028 902 3692, **f** 028 902 4923, *cavotagoo@hol.gr* (*A; lux*). The award-winning Cubist beauty , 'pour les lucky few', with seawater pool, beautiful view of Mýkonos, and the chance to rub shoulders with the stars.

**Aegean**, **t** 028 902 2869, **f** 028 902 4927 (*C; lux*). Well-appointed but still family run and friendly.

**Spanelis**, **t** 028 902 3081 (*D; exp*). Small, older hotel.

**Madalena**, **t** 028 902 2954, **f** 028 902 4302 (*C; exp*). Another lesser option, with a pool.

## North of Chóra: Toúrlos

**Rhenia**, **t** 028 902 2300, **f** 028 902 3152, *rhenia@otenet.gr* (*B; lux*). Tranquil, sheltered bungalows and pool, overlooking Chóra and Délos.

**Olia**, **t** 028 902 3123, **f** 028 902 3824 (*B; exp*). Pleasing, traditionally-styled rooms and pool nearer the sea.

**Sunset Hotel**, **t** 028 902 3013, **f** 028 902 3931 (*D; exp–mod*). Smaller, with a terrace café where they will cook to your order.

**Matthew Taverna**. Slick and well patronized.

## North of Chóra: Ag. Stéfanos

**Princess of Mýkonos**, **t** 028 902 3806, **f** 028 902 3031, *princes@myk.forthnet.gr* (*B; lux*). Favourite of Jane Fonda with pool, sauna, Jacuzzi and the works. It isn't in the heart of the action, but only a taxi-ride away.

**Vangeli**, just before Fanári at Choulakia Beach, **t** 028 902 2458, **f** 028 902 5558 (*exp*). Quiet, small and very Greek, with good restaurant.

**Artemis**, **t** 028 902 2345, **f** 028 902 3865 (*C; exp–mod*). Clean if uninspiring rooms with big balconies.

Take your pick from the various tavernas along the beach.

## South Coast Beaches: Ag. Ioánnis and Ornós

**Manoula's Beach**, at Ag. Ioánnis, **t** 028 902 2900, **f** 028 902 4314 (*C; lux*). Pretty bungalow complex where they filmed

Shirley Valentine. There are also a couple of tavernas, with boat trips and beach parties thrown in.

**Ornós Beach**, Ornós, **t** 028 902 3216, **f** 028 902 2243 (*B; lux*). Stylish, traditionally designed rooms, with a pool, private beach and wooden schooner available to guests for day trips.

**Kivotos**, Ornós, **t** 028 902 4094, **f** 028 902 2844, *kivotos1@hol.gr* (*C; lux*). One of the 'Small Luxury Hotels of the World' with Olympic squash courts, antique shops and a wet bar in the seawater pool.

**Yannaki**, away from Ornós centre, **t** 028 902 3393, **f** 028 902 4628 (*C; exp*). With a tranquil pool and mod cons.

## Platís Gialós

**Petinos Beach**, **t** 028 902 4310, **f** 028 902 3680, *george@petinos.myk.forthnet.gr* (*A; lux*). Ritzy pastel paradise with every facility, incl. pool and water sports.

**San Giorgio**, Parága, **t** 028 902 7474, *sangiorgio @gats.gr* (*A; lux*). Classy, with a sea-water pool and all comforts, incl. mini-bars.

**Zephyros**, Parága, **t** 028 902 3928, **f** 028 902 4902 (*C; lux–exp*). Has a pool at more manageable prices.

**Argo**, **t** 028 902 3405, **f** 028 902 4936, *argo@ otenet.gr* (*E; exp*). Friendly, clean and possibly a pool by the time you get there.

**Studios Katerina**, **t** 028 902 4086, **f** 028 902 7486 (*exp*). Pleasant self-catering facilities set back from the beach.

**Mýkonos Camping**, Parága Beach, **t** 028 902 4578. Preferable camping option, with good facilities and, again, minibus and boat service from Platís Gialós.

**Paradise Beach Camping**, **t** 028 902 2582, *paradise@paradise.myk.forthnet.gr.* Barracks-like, but there are a few cabins and good facilities, minibus and continuous boat service from Platís Gialós.

## Further East: Kalafátis and Áno Merá

**Anemoessa**, at Kalafátis, **t** 028 907 1420, **f** 028 907 2280 (*B; lux*). Built in the Cycladic style, with pool and Jacuzzi, and serves a big American buffet breakfast. It's a long way from the beach, though.

**Marcos**, at Kalafátis. Italian seafood restaurant – an old standby.

**Nikola's**, in nearby Ag. Ánna, at the end of the road that crosses the island. Authentic and a local favourite.

**Áno Merá**, at Áno Merá, **t** 028 907 1113, *gats-sa@gats.gr* (*A; lux–exp*). Cavernous building offering remarkable value given its Olympic-size pool, disco and restaurant, recommended for its meat dishes.

**Stavros**, on the square in Áno Merá. Good restaurant run by the Stavrokopoúlos family.

**Vangelis Taverna**. The other choice, set back from the square and more of a grill house, serving popular delights such as *exohikó*, *kléftiko* and suckling pig.

# Entertainment and Nightlife

Plunge into the old town's labyrinth for no end of quaint café/bars for that evening drink or ice cream; L'Unico is a nice one, opposite Ag. Kyriakí. An open-air cinema also operates in season. The international and gay set still bop the night away in venues ranging from the cosy to the crazy. The waterfront from Cathedral Square to Paraportiani is lined with inviting places for sunset connoisseurs:

**Galleraki Bar** and **Kástro's**, in Little Venice. Famous for sunset views, classical sounds and strawberry daiquiris.

**Bolero**. Good music and cocktails.

**Piano Bar**, above taxi square. Offers live music and snazzy cocktails; arrive early for a seat.

**Mona Lisa**, above taxi square. Plays lots of salsa and other Latin numbers.

**Astra Bar**. High-tech cool place to be seen.

**City Club**. Has a nightly transvestite show.

**Icarus**, above Pierro's (*see below*). Where the sexiest stuff provocatively struts its way along the bar.

**Mykonos Dancing Bar**. This perennial favourite plays Greek music.

**Zorba's**. Has live *rembétika*.

**Mad Club**, in taxi square. Tiny and popular.

**Pierro's**, just back from the main waterfront. The most frenzied of the lot, where hordes gyrate to the loud, lively music.

**Cava Paradiso**, on the rocks on Paradise Beach. Hosts superstar DJs.

**Super Paradise Beach Bar**. Starts pumping around noon.

## Mythology

In myth Mýkonos is best known as a graveyard, site of the rock tombs of the giants slain by Hercules and that of Ajax the Lokrian, a hero of the Trojan War. This Ajax was known as Little Ajax to differentiate him from Big Ajax, who committed suicide when the weapons of the dead Achilles were given to Odysseus rather than him. After the capture of Troy, Little Ajax proved himself just as pathetic a hero when he raped Priam's daughter Cassandra, who had sought protection in a Temple of Athena. Athena avenged this blasphemy by wrecking Ajax's ship off the coast of Mýkonos. Poseidon saved him in a storm but, defiant Ajax declared that he would have been perfectly able to save himself without the god's assistance. Poseidon's trident finished Ajax then and there, and his Mycenaean tomb can still be seen at Pórtes.

# Chóra

Prosperity has kept the homes of **Chóra** (ΧΩPA), the island's picture-postcard capital and port, gleaming and whitewashed, with brightly painted wooden trims. During the day it is a quiet place as everyone hits the beach; at night it vibrates. In the main square a bust of war heroine Mantó Mavrogenous guarded left luggage in simpler days; now dire little notices keep the backpacks away. Boats to Délos depart from further up the waterfront. The pelican mascot of Mýkonos, the successor of the original Pétros, may often be found preening himself in the shadow of the small church here. On the hill overlooking the harbour are several thatched **windmills**; one from the 16th century has been restored (*open June–Sept 4–6*). They are a favourite subject for the students at the School of Fine Arts, as is **Little Venice**, the quarter of Alefkándra, where the tall houses are picturesque and built directly on the sea, below the windmills; each abode now accommodates a cocktail bar for trendy sunset views.

Mýkonos claims to have 400 churches, some no bigger than bathrooms, and the most famous of these, beyond Little Venice, is the snow-white **Panagía Paraportianí**, an asymmetrical masterpiece of four churches melted into one. Just opposite, the **Folklore Museum** (*t 028 902 2591; open Mon–Sat 4–8, Sun 5–8*), houses old curiosities, a traditional bedroom and kitchen, and a gallery of 19th-century prints of sensuous Greek odalisques; downstairs is an exhibition, 'Mýkonos and the Sea'. **The Nautical Museum** (*t 028 902 2700; open summer 10.30–1 and 6.30–9.30; adm*), in the centre at Tria Pigádia, contains ships' models from ancient times and a collection of paintings and coins. Old anchors and copies of ancient tombstones of shipwrecked sailors fill the garden. Nearby, **Lena's House** (*t 028 902 2591; open April–end Oct, 7–9pm*) is a branch of the Folklore Museum: the 19th-century middle-class home of Léna Sakrivanoú, preserved with everything from her needlework to chamber pot. Towards the ferry quay, beyond Ag. Anna Beach, the **Archaeology Museum** (*t 028 902 2325; open Wed–Mon 9–3.30, Sun and hols 10–3; adm*) was built in 1905 in the jailhouse style to imprison boldly decorated ceramics from the necropolis islet of Rhéneia (*see* Délos, pp.251–3). The finest item was found on Tínos: a 7th-century BC funeral *pithos* with relief scenes from the Fall of Troy, like comic book strips, showing the death of Hector's son and a delightful warrior-stuffed Trojan horse, fitted with airplane windows.

# Around the Island

In ancient times Mýkonos was often the butt of jokes, especially about the baldness of its men, and even today the old fishermen never take off their caps. Despite all the changes, they've kept their sense of humour, and if you speak a little Greek they'll regale you with stories of the good old days – before all the tourist girls (and boys) began chasing them around. You may find a few old fellows to chat up at **Áno Merá** (ΑΝΩ ΜΕΡΑ), Mýkonos' other town, where the 16th-century **Panagía Tourlianí Monastery** with its sculpted marble steeple protects Mýkonos; it has a carved Florentine altarpiece, fine Cretan icons, an Ecclesiastical Museum and Farm Tool Museum (*ring ahead, **t** 028 907 1249*). Below, sandy **Panórmos Bay** was the site of one of Mýkonos' three ancient cities; here **Fteliá** and **Ag. Sostis** are wild beaches favoured by windsurfers. At **Linos**, by the airport, are the remains of a Hellenistic tower.

North of Chóra, the beaches at **Tagoo**, **Toúrlos** and **Ag. Stéfanos** have a lot of accommodation and people to fill it: **Fanári** to the north is considerably quieter. The nearest beaches south of Chóra are **Megáli Ámmos**, **Kórfos** and **Ornós**, all of which are built up, especially Ornós, with its cute little port. The biggest resort, however, is **Platís Gialós**, to the east, with boat excursions to the other beaches and Délos, while jet setters like to jet-ski at **Psaroú**, just before Platís Gialós. **Paradise**, with its campsite and diving school, and **Super Paradise** are the island's once notorious nudist beaches, both much less notorious now; little **Agrári**, east of Super Paradise, has somehow missed out on the exploitation. Eliá, a once quiet beach accessible by bus, is divided into straight and gay precincts; just inland sprawls **Watermania**, (*t 028 907 1685; open April–Oct*), the answer to all your aquatic desires. **Ag. Ánna** is a quieter beach, and there's the fishing hamlet and family beach at **Kalafátis**. At **Pórtes** you can spit on the 'tomb' of Ajax the troublemaker. **Tragonísi**, the islet off the east coast of Mýkonos, has numerous caves, and if you're lucky you may see a rare monk seal in one of them.

# Délos (ΔΗΛΟΣ)

*Many are your temples and shaded groves*
*Every peak, cliff and mountain high*
*Are loved by you, and the rivers that flow to the sea*
*But Phoebus, Délos is your heart's delight.*

Homeric Hymn to Apollo (8th century)

## Getting There and Around

**By sea: tourist boats** from Mýkonos leave between 8.30am and 1pm daily (except on Mon), returning between 12noon and 3pm, for around €6 return. Guided tours (€15) are available from agencies, or alternatively hire a **private boat** at the main harbour.

## Where to Stay and Eat

It isn't possible to stay on Délos at all. Near the museum there is an overpriced café designed to trap tourists. Don't be caught out; bring your own snacks and plenty of water with you.

# Délos

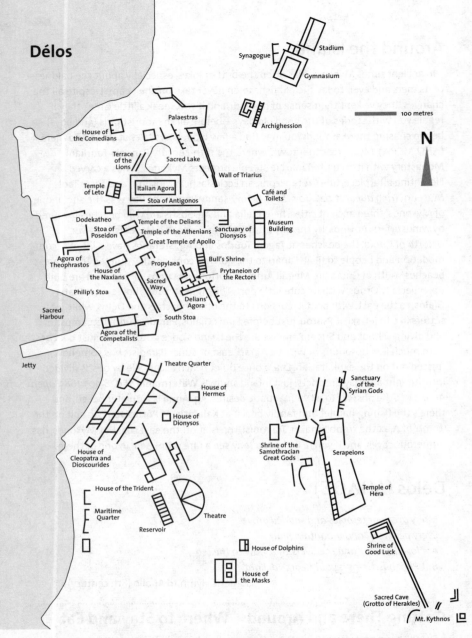

Synagogue · Stadium · Gymnasium · Archighession · Palaestras · House of the Comedians · Terrace of the Lions · Sacred Lake · Wall of Triarius · Café and Toilets · Temple of Leto · Italian Agora · Stoa of Antigonos · Dodekatheo · Temple of the Delians · Sanctuary of Dionysos · Museum Building · Stoa of Poseidon · Temple of the Athenians · Great Temple of Apollo · Agora of Theophrastos · Propylaea · Bull's Shrine · House of the Naxians · Sacred Way · Prytaneion of the Rectors · Philip's Stoa · Delians' Agora · Sacred Harbour · South Stoa · Agora of the Competalists · Jetty · Theatre Quarter · House of Hermes · Sanctuary of the Syrian Gods · House of Dionysos · Shrine of the Samothracian Great Gods · Serapeions · House of Cleopatra and Dioscourides · Temple of Hera · House of the Trident · Maritime Quarter · Theatre · Reservoir · House of Dolphins · Shrine of Good Luck · House of the Masks · Sacred Cave (Grotto of Herakles) · Mt. Kythnos

100 metres

N

Mýkonos could have no greater contrast than its little neighbour Délos; holy island of the ancient Greeks, centre of the great maritime alliance of the Athenian golden age, and hub of the Cyclades. It is now a vast open-air museum. A major free port in Hellenistic and Roman times that controlled much of the east–west trade in the Mediterranean, today it is completely deserted except for the lonely guardian of the ruins – and the boatloads of day-trippers. Even though the ancients allowed no burials on Délos, the islet is haunted by memories of the 'splendour that was Greece'; the Delians themselves seem to have been reincarnated as little lizards, darting among the poppies and pieces of broken marble.

## History

In the 3rd millennium BC Délos was settled by people from Caria in Asia Minor. By 1000 BC the Ionians had made it their religious capital, centred around the cult of Apollo, the father of Ion, the founder of their race – a cult first mentioned in a Homeric hymn of the 7th century BC. Games and pilgrimages took place, and Délos was probably the centre of the Amphictyonic Maritime League of the Ionians. In 550 BC Polycrates, the Tyrant of Samos, conquered the Cyclades but respected the sanctity of Délos, putting the islet Rhéneia under its control, and symbolically binding it to Délos with a chain. With the rise of Athens, notably under Pisistratos, Délos knew its greatest glory and biggest headaches. What was once sacred became political as the Athenians invented stories to connect themselves to the islet – did not Erechtheus, the King of Athens, lead the first delegation to Délos? After slaying the Minotaur on Crete did not Theseus stop at Délos and dance around the altar of Apollo? In 543 BC the Athenians even managed to trick (or bribe) the oracle at Delphi into ordering the purification of the island, which meant removing the old tombs, a manoeuvre

## Mythology

Zeus, they say, once fancied an ancient moon goddess named Asteria. She fled him in the form of a quail, and Zeus turned himself into an eagle to pursue her. The pursuit proved so hot that Asteria turned into a rock and fell into the sea. But in an older version of the story, Asteria was actually the sacred ship of the sky, crewed by the first Hyperborians, who after thousands of years alighted in Egypt and sailed up the Nile to this spot. The ship-rock was called Ortygia ('quail') or Adélos, 'the invisible', as it floated all over Greece like a submarine just below the sea's surface.

Zeus subsequently fell in love with Asteria's sister Leto, and, despite the previous failure of the bird disguise, succeeded in making love to her in the form of a swan – the subject of some of the most erotic fancies produced by Michelangelo and other Renaissance artists. But Zeus' humourless, jealous, Thurberesque wife Hera soon got wind of the affair and begged Mother Earth not to allow Leto to give birth anywhere under the sun. All over the world wandered poor, suffering, overripe Leto, unable to find a rock to stand on, as all feared the wrath of Hera. Finally in pity Zeus turned to his brother Poseidon and asked him to lend a hand. Poseidon thereupon ordered Ortygia to halt, and anchored the islet with four columns of diamond. Thus Adélos the Invisible, not under the sun but under the sea, became Délos, or 'visible'. Délos was still reluctant to host Leto, fearing her divine offspring would give the island a resounding kick back into the sea. But Leto promised the islet that her son would make it the richest sanctuary in Greece. Délos conceded, and Leto gave birth first to Artemis, goddess of the hunt and virginity, and then nine days later to Phoebus Apollo, the god of reason and light.

designed to alienate the Delians from their past and diminish the island's importance in comparison to Athens.

In 490 BC the population of Délos fled to Tínos before the Persian king of kings, Darius, who, according to Herodotus, not only respected the sacred site and sacrificed 300 talents' worth of incense to Apollo, but allowed the Delians to return home in safety. After the Persian defeat at the Battle of Salamis the Athenians, to counter further invasions, organized a new Amphictyonic League, again centred at Délos. Only the Athenian fleet could guarantee protection to the islands, who in return were required to contribute a yearly sum and ships to support the navy; Athenian *archons* administered the funds. The Delian alliance was effective, despite resentment amongst islanders who disliked being bossed around by the Athenians. No one was fooled in 454 BC when Pericles, in order better to 'protect' the league's treasury, removed it to Athens' Acropolis; the money went not only to repair damage incurred during the previous Persian invasion, but to beautify Athens generally. Shortly afterwards, divine retribution hit Athens in the form of a terrible plague, and as it was determined to have been caused by the wrath of Apollo, a second purification of Délos (not Athens, mind) was called for in 426 BC. This time, not only did the Athenians remove all the old tombs, but they forbade both birth and death on Délos, forcing the pregnant and the dying to go to Rhéneia and completing the alienation of the Delians. When the people turned to Sparta for aid during the Peloponnesian War, the Spartans remained unmoved: since the inhabitants couldn't be born or die on the island, they reasoned that Délos wasn't really their homeland, and why should they help a group of foreigners? In 422 BC Athens punished Délos for courting Sparta by exiling the entire population (for being 'impure') to Asia Minor, where all the leaders were slain. Athenian settlers moved in to take the Delians' place, but Athens herself was punished by the gods for her greed and suffered many setbacks against Sparta. After a year, hoping to regain divine favour, Athens allowed the Delians to return. In 403 BC, when Sparta defeated Athens, Délos had a breath of freedom for 10 years before Athens formed its second Delian alliance. It was far less forceful, and 50 years later the Delians had plucked up the courage to ask the league to oust the Athenians altogether. But the head of the league at the time, Philip II of Macedon, refused the request, wishing to stay in the good graces of the city that hated him most.

In the confusion following the death of Philip's son, Alexander the Great, Délos became free and prosperous, supported by the pious Macedonian general-kings. New buildings and shrines were constructed and by 250 BC Délos was a flourishing cosmopolitan commercial port, inhabited by merchants from all over the Mediterranean. When the Romans defeated the Macedonians in 166 BC they returned the island to Athens, which once again exiled the Delians. But by 146 BC and the fall of Corinth, Délos was the centre of all east–west trade, and declared a free port by the Romans in order to undermine the competition at Rhodes. People came from all over the world to settle in this ancient Greek Hong Kong, and set up their own cults in complete tolerance. Roman trade guilds centred on the Italian Agora. New quays and piers were constructed in order to deal with the heavy flow of vessels. The slave markets thrived. But in the battle of the Romans against Mithridates of Pontus in 88 BC, Délos was robbed of many treasures; 20,000 people were killed, and the women and children enslaved. This was the beginning of the end. Sulla regained the island, but 19 years later Délos was again pillaged by pirates allied to Mithridates, who once more sold the population into slavery. General Triarius retook and fortified the island and Hadrian attempted to revive the waning cult of Apollo with new festivities, but by this time Délos had fallen into such a decline that, when Athens tried to sell it, no one offered to buy. In AD 363, Emperor Julian the Apostate tried to jumpstart paganism on Délos until the oracles warned: 'Délos shall become Adélos.' Later Theodosius the Great banned heathen ceremonies. A small Christian community survived until the 6th century, when it was given over to the rule of pirates. House-builders on Tínos and Mýkonos used Délos for a marble quarry, and its once busy markets became pasture.

After the War of Independence, Délos and Rhéneia were placed in the municipality of Mýkonos. Major archaeological excavations were begun in 1872 by the French School of Archaeology in Athens under Dr Lebeque, and work continues to this day.

## The Excavations

*A trip to **Délos** (t 028 902 2259; open Tues–Sun 8.30–3) begins as you clamber out of the caique and pay the €5 entrance fee. Sensible shoes, sunhat, and water are essential. Major sites are labelled, badly translated guidebooks are on sale, and everything of interest can be seen in 2–3 hours. Think of the summer crowds talking in a dozen languages as a fair reconstruction of what Délos was like in its heyday! To get your bearings head up the hill, **Mount Kýthnos**, which has a great view over the site and the neighbouring islands of Mýkonos, Tínos and Sýros.*

To your left from the landing stage is the **Agora of the Competalists**. *Compita* were Roman citizens or freed slaves who worshipped the Lares Competales, or crossroads gods. These Lares gods were the patrons of Roman trade guilds, while others came under the protection of Hermes, Apollo or Zeus; many of the remains in the *agora* were votive offerings built to them. A road, once lined with statues, leads to the sanctuary of Apollo. To the left of the road stood a tall and splendid Doric colonnade called **Philip's Stoa**, built by Philip V of Macedon in 210 BC, and now marked only by its foundations; it once held a votive statue dedicated by Sulla after his victory over Mithridates. The kings of Pergamon built the **Southern Stoa** in the 3rd century BC, and you can also make out the remains of the **Delians' Agora**, the local marketplace.

The **Sanctuary of Apollo** is announced by the **Propylaea**, a gateway built of white marble in the 2nd century BC. Little remains of the sanctuary itself, once crowded with temples, votive offerings and statues. Next door is the **House of the Naxians** (6th century BC). A huge *kouros*, or statue of Apollo as a young man, originally stood here, of which only the pedestal remains. According to Plutarch, the *kouros* was crushed when a nearby bronze palm donated by Athens (symbolic of the tree clutched by Leto in giving birth) toppled over in the wind.

Next are three temples in a row. The first and largest, the **Great Temple of Apollo**, was begun by the Delians in 476 BC. The second was an **Athenian Temple** of Pentelic marble, built during the Second Purification, and the smallest, of porous stone, the **Temple of the Delians**, was made by the 6th-century Athenian tyrant Pisistratos to house the sacred Asteria, the 'ship of the sky', represented by a moon setting in the sea. Dimitrios the Besieger contributed the nearby **Bull's Shrine**, which held a model of another ship, a *trireme* in honour of the sacred Athenian delegation ship – the one Theseus sailed in on his return to Athens after slaying the Minotaur, and whose departure put off executions (most famously that of Socrates) until its return to Athens. Other buildings in the area were of an official nature – the **Prytaneion of the Rectors** and the **Councillor's House**. Towards the museum is the **Sanctuary of Dionysos** (4th century BC), flanked by lucky marble phalli. The **Stoa of Antigonos** was built by a Macedonian king of that name in the 3rd century BC. Outside is the **Tomb of the Hyperborean Virgins**, who came to help Leto give birth to Apollo and Artemis – a sacred tomb and thus the only one to stay put during the purifications.

On the opposite side of the Stoa stood the **Abaton**, the holy of holies, where only the priests could enter. The **Minoan Fountain** nearby is from the 6th century BC. Through the **Italian Agora** you can reach the Temple of Leto (6th century) and the **Dodekatheon**, dedicated to the 12 gods of Olympos in the 3rd century BC. Beyond, where the **Sacred Lake** once hosted a flock of swans, is the famous **Terrace of the Lions**, ex-votos made from Naxian marble in the 7th century BC; originally nine, one now sits by the arsenal in Venice and three have permanently gone missing. The site of the lake, sacred for having witnessed the birth of Apollo, is marked by a small wall. When Délos' torrent Inopos stopped flowing, the water evaporated. Along the shore are two **Palaestras** (for exercises and lessons) along with the foundation of the **Archigession**, or temple to the first mythical settler on Délos, worshipped only here. Besides the **Gymnasium** and **Stadium** are remains of a few houses and a **synagogue** built by the Phoenician Jews in the 2nd century BC.

A dirt path leads from the tourist pavilion to Mount Kýthnos. Along the way stand the ruins of the **Sanctuary of the Syrian Gods** of 100 BC, with a small religious theatre inside. Next is the first of three 2nd-century BC **Serapeions**, all temples dedicated to Serapis, the first and only successful god purposely invented by man – Ptolemy I of Egypt, who combined Osiris with Diónysos to create a synthetic deity in order to please both Hellenistic Greeks and Egyptians; syncretic Délos was one of the chief centres of his worship. Between the first and second Serapeions is the **Shrine to the Samothracian Great Gods**, the Cabiri or underworld deities. The third Serapeion (still housing half a statue) was perhaps the main sanctuary, with temples to both Serapis and Isis. In the region are houses with mosaic floors, and a **Temple to Hera** from 500 BC. **The Sacred Cave**, where Apollo ran one of his many oracles, is en route to the top of Mount Kýthnos, later it was dedicated to Heracles. On the mountain itself is the **Shrine of Good Luck**, built by Arsinoë Philadelphos, wife of her brother, the King of Egypt. On the 370ft summit, signs of a settlement dating back to 3000 BC have been discovered, but better yet is the view, encompassing nearly all the Cyclades.

The exclusive **Theatre Quarter** surrounded the 2nd-century BC **Theatre of Délos**, with a 5,500 capacity; beside it is a lovely eight-arched **reservoir**. The houses here date from the Hellenistic and Roman ages and many have beautiful mosaics, such as in the

House of the Dolphins and the House of the Masks. All have a cistern beneath the floor and sewage systems. Some are built in the peristyle 'style of Rhodes', with a high-ceilinged guest room and colonnades surrounding the central courts. Seek out the mosaics of the House of the Trident and the House of Dionysos and the House of Cleopatra and Dioscourides, where the headless statues stand guard.

Surrounding Délos are the islets Ag. Geórgios, Karavoníssi, Mikró and Megálo Rematiáris. Rhéneia lies west of Délos and is just as uninhabited. Here came the pregnant or dying Delians – a large number of little rooms were excavated in the rock to receive them, before they moved into the realm of tombs and sepulchral altars. A necropolis near the shore was the repository of the coffins which the Athenians exhumed in the second purification. On the other side of Rhéneia are the ruins of a *lazaretto* (leprosy hospital), once used by Sýros-bound ships sent into quarantine.

# Náxos (ΝΑΞΟΣ)

Náxos is a big fish in a little pond, the largest of the Cyclades (4,48sq km), and the highest, thanks to Mount Zas at 3,295ft and the most fertile: its 17,000 year-round residents grow much of their own food, in valleys that remain a refreshing green even in the height of the sizzling summer. It can also claim to be the most sacred to Dionysos: Náxos makes excellent wine, as well as Kítron, a fragrant liqueur distilled from citron leaves, but seed potatoes are the main export. The west coast is almost one uninterrupted beach of silvery sands. Náxos was Byron's favourite island, perhaps because it comes in romantic proportions: rugged mountains and lush valleys, sprinkled with the ruins of the ancient Greeks, the gilded Byzantines and his beloved Venetians. There are plenty of tourists, especially Germans and Scandinavians, but they stay by the beaches, leaving the rest of the big island to wanderers and poets.

## History

Náxos was one of the major centres of the Neolithic Cycladic civilization. Around 3000 BC, the main settlements were near Chóra, on the hill of the Kástro and at Grótta, where the remains of the houses can still be seen in the clear water. Tradition has it that the island was later colonized by a party from Karia, led by a son of Apollo named Náxos. Although these Naxians were Ionians, their most troublesome enemy was Miletus in Ionia proper, where Naxian refugees, eager to take back the island for themselves, fomented trouble. At the time, the most important citadel on the island was Delion, of which a few vestiges remain. Once when Miletus attacked Náxos and the alarm was raised, a beautiful islander named Polykrite arrived too late and found the gate at Delion closed against her. One of the Miletan leaders found her, fell in love and proved it by telling her of all his armies' movements. His information enabled the Naxians to make a sudden attack on the Miletians, but in the confusion of the battle Polykrite's lover was killed, and the girl died of sorrow the next day.

Náxos was one of the first islands to work in marble. In the Archaic period sculptors produced the lions of Délos and the largest *kouros* statues ever found. But big was

# Náxos

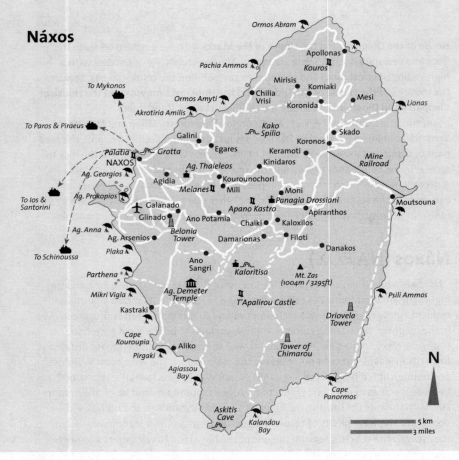

beautiful on Náxos; in 523 BC the tyrant Lugdamis declared he would make Náxos' buildings the highest in Greece, but only the massive lintel from the Temple of Apollo survives to tell the tale of his ambition. Náxos next makes the history books in 1207 when the Venetian Marco Sanudo captured the island's Byzantine castle, T'Apaliroú, and declared himself Duke of Náxos, ruler over all the adventurers who'd grabbed up islands after the conquest of Constantinople in 1204. In 1210, when Venice refused to grant Sanudo the status he desired, he hitched his wagon to the Roman Emperor and took the title Duke of the Archipelago ('Archelopelago' was a corruption of 'Aegean' as it appeared on Byzantine sea charts, Aigaíon Pélagos; under Sanudo's successors, the word gained its current meaning as a group of islands). Even after the Turkish conquest in 1564, the Dukes of Náxos remained in nominal control of the Cyclades.

# Náxos Town

The island's port and capital, **Náxos**, is a bustling place sprawling at the foot of the old town piled over a low conical hill. By the port, the island's P-shaped trademark, the **Portára** of Lugdamis' unfinished **Temple of Apollo** (522 BC), stands like an ancient version of the enigmatic monolith in *2001: A Space Odyssey*, a massive doorway to nowhere, or perhaps another dimension. Set on the islet of **Palátia**, linked by an ancient causeway to the port, it comes in handy as a frame for cheesy sunset photos. The ancient **harbour mole** was rebuilt by Marco Sanudo; in front of the port. Statues

## Getting There and Around

**By air**: 2–3 flights a day from Athens with Olympic Airways; charters from London and Manchester. **Airport**: t 028 502 3292; close to town – take a taxi.

**By sea**: Náxos is one of the big ferry hubs all year round. In high season, **ferries** and **hydrofoils** connect several times a day with Piraeus; daily with Rafína, Páros, Íos, Santoríni, Mýkonos and Sýros; smaller craft almost daily with Amorgós via Heráklia, Schinoússa, Koufoníssi and Donoússa; less frequent connections with Sámos, Kos and Rhodes; daily excursion boats to Délos, Mýkonos, Páros and Santoríni. **Port authority**: t 028 502 2300.

**By road**: frequent **bus** services from Náxos Town, by the dock, t 028 502 2291, every ½hr down to Ag. Prokópios and Ag. Ánna Beach; 6 times a day to Filóti and Chalki; 5 times to Apíranthos; 4 times to Apollónas, Kóronos, Pirgáki, and Kastráki; 2–3 times to Komiáki and Mélanes. **Taxi** rank by the bus station, t 028 502 2444. Taxis are not metered, so agree on a price first. **Car** and **motorbike** rentals abound along the waterfront. Try **Tourent a Car**, t 028 502 3330, f 028 502 3419 or **Moto Falcon**, over towards Ag. Geórgios, t 028 502 5323, f 028 502 5035, for motorbikes and bicycles.

## Tourist Information

Popular Náxos is very tourist friendly.
**Tourist Information Centre**, by the quay, t 028 502 5201, f 028 502 5200, *chateau-zevgoli@nax.forthnet.gr*. Organizes accommodation; also luggage-storage and laundry facilities.
**Zas Travel**, nearby, t 028 502 3330, f 028 502 3419, *zas-travel@nax.forthnet.gr*. Handles Olympic Airways.
**Naxos Tours**, t 028 502 3043, f 028 502 3951, *naxostours@naxos-island.com*. Another helpful source for accommodation, car rentals and excursions.

**Zoom Bookstore**, on the waterfront. Excellent selection of maps and guides, incl. Christian Ucke's helpful *Walking Tours in Náxos*.

## Internet

Náxos is well connected.
**Potikian Internet Café**, by the quayside, *potikian@nax.forthnet.gr*. This is the handiest café.

## Festivals

**23 April**: Kinídaros.
**1 July**: Sangrí.
**14 July**: the biggest of all for Ag. Nikódimos, patron saint of Náxos, with a procession of the icon and folk festival.
**17 July**: in Kórono.
**first week of Aug**: the Dionýsia festival in Náxos Town, with folk dancing in local costume and free food and wine.
**15 Aug**: Filóti.
**23 Aug**: Trípodes.
**29 Aug**: Apóllon and Apíranthos.

## Where to Stay and Eat

**Náxos** ✉ 84300
If you don't book, the **Hotel and Rooms Association** on the quay has a kiosk with photos of everything on offer; next to it, another kiosk has camping information. Ferries are met by campsite and room owners, with minibuses. Beware that many of their rooms are in Néa Chóra (10–15min walk from the ferries), unlovely but handy for the beach; if you stay there, make sure you can find your way 'home' through its anonymous streets.

### Náxos Town
Staying in car-free Chóra, behind the waterfront promenade, is delightful.

of two famous sons of Náxos greet you: Michaeli Damiralis (d. 1917), who translated Shakespeare into Greek, and the disappointed-looking Pétros Protopapadákis, who planned the Corinth Canal but had the misfortune of serving as Minister of Economics during the 1920–22 catastrophe in Asia Minor; he was executed with five other ministers as scapegoats by the subsequent regime.

**Château Zevgoli, t** 028 502 6123, *chateau-zevgoli@forthnet.gr* (*C; exp*). Spoil yourself in this plush old mansion, small and exclusive with roof garden, antique décor and a four-poster for honeymooners. Run by the manager of the Náxos Tourist Information Centre; enquire there.

**Grotta,** in Grótta, the northern suburb of Chóra, **t** 028 502 2215, *info@hotelgrotta.gr* (*C; exp*). Another blue and white creation with wonderful sea views; the owner will collect you from the quay.

**Nikos Verikokos,** on the Kástro hill, **t** 028 502 2025 (*rooms, mod; studios, exp*). A less expensive choice by the Pantanássa church, offfering views.

**Anixis,** up by the Kástro, **t** 028 502 2932, *hotelanixis@nax.forthnet.gr* (*D; mod*). Very moderate, overlooking the sea from its verandas and terraces.

**Boúrgos,** Amphitris St, in Boúrgos, **t/f** 028 502 2979 (*C; mod*). Another pleasant choice, especially the airy studio off the roof terrace.

**Iliada Studios,** in Grótta, **t** 028 502 3303, *iliada @naxos-island.com* (*mod*). Overlooking the sea.

**Pantheon,** just up from the entrance to the Kástro hill, **t** 028 502 4335 (*D; mod*). Run by a lovely couple, one of these 6 en suite rooms is the closest you'll get to what 'living' in the old town is like for the everyday inhabitant.

**Panorama,** Amphitris St, in Boúrgos, just outside the Kástro's walls, **t/f** 028 502 4404 (*C; inexp*). Pleasant small hotel, with a marvellous sea view.

**Sofi,** a 3min walk from the docks, at the base of the Kástro hill, **t** 028 502 3077, **f** 028 502 5582 (*inexp*). Attractive place that has seen the same customers for 20 yrs, thanks to the friendly Koufópoulos family (*see* below).

**Delfini,** on the Kástro hill under the wall. Café/bar with a lovely garden setting, serving generous drinks, snacks, Indian and Thai curry dishes, incl. some for vegetarians.

The owner spent years in England, where he got hooked on Asian food.

**Kástro,** Bradóuna Square, just under the Kástro's walls, **t** 028 502 2005. Delicious rabbit *stifádo* and *exohikó*, filo parcels.

**Koutouki,** hidden away in a narrow Kástro street. Another hearty option.

**Oniro,** a few steps away from the Kástro, **t** 028 502 3846. Candlelit tables in a courtyard, and a roof garden with a dream view over town; try the *arni bouti yemistó*, lamb stuffed with garlic and bacon.

**Manolis,** in a quiet courtyard on Old Market St, in the old heart of Chóra. Good value traditional food: ask for the specials and try the homemade *rakí* (good in itself and even better in '*rakimelo*', warmed with honey and a great cure for coughs).

**Picasso,** in main Plateia Protodikíou, below the Kástro. Popular restaurant with Mexican specialities such as tortillas, guacamole and salsas. Also a second-hand book exchange.

**Apolafsis** by the waterfront. Fine Greek food with live Greek music.

**Karnayo,** by the water, **t** 028 502 3057. Decent fish taverna; everything's fresh – the owner, a fisherman, catches it himself – incl. the lobster, cooked to your order.

**Meltemi,** 5 mins from the docks towards Ag. Geórgios, **t** 028 502 2654. Excellent waterfront taverna which has been serving delicious Greek meals for 25 years.

**Gallini,** 10min stroll away, **t** 028 502 5206. Proper Greek fish tavern; friendly service.

**Probonas.** Shop on the waterfront, where you can taste the local Kítron liqueur (regular, mint or banana flavour); Náxos wine is good as well, but it is best drunk from a barrel in situ because it's famous for not travelling well.

## Néa Chóra and Ag. Geórgios

**Nissaki Beach Hotel, t** 028 502 5710, *nissaki@ naxos.island.com* (*C; exp*). Rooms circling the pool, with restaurant-bar.

On the waterfront, by the Agrarian Bank, the 11th-century church of **Panagía Pantanássa** was once part of a Byzantine monastery and famous for its very early icon of the Virgin. Lanes here lead up into old Náxos, a fine Cycladic town, although you may find its twisting streets bewildering, which is just as the natives intended, to confuse invading marauders. The town was divided into three neighbourhoods:

**Panos Studios**, 20m from the beach on a quiet street, t 028 502 6078, *studiospanos@in.gr* (*mod*). Spick and span, well-appointed studios, run by the wonderful Koufópoulos family, whose warm welcome includes a free *ouzo* or coffee as they dispense helpful advice from their vast knowledge of Náxos.

**St George Beach**, on the beach, t 028 502 3162, f 028 502 5233 (*E; mod*). Arched verandas.

**Irene Pension**, t 028 502 3169, *irenepension@hotmail.com* (*inexp*). Quiet, family-run, good value; with air-con.

**Camping Náxos**, by the beach, t 028 502 3500, f 028 502 3502. Has a pool.

**Kavouri**, on Ag. Geórgios Beach. An old favourite; good fish soup and other dishes with Naxian wine for over 40 years.

### Beaches South of Chóra: Ag. Prokópios

**Kavouras Village**, t 028 502 5580, f 028 502 5800 (*B; lux*). Flower-bedecked studios; pool.

**Camping Apollon**, t 028 502 4117.

### Ag. Ánna

**Iria Beach Apartments**, right by the beach, t 028 504 4178, f 028 504 2602 (*C; lux–exp*). Range of facilities incl. car hire. Upstairs studios have attractive balconies.

**Studios Anemos**, above the bakery, t 028 504 1919 (*mod–inexp*).

**Ag. Ánna**, right by the sea, t 028 504 2576, f 028 504 2704 (*C; inexp*). With verandas and fruits of the orchard to feast on.

**Camping Maragas**, t 028 502 4552. German-run and immaculate.

**Gorgonas**, on the beach, t 028 504 1007. For fishy dishes, incl. lobster and seafood pasta, in a courtyard setting.

**Paradise Taverna**. Tasty Greek dishes, a terrace shaded by a vast pine tree and an infectious atmosphere.

### Pláka, Mikri Vigla, and Kastráki

**Villa Medusa**, at Pláka, t 028 507 5555, f 028 507 5500 (*A; exp*). A favourite of sophisti-cated windsurfers; rooms are furnished with antiques, mini bars and satellite TV.

**Aronis Taverna**, on the Ag. Ánna–Pláka Beach road, t 028 504 2019, f 028 504 2021 (*mod–exp*). Clean studios by the sea and a hippy eatery; the road is lined with similar studios.

**Mikri Vigla**, at Mikrí Vígla, on the beach, t 028 507 5241, *www.euripiotis.gr* (*B; exp*). New low-rise mini-resort in Cycladic style, with a pool and surfing centre.

**Summerland Complex**, at Kastráki, t 028 507 5461, *summerland@ath.forthnet.gr* (*exp*). Relaxed apartments around two pools and bars, with gym, Jacuzzi and mini-market on site, good for entertaining kids.

**Yiannis**, at Kastráki, t 028 507 5413 (*mod*).

### Apollónas

**Flora's Apartments**, t 028 506 7070 (*mod*). Pleasant, built around a garden.

**Efthimios**, at Órmos Ábram, t 028 506 3244 (*inexp–mod*). If you want to get away from it all; it also has a taverna.

# Entertainment and Nightlife

Náxos has a buzzing nightlife with masses of bars.

**Veggera**, near the OTE. Smartish and popular.

**Med Bar**, adjacent to Veggera. With a terrace overlooking the water.

**Cocos Café** and **Rendezvous**, on the main waterfront. Relaxed places to sit.

**Lakridi Jazz Bar**, in Chóra, Old Market St. The mellowest of places in the evening.

**Ocean Club**, right on the sea. Dance the night away, watching the sun rise through the giant window.

**Cream**. 'A club that is always on top'.

**Super Island**, in Grotta. A thumping club.

**Enosis**, in Ag. Ánna, t 028 502 4644. Popular club in old warehouse playing Greek music.

## Mythology

After slaying the Minotaur (*see* pp.116–17) Theseus and Ariadne, the Cretan princess who loved him, stopped to rest at Náxos on their way to Athens. Yet the next morning, while Ariadne slept, Theseus set sail and abandoned her. This, even in the eyes of the male chauvinist Athenians, was dishonourable, especially as Theseus had promised to marry Ariadne in return for the assistance she had rendered him in negotiating the Labyrinth. Did he simply forget her or find a new mistress? Was she shot with arrows by Artemis in the Temple of Dionysos and left for dead, as the *Odyssey* says? or did the god Dionysos, who soon found the abandoned Ariadne and married her, somehow warn Theseus off? Everyone agrees that it was the jilted bride's curse on Theseus that made him forget to change his black sails to white to signal his safe homecoming, causing his father to commit suicide in despair. Ariadne lived happily ever after with Dionysos, who taught the Naxians how to make their excellent wine and set Ariadne's crown, the Corona Borealis, amongst the stars; the Celts called it Ariansrod, where their heroes went after death. The story inspired later artists as well, including Richard Strauss, who wrote the opera *Ariadne auf Náxos*.

**Boúrgos** where the Greeks lived; **Evraiki**, the Jewish quarter; and up above, **Kástro**, where the Venetian Catholic nobility lived. In Boúrgos, the Orthodox Cathedral, the **Metropolis of Zoodóchos Pigí**, was created in the 18th century out of an old temple and older churches; its iconostasis is by Dimítrios Valvis of the Cretan school. Archaeologists would gladly knock it down for a slam-bang dig if only the bishop would let them; as it is they've had to be content with the cordoned-off ruins of the Mycenaean town under the adjacent square (*open Tues–Sun 8–2*). The cathedral looks down over **Grótta**, the coast named for its numerous caves (naturally re-dubbed Grotty by Brits); if it's not windy you can see remains of the prehistoric Cycladic town and a road under the water; one hollow in the rock is the 'Bath of Ariadne'. Ancient **Fort Delion**, scene of starcrossed love, stood just to the east.

At the very top, the high-walled **Kástro** preserves one of its seven original towers, guarding one of three entrances into the district's jumble of stunning houses, flowers and dark alleys. Some 19 Venetian houses still bear their coats-of-arms – something you'll almost never see in Venice proper, where such displays of pride were severely frowned upon. Most of the Kástro's current residents claim Venetian descent, and many of their grandparents' tombstones in the 13th-century **Catholic Cathedral** boast grand titles. The cathedral, clad from head to toe in pale grey marble, was founded by Marco Sanudo, whose ruined palace is directly across the square.

During the Turkish occupation, Kástro was famous for its School of Commerce, run by friars and attended for two years by Níkos Kazantzákis. This is now the **Archaeology Museum**, at least until a new one is built (*t 028 502 2725; open Tues–Sun 8–2.30; adm*), with artefacts from the 5th millenium BC to 5th century AD, including a superb collection of Cycladic figurines, a Cycladic pig about to be sick in a sack from 2800 BC, Mycenaean pottery (note the hydria painted with fishermen) and a Roman mosaic of Europa. The nearby **Venetian Museum** (Domus Della-Rocca-Barozzi) preserves a traditional Kástro house (*t 028 502 2387; open Tues–Sun 10–3 and 6–10;*

*adm*) and offers guided tours in English of the area, ending with refreshments in the museum; in summer it hosts atmospheric concerts. A beautifully carved portico by the Kástro entrance leads to a choice terrace containing tables and chairs. Just below the museums, the Antico Veneziano antique shop is housed in an 800-year-old mansion, with lovingly restored 2,000-year-old Ionian columns original to the house in the erstwhile servants' quarters (now the shop); it also has fascinating photos of Náxos and Santoríni through the 20th century and a room exhibiting works by international artists.

# Around the Island

## The Southwest Coast

Further south following the waterfront, numerous hotels and a whole new suburb, Néa Chóra, have sprung up around popular **Ag. Geórgios** beach. Its shallow waters and long curl of sand are genteely lined with tavernas and hotels, forming a proper neighbourhood that contrasts with the beaches further south, where buildings have mushroomed up haphazardly. The road then skirts the fertile **Livádi** plain, where Náxos grows its famous spuds; here, near the airport at Iria, a **Temple of Dionysos** was discovered in 1986. The road continues to **Ag. Prokópios**, with nice, coarse non-sticky sand, and then **Ag. Ánna**, the most popular beach, well sheltered from the notorious *meltémi*, and **Pláka** just south, considered by many the best in Náxos, with a variety of watersports, and an alternative campsite. From Ag. Ánna, boats and bifurcating dirt roads hidden in the bamboo continue south to the beaches; by asphalt road you have to divert inland, by way of **Ag. Arsénios** (if you get off the bus here, you can take a lovely path down to the beaches, past windmills and a 30ft-high Hellenistic watch tower, the **Paleó Pírgos**). The vast white sandy beaches to the south begin at **Parthéna**, excellent for surfing and swimming, followed by **Mikrí Vígla**, where the sea is brilliantly clear; **Sahára** is well equipped for sea sports, and merges into **Kastráki**, again with sparkling sea and white sands, ideal for letting the kids run wild. Above the road stands **Pírgos Oskéllou**, a ruined Mycenaean fortress, built over the remains of a Cycladic *acropolis*. If the above beaches are too busy for your taste, there's a more remote strip of sand beyond Kastráki on either side of **Cape Kouroúpia**.

## Inland Villages: South of Náxos Town

A few kilometres east of Náxos Town the main inland road forks, the southerly right-hand branch heading first to **Galanádo**, site of the restored Venetian **Belonia Tower**, bearing the lion of St Mark, and the Venetian church of **St John**, with a Catholic chapel on the left and an Orthodox one on the right: an unusual arrangement, but one typical on Náxos. It is also seen in the island's first cathedral, the recently restored 8th-century **Ag. Mámas**, dedicated to the patron saint of thieves, located a short walk from the road, towards **Áno Sangrí** (ΣΑΝΥΚΡΙ). Consisting of three hamlets picturesquely spread out over the plateau, Áno Sangrí gets its name from 'Sainte Croix', as the French called the 16th-century tower monastery Tímiou Stavroú or True

Cross. There are many Byzantine frescoed chapels and medieval towers in the vicinity and, a pretty mile's walk south of Áno Sangrí, a 6th-century BC **Temple of Demeter**. A church on the site used much of the stone, but here at least archaeologists have taken revenge on the Christians and dismantled the church and scoured surrounding farms for other bits to fit the temple back together. A much more strenuous walk southeast of Áno Sangrí will take you up to the ruins of **T'Apaliróu**, the Byzantine castle high on its rock that defied Marco Sanudo and his mercenaries for two months.

## Inland Villages: The Tragéa and Slopes of Mount Zas

From Áno Sangrí the road rises up to the beautiful Tragéa plateau, planted with fruit trees and lilacs, flanked on either side by Náxos' highest mountains. Olive groves engulf the small villages in the valley, including **Chálki**, where both the Byzantines and Venetians built tower houses: the Byzantine **Frankópoulo**, in the centre, and up a steep path the 13th-century Venetian **Apáno Kástro**, used by Marco Sanudo as a summer hideaway. He was not, however, the first to enjoy the splendid panorama from the summit; the fortress sits on Cyclopean foundations, and Geometric era and Mycenaean tombs have been discovered to the southeast; rare for Greece, there's even a menhir nearby. In Chálki itself there are two fine churches with frescoes: 12th-century **Panagía Protóthronis** and 9th-century **Ag. Diasorítis**. A paved road leads up to a shady glade sheltering the most striking church on Náxos, **Panagía Drossianí**, built in the 5th century and crowned with ancient corbelled domes of field stones. Open most mornings (*offering expected*), it contains excellent frescoes of the Pantokrator, Virgin, and two saints. Chálki is also in the heart of Kítron territory; to see how it's made, visit the **Vallindras Náxos Citron distillery** (*t 028 502 2227; open mornings Mon–Fri and weekends in July and Aug*). Seven kms or so west of Chálki is lovely **Ano Potámia**, another well-watered town, whose taverna (Paradise Garden) is popular with Náxians wanting to escape the capital in summer.

The main road continues on to attractive **Filóti** (ΦΙΛΟΤΙ), on the slopes of Mt Zas, the largest village in the Tragéa, where contented ewes produce the island's best cheese; it also offers splendid views and the chance to eavesdrop on everyday village life away from the tourist mills. Monuments include the Venetian towerhouse of the De Lasti family, the churches **Koímisis tis Theotókou**, with a fine carved marble iconostasis, and **Panagía Filótissa**, with a marble steeple. Of the many scenic paths, one leads up the slopes of **Mount Zas**, passing by way of an ancient inscription ΟΡΟΣ ΔΙΟΣ ΜΗΛΩΣΙΟΥ ('Mount Zeus, Herd-Protector'). There's a sacred cave near the summit, where one story says baby Zeus (*see* p.116) was briefly deposited; be careful and bring a light if you want to explore – the only inhabitants now are bats. A three-hour, mostly paved path from Filóti follows the west flanks of the mountain south to the isolated and excellently preserved Hellenistic **Tower of Chimárou**, built by Ptolemy of Egypt of white marble blocks, lost in the wildest part of Náxos.

From Filóti the road skirts the slopes of Mt Zas on its way to **Apíranthos** (ΑΠΕΙΡΑΝΘΟΣ), where the Venetian families Crispi and Sommaripa built towers. Many contemporary families, however, are Cretan, descended from migrants who came during the Turkish occupation to work in Greece's only emery mines. It's the most beautiful village on Náxos, with narrow winding paths paved with marble; Byron loved it so much that he declared that he wanted to die in Apíranthos (there are a few rooms to rent if you feel the same way). The churches, to Saints Geórgios, Sofia and Ilias, are built on ancient temples to Ares, Athena and Helios respectively. A few women still weave on looms and farmers sell their produce, and there's a wonderful antique barber shop. In August, however, cocktail bars and revelry shake things up. Visit the small **Cycladic Museum**, devoted to Neolithic finds (*open 9–3; adm*), and a **Geological and Folklore Museum** (*same hours*) in the school. A road descends to the port of **Moutsoúna**, where emery, used in ancient times to polish Cycladic statues, is now brought down from the mountains near Kóronos by a rope funicular and loaded on to ships. Moutsoúna has a fine beach; from here a rather dodgy dirt road follows the east coast south to the remote beach of **Psilí Ámmos**.

## North of Náxos Town

The left branch of the main road from Náxos Town leads to **Mélanes** and the ancient marble quarries in the heart of Náxos; at Flerio, signposted off the road, lies a 7th-century BC 20ft-high *kouros* in a cypress grove. Inspired by monumental Egyptian sculpture, these Archaic statues – highly stylized, naked young men, invariably smiling, their arms hugging their sides, one foot stepping forward – were an early example of the Greek capacity to borrow ideas from others and make them their own. This one was abandoned because of a broken leg. At **Kourounochóri**, near Mélanes, stand ruins of a Venetian castle; **Ag. Thaléleos** in the same area has a monastery with a fine 13th-century church. Náxos' marble is almost as fine as Páros' and is still quarried to the east at **Kinídaros**. One of the most beautiful walks on Náxos begins here; the path descends past the chapel of the woodland goddess Ag. Artemis, and follows the lush Xerotakari River valley down to Egarés. The Xerotakari is the only river in the Cyclades to flow in August; it has little waterfalls and provides a pleasant home for turtles and eels, as well as drinking water for Náxos Town.

A paved road links **Kóronos** to **Liónas** Beach, while the main road north turns into a winding, hairpin serpent leading to pretty **Komiakí**, highest of the island's villages, with stunning views over terraced vineyards. The road leads back down to **Apóllonas** (ΑΠΟΛΛΩΝΑΣ), a dreary little town with a sandy beach and several tavernas heavily patronized by tour buses. Ancient marble quarries are carved out of the slopes of the mountain, and steps lead up to a colossal, 33ft *kouros*, abandoned in the 7th century BC because of flaws in the marble. Because Apóllonas was sacred to Apollo (an inscription is still visible on the marble wall) the statue is believed to have been intended for a long-vanished temple that stood here, which intriguingly was located to form part of a perfect equilateral triangle with the temples of Apollo on Délos and Páros. Apóllonas is as far as the bus goes; by car you can chance the road along the north coast back to Náxos Town, passing the isolated beaches of idyllic **Ormós Ábram** with a taverna, rooms and a curious giant marble head abandoned on a rock, and **Pachiá Ámmos** near the **Monastery of Faneroméni** dating from 1606. There are lovely beaches in this northwest coast, although when the *meltémi* roars you'll probably want to give them a miss.

# Páros (ΠΑΡΟΣ)

Despite the tens of thousands who descend on Páros each summer, the Cycladic houses, narrow alleys and balconies overflowing with potted plants seem to dilute their presence. The Parians have approached the boom in tourism with less fervour than their neighbours on Mýkonos, managing to maintain a Greek island atmosphere. For the most part, the inhabitants have remained fun-loving and hospitable and, if you can find a place to stay, it's a fine spot to while away a few days on golden beaches and charming villages, whose main building material comes from Páros' gentle mountain, Profitis Ilías (2,530ft) – some of the finest, most translucent marble in the world. Páros is one of the larger, more fertile Cyclades, with vineyards, wheat and barley fields, citrus and olive groves, and, unusually, pastures of grazing cattle and sheep. Apart from its beaches, the island has several other attractions, including a famous Byzantine cathedral and a valley filled with butterflies.

## History

With the trade in Parian marble, the island of Páros prospered early on. Its thriving Early Cycladic town was connected with Knossós and then with the Mycenaeans in the Late Cycladic period (1100 BC). In the 8th century BC Ionians moved in and brought about a second wave of prosperity. The 7th-century BC soldier poet Archilochos, the first to write in iambic meter and whose ironic detachment inspired Horace, was a son of Páros. During the Persian Wars, Páros defiantly supported the Persians at both

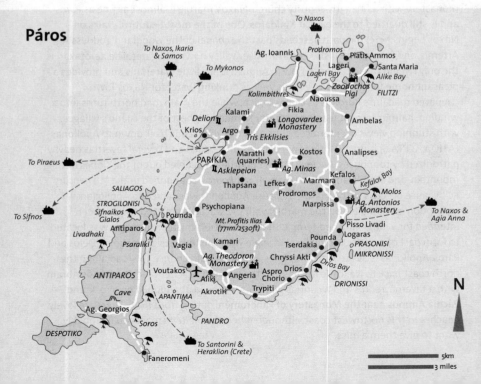

# Getting There and Around

**By air**: 2–7 flights daily in season from Athens with **Olympic Airways**, t 028 402 1900.
**Airport**: t 028 409 1256; frequent **bus** service to and from Parikiá, 14 kms away.

**By sea**: Páros is one of the great crossroads of the Aegean, with many daily **ferry**, **hydrofoil** and **catamaran** connections with Piraeus, Rafína, Náxos, Sýros, Tínos, Mýkonos, Íos and Santoríni; 3–4 times a week with Thessaloníki, Folégandros, Síkinos and Anáfi; 5 times a week to Amorgós and the Back Islands; several times a week with Sámos, Rhodes, Astypálaia, Kos and Kálymnos; twice a week with Crete, Sífnos, Sérifos, Kímolos, Mílos and Ikaría, once a week with Ándros. Hourly ferry from Poúnda (6kms south of Parikiá) to Antíparos, and many **day excursions** around Páros itself, Antíparos and other islands. **Port authority**: t 028 402 1240.

**By road**: very frequent **buses** depart from the port to all the towns and villages, and all nooks and crannies, with the exception of the south coast between Dríos and Alíki; KTEL in Parikiá, t 028 402 1395, in Náoussa, t 028 405 2865. If you want to hire a **car** or **bike**, there are signs everywhere in Parikiá, but beware of rip-offs; **Cyclades**, on the waterfront towards Livádia, t 028 402 1057, f 028 402 1056, and **Páros Europecar**, by the port, t 028 402 4408, f 028 402 2844, are among the most reliable. **Taxis** congregate by the dock and bus kiosk, and rates are pretty reasonable (€7 to Náoussa), but agree a price beforehand.

# Tourist Information

**Tourist police**: Plateía Mavroyénous, Parikiá, near the ferry dock, t 028 402 1673.
**Parikiá Information Center**, by the windmill. It's a bit of a dud.
**Cycladic Tourist Agency**, 3 mins from the port by the park, t 028 402 1738, f 028 402 2146, mpizas@otenet.gr. Helpful staff who can find you a room, rent you a car or bike, arrange excursions and horse riding.
**Vacances Horizon International**, t 028 402 4968, f 028 402 4969, vhigr@yahoo.com. For day excursions around Páros.
**Information Office** by the bus station in Náoussa, t 028 405 2158, f 028 405 1190;

open 10.30–2.30 and 5–9 but potentially all day soon. For up-to-date details of events, bus schedules and ex-pat chit-chat, pick up a copy of *The Foreigner*.
**Perantinos Travel**, Písso Livádi, t/f 028 404 1135, perantinos@par.forthnet.gr. Help with accommodation and other travel queries; open Easter–mid-Sept.
**Post office**, on the waterfront, between the port and Livádia.
**Left luggage**, next door to the quayside Kondes Hotel; open 8am–2am.
**Santa Maria Diving Club**, in Náoussa, t/f 028 405 3007, gcalligeris@hotmail.com. For scuba diving.
**Surfing Beach**, on Santa Maria Beach, t 028 405 1013, f 028 405 1937, winter t 010 922 2254. Also good for scuba diving.

# Internet

There are several waterfront cafés in Parikiá
**Calypso Café**, in Náoussa.
**Wired Café**, Main Market St, t 284 22003, St_Nicola@bigfoot.com.

# Festivals

**23 April**: Agkairia.
**21 May**: Parikiá.
**Good Friday–Easter**: Márpissa, with re-enactments of the Crucifixion.
**40 days after Orthodox Easter**: Písso Livádi.
**15 Aug**: Parikiá.
**23 Aug**: Náoussa sea battle.
**29 Aug**: Léfkas.

# Where to Stay and Eat

Páros is packed in July and Aug, and it may be hard to find a place if you just drop in, but the various well-organized reservations desks on the quay will do their best to find you a place to flop. It's also worth trying **Rooms Association**, t/f 028 402 4528 and **Hotels**, t 028 402 4555.

Most hotels and rooms operate April–Oct. Room owners meet the ferries, but not in the numbers they do on Náxos. Beware – in season prices are high; you can pay twice as much for the same room in Aug as in June.

At some point, try Páros' dry white, red or rosé labelled ΚΑΥΑΡΝΙΣ.

## Parikiá ✉ 84400

**Iria**, 3km from the centre on Parasporos Beach, **t** 028 402 4154, **f** 028 402 1167 (*A; exp*). Fanciest place here; a good family choice with air-con bungalows, playground, tennis, pool and big American breakfasts.

**Argo**, on Livádia Beach, **t** 028 402 1367, **f** 028 402 1207 (*C; exp*). For a cheaper pool, with billiards thrown in.

**Argonauta**, back from the waterfront, **t** 028 402 1440, *hotel@argonauta.gr* (*C; mod–exp*). Pleasant, with a lovely first-floor courtyard littered with *amphorae*.

**Helliniko**, Livádia, **t** 028 402 1429, **f** 028 402 2743 (*C; mod–exp*). At the lower end of the expensive range.

**Vayia**, set back on the Náoussa road, **t** 028 402 1068, **f** 028 402 3431 (*C; mod*). A small family-run hotel, surrounded by olive trees.

**Dina**, in the old town, **t** 028 402 1325, **f** 028 402 3525 (*mod*). A more modest, charming place with simple rooms.

**Kapetan Manolis**, also in the old town, **t** 028 402 1244, **f** 028 402 5264 (*C; mod*).

**Eleni**, near the beach, **t** 028 402 2714, **f** 028 402 4170 (*mod*). Attractive balconied rooms.

**Kondes**, on the quay, **t** 028 402 1096, **f** 028 402 2390 (*inexp–mod*). A done-up oldie with fridges, TV and air-con in each room.

**Oasis**, next to Kondes, **t** 028 402 1227, **f** 028 402 2390 (*inexp–mod*). Overlooks the busy port, so there's plenty to look at.

**Antoine**, in the old town near the port, **t** 028 402 4435 (*inexp*). Run by a helpful architect.

**Katerina Restaurant** in Livádia, **t** 028 402 2035 (*inexp*). Also has rooms.

Páros is especially popular among campers. Most sites have minibuses that meet ferries:

**Camping Koula**, near Parikiá, **t** 028 4022 082. For the laid back.

**Parasporos**, near Parikiá, **t** 028 402 1100. Friendly location.

**Krios Camping**, at Kríos Beach, opposite the port, **t** 028 402 1905.

**To Tamarisko**. Good international cuisine in the secluded garden at reasonable prices.

**Argonauta**, in the big square by the National Bank, **t** 028 402 3303. Well known for its fresh food and grills.

**Happy Green Cow**, behind the bank. Vegetarians can find so-so sustenance here, including *falafel* and *humous*.

**Levanti**, back from the harbour, right of the Venetian castle walls. Good Greek, French and Lebanese dishes like *falafels*.

**Porfyra**, by the ancient cemetery, **t** 028 402 3410. In a courtyard under vines, serving a wide array of seafood delicacies, including various shellfish and pasta dishes.

**Páros**, signposted from Ekatoapylani. Simple home cooking and seafood under a trellis.

**Amoras/Aromas**, in a couple of streets from the windmills. Large selection of vegetarian and vegan dishes, many made to order.

**Distrato Bar**. Crêpes accompanied by jazz in a shady, old-town square.

Alternatively, follow the road round through Livádia to **Argo** for relaxed beach tavernas.

## Náoussa and Around ✉ 84401

**Astir of Páros**, Kolymbíthres Beach, **t** 028 405 1976, *astir@mail.otenet.gr* (*A; lux*). The island's most luxurious hotel; all your heart's desires, VIP suites and gourmet restaurant.

**Antrides**, **t** 028 405 1711, **f** 028 405 2079 (*B; lux*). Posh neo-monastic, comfortably constructed around a pool.

**Atlantis**, **t** 028 405 1340, **f** 028 405 2087 (*C; exp*). Rooms with verandas facing on to a quiet pool and Jacuzzi.

**Petres**, 2km out of town, **t** 028 405 2467, **f** 028 405 2759 (*C; exp*). Comfy rooms with air-con and a pool.

**Kalypso**, Ag. Anargiri Beach, **t** 028 405 1488, *kalypso@otenet.gr* (*C; mod–exp*). Rooms, studios and suites.

**Stella**, in the old town, **t/f** 028 405 1317, *hotel-stella34@hotmail.com* (*D; mod*). Plain, clean rooms round a shady courtyard.

**Senia Apartments**, **t** 028 405 1971 (*mod*). New and airy, with large balconies.

**Miltiadis**, just east in Ambelas, **t/f** 028 405 2020 (*mod*). Rooms and apartments in a lush garden.

**Galini**, **t** 028 405 1210 (*C; inexp–mod*). Plain rooms with balcony.

**Flora and Maria Pouliou**, **t** 028 405 1118 (*inexp–mod*). Rooms with fridge and balcony; also apartments.

Náoussa is one of the most picturesque places to eat in all Greece with *ouzeries* chock-a-block by the water, and a place to rub shoulders with celebrities.

**Papadakis, t** 028 405 1047 (€15–22; *book in season*). A wonderful waterfront fish restaurant, with a varied menu, incl. stuffed onions and *paella* starters, freshest of fish and lobster dishes, plus good desserts.

**Barbarossa, t** 028 405 1391. *Ouzerie*-cum-restaurant, serving tasty mussel soup.

**Christos, t** 028 405 1901 (€20–30). Lovely courtyard dining, with Greek and international dishes. People come here to be seen.

**Diamantis,** just up the hill. Good food at good prices, with draught wine.

**Meltemi, t** 028 405 1263. Cretan specialities and views of the sea.

## Písso Livádi and East Coast Beaches
✉ 84400

**Paros Philoxenia,** Tserdakiá Beach, **t** 028 404 1778, **f** 028 404 1978 (*B; lux*). Hotel-bungalow complex with surf club, sea sports, and pool.

**Silver Rocks,** near Tserdakiá Beach, **t** 028 404 1244, *silverrocks@email.com* (*C; exp*). Good facilities and kiddies' playground.

**Poseidon,** in Chryssí Aktí, **t** 028 404 2650, *poseidon@otenet.gr* (*lux*). Luxurious apartment complex set in spacious grounds.

**Elena Studios and Apartments,** above town, **t** 028 404 1082, **f** 028 404 2363 (*exp*). A nice set-up, with playground.

**Albatross,** south in Logarás, **t** 028 404 1157, *albapar@otenet.gr* (*C; exp*). Family-oriented bungalow complex with pool.

**Afendakis Apartments,** up in Márpissa, **t/f** 028 404 1141, *info@hotelafendaki.gr* (*C; exp*). Beautifully appointed accommodation.

**Anezina,** in Driós, **t** 028 404 1037, **f** 028 404 1557 (*C; mod*). Nice choice with an elegant romantic garden restaurant. Apart from this option, Driós has plenty of Cycladic-style accommodation and a good taverna on the beach.

**Aloni, t** 028 404 3237, **f** 028 404 2438 (*C; mod–exp*). A nicely-done complex with cool blue rooms and some bird's-eye views.

**Elina Residence, t** 028 442 3180 (*mod*). Lovely British-owned apartment overlooking the bay with views of Náxos.

**Anna Agourou, t** 028 404 1320, **f** 028 404 3327 (*mod*). Air-con rooms and apartments with good watery views.

**Vrohaki,** just up the hill, **t** 028 404 1423 (*mod*). Attractive peaceful rooms and studios for blissful relaxation.

**Free Sun,** Logarás, **t** 028 404 2808, **f** 028 404 2809 (*mod*). Modest accommodation.

**Captain Kafkis Camping,** on the way into town, **t** 028 404 1392.

**Mouraghio,** Písso Livádi. This is the place to eat excellent fish.

**Stavros** and **Vrochas** in Písso Livádi are other favourite tavernas.

**Fisilani's,** Logarás. A good bet for food.

**Haroula's,** in the old town. As the name promises, dining is a joy here.

**Laini,** just off the main road. Grills, and often live Greek music.

**ΘEA,** in Messádha. Family taverna that makes tasty dishes from home-grown fare.

# Entertainment and Nightlife

Páros has something for everyone, from the rowdy waterfront bars at Parikiá to the more sophisticated haunts of Náoussa.

**Cine Paros,** set back from the waterfront. Parikiá's outdoor cinema.

**Rex, Black Barts** and **Salon d'Or.** Parikiá cocktail bars on the strip.

**Pirate's,** in Parikiá. For jazz.

**Páros Rock Complex.** A quad complex of four disco bars incl. the **Dubliner.**

**Pebbles** and **Evinos,** on Parikiá's waterfront. The music is altogether gentler and more classical.

**Simposium,** in Parikiá's old town. An august setting for a late ice cream.

**Varrelathiko,** along Náoussa's trendy nightclub strip. This is the summer headquarters of the hippest club in Athens, and plays Greek music.

**Café del Mar,** on Náoussa's waterfront. A very popular drinking hole with the fashionable set.

**The Golden Garden,** at Chryssí Aktí. Popular, laid-back garden bar with a wide range of international sounds.

**Remezzo,** in Písso Livádi. A favoured watering hole.

**Captain Yannis,** in Písso Livádi. Offers endless sea views.

Marathon and Salamis; when Athens' proud General Miltiades came to punish them after Marathon, they withstood his month-long siege, forcing Miltiades to retire with a broken leg that developed into the gangrene that killed him. The island produced the great sculptor Skopas in the Hellenistic period and did well until Roman times, exporting marble to make the Temple of Solomon, the *Venus de Milo*, the temples on Délos and, much later, part of Napoleon's tomb. When the Romans took Páros, their main concern was to take over the marble business.

Later invasions left the island practically deserted, and after 1207 the Venetian Sanudos ruled Páros from Náxos. Barbarossa captured the island in 1536 and the Turks ruled by way of their proxy, the Duke of Náxos; however, his control was often shaky, especially in the 1670s, when Páros was the base of Hugues Chevaliers, the inspiration for Byron's *Corsair*. In 1770, the Parians had to put up with more unlikely visitors when the Russian fleet wintered on Páros. During the War of Independence Mandó Mavroyénous, whose parents were from Páros and Mýkonos, led guerrilla attacks against the Turks throughout Greece; afterwards she returned to Páros.

# Parikiá

**Parikiá** (ΠΑΡΟΙΚΙΑ), the island's chief town and main port, still greets arrivals with its old, now empty windmill. Behind it, however, the town has quintupled in size in the last couple of decades, so obscuring the original version that it's almost been forgotten; the locals have put up signs pointing the way to the 'Traditional Settlement'. Once you've found it, just south of the port, Parikiá shows itself to be a Cycladic beauty, traversed by a long, winding main street that invites leisurely exploration, without having to trudge up stairs. The centrepiece in the heart of town is the walls of the **Venetian Kástro**, built out of the white marble temples of Apollo and Demeter into an attractive collage of columns and pediments; a tiny white chapel tucked underneath adds to the effect. Three more windmills close off the waterfront on the south end of town, where the *ouzeries* are a popular evening rendezvous.

Most of Parikiá's sprawling, in the form of hotels, bars and restaurants, has happened in the direction of **Livádia** and its tamarisk-lined beach, although if you continue along the strand past the main tourist ghetto to Argo, café life becomes much more relaxed. While digging here in 1983, part of the **ancient cemetery** was uncovered, in use from the 8th century BC to the 3rd AD; it lies below sea level and has to be constantly drained. More recently, in the course of building a new pier, a Doric-style temple with foundations the size of the Parthenon has been unearthed.

## The Church of a Hundred Doors and the Archaeology Museum

Set back between Livádia and the 'Traditional Settlement' is Páros' chief monument, the cathedral **Ekatontapylianí** or 'Hundred Doors', hidden behind a modern wall (*open 8–1 and 4–9; robes provided for the scantily clad*). In 326, St Helen, mother of the Emperor Constantine, was sailing from Rome to the Holy Land when her ship put into Páros during a storm. She prayed that if her journey was a success and she found the

True Cross, she would build a church on Páros. She did, and told Constantine her promise, and he dutifully built a church. What stands today is a 6th-century building by the Byzantine Emperor Justinian. The story goes that he hired an architect named Ignatius, an apprentice of the master builder of Ag. Sophia, and when the master came to view his pupil's work, he was consumed by jealousy and pushed Ignatius off the roof – but not before Ignatius had seized his foot and dragged him down as well. They are represented by two bizarre figures under the columns of the marble gate to the north of the church, one holding his head and the other covering his mouth.

In 1966, the church, far more human in scale than Ag. Sophia, was restored to its 6th-century appearance, with its dome on pendentives and a women's gallery along the nave. Originally the interior was covered with gleaming white marble. Another story says that only 99 entrances have ever been found but once the 100th is discovered, Constantinople will return to the Greeks. In fact, the name itself is a 17th-century fantasy; the original was probably *Katapoliani*, 'towards the ancient city'.

The marble iconostasis has a venerated icon of the black Virgin, silver-plated and worked all around with intricate little scenes made in Bucharest, in 1788; you can see frescoes and a marble ciborium, with a *synthronon* or little marble amphitheatre behind – in the earliest churches, before the iconostasis totally blocked the view of the sacred area, the high priest and clergy used to stand and sit here. In an alcove in the north wall is the tomb of the 9th-century Ag. Theóktisti. A nun captured by pirates on Lésbos, Theóktisti managed to flee into the forests of Páros when the ship landed for water. For 35 years she lived a pious existence in the wilderness. A hunter finally found her, and when he brought her the communion bread she requested, she lay down and died. Unable to resist a free saintly relic, the hunter cut off her hand and made to sail away, but he was unable to depart until he had returned it to the saint's body. The **Baptistry** to the right of the church has a 4th-century sunken cruciform font – the oldest one in Orthodoxy – adult-size, with steps leading down, and a column for the priest to stand on; baptism of children only began in the reign of Justinian.

Off the courtyard in front of the church is the **Byzantine Museum** (*t 028 402 1243; open 9–1 and 5–9; adm*); behind the church and next to the school, a row of sarcophagi marks the **Archaeology Museum** (*t 028 402 1231; open Tues–Sun 8.30–2.30; adm*), containing a section of the renowned 'Parian Chronicles' – an artistic history of Greece from Kerkops (*c.* 1500 BC) to Diognetos (264 BC) carved in marble tablets and discovered in the 17th century; to read the rest you'll have to go to the Ashmolean in Oxford. There are finds from the Temple of Apollo: a mosaic of the Labours of Hercules, found under the Ekatontapylianí, a 5th-century BC Winged Victory, a 7th-century BC amphora with the Judgement of Paris and swastikas (ancient solar symbols) going every which way, and a segment of a monument dedicated to Archilochos, who took part in the colonization of Thássos by Páros before he turned to lyric poetry. Archilochos was buried along the road to Náoussa; in the 4th-century BC a *heröon*, or tomb-shrine of a hero was erected over his tomb, and in the 7th-century, the basilica **Tris Ekklisíes** (or Ag. Charálambos) was built over the site. Northeast of Parikiá, the marble foundation and altar mark the **Temple of Delian Apollo**, which was lined up with temples to Apollo on Délos and Náxos to form a perfect equilateral triangle. One of the triangle's altitudes extends to Mycenae and Rhodes Town, site of the Colossus – the biggest statue of Apollo. Another heads up to holy Mount Áthos.

# Náoussa

Frequent buses connect Parikiá with the island's second port, the lovely fishing village turned jet-set hang-out of **Náoussa** (ΝΑΟΥΣΑ). In 1997 it made history as the first place where the Greek Government at last clamped down on shoddy building. Near the harbour stand the half-submerged ruins of the Venetian castle, with colourful caiques bobbing below and octopuses hung out to dry. The wetlands west of town are a winter flamingo haven. On the night of 23 August, 100 boats lit by torches re-enact the islanders' battle against the pirate Barbarossa, storming the harbour, but all ends in merriment, music and dance. Náoussa's church **Ag. Nikólaos Mostrátos** has an excellent collection of icons. There are more in the **Byzantine Museum** (*t 028 405 3261*), while traditional Cycladic life is covered in the small **Folk Art Museum** (*t 028 405 3453*). There are beaches within walking distance of Náoussa, or you can make sea excursions to others, including **Kolimbíthres**, with its bizarre rocks, **Ag. Ioannis** (Monastiri Beach) and nudist **Lágeri** (take the caique from Náoussa harbour, then walk to the right for about 10 minutes). **Santa Maria** is further around the coast, with a good windsurfing beach; the fishing village of **Ambelás** has sandy coves and an ancient tower. Páros' main wine growing area is just south.

# Southeast of Parikiá: Into the Land of Marble

From Parikiá, the main road east leads to Páros' ancient marble quarries at **Maráthi**, not far from the abandoned Monastery of Ag. Mínas. The quarries, re-opened in modern times for the makings of statues and decorations for Napoleon's tomb, are still in use. They produce the finest white marble, called 'Lychnites' by the ancients, or 'candlelit marble', for its translucent quality, admitting light 3.5cm into the stone (light penetrates the second most translucent Carrara marble only 2.5cm). The *Venus de Milo*, the *Victory of Samothrace* and the *Hermes of Praxiteles* are all made of the stuff. Blocks and galleries, some with ancient inscriptions, lie off the road.

The road continues to Páros' attractive medieval capital **Léfkes**, with churches from the 15th century and one made of marble: Ag. Triáda. There's also a **small museum** (*t 028 404 1605; open in season*) dedicated to another local speciality – ceramics – and good walks to be had along the Byzantine road. East of Léfkes, **Mármara** village lives up to its name ('marble') – even some of the streets are paved with it. Prettiest of all is shiny white **Márpissa**, laid out in an amphitheatre. Above its windmills are the ruins of a 15th-century Venetian fortress and the 16th-century **Monastery of Ag. Antónios**, constructed out of ancient marbles and containing lovely frescoes (note the 17th-century *Second Coming*, which seems a bit out of place in *bon-vivant* Páros).

Down on the east coast **Písso Livádi** served as the port for these villages and the marble quarries, and now has excursion boats to Náxos, Mýkonos and Santoríni. It is the centre of Páros' beach colonies: at **Mólos**, just north, luxurious villas line the bay where the Turkish fleet used to put in on its annual tax-collecting tour of the Aegean, while just south at **Poúnda** (not to be confused with the ferry port for Páros) beautiful people flock to a hip nightclub even bigger than the beach. The winds on Páros blow fiercely in July and August, and the next beach, **Tserdakia** (or **Néa Chryssí Aktí**) in particular has become a Mecca for serious windsurfers; every August since 1993 it has hosted the Professional Windsurfers' World Cup as well as the 'Odyssey' (a windsurfing relay race). Just to the south is the island's best beach, **Chryssí Aktí**, 'Golden Beach' with half a mile of sand. Further south, **Driós** is a pretty green place with a duck-pond, tavernas and sandy coves, and the remains of ancient shipyards.

## Southwest of Parikiá

Just south of Parikiá, by a spring, are the ruins of a small classical-era **Asklepeion** (dedicated to the god of healing); originally a Temple to Pythian Apollo stood nearby. The road south continues 6km to **Psychopianá** ('Valley of the Butterflies'), where swarms of tiger moths set up housekeeping in July and August. Petaloúdes/ Psychopianá has the ruins of a Venetian tower, while just outside the village stands the convent of Páros' second patron saint, **Ag. Arsénios**, the schoolteacher, abbot and prophet who was canonized in 1967. The saint is buried here, but this time men are not allowed in. At **Poúnda** there is a beach and the small boat that crosses to Antíparos. There's another beach at **Alikí** – and the airport, and now, inevitably, a roadside attraction, the **Historical Museum Scorpios**, with 'animated handmade miniatures' depicting the old days on Páros (*t 028 409 1129; open daily 10–2; adm*).

## Antíparos (ΑΝΤΙΠΑΡΟΣ)

A mile to the west, mountainous little Antíparos (meaning 'opposite Páros'), was known as Oliaros when it was first mentioned as a base of Phoenician merchants of Sidon. A deep cave full of stalactites was discovered on Antíparos in antiquity (tradition has it that Antilochos was the first to carve his name on a stalactite in the 6th century BC) and ever since it's been a must stop for every traveller in the region. Antíparos is also the octopus capital of Greece, and it may be that the tasty mollusc is an unsung aphrodisiac, considering the little island's current reputation. Even the local year-round population is rising, and that, in the Cyclades, is rare.

### Kástro and the Cave

Lacking any defences, Antíparos was uninhabited after the fall of Rome until the Venetians, under Leonardo Lorentani, built a small castle, its thick walls forming the outer walls of the houses; **Kástro** is the alternative name of the main settlement. Everyone tos and fros down the Kampiara, the wide street linking the port to the charming square, lined with *ouzeries* and bars. Kástro has a good beach, **Psaralíki**, just south, and another one for skinny-dippers a 5-minute walk north by the campsite.

## Getting There and Around

Every 2 hrs by **caique** from Parikiá (Páros) and hourly **car ferry** from Poúnda (Páros). Buses link the port with the cave. **Port authority** (Páros): **t** 028 406 1202. **Vacances Horizon International** island cruises (p.265).

## Where to Stay and Eat

### Antíparos ✉ 84007

Antíparos has a desk at Parikiá port, so you can book accommodation before you go – prices have risen to match big sister Páros.

**Artemis**, 500 yards from the port, **t** 028 406 1460, **f** 028 406 1472 (*C; exp–mod*). Newish; rooms have fridges and sea-view balconies.

**Mantalena**, on the waterfront, **t** 028 406 1206, **f** 028 406 1550 (*C; exp–mod*). Attractive, tidy rooms, all with bath.

**Chryssi Akti**, on the beach, **t** 028 406 1220 (*C; mod*). Small, elegant hotel.

**Bergleri**, just in from the beach, **t** 028 406 1378, **f** 028 406 1452 (*D; mod*). With a decent taverna and library of bestsellers.

**Antíparos**, **t** 028 406 1358, *antiparos1@otenet .gr* (*E; mod*). Simple, all rooms with shower.

**Korali**, **t** 028 406 1236, **f** 028 406 1369 (*E; inexp*). About the cheapest, with a restaurant.

**Antíparos Camping**, **t** 028 406 1410, **f** 028 406 1221. Laid-back campsite, clothes optional; freelancers are tolerated away from town.

**Garden** and **Anargyros**. Both have good food. **Time Marine Beach Bar, Café Yam, Captain Pipinos**. All popular summer hang outs.

In the late afternoon everyone wanders over to **Sifnaíkos Gialós**, also known as Sunset Beach. The best beach, **Ag. Geórgios**, south of the cave, is being developed as a resort.

The **cave** (*open daily 10.45–3.45; adm*) remains Antíparos' star attraction, and frequent buses in summer now do the old donkey work of getting you there from the village. Some 400 steps descend 210ft into the fantastic, spooky chamber. The cave is really about twice as deep, but the rest has been closed as too dangerous. Perhaps to make up for breaking off the stalactites, famous visitors of the past have smoked and carved their names on the walls, including Lord Byron and King Otho of Greece (1840). One stalagmite attests in Latin to a Christmas mass celebrated in the cavern by the French ambassador Count Novandel in 1673, attended by 500 (paid) locals. Another (now lost) from the 4th century BC, stated that the authors declared that they were hiding in the cave from Alexander the Great, after he accused them of plotting an assassination attempt. Many inscriptions were lost in 1774, when Russian officers chopped off stalactites as souvenirs, and in the last war, when the Italians and Germans shot up the cave. The church by the entrance, **Ag. Ioánnis**, dates from 1774.

Of the islets off Antíparos, **Strogilónisi** and **Despotikó** are rabbit-hunting reserves. On **Sáliagos**, a fishing village from the 5th millennium BC has been excavated by John Evans and Colin Renfrew, the first Neolithic site discovered in the Cyclades.

# Santoríni/Thíra (ΣΑΝΤΟΡΙΝΗ/ΘΗΡΑ)

*...We found ourselves naked on the pumice stone*
*watching the rising islands*
*watching the red islands sink*
*into their sleep, into our sleep.*
George Seféris, *Santoríni*

As many people's favourite Greek island, the pressure is on Santoríni to come up with the goods. And it does. The mixture of sinister dusky precipices, dappled with the most brilliant-white, trendiest bars and restaurants in the country, gives the island a splendid kind of schizophrenia; forget *Under the Volcano*, here you're teetering on the edge. Usually bathed in glorious sunshine, but occasionally lashed by high winds and rain, everything seems more intense on Santoríni, especially daily life. Some call it Devil's Island, an exhilarating but disturbing place where the scent of sulphur occasionally breaks through, and where the inhabitants, through centuries of experience, are such experts in dealing with the undead (the *vrykólakes*), that other islanders send their troublesome corpses here. Which doesn't seem to get in the way of it being the honeymoon capital of Greece.

Nothing beats arriving by sea. As your ship sails into the caldera, Santoríni looms up like a chocolate layer cake with an enormous bite taken out of it, frosted with coconut cream towns sliding over the edge, while the islets opposite look as infernal as the charred gunk in your oven. This little archipelago has, literally, had its ups and downs, rising and disappearing under the waves. Human endeavours have fared similarly: you can visit three former 'capitals' – the Minoan centre of Akrotíri, a favourite candidate for Metropolis, the capital of Atlantis; the classical capital Thíra at Mésa Vouno;

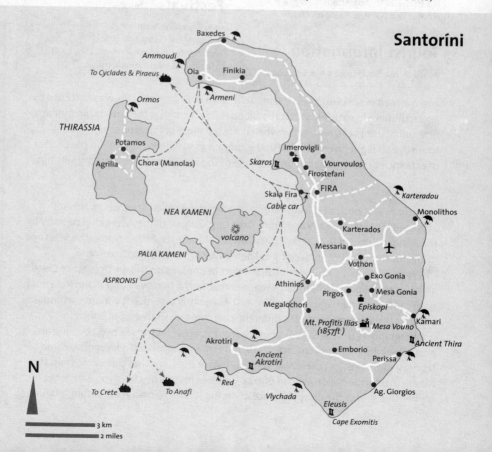

**Santoríni**

## Getting There and Around

**By air**:daily **flights** from Athens; 4 a week from Mýkonos; 3 a week from Thessaloníki; 2 a week in season from Heráklion (Crete) and Rhodes. The **Olympic Airways** office is at Fíra, **t** 028 602 2493; **airport: t** 028 603 1525. **Aegean Airlines: t** 028 602 8500. Catch a regular bus from the airport to Firá, or take a taxi (€7).

**By sea**: daily **ferry** connections with Piraeus, Íos, Páros, Náxos and Mýkonos; frequent (3–4 times a week) **hydrofoil** connections with Rafina and other Cyclades; 2–3 times a week with Heráklion (Crete), Kássos, Kárpathos, Chálki; twice a week with Thessaloníki and once a week with Skiáthos. **Port Authority**: **t** 028 602 2239.

**By road**: Santoríni has an efficient if often crowded **bus** service to all villages. In Fíra the bus stop is opposite the museum, down from Plateía Theotokopoúlou. **Taxis: t** 028 602 2555 (€8 from Fíra to Oía). Alternatively, rent a **scooter** and you'll be spoilt for choice.

## Tourist Information

**Police**: 25 Martíou Street, **t** 028 602 2649.

**Post office**: opposite the police; *open 8–2*.
**Kamári Tours**, in Kamári and with offices in every village on the island, **t** 028 603 1390, *kamaritours@san.forthnet.gr*. Arranges accommodation, tours and cruises.
**Markozanes Tours**, main office in the plateía in Fíra, **t** 028 602 3660. Also very helpful.
**Walking**: there are wonderful walks along the northern coast; consult **Ecorama** in Oía.
**Diving**: Paul Stefanidis runs the Mediterranean Dive Club from Perissa Camping, **t** 028 608 3080, *www.diveclub.gr*. Offers all sorts of volcano and wreck dives, as well as courses.

## Internet

**PC World**, in the main square in Fíra; *open 9–9*.
**Ecorama**, in Oía.

## Festivals

**19** and **20 July**: Profítis Ilías.
**15 Aug**: Mésa Goniá and Fíra.
**Sept**: Santoríni Music Festival, in Fíra, with Greek and international music.

and the medieval Skáros. Even the modern town of Firá, on the rim, was flattened by an earthquake in 1956. Although the island is now firmly on the cruise ship itinerary, older inhabitants can remember when it hosted more political prisoners than tourists, and nights were filled with the rumour of vampires rather than the chatter of café society, watching the sunset in one of the world's most enchanting settings.

### History

Santoríni was once a typically round volcanic island called Strogyle. Its rich soil attracted inhabitants early on – from Karia originally, until they were chased away by the Minoans. One of the Cretan towns was at Akrotíri. Its discovery resulted from one of the most intriguing archaeological detective stories of the 20th century.

In 1939, while excavating Amnisós, the port of Knossós on the north coast of Crete, archaeologist Spirýdon Marinátos realized that only a massive natural disaster could have caused the damage he found. At first Marinátos assumed it was an earthquake, but over the years evidence of a different kind came in: southeast of Santoríni oceanographers discovered volcanic ash from Strogyle on the sea bed, covering an area of 900 by 300km; on nearby Anáfi and Eastern Crete itself a layer of volcanic tephra 3–20mm thick covers Minoan New Palace sites. Another clue came from the Athenian reformer Solon, who in 600 BC wrote of his journey to Egypt, where the scribes told him of the disappearance of Kreftia (Crete?) 9,000 years before, a figure

Solon might have mistaken for a more correct 900. The Egyptians, who had had important trade links with Minoan Crete and Santoríni, told Solon about the lost land of Atlantis, made of red, white and black volcanic rock (like Santoríni today) and spoke of a city vanishing in 24 hours. In his *Critias*, Plato described Atlantis as being composed of one round island and one long island, a sweet country of art and flowers connected by one culture and rule (Santoríni and Crete, under Minos?). Lastly, Marinátos studied the eruption of Krakatoa in 1883, which blew its lid with such force that it could be heard 3,000 miles away in Western Australia. Krakatoa formed a caldera of 8.3sq km, and as the sea rushed in to fill the caldera, it created a *tsunami* or tidal wave over 200m high that destroyed everything in a 150km path. The caldera left by Strogyle (the present bay of Santoríni) is 22sq km – almost three times as big.

In the 19th century French archaeologists had discovered Minoan vases at Akrotíri, and it was there that Marinátos began to dig in 1967, seeking to prove the chronology of his theory: that Minoan civilization owed its sudden decline to the eruption, earthquakes, and tidal waves caused by the explosion of Stogyle in c. 1450 BC. Marinátos hoped to unearth a few vases. Instead he found something beyond his wildest dreams: an entire Minoan colony buried in tephra, complete with dazzling frescoes.

The island returned to history in the 9th century BC, when the Dorians settled the island, and named it Thera. Herodotus offers a rare early account of how the Therans in turn founded the much richer colony of Cyrene in Libya: in 631 BC, a certain Battos went to Delphi to see how he could cure his stutter, the oracle suggested a unique cure: colonizing Libya. The stutter was a code for the more serious problem Thera was having feeding its mouths, as Greeks divided land equally among their sons. One brother from each family was chosen by lot, and ordered to give the colony a try for five years; when they were discouraged and tried to come home, the Therans shot at their ships to keep them from landing, so they went on to found Cyrene.

The Byzantines covered the island with castles, but the Venetians under the Crispi got it anyway. Skáros near Imerovígli was their capital and Irene their patron saint, hence the island's second name, Santoríni, which has stuck as hard as volcanic rock as officialdom tries to change it back to the classical era Thíra.

# Firá (ΦΗΡΑ)

After arriving by air or at the island's port **Athiniós**, the bus to **Firá** leaves visitors in Plateía Theotóki, a zoo of a modern square to be processed and fattened on fast food before being sacrificed to the volcano god. Cruise ships rather more pleasantly anchor beneath the towering cliffs at Firá, where motor launches ferry passengers to the tiny port of **Skála Firá**; there, donkeys wait to bear them up the winding path to town, 885ft above. An Austrian-built **cable car** (*every 15 mins from 6.45am to 8.15pm; €3*), donated to the island by ship-owner Evángelos Nomikós does the donkey-work in two minutes. Profits go to a community fund – and to the donkey drivers.

Those who remember Firá before 1956 say that the present town can't compare to its original, although it's pleasant enough – perfectly Cycladically white, spilling down

# Where to Stay

### Firá ✉ 84700

Firá isn't the only village with hotels on the caldera rim, but it's the most expensive. Just out of season, in early July even, you can wheel and deal with the room owners who mug you as the Athiniós bus pulls into town. Most accommodation is open April–Oct.

**Aigialos,** t 028 602 5191, f 028 602 2856 (A; lux). For all the mod cons (incl. a counter swim unit in the pool) in a traditional, antique furnished cliff side skaftá.

**Atlantis,** t 028 602 2232, atlantissa@otenet.gr (A; lux). The oldest hotel on the island and the most photographed building. It's classy, but its rooms are on the small side. The views from the balconies overlooking the volcano are stunning. Pool and all mod cons.

**Efterpi Villas,** t 028 602 2541, f 028 602 2542 (D; lux). More affordable luxury in traditional apartments.

**Kavalari,** t 028 602 2455, f 028 602 2603 (C; lux). Attractive rooms dug out of the cliff.

**Santoríni Palace,** Firostefáni, t 028 602 2771, spalace@otenet.gr (A; lux). Modern, with pool and panoramas of the sea and town.

**Sun Rocks,** on the cliff edge at Firostefáni, t 028 602 3241, info@sunrocks.gr (B; lux). Stylish, couples only, with pool and views.

**Tsitouras Collection,** Firostefáni, t 028 602 3747, tsitoura@otenet.gr (A; lux). As exclusive as it gets. Suites in 5 beautifully restored Venetian houses, each with its own name and theme, centred around a courtyard. The House of Nureyev has the view.

**Lucas,** t 028 602 2480, loucasason@ath .forthnet.gr (B; lux–exp). Similar to Kavalari.

**Galini,** t 028 602 2095, galini-htl@otenet.gr (C; exp). Nice rooms with caldera views, and transfers to the port. Open Mar–Nov.

**Kafieris Apartments,** t 028 602 2059, f 028 602 2551 (C; exp). Fully equipped.

**Porto Carra,** faces the volcano from the central square, t 028 602 2979, kavalht@otenet.gr (C; exp).

**Pelican,** t 028 602 3113, f 028 602 3514 (C; exp). Air-con rooms, and a tank of odd fish in the lounge.

**Argonaftis,** t 028 602 2055 (mod). Friendly with breakfast served in the garden.

**Tataki,** in the centre, t 028 602 2389 (D; mod). View-less and bohemian.

**Stella's,** t 028 602 3464 (inexp). Rooms are plain but with kitchen and views to the other side of the island.

**International Youth Hostel,** 5min's walk from centre, t 028 602 2387. Doubles and dorms.

**Camping Santoríni,** nearby, t 028 602 2944. Superb site with pool.

# Eating Out

Besides wine, Santoríni is famous for its fava bean soup (puréed, with onions and lemon) and pseftokeftédes, 'false meatballs', made of deep-fried tomatoes, onion and mint; the tiny tomatoes of the island are said to be the

---

the volcano's rim on terraces, adorned with blue-domed churches, all boasting one of the world's most magnificent views. Understandably, the families who sold their damaged properties for peanuts after the quake have been kicking themselves; the little lanes are now chock-a-block with shops, bars, hotels and restaurants. Firá blends into quieter **Firostefáni**, one km to the north; here are some magnificent old skaftá, barrel-roofed cave houses, Santoríni's speciality, now equipped with all mod cons.

The old **Archaeology Museum** (t 028 602 2217; open Tues–Sun, 8.30–3; adm) is near the cable car on the north side of town and houses finds from ancient Thíra at Mésa Vouno, some going back to the 9th century BC. Opposite the bus station, the new **Museum of Prehistoric Thíra** (t 028 602 3217; same hrs ) has Early Cycladic figurines found in the local pumice quarries and lovely vases, ceramics, jewellery and a few frescoes from Akrotíri. Among the frescoes moved here from the National Archaeology Museum in Athens is the famous 17ft-long freize of a flotilla, a unique record of sailing in the prehistoric Aegean. The handicraft workshop founded by Queen Frederíka,

tastiest in Greece. There are no shortage of places to eat, but to enjoy dining to its fullest, be prepared to splash out.

**Meridiana**, up on top of the Fabrica Shopping Centre, **t** 028 602 3247. Claims to be the only restaurant on the island with views of both sides of the island, as well as gourmet and Thai cuisine and live jazz most evenings. *Open from lunch until 3am.*

**Kástro**, near the cable car. Big views will set you back a bit for one of its lavish spreads.

**The Roosters**, on the main street. Try and squeeze in at this fun little restaurant with tasty Greek dishes, and an inquisitive owner.

**Nikolas, t** 028 602 4550. Good place for excellent Greek food. Locals swear by it, proved by frequent queues for tables.

**Selini, t** 028 602 2249 (€25–35). Long-established and much-loved restaurant, which makes original and delicious use of the island's produce, especially the small tomatoes, cheese and capers in many of its dishes. Some specialities include lamb with *fava* sauce and *fava* rissoles. The food – and the view – will make you linger.

**Sphinx, t** 028 602 3823 (€30). Another romantic caldera setting; excellent seafood, much of it with pasta, some meat dishes.

**Alexandria**, on the caldera. Very expensive but even serves up ancient Greek specialities.

**Bella Thira**. Italians flock here for freshly made pasta and pizzas.

**Poseidon**, under the bus stop. A 24-hr diner, with reasonably priced filling food.

**Señor Zorba's**, on the caldera, south of town. Mosey on down here for tacos and other Mexican fare.

If you can't afford the dinner table views, there are plenty of quick snack and *gýro* places around Plateía Theotóki.

# Entertainment and Nightlife

Café and bar life takes up as much time as eating in Santoríni.

**Bebis**. The watering hole for a pleasantly loony young crowd.

**Two Brothers**. Draws the backpackers and is a hot spot for rock.

**Kira Thira**. Appeals to all ages for jazz, blues and sangria.

**Alexandria**. More sedate, attracts an older set.

**Franco's**. Playing gentle classical music, this is still the place to laze in deckchairs for sunset, even if the price of a coffee is sky-high. Cocktails are works of art, but a bottle of wine and *mezédes* are the best deal.

**Enigma bar**, on the rim. Pleasant place to contemplate volcanoes.

**Enigma**. This club is the hippest place to dance through the night.

**Koo Club**, next door. Also big, central and packed.

**Mamounia Club**. Lively, plays Greek hits.

**Tithora Club**, in the main square. Good for rockers.

where women weave large carpets on looms, is also worth a visit. The **Mégaron Gýzi Museum** (*t 028 602 2244; open daily 10.30–1.30 and 5–8pm, Sun 10.30–4; adm*), located in a beautiful 17th-century mansion, houses exhibits on the island's history – manuscripts from the 16th to 19th centuries, costumes, old maps of the Cyclades and photographs of the town before the 1956 quake. Another, privately run **Folklore Museum** (*t 028 602 2792; open 10–2 and 6–8; adm*) occupies a cave house of 1861, with all of the owner's uncle's belongings on display.

# Way Down South: Minoan Akrotíri

**Akrotíri** (ΑΚΡΩΤΗΡΙ), a pleasant wine village on the south tip of the island, was a Venetian stronghold, and although damaged in the earthquake the fort still stands at the top of the town. There are beaches nearby on either coast, and a pretty path along

# Where to Stay and Eat

## South: Akrotíri/Megalochóri ✉ 84700

**Vedema**, in Megalochóri, **t** 028 608 1796 (*A; lux*). One of the 'Small Luxury Hotels of the World', a former winery, offering every amenity, art gallery, marble baths, in-house movies and a private beach 3km away with minibus service. Its restaurant (€*40*), cut into the rock and cavernlike, promises fine dining, and doesn't disappoint.

**Villa Mathios**, **t** 028 608 1152, *vmathios@ otenet.gr* (*exp Aug; otherwise good value*). Friendly and comfortable, with a pool overlooking the island, air-con and TVs in the rooms. Travel agency in reception to organize your whole holiday.

**Villa Kalimera**, **t** 028 608 1855, **f** 028 608 1915 (*exp*). Next door; similarly priced, but offering slightly less.

**Pension Karlos**, **t** 028 608 1370, **f** 028 608 1095 (*mod*). Clean rooms with balconies.

**Panorama**. Cliffside dining with sunset views over all Santoríni.

**Glaros**, down near the Red Beach. Good fish.

**Villa Mathios**. Reasonable menu and homemade wine.

**Pyrgos Taverna**, in Pirgos, **t** 028 603 1346. Occupying a huge panoramic terrace just below town, a favourite for Greek parties and weddings.

## Períssa ✉ 84700

A gentle swathe of tavernas, bars and accommodation lines Períssa's strand.

**Veggera**, right on the black sands, **t** 028 608 2060, **f** 028 608 2608 (*lux*). Comfortable, fully equipped rooms with a Neoclassical touch, pool and laundry.

**Sellada Beach**, next door, **t** 028 608 1859, **f** 028 608 1492 (*exp*). Handsome traditional rooms and flats with pool.

**Ostria**, by the sea, **t/f** 028 608 2607 (*mod*). Good value apartments.

**Blue Albaco**, next door, **t** 028 608 1654 (*mod*). Similar to the Ostria; cheap out of season.

**Períssa Camping**, near the beach, **t** 028 608 1343, **f** 028 608 1604.

**Taverna Markos**, in a shady corner at one end of the strand.

**Yazz Club**. Where you can contemplate beach life from a hammock.

## Kamári ✉ 84700

**Kamári Beach**, smack on the black sands, **t** 028 603 1243, **f** 028 603 2120 (*C; exp*). With a large pool; all rooms have big verandas.

**Matina**, **t** 028 603 1491, *info@matina.gr* (*C; exp–mod*). Comfortable.

**Sunshine**, next to the sea, **t** 028 603 1394, **f** 028 603 2240 (*C; exp–mod*).

**Andreas**, **t** 028 603 1692, **f** 028 603 1314 (*D; mod*). Modest but has a lush garden.

**Sigalas**, at the end of the beach, **t** 028 603 1260, **f** 028 603 1480 (*D; mod*). Quiet with a shady garden and taverna.

**Kamári Camping**, up the main road from the beach, **t** 028 603 1453.

**Almira**, next to the sea. Good selection of starters and lemon chicken.

**Camille Stefani**, on the beach. One of the island's best restaurants with a French-influenced Greek menu and its very own wine label.

**Kamári**. Good, inexpensive family-run taverna, serving *fáva* soup.

**Taverna Galini**, Monolíthos. Where locals drive out for good cheap home cooking, fish and *pseftokeftédes*.

## Messariá ✉ 84700

**Archontiko Argyrou**, **t** 028 603 1669, **f** 028 603 3064 (*A; exp*). Occupying a lovely 1860s mansion with rooms on the ground floor. The first floor houses its own museum.

**Agapi Villas**, north of Messariá at Karterádos, **t** 028 602 2694 (*exp–mod*). Run by friendly, helpful people; apartments, studios and rooms, with a garden and fountain.

# Entertainment and Nightlife

**Kamári** throbs with bars:

**Hook**. Its tangerine chairs are a pleasant place to sit with mellow music.

**Uta**. Beer garden serving all sorts of frothy broths.

**Valentino's**. Good Greek music, always has a large crowd.

**Dom Club**. The place to strut your stuff.

**Albatross**. The venue to dance till dawn – there's very little point in trying to get an early night anyway.

the caldera rim. The first clues that something else may have once been here came in the 1860s; while digging pumice for the rebuilding of Port Said, ancient walls kept getting in the way. French archaeologists came and unearthed carbonized food, vases, frescoes and a pure copper saw. In 1967 Spyrídon Marinátos, following his hunch about the destruction of Minoan Crete (*see* 'History', above), returned to the site. The trenches were disappointing until, 15ft below the surface, they suddenly broke through into rooms full of huge storage vases, or *pithoi*, belonging to what turned out to be the best preserved prehistoric city in Greece.

The strange and wonderful **Minoan city**, buried in *c.* 1550 BC (*buses from Firá end up here; t 028 608 1366/2217; open Tues–Sun 8.30–3; adm*) is laboriously being liberated from its thick sepulchral shell of tephra – the same material used to make cement for tombstones. Protected by its huge modern roof, a carpet of volcanic dust silences footsteps on paved lanes laid 3,500 years ago, amid houses that stand up to three storeys high, some of rubble masonry, some in fine ashlar, with stone stairways and intact doors and windows. Although it has no street plan, the city's sophisticated drainage makes older Greek visitors laugh because of its resemblance to the sewage systems in the villages they grew up in. Some rooms still contain their giant *pithoi*, and in general the size of the storage areas and cooking pots suggests a communal life and collective economy. The residents must have had ample warning that their island was about to blow its top: no jewellery or other valuables were found, and the only skeleton found so far belonged to a pig. As they escaped they must have shed more than a few tears, for life at Akrotíri was sweet, judging by the ash imprints of their elaborate wooden furniture, their beautiful ceramics and the famous frescoes full of colour and life – every house had a least one frescoed room; one, unique in peace-loving Minoan art, shows a sea battle. In one of the houses is the grave of Marinátos, who died after a fall on the site and requested to be buried by his life's work. For more, pick up *Art and Religion in Thíra: Reconstructing a Bronze Age Society*, by his son, Dr Nannó Marinátos, which is sold at the entrance.

Below the site, the road continues to Mávro Rachidi, where cliffs as black as charcoal offer a stark contrast to the white chapel of Ag. Nikólaos; a path over the headland leads to **Kókkino Paralía** or Red Beach, with sun beds under startling blood-red cliffs.

## The Southeast: Embório, Veríssa and Ancient Thíra

East of Akrotíri, farming villages encircle Mount Profítis Ilías. **Megalochóri**, 'big village', actually has a tiny, resolutely old Greek core, with a tiny outdoor taverna. **Embório** (ΕΜΠΟΡΕΙΟ) still has its Venetian *goulas*, or fort; with its lone palm, it looks like something out of the Sahara. A modern church here replaces the Byzantine one to St Irene, the island's namesake and patroness of the Greek police. Outside of the village, the church of Ag. Nikólaos Marmarinós was a 3rd-century BC Temple of the Mother of the Gods, and still uses the original ceiling. Another 3km east of Embório, in a pretty setting under the seaside mountain Mésa Vouno, the black sands of **Veríssa** (ΠΕΡΙΣΣΑ) have attracted a good deal of development, and can be pleasant at either end of the season because the sand warms quickly in the sun. Eucalyptus groves provide shade; bars and clubs provide for plenty of nightlife; and a Byzantine church is being excavated on the edge of town. The coastal road south of Períssa leads around to **Cape Exomítis**, past Perivolos Beach, guarded by one of the best-preserved Byzantine fortresses of the Cyclades; submerged nearby are the ruins of the ancient **Eleusis**. The road ends by the wild cliffs and often big waves at **Vlycháda**, with a pretty beach, snack bar and world's end air, in spite of nearby smokestacks.

**Pírgos** (ΠΥΡΓΟΣ) shares with Embório the title of the oldest surviving village on the island, with interesting old barrel-roofed houses, Byzantine walls, and a Venetian fort. Much of the surrounding country is covered in vineyards, which swirl up the white flanks of **Mount Profítis Ilías**, Santoríni's highest point (1,857ft). On a clear day you can see Crete from here, and on an exceptionally clear day, Rhodes hovers faintly on the horizon. The locals say the monastery of 1712 (*make sure your knees and shoulders are covered*) is the only place that will protrude above sea level when Santoríni sinks into the sea to join its missing half. It has an interesting little museum and frescoes at the gate showing the narrow road to heaven and the considerably wider one to hell, where the devil whiles away time playing the *laouto*. At the foot of Profítis Ilías, by the village of Mésa Goniá, the 11th-century **Panagía Episkopí** (note how all the churches on Santoríni proudly fly the Greek flag) has fine Byzantine icons, although 26 that managed to miraculously survive earthquakes and fires were stolen in 1982. On 15 August it holds the biggest *panegýri* on the island. North, another black beach and a million sun beds and umbrellas announce **Kamári** (ΚΑΜΑΡΙ), with 300 hotels and pensions, and just as many tavernas, bars, and tourist shops, while a mile away women in big straw hats calmly thresh *fava* beans in the field.

Kamári was the port of **Ancient Thíra** (ΠΑΛΑΙΑ ΘΗΡΑ) spread over its great terraces on the rocky headland of Mésa Vouno, reached by a cobbled path or road (*open Tues–Sun 9–3*). Although inhabited since the 9th century BC, most of what you see dates from the Ptolemies (300–150 BC), who used Thíra as a base for meddling in the Aegean, or from Byzantine times: the chapel by the entrance, Ag. Stéfanos, stands over a 5th-century basilica. The north side of the city, with the Ptolemies' barracks, a gymnasium and governor's palace, are reached by way of the Temenos of Artemidoros of Perge, a sacred area dedicated by an admiral of the Ptolemies, and decorated with symbols of the gods in relief. In the garrison area, a statue of Demeter once sat on the throne carved in a niche, while another little sacred cave was converted into a church.

Below, Thíra's long main street passes through impressive remains of the vast *agora*, with the base of a Temple of Dionysos and altar of Ptolemy Philometor. The long **Royal Stoa** with its Doric columns was last restored in AD 150; behind it, the tidy Hellenistic houses have mosaics and toilets; note the one with a phallus dedicated 'to my friends.' The nearby theatre has a dizzying view down to the sea. The road along the headland passes Roman baths past the **Column of Artemis** and the **Temple of Apollo Karneios**, built in the 6th century: one of the most important Doric deities, associated with rams, his summer festival was celebrated by dancing and a race that was more of a hunt of a runner dressed in wool fillets; if he was caught, he'd cry out in delight and it would bode well for the city. Some of the oldest graffiti in Greek, going back to the 7th century BC, may be seen on the Terrace of Celebrations, recording the writers' admiration and homosexual relations with the naked dancers (the *gymno paidiai*).

## Santoríni in a Glass

Santoríni is one of Greece's premier white wine producers. Because of its exclusively volcanic soil, its vines were among the few in Europe to be spared the deadly plant lice *phylloxera*, so the original rootstock remains intact; the average age of an *assyrtiko* vine, the main variety of grape, is 70 years, and the oldest vines, near Akrotíri, go back over 150 years. *Assyrtiko* yields everything from a bone dry light wine to a sweet aged Vinsanto from sun-dried grapes. Because of the wind the vines are kept low and often protected by woven cane; some fields look as if they're growing baskets. Moribund for many years, churning out high-alcohol, low-quality plonk, the Santoríni wine industry has recently had a shot in the arm from the forward-thinking national winemaker Boutari, who in 1988 built a new domed winery, restaurant, and accessory shop at Megalochóri (*t 028 608 1011*). A second winery, Koutsoyanópoulos (*t 028 603 1322*), on the road to Kamári, also offers tastings. While connoisseurs are most welcome, the emphasis is on having a good time.

The coastal road north leads past the airport to **Monolíthos**, a soft grey sandy beach, with a big isolated lump of a rock draped with a few ruins, tamarisks along the shore, windsurfing and a few places to stay and eat. **Messariá**, an important wine and market village, has the **Archontiko Argyrou Museum**, in a 19th-century Neoclassical mansion owned by a wealthy vintner, with murals and traditional furnishings (*t 028 603 1669; tours April–Oct at 11, 12, 1, 5, 6, and 7; adm*); you can stay there, too.

# North of Firá to Oía

**Imerovígli** is on the verge of merging into Firostefáni and can be a good base if you prefer your caldera minus the crowds and paraphernalia. A traditionally Catholic village, it has views as magnificent as Firá or Oía, this time over a startling great big lump of volcanic crud with a knob on top in the foreground. This, incredibly, was the site of **Skáros**, the island's medieval capital, once defended below by an impregnable **castle** of 1207 built by Marco Sanudo; another fortress, the Rocca, sat on the top of the rock until a volcanic eruption in 1650 destroyed the town. A path (do it first thing in the morning, before it gets too hot; don't do it all if you're subject to vertigo) leads in about half an hour to the site of the Rocca, now occupied by a little white chapel. The views are sublime, awe-inspiring, terrifying. Other ruins belong to a Catholic convent, where the nuns stuck it out in extreme hardship until 1818 when they moved to the new **Ag. Nikólaos**. In the 19th century it was one of the biggest convents in Greece, and has a fine collection of bishops' portraits.

The road north continues to that trendy mouthful of vowels called **Oía**, or Ía (OIA), the third port of Santoríni, although these days only yachts and caiques to Thirassía call here. In 1900, 9,000 people lived here, mostly seamen. The 500 who remain are fiercely independent of Firá although, ironically, vastly outnumbered in season by Athenians milking the tourist trade. Half-ruined by the earthquake, its houses, painted in rich, Fauvist colours are nearly all restored now (some have won major

# Where to Stay and Eat

## Imerovígli ✉ 87400

**Heliotopos, t** 028 602 3670, *helio@hol.gr* (*A; lux*). Intimate, elegant Cycladic hideaway, with a restaurant and grand views. Large rooms, all with kitchenette.

**Villa Spiliotica, t** 028 602 2637, **f** 028 602 3590 (*exp*). Similar views, lower prices for its apartments and studios; publicizes the ceiling mirrors of its honeymoon suites.

**Katerina's Castle, t** 028 602 3111, **f** 028 602 2014 (*E; mod*). Simple rooms on the caldera.

**Tholos Villas, t** 028 602 3967, **f** 028 602 4549 (*B; mod*). Traditional architecture and views.

**Blue Note.** Good bet for dinner with grand views.

**Marilos,** near the car park. For something Greek, simple, and much cheaper. No views, but is run by a kindly old gent.

**Skaros Fish Taverna.** Also excellent.

## Oía ✉ 84702

**Ecorama Travel Agency,** by the bus stop, **t** 028 607 1507, *ecorama@otenet.gr*. Very helpful agency, with a range of accommodation, maisonettes and cheaper rooms.

**Fanari Villas,** below the windmill, **t** 028 607 1008, **f** 028 607 1235 (*lux*). Swishest place to stay, the luxury *skaftá*, with small bar, and steps down to Ammoúdi Bay.

**Katikies,** just out of town, **t** 028 607 1401, **f** 028 607 1129 (*lux*). Beautifully decorated rooms and apartments with great views, spectacular pool and breakfasts on the terraces.

**Zoe-Aegeas Traditional Houses, t/f** 028 607 1466, *zoe-aegeas@otenet.gr* (*B; lux*).

4 caldera-rim double studios and 4 flats sleeping up to 6.

**Ammoudi Villas, t** 028 607 1507, **f** 028 607 1509 (*exp*). Tranquil, offering all mod cons in traditional apartments with verandas and a café providing breakfast and excellent handmade ice cream.

**Perivolas, t** 028 607 1308, *perivolas@san .forthnet.gr* (*A; exp*). 14 lovely traditional houses, with a unique pool.

**Youth hostel, t** 028 607 1465, **f** 028 607 1965. Cheap dorm beds, breakfast and a pleasant terrace.

**1800,** on the main street, **t** 028 607 1485 (€25–35). For a romantic dinner by candlelight, in a shipowner's house, serving imaginative international cuisine, and taking Greek cuisine to new heights.

**Blue Sky Taverna,** a bit further down. Reasonable and deservedly popular.

**Amvrossia, t** 028 607 1413 (€25–35). Intimate dining, with nouvelle cuisine (sea bass in champagne and saffron sauce) dishes.

**Kástro.** If you want aperitifs and dinner by the sunset, arrive early to get a table.

**Neptune** and **Thalami,** in town. Good for fish .

**Katina,** descend to Ammoúdi (€10–15). This taverna serves up the excellent fresh catch of the day and island specialities. After all, the President of Greece likes it. He probably likes the prices, too.

**Palea Orihia** ('Old Mines') and **Ether Club,** on the road to Ammoúdi. Both are places to escape the tourist throng and enjoy the great views.

**Pelecanos Café.** Popular drinking haunt; its terrace overlooks that crater.

international restoration prizes) and piled on top of one another over the jumble of broken red and white cliffs; the roofs of the lower houses provide terraces for the houses above. There's a half-ruined Venetian lookout fort and working windmills; if you want the sea, it's 286 steps down to **Arméni** Beach with a little clutch of houses, or 214 steps down to **Ammoúdi** Beach with tavernas and a hotel, where you can fill your pockets with pumice-stone souvenirs. The third option is a 3km bus trip to **Baxédes,** with coarse blackish sand and shade. An old mansion in Oía houses the **Nautical Museum** (*t 028 607 1156; open Wed–Mon 12.30–4 and 5–8.30; adm*), created by an old sea captain; it has ships' models and figureheads, and rare instruments. Oía is reputedly haunted, although most of the spirits these days seem to come out of bottles, especially when everyone gathers down on the tip by the Kástro to watch the sun call it a day.

# Islets Around the Caldera

Crusts of land mark the rim of Santoríni's spooky 10km wide and 1,250ft deep caldera. The largest, curving around the northwest, is **Thirassía**, part of Santoríni until the two were blasted apart in 236 BC. In one of its pumice quarries a Middle Cycladic settlement was discovered, pre-dating Aokrotíri, though there are no traces of it now. The main business on Thirassía (pop. 245) is growing tomatoes and beans on the fertile plateau; the largest village, **Manolás**, has tavernas and rooms to rent. Excursion boats from Oía make trips out to the 'burnt isles', **Palía Kaméni** (appeared in AD 157) and **Néa Kaméni** (born in 1720), both still volcanically active, especially the Metaxá crater on Néa Kaméni, which last erupted in 1950. However, even though a local brochure promises 'the strange volcano which cause you greatness', be forewarned that most people come away disappointed. The tourist trail up the mountain is rubbish-strewn and stinks of sulphur. Other excursions take people to swim in the 'healthy' sulphurous mud nearby and hot volcanic waters around Palía Kaméni, which makes an unusual chat-up line ('Gosh, you stink!') in the bars.

# Sérifos (ΣΕΡΙΦΟΣ)

Where its neighbour Sífnos welcomes the visitor with soft green terraces and dovecotes, Sérifos, 'the barren one', tends to intimidate at first with its stark rocks. These were so rich in iron and copper mines, however, that in antiquity Sérifos minted its own coins, stamped with a frog. A violent miners' strike in 1916 followed by a decline in profitability led to the abandonment of the mines, and since the 1960s the population has drastically decreased to around 1,500. As for the rest, Sérifos is pure Cycladic; Chóra, high above the sea, seemingly inaccessible as it tumbles impressively down the steep slopes, was once fortified with a Byzantine-Venetian castle and walls. The appealing port Livádi provides an informal foreground to its dramatic setting, and has learned to cope with the arrival of yachties and a strong German and French contingent. Beware of water shortages in August.

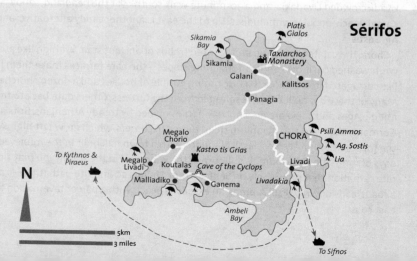

**Sérifos**

Platis Gialos

Sikamia Bay

Taxiarchos Monastery

Sikamia

Galani

Kalitsos

Panagia

Megalo Chorio

CHORA

Psili Ammos

Ag. Sostis

To Kythnos & Piraeus

Megalo Livadi

Koutalas

Kastro tis Grias

Cave of the Cyclops

Livadi

Lia

Malliadiko

Ganema

Livadakia

Ambeli Bay

N

5km

3 miles

To Sifnos

## Getting There

**By sea**: daily with Piraeus, Kýthnos, Mílos and Sífnos; 4 times a week with Kímolos, 3 times a week with Santoríni, Folégandros, Síkinos and Íos; twice a week with Mýkonos and Páros, once a week to Sýros and Tínos. **Port authority**: t 028 105 1470. Six **buses** go up to Chóra from Livádi; other villages are served once a day in the summer.

## Tourist Information

**Police**: Livádi, t 028 105 1300.
**Krings Travel**, Livádi, t 028 105 1164, *corglli@ mail.otenet.gr*. Very helpful with arranging all types of accommodation and travel tickets.

## Festivals

**5 May**: Koutalás.
**27 July**: Mount Óros.
**6 Aug**: Kaló Ábeli.
**15–17 Aug**: near the monastery and at a different village each day.
**7 Sept**: Livádi.
**23 Sept**: Ag. Theklas.

## Where to Stay and Eat

**Rent Rooms Association**, Livádi, t 028 105 1520. Helps all-comers.

### Sérifos ✉ 84005

Sérifos is well-known enough for its hotels and rooms to fill up in the summer. In Livádi, the further along the beach you go, the cheaper the prices.

### Livádi

**Asteri**, t 028 105 1891, *asteri@otenet.gr* (*B; exp*). Balcony with sea view for every room, TVs and a restaurant.
**Sérifos Beach**, t 028 105 1209, (*C; exp*). The island's biggest; nice taverna downstairs.
**Albatross**, further around the bay, t 028 105 1148 (*D; mod*). Smothered in oleander; the owner meets the ferry. *Open April–Oct*.
**Areti**, t 028 105 1479, f 028 105 1547 (*C; mod*). Handy for the ferries, with a quiet garden and comfortable rooms with terraces overlooking the sea. *Open April–Oct*.
**Maistrali**, t 028 105 1381, f 028 105 1298 (*C; mod*). Lovely airy rooms. *Open April–Sept*.
**Naias**, no distance from the beach, t 028 105 1749, *naias@otenet.gr* (*C; mod*). Blue and white, in true Cycladic style, with balconies.

# Livádi and Chóra

Most people stay in **Livádi** (ΛΙΒΑΔΙ), the port and island green spot, where many of the streets are still unpaved, behind a long pebbly-sandy beach lined with tamarisks and rooms to rent. There are two other beaches within easy walking distance from Livádi: crowded **Livadákia**, and a 30-minute walk south over the headland, sandy **Karávi Beach**, popular with nudists. **Lía** to the east is another sandy alternative, and **Ag. Sóstis**.

**Chóra**, the capital, is 6km up and is linked by bus or ancient stair. Set high like a whitewashed oasis over Sérifos' forbidding slopes – the bare terraces make them look like corrugated iron – Chóra is a fascinating jumble of houses and a dozen churches. Many of these are built of stone salvaged from the fortress; others date back to the Middle Ages and a few are now holiday homes owned by trendy Athenians, Brits and Germans. There are also geranium trees, tucked in corners, which grow 12ft high. At the top, there's a pretty Neoclassical square, with a **town hall** built in the moneyed days of 1908. The old windmills still turn in the wind, and in the spring you may find a rare carnation that grows only on Sérifos. From Chóra a 20-minute path (there is also a road) leads down to **Psíli Ámmos**, an excellent beach with a pair of tavernas on the east coast.

Captain George Rooms, near the square, t 028 105 1274 (inexp). Good value.

Kyklades, by the sea, t 028 105 1315 (E; inexp). Rooms and a restaurant serves delicious shrimp casserole with feta cheese and tomatoes. Open April–Oct.

Rent rooms, above the Cavo d'Oro supermarket, t 028 105 1160 (inexp).

Korali Camping, Livadákia Beach, t 028 105 1500. Good facilities.

Mokka, at the end of the port. Where the locals, yachties, tourists, various children and an assortment of cats and dogs mingle happily together. For a pleasantly zany atmosphere, with good, wholesome food (spaghetti, chicken curries) apart from the usual Greek fare.

Ouzerie Meltémi. For a karafáki (enough for 3–4 good drinks) and choice of tasty nibbles, incl. local cheeses and the mysterious 'single yellow pea' or 'married yellow pea'.

Stamati, round the bay. Sit right on the water and enjoy the excellent ready food, vegetarian dishes, or grilled meats.

Serfanto. Bargain Italian-based set menus.

Takis, on Livádi's waterfront under an enormous tamarisk. Popular with locals and tourists alike, offering excellent and inexpensive food and friendly service.

## Chóra

Apanemia, t 028 105 1717 (inexp). Some of the few rooms up here, all rooms kitted out with a fridge.

Petros, t 028 105 1302. Popular with locals, even those down in Livádi, for its traditional, reliable menu.

Stavro, by the bus stop. The owner's dad starred in a famous EOT tourist poster in the 60s, also serving food with accompanying view. Try their potent red wine, which the owners (and some locals) swear leads to wedding bells.

Zorba, on the top square by the town hall. Serving snacks with a view.

# Entertainment and Nightlife

There's a mix of nightlife in Livádi with several music bars and seasonal discos.

Metallein and Veggera. Both clubs play everything from heavy metal to pop.

Alter Ego. Features Greek music.

Captain Hook. This is another popular club.

Vitamin. Trendy pool hall bar.

Paradise, to the left of the ferry port. Enjoy the 'happenings' organized by these people.

# Around the Island

The road continues beyond Chóra to **Megálo Chorió**, which sits on the site of the ancient capital of Sérifos and is still guarded by a ruined marble Hellenist tower; below, **Megálo Livádi**, now visited for its beach and tavernas, once served as the loading dock for the iron and copper mined nearby. From Megálo Chorió the road continues around to **Koutalás**, with the ruins of another castle, the **Kástro tis Grías**. During mining operations, a cave, instantly dubbed the **Cave of the Cyclops**, was discovered near here, with two stalactite chambers and a small lake, and a floor of petrified seashells (bring a light). There are two beaches nearby, **Malliádiko** and **Gánema**, and a track back to Livádi.

A second road, now paved, passes **Panagía**, named after the oldest church on Sérifos, from the 10th century. At **Galaní** you can visit **Taxiárchos Monastery** (t 028 105 1027), built in 1500 and containing a precious altar, 18th-century frescoes by the painter Skordílis, and Byzantine manuscripts in the library, before continuing into the petrified island's corner of milk and honey, **Kalítsos**, where almonds, olives and vines prosper. There's a beach, Platís Giálos, just beyond the monastery. On the other side of Galaní, **Sikamiá Bay** is a good place to get away from it all, with a beach, taverna, rare bit of shade and fresh water.

## Mythology

Sérifos is a setting for one of the oldest Greek myths. When it was prophesied to Akrisios, King of Argos, that he would be slain by the son of his daughter Danaë, he locked the girl in an underground chamber. This failed to hide her from Zeus, however, who came to her in a shower of golden rain and fathered Perseus. Enraged but unable to put his daughter or grandson to death, Akrisios decided to leave the issue to fate and set them adrift in a chest. Zeus guided them to Sérifos, where a fisherman, Diktys, rescued and took them in. Polydektes, the King of Sérifos, lusted after Danaë but Perseus, as he grew older, stood in his way. One day, hearing the young man boast that he could kill Medusa, the only mortal of the three monstrous Gorgon sisters who lived beyond the Ocean and whose glance turned men to stone, Polydektes challenged him to do so, and threatened to take Danaë captive if he failed. Perseus succeeded, thanks to Athena and Hermes who helped him procure winged shoes to fly, a cap of invisibility, and a pouch to hold the head. Perseus then returned to Sérifos (rescuing Andromeda on the way), to find that his mother had been abused by Polydektes. Perseus then surprised the king at a banquet and presented him with the head, instantly turning him to stone. Diktys was declared King of Sérifos in his stead, and Danaë and Perseus went home to Argos. Fearing the old prophecy, Akrisios fled before them. But fate finally caught up with him in another town, where Perseus was competing in a game and accidentally killed his grandfather with a javelin in the foot.

# Sífnos (ΣΙΦΝΟΣ)

Sífnos in recent years has become the most popular island in the western Cyclades, with good reason – it is an island of peaceful serendipity, with gentle green hills, vineyards, watermelon patches and olives, charming villages and long sandy beaches, beloved by its 2,000 inhabitants who keep it spick and span. It is famous for its pottery and its cooks, ever since Sifniot Nikolas Tselemntes wrote the first modern Greek cookery book (to this day any cookbook in Greece is a *tselemntes*). Sífnos produces the best olive oil in the Cyclades, and the people speak with a sweet singsong lilt. One of the best things to do on Sífnos is walk: the landscape is strewn with Venetian dovecotes, windmills, 300 little chapels, and 52 ancient towers (more than the rest of the Cyclades combined) left over from a sophisticated signalling system devised in the 5th century BC – a bit after the fact in Sífnos' case.

## History: the Island that Laid Golden Eggs

Pliny, who often got it wrong, wrote that the Phoenicians called the island Meropia and were the first to mine its gold, but according to recent archaeological research, this time Pliny was right: the oldest gold, silver and lead galleries on Sífnos date back to the 3rd millennium BC – the oldest mines yet discovered in Europe. And when these first miners exhausted their galleries, the archaeologists note, they religiously filled them in to heal the wounds of the earth.

The Phoenicians were replaced by the Minoans, who founded Minoa near Apollonía, and who were in turn supplanted by Ionians who lived near Ag. Andreas and elsewhere. Meropia, meanwhile, had become famous for its gold; at one time, it is said, there was so much that the islanders simply divided it among themselves each year, and had enough extra in the 6th century to afford to pave their *agora* with the finest Parian marble. Apollo at Delphi heard rumours of this wealth and demanded that the island contribute an annual tithe of gold in the form of a solid egg. In 530 BC Meropia constructed a magnificent treasury at Delphi to house its golden eggs and adorned it with a fine frieze and pediment which can still be seen; for many years it was the richest of all the oracle's treasures. But one year the islanders, who began to have a reputation for greed and cunning, sent the god an egg of gilded lead. Apollo soon discovered he had been duped and cursed the island. This gave Polycrates, Tyrant of Sámos, a good excuse to extract a fine from Meropia; his 40 *triremes* plundered the island's gold, and Apollo's curse caused the mines to sink and give out. Thus the island became empty or, in Greek, *sifnos*. Nowadays most of the ancient mines at Ag. Mína, Kapsálos and Ag. Sostis are underwater, or just barely above the sea.

With egg on its face, Sífnos went into decline. In 1307 the Da Coronia family ruled the island for Venice; in 1456 Kozadinós, the Lord of Kýthnos, married into the family and his descendants ruled Sífnos until the Turks took the island in 1617. Towards the end of the 17th century the Sultan, thinking to reopen the mines, sent out experts to examine them. When they heard that they were coming, the islanders hired French pirates to sink the Sultan's ship. The experts, in turn, heard of the deal with the pirates, and simply went home. Later the French themselves exploited the local deposits of iron ore and lead; mining ended in 1925.

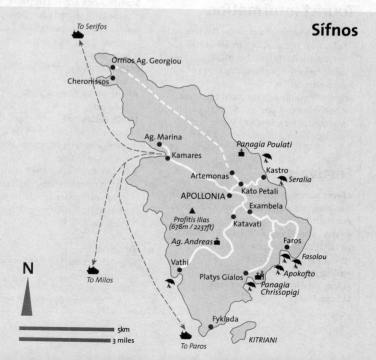

Sífnos has also made an important contribution to Greek letters. In the late 1600s, the 'School of the Holy Tomb' was founded in an attempt to keep alive ancient Greek and the classics, drawing students from all over Greece. Nikólaos Chrysoyélos, the most famous headmaster, led a contingent of Sifniots in the War of Independence, and, subsequently, he became modern Greece's first Minister of Education. Another

## Getting There and Around

**By sea**: daily with Piraeus, Kýthnos, Sérifos and Mílos; 4 times a week with Kímolos, 2–3 times a week with Íos, Santoríni, Folégandros and Síkinos, once a week with Páros, Tínos, Karystos (Évia) and Rafína. **Excursion boats** from Kamáres to Váthi and Cherónissos; also round the island tours. **Port authority: t** 028 403 1617.

**By road**: frequent reliable **buses** between Kamáres, Apollonía, Artemónas, and from there to Platýs Gialós; not quite as often to Fáros, Káto Petáli, Kástro and Váthi. Pick up the detailed schedule at the tourist office. **Taxis: t** 028 403 1656/1793/1626. For car or moped rental, try **Krinas**, on the waterfront in Kamáres, **t** 028 403 1488, **f** 028 403 1073. Kiosks and shops stock an excellent map showing all the island's footpaths.

## Tourist Information

**Municipal Tourist Office**: run by the helpful Sofia, near the quay in Kamáres, **t** 028 403 1977. In Apollonía, another municipal tourist office has a list of all availble types of accommodation.

**Aegean Thesaurus**, in the main square in Apollonía, **t** 028 403 3151, **f** 028 403 2190, *thesauros@travelling.gr*. Helpful and offers guided walking tours around the island.

## Festivals

**2 Feb**: *Lolopangyrio* 'Crazy festival' of pagan origins, at Panagía Ouranofóra, Apollonía.
**25 March**: Panagía tou Vouno.
**40 days after Greek Easter**: Chrissopigí.
**20 July**: Profítis Ilías near Kamáres.
**15 Aug**: Panagía ta Gournia.
**29 Aug**: Ag. Ioánnes near Váthi.
**31 Aug**: Ag. Simeon near Kamáres.
**14 Sept**: Fáros.

## Where to Stay and Eat

**Sífnos** ✉ 84003
 Most accommodation is open April–Oct. Sifnos is famous for *revithia tou foúrno*, oven baked chick peas, served only on Sun; *revithokeftedes*, chick pea patties; *xynomyzíthra*, a hard sheep's-milk cheese, steeped in wine and kept in barrels until it stinks but tastes great; *stamnás*, meat, cheese and potatoes in a clay pot; and *ambelofásoula*, made from green beans. Fresh dill is the island's favourite herb.

### Kamáres

**Boulis, t** 028 403 2122, **f** 028 403 2381 (*C; exp–mod*). By the beach, with a surprisingly green lawn.

**Kamari Pension**, on the waterfront, **t** 028 403 3383, **f** 028 403 1709 (*C; mod*). A decent option.

**Stavros, t** 028 403 1641 (*C; mod*). Basic rooms, some with shared bath. *Open all year.*

**Dimitris and Margarita Belli, t** 028 403 1276 (*inexp*). Good little rooms with sea-view balconies.

**Makis Camping**, just behind the beach, **t** 028 403 2366.

**Argyris**, in Ag. Marína. Right on the sea with good grills.

**Boulis Restaurant**, on the road. Good value rooms above (don't confuse it with the hotel) and serves traditional, excellent and cheap Greek fare.

**Kapetan Andreas**, on the harbour, **t** 028 403 2356 (€*12–18*). Serving the freshest of fish, including lobster, caught by Captain Andrew himself from his own boat. No frills, just good food.

### Apollonía

**Angelo's Rooms, t** 028 403 1533 (*inexp*). With garden views.

**Sofia**, set on a quiet little square, **t** 028 403 1238 (*C; inexp*). *Open April–Sept.*

islander, the 19th-century poet-satirist Cleánthis Triandáfilos, who wrote under the name Rabágas, was a thorn in the side of the monarchy until he was imprisoned and committed suicide. Ioánnis Gypáris (d. 1942), another Sifniot, was, along with Caváfy, the first to espouse the use of demotic Greek (as opposed to the formal *katharévousa*) in literature.

**Sífnos, t** 028 403 1624, **f** 028 403 3067 (*C; mod*). Another good choice.

**Orea Sifnos,** by the bus stop, **t** 028 403 3069. Tasty traditional food and barrelled wine.

## Artemónas

**Artemónas,** in Artemónas, **t** 028 403 1303, **f** 028 403 2385 (*C; mod*). This little guest house is one of the most charming places on Sífnos, with a cool courtyard. *Open April–Sept.*

**Artemón, t** 028 403 1303 (*mod*). Under the same management, but bigger and has a garden restaurant.

**Apostolidis, t** 028 403 2143. Recently renovated furnished apartments incl. mini-bars in every room and views over Platýs Giálos. It also has a café.

**Liotrivi** ('Olive Press'), on the main square, **t** 028 403 2051/1246. One of the best restaurants in the Cyclades, with delicious wholesome and satisfying dishes. Among the specialities are *kápari*, local capers, *revíthia* and other Sifniot specialities; it's also high on atmosphere and has a good choice of wine.

## Kástro

**Leonidas** and **Sifakis.** Both have rooms to rent.

**To Astro, t** 028 403 1476. Set in the backstreets, with a terrace, serving Sifniot dishes. The lamb in red wine is their speciality.

## Fáros/Chrissopigí

**Blue Horizon, t** 028 407 1442, **t** 028 407 1441 (*B; lux*). 10 new furnished apartments.

**Sifneiko Archontiko, t** 028 407 1454, **f** 028 407 1454 (*D; mod–inexp*). The old standby; some of the cheapest rooms on the island.

**Flora,** at Chrissopigí, **t** 028 407 1278, **f** 028 407 1388 (*B; inexp*). Small and family-run, with great views.

**Faros,** amid the clutch of jolly tavernas, **t** 028 403 1826. Charcoal grilled lobster, octopus and fish.

**Lembesis.** Serves excellent traditional food.

**On the Rocks.** Great bar and *crêperie*, especially nice for sunset views.

**Zambelis,** on the water, **t** 028 407 1434. Offering delicious Sifniot specialities and a very tasty lamb casserole. Don't tell anyone, but the owner was Christina Onassis' personal chef.

## Platýs Gialós

**Alexandros Sífnos Beach, t** 028 403 1333, **f** 028 407 1303 (*B; lux*). Smart with bungalows on the hillside above the beach.

**Platýs Yialos Beach, t** 028 407 1324, **f** 028 407 1325 (*B; lux*). Built in traditional Cycladic style with well-equipped air-con bungalows, all facilities and sports.

**Angeliki,** near the bus stop, **t** 028 403 1288 (*mod*). Nice little place with several well-presented rooms.

**Camping Platýs Yialos,** in an olive grove set back from the beach, **t** 028 407 1286.

**Mama Mia.** Popular for Italian (well, almost Italian) food.

**Sofia, t** 028 407 1202. For Sifniot dishes, suckling pig, lobster with spaghetti and some good wines.

# Entertainment and Nightlife

Nightlife in **Kamáres** centres on beachside cocktail bars and discos.

**Café Folie.** Lovely for a sundowner.

**Collage Bar,** overlooking the sandy beach. Another relaxing choice.

**Aloni,** in Apollonía, **t** 028 403 1543. Often has live Greek music.

**Argo** and **Doloma,** in Apollonía. Also very attractive bars.

**Castello** and **Remezzo,** in Kástro. Both trendy.

**Sifniot Cultural Society,** at Artemónas. Presents summer concerts, for those who fancy a spot of culture.

# Kamáres and the North Coast

The island's port, shady **Kamáres** (ΚΑΜΑΡΕΣ), has become a typical waterside jumble of tourist facilities. Situated between two steep, barren cliffs that belie the fertility inland, Kamáres has a sandy beach safe for little kids, with some shady places to camp, and a range of cafés and tavernas. Two pottery workshops specialize in decorative glazed chimney pots. The exceptionally fine clay on Sífnos has been used for ceramics since pre-Cycladic times, and the islanders are expert potters. In the early 19th century, there were so many that they emigrated to other corners of Greece, to the extent that someone has discovered that every Greek potter has a Sifniot in his or her family tree. Just after the war, there were still some 90 workshops in the island, employing 600 potters, and after nearly dying a death, the old tradition is undergoing something of a revival.

**Cherónissos** on the island's windy northern tip is another pottery centre, best reached by boat, although there's a rough road (most car hire firms make you promise not to use it, however). Here master potter Kóstas Depastás upholds the island's old ceramics tradition with local clay, his kiln fired by driftwood. There's a taverna if you feel peckish.

# Apollonía and Around

The bus makes the dramatic climb up from Kamáres to the capital **Apollonía** (ΑΠΟΛΛΟΝΙΑ), a Cycladic idyll of two-storey houses and bougainvillaea, spread out across the hills, a circle of white from the distance; note how most of the houses have terraces on the side, designed for talking; the Sifniots are a sociable lot. The town's name comes from a 7th-century BC Temple of Apollo, superseded in the 18th century by the church **Panagía Ouranofóra** (Our Lady of Heavenly Force) in the highest part of town. Fragments of the temple can still be seen, and there's a marble relief of St George over the door. Another church, **Ag. Athanásios** (next to the pretty square dedicated to Cleánthis Triandáfilos) has frescoes and a carved wooden iconostasis. In the square containing the bus stop, the **Museum of Popular Arts and Folklore** houses a fine ethnographic collection of Sifniot pottery, embroideries and costumes (*hours depend on who has a key*).

Artemis is Apollo's twin sister; similarly **Artemónas** (ΑΡΤΕΜΩΝΑΣ) is Apollonía's twin village and the second largest on Sífnos, a pretty mile's walk away. Beneath its windmills, cobblestoned lanes wind past the island's most ambitious Neoclassical residences and churches. The church of **Kochí**, with its cluster of domes, occupies the site of a Temple of Artemis; little 17th-century **Ag. Geórgios tou Aféndi** contains several fine icons from the period, and **Panagía ta Gourniá**, near the bridge, has a beautiful interior (*keys next door*). **Panagía Pouláti**, down on the coast, is in a superb setting overlooking the sea and cliffs, with a beach down below.

**Kástro** (ΚΑΣΤΡΟ), on the east coast, is 3km from Artemónas by road or the old scenic coastal path. The ancient and medieval capital of Sífnos, Kástro is a charming village overlooking the sea, if a bit forlorn with only 30 families in residence. Byzantine walls form the backs of the tall narrow houses, many sporting wooden balconies and their Venetian coats-of-arms. Ruins of the Classical *acropolis* and walls remain, and many churches have attractive floors, among them **Panagía Eleoússa** (1653); **Ag. Ekateríni** (1665) and **Panagía Koímmissi** (1593), where the altar is decorated with Dionysian bulls' heads. An old Venetian church of St Anthony of Padua houses the **Archaeology Museum** (*t 028 403 1022; open Tues–Sun, 9–2; out of season, ask the lady opposite*). The site of the School of the Holy Tomb, closed in 1834, is now Kástro's cemetery. At Kástro there's plenty of deep blue sea to dive into from the rocks, but if you prefer sand, a path from Kástro leads down to **Serália**, with remnants of the medieval port, and a lovely beach.

Just south of Artemónas the bus passes through **Exámbela**, a quiet flower-filled village famous for its songs. In the middle of one of the island's most fertile areas, the **Vrísi Monastery** (1612) is surrounded by springs and contains old manuscripts and art. On the road to Platýs Gialós the **Monastery of Ag. Andréas**, sitting on a hill, has some ruins of the double walls that once encircled the ancient citadel, and a little further north, a path from Katavatí continues up in two hours to Sífnos' highest peak (2,237ft). This is named after **Profítis Ilías Monastery**, built in the 8th century, with thick stone walls, a small network of catacombs and cells and a 12th-century marble iconostasis in the church (*check opening hours before setting out*); the views over the white villages below are delightful.

# Panagia Chrissopigí, Platýs Gialós and the South Coast

Further south, the old seaside village of **Fáros** with its sandy beaches is a friendly, low-key resort with cheap accommodation and good tavernas. There's a footpath to the island's most famous monastery, **Panagía Chrissopigí**, built in 1650 on a rocky cape. The story goes that two girls accidentally disturbed some pirates napping in the church. With the pirates in hot pursuit, the girls desperately prayed to the Virgin, who saved them by splitting the cape in the pirates' path – it is spanned in these pirate-free days by a bridge. The long beach here, **Apókofto**, has golden sands, while **Fasoloú** is popular with nudists; both have tavernas.

**Platýs Gialós** (ΠΛΑΤΥΣ ΓΙΑΛΟΣ) with its broad sandy beach – said to be the longest in the Cyclades – is the island's busiest resort. You can escape its worldly concerns by lodging in the serene cliff top Convent of **Panagía tou Vounoú**, affording a gorgeous view over the bay below. The last nuns left nearly a century ago, but the church with its ancient Doric columns is still used for island *panegýria*. Platýs Gialós has one of the island's oldest active potteries, Franzesko Lemonis, founded in 1936. There are boat excursions from Kamáres and now buses to the lovely pottery and fishing hamlet of **Vathí**, probably the prettiest place to stay on Sífnos, with a few rooms to rent, a lovely clean beach and shallow water.

# Síkinos (ΣΙΚΙΝΟΣ)

If you want to escape the outside world, its newspapers and noise or just practise your Greek, you always have Síkinos, Folégandros' little sister, with a sleepy port and stunning white villages of Chóra and Kástro perched high above. Declared an 'Ecosystem of European Importance', its shores host wild pigeons, black-headed hawks, and sea birds; monk seals (see p.603) live in its sea caves, rare cat vipers and sand snakes slither about on land; little wheat fields and vines in the terraces and valleys and fishing are still the island's mainstay. Light years away from neighbouring Íos – although there are day trips from the fleshpots – Síkinos is the place to savour the simple pleasures of old-fashioned island life, although things pick up in August with returning Greeks. Named after the child of banished Limnian Thoas who was set adrift in a tea chest and saved by a local nymph, in ancient times Síkinos was also one of several islands called Oenoe, or 'wine island', and the local stuff still packs a punch.

## Villages and Walks Around Síkinos

Ferries dock at Síkinos' port, **Aloprónia** (ΑΛΟΠΡΟΝΙΑ) or **Skála**, where you'll also find a sandy beach and shallow sea, ideal for children; bobbing fishing boats, a few tavernas and a shop-cum-café, a scattering of holiday homes behind the port, and a new hotel complex sums up the rest. **Chóra** (ΧΟΡΑ), the capital, is one of the most

## Getting There and Around

**By sea: ferry** connections 5 times a week with Piraeus, 3 times a week with Sífnos, Sérifos, Mílos, Kímolos and Íos, twice a week with Anáfi, Kýthnos, Náxos, Páros and Sýros; daily summer tourist **boats** to Folégandros and Íos; **excursion boats** to the beaches in summer. **Port authority: t** 028 605 1222.

**By road:** the island **bus** meets most ferries and runs hourly to Chóra and Kástro.

## Where to Stay and Eat

### Síkinos ✉ 84010

#### Aloprónia

**Porto Síkinos**, right on the beach, **t** 028 605 1247, **f** 028 605 1220 (*B; exp*). Smart and prettily laid out in traditional island design, with bar, restaurant and tourist office.

**Flora**, up the hill, **t** 028 605 1239/1214 (*C; mod*). Lovely Cycladic-style development of 8 self-contained rooms built round a courtyard with wonderful views.

**Kamáres, t/f** 028 605 1281 (*mod*). Charming traditional rooms, all with bath and phones.

**Loukas**, above the fish restaurant, **t** 028 605 1076, **f** 028 605 1075. Basic harbourside rooms .

**Panayiotis Kouvdouris**, by the sea, **t** 028 605 1232. Simple rooms.

There are several seasonal tavernas but if you go after late Sept, everything is closed.

**Flora's Shop**. Doubles as a makeshift taverna.

**Braxos Pizzaria**, aka **The Rock Café**. Serves simple pizza and drinks.

*Meltémi*. Where the fishermen gather, for a simple lunch, coffee or *ouzo*.

#### Chóra

There are a few rooms:

**Haroula** and **Dimitris Divolis**, on the way to the post office.

**Nikos**, over one of the *kafeneía*.

**Klimateria**. Pretty vine-covered restaurant and *kafeneíon* which does meals, snacks and omelettes.

**To Kástro**. The main taverna with a roof garden and excellent home-cooking.

**To Liotrivi**. The main nightspot; a trendy music/dancing bar converted from an olive press.

**Themonies**, halfway to Aloprónia. Fun disco.

authentic villages in the Cyclades and a good hour's walk up if the bus hasn't put in an appearance. Looming over the village is the ruined 18th-century **Monastery of Zoodóchos Pigí**, fortified against the pirates. The 300 inhabitants are most proud, however, of their 'cathedral' with icons by the 18th-century master painter Skordílis. In the main square, bees buzz furiously in the trees by the church of the **Pantánassa** and the 18th-century stone **mansions**, some with brightly painted wooden balconies as in Folégandros; one ruined marble portico has intricately carved grapes and Byzantine symbols.

A few minutes' walk up the next hill, **Kástro** (ΚΑΣΤΡΟ) with its labyrinthine lanes, ruined windmills, tiny little rooms and *kafeneíons* is a last relic of what most Cycladic villages looked like in the pre-tourism era. Some nationalist goofball has brightly illustrated his opinions on his walls and there is a delightful little **folk museum** close by run, by expat American John Margétis in memory of his mother, Kalíope (*open July–Aug afternoons only*).

From **Chóra** a new paved road leads past ruined **Cyclopean** walls south west to **Moní Episkópi**. Originally a 3rd-century mausoleum, it was converted in the 7th century to the Byzantine church of Koimísis Theotókou, and remodelled again in the 17th century after an earthquake. A rough path to the northeast leads in about an hour and a half to the rather scant remains of a Classical fortress at **Paliókastro**, near the nice sandy beach of **Málta**. Tracks from this path lead south to the sandy beaches of **Ag. Geórgios** (with a taverna) and **Ag. Nikólaos**, but there is also a caique in summer. From the harbour beach you can walk up over the mountain to the next cove at **Gialiskári**, while the pebble beach at **Ag. Panteleímonas** is about 40 minutes away and site of a big *panegýri* on 27 July.

# Sýros (ΣΥΡΟΣ/ΣΥΡΑ)

Inhabitants of Sýros (locally known as Sýra) affectionately call their island home 'Our rock', and it's as dry and barren a piece of real estate as you can find. But at the beginning of the Greek War of Independence in 1821 it was blessed with three important qualities: a large natural harbour, the protection of the King of France, and a hardworking population. The result is Sýros' capital, Ermoúpolis, once the premier port in Greece, and today the largest city and capital of the Cyclades. Don't come here looking for Cycladic sugar cubism: Ermoúpolis is the best-preserved 19th-century Neoclassical town in the whole of Greece.

A sophisticated island, with many Athenians working there in law or local government, Sýros can afford to snap its fingers at tourism, but it's booming nonetheless. However, it remains very Greek and tourists are treated more like guests rather than customers – except when it comes to *loukoúmia*, better known as Turkish Delight (both the Greeks and the Turks claim to have invented it; no one really knows). These sweet, gummy squares, flavoured with roses, quinces or pistachios and smothered in icing sugar, are an island speciality, along with gorgeous *halvadópittes*, which resemble nougat.

# Sýros

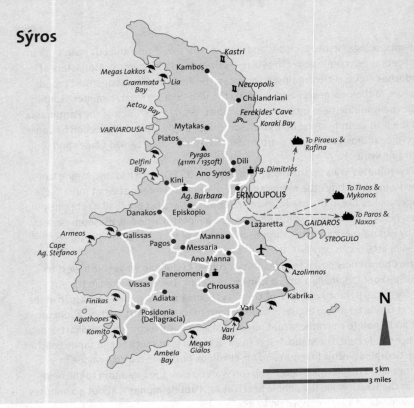

## History

Homer's swineherd Eumaeus, who helped Odysseus when he finally returned to Ithaca, was actually a prince of Sýros who had been captured by Phoenician pirates, and he described his native island as a rich, fertile place where famine and disease were strangers, and inhabitants died only when they were struck by the gentle arrows of Apollo or Artemis after living long, happy lives. The first inhabitants, who may have been the same Phoenicians who made off with Eumaeus, settled at Dellagrácia and at Fínikas. Poseidon was the chief god of Sýros, and in connection with his cult, one of the first observatories in Europe, a heliotrope (a kind of sundial), was constructed in the 6th century BC by Sýros' own philosopher, Ferekides. Ferekides was a keen student of ancient Chaldaean and Egyptian mysteries, and he spent two years in Egypt being initiated into secret cults; on his return to Greece, he became Pythagoras' teacher, imparting a mix of astrology and philosophy, and beliefs in reincarnation and the immortality of the soul; he was also the first Greek to write in prose. In Roman times the population emigrated to the site of present-day Ermoúpolis, at that time known as 'the Happy' with its splendid natural harbour and two prominent hills. After the collapse of the pax Romana, Sýros was abandoned until the 13th century, when Venetians founded Áno Sýros on one of the hills.

Because Áno Sýros was Catholic, the island enjoyed the protection of the French, and it remained neutral at the outbreak of the Greek War of Independence in 1821.

However, war refugees from Chíos, Psará and Smyrna brought their Orthodox faith with them and founded their own settlements on the other hill, Vrondádo, and down by the harbour. This new port town boomed from the start, as the premier 'warehouse' of the new Greek state where cotton from Egypt and spices from the East were stored. It also played an important role as the central coaling station for the eastern Mediterranean. When the time came to name the new town, Ermoúpolis – 'the city of Hermes' (the god of commerce) – was the natural choice. For 50 years Sýros ran much of the Greek economy, and great fortunes were made and then spent on elegant mansions, schools, and public buildings. Ermoúpolis built the first theatre

## Getting There and Around

**By air**: at least 3 daily **flights** from Athens with Olympic. **Olympic's office** is at 52 Andistasios, on the harbour, **t** 028 108 2634. **Airport: t** 028 108 7025. **Taxis** into town cost around €5.

**By sea**: several times daily with Piraeus, Tínos, Mýkonos, Páros, and Náxos; at least twice a week to Amorgós and the Back Islands, Kýthnos, Kéa, Folégandros, Síkinos, Santoríni, Crete and Astypálaia; at least once a week to Pátmos, Léros, Kálymnos, Tílos Sými and Rhodes. In summer, daily **hydrofoil** connection with Rafína and **day excursions** to Délos. **Doudouris, t** 028 108 3400, has caiques for hire. **Port authority: t** 028 108 8888.

**By road**: good **bus** service around the island, **t** 028 108 2575, departing from the ferry port. One way to see Sýros is to take one of the buses which circle the island, by way of Azólimnos, taking about an hour and passing through all the beach villages except Kíni, which has a separate service from the port. **Taxi** rank: **t** 028 108 6222.

## Tourist Information

**EOT Information Office**: Dodekanesou St, by the bus station, **t** 028 108 6725, **f** 028 108 2375; open weekdays 7.30am–2.30pm. **Police: t** 028 108 2610. **Post office**: between the port and main square, on Proto Papadhaki. **Teamwork Travel Office**, in the port, **t** 028 108 3400, teamwork@otenet.gr. Very helpful at organizing accommodation, travel and guided tours of Ermoúpolis, as well as car and bike rentals. Look out for Welcome to

Sýros, a free booklet with good maps of Sýros and Ermoúpolis. **Galissás Tours**, by the bus stop in Galissás, **t** 028 104 2801, galtours@syr.forthnet.gr. Very helpful.

## Internet

**Net Café**, by the town hall. Has smart surfing facilities.

## Festivals

**Carnival**: with dancing to the ancient tasmbouna and toubi, in Áno Sýra. **Last Sun in May**: celebrating the finding of the icon at Ag. Dimitríou. **June**: folklore festival in Azólimnos with 3 days of dancing, wine and song. **Late July/Aug**: Ermoúpoleia Arts Festival. **24 Sept**: Orthodox and Catholic celebration in Faneroméni. **6 Dec**: Ag. Nikólaos in Ermoúpolis.

## Where to Stay and Eat

**Sýros ✉ 84100**

Sýros has some refined, stylish new hotels in restored Neoclassical buildings. A tempting option is to stay in town and head for a different beach every day, especially as prices in town are reasonable, with big discounts outside of July and Aug. There are plenty of acceptable rooms for rent on the waterfront, but Sýros has some gems worth searching for. The **Rooms and Apartments Association, t** 028 108 2252, has a booth near the port and publishes an excellent booklet with a map.

in modern Greece and the first high school, financed by the citizens and government; when the Syriani died the citizens were so pleased with themselves that the most extravagant monuments ever to be seen in any Greek cemetery were erected in their memory. By the 1890s, however, oil replaced coal, and Piraeus, with the building of the Corinth Canal, replaced Ermoúpolis as Greece's major port. Sýros declined, but always dominated the Cyclades, supporting itself with shipyards and various industries, prospering just enough to keep its grand old buildings occupied, but not enough to tear them down to build new concrete blocks. The result is that today Ermoúpolis is a National Landmark.

## Ermoúpolis

**Palladian**, Stamatoú Proioú, one street back from the waterfront, **t** 028 108 6400, **f** 028 108 6436 (*C; lux*). Stylish, with a quiet internal courtyard terrace.

**Diogenis**, Papágou Square, just to the left of the ferry dock, **t** 028 108 6301, **f** 028 108 3334 (*B; exp*). Swish and new, with 43 Neoclassical style rooms; air-con, TV and the works.

**Hermes**, on the harbour near Plateía Kanári, **t** 028 108 3011, **f** 028 108 7412 (*C; exp*). Smart rooms with bath and balconies over the sea.

**Omiros**, 43 Omirou St, leading from Plateía Miaoulis up to Áno Sýros, **t** 028 108 4910, **f** 028 108 6266 (*A; exp*). For deep pockets and strong legs, the pick of several on this street; a gorgeous 150-year-old Neoclassical mansion, the elegantly restored family home of sculptor Vitalis.

**Sea Colours Apartments**, on the north side of town, beyond Kanári Square, **t** 028 108 1181, **f** 028 109 3509 (*A; exp*). Luxurious and modern with marble terraces and wonderful views. Can be booked through Teamwork Travel on the quay.

**Ypatia**, in the same area, 3 Babagiotou, **t** 028 108 3575 (*B; exp*). Super Neoclassical mansion with brass bedsteads. *Open summer mths only*.

**Ariadne**, 9 Filini, just off the waterfront by the bus depot, **t** 028 108 0245 (*mod*). Clean rooms and convenient if you arrive at an ungodly hour.

**Avra Rooms**, 7 Afrodíti, near to the port, **t/f** 028 108 2853 (*mod*). Friendly management, good rooms with air-con, TV and hair dryers.

**Paradise**, 3 Omirou St, nearer the square, **t** 028 108 3204, **f** 028 108 1754 (*mod*). Well-appointed rooms with a quiet flower-filled courtyard and fabulous roof terrace with panoramic views of the entire town. Good off-season discounts.

**Silvia's**, 42 Omirou St, **t** 028 108 1081 (*mod*). Rooms are elegantly furnished, good value and quiet, in yet another old mansion. Culinary specialities on Sýros incl. smoky San Michaeli cheese, *loúza*, salt pork, various sausages and the excellent Vátis wines – and there is no shortage of restaurants in which to find them.

**Archotariki**, just east of the main square. One of many small tavernas lurking in the maze of small alleys here.

**Bouba's**, opposite the ferry port. A fine old island *ouzerie*, serving exquisite barbecued octopus, local sharp *kopanistí* cheese on *paximádia* bread rusks, and the biggest slabs of feta you're likely to find on a Greek salad.

**Haravgi**, by the sea north of town, towards Ag. Dimítrios. Excellent fare.

**Lilli's**, in Áno Sýro. Famous for its wonderful views, excellent food (try the *louza*) and *rembétika* music at weekends.

**Mavros**, Plateía Miaoulis, **t** 028 108 2244. Comfortable place serving pizza, omelettes and *loukoumádes*, and a good place to take in the scene.

**Muses**, in the casino. Good food, although tables by the water can get a bit whiffy.

**Ta Yiannena Psistaria**, along the quay, **t** 028 108 2994. For the best roasts and barbecues as well as take-aways, with *kokorétsi*, chicken and some imaginative vegetable dishes too.

**Thea**, near Plateía Miaoulis. For good food with a view, as the name suggests.

**To Pétrino**, just east of the main square. Another good choice.

# Ermoúpolis

*Greece was reborn in Ermoúpolis.*

Elefthérios Venizélos

As you sail into the **commercial port**, Ermoúpolis (ΕΡΜΟΥΠΟΛΗ), pop. 12,000, presents an imposing, unexpected sight much commented on by early travellers: a sweeping crescent meringue rising in twin peaks, one for each religion; older Catholic **Áno Sýros** to your left (or north), and **Vrondádo**, on the right, the Orthodox quarter. Stately elegant buildings have been re-painted their original colours and, softly

## Kíni

**Sunset**, right on the sea, t 028 107 1211 (*C; mod*). With fine views of you know what.

**Harbour Inn**, t 028 107 1377, *tboukas@otenet.gr* (*mod-inexp*). 6 rooms close to the water.

**Delfini's**. Good place to enjoy delicious stuffed aubergines at the twilight hour.

**Zalonis** and **Alfonsos**. Two tavernas popular with locals, both with sea-views.

## Galissás

**Akti Delfiniou**, t 028 104 2924, f 028 104 2843 (*A; lux–exp*). Complex of apartments with everything from volleyball to a disco.

**Benois**, t 028 104 2833, f 028 104 2944 (*C; mod*). Newish; *open all year*.

**Semiramis**, near the beach, t 028 104 2067, f 028 104 3000 (*C; mod*). Family-run.

**Dendrinos**, near Akti Delfiniou, t/f 028 104 2469 (*mod–inexp*). Friendly, family-run place; rooms have fridges and a *máti* (electric ring for making coffee).

**Petros**, also near the beach, t 028 104 2067, f 028 104 3000 (*E; mod–inexp*).

**Two Hearts Camping**, t 028 104 2052/2321. With bungalows, mini-golf, motorbike hire and a minibus to meet ferries.

## Posidonía and Around

**Eleana**, on the beach, t 028 104 2601, f 028 104 2644, (*C; mod*). Very pleasant with lovely grounds.

**Willy**, t/f 028 104 2426 (*mod*). 8 rooms.

**Acapulco**, on Fínikas Marina, a 10min drive away, t 028 104 3008. A wonderful array of fish dishes on offer.

**Barbalias**, Fínikas, on the water, t 028 104 2004. Serving excellent fish and meat dishes.

**Chroussa**, up in the little village of the same name. The best food on Sýros; the menu changes weekly.

# Entertainment and Nightlife

There's no shortage of either on Sýros. The waterfront buzzes with a huge range of bars, from sophisticated to rowdy.

**Apóllon Theatre**. For a cultural night out.

**Pallas Outdoor Cinema**, near the market. There's also a winter indoor cinema.

**Aegean Casino**, by the ferry port. Occupies 2 buildings, the old Europa Hotel and a portside warehouse; both the games tables and restaurant are the rage.

**Miaoúlis Square**. The evening *vólta* up and down is still important; at one time the square was even specially paved so that the unmarried knew on which side to stroll to show they were available!

**Traffic**. A bar for ex-pats.

**Highway**. For loud music.

**Cotton Club** and next-door **Cocoon**. Both good for laid-back drinks.

**Kimbara** and **Archaeo**, at the port. Popular.

**Enigma** on Androu, just back from the waterfront. A metal hang-out.

**Rodo Club**, 3 Arcimidous, 2 km out of town, behind the Neorion shipyards. Trendy Ermoúpolis flocks to this half-ruined, half-beautifully restored building.

**Neos Oikos**, nr Iroon Square. The biggest club.

**Lilli's** and **Xanthomalis** in Áno Sýros. For *rembétika* music.

**Argo Café**, next to the beach in Galissás. Has live Greek music.

illuminated by old street lamps, with the silhouettes of palms outlined against the moon, form a rare urban idyll – 'Who could ever imagine finding such a city on a rocky island of the Aegean sea!' Gautier marvelled, when he visited it back when it was new. Yet at the same time there's no doubt that the city works for a living; prominent on the harbour are the Neórion shipyards.

Ermoúpolis' central square, **Plateía Miaoúlis**, is the most elegant in Greece, with its marble band stand and palms, its worn, lustrous marble pavement, and its cafés and statue of Admiral Miaoúlis, revolutionary hero and old sea-dog, looking down to the port, the whole embraced by fine Neoclassical buildings and wrought-iron balconies. In *Aegean Greece*, Robert Liddell wrote that he could think of no square 'except St Mark's that more gives the effect of a huge ballroom, open by accident to the sky.' Grandest of all is the Neoclassical **town hall**, designed in 1876 by the German architect Ziller; you can pop inside for a coffee and have a look at the old fire engine in the courtyard. The **Archaeology Museum** (*t 028 108 8487; open Tues–Sun 8.30–3*) up the steps to the left, contains Proto-Cycladic to Roman era finds from Sýros and other islands: note the Hellenistic era 'Votive relief to a hero rider from Amorgos' with a snake crawling on the altar as a sheep is led to sacrifice, and more snakes on a marble plaque referring to Homer, from Íos. The **Historical Archives**, by the town hall, host the Ermoúpolis Seminars in summer, when the archives are on show (*same hours*). To the right, behind the square, the **Apóllon Theatre**, a copy of La Scala, Milan, was the first ever opera house in Greece; until 1914 it supported a regular Italian opera season, and has now been restored after a botched repair that wrecked more than it fixed in 1970. Up the street a little way from here, the **Velissarópoulos Mansion**, now housing the **Labour Union**, is one of the few places you can get in to see the elaborate ceiling and wall murals characteristic of old Ermoúpolis. In the lanes above the square, the **Metamórphosis** is the Orthodox Cathedral, with a pretty *choklakía* courtyard and surprising, ornate Baroque interior. Chíos Street, descending towards the port, has the town's bustling **market**. Down towards the port, just up from the bus terminal, the church of the Annunciation, built by refugees from Psára, contains the rare icon of the *Assumption* painted and signed by Doménicos Theotokópoulos (aka El Greco) after he left for Venice. Nearby the old Europa Hotel on the waterfront with another lovely *choklakía* courtyard is now part of Sýros' new **Casino**.

Stretching off to the northeast, the elegant **Vapória** quarter is chockablock with old shipowners' mansions with marble façades, lavishly decorated inside with frescoes and painted ceilings. The main square here has one of Ermoúpoli's best churches, blue and golden-domed **Ag. Nikólaos**, dedicated to the patron saint of the city and boasting a carved marble iconostasis by the 19th-century sculptor Vitális of Tínos. In front of the church, a memorial topped by a stone lion, also by Vitális, is the world's first **Monument to the Unknown Soldier**. Vapória's grand houses hug the coastline above the town beaches of **Ag Nikólaos**, **Tálliro** and **Evangelídis** which have marble steps down from the street.

Crowning **Vrondádo Hill** (take the main street up from behind Plateía Miaoúlis), the Byzantine church **Anástasis** has a few old icons and superb views stretching to Tínos and Mýkonos. Come at night, when Vrondádo's excellent tavernas spread over its steps. More remote – 870 cobbled steps, or a hop on the bus or taxi and then walk back down – is its older twin, **Áno Sýros** (Apáno Chóra), where 'the houses seemed clinging around its top as if desperate for security, like shipwrecked men about a rock beaten by billows,' as Melville wrote after a visit in 1856. A whitewashed, Cycladic pedestrian-only enclave, this close-knit community has been mostly Catholic since the Crusades; the same families have lived in the same mansions for generations and worshipped at the **Catholic Cathedral of St George**, or **Ai-Giórgi**, on top of the rock. The main entrance to Áno Sýros, the **Kámara**, is an ancient vaulted passageway which leads past tavernas and little shops to the main street or **Piátsa**. There's a town hall, the **Women's Association of Handicraft Workers** with a folklore collection and work-shop, the **Cultural Centre** and **local radio station**. The large, handsome **Capuchin Convent of St Jean** was founded there in 1635 by France's Louis XIII as a poorhouse and contains archives dating from the 1400s; the Jesuits, just above at 16th-century **Panagía Karmilou**, have a cloister from 1744 with an important library. The famous *rembétiko* composer Márkos Vamvakáris was born in Áno Sýros; his bust graces his square. On your way down the hill, don't miss the **Orthodox cemetery of Ag. Geórgios**, with its elaborate marble mausoleums and dolorous damsels pining over wealthy shipowners.

A 45-minute walk from Ermoúpolis leads to the pretty seaside church of **Ag. Dimítrios**, which was founded after the discovery of an icon there in 1936. All ships coming into port hoot as they pass and a bell is rung in reply – cup your hand and you'll hear it. In **Díli**, just above, are the remains of a **Temple of Isis** built in 200 BC. Across the harbour at **Lazarétta** stood a 5th-century BC Temple of Poseidon, although the only traces of it are a few artefacts in the museum; it may have been the Poseidonia mentioned in the *Odyssey*.

# Around the Island

'Our Rock' is a wild place on the whole but it isn't quite as barren as it sounds; olives, pistachios and citrus fruit grow here, and the bees make an excellent thyme honey. Other ancient sites are in the quiet, seldom visited north side of the island. At lagoon-like **Grámmata Bay** (reached only by boat), sailors from Classical to Byzantine times who found shelter from storms engraved epigrams of gratitude, still legible on the rocks. If you want a beach away from it all this is the place; sea-lilies grow here and on the beaches of **Lía** and **Mégas Lakkos**. Towards the east coast, the wealth of grave-goods discovered in 1898, at the Bronze Age necropolis of **Chalandrianí** (2600–2300 BC) contributed much to the understanding of Early Cycladic civilization. **Kástri**, an hour's walk north, was the Bronze Age citadel: its walls, six towers, and foundations of houses remain in the undergrowth. The **cave** where philosopher Ferekides whiled away the summer may be seen just south of Chalandrianí.

Buses from Ermoúpolis travel to the main seaside resorts: **Kíni** (KINI), a small west coast fishing village with two sandy beaches, is a popular rendezvous for sunset-watching, and home to a famous singing family who play authentic *bouzouki* music at their beachside taverna. North over the headland is **Delfíni Beach** for that all-over tan. In the middle of the island, **Episkópio** boasts the oldest Byzantine church on Sýros, **Profítis Ilías**, prettily set in the pine-covered hills. The Orthodox Convent **Ag. Barbára**, inland from Kíni, has a school of arts and crafts with needlework on sale. The walls of the church are decorated with frescoes depicting Barbára's martyrdom – her father locked her in a tower and put her to death, but immediately afterwards was struck down by a thunderbolt, making her the patron saint of bombardiers.

The foreign tourists who come concentrate in **Galissás** (ΓΑΛΗΣΣΑΣ), which has the best sheltered beach on the island, a sweeping crescent of sand fringed by tamarisks, with the island's two campsites. You can hire sail boats; on shore, however, it's all mini-markets and heavy metal, backpackers and bikers. Nearby **Arméos** is for nudists. Further south, **Fínikas** (ΦΟΙΝΙΚΑΣ), 'Phoenix', originally settled by the Phoenicians and mentioned in Homer, is another popular resort with a gritty roadside beach.

The grandees of Ermoúpolis built their ornate summer houses at **Dellagrácia** or **Posidonía** (ΠΟΣΕΙΔΩΝΙΑ), a genteel resort with a serene film-set atmosphere of ornate Italianate mansions and pseudo castles, and a blue church. Further south, quieter **Agathopés** has a sandy beach and islet opposite and you can take the track from here to **Kómito**, a stony stretch in front of an olive grove. **Mégas Gialós** (ΜΕΓΑΣ ΓΙΑΛΟΣ) is a pretty family resort, with shaded sands. **Vári** (ΒΑΡΗ) to the east, first settled in the Neolithic era, is now a major resort, but still has its fishing fleet. **Azólimnos** is particularly popular with the Syriani for its *ouzeries* and cafés, and has three hotels and some rooms. Inland, **Chroússa** is a pleasant, pine-shaded village, home to more shipowners' villas, while nearby **Faneroméni** ('can be seen from everywhere') itself has panoramic views of the island.

# Tínos (ΤΗΝΟΣ)

If Délos was the sacred island of the ancient Greeks, Tínos, the Lourdes of Greece, occupies the same place in the hearts of their descendants. Ancient Délos probably had much the same atmosphere as Tínos – a harbour with a permanent carnival atmosphere, inns and mediocre restaurants, shaded *stoas* (here awnings over the street) merchants selling holy pictures, *támata* (votives) and backscratchers to throngs of pilgrims. The terraces of Tínos are dotted with 1,007 Venetian dovecotes, little white embroidered towers inhabited by clouds of white doves. You almost believe the locals when they say there's a hole in the ozone layer giving them a direct line to the Almighty – if chapels are God's phone booths, Tínos has one for every ten inhabitants. Sinners disturbing the peace will be politely but firmly placed on the first ferry – to Tínos' glitzy neighbour, Sodom and Gomorrah.

## History

Originally infested with vipers (its name comes from the Phoenician *Tunnoth* 'snake') Tínos was settled by the Ionians in Archaic times. A sanctuary of the sea god Poseidon was founded here in the 4th century, after he sent a flock of storks over to

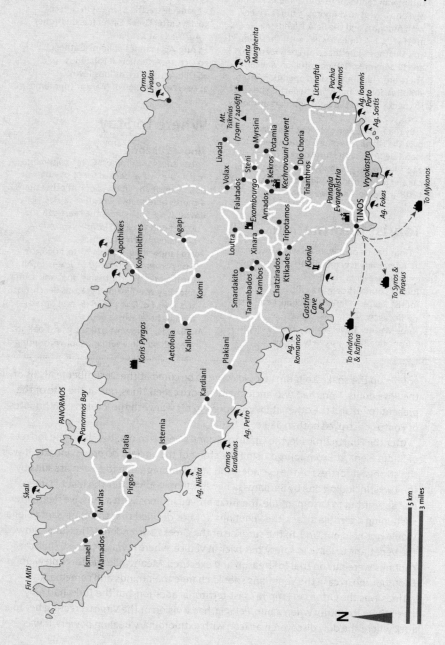

Tínos

## Getting There and Around

**By sea**: several daily **ferry**, **hydrofoil** and/or **catamaran** connections with Piraeus, Rafína, Mýkonos, Sýros, and Ándros; 5 times a week with Amorgós and the Back Islands via Náxos and Páros, 2–3 times a week with Thessaloníki and Skiáthos. Note that ships between Tínos and Piraeus are often brim-full on weekends. There are 2 landing areas in operation, often simultaneously, and when departing be sure to check you find the right one. **Port authority**: t 028 302 2220.

**By road**: there's an excellent **bus** service all over the island from the big square near the Hotel Delfinia by the ferry dock, t 028 302 2440, and plenty of **taxis**: t 028 302 2470. For **car** and **bike** rental, try **Vidalis**, 16 Aiavanou St, t 028 302 3400, f 028 302 5995.

## Tourist Information

Tínos has its own website, *www.pigeon.gr*, updated every few mths with information on museums, events and hotels.

**Tourist Council**: t 028 302 3780.
**Tourist Police**: 5 Plateía L. Sóchou, t 028 302 2180/2255.
**Tínos Mariner Travel Agency**, on the waterfront, t 028 302 3193. Very helpful.

## Festivals

**19 Jan**: Megalómatas at Ktikádes.
**25 March** and **15 Aug**: at the Panagía Evangelístra, the 2 largest in Greece.
**50 days after Greek Easter (i.e. mid-June)**: Ag. Triáda at Kardianí.
**29 Aug**: Ag. Ioánnes at Kómi (Catholic).
**20 Oct**: Ag. Artemíou at Falatádos.
**26 Oct**: Ag. Dimítri in Tínos Town.
**21 Dec**: Presentation of Mary at Tripotámos.

## Where to Stay

**Tínos** ✉ 84200
To witness the greatest Greek pilgrimage, make sure you've booked for 14–15 Aug, but don't expect any elbow room. At other times, a chorus of room owners greet ferries.
**Cavos**, at Ag. Sóstis, near the sea, t 028 302 4224, f 028 302 2580 (*B; lux–exp*). Airy bungalows with kitchens.
**Porto Tango** at Ag. Ioánnis Pórto, t 028 302 4411, *portango@otenet.gr* (*A; lux–exp*). All the major comforts; tennis, pool, and sauna.
**Aeolos Bay**, overlooking Ag. Fokás Beach, t 028 302 3339, f 028 302 3086 (*B; exp*). Smart, friendly hotel with a pool.
**Alonia**, east of town, t 028 302 3541, f 028 302 3544 (*B; exp*). In a verdant spot with springs.

gobble up the snakes; pilgrims would come to be cured at the December festivals of the Poseidonia. Tínos had two ancient cities, both called Tínos, one at the site of the present town and the other at Exómbourgo. In his war with the Romans, Mithridates of Pontus destroyed both in 88 BC.

After the Fourth Crusade, the Gizzi, the island's Venetian masters, built the fortress of Santa Elena at Exómbourgo, using the stone of the ancient *acropolis* and city. It was the strongest fortress of the Cyclades, and stood impregnable to eleven assaults by the Turks, including one by Barbarossa himself. In 1715, long after the rest of Greece had submitted to Ottoman rule, the Turks arrived in Tínos with a massive fleet. After sustaining a terrible attack, the Venetian captains decided that this time Santa Elena would not hold out, and, to the surprise of the Greeks, surrendered. The Turks allowed the Venetians to leave in safety, but back in Venice, where it was a crime to fail, the captains were put on trial for treason and executed. Meanwhile the Turks blew up Exómbourgo in case the Venetians should change their minds and come back.

Tínos was the Ottoman Empire's last territorial addition, but the Turks had only been there a century when a nun, Pelagía, had a vision of the Virgin directing her to a rock where she duly discovered an icon with extraordinary healing powers. It was

**Golden Beach**, at Ag. Fókas, t 028 302 2579, f 028 302 3385 (*C; exp*). Offers well-furnished studios and a shuttle bus into town.

**Tinion**, on the left of the harbour as you sail in, t 028 302 2261, *kohatzi@ath.forthnet.gr* (*B; exp–mod*). The Grande Dame of Tínos' hotels, with brass beds in hospital-like rooms.

**Vincenzo Rooms**, t 028 302 2612, *vincenzo@pigeon.gr* (*exp studios, mod rooms*). Friendly owners, who know everything about Tínos, will give you a warm welcome and, if they like your kids, they'll even babysit.

**Aphrodite**, t 028 302 2456 (*C; mod*). Handy for ferries.

**Argo**, a little out of town, by the sea at Agiali, t 028 302 2588, f 028 302 3188 (*C; mod*). Another good bet.

**Delfinia**, on the waterfront, near the port, t 028 302 2288, *dolfins@ath.forthnet.gr* (*C; mod*). Decent place.

**Favie-Souzane**, inland, t 028 302 2693, f 028 302 5993 (*C; mod*). Pleasant owners and rooms.

**Leandros**, 4 L. Lamera, t 028 302 3545, f 028 302 4390 (*C; mod*). A favourite, with friendly owners.

**Andriotis**, t 028 302 4719 (*D; inexp*). Rooms surrounding a charming courtyard with common kitchen and friendly owner.

**Camping Tínos**, south of town, t 028 302 2344 or t 028 302 3548. A good site.

## Eating Out

Restaurants are better than the mediocre waterfront efforts might suggest and prices are reasonable, if you're not going all out for fish. Try something cooked with the island's famous stinky garlic, which Aristophanes recommended for improving eyesight.

**Michaelis**, back from the harbour. Great for rabbit *stifádo*.

**Oi Pelekanoi**, in a side street. Offers all kinds of local goodies in a cosy atmosphere

**Palea Palada** near the fish market. With guess what on the menu.

**Pantelis**. Another authentic taverna.

**Platanos**, in Stení. Gastronomic gem, whose farmer/owner serves his own meat, veg and cheese, just the way the locals like it.

**To Koutouki tis Elenis**, nearby. Tiniot specialities, incl. tomatoes fried in batter.

**To Perivoli**, in beautiful Kardianí. Exotic and a popular haunt with Athenians.

## Entertainment and Nightlife

Although no one comes to Tínos for a wild time, there are some music bars; the best is **Kaktos**, 500m outside town, with a great view and mellow sounds.

1822, the second year of the Greek War of Independence, and to Greek minds the icon was evidence of divine favour for their cause. A church, Panagía Evangelístra, was built over the spot where it was found and it quickly became the most important pilgrimage site in Greece, and a national shrine. On 15 August 1940, during the huge annual pilgrimage, an Italian submarine sneaked into the harbour and sank the Greek cruise boat *Elli* – a prelude to Mussolini's invasion of Greece. Under the Colonels' regime the entire island was declared holy and women of Tínos had to wear skirts and behave at all times as if they were in church. No more.

# Tínos Town: Panagía Evangelístra

As your ship pulls into Tínos, the outline of the yellow church Panagía Evangelístra and its neon-lit cross floats above the town. The modern Sacred Way, Evangelístra Street, becomes a solid mass of pilgrims on the two principal feast days of the Virgin, 25 March and especially 15 August, when, on average, 17,000 descend on Tinos and the ceremonies are broadcast on national television. The icon itself goes out for an airing in a jewelled pavilion, carried by Greek sailors and accompanied by a military band and national dignitaries. Pilgrims stroke the passing pavilion. Many of the devout, elderly women in particular, cover the entire distance from the ferry to the church on all fours, with padded knees and arms, crawling in penance for the health of a loved one – a raw, moving and often disturbing sight.

At other times, do as the Greeks do: buy an ice cream and wander up Evangelístra, perusing the stalls full of candles, tin *támata*, holy water bottles and one of the finest displays of kitsch this side of Italy; sprawling ceramic nymphs with huge salt and pepper breasts and seashell frogs shooting pool mingle merrily among the icons and Panagía thermometers. When you reach the church, a red carpet covers the grand marble stair, where the only thing to do is join the queue to light a candle, kiss the icon and pray; the church employs men who do nothing all day but remove candles from the stands – the largest are the size of elephants' tusks. Through the smoke and incense, the church glimmers like Aladdin's cave with hundreds of precious offerings: an orange tree made of silver and gold, and lamps dangling ships (including one with a giant fish stuck in its side), heads, a foot, a truck and a bucket (blind pilgrims pledge to give the icon an effigy of whatever they first see if their sight is restored). The icon itself, the *Megalóchari*, or Great Grace, is so smothered in gold, diamonds and pearls that you can barely see the dark slip of the Virgin's face.

Around the courtyards, hostels have been built for pilgrims waiting for dreams of the Virgin or to be healed by the icon, but there is still not enough room to house them, and the overflow camp out patiently. The crypt, where Ag. Pelagía discovered the icon, is now the **Chapel of Evróseos** ('discovery'). Silver lines the spot in the rocks where the icon lay; the spring here is said to have curative properties. Parents from all over Greece bring their children here in August to be baptized in the font. Next to the chapel the victims of the *Elli* are interred in a mausoleum, next to a fragment of the fatal Fascist torpedo.

Enough art has been donated for the Panagía to fill several **museums** (*t 028 302 2256; all open 8–3.30*): an **art gallery**, with works from the Ionian school, a reputed Rubens, a dubious Rembrandt partially hidden by the radiator, and many 19th-century works; a museum devoted to the works of the Tiniot sculptor **Lázarou Sóchou**, and above it the **Sculpture Museum** housing pieces by Greek sculptors such as Ioánnis Boúlgaros and Vitális; old icons in the **Byzantine Museum**; and another museum containing items used in the church service.

## Around Tínos Town

There are more museums in town: parallel with Evangelístra Street, opposite a pine grove, the **Archaeology Museum** (*t 028 302 2670; open Tues–Sun 8–3*) contains artefacts from the Sanctuary of Poseidon and Amphitrite, including a sundial (a copy of Ferekides' Heliotrope on Sýros?), a broken sea monster and Archaic storage vessels. There's also a **Folklore Museum** on Loutrá Street (*open 9–12 and 4–7*).

The rest of the town is pretty much single-mindedly devoted to feeding and lodging pilgrims. From the port, buses go 4km west to **Kiónia** ('the columns'), with beaches and the **Sanctuary of Poseidon and Amphitrite** (*t 028 302 2670; open Tues–Sun 8–2*):

bits remain of two temples, treasuries, baths, fountains and inns for pilgrims; votive offerings in the museum show that like Panagía Evangelístra, Poseidon also was a great one for rescuing sailors, and his wife Amphitrite was known for granting fertility. Pilgrims to Délos often stopped here first to take a purifying bath. Further west, there's a little beach under **Gastriá Cave** with its stalactites. East of town, the closest and busiest beach is shingly nondescript **Ag. Fokás**; a few minutes further east, at **Vryókastro**, are the walls of an ancient settlement, and a Hellenistic tower. Further east at **Ag. Sostis** the beach tends to be less crowded, but sandy **Ag. Ioánnis Pórto** is now a busy resort.

## Around the Island

Buses wend their way north to the 12th-century **Kechrovoúni Convent**, one of the largest in Greece, with five churches and lanes lined with cells – it looks more like a village. It is here that Sister Pelagía, canonized in 1971, had her two visions, in which the Virgin told her where to find the icon. You can visit her old cell, with her little bed and box containing her embalmed head. The nearby villages **Arnados** and **Dío Choriá** are real charmers.

Tínos may be the centre of Orthodox pilgrimage, but of all the Cyclades it has the highest percentage of Catholics. Between the mountains and ravines, Tínos is all sloping terraces, lush and green until May (it is one of the few Cyclades naturally self-sufficient in water) and golden brown in the summer, brightened by the dovecotes and their white residents. Having a dovecote, once a privilege of the nobility (the doves gobbled the peasants' grain for free, and the master got nice plump birds for dinner and fertile guano to sell back to the peasants) was granted to all the islanders by the Venetians during their last decades on the island, and everyone wanted one. Nests filled each nook and cranny created by the intricate weave of stone slabs into geometrical patterns, stars, and suns; these days the doves, still prized for their fertilizer, are usually pets instead of lunch.

Dovecotes decorate all the villages encircling **Exómbourgo** (2,100ft), the great rocky throne of the Venetian fortress of Santa Elena; only ruined houses, a fountain and three churches remain in the walls, which afford a superb view over neighbouring islands, the Aegean, and Tínos' 50 villages. The road goes up from **Kámbos**, seat of the Catholic arch-diocese. From here, too, you can walk to the site of one of the two 8th-century BC towns called Tínos, where a large building and Geometric-era temple were discovered, and head up the valley to the charming villages of **Smardákito** and **Tarambádos**, with the island's most beautiful dovecotes. North of Exómbourgo, pretty **Loutrá** has a 17th-century Jesuit monastery where a school is run by the Ursulines; for wild scenery, continue around to little **Vólax**, where basket makers work in a landscape of granite outcrops and weird rock formations. **Mt Tskniás**, looming above, is no mere mountain, but the tomb of Calais and Zetes, the sons of Boreas the north wind, who puffed so hard that Jason and the Argonauts could not land to rescue Hercules at Mysia; the furious Hercules later killed them and buried them here, setting up the sombre crags as a marker. To this day the north wind keeps Tínos cool, even in August. From **Kómi**, another pretty village, a long valley runs down to the sea at **Kolymbíthres**, a horseshoe bay with sandy beaches.

A paved road follows the mountainous ridge overlooking the southwest coast. At **Kardianí** a driveable track winds down to a remote beach; otherwise, from **Istérnia**, a pleasant village with plane trees, you can drive down to popular **Ormós** or **Ag. Nikíta Beach**, the latter with rooms and tavernas. Often gusty, northern Tínos is famous for its green marble, and has a long tradition in working the stone, with some examples in a **sculpture museum** in Istérnia (*open Tues–Sun till 3*). Several Greek artists came from or have worked in Pírgos, a large traditional village, with a small **museum** and the **residence of sculptor Giannolís Halépas** (*open April–Oct daily 10–2 and 5–7.30; adm*). The old grammar school, built in the first flush of Greek independence, is now a School of Fine Arts. A shop near the main square exhibits and sells students' works – two-headed Byzantine eagles are popular. Below Pírgos, buses continue down to the beach at **Pánormos bay**, with a good fish taverna and rooms. **Marlás**, further north, is in the centre of the old marble quarries. From the wild, barren northwest tip of Tínos it's only one nautical mile to the island of Ándros; watch the red sunsets from here and be bowled over, by the drama – and the wind.

# The Dodecanese

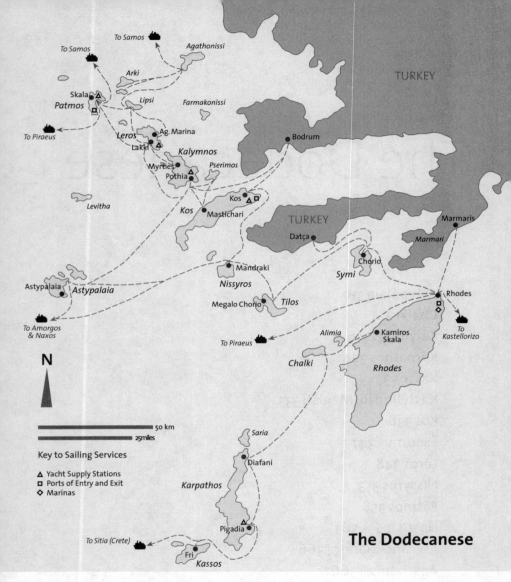

The Dodecanese

To Samos · To Samos · Agathonissi · Arki · Skala · Patmos · Lipsi · Farmakonissi · To Piraeus · Leros · Ag. Marina · Lakki · Kalymnos · Pserimos · Bodrum · Myrties · Pothia · TURKEY · Levitha · Kos · Kos · Mastichari · TURKEY · Datça · Marmaris · Marmari · Astypalaia · Astypalaia · Mandraki · Symi · Chorio · Rhodes · Nissyros · To Amorgos & Naxos · Megalo Chorio · Tilos · To Piraeus · Alimia · Kamiros Skala · To Kastellorizo · Chalki · Rhodes · N · Saria · Diafani · 50 km · 25 miles · Karpathos · Key to Sailing Services · △ Yacht Supply Stations · □ Ports of Entry and Exit · ◇ Marinas · Pigadia · To Sitia (Crete) · Fri · Kassos · **The Dodecanese**

Furthest from mainland Greece, the Dodecanese (ΔΩΔΕΚΑΝΗΣΑ), meaning 'twelve islands' (although there are actually 16 inhabited ones, and even that depends on how you count them), weren't added to Greece until 1948, although union only confirmed a sense of national identity, language, religion and traditions their inhabitants kept smouldering on the home fires for centuries. But their distance from the mainland, and long separation from the mainstream of Greek history, has dealt them a unique deck to play with – medieval knights, Ottoman Turks and 20th-century Italians, all of whom contributed to the distinct character and architecture of the Dodecanese. Add a sunny climate, long sandy beaches and the striking individualism of each island – including even one bright white Cycladic rock pile, Astypálaia – and the holiday possibilities on the Dodecanese are infinite, covering the gamut from the feverish high-calibre international resorts of Rhodes and Kos to the low-key, relaxed, very Greek pleasures of Lipsí, Chálki, Kárpathos or volcanic Níssyros. Striking Sými and Pátmos attract upmarket crowds; while Léros, Kálymnos and Tílos remain best-kept secrets of seasoned travellers. Kastellórizo has an end-of-the-world atmosphere that seems to draw more people every year; Kássos has a similar air but attracts nobody, if you're looking for a real getaway. Connections by ferry, hydrofoil and excursion boat are good between the islands, making it easy to get around and even to pop over to Turkey for a day or two (though *see* p.66).

## History

The Dodecanese flourished early in antiquity, populated by the elusive Carians (from Caria, on the nearby coast of Asia Minor). They were either subjugated by, or allies of, the seafaring Minoans, a connection reflected in the islands' myths. When Minoan Crete fell, the Mycenaeans took over and many of the Dodecanese sent ships to the Trojan War. In the various invasions that followed the fall of Troy, Aeolians, Ionians and Dorians swept through. By the Archaic period the last arrivals, the Dorians, had formed themselves into powerful city-states, particularly on Rhodes and Kos, states so prosperous that they established colonies and trading counters in Italy, France and Spain. The Persians were the next to invade, but once they were defeated at Salamis in 480 BC, the Dodecanese joined the maritime league at Délos as a hedge against further attacks. Their greater distance from Athens automatically gave them more autonomy than the other islands, and they produced a dazzling array of artists, scientists and intellectuals – including Hippocrates, the father of medicine.

After the death of Alexander the Great, his general, Ptolemy of Egypt, inherited the Dodecanese, leading to one of the greatest sieges in antiquity, when a rival general, Antigonos, sent his son Dimitrios to take Rhodes. Emboldened by its victory over Dimitrios, Rhodes erected its proud Colossus (164 BC) and made an alliance with Rome, enabling her to acquire her own little empire of Greek islands. Some two hundred years later Rome sent Jesus' disciple John into exile to another Dodecanese island, Pátmos, where he converted the inhabitants and got his own back by penning the *Book of Revelations*, where Rome comes out as no less than 'Babylon the Great, Mother of Harlots and of earth's abominations'.

In 1095, the islands had their first taste of a much more aggressive brand of Christianity, when Crusaders en route to the Holy Land made them a port of call. The Crusaders' odd bit of pillaging and piracy climaxed in the capture of Constantinople, on Venice's orders, in 1204; but in 1291 the tables turned when Jerusalem fell to the rising star of the east: the Ottomans. This disrupted, among other things, the work of the Knights of St John, or the Knights Hospitallers, an exclusive order made up of the second and third sons of Western Europe's aristocracy, who took vows of chastity, poverty and obedience, and operated a hospital in Jerusalem for pilgrims founded by Italian merchants in the 11th century. Forced to leave, the Knights, who were never as poor as their vows suggested, purchased the Dodecanese from a Genoese pirate, Admiral Vinioli. They set up headquarters on Rhodes, built a new hospital, fortified the big island and most of the smaller ones against the Turks, and communicated by means of carrier pigeons and smoke signals, while raiding the coast in swift vessels made on Sými, letting Christian pirates pass through their territory unmolested, but hijacking ships carrying Moslem pilgrims. In 1522 Sultan Suleiman the Magnificent had had enough of the pests and attacked Rhodes with an enormous army. All the men of the Dodecanese rallied to its defence, but after a bitter siege the Knights were betrayed by a disgruntled German and forced to surrender (*see* p.373).

Turkish occupation of the Dodecanese lasted until 1912, when Italy opportunistically took 'temporary possession' of the islands. This occupation was made 'permanent' after the Greek débâcle in 1923 by the second Treaty of Lausanne. Mussolini poured money into his new colonies, sponsoring massive public works (most of his public buildings are still scattered across the islands, for better or worse), reforestation, archaeological excavations and historical reconstructions. While Turkish rule had been depressing, negligent and sometimes brutal, the Fascists, in spite of their lavish expenditure, were even worse in the eyes of the islanders, outlawing their Orthodox religion and Greek language, to the extent that even today you can find older people on the Dodecanese who are more comfortable speaking Italian.

With Italy's surrender in 1943, Churchill sent in the British troops to withhold German occupation, but lacked sufficient numbers to do the job. In May 1945 they returned in the subsequent vacuum; many islanders claim to this day that Churchill meant the British occupation to be as 'temporary' as the Italian, but a treaty signed in March 1948 united them with Greece. The union has yet to be recognized by Turkey, which never signed the Treaty of Lausanne, and claims the Dodecanese were not Italy's to concede, creating a climate of mistrust and tense incidents such as the quarrel that almost led to war over rock piles near Kálymnos, Ímia/Kardak, in 1996.

# Astypálaia (ΑΣΤΥΠΑΛΑΙΑ)

Butterfly-shaped Astypálaia, the most westerly of the Dodecanese, halfway between Amorgós and Kos, offers the perfect transition from the Cyclades – in fact, it would be perfectly at home in the latter, with its austere rocky geography and dazzling sugar-cube houses spilling down from the citadel on the hill. Yet there's more here than meets the eye: the island nurtures a rich, fertile, very Dodecanesian valley called Livádia in its bosom, which led Homer to call it 'the Table of the Gods', and equally fertile fishing in the sheltered nooks and crannies of its wildly indented coastline – in antiquity Astypálaia was called Ichthyoessa, 'fishy island'. Besides the lure of seafood, Astypálaia's relative inaccessibility makes it a good place to escape the worst of the summer crowds. It now has a tiny airport, offering the chance to skip the long ferry slog from Piraeus or hops over from Kos. Most of all, although it gets busy in August, it remains a jovial, relaxed island that moseys along at its own pace.

## History

Astypálaia means 'old city', but mythology claims that the name is derived from a sister of Europa, the mother of King Minos. In classical times the island was most famous for its lack of snakes and a tragically short-tempered boxer named Kleomedes, who, when competing in the Olympics, killed his opponent, which even then was enough to merit instant disqualification. Kleomedes returned to Astypálaia seething with rage and took his disappointment out on the local school, knocking it down and killing all the pupils.

## Skála and Chóra

The capital of the island consists of two parts: **Skála** (or **Pera Gialós**), the port, and **Chóra**, the old town, which curls gracefully down from the Venetian castle to a sandy beach. In the morning or evening in Skála you'll see the fishermen's mascots, a pair of pelicans, currently named Iannis and Carlos, although those hoping for romance think Carlos is really a Jenny. Skála has everything you need if you don't want to go any further, including an antique shop selling foreign papers and an ATM machine. Just above the bus stop, the **Archaeology Museum** (*open in season Tues–Sun 10–2 and 6–10; adm*) contains finds from Kástro as well as four Mycenaean chamber tombs discovered in the 1970s by shepherds, classical *steles*, a 6th-century Byzantine chancel screen and the Quirini coat of arms. The best architecture, however, is up the character- and thigh-building flights of steps (or more circular road) in the upper town of **Chóra**, marked by a file of eight restored windmills standing sentinel along the ridge

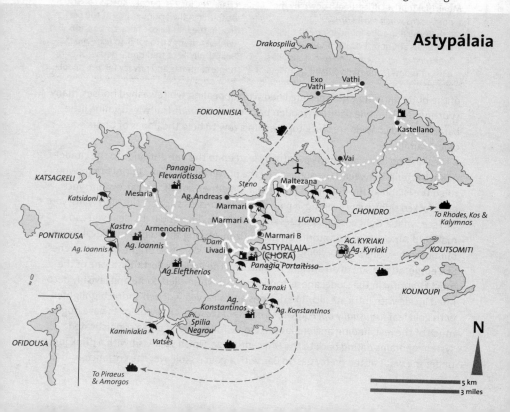

## Getting There and Around

**By air**: 4 **flights** a week from Athens: book early in season. **Olympic Airways**: **t** 024 306 1328/1588; **airport**: **t** 024 306 1665. Buses run between Skála, Chóra and the airport; a **taxi** costs around €10.

**By sea**: **ferry** connections 4 times a week with Piraeus, 3 times a week with Kos, twice a week with Rhodes, Kálymnos, Náxos, Páros and Amorgós, once a week with Níssyros and Donoússa; **hydrofoil** once a week from Rhodes; **excursion boats**: from Skála to south coast beaches of Ag. Konstantínos, Vatsés, and Kaminiakia, and to the islets of Ag. Kyriáki and Koutsomíti. **Port authority**: **t** 024 306 1208.

**By road**: there are 2 **buses** a day between Skála, Chóra, Livádia and Maltezána. **Taxis** are also available at reasonable rates; fares are posted. Skála has 3 **car** rental agencies, as well as **bikes** of varying description.

## Tourist Information

**Municipal Tourist Office**: booth down by the port; *opens when ferries arrive.* Otherwise it may be found in one of the windmills at Chóra, **t** 024 306 1412; *open June–end of Sept 9.30–1 and 6–9.* It also has a list of rooms if you find yourself homeless.

**Police**: **t** 024 306 1207.
**Astypalea Tours**, **t** 024 306 1571, under Vivamare Hotel. Very helpful.

## Festivals

**15 Aug**: Panagía Portaïtíssa in Chóra.

## Where to Stay and Eat

### Astypálaia ✉ 85900

In past years there was a building spree around Skála, but the pace has eased and bargains are relatively easy to find, especially outside of July and Aug, when the going rate for accommodation can drop by up to half. If you're feeling ill, eat the local snails; in ancient times they were said to have curative powers.

### Skála/Chóra

**Kostas Vaikousis**, just under the Kástro up in Chóra, **t/f** 024 306 1430 (*exp–mod*). Two charming traditional houses, with lots of character, for 2–6 people. Kostas can usually be found in the antique shop at the port.
**Titika**, in the middle of Chóra, **t/f** 024 306 1677, winter: Athens **t** 010 771 1540 (*exp–mod*). Beautifully-kept traditional house, offering home comforts and privacy for 2–6 people.

of the butterfly wing. The lanes are lined with appealing whitewashed houses, many sporting Turkish-style painted wooden balconies (*poúndia*). Halfway up, nine little barrel-vaulted chapels are stuck together in a row to hold the bones of Chóra's oldest families.

The winding lanes and steps eventually lead up to the one entrance to the citadel, or **Kástro**, built between 1207 and 1522 by the powerful Venetian Quirini family who ruled the island as the Counts of Stampalia. On either side of the narrow entrance, once locked tight every evening, a pair of new buttresses support the high walls; you can see what a tight corset squeezes Astypálaia's middle, and if it's clear you can make out Amorgós and Santoríni on the horizon. Among the ruined medieval houses built into the walls and surviving Quirini coat-of-arms are two bright white churches: **St George**, on the site of an ancient temple, and the **Panagía Portaïtíssa**, one of the most beautiful in the Dodecanese, topped with a white-tiled dome and lavishly decorated inside with intricate lace-like designs and a carved wooden shrine highlighted with gold leaf (*unusually open late afternoons in season*). Archaeologists have dug up much of the rest, finding ancient lanes, temple foundations, and a sophisticated system of drains dating back to the 6th century BC. Finish your visit with a drink just under the walls at the pretty Castro Bar, with a goat's skull over the entrance.

**Afroditi Studios**, above the harbour, t 024 306 1478 (*mod–inexp*). Good port and sea views from the verandas, incl. kitchen and phone.

**Anatoli Studios**, way up in Chóra, t 024 306 1680/1066 (*mod–inexp*). Soaring castle views from higher rooms.

**Astynea**, right on the port, t/f 024 306 1209 (*C; mod–inexp*). Fine, clean rooms with balcony.

**Maistrali**, t 024 306 1691 (*mod–inexp*). Attractive, charming hostelry in classic island style; with a restaurant.

**Vivamare Hotel**, inland from the harbour, t 024 306 1571, f 024 306 1328 (*C; mod–inexp*). Comfortable studios with a kitchen and good views thrown in.

**Karlos**, on the sea, t 024 306 1330 (*inexp*). Another rooms and restaurant combo, a decent option if all else fails.

**Camping Astypálaia**, just out of town, t 024 306 1338. A minibus usually meets ferries.

**Akroyiali**, on the beach at Pera Gialós. A tourist favourite, with fine food and lovely views up to Chóra after dark when the Kástro is bathed in golden light.

**Monaxia** (or Vicki's), in a small street back from where the ferry docks. Good simple taverna with excellent home cooking.

**Pizzeria Aeolos**, up by the windmills. All the pizza favourites, plus 'Lenten Pizza' without meat or cheese (only in Greece!).

**Meltémi** and **Eva**, on the way into Chóra. Known for their sweet things.

### Livádi

**Gerani**, t 024 306 1484, *gerani72@hotmail.com* (*inexp*). Small and attractive; studios with bath and fridge, and common living room. The restaurant has tasty homemade dishes and fish, served on its airy tamarisk terrace.

**Stefanida**, on the beach, t 024 306 1510. Fresh lobster, fish and local meat dishes.

### Maltezána

**Ovelix**, 150m from the sea, t 024 306 1260 (*inexp*). Studios and rooms. The restaurant prides itself on its fish and local recipes.

## Entertainment and Nightlife

Astypálaia is not exactly the place to rave it up, but there are some relaxed bars:

**Panorama** and **Aiyaion**, in Chóra. The latter is good for backgammon.

**Excite**, near the water.

**Magazi**, below the windmills. Wonderful views of Chóra and the sea, homemade sweets. A great place to savour your slice of island life at sunset.

## Around the Island

Set in a wide lush valley, **Livádi** (ΛIBAΔI) is downhill from the windmills to the west; its shingly, sandy beach gets busy with Greek families in high season. Little roads through farms lead back eventually to the barren mountains, where in 1994 EU funds built a dam to create a rather unexpected little **lake**, which the locals have planted trees around. Follow the coast along to the south and you can cast your clothes to the wind on the unofficial nudist beach at **Tzanáki**, or continue along the track to **Ag. Konstantínos**, one of the island's best beaches; other sandy strands, at **Vatses** (with a stalactite cave, **Negrou**, just behind) and **Kaminiakia** can only be reached by boat. An unpaved road starting at the windmills goes to **Ag. Ioánnis** on the west coast, a lush spot with orchards, a whitewashed church, ruined Byzantine castle and an excellent beach, calling in at the Monastery of **Panagía Flevariótissa** en route.

The paved road north of Skála passes a few beaches, all called Mármari. Just over on the north coast, ferries dock at **Ag. Andréas** if the wind is up. The road passes over the waist of the butterfly, or Steno (barely 50 yards wide at its narrowest point), and ends up after 9km near the airport at wannabe resort Análypsi, or more commonly, **Maltezána**. This was once a lair of Maltese pirates, where in 1927, during the War of

Independence, the French Captain Bigot died when he set fire to his corvette to avoid capture. The next cove is popular with nudists and on the fringe of the surrounding olive groves look out for the remains of the **Roman baths** with their well-preserved zodiac floor mosaics. On the far wing, the lost lagoon of **Vathí** (ΒΑΘΗΣ) is a favourite if lonely summer yachting port, a tiny fishing hamlet with an excellent fish taverna and rooms to rent, accessible only by sea or path and heading a deep, fjord-like bay. From here it's possible to visit the stalagmite caves of **Drákospilia** by boat, but take a torch; a path leads south to **Kastéllano**, built by the Italians between the wars.

# Chálki (ΧΑΛΚΗ)

With its Neoclassical pastel houses overlooking a horseshoe harbour, Chálki is a miniature version of nearby Sými, topped by a fairytale Crusader castle on a pointed peak like something out of Walt Disney. It is arid and rocky, and water may run short in summer. But traditional island life ambles on, fishing and goat-herding providing most of the income, as well as small-scale tourism. Chálki is famous for keeping its old music traditions alive, and on occasion you'll hear singers improvise *matinádes*, impromptu songs with 15-syllable verses. Pronounce their island 'Chalky' at your own risk. The name actually comes from *chalkí*, 'copper', which used to be mined here.

Chálki was designated the 'Island of Peace and Friendship of Young People of All Nations' in 1983 under a joint UNESCO and Greek Government scheme. The idea was to launch an international youth centre with annual conferences, and there was an allied municipal project, ADEK, to renovate the local houses that had been left to crumble after the mass exodus earlier this century, when the local sponge beds fell prey to rot. A Xenía hotel was built to serve the visiting groups and bureaucrats, but in the end the scheme went sour as youths and bureaucrats alike abused the little island's hospitality. Peace and friendship between Chálki and UNESCO at a definite end, in 1987 a British package holiday company was invited to set up a programme using the restored houses. Since then tourism has slowly grown and other owners have returned to convert their ruined family homes into studios and apartments. Although there is the odd hydrofoil excursion from Rhodes, Chálki doesn't suffer from surfeits of day-trippers like Sými. There are no newspapers, 300 inhabitants and a few pick-up trucks and bikes which head up the grandly named Boulevard Tarpon Springs.

## Emborió and Around

The main claim to fame of **Emborió** is that its church of Ag. Nikólaos has the tallest campanile in the Dodecanese, and it also has a magnificent pebble mosaic (*choklákia*) courtyard. There's the usual Italianate customs house and police station, a row of ruined windmills and a small army barracks. Sleepy by day, with fishermen mending their nets, the harbour buzzes with the traditional stroll or *vólta* in the evening.

From Emborió a 15-minute walk along Boulevard Tarpon Springs, just wide enough for a donkey train and single delivery van, takes you to sandy **Póndamos Beach**, a strand constantly being enlarged by the locals. The rocky coves a bit further on make

## Getting There

By sea: 3–4 times a week with Rhodes; twice a week with Piraeus (30hrs!), Kárpathos and Kássos, once a week with Kos, Kálymnos, Mílos, Sitía (Crete), and Ag. Nikólaos (Crete). Daily **boat** to and from Kámiros Skála, Rhodes, connecting with the **bus** to Rhodes Town. In summer once a week **hydrofoil** connection with Rhodes and Tílos (*July–Aug only*). You can also hire a caique: t 024 604 5309/5266. **Port authority**: t 024 604 5220.

## Tourist Information

Regular police: t 024 604 5213.
Halki Tours: t 024 604 5281.

## Festivals

**5 Aug**: Ag. Sotíris.
**15 Aug**: Panagía.
**29 Aug**: Ag. Ioánnis Pródromos, John the Baptist.
**14 Sept**: Ag. Stávros.

## Where to Stay

**Chálki** ✉ 85110

Most accommodation is now taken up by the holiday companies.

**Captain's House**, t 024 604 5201 (*mod*). Small but welcoming turn-of-the-century Chálki mansion; 3 lovely rooms with en suite bathrooms and fridges; run with nautical precision by Alex Sakellarídes, ex-Greek Royal Navy, and his English wife Christine – there's even a crow's nest; breakfast served on the cool terrace beneath the trees, often with classical music.

**Kleanthi**, near the school, t 024 604 5334 (*B; mod*). Rooms and studios in a traditional stone house newly restored.

**Manos** (*mod*). 6 rooms in the ex-sponge factory.

**Argyrenia**, on the way to the beach, t 024 604 5205 (*inexp*). Self-contained chalets set in shady gardens.

**Markos**, t 024 604 5347 (*inexp*). Newer furnished flats.

**Nick Pondomos**, overlooking the bay, t 024 604 5295 (*inexp*).

**Xalki**, to the left of the harbour, t 024 604 5390, f 024 604 5208 (*C; inexp*). The former scheme hotel and converted olive factory, offering a sun terrace, snack bar/restaurant, and swimming off the rocks.

## Eating Out

**Maria**. Maria and her triplet daughters serve Greek oven dishes and good *souvláki*.

**Mavri Thalassa** ('Black Sea'), in from the (Aegean) sea. An assortment of Greek and international cuisine, popular with all.

**O Houvardas**. Once arguably one of the best tavernas in the Dodecanese, it has never quite been the same under the new management. It's still a good eatery, popular with yacht people, but the standard depends on who's in the kitchen.

**Omonia**. The place for fresh fish, seafood and grills.

**Pondamos Taverna**, a step from the sands. Popular lunchtime haunt, with a tasty menu.

**Remezzo**. Some pasta dishes, but mostly pizza.

**Stanagia**, on its own beach behind the Halki Hotel. Excellent Greek dishes and grilled fish.

If you are self-catering there are three small general stores – **Petros** has everything – and a good bakery specializing in cheese and spinach pies, and honey pancakes.

## Entertainment and Nightlife

Nightlife on Chálki tends to be spontaneous, with outbreaks of traditional dancing in the bars. Some of the young people are learning the old instruments like the *lýra* and have put out a Chálki cassette. Easter and festivals are times for determined merrymaking, with live music and dancing, sometimes in costume.

**Nikola's To Steki**. Often the scene of local merriment.

**Areti's**. Enjoy a drink at this café-bar.

**Kostas**. An old favourite amongst café-bars.

**Vokolia**. Also does delicious cakes.

for rather more secluded sunbathing and snorkelling. Determined sightseers should continue walking uphill another hour for **Chorió**, the ghost-town capital of Chálki, abandoned in 1950, although a few cement mixers suggest it might not stay empty forever. Here the Knights of St John built a castle on the earlier *acropolis* and recycled most of the ancient building stone. Chorió's church of the **Panagía** has a few Byzantine frescoes and is the centre for the big festival on 15 August. On a very clear day there are stunning views down to Kárpathos and Crete from the castle.

A new road has been blasted through from Póndamos over the hill past the cemetery and barracks to the Xalki Hotel, and another now makes the once-gruelling cross-island trek to the **Monastery of Ag. Ioánnis Pródromos** less of a slog. It can still take from three to five hours by foot: it's best to go at dawn, or in the late afternoon and stay overnight in one of the cells. A track off the Póndamos road, past the water tank on the hill, descends to the pebbly cove of **Kánia** with its shady fig trees and little Garden of Eden. Unfortunately the locals have plonked a filling station at the end of the track and you can get strong whiffs of petrol at times.

Fishing is still the main way of life, and some fishermen, getting into the swing of tourism, offer trips round the island. The new high-speed launch *Yiánnis Express*, with brothers Michális and Vassílis Pátros, can whisk you to quiet swimming coves – Aréta, Kánia, Giáli and Trachiá are among the best. The most scenic excursion is to the green isle of **Alimniá**, which has another Crusader castle and a deep harbour where Italian submarines hid during the Second World War. The islanders abandoned it and moved to Chálki after British Special Boat Services commandoes sent to scupper the submarines in 1943 were captured by Nazis on the beach, then taken to Rhodes and executed. You can see the machine-gun strafing on the walls of some of the buildings as well as paintings of submarines done by troops in the ruined houses. Although it has a better water supply than Chálki, the islanders, appalled by the executions, vowed never to return, leaving Alimniá to grazing sheep and barbecuing holiday-makers; all in all a beautifully tranquil place in which to laze about, swim and picnic.

# Kálymnos (ΚΑΛΥΜΝΟΣ)

Sailing into Kálymnos from Kos just as the sun sets and the moon rises in the east is sublime. Even if you aren't lucky enough to arrive at the proper twilight hour, you may want to breathe a sigh of relief when you get to the port Pothiá – for, unlike Kos, this is the Real Greece. Although the bustling waterfront has all the usual tavernas and souvenir shops for the trippers, venture one street back and you're in the thick of a busy Greek town. Carpenters hammer, tailors stitch, and grocers have the old spicy Greek smell of coffee and herbs. Kálymnos also strikes a geographical equilibrium: emerald valleys wedged into its dry rocky face (its highest point, Mount Profítis Ilías, is the driest spot in all the Dodecanese) sweeping down to Scottish-style lochs. The inhabitants are known for being down to earth, and like to tell the story of Aristotle Onassis' visit to an island school. 'I'll give three million drachmae to any child who can tell me what I'm worth,' announced the shipping magnate. The guesses went higher

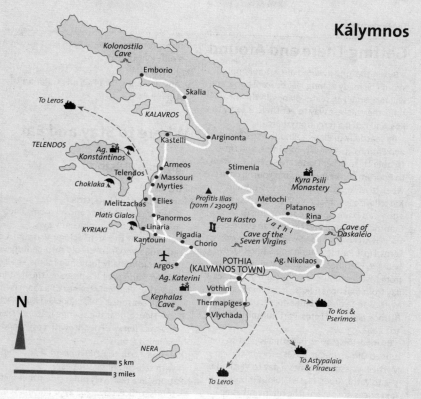

# Kálymnos

*(Map labels:)*

Kolonostilo Cave
Emborio
Skalia
To Leros
KALAVROS
Kastelli
Arginonta
TELENDOS
Ag. Konstantinos
Armeos
Stimenia
Telendos
Massouri
Myrties
Choklaka
Kyra Psili Monastery
Melitzachás
Elies
Profitis Ilias (701m / 2300ft)
Metochi
Platis Gialos
Platanos
Panormos
Pera Kastro
Vathi
Rina
KYRIAKI
Linaria
Cave of Daskaleio
Kantouni
Pigadia
Chorio
Cave of the Seven Virgins
Argos
POTHIA (KALYMNOS TOWN)
Ag. Nikolaos
Ag. Katerini
N
Vothini
Kephalas Cave
Thermapiges
Vlychada
To Kos & Pserimos
NERA
5 km
3 miles
To Astypalaia & Piraeus
To Leros

and higher until one little girl stood up and said: 'Mr Onassis, at the end of the day you're worth a six-foot hole in the ground.' Onassis could only agree and poneyed up.

Even the most fleeting visitor can't help but notice that this island is preoccupied with sponges: Kálymnos has Greece's last fleet of sponge-divers, employing 400 people. Such was its greatest claim to fame until March 2001, when word leaked out about the biggest archaeological find in years: the accidental discovery, by shepherds, of a trove of sculpture that the Christians in the 4th century had gathered from the island's pagan temples and buried in a pit under a now ruined basilica. So far the site has only been partially excavated, but has already yielded (according to a *Guardian* reporter, one of the few outsiders to be allowed a peek) a beautiful 6th-century BC *kouros*, unusually clothed, a giant head of Asklepios and a hermaphrodite. The czars of the cultural ministry in Athens demanded that Kálymnos cough them up, but so far the island's mayor, Dimítris Diakomichális, has dug his heels in and is doing all he can to keep them on the island, to put them on display in a museum here, citing the same arguments the Greek Government has been using for the return of the Elgin marbles.

## History

In mythology Ouranos (Heaven) angrily flung Kalydnos, one of his sons by Gaia (Earth), into the sea, but he landed on some bits of his mother that rose up to become the Kalydna islands, the largest of which became known as Kálymnos. Mycenaean

# Getting There and Around

**By air**: the long awaited airport at Kanoúni should be ready at long last by April 2002, and will take small 45 seater planes. In the meantime, the quickest way to get there is to fly to Kos, and catch a ferry from there.

**By sea**: daily to Piraeus, Rhodes, Kos, Léros, and Pátmos; 4–5 weekly to Sámos, and Lipsí; frequently to other Dodecanese, twice a week to Bodrum (Turkey), Ikária, and Fourní; once a week to Mýkonos, Sýros, Náxos, Páros and Kastellorízo (contact ANEM Lines, **t** 024 302 2909 and Dane Lines, **t** 024 302 3043). Summer **hydrofoil** and **catamaran** connections with Kos, Rhodes, Sými, Tílos, Níssyros, Léros, Lipsí, Pátmos, Ikaría and Sámos. Daily boats to Psérimos, Platí and Vathí, daily caique from Myrtiés to Xirókambos (Léros); 3 ferries a day from Mastichári (Kos); local caiques from Myrtiés to Télendos, Emborió; excursions to Pátmos, Lipsí, and Léros. **Port authority**: **t** 024 302 4444/9304.

**By road**: the station in Pothiá is next to the domed Dimarcheion. Buses every hr to Myrtiés, Massoúri, 5 times a day to Vlycháda, 3–4 to Vathí, Árgos, Platís Giolos Emboriós. **Taxi** prices are posted (the main rank is up Venizélou St, in Plateía Kýprou) but may make you wait until the car is full before setting off; other drivers offer guided tours of the island, **t** 024 302 9555/4222.

# Tourist Information

**Information Booth**, next to Olympic Hotel on Pothiá's waterfront **t** 024 302 9310, *www.kalymnos-isl.gr* (Note the advert for an excursion to Turkey: 'Come to the beautiful town of Bordum [sic] and view the unspoiled lovely bitches.'); *open April–Oct, Mon–Fri 7–2.30.*

**Premier Travel**, Myrtiés. Especially helpful, **t** 024 304 7830, **f** 024 304 8035.

# Festivals

**Easter**: lively Carnival celebrations, and ear-splitting in Pothiá.

**Week after Easter**: the Iprogrós (Sponge Week). Other celebrations are held when the divers return, although each boat arrives at a different time.

**27 July**: Brostá.

**15 Aug**: Télendos, Kyrá Psilí and Galatianí at Arginónta.

# Where to Stay and Eat

## Kálymnos ✉ 85200

### Pothiá

**Panorama**, in the back streets, **t** 024 302 3138 (*C; mod*). Lovely décor, and all rooms have balconies with magnificent views.

**Themelina**, by the Archaeology Museum, **t** 024 302 2682 (*mod*). Lovely old 19th-century villa with traditionally furnished rooms, shady gardens and pool. It's probably the best in town but your only chance of a room is in the off season; it's block-booked May–Oct.

**Greek House**, near the sponge factory, **t** 024 302 3752 (*inexp*). Friendly with cosy wood-panelled rooms.

**Katerina**, **t** 024 302 2186 (*inexp*). A good bet with self-catering facilities.

**Patmos**, in a relatively quiet side street by the tourist office, **t** 024 302 2750 (*inexp*). Self-catering faciliites.

**Johnny's Studios**, above the port. Commanding views over Pothiá.

In Pothiá, most of the restaurants are on 'Octopus Row' at the far end of the quay, beyond the administration buildings, and specialize in tasty octopus *keftédes*.

**Argos**, in Árgos. Authentic Kalymniot food; try the *moori*, lamb cooked overnight in a ceramic pot.

**Café Stoa**. Has internet access.

**Nauticos Omilos**, behind the port police. Tasty homemade food, but come in the evening, when all the daytrippers from Kos have left, leaving you in peace to enjoy dinner.

**O Barba-Petros**, at the end of the port. Popular dining spot with Kalymniots, who come for the fish and seasonal dishes.

*Ouzerie* **Athinas**, on the waterfront. Large portions of fresh shrimp at a kind price.

**Vouvali's**. Decorated with nautical bric-à-brac with seawater tanks from where you can choose your own lobster or fish – otherwise try their excellent fish casseroles.

**Xefteries**, in a back street near the Metropolis church. In the same family for over 85 yrs, and recommended by locals. Sit in the garden and enjoy the fresh fish and roast lamb, or try their *dolmádes* and *stifádo*; prices can be a little steep.

## Kantoúni/Pánormos/Eliés

**Elies**, near Panórmos, t 024 304 7890 (*B; mod*). With a restaurant, two bars and a pool.

**Kaldyna Island**, set back from the sea, t 024 304 7880 (*B; mod*). With pool and sea sports.

**Domus**, Kantoúni Beach, t 024 304 7959. Terrace dining with superb view, serving island specialities and international fare.

**Taverna Marinos** in Eliés. Specializes in roast stuffed lamb in the evenings.

## Myrtiés

**Delfini**, t 024 304 7514 (*C; mod*). Very central.

**Hermes**, t 024 304 7693, f 024 304 8097 (*C; mod*). Also a good bet.

**Myrties**, t 024 304 7512 (*D; inexp*).

**Drossia**. Psarotaverna renowned for swordfish.

**Babis Bar**, in the square. Good snacks and breakfast and the perfect place to wait for buses, taxis and the boat to Télendos.

**Nectar**. Restaurant with international menu.

## Massoúri

**Niki's Pension**, between the two resorts, t 024 304 7201 (*mod*). Great views but is set up steps over rough terrain.

**Plaza**, in the more peaceful Arméos area, t 024 304 7134 (*B; mod*). Perched high over the bay with a pool and fine views.

**Studios Tatsis**, t 024 304 7887 (*C; mod*). Stylish with great views over Télendos.

Massoúri has many eating places from fast-food joints to good tavernas, some of which look like tacky takeaways:

**Kokkinidis**. Looks like a pretty taverna but gets very mixed reviews.

**Mathaios**. Does all the Greek favourites well.

**Noufaro**, in the north part of town, t 024 302 7988. Worth a stroll up here for a hint of sophistication, friendly service and view; Greek and international dishes.

*Ouzerie* **Psaras** and **Sopiarkos**, on the way to Kastélli. Popular with locals.

**Punibel**, near the square, t 024 304 8150. Good Greek dishes, but the emphasis is on pizza.

**To Iliovasilema** ('The Sunset'). Owned by local butcher; dishes here used to walk, not swim.

## Télendos Islet

**Café Festaria**, further along, t 024 304 7401 (*inexp*). Decent doubles with en suites.

**Dimitrios Harinos**, t 024 304 7916 (*inexp*). Village rooms set back in a pretty garden.

**Pension Rita**, over the friendly cafeteria, t 024 304 7914 (*inexp*). Cakes baked below.

**Pension Uncle George's**, above the excellent restaurant, t 024 304 7502 (*inexp*).

**Ta Dalinas**. Good value taverna with Greek music on Weds and Sats.

## Emborió

**Harry's Pension/Taverna Paradise**, t 024 304 7483 (*C; mod*). Lovely secluded gardens.

**Xaris Apartments**, t 024 304 7434.

## Vathí

**Galini**, in Rína, t 024 303 1241 (*C; inexp*). Immaculate rooms and home-baked bread, served on a restful terrace overlooking the fjord-like harbour; good spot for lunch.

**Pension Manolis**, higher up to the right, t 024 303 1300 (*inexp*). Communal kitchen and nice garden. Manólis is an official guide and mine of information.

**Harbour Taverna**. Excellent seafood.

# Entertainment and Nightlife

**Apollo**, in Pothiá. Waterfront bars like this are popular after dark.

**Apothiki**, in Pothiá, near the cathedral. Live music venue.

**Nea Afrikaner**, in Pothiá. Traditional *bouzouki* club.

There are numerous bars in the resorts belting out music:

**Domus Bar** and **Rock and Blues Pub**, at Kantoúni.

**Babis Bar**, at Myrtiés. For a cocktail or game of backgammon.

**Smile Pub**, **NoName Pub**, **Paradise Bar**, **Ambience** (the current favourite), **Rebel Saloon**, and **Look Disco** (near Kastélli), all in Massoúri. For night owls and occasionally lager louts.

Argos sent colonists to the island, who named their capital after their mother city; the Dorians who followed had their city just northeast of Pothiá, at Dímos. An ally of Persia, the Queen of Halicarnassus, conquered the island at the beginning of the 5th century BC, but after Persia's defeat Kálymnos joined the maritime league at Delos.

Kálymnos next enters history in the 11th century, when Seljik Turks launched a sudden attack on the island and killed almost everyone. The Vinioli of Genoa occupied Kálymnos, but later sold it to the Knights of St John, who strengthened the fortress of Kástro. In 1522 the Knights abandoned it to succour Rhodes, leaving the Turks to quickly take their place. During the Italian occupation, attempts to make the Orthodox church toe the Fascist line and close down the Greek schools resulted in fierce opposition; prominent citizens were either jailed or exiled. The women of Kálymnos, who over the centuries had become fiercely independent with their menfolk away at sea for so long held protest marches in the centre of Pothiá, and in

## To Sponge, or Not to Sponge

In their natural state, sponges are foul, smelly and black, and have to be stamped, squeezed and soaked until their skeletons (the part you use in the bathtub) are clean. Many are then bleached in vitriol, acid and permanganate, to achieve the familiar yellow colour – but if you're out to buy, opt for the natural brown versions, which are much stronger. Look for the densest texture, the smallest holes. The seller should have a bucket of water on hand so you can feel and squeeze your potential purchase.

Diving for these primitive plant-like porifers is a difficult and dangerous art. In ancient times, divers strapped heavy stones to their chests to bear them down to the sea bed, where they speared the sponges with tridents, then, at a signal, were raised to the surface by a lifeline. As modern equipment permitted divers to plunge to new depths, cases of the 'bends' were frequent; old-timers on Kálymnos remember when it was common to see sponge-divers crippled, paralysed, or made deaf. These days divers wear oxygen tanks, attack the sponges with axes, and surface with decompression chambers. Politics limiting access to sponge beds (especially Libya's), a deadly sponge virus, overfishing and synthetic substitutes have undermined Kálymnos' traditional livelihood. In the last century, many divers emigrated to Florida to exploit sponge beds off Tarpon Springs. Many of the cheaper sponges are the big holey kind from the Caribbean; they feel synthetic and never last very long.

In the past Kálymnos's sponge fleet left home for seven months to work off the coast of North Africa. Today, only a few boats depart for a four-month tour, sticking mostly to Aegean and Cretan waters. On Kálymnos, the week before departure (traditionally just after Orthodox Easter, but it varies with the weather) is known as the Iprogrós or Sponge Week, devoted to giving the sponge-divers a rousing send-off, with plenty of food, free drinks and traditional dances – including the *mechanikós*, which mirrors the divers' often tragic life, from young and robust to stricken with the bends, although in the dance the diver makes a miraculous recovery. The last night is tenderly known as *O Ípnos tis Agápis*, the 'Sleep of Love'. It ends with the pealing of church bells, calling the divers to their boats. A local resident, Faith Warn, has written a book about the sponge divers called *Bitter Sea*, available in island bookshops.

a show of defiance painted everything in sight the blue and white of Greece. In 1996, Kalymniot patriotism nearly landed Greece in the soup with Turkey, over two tiny uninhabited islets to the east near Bodrum; fortunately level heads, and intense diplomatic pressure from Washington prevailed and the warships were sent home.

# Pothiá (Kálymnos Town)

Colourful **Pothiá** (ΠΟΘΙΑ), third largest city in the Dodecanese, is wrapped around the hills over the port and stretched along the big valley back to the old capital Chório. Pines close off one end, white churches hang on to cliffs as dry as biscuits. By the waterfront are the first two of the 43 bronzes that local sculptors Michail Kókkinos and his daughter Irene have made to decorate their island: a *Poseidon* by the Olympic Hotel and the waterfront *Winged Victory*, with the history of sponge-diving in relief. Here too the police occupy one of Kálymnos' most fanciful confections, a domed pink Italian villa that once served as a governor's mansion, rivalled only by the silver domes of 18th-century Cathedral **Chrístos Sotíros**, full of works by local painters. Pothiá's oldest quarter is just behind here, while by the Italian administration buildings (looking distinctly unloved), you'll find an old stone building housing the **sponge-diving school**. Being born to such a risky career has made the Kalymniots tough hombres. They fish illegally with dynamite and can regale you with stories of friends who blew themselves to smithereens; at Easter Pothiá becomes a war zone as rival gangs celebrate the Resurrection with dynamite and home-made bombs; some of the many crosses you see in town are in memory of the reckless. Think twice, too, before accepting a ride on their omnipresent motorbikes.

Perhaps not surprisingly, Pothiá has an excellent hospital and one of Greece's few orphanages, where Orthodox priests, before they were ordained, once came to choose a dowryless bride. On the waterfront, culture gets a say in **The Muses Reading Room**, with its Corinthian columns and bronze reliefs, founded in 1904 as a club to further Greek education and preserve national identity during the Turkish occupation. The Italians destroyed all Greek books and art and turned it into the Café Italia, which was damaged in the war. The club started up again in 1946, and in 1978 their building was restored to house historical documents and books, including some in English.

Lovely old mansions and walled orchards rise along its back streets. A five-minute walk up from the waterfront – allow fifteen for getting lost in Pothiá's higgledy-piggledy lanes – the **Archaeology Museum**, (*t 024 302 3113; open Tues–Sun 10–2*) is housed in a lovely Neoclassical mansion belonging to the Vouvális family, the first merchants to export sponges overseas, in 1896; the 'Victorian' furnishings, portraits, and panoramas of Constantinople tend to stick in the mind more than the miscellany of prehistoric finds. At the time of writing, the Kalmynian marbles sit in crates here, waiting for a brand new museum built just for them – that is, if the mayor wins his war against the cultural bureaucrats in Athens.

At night Pothiá's landmark is a huge illuminated cross in a hilltop 'sacred wood', near the Monastery of All Saints, **Ag. Pánton**. Here lie the remains of Ag. Sávvas, a monk who ran the secret school during the Turkish occupation. Sávvas is the local answer to fertility drugs: his reliquary has a fine collection of wax effigies of babies. Recently an icon of the Panagía in the school by the monastery dripped blood, but it's not Kálymnos' only miracle in the past few years: an X-ray of a man's lung distinctly showed the face of Christ.

There is a small **beach** near the yacht club, and beyond that a spa at **Thérma**, with waters good for rheumatism, arthritis and kidney disorders. Around the headland, the beach at **Vlycháda** is one of the island's nicest spots and has a wonderful museum dedicated to Aegean marine life. From Pothiá caiques sail south to **Néra** islet, with a monastery and to **Képhalas Cave**, a 30-minute walk from the sea (or taxis go as far as the **Monastery of Ag. Kateríni**, where you can pick up a 2km path). Discovered in 1961, the cave has six chambers full of colourful stalactites and stalagmites, and was once a sanctuary of Zeus; a huge stalagmite looks like the king of the gods enthroned.

## Vathí: the Fjord of Kálymnos

Nothing on the island properly prepares you for the sudden vision of 'the Deep', **Vathí** (ΒΑθΥΣ), the beauty spot of Kálymnos: a lush volcanic valley containing three charming, lush villages, **Rína**, **Plátanos** and **Metóchi**, superbly situated at the mouth of a magnificent fjord. Fragrant groves of mandarins, lemons and vegetable gardens (the tomatoes are famous) provide the valley's income, and houses and white-walled roads fill in the gaps between the trees. Rína, named after St Irene, has a pretty harbour with a few tavernas and hotels, a working boatyard and a mysterious 'throne' carved in the rock. The middle village, Plátanos, named for its enormous plane tree, has Cyclopean walls. North of Vathí you can walk to the Monastery of Kyrá Psilí, the 'Tall Lady'. Near the mouth of the fjord is the Cave of Daskaleío, accessible only by sea. A trove of Neolithic-to-Bronze Age items was found in its inner stalactite chamber.

## Up to Chorió and Árgos

Inland, Pothiá's suburb **Mýli** got its name from three monumental derelict windmills looming over the road. On a hill to the left stands the ruined Castle of the Knights of St John, or **Kástro Chryssochéria** ('Golden-handed'), named after the church of the Virgin built within its walls, over an ancient temple of the Dioscuri. Treasure was once discovered there, and the area has been combed on the off-chance of more.

Mýli blends imperceptibly into the pretty white town of **Chorió**, the old capital of Kálymnos. It grew up around the citadel **Péra Kástro**; on a gloomy day it looks more Transylvanian than Greek. The ruined village inside the walls was inhabited from the 11th to the 18th centuries. The only intact buildings are nine chapels kept freshly whitewashed by the women of Chorió; the views from the top, over the coast, are well worth the trouble of climbing up. The **Shelter of the Nymphs** or **Cave of the Seven Virgins**, at the foot of Mount Flaská near Chorió's hospital, has never been thoroughly explored, but take a torch and you can see traces of ancient worship: holes in the rock where supplicants poured libations to the nymphs. Legend has it that seven maidens took refuge there during a pirate raid and were never seen again, lost in the bottomless channel in the depths of the cave.

The island's old cathedral, **Panagía tis Kechaitoméni**, contains columns from a Hellenistic Temple of Apollo. Traces of the temple remain just beyond Chorió and the Árgos crossroads: most of its stone went into the 6th-century church of **Christós tis Ierúsalim**, built by the Byzantine Emperor Arkadios in gratitude for his shelter at Kálymnos during a terrible storm; now only part of the apse and the mosaic floor survives. There are rock-cut Mycenaean tombs in the area, not surprising as **Árgos** is to the west. Scholars doubt, however, whether the ancient city stood precisely here.

# West Coast Beaches and North Kálymnos

North of Chorió the tree-lined road dips down to the island's beaches, small fringes of grey shingly sand shaded with tamarisk trees, which are nothing to write home about, although the deep blue coves offer excellent swimming. Strung along the coast, Kálymnos' resort strip starts at **Kantoúni**, with a sandy beach enclosed by hills, and **Panórmos**, the latter running into **Eliés**, named after its olive groves, although these are fast becoming package-tour playgrounds. **Linária** is the next resort, with a small square home to a few bars and tavernas and a path down to a small harbour and seaweedy bay. A little further along, beyond the giant rock on the coastline, the beaches at **Platís Giálos** and **Melitzáchas** are quieter and more upmarket.

The road plunges down to **Myrtiés** (ΜΥΡΤΙΕΣ), the heart of the island's tourist strip, where the blood-red sunset over the islet of Télendos opposite is one of the wonders of the Dodecanese. Myrtiés blends into **Massoúri** to become a loud Golden Mile with neon-sign bars belting out music and local lads racing up and down on motorbikes. Brash fast-food, jewellery shops and 'English breakfasts' are in full expansion. Yet the far end of Massoúri towards **Arméos** is less frenetic: goatbells tinkle from the rocks above and women crochet as they mind their souvenir shops.

From Myrtiés jetty, a good half-hour's walk from Massoúri (buses every hour from Pothiá), frequent caiques make the short trip to the craggy islet of **Télendos** (ΤΕΛΕΝΔΟΣ), which broke off from Kálymnos in a 6th century AD earthquake. Its nickname, the Lady of Kálymnos, comes from its profile (best viewed from Kastélli, *see* below) looking out to her lover, the prince of Kastélli. He was supposed to send her a lighted candle to prove his love. But it blew out en route and she turned into marble, eternally waiting. On the islet, a derelict Byzantine monastery and fort face the strait. Up a narrow lane from the port you'll find the pretty church of the Panagía, ruins of Roman houses and, high above the beaches, the Byzantine Monastery of Ag. Konstantínos. Of several small pebble beaches, **Chokláka** (through the village and down steep steps in the cliff) is the most popular, while the shingly coves, reached from the track beyond the waterside tavernas towards Pothiá, are nudist haunts. Most of the islanders are fishermen and, apart from its daytime visitors, Télendos is a good place to get away from it all and sample some excellent seafood.

North of Massoúri, **Kastélli** was the refuge of survivors of the terrible 11th-century Turkish massacre, and overlooks the sea in a landscape of cave-mouths full of fangs. There are steps down to the church of the Panagía below. North of here, limestone cliffs plunge abruptly into the sea, attracting many rock climbers; a new route has recently been set up one crag known as the Priapus. The coastal road is spectacular, overlooking fish farms in the bay on its way to the fjord-like inlet at **Arginónta**. The hamlet lends its name to the entire northern peninsula, the perfect place for strenuous treks in the quiet hills. The small beach is pebbly and peaceful, and the taverna is perfect for lunch. The northernmost village on Kálymnos, **Emborió** (ΕΜΠΟΡΙΟΣ), is a pretty fishing hamlet with a small beach (bus twice a day from Pothiá, caiques from Myrtiés), within walking distance of some exceptional countryside and terraced hills. The **Kolonóstilo Cave** (or Cyclops Cave) is nearby, sheltering vast curtains of stalactites resembling columns; unfortunately treasure-hunters have damaged it with dynamite. The remains of a **Venetian castle** and a tower are close by. The tower is believed to have been a Neolithic temple; a sacrificial altar was found in the vicinity.

# Kárpathos (ΚΑΡΠΑΘΟΣ)

Halfway between Crete and Rhodes, on the same latitude as Malta and Casablanca, Kárpathos has for decades been an island-hopper's best-kept secret: hard to reach, but worth it for its beauty spots and distinct character, strongly marked by the affection it inspires in its inhabitants; although many have been forced to go abroad to make a living, they come back as often as possible, and even ship their bodies home to be buried on the island. They have the money: Kárpathos' sons and daughters have one of the highest rates of university education in Europe. And the climate gets a gold star, too, for people suffering from respiratory diseases.

Kárpathos offers two islands for the price of one: long and thin, austere and ruggedly mountainous in the north, and fertile, softer, beach-fringed and 'European' in the south, linked by a giant's vertebra of cliffs which culminates in two wild mountains over 3,000ft in height. These distinct geographical personalities extend to the population; the northerners and southerners may have descended from different ancient races. For centuries the little contact they had with one another was by sea. The isolation of the northern village of Ólympos left it a goldmine of traditions lost a century ago in the rest of Greece. Songs, dances and celebrations like Easter remain unchanged; women still bake their bread in outdoor ovens and dress in their beautiful traditional costumes. A rough road connecting the south to Ólympos was finished in 1979. Once limited to jeeps, coaches now ply it, and every year the Olympians somehow find more 'handicrafts' to sell to tourists.

## History

One ancient name of Kárpathos was Porfiris, or 'Red', after a red dye once manufactured on the island and used to colour the clothes of kings; another was Tetrapolis, after its four ancient cities of Vrykous, Possidion, Arkessia and Nissyros. Homer called it Kárpathos, perhaps from *Arpaktos*, or 'robbery'; from the earliest days, Vróntis Bay hid pirate ships that darted out to plunder passing vessels. The Venetians slurred it into 'Scarpanto', a name you may occasionally spot on maps.

Off the coasts, the prized *scarus* (or parrot fish, which, as Aristotle noted, ruminates its food) was so abundant that the Roman emperors hired special fleets to bring them back for the imperial table. Not long after, pirates made the island their head-quarters and one town, Arkássa, their chief slave market. The bays at Vróntis and Arkássa are said to be riddled with sunken treasure. Things were so rough that even the Turks didn't really want Kárpathos, and sent only a *cadi*, or judge, several times a year; he never stayed longer than a few days, and depended entirely on the Greeks to protect him. In the last war, 6,000 Italians used Kárpathos as a base to attack Egypt.

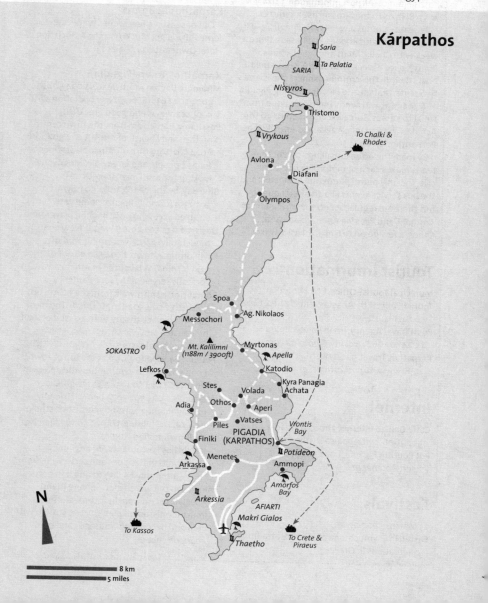

# Kárpathos

Saria
Ta Palatia
SARIA

Nissyros

Tristomo

Vrykous

Avlona

Diafani                To Chalki & Rhodes

Olympos

Spoa

Ag. Nikolaos

Messochori

Mt. Kalilimni
(1188m / 3900ft)        Myrtonas
SOKASTRO                         Apella

Lefkos                          Katodio

Stes                            Kyra Panagia
        Volada                  Achata
Adia    Othos
                Aperi
Piles           Vatses          Vrontis
Finiki    PIGADIA               Bay
          (KARPATHOS)
                                Potideon
        Menetes
Arkassa                 Ammopi

                        Amorfos
                        Bay
        Arkessia
                AFIARTI
                Makri Gialos

N

To Kassos                       To Crete &
        Thaetho                 Piraeus

8 km
5 miles

# Getting There and Around

**By air:** 2 daily connections with Rhodes, daily with Athens, twice a week with Kássos (the shortest scheduled flight in the world: it takes 5 mins) and twice a week with Sitía (Crete); also charters – even from Slovenia. There's an **Olympic Airways** office in town, by the main square, **t** 024 502 2150, run by the very helpful Kostis Frangos. **Airport information: t** 024 502 2057/8. **Taxis** to the airport cost around €12.

**By sea:** 2–3 times a week with Piraeus, 3–4 times a week with Rhodes and Kássos, twice a week with Chálki, Mílos and Ag. Nikólaos (Crete), once a week with Sitía (Crete); small boats daily in the summer connect the island's two ports, Diafáni and Pigádia, leaving Pigádia at 8.30am; at weekends there's a caique from Finíki to Kássos. Some **excursion boats** go to Acháta, Kýra Panagía, Apélla and Ag. Nikólaos. **Port authority: t** 024 502 2227.

**By road:** The often appalling state of the roads makes **car** and **motorbike** hire expensive, the only petrol pumps are in Pigádia, and the **bus** service seems like an afterthought, but there are regular services from Pigádia to Ammopí, and Pilés via Apéri, Voláda and Óthos; a few go on to Finíki, Arkássa, Lefkós.

# Tourist Information

**Municipal Tourist Office: t** 024 502 3841.
**Tourist Police:** Eth. Anastasis, in Pigádia, **t** 024 502 2218.
**Possi Travel Agency,** Iroon Polytechniou Sq., **t** 024 502 2627, *possitvi@hotmail.com*
**Karpathos Travel,** 9 Dimokatrias, **t** 024 402 2148, *www.karpathostravel.gr*

# Internet

**Caffe Galileo Internet 2000,** in Pigádia, **t** 024 502 3606, *caffe_galileo@yahoo.com*
**Pot Pouri,** in Pigádia, **t** 024 502 3709, *xpert@otenet.gr*

# Festivals

**25 March:** Pigádia.
**Easter:** in Ólympos, one of the most traditional celebrations in Greece.

**1 July:** Menetés.
**15 Aug:** Apéri and Menetés.
**22–23 Aug:** Kyrá Panagía and Myrtónas.
**27–29 Aug:** Vourgounda.
**6 Sept:** Pigádia.
**8 Sept:** Messóchorio.

# Where to Stay and Eat

**Kárpathos** ✉ 85700
Out of season a few room-owners meet ferries; if you get stuck, ring the **Association of Hotel Owners, t** 024 502 2483.

### Kárpathos Town (Pigádia)
**Miramare Bay,** on Affoti Beach, **t** 024 502 2345, **f** 024 5022 631 (*B; exp*). New operation, with pool, sea-views and good breakfast.
**Possirama Bay,** 400m from the town centre, on the sandy beach of Affoti, **t** 024 502 2916, **f** 024 502 2919 (*A; exp*). Air-con apartments for 2–4 people and large balconies overlooking the sea. *Open April–Oct.*
**Blue Bay,** by the beach, **t** 024 502 2479, **f** 024 502 2391 (*C; mod*). Rooms (some with disabled access), a pool, bar and playground.
**Oasis, t/f** 024 502 2915 (*C; mod*). New and moderately-sized, welcoming studios.
**Pavillion,** up in town, **t** 024 502 2818, **f** 024 502 3319 (*C; mod*). A favourite of Americans, with cocktails served in the roof garden.
**Romantica,** a short walk from the beach, **t** 024 502 2461, **f** 024 502 3267 (*C; mod*). The most charming place to stay, with 49 studios, halfhidden in a grove of citrus trees; it serves delicious breakfasts.
**Fotoula Georgiadou's,** up at the top of town, **t** 024 502 2519 (*inexp*). Among the quietest.
**Kárpathos, t** 024 502 2347 (*D; inexp*). Older.
**Mertonas, t** 024 502 3079 (*inexp*). Friendly management; pleasantly furnished studios.
**Rose's,** on the hillside, **t/f** 024 502 2284 (*inexp*). Well-maintained studios.

Kárpathos' restaurants are beginning to revive traditional recipes and serve wine from Óthos – although it's rare to find it in bottles.
**Aeraki,** on the waterfront. Serving island specialities – pumpkin fritters, stuffed mushrooms, onion pies, chicken stuffed with feta and bacon, local sausages and mild *manouli* cheese.

**Anemoussa**, upstairs, run by the same owners as Aeraki. Good Italian dishes.

**Café Kárpathos**, just off the waterfront towards the ferry. A good cheap place for breakfast or a snack.

**Kafeneíon**. A popular place to survey the scenery, with hearty evening fare accompanied by live music.

**Kali Kardia**, towards the beach. Big on fish.

**Mike's**, in a narrow lane in the centre. An old favourite place to eat.

**Oraia Kárpathos**, on the waterfront. The best *makarounes* (handmade pasta with fried onions and cheese) south of Ólympos.

## Ammopí

**Argo**, t 024 502 2589 (*C; mod*). A new beach addition.

**Long Beach**, t 024 502 3076, f 024 502 2095 (*C; mod*). With pool and tennis.

**Poseidon**, south of Ammopí, t/f 024 502 2020 (*C; mod*). In traditional style with a lovely garden terrace; ideal if you're a windsurfer.

**Ammopí Beach**, t 024 502 2723 (*inexp*). Simple, cheap rooms – help yourself to figs.

## Arkássa

**Arkesia**, t 024 506 1290, f 024 506 1307 (*B; mod*). The plush choice here, with all mod cons, pool and kiddies' playground.

**Dimitrios**, t 024 506 1313 (*B; mod*). Also comfortable, but with fewer facilities.

**Johnny's**, t 024 506 1310. For cheaper, but adequate rooms.

## Finíki/Lefkós

**Fay's Paradise**, near the harbour, t 024 506 1308 (*inexp*). Lovely rooms.

**Cuckoo's Nest**. *Ouzerie* with an all-blue interior for pre-dinner imbibing.

**Dimitrios'**. One of the good fish tavernas here.

**Pine Tree**, north in Adia. Great pasta, chick pea soup and fresh-baked bread.

**Small Paradise**, in Lefkós, t 024 507 1171. Good food; ask about their beach-side studios.

## Kyrá Panagía

Book to have a chance at any of these.

**Kyrá Panagía Studios**, t 024 503 1473 (*B; exp*). Upscale, with a bar.

**Sofia's Paradise Taverna**, t 024 503 1300 (*mod*). Pleasant rooms with bath and breakfast.

Run by a former New Yorker, also offering good home cooking, cheap fish, and figs drowned in *raki* to go with your coffee; boat available for private or group outings.

**Studios Acropolis**, t 024 503 1503 (*mod*). Popular, with lovely views.

**Klimateria**, up in Voláda. Traditional good taverna food under a pergola.

## Diafáni

**Chryssi Akti**, opposite the quay, t 024 505 1215 (*E; inexp*). Clean and basic.

**Delfini**, a bit further back, t 024 505 1391 (*inexp*). Quieter and friendly.

**Nikos**, t 024 505 1289 (*inexp*). Owned by Orfanos Travel; decent rooms.

**Taverna Anatoli**. A popular waterfront eatery.

## Ólympos

**Aphrodite**, t 024 505 1307 (*inexp*). Lovely views.

**Astro**, t 024 505 1378 (*inexp*). A good bet if the others are full.

**Mike's**, t 024 505 1304 (*inexp*). Rooms with a small restaurant serving island dishes.

**Taverna Ólympos**, t 024 505 1252 (*inexp*). 3 traditional rooms with en suite and great views; highly recommended.

**Milos Restaurant**, in the windmill. Try the delicious speciality of pasta stuffed with cheese and spinach.

# Entertainment and Nightlife

**Kafeneíon**, Apodi Kárpathos St. Impromptu Karpathian *lýra* of variable quality on summer nights under the pergola.

**Symposeio**, on the town waterfront. Popular music bar.

**Yuppy Bar**, near the church, in the skeleton of an unfinished building. Playing a mix of Greek and international music, or head for one of the panoramic bars over the bay.

**Filagri**, between Pigádia and Ammopí. Where locals and returned Karpathians dance the summer nights away.

**Kafeneíon**, in Finíki. Every Wed night the locals get together and play traditional music.

**Platania Bar**, in Apéri. Popular bar in a restored old house, playing Greek music and international hits.

For all its rough and ready past, Kárpathos has a strong tradition of delicately lyrical poetry, and, as in Crete, people like to compete in impromptu singing contests of *matinades*, or 15-syllable couplets. Two Austrians, Rudolph Maria Brandl and Diether Reinsch, spent 10 years on the island studying its songs, and wrote the monumental *Die Volksmusik der Insel Kárpathos* (Edition Re 1992), with transcribed songs and cassettes. One of the prettiest old songs was collected in the 19th century:

> A little bird was singing high up on the rough hillside,
> And a king's daughter listened from her window,
> 'Ah, bird, that I had thy beauty, and would I had thy song,
> And would I had such golden plumes for hair upon my head!'
> 'Why dost thou crave my beauty? Why dost thou crave my song?
> Why dost thou crave my golden plumes for hair upon thy head?
> For thou hast cakes to feed on, as many as thou wilt,
> I eat my scanty portion from herbage in the fields;
> Thou sleepest on a lofty couch, with sheets of thread of gold,
> But I lie out in solitude among the dews and snows;
> And when thou drinkest water thou hast a gleaming cup,
> But I must drink my water from the spring thou bathest in;
> Thou waitest for the priest to come thy way to bless thee,
> But I await the huntsman, who comes to shoot me down.'

# Kárpathos Town (Pigádia)

The island capital and southern port, Kárpathos or more properly **Pigádia** (ΠΥΓΑΔΙΑ) is attractively sheltered in that old pirate cove, mountain-ringed Vróntis Bay. Once the ancient city of Possidion, it was abandoned in the Byzantine era, and all that remains of its predecessor is a clutch of Mycenaean tombs and a few stones of a Temple to Lindian Athena on the rocky outcrop to the east. It's no accident that the local National Bank branch in the modern town has such an air of prosperity: Kárpathos receives more money from its emigrants than any other Greek island. New hotels and apartments are mushrooming up in Pigádia and along the sands outside town, and although German and Scandinavian holiday companies thrive, the town still has a relaxed, friendly feel to it; with all those dollars from Pittsburgh and Baltimore in the bank, the islanders don't have to be obsequious towards tourists.

Beyond the pretty Mussolini port authority building, it's a short walk to the 3km stretch of fairly good beach that rims **Vróntis Bay**. Within an enclosure several columns have been re-erected of a 5th-century basilica, **Ag. Fotiní**. Across the bay stands the chapel of **Ag. Nikólaos**, the saint who replaced Poseidon as the protector of sailors; a sacred cave nearby called Poseidona has sweet water. On the south side of Vróntis Bay, another ancient site, **Ag. Kiriakí** (the track is signposted from the road) had a 7th-century BC Geometric-era sanctuary dedicated to Demeter; a few years back one of the tombs hewn in the rock yielded a golden statuette.

# Around the South and up the West Coast

South of Pigádia, the land is flat and desolate. The wild coast softens after 7km at **Ammopí**, a pair of sandy coves decorated with great rocks and a popular family resort. Further south, a forlorn ship that ran aground in 1985 is like an advertisement for Kárpathos' windblasted windsurfing 'paradise', **Afiárti**, with accommodation and rentals duly springing up; Homer, after all, called the island, Anemoussa, the 'windy one'. The airport is further south, by the desolate site of the ancient city of Thaetho.

Colourful **Menetés** (ΜΕΝΕΤΕΣ), set in gardens on the flanks of Mount Profítis Ilías above Ammopí, has a small Ethnographic Museum (*ask at Taverna Manolis to visit*) and a church in a dramatic setting. Beyond, the road continues down to the west coast and **Arkássa** (ΑΡΚΑΣΑ), with its little beaches and big hotels in a picturesque setting at the mouth of a jagged ravine, cliffs riddled with caves that once sheltered shepherds. A paved road will take you south to the ruins of its predecessor, ancient **Arkessia**, where the Mycenaean *acropolis* with Cyclopean walls stands on the rocky headland of Paleokástro. The city was inhabited into late Byzantine times; the coloured geometric mosaic floor of a 5th-century church, **Ag. Anastásia**, is just under a fine layer of weeds, although the best sections have been moved to Rhodes.

Just north, **Finíki** is a bijou little fishing harbour with a good restaurant and sandy beach nearby; the sponge divers of Kálymnos call here, and caiques depart for Kássos, if the sea isn't too rough. The asphalted road north passes several tempting strands and mini fjords far below in the pines (one spot, **Adia**, has an excellent taverna), en route to **Lefkós** (ΛΕΥΚΟΣ), the nicest beach on the west coast – reached by a daily bus from Pigádia. Tucked in the rocks, Lefkós has white sandy beaches, piney groves and a scattering of antiquities, including a large stone that resembles a menhir. Packagers have arrived, but so far nothing too drastic. A short walk away are the ruins of a medieval fort; there was another on the offshore islet of **Sokástro**.

# Inland Villages and the East Coast

The beautiful road north of Pigádia rises first to opulent **Apéri** (ΑΠΕΡΙ). The capital of Kárpathos up to 1896, it is reputed to be the richest village in Greece per capita; nearly everyone (90 of whom are doctors) has lived in New Jersey, including the family that gave the world the late Telly 'Kojak' Savalas. One *kafeneíon* still proudly displays a picture of Roosevelt. In the new cathedral built over the Byzantine cemetery, you can pay your respects to Kárpathos' miracle-working icon. If you get the chance to peek in a house don't miss it; the Karpathiots have lavish tastes, and traditionally furnish their homes with colourful carpets, mirrors, portraits, antiques and elevated carved wood beds, or *souphas*; they also keep exquisitely tended gardens.

The other central villages are just as houseproud. Delightful whitewashed **Voláda** has pretty lanes, and a ruined castle built by the Cornaros of Venice, who owned the island until 1538. From here the road climbs to **Óthos**, at 2,133ft the highest village of Kárpathos and also one of the oldest, its houses decorated with carved wooden balconies; you may need a pullover, even in summer. If you're game for a tipple, try the fine local red wine, *othitikó krasí*. A 150-year-old house has been opened as a small **Ethnographic Museum**, run by the excellent Ioannis T. Hapsis, ex-barber, ex-shoe-maker and *lýra* player, who now paints pictures, which he sells for €6–60, solely by the size. To the west coast, the pretty village of ΠΥΛΕΣ, whose name in Roman letters unfortunately reads **Pilés**, has fine views over Kássos, with the profile of Crete as a backdrop, and makes delicious honey.

Caiques from Pigádia call at the east coast beaches, although you can brave some of them by road. A steep zigzag from Apéri leads down to **Acháta**, a lovely, empty white pebbly beach with fresh water, closed in a rocky amphitheatre. The road north of Apéri takes in the increasingly majestic coast. A serpentine paved by-road winds from Katodio to **Kyrá Panagía**, a pretty red-domed church by a wide beach, which varies from fine white sand to large pebbles. Rooms and tavernas are sprouting apace and fill up in the summer; an easier way to get there is by a 45-minute walk down through the lush greenery from the mountain village of Myrtónas. Another rotten road descends from **Myrtónas** to **Apélla**, the most beautiful beach: a crescent of fine sand, turquoise water and dramatic scenery, set in boulders furiously ravaged and rolled in the Clash of the Titans. Myrtónas is the place to be on 22 August, when it hosts the best *panegýri* on the island with all-night music and folk-dancing. The east coast road ends at **Spóa**, at the crossroads of the road to Ólympos; massive forest fires in the 1980s have left large patches between Spóa and Diafáni denuded and melancholy. A track from Spóa descends to the beach of **Ag. Nikólaos**, with too much new building, and in summer too many people.

Another unpaved, narrow Wild West road from Spóa circles Kárpathos' tallest mountain, **Kalílimni** (3,900ft), the highest point in the Dodecanese. Anticlockwise from Spóa, the road descends on a corniche to **Messochóri**, set in an amphitheatre facing the sea. Here you'll find the pretty 17th-century church of Ag. Ioánnis, with a carved iconostasis and frescoes. From here a road descends to Lefkós (*see* above).

## Ólympos and Northern Kárpathos

The easiest and least expensive way to reach **Ólympos** (ΟΛΥΜΠΟΣ) from Kárpathos is by caique to Diafáni, the village's laid-back little port, from where a minibus makes the connection to Ólympos. There's a beach with flat rocks nearby, and several others within walking distance; boats make excursions to ones further afield.

**Ólympos**, one of the most striking villages in Greece, is draped over a stark mountain ridge, topped by ruined windmills lined up as neatly as teeth; two of the 40 still work, grinding wheat and barley for the local bread. To the west are magnificent views of mountains plunging headlong into the sea. Decorative painted balconies, many incorporating two-headed Byzantine eagles (one head Rome, one Constantinople), adorn the houses, often stacked one on top of another and opened with wooden locks and keys that Homer himself might have recognized. The frescoes and recently cleaned iconostasis in the church date back to the 18th century.

As the Byzantines lost control of the seas, Ólympos became the refuge for all the inhabitants in the north. The area was isolated for so long that linguists in the 19th century were amazed to find people here using pronunciations and expressions that could be traced back to ancient Doric and Phrygian dialects. Women are more visible than men, because of emigration; many of the men who remain are noted musicians, playing the *lýra* with a bell-covered bow, the *laoúto*, and *tsamboúna* (goatskin bagpipes). Likewise, a mother's property goes to the eldest daughter, the *kanakára*; if you're in Ólympos during a *panegýri* or wedding, you can recognize a *kanakára* by the gold coins she wears on chains – coins that her forefathers earned abroad.

Ólympos' population was 1,800 in 1951, but is down to 340 today. Before the new road was built, visitors were so few that they had no effect on the village's traditional life, however, tens of thousands a year are another story. To get a feel for old Ólympos, stay overnight, or come in the off-season. On weekend evenings the *kafeneíons* still fill with live music. One owner displays a certificate from the Governor of Alabama, thanking him for his service in the state militia.

From Ólympos you can drive most of the way to **Avlóna**, a village that wouldn't look out of place in Tibet but is inhabited only during the harvest season by farmers from Ólympos; some of the tools they use are more commonly seen in museums. From Avlóna it is a rough walk down to **Vrykoús**, the ancient Phrygian city of Vourkóunda, remembered today by a stair, a breakwater, rock-cut burial chambers and walls; a tiny chapel sits out on the rocks. In a cavern in Vrykoús the chapel of **Ag. Ioánnis** hosts the largest *panegýri* in north Kárpathos, a two-day event where everyone sleeps out, roasts meat over an open fire and dances to the haunting music. Another two hours north of Avlóna, in the bay of the 'three-mouthed' **Tristomo**, are the submerged remains of the ancient city of Níssyros, colonized by the island of Níssyros to exploit the iron and silver mines at Assimovorni. Boats from Diafáni sail to **Sariá**, the islet that dots the 'i' of long, narrow Kárpathos. The ruins known as **Ta Palátia** (the palaces), are a post-Byzantine pirate base, with dolmus-style houses under barrel-vaulted roofs.

# Kássos (ΚΑΣΣΟΣ)

The southernmost of the Dodecanese and one of the most remote islands, Kássos (pop. 1,500) is a barren rock with steep coasts, ravines, and grottoes, with the odd beach wedged in between. Practically untouched by tourism, it can be the ideal place if you've been seeking the simple, friendly atmosphere of pre-mass-tourism Greece. The port, **Fri**, is small, and if the sea is rough, simply landing can be a big headache.

## History

Homer mentions Kássos in the *Iliad's* Catalogue of Ships. The ancient city stood at the site of the present village of Póli, and at Hellenokamára Cave there are Mycenaean walls. During the Turkish occupation, Kássos was practically autonomous, especially with regard to its fleet, which it quickly put at the disposal of the Greeks in the War of Independence. For the first three years of the conflict the Greek sailors

## Getting There and Around

**By air**: 3 flights a week to and from Rhodes, 1 a week to Athens and 4 twice a week to Kárpathos (world's shortest scheduled flight takes 5mins) **Olympic Airways, t** 024 504 4330.

**By sea**: 2–3 connections a week with Piraeus, 3–4 times a week with Rhodes and Kárpathos, twice a week with Chálki, Mílos and Ag. Nikólaos (Crete), once a week with Sitía (Crete); weekend caique from Finíki, Kárpathos. All are likely to skip Kássos if the wind's up. **Port authority: t** 024 504 1288.

**By road**: 3 taxis and an irregular summer **bus** service are all you get; there are **motorbikes** to rent, and occasional **boat excursions**.

## Tourist Information

**Kássos Maritime Tourist Agency: t** 024 504 1323, *www.kassos-island.gr*.
**Police: t** 024 504 1222.

## Festivals

**23 April**: Ag. Geórgios.
**7 June**: Fri.
**17 July**: Ag. Marína.
**14 Aug**: at Panagía.

## Where to Stay

**Kássos** ✉ 85800

**Anagennissis, t** 024 504 1323, **f** 024 504 1036 (*C; mod–inexp*). Comfortable and run by an engaging Kassiot-American. You'll pay more for the rooms facing the sea, less for those in the back. *Open all year.*

**Anessis**, 9 G. Mavrikáki St, **t** 024 504 1201 (*C; mod–inexp*). Similar, but you'll pay a bit less. *Open all year.*

**Borianoula Apartments, t** 024 504 1495, **f** 024 504 1036. A self-catering option. *Open May–Oct.*

**Manouses Apartments, t** 024 504 1047, **f** 024 504 1747 (*mod*). Similar to the above.

## Eating Out

**Oraia Bouka**, overlooking the port in Fri. As good as it looks.

**Kassos**, by the town hall. Newly refurbished, serving good standard dishes.

**Milos**, facing the sea, **t** 024 504 1825. Excellent fish menu.

**Karayiannakis**, behind the Anagennissis, **t** 024 504 1390. Good Greek classics and fish. There are also a couple of tavernas in Emborió.

generally came out ahead in the struggle, but the Sultan prepared a powerful counter-attack through his ally, Ibrahim Pasha, son of Ali Pasha (the Ottoman Empire's Governor of Egypt). In June 1824 Ibrahim left with a massive fleet to crush the Greek rebellion. His first stop was Kássos, which he decimated, slaying all the men and taking the women and children as slaves. The few who escaped went either to Sýros or Gramboúsa, an islet off the northwest coast of Crete, where they turned to piracy for survival, defiantly flying the Greek flag in Turkish waters. But Capodístria and his allies put a stop to their activities, and their refuge, Gramboúsa, was returned to Turkish rule. In spite of the massacre, thousands of Kassiots later emigrated to Egypt to work on the Suez Canal. Most now prefer America.

### Around the Island

There are five villages on Kássos and small, charmingly woebegone **Fri** (ΦΡΥ) is their capital, where the main occupation, fishing, is much in evidence in the little port of **Boúka**. Every year on 7 June a ceremony is held there in memory of the massacre of 1824, and many people from Kárpathos also attend. Swimming at Fri isn't brilliant, but boats make the excursion out to **Armathiá**, an islet north of Kássos, with a choice of five decent beaches; a long stretch of sand dignifies the other islet, **Makrá**.

Apart from a few olives, trees on Kássos never recovered after Ibrahim Pasha set the island ablaze, but many lighthouses, testimony to the tricky seas, stick out above the rocky terrain. A road and the one bus link Fri with Kássos' four other dinky villages, on a 6km circuit. There's **Emborió**, another fishing hamlet whose old commercial port packed up with silt, and above it **Panagía**, where proud ship captains' houses erode; the 18th-century church that gave the village its name is the oldest on Kássos. **Póli** is built on the island's *acropolis*, and has a crumbling Byzantine castle and church with inscriptions. At **Ag. Marína**, near the airstrip and Kássos' most accessible if mediocre beach at **Ammoúa**, there is a lovely stalactite cave called **Hellenokamára**, where signs of worship go back to Mycenaean and Hellenistic times. From Ag. Marína or **Arvanitochóri** you can spend a day walking across Kássos, the lonely track passing the Monastery of Ag. Giórgios, where you can find water, to the beach at **Chelathrós Bay**.

# Kastellórizo/Mégisti (ΜΕΓΙΣΤΗ)

The easternmost point of Greece, oddball Kastellórizo is six hours – 110km – east of Rhodes, within spitting distance of Turkey. It is the smallest inhabited island of the Dodecanese, 3 by 6km, yet the mother hen of its own small clutch of islets; hence its official name, Mégisti, 'the largest'. They say the Turks know it as Meis Ada, 'eye-land', for one nautical mile away is their town of Kaş ('eyebrow'), but the most commonly heard name is Kastellórizo, in memory of the days when the Neapolitans called it the 'Red Castle'. Dry, depopulated, more than half ruined by a long streak of bad luck, its once very lonely 170–200 permanent inhabitants now have an airport to bring them in closer contact with the rest of Greece. Athens has officially adopted the island and sends it contributions and gifts, including recently 20 council houses. Its success as a film set – for the award-winning Italian film *Mediterraneo* – has given the economy, based on government stipends and fishing, a new life as a tourist resort, as swarms of Italians now come to Kastellórizo; landladies cry '*Stanza? Stanza?*' as the ferry arrives. Some of the old houses are being repaired, mostly by returned Australian emigrants. However, it remains a quirky backwater, surrounded by a crystal sea brimming with marine life – including oysters, a rarity on Greek islands. And while there aren't any sandy strands, the locals will show you the rocks on which to catch some rays.

## History

According to tradition, the island was named for its first settler, King Meges of Echinada. Neolithic finds suggest an early arrival for Meges, and Mycenaean graves coincide with the mention in Homer of the island's ships at Troy. Subsequently, the Dorians built two forts on the island, the Kástro by the present town and one on the mountain, called Palaeokástro – the ancient *acropolis*, where Apollo and the Dioscuri were the chief deities. Diónysos was another favourite: recently 42 rock *patitíria* or grape-trampling presses were discovered, linked to conduits that fed the juice into underground reservoirs. The little island had a large fleet of ships and traded with Lycia on the mainland, transporting its timber to Africa and the Middle East. From 350 to 300 BC Kastellórizo was ruled by Rhodes, and in Roman times the pirates of Cassius used it as their hideout. The island was converted to Christianity from the time of St Paul, who preached along the coast of Asia Minor at Myra.

The Byzantines repaired Kastellórizo's fortifications, and their work was continued by the Knights of St John, who named the island after the red rock of the castle, where they imprisoned knights who misbehaved on Rhodes. The Sultan of Egypt captured Kastellórizo in 1440, but ten years later the King of Naples, Alfonso I of Aragon, took it back. Although Kastellórizo belonged to the Ottoman Empire by 1512, the Venetians later occupied it twice, in 1570 and in 1659. Despite all the see-sawing, the little island was doing all right for itself; at the beginning of the 19th century it had a population of 15,000 who lived from the sea or their holdings along the coast of Asia Minor.

Things began to go seriously wrong with the outbreak of the Greek War of Independence. The islanders were the first in the Dodecanese to join the cause and, taking matters into their own hands, seized their two fortresses from the Turks. The Great Powers forced them to give them back in 1833. In 1913 Kastellórizo revolted again, only to be put down this time by the French, who used the island as a base for their war in Syria – hence drawing bombardments from the Turkish coast. In 1927 an earthquake caused extensive damage but the Italians, then in charge, refused to do any repairs, as Kastellórizo had failed to co-operate with their programme of de-Hellenization. Another revolt in 1933 was crushed by soldiers from Rhodes. In spite of

## Getting There

**By air:** 3 flights a week from Rhodes. **Olympic Airways, t** 024 104 9241. **Airport: t** 024 104 9238. A bus meets planes.

**By sea:** 'Europe begins here' proclaims the sign by the quay. Twice a week from Rhodes; once a week with Sými, Tílos, Níssyros, Kos, Kálymnos, Léros and Piraeus. Also an over-priced, unofficial boat to Kaş (as Kastellórizo is not an official port of entry). **Port authority: t** 024 104 9270.

## Tourist Information

**Regular police:** in the harbour by the post office, **t** 024 104 9333.

## Where to Stay

**Kastellórizo** ✉ 85111
The island has 400 beds, but if you want a chance at one in Aug, book ahead.
**Megisti,** overlooking the harbour, **t** 024 104 9272, **f** 024 104 9221 (*C; exp–mod*). The most comfortable place to stay. *Open all year.*

**Blue and White Pension,** to the west of the bay, **t** 024 104 9348 (*mod–inexp*). Featured in *Mediterraneo*. Book via Taverna International.
**Mavrothalassitis, t** 024 104 9202 (*inexp*). Simple with en suite facilities.
**Paradeisos, t** 024 104 9074 (*inexp*).
**Polos, t** 024 104 9302 (*inexp*).

## Eating Out

Most eateries are in the harbour clustered round the Plateía Ethelontón Kastellórizon. Prices, always dear because of transport charges, have rocketed and fish is expensive, although it's fresh and the only thing that doesn't have to be shipped in.
**Evtychia.** Reasonably priced.
**Kaz-Bar,** in the harbour. Grilled fish, octopus.
**Mikro Parisi,** 'Little Paris'. The place for afford-able fish, but concentrating on yachties.
**O Meyisteas,** behind the market building arches. More ethnic fare and local ambience; good meat and *mezédes*.
**Oraia Mégisti,** opposite Evtychia. Good choice.
**Platania,** up the hill on Choráfia Square. Unpretentious, with tasty island dishes.

its port serving as a refuelling station for long-distance sea planes from France and Italy, Kastellórizo was in sharp decline – in 1941 only 1,500 inhabitants remained.

But the saga of Kastellórizo's misfortunes continues. During the Second World War, the isolated Italian garrison was captured by the Germans (subject of the film *Mediterraneo*). When the Allies shipped the entire Greek population for their safety to refugee camps in the Gaza Strip, the occupying British pillaged the empty houses. To hide their looting, the British (or, the British claim, Greek pirates, doing some looting of their own) ignited the fuel dump as they pulled out, leading to a fire that destroyed more than 1,500 homes and nearly all the islanders' boats. Then the ship carrying the refugees home after the war sank. Those who survived to return to Kastellórizo discovered that, although they had finally achieved Greek citizenship, they had lost everything else, and there was nothing to do but emigrate, some to Athens but most to Australia, where an estimated 12,000 to 15,000 'Kazzies' now live. The immediate postwar population was reduced to five families, who owed their survival to the Turks in Kaş, who sent over food parcels. British compensation for wartime damages came in the 1980s, but there are still bad feelings over the way it was distributed; none actually went to the people who stuck it out on the island.

The rare spirit of Greek-Turkish friendship continues. In 1992, all the Kastellorizans were invited over to spend Christmas in Kaş hotels, were taken on excursions, and given a two-day feast. It was Kaş' way of thanking Kastellórizo for its role in the underground railroad that brought Kurds from Kaş to Kastellórizo and a large refugee camp near Athens. Since the demise of Papandréou, the relationship has improved again. Almost all the Greeks, however, want to leave, and the only reason they stay is to keep the island firmly Greek. The government has built a desalination plant, and has bent over backwards to bring television and an airport to the island.

# Kastellórizo Town

There is only one town on the island, also called Kastellórizo, full of ruined houses, some burnt, others crumbling from earthquakes or wartime bombing. One can see how wealthy some of the inhabitants once were from the remaining elegant interiors. Some are being restored, others are inhabited by cats and chickens. Small tavernas line the waterfront, in high season packed with Italians and yachties. A hotel occupies one lip of the harbour mouth, while on the other sits the **fort** (*kástro*), last repaired by the eighth Grand Master of the Knights of St John, Juan Fernando Heredia; his red coat-of-arms is another possible explanation for the name of the island. The ladder to the top leads to a fine view of the sea and Turkish coast; every day an islander, and a lame one at that, climbs up to raise the flags of Greece and the EU at the easternmost extremity of both. A Doric inscription discovered at the fort suggests the existence of an ancient castle on the same site. A tomb nearby yielded a golden crown, and in the castle keep the small **museum** (*open Tues–Sun 7.30–2.30*) exhibits photographs of the prosperous town before everything went wrong, a few frescoes, costumes and items found in the harbour – including Byzantine tableware.

The walking path along the shore leads up to a **Lycian tomb** cut into the living rock and decorated with Doric columns; the whole southwest coast of modern Turkey is dotted with similar tombs, but this is the only one in modern Greece. The **Cathedral of Ag. Konstantínos and Heléni** re-uses granite columns lifted from a Temple of Apollo in Patara. From the town a steep path leads up to four white churches, a monastery and **Palaeokástro**, the Doric fortress and *acropolis*. On the gate there is a Doric inscription from the 3rd century BC referring to Mégisti; walls, a tower and cisterns also remain.

## Kastellórizo's Grotto Azzurro

There are no beaches on Kastellórizo, but the sea is ideal for snorkelling, and there are a multitude of tiny islets to swim out to. The excursion not to be missed is to the **Blue Cave**, or **Perásta**, an hour by caique from the town. The effects are best in the morning when some light filters in; the entrance is so low you'll have to transfer to a raft. As in the famous Blue Grotto of Capri, the reflections of the water inside dye the cavern walls and stalactites blue; wear your swimming gear. The same excursion boats often go out to **Rho**, a hunk of rock with a beach, a hundred goats and a flag-pole, where a cranky old lady became a nationalist heroine by daily raising the Greek flag to show those Turks what was what; after her death in 1982, she was buried on Rho, but her flag is still raised every day by a caretaker paid by the Greek Government.

# Kos (ΚΩΣ)

Dolphin-shaped Kos, with its wealth of fascinating antiquities, flowers and orchards, sandy beaches and comfortable climate, is Rhodes' major Dodecanese rival in the tourist trade. In other words, don't come here looking for anything very Greek – the *kafeneíon* and *ouzerie* serving octopus sizzling from the grill have long been replaced with fast-food joints and Euro-cafés. The streets are packed with T-shirt and tatty gift shops; where garlanded donkeys once carried their patrons home from the fields, swarms of rent-a-bikes rev. In high season English, German and Swedish tourists fill the island's myriad big, self-contained resort hotels and countless discos. Even the architecture isn't particularly Greek, partly owing to an earthquake in 1933: the Italians contributed some attractive buildings, and the pair of minarets rising from the mosques add an aura of elegance and *cosmopolitana* to the capital. Inland, Kos in summer looks uncannily like a mini-California: sweeping golden hills, with a few vine-yards, groves and orchards, grazing cattle and sheep, and pale cliffs, but otherwise empty, contrasting with the rashes of building – pseudo-Spanish villas seem to be the rage – crowding the countless sandy coves that ruffle the coasts.

## History

Evidence in Áspri Pétra Cave suggests people have been living on Kos since 3500 BC. A Minoan colony flourished on the site of the modern city; the Mycenaeans who superseded them traded extensively throughout the Mediterranean. The island went through a number of name changes, including Meropis, after its mythical king; Karis, for its shrimp shape; and Nymphaeon, for its nymphs. Kos, which finally won out, is either from a princess named Koon or a crab, an early symbol. In the 11th century, the Dorians arrived and made Astypálaia their capital, and in 700 BC they joined the Dorian Hexapolis: a political, religious and economic union that included the three cities of Rhodes, Cnidos and Halicarnassus on the Asia Minor coast.

Poised between East and West (Asian Turkey is, after all, just over the channel), Kos flourished with the trade of precious goods – and revolutionary ideas. Halicarnassus was the birthplace of Herodotus, the 'father of history', the first to attempt to distinguish legend from fact; in the 5th century BC Kos produced an innovating papa of its own: Hippocrates, father of medicine. Believing that diseases were not punishments sent from the gods but had natural causes, Hippocrates suggested that doctors should learn as much as possible about each patient and their symptoms before making a diagnosis. His school on Kos, where he taught a wholesome medicine based on waters, special diets, herbal remedies and relaxation, was renowned throughout the ancient world, and he set the standard of medical ethics incorporated in the Hippocratic oath taken by doctors to this day. When Hippocrates died, the Asklepeion (dedicated to Asklepios, the healing god) was founded, and people from all over the Mediterranean came to be cured in its hospital-sanctuary.

In 411 BC, during the Peloponnesian War, the Spartans played a nasty trick on the island; pretending to be friends, they entered the capital Astypálaia and sacked it. In 366 BC the survivors refounded the old Minoan/Mycenaean city of Kos, conveniently near the by-now flourishing Asklepeion. The next few centuries were good ones;

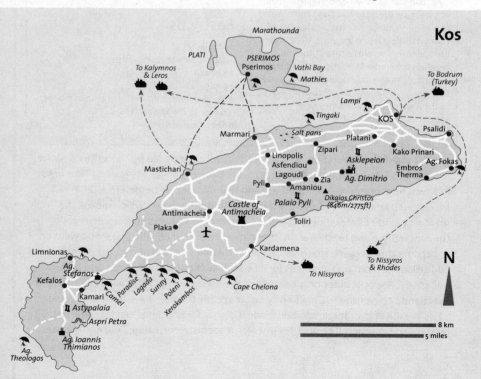

## Getting There and Around

**By air: charters** from London and other European cities; 4 flights a day from Athens. **Olympic Airways**, 22 Leof. Vass. Pávlou, **t** 024 202 8331. For one-way tickets home, try Plotin, in town, **t** 024 202 2871, **f** 024 202 5154. The **airport** is 26km from town. Olympic airport **buses** from Kos Town depart 2hrs before each flight and transport arriving Olympic passengers into town or Mastichári. There are infrequent **public buses** (the stop is outside the airport gate – ask for Taverna Panorama) to Kos Town, Mastichári, Kardámena and Kéfalos. **Airport: t** 024 205 1229.

**By sea:** daily **ferry** connections with Piraeus, Rhodes, Kálymnos and Pátmos, 6 times a week with Léros, 3–4 times a week with Astypálaia, Níssyros, Tílos and Sými, less frequently with Kastellórizo, Chálki, Agathónissi, N.E. Aegean islands (Ikaría, Foúrni, Sámos, Chíos, Mytilíni and Límnos) and Cyclades (Náxos, Páros and Sýros); daily excursions sail to Psérimos from Kos Town, as well as Mastichári, Kardámena, Bodrum (Turkey), Níssyros, Platí and Léros. **Port authority: t** 024 202 6594.

**By road:** flat Kos Town and the small roads out west are suited to bikes and there are no lack of hire shops, as well as an abundance of **car** rental agencies on the waterfront. The city **bus** runs every 15 mins at peak times and regularly otherwise from the centre of the waterfront (7 Akti Koundouriotou, **t** 024 202 6276) to Ag. Fokás and Lampi; roughly every hr to the Asklepeion; and 8 times a day to Messaria (buy tickets in the office before boarding). Buses to other points on Kos, **t** 024 202 2292, leave from the terminal behind the Olympic Airways office, but they get packed so arrive early; otherwise you'll find yourself in a long queue waiting for a taxi. In theory, at least, you can summon a **radio cab, t** 024 202 3333/7777, but watch the meter.

## Tourist Information

**Municipal Tourist Office**, on Vass. Georgíou just before the hydrofoil berth, **t** 024 202 6585/8724, **f** 024 202 1111. Very helpful; *open Mon–Fri 8am–8.30pm, Sat–Sun 8am–3pm.*
**Tourist police: t** 024 202 6666. Shares the yellow edifice with the clocktower opposite the main harbour with the **regular police**, **t** 024 202 2222, and **EOT, t** 024 202 4460.
**Post office:** 14 Venizélou.
**British consulate:** in Aeolos Travel, 8 An. Laoumtzi St, **t** 024 2026 203.

## Internet

**Café del Mare**, 4a Alexandrou. Offers pricey access in pleasant surroundings.

## Festivals

**23 April:** Pylí.
**24 June:** bonfires everywhere.
**29 June:** Antimácheia.
**29 Aug:** Kéfalos.
**Aug:** the Hippocratia features art exhibitions, concerts, theatre and films.
**8 Sept:** Kardaména.

besides physicians, Kos produced a school of bucolic poetry, led by Theocritus, a native of Sicily (319–250 BC) and the most charming of ancient poets. His *Harvest Time in Kos*, in which he evokes a walk across the island to drink wine by Demeter's altar, and meeting a poetic goatherd on the way, gave English the word 'idyllic'. Apelles, the greatest painter of Alexander's day, was a native of Kos, as was Philetas, inventor of the Alexandrine and teacher of another native, Ptolemy II Philadelphos, who went on to become king of Egypt; many subsequent Ptolemies were sent over to Kos for their education. The Romans prized Kos for its translucent purple silks, wines and perfumes and gave it a special autonomy because of the Asklepeion. St Paul called in and began the island's conversion to Christianity; so far 21 early basilicas have been discovered.

Kos' wealth and strategic position made it a prize for invading Persians, Saracens, pirates and Crusaders. The gods themselves, it seems, were jealous, and earthquakes in AD 142, 469 and 554 levelled most of the island's buildings. In 1315 the Knights of St John took control, and in 1391 began fortifications using the ancient city as a quarry, incorporating marble statues from the Asklepeion in their walls. In 1457 and 1477 the Turks besieged Kos without success, but they gained the fortress in 1523 by treaty after the fall of Rhodes. After almost 400 years, the Italians toppled the Turks. The Germans took over in 1943; when the 'thousand-year Reich' fell two years later, Kos was left in British custody. It was united with the rest of Greece in 1948.

## Kos Town

Bustling **Kos**, capital city and main port, is roughly in the region of the dolphin's eye. As you sail into the harbour it looks magical, especially at twilight: a medieval castle by the port, the silhouettes of mountains behind, in the foreground a lush garden

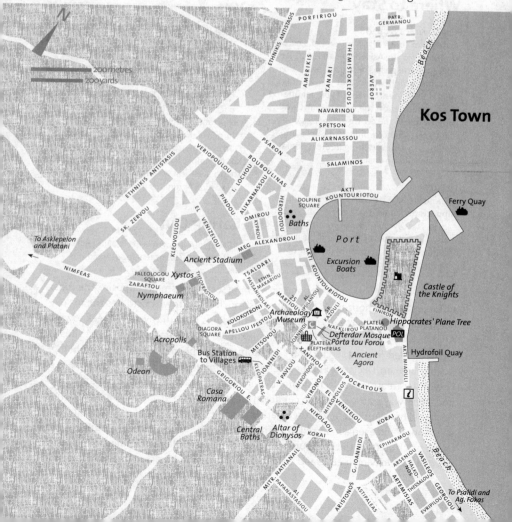

## Sports

**Diving**: certified instructors at the **Kos Diving Centre**, 5 Koritsas Square, t 024 202 0269/2782; if you already know how to dive, go out with the **Dolphin Divers**, t 024 209 454 8149, whose *Happy Puppy* boat is moored every evening with the excursion craft. The proximity of Turkey and other islands makes for lovely diving.

**Sailing**: **Sunsail**, 3 Artemisias, t 024 202 7547, or **Kavos Moorings**, 7 Themistokleous, t 024 202 7115, f 024 202 7116.

**Riding**: go in Mármari (*see* below).

## Where to Stay

### Kos Town ✉ 85300

In days of yore, visitors in need of a cure would stay in the Asklepeion and sacrifice a chicken to the gods. These days, beds can be so scarce in high season that you still might need that chicken. Book, or if you get offered a room as you get off the ferry, take it. If you want to stay in the centre *and* get a good night's sleep, buy earplugs. Package companies block book everything in the moderate range, so splurge or slum.

### Luxury

These are all A class and out in Psalídi.

**Hippocrates Palace**, t 024 202 4401, f 024 202 4410. The Olympic Health Centre spa, indoor and outdoor pools, tennis, and the largest conference hall in southeastern Europe. Owned by Kipriotis. *Open April–Oct.*

**Kipriotis Village**, t 024 202 7640, *www.kipriotis .com*. New, huge and packed with amenities: 2 pools, tennis, Jacuzzi, gym. It also has rooms for the disabled. *Open April–Oct.*

**Oceanis**, t 024 202 4641, *www.oceanis-hotel.gr*. Beachside complex set in a tropical garden; 370 rooms and 4 pools, incl. 2 sea water.

**Platanista**, nearby, t 024 202 7551, *www .platanista.gr*. Neo-Venetian palazzo, with tennis, pool, gym, tennis and kid's activities; rated one of the world's top 4-star hotels.

**Ramira Beach**, t 024 202 2891, f 024 202 8489. Slightly more affordable and still well endowed with facilities.

### Inexpensive

**Afendoulis**, 1 Evripílou, in a quiet road near the sea, t 024 202 5321, f 024 202 5797 (C). Friendly and comfortable guest house with a fragrant terrace run by Ippokrátis.

**Manos Hotel**, 19 Artemisias, t 024 202 8931, f 024 202 3541 (C). Rooms with balcony.

**Pension Alexis**, 9 Irodótou, t 024 202 8798, f 024 202 5797 (E). The Mecca for backpackers and full of character. Alex, brother of Ippokrátis (above), is amazingly helpful; the large veranda positively reeks of jasmine of an evening from the overgrown creeper.

**Kos Camping**, 3km from the port, t 024 202 3910. Well-run with facilities from laundry to bike hire. A minibus meets the ferries.

## Eating Out

Eating out in town is like playing Russian roulette if you want real food. Avoid the

setting, with stately palm trees and an evening scent of jasmine; opposite, the coast of Turkey fills the horizon. At close quarters, much of the town postdates the 1933 earthquake and this means more Art Deco buildings than the average Greek town. Another side-effect of the quake: when the rubble was cleared away, ancient sites were revealed, leaving serene Greek and Roman ruins peppered amongst throbbing holiday bedlam. Declared 'European City of 1995' for its self-improvements, Kos has a new water treatment system guaranteeing pristine beaches, new pedestrian areas and a one-way traffic system to cut down on some of the cacophony. But the tourist fleshpots have not lost any of their garishness: there's no lack of fast food, touts, T-shirt shops, and even a hard sell from the excursion boats all lit up along the front.

One block up from the harbour, the city's main square, **Plateía Eleftherías** has been freed of cars, leaving it eerie and empty, like a Pirandello character in search of a play.

harbour-front, where waiters aggressively *kamáki* or 'harpoon' punters in.

**Anatolia Hamam**, 3 Diagora Square, over-looking the Western Excavations, t 024 202 8323 (*€18–22*). One of the lovelier places to dine in the sumptuously restored Turkish bath with a garden terrace.

**Kástro**, near the ancient Agora on 15 Hippocratous, t 024 202 3692. Pricey French food in an alluring setting.

**Taverna Petrino**, nearby, t 024 202 7251 (*€15–20*). Set in a classy terrace courtyard, and serving huge salads.

**Otto e Mezzo**, 21 Apellou, t 024 202 0069 (*€15–20*). Fresh pasta dishes that Mama would approve of; intimate indoor dining and summer garden.

**Platanos**, in the square around Hippocrates' beloved tree, t 024 202 8991. Atmospheric creeper-draped dining; expensive international and traditional dishes and live music.

**Antonis**, Koutarys St, behind Hotel Anna. A real neighbourhood taverna with good food, big portions, and low prices.

**Taverna Ambavri**, 10min walk south of the Casa Romana. Very good traditional dishes.

**Nick the Fisherman**, cnr of Averof and Alikarnassou, t 024 202 3098. So-so setting, but Nick's catch comes at good prices, often accompanied by *bouzouki*.

**Kohili**, 9 Alikarnassou. An *ouzerie* with the finest *mezédes*, but they don't come cheap.

**Arap**, outside town in Platáni. The best of the handful of tavernas here serving Turkish food; excellent aubergine with yoghurt, *borek*, shish kebab and chicken.

**Mavromatis**, on the way to Psalídi, near the Ramira Beach Hotel. Tranquil place with traditional food.

**Spitaki**, in Psalídi, t 024 202 7655. Beachside taverna with pasta and grills.

**Nestoras**, near the campsite. Reliable taverna.

# Entertainment and Nightlife

Kos is one big party at night. The *agora* is alive with the thumping sound of house music from 'Disco Alley' on pedestrian Navklírou St, where every establishment is a pumping bar. Discos go in and out of fashion every season. Alternatively, try your feet at Greek dancing classes, advertised in many restaurants.

**Kalua** and **Heaven**, at Lámpi on Zouroudi. Both discos have a watery backyard and garden, and remain popular.

**Aesolos**, on the waterfront nearby. A café-bar playing mellow music at night and serving excellent Baileys *frappés*.

**Happy Club**, 1 Navarinou. For Greek music and *rembetíka*.

**Jazz Opera**, 5 Arseniou. A great place playing jazz, funk, reggae and the blues.

**Orpheus Cinema**. Films play at the indoor screen in Plateía Eleftherías and the outdoor screen along Vas. Georgíou St, t 024 202 5713.

**Taurus Bar**, 9 Mandilara St. For anyone homesick for football, rugby, cricket, or just about any other sport, this venue keeps up with all the scores and shows many matches live.

Here you'll find the 18th-century **Defterdar Mosque** (*still used by the 50 or so Muslim families on the island, but not open to the public*), and two Italian Art Deco buildings. One, laid out like a Roman house, holds the **Archaeology Museum** (*t 024 202 8326; open Tues–Sun, 8.30–3; adm*). Fittingly, the prize exhibit is a 4th-century BC statue of Hippocrates with a noble, compassionate expression. Other items include an intriguing fragment of an archaic Symposium; a 2nd-century AD seated Hermes, with a little pet ram and red thumb; a statuette of a pugilist with enormous boxing gloves; and another of Hygeia, the goddess of health, feeding an egg to a snake. There are also fine mosaics, of a fish and of the god Asklepios with his snake, stepping from a boat and welcomed by Hippocrates.

Plateía Eleftherías also has the city's **market**, with fruit, vegetables and seashell kitsch – walk through it to Ag. Paraskévi Square, with its shady cafés and superb bougainvillaea arching over the back of the market. Buying and selling is old hat here; in Plateía Eleftherías you'll find the entrance into the ancient *agora*, by way of the **Pórta tou Foroú**, draped with another massive bougainvillaea. This was where the Knights of St John built their town and auberges, just as in Rhodes (*see* pp.372–3). When these collapsed in the earthquake, they revealed not only the market, with the re-erected columns of its *stoa*, but the harbour quarter of the ancient city, a Temple of Aphrodite Pandemos, and a 5th-century Christian basilica, all sprinkled with trails of dried cat food scattered by the Kos Animal Protection League.

On the northern end of the *agora*, Plateía Platánou is almost entirely filled by **Hippocrates' plane tree**, its trunk 52ft in diameter, its huge boughs now supported by an intricate metal scaffolding instead of the marble columns that once kept the venerable tree from disaster. At an estimated 700 years old it may well be the most senior plane in Europe. Hippocrates may well have taught under its great-grand-mother, for he believed, as do modern Greeks, that of all the trees the shade of the plane is the most salubrious. The Turks loved the old plane just as much, and built a fountain with a sarcophagus for a basin and the lovely **Mosque of the Loggia** (1786) to keep it company. On 1 September the citizens of Kos pluck a leaf from the tree to include in their harvest wreaths as a symbol of abundance.

## The Castle of the Knights

A stone bridge off Plateía Platánou crosses the former moat (now the Finikon, or palm grove) to the **Castle of the Knights of St John** (*t 024 202 8326; open Tues–Sun 8.30–3; adm*). Combined with the fortress across the strait in Bodrum, this was the premier outer defence of Rhodes. After an earthquake in 1495, Grand Master Pierre d'Aubusson rebuilt the walls and added the outer *enceinte*, and the tower overlooking the harbour bears his name and coat-of-arms. Since d'Aubusson mostly used stones from the *agora*, the masonry is a curious patchwork quilt of ancient inscriptions and coats-of-arms. Some have been removed to the castle's **antiquarium**, to join other stacks of defunct columns and marble that nobody seems to know what to do with. The castle's dishevelled weeds and wildflowers, and the stillness of the noonday sun, attracted director Werner Herzog. He set his first black and white film, *Signs of Life* (1966), within its walls; the elaborate cockroach traps and hypnotized chickens that played a major role are, however, no longer in evidence.

## Roman Kos

From Plateía Eleftherías, Vas. Pávlou leads to Kos' other archaeological sites. In the quarter called the Seraglio (don't expect any harem girls), Minoan, Mycenaean and later houses were discovered. Opposite the Olympic Airways office stands a ramped Hellenistic **Altar of Diónysos**, and across Grigoríou Street, the ruins of the **Central Baths** (site of the Vourina spring, praised by Theocritus) and the **Casa Romana** (*t 024 202 3234; open Tues–Sun 8.30–3; adm*); both were victims of the earthquake of AD 554, and were excavated and reconstructed in grim concrete shell by the Italians in 1940. The house, begun in the Hellenistic era, has well-preserved mosaics – the owner was fond of panthers – and offers a fair idea of the spacious elegance to which the wealthy could aspire; even on the hottest days it remains cool inside. West along Grigoríou Street, by the Catholic church, the **Roman Odeon**, or concert hall, has rows of white marble seats, partially restored by the Italians; the statue of Hippocrates was discovered under its arches. Besides this the city had three other theatres and a music school. As Strabo wrote, 'The city of the Koans is not large, but one lives better here than in others, and it appears beautiful to all who pass it by in their ships'.

Some of this good living is evident in the **Western Excavations** just opposite. Great Hellenistic walls were built around the *acropolis* (now studded with a minaret); on the other side you can pick out the marble-paved **Cardo and Decumanus**, the main arteries of Roman Kos, lined with ruined houses. Although the Italians took many of the best mosaics off to Rhodes, some good bits remain (often under a protective layer of sand), especially the **House of Europa**, on the *Decumanus*. Just north of this, lining the *Cardo*, is an elegant 3rd-century BC **nymphaeum**, or fountain house, which supplied running water to the nearby **public lavatory** with marble seats. The gymnasium has a **xystos**, a running track covered by a marble colonnade, used in the winter months – a luxury that even Kos' most luxurious beach hotels lack. The Romans also had a heated pool, near the brick **baths** (the *thermae* still survive). Part of this was transformed into a Christian basilica in the 5th century; the lintel has been rebuilt and the baptistry has a well-preserved font. At the north end, an unidentified 3rd-century BC building contains mosaics of battling bulls, bears and boars. The **Stadium** is along Tsaldári St; only a few of the seats have been excavated and work continues, but on the far side near the church is a well-preserved *aphesis*, or starting gate.

## Beaches near Kos Town

Since the advent of the water treatment plant these have won blue flags, but that's about the nicest thing you can say about them. The sandy and pebbly town beaches are packed with sunbeds and umbrellas; in places along Vas. Georgíou the smell of sun lotion is overpowering. The city bus will take you in a few minutes to better, less crowded beaches north of town at **Lampí** (ΛΑΜΠΙ), now occupied by package tourists rather than the military; the closest strands to the south are at **Psalídi** (ΨΑΛΙΔΙ), 3km away, and **Ag. Fokás** (8km). For something more remote, get your own transport to continue to **Embrós Thermá** (13km), where volcanic black sands and thermal springs make the bathing a few degrees warmer; a new spa is planned to replace the old hot pit where the water oozes out.

## The Asklepeion and Platáni

A city bus or short bike climb will take you up to the **Asklepeion** (ΑΣΚΛΕΠΕΙΟΝ) (*t 024 202 8763; open Tues–Sun 8.30–3; adm*), 4km west of the city. The German archaeologist Herzog, following Strabo's description, discovered it in 1902, and it was partially restored by the Italians during their tenure. This was one of the ancient world's most important shrines to the healing god Asklepios, served by the Asklepiada, a secret order of priests (Hippocrates was one) who found that good water, air and relaxing in beautiful surroundings did much to remedy the ills of body and soul. The cult symbol was the snake, the ancestor of the same one on the modern medical symbol, twining itself around the caduesis. Snakes, sacred intermediaries between the living and the dead (they were always found in holes in cemeteries, eating mice fattened on grave offerings), were believed to have a knack for seeking out healing herbs and transmitting dreams, which were part of the therapy, along with hallucinogens and the power of suggestion. The sanctuary on Kos was built after the death of Hippocrates, who left a school of disciples behind him, but most of the buildings visible today date from the Hellenistic age, when the earthquake-damaged Asklepeion was last reconstructed. Many of the structures were cannibalized by the Knights, who found it too convenient a quarry.

Set on a hillside, the Asklepeion is built in a series of terraces split by a grand stair. On the lowest level are Roman baths, built in the 3rd century AD. The next level, once surrounded by a huge portico, has the main entrance and another large bath; here was the medical school, and the museum of anatomy and pathology, with descriptions of cures and votive offerings from grateful patients. Near the stair are the remains of a temple dedicated by the Kos-born physician G. Stertinius Xenophon, who served as the Emperor Claudius' personal doctor and murdered his patient by sticking a poisoned feather down his throat, before retiring on Kos as a hero (so much for the Hippocratic oath!). On this level, too, was the sacred spring of the god Pan, used in the cures. On the next terrace is the Altar of Asklepios, and Ionic temples dedicated to Apollo and Asklepios (a few columns have been reconstructed by the Italians); on the top stood a Doric Temple of Asklepios from the 2nd century BC, the grandest and most sacred of all, and enjoying a view that in itself might shake away the blues. In August, for the Hippocratia, the teenagers of Kos get off their motorbikes to don ancient *chitons* and wreaths to re-enact the old rituals and recite the Hippocratic oath.

Just up the road, the modern **International Hippocrates Foundation** is dedicated to medical research. In 1996, several Nobel Prize winners and other leading lights attended the first 'International Medical Olympiad' here, and no, they didn't hold brain surgery races but gave out awards and held conferences. The five rings of the Olympic symbol were used to sum up Hippocratic philosophy: 'Life is short. Science is long. Opportunity is elusive. Experiment is dangerous. Judgement is difficult.'

On the way back down to Kos Town, along the cool cypress-lined avenue, stop for refreshments in **Platáni**, Kos' main Turkish settlement. It's busy and a bit touristy, like everything on Kos, but the Turkish food is excellent and relatively cheap. A little out of Platáni, on the road back to the harbour, the **Jewish Cemetery** stands in a pine grove.

# Around the Island

The northeast of Kos is flat and very fertile, with fields of watermelons and tomatoes. Beyond Lampí and the reach of the town bus, **Tingáki** (ΤΙΓΚΑΚΙ) is a smart little resort overlooking the island of Psérimos, and still has a village feel, especially when the day-trippers have gone. Boat Beach (so nicknamed by locals because of the beached whale of a vessel there), before Tingáki, is quiet and has a taverna. In March and April, the nearby salt pans, Alíkes, are a favourite port of call for flamingoes and numerous migratory birds, while the sandy coast and estuary are loggerhead turtle nesting areas. At the far end of the wet lands, **Marmári** (MAPMAPI) is increasingly packaged, but offers a generous sandy beach and a chance to explore local byways on horseback at the **Marmári Riding Centre**, (*t 024 204 1783*). Just inland, two ruined Byzantine basilicas (Ag. Pávlos and Ag. Ioánnis) lie on the outskirts of **Zipári**; above, Kos' spinal ridge has a bumpy, curiously two-dimensional profile.

But these are real mountains, not a child's drawing. From Zipári, the road ascends to **Asfendíou**, a cluster of five peaceful hamlets set in the woods, with whitewashed houses and flower-filled gardens, many now being turned into holiday homes. The highest of the five hamlets, **Ziá** is a pretty place, of fresh springs, fruit and walnut groves – the bucolic Pryioton described by Theocritus – now a converted 'traditional village' for coach parties, who come for the absolutely spectacular sunsets and a 'Greek Night' in the schlocky tavernas; but there are others, too, such as the excellent

# Where to Stay and Eat

## Tingáki ✉ 85300
**Park Lane**, 150m back from the beach, t 024 206 9170 (*B; mod; book through Aeolos Travel in Kos Town t 024 202 6203*). Package-dominated family hotel, with pool, playground.
**Meni Beach**, close to the sea, t 024 206 9217, f 024 206 9181 (*C; inexp*). With a pool.
**Paxinos**, t 024 206 9306 (*C; inexp*).
**Alikes Taverna**, on the edge of town. Should satisfy your appetite.

## Marmári ✉ 85300
**Caravia Beach**, a little out of town, t 024 204 1291, f 024 204 1215 (*A; exp*). Super club hotel set in beautiful grounds with a vast range of facilities. *Open May–Oct.*
**Tam Tam Beach Taverna**, between Marmári and Mastichári, by Troulos Beach. A lovely place for lunch or dinner.

## Kardámena ✉ 85302
Kardámena has scores of hotels, but unless you go on a package you may only find rooms on the edges of the season. Kardámena lives it up with happy hours and has something for night owls of all ages, seasoned with good old-fashioned seaside Brit vulgarity.
**Porto Bello Beach**, t 024 209 1217, *portobello@ kos.forthnet.gr* (*A; exp*). Luxurious setting with views of Níssyros, a huge pool and private beach, and its original flooring.
**Restaurant Andreas**. Refuses to pander to tourists and has good ethnic dishes.

**Christopoulos Taverna**, by the beach. Also recommended.

## Mastichári ✉ 85301
**Mastichari Bay**, t 024 205 9300, f 024 205 9307 (*A; exp*). Good for families, with lots of activities, nice pool and beach, playground, floodlit tennis and open-air theatre.
**Arant**, just back from the road and very close to the beach, t 024 205 1167 (*C; inexp*).
**Evagelia Argoula**, t 024 205 9047 (*inexp*). Cheap, clean and cheerful studios.
**Mastichari Beach**, near the harbour, t 024 205 9252 (*C; inexp*). Plain, clean, with sea-views.
**Kalikardia**. The first taverna in town, and still good.
**Taverna Makis**, just off the waterside. Long-established and popular.

## Kéfalos ✉ 85301
**Panorama**, perched above packageville overlooking Kastrí island, t/f 024 207 1524 (*inexp*). Quiet studios that live up to the name and a garden; incl. breakfast.
**Paradise Pension**, down in town, t 024 207 1068 (*inexp*). Cheap rooms with fridge, kettle, balcony and a café below.
**Esmeralda**, in the hill village. Quails and liver as well as more usual Greek fare.
**Kastro**. Good view of the bay.
**Stamatia** by the sea. Wide selection of fish, incl. 'dogs' teeth' for adventurous diners.
**Milos Taverna**, above the tiny fishing port of Limniónas. Worth the journey if you have wheels; serves up a fishy feast.

Olympiada, minus dancing 'ópa ópa' waiters. Kos' ancient sculptors came up here to quarry marble from Kos' highest peak, **Díkaios Christós**, 'Justice of Christ' (2,775ft). It can be reached without too much difficulty in about three hours from Ziá, and well worth it for the god-like views of Dodecanese and Turkish geography.

From the Asfendíou a road runs across country to **Lagoúdi** and continues from there to **Amaníou**, where there's a turn-off to **Palaío Pýli**, the Byzantine capital of Kos, now a ghost town on a crag surrounded by concentric walls camouflaged in the rocks. Within its walls is the church of Panagía Ypapandí, built in the 11th century by the Blessed Christódoulos before he made a trade for land on Pátmos; it and two others, Ag. Antonio and Ag. Nikólaos, have 14th-century frescoes. Another side lane, just west of Amaníou, leads to the **Charmyleion**, a *tholos* tomb hero shrine with twelve little vaults, re-used as a church crypt. The grotty village of **Pýli** below is a major agriculture centre, although the upper part of town has a great place to stop for lunch, in the taverna by a handsome spring-fed fountain (or *pygí*) built in 1592. On 23 April, for the feast of St George, Pýli holds a horse race, with an Easter egg as prize, cracked on the forehead of the winning horse – a custom going back to remote antiquity.

Further west, in a wild setting, the **Castle of Antimácheia** was built by the Knights as a prison for bad knights in the mid-14th century. Within its great, battlemented triangular walls are two churches (one with a fresco of St Christopher carrying baby Jesus), a few surviving cisterns and, over the gateway, the arms of Pierre d'Aubusson. The sprawling village of **Antimácheia**, near the airport, has the island's last opera-tional windmill as its landmark. Opposite is a traditional house (*open 8–4.30*); the typical boxed-in beds were often even higher than this so olives and wine could be stored underneath. Even better, head up to **Pláka**, on a paved road from the airport: a green oasis and favourite picnic ground, with wild peacocks and more great sunsets.

There are more beaches on either coast: to the south, the sand stretches between **Tolíri** and much hotter **Kardámena** (ΚΑΡΔΑΜΑΙΝΑ), once a charming fishing village famous for its ceramics and now a heaving resort. Commercialized to Costa Brava proportions, it's very much the Brit and Scandinavian family package destination, complete with pubs, chips and *smorgasbord*. But there is also golden sand, boats to Níssyros, and watersports and entertainment for all ages. On the north coast, **Mastichári** (ΜΑΣΤΙΧΑΡΙ) is quieter, and has frequent boats for Kálymnos and Psérimos, and, a 20-minute walk beyond the Kanari Beach Hotel, the ruins of a 5th-century **basilica of Ag. Ioánnis** with a fine mosaic floor.

There are more mosaics (again, under a layer of sand), Ionian columns and remains of an atrium and baptistries with the extensive ruins of the lovely twin 5th-century basilicas of **Ag. Stéfanos**, near the beach at **Kamári**, towards the dolphin's tail. In the bay you can contemplate the islet of **Kastri**, a natural volcanic bulwark, often surrounded by the butterfly wings of windsurfers skimming over the blue sheet, with a Club Med complex as a foreground. A long fringe of sand runs under the cliffs to the east with a few access roads; the steepest descent is to pretty **Camel Beach**, by pictur-esque rocks, and the easiest to **Paradise Beach** (or 'Bubble Beach' after the bubbles that rise to the surface through the clear waters at one end of the bay); it's perfect for children, although they'll have to fight their way through the forest of sunbeds to get to the water. Further along the headland to the left, the beaches **Lagáda** (or Banana – the most beautiful with its dunes), **Sunny**, attractive **Poléni** (or Magic) and **Xerókambos** are much quieter although still offering sunbeds, parasols and cantinas.

The road twists up to **Kéfalos** (ΚΕΦΑΛΟΣ) to the west, high up on the headland of the dolphin's tail. This is where the bus terminates and, when the hotels are bursting full elsewhere, you may just find a room here. Another Knights' castle looks over Kamári and isn't particularly impressive, although it inspired many travellers' tales in the Middle Ages, all involving a dragon; Mandeville in his *Travels* claims the serpent was none other than Hippocrates' daughter, enchanted by Artemis and awaiting a knight brave enough to kiss her to transform her back into a maiden. South, just off the road, there's a Byzantine chapel of the Panagía built out of a temple that once belonged to the ancient capital of Kos, **Astypálaia** (signposted Palatia), the birthplace of Hippocrates. A few bits of the ancient city remain, including a theatre. Isthmioton, another ancient city on the peninsula, was important enough in the past to send its own delegation to Délos, but not a trace of it remains. A paved road descends to **Ag. Theológos** Beach, offering some of the island's most secluded swimming (but often big waves) and a nice taverna. Neolithic remains from 3500 BC were found in the **Áspri Pétra Cave** just south, reached by an (unmarked) path. The road passes through dramatic scenery, past sheer cliffs and a telecommunications tower, then ends at the charming **Monastery Ag. Ioánnis Thimianós**, 6km from Kéfalos.

# Psérimos (ΨΕΡΙΜΟΣ)

**Psérimos**, wedged between Kos and Kálymnos, has a beautiful sandy beach, which its 70 residents have come to regard as a curse, as day in and day out during high season it becomes invisible under rows of day-trippers like well-oiled sardines. Even in September, excursion boats from Kos Town, Mastichári and Kálymnos queue up to dock, the tavernas are thronged and the islanders short-tempered. It becomes even more crowded on 15 August, when hundreds of pilgrims attend the *panegýri* at its Monastery Grafiótissa. If you are staying any length of time (when the day boats have gone the people become quite friendly), you'll probably want to take to the interior by day, or hunt up one of the smaller pebbly strands on the east coast; the main beach can be murder. Some boats now head instead to the adjacent islet of **Platí**, with another sandy beach, and make a day of it by stopping for lunch in Kálymnos.

## Where to Stay and Eat

**Psérimos** ✉ 85200

If the rooms are full, you can sleep out on one of the island's more distant beaches, a kilometre from the village.

**Pension Niki-Ross**. Worth a try (Ross is Australian Greek).

**Tripolitis**, on the sea, located over Mr Saroukos' taverna, t 024 302 3196. Pleasant.

**Glynatsis**, t 024 302 3596.

**Katerina Xiloura**, t 024 302 3497. Rooms in the village.

The **monastery** has simple accommodation for up to 10 people.

Most of the tavernas on the main beach are packed, and the service in them surly at lunchtime. The unnamed one with the garden area does excellent and reasonably priced fresh *kalamári*.

# Léros (ΛΕΡΟΣ)

With its wildly serrated coastline like an intricate jigsaw puzzle piece, sweeping hills, tree-fringed beaches and unspoiled villages, Léros is a beautiful and much misunderstood island. Few places have had such a bad press, both as an isle of exile and home to Greece's notorious mental institutions. Perhaps to make amends, the people are welcoming and visitors who discover the island's charms are often hooked.

Léros has long been the butt of jokes in Greece, where its name evokes the same reaction as 'Bedlam' in Britain; to make matters worse, Léros sounds like *léra*, 'filth' or 'rogue'. The 1989 Channel 4 documentary exposing the grim conditions in the hospitals was another blow, but at the same time it prodded the authorities to get their act together. Dutch medical teams have been working to improve conditions; a care-in-the-community scheme was set up and you might see patients in the villages. But they are not intrusive, and, to be frank, you're likely to see even more lost souls wandering the city streets back home.

Léros is not a dreary or downbeat island. Green and pretty, its indented coastline offers little strands of shingly sand, very clear waters, excellent fish tavernas, and a lively but very Greek nightlife. It is an exceptionally musical place, home of the famous Hajiadákis Dynasty whose folk songs have influenced Greece's leading composers; it's not at all rare to hear the hammer dulcimer (*sandoúri*), or the bagpipes (*tsamboúna*), as well as the more usual instruments playing dances such as

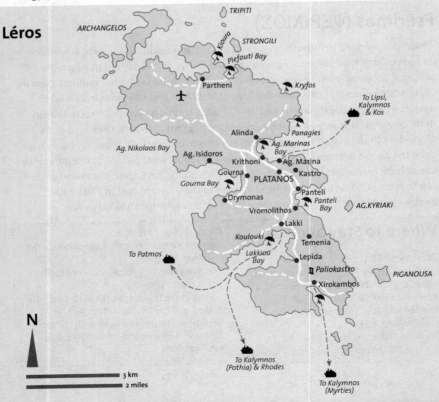

the Issós Lérikos, Soústa, Stavrotos, Passoumáki and the ancient Dance of the Broom. The ancient island of Artemis, Léros has a special atmosphere you either love or hate; and the bad press shields the island from the masses, which helps preserve its charm.

## History

On the death of the hero Meleager (of Chalydonian boar hunt fame), his sisters mourned him so passionately that Artemis turned them into guinea fowl and put them in her temple on Léros. This worship of the goddess of the chase and guinea fowl might be traced back to Ionians from Miletus who colonized Léros; Robert Graves notes that, because of their conservatism and refusal to adopt the patriarchal religion of Ólympos, the island had a bad press even in ancient times: the Greeks called the Leriots 'evil-livers' (an epigram went, 'The Lerians are all bad, not merely some Lerians, but every one of them – all except Prokles, and of course he is a Lerian too'). Fittingly for an island dedicated to Artemis, property has been passed down through the female line, so that most of Léros is owned, at least on paper, by women.

Homer included Léros with Kálymnos as the 'Kalydian isles' in his Catalogue of Ships. The island sided with Sparta in the Peloponnesian War, despite its Ionian ancestry. Under the Romans, pirates preyed among the islets that surround Léros; some nabbed a handsome young lawyer named Julius Caesar on his way back to Rome from Bithynia, where according to rumour, he had a dissolute affair with the governor; released after a month when his ransom was paid, Caesar took his revenge by capturing and crucifying every brigand around Léros. Under the Byzantines, the island was controlled by Sámos, but in 1316 it was sold to the Knights of St John and governed by the Duke of Náxos as part of the monastic state of Pátmos.

Léros paid a high price for its excellent anchorages in the Second World War. After 1912, the occupying Italians built their main air and naval ordnance bases at Lépida. Their Eastern Mediterranean fleet was based in Lakki Bay; when Churchill sent the British to occupy the island after the Italian surrender in 1943, Hitler sent in an over-whelming force of paratroopers to take it back, causing a good deal of damage in the Battle of Léros (12–16 November); see the photos displayed in the Kastis Travel Agency. The Allies in turn bombed the German fleet at Lakkí, and for three years after the war the British fleet held the fort. When the *junta* took power in 1967, Communist dissidents were imprisoned in the notorious camp in Parthéni; during the later Cyprus dispute the Greek Government dismantled its military installations to show that it had no warlike intentions against Turkey. One of the brightest lights in Australian poetry, Dimítris Tsaloúmas, was born on Léros and emigrated to Melbourne in 1952; his work explores the bittersweet feelings of emigrants in the Greek diaspora and explains why so many hotels and restaurants are named *Nostos*, a longing for home.

# Lakkí and South Léros

Arriving at **Lakkí** (ΛΑΚΚΙ), by ferry, usually at night, is quite an experience, its extraordinary Fascisti Art Deco buildings reflected in the gulf. If Fellini had been

# Getting There and Around

**By air**: daily from Athens with **Olympic, t** 024 702 2844/4144. **Airport: t** 024 702 2777; it is best reached by taxi.

**By sea: ferry** connections 6 times a week with Piraeus, Patmos, Kálymnos, Kos and Rhodes, once to twice a week with Níssyros, Tílos, Sými, Lípsi, Arkí, Kastellórizo, Sámos, Náxos, Páros and Sýros; **excursion boats** from Ag. Marína to Lipsí, Arki, Maráthi, Tiganákia and Pátmos (contact **Lipsos Travel, t** 024 704 1225). Caique once a day in high season from Xirókambos to Myrtiés, Kálymnos. **Port authority**: Lakkí, **t** 024 702 2234.

**By road: taxi** ranks: **Lakkí t** 024 702 2550, **Ag. Marína t** 024 702 3340, **Plátanos t** 024 702 3070 (prices are more or less fixed and reasonable). Buses run 5 times daily in season between Plefoúti, Parthéni, Alínda, Plátanos, Lakkí and Xirócampos; alternatively, rent a scooter in any of the main towns.

# Tourist Information

**Municipal Tourist Office**: at the quay in Ag. Marína; *open daily 8.30–noon and 3–4.30, Wed 2.30–3.30.*

**Apocalypsis Travel**, in Plátanos, **t** 024 702 4828, **f** 024 702 5775, *apcalyps@12net.gr*

**Kastis Travel** in Lakkí, **t** 024 7022 500, **f** 024 7023 500 (also in Ag. Marína, **t** 024 702 2140, and Alínda, **t** 024 702 2305). Help with accommodation and tickets.

# Festivals

**Pre-Lent Carnival**: children don monks' robes and visit the homes of the newly married, reciting verses made up by their elders.

**16–17 July**: Ag. Marína.

**First 10 days of Aug**: in Alínda, the Alintia regatta run since 1907 with sailing races.

**6 Aug**: Plátanos.

**15 Aug**: at the Kástro (Plátanos).

**20 Aug**: foreign tourist day in Alínda.

**24–25 Sept**: Lakkí.

**26 Sept**: 3 days of memorial services are held for those who tragically lost their lives on the Queen Olga ship; Greek naval vessels always attend.

# Where to Stay and Eat

## Léros ✉ 85400

The lushness of Léros translates into an airborne division of Lilliputian vampires by night so bring big bug-goo, especially if you sleep under the stars.

## Lakkí/Xirókambos

**Katikíes, t** 024 702 3624, **f** 024 702 4645 (*A; exp*). Lovely studios and apartments in traditional style, set away from the road and sleeping up to 6.

**Efstathia**, in Xirókambos, **t/f** 024 702 4199 (*C; mod*). Roomy studios and apartments with pool.

**Katerina, t** 024 702 2460, **f** 024 702 3038 (*E; inexp*). All in cool marble.

**Miramare**, nearby, **t** 024 702 2053, **f** 024 702 2469 (*D; inexp*). Gilds the lily with its gold cornicing, but is central and comfortable.

**Villa Maria, t** 024 702 2827 (*inexp*). Another comfortable choice.

**Camping Léros**, up the road, **t** 024 702 3372.

**Merikia**, just out of town, at the eponymous beach just past the Kouloúki strands. A good bet for fish.

**Petrinos, t** 024 702 4807. A touch of class, specializing in refined meat dishes influenced by the time owner-chef Giorgos spent in Belgium; Lerians flock here all year.

## Vromólithos

**Tony's Beach, t** 024 702 4742, **f** 024 702 4743 (*C; inexp*). Often has rooms in Vromólithos, although the rest tend to be block-booked.

**Frangos**, slap on the beach. Legendary for traditional food.

**Paradisos**. A good menu but slow service in high season.

## Pantéli

**Aegean Sky Apartments**, up the lane back towards Plátanos, **t** 024 702 4722 (*inexp*). Another decent, friendly possibility.

**Cavos, t** 024 702 3247 (*inexp*). Marginally preferable alternative with rooms and studios (the same family also owns Pension Anastasios, in Vromólithos).

**Pension Afroditi, t** 024 702 2031 (*inexp*). Rooms and studios, some with pretty sea-views.

Rosa, t 024 702 2798 (*inexp*). One of the several good pensions overlooking the picture-postcard harbour at Pantéli.

Drossia, opposite Pension Rosa. Less touristy than some, with fish almost leaping from the family nets.

Patimenos. Good food and *frappés*.

Psaropoula, on the beach, t 024 702 5200 (€15–20). As the name suggests, it's bites from the briny on the menu; try the seafood with rice.

Taverna Maria, at the eastern end of the strand. Best for atmosphere and popular with the local fishermen. Gold-toothed Maria will rustle you up a huge dish of small whitebait-style *marídes* or *kalamári* fresh from their caiques.

Zorba's. Popular beach eatery.

### Plátanos/Ag. Marína/Krithóni

Krithóni Paradise, in Krithóni, t 024 702 5120, f 024 702 4680; winter t 010 412 8247 (*B; exp*). Swish complex with references to traditional architecture; pool, landscaped gardens and piano bar. Very relaxing.

Eleftheria, in Plátanos, t 024 702 3550 (*C; mod*). Pleasant and quiet family apartments as well as decent doubles, owned by Antónis Kanáris of the local Laskarina Travel agency, confusingly unconnected with the British holiday company.

Nefeli Apartments, t 024 702 4001, f 024 702 2375 (*C; mod*). Tasteful, upmarket establishment designed by a woman architect.

Esperides, next to the Paradise, t 024 702 2537. A tasty taverna.

Glaros. Corners the pizza market.

Kapaniri, in Ag. Marína. The place to sample a selection of *mezédes* with your *ouzo*.

Neromylos, just outside town. Newly opened and popular with locals and tourists alike for its traditional food.

### Álinda

Ara, t 024 702 4140, f 024 702 4194 (*C; mod*). Set up high with lofty views of both 'seas'; studios and apartments, restaurant, pool and Internet access.

Archonitkó Angelou, t 024 702 2749, f 024 702 4403 (*C; mod*). Built in 1895, lovingly restored and set in a cool, flowery garden.

Boulafendis Bunglalows, t 024 702 3515, f 024 702 4533 (*C; mod*). Pleasant, spacious studio development around a traditional mansion and pool-bar area.

Chryssoula, t 024 702 2451 (*C; mod*). Bright white studios overlooking a pool and the sea, 300m away.

Marilen, t 024 702 4100, *marilen@otenet.gr* (*C; mod*). Studios overlooking a pool-bar area, with a convenient mini-market.

Papafotis, t 024 702 2247 (*inexp*). Friendly owner; clean rooms and studios; the ones facing the mountains are fanned by the *meltémi* and are, thus, cooler when it swelters.

Finikas, t 024 702 2695. An old seaside favourite.

Álinda, t 024 702 3266. The best taverna for traditional fare, served on the veranda or in the courtyard.

## Entertainment and Nightlife

There are a number of cultural events during the summer months, incl. performances by the **Léros Theatre Group** and **Artemis**, a society dedicated to the revival of the island dances in beautiful traditional costumes.

*Bouzouki* club, on the road up to Plefoútis.

Savanna, in Pantéli at the end of the harbour. A cool bar. Pantéli also has a disco.

Nectar and Café Continent. Another couple of decent watering-holes.

Apothiki and Apokalipsi, in Ag. Marína. Both are happening places.

Faros, in Ag. Marína. Plays great international music.

Seagull. Mellow café/bar with marble tables on the port and good *frappés*.

Palatino, in Alínda. Waterfront bars such as this cater for a range of musical predilections. Succumb to a sundae with good music and the live Greek variety on summer weekends.

Cosmopolitan. Also offers live music and international DJs in season.

Puerto Club, in Lakki. For a bit of a dance, locals and tourists head here.

Greek, Lakkí would have been one of his favourite sets. The streets are perfectly paved and wide enough to accommodate several lanes of traffic, although they're usually empty except for a few lone bikers rumbling through, while what remains of Mussolini's dream town, a tribute to Italian Rationalism and the International Style, crumbles away, dilapidated but still weirdly compelling. The grandiose cinema and school are defunct, as is the old Hotel Roma, later the **Leros Palace**, now stuffed with litter. Lakkí's style was dubbed 'Ignored Internationalism' by Greek scholars when the Lerians decided to abandon the town and make the more convivial Plátanos the capital. Many islanders commute to Lakkí to work in the three mental hospitals, set up during the Italian occupation across the bay. These days the park around the institutions is open to visitors; one building was intended as the Duce's summer retreat.

Near the waterfront there's a monument to the many who perished in 1943 when a Greek ship, the *Queen Olga*, was bombed by German planes and sank in Lakkí's harbour. A path leading up from the jetty goes to the nearest beach at **Kouloúki**, with a taverna and unofficial camping under the pines. At **Lépida**, across the harbour, the **Moní Panagía** is built on the ruins of an old lighthouse, and further south, overlooking **Xirókambos** (ΞΗΡΟΚΑΜΠΟΣ), is the fort **Paliokástro**, built near an older fortification dating back to the 3rd century BC. The church inside has mosaics, and Xirókambos itself, a simple fishing village, has a pleasant sandy beach to the west. In summer the caique goes over to Myrtiés on Kálymnos once a day. There are also secluded pebbly coves accessible from a track beside the chapel.

# Pantéli, Plátanos and Ag. Marína

Up the tree-lined hill from Lakkí, it's only 3km to the very popular coarse sandy beach of **Vromólithos** ('Dirty Rock'), with sunbeds and tavernas, prettily closed in by deeply wooded hills. There are more places to stay just around the bay at **Pantéli** (ΠΑΝΤΕΛΙ), a working fishing village by day with its little harbour full of caiques and passing yachts, and by night the rendezvous of Léros' seafood-lovers, with tables spilling on to the small, tree-fringed beach.

Up hill, the capital **Plátanos** (ΠΛΑΤΑΝΟΣ) is as near the centre of Léros as possible. A pretty place with a smattering of Neoclassical houses mixed in with traditional ones, it has views over Pantéli that are especially stunning at night. Overhead the ancient *acropolis* was taken over by the **Kástro**, a Byzantine fortress renovated by the Venetians, the Knights and the Greek military, who have recently upped sticks for another hill. A winding, rough asphalt road rises to the top, but the alternative 370 steps, lined by houses with fragrant flower gardens, will make you feel more righteous. From the top, the 'four seas' of Léros are spread at your feet: the bays of Pantéli, Ag. Marína, Gourná and Lakkí. Within the walls, the church of the **Megalóchari Kyrás Kástrou** (*open 8.30–12.30 and Wed, Sat and Sun 3.30–7.30*) houses a miraculous icon of the Virgin. The story goes that during the Turkish occupation the icon set sail from Constantinople on board a boat lit by a sacred candle, and turned up on Léros. The inhabitants, led by the bishop, carried it in great procession to the cathedral. The next day, however, the icon had vanished and the Turkish captain of the Kástro found it, candle still blazing, in his gunpowder store, even though the door had been locked. The icon was taken back to the cathedral, but the following nights decamped to the arsenal again and again, until the Turkish governor was convinced it was a miracle and gave the storeroom to the Christians. They cleaned it up, and the wilful icon has been happy ever since. **Ag. Marína** (ΑΓ. MAPINA), the seaside extension of Plátanos, is easily reached by the main street, Ódos Xarami, but if you want to avoid the motor- bike Grand Prix, take the quiet lane that runs parallel down to the pottery. Ag. Marína is a windswept harbour, full of fishermen and excursion boats from Lípsi and Pátmos; there are tavernas, and accommodation up the road at **Krithóni**.

## Álinda and the North

**Álinda** (ΑΛΙΝΤΑ), once the old commercial port of Léros, is the island's oldest resort and principal package destination, although still low-key by Kos standards. There's a long sandy beach, with water sports and seafront tavernas. The pretty mosaics of an Early Christian basilica, **Panagía Galatiani**, may be seen in the forecourt of the town hospice. Nearby, the immaculate **British War Cemetery**, where 183 soldiers lie, looks out over the crystal bay – next to a motorbike rental shop, where boys the age that they died are known as the *kamikazi*. Léros has strong links with Egypt as many nota- bles fled to Cairo in the twenties, and Álinda's folly, the **Bellini Tower**, was built by one of them, Paríssis Bellínis; it now houses a good **Historic and Folk Museum** (*open daily 10–1 and 6–9; adm*). North of Alínda, a track leads to the secluded beaches at **Panagíes** and sandy **Kryfós**, where you can skinny-dip. There's a large sandy beach just over the isthmus at **Gourná**, but it tends to be windblown; you're better off seeking out one of the small coves leading to Léros' answer to Corfu's Mouse Island, **Ag. Isidóros**, a white chapel perched on an islet reached by a causeway. If you fancy a long walk off road, there are sandy beaches at **Ag. Nikólaos** further along the coast.

From Alínda there's a road north to **Parthéni** ('the Virgins'), former centre of guinea fowl worship, now a military base and used in the 1960s as a detention centre for political dissidents. Above, only a few ruins remain of the ancient **Temple of Artemis** (near the present church of Ag. Kyrás) but they still enjoy a superb setting, where you can linger under a sacred myrtle tree. There's a popular family beach at **Plefoúti**, in a lake-like bay, while over the headland at **Kioúra** there are quiet pebble coves reached via the chapel gates. You can easily do a round-island trip by car past **Drymónas** with lovely coves and an oleander gorge, then over the mountain back to Lakkí.

## Níssyros (ΝΙΣΥΡΟΣ)

In the great war between gods and giants, one of the casualties was the fiery Titan Polyvotis, who so irked Poseidon that the sea god ripped off a chunk of Kos and hurled it on top of him as he attempted to swim away. This became the island of Níssyros, and the miserable Polyvotis, pinned underneath, sighs and fumes, unable to escape.

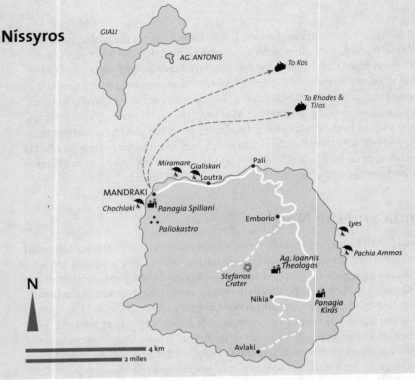

# Níssyros

The story is geologically sound: Níssyros was indeed once part of Kos, and one of the craters of its volcano, the only one in the Dodecanese, is named after the giant, still struggling to break free. Níssyros sits on the same volcanic line as Áegina, Páros, Antíparos, Mílos, Santoríni and Kos. Almost round, the island was once crowned by a 4,593ft peak. When it erupted in 1422, the centre imploded, forming the fertile Lakkí plain, which looks like a moonscape in places with its ashy slag heaps and yellow sulphurous rocks. Dormant these days – the last eruption was in 1933 – the volcano dominates the island's character as well as its tourist industry. Its rich soil holds tight to water so Níssyros is lush and green, its terraces thick with olives, figs, citrus groves and almond trees (someone once called it the Polo mint island – green outside, white inside with a hole in the middle). Quarrying the gypsum and harvesting the pumice, both on Níssyros and its little sister islet Giali, keep the ecomony going year round. The coast is a jumble of black volcanic boulders and pebbly or grey sandy beaches, and although Giali is an industrial centre, it also has some lovely golden sands. Drinking water is a problem on Níssyros, and although there is a desalination plant, it isn't always working and tap water is ghastly.

## Mandráki

Life revolves around the cafeteria on the quay in **Mandráki** (MANΔPAKI), the capital and port, where agents set up tables selling tickets for trips to the volcano and buses

# Getting There and Around

**By sea**: ferry several times a week to Kos, Kálymnos, Tílos, Sými and Rhodes, and 1–2 a week to Astypálaia, Léros, Pátmos, Piraeus, Sými, Sýros, Páros and Náxos; daily **taxi boat** and *Nissiros Express* to Kardámena (Kos); **hydrofoil**: almost daily from Rhodes and Tílos, regular but variable services to Kos, Kálymnos and Sými. You can hire a **caique** from **Manolis Melianos**, **t** 024 204 1221 or **Manolis Manis**, **t** 024 204 1218. **Port authority**: **t** 024 203 1222.

**By road**: there is a regular bus service, **t** 024 203 1204, from the harbour to Páli via White Beach but buses for the village of Emborió and Nikiá leave early morning and return mid-afternoon only. Níssyros also has 2 **taxi** firms, **Bobby's**, **t** 024 203 1460, and **Irene's**, **t** 024 203 1474. A round-island tour will cost about €20; to the volcano €14.

# Tourist Information

**Enetikon Travel**, on the right as you head up from the harbour, **t** 024 2031 180, **f** 024 203 1168. Particularly helpful, offering a range of excursions.

# Festivals

**23 April**: Ag. Geórgios.
**29 June**: Páli.
**27 July**: Nikiá.
**15 Aug**: Mandráki.
**25 Sept**: Nikiá.

# Where to Stay

**Níssyros** ✉ 85303

It can be very difficult to find a room in July and Aug and there is no official campsite so book ahead. Prices tend to be lower than on the other Dodecanese islands.

**III Brothers**, by the sea, **t** 024 203 1344 (*mod*). Pleasant place with a decent restaurant.

**Haritos**, over the road, **t** 024 203 1322, **f** 024 203 1122 (*C; mod*). Friendly pension with spacious rooms and sea-view balconies.

**Hellenis**, in Páli, **t** 024 2031 453 (*mod*). Has a decent restaurant.

**Miramare Apartments**, on the coast road to Páli, **t** 024 203 1100, **f** 024 203 1254 (*mod*). New and luxurious by island standards, beautifully appointed with a sea-view terrace.

**Porfyris**, further into the village opposite the orchard, **t** 024 203 1376 (*C; mod, incl. breakfast*). The most comfortable and well-priced bet with a pool and views to Gialí.

**White Beach**, at Gialiskári, **t** 024 203 1497/8, **f** 024 203 1389 (*C; mod*). Ungainly, but right on the sands – which are black.

**Xenon**, in Mandráki harbour, **t** 024 203 1011 (*mod*). By the seaside; handy for ferries.

**I Drossia**, **t** 024 203 1328 (*inexp*). One of the cheapest in the village, and the waves crash on the black rocks beneath your balcony.

# Eating Out

Níssyros has 13 tavernas and 10 bars at the last count, ranging from waterside tavernas to village favourites in Mandráki's Elikioméni Square.

**Angistri**, in Páli, on the far edge of the beach. Mama makes a knock-out moussaka.

**Aphroditi**. Excellent with home-made desserts.

**Captain's Taverna**, along the front. Excellent home-made dishes incl. mouthwatering *pittiá* and wild caper salad made to Granny's recipe.

**Hellenis**. With music when the owner's husband is playing his *lýra*.

**Irini**, in lively Platéia Elikioméni, the centre of Mandráki nightlife. Good value and a wide menu from *laderá* to roasts.

*Ouzerie* **Paradeiso**, just beyond the harbour. Set back off the road in a lovely garden and aptly named; it's great for an atmospheric evening aperitif.

**Panorama**. Gets very busy at night so you could have a long wait for a table. The food is good but a bit pricey.

**Taverna Nikiá**, at Nikiá. Great views over the crater and out to Kos.

**Taverna Níssyros**, spilling out into a narrow alley in the village centre. One of the most popular and authentic eateries with its vine-clad canopy and jolly atmosphere. It's packed at night; the food is good but portions small.

wait to take groups arriving on the excursion boats. A short walk from the quay leads down the narrow road towards the village and a wide choice of seaside tavernas. Despite the boatloads of day-trippers from Kos, the centre of Mandráki manages to retain its charm, especially in the higgledy-piggledy **Langadáki** district. The little lanes, cobbled or picked out with pebble mosaic patterns, twist under the wooden balconies of the tall, narrow, brightly painted houses. Designed to confound marauding pirates, there's still an air of being closed to outsiders, especially during siesta-time, with the shutters pulled tight over the traditional embroidered curtains. But at night what looked like ordinary houses, suddenly open up as shops by day, selling drapery and baby clothes.

Seawards the lanes aim for **Plateía Ilikioméni** with its bars, while others weave inland past the public orchard or *kámbo* into a succession of shady squares. Signs point the way to major attractions: up to the ancient **Kástro** (or **Enetikon**), taken over in 1315 by the Knights, and, within its walls, the monastery of 15th-century **Panagía Spilianí**, Our Lady of the Cave (*open daily 10.30–3*). A finely carved iconostasis holds a venerated icon of the Virgin, loaded with gold and silver; the church's fame grew after raiding Saracens failed to find its secret trove of silver, worked into the rich collection of Byzantine icons. There are guest rooms in the monastery and fantastic views from ruined walls out over the village at sunset.

On the stairway up to the monastery a small **Historical and Popular Museum** (*open when the owner's around*) houses various exhibits and a reconstructed traditional kitchen. Higher up, a rough path leads from the Langadáki quarter, crossing fields and olive groves to the 7th century BC Doric **Paliokástro**, a spectacular site with vast Cyclopean walls hewn from volcanic rock. The *acropolis* of ancient Níssyros, a mighty bastion, dates back 2,000 years and you can walk along the top of the wide walls – from where they used to pour boiling oil on attackers – and look out to Gialí and Kos.

### Beaches and Hot Springs Around Mandráki

There are a few sandy strands along the front, usually packed with trippers, and the nearest (but often windswept) to town is **Chochláki**, under the monastery cliffs, reached by a daisy-patterned pathway. The beach has blue-black volcanic pebbles and boulders, that give way to shale further along. A pen of pigs guarded by a watchdog occupy one end, while at the other there's a wacky beachcomber's house-cum-bar made from driftwood and all kinds of flotsam and jetsam. A 10-minute walk from Mandráki takes you to **Miramare** Beach, nicer for fish tavernas than bathing. Further along, **Gialiskári** (alias **White Beach**) is a better bet, with its black and white crystals, by the thermal spa of **Loutrá** (*open June to October*), where the hot springs straight from the volcano ease arthritis and rheumatism.

# Around the Island

Further along the coast the pretty fishing village of **Páli** (ΠΑΛΟΙ), has a succession of dark volcanic sandy beaches, some shaded by trees, and some rudimentary early

Christian catacombs. Fishing boats in the harbour are often surrounded by masses of bobbing pumice stones – great souvenirs for the bath. Páli has an incongruous central roundabout and good fish tavernas. Follow the beach road, hung over with fig trees, and you'll come to another spa in the throes of construction, which looks like an abandoned jail. In August the *meltémi* blows fiercely on Níssyros and the beaches can be littered with junk and rutting piglets. About an hour's walk, or 20 minutes by moped along the road brings you to the island's best beaches: **Lýes** with its Oasis cantina and free camping, and **Pachiá Ámmos** over the headland. With mining operations for a backdrop, the islets **Gialí** and **Ag. Antónis** have white crystal sand and are great for swimming and snorkelling, with their curious rocks; on the former is 'Miaoulis' Well', dug by the admiral's sailors in 1821 while hiding out from the Turks.

## Into the Volcano

The excursion not to be missed on Níssyros, however, is to the volcano (be sure to wear sturdy shoes). It has five craters – Polivótis, Aléxandros, Logothétis, Achilles and the biggest, Stéfanos, 80ft deep and 1,150ft across. Buses leave the port in succession as the tourist boats arrive; if you want more time and a bit of solitude, take the village bus to **Nikiá** (*see* below) in the morning and walk down. There are wonderful views from the winding road, where the greenery and neat terraces offer a stunning contrast to the vast plain below, an extra-terrestrial landscape of pale greys and yellows, the smell of sulphur so pungent that you can almost see cartoon stink lines curling up out of the crater. After passing several geothermal pools, the bus stops near the great fuming heart of **Stéfanos**. A slippery zigzag path descends to the floor of the crater, with bubbling fumaroles all around. You can feel the great heat and turmoil of the gases beneath the crust; in some places the crust is so fragile that your foot could go through, so if you have children in tow make sure they don't stray. After the steam and the stench, you can join the queues to quench your thirst at the café on the rim of the crater.

## Emborió and Nikiá

The villages of Emborió and Nikiá cling to the rim of the crater. **Emborió** (ΕΜΠΟΡΕΙΟΣ) above Páli (linked by an old cobbled pathway) only has a handful of inhabitants who haven't emigrated to Australia or America, but the population rises in the summer, as houses are being restored as holiday homes. Many of these come with a free mod con in the basement: natural volcanic saunas. If you want to partake, there's a public sauna in a cave on the outskirts of the village. A ruined Byzantine fort offers memorable views of the crater 1,000ft below. In contrast pretty **Nikiá** (ΝΙΚΑΙΑ) is lively with dazzling blue and white paintwork, bright gardens and views over Tílos as well as the crater in all its ghostly enormity far below. The village square has a lovely *choklákia* mosaic and there are a couple of *kafeneía* and a taverna, plus a hostel if you want to stay. The path down to the volcano is steep but clearly marked and takes about 40 minutes. On the way, watch out for the **Calanna** Rock, said to be a witch who was turned to stone; a safer place to rest is the **Monastery of Ag. Ioánnis Theológos**, with shady trees and picnic benches as well as icons and frescoes.

# Pátmos (ΠΑΤΜΟΣ)

Of all the Greek islands, dramatically beautiful Pátmos is the most sacred to Christians, both Orthodox and Western alike; here St John the Theologian received the vision he described in the *Apocalypse*, or *Book of Revelations*, and here, in the 11th century, the Blessed Christódoulos founded a monastery more wealthy and influential than any in Greece except for Mount Áthos. Although by day the harbour is thronged with day-trippers and cruise passengers being hauled up to the monastery, and there are plenty of cafés, restaurants and stylish gift shops to make sure they don't leave thirsty or empty-handed, Pátmos still maintains something of its otherworldly feel, especially in the evening, and outside July and August. But even in the height of summer it maintains certain standards: there's a law banning 'promiscuity and looseness', and although it may seem appropriate in theory, don't come to the island of the Apocalypse to rave, rave, rave against the dying of the light.

## History

Pátmos was inhabited from the 14th century BC, its main settlement near present-day Skála and its *acropolis* and fortifications at Kastélli. It was a subject to Asia Minor

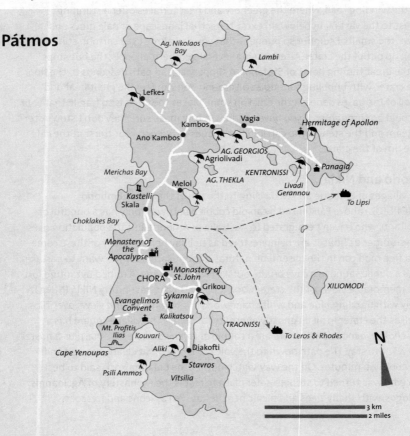

Pátmos

and not terribly important. In AD 95, however, the island's destiny was forever altered with the arrival of St John, the beloved apostle of Jesus (known variously as the Theologian, the Evangelist or the Divine). After the Crucifixion he spent most of his life in Ephesus as Jesus' appointed guardian of his mother Mary; tradition has it that during Domitian's persecution of Christians he was transported to Rome and cast into a pot of boiling oil, from which he emerged without a burn, before being exiled to desolate Pátmos, where he lived in a cave, perhaps wrote his gospel, and received his end-of-the-world *Revelations*. He may have only spent a year or so on Pátmos before returning to Ephesus, but in that time John provided not only a fairly accurate prophecy of the fall of the Roman Empire, but enough material to keep fire-eating preachers and literal-minded crank interpreters going for the next 1,900 years.

Barren volcanic Pátmos was abandoned from the 7th century until the late 11th century, when in Constantinople things were going badly for Alexis Comnenus – 'born to the purple', but so battered by fate and politics, he had nothing but the blues. Nevertheless, a saintly hermit named Christódoulos predicted his ascent to the throne, and the miserable Alexis promised him a wish should it come true. Of course it did, and in 1088 Christódoulos asked the Emperor for the island of Pátmos, to found a monastery on the site of an ancient Temple of Artemis. Emperor Alexis provided not only the island but the building funds, as well as tax exemptions and the right to engage in sea trade.

The island remained under absolute control of the monastery for centuries, against poverty, pirates and a thousand other afflictions. The Venetian Dukes of Pátmos were content to leave it as an autonomous monastic state. The Turks respected its imperial charter, leaving Pátmos to flourish from the 16th to the 19th century; its school of theology and liberal arts, founded in 1713, was one of the few able to function in the open. Monastic control lessened as the islanders took over the sea trade, and in 1720 the monks and laymen divided the land between them. After that, Pátmos prospered to the extent that it established colonies in the Balkans, although the invention of the steamship nipped its imperial ambitions in the bud.

# Skála

All boats drop anchor at **Skála** (ΣΚΑΛΑ), the island's main resort, and a smart and upmarket one it is too, thanks to the cruise ships. One of the first things you'll see in Skála is a statue of Protergatis Xanthos Emmanuel, who led an uprising against the Turks in 1821. Skála didn't even exist until that year, so fearsome were the pirate raids. Near the beach, marked by a red buoy, is a reminder of another troublemaker, the evil magician Yenoúpas, who at the urging of priests from the Temple of Apollo challenged St John to a duel of miracles. Yenoúpas' miracle was to dive into the sea and bring back effigies of the dead; John's was to ask God to petrify the submerged magician, which abruptly ended the contest. Even petrified, Yenoúpas is a menace to shipping and stinks of overpowering sulphur, but all attempts to dislodge him so far have failed miserably.

# Getting There and Around

**By sea**: **ferries** connect daily with Piraeus, Kálymnos, Léros, Kos and Rhodes; 4 times a week with Sámos, 3 times a week with Ikaría and Agathónissi, and twice a week with Arki, once with Níssyros, Náxos, Páros, Sýros Chálki, Kárpathos, Kássos; **hydrofoil**: regular summer services to Léros (Ag. Marína), Kálymnos, Kos, Lipsí, Kálymnos, Ikaría and Sámos' 3 ports; **excursion boats** leave Skála for most beaches as well as to Arki, Maráthi and Sámos (Pythagório) and Lipsí. To hire a **caique** contact **Apollon**, t 024 703 1324. **Port authority**, t 024 703 1231/4131.

**By road**: **buses** depart from the ferry dock in Skála to Chóra, Gríkou and Kámbos. **Taxis**, t 024 703 1225, from the rank on central square; to avoid being ripped off, agree on prices before setting out.

# Tourist Information

**Municipal Tourist Information Office**: in Skála, t 024 703 1666/1158. Very helpful and has a good range of leaflets and timetables.
**Astoria Travel**, in Skála, t 024 703 1205, *www.astoria.gr*. Help with accommodation.

# Festivals

**Maundy Thursday**: Niptíras ceremony.
**8 May**: service for St John.
**26 Sept**: another service for St John.
**15 Aug**: Kámbos.

# Where to Stay and Eat

## Pátmos ✉ 85500

### Skála

Owners meet the ferries offering *domátia*, and on the whole the rooms are better value than the hotels, although beware – many are out in the boondocks.

**Romeos**, 500m from the port, t 024 703 1962, *romeosh@12net.gr* (*B; exp–mod*). Traditional style rooms, all with sunset views; also a pretty pool.

**Skála**, 2mins from the ferry, t 024 703 1343, *skalahtl@12net.gr* (*B; exp–mod*). Set in attractive gardens with a pool and restaurant.

**Blue Bay**, on the road to Gríkou, t 024 703 1165, *bluebayhotel@yahoo.com* (*C; mod*). All the mod cons in a quiet waterside spot. *Open April–Oct*.

**Galini**, in the Choklaká district overlooking the bay, t 024 703 1240 (*C; mod*). A little upmarket.

**Hellinis**, right on the waterfront, t 024 703 1275, *skalahtl@12net.gr* (*C; mod*). Nice en suite rooms with views of the monastery. *Open April–Oct*.

**Kasteli**, t 024 703 1361, f 024 703 1656 (*C; mod*). Commands fine views from the upper part of town.

**Summer**, in Choklaká, t 024 703 1769 (*C; mod*).

**Asteri**, by the harbour, t 024 703 2465 (*mod–inexp*). Pleasant garden setting. Simple rooms with fridge; some have air-con.

**Byzance**, on the edge of Skála, t 024 703 1052 (*C; mod–inexp*). Roof garden with a small restaurant and lovely views over the port.

**Efi**, at Kastélli, t 024 703 2500, f 024 703 2700 (*C; mod–inexp*). Comfortable rooms.

**Maria**, in Choklaká, t 024 703 1201 (*C; mod–inexp*).

**Australis**, t 024 703 1576 (*inexp*). Friendly and prettily decorated.

**Arion Café**, on the waterfront. Good place to watch the world go by over a nightcap.

**Aspri**, at Aspri Beach, t 024 703 2240 (*€16–22*). Fish taverna with a wonderful view of the castle; specialities include lobster with pasta and *kalamári* risotto.

**Benetos**, just outside town, on the waterfront, t 024 703 3089 (*€16–22*). Head here if your

Behind Skála one of the world's largest desalination plants has been replaced by a reservoir, but water can still be short in high summer. You can also hike up to the site of the ancient city, **Kastélli**, in about 20 minutes give or take the heat, a walk rewarded more by stunning views than any bits of old stone. The remains of a Hellenistic wall and the chapel of **Ag. Konstantínos** are perched on the summit. Go in the evening for a wonderful sunset.

taste buds tingle for the unexpected. Chef Benetos flies over from his winter stint in top restaurants in Miami to create some of the most original dishes on the islands.

**Byblos**. Fashionable evening watering hole.

**Grigoris**, opposite the ferry dock. Tasty, cheap and cheerful with excellent charcoal-grilled fish and meat.

**Taverna O Vrachos**, north of the waterfront. Good for fish.

## Chóra

**Archontika Irini**, t 024 703 2826 (*exp*) Old stone mansion, with traditional furniture, fireplaces and wood burning stove, sleeps 6–10.

**Aloni**. Traditional *bouzouki* and dancing in the evenings.

**Olympia**, Plateía Ag. Leviás, t 024 703 1543. Good Greek food, and plenty to look at while you wait for it to come.

**Patmian House**, t 024 703 1180 (€*30–40*). You'll definitely need the phone number for reservations – this place is booked solid in season by visiting dignitaries and Athenian glitterati entertaining their Hollywood counterparts. Excellent local dishes on the menu.

**Vangelis**, Plateía Ag. Leviás, (follow the little signs), t 024 703 1967 3 (€*16–24*). Lovely view from the terrace, but no culinary surprises here; solid Greek fare, although bigger boned bodies might find the portions rather small.

## Méloi (Giordami)

**Porto Scoutari**, overlooking the bay, t 024 703 3123, f 024 703 3175 (*B; exp*). Pretty apartments, romantic and quiet, with big beds, TVs, a pool and a regular minibus service into civilization.

**Rooms and Taverna Méloi**, known to all as **Stefanos**, almost on the beach, t 024 703 1888. Basic facilities, but serving good, reasonably priced food.

**Campsite**, t 024 703 1821. Bamboo-shaded pitches, mini-market, cafeteria, cooking and washing facilities.

## Kámbos

**Pátmos Paradise**, 200m from Kámbos, t 024 703 2624, f 024 703 2740 (*B; exp*). In traditional style, this complex offering the works: an à la carte restaurant, buffet breakfast, swimming pool, squash, tennis courts, sauna and fitness centre. There are also very attractive rooms to retire to after working up a sweat.

## Gríkou

**Petra Hotel and Apartments**, just back from the beach, t 024 703 1035 (*C; lux–exp*). Huge panoramic terraces; air-con rooms with minibars and phones.

**Golden Sun**, overlooking the bay, t 024 703 2318, f 024 703 2319 (*B; mod*). Family-run and friendly.

**Joanna Hotel and Apartments**, t 024 703 1031, f 024 703 2031, book in Athens t 010 981 2246 (*mod*). Newly renovated; a nicely-done complex with self-catering, air-con studios and apartments.

**Athena**, on the hillside, t 024 703 1859, f 024 703 2859. An attractive, family-run place with lovely views from its room balconies and it isn't block-booked in the summer by package companies.

**Panorama Apartments**, by the sea, t 024 703 1209, *panorama-patmos@excite.com*. Old favourites renovated in 1999. Minibus service.

**Flisvos**, up on the hill. Small and family-run, taverna with well-cooked Greek staples, fish dishes at affordable prices and a few rooms (*inexp*).

**Stamatis**, near the harbour, t 024 703 1302. Family-run taverna serving traditional favourites such as moussaka and stuffed tomatoes.

# Chóra

From Skála you can see whitewashed **Chóra** (XOPA) clinging to the mighty castle walls of the monastery. Buses and taxis make the ascent in a few minutes, but if you have the time it isn't too strenuous to walk up the old cobbled path from Skála, to enjoy the ever-widening panorama spread out below. Chóra is a lovely, almost

Cycladic village, with a maze of narrow alleyways, masses of chapels and mansions built by the owners of Pátmos' merchant fleet. Try to get a glimpse inside these: most have startlingly lavish interiors.

## Monastery of St John the Theologian

*t 024 703 1398; opening times vary; at the time of writing May–Nov daily 8–2 and Tues, Thurs, Sun 4–6; adm for the Treasury. Get there first thing in the morning before the cruise passengers. Shorts prohibited, women must wear skirts.*

The usual gauntlet of trinket-vendors marks the entrance to Pátmos' prime attraction, and once you get past them and through the walls that stood up to every invader and marauder for centuries, expect, alas, a grumpy welcome; apparently no one told the monks when they took their vows that dedicating their lives to God meant spending their days as museum guards and dress code enforcers.

The intimate scale and intricate little corridors are delightful – but can easily become unbearably crowded with groups marching through. A charming court of 1698 incorporates the outer, or exo-narthex of the church; just inside this is the chapel-tomb of its founder, the Blessed Christódoulos. Designed as a Greek cross set in a square, the church still retains its original marble floor; its icon of St John was a gift from Alexis Comnenus. Frescoes cover every surface, although only those in the 12th-century **Chapel of the Theotókos** are as old as the church; others are in the Refectory, off the inner courtyard. The **Treasury Museum** displays the original monastery deed – a *chrysobul*, signed and sealed, from the Emperor; an inscription from the Temple of Artemis, stating that Orestes sought refuge here from the Furies; exquisite gifts to the monastery – gold and silver crosses, croziers and stoles; superb icons, including a rare one from the 11th century, brought here by Christódoulos, and ship pendants made of diamonds and emeralds donated by Catherine the Great. The library contains hundreds of rare codices and manuscripts, including the 6th-century *Codex Porphyrius*, St Mark's gospel written on purple vellum, but may only be visited with permission from the abbot. Lastly, if it's open, climb up to the roof terrace for a commanding view over the Aegean.

## Around Chóra and down to the Monastery of the Apocalypse

After the monastery, you could spend a day finding the 40 or so churches wedged in the narrow lanes of Chóra: especially good are the **Convent of Zoodóchos Pigí** (1607) with fine frescoes and icons (*open mornings and late afternoons*), the **Convent of the Evangelismós** (*follow the signposts west of town, open mornings*) and 11th-century Ag. Dimítrios, contemporary with the monastery, but likely to be locked like the others. Nor is hunting out the caretaker easy, as Chóra is one of those very old, silent places where the streets always seem to be deserted, especially once the trippers have gone.

This changes dramatically on Orthodox Maundy Thursday, when Chóra is packed with visitors and even TV crews for the *Niptíras* ceremony, when the abbot re-enacts Christ's washing of his disciples' feet – a rite once performed by the Byzantine emperors. Depending on the weather, it takes place either in Plateía Ag. Leviás or

Plateía Lóza. It's a short walk down from Chóra to the **Monastery of the Apocalypse** (*open Mon, Tues, Thurs and Sun, 8–2 and 4–6; other days 8–2*), where a stair covered with flower pots leads down to the cave where St John lived and dreamed, and dictated what he saw to his follower, Próchoros. The cave has been converted into a church, where you can see the rock where the good saint rested his head and hand (he must have been a contortionist to manage it), and the massive overhanging roof, split in three sections by the voice of God, symbolizing the Holy Trinity. If you're walking up from Skála, the cave is marked with signs saying ΑΠΟΚΑΛΥΨΟΣ.

## Beaches and Villages around Pátmos

The closest beach to Skála, **Méloi**, is 2km north and pleasantly tree-shaded, but tends to get crowded; if you want something more peaceful if less shady, look for the sign to **Agriolivádi**, a quiet, if rocky cove with some sand and a pair of tavernas. Pátmos is great walking country, with much of it around the dramatic shore here, with **Áno Kámbos** at the centre of the network. Surrounded by Pátmos' most fertile fields, it is the only other real village on the island and the end of the bus line; many long-term residents rent houses in the valley, where a hippy commune thrived back in the seventies before being evicted by the anti-promiscuity squads. There are beaches in every direction: one at least will be sheltered from the prevailing winds. **Kámbos** to the east is popular and sandy, with watersports; **Léfkes** to the west is often wild and windswept; to the north, **Lámbi**, also reached by excursion boat, is famous for its subtle, multi-coloured pebbles. Further east there are secluded **Vagiá** and **Livádi Gerannoú**, with shade and a cantina. If you need a goal for a stroll, there's the 19th-century **Hermitage of Apollon**, near a small mineral spring.

Roads from Skála and Chóra go to Pátmos' principal beach resort, **Gríkou** (ΓΡΙΚΟΥ), overlooking a beautiful bay, which has windsurfers and water skis for hire. On the south end of the bay, the **Kalikátsou Rock** has carved rooms and stairs in unlikely places and may have been the 11th-century hermitage mentioned in the writings of Christódoulos. Inland, at **Sykamiá**, there's an old Roman bath said to have been used by St John to baptize his converts. The south road peters out at the **Stávros** chapel, at Diakofti, where Pátmos is only a few hundred yards across. There's a beach here, but a half-hour's tramp (or caique from Skála) will take you to lovely **Psilí Ámmos**, with fine white sand. West of here, a seaside grotto on **Cape Yenoúpas** was the home of the evil magician (*see* above), and even today it's unpleasantly hot and smelly inside.

## Lipsí/Lipsos (ΛΕΙΨΟΙ)

Lipsí is a little gem of an island midway between Léros and Pátmos, and it's not surprising that Odysseus put off his homecoming for seven years to linger here, beguiled by the charms of the enchantress Calypso. If opinions differ on whether Lipsí really is Homer's isle of Ogygia, no one can deny that it has a certain unworldly magic. For centuries most of the land was owned by the monastery on Pátmos, and the blue

# Getting There

**By sea**: **ferry** connections 3 times a week with Piraeus, Sámos, Pátmos, Léros and Kálymnos, twice a week with Kos and Agathónissi, Arkí, once a week with Níssyros, Tílos, Sými, Rhodes and Ikaría; daily **excursion boats** *Anna Express* and *Rena II* to Ag. Marína, Léros and Skála, Pátmos; **hydrofoils** from Pythagório, Sámos (closest air connection) Kos, Kálymnos, Léros, and Pátmos. Boat excursions around the island and to Arkí, Maráthi and Makrónissi caves. You can also hire your own caique from Manolis Melianos, **t** 024 704 1221. **Port authority**: **t** 024 704 1240.

**By road**: Lipsí's old fleet of pickup trucks-cum-taxis has been replaced with a new municipal **bus** service in the harbour square, with almost hourly departures in high season as far as Platís Gialós Beach and Katsadiá Beach.

# Tourist Information

**Town Hall**, **t** 024 704 1209.
**Laid Back Holidays**, **t** 024 704 1141, **f** 024 704 1343, *www.otenet.gr/lbh*. Friendly Nico and Anna Christódoulou are a mine of information about Lipsí, and change money at bank rates, sell newspapers, and hire out motorbikes and mopeds.

# Festivals

**23–24 Aug**: Pilgrims from the surrounding islands pour in for 'the ninth day of the Virgin'.
**Mid-Aug**: the islanders also host a wine festival.

# Where to Stay

## Lipsí ✉ 85001
Landladies still meet the boats if they have a free room.
**Aphrodite**, right on the beach, 100m from the port, **t** 024 704 1000, **f** 024 704 1002 (*mod*). All rooms kitted out with kitchenettes and balconies.

**Kalypso**, on the harbourside, **t** 024 704 1242 (*C, inexp*). With an information service.
**Glaros Rooms**, **t** 024 704 1360. A good bet, perched high with views over the bay.
**Pension Manolis**, south of the harbour, **t** 024 704 1306. Overlooks the fishing boats.
**Rena's Rooms**, **t** 024 704 1242. Immaculate; owned by John and Rena, who lived in America and run the *Rena II*.
**Studios Dream**, past Lendoú Beach, **t** 024 704 1271. Rooms have kitchenettes and balconies.
**Studios Kalymnos**, on the far side of the village, a 2min walk from the centre, **t** 024 704 1102/1141. Peaceful, set in a garden and lovely views over the countryside.

# Eating Out

There's little to choose between the waterfront tavernas, all offering reasonable fish (incl. lobster) and oven dishes: among the specialites are *revythokeftédes* and fish *croquettes* in mustard sauce. Places nearest the day-boats tend to be more touristy. Several *kafeneía* do breakfast; visit the bakery for superb cheese pies and breads.

**Asprakis** *Ouzerie*, near the excursion boats. Doubling as shop and bar; great for local atmosphere, grilled octopus and *ouzo*.
**Kali Kardia**, towards the ferry dock. Popular, with a lovely terrace and cooking by the redoubtable Vassiléa and family.
**Kalypso Restaurant**. Under shady vines, run by the famous Mr Mungo, with a certain dishevelled style.
**Maria**. Excellent. Less frenetic at lunchtime.
**Taverna O Theologos**. Specializes in fish, and prices won't break the bank.

# Entertainment and Nightlife

If you're a party animal, forget it – unless there's a wedding, when the whole island celebrates with a joyous all-night dance marathon. There's a new club at the far end of the harbour that plays Greek music all year round. Otherwise, the action centres on the waterfront, where someone might start gently hammering their *santoúri*.

domes of the Cycladic-style churches from that period bubble over a horizon of soft, green hills, while the village houses are painted in wild fauvist colours.

Lipsí is one of an archipelago of tiny islets, and its lovely beaches a magnet for day excursions from Pátmos and Léros, yet once the trippers have gone it quickly regains its tranquillity. Above all, it's a great place to do nothing. The 650 inhabitants are friendly and go about their lives as they have for centuries, fishing and farming. Lipsí is well-known for its special cheese made from sheep's and goat's milk – there are more goats than people – even donkeys outnumber the wheeled transport.

## Around the Island

Lipsí village greets arrivals with a tidal splash of colour and a smattering of tavernas around the bay and odd front-room cafés which double as shops. Everything is neatly signposted from the harbour, and everything is kept new-pin bright, as if the locals were entering a best-kept island contest. If most of the trippers head straight for the beaches, you may want to follow the Greeks and first visit the famous blue-domed church of **Ag. Ioánnis** to pay your respects to its miraculous icon of the Panagía. The story goes that a woman prayed to the Virgin to help her son and the Virgin granted her prayer. Being poor, she had nothing to offer in return but a lily, which she humbly placed near the icon. In time the lily withered, but miraculously, on the day of the Virgin's acceptance into Heaven, 24 August, it sprang into full bloom and has flowered on that day ever since. The ancient lily stalk can clearly be seen under the glass of the icon and dutifully in early August it bears small white buds which burst into flower right on time. Dried flowers are also supposed to spring to life on the day at the **Panagía tou Chárou** chapel (Our Lady of Death (!) but actually named after the man who built it) which stands at Lipsí's highest point.

Opposite the church in the Dimarchíon there's the small if grandly titled **Nikoforeion Ecclesiastical Museum** (*open Mon–Fri 9.30–1.30 and 4–8, Sat and Sun 10–2*), a collection of motley stuff, from the ridiculous to a letter from Admiral Miaoúlis written to a cousin on the night of his famous sea battle. There is also a **carpet factory** to visit, one of a score set up across Greece employing young women in rural areas to work on the traditional looms, but all their handiwork is sold in Athens.

Lipsí is a miniature world, only six square miles, so you can walk across it in two hours, taking in its well-tended walled fields and thirty-odd blue and white chapels, as well as views of neighbouring islands Arkí, Maráthi and Agathónissi. The town beach at **Lendoú** is shaded by trees but gets busy with Greek families in high season, and you'll find more peaceful sands by walking over the dusty headland track to **Kámbos** or beyond to **Kimissí** and you could even have the sands to yourself. The buses will deposit you on the island's best-known beach, the white cove of **Platís Gialós** (3km) which has a pretty church and taverna, or take you south to **Katsadiá**, with its succession of sandy coves and a good taverna, Adonis, while on the east coast **Monodéndri** is the unofficial nudie beach.

There are vineyards in the valley beyond the town where a good local wine is produced. And with a bottle of this, and some octopus grilled at the harbourside, the island casts a gentle spell once the day-trippers have been herded away.

# Arkí (APKOI) and Maráthi (MAPAΘI)

**Arkí**, a hilly little island just 4km long and 1km wide with 40 inhabitants, sees occasional caiques from Pátmos and Lipsí as well as one or two ferries a week between Agathónissi, Kálymnos, Pátmos, Sámos, Léros and Lipsí. With its few scattered houses, it attracts yachts and adventurous travellers. Facilities are minimal – there's no place to change money, for instance, and water must be shipped in; a little solar plant provides some electricity. There are some quiet coves and a **Blue Lagoon**, if not a rival to Capri's, just as good for snorkelling and swimming in the vivid waters. The harbour of **Port Augusta** has two tavernas and the Taverna Asteria also has inexpensive rooms and the island's one phone (*t 024 703 2371*).

Even smaller **Maráthi** has a natural harbour popular with fishermen from surrounding islands as well as yachts, but no ferry calls in; once or twice a week excursion boats from Pátmos and Lipsí provide most of the transport and can strand you if the weather turns, so don't wait till the last moment if you have to catch a flight. Maráthi has a long sandy beach and two tavernas with rooms, **Pantelís Marathi Restaurant** (*t 024 703 2609; inexp*), run by Mr Pantelís from Arkí via Australia, who bases himself plus family on Maráthi for the summer, with comfortable, very reasonable en suite rooms and serving up tasty dishes; the second, **Mihalis Kavouras** (*t 024 703 1580; inexp*), is a bit more basic, with its own charm, owing to a Golgotha of goat skulls used for decoration in the trees. Goats leap all over the island and they're often on the menu as well.

# Agathónissi (ΑΓΑΘΟΝΗΣΙ)

Northeast of Pátmos, steep little Agathónissi (pop. 130) may be alphabetically the first Greek island but few people have ever heard of it, tucked up as it is next to Turkey. It may be the ticket if you've been seeking a very Greek island with a tad of civilization, or quiet sheltered coves to park the yacht.

### Around the Island

Literally 'thorny island', Agathónissi has its share of thorn bushes as well as other small trees, but water is scarce and limited to rainwater cisterns: bring enough money

## Getting There

**By sea**: the **ferry** *Níssos Kálymnos* links Agathónissi with Sámos (Pithagório), Pátmos, Lipsí, Léros, Kálymnos, and Kos, twice a week; there is a **hydrofoil** service once a week to Kos, Kálymnos, Léros (Ag Marína), Pátmos, and Sámos (Pythagório), the latter which also runs excursion boats to the island about once a week. **Port authority** (and police), near Megálo Chorió: t 024 702 3770.

## Where to Stay and Eat

**Agathónissi** ✉ 85001
**George's Taverna**, Ag. Giórgios, t 024 702 4385 (*inexp*). Also has excellent food.
**Maria Kamitsi**, Ag. Giórgios, t 024 702 3690 (*inexp*). Beautiful flower-filled garden.
**Theologia Yiameou**, Ag. Giórgios, t 024 702 3692 (*inexp*). With use of the kitchen.
**Dekatria Adelfia**. Serves good cheap food.
**Ioannis Taverna**. Excellent grilled fish.

for your stay and a bag of fresh fruit. The island has three villages, the port of **Ag. Giórgios**, pleasant **Megálo Chorió**, where most people live, and **Mikró Chorió**, with only about ten inhabitants, linked by a cement road and a rickety three-wheeler or maybe a van. Ag. Giórgios has a pebbly, grotty beach but there's a better one at **Spília**, a sheltered cove to the west. There are boat trips in high season to remote beaches, or else don stout shoes and walk: even paths are something of a luxury. There are the remains of a medieval granary at **Thóli**, and an excellent place to swim. It's worth taking the walk, about 90 minutes, to **Choklakiá**, or to the deserted fishing village of **Kathóliko** either via the **Mikró Chorió** road or over the old goat paths in the hills, with views of Sámos and Turkey. There's a beach, so you can take the plunge on arrival.

# Rhodes/Ródos (ΡΟΔΟΣ)

Rhodes, 'more beautiful than the sun' according to the ancient Greeks, is the largest and most fertile of the Dodecanese, ringed by sandy beaches, bedecked with flowers, blessed with some 300 days of sun a year, dotted with handsome towns and villages full of monuments evoking a long, colourful history – in a nutshell, all that it takes to sit securely throned as the reigning queen of tourism in Greece. As a year-round resort for cold northerners and top international package destination (in increasingly swanky packages) it's not fair to compare it with Greece's other islands. Rhodes is a holiday Babylon, Europe's answer to Florida, a glittering, sun-drenched chill pill in the sea where people shed their inhibitions with their woollens, if not always their black socks with their sandals. Germans, Brits and Scandinavians outnumber everyone (there's even a special post box for Sweden at the central Post Office) but Israelis, Czechs and Turks are now adding some different accents to the Babelling brew.

When and if you get fed up with the hordes, head inland, or for the south, beyond Líndos, and watch the sun set to see if you can find any lingering hints of the island evoked by Lawrence Durrell in his *Reflections on a Marine Venus*, written just after the war: 'Ahead of us the night gathers, a different night, and Rhodes begins to fall into the unresponding sea from which only memory can rescue it. The clouds hang high over Anatolia. Other islands? Other futures? Not, I think, after one has lived with the Marine Venus. The wound she gives one must carry to the world's end.'

## History

As on many islands, the founding myths echo early Rhodian history. The island was colonized by the Minoans, who built shrines to the moon at Filérimos, Líndos and Kámiros. In the 15th century BC, the Mycenaeans took over their colonies and founded the town of Achaia. Before settling on Rhodes for its name, the island was known as Telchinia (*see* 'Mythology'), or Ophioussa, for its numerous vipers; even today villagers wear snake-repelling goatskin boots when working in the fields. The Mycenaeans were supplanted in the 12th century BC by the Dorians, whose three cities – Líndos, Ialysós and Kámiros – dominated the island's affairs. Positioned along the main Mediterranean trade routes, Rhodes soon became a major trading and naval power.

# Rhodes

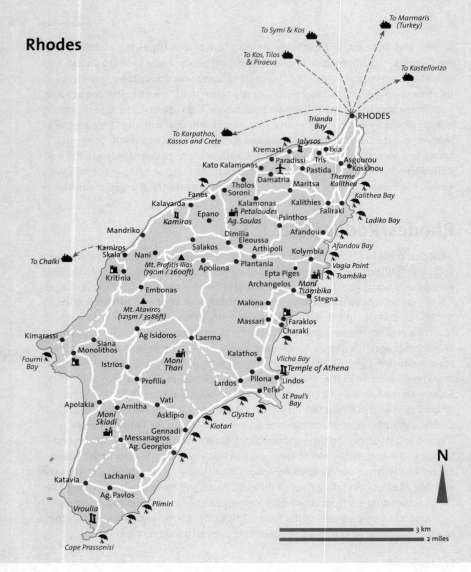

To Marmaris (Turkey)
To Symi & Kos
To Kos, Tilos & Piraeus
To Kastellorizo
RHODES
Trianda Bay
To Karpathos, Kassos and Crete
Ialysos
Kremasti
Ixia
Paradissi
Tris
Asgourou
Kato Kalamonas
Pastida
Koskinou
Damatria
Therme Kalithea
Tholos
Maritsa
Soroni
Kalithies
Kalithea Bay
Fanes
Kalamonas
Kalavarda
Petaloudes
Faliraki
Epano
Ag. Soulas
Psinthos
Ladiko Bay
Kamiros
Mandriko
Dimilia
Afandou
Kamiros Skala
Eleoussa
Nani
Salakos
Arthipoli
Afandou Bay
To Chalki
Kolymbia
Mt. Profitis Ilias (790m / 2600ft)
Plantania
Vagia Point
Kritinia
Apollona
Epta Piges
Tsambika
Embonas
Archangelos
Moni Tsambika
Mt. Ataviros (1215m / 3986ft)
Malona
Stegna
Massari
Faraklos
Kimarassi
Charaki
Siana
Ag Isidoros
Laerma
Monolithos
Fourni Bay
Kalathos
Vlicha Bay
Istrios
Moni Thari
Temple of Athena
Profilia
Lardos
Pilona
Lindos
Vati
Pefki
St Paul's Bay
Apolakia
Asklipio
Glystra
Arnitha
Moni Skiadi
Kiotari
Gennadi
Messanagros
Ag. Georgios
Katavia
Lachania
Ag. Pavlos
Plimiri
Vroulia
Cape Prassonisi

N

3 km
2 miles

Around 1000 BC, in response to the first Ionian confederacy, the island's three cities formed a Doric Hexapolis along with Kos, Cnidos and Halicarnassus, a prototype EU uniting the six city-states politically, religiously and economically. For four centuries the Hexapolis prospered, establishing trade colonies from Naples to the Costa Brava.

## The Founding of Rhodes City, and its Colossus

Rhodes sided with the Persians in both their major campaigns against Greece, but upon their defeat, quickly switched sides and joined the Delian confederacy. In 408 BC, in order to prevent rivalries and increase their wealth and strength, Líndos, Ialysós and Kámiros united to found one central capital, Rhodes ('the Rose'). Hippodamos of

Miletus, the geometrician, designed the new town on a grid plan similar to Piraeus, and the result was considered one of the most beautiful cities of ancient times. Celebrated schools of philosophy, philology and oratory were founded, and the port had very advanced facilities. Although Líndos, Kámiros and Ialysós continued to exist, they lost their importance and most of their populations to the thriving new capital.

One reason for this prosperity was its unabashedly expedient foreign policy. During the Peloponnesian War, Rhodes sided with whichever power was on top, and later hitched its wagon to the rising star of Alexander the Great in 336 BC. Alexander in turn favoured Rhodes at the expense of hostile Athens, and enabled the island to dominate Mediterranean trade; like Athens in classical times, the Rhodian navy ruled the waves of the Hellenistic era, and founded trading counters all over the known world; its trade and navigation laws were adopted by the Romans and remain the basis of maritime trade today. The proud Rhodians were also famous braggarts.

# Getting There and Around

## By Air

Rhodes airport (t 024 108 3400), the third busiest in Greece, has recently been enlarged. There are numerous UK, German and Scandinavian direct charters from April to mid-Oct and nearly a million charter tourists during the season. From Athens, there are at least 5 daily flights with Olympic and 2 with Aegean; from Crete (Heráklion), Olympic and Aegean have 3 weekly flights; from Thessaloniki, Olympic has 2 a week and Aegean has 3; Olympic also has flights from Mýkonos (twice a week), Santoríni (5 a week), Kárpathos (twice a day), Kastellórizo (once a day) and Kássos (3 a week). **Olympic** is at 9 Iérou Lóchou, Rhodes Town, t 024 102 4571; **Aegean** is at the airport, t 024 109 8345 and at No.525 Martíou, Rhodes Town, t 024 102 5444/4400. **Airport Flight Information Desk**: t 024 108 3214, 024 108 3200 or 024 108 3202. The **bus** to Parádissi passes near the airport every 30 mins until 11pm; **taxi** fares to town are around €8–10. If your return flight is delayed – charters always seem to be – it's only a 3min walk to the nearest bar and taverna (Anixis, *open until 2am*) in Parádissi.

## By Sea

**Ferry** connections daily with Piraeus, Kos, Kálymnos, Léros and Pátmos, 4–5 times a week with Chálki, Níssyros, Sými and Tílos, 3 times a week with Kárpathos, Kássos and Sitía (Crete), twice a week with Kastellórizo, Mílos and Ag.

Nikólaos (Crete), once a week with Sámos, Chíos, Mytilíni and Límnos. Daily **excursion boats** and *Sými I* and *Sými II* ferries from Mandráki harbour to Líndos, Sými (also by hydrofoil) and beaches at Lárdos, Tsambíka, Faliráki, Kalithéa, Ladiko and Kolymbia. Daily caiques ply their way from Kámiros Skala on the west coast to Chálki; for Marmaris, Turkey, there are daily **hydrofoils** (around €42 return) and ferries. Port authority: t 024 102 8695 and 024 102 8888.

## By Road

There is a frequent **bus** service. East coast buses (t 024 102 4129) are yellow and depart from Plateía Rimini in Rhodes Town; they service Faliráki (18 times daily), Líndos and Kolymbia (8–10 times), Genadi and Psinthos (3–5 times). West coast buses (t 024 102 7706) are white and blue, departing from around the corner by the market; these travel to Kalithéa Thermi (16 times), Koskínou (10 times), Salakós (5 times), and Kámiros, Monólithos and Embónas (once). **Taxis** are plentiful and reasonably priced. The central rank is in **Plateía Alexandrias**, Rhodes Town, t 024 102 7666. **Radio taxis** are a bit more expensive, t 024 106 4712, 024 106 6790 or 024 106 4734. To get off the beaten track, anything from four-wheel-drive beach buggies to motorbikes are available for hire; out of high season prices are negotiable. Note that petrol stations are closed Sun, hols and after 7pm.

**The Dodecanese Association of People with Special Needs**, t 024 107 3109, will, with 48-hrs

Egypt was one of Rhodes' most lucrative trading partners, and in the struggles between Alexander's Successors, Rhodes allied itself with Ptolemy, who had taken Egypt as his spoils. When another of Alexander's generals, the powerful Antigonas of Syria, ordered Rhodes to join him against Ptolemy, the Rhodians refused. To change their minds, Antigonas sent his son Dimitrios Poliorketes (the Besieger) at the head of an army of 40,000 and the Phoenician fleet. The ensuing year-long siege (305–304 BC) by a great general against the greatest city of the day has gone down in history, as a contest of strength and a battle of wits. As often as Dimitrios invented a tactic or ingenious machine, such as the 10-storey Helepolis siege tower, the Rhodians (who tripped up the Helepolis with a hidden, shallow ditch) foiled him, until after a year both sides wearied of the game and made a truce.

So Dimitrios departed, leaving his vast siege machinery behind. This the Rhodians either sold or melted down to construct a great bronze statue of Helios, their patron

warning, provide free transport in special vans to any destination on Rhodes, btwn 7am–3pm.

## Tourist Information

Hotels and tourist offices have copies of the free English-language newspaper *Ródos News*.
**EOT**: cnr of Papágou and Makaríou Sts, Rhodes Town, t 024 102 1921, *eot-rodos@otenet.gr*. Very helpful multilingual staff and a wide range of maps, leaflets and information; *open Mon–Fri 8–3*.
**Tourist police**: t 024 102 7423. This is a 24-hr multilingual number for any information or complaints.
**City of Rhodes Tourist Information Centre**: Plateía Rimini, t 024 103 5945. Mostly a money exchange; *open Mon–Sat 9–8, Sun 9–noon*.
**Post office**: on Mandráki harbour, Rhodes Town; *open Mon–Fri 7.30am–8pm*.
**American consulate**: the Voice of America station at Afándou, t 024 105 2555.
**British consulate**: Mr and Mrs Dimitriádis, 3 P. Méla, t 024 102 7247.
**Irish consulate**: Mr Skevos Mougros, 111 Amerikís, t 024 102 2461.

## Internet

**Mango café-bar**, Plateía Doriéos, in Rhodes Old Town.
**Rockstyle**, 7 Dimokratías, near the stadium. (For Líndos, *see* that section.)

## Festivals

**Just before Easter**: Lenten carnival.
**14 June**: Faliráki.
**20 June**: Scandinavian midsummer festivities in Rhodes Town (yes, really).
**28 June**: Líndos.
**First 10 days of July**: Musical Meetings in Rhodes.
**29–30 July**: Soroní, with donkey races.
**26 July**: Siána.
**Late July–early Aug**: Rhodes Wine Festival.
**Aug**: dance festivals in Kallithiés, Maritsa and Embónas.
**14–22 Aug**: Kremastí.
**7 Sept**: in Moní Tsambíkas (for fertility).
**13 Sept**: Apóllona and Kallithiés.
**26 Sept**: Artamíti.
**18 Oct**: Afándou.
**7 Nov**: Archángelos.

## Watersports

The only permitted **diving** is at Kallithéa. Contact:
**The Diving Centre**, 33 Lissávonas, t 024 106 1115, f 024 106 6584.
**Waterhoppers**, 45 Kritiká in Ixiá, t/f 024 103 8146.
**Scuba-Diving Trident School**, 2 Zervoú, t/f 024 102 9160.
Cape Prassonís is the place for excellent **windsurfing**:
**Procenter**, t 024 109 1045, *procenter.prasonisi@eunet.at*. Operates April–Oct.

## Mythology

In myth, Rhodes is the subject of ancient and contradictory traditions. According to one, the first inhabitants were the Children of the Sea, the nine dog-headed enchantresses called Telchines. In spite of having flippers for hands, they made the sickle that Cronos used to castrate Uranus, carved the first statues of the gods, and founded Kámiros, Ialysós and Líndos before moving to Crete. There Rhea, the Earth, made them nurses of her son Poseidon, and they forged the sea god's trident.

Poseidon fell in love with the Telchines' sister, Alia, and had six sons and a daughter by her. The daughter, the nymph Rhodos, became the sole heiress of the island when Zeus decided to destroy the Telchines for meddling with the weather, although their real crime was belonging to a pre-Olympian matriarchal religion. He flooded Rhodes, but the Telchines managed to escape in various forms.

The same cast of characters are on stage in a later version of the myth, which made the clever Telchines change sex and shed their dog heads and flippers. The sons of Pontos and Thalassa (the sea), they were artisans, magicians and ministers of Zeus, with the same sister, Alia, who was loved by Poseidon and gave birth to Rhodos and a number of sons. When these sons refused to let Aphrodite dock as she sailed between her favourite islands of Kýthera and Cyprus, the goddess of love put a curse of incestuous passion on them and they raped their mother Alia. In despair Alia flung herself into the sea and became 'Lefkothea' (the White Goddess). The wicked sons hid in the bowels of the earth and became demons, as Poseidon in his wrath flooded Rhodes (the Telchines, tipped off by Artemis, again escaped before the deluge).

The sun god Helios later fell in love with Rhodos, evaporated the stagnant waters with his hot rays and married the nymph. They had a daughter and seven sons, known as the Heliades. Athena gave them wisdom and taught them nautical and astrophysical lore. But the wisest of the Heliades, Tenagis, was killed in a jealous fit by four of the brothers, who then fled. The two innocent brothers, Ohimos and Kerkafos, remained and founded the city of Achaia; one had three sons, Líndos, Kámiros and Ialysós, who founded the three city-states that bear their names.

A later, tidier version relates that while the gods were dividing up the world, Zeus realized that he had forgotten to set aside a portion for Helios. Dismayed, Zeus asked Helios what he could do to make up for his omission. The sun god replied that he knew of an island just re-emerging from the sea off the coast of Asia Minor which would suit him admirably. Helios married Rhodos and one of their sons, or perhaps Tlepolemos (who led the ships of Rhodes to Troy), founded the ancient cities.

Kámiros even has another possible founder: Althaemenes, son of the Cretan King Katreus and grandson of Minos. When an oracle predicted that Katreus would be slain by his offspring, Althaemenes fled to Rhodes, where he founded Kámiros and surrounded it with metal bulls that would bellow if it were invaded. In later life Katreus sailed to Rhodes to visit his son, but arrived at night, and what with the darkness and the bellowing of the metal bulls, Althaemenes failed to recognize his father and fellow Cretans, and slew them. When he realized his error in the morning he piteously begged Mother Earth to swallow him up whole, which she did.

god of the sun. The famous sculptor from Líndos, Chares, was put in charge of the project, and in 290 BC, after 12 years of work and at a cost of 20,000 pounds of silver, Chares completed the Colossus, or didn't quite: he found he had made a miscalculation and committed suicide just before it was cast. Standing somewhere between 100 and 140ft tall (at her crown the Statue of Liberty is 111ft), the Colossus did not straddle the entrance of Rhodes harbour, as is popularly believed, but probably stood near the present Castle of the Knights, gleaming bright in the sun – one of the Seven Wonders of the Ancient World. But of all the Wonders the Colossus had the shortest lifespan; in 225 BC, an earthquake brought it crashing to the ground. The Oracle at Delphi told the Rhodians to leave it there, and it lay forlorn until AD 653 when the Saracens, who had captured Rhodes, sold it as scrap to a merchant from Edessa. According to legend, it took 900 camels to transport the bronze to the ships.

In 164 BC, when they had repaired their city and walls, the Rhodians signed a peace treaty with Rome. Alexandria was their only rival in wealth, and tiny Délos, with all its duty-free trade concessions, their only rival in Mediterranean trade. The island's School of Rhetoric taught Pompey, Cicero, Cassius, Julius Caesar, Brutus, Cato the Younger and Mark Antony. When Caesar was assassinated, Rhodes as always backed the right horse, in this case Augustus, only this time the wrong horse, Cassius, was in the neighbourhood; he sacked the city, captured its fleet, and sent its treasures to Rome (43–42 BC). It was a blow from which Rhodes never recovered. She lost control of her colonies and islands, and other Roman allies muscled in on her booming trade. In AD 57 St Paul preached on the island and converted many of the inhabitants; by the end of the Roman empire, Rhodes was a sleepy backwater.

## Two Hundred Years of Knights

Byzantium brought many invaders and adventurers to Rhodes: Arabs and Saracens (including in 804 a siege by Harun al Rachid, of *Arabian Nights* fame), Genoese, Venetians and Crusaders all passed through; in 1191 Richard the Lionheart and Philip Augustus of France came to recruit mercenaries. After the fall of Jerusalem in 1291, the Knights Hospitallers of St John, dedicated to protecting pilgrims and running hospitals in the Holy Land, took refuge on Cyprus, but by 1306 they had become interested in Rhodes. They asked the Emperor Andronicus Palaeológos to cede them the island in return for their loyalty, but after 1204 the Byzantines had learned better than to trust the Franks. The Knights, under Grand Master Foulques de Villaret, then took the matter into their own hands and purchased the Dodecanese from their current occupants: Genoese pirates. The Rhodians weren't impressed, and the Knights had to spend their first three years subduing the natives.

By 1309, with the help of the pope, the Knights were secure in their possession and began to build their hospital and inns in Rhodes Town. They built eight inns or auberges in all, one for each of the 'tongues', or nationalities, in the Order (England, France, Germany, Italy, Castile, Aragon, Auvergne and Provence). Each tongue had a bailiff, and the eight bailiffs elected the Grand Master, who lived in a palace. There were never more than 650 men in the Order and, although as always dedicated to the care of pilgrims, their focus shifted to their role as freebooting, front-line defenders of

Christendom. Already wealthy, they were given a tremendous boost in 1312, when Pope Clement V and Philip the Fair of France dissolved the fabulously wealthy Knights Templars, confiscated their fortune and gave the Hospitallers a hefty share. With their new funds, the Knights of St John replaced the fortifications – and continued to replace them up until the 16th century, hiring the best Italian engineers to build one of the most splendid defences of the day.

Meanwhile, the knights had made themselves such a thorn in the side of Muslim shipping that they were besieged by the Sultan of Egypt in 1444 and by Mohammed II the Conqueror in 1480 with 70,000 men, both times without success, thanks to those tremendous walls. Then in 1522 Suleiman the Magnificent moved in with 200,000 troops; the Rhodians (there were 6,000 of them, plus 1,000 Italian mercenaries, and 650 knights) bitterly joked that the Colossus was now coming back at them, in the form of cannon balls. After a frustrating six-month siege, Suleiman was about to abandon Rhodes when a German traitor informed him that, of the original Knights, only 180 survived, and they were on their last legs. The sultan redoubled his efforts and the Knights were forced to surrender. In honour of their courage, Suleiman let them leave in safety, with their Christian retainers and possessions. They made their new headquarters in Malta – at the nominal rent of a falcon a year – and in 1565 they withstood a tremendous all-out assault by the Ottoman fleet. After caving in to Napoleon, in 1831 the Knights re-formed as a benevolent charity in Rome, from where they still fund hospitals; the English Order established the St John Ambulance, as well as the St John Ophthalmic Hospital back where it all started, in Jerusalem.

### Ottomans and Italians

The Greeks of Rhodes were forced to move outside the walls, which became the exclusive domain of the Turks and Jews. The Ottomans loved Rhodes as a pleasure island, and when the Rhodians attempted to join the War of Independence in 1821, the Turks reacted with atrocities; their popularity dropped even more in the Great Gunpowder Explosion of 1856, when lightning struck a minaret and exploded a powder magazine, destroying much of the Old Town and killing 800 people. During the confusion of the Balkan Wars in 1912, the Italians besieged and took Rhodes, claiming the island as their inheritance from the Knights of St John. After 1943 the Germans took over and sent most of the island's 2,000 Jews to the concentration camps. Rhodes, with the rest of the Dodecanese, joined Greece in 1948, whereupon the government declared it a free port, boosting its already great tourist potential.

# Rhodes Town

Spread across the northern tip of the island, Rhodes (pop. 55,000), the capital of the Dodecanese celebrated its 2,400th birthday in 1993. It divides neatly into Old and New Towns. Tourism reigns in both, although these days the New Town is filling up with designer boutiques aimed at the Rhodians and visiting Greeks who come to shop – VAT is five per cent lower than on the mainland. The medieval city is so

# Rhodes Town

Aquarium

Aquarium

KALIMNOU-LEROU

PL. VAS. PAVLOU

KASSOU

KASTELORIZOU

Windy

AKTI MIAOULI

G. GRIVA

ION.

KATHOPOULI

NIKIFOROU

ORFANDIOU

KRITIS

G. LEON

DRAGOUMI

MANDILA

DIL PERAKI

FANOURAK

Psaropoula

PSAROPOULA

28 OKTOVRIOU

FANOURAK

ALEXANDROU

AMOHOSTOU

A. ZERVOU

ALEXANDROU

ETHN. MAKARIOU

AKTI KANARI

PAPALOUKA

EL. VENIZELOU

VORIOU IPIROU

KENNEDY

RIGA FEREOU

VORIOU IPIROU

PINDOU

NAVARINOU

ENOPLON DINAMEON

HIMARAS

DIAGORIDON

AGIOU IOANNOU

Ancient
Theatre

Monte
Smith

Ancient Stadium

KENNEDY

PAVLIDI

Temple of Pythian
Apollo

400 m
400 yds

N

Elli

SOK

PAPANIKOLAOU G

Murad Reis
Mosque

PLATEIA
KOUNDOURIOTI

Governor's
Palace

Town
Hall

G. EFSTATHIADI

IRON POLITEHNIOU

IEROU

LOHOU

ARA

Evangelismos

PLVAS.
GEORGIOU

25 MARTIOU

PL. ELEFTHERIAS

Mandraki

Ag. Nikolaos
Fort and
Lighthouse

AKTI BOUMBOULI

AMERIKIS

MAKARIOU

SOF. VENIZELOU

LAMBRAKI

PL.
KYPROU

THEO DOKAS

New Market

To Marmaris

POL

West Coast
bus station

PLATEIA
ALEXANDRIAS

PALAMA

PAPAGOU

East Coast
bus station

PL.
RIMINI

PILI ELEFTHERIAS

PILI AMBOUAZ

Sound
and Light

PLATEIA
SYMIS
PLATEIA
ARGYROKASTRO

PILI NAVARCHIO

Temple of Aphrodite

PILI TILEVOLON

PISSANDR

Palace of the
Grand Masters

Museum of
Decorative
Arts

IPPOTON

Inn of Auvergne

Kolona Harbour

DIMOKRATIAS

Loggia

Roloi

IPARHOU

ORFEOS

Archaeology
Museum

Byzantine Museum

PLATEA
MOUSSIOU

Commercial
Harbour

Suleiman's
Mosque

APOLONION

POLIDOROU

EVDIMOU

PILI AG.
EKATERI

PILI MILON

TIMOKREONDOS

SOKRATOUS

Kastellania

MENEKLEOUS

ARISTOTELOUS

AKTI SACHTOURI

PILI
PANAGIAS

RODIOU K.

EOLOU

PILI AG.
GEORGIO

ALEXANDIADOU

PODARMOU

ARCHELAOS

ERGIOU

THOUKIDIDI

PLATONOS

EVKIPID

Admiralty

MARTYRON

DOSSIADOU

PINDAROU

THISSEOS

KISTHINIOU

Acandia

PL.
Arionos

ZINONOS

PL. ATHINAS

SOFOKLEO

Ibrahim
Pasha
Mosque

PERIKLEOUS

DIMOSTHENOUS

Our Lady of
the Bourg

FIDIA

Mustafa Hammam

OLD TOWN

AG. FANOURIOU

Redjep Pasha
Mosque

PITHAGORA

PRAXITELOUS

EVRIAKI

CAVALA

PILI KARETOU

Ag. Nikolaos/Folk
Dance
Theatre

Ag. Fanourios

OMIROU

TLIPOLEMOU

EKATONOS

PILI AG.
ATHANASIOU

ARH. EFTHIMIOU

IRINIS

VIRONOS

KOMNINON

FILELINON

PILI AG. IOANNOU

DIMOKRATIAS

Stadium

To Rodini Park

# Shopping

Rhodes' duty-free status has made for some odd sights; it may be the island of the sun, but nowhere on earth will you find more fur shops, or umbrella shops: a popular model opens up to reveal Michael Jackson's mug in alarming proportions. The New Town near Mandráki is full of designer shops and even a Marks and Spencer's.

**Platéia Kýprou**, for shoes.

**Kakakios Brothers**, 47 G. Lambráki. For a reasonably priced tailor-made suit made from British fabrics. These brothers made them for the likes of Gregory Peck and Anthony Quinn.

**Market**, on Zefiros St (by the cemetery). The biggest market in the Dodecanese takes place every Sat morning; get there early to find a bargain.

**Market**, on Vironos St by the Stadium. This smaller market takes place on Wed.

# Where to Stay

## Rhodes Town ✉ 85100

Rhodes has a plethora of accommodation in every class and price from one of the most expensive hotels ever to be built in Greece to humble village rooms. Most places are booked solid by holiday package companies, some for winter breaks too, so if you're island-hopping in high season it's definitely worth phoning ahead.

On the Internet: *www.helios.gr/dis/rhodes* has more info on hotels, and sights, while *www.helios.gr/hotels* offers on-line descriptions and bookings for a selection of luxury to C-class hotels across the island. Most of the luxury hotels are in Ixiá and Triánda.

### Luxury

**Grand Hotel Rhodes**, Aktí Miaoúli, t 024 102 6284, f 024 103 5589 (*L*). With one of the island's casinos, a nightclub, tennis courts and what's reputed to be the largest swimming pool in the country.

**Rodos Park**, next to the historic centre at 12 Riga Fereou, t 024 102 4612, f 024 102 4613 (*L*). Overlooking the park, mega-luxury, 7-star suites provide some of the opulence in town, with private Jacuzzis, pool, health club, and ballroom.

### Expensive

**Chryssos Tholos**, 15 Kistiniou, t 024 107 7332, f 024 103 6980 (*B*). Small hotel in a beautifully restored mansion, 100m from the sea. *Open Mar–Oct*.

**Marie**, 7 Kos, near Élli Beach, t 024 103 0577, f 024 102 2751 (*C*). Recently renovated, offering a swimming pool, sea sports, and satellite TV.

**S. Nicolis**, 61 Ippodámou, t 024 103 4561, f 024 103 2034 (*E*). Offers atmospheric accommodation in a lovely old house in the heart of the Old Town; excellent bed and breakfast, large garden and rooftop terrace with great views. The Greek-Danish proprietors also have new apartments to sleep 4 people nearby and a cheaper pension; booking is essential.

**Plaza Hotel Best Western** on Ieroú Lóchou, t 024 102 2501, f 024 102 2544, *plaza@otenet.gr* (*A*). Centrally situated and refurnished with a pool, baby-sitting and English buffet breakfast.

### Moderate

**Cavo d'Oro**, 15 Kisthiníou, near the commercial harbour, t 024 103 6980. Well worth a try; it was good enough for Michael Palin on his *Pole to Pole* jaunt. The delightful 13th-century house has been beautifully restored by the owner and his German wife; he'll even meet you from the ferry.

**Paris**, 88 Ag. Fanouríou, t 024 102 6356, f 024 102 1095 (*D*). Nice rooms and a quiet courtyard with shady orange and banana trees, and prices at the bottom of this range.

**Popi**, Stratigou Zisi and Maliaraki 21, near the Old Town, t 024 103 3479, f 024 103 3453. Studios in the old fashioned Greek style, each sleeping 4.

**Victoria**, No.22 25 Martiou, t 024 102 4626, f 024 103 6675 (*C*). Central, family-run, and the owner's son, a UK-trained doctor, has consulting rooms next door.

### Inexpensive

**Ambassadeur**, 53 Othonos and Amalías, t 024 102 4679, f 024 102 4679 (*C*). One of the best for value in this category.

**Attiki**, Haritos and Theofiliskou, **t** 024 102 7767 (E). In a medieval building in the heart of the Old Town, quietly tucked away in the corner; a bit dishevelled but children welcome. *Open all year.*

**Iliana**, 1 Gavála, **t** 024 103 0251 (E). In an old Jewish family house, with a small bar and terrace; no charge for childen under 10 and cheap for everyone else.

**La Luna**, next to a tiny church on Ierokléous, just off Orfeos, **t/f** 024 102 5856 (E). With a bar, in a perfectly quiet courtyard with *hammam. Open all year.*

**Maria's Rooms**, on Menekléous, **t** 024 102 2169. Comfortable choice around a quiet courtyard.

**Minos Pension**, 5 Omírou, **t** 024 103 1813. Pristine and offers panoramic roof-garden views.

**Spot**, Perikléous 21, **t** 024 103 4737 (E). One of the better cheap backpackers' haunts; good value with light, airy rooms plus en suite bathrooms.

# Eating Out

Rhodes Town has a cosmopolitan range of eating places from luxury hotel restaurants (for these, *see* the list below) to real dives selling tripe (*patsás*). The Rhodians are to the Greek islands what the Parisians are to France. They are very fashionable, often fickle, and love new food trends. In the New Town, with its strong Italian influence, you can eat great authentic pizza and pasta, or alternatively, there's Danish, Swedish, Indian, Chinese, French, Mexican, or Yorkshire cuisine. There's even Greek...

Be sure to try Rhodes' own wines: Chevaliers de Rhodes; Ilios; Archontiko, the prize-winning premium red from XAIP; Villaré, an excellent Emery white.

## New Town

**Christos**, out in the suburb of Zéfiros beyond the commercial harbour. This is one of the best and most authentic tavernas for a hearty lunch; it is a favourite with local families and taxi drivers – there'll be no problem finding it – the food is excellent, good value and is accompanied by an astonishing range of *ouzos*.

**Dania**, 3 Iroon Polytechniou, near the Royal Bank of Scotland, **t** 024 102 0540. For a real taste of Denmark; serving traditional herring dishes and a running *smorgasbord* on Sun evenings.

**Ellinikon**, 29 Alexándrou Diákou, **t** 024 102 8111 (€15–20). Another popular choice with the locals, serving a choice of Greek and international dishes and excellent desserts.

**Palia Istoria** ('Old Story'), on the corner of Mitropóleos and Dendrínou, south of the new stadium, **t** 024 103 2421 (€18–25). With the best *mezédes* on the island served under a pergola, this award-winning restaurant isn't cheap but you get what you pay for – an imaginative array of dishes from celery hearts in *avgolémono* sauce to scallops with mushrooms and artichokes, and a good choice of vegetarian dishes; the fruit salad has 20 kinds of fruit. The food is complimented by an excellent Greek wine list; booking is advisable; splurge for a taxi.

**Steno**, 29 Ag. Anargíron, just south of Ag. Athanasíou gate. Another genuine, friendly *ouzerie*, deservedly popular.

**7.5 ΘAYMA** ('Wonder'), Dilperáki 15, **t** 024 103 9805 (€18–25). Wacky establishment, advertising 'food, drink and party hats since 292 BC'; turns out to be Swedish chefs, ancient Greek décor, Eastern-inspired dishes and seriously good food served in a secret garden.

For something cheap, the New Market is full of holes in the wall offering good 'n' greasy *gýros* with outdoor tables.

## Old Town

After an aperitif, plunge into the maze of backstreets, which are almost deserted after about 8pm – in some industrious shops you'll see tailors and cobblers still hard at work and you'll find a wide range of eating places, some still untouristy and authentic, others all the rage with trendy locals.

**Alexis**, 18 Sokrátous, **t** 024 102 9347 (€30). Good fish and seafood, but quite expensive.

**Araliki**, 45 Aristofánous. Greek home cooking, offering superb *mezédes* in a medieval setting.

**Cleo's**, on Ag. Fanouríou, **t** 024 102 8415 (reservations recommended). One of the most elegant places to dine in the heart of the medieval city, serving upmarket Italian and French cuisine.

**Dinoris**, 14 Plateía Moussíou, **t** 024 103 5530. An old but pricey favourite, tucked down a narrow alley by the museum, with a romantic garden patio and more lovely fish.

**Dodekanissos**, 45 Plateía Evrión Martyrón, **t** 024 102 8412. Homely atmosphere, moderately-priced seafood and an exceptional shrimp *saganáki*.

**Fotis**, 8 Menekleóus St, **t** 024 102 7359 (€*20–30*). Courtyard dining, with excellent grilled fish – simple and delicious, plus 1 or 2 delicacies such as sea urchin salad and steamed mussels.

**Fotis Melathron**, Parodos Sokrátous, **t** 024 102 4272 (€*16–22*). One of the best restaurants on the island. Set in an elegantly refurbished building, there are some private rooms (for larger parties; book in advance) with drinks and humidor. The menu is both Greek and international, but the Greek dishes are by far the best.

# Entertainment and Nightlife

Rhodes has something for everyone, with around 600 bars in Rhodes Town alone. There are discos, laser shows and swimming pools; Irish pubs; theme bars; super-cool cocktail bars or live-music tavernas in restored Old Town houses; bars full of gyrating girls and wet T-shirt nights; and even simple *ouzeries* where a game of backgammon is the high spot (notably at 76 Sokrátous St). The island has all kinds of music from traditional folk to funk, soul, house and rap to vintage Elvis.

*Bouzoúki* club at Élli Beach. Traditional Greeks head here for the late-night music.

**The Grand Hotel** on Aktí Miaoúli. Caters for those wanting more sophisticated Greek sounds, at the **Moons Rock**, featuring top singers and musicians. There's also a **casino**, **t** 024 102 4458 (no jeans or shorts), although it now has to compete with a new casino operated by Playboy International in the Hotel des Roses, a 1930s landmark.

**Christos**, 59 Dilperaki. Ideal for a romantically intimate garden evening among the jasmine.

**Orfanídou St**, just in from Akti Miaoúli is known as the street of bars:

**Flanagan's.** Full of Irish flavour.

**Colorado.** With pub, club and bar.

**Hard Rock Caffé** (sic).

**Down Under Bar**, 36 Orfanidou. Currently another popular bar.

**Diákou Street** to the south is also heaving with nightlife, British and Scandinavian tourists spilling out of the bars into the street in high season.

**Sticky Fingers**, 6 A. Zervou, south of Psarópoula. Rockers should head for this ever popular bar.

**Blue Lagoon Pool Bar**, No. 25 Martíou. A place to live out your fantasies in a totally themed and tropical environment.

**O Mylos**, just off Sokrátous, in the Old Town. A pretty open garden music bar.

**To Roloi**, up the ramp on Orféos. Join the smart set in this impressive, distinctly pricey clocktower.

**Karpouzi**, off Sokrátous in the Old Town. Follow the cognoscenti to this fabulous medieval building with *rembetíka*, wine and *mezédes*.

**Café Besara**, 11 Sofokléous. For an Antipodean atmosphere, never dull and featuring live music 3 times a week.

You can take in a **film** (most often subtitled, in the original language) at one of the many great open-air cinemas (indoors out of season):

**Metropol Cinema**, corner of Venetoken and Vironos Streets, near the stadium.

**The Pallas Cinema**, nearby on Dimokratías.

**The Muncipal Cinema**, by the town hall. With artier fare.

**The Son et Lumière Show**, in the Palace of the Grand Masters, **t** 024 121 922 (*in English on Mon and Tues at 8.15pm, Wed, Fri and Sat at 9.15pm, Thurs 10.15pm*). The history of Rhodes unfolds here.

**Traditional Greek folk dances** by the Nelly Dimogloú Company in the Old Town Theatre, Androníkou, **t** 024 102 0157 or 024 102 9085 (*May–Oct Mon, Wed and Fri 9.20pm–11pm*). Real if coolly professional traditional dancing. Dance lessons also available.

**Le Palais disco**. Bop till you drop.

**Privato disco**, 2 Iliadon, **t** 024 103 3267.

remarkably preserved it looks like a film set in places, and has often been used as such (for example, *Pascali's Island*).

Rhodes presents an opulent face to the sea and sailing in is much the prettiest way to arrive. The massive walls of the Old Town, crowned by the Palace of the Grand Masters, rise out of a lush subtropical garden; graceful minarets and the arcaded waterfront market, bright with strings of lights at night, add an exotic touch. Monumental pseudo-Venetian public buildings trying to look serious decorate the shore to the left, while opposite, three 14th-century **windmills** (down from the original 15) turn lazily behind a forest of masts. Yachts, smaller ferries and excursion boats dock at the smallest of three harbours, **Mandráki** (ΜΑΝΔΡΑΚΙ). The entrance to Mandráki is guarded by the lighthouse and fort of **Ag. Nikólaos**, built in the 1460s to bear the brunt of the Turkish attacks, and a **bronze stag and doe**, marking where the Colossus may have stood. Under the Knights, a chain crossed the port here, and every ship that entered had to pay a two per cent tax of its cargo value towards the war effort. Hydrofoils leave from Kolona harbour further on, and larger ferries, any craft to Turkey, and cruise ships enter the **commercial harbour** (ΕΜΠΟΡΙΚΟΣ ΛΙΜΕΝΑΣ) nearer the Old Town walls.

These **walls** are a masterpiece of late medieval fortifications, but access is by guided tour only (*Tues and Sat, meet in front of the Palace of the Grand Master at 2.30; adm*). Alternatively, you can get a good free squiz at them by walking round the bottom of the dry moat: the main entrance is off Plateía Alexandrías. Constructed over the old Byzantine walls under four of the most ambitious Grand Masters (d'Aubusson, d'Amboise, del Carretto and Villiers de l'Isle Adam), they stretch 4km and average 38ft thick. Curved the better to deflect missiles, the landward sides were safeguarded by the 100ft-wide dry moat. Each national group of Knights was assigned its own bastion and towers to defend, except the Italians, who as the best sailors were put in charge of the Knights' fleet.

Of the many gates that linked the walled Old Town with the village outside, the most magnificent is the Gate of Emery d'Amboise (**Píli Ambouaz**, in Greek) near the Palace of the Grand Masters, built in 1512 (entrance off Papágou Street). Under the Turks, all Greeks had to be outside the walls by sundown or forfeit their heads.

## The Old Town (ΠΑΛΑΙΑ ΠΟΛΗ)

The town within these walls was fairly dilapidated when the Italians took charge. They restored much, but fortunately lost the war before they could get on with their plan to widen all the streets for cars and build a ring road. To keep any such future notions at bay, UNESCO has declared the Old Town a World Heritage Site, and is providing funds for historical restoration and infrastructure, and burying electric and phone cables.

Entering the aforementioned Gate d'Amboise, passing the tablecloth sellers and quick-draw portrait artists, you'll find yourself in the inner sanctum, the **Collachium**, where the Knights could retreat if the outer curtain walls were taken. By the gate, at the highest point, a castle within a castle, stands the **Palace of the Grand Masters** (*open Tues–Fri 8–7, Sat and Sun 8–3, Mon 12.30–7; adm*), built over a Temple to Helios;

some scholars believe that the Colossus actually stood here, overlooking the harbour. Construction of this citadel was completed in 1346, modelled after the Popes' Palace in Avignon – not by accident: 14 of the 19 Grand Masters on Rhodes were French and French was the official spoken language of the Order. Underground rooms were used as storage and as a refuge for the civilian population in case of attack. The Turks used the whole as a prison, even after the Great Gunpowder Explosion of 1856, when the first floor caved in, and the Italians did the same until Mussolini ordered that it be reconstructed as one of his summer villas. The Italians covered the floors with lovely Roman mosaics from Kos, a hotch-potch of Renaissance furniture, and installed a lift and modern plumbing, but war broke out and ended before the Duce could swan around its 158 rooms (don't panic: only a tenth are open to the public). Note the huge marble coat-of-arms on one of the fireplaces: 'Restored by Vitt. Eman. III, King and Emperor 1939.' On the ground floor, two excellent permanent exhibitions have been set up: **The City of Rhodes from its Foundation to the Roman Period** and **Rhodes from the 4th Century to its Capture by the Turks**, with English translations and full of curious sidelines on lightweight Rhodian bricks (used for the dome of Ag. Sophia in Constantinople) and the Knights' production of sugar, an item worth its weight in gold in the Middle Ages. There's a collection of detached frescoes, coins, icons and the tombstone of the Grand Master Villier de l'Isle Adam, who defied Suleiman for six months even though outmanned nearly 40 to one.

The main street descending from the palace into the heart of the Collachium is a favourite of film makers: quiet, evocative, cobblestoned **Odós Ippotón** (Knights' Street), beautifully restored by the Italians. It passes under the arcaded **Loggia** that originally linked the Palace to the Knights' 14th-century Cathedral of St John, where the Grand Masters were buried; after being shattered in the Gunpowder Explosion, a Turkish school was built in the midst of the ruins. Ippotón is lined with the Knights' inns, where they had meetings and meals. There were eight, each housing a 'tongue' and emblazoned with the arms of the Grand Master in charge when it was built: the **Inn of Provence** on the left and the two buildings of the **Inn of Spain** on the right, then the French chapel and elaborate **Inn of France** (1509), adorned with escutcheons and crocodile gargoyles; as there were always more French knights than any other 'tongue', their inn was the most spacious. Next door stands a townhouse, belonging to Villier de l'Isle Adam; opposite was the Knights' entrance to the hospital. The **Inn of Italy** (1519) stands at the foot of the street.

Two squares open up at the end of the street; just to the right, on the corner of Plateía Moussion, stands the much restored **Inn of England** (1483), abandoned in 1534, when the Pope excommunicated Henry VIII. It was hit by an earthquake in 1851, rebuilt by the British, bombed and rebuilt again in 1947. The British consul of Rhodes (*see* box above for the address) has the key. Opposite stands the Flamboyant Gothic hospital of the Knights, built between 1440 and 1481 and restored by the Italians in 1918, now home to the **Archaeology Museum**, still awaiting a much needed overhaul (*open Tues–Sun 8–2.30; adm*). The long arched ward where the Knights' surgeons (from the ranks of commoners) cared for patients in elaborate canopy beds, still has its heraldic devices. The star attraction is Lawrence Durrell's beloved 3rd-century BC *Marine Venus* (marine and a bit eroded because she was found in the sea) and the pretty kneeling *Aphrodite of Rhodes* (90 BC), combing out her wet hair; also note the bust of Helios from the 2nd century BC, complete with holes in the head to hold his metal sunrays. Ceramics, *stelae*, Mycenaean jewellery found in local tombs, and mosaics round off the collection. In the adjacent square, 11th-century Panagía Kástrou, used by the Knights as their Cathedral of St Mary until they built their own, now contains a little **Byzantine Museum** (*open Tues–Sun 8.30–3; adm*), with frescoes and icons from disused churches across the island and Chálki.

Through the arch, charming Plateía Argyrokástro has the loveliest inn, the 15th-century **Inn of Auvergne** (now a cultural centre), with a **fountain** made from a Byzantine baptismal font. Here, too, is the 14th-century **Palace of the Armeria**, constructed by Grand Master Roger de Pins as the Knights' first hospital on Rhodes, and the **Museum of Decorative Arts** (*open Tues–Sun 8.30–3; adm*) with folk art and handicrafts from all over the Dodecanese, including costumes, embroideries and a reconstruction of a traditional room. Nearby, in Plateía Sýmis, the **Municipal Art Gallery** (*open Tues–Sun 8–2*), houses 20th-century Greek paintings and engravings. Also in the square are the ruins of a 3rd-century BC Temple of Aphrodite, discovered by the Italians in 1922. Fragments of another temple of the same epoch, dedicated to Diónysos, are in a corner behind the Ionian and Popular Bank. The Italians reopened the two harbour gates that the Turks had blocked up, **Píli Eleftherías** ('Freedom Gate'; the Italians regarded themselves as Rhodes' liberators) to Mandráki and **Píli Navarchio** (or Arsenal Gate) to the marina and commerical harbour.

## The Turkish Town

South of the Collachium of the Knights is the former Turkish bazaar, where all the streets have been renamed after Greek philosophers and poets; bustling **Sokrátous**, the main street, is thick with tourist and duty-free luxury shops. Midway along, at No.17, the Turkish-owned *kafeneíon* has remained steadfastly unchanged for the past century: some say, ditto its coffee-drinking, backgammon-playing clientèle. At the top of Sokrátous Street stands the slender minaret of the lovely, faded **red Mosque of Suleiman** (*now closed*), built in 1523 by Suleiman the Magnificent to celebrate his conquest of Rhodes. The **Muselman Library** (*open Mon–Fri 7.30–2.30 and 6–9, Sat and Sun 8–noon*) opposite (1793) contains rare Persian and Arabian manuscripts, and illuminated copies of the *Koran*. Two precious 700-year-old *Korans* stolen in 1990 and worth €300,000 have now been recovered and are back on show. Behind Suleiman's mosque, the Byzantine clock tower, **To Roloi**, has splendid views over the town if you're lucky enough to find it open.

South of Sokrátous Street, the Turkish Quarter dissolves into a zigzag of narrow streets, where charming Turkish balconies of latticed wood project beside crumbling stone arches and houses built directly over the street. On scruffy Plateía Arionos, off Archeláos Street, the **Mustafa Mosque** keeps company with the atmospheric **Mustafa Hammam**, (*t 024 102 7739; open Tues–Fri 11–5, Sat 8–7; bring own soap and towel; adm*) built in 1558 and remodelled in 1765. Heated by a ton of olive logs a day, it has mosaic floors, marble fountains and a lovely ceiling, divided into men's and women's labyrinthine sections. Another old mosque, **Ibrahim Pasha** (1531), is off Sofokléous Street; executions took place in front of it.

On Hippocrátes Square, where Sokrátous turns into Aristotélous Street, stands the picturesque Gothic-Renaissance **Kastellania**, built by Grand Master d'Amboise in 1507, perhaps as a tribunal or commercial exchange for the Knights. It stands at the head of Pithágora Street, the main street of **Evriakí**, the Jewish quarter; according to the historian Josephus, the community dates from the 1st century AD; later chronicles cite them among Rhodes' defenders against the Turks. To the east along Aristotélous Street, the Plateía Evrión Martyrón (the Square of Hebrew Martyrs) honours those sent to die in the concentration camps. Just south stands Rhodes' remaining synagogue, highly decorated and still in use; commemorative plaques pay homage to the deported Jewish population and a small display at the back illustrates the Rhodian Jewish community and its diaspora.

The so-called **Admirality** (more likely the seat of Rhodes' Catholic bishop) is back on the square, behind a charming bronze seahorse fountain. From here, Pindárou Street continues to the impressive ruins of **Our Lady of the Bourg**, built by the Knights in thanksgiving for their defeat of the Turks in 1480, but never the same after it took a British bomb in the war. The Turkish and Jewish Quarters offer other cobbled lanes to explore, dotted with old churches converted into mosques and converted back again: one, off Omírou St, is little 13th-century **Ag. Fanoúrios** with fine frescoes, hidden behind a modern building, near the abandoned **Redjep Pasha Mosque** (1588), which was once coated with colourful Persian tiles. The gate at the end of Pithágora Street, **Píli Ag. Ioánnou**, or Red Door, is another demonstration of the walls' strength.

## The New Town

Outside the walls, the overpriced seafront cafés look enticingly over Mandráki harbour. Just behind them, in the Italian-built octagonal **New Market**, tomatoes and watermelons have been replaced by *gýros* and *souvláki* stands. Further along Mandráki is an austere ensemble of Fascist public buildings from the 1920s – post office, theatre and town hall. The Italians also left Rhodes some more lighthearted architecture: the **Governor's Palace**, a pseudo-Doge's Palace decorated with a garish red diaper pattern, and the **Evangelísmos** Cathedral, a copy of the one blown up in the Gunpowder accident. The Gothic fountain is a copy of Viterbo's Fontana Grande.

The Turks regarded Rhodes as an island paradise, and many Muslim notables in exile (including a Shah of Persia) chose to spend the rest of their lives here. Many lie buried in the cemetery north of the municipal theatre, next to the **Mosque of Murad Reis**, named after the admiral of the Egyptian sultan who was killed during the siege of Rhodes in 1522 and is buried in a turban-shaped tomb, or *turbeh*. The mosque has a lovely minaret reconstructed by the last people you would guess – the Greek Government. Stretching along the shore from here is Rhodes' busiest strand, shingly **Élli Beach**, sheltered from the prevailing southwest winds and packed chock-a-block with parasols and sunbeds; signs everywhere warn about illegal beach touts poisoning people with out-of-date food. There's a diving platform for high divers and a lifeguard, but people floating on airbeds should beware of being swept out to sea.

At the northernmost tip of the island is the **Aquarium** (*open daily in season 9–9, otherwise 9–4.30; adm*), built by the Italians in 1938, with tanks of Mediterranean fish and sea turtles, a pair of which are over 100 years old, and a startling collection of stuffed denizens of the deep, their twisted grimaces the result not of any prolonged agony but of amateur taxidermy. In the same vein, local farmers have contributed an eight-legged calf and four-legged chicken. On the headland, **Aquarium Beach** has deep water, but its breezes make it more popular for windsurfing and paragliding than sunsoaking; ditto **Windy Beach**, which stretches down to Aktí Miaoúli. A bit further south, **Psaropoúla** is a safe, sandy beach running from the Hotel Blue Sky to the Belvedere. Although often breezy, the biggest danger is crossing the busy road to get to it. South of Psaropoúla are numerous small coves with safe swimming unless the wind is strong. Women should beware another drawback: the area is nicknamed Flasher's Paradise.

### Just Outside Rhodes Town

City bus no.5 heads south of the New Town to the *acropolis* of ancient Rhodes, now known as **Monte Smith** after Admiral Sydney Smith who in 1802 kept track of Napoleon's Egyptian escapades from here; today most people come up for the romantic sunset. On the way (North Epírou Street) are the ruins of an **Asklepeion**, dedicated to the god of healing, and a **Cave of the Nymphs**. On the top of Monte Smith, the Italians have partly reconstructed a 2nd-century BC Doric **Temple of Pythian Apollo**, who was associated with Helios, and a 3rd-century BC **Stadium**, which sometimes hosts classical dramas in the summer. A few columns remain of Temples of Zeus and Athena. The adjacent, reconstructed **Ancient Theatre** is the only square one found on the islands.

City bus no.3 will take you the 2km out to **Rodíni Park**, with its cypresses, pines, oleanders, maples, peacocks and **Deer Park** (the Delphic oracle told the ancient Rhodians to import deer to solve their snake problem, and they have been here ever since). Rodíni Park marks the spot where Aeschines established his celebrated School of Rhetoric in 330 BC, where the likes of Julius Caesar and Cicero learned how to speak – there's a rock-cut tomb from the 4th century BC, the so-called 'Tomb of Ptolemy', and ruins of a Roman aqueduct. The Knights grew their medicinal herbs here, and merry drinkers can join Rodíni's peacocks for the **Rhodes Wine Festival**, recently resurrected by the council during three weeks in late July–early August with music, dance and food. Special buses transport revellers to and from Mandráki harbour.

# Western Suburbs:
# Rhodes Town to Ancient Ialysós and Mt Filérimos

On your way out of town, look out for the little houses on the left at **Kritiká**, built by Cretan Turks in 1923, facing their old homeland. **Triánda** (ΤΡΙΑΝΤΑ) or Tris, the modern name for Ialysós, has become the island's prime hotel area, and Ialysós Avenue, which runs via **Ixiá** into Rhodes Town, is lined with apartments, hotels and

# Where to Stay

## Rhodes Town ✉ 85100

The Ixiá and Triánda strip is one long stretch of hotels, with the prime luxury compounds to be found in Ixiá.

**Grecotel Rhodos Imperial, t** 024 107 5000, **f** 024 107 6690 (*L; lux*). Vast, luxurious 5-star hotel, with a range of top restaurants, watersports centre, fitness club, children's mini club, and every delight from *syrtáki* dance lessons to Greek language courses, squash to cabaret.

**Miramare Wonderland, t** 024 109 6251/4, **f** 024 109 5954 (*L; lux*). Built for those 'seeking paradise on earth', with swish cottages slap on the beach, all facilities and even a train around the complex.

**Ródos Palace, t** 024 102 5222, **f** 024 102 5350, *www.rodos-palace.com* (*L; lux*). Another rival, one of the most up-to-date hotels in the Med, with twin digital state-of-the-art communications systems and catering for the conference trade and meetings of European heads of state. The striking domed, heated Olympic-size indoor pool is partly built with Sými's former solar water still; you'll also find three outdoor pools, a sauna, gym, tennis courts and plenty more trimmings.

**Ródos Bay, t** 024 102 3661, **f** 024 102 1344 (*A; exp*). Sprawling over a hillside, with a pool and bungalows by its private beach, while the rooftop restaurant has one of Rhodes' finest views.

Scores of A- and B-class hotels and apartments, plus cheaper pensions, are available all along the road from here to the airport.

**Galini Hotel Apartments** in Ialysós, **t** 024 109 4496, **f** 024 109 1251 (*B; mod*). Apartments for 2–6 people, pool, children's pool and playground. *Open May–Oct.*

# Eating Out

Two of the island's gourmet citadels are located here.

**La Rotisserie**, in the Ródos Palace, **t** 024 102 5222 (€*30–40*). The place for French and Greek *nouvelle cuisine*, with an exquisite wine list, followed by dessert trolley and a cigar from the humidor; the Rhodians love the set-price lunch, which changes daily.

**Sandy Beach Taverna**, right on the beach in Ialysós. Favourite lunchtime haunt with a garden terrace; try its *kopanisti*, cheese puréed with cracked olives.

**Ta Koupia**, in Triánda by Ialysós (take a taxi), **t** 024 109 1824 (€*25–35*). Simply the cat's pyjamas among Rhodian trendies and visiting movie stars. Wonderfully decorated with antique Greek furniture, the food matches the décor in quality – excellent *mezédes* and upmarket Greek dishes with an Eastern touch.

**Trata** on Triánda Beach (€*16–22*). Extremely good fish and other dishes, and much kinder to the pocket.

**Tzaki**, in Ixiá. Known for its *mezédes* and *bouzouki* music.

luxury complexes out for the conference trade all the year round, as well as catering for rich summer clientèle. The beaches along here are a favourite of windsurfers (nearly every hotel has a pool for calmer swims), the sea is a lovely turquoise colour, and there are views across to Turkey. This coast was settled by Minoans in 1600 BC, and may have been damaged in the eruptions and tidal wave from Santoríni; more recently this golden mile has been devastated by neon-lit bars, fast-food places, and signs for English breakfasts and *smorgasbord*.

Triánda village occupies the not completely excavated site of **ancient Ialysós**, the least important of the three Dorian cities of Rhodes. When the Phoenicians inhabited Ialysós, an oracle foretold that they would leave only when the crows turned white and fish appeared inside the water jars. Iphicles, who besieged the town, heard the prediction and with the help of a servant planted fish in the *amphorae* and daubed a few ravens with plaster. The Phoenicians duly fled (and whatever the ancient Dorian word for 'suckers' might have been, we can be sure Iphicles said it). Ialysós was the birthplace of the boxer Diagoras, praised by Pindar in the Seventh Olympian Ode, but with the foundation of the city of Rhodes it went into such a decline that when Strabo visited in the 1st century AD he found a mere village.

The main interest in Ialysós lies in the beautiful garden-like *acropolis*-citadel above Triánda, on **Mount Filérimos** (*open Tues–Sun 8–6; adm; wear modest dress to visit the monastery*). Historically this has been a busy place. Suleiman the Magnificent made it his base during the final assault on the Knights in 1522, and it may have been the nucleus of the Mycenaean city of Achaia; the nearby cemetery yielded the Mycenaean jewellery in the Archaeology Museum. Built over the foundations of a Phoenician temple are the remains of the great 3rd-century BC **Temple of Athena Polias and Zeus Polieus**, in turn partly covered by Byzantine churches. A 4th-century **Doric fountain** with lionhead spouts has been reconstructed, but the main focal point now is the Monastery of **Our Lady of Filérimos**, converted by the Knights from a 5th-century basilica church and heavily restored by the Italians. Reached by a cypress-lined flight of steps, the monastery and its domed chapels wear the coat-of-arms of Grand Master d'Aubusson, under whom the church had both Catholic and Orthodox altars. Beneath the ruins of a small Byzantine church with a cruciform font is the tiny underground chapel of **Ag. Geórgios**, with frescoes from the 1300s. The monks will be pleased to sell you a bottle of their own green liqueur called Sette, which is made from seven herbs.

For more wonderful views, there's an uphill path from the monastery lined with the Stations of the Cross. In 1934 the Italian governor erected an enormous Cross on the summit, although seven years later the Italians themselves shot it down to prevent the Allies from using it as a target. In 1994 the Lions Club financed the current one, 52ft high, dominating an otherwise very secular coast.

## Down the East Shore to Líndos

Like the windier west shore, the sandy but not so clean shore southeast of Rhodes Town is lined with modern luxury hotels, beginning with the Blue Flag beaches of **Réni Koskinoú**, popular with families. The inland village of **Koskinoú** is known for its houses with decorative cobblestoned floors and courtyards in pebble mosaics, or *choklákia*, a technique introduced by the 7th-century Byzantines. En route, industry has taken over the Turkish village of **Asgouroú**; the mosque here was originally a church of St John.

Further along the coast the coves of **Kalithéa** are a popular spot for swimming and snorkelling. Kalithéa's waters were personally recommended by Hippocrates, and now the old, disused thermal spa, in a magnificent kitsch Italianate-Moorish building from the 1920s, is being restored at great expense by EOT. There's a small lido here and scuba-diving as well. Beyond here, holiday La-La Land begins in earnest with **Faliráki Bay North**, a massive development of upmarket hotel complexes along the sandy beach, complete with a shopping mall. Bad enough, if that's what you've come to a

# Where to Stay and Eat

## Koskinoú ✉ 85100

Most tavernas are like the village itself, small and typically Greek.
**O Yiannis**. Once cheap and cheerful, it has now become the place to see and be seen. There'll be queues but it's definitely worth the wait.

## Faliráki ✉ 85100

**Esperos Village**, between Kalithéa and Faliráki, t 024 108 6046, f 024 108 5741 (*L; lux*). Set high in its own grounds with Disney-inspired castle gates, it is so Cycladic it looks as if it escaped from Tínos; facilities on offer incl. a conference centre, swimming pools and tennis courts.
**Ródos Palladium**, right on the beach, t 024 108 6004, f 024 108 6424, *www.rodospalladium.gr* (*L; lux*). Newest all-in luxury hotel on the island (1998), with every amenity and service to spoil you rotten.
At the other end of the scale there are droves of C-class hotels (any package operator can set you up).

**Faliráki Camping**, t 024 108 5516. Now the island's only official campsite, which has every comfort.

## Afándou ✉ 85103

**Lippia Golf Resort**, t 024 105 2007, f 024 105 2367 (*A; exp–mod*). An all-inclusive air-con resort hotel, with indoor and outdoor swimming pools and tennis courts.
**Reni Sky**, t 024 105 1125, f 024 105 2413 (*B; inexp*). With a pool and good value rooms.
**Reni's**, t 024 105 1280. The jet-set head here for exceptional fish dishes, probably the best on the island.

# Entertainment and Nightlife

After dark, Faliráki is one big party.
**Champers**, t 024 108 5939. This is the 8th wonder of the world for young package ravers: karaoke and dancing on giant barrels are among the attractions.
**Slammer's Pub**. Also attracts the young sun-and-fun crowds.

Greek island to escape from, but reserve judgement until you meet the original **Faliráki**, the vortex, with its sweeping golden sands. A playground for the 18–30s predominantly Brit crowd, fur and jewellery shops rub shoulders with bars featuring wet T-shirt contests and local supermarkets that call themselves Safeway, ASDA and Kwik Save, copying the logos from UK carrier bags. If the beach to the south is for nudists, the rest of Faliráki attracts families with Godzilla's Meccano set, otherwise known as **New World Bungy** (*t 024 107 6178*), the **Faliráki Snake House** with tropical fish and live reptiles (*open 11am–11pm; adm*) and **Aqua Adventure**, 'the longest water-slide in Greece!' located in the grounds of the Hotel Pelagos. Yet as Faliráki struggles hard to become the Blackpool of the Aegean, some exclusive hotel complexes in Cycladic village style are springing up in the area. Faliráki also has the island's only campsite. The town's backdrop is all the bleaker due to recent fires which scorched the scrub from here heading south.

**Ladiko Bay** just south is a small rocky cove also known as Anthony Queen Beach (sic) after the late actor who bought land from the Greek Government (or thought he did – he could never get the title) while filming *The Guns of Navarone* at Líndos; some scenes were shot on the beach. Next door, the hidden village of **Afándou** is less frenetic and has the ultimate rarity in this part of the world – an 18-hole golf course by the sea (*t 024 10 5 1255/6*), as well as tennis courts. Once known for its carpet-weaving and apricots, Afándou now has a little tourist choo choo train and a Chinese takeaway, thanks to its 7km pebble beach, deep crystal waters and excellent fish tavernas; a few people also work at the 'Voice of America' radio station. By this point you may have noticed a plethora of roadside ceramic 'factories' with coach-sized parking lots, which are exactly what they seem to be.

Next comes **Kolýmbia**, a soulless, rapidly developing resort. A scenic avenue of eucalyptus trees leads to **Vágia Point** with some great beaches south of the headland. Local farms are irrigated thanks to the nymph-haunted lake fed by the **Eptá Pigés**, the 'Seven Springs', 5km inland. A wooded beauty spot with scented pines, it's a tranquil place to escape the sun, with strutting peacocks, lush vegetation and a wonderful streamside taverna. You can walk through ankle-deep icy water along the low, narrow, tunnel dug by the Italians (claustrophobes have an alternative route, from the road) which opens out into the spring-fed lake. But beware: the Greeks tend to wade back up again, colliding with everyone.

The long sandy bay at **Tsambíka** is very popular (although bereft of accommodation), with its tiny white monastery perched high on the cliffs above. Rhodes' answer to fertility drugs, the monastery's icon of the Virgin attracts childless women who make the barefoot pilgrimage and pledge to name their children Tsambíkos or Tsambíka, names unique to Rhodes but common enough in the phone book to prove that it works. The road leads on to **Stégna**, where charming fishermen's houses are being engulfed by tourist development. There's a shingle beach set in a pretty bay. The rugged coastal path, redolent of Cornwall, offers rewarding walks: from Tsambíka to Faraklós takes around three hours.

Next stop on the main road, **Archángelos** (pop. 3,500) is the largest village on Rhodes, with a North African feel, its little white houses spread under a chewed-up castle of the Knights, although much of its charm has been lost to tourism. Its churches, **Archángelos Gabriél** and **Archángelos Michaél**, are two of the prettiest on the island; another nearby, **Ag. Theodóroi**, has 14th-century frescoes, but all three are usually shut. Fiercely patriotic, the villagers have even painted the graveyard blue and white. Archángelos is famous for its ceramics and has several potteries, which double as gift shops. The villagers speak their own dialect, and also have a reputation for their musical talent, carpet-making and their special leather boots that keep snakes at bay. Local cobblers can make you a pair to order; they fit either foot but be warned, they don't come cheap.

Once one of the strongest citadels on Rhodes, the ruined **Castle of Faraklós** is dramatically positioned on the promontory below **Malóna**, overlooking Charáki and **Vlícha Bay**. It was originally occupied by pirates, until the Knights gave them the boot, repaired the walls and used the fort as a prison. Even after the rest of the island fell to Suleiman, Faraklós held, only surrendering after a long, determined siege. The nearby fishing hamlet of **Charáki** has a pretty shaded esplanade running along a small crescent-shaped pebble beach, and makes a welcome stop after the coastal walk. There are good waterside fish tavernas, excellent swimming and postcard views of Líndos. In **Mássari**, just inland, one of the Knights' sugar refineries was discovered where olives and orange groves now reign.

# Líndos

Dramatically situated on a promontory high over the sea, beautiful **Líndos** (ΛΙΝΔΟΣ) is Rhodes' second town, with a year-round population of 800. With its sugar-cube houses wrapped around the fortified *acropolis*, it has kept its integrity only because the whole town is classified as an archaeological site, unique in Greece; even painting the shutters a new colour requires permission, and no hotels are allowed to be built within sighting distance of the windows. Líndos was a magnet for artists and beautiful people back in the swinging sixties, when, they say, you could hear the clink of cocktail glasses as far away as Rhodes Town. It still has a few showbiz Brits (Pink Floyd's Dave Gilmour), Italians, Germans and Saudi princes and diplomats – who have

## Getting Around

Besides daily **boats** from Rhodes Town, Líndos has its own direct **hydrofoil** to Sými and to Marmaris (Turkey); book through **Pefkos Rent-a-Car, t** 024 403 1387. **Donkey taxis** to the Acropolis cost €5; the possibility of buying a photo of the experience comes with the deal. If you're staying, 3-wheeled vehicles will transport your luggage.

## Tourist Information

**Municipal Tourist Office**: Plateía Eleftherías, **t** 024 403 1900, **f** 024 403 1282; *open daily 7.30am–10pm.*

## Internet

**Lindianet**, by the post office, **t** 024 403 2142.

## Where to Stay

**Líndos** ✉ 85107

In Líndos, where it's illegal to build, nearly every house has been converted into a holiday villa, all but a few with the name of a British holiday company on the door: **Direct Greece** is one of the bigger operators (book from the UK; *see* p.88). Locally run **Pallas Travel, t** 024 403 1494, **f** 024 403 1595, can also arrange villas and rooms. If you prefer to take pot luck, you may be offered a room on arrival. If not, try this range:

**Nikolas, t** 024 404 8076 (*exp*). Pricey apartments sleeping 2–6.

**Líndos Sun, t** 024 403 1453, **f** 024 402 2019 (*C; exp–mod*). Offering tennis and pool. *Open April–Oct.*

**Kyria Teresa's, t** 024 403 1765 (*mod*). More modest, pretty garden rooms.

**Electra, t** 024 4031 266 (*mod–inexp*). Its shady garden wins the day.

**Katholiki**, adjacent, **t** 024 403 1445 (*inexp*). Rooms in a traditional house built in 1640; with a shared bathroom.

### Vlícha Bay

Outside Líndos going north, several excellent hotels are beautifully positioned on Vlícha Bay, 3km from town.

**Atrium Palace**, Kálathos, **t** 024 403 1601, **f** 024 403 1600, *atrium@otenet.gr* (*L; lux*). This is the big noise here, with every conceivable amenity.

**Líndos Bay**, on the beach, **t** 024 403 1501, **f** 024 403 1500 (*A; lux*). With great views of Líndos, tennis, watersports, swimming pool and wheelchair access.

**Líndos Mare, t** 024 403 1102, **f** 024 403 1131 (*A; exp*). Another fancy place, with a pool overlooking the sea.

**Steps of Lindos, t** 024 403 1062, **f** 024 403 1067 (*A; exp*). Luxury rooms and facilities, and offering a variety of watersports.

### South of Líndos

There are plenty of rooms for rent and pensions south of Líndos – just look out for the signs on the road.

**Lydian Village**, outside Lárdos, **t** 024 404 7361, **f** 024 404 7364 (*B; lux–exp*). Stylish club-type complex, exquisitely designed, with white Aegean-style houses clustered around paved

snapped up many of the lovely old captains' houses. Incredibly beautiful as Líndos is, there's little left of real village life apart from locals selling a few vegetables and produce in the early morning when most people are sleeping off the night before. In July and August the cobbled streets are heaving with day-trippers and you can literally be carried along by the crowds – around half a million visitors are siphoned through each year. If you want to avoid the hordes, visit in the off season; Greek Easter is wonderful in Líndos. But if you can't take the heat, be warned: Líndos is the frying pan of Rhodes and temperatures can be unbearable in August (several places rent out electric fans). The nightlife also sizzles.

Líndos was the most important of the three ancient cities of Rhodes, first inhabited in c. 2000 BC; the first temple on its magnificent, precipitous *acropolis* was erected in

courtyards. Furnishings are luxurious but with an ethnic feel: rooms are decked out with pale blue wooden taverna chairs and old ceramics. There's every facility, and it's right on the beach, with hills behind.

## Eating Out

International cuisine rules in town; prices are high and a traditional Greek coffee is as scarce as gold dust.

**Agostino's.** A very romantic roof garden, offering tasty grills, village dishes and Embónas wine by the carafe. *Open for breakfast and brunch.*

**Anna's Garden Taverna**, in the main square at Lárdos. As pleasant and tranquil as it sounds.

**Argo**, venturing north to Charáki, t 024 405 1410. Well worth the effort for the excellent food.

**Butcher's Grill**, at Péfki. Run by family butchers from Lárdos. Excellent fresh meat and traditional village cooking.

**Diónysos Taverna**, in the centre of town. All the usual Greek favourites in a beautiful rooftop setting, catering for a more modest budget.

**Haraki Bay**, in Charáki, t 024 405 1680. With an enormous *mezédes* selection.

**Líndos Restaurant**, bang in the centre by the bank. Good, reasonably priced tourist fare in a two-tiered roof garden.

**Mavriko's**, just off the square, t 024 403 1232 (€18–25). Established in 1933; an imaginative menu with exceptionally good Greek, French and Italian dishes.

**To Spitaki**, an old house in the village centre. Greek dishes with a *cordon bleu* touch in peaceful gardens.

## Entertainment and Nightlife

Líndos has all types of bars that come into their own once the day-trippers have disappeared, many in converted sea captains' mansions.

**The Captain's House**. It has the most elaborate doorway in Líndos, decorated with birds, chains and pomegranate flowers (the symbol of Rhodes); this is a charming, friendly and tranquil place for an evening tipple.

**Lindian House**. This 400-year-old building, with painted ceiling and lovely windows, is a grand place.

**Socrates**, opposite Lindian House. In another attractive captain's house.

**Jody's Flat**. Encompassing a tree, with English papers and board games, this popular place is full of character.

**Lindos By Night**, just above the donkey station. This is quite an institution, on 3 floors with lovely roof gardens, laying out superb *acropolis* views, but lost in thumping music in season.

Some nightclubs also reverberate through the town at night:

**Akropolis**, halfway down to the beach.

**Namas**, nearby.

**Amphitheatre**, on the hillside.

**Lárdos** has a good selection of music bars as well.

1510 BC. The city grew rich from its many colonies, especially Parthenope (modern Naples). Ancient Líndos, four times the size of the present town, owed its precocious importance to its twin natural harbours, the only ones on Rhodes, and to the foresight of its benevolent 6th-century BC tyrant Cleoboulos, one of the Seven Sages of Greece; he was a man famous for his beauty, his belief in the intellectual equality of women, and his many maxims, one of which, 'Measure is in all the best' (moderation in all things), was engraved at Delphi. The reservoir and rock tunnels dug by his father, King Evander, supplied water to Líndos until only a few years back. St Paul brought Christianity to the Lindians; the Knights fortified Líndos, and during the Turkish occupation, Lindian merchants handled most of the island's trade. To this day there is a rivalry between the people of Rhodes and Líndos, and the Lindians are still known for their great business acumen.

## A Walk Around Town

The serpentine pebbled lanes and stairs of Líndos are lined with elegant sea captains' mansions built between the 15th and 17th centuries. Usually constructed around courtyards with elaborate pebbled mosaics (*choklákia*), secluded behind high walls and imposing doorways, the houses have high ceilings to keep cool and raised living rooms (*sala*), while beds are often on sleeping platforms. The number of cables carved around the doors or windows represented the number of ships owned by the resident captain. Many are now holiday homes or bars, which take full advantage of their flat roofs: great for sunbathing and admiring the views. Some houses still have collections of Lindian ware, delightful plates painted with highly stylized Oriental motifs first manufactured in Asia Minor; legend has it that the Knights of St John once captured a ship full of Persian potters and would not let them go until they taught their craft to the islanders. This Lindian ware used to be displayed in the **Papakonstandís Mansion**, once the museum, now the Museum Bar. As some compensation, stop in at the Byzantine church of the **Assumption**, built on the site of a 10th-century church and restored by Grand Master d'Aubusson in 1489–90. It may take a few moments for your eyes to adjust to the dim light to see its frescoes of the Apostles, painted by the artist Gregory of Sými in 1779 and refurbished in 1927. One, oddly, has a camel head. The back wall of the church is covered with a scene of the *Last Judgement*, with St Michael weighing souls and a misogynist St Peter welcoming the Elect into heaven's gate.

## The Acropolis of Líndos

Floating high over Líndos, the **Temple of Lindian Athena** (*open in season Mon 12.30–6.40, Tues–Fri 8–6.40, Sat and Sun 8.30–2.40; rest of the year Tues–Sun 8.30–2.40; adm*) is one of the most stunningly sited in Greece, accessible on foot or by 'Lindian taxi' – hired donkey. The steep route up is lined with a guantlet of billowing blouses, embroidered tablecloths and other handicrafts, and saleswomen mugging passersby. Líndos' reputation for embroidery dates back to the time of Alexander the Great: if you look hard you may find some hand-made work, but the vast majority is massproduced, imported and overpriced.

Just before the Knights' stairway, note the prow of a *trireme* carved into the living rock. This once served as a podium for a Hellenistic statue of Agissándros, priest of Poseidon, sculpted by Pythokretes of Rhodes, whose windblown *Victory of Samothrace* now graces the Louvre. The inscription says that the Lindians gave Agissándros a golden wreath as a reward for judging their athletics events. At the top of the stair are two vaulted rooms, and to the right a crumbling 13th-century church of **St John**. Continue straight on for the raised Dorian arcade, or **Stoa** of Lindian Athena, the patron goddess of the city. She was a chaste goddess; to enter beyond here, any woman who was menstruating or had recently made love had to take a purifying bath, heads had to be covered, and even men were obliged to have clean bare feet, or wear white shoes that were not made of horsehair.

From here the 'stairway to Heaven' leads up to the mighty foundations of the **Propylaea** and, on the edge of the precipice, the **Temple of Athena** itself, of which only seven columns are standing. Both were built by Cleoboulos, rebuilt after a fire in 342 BC and reconstructed by the Italians; the reconstructions are now being restored in turn. The temple was celebrated for a primitive wooden statue of Athena, capped with gold, and its golden inscription of Pindar's Seventh Olympian Ode, now gone without a trace. On the northern slope of the Acropolis, the **Voukópion** is a small sanctuary in the recess of the rock which was used to sacrifice bullocks in honour of Athena.

The views from the Acropolis are stunning, especially over the azure round pool of the small harbour, **St Paul's Bay**, where St Paul landed in AD 58; the diminutive beach gets quite busy despite encroaching pollution. Below this, the **Grand Harbour** with the decent town beach and small but trendy **Pallas Beach** was the home port of ancient Líndos' navy, 500 ships strong. On the far end of this, the cylindrical **Tomb of Cleoboulos** intriguingly actually pre-dates the king, and in the Middle Ages was converted into the church of Ag. Ailiános.

## Villages and Beaches Around Líndos

**Péfki** (ΠΕΥΚΟΙ), just south of Líndos, has a narrow sandy beach fringed by the pine trees which give it its name along with holiday apartments, mini-markets, cocktail bars, some good tavernas, fish and chips and a Chinese restaurant. Sprawling **Lárdos** (ΛΑΡΔΟΣ), inland west of Líndos, has a pretty valley village as its core, with a charming central square where you can watch the local world go by. Just to the southwest, in the valley of **Keskinto**, farmers in 1893 dug up half of a stone *stele* from c. 100 BC with references to the orbits of Mercury, Mars, Jupiter and Saturn. Keskinto, situated on the same latitude as the Pillars of Hercules (*aka* Gibraltar), was the site of the observatory believed to have produced the famous Antikýthera Mechanism (*see* pp.466–7).

If you're under your own steam, you may want to head 12km inland to **Laerma**, turn 2km down the Profila road and travel another 2km on a dodgy road to **Moní Thari**, founded in the 9th century – the oldest surviving religious foundation on Rhodes, well hidden from pirates and now reoccupied by monks from Pátras. The church has some of the finest frescoes on Rhodes, dating back to the 12th century; in places they are four layers thick. Among the more unusual scenes are the *Storm on the Sea of Galilee* and the *Encounter with the Magdalene*.

South of Lárdos, the beach on sweeping **Lárdos Bay** has sand dunes bordered by reeds and marshes. This area is being developed with upmarket village-style hotels, but you can still find very peaceful, even deserted beaches further along the coast: **Glystra** is a gem, with a perfect sheltered cove. **Kiotári** now has sophisticated hotel complexes isolated in the surrounding wilderness, while its beach stretches for miles, with a hilly backdrop, stylish international holidaymakers and laid-back seafront tavernas. A detour inland leads to the medieval hill village of **Asklipío** (ΑΣΚΛΗΠΙΕΙΟ), huddled beneath the remains of yet another crusader castle. The church of the recently restored **Monastery of Metamórfossi** dates from 1060, and has frescoes from the 15th century depicting stories from the Old Testament, arranged like comic-strips around the walls (*open daily 9–6*).

Further south, buses go as far as **Gennádi**, an agricultural town with a beach which looks like a vast pebble mosaic. Nearby **Ag. Geórgios** has water sports and refreshments; inland, **Váti**, with its huge plane tree in the centre, is typical of the new Rhodes; only 35 people hold the fort during the week, while everyone else has a flat in the city and returns at weekends. A Bohemian, arty crowd of mostly German ex-pats have livened up the similar one-horse village of **Lachaniá Plimíri** (ΠΛΗΜΥΡΙ) has a spanking-new marina, a fish farm and a popular fish restaurant as well as some wonderful deserted beaches along a California-like coast.

## The Far South: Windsurfing and Weddings

**Kataviá** (ΚΑΤΤΑΒΙΑ), the southernmost village on Rhodes, has an end-of-the-line atmosphere, and, more importantly, a petrol station. In July and August it gets invaded by migrating windsurfers who adore the southernmost tip of Rhodes, **Cape Prassonísi**, 'the Green Island', reached by road from Kataviá. The desolate landscape may as well be the end of the world. The narrow sandy isthmus which links Prassonísi with Rhodes partially disappeared after storms, although one side remains wild and wavy, the other perfectly calm; take a caique to reach the very tip. There are a couple of tavernas, rooms and unofficial camping. Near the isthmus, Danish archaeologists discovered ruins of a 7th–6th-century BC walled settlement at **Vroulia**, set on a panoramic shelf over the sea.

For more grand views over both coasts of Rhodes, take the high corniche road from Kataviá up to **Messanagrós**, an old-fashioned mountain village. Just west, if you get stuck, you can spend the night (ask on arrival) at **Moní Skiádi**, a hilltop monastery sheltering a miraculous icon of the Panagía which was said to have flowed blood when a 15th-century heretic stabbed the Virgin's cheek. The wound, and stains, are still visible. The unpaved road continues down to the west coast, where there are spectacular views but a wind-battered sea. Sheltered in a valley, **Apolakiá** (ΑΠΟΛΑΚΚΙΑ) is a modern, unexceptional town with a few tavernas and rooms to rent, but producing the best watermelons and marriage feasts on Rhodes.

## Getting Hitched on Rhodes

As marriages and renewing-wedding-vows ceremonies become big business on Rhodes, traditional Rhodian weddings, common only 50 years ago, have become the stuff of legend. The ceremony began with gifts: the bridegroom presented his fiancée with a braided jacket, a veil embroidered with gold, a skirt and shoes, and the bride reciprocated with a shirt and tobacco pouch she had embroidered herself. To show she was no longer available, the bride's long hair was cut in front in a fringe, while the rest was gathered in numerous small plaits. Her hands were anointed with cinnamon. When she was ready, the wedding musicians were brought in to pass their instruments over her head (a somehow meaningful gesture repeated several times during the wedding day). The bridegroom was given much the same treatment.

After the wedding, the young couple were led to their new home. The new husband then dipped his finger in a pot of honey and made the sign of the cross on the door, while all the guests cried: 'Be as good and sweet as this honey!' He next stamped on a pomegranate placed on the threshold, its bursting seeds promising fertility, while the guests showered the couple with corn, cotton seeds and orange flower water. After the musicians had sung the praises of the bride and groom, the bride knelt before the father and mother of the groom and kissed their hands, then was led away by her female friends to eat at a neighbour's house to the wild crashing of cymbals and song. The dancing would begin at night and last for two days.

# Up the West Coast: Monólithos, Embónas and Mount Atáviros

**Monólithos** is the most important village of the region, the monolith in question a fantastical 700ft rocky spur rising sheer above the sea, capped spectacularly by a **castle** built by the ubiquitous Grand Master d'Aubusson. A precarious stairway winds to the top and, within the castle walls, there's the little 15th-century chapel of **Ag. Geórgios** with frescoes. There are fabulous views, especially at sunset, across to the islands of Alimnia and Chálki; a couple of panoramic tavernas make the viewing easier. There are strong currents off Cape Monólithos, but 5km below the castle, down a tortuous road, the shady bay of **Foúrni** has a sandy beach and a seasonal cantina. There are early Christian cave dwellings round the headland.

The road continues through **Siána**, an attractive old stone village built on a hillside, offering a superb view of the coast and islets. Siána is famous for its wild honey and *suma*, a local firewater reminiscent of schnapps. You can sample both at roadside cafés in the village, where the oldest houses have roofs made of clay. The church of **Ag. Panteléimon** has a beautiful interior and basil growing at the doorway.

Renowned for its wine, olives, tobacco, dancing and festivals, the mountain village of **Embónas** (ΕΜΠΩΝΑΣ) has tried to preserve its traditional ways. The dances of the women are exceptionally graceful and the *panegýri* in August are among the best on the island, fuelled by the local vintages. Some of the older people still wear local costumes, but only those who don't mind being camera fodder for the Greek Nights

## Where to Stay and Eat

**Thomas**, in Monólithos, **t** 024 606 1291, **f** 024 102 8834 (*D; inexp*). *Open all year.*
To escape from the sun-and-fun crowds, head for the hills and the village of **Sálakos**, where there are rooms and where they bottle Rhodes' natural spring water.
**Nymfi**, in Sálakos, **t** 024 602 2206 (*B; mod*). A real oasis with 4 traditional rooms: the perfect island hideaway. *Open all year.*
The village of **Kámiros Skála** is popular for fresh fish, especially at weekends, with several tavernas overlooking the sea:

**Loukas**, at the harbourside. Good food and a jolly place to wait for the Chálki ferry.
**Taverna New Kámiros**, by the sea on the old Kámiros road. Not much to look at but serves good seafood and a variety of meat dishes.
**Psinthos** and **Pigi Fasouli**, near Arthípoli, under the plane trees. These 2 restaurants are favourites, especially for a cool, shady prolonged Sun lunch.
**Artemida**, near Arthípoli. With charcoal grills and good house wines.
**Taverna Oasis** at Eleoússa. Another fine choice, lost in the trees.

and Folk Dance busloads from Rhodes Town. Embónas is the centre of the Rhodes winemaking co-operative, **CAIR** (their sparkling white makes a superb Buck's Fizz), and **Emery Winery**, founded by the Triantafýllou family in the 1920s. Visitors are welcome in their handsome tasting room (*t* 024 604 1208; open Mon–Fri 9–3). Their mighty red Cava (12.5°) is made from a local grape, *mandilari* (or *amoryianí*), but the wine that has really made them famous, white Villaré, owes its distinctness to indigenous grape *athiri* that refuses to grow well outside its own microclimate, at 2,296ft altitude, on the slopes of the island's highest peak, **Mount Atáviros** (3,986ft); the summit is a tough three-hour climb from Embónas. Here Althaemenes (*see* p.371) built the Temple of Zeus Atavros, although little remains to be seen, besides eagle-eye views of the whole island – you can, they say, see Crete on a clear morning. Poor Althaemenes used to come up here when he longed, like all Cretans, for his mother island.

While up on the roof of Rhodes, head around to **Ag. Isidóros**, like Embónas minus tourists, with vineyards and tavernas. Legend says Althaemenes founded the white hillside village below Embónas, **Kritinía**, which he named in honour of Crete. Just below Kritinía lies **Kámiros Skála** (ΣΚΑΛΑ ΚΑΜΙΡΟΥ), a fishing harbour with two good tavernas that served as the port of ancient Kámiros, 16km north. These days it's where the local ferries depart for Chálki. The ferries link with the buses to and from Monólithos and Rhodes Town, taking the children of Chálki to school and the islanders shopping. Towering high above Kámiros Skála, the **Kastéllo** (signposted Kástro Kritinías) is one of the Knights' most impressive ruins, set above lemon groves and pinewoods, and affording spectacular views.

### Ancient Kámiros

Althaemenes' most celebrated foundation, however, was **Kámiros** (ΚΑΜΙΡΟΣ) (*open Tues–Sun 8.30–5; adm*), one of Rhodes' three Dorian cities, built in terraces up the hillside. Destroyed by an earthquake in the 2nd century BC, the city was simply abandoned and forgotten, covered with the dust of centuries until no one remembered it was there. In the 19th century, local farmers discovered a few graves, and in 1859 the improbably named British Consul and French archaeologist, Biliotti and Alzman respectively, began excavating. The city they eventually brought to light was the Pompeii of Rhodes, and yielded many beautiful items now in the British Museum. An excellent water and drainage system, supplied by a large reservoir, served around 400 families in the excavated Hellenistic-era houses. A second dig in 1914 carried out by the Italians uncovered most of the ancient city: the baths, the *agora* with its rostrum for public speeches, the *agora*'s Great *Stoa* with its Doric portico, Roman houses, two temples – one 6th-century BC dedicated to Athena of Kámiros and the other Doric from the 3rd century – and an altar dedicated to sunny Helios.

Down on the coast at the modern town of Kámiros there are some tavernas for necessary pit-stops. **Fanés**, further north from here, has a long, narrow stony beach with a few tavernas.

Inland, on a high hill over the village of **Sálakos**, are the ruins of another medieval fort; Sálakos itself is beloved for its shade and fresh water from the Spring of the Nymphs. This region of Rhodes, with its cedar and pine forests, and views of the sea, is one of the prettiest for walks. Further up, the road leads to **Mount Profítis Ilías** (2,600ft) and its two derelict Swiss chalet hotels. The trees here belong to the Prophet Elijah, who according to legend strikes down any sinner who dares to cut one down. The chief settlements on its slopes are **Apóllona** with a museum of popular art and Eleoússa with a pretty Byzantine church. Nearby Arthípoli, with its good tavernas, is a favourite green oasis for lunch.

## Back on the Northwest Coast

**Theológos** (or **Thólos**) announces the proximity of Rhodes Town with hotels and a collection of roadside supermarkets and tavernas. Beyond is the straggling village of **Paradíssi** (ΠΑΡΑΔΕΙΣΙ), next door to the **airport**. Hardly heaven, it's still a useful place for an overnight stay after a night flight – plenty of 'rooms to let' signs – and there's a small beach, constantly zapped by roaring planes. The strip in neighbouring **Kremastí** (ΚΡΕΜΑΣΤΗ) bustles with foreign tourists and Greek soldiers from the island's barracks. The village itself is famous for its wonder-working icon, **Panagías Kremastí**, occasioning one of the biggest *panegýri* in the Dodecanese (from 15–23 August), complete with a funfair, *souvláki* stands and hawkers selling their wares. At the climax on 23 August, the villagers don beautiful traditional costumes and dance a very fast *sousta*.

Inland, a road between Theológos and Paradíssi leads to **Káto Kalamónas** and from there to one last enchanting spot, more so if you manage to get there before or after the coach parties: **Petaloúdes**, the **Valley of the Butterflies** (*open May–Sept daily 8.30–7; adm*). Sliced by a stream and waterfalls, the narrow gorge is crowned by a roof of fairytale *storax* trees, whose vanilla-scented resin is used to make frankincense. From June to September rare Quadrina butterflies (actually moths, *Callimorpha quadripuntaria*, named for the Roman numeral IV on their black, brown, white and red wings) flock here, attracted by the resin. This is one of their two breeding grounds in the world, and in recent years their numbers have declined because of tourists clapping their hands to see their wings: every flight weakens them, so resist the urge.

You can follow the trail up the valley to the Monastery of the **Panagía Kalópetra**, built in 1782 by Alexander Ypsiléntis, grandfather of the two brothers who wanted to be kings at the start of the 1821 Greek War of Independence. It's a tranquil place well worth the uphill trek, with wonderful views and picnic tables in the grounds. From here another wooded trail leads to the **Monastery of Ag. Soúlas**, just off the road down to Soroní. Here they have a giant festival on 30 July with donkey races and folk dancing immortalized in *Reflections on a Marine Venus*.

# Sými (ΣΥΜΗ)

Inevitably, there's a fusillade of clicking camera shutters and purring of camcorders when the ferries swing into Sými's main harbour, Gialós. Few islands have Sými's crisp brightness and its amphitheatre of Neoclassical mansions, in soft ochre or traditional deep shades, stacked one on top of the other right up the barren hillsides. There are few trees to block the sun, for unlike its neighbour Rhodes, Sými is an arid island. Most visitors arrive on the numerous daily excursion boats from Rhodes, when pandemonium reigns in several languages, as groups are herded along the waterfront or head for the small town beach at Nos. When the boats have at last sounded their sirens and the invaders departed, Sými regains much of its serenity; at night when the lights come on it is pure romance. As its lovely houses are all bought up and immaculately restored, the island has become a very trendy place, with a major cultural festival for two months each summer and many fancy restaurants. Sými is also very popular with the sailing fraternity, who fill the harbour with their yachts, flotillas and cruisers flying the colourful flags of all nations. Avoid August when the island is heaving, rooms are expensive and tempers frayed in the heat; because it's in a basin and the heat bounces off the rocks, Sými sizzles like a cat on a hot tin roof from July to September.

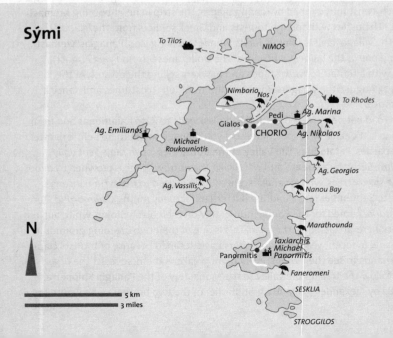

**Sými**

# Getting There and Around

**By sea**: **ferry** connections with the island's own ferries, *Sými I* and *Sými II*, leave Mandráki harbour (Rhodes) daily in the early evening and then return to Rhodes in the early morning. There are at least 3 daily **tourist boats** from Rhodes, some calling at Panormítis Monastery, and also a daily **hydrofoil**. Local **excursion boats** visit different beaches, and the islets of Sesklía and Nímos; lovely old caiques like the *Triton* circle the island, plying you with *ouzo* and *retsína* on the journey. **Water taxis** go to Nimborió from Gialós and Ag. Nikólaos from Pédi Beach. There's a weekly excursion to Datcha (Turkey) that's run by **Sými Tours, t** 024 107 1307. **Port authority**: **t** 024 107 1205.

**By road**: the **taxi rank** and **bus stop** are to be found on the east of the harbour, **t** 024 107 2666; the island has 4 **taxis** and the Sými **Bus**, departing every hr from 8.30am to 10.30pm from Gialós to Pédi via Chorió. Various places rent **motorbikes** and **scooters** nearby at a cost – shop around.

## Tourist Information

**The police** share the **post office** building near the Clock Tower, in Gialós, **t** 024 107 1111. Pick up a copy of the free *Sými Visitor* for helpful tips on the island. Also, look out for Mr Noble's *Walking on Sými*.

**Kalodoukas Holidays**, at the foot of the Kalí Stráta, **t** 024 107 1077, **f** 024 107 1491. Has character properties to let, excursion programmes, and also runs a second-hand book exchange.

**Sými Tours, t** 024 107 1307, **f** 024 107 2292, *www.symi-island.com*. Villas and rooms to rent. Also organizes a range of walking excursions.

## Internet

**Vapori Bar**, near the start of the stairs to Chorió.

## Festivals

**July–Sept**: Sými Festival, with big-name performers, especially in music.
**8 Nov**: at the monasteries of Panormítis and Roukouniótis.

## Where to Stay and Eat

### Sými ✉ 85600

Most of the island's accommodation is in Gialós but there are also rooms to let in Chorió and Pédi. Sými is very expensive in July and Aug, and suffers from cockroaches then anyway. Cheaper rooms are often let on condition that you stay 3 nights or more, to economize on sheet-washing. There's no campsite but unofficial camping is tolerated on remote beaches.

### Gialós

Two of the most stylish places to stay on the island are both old sea captains' mansions, lovingly restored and decked out with fine wood interiors:

**Aliki**, **t/f** 024 107 1665 (*A; lux–exp*). With an attractive roof garden, and air-con in some of the rooms.

**Dorian**, up the steps just behind the Aliki, **t** 024 107 1181, **f** 024 107 2292 (*A; lux–exp*). 9 decent self-catering studios.

On the other hand, it stays wonderfully warm into October and is particularly lovely in the cooler months of spring.

## History

According to legend, Sými was a princess (daughter of King Ialysos on Rhodes), who was abducted and brought here by Glaukos, an eminent sponge-diver and sailor who also built the Argo for Jason. The islanders inherited Glaukos' shipbuilding skills: throughout history Sými was famous for its ships. Sými was also known as Metapontis, or Aigle, after a daughter of Apollo and mother of the Three Graces.

**Grace, t** 024 107 1415 (*B; exp*). One of the many traditional houses with recently added smart studios.

**Nereus**, near the Dorian, **t** 024 107 2400, **f** 024 107 2404 (*C; exp*). Sympathetically restored and wonderfully painted in traditional colours.

**Opera House**, set back from the harbour, **t** 024 107 1856, **f** 024 107 2035 (*A; exp*). Lovely family suites with air-con and surrounded by a well-kept garden.

**Albatros** in the marketplace, **t** 024 107 1707, **f** 024 107 2257 (*C; mod*). For more modest but recommended rooms, well decorated and with air-con.

**Kokona, t** 024 107 1451, **f** 024 107 2620 (*mod*). Decent en suite rooms, but unfortunately, no sea-view.

**Les Katerinettes, t** 024 107 2698 (*mod*). For stunning views over the harbour, especially at night, this old favourite takes some beating; situated above the restaurant in an eccentric traditional house with pleasingly painted ceilings. Downstairs, try the octopus and *pikilía*, or the wide selection of tasty *mezédes*.

**Egli**, at the base of the stairway to Chório, **t** 024 107 1392 (*inexp*). Clean, no frills rooms; *usually only open in high season*.

**Katerina's Rooms, t** 024 107 1813. Scenic location, with kitchen facilities and tremendous vista.

The eateries in Sými fall into 2 clear-cut categories: really good and genuine, and tourist traps along the harbour.

**Meraklis**, in the backstreets beyond the bank. Away from all the frippery, this is one of the island's most authentic tavernas with excellent Greek cooking and very reasonable prices.

**Neraida**, behind Hotel Glafkos. Delicious untouristy food at budget prices.

**Mylopetra, t** 024 107 2333 (€25–35). Friendly German owner; elegant atmosphere with good Greek and Mediterranean dishes, incl. homemade bread and pasta. Part of the floor is made of glass, and looks down onto the site of a 50 BC tomb, the finds of which are in Rhodes Museum.

**Ellinikon**, just back from the bridge, **t** 024 107 2455 (€18–22). Unusual *mezédes* and main courses (try sea bass with pesto sauce), and 150 Greek wines.

**Taverna Yiannis**, over the bridge. Another good place where you might be lucky enough to be treated to some impromptu Greek music.

**O Tholos**, out on the headland, **t** 024 107 2033. An impressive menu in a romantic setting, serving great *mezédes* and fresh grills.

**Dimítris**, on the way out of town. Family-run *ouzerie* with a scrumptious variety of fish dishes.

**Vapori Bar**, near the square, at the start of the stairs to Chorió. Send an e-mail home, or read the quality UK newspapers and magazines over baked potatoes or home-made chocolate cake.

## Chorió

**Horio, t** 024 107 1800, **f** 024 107 1802 (*B; exp–mod*). Built in traditional style with smart rooms ( incl. air-con and breakfast) and stunning views, surrounded by fields, plus goats and donkeys.

**Metapontis**, in upper Chorió, **t** 024 107 1491 (*B; exp–mod*). In a very old Sými house cleverly converted to keep many of the traditional wooden features like the *moussandra* sleeping gallery.

In another myth, Prometheus modelled a man from clay here, angering Zeus so much that he turned the Titan into a monkey for the rest of his natural days on the island – hence simian.

Pelasgian walls in Chorió attest to the prehistoric settlement of Sými. In the *Iliad* Homer tells how the island mustered three ships for Troy, led by King Nireus. After Achilles, Nireus was the most beautiful of all the Greeks, but, as in Achilles' case, beauty proved to be no defence against the Trojans. In historical times Sými was part of the Dorian Hexapolis, but dominated by Rhodes. The Romans fortified the *acropolis*

Fiona, lower down the village, t 024 107 2088 (*mod*). Comfortable and tasteful bed and breakfast; the owner plays the *sandouri* – Zorba's instrument.

Jean and Tonic Bar, t 024 107 1819, f 024 107 2172 (*mod*). Affable Jean also has several well-situated traditional-style houses to rent.

Taxiarchis, t 024 107 2012, f 024 107 2013 (*C; mod*). Elegant Neoclassical development of family-run apartments with a small bar, breakfast terrace, and breathtaking panorama of Pédi (as well as the occasional package group).

Georgio's Taverna. An institution at night, famous for exquisite Sými shrimps and the man himself on the accordion.

### Pédi

Lemonia, t 024 107 1201, f 024 107 2374 (*exp*). Small, pretty and blue, with views of the village and bay below; rooms with balcony, sitting area, kitchenette, ceiling fans and phone.

Pédi Beach, t 024 107 1870, f 024 107 1982 (*B; exp–mod*). Usually booked solid by package holiday operators. Otherwise there are a few rooms to let.

Taverna Tolis, on the beach, next to the boat yard. The best for food and atmosphere among the several eateries.

Kamares. The next best decent choice.

### Nimborió

Taverna Metapontis, t 024 107 1820 (*mod*). Besides being a pretty spot for lunch (their taxi boat *Panagióta* will take you back to Gialós), try the rooms to let if you really want to get away from the crowds for a few days.

# Entertainment and Nightlife

Sými buzzes at night, the lights from the houses and the bars reflecting their colours in the harbour like stained glass.

Paco's. The island's old *ouzerie* is still a favoured institution.

Elpida, across the water in Mouragio. A rival for Paco's; this is a smart new *ouzerie* doing traditional *mezédes*.

Nightlife revolves around the bars off the square, popular with locals and tourists alike.

Mina's and former rival bar Vapori next door have finally clubbed together now, jointly attracting yachties and up-market Brits.

*Meltémi* Bar. For less conspicuous rivalry and conflicting sounds make your way to this laid-back bar.

Τεμβελα Σκαλα ('Lazy Steps'), along the harbour. An excellent bar where locals sometimes play traditional Greek music if the mood takes them.

The Roof Garden. Attracts the yachting crowd and sophisticated night owls, for snacks, mellow sounds and romantic views.

Kalí Stráta, just down the steps. Panoramic views from this venue.

Jean and Tonic, in Chorió. There are a few bars in town, but this friendly one caters for locals as well as tourists and still reigns supreme for early outdoors happy hour and late nightcaps.

The Club dancing bar, in Gialós. Great for a good bop.

Alethini Taverna on the road to Pédi. Real *bouzouki* nights with traditional music and dance.

Valanidia, further along. Also has *bouzouki* with top singing stars in high season.

at Chorió; the Byzantines converted it into a fort, which was renovated by the first Grand Master of the Knights of Rhodes, Foulques de Villaret. From Sými's Kástro the Knights could signal to Rhodes, and they favoured swift Sýmiot skiffs or *skafés* for their raiding activities.

Thanks to the Knights, Sými prospered through shipbuilding and trade. When Suleiman the Magnificent came in 1522, the Sýmiots, known as the most daring divers in the Aegean, avoided attack by offering him the most beautiful sponges he had ever seen. In return for a relative degree of autonomy, Sými sent a yearly consignment of sponges to the sultan's harem. Like the Knights, the Turks made use of the swift Symiot ships, this time for relaying messages. In order to keep Sými thriving, the sultan made it a free port and allowed the inhabitants to dive freely for sponges in Turkish waters.

Little Sými thus became the third richest island of the Dodecanese, a position it held from the 17th to the 19th centuries. Large mansions were constructed; shipbuilders bought forests in Asia Minor; schools thrived. Even after certain privileges were withdrawn because of its participation in the 1821 revolution, Sými continued to flourish. The Italian occupation and the steamship, however, spelt the end of its luck: the Italians closed the lands of Asia Minor and the steamship killed the demand for wooden sailing vessels altogether; during the Italian tenure the population of Sými nosedived from 23,000 to 600 by the outbreak of the Second World War. At its end, the treaty giving the Dodecanese to Greece was signed on Sými on VE Day, 8 May 1945, later ratified on 7 March 1948.

## Gialós and Chorió

Sými divides into down, up and over – Gialós situated around the harbour, Chorió, the older settlement high above it, Kástro even higher, on the site of the ancient *acropolis*, and Pédi clustered round the bay over the hill. In **Gialós** (a derivation of its ancient name Aigialos), arrivals are greeted by the elaborate free-standing bell tower of Ag. Ioánnis, surrounded by beautiful *choklákia* pavements, and most of Sými's tourist facilities, tavernas and gift shops. Many harbour stalls sell sponges and locally-grown herbs, filling the air with the pungent scent of oregano and spices. In honour of the island's shipbuilding tradition and the signing of the Treaty of the Dodecanese, a copy of the *trireme* from Líndos has been carved into the rock with the inscription: 'Today freedom spoke to me secretly; Cease, Twelve Islands, from being pensive. 8th May, 1945.' The Treaty of the Dodecanese was signed in the nearby restaurant, Les Katerinettes. Behind the small recreation ground next to the bridge which links the two halves of the harbour, a Neoclassical mansion houses the **Nautical Museum** (*open Mon–Sat 10–3; adm*), with models of Sými's sailing ships, sponge-diving equipment, old photos and a stuffed heron.

At the end of the harbour, behind the clock tower and bronze statue of a little boy fishing, the road leads to shingly **Nos Beach** via **Charani Bay**. It is still a small hive of industry where wooden caiques are built or repaired, while chickens strut about and cats lurk under the beached prows. Heavily bombed during the Second World War, many of the houses here are now being renovated in traditional Sými style with elegant plasterwork in blues, greys, yellows and Venetian red. **Nos**, complete with waterside taverna and omnipresent sun-loungers, is a small strand that is popular with families. But it's also the first place the day-trippers hit, so it soon gets extremely packed. It's a better idea to walk further along the coastal path to the flat rocks and small coves popular with nudists, on the way to **Nimborió**, a pretty tree-shaded harbour with a good taverna, yet more loungers and a rather pebbly shore. Sand has been imported further round the bay to create **Zeus Beach**, which also has a cantina for those in need of refreshment.

Most of the Neoclassical houses in Gialós date from the 19th century, while older architecture dominates the **Chorió**. The lower part can be reached by road from the port; the alternative is a slog up the 375 steps of the **Kalí Stráta**, a mansion-lined stairway which starts near the Kaloudoukas agency off Plateía Oekonómou (or Plateía tis Skálas), to reach the houses in the maze of narrow lanes in the high town. Worn smooth and slippery over the years, the steps can zap even the fittest in the heat of high summer, even though local grannies trip up and down like mountain goats. The stairway can be sinister after dark: a torch is a must. In the centre of lower Chorió near the derelict windmills, a **stone monument** was erected by the Spartans for their victory over the Athenians off the coast of Sými. On the headland overlooking Pédi Bay are the Pillars of Sými, dating from when the island was an important part of the Dorian Hexapolis.

Now mostly restored, the houses in Chorió are crammed together, often forming arches and vaults over the narrow lanes. They are built in the Aegean sugar-cube style, small and asymmetrical, but with Neoclassical elements incorporated into their doorways and windows. Many have lovely interiors with carved woodwork and Turkish-style *moussándra*, beds on raised platforms. Buildings to look out for are the **19th-century pharmacy** with a remedy for every malady in its many drawers and jars; the fortress-mansion **Chatziagápitos**; and the churches of **Ag. Panteleímon** and **Ag. Giórgios** with their intricate pebble mosaics of evil mermaids sinking hapless ships. Follow the signs to the island's **museum** (*t 024 107 1114; open Tues–Sun 10–2; adm*), which houses icons, coins, pottery, a reconstructed 19th-century Symiot room and bits and bobs going as far back as the 5th century AD. Up at the top, the **Kástro** sits on the ancient *acropolis*; its Byzantine and medieval walls top a Temple of Athena; the coat-of-arms belongs to d'Aubusson, the Grand Master supremo. Within the Kástro's fortifications the church of **Megáli Panagía** has good frescoes and post-Byzantine icons. The orginal church was blown up by the Germans when they discovered an arms cache hidden inside. As a memorial, one of the church bells is made from the nose-cone of a bomb.

# Around the Island

From Chorió it's an easy half-hour walk downhill to **Pédi** (ΠΕΔΙ) along a shady avenue of eucalyptus trees. This being the most fertile area of the island, there are smallholdings all along the way, herds of goats, a few donkeys and fig trees in the fields. A petite sandy beach and boatyard plus excellent taverna await you to the left where the road forks, while to the right past the church you'll find some rooms to let and a more developed beach with cafés, the Pedi Beach Hotel, and typical fishermen's cottages edging the bay. From here you can follow the left-hand path up over the headland to **Ag. Marína**, with a chapel-topped islet within swimming distance. This was the site of a famous secret school before the Greek War of Independence broke out in 1821. Water taxis from Pédi buzz to the 18th-century church of **Ag. Nikólaos** with its shingly tree-fringed beach and cantina. Otherwise follow the goat-track, marked with daubs of red paint, which begins to the far right of the bay, and takes you up and over the headland.

A road from Chorió now goes to the extreme southern tip of the island to the vast 18th-century **Monastery of Taxiárchis Michael Panormítis** (*open daily 9–2 and 4–8*), set against a backdrop of cypresses and pine. In the summer, tourist boats from Rhodes descend on it for an hour at 11am, making for massive crowds. Archangel Michael of Panormítis Bay is Sými's patron, a favourite of all Greek sailors, and the monastery is the goal of pilgrimages throughout the summer – hence the seaside guest rooms, where the underwear of Greek families flaps merrily by signs demanding modest dress. The monastery's landmark colourful Neoclassical bell-tower was built in 1905; its *choklákia* courtyard is strewn with flags; the church, coated with smoke-blackened frescoes has, on a remarkable wooden **iconostasis**, the stern, larger-than-life silver-plated icon of St Michael, painted by Ioánnis of the Peloponnese in 1724. Taxiárchis Michael is a busy archangel: at once heaven's gener-alissimo, slayer of the satanic dragon, weigher of souls (one of his nicknames on Sými is *Kailiótis* because of the pain he brings mortal hearts), and patron saint of the Greek Air Force, he can also be called upon to come through in storms and induce fertility. You can hardly miss the gold and silver ship ex-votos, and the wax babies left behind by the grateful faithful.

There are two small **museums** (*adm*), one filled with more rich gifts from sailors, model ships and prayers in bottles which miraculously found their way to Panormítis bearing money for the monastery, Chinese plates and ivories donated by Symiots living in Africa, stuffed crocodiles, a weasel and a mongoose. The second contains household furnishings, and the radio for British commandoes operated by the abbot and two members of the Resistance, who were executed by the Germans in 1944. Outside, there's a small shop/*kafeneíon* with miserable service, a bakery selling white and 'brawn' bread, a decent taverna with wonderful sunset views (with a memorial to the abbot), a small sandy beach, and an army barracks. You can walk in the woods surrounding the monastery, or follow the forest trail to the pebbly beach at **Marathoúnda**, with resident goats.

**Sesklía**, the islet facing Panormítis, also belongs to the monastery. Its ancient name was Teutlousa, and Thucydides writes that it was here that the Athenians took refuge after their defeat by the Spartan navy during the Peloponnesian War. A few Pelasgian walls remain and there are regular barbecue trips from Gialós. Sesklí has a long pebbly beach shaded with tamarisk trees, and crystal waters. There are a few ruins on the nearby islet **Stroggilós**, while boat trips also visit the islet of **Nímos**, a stone's throw from the Turkish coast.

Sými has 77 churches altogether, many of which are dedicated to Archangel Michael. One of the most interesting is **Michael Roukouniótis**, an hour's walk from Gialós. Built in the 18th century, this church is a curious combination of Gothic and folk architecture, and holds its feast day beneath an old umbrella-shaped cypress tree. **Ag. Emiliános** is on an islet in the bay of the same name, connected to the shore by a causeway with a pleasant pebbly beach nearby. On the east coast, best reached by caique, **Ag. Giórgios** has a tree-shaded sandy beach and **Nánou Bay** has an excellent shingly one, fringed by delightful trees – another favourite barbecue spot. There's a small chapel and masses of wild herbs to flavour the food. Other beaches include **Faneroméni** opposite Panormítis and the scenic bay of **Ag. Vassílis**, a two-hour-plus walk across the island.

# Tílos (ΤΗΛΟΣ)

Tílos has been one of the best-kept secrets in the Dodecanese for some time, with good unspoiled beaches, friendly people and wonderful walking country: a tranquil antidote to Kos and Rhodes. Although at first glance the island looks rugged and barren, inland it shelters groves of figs, almonds, walnuts, pomegranates and olives, and small farms growing vegetables and tobacco, watered by fresh springs. It's even a lot cheaper than neighbouring islands like Sými. The harbour Livádia isn't the prettiest you'll ever find but it has a certain charm that soon grows on you. Village life goes on with few concessions to tourism, although it's beginning to trickle in: a package holiday programme, a few day trips and hydrofoil links with other islands have inspired a bit of new holiday development. But so far, nothing overwhelming. It's as fine a place as any to do nothing, to birdwatch; a dreaminess surrounds all practical activities and the visitor who neglects to wind his watch is in danger of losing all track of time.

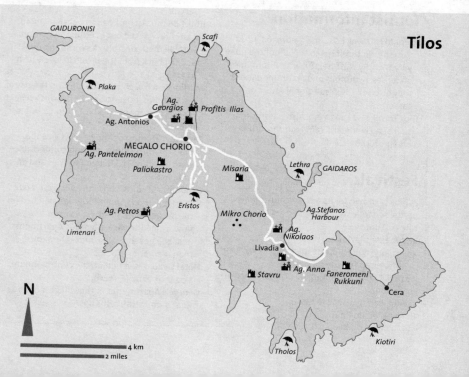

# Getting There and Around

**By sea: ferry** connections 4–5 times a week with Rhodes, Kos and Kálymnos; 3–4 times a week with Sými and Níssyros; twice a week with Piraeus, Pátmos, Léros and Kastellórizo; once a week with Náxos, Páros and Sýros. In addition, by **hydrofoil** there are regular links with the islands of Rhodes, Níssyros, Kos, Kálymnos, Sými and Chálki. **Port authority**: t 024 104 4350. **Excursion boats** do the rounds of the island's more remote beaches. (*see* Blue Sky Taverna for details), but be warned, the fares can be expensive.

**By road**: there's a regular **bus** service from Livádia to Megálo Chorió, Ag. Antónis and Éristos. You can also hire **mopeds** and **motorbikes** from various outlets in town. If you come across a **yellow taxi** in high season it will be an Athens cabbie on holiday. You could try your luck at flagging him down. Otherwise you're on foot, but fortunately, Tilos is very good for walkers, with plenty of tracks to follow and excellent locally-researched walking maps.

# Tourist Information

**Stefanákis Travel**, t 024 104 3310/4360, f 024 104 4315, on the steps to the left of the quay. Very friendly staff, helpful with information on ferries, hydrofoils and accommodation; they also sell Tílos' traditional music on cassette.

**Tílos Travel**, t 024 105 3259. Also has information of all kinds, and rents out motorbikes and motorboats.

# Festivals

Tílos is known for its ancient music played on the *sandoúri* and violin, dances, and elaborate costumes.

**28 June**: Ag. Pávlos.

**25–27 July**: huge 3-day festival or *panegýri*, Ag. Panteleímon at the monastery.

**28 July**: Taxiárchis at Megálo Chorió, dance of the Koúpa.

**15 Aug**: Panagías, Mikró Chorió.

**8 Nov**: Megálo Chorió.

# Where to Stay and Eat

**Tílos ✉ 85002**

There's an accommodation booth by the quay that opens when the ferries and hydrofoils arrive in the port. Property owners with free rooms may meet the ferries, but it's best to make a reservation in the summer months. Everyone on the island seems to own at least a hundred goats, which provide the main ingredient of the delicious local speciality – kid stuffed with rice: a mix of local herbs, tomatoes and chopped liver, baked in the oven.

## Livádia

**Tílos Mare**, t 024 104 4100, f 012 104 4005 (*B; exp*). New, furnished studios, all with air-con; there's also a swimming pool and excellent restaurant.

**Castellos Beach**, t 024 104 4267 (*mod*). Family-run; luxurious, modern rooms with fridges and fans, overlooking the sea.

**Eleni**, right on the beach, t 024 104 4062, f 024 104 4063 (*C;mod*). Pleasant, new development; blue and white and with a minibus service.

**Irini**, t 024 104 4293, f 024 104 4238 (*C; mod*). Tastefully tricked out in ethnic style, rooms with all mod cons; also a swimming pool. Set just back from the beach in lovely lush gardens.

**Marina Beach**, a 20min walk around the bay at Ag. Stéfanos, t 024 104 4064 (*mod*). Excellent A-class rent rooms, if a bit far-flung, but also does good food.

**Paraskevi Studios**, on the beach, t 024 104 4280 (*mod*). A couple of clean comfortable apartments, with kitchen facilities and en suite bathrooms.

**Panorama Studios**, above the village, t/f 024 104 4365 (*mod*). Smart lodgings, perched on the hillside, with great views from the flower-filled terrace. **Olympus Apartments**, near the beach, is also under the same management.

**Hotel Livadia**, just behind the central square, t 024 105 2202 (*E; inexp*).

**George's Apartments**, in the village, t 024 104 4243. Comfortable studios.

**Spiros**, on the row of rooms to let at the western end of the beach, t 024 105 3339. This one has en suite rooms.

**Stefanakis Apartments**, behind the bakery, t 024 104 4310/4360, f 024 104 4315. Comfortable option with convenient daily maid service.

**Blue Sky Taverna**, above the jetty. Wonderful harbour views. They also organize around the island boat trips, visiting various small beaches.

**Irina**, on the beach. Good Greek home cooking, a wide choice of dishes and cheap beer. Great for lunch with tables on the sand shaded by trees.

*Kafeneíon* **Omónia**, near the post office. Very Greek and good for a cheap filling breakfast and snacks, although food can be scarce at night; it's also the place for a pre-dinner *ouzo*.

**Michaelis Taverna**, not far from the central square. Specializing in mouthwatering spit roasts.

**Sophia's Taverna**, along the beach road. Excellent food and friendly service, popular with Brits.

**Trata**. First choice for fish and seafood, but a bit pricier than most.

### Megálo Chorió

**Miliou Rooms and Apartments**, in the village centre, t 024 102 1002, f 024 104 4204 (*mod*). Pleasant rooms with a traditional Greek touch set in a lush garden. The complex even has an aviary full of lively budgies to keep you company.

**Pension Sevasti**, next door to the excellent Kali Kardia Taverna, t 024 105 3237 (*inexp*). Decent rooms for those on a more modest budget.

**Konstantina's**. All the tavernas here are good. This is a friendly place, from whose terrace you can watch the hawks floating over the valley below.

### Éristos

**Éristos Beach Apartments**, right on the beachfront, t 024 104 4336, f 024 104 4024 (*inexp*). A new, simple development, but all apartments come equipped with fans and verandas.

**Nausika Taverna**, set back from the beach. Standard fare on the menu. Also has inexpensive but comfortable rooms.

**Tropicana Restaurant and Rooms**, t 024 105 3242. Peaceful haven in a tropical garden with chalet-type rooms. Good for fresh seafood and local vegetable dishes served in a beautiful rose-covered arbour. Great for romantic al fresco dining.

Éristos Beach is a good option for freelance camping, with its facilities block. Plaka Beach is also a camping spot, but you need your own wheels to get there, and it doesn't have any drinking water.

### Ag. Antónios

**Hotel Australia**, right on the beach, t 024 105 3296 (*D; inexp*). Immaculate, informal place; run by a couple of Greek Australian brothers who meet guests from the ferries with their own transit van.

**Delfini Fish Restaurant**. Owned by fishermen; they also do stuffed kid.

## Entertainment and Nightlife

Nightlife in Tílos centres around the inviting tavernas and bars.

**Yiorgo's**. People sit here in the square, happily watching the world go by.

**Omónia**. Another good central choice for a nightcap.

**La Luna Bar**, on the quay. New venue that plays an eclectic mix of international and Greek music and attracts a young lively crowd.

**Mikró Chorió**. Night owls with plenty of energy head for this deserted town, where a group of friends have recently set up a unique dancing bar in a restored traditional house. They light up the ruins at night to give the impression that the village has come alive again. The action kicks in at midnight, with rock music until 1.30am, and following this, Greek music and dancing often goes on until dawn creeps magically over Livadía – and the beauty of it is, there are no neighbours to complain about the noise.

## History

Tílos was joined to Asia Minor six million years ago. When it broke away *c*. 10,000 years ago, elephants were trapped on the island and adapted to the limited supply of food by shrinking. In the Grotto of Charcadio, a deep ravine in the Mesaria area, the bones of these mini-elephants and the remains of deer and tortoises left over from other feasts were found alongside Stone Age pottery. Nearby, pumice cliffs and volcanic debris came from the eruption on Níssyros.

In mythology, Tílos was named after the youngest son of Alia and Helios, the sun god. When his mother fell ill, Tílos came to the island to gather healing herbs for her. When she recovered he built a sanctuary to Helios Apollo and Poseidon in gratitude and became a priest, and ever after local priests bore the title of Holy Servants of Helios. The main town on the island up to early Christian times was the Kástro at Megálo Chorió. In the 7th century BC Tílos was prosperous enough to found Gela, an important colony in Sicily under the leadership of Tilinis. The island minted its own coins from the 4th century, became an ally of Rhodes, and at the summit of its fortunes, it was famous for its variety of perfumes and the poetess Erinna, 'the female Homer' whose work was said to rival that of Sappho. Sadly, she died very young and little of her poetry survives, but her famous work *The Distaff* gives an insight into her life and friendships.

In the dark age following the Romans, Tílos became so irrelevant that it was often confused with Teftlousa, the island of Sesklí near Sými. History returns with the Knights of St John in 1309, who strung seven castles across Tílos. In the 17th century, Venetian admirals and Christian pirates raided the island; what bits survived them fell prey to raiders from Mýkonos and Spétses from 1821 onwards in the name of the Greek Revolution.

Tílos in the 1990s is *the* Green island of the Dodecanese. The mayor, who is a member of Greenpeace, banned hunting on the island, declaring it to be a wildlife refuge. In 1997 it hosted a major Mediterranean environmental conference (not bad for an island with a permanent population of only 300), attracting the likes of Gina Lollobrigida, although the expected guest of honour, Jacques Cousteau, unfortunately died before it began.

# Livádia and Megálo Chorió

Although there used to be nine villages on the island, only the port **Livádia** (ΛΙΒΑΔΙΑ) and the capital Megálo Chorió are inhabited, and Livádia only since the 1930s. Popular with Greek families in the high season, it has a mile of tree-fringed pebble beach and water that's as clear as gin. Village life revolves around the little central square, near a couple of embryonic supermarkets and an excellent bakery selling wonderful pastries. Spirits are fed by the pretty blue and white church of **Ag. Nikólaos**, situated right on the waterfront. Further along the beach road the tiny early Christian basilica of **Ag. Panteleímon** and **Polýkarpos** has a beautiful mosaic floor, while **Ag. Anna**, further back on the hillside, has some 13th-century frescoes.

At the far side of the bay the little sheltered harbour of **Ag. Stéfanos** often hosts a handful of yachts. The track from the harbour leads over the headland to the pebbly beach at **Lethrá**, about an hour's walk away and quiet even in August. Fishermen may take you out to the other beaches: two red sandy coves opposite Gaidaros islet, and Ag. Nikólas Bay to the north.

**Megálo Chorió** (ΜΕΓΑΛΟ ΧΩΡΙΟ), 8km uphill from Livádia, stands on the site of ancient Tílos, and near the castle you can see Pelasgian walls built by the earliest known residents (if you discount the elephants, that is) dating back to 1000 BC. The pretty whitewashed village is a maze of narrow alleys and lovely flower-filled gardens and looks over a fertile plain. The town hall has the key to the church of **Archangel Michael** (1826), with a little double Arabic arch and other bits built into the walls, and a 16ft Hellenistic wall just behind it; its fine iconostasis has the silver icon from the original Taxiárchis church in the Kástro. Festivals are held in the church courtyard on 8 November and 28 July when women dance the ancient dance of the *koúpa* or cup. The small **museum** contains pygmy elephant bones and a video about the island, accompanied by an ancient song by Erinna. The **Kástro**, which is currently being restored, was built by the Venetians, who incorporated a Classical gateway and stone from the ancient *acropolis*.

The road drops down to the fertile plain and meanders along to the long sandy beach at **Éristos** (ΕΡΥΣΤΟΣ), where at the far end you can retire for an all-over tan. Further north is the deserted village of **Mikró Chorió**, an amphitheatre of ruined houses that looks especially sad as the owners took their roofs with them when they moved down to Livádia in the 1950s. Below here, in a cave by a river gully the elephants bones, measuring only 4ft high, were discovered in 1971. They co-existed with Tílos' stone age dwellers, but the humans killed them all – the last elephants in Europe – by 4000 BC.

The old church of **Timía Zóni** has charming 18th-century frescoes, and the newer church, a glorious pink confection, is the hub of all celebrations on August 15 when the deserted village comes alive again for the Assumption of the Virgin Mary. There are stunning views from the ghost town and the churches of **Sotíras**, **Ag. Elesas and Prodrómos** have impressive 15th-century frescoes. The area is locally famous for a plant called *rouvia* that is used to dye the Easter candles red; its gathering is the subject of an ancient ritual, in which children play the part of Lazarus and hide under twigs, until told to rise up from the dead; the aim of the game is to hop up before being hopped on.

From Megálo Chorió the road runs to windswept **Ag. Antónios**, which has a grotty beach, the island's one gas pump (*open afternoons only, 3–5*), a small chapel and an enormous tamarisk tree in the square. The main attraction along the beach is Tílos' other fossils – the petrified remains of human skeletons 'baked' into the rock, which are thought to belong to sailors caught in the lava when Níssyros erupted in 600 BC. A rough track leads from here to the isolated beach at **Pláka**, while another track winds its way up into the mountains to the lovely Byzantine **Monastery of Ag. Panteleímon**, founded in 1407, with red pantiled roof, set in a lush oasis of shady trees and gushing water. The fortified monastery, defended by a tall stone tower and even taller cypress trees, is perched more than 660ft above the west coast and enjoys stunning views. It has fine 15th-century frescoes, including one of the founder holding the monastery in his hand, others of Paradise, and a beautiful old marble drinking fountain fringed by pots of basil. The bus driver arranges trips up to the monastery on Sundays; the sunsets are superb.

# The Ionian Islands

12

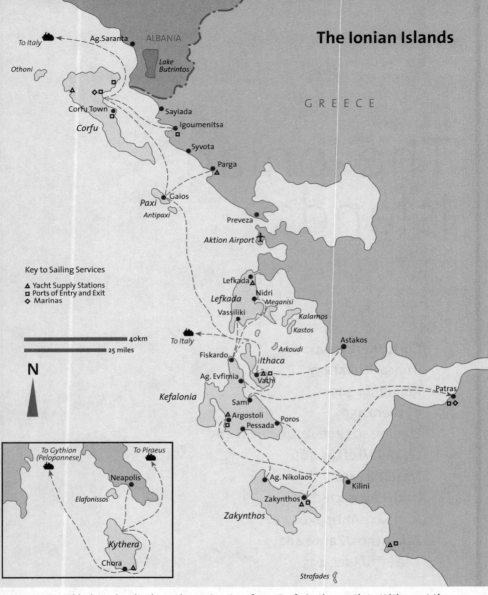

# The Ionian Islands

**Key to Sailing Services**

△ Yacht Supply Stations
□ Ports of Entry and Exit
◇ Marinas

40km
25 miles

N

Sprinkled randomly along the Ionian Sea, from Corfu in the north to Kýthera at the southern end of the Peloponnese, the Ionians are known in Greek as the Eptánissa, the Seven Islands. Politically lumped together since Byzantine times, they share a unique history and character; in general, they are more Italianate, more luxuriant than the Greek island stereotype, swathed in olive groves and cypresses and bathed in a soft golden light very different from the sharp, clear solar spotlight that shines on the Aegean. In temperament, too, the Seven Islands beg to differ: they are more gentle and lyrical, less prone to the extremes that bewitch and bedazzle the rest of the country. They also get more rain, especially from October to March, only to be rewarded with a breathtaking bouquet of wild flowers in the spring and autumn, especially on Corfu. Summers, however, tend to be hot, lacking the natural air-conditioning provided by the *meltémi* in the Aegean.

Weather and history aside, each of the Ionian islands has a strong, distinct personality. Connections between them are not the best, but with a little forward planning you can hop from one to the next depending on your mood, whether you want to boogie the night away in a Zákynthos nightclub, windsurf below the cliffs at Lefkáda, hike among the olive groves of bijou Paxí, swim under the white cliffs of Kefaloniá, or seek Odysseus' beloved home on Ithaca. Corfu, like Rhodes, is a major international resort destination, with its gorgeous beaches and historic town, once labelled in the British Press as a 'Venice without canals, Naples without the degradation.' Only beautiful and distant Kýthera remains aloof and today belongs to the district of Piraeus.

## History

Little remains of the ancient past on the islands, but they were probably settled in the Stone Age by people from Illyria (present-day Albania) and then by the Eretrians. Homer was the first to mention them, and were he the last they would still be immortal as the homeland of Odysseus. In the 8th century BC, mercantile Corinth colonized the islands. As trade expanded between Greece and the Greek colonies in southern Italy and Sicily, the Ionians became more important; Corfu, the richest, grew so high and mighty that she defeated mother Corinth at sea, and proclaimed herself the ally of Athens. This forced Sparta, Corinth's ally, either to submit to this expansion of Athenian influence and control of western trade routes through the Ionian islands, or to attack. They attacked. The result was the disastrous Peloponnesian War.

The Romans incorporated the Ionian islands into their province of Achaia. After the fall of the Roman Empire, Ostrogoths from Italy overran the islands, only to be succeeded by the Byzantines, who prized them for their strategic importance as a bridge between Constantinople and Rome. In 1084, during the Second Crusade, the Normans under Robert Guiscard, Duke of Apulia, captured the islands by surprise and established bases to plunder the rest of Greece. With difficulty the Byzantines succeeded in dislodging them, although the Normans were no sooner gone than the

## Mythology

If the Ionian islands spent centuries out of the mainstream of Greek politics, their inhabitants have been Hellene to the core from the beginning. Not to be confused with Ionia in Asia Minor (named after the Ionian people's legendary father Ion, son of Apollo), the Ionian Sea and islands are rather named after lovely Io the priestess, who caught the roving eye of Zeus. When the jealous Hera was about to catch the couple in flagrante delicto Zeus changed the girl into a white cow, but Hera was not to be fooled. She asked Zeus to give her the cow as a present, and ordered the sleepless hundred-eyed Argus to watch over her. When Hermes charmed Argus to sleep and killed him, Io the cow escaped, only to be pursued by a terrible stinging gad-fly sent by Hera. The first place she fled to was named after her, the Ionian Sea.

Venetians claimed the Ionians in the land-grab after the Sack of Constantinople in 1204. Once the Venetians deposed of the islands' Sicilian Norman pirate king, Vetrano, by crucifying him, the southern islands became the County Palatine of Kefaloniá. Fate, however, dealt Corfu into the hands of the Angevins for 150 years, a rule so bitter that the inhabitants willingly surrendered their island to the 'protection' of Venice.

Venetian rule was hardly a bed of roses. The average Greek in fact preferred the Turks to the bossy Catholic 'heretics': if nothing else, the Turks allowed the people a measure of self-government and demanded fewer taxes. Some of the Ionians actually came under Turkish rule until 1499, and the Ottomans renewed their assaults as the Serenissima weakened: life was never secure. Yet for all their faults, the Venetians were more tolerant of artists than the Turks, and in the 17th century the Ionian islands became a refuge for painters, especially from Crete. The resulting Ionian school was noted for its fusion of Byzantine and Renaissance styles.

In 1796, Napoleon conquered Venice, and as the Ionian islands were of the utmost importance to his schemes of conquest, he demanded them in the Treaty of Campo Formio. In 1799 a combined Russo-Turkish fleet took the islands from him, and the Russians created the independent Septinsular Republic under their protection – shielding the islands not only from the French but from the designs of the notorious tyrant of Epirus, Ali Pasha. Although the Septinsular Republic was nullified by the 1807 Treaty of Tilsit which returned the islands to Napoleon, it was the first time in almost four centuries that any Greeks had been allowed a measure of self-rule, and the experience helped to kindle the War of Independence in 1821.

In 1815 the British took the Ionian islands under military protection and re-formed the quasi-independent Septinsular Republic. Sir Thomas Maitland, the first High Commissioner, has gone down in history as one of the most disliked British representatives ever; he assumed dictatorial powers, and deeply offended the Greeks by giving the city of Párga, an important port on the mainland, to Ali Pasha, obeying an obscure clause in the 1815 treaty that everyone else had forgotten. Although other High Commissioners were more palatable, and some were actually very well liked, the Ionian State never stopped demanding or conspiring for union with Greece. Once they had Cyprus as well as Malta to use as Mediterranean ports, the British agreed and ceded the islands to Greece in 1864 – but only after blowing up all the fortresses on Corfu. During the Second World War Italy took the islands, but Mussolini's dream of creating a new Ionian State under Italian protection was shattered in 1943 when the Germans occupied the islands. Large numbers of Italian troops joined the Greeks in fighting the Nazis, only to be slaughtered by their former Axis allies. When the news reached Italy, it contributed to the collapse of the Fascist government.

# Corfu/Kérkyra (ΚΕΡΚΥΡΑ)

Corfu is a luxuriant Garden of Eden cast up in the northwest corner of Greece, a sweet mockery of the grim, grey mountains of Albania, so close and so unenticing. Its Venetian city-capital is one of the loveliest towns in Greece; the beaches that have managed to escape the infectious claw of package tourism are still gorgeous; the gentler mountain slopes, sprinkled with pastel villas and farms, could be in Tuscany.

Corfu's reputation as a distant paradise began with Homer, who called it Scheria, the happy isle of the Phaeacians, beloved of the gods, where the shipwrecked Odysseus was found washed up on a golden beach by the lovely Nausicaä. Shakespeare had it in mind when creating the magical isle of *The Tempest*, even if Prospero offered a different sort of hospitality to his shipwrecked guests. Edward Lear and brothers Gerald and Lawrence Durrell evoked its charms so delightfully that it

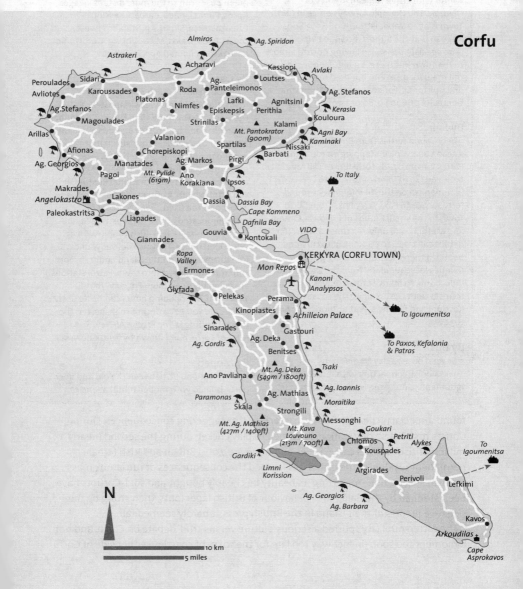

# Corfu

# Getting There and Around

## By Air

Frequent charter flights from London, Manchester, Glasgow and other UK airports; also regular flights from many European cities; 4 flights a day from Athens, 2 in the winter with either Aegean Airlines or Olympic. The **Olympic Airways** office in Corfu Town is at 20 Kapodistríou, **t** 066 103 8694; **Aegean** is at the airport, **t** 066 102 7100. There is no special bus service linking Corfu's airport to the town but there is a regular bus stop on the main road, several hundred metres away, or a taxi for €5. For general **airport information**, call **t** 066 103 0180 or **t** 066 103 7398.

## By Sea

Year-round **ferries** from Brindisi, Bari, Ancona and Venice, stopping en route to Pátras (*see* pp.67–8). Local ferries sail regularly between Corfu Town or Lefkími to Igoumenítsa on the mainland; year-round ferry service to Paxí. Ferry links from Corfu Town to the small islands of Eríkousa, Othoní and Mathráki are only 2–3 times a week (for details call **t** 066 103 6355), but **excursion boats** go there from Sidári and Ag. Stéfanos. Caiques leave regularly from the Old Port for Vído, home to many Serbian graves, and take tourists from Dassiá along the coast to Kassiópi and Benítses. **Port authority: t** 066 103 2655.

## By Bus

Several buses a day from Athens and Thessaloníki, connecting with ferries from Igoumenítsa (luggage is checked right through to Corfu); for travel on Corfu, there are two bus stations: the bus depot in Plateía G. Theotóki–San Rócco Square – **t** 066 103 1595, has blue KTEL buses to villages just beyond Corfu Town (Kanóni, Pótamos, Kontokáli, Goúvia, Dassiá, Pérama, Ag. Ioánnis, Benítses, Pélekas, Kastelláni, Kouramádes, Áfra, Achilleíon and Gastoúri). From the depot in Avramíou St, **t** 066 103 9985 or **t** 066 103 0627, green buses run to the more distant villages (Ipsos, Pírgi, Glyfáda, Barbáti, Kassiópi, Paleokastrítsa, Sidári, Ag. Stéfanos [west coast], Róda, Kávos, Messóghi, Ag. Górdis, and both resorts named Ag. Geórgios).

## By Car

Although lately much improved, Corfu's roads are not always well signposted, and there seem to be more than the usual number of Greek island hazards: dangerous curves and farm vehicles, careless tourists on motorbikes or sudden deteriorations in the surface. Road maps often confuse donkey tracks with unpaved roads. Try **International Rent A Car** if you want wheels, **t** 066 103 3411 or 066 103 7710, **f** 066 104 6350, *slemis@otenet.gr*, centrally located at 20a Kapodistríou St and run by a friendly Greek-Irish couple with 35 years' experience. They will deliver your car free to anywhere on the island and transport you from the airport into town. Petrol stations are generally open Mon–Fri 7am–7pm, Sat 7am–3pm, but opening hours can be flexible. Make sure you get a decent map; best at the time of writing is *The Precise All New Road Atlas of Corfu*, hand drawn by S. Jaskulowski.

## By Moped

Xen. Stratigoú St, between the old and new ports, is lined with moped rental agencies.

found a special niche in the English heart – with staggering consequences. During Corfu's first British occupation, it learned to play cricket; during the second (nearly a million British tourists come a year, and there are 7,000 British and Irish female permanent residents), the island has learned the consequences of run-amok mass tourism speculation – of letting its beauty be cheaply bought and sold. Corfiots have been stunned by the Calibanish behaviour of British lager louts, then stung by the negative reports of their island in the British press. It hardly seemed fair.

The rotten publicity spurred a serious 'culture versus crud' debate on Corfu, and not a moment too soon (in fact way too late for the 10km of coastline either side of Corfu

## By Bicycle

There are many bike rentals in town:

**Dutch Bicycle Company**, Ag. Ioánnis Tríklino, t/f 066 105 2407. Rents out mountain bikes for exploring the hidden corners of Corfu.

**Corfu Mountainbike Shop**, in Dassiá, t 066 109 3344, f 066 104 6100. Also rents out bikes galore and organizes tours of all levels of expertise.

## On Foot

The ubiquitous Mrs Paipeti has also written a book on hidden trails across the island; you can purchase it at Likoudis bookstore, next to the National Bank.

## Tours

Travel agents in Corfu offer one-day Classical tours to the mainland: to Epirus to visit the Oracle of the Dead (consulted by Odysseus after crossing the perilous River Styx), and the ancient cities of Kassopea and Nicopolis, founded by Augustus after the defeat of Mark Antony and Cleopatra in 31 BC. A second tour takes in Dodóni, with its ancient theatre, and Ioannína, the modern capital of Epirus, with its island of Ali Pasha and museum. Excursions to Albania to visit the ancient Roman city of Saranda have recently been resumed. Contact friendly and efficient Mrs Charitos at **Charitos Travel**, t 066 104 4611, f 066 103 6825, *charitostravel@otenet.gr*.

## Tourist Information

**EOT**: 7 Rizospaston Voulefton, t 066 103 7520, f 066 103 0298; *open weekdays 8–2*.

**Tourist police**: Samartzi St, near San Rocco Square, t 066 103 0265; *open Mon–Fri, 8–2*.

**Post office**: 26 Alexándras Avenue, t 066 103 9265; *open Mon–Fri, 8–8; Sat 7.30–2.30; Sun 9–1.30*.

**UK Consulate**: 1 Penecratous, t 066 103 0055/7995.

**Ireland Consulate**: 20a Kapodistríou St, t 066 103 2469/9910.

**Hospital**: 1 Andreádi St, t 066 108 8200. Some staff speak English.

**Scuba-diving**:

**Waterhoppers**, Ípsos, t 066 109 3867, Paleokastrítsa t 066 103 7118.

**Corfiot Diving Centre**, t 066 103 9727.

## Internet

**Café Online**, 28 Kapodistríou St, t 066 104 6226; *open 9am–12am*. Many terminals on offer in pleasant surroundings.

## Festivals

**Palm Sunday, Easter Saturday, 11 Aug and first Sunday in Nov**: Procession of Ag. Spyrídon in Corfu Town.

**Holy Saturday**: celebrated in Corfu Town with a real bang – the sound of everyone enthusiastically tossing out their chipped and cracked crockery.

**First Friday after Easter**: Paleokastrítsa.

**21 May**: Union with Greece.

**5–8 July**: Lefkími.

**10 July**: Kávos.

**14 Aug**: the beautiful Procession of Lights in Mandoúki.

**15 Aug**: Kassiópi.

**Sept**: the Corfu Festival brings all kinds of concerts, ballet, opera and theatre to the island.

Town, where a depressing jerry-built sprawl litters the road and pebble beaches). A new sewage system has sorted out most of the sea pollution complaints. Stricter zoning and licensing laws are being enforced, and a spit and polish of Corfu Town has begun to set the tone for a classier, more genteel Corfu. An Autumn Chamber Music Festival has been added to its successful annual Spring Chamber Music Festival (three quarters of the musicians in the Greek National Orchestra are from Corfu), and the Art Café and the Old and New Fortresses now host innovative art exhibitions, subsidized by the municipality. Count Spíros Flambouriári, member of an old Corfiot family ennobled by the Venetians, has begun an island 'National Trust' to restore its lovely but mouldering country estates. They are beautifully photographed in his book *Corfu: The Garden Isle*.

These gentry estates are scattered in the gorgeous hinterland (especially to the north of Corfu Town), where villages are free of monster concrete hotels, enclaves of expensive villas, and tourist compounds. In some of Corfu's more distant nooks and crannies are lovely beaches that somehow slipped past the cement mixer. Come in the early spring, when the almond trees blossom, around Palm Sunday or the first part of November (coinciding with the colourful celebrations of Ag. Spyrídon). Seek out the old cobbled donkey paths that once provided the main link between villages – you'll be rewarded with a poignant vision of the old Corfu, strewn with wild flowers (43 kinds of orchids), scented with the blossoms of lemons and kumquats, and silvery with billowing forests of ancient olives interspersed with towers of straight black cypresses. The olive trees still outnumber tourists by three and a half million.

## History

In ancient times Corfu was Corcyra, named after a mistress of the sea god Poseidon, and their son Phaeax became the founder of the gentle and noble Phaeacian race. Archaeological evidence suggests that the Phaeacians were quite distinct from the Mycenaeans, and had much in common not with any people in Greece but with cultures in Puglia, in southern Italy. In 734 BC the Corinthians sent a trading colony to the island and founded a city at Paliaopolis (the modern suburbs of Anemómylos and Análypsis). A temple there housed the sickle that Zeus used to castrate his father Cronos, whose testicles fell to form the two hills around the Old Fortress (*corypho* in Greek means 'peaks'). A prophecy current in Classical Greece foretold that Apollo would one day fetch the sickle to do the same to his father Zeus.

Although Corcyra soon became the richest of the Ionian islands, it was cursed with violent political rivalries between its democrats and the oligarchs. According to Thucydides, the Corcyrans fought the first sea battle in Greek history, against mother Corinth in 664 BC. In 435 BC, after the same two quarrelled over a colony in Albania in the Battle of Sybota (the dispute that set off the Peloponnesian War), internal strife left Corcyra so weakened that it was captured by Syracuse, and then by King Pyrrhus of Epirus, and in 229 BC by the Illyrians. In the first century BC, Corcyra was loyal to Mark Antony – he left his wife Octavia here before sailing off with Cleopatra – and as a reprisal Octavian's army under Agrippa destroyed every civic monument on the island. Yet whatever the turmoil, ancient Corcyra never lost its lofty reputation for fertility and beauty; Emperor Nero paid it a special visit in AD 67 to dance and sing at the Temple of Zeus in modern Kassiópi.

The remnants of the population that survived the ravages of the Goths in AD 550 decided to rebuild their town on the more easily defensible site of the Old Fortress and two hills of Cape Sidáro. This failed to thwart the Normans in 1081, but in 1148, when their raids menaced the Byzantium, Emperor Emmanuel Comnenus sent a special force and fleet to dislodge them, and then came to lead the attack in person. They were no match for Byzantine subtlety: by craftily seeding subversion and distrust among the Norman ranks, the emperor won back the island.

## Venetian Corfu

In 1204, when Venice came to claim Corfu as part of its spoils in the Fourth Crusade, the inhabitants put up a stiff resistance. Although the Venetians captured the island's forts, the Corfiots aligned themselves with the Orthodox Despotat of Epirus. Fifty years later, however, the King of Naples, Charles I of Anjou, snatched Corfu and the Peloponnese when his son married the Princess of Villehardouin. Angevin rule, already infamous for provoking the Sicilian Vespers, was equally intolerant and hated on Corfu. In 1386, the Corfiots swallowed their pride and asked Venice to put them under the protection of the Republic.

In 1537 a serious threat, not only to Corfu but to all of Europe, landed at Igoumenítsa. Suleiman the Magnificent, the greatest of the Ottoman sultans, already had most of the Balkans in his pocket and was determined to take Corfu as a base for taking Italy and western Europe. Thanks to a peace treaty with Venice, Suleiman was able to plot his attack in the utmost secrecy. When the Corfiots discovered with only a few days' warning what was in store for them, they tore down their houses for stone to repair the fortress and leave nothing behind for the Turks. The terrible Barbarossa was the first to arrive and begin the siege. Thousands who had been pitilessly abandoned outside the fortress were caught in the Venetian and Turkish crossfire, and fell prey to Barbarossa's fits of rage at his continual setbacks and massive losses. Those who survived were carted off to the slave markets of Constantinople when Suleiman, discouraged by his losses and the bad weather, ordered the lifting of the siege.

Only 21 years later Venice, under pressure from the Corfiots, expanded the island's fortifications to include the town. Many houses remained unprotected, however, and when the Turks reappeared in 1571 under Ouloudj Ali, these and the rest of the villages, trees and vineyards of Corfu were decimated. This time the Turks took no prisoners and massacred whoever they caught. A final blow was struck two years later by another pirate admiral, Sinan Pasha: of the entire Corfiot population, only a tenth remained on the island after 1573.

In 1576, Venice finally undertook to protect all the surviving islanders. Renaissance fortifications expert Micheli Sammicheli, master of the bastions around Heráklion, designed the New Fortress and other walls that were superb, state-of-the-art defenses. The Venetians also restored Corfu's economy, most notably by offering a bounty of 42 *tsekínia* for every olive tree planted (today there are an estimated 4.5 million trees, producing three per cent of the world supply of oil). To ingratiate themselves further, they allowed wealthy Corfiots to purchase titles, creating a class society in Greece unique to the Ionian islands. Sammicheli's walls were given the ultimate test in 1716, when Turks staged furious attacks for one terrible month before being repulsed by the stratagems of a German mercenary soldier, Field Marshal Schulenberg, and a tempest sent by Corfu's guardian, St Spyrídon.

After Napoleon captured Venice, the French duly occupied Corfu, immediately improving the education system and setting up the first public library (1797), but they lost the island two years later in a fierce battle against the Russo-Turkish fleet. When Napoleon finally got it back, he personally designed new fortifications for the town; he loved Corfu, 'more interesting to us than all of Italy put together'. Napoleon's walls were so formidable that the British, when allotted the Ionian islands after Waterloo, did not care to argue the point when the French commander Donzelót refused to give them up. Paris finally had to order Donzelót home and, in 1815, with the signing of the Treaty of Vienna, Corfu and the other Ionians became a British Protectorate, with the blessing of Count John Capodístria. Capodístria, soon to be the first president of Greece, was a native of Corfu and, like many of the island's noblemen and scholars, had been in the employ of the tsars after 1799.

## British and Greek Corfu

While Capodístria had requested 'military protection', the British took it upon them-selves to run all the affairs of the Ionian State, which they 'legalized' by a constitution imposed by the first Lord High Commissioner, Sir Thomas Maitland, whose high-handed behaviour earned him the nickname 'King Tom'. One of his first acts was to demolish part of the Venetian walls to build new, stronger ones in their place, calling upon the Ionian Government to cough up more than a million gold sovereigns to pay for it. Maitland made himself even more disliked by forcing neutrality on the islands as the Greek War of Independence broke out, disarming the population and impris-oning – and executing – members of the secret patriotic Society of Friends. His constitution ensured that the peasantry lived in near-feudal conditions, while denying Corfu's educated and middle classes any political role; the Ionians weren't even given favourable trade status with Britain. It was, as one British High Commissioner put it, 'a sort of middle state between a colony and a perfectly inde-pendent country, without possessing the advantage of either.' Yet the British also built new roads, schools and a university (the 'Ionian Academy', founded by Hellenophile Lord Guilford), and established a permanent water supply to Corfu Town. The locals took up cricket, and Edward Lear spent months on the island, painting pretty water-colours and writing in his journal.

In 1858, with the political situation growing increasingly uncomfortable, Gladstone was sent down to resolve the crisis, but constrained by British distrust of King Otho and Greek support of Russia (Britain's enemy in the Crimean War), he had little to propose. The overthrow of Otho (1862) gave Britain a chance to cede the islands gracefully to Greece, on condition that Greece found an acceptable king. This was Prince William of Denmark, crowned George I; on 21 May 1864 the Ionians were presented as the new king's 'dowry'. There was one ungracious hitch: that the British ensure the island's neutrality by destroying the fortresses of Corfu – not only the walls they themselves had just made the Corfiots pay for and build, but also the historical Venetian buildings. A wave of protest from all corners of the Greek world failed to move the British, and the bulk of the fortifications were blown sky high.

In 1923, Mussolini gave a preview of his intentions when he bombarded and occupied Corfu after the assassination of an Italian delegate to the Greek-Albanian border council; the Italians left only when Greece paid an indemnity. An even worse bombardment occurred in 1943, when the Germans blasted the city and its Italian garrison; a year later, the British and Americans bombed the Germans. At the end of the war, a quarter of the old city was destroyed, including 14 lovely churches.

# Corfu Town

Corfu Town, or Kérkyra (pop. 40,000), the capital of the Ionian islands, was laid out by the Venetians in the 14th century when the medieval town, crowded onto the peninsula of Cape Sidáro (where the Old Fortress now stands), had no room to expand. They began with the Campiello (from *campo*, Venetian for 'square'), where three- or four-storey houses loom over the narrow streets, as they do back in the lagoon capital. By the time the new walls were added in the 16th century, the Venetians built in the more open style of the Renaissance, laying out an exquisite series of central streets and small squares. Some of the finest houses, their arches

## Shopping

Shops with a predominantly touristy clien-tèle hardly ever seem to close, but non-tourist shops are closed every evening except Tues, Thurs and Fri.

**Xenoglosso**, 45 Ger. Markóra, near San Rocco Square. Has a good selection of books in English.

**Mrs Paipeti's antiques** shop, next to the Cavalieri Corfu Hotel. Sells antique prints, maps, postcards and watercolours.

**Panton**, on Panton St. There are a number of high-fashion shops, of which this is probably the most famous. It's the main outlet of Corfu designer Lisa Palavicini, whose clothes have been featured in *Vogue* and are sold in outlets in Athens, London and Jordan.

## Where to Stay

### Corfu Town ✉ 49100

If you arrive without a booking, the **association of owners of private rooms and apartments**, 24 Adr. Iakovou Polyllá, t 066 102 6153, f 066 102 3403, can help.

### Luxury

**Cavalieri Corfu**, on the end of the Esplanade at 4 Kapodistríou, t 066 103 9336, f 066 103 9283 (*A*). In a renovated French mansion, for old-style elegance no hotel on Corfu can compete; comfortable, with air-con and a magnificent roof garden, open for drinks to non-guests and overlooking the town in all directions. *Open all year.*

**Corfu Palace**, 2 Dimokratías, just south of the centre, t 066 103 9485, f 066 103 1749,

cfupalace@hol.gr (*L*). Enormous, with 2 swimming pools and all the trimmings, from baby sitting to 24-hr room service. Most rooms have sea-views but can cost a fortune in high season. *Open all year.*
There's also a cache of luxurious high-rise palaces in Kanóni:

**Corfu Holiday Palace** (née Hilton), 2 Nafsiká St, t 066 103 6540, f 066 103 6551 (*L*). Hotel and bungalow complex with casino, bowling alley, indoor and outdoor pools, water sports, etc; rooms have either sea or lake views. *Open all year.*

### Expensive

**Arcadion**, 44 Kapadistríou, t 066 103 7671, f 066 104 5087, arcadion@otenet.gr (*C*). Very central, overlooking the Esplanade and Old Fortress, and comfortable – rooms at the back are quietest. *Open all year.*

**Astron**, 15 Donzelót, t 066 103 9505, f 066 103 3708 (*B*). In an old building overlooking the Old Port and the New Fortress; most rooms have balconies but are a bit basic for the price, despite good bathrooms. *Open all year.*

**Bella Venezia**, just back from the Esplanade at 4 Napoleon Zambeli, t 066 104 4290, f 066 102 0708, belvnht@hol.gr (*B*). Renovated salmon-coloured old mansion in a relatively quiet, yet central, part of town, with a pretty garden terrace in which to linger over the sumptuous buffet breakfasts. *Open all year.*

**Konstantinoupolis**, 11 Zavitsianou St, on the waterfront in the Old Port, t 066 104 8716/7, f 066 104 8718 (*C*). A very good choice, the building was originally established as a hotel in 1878 and very well refurbished in 1997. *Open all year.*

decorated with masks and half-moon windows over the door, can be seen along the upper Esplanade, and everywhere you look there are gentle shades of Savoy red and pink peeling off gracious Venetian façades. The British knocked down the Venetian walls to allow the pent-up town to grow again, and then added a set of elegant Georgian public buildings.

Besides Campiello, the old city is divided into smaller quarters such as Garítsa, the 19th-century residential district to the south. The Old Port, on the east side of the New Fortress, is now used only by the excursion boat to Paxí; all the other ferries and excursion boats come in and out of town through its back door at Mandoúki, or New Port, west of the New Fortress.

### Moderate

**Ionian**, 46 Xen. Stratigoú, in between the old and new ports, **t** 066 103 9915, **f** 066 104 4690 (C). Conveniently located; plain but decent, with en suite baths.

**Royal**, 110 Paleopolis St, in Kanóni, **t** 066 103 5345, **f** 066 103 8786 (C). Enjoys a commanding position and could be a class higher, with its 3 swimming pools on descending levels, and roof garden with views over Mouse Island and the airport.

### Inexpensive

**EOT**, 7 Rizospaston Voulefton, **t** 066 103 7520. For something cheap, try their list of rooms to rent. Most of these are in the old quarters and cost €18 upwards for a bed in season.

**Europa**, 10 Gitsiáli, at the New Port, **t** 066 103 9304 (D). One of the better modern choices.

**Hermes**, 4 Ger. Markóra on the inland side of the New Fortress, **t** 066 103 9268, **f** 066 103 1747 (C). Away from the tourist crowds but next to the early-morning food market.

## Eating Out

Corfu shows its Venetian heritage in the kitchen as well as in its architecture. Look for *sofríto*, a veal stew flavoured with garlic, vinegar and parsley; *bourdétto*, a fish stew, liberally peppered; and *pastitsátha*, a pasta and veal dish. The island's own sweet is *siko-maeda*, or fig pie. Eating out on the genteel Listón, with front-row seats on the crowds, can be expensive unless you stick to pizza.

**Averof**, at Alipíou and Prossalendíou. A long-established favourite of tourists and locals alike.

**Barbathomas**, near Taverna Tripa, on the Achilleion road (about 7km from town). With live music and great meat specialities.

**Becchios**, in Mandoúki, opposite the ferries to Igoumenítsa. For carnivores: splendid char-coal-grilled meats.

**La Famiglia**, 30 Arlioti, Kantouni Bizi, in the heart of town, **t** 066 103 0270 (€18–22). Delicious Italian food in small, cosy surroundings; excellent *linguini alle vongole*. *Open Mon–Sat.*

**Faliraki**, on the seafront below the Palace of St Michael and St George, **t** 066 103 0392. Tucked away in a historic spot where the steam passengers used to disembark; now an *ouzerie*/restaurant, it has mesmerizing views of the sea, old walls and the off-shore yacht club, but average fare.

**Il Giardino**, 4B Vraila St, **t** 066 103 0723 (€20–25). Considered the best Italian restau-rant in town, in a pleasant garden setting.

**Loutrovio Restaurant**, in Kefalomandoukó, on the hill overlooking 'disco strip'. Good food accompanied by the best live Greek music, with dancers and the works.

**Nausicaä**, out in Kanóni, 11 Nafsiká, **t** 066 104 4354. Delicious Greek, French and Eastern dishes under the garden trellis (fairly dear, but they take credit cards).

**Nicholas**, in the suburb of Potamós. Excellent and reasonable traditional fare.

**Orestes**, by the New Port in Xen. Stratigoú St. Smart dining inside and in a pleasant little garden opposite; good seafood specialities.

**Pontis**, near Taverna Tripa, on the Achilleion road (about 7km from town). Live music and a big selection of *mezédes*, spit-roasted lamb, charcoal grills and delicious local dishes.

## The New Fortress

The mass of walls that dominates the view if you arrive by sea is the New Fortress, or Néo Froúrio (*open daily 9–8.30; adm; entrance from Solomóu St*), built after 1576 by the Venetians following the Ottomans' third attack. It bore the brunt of the siege of 1716, and although most of the walls were dynamited by the British, enough masonry survived for the installation of a Greek naval base. Over the gates, Lions of St Mark and inscriptions genteelly erode away; there are excellent views of Corfu Town from its bastions, and two underground tunnels to explore. The town **Market** is in the old moat (*G. Markorá St*); if you're self-catering or planning a picnic, try to come early to get the pick of the fresh fish and produce. Quite a bit further west, beyond the

**Porta Remounda**, Guilford St. Has a well-earned reputation for fish.

**Rex**, 66 Kapodistríou, one street back from the Listón, t 066 103 9649. Inexpensive, reliable and good varied menu – try the *pastitsátha*, *sofríto* and other Corfiot dishes.

**Taverna Pelargos**, close neighbour to the Nausicaä. Corny-looking from the outside but serves a vast array of well-prepared Greek dishes: the *stifádo* and *sofríto* are superb.

**Taverna Tripa** ('Hole in the Wall'), in Kinopiástes, 3km from Gastoúri, t 066 105 6333 (*€25*). Run by the Anyfantís family since 1947. Something of a monument, completely cluttered inside with bottles, knick-knacks, a hurdy gurdy and photos (mostly of the late Spiros Anyfantís with celebrity diners), while up on the ceiling strings of salamis, sausages, peppers and garlic are linked by cobwebs. Greek nights here are renowned, with up to 10 courses served; although it's not cheap, the food and service are excellent and the costumed waiters put on a folk-dancing show to boot.

**Traditional**, 20 Solomoú. As authentic an old Greek taverna as you could hope for, with old pots bubbling away in the kitchen and oven-ready dishes; try their pickled octopus (*ochtapóthi xytháto*).

**Venetian Well**, in Kremastí Square, t 066 104 4761 (*€22–28*). Upscale and stylish in a romantic setting, with a varied and international menu and a wide choice of costly Greek wines, but it's the Martini ad ambience that attracts.

**Xenichtes**, on the road to Paleokastrítsa, t 066 102 4911 (*€18–22*). Elegant restaurant serving excellent Greek food with a sprinkling of

dishes from other countries for 20 years; fresh salmon is delivered every morning on the Oslo–Corfu flight.

**Yannis**, in Garítsa, near Ag. Iássonos and Sosipater. One of the few remaining tavernas where you are still invited to go into the kitchen, lift lids off pots and choose your food.

**Yoryias**, Guilford St. Popular traditional taverna, with cheery staff and atmosphere.

# Entertainment and Nightlife

Pick up a copy of the monthly *The Corfiot* for local news and a calendar of events; published primarily for ex-pat residents, it makes interesting reading. Other media are even better served: Corfu has 3 cable TV stations, 17 radio stations, and a flip through the FM dial may even dig up an English-speaking DJ.

Apart from the disco ghettoes north of town and, a bit less brash, in Kanóni, most of Corfu's nightlife revolves around the Listón, with a smattering of music bars:

**Magnet Bar**. A good choice to be drawn to.

**Karnayio**. Dancing until the wee hours.

**Coca** and **Bora Bora**. Two of the most popular bar/clubs.

**The Gallery**, on Ag. Spyrídon St. A favourite watering hole of Greeks and ex-pats.

**Remezzo**. Fun for late-night ice-cream.

**The café/bar**, perched up in the Old Fort. Also a scenic spot, with music and an alluring view. *Open 9am–2am.*

**The Pallas Cinema**, on Theotoki and **The Orfeus Cinema**, on Aspioti. Both show undubbed English-language films.

# Corfu Town

Vido Island

OLD PORT

ARSENIOU

DONZELOT

SPILIA

ZAVITSIANOU

PROSFOROU

CAMPIELLO

Solomos Museum

Byzantine Museum

RARTOUROU

APOLODOROU

DOUSMANI

AG. ELENIS MANESSI

AG. EKATERINIS LEONDOS

AG. THEODORA

AG. NIKOLAOU

THEMISTOKLEOUS

PALEOLOGOU

PROSALENDIOU

MITROPOLEOS

THEODOSSIOU

Palace of St Michael and St George

MANDRAKI

POL

PLATEIA SOLOMOU

SOLOMOU

Cathedral

N. THEOTOKI

AG. SPIRIDONOS

PHILARMONIKIS

AG. Spyridon

PARGAS

Offshore Sailing Club

NEW VENETIAN FORTRESS

TENEDHOU

VELISSARIOU

HISTORICAL CENTRE

AG. PATERON

N. THEOTOKI

SEVASTIANOU

AG. PANTON

LISTON

Cricket Ground

Sound and Light

OLD VENETIAN FORTRESS

Cape Sidaro

National Bank

PLATEIA M. THEOTOKI

VOULGAREOS

Town Hall

Buses for Kanoni

Statue of Schulenburg

DOUSMANI

ESPLANADE (SPIANADA)

PALEOLOGOU

VOULGAREOS

PANDOVA

DIKASTIRION

MANOU

EPARHOU

KAPODISTRIOU

G. MARKORA

Market

DESSILA

Municipal Theatre

G. THEOTOKI

MANTZAROU

N. POLITI

N. ZAMBELI

ARISTOTELOUS

MOUSTOXIDI

Maitland Rotonda

To Avrami Hill and KTEL Long Distance (Green) Bus Station

I. THEOTOKI

PLATEIA SAN ROCCO

City (Blue) Bus Terminal

SAMARA

ALEXANDRAS

RIZOSPASTON VOULEFTON

G. ASPIOTI

MAVILI

GUILFORD

SOULIOU

DIMODOKOU

AKADIMIAS

Corfu Nautical Club

MITROPOLITI METHODIOU

ZAFIROPOULOU

MARASLI

I. ROMANOU

VRAILA

POLILA

Tennis Courts

Archaeology Museum

Garitsa Bay

British Cemetery

G. KALOSGOUROU

DIMOKRATIAS

Tomb of Menecrates

Prison

MENEKRATOUS

KIPROU

ALKINOU

MARASLI

M. ATHANASIOU

GARITSA

To Kanoni

Ag. Georgios

300 m
300 yds

N

hospital on Polichroni Konstantá Street, the **Monastery of Platýteras** contains two beautiful icons given to the island by Catherine the Great in honour of Count Capodístria, who is buried here; also note the silver and gilt columns by the altar, a typical Russian feature.

To the east of the New Fortress in Spiliá, near New Fortress Square, stands the 1749 Catholic **church of Ténedos**, named after an icon brought to Corfu by the Venetians from the now Turkish island of Ténedos. You can reach the centre of town from the Old Port through the 16th-century Spiliá Gate, incorporated into a later structure, or take the narrow steps up into the medieval Campiello Quarter (*see* below); the **Jewish Quarter**, equally old and picturesque, lies south of Plateía Solomóu. Although the Greek synagogue and a school remain in Velissáriou Street (the Italian synagogue was bombed and burned in 1943), only 170 out of the 1,800 members of the congregation sent to Auschwitz returned to Corfu after the war.

## The Esplanade (Spianáda) and the Listón

A series of long parallel streets – the main residential district of the Venetians – all lead to the town's centre, the great green space called the Spianáda, or Esplanade, one of the largest public squares in Europe. Originally a field left open for defensive purposes, it began to take its present form as a garden and promenade when Napoleon ordered the building of the arcaded **Listón** on the west edge of the Esplanade, in imitation of one of his proudest Paris creations, the Rue de Rivoli. At the time, it was the only place in all of Greece reserved exclusively for the aristocracy (or those on the list, hence the name). Then, as now, the Listón was a solid row of elegant cafés; at night the monuments and trees are floodlit for dramatic effect.

The northern end of the Esplanade is filled by the Georgian **Palace of St Michael and St George**, with its two grand gates. Designed by Sir George Whitmore, the palace was built as the residence of Sir Thomas Maitland, first High Commissioner of the Ionian State – note the symbols of the seven islands on its Maltese marble façade. In 1864 it became the summer residence of the King of Greece, then fell into disuse until it was renovated in 1953 to house a magnificent **Museum of Asiatic Art** (*t 066 103 0433; open Tues–Sun 8.30–3; adm*), one of the largest and most important privately formed collections in the world. A gift to Corfu from Greek diplomat Gregórios Mános, with further contributions from Michális Hadzivasilíou and others, the museum contains 10,000 masks, ceramics, armour and weapons, and much more from all the countries of the Far East, dating back to 1000 BC. At the **Art Café**, in a corner of the palace, you can linger over coffee and drinks and enjoy one of the local art exhibitions. Adjacent to the palace is the loggia of the **Reading Society** (*t 066 102 7277; open daily 9–1*), founded in 1836 by a group of young Corfiot idealists freshly returned from their studies in France; the library has a fine collection of books on the Ionian islands. Just in front of the palace is another British legacy – the **cricket ground**, where little boys play football until their older white-clad brothers chase them off the field. In the summer, matches pit the six local teams (which aren't at all bad) against visitors from Britain, the Greek mainland and Europe.

Numerous monuments embellish the Esplanade. In the centre of the Upper Plateía is the **memorial to Sir Thomas Maitland**, which Sir George Whitmore designed in the form of an Ionian rotunda, where local brass bands serenade the summertime crowds; you can often hear them practising in the evening in the old quarters. There is a marble statue of **Marshal Schulenberg**, the crafty and heroic soldier of fortune from Saxony who outwitted the Turkish High Admiral in the Great Siege of 1716 to spoil the last attempt of the Ottoman Empire to expand in the west. The **Guilford Memorial** is to Corfu's favourite Englishman, the Hellenophile Frederick North, Earl of Guilford (1769–1828), here dressed in ancient robes, a touch he would have appreciated. On the southern end of the Esplanade is a statue of his ambiguous and later assassinated Corfiot friend Capodístria, first president of Greece. Nearby, on Moustoxídi, one of the streets traversing Guilford, is a **Serbian War Museum** (*open 9–noon*). This is not at all what immediately springs to mind, but a collection of photographs and memorabilia from the First World War, and Corfu's role in aiding Serbian refugees (*see* below).

The **Old Fortress** (*t 066 104 8120; open daily 8.30–2.30; adm*) on Cape Sidáro is separated from the Esplanade by the moat, or *contra fosse*, dug over a 100-year period by the Venetians. The medieval town of Corfu was located on the two little hills of Cape Sidáro; scholars have identified the site with the Heraion *acropolis* mentioned by Thucydides. The walls, built over the centuries, were badly damaged by the British; others have fallen into decay. Part of the Old Fortress is still used by the Greek army, but you can wander about and explore the Venetian tunnels, battlements, drawbridge, well, cannons from 1684 and St George's, the bleached church of the British garrison, which is now an Orthodox chapel. The Old Fortress Café has an alluring vista out to sea from its privileged position; best of all, however, is the wonderful view of the city from the hills.

## Ag. Spyrídon

The church of Corfu's patron saint Ag. Spyrídon – the original Spíros – is in the old town, and easy to find: the campanile soars above the town like a ship's mast, bedecked with flags and Christmas lights. Spyrídon was a 4th-century Bishop of Cyprus, buried in Constantinople; when the city fell to the Turks, his bones were smuggled in a sack of straw to Corfu. The church was built in 1596 to house the relics, no longer in straw but in a silver Renaissance reliquary. According to the Corfiots, Spyrídon ('the Miracle-Worker') has brought them safely through many trials, frightening both cholera and the Turks away from his beloved worshippers. He even gave the Catholics a good scare when they considered placing an altar in his church; the night before its dedication, he blew up a powder magazine in the Old Fortress with a bolt of lightning to show his displeasure. He did, however, peacefully accept a large silver lamp from the Venetians in thanks for his divine intervention against the Turks in 1716. Four times a year (Orthodox Palm Sunday, Easter Saturday, 11 August and the first Sunday in November) his reliquary is brought out and the faithful gather from all over Corfu and the mainland, and queue to kiss the lid for good luck. In the church, amid mediocre Italianate frescoes blackened by smoke, the gold shimmers through in the flickering light of votive candles.

The nearby Ionian Bank houses a **Museum of Paper Money** (*t 066 104 1552; open Mon–Sat 9–1*), with a collection of banknotes from around the world and Greek notes dating from the nation's birth; upstairs, you can learn how they're printed. Across the square, the church of the **Panagía Faneroméni** (1689) contains some fine icons of the Ionian School. The square gives on to the pretty main street, Nikifórou Theotóki. From there, head up E. Voulgáreos Street to the elegant square with Corfu's Town Hall, a Venetian confection begun in 1691 that later did duty as the municipal opera house; grotesque faces grimace from the building and a bas-relief shows a triumphant Doge. The Catholic **Cathedral of St James** on the square was hit by German bombs in 1943. Only the bell tower survived intact; the rest has been reconstructed.

## Campiello

There are a number of buildings worth seeking out in the Campiello Quarter between the Old Port and the Esplanade, beginning with the **Orthodox Cathedral** (1577), its 18th-century façade rather unfortunately located next to the rudest T-shirt shop in town. The cathedral is dedicated to Ag. Theodóra Augústa, Empress of Byzantium (829–842), who was canonized for her role in restoring icons in the Orthodox Church following the Iconoclasm. Her relics were brought to Corfu along with those of Ag. Spyrídon and lie in a silver casket in the chapel to the right of the altar; if the priest in charge likes the look of you, he'll take you aside so you can kiss her and take home titbits of her slipper; donations are more than welcome. The gold-grounded icons are lovely, reminiscent of 13th-century Italian art.

The **Byzantine Museum of Corfu** (*t 066 103 8313; open Tues–Sat 8.45–3, Sun and hols 9.30–2; adm*) is near here, up the steps from Arseníou Street. The collection is housed in the beautifully restored 15th-century Antivouniótissa, a typical Ionian church with its single aisle, timber roof and exonarthex, or indoor porch, that runs around three sides of the building. Among the eminent Corfiots buried under the flagstones is Capodístria's sister, who was a nun here. The church has one of the elaborately decorated ceilings or *ourania* ('heaven') that the Ionians were so fond of, a stone iconostasis from a later date and very Italianate 17th-century murals on the Old Testament. Icons from all over Corfu have been brought here; among the finest are the mid-16th-century *SS. Sergius, Bacchus and Justine* by Michael Damaskinós, the 17th-century *St Cyril of Alexandria* by Emmanuel Tzanes, the 17th-century four-handed *Ag. Panteléimon* and icons by the 18th-century painter Geórgios Chrysolorás. On the same street is the **Solomós Museum** (*t 066 103 0674; open weekdays 9–1; adm*), with a collection of old photographs and memorabilia associated with the great Zákynthos poet Diónysos Solomós, who lived here in his later years (*see* p.488).

On a narrow stair off Philharmonikí Street, **Ag. Nikólaos** once served as the parish church of the King of Serbia. After the defeat of the Serbian army by the Austro-Hungarians in 1916, the king, his government and 150,000 Serbs took refuge on Corfu. A third died shortly thereafter from the flu and are buried on **Vído island**. Boats regularly make the trip to Vído; the Venetians fortified it after the Turks built a gun battery on it to attack the Old Fortress in 1537. The walls were demolished by the British. Today Vído is a quiet refuge with footpaths, a little beach and a memorial to the Serbs.

## Garítsa and the Archaeology Museum

South of the Old Fortress, Garítsa Bay became a fashionable residential district in the 19th century and is still dotted here and there with elegant Neoclassical mansions. On Kolokotróni Street, the beautiful, peaceful **British Cemetery** is famous as a natural botanic garden, where rare species of wild flowers bloom; the graves, with intriguing headstones, date from the beginning of the British protectorate.

Garítsa's star attraction is the **Archaeology Museum** (*t 066 103 0680; open Tues–Sun 8.30–3; adm*), with finds from the island and nearby mainland, flanked by outsized amphorae worthy of Pirandello. Opened in 1967, the museum has already been extended but is still too small to display all the recent discoveries. Among the new exhibits are bronze statuettes from Archaic to Roman times, a horde of silver *staters* (coins) from the 6th century BC, an iron helmet with silver overlay from the 4th century BC, and Cycladic sculptures, discovered in 1992 by a customs officer as smugglers attempted to spirit them abroad from Igoumenítsa. Upstairs are grave-offerings, Archaic *kore* and *kouros* statues, and two of Aphrodite, the favourite goddess of the lusty Corinthians; here, too, are the snarling, stylized 'Lion of Menecrates' from the Archaic tomb (*see* below), and the relief of a Dionysiac Symposium (*c.* 500 BC), showing the god Diónysos with a youth, lying on a couch; their eyes are focused intently on something lost forever. A lion sleeps under the couch; a dog comes striding up.

One room is given over to the striking wall-sized Gorgon Pediment (585 BC), discovered near the Temple of Artemis in Kanóni; the oldest preserved stone pediment, and one of the largest (56ft wide), it shows how advanced the Corinthians were in the early days of Greek monumental sculpture. The grinning Gorgon Medusa is powerfully drawn, running with one knee on the ground, flanked by her two diminutive children, Pegasus the winged horse and Chrysaor; according to myth they were born from her blood when she was slain by Perseus, although here she looks very alive indeed. Two large leopards on either side suggest that this is actually Artemis herself in her form of 'the Lady of the Wild Animals', a fearsome goddess who demanded an annual holocaust of the creatures she protected, burned alive on the altar; in the far corners of the pediment, much smaller scenes show the Clash of the Titans.

The circular, 7th-century BC **Menecrates tomb** was discovered in the 19th century in an excellent state of preservation. Its lower sections are intact in the garden of a building at the junction of Marásli and Kíprou Sts, three blocks south of the museum.

# South of Corfu Town

City bus no.2 from Corfu Town takes you to Mon Repos and the garden suburbs draped over little **Kanóni Peninsula** that dangles south of Garítsa Bay. Ancient Corcyra occupied much of this peninsula and had two harbours: what is now the Chalikiopóulos lagoon to the west, and the ring-shaped 'harbour of King Alcinous' (now filled in) in the northeastern corner of the peninsula, at Anemómylos. Here, a few lanes back, the handsome early 11th-century Byzantine church of Ag. Iássonos and

Sosipater is crowned by an octagonal drum and incorporates ancient columns; inside an original fresco has survived, along with the supposed tombs of the church's name-sakes, natives of Tarsus instructed by St Paul, who brought Christianity to Corfu in AD 70 and were martyred under Caligula.

The coastal road continues to the entrance of the little Regency villa of **Mon Repos**, built by Sir Frederick Adam, the second High Commissioner of the Ionian State, for his Corfiot wife. The Greek royal family later adopted it; Elizabeth II's consort, Philip, Duke of Edinburgh, was born here in 1921. In 1994 the Greek Government allowed Corfu to repossess the estate from King Constantine, and the beautiful wooded grounds are being developed as an archaeological park of ancient Corcyra. So far a Roman villa and Roman baths have been discovered, opposite the 5th-century basilica of **Ag. Kérkyra** of Paleópolis, made from the ruins of a Doric temple (by the crossroads, opposite the gate of Mon Repos). A minor road leads to the Doric **Temple of Artemis** (585 BC), source of the magnificent Gorgon Pediment in the Archaeology Museum. The large altar and the retaining wall of the Hellenistic *stoa* survive; some of its stones were cannibalized in the 5th century to build the adjacent convent of **Ag. Theodóri**.

Little **Mon Repos Beach** is just below if you need a dip, or follow the seaward wall of the villa to the path to the bucolic spring of **Kardáki**, which flows icy cold year-round from the mouth of a stone lion fountain; the Venetians and British used it to supply their ships, in spite of the inscription that warns: 'Every stranger who wets his lips here, to his home will not return.' From here it's an easy walk to the lush and lovely residential area of Análypsos.

At the southern tip of the lovely little peninsula, **Kanóni** is named for the old cannon once situated on the bluff, where two cafés now overlook the pretty bay, the harbour of ancient Corcyra. Two islets protected it: that of the oft-photographed Convent of **Panagía Vlacharína**, connected to the shore by a causeway, and **Pondikonísi**, 'Mouse Island' with its 13th-century chapel, Ag. Pnévmatos. Pondikonísi was the Phaeacian ship that brought Odysseus home to Ithaca, but on its way back to Corfu the angry Poseidon smote 'with his open palm, and made the ship a rock, fast rooted in the bed of the deep sea', according to the *Odyssey*. An airport runway built on a landfill site now crosses the west end of the shallow lagoon, and a collection of big new hotels has toadstooled nearby, in spite of noisy charter flights day and night.

## Pérama, Gastoúri and the Achilleíon

Past the Kanóni Peninsula and linked to it by a pedestrian causeway over the lagoon, **Pérama** claims to be the site of King Alcinous' fabled garden and is where the Durrell family first lived (for more details, pick up a copy of Hilary Whitton Paipeti's *In the Footsteps of Lawrence Durrell and Gerald Durrell in Corfu*). The pretty village of **Gastoúri** is the dreamy setting for a Neoclassical Neo-Pompeiian villa called the **Achilleíon** (*open for tours daily in summer, 8–3.30; adm*), with lovely views in all directions. The villa itself is more of a nightmare, sufficiently kitsch to be used as a location for the James Bond film *For Your Eyes Only*. Built in 1890 by the Empress Elisabeth ('Sissi') of Austria after the tragic death of her only son Rudolphe, the villa was named after Sissi's passion for the hero of Homer's *Iliad*; Sissi fancied herself as the immortal sea goddess Thetis, with Rudolphe as her son Achilles, idealized by a large marble statue she had made of the *Dying Achilles* for the garden. Ten years after Sissi was assassinated in 1898 by an Italian anarchist, Kaiser Wilhelm II purchased the Achilleíon and made it his summer residence from 1908 to 1914, and, true to character, had the *Dying Achilles* replaced with a huge bronze: *Victorious Achilles*, with the inscription 'To the Greatest of the Greeks from the Greatest of the Germans.' Among the bevy of more delicate statues, note the Grace standing next to Apollo, sculpted by Canova using Napoleon's sister Pauline Borghese as his model. The small museum contains, among its collection of imperial mementoes, one of the Kaiser's swivelling saddles, from which he dictated plans for the First World War, and photos of him swanning around on his huge yacht, the *Hohenzollern*, which he used to anchor off the 'Kaiser's Bridge' just south of Pérama. Amid this fetid mix of bad art and power, note, over the gate of Troy in Franz Matsch's stomach-churning painting of the *Triumph of Achilles*, a prophetic little swastika.

# North of Corfu Town

The roads along the east coast of Corfu are fast moving and hotel developers have followed them every inch of the way. To the immediate north of Corfu Town begins a 10km stretch of beach, hotel, self-catering, campsite and restaurant sprawl, most intensely at Kontókali, Gouviá, Dassiá, Ípsos and Pírgi; yet if they all missed the boat in architecture and design, there's visual redemption in the dishevelled beauty of the surrounding green hills and olive groves. At 8km from Corfu Town, the coast road veers sharply right through **Gouviá** (ΓΟΥΒΙΑ), overlooking a lagoon once used by the Venetians as a harbour; in return, the impressive remains of the Venetian **arsenal** overlook Gouviá's popular marina. The pebble beach offers watersports and reasonable swimming. A bit further along the dual-carriageway, emerald Cape Komméno extends out, but looks better from a distance and has poor beaches to boot. A few kilometres further north on the still excruciatingly built-up main road, **Dassiá** (ΔΑΣΙΑ) has a long, narrow sand and shingle beach fringed by olive groves, a favourite for sports from waterskiing to paragliding; keep on heading north to avoid the seemingly endless pub/bar sprawl. Excursion boats from here run as far as Kassiópi (north) and Benítses (south).

**Ípsos** (ΥΨΟΣ) and **Pírgi** (ΠΥΡΓΙ), former fishing villages at either end of Corfu's 'Golden Mile' north of Dassiá, offer carousels of inflatable crocodiles and 'I ♡ Corfu' postcards on their long scimitar of shingle beach, leaving barely enough room for a good wiggle. From Ípsos, you can escape inland to **Áno Korakiána**, with its olive wood workshop and delightful exhibition of folk sculpture at the **Museum of Aristides Metalinós**, (*t 066 302 2317; open Tues–Sun 8.30–2.30*). The road into the Troumpétta range via Sokráki is an awesome series of hairpins through green and gorgeous country. From Pírgi, noodle up though Spartílas to Strinílas for lunch and excellent local wine in the beautiful square; or browse through olive wood shops, like family-run 'Pantokratora', with its workshop at the entrance to the village.

# Where to Stay and Eat

## Gouviá ✉ 49100

**Grecotel Corfu Imperial, t** 066 109 1481, gman_ci@ci.grecotel.gr (L; lux). Occupying a private peninsula overlooking Komméno Bay with no fewer than 5 bars, a disco, tennis, pool and watersports. *Open April–Oct.*

**Debonos, t** 066 109 1755, f 066 109 0009 (A; exp). Garden with a pool. *Open Mar–Oct.*

**Louvre, t** 066 109 1506, f 066 109 1979 (C; mod). Cheaper, with pool, but don't expect any masterpieces.

**Bella Mama**, on the edge of the strip. Greek owned and run, in spite of its name, serving delicious *sofríto*, lamb *kléftiko*, chicken, with a house wine to quaff.

**La Bonita**. Good Italian place.

**Gorgona, t** 066 109 0261 (€18–25). Ordinary-looking place but serves delicious seafood, including *pastitsátha* with lobster.

**O'Kapetanios**. A good fish option.

**Tartufo**, up the hill. Owned by the same family as Bella Mama and similar, but set in a quieter area.

**Whistles**, next door to O'Kapetanios. Reasonable for a tipple, otherwise bars aren't exactly tranquil here.

## Dassiá ✉ 49100

**Corfu Chandris** and **Dassiá Chandris**, on the beach, t 066 109 7100, www.chandris.gr (A; lux). Huge double resort; their bungalows and villas in the environs also have use of the pools, tennis, playground, restaurants and a free shuttle service into Corfu Town. The Corfu is currently the most recently renovated; ask for a se-view since the so-called mountain view faces right onto the hideous main road. *Open April–Oct.*

**Scheria Beach, t** 066 109 3233, t 066 109 3289 (C; mod). Rather more modest but perfectly pleasant and family-run; try to get a sea-facing balcony. *Open June–Sept.*

**Camping Karda Beach, t** 066 109 3595. Both campsites offer ample facilities, incl. pool.

**Camping Kormari, t** 066 109 3587.

**Etrusco**, in Kato Korakiana, inland between Dassiá and Ípsos, t 066 109 3342 (€22–35). Corfu has many jewels in its crown, and this restaurant belongs up there with them. Since 1992 the Botrini family have been running this temple to Italian cuisine, serving fresh pasta delicacies such as *papardelle* with duck and truffles, black *tagliolini* and pasta with heady brunello wine, rosemary and garlic, plus some mouthwatering desserts, incl. melon mousse. Extensive wine list (over 200 labels), service is excellent and the courtyard setting sublime. *Evenings only.*

## Ípsos ✉ 49083

**Costas Beach, t** 066 109 3205, f 066 109 7693 (D; mod). One possibility on the seafront. *Open April–Oct.*

Although no longer allowed to boom all night, there are still plenty of young bars in Ípsos, incl. **Hector's Club** and **B52**.

## Nissáki/Kalámi/Ag. Stéfanos/Agní ✉ 49100

This is the perfect area for a glimpse of the old Corfu and you can rent from an exquisite selection of villas, incl. the upstairs of Lawrence Durrell's **White House** in Kalámi; book through **CV Travel** in London, t (020) 7581 0851 (see p.88).

**Sol Elite Nissáki Beach Hotel, t** 066 309 1232, nissaki@otenet.gr (A; lux). The only big hotel

# The Northeast Corner: Barbáti to Ag. Spirídon

Continuing north, **Barbáti** (ΜΠΑΡΜΠΑΤΗ) has a long stretch of pebbles and every conceivable facility to go with it, but from here on there is a gentle and welcome gear-change; as the coastal road wiggles its way up from the sea, the resorts below become smaller and cosier, and hints of traditional village charm peek through. The first, **Nissáki**, is a fishing hamlet which trickles along the main road; below, goat tracks lead to quiet coves. Its tiny beach has two good tavernas, and a good arts and crafts shop (The Loom), so tends to get pretty full. Even if you don't venture off the main road, it is worth pausing at Nissáki's olive wood shop, opposite the Hotel Ilios.

on this stretch of coast; despite being a mammoth eyesore, it offers great views, a pool, gym, shops, restaurants and good facilities for kids. *Open April–Oct.*

**Mitsos**, on Nissáki Beach. Always busy for lunch, with good reason.

**Vitamins**, up on the coast road through Nissáki. Smart and friendly taverna with excellent food and a lovely terrace.

For a taste of romance on a moonlit evening, take a water-taxi from Kalámi to any one of the 3 excellent tavernas in Agní (or drive there for a long lazy lunch):

**Agní, t** 066 309 1142. Attracts the glitterati.

**Nikolas, t** 066 309 1243. Offers wondrous fare.

**Toulas**. Next door to Agní. With traditional Greek cuisine.

## Kassiópi ✉ 49100

Kassiópi bulges with Italians in Aug and, unless you are pre-booked (*see* the specialist companies on pp.75–6), forget it. Even at other times of the year, the hotel situation is pretty meagre.

**Kassiópi Travel Service, t** 066 308 1388.

**The Travel Corner, t** 066 308 1220, **f** 066 308 1108. Both may be of some help.

**Villas Elli, t** 066 308 1483 (*mod, but exp in high season*). Worth calling or asking to see if they have a free apartment.

**Manessis Apartments**, right on the port, **t** 066 308 1474, *diana@otenet.gr* (*mod*). Delightful exception in a building overflowing with vines and bougainvillaea, run by friendly Irish Diana.

**Cavo Barbaro**, on Avláki Beach. Good choice for food.

**Imerólia Beach Taverna**, at Imerólia, the nearest beach. Good food, and dancing every other night.

**Kassiópi Star** and **The Three Brothers**, on the waterfront. Greek and Corfiot specialities.

**Porto**, next door to Kassiópi Star. Serves more fishy fare.

## Ag. Spirídon ✉ 49100

**St Spirídon Bay**, 100m from the sea, **t** 066 309 8294, *norcorfu@otenet.gr* (*B; mod*). Tucked away in the olive groves; quiet, unpretentious bungalow complex with pool. *Open in high season.*

**Olive Bar**, opposite. Mellow place to eat, with good fresh fish and the beach nearby; ask here if you're looking for a room.

## Róda/Agnos/Astrakéri ✉ 49081

In season nearly every room in Róda is block-booked.

**Angela Beach Hotel**, in Agnos, 1km from Róda, **t** 066 303 1291, **f** 066 303 1279 (*C; mod*). Uninspiring package development, but does offer a pool by the gently shelving sands and is 2 mins from a couple of good value fish tavernas.

**Aphrodite, t** 066 306 3125, **f** 066 306 3125 (*C; mod*). Tends to be booked with package tours in high season.

**Village Roda Inn, t** 066 306 3358 or in the UK **t** (01332) 776353 (*C; mod*). Friendly Greek-Canadian-run hostelry; they'll organize a boat trip on one of George's Dreamer Cruises for you, too.

**Róda Beach Camping, t** 066 306 3120. An alternative if everything else is full.

**Kind Hearted Place**, at the eastern end of Róda waterfront. Once the only taverna in town, offering a good, if limited, Greek menu; a small back terrace overlooks the water.

**Three Brothers**, west along the strand at Astrakéri. Taverna offering traditional fare.

Just on from Nissáki, you can drive down to **Kamináki**: a pebbly bay bordered by villas, with the clearest of water, perfect for snorkelling. There are some watersports here, boat hire and two beach tavernas. Still heading north is the picturesque and unspoilt bay of **Agní**, with crystal-clear waters and three outstandingly good tavernas, all with sunbeds on the beach for collapsing after lunch. The next little resort is built around the popular pebble beach of **Kalámi** (ΚΑΛΑΜΙ), one of the biggest self-catering compounds on Corfu. Kouloúra, a kilometre or so from the rugged Albanian coast, is a lovely seaside hamlet on a narrow horseshoe bay with a shingle beach, which has not yet succumbed to the developers; the brothers Durrell spent their youth here. **Kouloúra** was also favoured by Venetians: note the 16th-century **Koúartanou Gennatá**, part villa and part fortified tower, and two 17th-century mansions, **Vassilá** and **Prosalenti**. The next beach north is **Kerásia**, a pretty strand of white pebbles with shade and a taverna, most easily reached by doubling back 2km from beautiful, pricey South Kensington-on-Sea, known locally as **Ag. Stéfanos** and hiding the exclusive villas of the Rothschild set.

**Kassiópi** (ΚΑΣΣΙΟΠΗ), an important Hellenistic town founded by Pyrrhus of Epirus (the famous generalissimo of pseudo-victories), is now the largest and busiest resort on the northeast coast. The Romans surrounded it with great walls; its famous shrine of Zeus Cassius was visited by Cicero and Nero, and Tiberius had a villa here. The Byzantine fortress was the first place in Greece to fall to Robert Guiscard's Normans, who invaded from Calabria after first pillaging Rome. As every subsequent marauder from the north passed by Kassiópi to reach Corfu Town, it bore the brunt of their attacks. When after a long struggle the Venetians finally took the fortress, they rendered it useless in a fit of pique. Without any defences the Kassiopiots suffered terribly at the hands of the Turks and the town lost all its importance.

The ruined fortress still stands, guarding only wild flowers and sheep. Although still a fishing village with a pretty waterfront, Kassiópi's main shopping street now positively groans with touristy trinkets; however, on the road skirting town 'Barbara's' is worth a peek if you're after locally designed ceramics. Four small, well-equipped beaches with windsurfers can be reached by footpath from the headland. Two of Corfu's most tastefully developed beaches, **Avláki** and **Koyévinas**, are a quick drive, or 20–30-minute walk, south of Kassiópi; both beautiful white pebble bays, Koyévinas sports a taverna, while Avláki has two, along with boats, pedalos and windsurfers.

Continuing west beyond the grey sand beach of **Kalamáki** (also with a taverna), a sign for Loútses and Perithía announces the way up the brooding slopes of 2,953ft **Mount Pantokrátor**, Corfu's highest point. You can take a car as far as **Perithía**, a charming cobblestoned village of stone houses, abandoned by all but three farming families, one of whom runs a taverna in the old village. Lost in a mountain hollow, Perithía's garden terraces have been slowly disintegrating since everyone left for the coast to seek their fortune. The path from here to the summit of Pantokrátor takes about an hour, and offers a wondrous display of flora even into the hot summer months, and a bird's eye view of emerald Corfu and the white-capped Albanian peaks on the mainland, a vista enjoyed daily by the single monk and his somewhat less orthodox pylon in the Pantokrátor's monastery. The rutted road from Perithía by way of Láfki takes in some of Corfu's most enchanting countryside.

Back down on the coast road, **Ag. Spirídon** may be the answer if you've been seeking a small sandy beach, a simple taverna or two and a handful of rooms to rent, although Corfiots converge on it on Sundays.

## The North Coast

**Almirós**, at the quiet east end of Corfu's longest beach, is a warm shallow lagoon with trees and migratory birds. The rest of the coast has been clobbered with the magic wand of package tourism, from **Acharávi** (ΑΧΑΡΑΒΗ), where the beach is framed by pretty scenery, to **Róda** (POΔA), where egg and chips seems to be everyone's special of the day, but at least there's enough sand to escape the worst of the crowds by walking a bit in either direction. **Astrakéri** and next-door **Agnos**, at the west end, have a downbeat feel but might have free rooms.

Inland from Acharávi, **Ag. Panteléimonos**, has a huge ruined tower mansion called **Polylas**, complete with prisons used during the Venetian occupation; another Venetian manor lies further up in **Episkepsís**. Inland from Róda, **Plátonas** is in the heart of Corfu's kumquat country. Introduced from the Far East half a century ago, kumquats look like baby oranges but are too sour for most tastes; the annual harvest of 35 tonnes produced by 70 farmers is distilled into kumquat liqueur (using both blossoms and fruit) and preserved as kumquat jams and conserves. Inland from Astrakéri, **Karoussádes** is a pretty agricultural village with the 16th-century Theotóki mansion as its landmark.

**Sidári** (ΣIΔAPI) has rolled over and surrendered wholesale to package tourism and mosquitoes. If you're passing through, you may want to take a dip in the **Canal d'Amour**, a peculiar rock formation said to be two lovers – swim between them and you are guaranteed eternal love. If you have your own transport, less crowded beaches await west of Sidári below the village of **Perouládes**; the wind-sculpted tawny cliffs are high enough to cast the sandy beach in shade in the early afternoon.

# Islands near Corfu: Othoní, Eríkousa and Mathráki

Northwest of Sidári, three sleepy islets, Othoní (the largest), Eríkousa and Mathráki, comprise the westernmost territory of Greece. Transport to them is not always reliable: there are organized excursions from Sidári (caiques run most of the year, depending on demand and weather), ferries from Corfu Town, or a summer excursion from Ag. Stéfanos. The population is disproportionately feminine, the wives of husbands who fish, or work in the USA. Olives and aromatic table grapes are produced locally, and fresh fish is nearly always available; each island has rooms to rent, but food supplies can be scarce.

Of the three, **Othoní** is the largest and driest, but has the friendliest atmosphere and the most to offer if you like to ramble. There are a handful of shingle beaches and donkey trails up to the pretty, nearly abandoned villages and a well-preserved medieval fort on a pine-covered hill. Most of the excursions make for **Eríkousa**, which has the best sandy beach and a pair of villages set in the cypresses and olives. **Mathráki**, the smallest island, also has a sandy beach – a nesting place for loggerhead turtles (*see* p.490) – and very limited facilities.

## Where to Stay and Eat

**Othoní/Eríkousa/Mathráki** ✉ **49081**
**Locanda dei Sogni**, on Othoní, t 066 307 1640.
Pretty rooms (but it's essential to book early) and good Italian food.

**Rainbow**, on Othoní. Another good taverna serving traditional Greek dishes, very friendly owners .

**Eríkousa**, directly on the beach, t 066 307 1555 (*C; inexp*). This hotel is the only accommodation of any sort on Eríkousa.

# Western Beaches: North to South

The northwest corner of Corfu is covered with forests, and once off the beaten track, the 'roads' can bottom out the best shock-absorbers. The main good coastal road from Sidári cuts off the corner en route to **Ag. Stéfanos** (not to be confused with the Ag. Stéfanos on the east coast), a large and uninspiring bay with brown sand and windsurfing; **Aríllas** just south has a wide, sandy, steep bay with an attractive backdrop of green hills. The village of **Afiónas** is on a headland with magnificent views in either direction, its sandy beach steadily developing. Best of all is **Ag. Geórgios** (Pagoí), a long, magnificent stretch of beach under steep cliffs. As yet it is not over-developed, but already offers watersports (especially windsurfing), tavernas, discos and some rooms to rent; during the day it fills up with day-trippers from Paleokastrítsa.

One of Corfu's celebrated beauty spots and the major resort in west Corfu, **Paleokastrítsa** (ΠΑΛΑΙΟΚΑΣΤΡΙΤΣΑ) spreads out from a small horseshoe bay, flanked by sandy and pebbly coves, olive and almond groves, mountains and forests. Although chock-a-block in the summer, if you come in the early spring, you can believe its claim to have been the fabled home of King Alcinous and Princess Nausicaä. The sea is said to be colder here than anywhere else in Corfu. On a promontory above town, **Zoodóchos Pigí** (or Paleokastrítsa) Monastery was built in 1228 on the site of a Byzantine fortress, and tarted up by an abbot with rococo tastes in the 1700s. Tour groups queue up to buy a candle (the price of admission) as a monk hands out black skirts and shawls to the underclad. Inside, a one-room museum contains very old icons and an olive press; outside, there's a peach of a view of the sapphire sea below. An even more spectacular view of the magnificent coastline is a steep climb (or drive) out of Paleokastrítsa through cypress and pines north to the traditional village of **Lákones** and its Bella Vista Café, affording nothing less than 'the Most Beautiful View in Europe'.

Lákones itself is the hub of some of the loveliest walks on Corfu, especially to Kríni and the formidable **Angelókastro** (you can also walk from Paleokastrítsa). Built in the 13th century by the Despot of Epirus, Michael Angelos, Angelókastro is mostly ruined, but makes an impressive sight clinging to the wild red rocks over a 1,000ft precipice. Angelókastro played a major role during the various raids on the island, sheltering the surrounding villagers (as well as the Venetian governor, who lived there). If you have a car, the mountain roads from Lákones north to Róda through the little villages of **Chorepískopi**, **Valanión** (3km on a by-road) and **Nímfes** offer a bucolic journey through the Corfu of yesteryear, and in spring and early summer the air is laden with the aromatic perfumes of the wild herbs and flowers; little old ladies line the road tempting you with oregano, honey, almonds and olive oil for sale.

South of Paleokastrítsa stretches the fertile, startlingly flat **Rópa Valley**, where Homer's description of the island rings true: 'Pear follows pear, apple after apple grows, fig after fig, and grape yields grape again.' Along with orchards, Rópa has the **Corfu Golf Club** (*t 066 109 4220; green fees €38–44; club hire available*), 18 holes designed by Harradine and Pencross Bent, rated one of the 100 top courses in the world; its Riding Club organizes rides out in the countryside. Westwards on the coast,

# Where to Stay and Eat

## Paleokastrítsa ✉ 49083

Prices have come down here, but so have standards; most apartments are pre-booked and the choice of hotels isn't riveting.

**Akrotiri Beach**, 5 mins uphill from the beach, t 066 304 1237, f 066 304 1277, *belvnht@hol.gr* (*A; lux*). Enjoys some of the best views in town, and there's a seawater pool for those who don't want to commute to the real thing.

**Casa Lucia**, 12 km from Paleokastrítsa, t 066 109 1419, f 066 109 1732 (*exp–mod*). Charming group of small houses belonging to a converted olive press; lovely garden with swimming pool; houses are nicely done out and come with kitchens. An ideal choice for young families and good value for money all round.

**Odysseus**, above the beach, t 066 304 1209, f 066 304 1342, *info@odysseushotel.gr* (*C; exp–mod*). A smart complex with a swimming pool.

**Apollón**, t 066 304 1124, f 066 304 1211 (*C; mod*). A more modest affair, with balconies facing the sea.

**Astacos** ('Lobster'), t 066 304 1068. Restaurant popular with residents and long-term visitors; also has quiet, good value rooms (*inexp* rooms, not so for the lobster).

**Diving Centre**, just past Astacos. Also has rooms.

**Paleokastrítsa Camping**, t 066 304 1204. Probably the nicest campsite on Corfu.

**Chez George**. Seafood restaurant, commanding the prime location and the highest prices.

**Smurf's**, along the main beach. An alternative for fish dishes, if you can stomach the naff name.

## Ermónes ✉ 49100

**Ermónes Beach**, t 066 109 4241, f 066 109 4248, *ermones@otenet.gr* (*A; exp*). Huge bungalow complex, with every conceivable facility.

**Athena Hermones Golf**, near the golf course, t 066 109 4236, f 066 109 4605 (*C; mod*). A much more intimate choice of accommodation.

## Glyfáda/Pélekas ✉ 49100

**Pélekas Country Club**, a few mins from Pélekas, t 066 105 2239, f 066 103 3867 (*A; lux*). A touch of genteel, rural Corfu, with plenty of peace and quiet in the middle of wooded grounds, with pool and tennis courts. Elegant rooms with bath, kitchen, TV and phone.

**Louis Grand Hotel Glyfáda**, t 066 109 4140, f 066 109 4146 (*A; lux–exp*). Its many watersport activities dominate the beach.

**Levant Hotel**, Pélekas, t 066 109 4230, f 066 109 4115. *levant@otenet.gr* (*A; exp*). Perched on top of Pélekas by the Kaiser's Throne; superb views and a pool, away from it all. *Open all year*.

**Glyfáda Beach**, t/f 066 109 4257 (*B; mod*). A cool, pleasant alternative.

**Ermónes**, with its pebble beaches and hotels, is another candidate for Odysseus' landing point; Nausicaä and her servants would have been washing the palace laundry in a little cascade, near the present-day Snackbar Nausicaä. **Pélekas**, a 17th-century village up on a mountain ridge, was Kaiser Wilhelm II's favourite spot to watch the sunset; busloads of people arrive every evening in the summer to do the same, from a tower called the **Kaiser's Throne**. Pélekas was one of Corfu's nudie beaches until a road built from Gialiskári brought in crowds of trippers; now the completely unadorned walk down the steep track to lovely **Mirtiótissa** Beach (the other half of the beach, by the monastery, is not nudist). After sunset the village throbs to the sound of disco music. **Glyfáda**, one of the island's best beaches, is a long gentle swathe of golden sand. It fills up during the day with hotel residents and day-trippers, but early evening is perfect for a swim here, with steep cliffs dropping straight down into the blue bay.

# Southern Corfu

The southern half of the island has attracted the worst excesses of tourism. For years **Benítses** (ΜΠΕΝΙΤΣΕΣ) was the numero uno offender, a British package resort bubbling with hormones and devouring a little Greek fishing village (with its permission, of course). More recently, tour operators have pulled out and Benítses is an altogether gentler place again, but the damage is done. The patches of beach it offers will always be too close to the coastal highway and the rowdies seem to have chased the resort's former enthusiasts away for good. But if you look hard enough, there are a few remnants of Benítses' more aesthetic past. The arches and mosaics just behind the harbour belonged to a Roman bathhouse. And you can walk through the old, residential quarter of the village, past the local cemetery through delightful rural scenery towards **Stavrós**, where the Benítses Waterworks were built by Sir Frederick Adam, British High Commissioner from 1824 to 1832. Originally, the waterworks supplied Corfu Town; now Benítses manages to use it all, even though few people there would be caught dead drinking from it. Benítses also currently houses the itinerant **Corfu Shell Museum**, (*t 066 107 2227; open daily 10–8; adm*), with its thousands of beautiful sea treasures. Further south, the nearly continuous resort sprawls past the beaches of **Moraítika** (ΜΟΡΑΙΤΙΚΑ) and **Messónghi** (ΜΕΣΣΟΓΓΗ), a cut above Benítses. If you're down here for the scenery, skip the coast and take the inland route, beginning at Kinopiástes (near Gastoúri), passing by way of Ag. Déka (one of Corfu's prettiest villages), Makráta, Kornáta and Strongilí.

The more inaccessible west coast is also worthwhile: **Ag. Górdis** (ΑΓ.ΓΟΡΔΗΣ) is one of Corfu's more attractive village-resorts with a lovely, sheltered 2-mile-long beach of soft golden sand and minimal waves, although it is increasingly dominated by package-holiday operators. Inland, **Sinarádes** is a large and pretty village surrounded by vineyards and home to a fine **Folk Museum** (*t 066 105 4962; open Tues–Sun 9.30–2.30; adm*). The road south to **Ag. Mathias** is a delightful meander through olive groves and cypresses; stop at Golden View café to admire the view. Ag. Mathias, planted on its own mountain, is a serene place to daydream under the plane tree and write up your diary, disturbed only by the occasional roar of hired scooters and jeeps as they zip through the village. The village remains delightfully Greek – full of old houses with wonky wooden verandas overflowing with geraniums and bougainvillaea, and reverberating with birdsong – and the locals are more concerned about their olive crop than threatened decreases in tourist numbers. There are 24 churches in or near the village, and by asking around you can find your way down the steep slopes to the really peaceful beaches of **Tría Avlákia**, **Paramónas** and **Skithi**, with a few rooms and the odd taverna. An octagonal Byzantine castle at **Gardíki**, south of Ag. Mathias, was another work by the despot of Epirus, Michael Angelos II. This is one of the most unspoilt areas of Corfu, and is a good starting point for some excellent walks. A minor road by Gardíki leads in 4km to one of Corfu's few lakes, the lagoony **Límni Korissíon**, which is separated from the sea by a long stretch of huge, wild dunes; in spring and autumn it fills with migratory birds. Take your mosquito defences, however; they grow as big as pterodactyls here and have

# Where to Stay and Eat

## Benítses ✉ 49084

**All Tourist Services, t** 066 107 2223, on the main road. Can find you a private room.

**Marbella,** past Benítses at Ag. Ioannis, **t** 066 107 1183, *marbella@otenet.gr* (*A; lux*). One of the most luxurious establishments along the coastal strip; recently refurbished in grand style, it exudes tranquil opulence. With reasonable à la carte restaurant.

**San Stefano, t** 066 107 1112, *sanstefano@hol.gr* (*A; lux*). Spread across terraces, overlooking the sea, with the largest swimming pool on the island, sea sports and other facilities.

**Corfu Maris,** on the beach at the south end of town, **t** 066 107 2129, **f** 066 107 2035 (*C; mod*). More modest rooms.

Benítses is not known for its cuisine, but there are a few decent choices.

**Marabou.** Tasty local dishes.

**Paxinos,** in the old village, **t** 066 107 2339. Serves traditional fare.

**Disco Valentino**. After eating your fill, you can try your voice at laser karaoke or dance the night away.

## Ag. Górdis ✉ 49084

**Karoukas Travel, t** 066 105 3909, *karoukas@otenet.gr*, on the main street. May be able to fix you up with a room or apartment if you don't want to plod around looking.

**Yaliskari Palace,** 3km from the beach, **t** 066 105 4401, *rizosresorts@sympna.com* (*A; exp*). Vast complex with a pool, tennis and sea sports.

**Ag. Górdis,** right on the sand, **t** 066 105 3320, **f** 066 105 2237 (*A; exp–mod*). Similarly large, ultra modern and endowed with facilities.

**Dandidis Pension-Restaurant,** on the beach, **t** 066 105 3232 (*mod*). Plain doubles with fridge and balcony.

**Pink Palace, t** 066 105 3103 (*E; inexp*). Resort complex run by Americans for backpackers who want to party the night away.

**Michali's Place** or **Alex in the Garden.** Two established eateries keeping locals' and visitors' taste buds happy.

## Moraítika ✉ 49084

It's fairly easy to find a room to rent here. Ask at **Vlachos Tours,** by the pharmacy, **t** 066 107 5723.

**Miramare Beach, t** 066 107 5224, *cfumiram1@otenet.gr* (*L; lux*). Superior complex set in old olive groves and citrus orchards, with pool, tennis, theatre and disco.

**Koryfo Apartments,** 400m from the sea, **t** 066 107 5511, in Athens, **t** 010 981 8889, **f** 010 982 2445 (*exp*). Pretty flats.

**Margarita Beach Hotel, t/f** 066 107 5267 (*C; mod*). Offers more modest seaside doubles with balcony.

**Bella Vista,** up in the old village. Promises a calm evening in a garden with views and good food.

**Islands,** on the main road in Moraítika. A good restaurant option.

## Messónghi ✉ 49080

**Apollo Palace, t** 066 107 5433, *apollopl@mail.hol.gr* (*A; exp*). One of the grander places here, in a relatively tasteful way, offering all facilities and half-board.

**Messónghi Beach Hotel and Bungalows, t** 066 107 6684, *aktimess@otenet.gr* (*B; exp*). Giant, self-contained complex that's very suitable for family activities.

## Ag. Mathiás ✉ 49084

**Paramónas,** on Paramónas Beach, **t** 066 107 6595, *paramonas@otenet.gr* (*B; mod*).

**Mouria**. Grill house worth a try.

appetites to match. **Lagoúdia**, two islets off the southwest coast, are home to a tribe of donkeys; some of their ancestors were eaten by a boatload of Napoleon's troops who were wrecked there for three days.

The scenery from here down to Corfu's tail is flat and agricultural, but the beaches are sandy and clean. South of Límni Korissíon a busy family resort has grown up around (another) **Ag. Geórgios**. **Linía**, the northern extension of Ag. Geórgios Beach, is more tranquil and backed by dunes; the beach of **Marathiás** is the southern extension of the same strand, with a few tavernas. In the centre of a large fertile plain, **Lefkími**, the largest town in the south, is dusty and uninviting; the nearest beaches, **Mólos** and **Alykés**, 2km away on the east coast, are flat and grey, set amid salt pans.

**Kávos** (ΚΑΒΟΣ) is a one-time fishing village turned all-day-and-night package holiday rave party where things have got so out of hand that locals now refuse to work there. At the southernmost tip of Corfu, the quieter beaches of **Asprókavos** and **Arkoudílas** (near a ruined monastery, reached by a path from Sparterá) have white sand and tavernas; the pretty beach below Dragotiná is a long walk from the village but never crowded.

# Ithaca/Itháki (ΙΘΑΚΗ)

*Every traveller is a citizen of Ithaca.*

sign in the port

Ithaca is a compelling and universal symbol, although many who have heard of it have no idea where it is, and those who do visit it often have a hard time reconciling the island's reality with their idea of Odysseus' beloved home. But re-read your Homer before you come, and you'll find that nearly all of his descriptions of Ithaca square with this small, mountainous island – it is indeed 'narrow' and 'rocky' and 'unfit for riding horses'. Some ancient and modern scholars have theorized that Homer's Ithaca was elsewhere – Lefkáda and Kefaloniá are popular contenders. Don't believe them. Itháki, as the locals call their home, the eternal symbol of all homes and journey's end, is the real thing, and 'even if you find it poor,' as Caváfy wrote, 'Ithaca does not deceive. Without Ithaca your journey would have no beauty.'

Ithaca has a jagged, indented coast (as Homer says), with no exceptional beaches, but its harbours make it a big favourite with sailors. Best of all, it has changed little over the years; the atmosphere is still relaxed and low-key.

## History

On Pilikata hill near Stavrós a road, buildings and walls show that communal life was established on Ithaca by the early Helladic era (3000–2000 BC). The Cave of Loízos was the centre of cult activity, used by both the inhabitants and passing sailors. By Mycenaean times, settlements had relocated further south as Arkikious (*see* 'Mythology') organized a kingdom (*c.* 1200 BC) that included Kefaloniá, Zákynthos, Lefkáda and part of the Peloponnesian coast. Ithaca was the capital, and under Odysseus the kingdom reached its prime, sending 12 ships to Troy.

In the last 200 years archaeologists have combed Ithaca for signs of Odysseus. Schliemann came after his great discovery of Troy, and since Schliemann always found what he sought, he unearthed a large structure he immediately labelled 'Odysseus' Palace'; although it dates from only 700 BC, the name has stuck. Later finds, while failing to produce any concrete evidence of the Crafty One's existence, at least indicate that the ancients considered Ithaca Homer's Ithaca: inscriptions show that Odysseus was worshipped as a divine hero, ancient coins bore his picture, and pottery was decorated with his cockerel symbol. Homer describes the palace of

# Ithaca

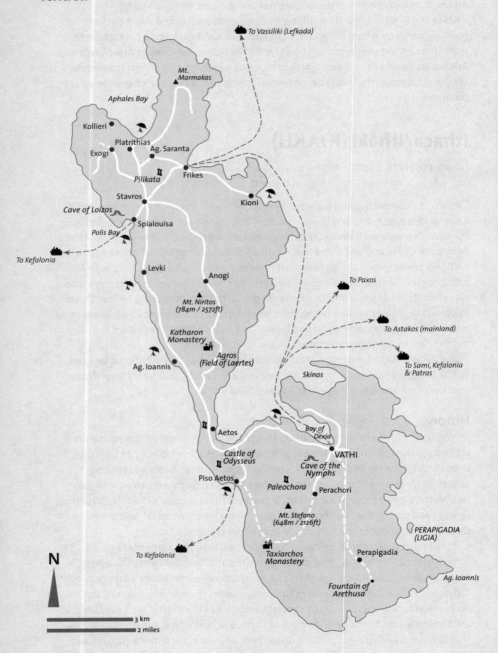

To Vassiliki (Lefkada)

Mt. Marmakas

Aphales Bay

Kollieri

Platrithias

Exogi

Ag. Saranta

Pilikata

Frikes

Stavros

Kioni

Cave of Loizos

Spialouisa

Polis Bay

To Kefalonia

Levki

Anogi

To Paxos

Mt. Niritos
(784m / 2572ft)

To Astakos (mainland)

Katharon
Monastery

Agros
(Field of Laertes)

To Sami, Kefalonia
& Patras

Ag. Ioannis

Skinos

Aetos

Bay of
Dexia

Castle of
Odysseus

VATHI

Cave of the
Nymphs

Piso Aetos

Paleochora

Perachori

Mt. Stefano
(648m / 2126ft)

PERAPIGADIA
(LIGIA)

To Kefalonia

Taxiarchos
Monastery

Perapigadia

Fountain of
Arethusa

Ag. Ioannis

N

3 km

2 miles

Odysseus as above 'three seas' and the hill near Stavrós fits the description, over-looking three bays. In 1930 two ruined towers were discovered that may have been used to signal the palace. Other Homeric sites have been tentatively identified, such as the Fountain of Arethusa, where Odysseus met his faithful swineherd Eumaeus, and the cave where he hid the treasure given to him by the Phaeacians. A manuscript kept on Mount Áthos claims that Homer himself was born in Ithaca; one tradition says that, although born in Smyrna, he was invited as a young man to stay in Ithaca and knew first hand the places he described.

After the Mycenaeans, Ithaca lost its importance and even its name; for a period it was humiliatingly known as 'Little Kefaloniá'. By the time of the Venetians, it was all but abandoned because of pirates, and the Venetians offered generous incentives to anyone who would settle and farm there. Once again Ithaca prospered, but, unlike the

## Getting There and Around

**By sea**: Ithaca has 3 ports, Váthi, connected at least twice a day by **ferry** with Sámi (Kefaloniá), Pátras and occasionally with Astakós (on the mainland); Píso Aetós, 7km west of Váthi has a faster, cheaper regular **car ferry** to Sámi (Kefaloniá), and occasionally to Fiskárdo (Kefaloniá) and Vassilikí (Lefkáda). Fríkes, in the north of Ithaca, connects with Lefkáda and Sámi (also daily **caiques** between Váthi and Fríkes). Ferry routes are often subject to change. **Port authority**: Váthi, t 067 403 2209, Píso Aetós, t 067 403 2104.

**By road**: for 10 mths a year one (school) **bus** a day plies its route once a day up and down the island (times depending on school hours) from Kióni to Váthi and back. In July and Aug, the service extends to twice a day. **Taxis** abound (Kióni to Váthi €15–20, Váthi to Píso Aetós €8). For **car** rental, try **Mr Koutavás**, by the town hall in Váthi, t 067 403 2702 and for **motorbikes Mákis Grívas**, by the port, t 067 403 2840.

**On foot**: off the road, there are some wonderful **walks** as outlined in an excellent free pamphlet, 'Trails of Ithaca'. Long-term resident Ian Peters, PO Box 2 Váthi, t 067 403 3592, offers unique walking tours privately, or through **Headwater Holidays** (*www.head-water-holidays.co.uk, see* p.75)

## Tourist Information

Tourist police: *see* regular police at Váthi, **t** 067 403 2205.

For car rentals, boat rental and tickets, contact:

**Polyctor Tours**, in the square in Váthi, **t** 067 403 3120, *polyctor@otenet.gr*.

**Dela Tours**, in the square in Váthi, **t** 067 403 2104, **f** 067 403 3031, *delas@otenet.gr*.

**Kiki Travel**, in Fríkes, **t** 067 403 1387, **f** 067 403 1762, *kikitrav@otenet.gr* is friendly.

## Festivals

**1 May**: Taxiárchos.
**24 June**: Kióni.
**Aug**: wine festival, in Peráchori.
**5–6 Aug**: Stavrós.
**14 Aug**: Anogí.
**15 Aug**: Platrithias and Kathará Monastery.
**Mid-Aug to mid-Sept**: theatre and cultural festival at Váthi.

## Where to Stay and Eat

Ithaca is building new hotels, although the island resolutely shuns large tourist complexes. For help with rooms or apart-ments, contact **Polyctor Tours** (*see* above), or **Greek Islands Club**, **t** (UK) (01932) 220 477, which has the scoop of the prettiest self-catering properties.

### Váthi ✉ 28300

**Perantzada**, 821 Odyssea Androutsou, over-looking the port, **t** 067 403 3496, **f** 067 403 3493, *arthotel@otenet.gr* (*A; lux*). Classy modern 'art' hotel where brightly-coloured fabrics, furnishings, rugs and lighting are the

other Ionian islands, it never had an aristocracy. Ironically, union with Greece in 1864 initiated a great migration, many Ithakians going to Romania, Australia, South Africa, and perhaps to Ithaca, New York. Like their countryman Odysseus, they are known as great sailors, and even those who call Ithaca home spend much time away at sea.

# Vathi (ΒΑΘΥ)

Váthi, built at the bottom of a long horseshoe bay, has been the capital of the island since the 16th century. Its beautiful harbour, surrounded by mountains, embraces a wooded islet called **Lazaretto** after a quarantine station established in 1668 by the Venetians and converted into a prison before earthquakes destroyed it; now there's

focus; each room decorated in individual style, and hand-painted poems on each wall. A good place for home-makers looking for ideas, much less so for families with ice cream-covered kiddies. *Open all year*.

**Mentor**, Georgíou Drakoúli St, just east of the port, **t** 067 403 2433, **f** 067 403 2293 (*B; exp*). The old standby, standing sentinel; plain but pleasant.

**Odyssey**, just east of town, **t/f** 067 403 2268 (*exp*). Wonderful view, well equipped and roomy.

**Penelope Studios, t** 067 403 3134 (*exp*). Self-catering option.

**Odysseus, t** 067 403 2381, **f** 067 403 2587 (*C; mod*). Also pleasant and a bit cheaper. There's good dining here, too.

**Maroudas Rooms, t/f** 067 403 2451. Studios (*mod*) and rooms (*inexp*).

**Captain Yiannis**, east across the bay from the hub of the town, **t** 067 403 3173, **f** 067 403 2849 (*C*). Appealing bungalow complex with kitchenettes etc, pool and tennis.

There's a good smattering of tavernas around the harbour and back lanes, all serving good food. Ithaca isn't a take-your money-and-run kind of place – 'Run where?' cynics may ask – and locals genuinely want your stay to be as pleasant as possible.

**Grill Restaurant**, Plateía Polytechneíou. Offering Ithaca's version of surf'n'turf: delicious grilled octopus and *kokorétsi* – lamb's offal on a spit.

**Kandouni**, on the waterfront, **t** 067 403 2918. Plain taverna, but the kitchen has a few treats, *soutzoukákia* and pasta with lobster among them.

**Sirines** ('Sirens'), **t** 067 403 3001. No noise here – classical or modern – but you may be lured nonetheless by its romantic courtyard setting; tasty *mezédes* and hearty main dishes.

**Trexandiri**, set back from the port. Small and reasonable with good local food.

**Tsibiris**, 800m east of the ferry dock. Fresh fish by the water, with a view of town.

For a nightcap, and a chance to reflect on whether it was worth a ten-year journey to get here, head for the pleasant...you guessed it, **Odyssey** bar.

## Fríkes/Kióni ✉ 28301

For the handful of rooms and apartments to rent, contact **Kiki Travel** in Fríkes (*see* above).

**Kionia**, up in Kióni, **t/f** 067 403 1362 (*lux*). Tends to be block-booked by package companies.

**Maroudas Apartments**, in Fríkes, **t** 067 403 1691, **f** 067 403 1753 (*mod*). Pleasant self-catering option that may have vacancies in season. *Open all year*.

**Nostos Hotel**, in Fríkes, **t** 067 403 1644, **f** 067 403 1716 (*C; mod*). Set back from the beach.

**Symposium**, smack on Fríkes' waterfront. Serving fish, and carafes of local wine, although old favourites 'Odyseas Meat-pie' and the 'Brides' Salad (Magical callings of a mythical world) are no longer on the menu.

**Taverna Ulysseus**, by the sea in Fríkes. Good fresh fish (and other dishes), its name obviously evidence of a great reconciliation with Poseidon.

Kióni has 3 tavernas, and a *kafeneíon*, cleverly renovated to attract the boaties without losing the approval of locals.

## Mythology

A king of Kefaloniá, Kefalos, had a son named Arkikious who annexed Ithaca and made it the centre of his realm; his son was Laertes, who participated on the voyage of the Argo and married Anticleia, who gave birth to Odysseus. But a strong tradition says that two crafty shepherds, Autolykus, a son of Hermes, and Sisyphus, used to graze their flocks next to each other, and through trickery would steal one another's sheep. Autolykus thought that if he married his daughter Anticleia to Sisyphus, their child would inherit cunning from both sides of the family and be the ultimate trickster. Sisyphus was equally keen and had his evil way with Anticleia even before their wedding; but during the interval, King Laertes asked to marry her, and did. She was already pregnant by Sisyphus, and Autolykus, the child's grandfather, named him Odysseus, which means 'angry' or 'he who is hated by all', as Homer explains it.

Odysseus sought Helen's hand in marriage, then wed Penelope instead and had a son, Telemachus. Having been warned by an oracle that if he went to Troy he would be absent for 20 years and return alone without booty, Odysseus pretended madness by ploughing the sand and sowing it with salt when the Greek representatives came to fetch him; to test him, the Greeks placed his baby son Telemachus in front of his oxen. Odysseus diverted their course, and was constrained by his promise as one of Helen's ex-suitors to depart for Troy and bring her back. After his homecoming in disguise, the murder of Penelope's suitors, and recognition by his wife, Homer's story ends, but there are two accounts of Odysseus' death: one, that the families of the suitors forced him to live in exile, and that he died at a ripe old age in Italy; another, that Odysseus was not permitted to die until he appeased the anger of his old enemy Poseidon, and the only way to do so was to take an oar and walk until he came to a land where people asked him what he carried. Then, after a sacrifice to the sea god, he sailed home, and was drowned on the way.

only a chapel. Two ruined forts, **Loútsa** and **Kástro**, built in 1805 by the French, stand at either side of the harbour entrance; there's a small bathing beach on the east side.

Although shattered by the 1953 earthquake, Váthi (pop. 1,800) was reconstructed as it was with red tile roofs and is considered a 'traditional settlement', which ensures that all new building must conform to the local style. One building that survived is the Neoclassical mansion of the Drakoúlis family, who brought the first steamship, the *Ithaka*, to Greece. The **Archaeology Museum** (*t 067 403 2200,; open Tues–Sun 8.30–2.30*) behind the Mentor Hotel houses a collection of Mycenaean and Classical artefacts. One of the prizes in the library of the adjacent **Cultural Centre** is a Japanese edition of Homer's works printed in 1600. For an insight into local history, the little **Folklore Museum**, near Polyctor Tours (*t 067 403 3398; open 8.30–2*), displays bedrooms and sitting rooms of old Ithaca. The church of the **Taxiárchos** contains an icon of Christ attributed to the young El Greco. Every four years since 1981, Váthi's Centre for Odyssean Studies has hosted an International Congress on the *Odyssey*. But if it's a swim you need, make use of the caique services in Váthi port for Gidáki Beach. Some small pebble beaches are accessible by car to the east of Vathí.

## Southern Ithaca: on the Odysseus Trail

Some sites identified with places in the *Odyssey* make pretty walks from Váthi. West of Váthi, it's a 4km walk (or drive) to the **Cave of the Nymphs** or Marmaróspilia (*signposted, but often closed at the time of writing while excavations are being carried out*), where Odysseus is said to have hidden the gifts of King Alcinous. The cave has a hole in the roof – 'the entrance of the gods' – which permitted the smoke of the sacrifices to rise to heaven. Stairs lead down through the narrow entrance into a small stalactite chamber. Below, the narrow **Dexiá** inlet may be the 'Harbour of Phorcys' where the Phaeacians gently put the sleeping Odysseus on shore.

South of Váthi, an unpaved road runs 7km to the pretty Maráthias plateau. About 4km along, a donkey path to the left is signposted to the **Fountain of Arethusa** (KPINI APEΘΥΟΣΑ), an hour and a half walk. According to the myth, Arethusa wept so much when her son Corax 'the raven' was killed that she turned into a spring; the water flows (in the summer, dribbles) from under the towering rock Corax and is good to drink, although beware that it has a reputation for making you as hungry as a bear. Just to the south, at **Ellinikó**, Odysseus, disguised as a beggar, met the swineherd Eumaeus; excavations at Ellinikó duly uncovered some Mycenaean odds and ends. From the Arethusa Fountain a rocky scramble descends to the pretty little beach, facing the islet of **Perapigádia** (the Homeric Asteris), where the murderous suitors hid, awaiting to ambush young Telemachus on his return from Pýlos.

The only other real village in the south of Ithaca is **Perachóri** (ΠΕΡΑΧΩΡΙ), occupying a 984ft-high fertile balcony 2km from Váthi, where most of Ithaca's wine is produced. The village dates from the Venetians, although the first fortified houses were built in the walled confines of **Paleochóra**, Ithaca's first capital; among their ruins is a church minus its roof but still adorned with fading Byzantine frescoes. Follow the signposts, or in Perachóri the villagers will show you which path to take; the view is superb. Another road – it's for four-wheel-drives only – climbs 3km from Perachóri to the **Monastery of the Taxiárchos** (1645) near the top of Mount Stéfano. Although the earthquakes have blasted it, the views from the monastery and the road are lovely. Perachóri has a pair of small high season tavernas with panoramic views, serving local wine and *tserépato*, meat slowly roasted in a special clay pot.

## North of Váthi

Ithaca has an hourglass figure with a waist, the narrow mountain stretch of **Aetós**, only 500m wide. Overlooking the two bays below is what the locals (as well as Schliemann) have always called the **Castle of Odysseus**, although it's apparently the citadel of the 8th-century BC town of Alalkomenes, which was abandoned in Roman times. Impressive Cyclopean walls and the foundations of a temple remain. Since 1984 the 'Odysseus Project', sponsored by the Archaeological Society of Athens, Washington University and the National Geographic Society, has concentrated its excavations around Aetós' church of Ag. Geórgios, a site has been continuously occupied since the 13th century BC. There's a pebble beach in the bay below to the east and another small, excellent, usually deserted one at the little bay of **Píso Aetós** in the west, where the ferry boats come in.

Just north of Aetós, near Agrós, is the **Field of Laertes**, where Odysseus encountered his father after killing the suitors; note the massive 2,000-year-old 'Laertes' olive'. From here a road ascends the slopes of 2,572ft **Mount Níritos** (formerly Korifí – Ithaca is slowly reclaiming its Homeric names) to the **Monastery of the Katharón**, 'of the dry weeds' (**t** 067 403 3460), built on the site of a Temple of Athena. One far-fetched story says it was built by the heretical Cathars; another explains that farmers were burning dry weeds here when they found an icon of the Birth of the Virgin attributed to St Luke, which holds pride of place in the church of the **Panagía Kathariótissas**. When Byron visited in 1823 a special mass was held in his honour. Nowadays many faithful spend the night of 14 August here, walking from Vathí. From its lighthouse of a bell tower you can see the Gulf of Pátras on a clear day.

From Moni Katharón, a paved road continues 3km up to **Anógí**, 'at the top of the world', passing odd-shaped boulders, including a very phallic 25ft monolith named Araklís, or Heracles. The village retains some Venetian ruins, including a sturdy grey campanile and a restored 12th-century church dedicated to the **Panagía** (*ask at the kafeneíon for the key, or call* **t** 067 403 1306) with Byzantine frescoes; note the clay amphorae embedded in the walls to improve the church's acoustics.

The second and easier road from Agrós follows the west coast. At Ag. Ioánnis, just opposite Kefaloniá, is a lovely, seldom-used white beach, Aspros Gialós. **Lévki**, the small village to the north, was an important port for the resistance movement during the war, and when it was destroyed by the 1953 earthquake, Britain helped rebuild it. There are small beaches below and a few rooms to rent on the main road.

## Stavrós and the North

The two roads meet at Stavrós, the most important village in the north, overlooking lovely Pólis Bay ('city bay'), its name referring to the Byzantine city of Ierosalem, which sank into it during an earthquake in AD 967; Robert Guiscard (*see* p.458) was told by a soothsayer that he would die after seeing Jerusalem, but he didn't think 'Jerusalem' would be the ruins of a town on Ithaca. A bust of Odysseus in the centre of Stavrós looks sternly out over the bay. The **Cave of Loízos** to the right of the bay was an ancient cult sanctuary; some believe it was Homer's Cave of the Nymphs. Prehistoric pots, Mycenaean amphorae, bronze tripods from 800–700 BC, ex-votos of nymphs and an inscription dedicated to Odysseus were found here before the cave collapsed.

Another plausible Odysseus' palace is **Pilikáta**, or the Hill of Hermes, just north of Stavrós. The site fits the Homeric description almost perfectly, in sight of 'three seas' (the bays of Frikés, Pólis and Aphales) and 'three mountains' (Níritos, Marmakás and Exógi or Neion). Although the ruins are of a Venetian fort, under it excavators found evidence of buildings and roads dating back to Neolithic times, and a pit containing sacrifices and two ceramic shards engraved in Linear A, from c. 2700 BC. In 1989, Prof. Paul Fauré attempted a translation of them, based on Linear B and the index of symbols established for Linear A, written in an Indo-European language – a very, very early form of Greek – called Kreutschmer by the linguists: Fauré translates one as

'Here is what I, Aredatis, give to the queen, the goddess Rhea: 100 goats, 10 sheep, 3 pigs' and the other as: 'The nymph saved me.' The other finds from Pilikáta and the Cave of Loízos are in the small but interesting **Stavrós Archaeology Museum** (*t 067 403 1305; open Tues–Sun 9–2*) on the Platrithiás road.

From Stavrós a road leads north to Ithaca's remotest village, called **Exógi** ('beyond the earth'). Set high up on terraces, the village is deserted, but there are beautiful views; above the village is Ithaca's oddball attraction, three narrow pyramids built in 1933 by a pyramid-fancier named Papadópoulos. He's buried under one, his mother under another, while the third has a jar with his coin collection. Another 2km up, the disused Monastery of Panagía Eleoússa offers extraordinary views over the Ionian islands. Between Exogi and Platrithiás is an area known as '**Homer's School**'; the ruined 7th-century church of Ag. Athanásios has hewn blocks reused from an ancient wall. By the Melanydrus spring there's a stepped well that the locals call 'Penelope's Bath' – it's actually a Mycenaean tomb. This fertile area is one of the most pleasant on the island; it was here that Odysseus was ploughing his field when he was dragged off to Troy. **Platrithiás** is the biggest hamlet; another, **Kóllieri**, greets wayfarers with an outdoor 'folklore museum', with stone obelisks made out of millstones.

### Fríkes and Kióni

North of Stavrós, **Fríkes** (ΦΡΙΚΕΣ), a favourite pirates' lair into the 19th century, is now a tiny fishing village and popular port-of-call for flotilla yachts. About 100 people live there year-round; there are two tiny beaches nearby, Limenária and Kourvoúlia, and a new hotel and tavernas. The road continues to **Rachí**, a tiny hamlet of old stone houses, and continues down to the pretty village of **Kióni**, built around a tiny harbour, guarded by three ruined windmills. Twice the size of Frikés, it too is popular with the yachting set; landlubbers can hire motorboats to the surrounding beaches. Kióni means 'column', and an ancient one still stands on the altar in the church of Ag. Nikólaos. There are more Cylopean walls nearby, at a site called Roúga.

# Kálamos (ΚΑΛΑΜΟΣ) and Kástos (ΚΑΣΤΟΣ)

Kálamos and Kástos, two mountains in the sea east of Meganísi, are under the jurisdiction of Lefkáda, but can only be reached on a daily regular basis by way of Mítikas on the mainland; occasionally Kálamos is connected to Sámi, Ithaca, the port Astakós and Meganísi, as well as Nidrí and Vassilikí on Lefkáda. Kálamos lives primarily by fishing and most people live in the attractive north coast village of Kálamos (Chóra), where there are a few rooms to rent. It has all the essentials of village life, even a pair of tavernas on the town beach, and tolerates rough camping. Better beaches may be found towards **Episkopí**, but are most easily reached by boat. A donkey path leads up from Chóra to the abandoned walled village of **Kástro**, where everyone used to live. Only two or three families live on **Kástos**, now unable to care for all the vineyards which once produced a fine wine. There aren't any regular connections; you'll have to hire a caique from Mítikas, but there's a taverna and a room or two if you're lucky.

# Kefaloniá (ΚΕΦΑΛΟΝΙΑ)

'The half-forgotten island of Cephallonia rises improvidently and inadvisedly from the Ionian Sea,' writes Dr Iannis in Louis de Bernières' *Captain Corelli's Mandolin*. Its Jabberwocky silhouette contains 781 square kilometres of ruggedly beautiful mountains, making it the largest of the Ionian islands, although it supports a mere 30,000 people (and many of these live in Athens in the winter). Kefalonians are famous for wandering (one, Constantine Yerákis, made a fortune in the British East India Company and became Regent of Siam), and it's not uncommon to meet someone whose entire family lives in Canada, Australia or the United States. Most Kefalonians are good-humoured and clever, but have the reputation of being cunning, eccentric, tight with their money and the worst blasphemers in Greece. Other Greeks say the Kefalonians have drunk a toast with the devil himself.

## Getting There and Around

**By air**: daily flights from Athens and frequent charters from Britain. The **Olympic Airways** office is in Argostóli, at 1 R. Vergotí, t 067 102 8808/8881; the **airport** is 9km south of Argostóli, t 067 104 1511, and reachable by taxi (€10–12).

**By sea**: Kefaloniá has 5 ports. Starting at the top, Fiskárdo has **ferry** links to Ithaca and Lefkáda; Sámi with Ithaca and Pátras; Póros with Killíni (Peloponnese); Pessáda, in the south, with Zákynthos; finally, Argostóli with Killíni. In summer there are also connections with Astakós on the mainland. Ferry schedules are subject to frequent changes; call the following **Port authority** numbers for information: Fiskárdo, t 067 404 1400, Sámi, t 067 402 2031, Póros, t 067 407 2460, Pessáda (EOT), t 067 102 2248, Argostóli, t 067 102 2224. There's a ferry between Argostóli and Lixoúri which goes every half-hour in season and otherwise hourly.

**By road: bus** services are not frequent and schedules change often; in Argostóli, the **bus station** is at 4 Tritsi (to the left of the causeway as you enter town), t 067 102 2281, in Lixoúri, t 067 109 3200. From Argostóli there are 6 buses a day to and from Lassi in the high season, 2 or more to Fiskárdo, Ag. Evfimía, Sámi and Skála. **KTEL Travel**, next door to the bus station in Argostóli, t 067 102 2276, offers day trips around the island and to the mainland. No lack of **taxis**, **car** and **moped** rentals; in Argostóli, try Neptune (near the Star Hotel), t 067 102 4092, f 067 102 4174, with good rates.

## Tourist Information

**EOT**: Argostóli, on the waterfront across from the Star Hotel, t 067 102 2248, f 067 102 4466. Helpful and distributes freebies like *Kefaloniá Tourist News; open weekdays 8–2*.

**Tourist police**: Argostóli, t 067 102 2815.

**Filoxenos Travel**, 2 Vergoti, t 067 102 3055, *filoxenos-travel@galaxy.gr*.

**Proper Cefalonian Travel**, 13 Rizopaston, t 067 102 6924, *ecco@ath.forthnet.gr*. Arranges rooms, tours, dives and yacht rentals.

## Festivals

**Last Sun and Mon before Lent**: Carnival celebrations.

**Easter**: festival in Lixoúri.

**23 April**: Ag. Geórgios.

**21 May**: Festival of the Radicals (celebrating union with Greece) in Argostóli.

**23 June**: Argostóli.

**15 Aug**: Markópoulo (with the little snakes).

**16 Aug** and **20 Oct**: Ag. Gerásimos.

**First Sat after 15 Aug**: Robóla festival of wine in Fragáta.

Although the earthquake in 1953 shattered all but a fraction of Kefaloniá's traditional architecture and all the charm that goes with it, the big, sprawling island has lost none of its striking natural beauty. It has fine beaches (one of which, Mýrtos, is perhaps the most dramatic in all of Greece), two of the country's loveliest caves, lofty fir forests, splendid views and Robóla wine. But by no means is the island undiscovered, thanks in no little part to the popularity of Captain Corelli, book and film, which was shot on location. Northern Kefaloniá in particular has been consumed by package tourism – albeit genteel – and in July and August bursts at the seams. The last enclaves of accommodation for the independent are around Argostóli, Sámi and Póros. The island's bus service is pretty sub-standard, so you'll need wheels to see the best of the island, although driving distances can be tiring.

### History

Fossil and tool finds in Fiskárdo, Sámi and Skála go back to at least 50,000 BC and perhaps earlier, making Fiskárdo man (and woman, one supposes) among the earliest known inhabitants in Greece. Later inhabitants appear to have been culturally related to the 'Pelasgians' in western Sicily and Epirus; their skulls, all banged about, suggest that Kefalonians have always been a feisty lot. Mycenaean culture was imported from the Peloponnese in the 14th century BC; Krani, near Argostóli, was their most important colony. Although the name Kefaloniá does not occur in Homer, scholars believe that the 'glittering Samos' of the *Odyssey* actually refers to Kefaloniá's town of Sámi. Others believe Homer doesn't mention Kefaloniá because, as part of the kingdom of Odysseus, he simply calls it Ithaca. The recent discovery of a major Mycenaean tomb near Póros has given the argument new weight as archaeologists scramble to locate the big jackpot – the Palace of Odysseus.

The first sure references to Kefaloniá are in Herodotus. Thucydides describes its four city-states – Sámi, Pali, Krani and Pronnoi – allies of Corinth who spent much of their history fighting for their independence from Athens. In Byzantine times the island prospered, in spite of attacks by pirates from Spain and Sicily, and in the 9th century was made the capital of its own *theme*. In 1085, Normans based in southern Italy unsuccessfully besieged Kefaloniá's Byzantine forts; their duke, Robert Guiscard, died of fever in the village that has taken his name – Fiskárdo (*see* below). If the Kefalonians breathed a sigh of relief, it was way too soon; for the next 800 years the island, like its sisters, would be the plaything of the Normans, of Venice and of the Vatican (but mostly the Venetians), as well as a motley assortment of dukes and counts, including the colourful pirate Count Matteo Orsini, who founded a murderous, dowry-snatching dynasty at the end of the 13th century. In 1483 the Turks captured the island, but lost it again in 1504 when Venice and Spain, under the Gran Capitan, Gonzalo Fernández de Córdoba, took the fort of Ag. Geórgios and slaughtered the Turkish garrison. In 1823, Byron spent three months on Kefaloniá (along with a retinue including his faithful Venetian gondolier, Tita) working as an agent of the Greek Committee in London before going to die a pathetic death from fever in Messolóngi. During the British occupation, the Kefalonians demanded union with Greece and revolted; 21 nationalists were hanged in 1849.

Ioánnis Metaxás, Prime Minister-Dictator of Greece from 1936 to 1941, came from Kefaloniá, and for all his faults has gone down in history for laconically (and, apparently, apocryphally) saying 'No' to Mussolini's ultimatum at the beginning of the Second World War – celebrated nationally on 28 October as *Ochi* ('No') Day. In 1943, after the surrender of Italy, the occupying Italian Acqui Division joined the Greeks and for seven days fought the Germans. Five thousand Italians, or perhaps twice that many, died in the subsequent mass executions ordered, it is said, by Hitler himself; their bodies were all burned to hide the evidence; the Greeks call them the Kefaloniá martyrs – all now familiar to the world through Captain Corelli (although the islanders consider the novel's portrayal of events as too one-sided).

A decade later nature itself struck Kefaloniá a blow which made all the previous earthquakes seem like mere cocktail shakers. For five days in August 1953, 113 tremors reduced the island's 350 towns and villages to dust; the first, deadliest earthquake had the estimated force of 60 atom bombs. As the dust slowly cleared, money for reconstruction poured in from all over Europe and the tens of thousands of Kefalonians who live abroad.

# Argostóli (ΑΡΓΟΣΤΟΛΙ)

Magnificently set on a thumb in the island's west bay, Argostóli (pop. 10,000), is a big, busy Greek town, with a surprisingly sophisticated centre. It started out as a smugglers' hamlet under the Venetians and gradually grew up around vast warehouses full of raisins, where ships from all over Europe would fill their holds; the port is especially deep and safe, and to this day is used for winter berthing of yachts and larger ships. As Ag. Geórgios, the Venetian capital, declined, the residents petitioned Venice to make Argostóli capital and in 1759 their wish was granted, to the everlasting disgust of archrival Lixoúri. After the earthquake of 1953, the Kefalonians abroad lavished money to rebuild the town as a proper provincial capital, with public buildings grouped neatly around the large, central and palmy **Plateía Vallianóu**.

## Where to Stay

**Argostóli** ✉ 28100

**Mediterranée**, on the beach at Lassí, t 067 102 8760, f 067 102 4758 (*A; lux–exp*). Caters for the fat wallets of a youngish crowd in an international bland fashion; it has all mod cons, and a variety of land and sea sports. *Open April–Oct.*

**White Rocks**, at Platís Gialós Beach, 3km from Argostóli, t 067 102 8332, f 067 102 8755 (*A; lux–exp*). The other swanky choice, appealing to a slightly older clientèle; just as well equipped. *Open April–Oct.*

**Miramare**, by the sea on the edge of Argostóli towards Lassí, t 067 102 5511, f 067 102 5512 (*exp–mod*). Large, classy and comfortable.

**Cefalonia Star**, 50 Metaxá St, t 067 102 3181, f 067 102 3180 (*C; mod*). At the quieter end of the waterfront in a clean modern block.

**Ionian Plaza**, in central Plateía Valliánou, t 067 102 5581, f 067 102 5585 (*C; mod*). Stylish hotel, each room with a balcony.

**Ionis**, at Peratáta, 8km south of Argostóli t 067 106 9322, f 067 106 9770 (*C; mod*). In the shadow of Ag. Geórgios Castle, a new hotel with a pool, a good place to try if Argostóli is full up. Peratáta also has many rent rooms.

**Irilena**, on the Lassí Peninsula, t 067 102 3118 (*C; mod*). Family-run, cosy, pleasant choice near a little beach. *Open May–Oct.*

**Tourist**, on the waterfront, t/f 067 102 2510 (*mod–inexp*). Comfy en suite rooms, with TV.

**Hara**, 87 Leof. Vergotí, t 067 102 2427 (*D; inexp*). Basic, but cheap. *Open all year.*

**Argostóli Beach Camping**, 2km north of town, by the lighthouse, t 067 102 3487/4525.

## Eating Out

Argostóli has some terrific restaurants.

**Captain's Table**, by Plateía Vallianoú, t 067 102 3896. Upscale and nautical, with live music.

**Casa Grec**, 10 Metaxas, t 067 102 4091 (*€18–22*). Best place for dinner on the island. Elegant dining room and attractive courtyard, dishes range from *tagliatelle primavera, cordon bleu* chicken and pepper steak to Caesar salad and shrimp Newburg.

**Elliniko**, t 067 102 3529, down from Plateía Vallianoú. Famous for its version of Kefalonian *kléftiko*.

**Indian Queen**, 2 Lavranga St, t 067 102 2631 (*€20*). If it's hot'n'spicy you crave, now's your chance, and you won't get many on the islands. Run by a British family, serving a selection of Asian dishes in an Oriental courtyard setting.

**Mythos**, 13 Rizopaston, t 067 102 2663 (*€18–22*). Dine under the palms on some delicious offbeat international and Greek dishes, some with a touch of the ancient world, *panzeta* in vinegar, honey and thyme – or sweet 'n' sour pork, if you prefer.

**Patsouras**, 26 I. Metaxas, opposite the Sailing Club, t 067 102 2779. Long-established and popular for its local meat dishes, spicy sausage, and *panzeta* (smoked pork).

**Diana** on the waterfront near the fruit market. Does good moussaká and *kreatópita* (Kefalonian meat pie), beef and pork with rice in filo pastry.

**Oscars**, en route to Lassí. Costumed waiters perform Greek dances in a grandiose but pretty setting.

Pre-earthquake Argostóli was famous for its bell towers, two of which have been rebuilt – there's something vaguely German Expressionist about the one by the Catholic Church near the square.

Argostóli itself has two museums: the **Koryalenios Historical and Folklore Museum** (*t 067 102 8835; open Mon–Sat 9–2; adm*), below the library on Ilía Zervoú Street, is one of the best of its kind, giving great insight into the island's history and the devastation of the earthquake. It contains the Venetian records of the island, including its Libro d'Oro listing the local nobility, photos of old Kefaloniá icons and of pre-1953 Argostóli, a traditional bedroom, memorabilia recalling Kefaloniá's early love affair with opera and theatre, and a carved ebony desk that belonged to Ferdinand Lesseps, the mastermind behind the Suez Canal. The library itself is the ground floor of an elegant rebuilt mansion. The **Archaeology Museum** (*t 067 102 8300; open Tues–Sun 8.30–3; adm*), on R. Vergóti, contains ex-votos to the god Pan from the Cave of Melissáni, a room of Mycenaean finds (bronze swords, vases with spirals, and gold and ivory jewellery), coins from the four ancient cities of Kefaloniá and a startlingly modern bronze bust of a man from the early 3rd century AD. The island's first theatre, the Kéfalos, has been reconstructed above the museum. Five km north, at Davgata, the low-key **Museum of Natural History of Cephalonia and Ithaca** (*t 067 102 8835; open Mon–Sat 9–1 and 6–8, Sun 9–1 only*), has educational exhibits and a library.

The one structure to survive the earthquake in one piece was the 800m **Drapanós Bridge**, built by the British in 1813 over the shallowest part of the bay, punctuated with a commemorative obelisk. Cross it to join the road to Sámi; a few minutes on by car, the picturesque church of **Ag. Barbára** peers from the rockface over a little bridge. About 1km further, at Razáta, a dirt road leads up to ancient **Krani** (Paleókastro), where the huge stone blocks of the 7th-century BC Cyclopean walls snake through the trees. There are some fragments of a Doric Temple to Demeter and a rectangular hollow carved out of the top of the hill called the Drakospilia, or Dragon's Lair, although it was probably really just a Roman tomb.

## The Lassí Peninsula

One thing to do in Argostóli is to shoot the loop on foot, by bike, car or bus around the little Lassí Peninsula, just north of the city. There are a number of sandy beaches and a clutch of bars and tavernas around the **Katovothri**, or swallow holes, where the sea is sucked into two large tunnels deep under the ground. Where the water actually went was a big mystery until 1963, when Austrian geologists poured 140 kilos of green dye into the water. Fifteen days later the dye appeared in the lake of the Melissáni Cave and at Karavómylos, near Sámi, on the other side of the island. Sea mills to harness the rushing water for electricity were destroyed by the earthquake (which also greatly diminished the suction). One has been reconstructed, mainly for decoration, although the site now seems rather woebegone. At the tip of the peninsula, the lovely **lighthouse of Ag. Theódori** in a Doric rotunda was built by one of Kefaloniá's great benefactors, British High Commissioner Charles Napier, and reconstructed after the 1875 earthquake. A 20-minute walk inland is a memorial to the Italian troops who hid nearby but were found and slaughtered by the Germans.

The coastal strip south of Argostóli with its huge beaches, **Platís Gialós** and **Makris Gialós**, was once a place of great natural beauty. Now the locals steer clear and leave it for the razzle-dazzle of package tourism, but since Kefaloniá is hardly lacking in beautiful places to swim, don't feel deprived if you give it a miss.

# Lixoúri and the Palikí Peninsula

Ferries trundle regularly across the bay from Argostóli to the bulging Palikí Peninsula and **Lixoúri** (ΛHXOYPI), Kefaloniá's second city, all new houses on wide streets. Lixoúri is known for its sense of humour, and in its central square near the waterfront the town has put up a dapper **statue of Andréas Laskarátos**. Born into the island aristocracy, Laskarátos (1811–1901) was a poet and satirist who directed most of his broadsides at the Orthodox Church; he heckled the clergy so much that they finally excommunicated him – in Greek, *aforismós*, meaning that the body will not decompose after death. When Laskarátos found out, he collected his innumerable children's decomposing shoes and returned to the priest, asking him to please excommunicate the footwear, too. You can get a glimmer of what pre-earthquake Lixoúri was like at the west end of town at the **Iakovátos Mansion** (*t 067 109 1325; open Mon–Fri 8–1.30, Sat 9.30–12.30*), a rare survivor and now a library and museum of icons attributed to Mikális Damaskinós. Fresco fragments and an iconostasis salvaged from the earthquake have been installed in the town's newer churches. North of Lixoúri, the unexcavated ancient city of Pali (or Pale) stood on the hill of Paliókastro.

The Palikí Peninsula is well endowed with beaches. **Ag. Spyrídon** is north of town and safe for children, while 4km south are **Michalitsáta** and **Lépeda**, both sandy, the latter near the abandoned cave-monastery (now church) of Ag. Paraskeví. In the same area, **Soulári's** church of Ag. Marína has fine icons and a handsome Venetian doorway; the next village, **Mantzavináta**, has good frescoes in its church of Ag. Sofía. From here a road leads south to the lovely beach of **Ag. Geórgios** (or **Miá Lákko**), a long stretch of golden-red sand, which merges to the west with the Palikí's preferred beach, **Xi**, a long crescent of pinkish sand, with sun beds and a taverna; buses run there in summer. Just south of it is the famous **Kounópetra**, a huge monolith a few inches from the shore that rocked to and fro, pulsating at the rate of 20 times a minute. The earthquake of 1953 fouled up the magic by stabilizing the sea bed beneath and likewise destroyed the houses on pretty, now deserted **Vardianá islet**.

## Where to Stay and Eat

**Lixoúri** ✉ 28200

**Cefalonia Palace**, by Xi Beach, **t** 067 109 3178, in winter, **t** 067 109 2555, *cphotel@compulink.gr* (*A; lux*). New hotel offering half-board accommodation with pools; all rooms with sea-view and balcony. *Open May–Oct*.

**Summery**, **t** 067 109 1771, *summery@otenet.gr* (*C; exp–mod*). Although used by tour opera-tors, a tranquil place to stay, with a pool; taxi transfers from the airport are provided.

**La Cite**, 28 Octovríou, **t** 067 109 3501 (*mod*). Quiet, relaxed and friendly, with a pool and palm-fringed garden; rooms are standard but all have air-con.

The main square in Lixoúri provides ample cafés for gentle navel gazing.

**Akrogiali**. Good fish in season.

**Zorbas**. Nice terrace garden.

A paved by-road west of Lixoúri passes the abandoned **Tafíon Monastery**, en route to **Kipouríon Monastery**, rebuilt as it was before the quake in the 1960s and perched on the west cliffs, with spectacular sunset views. The peninsula is shot full of caves: the best, **Drákondi Spílio**, 130ft deep, can be reached from the monastery with a guide.

The sparsely populated northern part of the Palikí has a scattering of pretty villages such as **Damoulináta**, **Delaportáta** and **Kaminaráta** (the latter has a small Folk Museum in an old olive press and is famous for its folk dances), and more beaches: the large, lovely white sands of **Petáni** are rarely overcrowded and are known as Paralía Xouras ('Old Geezer Beach', after the old man who used to run the taverna). Even more remote is sandy **Ag. Spyrídon**, tucked into the northernmost tip of the Palikí Peninsula, reached via the village of Athéras.

# South Kefaloniá

## Southeast of Argostóli: The Livathó and Mount Aínos

Most of Kefaloniá's rural population is concentrated southeast of Argostóli in the fertile region of valleys, gardens and rolling hills called the Livathó – well worth exploring if you have your own transport. After Platís Gialós Beach, emerging free from the tourist tinsel is **Miniés**, home to a ruined Doric temple from the 6th century BC and some of Greece's finest white wine.

The coastal road south of Miniés continues to **Svoronáta**, where the red sands of **Avithos Beach** (with a *cantina* and taverna) look out to the tiny islet of Días. This is named after a tiny islet off the coast of Crete, and like that one had an altar to Zeus: sacrifices were co-ordinated by smoke signals with those on Mount Aínos. **Domáta**, the next village east, boasts Kefaloniá's oldest olive tree (able to squeeze 20 people in the hollow of its ancient trunk) and the beautiful church of the **Panagía**, with a pretty reconstructed Baroque façade and a giant 19th-century carved iconostasis gilded with 12,000 melted gold sovereigns.

Nearby **Kourkomeláta** was rebuilt by the wealthy Kefalonian shipowner Vergotís; everything is as new and pastel-coloured as a Californian suburb, complete with an arty Neoclassical cultural centre. To try the product of the surrounding vineyards, follow the sign 'visit the familiar farm – free wine tasting'. At **Metaxáta**, where printing was introduced to Greece, Byron rented a house for four months in 1823, finished *Don Juan*, his satirical rejection of romanticism, and dithered over what to do as the representative of the London Committee while each Greek faction fighting for independence jostled for his attention – and his money. Just northwest, **Lakídra**, rebuilt by French donations after the earthquake, is the most important village of the Livathó and believed by some archaeologists to be the site of Odysseus' palace; in the suburb of Kallithéa, near the plain little church of **Ag. Nikólaos ton Aliprantídon**, four Mycenaean tombs yielded a good deal of pottery from 1250 to 1150 BC. Byron used to come here and sit on a rock, inspired by the views, and a line from the poem he wrote is inscribed on a plaque: ΑΝΕΙΜΑΙ ΠΟΙΗΤΗΣ ΤΟ ΟΦΕΙΛΩ ΕΙΣ ΤΟΝ ΑΕΡΑ ΤΗΣ ΕΛΛΑΔΟΣ ('If I am a poet, I owe it to the air of Greece').

# Where to Stay and Eat

## Pessáda ✉ 28083

**Sunrise Inn**, 1.5km from the port, t 067 106 9586, f 067 106 9621 (*B; lux*). Comfortable and with air-con, set in the trees, with a pool and children's activities.

**Karavados Beach Hotel**, near Ag. Thomas Beach, t 067 106 9400, f 067 106 9689 (*B; exp*). Offers 2 pools, tennis and a minibus service to Argostóli.

**Poseidon**, in nearby Spartiá, t 067 108 6475, f 067 106 9649, book in Athens t 010 895 9899 (*exp–mod*). Apartments with sea-view balconies, tennis court, pool and a large garden.

## Lourdáta ✉ 28083

Lourdáta looks like Lassí in miniature – chock full of rent rooms owned by tour companies, car hire firms, stores, bars and 6 or 7 tavernas stretched along the beach. Pre-book via a travel agent or try:

**Lara**, a few mins from the sea, t 067 103 1157, *lara@hol.gr* (*C; exp–mod*). Pleasant moderate-sized hotel with a pool and play-ground, set in greenery. *Open May–Oct.*

## Skála ✉ 28082

**Nine Muses**, by the beach, t 067 108 3563, f 067 108 3560 (*exp*). Spacious rooms and suites in a tasteful bungalow village mini-complex, set in lush gardens with a pool.

**Tara Beach**, by the beach, t 067 108 3341, *tarabeach@tarabeach.gr* (*C; exp–mod*). Rooms and bungalows. *Open May–Oct.*

**Aliki**, overlooking the sea, t 067 108 3427, f 067 108 3426 (*B; mod*). Good value and with a large garden.

## Póros ✉ 28082

**Pandelis Rooms**, on the busy waterfront, t 067 407 2484, *pantelis-rest@usa.net* (*mod–inexp*). Large, basic rooms with fridge, air-con and sea-views; a bargain, except in Aug. They have 2 apartments. The large restaurant is one of the island's best.

**Seagull Holidays**, t 067 407 2001, f 067 407 2002, *seagull@otenet.gr* (*inexp*). Offer 10 simple rooms with balconies; they can fix you up with rental cars or bikes. *Open April–Oct.*

**Romanza**. Restaurant perched one flight up on a rock in the village. Offering Greek cuisine and the best view.

## Inland: Ag. Andréas, Ag. Geórgios and Ag. Gerásimos

North of Metaxáta is the Byzantine convent of **Ag. Andréas**, originally known as Panagía Milapídia (the Apple Virgin) after an icon discovered on an apple tree trunk. Perhaps the one and only good deed done by the quake of 1953 was to shake loose the whitewash on the walls, revealing frescoes that date back to the 13th century (in the chancel) and the 17th and 18th centuries (along the nave). Now the **Ag. Andréas Monastery Museum** (*t 067 106 9700; open Mon–Fri 9–1.30 and 5–8, Sat 9–1.30; adm*), it also houses icons, fresco fragments and relics orphaned by the earthquake, among them the Veneto-Byzantine icon of Panagía Akáthistos, painted in 1700 by Stéfanos Tsankárolos from Crete. After the earthquake, a new Basilica of Panagía Milapídia was built next door to house its prize: the sole of St Andrew's right foot, donated in the 17th century by Princess Roxanne of Epiros.

Above the church looms the tree-filled polygonal **Castle of Ag. Geórgios** (*open June–Oct Tues–Sat 8.30–3, Sun 9–3*), spread over a 1,050ft hill, with a grand view of the surrounding plains and mountains. Founded by the Byzantine emperors, the citadel was completely rebuilt by the Venetians and Greeks under Nikólaos Tsimarás, after the fierce seige of 1500 dislodged the Turks. The island capital until 1757, Ag. Geórgios once had a population of 14,000. Storerooms, prisons, Venetian coats-of-arms, a ruined Catholic Church and a bridge built by the French during their brief occupation crumble away within the battlements; of the 15 churches, the **Evangelístria**, with Byzantine icons, still stands.

To the east lies the green **plain of Omalós** and the **Monastery of Ag. Gerásimos**, where the bones of Kefaloniá's patron saint rest in a silver reliquary, in a church built over his little grotto hermitage. If half of the male population of Corfu are named Spíros after St Spyrídon, half of all male Kefalonians are named Gerásimos. The saint's speciality is intervening in mental disturbances and exorcizing demons, especially if the patient keeps an all-night vigil at his church on his feast day (20 October), but pilgrims from all over Greece pour in year round. The monastery is dwarfed by an enormous plane tree and its tall, pseudo-rococo freestanding belfry. Opposite is a local winery, **Si.Ro.Ke**, sometimes open for tastings.

From the Argostóli – Sámi road, a branch winds up the slopes of **Mégas Sóros** (5,341ft), the highest of the majestic Aínos range, covered with snow from December to March. The road goes as far as the tourist pavilion (4,265ft), and from there you can easily hike the rest of the way, among the tall, scented trees, seemingly on top of the world. On a clear day, the Peloponnese, Zákynthos, Ithaca, Lefkáda, the Gulf of Pátras and Corfu are spread out below as if on a great blue platter. At one time the Aínos was blanketed with *Abies cefalonica*, the island's indigenous black firs, which have a distinctive bushy appearance and upward-pointing branches; the forests were so dense that Strabo called the island Melaina ('the Dark'). Ancient Kefaloniá exported timber far and wide; even the Minoans used firs for the pillars of the labyrinth. Venetian shipbuilders over-harvested the trees, but two disastrous fires, in 1590 and 1797, share the blame for destroying nine-tenths of the forest; the second fire burned for three months. In 1962 what remained of the forest was made into Mount Aínos

## Kefaloniá in a Glass

Kefaloniá is one of the most important islands for wines, especially Robóla, a grape variety introduced by the Venetians in the 13th century that ferments into distinctive lemony dry white wines. Lately it's been better than ever: the Robóla from Gentilini, a small vineyard in Miniés owned and operated by Nichólas Cosmetátos, has been something of a revalation in the country, demonstrating just how good Greek wines can be when made with the latest techniques and *savoir faire*, even when starting from scratch. In 1978, Cosmetátos purchased an estate in these limestone hills, planted his first vines, built a small but ultra-modern winery, and carved a cellar out of the cliffs to attain the perfect storage temperature. Each year his vintages improve: pale gold Gentili Animus, 100 per cent Robóla, is a crisp, delicious wine well worth looking out for; Gentili Fume is a Robóla aged in oak casks, with an oaky fragrance. Gentili also does a fine Muscat fortified dessert wine (Amando) and a lovely apéritif wine (half Muscat, half Robóla) called Dulcis, which goes perfectly with fresh fruit. Another label to look for, Calligas, was founded in the early 1960s, and produces lovely Robólas and other dry whites and reds, and occasionally the very rare Thiniatikó – a velvety port-like wine. In fish tavernas, the common house wine is Tsoussi, made from a white grape unique to Kefaloniá. You may also see Mavrodáphni Kefalinías, another sweet wine.

National Park, where a handful of wild horses, descendants of ancient stock, still gallop free. Hesiod mentioned the 8th-century BC sanctuary of **Aenesian Zeus**, the lord of the mountain, the foundations of which are just below Mégas Sóros; until recently you could see the ash piles from the animal sacrifices that took place there.

## The South Coast: Beaches and the Virgin's Little Snakes

The south coast of Kefaloniá is trimmed with sandy beaches shielded from the north winds by Mégas Sóros. There are good strands just down from **Spartiá**, under sheer white cliffs, and at **Trapezáki**, 1.5km from the tiny harbour of **Pessáda** (ΠΕΣΑΔΑ) – Kefaloniá's chief link to Zákynthos (with a summer *cantina* but no telephone for the unwary foot passenger to ring for a cab, so be first off the boat and grab one that's waiting). East, below **Karavádos**, is another pretty little sand beach with a taverna perched above, and plane trees and reeds spread behind.

The longest and most crowded beach, **Lourdáta** (ΛΟΥΡΔΑΤΑ) was named after the English lords who came here in the 19th century, perhaps attracted by the village's warm microclimate. Its main square, with a spring and an enormous plane tree, is the beginning of Kefaloniá's first nature trail, blazed with funds from the WWF. It takes about 2½ hours to walk and passes through a representative sample of the island's flora – orange and olive groves, *macchia* shrubs and scrubby *phyrgana*, pine woods and kermes oaks, and masses of wild flowers in the spring. The path goes by the ruined **Monastery of Síssia**, founded in 1218 by St Francis of Assisi (hence its name) on his return from the Crusades in Egypt, and converted to Orthodoxy in the 16th century; a new monastery was built just above after 1953.

**Káto Kateliós** is a small resort, a pretty place with springs, greenery and a beach that curves along Moúnda Bay. Just east, Potomákia Beach, below Ratzaklí, is a favourite nocturnal nesting place of loggerhead turtles (*see* p.490) from June to mid-August; stay off the beaches at night during this period, as the nesting mothers are easily scared off and may just dump their eggs at sea.

Just inland, Kefaloniá's most curious religious rite takes place in the village of **Markópoulo**, set over the sea on a natural balcony. During the first 15 days of August, small harmless snakes with little crosses on their heads, 'inoffensive to the Virgin Mary', suddenly appear in the streets. Formerly they slithered into the church (rebuilt in exactly the same place after the earthquake) and mysteriously disappeared near the silver icon of the Panagía Fidón ('Virgin of the Snakes'). Nowadays, to keep them from being run over, the villagers collect them in glass jars and bring them to the church, where they are released after the service and immediately disappear as they did in the past. Although sceptics believe that the church is simply along the route of the little snakes' natural migratory trail, the faithful point out that the snakes fail to appear when the island is in distress – as during the German occupation and in 1953, the year of the earthquake.

**Skála** (ΣΚΑΛΑ), with its long beach and low dunes, is the biggest resort in this corner, with plenty of watersports, sunbeds, bars – the works – but still relatively low key. The Romans liked the area; a Roman villa was excavated near Skála, with 2nd-century AD mosaic floors, one portraying Envy being devoured by wild beasts and two men making sacrifices to the gods. Two kilometres north of Skála, a 7th-century BC Temple of Apollo has also been discovered, though most of its porous stone was cannibalized to build the nearby chapel of Ag. Geórgios.

Pronnoi, one of the four ancient cities of Kefaloniá, was located inland, above the village of **Pástra**, although only a necropolis and some walls of the *acropolis* have survived. In the nearby hamlet of **Tzanáta**, signs point to a vineyard where in 1992 Danish and Greek archaeologists uncovered a huge 12th-century BC domed tomb 23ft underground, the most important ever discovered in western Greece. The bones, gold jewellery and seals it yielded are now being studied at the University of Pátras, but the discovery (the Kefalonians immediately declared it the tomb of Odysseus) has added new fuel to the 'where was Ithaca really?' debate.

From Tzanáta the road descends through the wild and narrow 'Póros Gap', carved, according to myth, by Heracles, who ploughed his impatient way through the mountains. **Póros** (ΠΟΡΟΣ), built on three shallow bays, with direct ferry links to Killíni, was originally the port of Pronnoi. In the 1820s, British High Commissioner Napier settled Maltese farmers here to create a model farming community called New Malta. It never got off the ground. Now the village, set over clear turquoise waters, is probably the most Greek of the resort towns on the island, with a pleasant waterfront, long shingle beach, rooms for rent and good Greek food.

# North Kefaloniá: Caverns and Castles

**Sámi** is the port for ships to Pátras, Corfu and Italy, and although the bay, with mountainous Ithaca as a frontdrop, is not unattractive, the town and its beach are of little interest. Cinema goers may not recognize it on arrival, but Sámi suffered a modern siege for the shooting of the film version of *Captain Corelli's Mandolin*, when a wonderful mock-Venetian waterfront façade was constructed; for the first time in almost 60 years, Italian Second World War artillery was seen thundering through the streets. Many older residents were dewy eyed when they saw the realistic reconstruction. It remains to be seen what the eventual impact will be on Sámi, as it copes with a new invasion – holidaymakers, inevitably – in search of peace and quiet to finish reading the book they began on the charter flight over. Five km east of Sámi, there's an exquisite pebble beach, **Andisámos**, set in a bay of exceptional beauty with forested hills spilling down to the postcard-clear water; yet because facilities don't stretch beyond a simple *cantina*, the crowds stay away.

On the two hills behind Sámi are the town's **ancient walls**, where the citizens put up a heroic four-month resistance to the Romans in 187 BC before their inevitable defeat and sale into slavery. Sámi is also close to Kefaloniá's magnificent grottoes. The **Drogaráti Cave** (*t 067 102 2950; open 9–6, closed after Oct; adm*), near the hamlet of Chaliotáta, is a lugubrious den of orange and yellow stalactites and stalagmites; one of its great chambers has such fine acoustics that Maria Callas came here to sing. The other, the magical sheer-sided **Melissáni** (*'purple cave'; t 067 102 2997; open 9–6,*

# Where to Stay and Eat

## Sámi ✉ 28080

A good base for exploring, Sámi has accommodation not geared exclusively to package tours.

**Sámi Travel**, by the dock, t 067 402 3050, samitrvl@otenet.gr. Can help find rooms and issue tickets.

**Aris Rent A Car**, t/f 067 402 2239. Cars and motorbikes at cheap rates by Kefalonian standards.

**Pericles**, on the edge of town, t 067 402 2780, f 067 402 2787 (B; exp). Large-ish unexceptional complex with 2 round swimming pools, tennis courts and a nightclub. Open May–Oct.

**Kastro**, t 067 402 2656, f 067 402 3004 (C; mod). Sea-view balconies and convenient for ferries. Open April–Oct.

**Melissáni**, set back from the waterfront in greenery, t/f 067 402 2464, in Athens t 010 417 5830 (D; mod). Small and friendly hotel . Open April–Oct.

**Karavomilos Beach Camping**, 1km from town, t 067 402 2480. Well equipped.

The taverna selection is unexciting, though **Delfini**, **Adonis**, **Port Sámi** and **Diónysos** are pretty reliable. Look out for local specialities such as octopus pie and meat cooked in a ceramic stámna.

## Ag. Evfimía ✉ 28081

**Gonatas**, Paradise Beach, a 5min amble from the port, t 067 406 1500, f 067 406 1464 (B; exp). Family-run and smartest, with a pool and sea-views. Open May–Oct.

**Logaras**, t/f 067 406 1202 (C; exp). Apartments in a floral setting, but may be package-booked. Open April–Oct.

**Pyllaros**, on the waterfront, t 067 406 1800, f 067 406 1801 (C; exp). Rooms and suites full of dark repro furniture, as well as boat hire and tennis. Open all year.

**Moustakis**, t 067 406 1060, f 067 406 1030 (C; mod). An institutional alternative if everything else is booked up. Open April–Sept.

**Finikas**, on the waterfront in the village. For pizza and traditional food .

July–Aug 9–9; adm, closed after Oct), is a half-hour walk from Sámi; small boats paddle you across its salt water lake (supplied by the swallow holes near Argostóli; see p.449), immersing you in a vast shimmering play of blues and violets caught by the sun filtering through a hole in the roof, 100ft overhead. According to the school of thought that Homer's 'Ithaca' consisted of both Itháki and Kefaloniá, this was the Cave of the Nymphs, where the Phaeacians deposited Odysseus. There are other, undeveloped caves for spelunkers only in the vicinity of Sámi, many with lakes and dangerous, precipitous drops; the best of them is **Angláki Cave**, near Pouláta, a few kilometres from Sámi Town.

At the base of Kefaloniá's northernmost peninsula, pretty **Ag. Evfimía** (ΑΓ. ΕΥΦΗΜΙΑ) is a far cosier resort base than Sámi, although there are still a number of simple rooms for rent in the town. There's good swimming off a scattering of white pebbly beaches along the Sámi road. A mosaic uncovered in Archeotíton Street is believed to have been the floor of the early Byzantine church of Ag. Evfimía, and the pretty village of **Drakopouláta**, a few kilometres above the port, was spared by the earthquake. Further west, scattered across the slopes of Mount Ag. Dinatí, are more of Kefaloniá's traditional villages – and goats with silver-plated teeth, owing to the high mica content in the soil.

## Up the Northwest Coast: To Mýrtos, Ássos and Fiskárdo

The journey from Argostóli north to Fiskárdo is magnificently scenic – perhaps a good reason to take the bus, so you don't have to keep your eyes on the road,

**Paradise** (also known as Dendrinos, after its owner), at Paradise Beach, **t** 067 406 1392. Taverna which has earned itself a big reputation for Greek and international dishes, but stick to the Greek fare.

## Ássos ✉ 28084

Beds fill up fast in the summer; book well ahead through a package company or try:

**Linardos Apartments, t** 067 405 1563 or winter in Athens, **t** 010 652 2594.

**Platanos.** Excellent food and the English-speaking owner is a mine of information, and typical Kefalonian irony.

## Fiskárdo ✉ 28084

In the off season, head for the streets behind the port for rooms; in season, check out the package companies.

**Pama Travel, t** 067 404 1033, *pamatravel@ compulink.gr*. Can help with all your accommodation needs, down to yacht rentals.

**Kiki Apartments**, up on the waterfront in the back bay, **t** 067 404 1208 (*exp*). Attractive complex.

**Stella**, right on the water, **t** 067 404 1211, *stella@kef.forthnet.gr* (*B; exp–mod*). Furnished apartments.

**Nikolas**, perched above the harbour, **t** 067 404 1307 (*A; mod*). Has a fine location, rooms and food – with nightly Greek dancing to boot.

**Regina**, in the new main square over the port, **t** 067 404 1125 (*mod*).

**Dendrinos**, just out of town, **t** 067 404 1326 (*mod–inexp*). Renovated in the traditional style.

**Nitsa, t** 067 404 1143 (*A; inexp*). Cheaper rooms and a studio.

**Sotiria Tselenti**, over the Fiskárdo bakery, **t** 067 404 1204 (*inexp*).

**Lagoundera**, in a square just back from the water, **t** 067 404 1275. Good, friendly grill house; try the fresh anchovies when they are in season.

**Tassia**, in the heart of the hearbour, **t** 067 404 1205 (€25–30). Rub shoulders with visiting celebrities – or pretend you are one – at this restaurant nestling amongst the yachts. Seafood is the order of the day, incl. pasta with lobster.

although there are some very tempting stops along the way. The first good beach, white pebbly **Ag. Kiriakí**, with several bars and tavernas, rims the crotch of land linking the Palikí Peninsula to the rest of Kefaloniá, a few kilometres below the village of **Zóla**. An unpaved road links Zóla to **Angónas** (it's also on the main Argostóli road), where local folk artist Razos has decorated the village square with paintings. Eight km to the north and 2km below **Divaráta** curves the U-shaped bay of **Mýrtos**, where sheer white cliffs carpeted with green maquis frame a stunning crescent of tiny white pebbles and patches of sand against a deep sea so blue it hurts. There are sunbeds, but if you want to make a day of it bring provisions (and a hat – there's no shade in the afternoon) or settle for a pricey sandwich at the beach café.

The road winds along a corniche to another famous stunning view, over **Ássos** (ΑΣΟΣ), where the Venetian citadel and colourful little fishing hamlet tucked under the arm of the isthmus look like toys. The village was rebuilt by the French after the earthquake and, more recently, by package tour companies. The once pristine causeway to the fortress now resembles the Ponte Vecchio in Venice, with wall-to-wall holiday villas. Don't come here on spec in high season looking for a room – but a day trip is recommended, for the lovely bay and inviting translucent waters. The **Venetian fortress** – a favourite sunset destination, on foot or, much more easily, by car – dates from 1585, when the Turks occupied Lefkáda and began raiding this coast; it was the seat of the Venetian *proveditor* until 1797. His house survives in ruins, along with the church of San Marco and a rural prison, used until 1815. The venerable olive tree in principal Plateía Paris shaded the open-air sermons of St Cosmás the Aetolian,

## Genius and Extrovert

The name Fiskárdo comes from Robert Guiscard, the *terror mundi* of his day, whose very name made popes, emperors and kings tremble in their boots. Born in 1017, the sixth of 13 sons of a minor Norman nobleman named Tancred de Hauteville, Robert began his career as a mercenary adventurer working for (and against) the Byzantines and Lombards in Italy. By a mix of adroit military leadership, an eye for the main chance and cunning (his nickname *Guiscard* means 'crafty'), he made himself Duke of Apulia, master of southern Italy. Other Hauteville brothers came to join him; the most successful was the youngest, Roger, who married a cousin of William the Conqueror, defeated the Arabs of Sicily and founded a remarkable dynasty of Norman-Sicilian kings.

In 1085, having just sacked Rome after defeating Emperor Henry IV's attempt to dethrone Pope Gregory VII (Hildebrand), Robert Guiscard and his Normans were on their way to do the same to Constantinople, on the excuse Emperor Michael VII had locked his empress – Guiscard's daughter – up in a convent. Guiscard had just scored a major victory over the Venetians (then Byzantium's allies) at Corfu, when a typhoid epidemic laid low the 68-year-old warrior; Guiscard was brought ashore here and died in the arms of his Lombard warrior wife, Sichelgaita. His body was preserved in salt and sent back to Italy to be buried with his brothers; the coffin was washed overboard in a storm, but later recovered off Otranto and the messy remains of Guiscard were buried at Venosa. As John Julius Norwich wrote in *The Normans of the South*: 'He was that rarest of combinations, a genius and an extrovert...a gigantic blond buccaneer who not only carved out for himself the most extraordinary career of the Middle Ages but who also, quite shamelessly, enjoyed it.' Such was the power of his name that the old pirate was granted a posthumous and false reputation as a virtuous Crusader, and two centuries after his death Dante installed him in *Paradiso*.

an 18th-century missionary; at one point, the story goes, his words were being drowned out by the buzzing cicadas. Cosmás told the insects to hush, and they did.

East of the main road, an unpaved road rises up through the inland villages of the peninsula. One, **Varí**, has by its cemetery a late Byzantine church called Panagía Kougianá, with frescoes by a folk artist who decorated the left wall with scenes from hell, and the right one with scenes of paradise. The church is usually locked, so ask in the village for the key.

Continuing up to Cape Dafnoudi, the northernmost tip of Kefaloniá, the road passes the white rocky beach of **Chalikéri**, where people come to soak in the exceptionally briny water and leave pleasantly pickled. In **Ántipata Erissóu**, the unusual Russian church of 1934 was built by a Kefalonian who made a fortune in the Soviet Union; opposite, by the pine tree, there are good *mezédes* at the bar.

**Fiskárdo** (ΦΙΣΚΑΡΔΟ) is by a landslide the most picture-postcard-perfect, trendiest and most expensive village on the island, its 18th-century houses gathered in a brightly coloured apron around a pretty yacht-filled port. A fluke in its innermost geological depths spared it from the 1953 earthquake, and it's a poignant reminder of the architecture Kefaloniá once had. This and its setting have inspired a building fever, and now the entire north cape is dotted with villas and studios. In town, some of the old houses have been fixed up for guests; others are decorated with folk paintings of mermaids and ships. Four carved stone sarcophagi and the ruins of a Roman bath are fenced off by the Panormos Hotel. The tiny **Nautical and Environmental Museum**, at the top of the village (*open 10–2 and 5–9*), displays objects trawled up from the depths (including the Bristol Beaufighter, a plane shot down in 1943), as well as marine life and current projects. Fiskárdo's beaches are not top notch, but there are day trips on caiques to other beaches, as well as to Itháca and Lefkáda.

# Kýthera (ΚΥΘΗΡΑ)

Tucked under the great dangling paw of the Peloponnese, Kýthera, the isle of the goddess of love, is on the way to nowhere, and owes a good part of its attraction to that fact. The opening of the Corinth Canal doomed even the minor commercial importance Kýthera once had by virtue of its position between the Ionian and

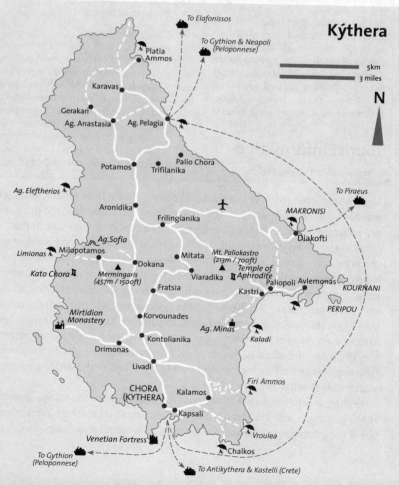

# Getting There and Around

**By air:** 3 flights a day from Athens in season; airport information: t 073 603 3292; tickets from the **Olympic Airways** office at 49 El. Venizélou, Pótamos, **t** 073 603 3362, or try **Porfyra Travel** in Livádi (*see* below).

**By sea:** Kýthera has 2 ports, small Ag. Pelagía and the newer Diakófti. Sometimes in bad weather a **ferry** may switch ports, so check before departure; in season daily ferry from Neápoli (Peloponnese), 3 times a week from Gýthion (Peloponnese); June–Sept Minoan Flying Dolphins have hydrofoils from Piraeus, some making the trip in 3½ hrs. **Port authority:** Diakófti, **t** 073 603 4222, Ag. Pelagía, **t** 073 603 3280. In Kapsáli, a **caique** visits nearby beaches and little Avgo Island.

**By road:** in the absence of buses, expect to rely on **taxis**, which charge set fees (eg Diakófti–Kapsáli €18). If there are no taxis on arrival, ask the port authority to call one. At Ag. Pelagía, Pótamos and Kapsáli there are **cars** and **mopeds** to hire. Try **Panayiotis** in Kapsáli, **t** 073 603 1600, *panayioti@otenet.gr*, in Ag. Pelagía, **t** 073 603 3194, and in Chóra, **t** 073 603 1551. The developed road network makes Kýthera ideal for touring by car or bike.

# Tourist Information

**Tourist police: t** 073 603 1206.

Kýtheros International, Livádi, **t** 073 603 1790, **f** 073 603 1688. For help with accommodation in the south of the island, try Yannis Fatseas.

**Porfyra Travel**, Livádi, **t** 073 603 1888, *porfyra@kythira.com*. Organize accommodation and walking tours of the island. The interesting tourist guide *Kythera* is freely available.

# Festivals

**29–30 May:** Ag. Trias in Mitáta.
**15 Aug:** Panagías Mirtidíon.
**24 Sept:** Mirtidión Monastery.

# Where to Stay and Eat

**Kýthera** ✉ **80100**

## Chóra (Kýthera)
**Margarita**, tucked away off the main street, **t** 073 603 1711, *fatseas@otenet.gr* (*C; exp*). Attractive blue and white hotel in a building that was once a bank, with an impressive wooden spiral staircase. *Open May–Oct*.
**Castello**, near the fortress, **t** 073 603 1069, **f** 073 603 1869 (*mod*). 3 studios and 6 rooms leading off a lovely walled garden; immaculate and well-designed, rooms all have telephone, fridge and overhead fans.

Aegean Seas; even today, unless you take the small plane from Athens, getting there is awkward, time-consuming and expensive, requiring a long overland drive and ferry or a long hydrofoil ride. Although sentimentally it continues to be one of the Eptánissa, or Seven Ionian Islands, with whom it shares a common history of Venetian and British occupation, politically it now belongs to Attica and is administered from Piraeus. In this century Kýthera's population has decreased dramatically, most emigrating to the other side of the world; some 100,000 people of Kýtheran origin now live in Australia or 'Big Kýthera' as the 3,000 who still live on Kýthera call it. All the emigrants who possibly can, return each summer, constituting its main tourist rush. Nor are many of them interested in developing the island's tourist potential; they like it fine the way it is. The non-Aussies who do visit are usually Italians or hardy Hellenophiles anxious to escape their own countrymen, or the wealthy who have scattered their villas all over Kýthera.

The drive south from either of its ports may at first seem forbidding – a narrow road snaking through a desert of scrub and rock – but don't let this first impression fool you. If the shimmering luxuriance of Watteau's sumptuous painting, *Pèlerinage à l'Ile*

**Ta Kýthera**, just inland at Manitochóri, **t** 073 603 1563 (*B; inexp*). Clean, pleasant double rooms. *Open June–Aug.*

**Belvedere**. Pizzeria-cum-grill house with a magnificent view.

**Mercato**, on the main road, **t** 073 603 1922. Serves crêpes.

**Mirtoon**, on the road to the port, **t** 073 603 1705. Good Greek staples.

**Zorba's**, in the main street. Old-fashioned. Chóra is also well endowed with shops selling local arts and crafts:

**Nikolaou**, on the road into town from the north. You can see rugs being woven and a fine selection of ceramics and ethnic-style jewellery.

**Stavros**. Known the island over for stocking a wide range of well-presented local produce – wine, jam, honey, chutneys, oils, vinegars, freshly baked sweets and an eclectic selection of books.

## Kapsáli

**Kalokerines Katikies Rigas**, **t/f** 073 603 1265 (*C; exp*). Upmarket furnished apartments.

**Raikos**, between Chóra and Kapáli, **t** 073 603 1629, **f** 073 603 1801 (*B; exp*). One of the island's posher places, with a pool. *Open May–Sept.*

**El Cime**, over the Vanillia coffee shop, right by the sea, **t** 073 603 1830/1886 (*exp–mod*). 4 apartments with air-con and TV.

**Iannis Avgerinos**, on the beach (*exp–mod*). Rooms and apartments converted from fishermen's huts, in an olive grove.

**Poulmendis Rooms**, **t** 073 603 1451 (*mod–inexp*). Clean and comfortable.

**Daponte Stella**, **t** 073 603 1841. Peaceful and private, with access to the gorgeous secluded beach of Sparagário.

**Porto Delfino**, over the campsite, **t** 073 603 1940. Very good.

**Camping Kapsáli**, **t** 073 603 1580. Good facilities and lovely site, set in amongst cypress trees.

**Filio**, in Kálamos, **t** 073 603 1054 (*inexp*). Rooms to rent at this impressive taverna where locals go to sample traditional Kythniot *cuisine*.

**Artena**, on the beach. Fresh fish, with the menu depending on the day's catch.

**Magos**, **t** 073 603 1407. Taverna with lovely views of Kapsáli, serving all the usual Greek specialities.

**Venetsianiko**. Blue and white, for that island feel. Try the *iadopaximado*.

## Livádi

**Aposperides**, in Livadi, **t** 073 603 1656, **f** 073 603 1688 (*C; exp*). Pristine hotel.

**Rousos**, in Káto Livádi, **t** 073 603 1124 (*mod*). Offers apartments.

**Eleni**, near the 'British bridge'. A favourite for *mezédes*.

*de Cythère* gilds the lily somewhat, Kýthera is in many places a green island whose very human landscape will delight you once you begin to explore.

## History

When Zeus took his golden sickle and castrated his father, Cronos, then ruler of the world, he cast the bloody member into the sea. This gave birth to Aphrodite, the goddess of love, who rose out of the foam on her scallop shell at Kýthera. She found it far too puny for her taste and moved to Paphos, Cyprus – hence her two names in antiquity, the Cypriot or the Kytherian. An ancient sanctuary dedicated to Aphrodite on Kýthera was the most sacred of all such temples in Greece, according to Pausanius, but scarcely a trace of it remains today.

Aphrodite was called Astarte by Kýthera's first settlers, the Phoenicians, who came for its murex shells, the source of a reddish purple dye for royal garments – hence the island's other early name, Porphyrousa. The Minoans, the first in Greece to worship Aphrodite, made Kýthera a central trading station at the crossroads between Crete and the mainland, and the Aegean and Ionian Seas. It was a spot on the map in great

**Lokanda**, 3km north in Karvoynádes. Good place for a pizza or snack.

**Pierros**, in Livadi. Probably the oldest and most traditional taverna on Kýthera, with authentic home cooking and kind prices.

### Avlémonas

There are plenty of decent self-catering apartments here:

**Poppy's**, t 073 603 3735 (*exp*). Catering for families.

**Mandy's**, t 073 603 3739 (*mod*).

**Manolis Stathis**, t 073 603 3732 (*mod*).

**Roulas**, t 073 603 3060 (*mod*).

**Skandia**, just outside nearby Paliópoli, t 073 603 3700. Greek specialities served under an enormous elm tree – a great place for lunch.

**Sotiris**, t 073 603 3722. Taverna prettily set in a small square overlooking the sea, preparing excellent seafood as fresh as can be, caught by the owners themselves.

### Diakófti

**Sirena Apartments**, right on the sea, t 073 603 3900, or winter in Athens, t 010 481 1185 (*A; exp*). For peace and quiet, with big verandas and kitchens.

**Kýthera Beach Apartments**, within spitting distance of the sea, t 073 603 3750, f 073 603 3054 (*C; exp*). *Open April–Oct.*

**Petroheílos**, t 073 603 4069 (*mod*). Rooms in an old mansion overlooking the sea.

**Maistali**, t 073 603 3760 (*inexp*). Simple, decent rooms.

**Manolis**, on the beach. Good fish taverna.

### Mitáta

**Michális**, in the village's main square. Informal taverna with panoramic views of the surrounding hills and valleys. People come from across Kýthera to eat here; Michális' wife cooks a number of island specialities, incl. cockerel and rabbit, prepared with vegetables from their own garden.

### Ag. Pelagía

In Ag. Pelagía, hotels and rooms are listed on a noticeboard near where the ferry docks.

**Filoxenia**, t 073 603 3800, f 073 603 3610 (*B; exp*). 27 furnished apartments with a swimming pool.

**Kýtheria**, t 073 603 3321, f 073 603 3825 (*D; exp–mod*). Nearest the pier, with 10 comfortable rooms; serving breakfast.

**Romantica**, t 073 603 3834, f 073 603 3915 (*exp–mod*). 9 well-laid-out apartments for 2–4 people, and a pool.

**Vernados**, t 073 603 4100. Rooms with air-con and satellite TV.

**Kaleris**, t 073 603 3461. Popular taverna with tables right on the sand.

**Amir Ali**, inland at Karavás. In the evening a lot of people end up at this piano bar, named after a Turk, but no one knows why.

demand: Kýthera was invaded 80 times in recorded history. Particularly frightful were the visits of the Saracens from Crete, so ferocious in the 10th century that the island was abandoned until Nikephóros Phokás reconquered Crete for Byzantium.

The rulers of Kýthera in the Middle Ages were the Eudhaemonoyánnis family from Monemvássia. The Venetians occupied the island in 1204, but with the help of Emperor Michael Palaeológos, Kýthera was regained for the Eudhaemonoyánnis and served as a refuge for Byzantine nobles until 1537 when Barbarossa stopped on his way home from his unsuccessful siege of Corfu and destroyed the island. The Venetians took over again in the 16th century and called the island 'Cerigo'. In 1864 it was ceded to Greece by the British with the other Ionian islands.

# Chóra (Kýthera)

**Chóra** (XΩPA), the capital of the island, is a pretty-as-a-picture-postcard blue and white Greek village, 900ft above the port of Kapsáli, and guarded by a mighty if ruined fortress, furnished by the Venetians in 1503. Its location was supposedly selected by pigeons, who took the tools of the builders from a less protected site; the views of the sea are worth the climb up. Ten old **Venetian mansions** in Chóra still retain their coats-of-arms, and a small two-room **museum** (*open Tues–Sun 8.30–2.30*) contains artefacts dating back to Minoan times. Below, a 20-minute walk down the hill, the port mini-resort of **Kapsáli** (ΚΑΨΑΛΙ) has a row of restaurants and two picturesque pebble and sand beaches, one very sheltered and boaty, the other only a tiny bit more exposed; pedalos will take you to other pebbly strands. The little 'egg islet', Avgó, offshore here is said to be the spot where Aphrodite was born.

**Kálamos**, just east, is within walking distance. One of its churches, Ag. Nikítas, has a pretty bell tower, and there is a restaurant and some rooms for rent by the square. Dirt roads continue across the rugged landscape to various beaches; nearest is pebbly **Chalkos**, set in a beautiful, almost enclosed bay, with a small summer snack bar.

# Around the Island

## Northwest of Chóra

From Chóra, the paved road heads north to **Livádi** (ΛΙΒΑΔΙ), where there's a stone bridge of 13 arches, built by the British in 1822 and proudly heralded as the largest in Greece. The story goes that its size is a result of the British engineer's love affair with a local girl and his desire to prolong his stay on the island. If you ring ahead (*t 073 603 1124*) you can visit the Roússos family ceramic workshop, where the ancient tradition of Kýthera pottery is kept alive, now into the fourth generation. Heading east from Livádi, you'll come across a good collection of Byzantine and subsequent pieces in Káto Livádi's **museum** (*t 073 603 1731; open Tues–Sun 8.30–2.30*). A 4km dirt road leads on to the dramatic beach and tiny snack shack of **Fíri Ámmos** ('red sands'), popular with snorkellers; in an ordinary car, the final descent is manageable, if a little hair-raising. West of Livádi via Drimónas is the important **Monastery of the Panagía Mirtidíon** with a tall carved bell tower, magnificently set on the wild west coast among cypresses, flowers and peacocks. The monastery is named after a gold-plated icon of the Virgin and Child, whose faces have blackened with age – a sign of special holiness that attracts huge numbers of pilgrims. Two small islets just offshore are said to be pirate ships that the Virgin turned to stone for daring to attack the monastery. Unfortunately she was unable to protect the surrounding landscape from a devastating fire.

North of Drimónas, **Milopótamos** (ΜΥΛΟΠΟΤΑΜΟΣ) is the closest thing to Watteau's vision of Kýthera, a pretty village criss-crossed by tiny canals of clear water – so much water, in fact, that the toilet in the valley is in a constant state of flush. The stream valley through the middle of town is called the Neraída, or Nymph; an old watermill lies along the somewhat overgrown path to the waterfall at Foníssa, named after the girl who took her life by jumping into it. It is surrounded by ancient plane trees, flowers and banana palms; on quiet evenings you can hear the nightingales sing. The ghost town **Káto Chóra** lies just below Milopótamos, within the walls of a Venetian fortress built in 1560. Above the gate there's a bas-relief of the lion of

St Mark gripping his open book, reading the angelic words '*Pax Tibi, Marce, Evangelista Meus*' that gave the Venetians a certain celestial legitimacy, at least in their own eyes. It welcomes you to a desolation of empty 16th-century stone houses and churches, although some are slowly being restored. A road descends steeply down to one of the island's best secluded beaches, white sandy **Limiónas**.

Signs from Milopótamos lead down to the **Ag. Sofía Cave** (*usually open Mon–Fri 3–8 in summer, weekends 11–5, but check in the village or call t 073 603 4062/3397*), Kýthera's most impressive, at the end of a rugged, declining track. In the past, the cave was used as a church, and inside there are frescoes and mosaics, as well as stalactites and stalagmites and small lakes that go on and on; some say it tunnels all the way under Kýthera to Ag. Pelagía. And at Ag. Pelagía a sign does indeed point down a rocky hill to a mysterious Ag. Sofía.

## The East Coast

From both Fratsiá and Frilingianiká, roads branch east towards **Paliópoli** (ΠΑΛΑΙΟΠΟΛΙΣ), a tiny village on the site of **Skandeia**, the port mentioned by Thucydides. The Minoan trading settlement was here, from 2000 BC until the rise of the Mycenaeans; their long-ago presence (ruins of the settlement may be seen at a place called **Kastrí**) has bestowed archaeological status on the long and lovely beach, which has kept it pristine except for a good taverna. In ancient times, devotees would climb to the Temple of Urania Aphrodite, 'Queen of the Heavens', to pay their respects to the goddess. Urania Aphrodite was often known as the 'eldest of the Fates', the daughter of the Great Goddess Necessity, whom even the great Zeus could not control. Pausanius wrote that her temple was one of the most splendid in all Greece, but the Christians destroyed it and built the church of Ag. Geórgios, with the temple's Doric columns (one remaining marble column from the holy of holies, the Temple of Aphrodite, can be seen by appointment, *call the Archaeological Society, t 073 603 1731*); now only the *acropolis* walls remain at the site, called **Paliokástro**.

From Paliópoli the coastal road descends to **Avlémonas** (ΑΒΛΕΜΟΝΑΣ), a fishing village with good restaurants. Locals can direct you to the so-called 'ruins' of Helen's throne, overlooking the ancient beach of Skandia, where she first met Paris. Nearby are boulders from the Mycenaean period, grooved to channel blood from sacrificed animals, and an ancient cave dwelling resembling a five-roomed house, with an early example of a column being used for structural support. By the sea is a small octagonal fortress built by the Venetians, who left a coat-of-arms and a few rusting cannons inside. A short drive and walk from the village is one of the island's finest beaches, **Kaladí**, featured on many a tourist office poster. Follow signs marked ΠΡΟΣ ΚΑΛΑΔΙ along 2km of dirt road which leads past a blissful little chapel and abruptly stops; from here there's a steep, but mercifully short, climb down to the glorious double-coved pebbly beach – definitely not for the faint-hearted, but well worth it in the end. Another dirt road leads north of Avlémonas, 7km to **Diakófti** (ΔΙΑΚΟΦΤΙ), a scrap of a resort popular with Greek families, which has taken over as the island's main port and has a strip of white sand, protected by a pair of islets, Makronísi and Prasonísi. The main road from Diakófti passes the airport; and to the south, near the

centre of Kýthera, **Mitáta** is a great place for picnics, surrounded by lovely green countryside and lemon trees; the cool clear water of its spring is delicious. It's also a good
spot to purchase delicious thyme honey, at about half the price of the rest of Greece;
one source is George and John Protopsáltis (*t 073 603 3614*).

## Palio Chóra and the North

**Palio Chóra** (or Ag. Dimitríou), is Kýthera's Byzantine ghost town, founded by the
noble Eudhaemonoyánnis clan in the Monemvassian style. Set high on the rocks, it
was carefully hidden from the sea in a magnificent gorge – according to legend, the
terrible Barbarossa found it only by capturing the inhabitants and torturing them
until they told him where it was. Beside the ruins of the fort is a terrible 330ft abyss,
where mothers threw their children before leaping themselves, to avoid being sold
into slavery by Barbarossa. For that reason it is known as Kakiá Langáda – 'bad gorge'.
Most of the island's ghost stories and legends are set here. The dirt road drive and the
scramble up are rewarded not only by views over the precipice, but also by a few frescoes in the haunted churches. You can walk the gorge in five hours and have Kakiá
Langáda Beach as your reward.

Palio Chóra is near **Potamós** (ΠΟΤΑΜΟΣ), which, despite its name, has no river. It is
the largest village in the north, all blue and white like the new Chóra. It has a bank
and an Olympic Airways office, but the largest building at the edge of town is
Kýthera's retirement home. Come on Sunday if you can, when the village hosts the
island's biggest market. West of Potamós, **Ag. Elefthéríos** is a lovely secluded beach,
and a pretty place to watch the sunset.

At **Gerakári** to the northwest you can see another tower, built by the Turks in the
early 18th century. From the pretty village of **Karavás**, the road continues to the fine
beach and taverna at **Platiá Ámmos. Ag. Pelagía** (ΑΓ. ΠΕΛΑΓΙΑ), Kýthera's northern
port, also has a long pebble beach and a few more facilities, if not a lot of soul, nor
even a lot of boats, since many have diverted to Diakófti's big, new harbour. There are
some excellent beaches to the south including a second by the name of **Fíri Ámmos**.

# Elafónissos (ΕΛΑΦΟΝΗΣΟΣ) and Antikýthera (ΑΝΤΙΚΥΘΗΡΑ)

From Ag. Pelagía you can look out across the Lakonian Sea to the islet of **Elafónissos**,
which until the 17th century was part of the Peloponnese, and is now connected daily
in the summer by caique every 40 minutes from Neápolis (*July–Sept*) or less often
from Ag. Pelagía (*call t 073 406 1177 for info*). The one village is mostly inhabited by
fishermen and sailors, but the main reason for visiting is 5km south of the village,
**Katá Nísso**, a twin bay endowed with two gorgeous white sandy beaches that go on
and on, as yet hardly discovered by tourists (a caique from the 'capital' makes the trip).
There are two tavernas and two small B-class pensions in the village (*open June–Sept*)
if you want to escape it all: **Asteri tis Elafónissou, t** 073 406 1271 and **Elafónissos, t** 073
406 1268; rough camping on the beach is another possibility.

## The World's Oldest Computer

Antikýthera is just a tiny smudge on the map, but thanks to the wild winds that churn the surrounding sea it is also a name familiar to any student of ancient Greek art. For on the 22nd day of the ancient Greek month of Mounichon, in the first year of the 180th Olympiad (5 May, 59 BC), a Roman ship sailing from Rhodes, laden with booty that included the magnificent 4th-century BC bronze statue known as the *Ephebe of Antikýthera* (one of the celebrities of the National Archaeology Museum in Athens), went down off the coast of Antikýthera. Now you might ask: how is it that anyone could even begin to know the precise date of a 2,000-year-old shipwreck? Pinpointing even the century of ancient finds is more often than not just an archaeological guessing game. The answer is that part of the booty from Rhodes included the world's first computer, and its timekeeping mechanism was stopped forever on the day the ship went down.

The wreck was discovered by chance in 1900 by sponge divers from Sými, who in a storm sheltered off the inaccessible coast of Antikýthera. After the storm, a few divers donned their weighted belts and went down to see if this remote seabed might in fact shelter a sponge or two. Instead they were startled to see a man beckoning to them – the famous Ephebe. The Greek archaeological service was notified, and sent down a small warship to haul up the bronze and marble statues, vases, and glass – the world's first underwater archaeological dig. One of the items was a lump; as the months passed and the sea mud dried, a wooden cabinet about a foot high was revealed. This quickly deteriorated on contact with the air, leaving a calcified

Another islet, the utterly remote **Antikýthera**, lies far to the south of Kapsáli, midway between Kýthera and Kastélli, Crete. If the *meltémi* isn't up, as it often is, ships call twice a week en route between Kýthera and Crete. Fewer than 100 people live in Antikýthera's two villages, **Potamós** and **Sochória**, and the rest is very rocky with few trees; curiously, like west Crete, the island is slowly rising. By Potamós, ancient **Aígilia** has walls dating back to the 5th century BC. There's a small beach at **Xeropótamo**, 5 minutes from Potamós by boat, or 30 minutes on foot. Water is a luxury, and the few rooms available are quite primitive; running water and toilets are rare. Potamós has a taverna, but food can also be scarce.

# Lefkáda/Lefkás (ΛΕΦΚΑΔΑ)

The island of Lefkás (more popularly known in Greece by its genitive form Lefkáda) was named after the whiteness (*leukos*) of its cliffs. It barely qualifies as an island; in ancient times Corinthian colonists dug what is now the 20m (66ft) wide Lefkáda ship canal, separating the peninsula from the mainland. This is kept dredged by the Greek Government and is easily crossed by a swing bridge; beyond the canal a series of causeways surrounds a large, shallow lagoon, where herons and pelicans figure among the migratory visitors. As on Kefaloniá, Ithaca and Zákynthos, a series of earthquakes – most recently in 1953 – destroyed nearly all of the island's buildings.

hunk of metal that broke into four bits. Archaeologists were astonished to see that they belonged to a mechanical device inscribed with ancient Greek script.

At first dismissed as a primitive astrolabe, the Antikýthera Mechanism, as it was known, soon proved to be much more complex. In 1958, a young British historian of science, Derek de Solla Price, was allowed to examine it and was the first to recognize it as an astronomical computer, which, by its setting, was made on the island of Rhodes in 82 BC. The days of the month and the signs of the zodiac were inscribed on bronze dials, with pointers to indicate the phases of the moon and position of the planets at any given time, operated within by a complex mass of clockwork: bronze cog wheels with triangular teeth, connected to a large four-spoked wheel (the most prominent part visible at the National Archaeology Museum in Athens) driven by a crown gear and shaft, which probably had some kind of key for winding. A moveable slip ring allowed for Leap Year adjustments and alignments. As far as anyone can judge, it was last set by the Roman sea captain on the day his vessel went down. He may have been bringing it to Rome on the special order of Cicero, who knew of the 'future-telling astronomical device' from his school days at Rhodes' famous School of Rhetoric. 'It is a bit frightening to know,' concluded Derek Price, 'that just before the fall of their great civilization, the Ancient Greeks had come so close to our age, not only in their thought, but also in their scientific knowledge.' The next similar device to be noted anywhere was in 11th-century India, by the Iranian traveller al-Biruni. (For all the details, pick up a copy of Victor Kean's *The Ancient Greek Computer from Rhodes*, Efstathiadis Group, 1991.)

Lefkáda is not a love-at-first-sight island; the approach from land is unpromising, and first impressions may be disappointing. This changes once you make your way down the coast, where the island's long sandy beaches make a rich blend with the natural beauty and traditionalism of the interior. Lefkáda is especially well known for the laces and embroideries produced by its women, some of whom still keep a loom in the back room of their house; it is just as famous for its perfect windsurfing at Vassilikí and sailing through the enchanted isles off Nidrí. Dolphins seem to like it, too: there are more varieties seen off the coasts of Lefkáda than anywhere else, including the rare *Delphinus delphis*.

## History

Although inhabited at least as far back as the late Paleolithic era (8000 BC), Lefkáda first enters recorded history as part of ancient Akarnania, site of the 'vast' city Nerikus, located under the farms and houses of modern Kallithéa. In 640 BC, the Corinthians used a ruse to snatch Nerikus from the Akarnanians; they founded the city where it is today and dug the channel making Lefkáda an island. During the Peloponnesian War, Lefkáda, as a loyal ally of Corinth, sided with Sparta and was devastated twice, by the Corcyraeans and the Athenians.

The biggest blow came with the war between Macedonia and Rome in the mid-3rd century BC, when the island was punished for siding with Macedonia. Another dark

# Lefkáda

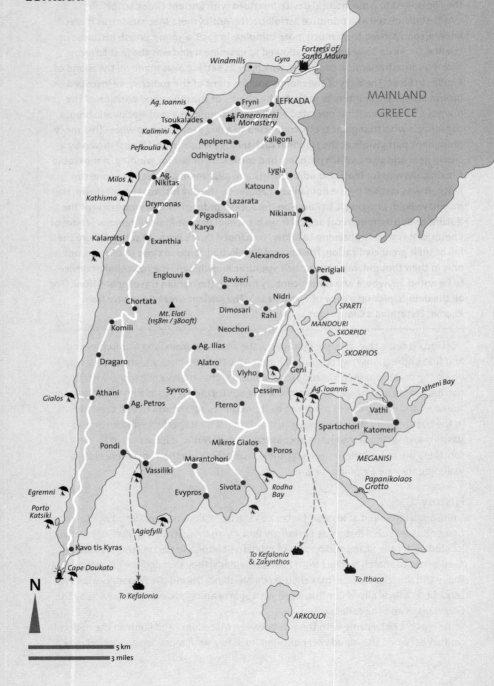

Windmills
Gyra
Fortress of Santa Maura

MAINLAND GREECE

Ag. Ioannis
Fryni
LEFKADA
Tsoukalades
Faneromeni Monastery
Kalimini
Apolpena
Kaligoni
Pefkoulia
Odhigytria
Lygia
Milos
Ag. Nikitas
Katouna
Kathisma
Lazarata
Drymonas
Nikiana
Pigadissani
Karya
Kalamitsi
Exanthia
Alexandros
Perigiali
Englouvi
Bavkeri
Nidri
SPARTI
Chortata
Dimosari
MANDOURI
Mt. Elati (1158m / 3800ft)
Rahi
SKORPIDI
Komili
Neochori
SKORPIOS
Ag. Ilias
Dragaro
Alatro
Atheni Bay
Vlyho
Geni
Athani
Syvros
Dessimi
Ag. Ioannis
Gialos
Ag. Petros
Fterno
Vathi
Spartochori
Katomeri
Pondi
Mikros Gialos
MEGANISI
Marantohori
Poros
Papanikolaos Grotto
Egremni
Vassiliki
Porto Katsiki
Evypros
Sivota
Rodha Bay
Agiofylli
To Kefalonia & Zakynthos
Kavo tis Kyras
To Ithaca
Cape Doukato
N
To Kefalonia
ARKOUDI

5 km
3 miles

moment was the Battle of Aktium, where Augustus outmanoeuvred the fleets of Mark Antony and Cleopatra and won the Roman Empire as his prize. To celebrate his victory, Augustus founded a new city, Nikopolis (near modern Aktion) which drained away Lefkáda's wealth and population.

Although Lefkáda was granted to Venice after the Fourth Crusade, it took the Venetians a century to wrench it from the Despot of Epirus. The inhabitants, exasperated by the fighting and pirates, received permission from Venice to built the fortress of Santa Maura, a name that soon came to refer to the entire island. When Constantinople fell in 1453, Helene Palaeológos, mother of the last emperor, Constantínos XI, founded a monastery within the walls of Santa Maura. When the Turks took Lefkáda in 1479, they turned the monastery into a mosque.

In 1500 the combined forces of Spain and Venice, under the Gran Capitan Gonzales de Cordoba, captured Lefkáda and Santa Maura, but the very next year Venice made a treaty with Turkey and returned the island. In 1684, Francesco Morosini, angry at losing his own fortress at Heráklion, Crete, was determined to win Lefkáda back for

## Getting There and Around

**By air**: flights 4 times a week from Athens and regular charters from England, to Aktion, 26km away on the mainland; from May–mid-Oct there are bus connections to Lefkáda from the airport. Another charter, Britannia, flies to Préveza. For **Olympic** information, t 064 502 2881; for Aktion/Préveza **airport**, t 068 202 2355.

**By sea**: in summer, **excursion boats** from Nidrí and Vassiliki to Sámi, Fiskárdo and Póros (Kefaloniá) and Kióni (Ithaca). Daily boat from Nidrí to Meganísi Islet. The *Ikaros*, based in Nidrí, does a plush **day trip** to Meganísi, Ithaca and Kefaloniá. **Ferries** leave Vassiliki once or twice a day for Kefaloniá and Ithaca. **Port authority**: Lefkáda, t 064 502 2322; **Nidrí harbour**: t 064 509 2509.

**By road**: there are 5 buses a day from Athens. The main bus station is located at the north end of Lefkáda Town; for information call t 064 502 2364. Routes to Nidrí, Ag. Nikítas, Vassiliki and the touristy west coast beaches are well plied, but to really see the island you need at least a moped; there are plenty to hire in Vassiliki and Nidrí.

## Tourist Information

**Tourist police**: 30 Iroon Politechníou in Lefkáda Town, a few blocks from the bus station, t 064 502 6450.

**Regular police**: in Vassiliki, t 064 503 1218, and Vlychó, t 064 509 5207.

**George Kourtis**, on Nidrí's main street, t 064 509 2494, f 064 509 2297. The first travel agent to set up on the island which can help with anything from transport to accommodation.

**Iris travel**, Akarmanias and Golemis St, in Lefkáda Town, t 064 502 1441. Very friendly agency with lots of information.

**Samba Tours**, in Vassiliki, t 064 503 1520, *sambatours@otenet.gr*. Can help with a variety of accommodation types and car rentals.

## Festivals

**50 days after Easter**: Faneroméni Monastery.

**26 July**: Ag. Paraskeví near Ag. Pétros, carnival festivities, with a parade.

**Aug**: Arts and Letters Festival and large International Folklore Festival, in Lefkáda Town.

**First 2 weeks of Aug**: Karyá, which is well known for its handmade lace and woven carpets, puts on a stream of festivities incl. a clarinet festival on the 11th (in the same vein, nearby Englouvi has a clarinet and lentil festival on 6 and 7 Aug) and 'Riganada', the re-creation of a traditional wedding, where everyone wears their finest old costumes.

**11 Nov**: Ag. Minás in Lefkáda Town.

Venice, which he did with the help of the Bishop of Kefaloniá, leading an army of priests and monks. Venice held on to the island until its own fall in 1796, but never managed to influence it as strongly as it did the other Ionian islands. The French and then the Russians grabbed Lefkáda; in 1807 the tyrant Ali Pasha of Epirus tried to purchase it from Russia, but was held back by the Russian-appointed Secretary of State, Count John Capodístria. Capodístria is said to have later sworn to support the cause of an independent Greece with the rebellious refugees on the island, among them Kolokotrónis.

# Lefkáda Town

Approaching Lefkáda over the floating bridge, the first thing you'll see as you cross the causeway over the lagoon is the massive Venetian and Turkish **Fortress of Santa Maura**, dipping its feet in the sea near Akarnania (as the region is still known) on the mainland. Although the buildings within the walls were blown to smithereens in an accidental powder explosion in 1888, the fortress continued to serve as a military camp, and then, for 10 years after the 1922 Asia Minor Disaster, it was used as a refugee camp.

Santa Maura has survived the periodic earthquakes that rattle the area better than the capital, **Lefkáda Town**, which collapsed like a house of cards in the earthquake in 1948, and was hit hard again in 1971. The rebuilt town is like no other in Greece: narrow lanes lined with brightly painted houses, stone on the ground floor, topped by a fragile wooden or more often corrugated metal upper storey as an antiseismic measure. Iron bell towers, rearing up like oil derricks, replace dangerous stone ones. For all this, it is a bustling market town with more genuine Greek atmosphere than anything you'll find in the resorts.

# Where to Stay

**Lefkáda** ✉ 31100

**Nirikos, t** 064 502 4132, *nirikos@lefkada.gr* (*C; exp*). Most rooms face the water, and there's a nice café-bar downstairs. *Open all year.*

**Pension Pirofani, t** 064 502 5844 (*mod*). Newly renovated; spacious, air-con rooms with balconies looking on to the pedestrianized main street.

**Byzantio, t** 064 502 1315, **f** 064 502 2629 (*E; inexp*). Basic but well-kept and friendly, at the waterfront end of the same pedestrianized street. *Open all year.*

# Eating Out

Restaurants are numerous and reasonably priced on Lefkáda, and portions seem to be larger than many other places elsewhere in Greece. If they are on offer in the tavernas and bars, try the increasingly rare local wines *vartsámi*, *kerópati* or *yomatári*.

In the quaint, central Plateía Antistási there are plenty of colourful cafés and atmospheric tavernas, which are very good for people-watching.

**Adriatika**, on the edge of town towards Ag. Nikítas. Set in a pleasant garden setting, this taverna is a little pricey, but has some good Greek specialities and excellent service to warrant it.

**Café Boschetto**, on the seafront. Pleasant place to vegetate.

**Taverna O Regantos**, on D. Vergoti, near the Folklore Museum, **t** 064 502 2855. Blue and white and cute, with solid fare at reasonable prices.

**Bosketo Park**, the large shady square near the end of the causeway, displays busts of Lefkáda's three great contributors to letters: Valaorítis, Sikelianós (for more on both, *see* below), and Lafcadio Hearn (1850–1904), whose British father and Kytheran mother named him after his birthplace. He went on to become a journalist in America, and in 1890 went to Japan, where he became an expert on Japanese language and culture, teaching the Japanese about Western literature and vice versa; every now and then Japanese tourists make the pilgrimage to the island to honour the man they know as Yakomo Kuizumi.

Lefkáda's churches, constructed mostly in the 18th century, are square, domeless and solidly built of stone, and have largely survived the tremors; you'll find fine examples of the Ionian school of painting in **Ag. Minás** (1707), and in the three icons in **Ag. Dimítrios** (1688), although the chances of finding either open are not good. Another church, the **Pantokrátor**, has a pretty façade, last reworked in 1890, with an atypical curved roofline. **Ag. Spyrídon** (17th century) has a fine carved wooden screen.

There are four small museums in Lefkáda Town. Near Ag. Spyrídon, the **Orpheus Folklore Museum** (*follow the little signs; closed for renovation at the time of writing*) has four rooms displaying the beautiful embroideries and weavings made on the island, dating back to the last century; there are also old maps, including a precious original map of Lefkáda made by the Venetian mapmaker Coronelli in 1687. The **Archaeology Museum** (*t 064 502 3678; open weekdays 10–1; adm*) has recently moved to a new building on the northwestern edge of the seafront and houses finds from cave sanctuaries and the 30 12th-century BC tombs discovered by Dörpfeld in Nidrí; the **Icon** (or **Post-Byzantine**) **Museum** (*open 10.30–12.30; adm*), with works of the Ionian school, is housed in the municipal library (*t 064 502 2502*); and, appropriately for the town that established the first municipal brass band in Greece (1850), the **Lefkáda Phonograph Museum**, beyond the square at 12–14 Kalkáni Street (*open in season 10–1.30 and 6.30–11*). The only museum of its kind in Greece, it contains old gramophones sent over by the collector's relatives from the United States, recordings of *cantades* and popular Greek songs of the 1920s, and one of the first discs recorded by a Greek company, 'Orpheon' of Constantinople, founded in 1914. The ancient Corinithian cemetery from 600 BC was discovered a few years ago on the outskirts of town, and is in a permanent state of excavation, and still not open to the public.

## Just Outside Town

The closest place to town for a swim is the **Gýra**, the long, sandy if often windy lido that closes off the west side of the lagoon, with a few tavernas. On the other side of the windmills, a second beach sometimes used by surfers, **Ag. Ioánnis Antzoúsis**, is tucked under a chapel, supposedly named after Angevin Crusaders. In the opposite direction, by the cemetery, stop at the Café Pallas for a refreshing glass of *soumáda* (almond milk) and watch the old men in the olive grove opposite play *t'ambáli*, Lefkáda's version of boules, played with egg-shaped balls on a concave ground, which as far as anyone knows is played nowhere else in the world. Two km south, set in a ruined monastery, the stone church of the **Panagía Odhigýtria** (1450) is the oldest on the island and the only one to have withstood all the earthquakes.

## Sikelianós and the Delphic Idea

Angelos Sikelianós, born on Lefkáda in 1884, was as romantically handsome as a poet should be. Although he duly followed his parents' wishes by going to law school in Athens, he left after a couple of years to join a theatre company with two of his sisters, Helen and Penelope. Penelope married the brother of Isadora Duncan, and through him Sikelianós met his own American spouse, Eva. All shared an interest in reviving the mythic passion and power of ancient Greece, in active artistic expression rather than in the dusty, pedantic spirit of the time. Sikelianós did his part by writing startling lyrical poetry, infused with Dionysian mysticism, yearning to join the world of the gods to the world of men.

In the 1920s, Sikelianós and Eva came up with the idea of reviving the 'Delphic Idea' of the arts, in the same spirit as the revival of the Olympics. Their goal was to create an International Delphic Centre and University, and stage a Delphic Festival of drama, dance, music, sports and crafts; this actually took place in 1927 and 1930, funded in part by a mortgage on the Sikelianós house and Eva's inheritance. But the Depression closed in, and the following years were bitter; Eva went back to America, and although they divorced she continued to support the 'Delphic Idea' and send Sikelianós money. Sikelianós remarried and sat out the war years in a small flat in Athens, in declining health. His finest moment came when he gave the funeral oration of the poet Palamas, declaring 'In this coffin lies Greece', and boldly led the singing of the banned Greek national anthem, even though he was surrounded by German soldiers. The dark years of the war and Greek Civil War added a tragic power to his poetry, but his progressive ideas barred him from membership of the Athens Academy, and, as they will tell you in Lefkáda, from winning the Nobel Prize, too, although he was twice nominated. In 1951 he died when he mistook a bottle of Lysol for his medicine.

Just above the town is the 17th-century **Faneroméni Monastery**, rebuilt in the 19th century after a fire. It is a serene place in the pine woods, with bird's-eye views over the town, lagoon and the walls of Santa Maura. On the islet with the ruined chapel of **Ag. Nikólaos** was a cottage where Angelos Sikelianós and his wife Eva would spend their summers.

# East Coast Resorts

The east coast of Lefkáda is as lovely, green and bedecked with beaches as the choice coasts of Corfu. Just a few kilometres south of Lefkáda Town at Kaligóni, on a hill near the shore, are the scant ruins of **ancient Nerikus**, the pre-Corinthian city, where Dörpfeld (*see* below) found Cyclopean walls, traces of roads, arches, a water-tank, and a pre-Roman theatre, as well as early Byzantine ruins, which can be seen after some scrambling through the olives. Further along is the once cute fishing village of **Lygiá**, now a sprawling resort with narrow beaches; **Nikiána**, spread out more attractively, has good striking views of the mainland.

Further south is **Perigiáli**, with a fine beach and some new hotels, and, two kilometres further on, **Nidrí** (ΝΥΔΡΙ), Lefkáda's busiest resort. Nidrí looks out over lovely Vlyhó Bay, closed in by the Géni Peninsula so that it resembles a lake, its still waters dotted with the privately owned wooded islets of **Mandourí**, **Sparti**, **Skorpídi** and **Skórpios**. The last still belongs to what remains of the Onassis family – Aristotle's granddaughter. From the sea you can spy Aristotle's tomb, and excursion boats now have permission to land on the beaches if no one is in residence. You may notice a little red caique taking over a small army of workers who maintain the island; Onassis stipulated in his will that they must be from Nidrí. His obsession with privacy and payoffs in the right places kept tourist facilities at Nidrí at a bare minimum during his lifetime, but the locals have since made up for lost time. By Lefkáda standards Nidrí is

# Where to Stay and Eat

**Lefkáda** ✉ 31100

## Nikiána

Besides those below, there are rooms to let in abundance, and a row of fish tavernas.

**Red Tower, t** 064 509 2951, **f** 064 509 2852 (*C; lux–exp*). Hotel-apartment complex, sitting high up like a castle with wonderful views over the water.

**Aliki, t** 064 507 1602, **f** 064 507 2071 (*C; exp*). Top-notch small apartment hotel in a superb location; pool and air-con rooms overlook the sea and its own small beach. *Open all year.*

**Pension Ionian, t** 064 507 1720 (*C; exp*). A stone's throw from the sea, slightly cheaper.

**Porto Galini, t** 064 509 2431, **f** 064 509 2672 (*B; exp*). Luxurious furnished apartments among the cypresses and olives, and watersports down on the beach.

**Konaki**, at Lygiá, **t** 064 507 1397, **f** 064 507 1125 (*C; exp–mod*). In a garden setting, overlooking a large pool.

**Kariotes Beach Camping**, just north of Lygiá, **t** 064 507 1103. With a pool but, ironically, no beach in sight.

## Nidrí

Lots of places are block-booked by package companies. **Direct Greece** (*see* p.88) has apartments and a hotel here, and **George Kourtis** can fix you up with a room (visit his agency on the main road, or call **t** 064 509 2494).

**Armeno Beach**, right on the beach, **t** 064 509 2018, **f** 064 509 2341 (*C; exp*). Modern rooms with air-con; watersports available.

**Scorpios**, 2km north in Perigiáli, **t** 064 509 2452, **f** 064 509 2652 (*C; exp*). Upmarket apartment complex with pool.

**Ta Nisakia**, 1km from Nidrí, **t** 064 509 2777, book in Athens, **f** 010 764 5440 (*A; exp*). Studio apartments with commanding views, 200m above the sea.

**Bella Vista**, 500m from Nidrí and 2 mins from the beach, **t** 064 509 2650 (*mod*). Set in a garden; studios have pretty views of Vlýho Bay.

**Gorgona, t** 064 509 2268, **f** 064 509 5634 (*E; mod*). Set back from the razzmatazz in its own quiet garden.

**Nidrí Akti, t** 064 509 2400 (*B; mod*). Good views. *Open all year.*

**Desimi Camping**, Simi Bay, near Vlýho at the end of the peninsula, **t** 064 509 5374.

**Charadiatika village**, just out of town. Popular with locals for its good quality meat and *mezédes*.

**Kavos**. Has consistently good food.

**Il Saporre**. Similar, is also worth a try.

**Olive Tree** and **Paliokatouna**, towards Neochóri. Both are also well liked.

## Póros/Sívota

**Okeanis** at Mikrós Gialós, on the beach, **t** 064 509 5399 (*mod*). A relatively quiet, peaceful place with comfortable rooms. *Open May–Sept.*

**Poros Beach Camping, t** 064 502 3203. Affording luxury for campers, with 50 sites, some bungalows, a bar, restaurant and swimming pool.

Sívota has rooms to rent, but is better known for its excellent fish tavernas, where you can pick a lobster from the sea cage.

cosmopolitan, commercial and smack on the main road; the tavernas are mostly lined up along the seafront, all of which can get very busy and noisy in the summer. Much of the old beach was sacrificed for the building of a quay, so most people head up to Perigiáli for a swim.

Sit at a café in Nidrí at twilight – there's one so near the shore you can sit with your feet in the sea – and, as croaking frogs drag out the motorbikes, watch Mandourí, 'the poet's island' as the locals call it, float above the horizon on a magic carpet of mist. Its mansion belongs to the family of the Aristotélis Valaorítis (1824–79), who was one of the first to write in demotic Greek rather than the formal *kathourévesa*. A member of the Ionian Parliament, he later served in the Greek Parliament, where he was renowned as a public speaker.

One of the nicest excursions from Nidrí is the 45-minute walk by way of the hamlet of Rahí to the **waterfall**, at the end of the Dimosári gorge. In the spring it gushes forth with enthusiasm; in the summer it is little more than a high altitude squirt, but it's wonderfully cool and refreshing, and there's a pool for a swim.

**Vlyhó**, the next village south, is a quiet charmer, famous for its traditional boat-builders. Sandy **Dessími** Beach, with a campsite, lies within walking distance, as does the **Géni Peninsula**, covered with ancient, writhing olive groves. Wilhelm Dörpfeld, Schliemann's assistant in the excavation of Troy, found a number of Bronze Age tombs behind Nidrí and instantly became a local hero, when he announced that they proved his theory that Lefkáda was the Ithaca of Homer. He died in 1940 and is buried near his house, by the Géni's white church of Ag. Kyriakí. Further south, **Póros** is near the very pretty white pebble beach of **Mikrós Gialós**, set under the olive trees. **Sívota**, the next town south, has an exceptionally safe anchorage that draws yacht flotillas; the nearest swimming is at **Kastrí**, to the west.

## Inland Villages: Lace and Lentils

At least venture into Lefkáda's interior, where traditional farming villages occupy the fertile uplands surrounded by mountains, and it's not unusual to encounter an older woman in her traditional costume of brown and black, with a headscarf tied at the back, sitting with distaff in hand, at her loom, or over her embroidery. Although many villages are suffering the usual rural exodus of their young people for the bright lights of the coast, **Karyá** is one large village to aim for, the centre of the island's lace and embroidery industry. Most of the women sell their goods direct, although don't come looking for bargains: look for signs reading KENTHMATA. The ethnographic **Museum**

### Where to Stay and Eat

**Karyá** ✉ 31080

**Karyá Village, t** 064 504 1030 (*B; mod*).
Pleasant rooms if you want to get away from the beach crowds (phone ahead out of season).

There are also rooms available, as well as tavernas and traditional lazy *kafeneíons* under the plane trees. In the event of homesickness, have some Tetleys and one of Brenda's toasties in the main square. After working for years as an island guide, she can answer most questions (and probably find you a room, too).

Maria Koutsochéro (*t 064 504 1590; open in high season 9am–8pm; adm*) is dedicated to the most famous embroiderer of them all, a woman from Karyá whose works were in international demand around 1900. Another traditional lace and embroidery town, **Englouví**, is the highest village on Lefkáda (2,395ft), tucked in a green mountain valley; it is even prouder of its lentils, which win prizes at Greek lentil competitions. In the interior there are several notable churches with frescoes, among them the Red Church (Kókkini Eklisía) and Monastery of Ag. Geórgios (from around 1620) near **Aléxandros**, a nearly abandoned village crumbling to bits, and the 15th-century church of Ag. Geórgios at **Odhigytría** (near Apólpena), its design incorporating Byzantine and Western influences. **Drymónas**, to the west, is a pretty village of stone houses and old tile roofs.

# Down the West Coast

The west coast of Lefkáda is rocky and rugged, and the sea is often rough – perfect for people who complain that the Mediterranean is a big warm bathtub. For under the cliffs and mountains are some of the widest and most stunning stretches of sand in the Ionians, that are only just beginning to be exploited. The road from Lefkáda Town avoids the shore as far as the farming village of **Tsoukaládes**, from where a 2km road leads down to narrow pebbly Kalímini Beach and the most turquoise water imaginable (take provisions and swimming shoes). The route down to the coast from Karyá is a superb approach offering stunning views down to the sea; from Karyá head back towards Lefkáda, turning right at the T-junction; then take the first left. The long sandy beach of **Pefkóulia** begins under the mountains and stretches around the coast to **Ag. Nikítas** (ΑΓ.ΝΙΚΗΤΑΣ). With only a cluster of hotels at the top, the nucleus of the village, with its pretty tile roofs and old tavernas, is off limits to developers; the narrow streets are overhung with flowers and vines. Beware that parking is a major headache, especially on summer weekends. With nothing between here and Italy, the sea is a crystal-clear pale blue and clean, but cold. Don't let your windsurfer run away with you, though – the odd shark fin has been spotted off the coast. Just south of here, 2km off the main road, **Káthisma** is another good, wavy place to swim, with a taverna and cantinas on the wide beach of golden sand, dotted with places to dive and little caves to explore. An unpaved road leads to yet another beautiful sandy beach below the village of **Kalamítsi**, set among giant rocks, with rooms and tavernas that make it a good quiet base.

## The Original Lovers' Leap, Vassilikí and Windsurfing

To reach Lefkáda's southwest peninsula, a secondary road from Kalamítsi crosses to the pretty leafy village of **Chortáta** and **Komíli**, where the road forks. Buses continue down the coastal road only as far as **Atháni**, a tiny village famous for its honey, that struggles to meet the demands of tourists heading further south to the superb beaches along the peninsula. The first, long and undeveloped **Gialós**, can be easily reached by a path from Atháni; the next, glorious golden **Egrémni**, requires a labour of

# Where to Stay and Eat

## Ag. Nikítas ✉ 31080

**Ag. Nikítas**, at the top of the village, t 064 509 7460, f 064 509 7462 (*C; exp*). Tastefully decorated, tranquil hotel with all the mod cons.

**Odyssey**, t 064 509 7351, f 064 509 7421, *filippas@otenet.gr* (*C; exp*). One of the island's nicest hotels, with a roof garden and swimming pool.

**Ostria Pension**, t 064 50 7483, f 064 509 7300 (*A; exp–mod*). Pretty blue and white house overlooking the bay.

**Captain's Corner**. The place to alcoholically survey the bays.

**Poseidon**, on the main street. Offers good fare.

**Sapfo**, on the beach. A tasty lunch option.

## Vassilikí ✉ 31082

**Ponti Beach**, above the bay, t 064 503 1572, f 064 503 1576 (*B; exp*). Smart option, rooms with air-con and fabulous views; also a pool.

**Billy's House**, 70m from the beach, t 064 503 1418 (*mod*). Nice rooms, private baths and kitchen.

**Christina Polete**, one field back from the sea, t 064 503 1440 (*mod*). Newly converted rooms and 2 small apartments in a beautiful house.

**Odeon**, near the beach, t 064 503 1917, f 064 503 1919, *www.vassiliki.net* (*C; mod*). Hotel and apartments, all with air-con; congenial breakfast on the large veranda and cocktails by the pool.

**Wildwind Aparments**, a few yards from the beach, t 064 503 1501, f 064 503 1610 (*mod*). With sailing and windsurf instruction and equipment, and volley ball and croquet for moments when the wind isn't gusting.

**Katina's Place**, t 064 503 1262 (*mod–inexp*). Simple, clean and tremendously hospitable place with great views over the village and port.

**Surf Hotel**, in Pondi, t 064 503 1740, f 064 503 1706 (*C; inexp*). New, with balconied rooms by the beach.

**Vassiliki Beach Campsite**, well located halfway along the bay, t 064 503 1308, f 064 503 1458.

**Miramare** and **Mythos**. Among the better tavernas in town.

Depending on how raucous you're feeling, there's a terrific choice in the way of nightlife. **Zeus** is the crazy late-night bar for young windsurfers.

love to reach from land – a long unpaved road followed by 200 steep steps. Sublime sandy **Pórto Katsíki** ('goat port') further south is magnificently set under pinkish white cliffs, reached by another long walkway-stair from the road (*fee for parking*) and is a popular excursion boat destination; there's a taverna too.

At the end of the road are the famous 190ft sheer white cliffs of **Cape Doukáto** or **Kávo tis Kyrás** (Lady's Cape), where Sappho, rejected by Phaon, hurled herself into the sea; one old tradition says that she was only imitating the goddess Aphrodite, who took the plunge in despair over the death of her lover Adonis. Later, Romans rejected by their sweethearts would make the leap – with the precaution of strapping on feathers or even live birds and employing rescue parties to pull them out of the sea. Young Greeks still soar off the edge, but now use hang-gliders instead of feathers.

Before becoming a cure-all for unrequited love, the leap was made by unwilling sacrifices to stormy Poseidon – prisoners or criminal scapegoats. When human sacrifices dropped out of fashion, priests serving at the Temple of Apollo Lefkáda 'of the Dolphins' (of which only the scantiest ruins remain) would make the jump safely as part of their cult, called *katapontismós* ('sea plunging'), rather like the divers at Acapulco, one imagines; no doubt the leaps were accompanied by animal sacrifices – read barbecues – for a pleasant ancient Greek outing. The white cliffs are a famous landmark for sailors and are now topped by a lighthouse. Byron, sailing past in 1812 during his first visit to Greece, was strangely moved, and put down the experience in *Childe Harold* (canto II):

> *But when he saw the evening star above*
> *Leucadia's far-projecting rock of woe*
> *And hail'd the last resort of fruitless love,*
> *He felt, or deem'd he felt, no common glow*
> *And as the stately vessel glided slow*
> *Beneath the shadow of that ancient mount,*
> *He watch'd the billow's melancholy flow,*
> *And, sunk albeit in thought as he was wont,*
> *More placid seem'd his eye, and smooth his pallid front.*

The left-hand fork in the road at Komíli passes through inspiring scenery, divinely scented by the wild flowers in late spring (no wonder the honey is so good), by way of the pretty farming village of **Ag. Pétros** on the way to **Vassilikí** (ΒΑΣΙΛΙΚΗ), Lefkáda's second biggest resort after Nidrí. Although not half so compromised by package tourism, it still gets very crowded in August, when it becomes a windsurfer's Mecca. A shady, charming village, Vassilikí has a little tree-rimmed port with cafés and shops that specialize in all types of boards for sale or hire. The long beach north of town is a favourite of surfers whizzing around the bay, their brightly coloured sails like butterflies skimming the water. On most days a gentle breeze blows up by mid-morning, perfect to teach beginners the fundamentals, and by mid-afternoon it's blowing strong for the experts; by evening, the wind, like a real gent, takes a bow and exits, allowing a pleasant dinner by the water's edge before the discos open; the nightlife is almost as exhilarating as the wind. For a swim, walk along the sand to Pondi or catch a caique from Vassilikí round the white cliffs of Cape Doukáto for the beach of Pórto Katsíki (*see* above) or the pretty white beach of **Agiofýlli**, accessible only by sea.

Lefkáda's highest peak, Eláti (3,800ft) cuts off the inland villages of the south, which can only be reached from Vassilikí or the Póros–Sívota road in the southeast. The road rises from the plain of Vassilikí, covered with olives and fields of flowers (flower seeds for gardeners are an important local product), to **Sývros**, one of the larger villages in the interior, with places to eat and Lefkáda's largest cave, **Karoucha**. From here the road tackles the increasingly bare slopes of Mount Eláti to lofty little **Ag. Ilías**, with magnificent views.

# Meganísi (ΜΕΓΑΝΗΣΙ)

Spectacular rocky and wild Meganísi, an hour and a half by daily ferry or excursion boat from Nidrí, lies off the southeast coast of Lefkáda. Believed to be the island of Taphos mentioned in the *Odyssey*, it was the main base of the semi-mythical Teleboans, sailors and pirates who at one point were powerful enough to take on the King of Mycenae. The population of 1,800 is still employed in traditional occupations – seafaring for the men, embroidery and lacemaking for the women. Ferries call at

**Váthi**, a pretty port with lots of good fish tavernas, rooms to rent and a campsite, packed to the gills for the *panegýri* of Ag. Konstantínos on 21 May. A road leads up to the cheerful flowery hamlet of Katoméri, where a track heads down to the beach of Polistafíon in narrow Athéni Bay, and there's even the small **Hotel Meganísi**, (*t 064 505 1049, f 064 505 1639; B; exp*). The paved road continues around to **Spartochóri**, with a couple of good tavernas and five rooms to rent, and back to Váthi. Excursion boats from Nidrí usually call at the yawning 90m-deep **Papanikólaos' Grotto**, said to be the second largest in Greece and named after the daring Greek resistance submariner who used to hide here and dart out to attack Italian ships, and at the sandy beach of **Ag. Ioánnis**, with a summer cantina.

# Paxí/Páxos (ΠΑΞΟΙ)

The island of 20 fabled secrets, Paxí (or Paxos) is the tiniest and one of the most charming of the canonical Seven Islands, its 8km transversed by a road that twists

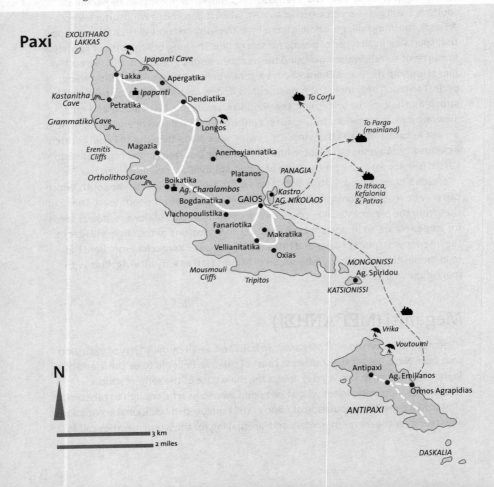

# Getting There

**By boat**: year round daily **ferry** connections with Corfu; twice a week (daily in season) with Párga on the mainland (in the summer months you will need to buy your ticket a day or two in advance), also infrequent ferry connections with Pátras, Kefaloniá and Ithaca. Connections are far less frequent in the off season. In summer you may well be asked to produce proof of a room reservation before boarding a ferry to the island, which is small, wooded, and very fearful of campers and their damaging fires.

The Paxos Express **excursion boats** circle the island, offering a look at the caves and dramatic cliff scenery, stopping at the better pebbly beaches and Antípaxi. **Port authority**: t 066 203 2259.

# Tourist Information

**Regular police**: in Gaiós, t 066 203 1222.

# Festivals

**10 Feb**: Ag. Charálambos.
**Easter Monday**: procession from Gáios to Vellianitatika.
**11 Aug**: Ag. Spyrídon.
**15 Aug**: Panagía.

# Where to Stay and Eat

**Paxí** ✉ **49082**
Be prepared for prices above the norm; transport costs add to the tariff, and supplies from the outside world can be cut off without warning whenever the wind kicks up. Restaurants take full advantage of the day-trippers who come from Corfu and the yachting set berthed in Gáios. Official accommodation is limited, rather expensive, and block-booked by tour operators in the summer. Everyone else stays in rent rooms (about €20–25), which are invariably pleasant, tidy and doubles. **Bouas Travel**, t 066 203 2401, *info@bouastours.gr*, can help with all types of accommodation.

## Gáios

**Páxos Club**, 1km from Gáios, t 066 203 2450, *paxosgr@otenet.gr* (*lux*). With a large swimming pool and very comfortable modern rooms.

**Páxos Beach Bungalows**, near the beach, t 066 203 1211, *www.geocities.com/paxosbeach* (*B; exp*). Pleasant, comfortable chalet bungalows, but only available in the off season.

**Naïs**. Offers a wide variety of croissants and sandwiches.

**Costa's** *Kafeneíon*. Good value grub.

**Taka Taka**. One of the handful of tavernas in Gáios serving solid Greek fare and fish.

Take the caique to **Mongoníssi** for the excellent restaurant there, and to while the day away on the beach.

## Lákka

**Ilios**, t 066 203 1808 (*E; inexp*).

**Lefkothea**, t 066 203 1408 (*E; inexp*). Both of these options are small, but fill up in season. *Open all year.*

**Sgarelios** and **Klinis**. You can eat well and reasonably at both of these pleasant tavernas.

**Italian Rosa**. Pretty little restaurant featuring a wide variety of pasta dishes.

and turns through immaculate groves of olives, source of the liquid gold that has won international medals; unlike Corfu, the olives here are rarely sprayed against the dreaded dacus fly, but are protected with ecologically sound sticky traps in plastic bags. Besides the beauty of the silvery trees (there are some 300,000 – each family owns at least 500) and the tidy stone walls, Paxí has some of the friendliest people you'll find in Greece. Together with little sister Antípaxi it has long served as an upmarket, small-is-beautiful escape from the mass tourism on neighbouring Corfu, although the Italians and yachties who descend on it in July and August strain the limited accommodation.

rooms he mentions, although it used to shelter monk seals. **Grammatikó** is the largest cave of them all. When sailing around the island, you can also see the **Moúsmouli Cliffs** and their natural bridge **Tripitos**.

The main road from Gáios that crosses the island was donated by Aristotle Onassis, a great fan of Paxí. The minibus (everything on Paxí is mini) runs north to **Lákka** (ΛΑΚΚΑ), a tiny port where the boats from Corfu usually call and sometimes cause traffic jams. Lákka is within easy reach of small, shady pebble beaches, and the Byzantine church in the village has particularly musical Russian bells, which you can ring if you find the villager with the key. Walk inland to the church of **Ípapanti**, topped by two odd stumpy, flat-topped domes, with a massive freestanding campanile on one side, crowned by an onion dome. The Venetian stone **Grammatikoú mansion** near Lákka is fortified with a tower.

Laid-back **Longós** (ΛΟΓΓΟΣ), Paxí's third minute port, is about midway between Gáios and Lákka, and gets fewer visitors; there's a pleasant rocky beach (and others within easy walking distance to the south of town) and a few bars. In tiny **Boikatiká** village, the church Ag. Charálambos contains an old icon of the Virgin, and in nearby **Magaziá** are two churches, Ag. Spyrídon and Ag. Apóstoli; the latter's churchyard affords an impressive view of the Eremitis cliffs. At **Apergatiká** the Papamárkou mansion dates from the 17th century.

## Antípaxi/Antípaxos

South of Paxí lies tiny Antípaxi, with only a few permanent residents. From June until September four or five caiques leave Gáios daily for the 40-minute trip to its port Ormós Agrapídias. Although both Paxí and Antípaxi were created with a resounding blow of Poseidon's trident, the two islands are very different in nature; the part of Antípaxi facing Paxí looks bare, almost as if it had been bitten off by a Leviathan. Rather than olive oil, Antípaxi produces good white and red wines, and rather than little pebble beaches, Antípaxi's gentle side is graced with fine sandy beaches: **Voutoúmi** and **Vríka** are 'softer than silk'. There are two tavernas in the itty bitty village and port at **Ormós Agrapídias**, but no accommodation on the islet; if you want to stay bring a sleeping bag, for Voutoúmi has a small campsite. This could be the uncontaminated paradise you've been seeking.

# Zákynthos/Zante (ΖΑΚΥΝΘΟΣ)

Of all their Ionian possessions the Venetians loved Zákynthos the most for its charm and natural beauty. *Zante, fiore di Levante* – 'the flower of the East' – they called it, and built a city even more splendid than Corfu Town on its great semi-circular bay, all turned to rubble by the earthquake of 1953. Nevertheless, the disaster did nothing to diminish the soft, luxuriant charm of the landscape: its fertile green hills and mountainsides, the valleys planted with vineyards and currant vines, olive and almond groves and orchards, or the brilliant garlands of flowers and beautiful beaches (the flowers are best in spring and autumn, a time when few foreigners visit the island). And if the buildings are gone, the Venetians left a lasting impression – many islanders have Venetian blood, which shows up not only in their names, but in their love of singing. The flip side of the coin is that the once politically progressive Zákynthos has bellied up to the trough of grab-the-money-and-run honky tonk tourism (choo choo train rides, reptile houses, porn and touts), to the extent of sabotaging efforts to preserve the beaches where the loggerhead turtles breed.

## History

Tradition has it that Zákynthos was named after its first colonist, a son of Dardanus from Arcadia, who brought with him the Arcadian love of music and festivals that would always characterize the island. Zákynthos fought under Odysseus in the Trojan War, although when he returned home and shot 20 of the island's nobles – Penelope's suitors – Zákynthos rebelled and became an independent, coin-minting state. It set up colonies throughout the Mediterranean, most importantly Saguntum in Spain, a city later demolished by Hannibal. Levinus took the island for Rome in 214 BC, and when the inhabitants rebelled, he burnt every building on the island. Uniting with the Aeolians, the islanders forced the Romans out, although in 150 BC Flavius finally brought them under control.

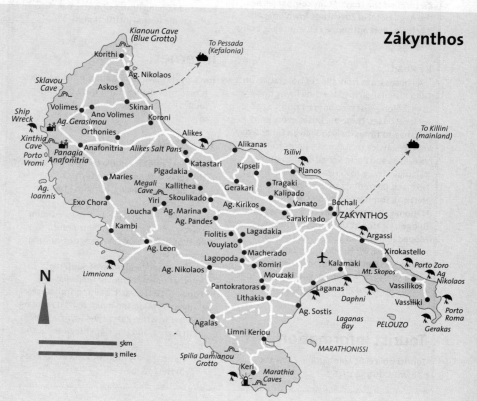

**Zákynthos**

Kianoun Cave
(Blue Grotto)

To Pessada
(Kefalonia)

Kórithi
Ag. Nikolaos
Sklavou Cave
Askos
Ship Wreck
Volimes
Ano Volimes
Skinari
Koroni
Ag. Gerasimou
Xinthia Cave
Orthonies
Porto Vromi
Panagia Anafonitria
Anafonitria
Alikes Salt Pans
Alikes
Alikanas
Tsilivi
To Killini
(mainland)
Maries
Katastari
Kipseli
Pigadakia
Planos
Ag. Ioannis
Megali Cave
Kallithea
Gerakari
Tragaki
Exo Chora
Yiri
Skoulikado
Kalipado
Loucha
Ag. Marina
Ag. Kirikos
Vanato
Bochali
Kambi
Ag. Pandes
Sarakinado
ZÁKYNTHOS
Fiolitis
Lagadakia
Argassi
Vouyiato
Ag. Leon
Macherado
Xirokastello
Lagopoda
Romiri
Kalamaki
Porto Zoro
Limniona
Ag. Nikolaos
Mouzaki
Mt. Skopos
Ag Nikolaos
Pantokratoras
Laganas
Vassilikos
Lithakia
Daphni
Vassiliki
Ag. Sostis
Laganas Bay
PELOUZO
Porto Roma
Agalas
Limni Keriou
Gerakas
MARATHONISSI
5km
3 miles
Spilia Damianou Grotto
Keri
Marathia Caves

N

# Getting There and Around

## By Air

Daily flights from Athens; the **Olympic Airways** office is located at 16 Alex. Róma, Zákynthos Town, **t** 069 502 8611. There are several charters from major European cities, incl. flights to various locations in the UK. For **airport information**, call **t** 069 502 8322. The airport is 6km from town; a taxi will set you back around €6.

## By Sea

6–7 **ferry** connections daily with Killíni on the Peloponnese; 1–2 a day from Pessáda (Kefaloniá) to Skinári-Ag. Nikólaos; from Zákynthos Town and Alikés, **excursion boats** regularly take tourists to the spectacular west-coast beaches; caiques sail several times a week from Laganás to the deserted Strofádes. There are also regular excursion boats from Skinári to Kianoún Cave, and from Kerí around the coast. Many companies near the Aegli Hotel in Zákynthos Town offer all-day tours. **Port authority:** 1 El. Venizélou, **t** 069 502 8117.

## By Road

All **buses** leave from the central station on Filíta Klavdianoú in Zákynthos Town, **t** 069 502 2255 for long-distance buses; **t** 069 504 3850 for local buses. There are buses every hr to Laganás, 10 times daily to Tsilivi, 4 times a day to Alikés, twice to Volímes, 3 times to Vassilikós and Porto Roma, 8 times to Kalamáki, twice to Kerí Lake and Skinári-Ag. Nikólaos. **Car** rentals are possible through **Hertz**, 58 Lombárdou, **t** 069 504 5706, **National**, 18 Lombárdou, **t** 069 504 3471, and **Budget**, located at the airport, **t** 069 504 3680. **Moped** rentals also abound on the island. If you're fresh off the boat and raring to get going, **Sáki Rentals**, 3 Leofóros Dimokratías, **t** 069 502 3928, will oblige with a wide range of vehicles and daily rates, which start at around €15.

# Tourist Information

**Tourist police:** 62 Lombárdou, Zákynthos Town, **t** 069 502 7367.

**Post Office**, on Tertséti St, 3 roads back from the bus station.

Be sure to pick up a free copy of the essential *Zante Moments*, issued every 10 days in the summer and available at all tourist agencies in Zákynthos Town.

**Friendly Tours**, 5 Foscolos, Zákynthos Town, **t** 069 504 8030, **f** 069 502 3769. They live up to their name and can help with accommodation of all types and budgets, boat excursions to remote island beaches the mainland. They will also organize car and moped rentals.

**Pilot U**, highly visible on the port at 78 Lombárdou, **t** 069 502 8207, **f** 069 502 8208. They also arrange scuba-diving and horse-riding, which make a welcome change from the rash of commercial 'fun parks' and 'bronco rides'.

**Scuba-diving** is restricted to certain areas around Laganás. Contact:

**Zante Diving**, **t** 069 505 2264. Organize courses of all ability levels.

**Barracuda Diving Club**, **t** 069 504 1125. Also offer professional instruction.

# Internet

**Top's**, by the town bus station. Internet access is readily available at this busy, bulbous joint.

# Festivals

**Two weeks prior to Lent**: a carnival initiated by the Venetians, known for its masked singers and vigorous dancing, remains strong in Zákynthos.

**Holy Week**: the inhabitants also give themselves over to infectious merriment.

**July**: the Zakýnthia, with a range of cultural activities.

**End of Aug** and **beginning of Sept**: the International Meeting of Medieval and Popular Theatre, with daily performances.

**24 Aug** and **17 Dec**: the major feast days of Ag. Diónysios, when Zákynthos Town is strewn with myrtle, and there are fireworks at the church.

**10 Nov**: the slightly more modest Zoodóchos Pigí in the town.

In 844 the Saracens based in Crete captured the island; the Byzantines expelled them, until 1182, when the Norman-Sicilian pirate Margaritone took Zákynthos, and made it part of his County Palatine of Kefaloniá. One of his successors ceded the island to the Venetians in 1209, who held on to it for almost 350 years, with a Turkish interval between 1479 and 1484. It was an eventful period: the privileges of the Venetians and wealthy Zantiotes provoked 'the Rebellion of the Popolari', when the commoners seized control of the island for four years. The influx of artists after the fall of Heráklion in Crete, in 1669, made Zákynthos the centre of a very productive Cretan-Venetian Ionian school of painting. The Cretan–Venetian influence in local music at this time gave birth to the island's serenades, the *kantádes*. Major poets were born on Zákynthos: the Greek-Italian Ugo Foscolo (d. 1827), Andréas Kálvos and Diónysios Solomós.

Fired by the French Revolution, the Zantiots formed a Jacobin Club and destroyed the rank of nobility, burning the Libro d'Oro that accredited the island aristocracy. In 1798, the Russians forced the French garrison and the inhabitants to surrender, and when the Septinsular Republic established an aristocracy of its own in 1801, populist, high-spirited Zákynthos rebelled again. During the War of Independence many rebels on the mainland, notably Kolokotrónis, found asylum on the island before Zákynthos joined Greece with its Ionian sisters in 1864.

## Zákynthos Town

When the time came to rebuild their earthquake-shattered town, the inhabitants gamely tried to incorporate some of the old city's delight and charm into the dull, uninspiring lines of modern Greek architecture. They didn't fully succeed. However Zákynthos Town, or Chóra (pop. 10,000), is saved from anonymity by its superb setting – the ancient *acropolis* hovering above, crowned by a castle, and the graceful sweep of the harbour, punctuated off to the right by the striking silhouette of Mount Skopós. Wrapped along the waterfront, the streets of the long, narrow town – Lombárdou Street by the sea, and the parallel streets of Filíta, Fóskolou, Alexándrou Roma and Tertséti – are sheltered by arcades (as they were before the earthquake). Houses are one-storey, painted clapboard, draped to the hilt with colourful bougainvillaea and hibiscus, and a few shops still sell the delicious local speciality, *mandoláto* (white nougat with almonds) amongst the figurines of coupling turtles and other foofaraws.

The rebuilders of Zákynthos Town failed where they should have done their best, in the seaside front parlour, **Plateía Solomoú**; although adorned with flowerbeds and a statue of the portly Diónysios Solomós, raising a hand in greeting, the square is too large and open for comfort, and its small cafés are overwhelmed by solemn formal buildings: the Town Hall (with another statue of another poet, Ugo Foscolo, and the inscription 'Liberty Requires Virtue and Daring'), the Cultural Centre, and the sailors' church, **Ag. Nikólaos tou Mólou** 'of the Mole' (1561), which was pieced together like a jigsaw after the quake.

# Where to Stay

## Zákynthos Town ✉ 29100

Outside Aug, accommodation in Zákynthos Town is usually feasible; if you have any difficulty finding a hotel or booking a room, the tourist police will have a list of rooms to let in the area.

**Bitzaro**, set right on the waterfront, t 069 502 3644, f 069 504 5506 (*C; exp*). Glamorous reception area, equally smart rooms with all the mod cons, incl. a balcony and a pleasant veranda to relax on.

**Reparo**, next door to the Bitzaro, t 069 502 3578, f 069 504 5617 (*B; exp–mod*). Similarly priced to the Bitzaro and extremely comfortable.

**Strada Marina**, 14 K. Lombárdou St, t 069 504 2761, f 069 502 8733 (*B; exp–mod*). Larger than the Reparo, less smart, although well located for where the ferries come in. *Open all year.*

**Apollon**, 30 Tertséti, t 069 504 2838, f 069 504 5400 (*C; mod*). Small, intimate hotel with lots of character, a good central choice. *Open April–Oct.*

**Dessy**, 73 N. Kolíva, t 069 502 8505 (*E; mod*). Another reasonable option near the centre of town.

**Phoenix**, Plateía Solomoú, t 069 504 2419, f 069 504 5083 (*C; mod*). Comfortable rooms, all with air-con and satellite TV. *Open all year.*

## Pórto Zóro–Vassilikós

**Matilda**, 200m above the sea, t 069 503 5430, f 069 503 5429 (*B; lux–exp*). A fancy-pants complex with two swimming pools and a wide array of sea sports on offer. *Open May–Oct.*

**Zante Royal Palace II**, t 069 503 5492, f 069 503 5488, *plus12@ath.forthnet.gr* (*A; lux*). One of the various decadent complexes in Vassilikós, that offers the works, replete with Watermania; guaranteed to keep the kids entertained.

**Aquarius**, t 069 503 5300, f 069 503 5303 (*B; exp*). Prettily set amongst lush greenery, and advertises itself as 'a place to forget the world'.

**Locanda**, by the beach at Argássi, t 069 504 5563, f 069 502 3769 (*C; mod*). Well-run family hotel.

The **Neo-Byzantine Museum** (*t 069 504 2714; open Tues–Sun 8–2.30; adm but free Sun*) contributes to Plateía Solomoú's stiff formality, but it can be forgiven this for the beauty of its contents: art salvaged from shattered churches across the whole of Zákynthos. The 17th century was a golden age for painting on the island, especially after the arrival of refugees from Crete in 1669, among them Michael Damaskinós, the teacher of El Greco. Italian influences were also strong, and by the late 18th and 19th centuries, local painters were producing rosy-cheeked fluff. But before turning into candy floss, the Cretan-Venetian-Ionian School left Zákynthos with some spirited, lovely works: namely, the iconostasis of Ag. Dimitrioú tou Kollás and another one from Pantokrátoras (1681), the latter completely covered with intricate wood carvings. The museum also contains marble fragments, ancient and Byzantine tombs, and excellent 16th-century frescoes from Ag. Andréa at Volímes, the apse showing Jesus in the cosmic womb, the side walls painted with New Testament scenes and every saint in the Orthodox calendar represented, the back wall covered with a *Last Judgement*, with a great tree branch emanating from hell and an empty throne awaiting, cupped by the hand of God. The icons, mostly from the 16th and 17th centuries, are superb, varying between Oriental and Western extremes. Other rooms in the museum display the creative talents of Damaskinós, Ioánnis Kýprios, Emmanuel Zána and Nikólas Kallérgis. The last bittersweet exhibit is a model of Zákynthos Town as it was before the terrible earthquake.

# Eating Out

**Aresti**, by the Krionéri lighthouse, t 069 502 7379 (€16–22). Here's where you'll find Zákynthos' finest dining, either inside surrounded by antiques and oil paintings, or outside on the terrace with views out over the sea. The chef is Brazilian, and her speciality is leg of pork with chili, mushrooms and Chinese-style rice.

**Aresti**, on the coast road near Stávros, t 069 502 6346. Yes, there are two. This one is also a very popular taverna, if a little more reasonable. It has a long musical, if not culinary, tradition. Onassis and Maria Callas came here often for the live Greek music and traditional Zákynthos *kantádes*, performed by male trios. If you do get a table, don't start humming while you wait for service – you'll be expected to sing.

**Karavomilos**, on the road to Argássi, near the basilica of Ag. Diónysos (€15–20). Has the name for the best fish on the island; the friendly owner will recommend the best of the day's catch.

**Malanou**, 38 Ag. Athanásou, t 069 504 5936. In a similar direction; locals in the know head to this delightful place for lunch, especially for the moussaká, lamb from the oven and veal *giovétsi*.

**O Adelfos tou Kosta**, in Vassilikós, t 069 503 5347. Traditional taverna with the opportunity to hear more wonderful *kantádes*. Some delicious starters, incl. *kolokithokeftédes* (courgette rissoles), *tirokrokétes* (cheese croquettes), and delicious rabbit and cockerel casserole.

**Panorama**. Very scenic spot up by the castle, with yet more live *kantádes* as well as traditional Zantiote dishes such as rabbit casserole and *moskári kokkinistó*, beef in tomato sauce.

**Pantheon**, 46 Lombárdou. Good Greek food and plenty to look at in the port as you wait for the ferry.

**Restaurant-Pizzeria Corner**, Plateía Ag. Márkos. Perfectly reasonable choice among some so-so expensive places on the main town square.

**Base Bar**, on Plateía Ag. Márkos in Zákynthos Town. This lively night spot has a jazzy ensemble.

**Kazino**, nearby. Another popular music bar.

Inland from Plateía Solomoú, you'll come across the smaller, triangular, marble-paved, pizzeria-lined **Plateía Ag. Márkou** – Zákynthos' Piazza San Marco. This is as lively as the bigger square is sleepy. It has been the social centre of town since the 15th century and was the site of the Romianiko Casino, which everyone loved but no one rebuilt after the earthquake. The Catholic church of San Marco, stripped of its art, occupies one end of Plateía Ag. Márkou, near the **Solomós Museum** (*t 069 504 8982; open daily 9–2; adm*), with mementoes of the poets and other famous Zantiotes, as well as photographs of the island before 1953. Adjacent are the mausoleums of Diónysos Solomós and Andréas Kálvos; the latter lived in London and Paris for much of his life, but was granted the wish he expressed at the end of his romantic ode 'Zante': 'May Fate not give me a foreign grave, for death is sweet only to him who sleeps in his homeland.'

Zákynthos' most important churches were reconstructed after the earthquake, among them little **Kyrá tou Angeloú** (1687) in Louká Karrer Street, containing icons by Panagiótis Doxarás of Zákynthos and a pretty carved iconostasis. Near the Basilica tis Análipsis on Alex. Róma Street is the boyhood **home of Ugo Foscolo**, marked by a marble plaque and angel; apparently he used to read by the light of the icon lamp in the shrine across the street from his home. Further south from here, the restored 15th-century **Faneroméni** church with its pretty campanile (located on the corner of Lisgara and Doxarádou Streets) was, before the earthquake, one of the most beautiful

## A Patriotic Perfectionist

Of the two poets, Solomós is the more intriguing character. Born in 1798, he was educated like many Ionian aristocrats in Italy and wrote his first poems in Italian. He then decided that it was time for Greece to have a Dante of its own, and like Dante, he rejected the formal language of the day (in Dante's day Latin, in Solomós' the purist Greek, or *katharévousa*) and chose instead the demotic everyday language. Nearly as important, he broke away from the slavery to the 15-syllable line that dominated Greek poetry from the 17th century, and introduced Western-influenced metres and forms.

Solomós concentrated on lyrical verse until the Greek War of Independence inspired in him deeper, and increasingly more spiritual works, especially in 'The Free Besieged', which he wrote after the heroic resistance of Messolóngi. His verse has a degree of beauty, balance and delicacy that has rarely been matched by other Greek poets – that is, whatever fragments have survived; highly strung and hyper-critical, Solomós destroyed nearly everything he wrote in his later years on Corfu, where he often used his great influence with the British to gain more lenient sentences for Greek nationalists on the Ionian islands. The first stanzas of his *Ode to Liberty*, which he composed upon hearing of the death of Lord Byron, are now the lyrics to the Greek national anthem:

Σε γνωρζω απο την κοψυ του σπαθιου την τρομερη
σε γνωρζω απο την οψη που με βια μετραει τη γη...

*I recognize you by the fierce edge of your sword;*
*I recognize you by the look that measures the earth...'*

churches in the whole of Greece. At the southern end of town a huge **basilica of Ag. Diónysios** was built in 1925 to house the bones of the island's patron saint, and was one of only three buildings in town left standing after the earthquake, thanks in small part to Dionysios' divine intervention but in large part to its solid concrete construction. New and Old Testament paintings decorate the walls, and an array of gold and silver ex-votos are witness to his influence; throngs of pilgrims pile in every year on 24 August.

## Upper Zákynthos Town: Bocháli

Filikóu Street, behind Ag. Márkou, leads up to Bocháli, affording an excellent view of the town and sea; further along, in Tsilívi, the small **Maritime Museum** (*t 069 502 8249 or t 069 504 2436, open 9–1.30 and 6–8.30*) may lure you in with its imposing torpedo display. Bocháli was a centre of the Greek independence movement: the church of Ag. Giórgios Filikóu was the seat of the local branch of the revolutionary Friendly Society, and from the Bocháli crossroads, a road leads to the hill Lófos Stráni, where a bust of Solomós marks the spot where the poet composed the *Ode to Liberty* during the siege of Messolóngi. Another road is signposted to the well-preserved **Venetian Kástro** (*t 069 504 8099; open Tues–Sun 8–2.30; adm*), a short taxi ride or 5-minute walk up an old cobbled path. Three gates, the last bearing the Lion of St Mark, guarded the medieval town. Ruins of churches and walls of the ancient *acropolis* still stand amid the pines. Cafés (notably the shady Diogenes) overlook the vista at the foot of the castle. Some neglected gardens in Akrotíri (take the north road at the Bocháli crossroads) recall long gone Venetian villas. This was the centre of Zante society into the period of British rule; the villa that belonged to Diónysios Solomós' father was the residence of the High Commissioner. At one house, the Villa Crob, the British laid out the first tennis court in Greece. Down in the north end of town, a romantically melancholy British cemetery is wedged next to the green cliffs (turn right at Bociari Street from N. Kolíva).

## Beaches under Mount Skopós

The town beach isn't really up to much – for better, cleaner swimming spots, try the beaches along the beautiful rugged eastern peninsula under Mount Skopós, beyond **Argássi** (ΑΡΓΑΣΙ), with a somewhat soulless assembly line of hotels and tavernas along its waterfront. Further along, there's wide, sandy **Pórto Zóro** (**Banana Beach**), strewn with sea daffodils, which send such a strong fragrance out to sea that they may have been the origin of the island's nickname, *Fiore di Levante*. This is followed by **Ag. Nikólaos, Mavrándzi** and the thinnish crescent at **Pórto Róma**, all with traditional tavernas. The 16th-century Domenegini Tower here was used during the Greek War of Independence for covert operations by the revolutionary Friendly Society, which sent men and supplies over to the Peloponnese. To keep busybodies away they spread word that the tower was haunted, and even installed a 'devil' at night to holler and throw stones at any passer-by.

**Vassilikós** (ΒΑΣΙΛΛΙΚΟΣ) is a tiny village at the end of the bus line, but bear in mind that services are infrequent and you may have to get back into town by taxi if you leave it too late in the day. **Gérakas**, right at the tip of the peninsula, has another long, lovely stretch of sandy beach, which is the finest of them all. Although popular with bathers, it's also a favourite spot with nesting loggerhead turtles (*see* box overleaf) and fortunately has been saved from any more encroaching hotels by its designation as a conservation area. Roads cross the peninsula for **Daphní** and **Sekánika**, two secluded, undeveloped beaches to the south, facing Laganás Bay, and both are equally popular with the turtles.

## Up Mount Skopós

From the edge of Argássi, a road leads up through the wildflowers, including several species of indigenous orchid, to the top of **Mount Skopós** ('Lookout'), the Mount Hellatos of the ancient Greeks and the Mons Nobilis of Pliny, who wrote of a cavern here that led straight to the Underworld. On the way note the picturesque ruins and mosaic floor of the 11th-century **Ag. Nikólaos Megalomátis**, built on the site of a Temple to Artemis. Views from the summit of Mount Skopós not only take in all of Zákynthos, but also the Peloponnese and the Bay of Navarino, where on 20 October 1827 the most famous battle of modern Greece was fought between the Turko-Egyptian navy and the Anglo-Franco-Russian fleet, leading directly to Greek independence. By the rocky lump summit or *toúrla* of Mount Skopós stands the

## Loggerheads over Loggerheads

A decade ago Zákynthos became the centre of an international stir when environmentalists themselves were at loggerheads with government ministries and the island tourist industry to protect Laganás Bay, the single most important nursery of rare loggerhead turtles (*caretta caretta*), who dig some 1,000 nests a year on 4km of beach. These sea turtles are among the oldest species on the planet, going back hundreds of millions of years, and as long as anyone can remember, they have gathered every June until September from all over the Mediterranean at Zákynthos to crawl up onto the beaches at night, dig a deep hole with their back legs, lay between 100 and 120 eggs the size of golf balls and cover them up again before lumbering back to the sea. For 60 days the eggs incubate in the warmth of the sands, and, when they hatch, the baby turtles make a break for the sea. It is *essential* that the nesting zones remain undisturbed as much as possible – that people stay away from the beaches between dusk and dawn, and not poke umbrellas in the sand, run vehicles over it, or leave litter. Even then the odds for the turtle hatchlings aren't good: the lights in the bay are liable to distract them from their all-important race to the sea, and they die of exhaustion.

Whether or not the turtles can co-exist with the local tourist economy remains to be seen. At first the going was rough; uncompensated for the beaches they owned, some Zantiotes did all they could to sabotage the efforts of the marine biologists and even resorted to setting fires on the beaches to keep the turtles away. In 1983, when the steep decline in nests was noticed, the Sea Turtle Protection Society of Greece (STPS) was formed to monitor the loggerheads and mark their nests. They have succeeded in heightening public awareness, in limiting sea traffic in Laganás Bay, and in finally establishing a Marine Park in December 1999 to protect the turtle rookery. However, opposition remains; in July 2000 a Greek turtle project co-ordinator was beaten up with an iron bar by two men who jet-skiied into the park's protected zone.

venerable white church of **Panagía Skopiótissa**, believed to replace yet another Temple to Artemis. The interior is decorated with frescoes and a carved stone iconostasis; the icon of the Virgin was painted in Constantinople, and there's a double-headed Byzantine eagle mosaic on the floor.

# Laganás Bay and the South

On the map, Zákynthos looks like a piranha with huge gaping jaws, about to devour a pair of crumb-sized fish in Laganás Bay. These small fry are **Marathoníssi** and **Peloúzo**, the former with a sandy beach that makes for a popular excursion destination, the latter colonized in 1473 BC by King Zákynthos. The island's most overripe tourist developments follow the sandy beaches step by step, starting at **Kalamáki**, on the east end of the bay at the beginning of currant country, with a beach under Mount Skopós. The next town, **Laganás** (ΛΑΓΑΝΑΣ) is set on a flat hard sandy beach

## Eating Out

**Kalamáki** ✉ **29100**

**Mikaélos**, just along the main Kalamáki–Zákynthos road, t 069 504 8080. This is one of the best tavernas in Zákynthos and, inevitably, also one of the most crowded. However, there's a convenient bar next door

if you have to wait for a table. *Open May–Oct.*

**Cave Bar**, also away from the coast, up a little road lined with lights. A very romantic place on various levels, perfect for a troglodyte cocktail.

**Vios**. This is more of a club, in a panoramic garden setting.

that overlooks curious rock formations by the sea. This is Zákynthos' Blatant Beast, Las Vegas on the Ionian, filled with British and German package tourists and about as un-Greek as it gets in Greece. Its 'Golden Mile' of open bars (with boorish touts to lure you in) throbbing with music and flashing neon lights, is the joy of revellers and ravers and the despair of the loggerhead turtles. A bridge leads out to the pretty islet of **Ag. Sostís**, its limestone cliffs falling abruptly where the earthquake of 1633 cleaved it from the rest of Zákynthos. Ag. Sostís is topped with pine trees and, this being Laganás, there's an omnipresent disco.

### A Gently Inclined Plain

Behind Laganás extends the lush plain of Zákynthos, a lovely, fairly flat region to cycle through, dotted with the ruins of old country estates wrapped in greenery. The chief village to aim for is **Pantokrátoras**, near three fine churches: the beautiful **Pantokrátor**, founded by Byzantine Empress Pulcheria; **Kiliómeno**, restored after the quake, with beautiful icons; and the medieval church of the Panagía, with a pretty bell tower and stone carvings. The picturesque ruins of the Villa Loundzis, once one of Zákynthos' most noble estates, are in **Sarakína** nearby. **Lithakiá**, south of

### The Belgian on the Beach

Not a few sunbathers at Laganás are keen students of the opposite sex's anatomy, so generously displayed and baked to a T. None, however, are as studiously keen as Vesalius (1514–64), the Renaissance father of anatomy, whose statue stands at the southern end of the beach. Born in Brabant, Vesalius studied in Paris, where he edited the 2nd-century AD anatomical works of Galen, the Greek physician to the gladiators and Emperor Marcus Aurelius. Vesalius went on to the University of Padua, and developed it into the leading school of anatomy in Europe, publishing in 1543 his milestone *De humani corporis fabrica*, the first thorough and original study of the human body since Galen.

In 1555 Vesalius became the personal physician to Philip II of Spain, only to be sentenced to death by the Inquisition for dissecting a dead Spaniard. Philip commuted the sentence to a pilgrimage to the Holy Land, and on the way home the doctor's ship was wrecked off the coast of Zákynthos at Laganás Bay. Vesalius, realizing a return to Inquisition-plagued Madrid would mean an end to his studies anyway, decided to spend the rest of his life in the now ruined Franciscan monastery at Faneró, which is on the road from Laganás to Pantokrátoras; his epitaph here is still intact.

Pantokrátoras, has another restored church, the 14th-century Panagía Faneroméni, containing works of art gathered from ruined churches in the vicinity. Lithakiá's long stretch of sand that has stayed resolutely Greek, with half a dozen tavernas (and not a baked bean sign in sight) and the pleasant **Michailitis** rooms for rent (*t* 069 505 1090, *f* 069 505 2710; *inexp*).

From Lithakiá the main road continues south over the Avyssos Gorge – a rift made by the 1633 earthquake – to the coastal swamp known as **Límni Kerioú**. If you look carefully at the roots of the aquatic plants, you can see the black bitumen or natural pitch that once welled up in sufficient quantity to caulk thousands of boats; both Herodotus and Pliny described the phenonemon and more recently an exploratory oil bore was sunk, but with negligble results. There are tavernas by the rather mediocre beach. From the sea (there are caique excursions from Kerí Beach) this coast is magnificent, marked by sheer white cliffs, a second Mount Skopós, deep dark-blue waters and two towering natural arches at Marathía.

At the end of the road is the mountain village of **Kerí** – with the cheapest rooms on the island (*for details, contact the tourist office in Laganás, t* 069 505 1270). It offers fine views, especially those at the white lighthouse 2km from the village. From the main road a secondary road winds westward to one of Zákynthos' more remote villages, **Agalás**, passing by way of the two-storey grotto called **Spiliá Damianoú**, where one formation resembles a horse. The legend goes that a giant named Andronia once lived in the area and continually pestered the good people of Agalás for food. His appetite was huge, and the people were at their wits' end when an old lady slipped him a poisoned pie. Down he fell at a place called Andronia, where you can see twelve 15th-century wells with their old well-heads. The giant's horse was so shocked it turned to stone.

# Heading Northwest

From Zákynthos Town the coastal road leads north, past the **Kryonéri Fountain**, built by the Venetians to water their ships; Greeks know the red rock overhead, which featured as a suicide leap in a popular novel, *Kókkinos Vráchos*. Beyond, the road turns abruptly west to reach a series of pretty sandy beaches, connected by short access roads and backed by orchards and vineyards. Holiday development is taking off with abandon, although it is still calm when compared to the babylonian crud along Laganás Bay: long and narrow **Tsiliví** (ΤΣΙΛΙΒΙ), a packaged paradise; **Plános** (over-looking **Tragáki Beach**); little **Ámpoula** with golden sand; **Pachiámmos**; **Drossiá**; **Psaroú**; **Ammoúdi**; and **Alikanás**, where a wonderful long stretch of sand sweeps around the bay west to **Alikés** (ΑΛΥΚΕΣ), named after the nearby salt pans, an area popular with windsurfers.

The rich agricultural interior is pleasant to explore, if directions can be a bit confusing. **Skoulikádo** rewards visitors with several handsome churches, among them the **Panagía Anafonítria**, with stone reliefs and a lovely interior, and **Ag. Nikólaos Megalomáti**, named after a 16th-century icon painted on stone of St Nicholas, with unusually large eyes. **Ag. Marína**, a rare survivor of the earthquake, has a cell behind the altar where the insane would be chained in hope of a cure from the saint. Inland from Alikés, **Katastári** is the island's second-largest town, marking the northern edge of the plain; from here the main road divides, one branch spiralling into the mountains, while a newer offshoot follows the sea all the way to Korithí. In its early stages, this coastline is a sequence of beautiful pebbled beaches, such as **Makri Aloú** and

# Where to Stay and Eat

### Tsiliví – Ag. Nikólaos ✉ 29100

To stay in Tsiliví or Alikanás, it's probably easiest to arrange it through a tour operator as package holiday firms dominate this coast. A plethora of throbbing bars/clubs around here will see you through the night and into the early hours.

**Caravel** at Plános, t 069 504 5261, f 069 504 5548 (*A; exp*). Sister to the one in Athens; it will most certainly lighten your wallet, but it does have all the glorious trimmings. *Open April–Oct.*

**Contessina**, t 069 502 2508, f 069 502 3741 (*C; mod*). This pleasant hotel might be able to squeeze you in if everything else is full in high season.

**Plessa**, t 069 502 2648 (*mod–inexp*). Decent en suite rooms.

**Olive Tree**, in Tsiliví. The first taverna in town and still going strong. It's one of the few places amongst the many catering for the package tourist hordes that's still playing traditional Greek music rather than English top-ten hits.

**Koukos**, just behind Popeye's. Another traditional taverna.

**Louis Plagos Beach**, at Ámpoula Beach, t 069 506 2800, f 069 506 2900 (*A; lux*). Big white hotel and bungalow complex, a stone's throw from the sea, with a swimming pool, tennis court and babysitting service on offer for guests.

**Camping Zante**, on Ámpoula Beach, t 069 506 1710. A basic campsite but kitted out with all the necessary facilities.

**Montreal**, in Alikés, t 069 508 3241, f 069 508 3342 (*C; exp*). One of many hotels here, just set back from the sea.

**Mantolina**, in Alikanás. Friendly family-run taverna offering appetizing traditional Greek food.

**Catacombs**, in Alikanás. Quiet, atmospheric post-prandial bar.

**Taverna Xikia**, on the coast road, not far from Koroni, t 069 503 1165. Worth a detour from the main road. Serving tasty Greek favourites in an idyllic clifftop setting, with great views.

**Peligoni Club**, further north, t 069 503 1511 or in the UK, t (01243) 511 499, *www.peligoni .com* (*exp*). Well away from the block-booked beach resorts; English-owned surf and sailing holiday haven set into the rugged volcanic coastline. Accommodation is in a sprinkling of villas, most with lovely swimming pools, within driving distance of the friendly clubhouse. The club caters just as well for watersports beginners and experts as it does for lazybones landlubbers with vast appetites and a talent for Scrabble. The club also runs very popular painting holidays and 'restoration' breaks for those in need of total stress-free relaxation and pampering.

**Camping Skinari**, not far from the Peligoni Club, t 069 503 1061. It's possible for some or all of your party to stay at this well-maintained campsite and, for a fee, to use the Peligoni Club's many facilities.

**Nobelos**, in Ag. Nikólaos, t 069 503 1400, f 069 503 1131 (*lux*). 5 sumptuous suites with every conceivable facility in a beautiful stonework villa, with paved courtyards, abundant flowers and an inviting sun platform by the sea. Book – and save up – well in advance for such a treat.

**Pension Panorama**, in Ag. Nikólaos, t 069 503 1013, f 069 503 1017 (*mod–inexp*). Pristine and, again, for a fee you can use the Peligoni Club's facilities on a more ad hoc basis. *Open May–Oct.*

**Astoria**, at Ag. Nikólaos. Serves good fish and overlooks the beautifully appointed harbour.

**Makrí Giálos**, becoming more dramatic, volcanic and inaccessible as it wends north-wards. The port of **Ag. Nikoláos**, where the little ferry from Kefaloniá calls, nestles in a bay with beautiful views of its eponymous islet; sadly, the uninspiring architecture doesn't live up to the natural setting. (*Note that buses are scant and, unless you find one waiting, taxis called in from afar can be pricey.*) The white coast around here is pocked with caves, cliffs, natural columns and arches, and most spectacularly of all, one hour by boat from Skinári, **Kianoún Cave**, the local version of Capri's Blue Grotto, glowing with every imaginable shade of blue; the light is best in the morning. Excursion boats from Ag. Nikólaos also run around the northern tip of the island and south to **Xinthia Cave**, with sulphur springs, evidence of the island's volcanic origins – with rocks and sand so hot that you need swimming shoes to protect your toes – and to the cave of **Sklávou**.

# Up the Southwest Coast

Unlike the low rolling hills and plain of the east, the west coast of Zákynthos plunges steeply and abruptly into the sea, some 1,000ft in places, and is a favourite place for caique excursions either from Zákynthos Town or Alikés. Taking the pretty road from Zákynthos Town, **Macherádo** is the last stop on the plain, where the church of **Ag. Mávra** has a very ornate interior, with a beautiful old icon of the saint covered with ex-votos and scenes in silver of her life and martyrdom; the Venetian church bells are famous for their clear musical tones. The 16th-century church of the Ipapánti has a handsome reconstructed campanile. Macherádo is also famous for wine; its Domaine Agria is the oldest winery in Greece, run by the Comoutós family since 1638 (*visits and tastings by appointment, t 069 509 2284*). The Comoutóses made their fortune in raisins and currants, and were ennobled in the Libro d'Oro; today their estate is divided between olive groves and vines that yield excellent reds, rosés, whites, and old-fashioned dessert wines. In nearby **Lagopóda** there is more wine, and the pretty crenellated Eleftherías Convent, where you can witness the nuns creating their fine needlework.

From Macherádo the road rises to **Koiloménos**, with a handsome stone belltower from 1893, attached to the church of Ag. Nikólaos and mysteriously carved with Masonic symbols; its original pyramidal crown broke off, giving it a stumpy look. A secondary road from here leads to the wild coast and the **Karakonísi**, a bizarre islet just offshore that resembles a whale, and even spouts great plumes of spray when the wind is up. At Ag. Léon (with another striking bell tower, this time converted from a windmill) there's another turn-off to the coast, to the dramatic narrow creek and minute sandy beach at **Limnióna**. Just before Exo Chóra, another road descends to **Kámbi**, where Mycenaean rock-cut tombs were found and two tavernas perched on the 650ft cliffs are spectacular sunset viewing platforms, although in summer you'll have to share them with coach parties from Laganás.

The main road continues to Anafonítria, where the 15th-century **Monastery of the Panagía Anafonítria** survived several earthquakes intact along with its time-darkened frescoes and cell of St Diónysos – he was abbot here and one of his claims to saint-hood was that he gave sanctuary to his brother's killer. Below is **Porto Vrómi**, 'Dirty Port' because of the natural tar that blankets the shore, although the water is perfectly clear. Around the corner is a perfect white sandy beach, wedged under sheer white limestone crags set in completely clear azure water – the setting for Zákynthos' notorious '**shipwreck**'. The scene that graces a thousand Greek postcards is a prime destination for excursion boats; although some tour guides let the punters fantasize that the wreck has been there for decades, the boat really belonged to cigarette smugglers in the late 1980s who ran the ship aground and escaped when they were about to be nabbed by the Greek coastguard. When word reached the inhabitants of the small villages above, immediate action was taken, and by the time the coastguard got back to the ship it was empty; the free smokes lasted for years. You can look down at 'shipwreck' beach from the path near the abandoned 16th-century Monastery of **Ag. Geórgios sta Kremná**. The path, ever more overgrown, leads to the narrow cave-chapel of **Ag. Gerásimou**.

The road passes through an increasingly dry landscape en route to **Volímes** (ΒΟΛΙΜΕΣ), the largest village on the west coast, permanently festive, with billowing, brightly coloured handwoven goods displayed for sale. Seek out the fine church of Ag. Paraskeví and the 15th-century Ag. Theodósios, with its stone carved iconostasis. On the village's main road, Diónysos' taverna is the place for top-notch spit-roast lamb and other excellencies. **Áno Volímes**, just above its sister town, is a pretty little mountain village.

# The Strofádes

A couple of times a week caiques from Laganás sail the 37 nautical miles south of Zákynthos to the Strofádes (there are two islets, **Charpína** and **Stamvránio**), passing over the deepest point in the entire Mediterranean Sea, where you would have to dive 1,449ft down to reach Davy Jones' locker. Strofádes means 'turning' in Greek: according to ancient myth, the Harpies, those composite female monsters with human heads, hands and feet, winged griffon bodies and bear ears, were playing their usual role as the hired guns of the gods, chasing the prophet Phineas over the little islets, when Zeus changed his mind and ordered them to turn around immediately and come back.

Although little more than flat green pancakes in the sea, the Strofádes offered just the right kind of rigorous isolation Orthodox monks and mystics crave, and accordingly in the 13th century Irene, wife of the Byzantine emperor John Láskaris, founded the **Pantochará** ('All Joy') Monastery on Charpína. Pirates soon proved to be a problem, and in 1440, just before Constantinople itself fell to the Turks, Emperor John Palaeológos sent funds to build high walls around it. As on Mount Áthos, no women or female animals were allowed, and the 40 monks who resided there (among them the future saint Diónysos) spent their days studying rare books. In 1530, however, the Saracens managed to breach the high walls, slew all the monks and plundered the monastery; in 1717 the body of Ag. Diónysos was removed to Zákynthos Town for safe keeping. The evocative, desolate citadel is now owned by the Monstery of Ag. Diónysos, and remains in a fine state of preservation, complete with a new pink tile roof, although the population has been reduced to migratory turtle doves and quails. If you have your own boat and provisions and have been looking for an out-of-the-way romantic destination, this may be it.

# The Northeastern Aegean Islands

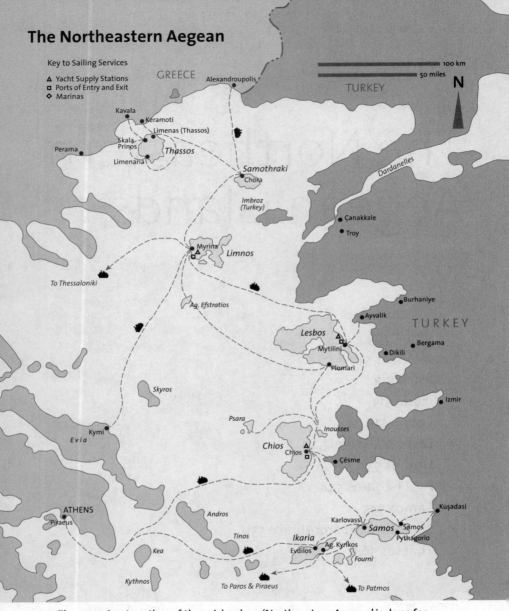

# The Northeastern Aegean

**Key to Sailing Services**
△ Yacht Supply Stations
□ Ports of Entry and Exit
◇ Marinas

GREECE
TURKEY

100 km
50 miles

N

Alexandroupolis

Kavala
Keramoti
Limenas (Thassos)
Skala Prinos
Perama
Limenaria
*Thassos*

*Samothraki*
Chora

*Imbroz (Turkey)*

Dardanelles

Çanakkale
Troy

Myrina
*Limnos*

To Thessaloniki

*Ag. Efstratios*

Burhaniye
Ayvalik
*Lesbos*
Mytilini
Dikili
Bergama
Plomari

TURKEY

*Skyros*

Izmir

*Psara*
Inousses
*Chios*
Chios
Çesme

ATHENS
Piraeus

*Evia*
Kymi

*Andros*

Karlovassi
*Samos*
Samos
Kuşadasi
Pythagorio

*Tinos*
*Ikaria*
Ag. Kyrikos
Evdilos
Fourni

*Kea*

*Kythnos*
To Paros & Piraeus
To Patmos

The grouping together of these islands as 'Northeastern Aegean' is done for convenience rather than for any higher cultural or historical consideration. What they have in common, besides their location off the coast of Turkey and Northern Greece, is a rugged individualism and strong character – although green and forested, the islands are rarely cat-calendar cute, and many of their big towns and main ports are frankly unattractive, at least at first glance from the ferry. However, just beyond the bustle and razzmatazz are deep, still villages and landscapes out of time, places to linger, to just be. With the exceptions of Sámos, with two decades of package-tour experience under its belt, and Thássos, long a favourite destination with its pine forests and ring of beaches, the Northeastern Aegean islands are the last frontier in Greek island tourism.

Most of these islands were colonized during the Dorian invasion in the 12th century BC, when the invaders forced the Ionians of mainland Greece to seek new homes in the east. The Ionians occupied the coastal regions of Asia Minor and the islands, and, between the 7th and 6th centuries BC, seeded much of what we call Western civilization: the islands alone produced talents like Pythagoras, Sappho and probably Homer himself. Their cities were among the most important in Greece in trade, in the production of wine and olive oil, and in religion. Samothrace is practically synonymous with its sanctuary of the gods of the underworld; Límnos was dedicated to the smithy god Hephaistos, and on Sámos the Temple of the goddess Hera was one of the wonders of the Ancient World. These prosperous and independent islands slipped into obscurity as they fell prey to the greater powers around them, first the Persians from Asia Minor and then the Athenians from the West, and then from Asia Minor again in the form of the Ottoman Empire. They were annexed to Greece only in 1912, following the Balkan Wars.

# Chíos (XIOΣ)

*Soak me with jars of Chian wine and say 'Enjoy yourself, Hedylus.' I hate living emptily, not drunk with wine.*

Hedylus, c. 280 BC

Chíos is a fascinating and wealthy island celebrated for its shipowners, friendly good humour and the gum mastic that grows here and nowhere else in the world. It offers the most varied geography of any Aegean island: lush fertile plains, thick pine forests, mainly unspoiled beaches, Mediterranean scrublands tufted with maquis and

## Mythology

Chíos was favoured by Poseidon, and is said to owe its name to the heavy snowfall (*chioni*) that fell when the sea god was born. Vine-growing was introduced to the island by Oenopion, son of Ariadne and Theseus. Oenopion pledged his daughter Merope in marriage to the handsome giant Orion, on the condition that he rid Chíos of its ferocious beasts, a task he easily performed – it was his boast that given time he could rid the entire earth of its monsters. Rather than give Orion his reward, however, Oenopion kept putting him off (for he loved his daughter himself), and finally Orion took the matter into his own hands and raped Merope. For this the king poked out his eyes. Orion then set out blindly, but the goddess of dawn, Eos, fell in love with him and persuaded Helios the sun god to restore his sight. Before he could avenge himself on Oenopion, however, Orion was killed when Mother Earth, angry at his boasting, sent a giant scorpion after him. Orion fled the scorpion, but his friend Artemis, the goddess of the hunt, killed him by mistake. In mourning, she immortalized him in the stars.

# Chíos

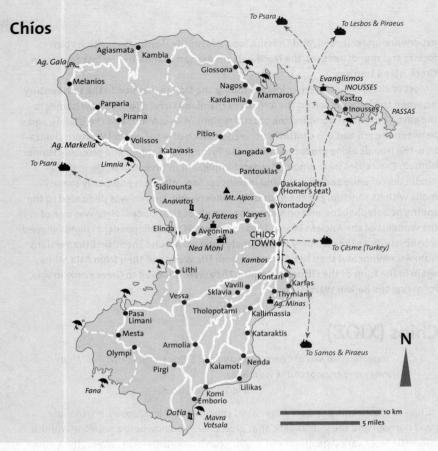

startlingly barren mountains that bring to mind the 'craggy Chíos' of Homer, who may have been born on the island. Its architecture is unique and varied, and its church of Néa Moní has some of the finest 11th-century Byzantine mosaics anywhere. Tourism, with charters and package companies, is fairly new to Chíos, and most of the islanders are still at the stage where they want visitors to share their deep love for the island rather than just take their money.

## History

Inhabited from approximately 3000 BC, Chíos was colonized by the mysterious seafaring Pelasgians who left walls near Exo Dídyma and Kouroúnia and a Temple of Zeus on top of Mount Pelinaío. The Mycenaeans followed, and were in turn usurped by the Ionians, from Athens according to one tradition, who had the longest-lasting influence on the island; one tradition asserts that Homer himself was born here in the 9th or 8th century BC. By then Chíos was a thriving, independent kingdom, founding trade counters or *emporia*, notably Voroniki in Egypt. It was famed for its mastic and wine (especially from the medicinal *arioúsios* grapes), and for its sculpture workshop and system of government, studied by Solon and adapted for use in his

Athenian reforms. Around 490, a Chiot sculptor Glaucus invented the art of soldering metals; on the minus side, Chíos was the first state in Greece to engage in slave-trading. One of the twelve cities of Archaic Ionic Confederacy, Chíos joined Athens in the Battle of Lade (494 BC) in an unsuccessful attempt to overthrow the Persian yoke, but after the Battle of Plateía, it regained its independence, and held on to it even after Athens made its other allies into tribute-paying dependencies, until 412 when it revolted, only to be crushed.

Chíos allied itself with Rome and fought the enemy of the Empire, Mithridates of Pontus (83 BC), only to be defeated and destroyed, although it was liberated after two

## Getting There and Around

The Northeastern Aegean islands were the last to be 'discovered', partly due to their great distance from Athens – Ikaría, the least far, is a 10hr journey by ship. Almost all the islands, however, now have airports, although anyone planning to fly there during the summer should reserve a seat as much as 2 months in advance. Connections between the islands have improved of late, particularly hydrofoil services.

### By Air

Olympic has 4 flights a day from Athens, 2 a week to/from Lésbos and Thessaloníki. **Olympic** at the airport: t 027 102 4515, in Chíos Town at 50 Leof. Aegeou, t 027 104 4727. The 4km journey between Chíos Town and the runway can be made by taxi (under €12) or the blue Kondári–Kaifas bus (around 10 a day).

### By Sea

Daily **ferry** connections with Piraeus, Lésbos and Inoússes; daily in summer to Çegme (Turkey), less frequently out of season; 3 times a week with Límnos and Psará; at least twice a week with Thessaloníki and Kavála; once a week with Ikaría, Kos, Rhodes, Mýkonos and Sýros; in summer one-day excursions to Psará and Inoússes (contact **Miniotis Lines**, 21 Neorion St, t 027 102 4671). Travel Agents also offer organized tours to Turkey. **Port authority**: Chíos Town, t 027 104 4433.

### By Road

**Blue buses** (t 027 102 2079) serve Chíos Town, making 5–6 trips daily to the Kámbos area, Karfás Beach, and Vrontádos. Green buses depart from next to the Homerium Cultural Centre near Plateía Vounáki (t 027 102

4257) 6–8 times daily to Pirgí, Mestá, Kalamotí, Katavakris and Nenita; 4 times to Kómi, Emborió, Kardámila, Lagáda and Ag. Fotía. **Taxi**: t 027 104 1111. **Car**, rather than bike, rental is more appropriate for getting around big Chíos; try **Avis**, at the airport, t 027 106 3080, or in town, at the Travel Shop, 56 Leof. Aegeou, t 027 104 1031, *travelshop@otenet.gr*. For **mopeds** and **motorbikes**, try **Mr Psaras** at 9 Omirou (by the Olympic office), t/f 027 102 5113, who offers reasonable daily rates (€12) and 7 days for the price of 6.

## Tourist Information

**Tourist Office**: 11 Kanári St, Chíos Town, t 027 104 4389, f 027 104 4343; *open Mon–Fri 7am–2.30pm and 7–10pm, Sat 10–1 and Sun 7am–10am; Nov–Mar Mon–Fri 7–2.30.*
**Tourist police**: at the far end of the quay, next to the regular police, t 027 104 4427.
**Post Office**: at the corner of Omirou and Rodokanáki. Offers a fax service.
**Hatzelenis Tourist Agency**, by the ferry dock, t 027 102 6743, *mano2@otenet.gr*. Helpful for accommodation, tickets and ferry info.

## Festivals

**Easter**: in Pirgí, featuring the slaughter of the lambs, if you have the stomach for it.
**22 July**: Chíos' most important *panegýri*, Ag. Markélla, takes place at Ag. Markélla Monastery, and in Volissos and Karyés.
**26 July**: Kástello.
**27 July**: Kalamotí.
**12 Aug**: Kallimasía.
**15 Aug**: Pirgí, Nénita, Kámbos and Ag. Geórgios.

years when Mithridates was defeated by Sulla. In the 4th century AD Chíos made the mistake of siding against Constantine the Great, who conquered the island and carried off to his new city of Constantinople many of Chíos' famous ancient sculptures, including the four bronze horses that eventually ended up on the front of St Mark's in Venice. In 1261 the Emperor Michael Paleológos gave Chíos to the Giustiniani, the Genoese family who helped him reconquer Constantinople from Venice and her Frankish allies. In 1344, the Giustiniani chartered a company called the Maona (from the Arabic *Maounach*, or trading company) of 12 merchants and shipowners, who governed until 1566 when Chíos was lost to the Turks.

The Sultans loved Chíos, especially its sweet mastic, and they granted it more privileges than any other Greek island, including a degree of autonomy. It became famous for its doctors and chess players; and elsewhere in Greece, the cheerfulness of the Chiots was equated with foolishness. This came to an abrupt end in 1822. Although the islanders had refused to join in the revolt, a band of 2,000 ill-armed Samians disembarked on Chíos, proclaimed independence and forced them to join the struggle. The Sultan, furious at this subversion of his favoured island, ordered his admiral Kara Ali to make an example of Chíos that the Greeks would never forget. This led to one of the worst massacres in history. In two weeks an estimated 30,000 Greeks were slaughtered, and another 45,000 taken into slavery; the Sultan's sweet tooth dictated that only the mastic villages survived. All who could fled to other islands, especially to Sýros (where they picked up useful lessons about owning ships), before moving to England, France and Egypt. News of the massacre deeply moved the rest of Europe; Delacroix painted his stirring canvas of the tragedy (now in the Louvre) and Victor Hugo sent off reams of rhetoric. On 6 June of the same year, the Greek Admiral Kanáris took revenge on Kara Ali by blowing him and 2,000 men up with his flagship. In 1840 Chíos attained a certain amount of autonomy under a Christian governor, but in 1881 suffered another tragedy in an earthquake that killed nearly 4,000 people. It was incorporated into Greece in 1912.

# Chíos Town (Chóra)

First-time visitors to Chíos arriving by ferry wonder what they've let themselves in for. The long harbour-front of Chíos Town (pop. 25,000) doesn't even try to look like a Greek island, with tall buildings holding half a dozen American pool halls, and a score of brightly lit bars and tavernas; throngs saunter and dawdle, and on summer evenings every single table is full. Badly hit by an earthquake in 1881, the town that arose from the rubble is slick and glossy, full of new apartment blocks and high-rise offices, and perhaps more fast-food joints run by Greek Americans than strictly necessary. Yet after the first surprise, the town – a sister city of Genoa, for old times' sake – is a very likeable place well worth a few hours' poking about.

Most of what survives from the Turkish occupation is enclosed within the Byzantine **fortress**, which more or less follows the lines of the Macedonian castle destroyed by Mithridates. After 1599 only Turks and Jews were allowed to live inside; the Greeks had to be outside the main gate or **Porta Maggiore** when it closed at sundown. Within the walls is a ruined **mosque** and a Turkish cemetery with the **tomb of Kara Ali**, 'Black Ali', author of the massacre of Chíos. The tomb's surprisingly unvandalized state is perhaps a testimony to the tolerant, easygoing nature of the Chiots, remarked on since antiquity. In a closet-sized **prison** by the gate, Bishop Pláto Fragiádis and 75 leading Chiots were incarcerated as hostages before they were hanged by the Turks in 1822. The **Kastro Justinian Museum**, nearby in Plateía Frouríou (*t 027 102 2819; open Tues–Sun 9–3; adm*), contains detached frescoes, carvings and early Christian mosaics.

The main square, **Plateía Vounakíou** (or **Plastíra**), with its cafés and plane trees, is a few minutes' walk away. It has a statue of Bishop Pláto Fragiádis, and in the municipal gardens behind the square is another of Kara Ali's avenging angel, 'Incendiary' Kanáris, a native of Psará. Plateía Vounakíou's crumbling mosque is marked with the *Tugra*, the swirling 'thumbprint of the Sultan' that denotes royal possession. *Tugras*, though common in Istanbul, are rarely seen elsewhere, even in Turkey, and this one is a mark of the special favour that Chíos enjoyed. Today the mosque houses the **Byzantine Museum** (*t 027 102 6866; open Tues–Sun 10–1, Sun 10–3; adm*), with a collection of art, tombstones and other old odds and ends too big to fit anywhere else.

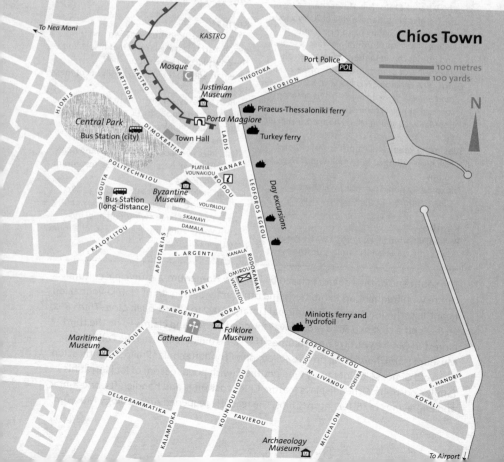

# Where to Stay

## Chíos Town ✉ 82100

**Chíos Chandris**, E. Chandrí, t 027 104 4401, f 027 102 5768, *www.chandris.gr (B; exp)*. The large harbourfront landmark where shipowners hobnob, in the light and airy downstairs with marble floors, and newly renovated (in 2000) comfortable rooms upstairs; many overlooking the port. *Open all year*.

**Diana**, 92 Venizélou, t 027 104 4180, f 027 102 6748 *(C; mod)*. Modern and utilitarian, but well-kept and friendly. Rooms at the back are much quieter and the bathrooms are better than most. *Open all year*.

**Kyma**, opposite the Chandris, t 027 104 4500, f 027 104 4600, *kyma@chi.forthnet.gr (C; mod)*. Convivial hotel owned by friendly Theodore Spordilis, who knows all there is to know about Chíos. The atmospheric core of the hotel is an Italianate villa built by a local shipowner; the lobby has a fine painted ceiling. A luscious buffet breakfast is served, and guests can help themselves to an all-day supply of orange juice and coffee.

**Fedra**, 13 M. Livanoú, t/f 027 104 1128 *(A; mod–inexp)*. Stylish place with handsome (if somewhat noisy) rooms, however no views; popular with young island hoppers. *Open all year*.

**Alexios**, 34 Rodokanaki, t 027 102 1113 *(inexp)*. Has high-ceilinged but small-windowed rooms.

**Filoxenia**, Roidou, t 027 102 2813 *(D; inexp)*. Clean, simple and cheap. *Open all year*.

## Kámbos

**Perleas**, Vitiadou St, t 027 103 2217, f 027 103 2364 *(A; exp)*. Friendly family guesthouse in a restored mansion with 5 rooms, set in citrus fruit groves, where the produce ends up on the table for breakfast marmalades. Serene, civilized atmosphere for those who really want to unwind.

**Villa La Favorita**, t/f 027 103 2265 *(A; exp–mod)*. Similar to Perleas. Charming Genoese villa with 13 beautifully furnished rooms with air-con, minibars and a waterwheel in the courtyard. *Open May–Oct*.

**Perivoli**, 11 Argénti, t 027 103 1513/1973, f 027 103 2042 *(A; mod)*. Quiet and serene traditional pension with 9 rooms and a good, popular restaurant, with music and dancing on Friday nights. *Open all year*.

**Villa Clio**, t 027 104 3755, f 027 102 9761 *(B; mod)*. Another renovated traditional place with studios, surrounded by banana and palm trees.

For something cheaper, ask the **Chíos Tourist Office**, t 027 104 4389, about rooms.

## Karfás

Near to the airport, Chíos Town and the beach, Karfás is the island's chief resort and the only place to have succumbed, unashamedly, to the dubious delights of mass tourism.

**Golden Odyssey**, on the road to Karfás, t 027 104 1500, f 027 104 1715 *(B; exp)*. Korean-run, but wouldn't look out of place in the USA; rooms have air-con, satellite TV and balconies overlooking the swimming pools, and there's an excellent Chinese restaurant. *Open April–Sept*.

**Golden Sand**, on the beach, t 027 103 2080, f 027 103 1700, *goldsand@compulink.gr (A; exp)*. Boasts a large swimming pool in a complex overlooking the sea; ask for a room with sea-view.

The south end of the square is closed by the new **Homerium**, a municipal cultural centre with frequent art exhibitions and other activities. South of Plateía Vounakíou near the cathedral, the **Koraï Municipal Library** (*t 027 104 4246; open Mon–Thurs 8–2, Fri 8–2 and 5–7.30 and Sat 8–noon*) was founded in 1792 and claims to be the third largest in Greece with 135,000 volumes; the same building houses the **Folklore Museum** (*same hours*), the private collection of London scholar Philip Argéntis, scion of an old Genoese-Chiot family who got tired (with good reason) of looking at his family's portraits. Other displays feature Chiot costumes and handicrafts, bric-à-brac, and engravings of 18th-century Chíos. The recently reopened **Archaeology Museum**,

Benovias, uphill from the beach, t 027 103 1457 (*mod*). With 8 one- or two-bedroom apartments available.

Markos' Place, t 027 103 1990, *www.marcosplace.gr* (*inexp*). For an altogether atmospheric and restful stay in an ex-monastery just south; essential to book. *Open May–Oct.*

## Eating Out

Besides mastic to masticate, Chíos has 2 specialities: Greek blue cheese, *kopanistí*; and a unique brown, wrinkly, nutty olive called *chourmádes*, the Greek word for dates. Chíos Town's lack of superficial charm means that, despite a smattering of fast-food yuck on the waterfront, it hasn't been overrun by below-par, overpriced eateries.

Aeriko, just uphill from the beach out in Karfás. Café in a pleasant spot.

Dolphins, in the middle of Prokyméa. A good Greek lunch guaranteed.

Hotzas, Chíos' oldest taverna, at 3 G. Kondíli St, a 15min walk from the harbour front, t 027 104 2787. It's advisable to ask for directions before heading out. The food's excellent, from the *mezédes* to aubergine simmered with tomatoes, delicious whitebait, and other standard Greek dishes, topped off with good barrelled *retsina*, a rare find on any island. *Open eves only.*

Karatza on Karfás Street, t 027 103 1221. Has a terrace where you can look over to Turkey while feasting on grilled or ready-prepared food.

Nox (Nautical Club of Chíos), on the southernmost quay, beyond hotels Chandris and Kyma. Well liked by locals for its simple oven dishes, grilled meats and fish.

Tassos Taverna, 20 yards further on from Nox. Tables set in a large, shady garden (but alas no sea-views); good for long, lazy lunches away from the frenetic portside strip.

Theodosiou, 33 Neorion, at the north end of the port. This is the best of the many waterfront restaurants, relying on really good food rather than designer décor for its very loyal clientèle.

Two Brothers, just in from the waterfront at 38 Livanoú St, t 027 102 1313. Ordinary-looking venue, but the surprise is the charming back garden and good, cheap food.

Votsalakia, at Kontári, t 027 104 1181. Serves some of the best food on Chíos.

## Entertainment and Nightlife

Loafing around the waterfront after the obligatory *vólta* takes up most evenings in Chíos Town.

Kavos, Remezzo and La Loca. Currently the bars to see and be seen in.

Kronos, 2 E. Argénti Street. Scoops out the best ice cream till the small hours.

Nifada, at Prokyméa. Serves a variety of tasty croissants for late night munchies.

Graffiti, on Enóseos Ave. For a drink and lively disco.

En Plo Rock Club, on Prokyméa.

B52 and Xandres, out at Kontári.

Club Base (Jungle), on the road to the airport. For serious groovers.

Stasis Bar, in Karfás. Another popular drinking haunt.

The Waterfront Alley, 120 Aegeou. If you wish to bowl the night away.

Cine Kipos, in central park. Alternatively check out this upmarket summer cinema.

5 Michálon Street, near the Chandris Hotel (*t 027 104 4139; open 8.45–3, Sun 9.30–2.30, closed Tues; adm*), contains typical island finds, some bearing the ancient Chíos symbol, the sphinx (the same as Thebes); there's also a letter from Alexander the Great addressed to the Chiots. The **Maritime Museum**, 20 Stefanou Tsouri (*open Mon–Sat 10–1*), is a shipping fanatic's fantasy, housed in the Patéras family pile.

## Kámbos: Genoese Gentility

The Genoese especially favoured the fertile, well-watered plain south of town they called the Campo, or **Kámbos**, where from the 14th-century they and the local Chiot aristocracy built villas and plantations of citrus fruit, mastic trees and mulberries for silk, an important source of income until the 19th century. Kámbos is an enchanting and evocative mesh of narrow lanes, full of secret gardens enclosed by tall stone walls, with gates bearing long forgotten coats-of-arms or the tell-tale stripes of the Genoese nobility. Outside the walls the flowering meadows, wooden bridges and ancient trees create a scene of elegaic serenity unique on the Greek islands, especially in the golden light at the end of day. Mastodon bones were found at **Thymianá**, which was the source of Kámbos' golden building stone and is now home to a women's co-operative producing rugs, towels and other woven goods. **Sklaviá**, named after the Greek slaves of the Genoese, is especially lush. Towards the modern village of **Vavíli**, the octagonal domed church **Panagía Krína** (1287) contains some fine frescoes by the Cretan school.

The nearest beach to Chíos Town and Kámbos is at **Karfás**, reached by frequent blue buses, and so far the only major concession to mass tourism on Chíos. The sand may be 'as soft as flour' but there's less of it to go around all the time as more and more new hotels and flats sprout up like *kudzu*; for a lower-key beach, continue south to **Kómi** (*see* below) beyond **Moni Ag. Minás** (*closed afternoons until 6*). During the massacre in 1822, women and children from the surrounding villages took refuge there; a small, hopeless battle took place before Ag. Minás was overrun and all 3,000 were slain, their bodies thrown down the well. Their bones are now in an ossuary; blood still stains the church floor.

# The Mastikochória: Mastic Villages of the South

Southwest of green Kámbos stretch the drier hills and vales of mastic land, where it often seems that time stands still. It must have special magic or secret virtue, for the bushy little mastic trees (*pistacia lentiscus*, a relative of the pistachio) refuse to be transplanted anywhere else in the world – even northern Chíos won't do; the bushes might grow, but not a drop of mastic will they yield. The bark is 'needled' three times a year between July and September, allowing the sweet sap to ooze from the fine wounds, glistening like liquid diamonds in the sun. Some 300 tons of gum mastic are produced annually, although since the advent of synthetics, the mastic market just isn't what it used to be. Considered a panacea in antiquity, good for everything from snake bite and rabies in mules to bladder ailments, mastic puts the chew in gum and the jelly in the beans that kept the bored inmates delicately chomping in the Turkish harems; Roman women used toothpicks made of the wood to sweeten their breath. In the more mundane West, mastic was used in paint varnish; the Syrians buy it as an ingredient in perfume. On Chíos they use it to flavour a devilishly sweet sticky liqueur, spoon sweets, chewing gum and MasticDent toothpaste, the perfect Chíos souvenir.

Nearly all the 20 villages where mastic is grown, the Mastikochória, date from the Middle Ages, and were carefully spared by the Turks in 1822. The Genoese designed them as tight-knit little labyrinths for defence, the houses sharing a common outer wall with few entrances; if that were breached, the villagers could take refuge in a central keep. Heading south from Chíos Town, the first of the Mastikochória is **Armoliá**, which also makes pottery, although not particularly the kind you'll have room for in your luggage. It is defended by the Byzantine **Kástro tis Oréas** (1440), a castle named after the beautiful châtelaine who seduced men only to have them executed. **Kalamotí**, once one of the most thriving villages, has tall stone houses on its narrow cobbled streets and a pretty Byzantine church, Ag. Paraskeví, and isn't far from the 12th-century church **Panagía Sikelia**. The closest beach to both towns is **Kómi**, a darkish stretch of sand with tavernas and rooms, reachable by bus. If Kómi gets too busy, **Lilikas** is a good pebbled alternative 2km further east.

The largest mastic village, **Pirgí** (ΠΥΡΓΙ) was founded in the 13th century. Uniquely, nearly every house is beautifully decorated with *xistá*, the local word for the *sgrafitto* decoration taught to the locals by the Genoese; walls are first covered with mortar

# Where to Stay and Eat

## The Mastic Villages ✉ 82102

Accommodation in the Mastic villages is quite sparse, but it's definitely worth the effort of trying to find a room for the unique atmosphere.

## Kómi

**Bella Mare**, above the restaurant on the beach, t 027 107 1226 (*mod*). Friendly and family-run; en suite rooms and a free supply of sun loungers and umbrellas. *Open May–Oct.*

**Mika's**, just south of town, t 027 107 1335 (*inexp*). An alternative option for those travelling on a budget. *Open May–Oct.*

**Nostalgia**, t 027 107 0070. Proudly advertises its 'free umprellas'. Fresh fish and lobster on the strand.

After dark, for a taste of the nightlife, everyone heads for a drink at beach bars such as **Kochili** or hip **Onar**, or out to **Blue** for a boogie.

## Pirgí

**Lila Rooms**, on the main road, t 027 107 2291, f 027 107 2107 (*mod–inexp*). Run by the dynamic Lila; en suite rooms with an attractive garden.

**Rita Valas Rooms**, near the main square, t 027 107 2479/2112 (*mod–inexp*). Quiet, clean rooms, with shared kitchen facilities.

**'Balcony'**, in Pirgí. Café/restaurant run by the municipality, housed in a traditional building decorated with *xistá*. Good for meals or just a snack with *ouzo*.

## Emborió

**Themis Studios**, just above the portlet, t 027 107 1810 (*inexp*).

**Vassiliki**, set back from the harbour, t 027 107 1422 (*inexp*). Decent apartments.

**Volcano**, t 027 107 1136. Highly recommended; not only does it serve delicious food but there's a shady terrace and interior dining room decorated with a wedding chest, photos, plates. It also has the prettiest loos in Greece.

## Mestá

**Lambriní**, t 027 10 7 6226 (*mod–inexp*); **Popi**, t 027 107 6262 (*mod–inexp*) and **Déspina Almiroúdi**, t 027 107 6388 (*mod–inexp*): all of these have rooms to rent within the fortress itself.

**Olga Merié**, in Liménas, t 027 107 6220 (*mod–inexp*).

**Messeonas**, in the square, t 027 107 6050. Sees more than its share of tourists, but the food is reliably good with some unusual dishes, especially out of high season.

**Pefkákia**, at the entrance to Mestá. This is the epitome of the family-run Greek taverna, set among whitewashed pine trees, with painted gourds hanging overhead. Fresh seafood and homemade Chiot cooking dominate the menu.

## Líthi

**Kira Despina Murina**, on the beach, t 027 107 3373 (*inexp*). Handful of rooms and great fish; fish soup and big breakfasts.

**Medusa Rooms**, t 027 107 3289, t 027 102 3634 (*inexp*). Traditionally furnished.

containing black sand from Emborió, then coated with white plaster, which the artist scrapes off into geometric, floral or animal-based designs; the main square is particularly lavish. Of the equally pretty churches, the 12th-century **Ag. Apóstoli**, a miniature version of Néa Moní, has frescoes from 1655 (*open most mornings*).

One of Chíos' 12 ancient cities was Levkonion, a rival of Troy that was later mentioned by Thucydides. Near the old mastic-exporting port of **Emborió** (ΕΜΠΟΡ-ΕΙΟΣ), 5km from Pirgí, archaeologists discovered a settlement that may well fit the bill, dating from 3000 BC. East of the port, under the chapel of Profítis Ilías are ruins of the 7th–4th century BC **Temple of Athena Polias** and the *enceinte* of an ancient *acropolis*. The wealth of amphorae found underwater here hint at the extent of Chíos' wine trade (Aristophanes wrote that the ancient Chiots tippled with the best of them; these days most of their grapes go into *ouzo* or a raisin wine not unlike Tuscan *vinsanto*). **Mávra Vótsala** Beach, five minutes from Emborió, is made up of black volcanic pebbles, but the effect is somewhat spoiled by the DEH's new power lines; around the headland is a second, better black beach which seems to have five or six names, but is confusingly best known as Mávra Vótsala too. Some way from the shore are the ruins of a 6th-century **Christian basilica** with a marble cross-shaped font and a few mosaics.

The last two mastic villages have impressive defences: **Olýmpi** (ΟΛΥΜΠΟΙ) built around a 68ft tower, with originally only one gate and **Mestá** (ΜΕΣΤΑ), the ultimate fortress or *kástro* village, with no ground floor windows facing out and only one entrance into its maze of lanes and flower-filled yards, now much beloved of film crews; at other times you can almost hear the silence. Two churches are worth a look: the medieval **Ag. Paraskeví** and the 18th-century **Mikrós Taxiárchis**, with a beautifully carved iconostasis. The southwest coast is dotted with exquisite wild beaches; **Fana**, to the south, owes its name to the ruins of a fountain recalling the Great Temple of Phaneo Apollo (6th century BC) that stood nearby. Alexander the Great stopped to consult its oracle; several of its Ionic columns are in the Chíos Archaeology Museum. The road north from Mestá to Chíos Town passes Mestá's port of **Liménas** (or **Pasá-Limáni**) and picturesque medieval **Véssa**, deep on the valley floor and worth exploring on foot. From here, another road leads north to **Lithí** (4½km), a pretty village with a so-so sandy beach below, tavernas and a few places to stay. Further up the west coast you can swim at the pebble coves near Elínda and circle back to Chíos Town by way of Avgónima and Néa Moní.

# Inland from Chíos Town: Néa Moní (NEA MONH)

A trip to **Néa Moní** perched high in the pines (*t 027 107 9370; open 8–1 and 4–8; women should wear knee-length skirts*) is the most beautiful excursion on Chíos, and easiest made by taxi if you don't have a car; blue buses only go as far as **Karyés**, a mountain village flowing with fresh springs, but a long 7km walk from the monastery.

Néa Moní was 'new' in 1042, when Emperor Constantine VIII Monomachos ('the single-handed fighter') and his wife Zoë had it built to replace an older monastery, where the monks had found a miraculous icon of the Virgin in a bush; not the least of its miracles was its prophecy that Constantine would return from exile and gain the throne. In gratitude, the emperor sent money, architects and artists from Constantinople. The church has a sumptuous double narthex and a subtle, complex design of pilasters, niches and pendentives that support its great dome atop an octagonal drum. Its richly coloured 11th-century mosaics shimmer in the penumbra: the *Washing of the Feet*, *The Saints of Chíos* and *Judas' Kiss* in the narthex and *The Life of Christ* in the dome, stylistically similar to those at Dáfni in Athens and among the most beautiful examples of Byzantine art anywhere – even though they had to be pieced back together after the earthquake of 1881 brought down the great dome. A chapel has the bones of some of the 5,000 victims (among them, 600 monks) of Kara Ali's massacre who sought sanctuary in the monastery.

From here, a rough road leads to the Monastery of **Ag. Patéras**, honouring the three monks who founded Néa Moní and rebuilt after the earthquake in 1890. Further up, **Avgónima**, a once nearly abandoned village, now has three tavernas and is full of Greek holiday homes. From here, a road zigzags up the granite mountain to the 'Mystrás of Chíos', the striking medieval village and castle of **Anávatos**. It saw horrific scenes in 1822; most of the villagers threw themselves off the 1,000ft cliff rather than wait to be slaughtered, and ever since then the place has been haunted. There are now only a handful of residents.

# Northern Chíos

Northern Chíos is the island's wild side, mountainous, stark and barren, its forests decimated by shipbuilders, and in the 1980s by fires. Many of its villages are nearly deserted outside of the summer. **Vrontádos** (ΒΡΟΝΤΑΔΟΣ), 4½km north of Chíos Town, is an exception, a bedroom-suburb village, where most of the island's shipowners have their homes, overlooking a pebbly beach and ruined windmills. The locals are proudest of the **Daskalópetra** (the Teacher's Stone), a rather uncomfortable rock throne on a natural terrace over the sea where Homer is said to have sung, and where his disciples would gather to learn his poetry, although killjoy archaeologists say it was really part of an ancient altar dedicated to the local version of Cybele. A curious local legend relates that the most famous Genoese of all, Christopher Columbus, stopped by and sat here before going on to America. The headquarters of the International Society of Homeric Studies is located in Vrontádos, and there is also a small **Folklore Museum** (*open daily 5–7pm*); the 19th-century **Monastery of Panagía Myrtidiótissa** nearby houses the robes of the martyred Gregory V, Patriarch of Constantinople.

Near Vrontádos stood Chíos' first church **Ag. Isídoros**, founded in the 3rd century on the spot where the saint was martyred. A later church to house the relics of St Isídoros (whose feast day only happens every four years, on 29 February) was built by Emperor Constantine, but it fell in an earthquake and was replaced by three successive structures, the last ruined by the Turks in 1822; mosaics from the

# Where to Stay and Eat

## Vrontádos ✉ 82100

**Kyveli Apartments** at Daskalópetra, t 027 109 4300, f 027 109 4303, *goldsand@compulink.gr* (*A; exp*). Large, bland apartments with swimming pool; try for an upstairs one for the harbour view. *Open April–Oct.*

**Ag. Markella**, in Vrontádos proper, t 027 109 3763, f 027 109 3765, *ag.Markel@otenet.gr* (*B; mod*). Quirky place with dinky pool.

**Velonas**, just up from the sea, t 027 109 3656, f 027 109 3656 (*inexp*). One of the many places with rooms for rent, with small, clean studios.

**Camping Chíos**, at the stony coved beach of Ag. Isídoros at Sikíada, t 027 107 4111. Chíos' only official, if inconvenient, campsite.

**Omiros**, in Daskalópetra. A good reasonable taverna.

**Pantoukios**, a short drive north in Pantoukias, t 027 107 4262. Outstanding for lobster.

**To Limanaki**, t 027 109 3647. Serves delicious fresh fish.

## Langáda ✉ 82300

Langáda has about a dozen waterside tavernas from which to choose.

**O Passos**. Popular all round for the best Greek food.

**Stellios**, next door, t 027 207 4813. For excellent octopus.

**Timoniera Club**. Will furnish you with the obligatory waterfront drink.

## Kardámila ✉ 82300

**Kardamyla**, t 027 202 3353, t 027 202 3354, *kyma@chi.forthnet.gr* (*B; exp*). A good base for exploring the unspoiled north, on its own shady beach with watersports. Although in a rather unprepossessing 1960s institutional block, the hotel is brought to life by its owner, the ever genial Theodore Spordilis. There is a restaurant and, as at his Hotel Kyma in Chíos Town, an endless free supply of orange juice and coffee. *Open April–Oct.*

## Volissós ✉ 82300

**Ta Petrina** ('The Stone Houses'), just below the Kástro, t 027 402 2128, f 027 402 1013 (*exp*). Beautifully restored houses in traditional Greek style, accommodating 6–8 people in each.

**Latini Apartments**, on the road to Límnos and the beach, t 027 402 1461, f 027 402 1871 (*exp–mod*). Apartments closest to the beach, with a lovely garden and terrace.

**Stella Tsakiri**, t 027 402 1421, f 027 402 1521 (*exp–mod*). English-speaking establishment with stylish, well-equipped renovated houses for rent in the village.

**Taverna Anemi**, near the plateia . Shady, and an adjacent bar with great music.

**Akroyálli**, in Límnos. Taverna with fresh fish dishes.

7th-century version are in the Byzantine Museum in Chíos Town. The church was never rebuilt, perhaps because the Venetians snatched Isídoros' relics in the 12th century and installed them in St Mark's. In 1967 Pope Paul VI ordered them to return one of Isídoros' bones, now kept in Chíos Cathedral.

Further north is **Langáda**, an attractive fishing village, popular with Greek tourists in July and August, and sporting an array of bars, cafés and fish tavernas. Jagged rocks surround **Kardámila** (ΚΑΡΔΑΜΥΛΑ), the largest village of northern Chíos and cradle of the island's shipowners. Kardámila is actually two villages, 2km from one another: the picturesque upper town and the seaside **Mármaros**, blessed with philanthropic gifts from the shipowners, including a statue of the Kardámila sailor on the beach. To the north, pretty **Nagós Beach** is set in a green amphitheatre and can get very busy in summer; its name is a corruption of *naos*, or temple, for there used to be one here, dedicated to Poseidon. At nearby Gióssona, named after Jason of the Argonauts, there's another pebble beach, longer and more exposed than Nagos, but with fabulous turquoise water and a taverna.

Taxis have a monopoly on transport to the striking and unspoiled mountain village **Pitiós**, which claims to be the birthplace of Homer; you can still see his 'house' and olive grove. A 12th-century tower dominates the village and there's usually something to eat at the café or at O Makellos, under an enormous plane tree on the edge of town. The landscape from Pitiós towards Chíos Town is lunar in its burnt emptiness, but just above the village is a lovely pine forest, filled with fire warnings.

Further west, the 13th-century **Moní Moúdon** is strikingly set in the barren hills near Katávasis. Byzantine nobles out of favour were exiled in the medieval fortress at **Volissós** (ΒΟΛΙΣΣΟΣ), founded by Belisarius, Justinian's great general, although what you see was rebuilt by the Genoese. The beloved 16th-century saint Markélla hailed from this little white village, which also lays claim to Homer; in ancient times it was the chief town of his 'descendants', the Homeridai, who said a local shepherd named Glaukos introduced Homer to his master, who then hired the poet as a teacher. Soon after Homer married a Volissós girl, had two daughters, wrote the *Odyssey* and set sail for Athens but died en route on Íos. Although renovation is under way, much of the old town up by the Kástro remains evocatively in ruins. The sandy beach below the town, **Skála Volissoú** or **Limniá**, is one of the island's finest and has two good traditional tavernas and a few rooms to let. Caiques go several times a week to Psará (the shortest way of getting there). There are other excellent beaches near here, just as minimally developed: pebbly **Chóri** just south, the unofficial nudist beach, and **Límnos**, on the road to the Monastery of **Ag. Markélla**, these days the island's favourite pilgrimage destination; one of Chíos' finest beaches lies just below.

Twice a week or so, buses brave the deserted roads north of Volissós. The westerly one climbs to little **Piramá**, with a medieval tower, and the church of Ag. Ioánnis with old icons. **Parpariá** to the north is a medieval hamlet of shepherds, and at Melaniós many Chiots were slain before they could flee to Psará in 1822. On the northwest shore, the village of Ag. Gála ('Holy Milk') is named after a frescoed 15th-century Byzantine church in a cave (*you'll have to ask for the key*), which drips whitish deposits, or milk (*gála*), said to be the milk of the Virgin; the chapel has a superb iconostasis. For more strange terrestrial secretions, make your way along the rough coastal road east to Agiásmata where Chiots come in the summer months to soak in the magic baths.

# Inoússes (ΟΙΝΟΥΣΣΕΣ)

A ferry leaves Chíos Town every afternoon for Inoússes, 'the wine islands', an archipelago of nine islets to the northeast. Only the largest, all of 30 square kilometres, is inhabited, but per capita it's the richest island in Greece: the Inoussians comprise some 60 of the 180 Greek shipowning families, including the Lemnos clan, the richest of them all. It's not for nothing that the Inoussians have a reputation for being tough and thrifty; most families began as goatherds or wine makers who spent centuries in Kardámila, Chíos, until it was safe to return to their defenceless rock pile. After losing everything in the Second World War they cannily parlayed a handful of wartime

Liberty ships into a fleet of 500 ships and tankers, not to mention some of the fanciest yachts in Greece that congregate in its sheltered little harbour every summer. The rest of the year they divide between Geneva, London and Athens.

For all that, the island's one town is surprisingly unpretentious, if extremely well kept. It has a pair of tavernas and the 11-roomed **Hotel Thalassoporos** (*t 027 205 1475; D; inexp; ring ahead if you mean to stay – you'll have to if you take the ferry rather than a day excursion*). The shipowners have created a little Maritime Museum by the quay, that opens when it feels like it. There are a few small, clean undeveloped beaches, the furthest a 30-minute walk away.

The one road on the island crosses to the western cliffs, where in the 1960s Katíngo Patéras, a member of one of the most prominent shipowning dynasties, built the multi-million-dollar Convent of the **Evangelismós** (*adm only to women with long sleeves, headscarves and long skirts*) after her pious 20-year-old daughter Iríni died of Hodgkinson's disease, having prayed to take the illness and die instead of her afflicted father. When, as custom has it, her body was exhumed after three years, she was found to be mummified. Her failure to decompose convinced her bereaved mother, now the abbess, that she was a saint (a fact recently confirmed by the Orthodox Church) and like Sleeping Beauty, she is kept in a glass case on display with the remains of her father, who died a few years later.

# Psára (ΨAPA)

**Psará**, one of Greece's martyr islands, is much further away than Inoússes: 54 nautical miles northwest of Chíos and connected once a day with the larger island – a good 4-hour journey depending on the weather unless you depart from the port of Limniá below Volissós, when it only takes half as long. The Mycenaeans were here in the 13th-century BC near Paliókastro, the same spot chosen by independent-minded Chiots wanting to escape even their benign Turkish rule. They knew this remote rock was largely neglected by the Sultan and over the years developed one of Greece's most important commercial fleets, rivalled only by Hýdra and Spétses. During the War of Independence (especially after the 1822 massacre on Chíos, which swelled the

## Getting Around

**Ferries** to Psára alternate: one day from Chios Town, one day from Volissós. For information contact the **ticket agency** in Chios: t 027 102 4670 or the Chíos **Port authority**: t 127 104 4433.

## Where to Stay and Eat

**Psará** ✉ 82104
**Xenonas Psaron**, t 027 406 1293 (*mod*). 5 rooms run by the EOT tourist office in an atmospheric 17th-century prison at Ag. Nikolaos; they also run the pleasant restaurant called **Spitalia** in the old naval quarantine hospital. It is renowned for serving up a good variety of Greek and international dishes.

**Psará Studios**, up by the football field, overlooking the town, only 350m from the sea, t 027 406 1180 (*mod*). 15 clean basic studios, with kitchenettes. Ideal as a base for family holidays.

**Bernardis**, t 027 406 1051 (*inexp*). Has 3 cheap but decent rooms available. Good for those travelling on a tight buget.

islet's population with refugees), Psára enthusiastically contributed its ships and one of the war's heroes, Admiral Kanáris, to the cause. Psára even invented a new weapon, the *bourléta*, which its captains used to destroy the Turkish fleet.

The Sultan demanded vengeance, and on 20 June 1824 he sent 25,000 troops to wipe Psára off the map with fire and sword. Most were blown to bits when they retreated with the Turks on their heels to the famous 'Black Ridge of Psára' where they set their powder stores alight. Only 3,000 of the 30,000 men, women and children managed to escape to Erétria, on Évia. The little island has never recovered: today only 500 people live on Psára, mostly fishermen and beekeepers. Although a few buildings have been restored, nearly everything was built after the massacre; the site of the house of Admiral Apostolis, a shipowner who fought in the war, is now a memorial square to the massacre. Your feet are your main transport to the island's beaches: the best is Límnos, a dandy sandy strand 20 minutes' walk away; you may have to bring your own provisions.

# Ikaría (IKAPIA)

Ikaría is one of the most mountainous islands in Greece, divided neatly in two by the dorsal range of Atheras, its peaks over 3,000ft high, often lost in billowing cloud. A giant sea cucumber on the map, 40km long and only 5 to 9km wide, it presents a forbidding, rocky face to the world. Yet both the wooded north coast (with a monopoly on the sandy beaches) and more rugged south coast (with pebbly beaches and rocks) are watered by mountain springs that keep them green under oak, pine and plane trees, with added natural air-conditioning from the wind. The Ikarían Sea is one of the wildest corners of the Aegean; if it's calm on one side of the island it's more likely than not blustery on the other, whipping up rainbows of sea mist. Forget the myth: it was the wind that downed Icarus here, not the sun. It certainly abetted the fire that began in a roadworks tar pot and incinerated the hills west of Ag. Kýrikos in 1993, causing 15 deaths in one of the worst forest fire tragedies in recent years.

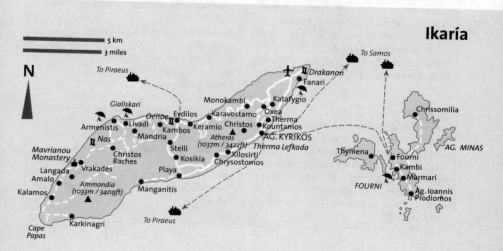

Don't come here if you're in a hurry or want to see big sights; life here is at such a slow pace that the locals joke about living in their own private Ikarian time zone. Development, too, has been slow here, partly for political reasons, partly by choice, and nearly all is in the traditional style; in recent years Ikaría has been held up as a model microcosm of environmental and economic sustainability. It helps that tourism is irrelevant to most of its 7,000 year-round inhabitants, who live in 60 villages, immersed in gardens, groves and orchards, and spend as much time as possible eating, drinking, singing and dancing.

## History

Ikaría has had more names than history. Originally called Dolichi ('oblong'), it was also known as Ichthyoessa ('fishy'), or Oenoe, for its wine. By Classical times it seems

## Getting There and Around

### By Air

The **airport** is at Fanári, t 027 502 2981, 13km east of Ag. Kýrikos; because of the wind, it has a unique north–south runway that can be approached from either direction. Olympic has connections 4 times weekly with Athens, 6 times in the summer (tickets t 027 502 2214). A bus (€3) links Ag. Kýrikos to flights.

### By Sea

Ikaría has 2 ports, and ships to the island serve one or the other. In summer, **NEL Superfast Ferries** (t 010 411 5015) from Piraeus take only 4½ hrs to either Ag. Kýrikos or Évdilos en route to Sámos, usually calling at Páros and Náxos on the way. Year-round **slow ferries** follow the same route daily, cost half as much, but take 12 hrs. Small tourist **excursion boats** from Ag. Kýrikos to Foúrni daily. Summer **hydrofoils** run 4 times a week to Pátmos, which can be visited as a day trip, and 3 times to Sámos. **Caiques** link Ag. Kýrikos to Manganítis and Karkinágri on Mon, Wed, and Fri. **Port authority**, Ag. Kýrikos, t 027 502 2207; Évdilos, t 027 503 1007.

### By Road

Buses run once or twice a day across the island from Ag. Kýrikos to Évdilos, with summer connections to Armenistís (the trip takes over an hr). **Taxis** are used to making long-haul trips and will estimate fares before setting out; sharing is common. There are plenty of **car** and **bike** hire places in both ports and Armenistís.

## Tourist Information

**Police**: in Ag. Kýrikos, t 027 502 2222, and in Évdilos, t 027 503 1222.
**Post office**: in Ag. Kýrikos and Évdilos; *open weekdays 7.30–2.30*.
**Ikariada Travel**, in Ag. Kýrikos, t 027 502 3322.
**Nas Travel**, in Évdilos, t 027 503 1947, and in Armenistís, t 027 507 1396.

## Festivals

In the **summer**, some of the most authentic *panegýria* in Greece occupy the attention of the whole island. Guests order a *próthesi* – a kilo of wild goat meat, a bottle of wine, a huge bowl of soup and a loaf of bread – enough to feed 4 people, and provide enough energy to dance until dawn.

**17 July**: the biggest festival of them all, in honour of Ikaría's fling with independence in 1912.
**8th Sun after Easter**: Ag. Pándas in Karavostamo.
**26 July**: Ag. Paraskeví in Xilosírti.
**27 July**: in Ag. Panteleímonos.
**6 Aug**: in Christós.
**15 Aug**: in Akamátra and Chrysóstomos.
**8 Sept**: in Plagiá and Manganítis.
**17 Sept**: Ag. Sofía in Mesokámbos.

As the place synonymous with the world's first hang-glider, Ikaría has been deeply involved since 1990 in setting up the **Ikaríada**, the Olympics of air-sports, to be held every 4 years in late June in different parts of the world.

## Mythology

After Theseus escaped Knossós with Ariadne (*see* pp.116–17) King Minos was furious at the great inventor Daedalus, who had given Ariadne the thread that enabled Theseus to find his way through the Labyrinth. Daedalus escaped from Knossós, but Minos ordered all outgoing ships to be watched to keep Daedalus on Crete. Unable to flee by land or sea, Daedalus made wings of feathers and wax for himself and his young son Icarus. Off they flew, but the boy, enchanted by flight, forgot his father's warning and flew too near the sun; the wax binding the feathers melted and Icarus plummeted to his death off the south coast of the island that took his name. In the 2nd century AD, Pausanius mentions that his grave could still be seen.

that the Phoenician name for the island, Ikor (also 'fishy') had been identified with the myth of Icarus. Under the Byzantines the island took on an extra N (many locals still call it Níkaria) and was used to exile court officials; over time the entire population began to take the airs of those 'born in the purple,' and to this day Ikarians have a reputation for mild eccentricity. As the Byzantines lost control in the 15th century, people fled high into the mountains, to practically independent villages such as Langáda that cannot be seen from the sea: the *afaneia*, or 'times of disappearance' lasted until the 1700s, when people slowly began to move back towards the sea.

In July 1912 during the Balkan War, the local doctor and priest led the inhabitants in liberating the island (they put the handful of Turkish administrators on a boat and said goodbye) and for five months Ikaría was an independent state with its own flag, stamps, and national anthem. Not long after it joined Greece, however, came the tragedy of 1922, followed by phylloxera that killed the vines, and many Ikarians emigrated, mostly to America. During the Civil War (1946-49) and junta (1967-74) Ikaría was a dumping ground for left-wing dissidents; at one point there were 15,000, twice the number of natives. Like the Byzantine exiles, their presence and ideas influenced the locals; although the Communists rarely win elections these days on the 'Red Rock', they are strong enough to decide who does.

# Ag. Kýrikos and the South Coast

**Ag. Kýrikos** (ΑΓ. ΚΗΡΥΚΟΣ) or just plain 'Ágios' as everyone calls it, is the biggest port and throbbing commercial heart of Ikaría, a town 'obviously designed by a drunken postman' according to Lawrence Durrell. It has a tiny centre of shops, rooms to let, banks, travel agents and a bakery unchanged since the 1930s. Outside of this little knot, forget urban density; like Candide, every Ikarian cultivates his or her own garden in the great mountain amphitheatre above. There's a pebble beach on the other side of the port, although the enormous 'Welcome to the Island of Radiation' sign on the breakwater has been changed to 'WELCOME TO THE ISLAND OF IKAROS'; the landmarks here are two tall girders holding a nose-diving metal Icarus as if in a pair of giant tweezers. Another work by local sculptor Ikaros, called the *Sképsi*, or 'Thinking Woman' on the west end of Ágios, looks as if she's sitting on the loo, and has been

# Where to Stay and Eat

## Ikaría ✉ 83000

The Ikarians are busily reviving their viticultural past, and are currently trying out a wide variety of grapes in tiny vineyards: the result may often be curiously brown in tone but tastes like nectar. The downside is that no one bottles it commercially, but you can often find it in tavernas. The islanders also make *kathoúra* cheese, honeys, fruit preserves (*Ikariaká glyká*), *ouzo*, and *raki* (*tsipoúra*).

## Ag. Kýrikos

**Adam's, t** 027 502 2418 (*C; mod*). Comfortable choice. *Open all year.*

**Kastro,** in the centre of Ágios, **t** 027 502 3480/3770, **f** 027 502 3700 (*C; mod*). A good bet, tastefully kitted out.

**Maria Elena,** on a slope just above town, **t** 027 502 2835, **f** 027 502 2223 (*B; mod*). Pristine

and pleasant pension with 16 simple airy rooms and 7 studios, all with balcony.

**Galini,** near the sea at Thérma Lefkáda, **t** 027 502 2530 (*E; mod–inexp*). *Open July–Sept.*

**Isabella's,** right in the centre, **t** 027 502 2839 (*E; inexp*). With a restaurant and pool.

**Filoti,** in the centre of Ágios. Specializing in excellent pizzas and pasta dishes.

**Kazalas,** in Glarédou, one of the mountain villages above Ágios (take a taxi). The best and most authentic taverna on the south side.

**Klimataria,** in the centre of Ágios. Reliable old restaurant serving delicious moussaká and old fashioned *ládera.*

## Thérma

**Marina, t** 027 502 2188 (*B; mod*). Airy and white in a handsome traditional building.

**Ikarion, t** 027 502 2481 (*D; inexp*). Recently renovated little hotel.

---

sadly abused by teenagers on their way to the local clubs, which open at 2am and close well after dawn.

For decades tourism on Ikaría has meant **Thérma** (ΘΕΡΜΑ), an archetypal beachside village 10 minutes' drive east of Ágios, where hot springs – the most radioactive in Europe – bubble up from the earth at 33–55°C and are used to treat chronic rheumatism, arthritis, gout and spondylitis; one spring, Artemidas, is so strong (790 degrees of radiation) that it's closed to the public. For better or worse, the baths (behind the sculpture of the goddess of health) haven't been improved since the 1950s, in spite of tales of miraculous cures.

For a long shingly-sandy beach safe for children, take the new airport road east out 10km to **Fanári**, a slice of old Greece with a row of ramshackle bars and tavernas overlooking the sea and tamarisk trees. A dirt road continues towards the very end of the cape, marked by one of the best preserved Hellenistic towers in Greece, round and whitish and from the 3rd or 4th century BC; until the War of Independence, an entire castle stood here, until Admiral Miaoúlis sailed by and used it for target practice. It protected the ancient town of **Drakanón**, sacred to Diónysos; only a few 5th-century BC walls survive on the *acropolis.*

The forbidding cliff-bound coast west of Ag. Kýrikos has more springs; one by the beach at **Thérma Lefkáda** (signposted 'hot water' by the road) bubbles out of the sea so hot that local picnickers use it to boil their eggs. The road then passes below the Neo-Byzantine **Evangelístrias** Monastery (1775), with a pretty slate-roofed church and exactly one nun, close to the new retirement home. Here too is a little theatre by the sea, first used in June 2001 to light the torch for the Ikaríada games (*see* 'Festivals' in box on previous page) in Valencia, Spain. Tucked on the coast beyond a huge granite spur, **Xilosírti**, is spread out among gardens and apricot orchards; a path leads down to a beach of big smooth pebbles, and at night there are a couple of places to eat, including little Argyro's famous *souvlaki* taverna, unchanged since 1957. People come to Xilosírti to fill up bottles of Athanató Neró (the 'immortal water', good for kidney stones), a small seaside spring on the east end of town, while to the west a rock by the beach at Livádi marks the spot where Icarus plummeted into the sea.

Above Xilosírti the road climbs to **Chrysóstomos** and **Playa**, with a handful of houses and a big yellow church. After a rough patch of road, there's a fork in it: the dramatic new paved road to the north side of Ikaría passes through wild west scenery on the way to Kosíkia, where the mountain pass is guarded by the ruined 10th-century Byzantine Nikariás Castle; or, if you have a 4 by 4, you can continue west along the south coast through a long tunnel to **Manganítis** (you can also get there by caique from Ágios). Built on a steep hillside with a pocket-sized port, it's a surprisingly lively little spot. The rubble from blasting the tunnel through the mountain has been made into a stunning if shadeless beach dubbed 'Seychelles'.

## Ikaría's North Coast

Ikaría's northern half attracts far more tourists with its pine forests, stream beds lined thick with plane trees, vineyards, sandy beaches and excellent roads. From Ag. Kýrikos a long winding road climbs up to the barren mountain pass, taking in breath-taking views of Foúrni, Sámos, Pátmos, Turkey and Náxos. One hamlet near the top, **Katafýgio** means 'shelter'. One day Turkish raiders came to Katafýgio, only to find all the villagers at church. The Turks decided to capture the people as they came out. They waited and waited, then impatiently broke into the church – to find it empty. The priest had opened the secret trapdoor in the floor, into a tunnel dug for just such an expediency, and everyone had escaped. Seven power-generating windmills mark the top of the pass; about 8km from there, as you descend, keep an eye out for a sign marking the short path up to little Byzantine Ag. Kýrikos, the oldest church on Ikaría.

After passing above villages immersed in the trees – Monokámbi, **Karavóstamo** (the biggest and most populous village on Ikaría, with a 17th-century church, **Ag. Pántas** and a dinky port) and Keramió – the road descends to **Évdilos** (ΕΥΔΗΛΟΣ), the pictur-esque ferry port of the north coast, with a town beach Fytema just to the west.

The road veers inland a bit for **Kámbos**, built on the site of **Oenoe**, the ancient capital of Ikaría, famous for its *pramnios oinos* mentioned by Homer. Some writers even made it the birthplace of Diónysos, the god of wine; an inscription found on Athens' Acropolis describes one Oenoe as being a major contributor to Apollo on Délos. Byzantine princelings in exile installed themselves here, renaming it Dolichi; the columns and arches of their palace remain, as well as their slate roofed church Ag. Iríni. The adjacent **museum** (*Vassilis Diónysos has the key; he may well throw in a free guided tour*) houses finds from Oenoe – pottery, clay figurines, coins, tools etc., and a 5th century BC inscription reading 'All Ikarians are liars', modified over the years to 'Jews' or 'Turks' or whoever was out of favour. In the nearby village of **Pygí**, the slate-roofed Moní Theoktisti has Ikaría's finest frescoes, by the Mount Áthos school.

# Where to Stay and Eat

## Évdilos ✉ 83302

**Atheras-Kerame**, in the centre, t 027 503 1434, f 027 503 1926, winter in Athens t 010 685 8096 (*B; exp–mod*). A handsome hotel, partly in a 19th-century building, with a restaurant and bar, pool, gym. They also have 20 apartments by the beach. It's a long walk from the ferry, but if you ring ahead, they'll collect you. *Open May–Oct.*

**Evdoxia**, up the hill overlooking the port, t 027 503 1502, f 027 503 1571 (*C; mod–inexp*). With 10 rooms, all with balcony, minibar and TV; plus a restaurant and laundry.

**Diónysos**, in Kámbos, t 027 503 1300 (*inexp*). Out by ancient Oenoe, comfortable rooms owned by the irrepressible and very knowledgeable Vassilis, one of Ikaría's great characters and a spontaneous entertainer.

**To Fytema** (tis Popis) by Fytema Beach, t 027 503 1928. Ikaría's prettiest taverna, in a lush garden, where the food is made from home-grown ingredients: try *soufikó* (Ikarian ratatouille), stuffed courgette flowers, and homemade pitta breads. *Open Mar–Nov.*

## Gialiskári and Armenistís ✉ 83301

**Cavos Bay**, t 027 507 1381, f 027 507 1380 (*C; exp*). Comfortable, with swimming pool, restaurant and sea-views.

**Erofili Beach**, near Livádi Beach, t 027 507 1058, f 027 507 183, *erofili@mailboom.com* (*A;exp*). Intimate, beautifully appointed hotel (most rooms have sea-views) with indoor sea water pool and Jacuzzi; huge buffet breakfasts. *Open May–Oct.*

**Messakti Village**, Gialiskári, t 027 507 1331, f 027 507 1330, in Athens t 010 621 9112, f 010 621 6684 (*B; exp–mod*). Attractive island architecture and slate floors; rooms have kitchenettes and overlook the pool and sandy beach; friendly management.

**Daidalos**, t 027 507 1390, f 027 507 1393, in Athens t 010 922 9034, f 010 923 5453 (*C; mod*). Traditionally furnished and set among

Further west along the coast, **Gialiskári** has Ikaría's most beautiful sandy beaches: **Messakti**, framed on one side by a tiny blue-domed church, linked by a spit to the shore and Livádi, over the next headland. The old fishing village of **Armenistís** (ΑΡΜΕΝΙΣΤΗΣ), is now Ikaría's biggest resort – big by local standards at any rate. Armenistís is the point of departure for the region of Rachés or 'hillsides', also known as the 'Little Switzerland of Ikaría', although some stretches of forest burned back in 1999. The main village, **Christós Rachés** (ΧΡΙΣΤΟΣ ΡΑΧΕΣ), is a charmer, the most Ikarian of Ikaría's villages: famous for keeping very late hours in its old-fashioned little shops and tavernas, and famous for wine. This is also one of the best places on the island for walks, with some 24km of excellent trails; a local group has produced a good map, with explanations in English. One possible excursion is the walk or drive east to the 13th-century convent at Mounté with wall paintings. An unpaved road off to the south leads towards Pezi and a pretty little **lake** and waterfall (in the winter, at any rate).

West of Armenistís, **Nas** (from *naos*, or temple), is marked by tavernas and a few rooms to rent, and a path leads down to a small pebble beach (swimming costume optional) in the ancient harbour, where you can swim around the corner into a series of caves for some excellent snorkelling. Behind, by the River Chalaris, are the platform and foundations of the 5th-century BC **Temple of Artemis Tavrópolio**. A marvellous statue of the goddess was discovered in the 19th century, with eyes that followed the viewer from every angle. The local priest immediately had it thrown in the nearest lime kiln. There's a pretty path along the river up into the mountains that takes four hours if you do the whole thing.

the cedars overlooking the sea, with a swimming pool, children's pool, large garden and restaurant.

**Dimitris Ioannidopoulos, t** 027 507 1310 (*inexp*). Hillside studios and apartments amongst a veritable forest of flowers.

**Atsahas,** above Livadi Beach, **t** 027 507 1049. A refreshing setting, serving light Ikarian delicacies such as carrot pies (*karotópita*) and other treats; excellent choice for vegetarians. They also have rooms. *Open May–Sept.*

**Charley Facaros, t** 027 507 1208. Charley (Kyriákos) has been on the waterfront for years; stop in for a simple meal or pizza. He also has inexpensive rooms.

**Delfini,** right by the sea, **t** 027 507 1254. Famous for its very tasty wild goat dishes. Also has rooms to rent.

**Kelari** (Kastanias), in Gialiskári, **t** 027 507 1227. This is the best of several fish tavernas overlooking the little port, patrolled by very well-fed cats.

**Paskalia** (aka Vlachos), **t** 027 507 1302. Some of the best food in Armenistís comes from this kitchen; it has good value rooms to rent above.

### Christós Raches ✉ 83301

**Raches,** in Christós Rachés, **t** 027 504 1269 (*B; mod*). The peace and quiet here is wonderful. It also offers meals in the evening. *Open June–Oct.*

There are 3 inexpensive places with rooms for rent in the village.

### Nas ✉ 83301

**Anna,** the first taverna on the right when coming from Armenistís, **t** 027 507 1489. Delightful owners serving excellent traditional Ikarian dishes, wine and fresh seafood.

**Astra,** in Nas, **t** 027 507 1255. Views over the beach and seafood (incl. tender octopus), courgette *beignets* and other delicious dishes, with local wine.

Beyond Nas, the road is unpaved but continues southwest to the little whitewashed **Monastery of Mavrianoú,** next to an old threshing floor; the village above, **Vrakádes,** has a pair of cafés and pretty views. A few kilometres further on, **Amálo** has summer tavernas (try the one back at Langáda). If you're feeling especially adventurous, carry on south to **Karkinágri,** Ikaría's most isolated village, with a tiny port (with a boat three times a week to Ag. Kýrikos), a summer taverna, a few rooms to rent and not much else. This whole area is a good place to find 'pirate houses', low free stone buildings often under huge boulders, where people lived in the 'times of disappearance'.

# Foúrni (ΦΟΥΡΝΟΥΣ)

Ikaría is too cosmopolitan for your taste, turn the clock back a couple of decades and head out to Foúrni (or Foúrnous) – a rugged, quiet, friendly and utterly Greek mini archipelago just about midway between Sámos and Ikaría. The larger, hook-shaped island embraces a huge sheltered bay that long hid a band of pirates, from where they would pounce on passing ships; modern Greeks, beginning with refugees from Turkish misrule, only dared to settle here in 1775. Foúrni by that time had been ruthlessly denuded by charcoal burners from Sámos and Ikaría. But the sea here is the η φωλια των ψαριων, 'the lair of fish', especially the much-loved *barboúnia* (red mullet) and clawless Mediterranean lobster (*astakós*), which, although plentiful, isn't cheap; Foúrni's fleet sends most of the catch to Athens. Many locals fish by night, using bright lamps that set the sea aglitter.

## Getting There and Around

Once or twice a week the Piraeus–Ikaría–Sámos ferry calls at Foúrni, augmented 3 times a week by a shopping **caique** from Ag. Kýrikos (Ikaría). In summer **hydrofoils** connect Ikaría and Foúrni 3 times a week. Caiques will ferry you to coves and beaches. **Port authority**: **t** 027 105 1207.

## Festivals

**15 Aug**: one of the two big *panegýri*.
**29 Aug**: Ag. Ioánni tou Thermastí.

## Where to Stay and Eat

**Foúrni** ✉ 83400
Finding a room is usually no problem, and you may well be met as you disembark.
**Spyrakos Rooms**, back from the sea, **t/f** 027 105 1235, in Athens **t** 010 261 9010 (*mod*). Nice rooms with mini-fridges and private baths.
**Eftychia Amorgiannou**, just inland, **t** 027 105 1364, **f** 027 105 1290 (*inexp*). Modern rooms.
**Markakis Rooms**, **t** 027 105 1268 (*inexp*). Rooms in a renovated pile by the port.
**Nikos**, among the tavernas near the port. This is the best for lobster and fresh fish.

### Foúrni's Villages

About half of Foúrni's 1,600 souls live around the port, also called **Foúrni**, a picturesque web of narrow lanes with a winsome ramshackleness and strong communal feeling: three times a day nearly everyone meets in the lovely square with its old fashioned *kafenía*. Just north, up the steps, a path leads to the beaches of **Psilí Ammo**, and **Kálamos**. Further north, the new road ends up at **Chrissomiliá**; if you've been looking for a retreat to write your next novel, this might be it, with beaches, a few rooms and a couple of tavernas.

A 15-minute walk south of the port will bring you to **Kámbi**, the 'capital', a pleasant little place scattered Ikarian-style under the trees, with a few rooms, a tamarisk-lined beach and a little cove full of yachts in the summer. From here you can arrange boat trips to **Marmári**, a cove just south, or sail further south to Vlycháda Beach. If Foúrni is too cosmopolitan, try its baby islet **Thýmena**, where you'll be stared at if you disembark; bring your own food and be prepared to sleep under the stars.

# Lésbos/Mytilíni (ΛΕΣΒΟΣ/ΜΥΤΙΛΗΝΗ)

Officially Lésbos, but often called Mytilíni after its principal city, Sappho's island (pop. 116,000) is the third largest in Greece after Crete and Évia and one of the more elusive and many-sided, hanging off the coast of Turkey like a plane leaf. Traditional life remains strong in the villages, 15 of which have been declared traditional settlements; its undulating hills support an astonishing 11–13 million olive trees, glistening in the sunlight, while the higher peaks are swathed in chestnuts and pines; in Sigri you'll find Europe's biggest petrified forest; vineyards produce Greece's best *ouzo*. It may have only pockets of that stellar pin-up beauty of some islands, but there's a bewitching magic to it. The people are friendly, easy-going, lyrical and fond of horses and drink, like Greek Celts, ready to sing and dance whenever the mood takes them. Lésbos has been a cradle of some of Greece's greatest musicians and poets, from Terpander, 'the father of Greek music', to the aristocratic Sappho and Alcaeus and Longus (the 3rd-century BC author of the romance *Daphnis and Chloe*) to Nobel

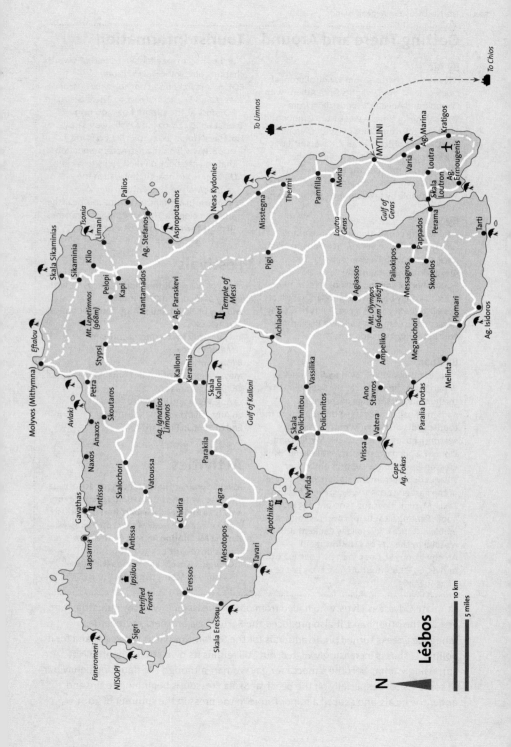

Lésbos

N

10 km
5 miles

To Chios

To Limnos

MYTILINI
Ag. Marina
Kratigos
Varia
Loutra
Skala
Loutron
Ag. Ermougenis
Moria
Pamfilla
Thermi
Neas Kydonies
Misstegna
Aspropotamos
Ag. Stefanos
Palios
Limani
Tsonia
Skala Sikaminias
Sikaminia
Klio
Pelopi
Kapi
Mantamados
Mt. Lepetimnos (968m)
Stypsi
Ag. Paraskevi
Keramia
Kalloni
Skala Kalloni
Petra
Skoutaros
Ag. Ignatios Limonos
Molyvos (Mithymna)
Eftalou
Avlaki
Naxos
Anaxos
Skalochori
Vatoussa
Parakila
Agra
Chidira
Apothikes
Gavathas
Antissa
Lapsarna
Antissa
Mesotopos
Tavari
Ipsilou
Petrified Forest
Sigri
Eressos
Skala Eressou
Faneromeni
NISIOPI

Pigi
Temple of Messi
Achladeri
Agiassos
Mt. Olympos (964m / 3162ft)
Ampeliko
Vassilika
Ano Stavros
Vrissa
Vatera
Nyfida
Cape Ag. Fokas

Gulf of Geros
Loutra Geras
Paliokipos
Messagros
Pappados
Perama
Skopelos
Megalochori
Paralia Drotas
Melinta
Plomari
Ag. Isidoros
Tarti

Gulf of Kalloni

Polichnitou
Skala Polichnitou
Polichnitos

## Getting There and Around

### By Air

Numerous charters from various European cities; at least 3 daily flights from Athens with Olympic and Aegean/Cronus; daily from Thessaloníki, 3 times a week from Límnos and twice a week from Chíos (all with Olympic). The **Olympic office** is at 44 K. Kavétsou, **t** 025 102 8660; Aegean/Cronus is only at the airport, **t** 025 106 1120; the **airport** is 8km from Mytilíni Town, **t** 025 106 1490 or **t** 025 106 1212, and reachable by taxi (around €8 from town).

### By Sea

Daily **ferry** connection with Piraeus and Chíos; 6–7 times a week with Sámos, at least once a week with Thessaloníki, Alexandroúpolis, Rafína, Ag. Efstrátios, Ikaría, Psará, Rhodes, Kos and Pátmos. In summer, there is a **daily boat** to the pleasant resort of Ayvalik in Turkey (with a possibility of a 3-day excursion to Bergama – ancient Pergamon). **Port authority: t** 025 102 4115.

### By Road

**Buses** from Mytilíni Town to distant villages depart from the station at the south end of the harbour, on the edge of the public gardens, **t** 025 102 8873; 3–4 buses a day to the tourist spots on the west of the island in season; 5 buses a day between Mytilíni and Plomári, 2 per day between Mytilíni and Skála Eressoú. Buses to the suburbs and closer villages depart from the station in the centre of the harbour, **t** 025 104 8725, every hr or so. **Taxis:** Mytilíni, **t** 025 102 3500 or **t** 025 102 5900; Renting a **car** helps cover Lésbos' considerable distances. Try **Holiday Car Rental**, in Mytilíni by the city bus station at 21b Archipelagous St, **t** 025 104 3311, **f** 025 102 9581, or **Avis**, 69 P. Kountouriótou St, **t** 025 104 1464, **f** 025 104 1465.

## Tourist Information

Lésbos has an excellent website that's worth checking out: *www.greeknet.com*.
**EOT**, 6 Aristarchou St, **t** 025 104 2511/2513; *open weekdays 8–2.30 and 6–8.30*. There is also an EOT desk at the airport, **t** 025 106 1279.
**Tourist police: t/f** 025 102 2776; *open 8–3*.
**Hoteliers' Union, t** 025 104 1787, **f** 025 104 0008, *www.filoxenia.net*. Accommodation that you can book on their website.
**ATMs:** There are holes in the wall in the capital, Mólyvos, Kallóni and Eressós.
**Post office:** in Mytilíni, up Vournazon, near the summer cinema. There are smaller branches in most towns and tourist villages.

## Festivals

Lésbos has great traditional *panegyría*, with plenty of food, drink and music.
**2nd day of Easter and 15 Aug:** famous Carnival in Agiássos.
**3rd Sun after Easter:** bull sacrifice in Mantamádos.
**8 May:** Ántissa.
**May:** 'Week of Prose and Drama', in the capital.
**26 July:** Ag. Paraskeví.
**15 Aug:** Pétra and Skópelos.
**26 Aug:** Paliókipos.
**End of Sept:** in Plomári.

## Activities

**Milelia Seminar House, t/f** 025 107 2030. Yoga courses with an international clientèle run by Gisa and Detlev Siebert-Bartling. British and Australian bodyworkers do therapies.
**Karuna Meditation Retreat Centre**, 3km outside town, **t** 025 307 1486, run by Geórgios (Greek) and Yosoda (Nepalese) Kassipides. More spiritual feeding.

Laureate Odysséas Elýtis, who hailed from one of the island's wealthy industrial families. On the other hand, it also produced the Barbarossa brothers, red-bearded renegade Greeks turned pirate admirals for the Sultan. Known as the Red Island for its politics, Lésbos is increasingly visited, but still retains its own strong identity. Not surprisingly, it has become a mecca for gay women, although the flaunting behaviour of some visitors, especially on the beach at Skála Eressoú, is beginning to tire and anger the locals, and caused a minor furore in the press in the summer of 2001.

# History

Like many of the islands that hug the coast of Asia Minor, Lésbos both enjoyed the benefits and suffered the penalties of its east–west location as early as the Trojan War; it was allied with Troy, and suffered raids by both Odysseus and Achilles. In the 10th century BC Aeolians from Thessaly, led by Penthilos, son of Orestes, colonized the island and Asia Minor coast. The Aeolians lacked the sharp intellectual curiosity of their Ionian neighbours to the south, but they made Lésbos a cultural centre, especially under its dictator Pittakos (598-79), one of the Seven Sages of Greece, who tried to heal the destructive rivalry between Lésbos' two city states, Mytilíni and Míthymna, and promoted trade with Egypt. From 527–479 it was under the rule of Persia, then joined the Delian League.

Míthymna, having lost the fight for island dominance, avenged itself on Mytilíni in 428 BC when the latter decided to leave the Delian League and join Sparta in the Peloponnesian War. Míthymna told Athens, and Athens in a fury sent troops to massacre the Mytilinians. However, once the ship set sail, the Athenians reconsidered (for once) and sent a second ship countermanding the massacre. It arrived in the nick of time, and the people were spared.

In the 4th century BC, Lésbos continued to change hands frequently, its most memorable ruler being the Greek eunuch and soldier of fortune Hermeias of Arteneus, who governed both the island and the Troad, or region around Troy, on the mainland. Hermeias attempted to rule on the precepts of the *Republic* and the ideal city-state, and invited Aristotle to found an academy like Plato's Academy in ancient Assos (just opposite Lésbos, in Asia Minor) and while living there Aristotle married Hermeias' niece Pythias and wrote most of the Politics; he later moved to Mytilíni for three years, where he set up another philosophical academy with his friend Theophrastus, a native of Lésbos, and became fascinated with biology, performing pioneering observations of the island's plant and animal life before departing to tutor Alexander in 342 BC. Later the island was occupied by Mithridates of Pontus, who was in turn ousted by the Romans in 79 BC in a battle that was Julius Caesar's first combat.

# Mythology

Even in myth Lésbos is connected with music and poetry. The mytho-historical musician Arion, accredited with the invention of the *dithyramb*, was a son of the island. His talents brought him great wealth – and headaches. After a musical contest in Italy, where he had won all the prizes, the crew of the ship returning him to Lésbos decided to throw him overboard and keep his prizes for themselves. Arion was allowed to sing one last tune, after which he dived into the sea. But his swan song had charmed the dolphins, and they saved his life, carrying him safely to shore, and the ship's crew were later executed for their treachery. Another myth deals with the great poet Orpheus, who was torn to pieces by the maenads of Diónysos and thrown into a river of Thrace. His beautiful head floated to Lésbos, where the inhabitants carried it to a cave. The head sang and prophesied so well that people stopped patronizing the Delphic oracle. This loss of business angered Apollo, who went to Lésbos to order the head to shut up.

Like Chíos, Lésbos in 1354 was given by the Emperor John Palaeológos to the Genoese captain Francesco Gattilusio for his help in restoring his throne. In 1462 Mohammed the Conqueror captured the island, despite the heroic resistance led by Lady Oretta d'Oria, and the island remained in Turkish hands until 1912.

# Mytilíni

The capital of Lésbos, **Mytilíni** (ΜΥΤΙΛΗΝΗ) is a town of 30,000, with magnificent old mansions, impressive public buildings and beautiful gardens. At the same time it manages to be dusty, higgledy-piggledy, cacophonous, and, outside of its cavernous dark waterfront ticket agencies and the odd hotel, not the slightest bit bothered with tourism. It has two harbours, one to the south, protected by a long jetty, and the abandoned one to the north. In ancient times a canal known as the 'Euripos of the Mytilineans' flowed between the two, a fact dramatically proved when a marble bridge, and then an ancient *trireme* was found under a street in the middle of town,

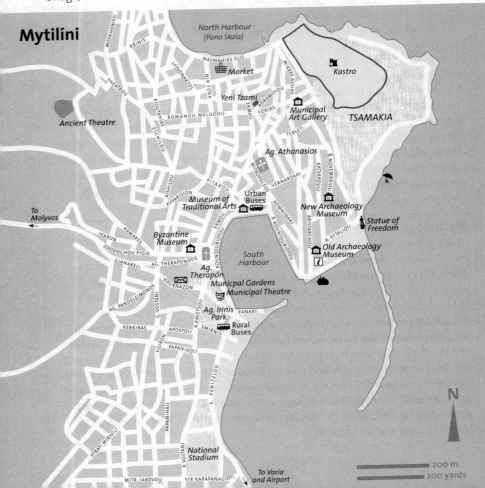

**Mytilíni**

North Harbour (Pano Skala)

MOSHONISSI

KRINIS

NAVMAHIAS ELIS

Market

NIK FOKA

LESVONAKTOS

THEATROU

KIOUTLAMIAS

ROMANOU MELODOU

ESCHILIOU

Ancient Theatre

MIKAS ASSIAS

Kastro

Yeni Tzami

ADRAMITIOU

ERMOU

FOKIAS

Municipal Art Gallery

TSAMAKIA

TERSETI

Ag. Athanasios

PITAKOU

MITROPOLEOS

VERNARDAKI

8 NOVEMBRIOU

KATSAKOULI

AISHILOU

KYPARISION

Museum of Traditional Arts

Urban Buses

ERMOU

KOMNINAKI

New Archaeology Museum

ARISTARCHOU

P. KOUNTOUROIOTOU

Statue of Freedom

To Molyvos

KAMARES

IKARON

ZOODOCHOU PIGIS

Byzantine Museum

KOUNTOUROIOTOU

GIANARELI

AG. THERAPONDOS

South Harbour

A. EFTALIOTI

Old Archaeology Museum

Ag. Therapón

VOURNAZON

Municpal Gardens

Municipal Theatre

AG. PANDELEIMONOS

G. VOSTANI

Ag. Irinis Park

FANARI

KAVETSOU

Rural Buses

KERKIRAS

APOSTOLI

SMIRNIS

FILIJON

PAPANIKOLI

E. VENIZELOU

PARAMI HALL

STRATI MIRIVILI

P. VOSTANI

National Stadium

MITR. IAKOVOU

VIR KARAPANAGIOTI

To Varia and Airport

N

200 m
200 yards

# Where to Stay

## Mytilíni ✉ 81100

Package-booked accommodation ebbs and flows here; it's a good idea to book. The **Tourism and Travel Agency**, near the bus station at 5 Konstantinoupoleos St, t 025 102 1329, f 025 104 1268, can arrange rooms in 16 villages. **Sappho Rented Rooms Association**, t 025 104 3375, has 22 owners offering rooms in town.

## Mytilíni Town

**Blue Sea**, 91 P. Kountouriótou, t 025 102 3994, f 025 102 9656 (*B; exp*). Smart, clean rooms with balconies overlooking the ferries, but not without noise. *Open all year.*

**Pyrgos of Mytilene**, 49 E. Venizélou, t 025 102 5069, f 025 104 7319. *www.pyrgoshotel.gr* (*A; exp*). Opened in 1999, it's the smartest mansion-hotel conversion, with 12 luxurious rooms meticulously done in the same romantic Second Empire style as the building, but complete with all mod cons; parking available.

**Sappho**, Prokimea St, back on the waterfront, t 025 102 8415 (*C; mod*). Lovely views from a modern block. *Open all year.*

**Heliotrope**, 2.5km from the centre overlooking Vigla Beach, t 025 104 5857, f 025 104 4272, *www.heliotrope.gr* (*B; mod–exp*). Combination of a new hotel and older studios sleeping up to 8, all with sea-views; the complex includes sea water swimming pool with a hydromassage, children's pool, restaurant, bars, and satellite TV.

**Villa 1900**, 24 P. Vostáni, a 10min walk south of the harbour, t 025 102 3448, f 025 102 8034 (*A; mod–inexp*). For a more tranquil time, one of Mytilíni's Neoclassical mansions, now run as an atmospheric guesthouse. *Open April–Oct.*

**Salina's Garden Rooms**, 7 Fokiás, t 025 104 2073 (*inexp*). The garden is lovely.

## Around Mytilíni Town

**Loriet**, in Variá, near the beach and Theóphilos Museum and en route to the airport, t 025 104 3111, f 025 104 1629, *loriet@hotmail.com* (*A; lux*). 10 suites charmingly situated in an old stone mansion, with pool and wheelchair access. *Open all year.*

**Silver Bay Hotel and Bungalows**, just over 5km west of the capital at Alifanta, t 025 104 2410, f 025 104 2860 (*B; exp*). Soulless complex but offers pool, tennis and sea-views. *Open all year.*

**Votsala**, north in Thermi, t 025 107 1231, f 025 107 1179, *votsala@otenet.gr* (*B; exp–mod*). For a more modest but delightful stay; relaxing garden by the water where you can contemplate the Turkish coast, and the friendly owner will ferry you to and from Mytilíni. *Open April–Oct.*

**Akrotiri**, t 025 102 6452 (*inexp*). Cheaper rooms on offer in Variá.

# Eating Out

Be sure to savour the island's famous fresh sardines and giant prawns; local specialities incl. *kakávia* (fish soup), *astakós magiátikos* (lobster with vegetables), *skoumbri foúrnou* (baked mackerel) and *kotópoulo me karýdia* (stuffed chicken with walnut sauce). The island being the home of Greece's best *ouzo*, you should try at least one *ouzerie* experience, not just a snack and glass on the hoof, but a chance to stop the clock, put down the guide book and see if you can match locals for lazy-day endurance.

**Apolafsi**, near To Fanari, t 025 102 7178. A good venue for delicious *mezédes*, grilled meat and fresh fish.

**Kalderimi**, 2 Thassou, at the central market. In an alley in the old town; mecca for Mytilíni *ouzerie* connoisseurs, as much for the *mezédes* as the street atmosphere and chance to hang out with some local celebs.

**Navagio**, on the waterfront at 23 Archipelagous, t 025 104 2609 (€18–24). First-floor restaurant with balcony and ambience that specializes in, well, everything, from sandwiches, shrimp and smoked trout to lamb *kléftiko* and pasta.

**To Fanari**, on the south end of the harbour, t 025 104 6417. One of the fish tavernas here, with a wide selection of wines; the owner will regale you with historical details about Mytilíni.

The harbour area, Variá and Neapolis are all popular bar venues where young Greeks aren't in the least inhibited about dancing a *zembékiko* when the mood strikes.

having been stranded in the accumulation of sand and sediment. For the last few years, half of the city's streets have been dug up to install a biological waste treatment system; every time the works hit an archaeological find it all grinds to a halt – a gift for the archaeologists and a curse for anyone in a car.

Standing on a traffic island amid the bustle of the waterfront, a prettily restored old white house, belonging to the harbourmaster, now holds the **Museum of Traditional Arts and Crafts** (*t 025 102 8501; open by request; adm*), with a collection of lace, weapons, ceramics, tools, engraved copper pans and costumes. A few streets back, the cathedral **Ag. Athanásios** (16th–17th century) has a finely carved wooden iconostasis. The lofty dome that dominates the skyline, however, belongs to **Ag. Therápon**, dedicated to a penniless but saintly doctor. Built over a Temple of Apollo, or perhaps even the School of Sappho, in the 5th century it became a Christian basilica; the present church dates from 1850. In front of the church the priest runs an interesting **Byzantine Museum** (*t 025 102 8916; phone to check when open; adm*) stocked with icons from the 13th to 18th centuries, including one by Theóphilos (*see* below). The **Municipal Gardens**, a delightful green and shady oasis with a scattering of cafés where everyone goes to escape the hurly-burly is nearby, along with the **Municipal Theatre** (1968). The quarters south of here (Sourada and Kióski) are dotted with grand and very un-Greek Victorian or Bavarian Neoclassical mansions ('*archontika*') built by olive oil and *ouzo* barons. Most have been beautifully restored and some are now upmarket hotels.

On the west side of the harbour, on 8 Novembriou Street, the **Archaeology Museum** (*t 025 102 8032; open Tues–Sun 8.30–3; adm*) is housed in another aristocratic mansion, and prides itself on reliefs found in a Roman house depicting scenes from the comedies of Menander, a statue of the Lion of Yéra, Greek mosaics found at Chórafa, Roman mosaics from Ag. Therapón and Páno Skála, and prehistoric finds from Thérma. Rescue finds, including some excellent mosaics, from Mytilíni Town fill a new annexe up the same street (*same hours*).

Novembriou Street continues up to the ancient *acropolis*, now crowned by a sprawling **Byzantine-Genoese** castle, or *kástro* (*t 025 102 7970; open 8–2.30; adm*), founded by Justinian in the 6th century, who blinded every prisoner he sent here. In 1373 the Genoese enlarged and repaired it with any available material, including columns from the 600 BC Temple of Apollo hastily crammed in between the stones like a collage. Inside are buildings left by the various occupants, one bearing the coat-of-arms of the Paleológos (the emperor John's sister married Francesco Gatilusio); there's also a Roman cistern and a Turkish *medrese* (Koranic school), prisons, and a *tekes*, the cell of a holy man. Recent excavations have revealed an Archaic **Thesmophorion**, where women held their annual festival and sacrificed piglets to Demeter for fertility. In July and August, some of the most popular performers in Greece put on concerts here; somewhat in the spirit of the Thesmophoria, the heart-throb *bouzouki* singer George Dalaras once memorably had his trousers ripped off by ardent female fans. There are picnic tables in the pine groves below and a pay beach run by EOT at **Tsamákia**, and a large statue of Freedom that greets arrivals by sea.

North of the *kástro*, the abandoned Old North Port or **Páno Skála** is a neighbourhood in the first stages of reinventing itself. In the centre, a ruined mosque, the **Yeni Tzamí**, and its truncated minaret stand forlorn, with trees growing out of the walls; carpenters and metalworkers work in the grimy shops; kids on bikes hurtle around the warren of lanes; a market adds its bustle. Now small antiques shops are moving in, worth a look if you fancy the unusual or bizarre. By the pine forest to the west, at the end of Theátrou Eschílou Street, the Hellenistic **Theatre** was one of the largest of ancient Greece with a capacity of 15,000 (*due to re-open in 2002 after extensive renovation*); Pompey, who loved the island, admired it so much that he was inspired to build his own theatre in Rome in 55 BC. Just south are the remains of a Roman aqueduct, and near the cemetery of **Ag. Kyriakí** are some of the walls of ancient Mytilíni.

## South of Mytilíni Town

Buses from the waterfront municipal station will take you hourly to **Variá** (BAPEIA), the birthplace of Theóphilos Hadzimichális (1873–1934), a former door guard at the Greek consulate at Smyrna who earned his *ouzo* in exchange for the most passionate and truest paintings modern Greece has produced, 'like the trembling of the dew', as Seferis described them – sometimes on walls of shops, or on tins or rags – whatever he could find. The old village school, set in an ancient olive grove a few minutes' walk from the main road, is now a charmingly rustic **Theóphilos Museum** (*t 025 104 1644; open Tues–Sun 9–2.30 and 6–8; adm*), founded by Tériade (*see* below) in 1964. Because he aimed for total lucidity, Theóphilos wrote long descriptions around each scene he painted so there's no mistaking what's going on, whether it is a scene from mythology, the lives of the saints, a postcard, the Greek War of Independence, current events (Vesuvius' eruption) or a local festival; smokestacks belch smoke over Lésbos, aeroplanes fly over it, steam boats call at its ports. Note how he painted frames around his paintings, since he couldn't afford them. The museum also has 19th-century studio photos, of Greeks posing in the same splendid costumes that Theóphilos loved to paint; he himself, dumpy and middle-aged, liked to dress up as Alexander the Great, followed by his 'Macedonians' or street urchins in carnival gear. Not surprisingly, most of his contemporaries thought he was a bit eccentric.

A stone's throw away, a modern building houses the **Tériade Museum and Library** (*t 025 102 3372; open Tues–Sun 9–2 and 5–8; adm*), founded in 1979 by Stratís Eleftheriádes, better known by his adopted French name Tériade. Born in Mytilíni in 1897, Eleftheriádes went to study law in Paris at the age of 18, where he was drawn to the lively, pioneering artistic world of the time. In 1937 he launched his own publishing house, *VERVE*, printing art books and a respected quarterly review of the same name that lasted until 1971. Inspired by medieval illuminated manuscripts, Tériade produced a series of 'Grands Livres' with lithographs by Picasso, Miró, Léger, Chagall, Rouault, Giacometti, Henri Laurens, and Juan Gris, handprinted on handmade paper in limited editions, many of which are on display here, along with minor paintings by the same names (although a burglary has put a dent in the collection). On the ground floor there's a room with more paintings by Theóphilos. Tériade 'discovered' him in 1930, but not in time to save the artist from dying unknown and penniless.

**Neápolis**, just south of Variá, has a beach and ruined 5th-century basilica, but the main attraction south of Mytilíni is a lovely pair of beaches at the extreme southern tip of the peninsula at **Ag. Ermougénis**, on either side of the eponymous chapel, and with an excellent taverna on the hill. From Skála Loutrón, a ferry crosses the Gulf of Géras, completely encompassed with dense olive groves, for Pérama; at nearby **Loutrá Géras** you can indulge in a relaxing warm soak in the gentlest of Lésbos' five spas, in pools segregated by sex (*open daily 8–8; adm*).

# North of Mytilíni

There are two roads to the north coast and its resorts. The longer, east-coast road passes **Mória**, where more arches of the Roman aqueduct remain intact, and **Thérmi**, a spa with hot iron-rich springs recommended by Galen (good for diseases of the

## Getting Around

**Excursion boats** run from Mólyvos to Skála Sikaminiás and beaches, or you can hire your own **caique** from Evangelos Pairaktaris, **t** 025 103 1766; from Sígri, caiques visit Nisiópi islet. A local **bus** now runs on a regular basis between Eftaloú and Náxos, stopping at Mólyvos, Pétra and the beaches in between. Pick up a timetable at the Mólyvos tourist office or at Petra Tours. Mólyvos **taxi** rank is opposite the bus station, **t** 025 107 1480; in Pétra, **t** 025 104 2022.

## Tourist Information

**Municipal Tourist Information Office**: on the main street in Mólyvos, **t** 025 307 1347/1069, *mithimna@aigaio.gr*. Very helpful and will help find you a room; *open weekdays 7.30–4.*
**Mólyvos Watersports, t** 025 107 1861. Parasailing, waterskiing, and windsurfing lessons.
**Donkey trekking** with Michaelis, **t** 025 307 1309. Day and evening treks with barbeque beach supper.

## Internet

**Café Central**, by the harbour in Mólyvos. During the day there are 'Internet Specials' (with breakfast, for example), while after 10pm emails are free with a drink; *open 10–3am.*
In **Pétra**, seek out the anonymous shop on an anonymous street; next to the wonderful clapboard barber's; around €4 per hr.

## Where to Stay and Eat

**Skála Kallóní** ✉ 81107
**Pasiphae, t** 025 302 3212, **f** 025 302 3154 (*B; exp*). Comfortable hotel with a saltwater pool, one of several large, family-orientated complexes on the gulf. *Open April–Oct.*
**Arivisi, t** 025 302 2456, **f** 025 302 3530 (*exp–mod*). With 10 decent apartments. *Open May–Oct.*
The fish tavernas are cheap and specialize in *avthrini*, rather like fresh sardines.

**Mólyvos/Eftaloú** ✉ 81108
There's plenty of accommodation here, but it can be pricey. Choose between 4 areas: just outside town; down to the beach, where there are some very attractive converted stone houses (but often block-booked by package companies in season); on the harbour; and pensions and rooms in the old town climbing up to the *kástro*, which is blissfully car-free but requires schlepping your bags.
**Panselinos**, by the sea in Eftaloú, **t** 025 307 1905, **f** 025 307 1904 (*B; lux*). With the works, incl. wheelchair access. *Open May–Oct.*
**Delfinia**, just outside Mólyvos, **t** 025 307 1373, *delfinia@otenet.gr* (*B; exp*). With a pool, tennis, beach sports and lazy terrace.
**Olive Press, t** 025 307 1646, **f** 025 307 1647 (*B; exp*). One of the more modest options by the beach; a lovely conversion of an olive press, with tennis court, charming café and dining terrace. *Open May–Oct.*
**Sun Rise**, 2km from Mólyvos, **t** 025 307 1713/1779, **f** 025 307 1791 (*B; exp*). One of the pricier options out of town; bungalow complex with pool, tennis, playground and

joints and skin, gynaecological ailments and rheumatoid arthritis), and the 12th-century Byzantine church of **Panagía Troullootí**. Thérmi was inhabited before 3000 BC; its five successive levels of civilization were excavated by Winifred Lamb between 1923 and 1933. Ancient Thérmi had connections with Troy, and it was burnt to the ground; the dates match the traditional dates of the Trojan War and the Homeric raids by Achilles and Odysseus (1250 BC). A large Turkish tower stands near the baths, and there are rooms, restaurants and a beach nearby.

After passing beaches at Néas Kydonies and Aspropótamos, this road leaves the coast for **Mantamádos** (ΜΑΝΤΑΜΑΔΟΣ), a large village of grey stone houses, famous for its yoghurt and a miraculous black icon of Archangel Michael that is said to smell of wildflowers, in the 18th-century church **Taxiárchis Michael**. One story has

minibus service to whisk you to the coast. *Open May–Oct.*

**Sea Horse**, t 025 307 1630, f 025 307 1374 (*C; exp–mod*). Variety of airy rooms; the bathrooms are alluring and front-facing rooms have good views of the day's catch. The cafeteria below has shady seating by the water's edge, while the owner runs boat trips from his travel agency next door. *Open April–Oct.*

**Adonis**, t 025 307 1866, f 025 307 1636 (*C; mod*). Attractive, set amongst trees. *Open all year.*

**Amfitriti**, 2 mins' walk inland, t 025 307 1741, f 025 307 1744 (*B; mod*). Mainly taken up by tour operators, but has a pool set in verdant grass surrounded by apricot trees. *Open April–Oct.*

**Mólyvos I**, by the beach, t 025 307 1496, f 025 307 1640 (*B; mod*). Cool terracotta-floored rooms in a converted traditional building with a spacious terrace overlooking the beach. *Open April–Oct.*

**Mólyvos II**, in Eftalóu, t 025 307 1534, f 025 307 1694 (*B; mod*). Playground, tennis, volleyball, pool and poolside bar, not to mention minibus service from sister hotel Mólyvos I in town. *Open April–Oct.*

**Evangelía Tekés**, at the port near the Sea Horse, t 025 307 1158, f 025 307 1233 (*mod–inexp*). Rooms with air-con, in a restored stone house.

**Malli**, up the hill in the old town, t 025 307 1010 (*inexp*). Equipped with a veranda offering spectacular views.

**Memma**, t 025 307 1734 (*inexp*). Charming place to stay in the warren of stone-clad streets, complete with its own garden.

**Posidon**, near the beach, t 025 307 1981, f 025 307 1570 (*C; inexp*). Quiet, good value and

some rooms have picture-postcard castle views. *Open May–Oct.*

**Studios Voula**, along the cobbled path to the castle, t 025 307 1305 (*inexp*). Simple studios, and a brand-new detached 'villa' with 2 double bedrooms, a spacious living area, cool stone floors and pine ceilings.

**Eftalóu Taverna**, t 025 307 1049. One of the best on Lésbos and the home of delicious stuffed courgette flowers and other delicacies, served in a shady garden, neither expensive nor touristy.

**Faros** at the end of Mólyvos harbour. Very good, serving tasty seafood specialities.

**Mermaid**. Famous for its fish and lobster 'with Lesbian sauces'.

**Onar**, t 025 307 2099. Small, but with a touch more style than some of the others; home-grown ingredients in its tasty specialities.

**Salguimi** *Kafeneíon*, in the *agora*. More traditional food and atmosphere, with a welcome respite from the tourist trash.

**T'Alonia Taverna**, outside Mólyvos near the Eftalóu road. Excellent, cheap and very popular with the locals; besides traditional Greek dishes it also cooks up breakfast.

**The Captain's Table**. Varied menu and a bit more expensive.

**To Panorama** beside the castle. Worth the strenuous hike up for the ultimate view; get there in time for a sundown drink or meal.

**To Pithari** (or O Gatos), up in the *agora*. Where prices are inching up while portions and quality are shrinking. But this is good and deservedly popular, with its balconies high on stilts and great views.

**To Xtapodi**. The harbour in Mólyvos is by far the most atmospheric, but inevitably

it that pirates killed all the monks except one, who collected the blood-soaked earth and moulded it into the icon; another says St Michael made it himself. The faithful press a coin to the icon; if it sticks, the wish they make will be granted. Mantamádos, like Ag. Paraskeví, ritually sacrifices a bull on the third Sunday after Easter, a feast that draws pilgrims from across the island. Further north, **Kápi**, one of several villages circling the 3,176ft Mount Lepétimnos, is the start of one of the new marked hiking trails on Lésbos that takes in some ravishing, luxuriant ravines. Further north lies the fetching village of **Sikaminiá** and, at the end of the road, the little fishing port of **Skála Sikaminiás**, in many ways the quintessence of a Greek island fishing village, locally renowned for its mild winters and good tavernas. The novelist Stratís Myrivílis was born in Sikaminiá, and next to the Restaurant Sikaminiá in Skála you can see the

touristy, place to eat fish: the 'Octopus' is authentic, good, and not overpriced, even though it appears on most of the island's postcards.

**Vafios** and **Ilias**, both in Vafiós (the village just above Mólyvos). Traditional meat tavernas with good pies and wine from the barrel.

**Pétra** ✉ 81109

**Clara**, at Avláki (1.5km from Pétra, with a shuttle bus), t 025 304 1532, *clara@ hellasnet.gr* (*B; lux–exp*). Hotel and bungalows around a seawater pool; all rooms have balconies and sea-views.

**Theofilos**, t 025 304 1080, t 025 304 1493 (*C; exp*). Large, with a pool. *Open April–Oct.*

**Michaelia**, on the beach, t 025 304 1730, t 025 302 2067 (*C; exp–mod*). Views and sports, but mainly tour operated. *Open May–Oct.*

**Studios Niki**, next to Michaelia, t 025 304 1601 (*inexp*). Plain, clean and quiet accommodation set in a garden of flowers and birds.

**Women's Agricultural Co-operative**, t 025 304 1238, f 025 304 1309, *womes@otenet.gr* (*inexp*). Now rents more than 100 rooms to visitors; starting at €20 for a double, all immaculately clean, tastefully decorated and good value. You are welcome to join in family life, fishing and working in the fields if you want; they also organize excursions to show visitors aspects of rural Greek life. Their taverna has some of the most scrumptious food on Lésbos, especially the delicious *mezédes* – try the fresh *dolmades* and mouthwatering aubergine jam, and reserve one of the dinky little balconies over the *plateía* if you can. *Open all year.*

**Niko's**. Recommended for seafood.

## Entertainment and Nightlife

Mólyvos has some more traditional summer entertainment – an open-air cinema opposite the taxi rank, a summer theatre festival with spectacular evening productions of ancient Greek drama and modern works, and music and dancing in the castle – as well as clubs.

**Gatelousi** (ΓΑΤΕΛΟΥΣΙ) between Mólyvos and Pétra (walkable from the latter). An amazing alfresco nightclub, resembling a cruise liner with its deck projecting from the rock face. It has a restaurant and a shuttle bus service that runs from 10pm to 5am.

**Pirates**. Plays the music of polite seduction.

**To Panorama** (the *agora* branch). Good for coffee and cake.

**Conga**. Open-air bar and club where you can sit by the waves.

**Bazaar**, nearer the harbour. Has an atmospheric little terrace.

**The Other Place**. Another dancing bar in the harbour, is happily sound-proofed in a very atmospheric old house, with Greek nights and traditional dancing on Thurs.

**The *Bouzouki* Taverna** down a track on the road to Eftaloú. Romantic gardens with good Greek musicians and singers and the chance to dance. Expensive drinks pay for the entertainment.

**Machine Dancing Bar**, in the former olive factory in Pétra. Oozes atmosphere with all the press machinery in view, and the top 2 floors engagingly derelict.

**Magenta Bar**. Bizarrely blue and yellow, pumps out a club sandwich of sounds until the early hours.

ancient mulberry tree ('*sikaminiás*' means mulberries) where the author used to sleep in a tree bed. His novel *The Mermaid Madonna* was inspired by the chapel of the **Panagía**, about which he once had a dream, although don't come looking for the icon that gave the book its name – Myrivílis invented it. Another novel, *The Schoolmistress with the Golden Eyes*, was based on a woman from Mólyvos who collaborated with the Germans, went mad and burnt her house down. Although you can swim at Skála Sikaminiás, the nearest good beach, a strand of rose-tinted volcanic sand (with tavernas and showers) is at **Tsónia** to the southeast, but you have to go by way of Klió to get there on wheels. There's a footpath through the olive groves from Skála.

## The Inland Route

The buses from Mytilíni to Mólyvos take the shorter, inland road (still, it takes an hour and 45 minutes). Keep your eyes peeled for a tree known as **Ag. Therapís Tzatzaliáris** (St Therapis of the Rags), where the superstitious hang bits of clothing belonging to ill relatives, hoping for a cure. The road passes near **Keramiá**, a village beloved for its cool springs and centuries-old trees; further along, it skirts the wide Gulf of Kallóni, where a lovely, intensely cultivated plain is dotted with Lombardy poplars. A signposted road leads to the Ionic **Temple of Mesi**, built in the 4th or 3rd century BC and dedicated to Aphrodite; the foundations and column drums remain. **Kalloní** (ΚΑΛΛΟΝΗ), the large village here, replaces the ancient city of Arisbe; its *acropolis* now hosts the medieval **Kástro**. Arisbe flourished until a few local swains abducted some girls from Míthymna. The girls' kinsfolk perhaps overreacted, destroying Arisbe and enslaving all its people. **Skála Kallóni** is a quiet family resort, its sandy beach ideal for small children. Famous for its sardines (eaten raw as a *mezé*) and anchovies, it's also a mecca for birdwatchers – a fad they say began here with the ever observant Aristotle – with many kinds of waders and visiting storks nesting on the chimney-pots.

West of Kallóni, the 16th-century Monastery of **Ag. Ignatios Limónos** was used as a secret Greek school under the Turks. Men only are allowed in to see the frescoes in the central church, but women don't have to feel hard done by: there are over 40 other chapels on the grounds, St Ignatius' own room, monks' cells, and the petrified wood, folk art and ecclesiastical artefacts in the excellent little museum. From Kallóni a road leads east up to the village of **Ag. Paraskeví**, where, in a rite going straight back to antiquity, a bull is bedecked with flowers and ribbons, paraded through the village, sacrificed and eaten in the three-day feast (in late May) of Ag. Charálambos, in conjunction with horse races – horse breeding being a serious island passion. Apart from having an unusually old-time feel (and an extraordinary number of men playing chess and backgammon, spilling out on to the street from the *kafeneíons*), the village is best known for making olive oil. Old presses adorn the surrounding countryside; some have been attractively converted into centres for conferences and local festivals. Further north, the green Ligona ravine below **Stýpsi**, on the slopes of Mount Lepétimnos, has the remains of 20 water mills and is a favourite venue for organized 'Greek Nights'.

## Mólyvos (Míthymna) and the North Coast Resorts

Up at the northernmost tip of the island is **Míthymna** (ΜΗΘΥΜΝΑ), although the locals still call it **Mólyvos** (ΜΟΛΥΒΟΣ), its Venetian name. By whatever name, it is the most popular and prettiest town on Lésbos, Mytilíni's arch-rival for centuries, although it has now dropped to third town on the island in terms of population. Míthymna was the birthplace of the poets Arion and Longus and the site of the tomb of the hero Palamedes, buried here during the Trojan War by Achilles and Ajax. Achilles besieged Míthymna, but with little success until the daughter of the king fell in love with him and opened the city gates, a kindness Achilles rewarded by having her slain for betraying her father.

Mólyvos is a symphony of dark-grey stone houses with red-tiled roofs, windows with brightly coloured shutters and gardens full of flowers, stacked above the lovely harbour and beach. For years a haunt of artists, and now of package tourists, Mólyvos has lost little of its charm: the steep cobbled lanes of the centre, known as the *agora*, are canopied with vines and lined with boutiques, while the taverna terraces are perched high on stilts with wonderful views across to Turkey. Climbing through the *agora*, you'll pass a small **Archaeology Museum** (*t 025 307 1059; open Tues–Sun 8.30–3*) on the way up to the striking **Genoese Castle** (*same hours*). In 1373, Francesco Gattilusi repaired this Byzantine fortress, but it fell to Mohammed the Conqueror in 1462. However, he didn't get it without a fight. Onetta d'Oria, wife of the Genoese governor, repulsed an earlier Turkish onslaught when she put on her husband's armour and led the people into battle. Note the Turkish inscription in marble over the gate. The fine, long pebble town beach lined with feathery tamarisks has loungers and watersports and becomes shingly sand at the far end, where nudists flock. East of Mólyvos, its sidekick **Eftaloú** has a tree-fringed beach, also popular with nudists, an excellent taverna and a bathhouse with very hot thermal springs.

## Pétra and Ánaxos

**Pétra** means rock, and in particular a sheer rocky spike, carved with 114 steps and crowned by the church of **Panagía Glykofiloússa**, 'Virgin of the Sweet Kiss' (1747). The icon of the same name belonged to a captain, but it insisted on staying atop this pinnacle, sneaking away every night even after the captain nailed it to his mast. He finally gave up and then the Virgin started bullying the mayor of Pétra to build her a church. When he gave in and the church was built, a special ceremony was held for its dedication. A boy bringing up a tray of *raki* for the workers slipped and fell over the precipice. But the Virgin wasn't far, and caught the boy in a puff of air and brought him back to the top of the cliff – not spilling a drop of the *raki*, either. No wonder, in spite of the heat, flocks of pilgrims tackle the climb up on 15 August, when they're rewarded with the traditional dish of *keskesi*, made of meat, grain, onions and spices. Below, the pretty village has winding lanes, Levantine-style wooden balconies, a fine beach rapidly being developed, and the **Women's Agricultural Co-operative**, which in 1985 launched its own taverna, where men have been spotted doing the washing-up.

Other beaches lie within easy striking distance of Pétra: **Avláki**, 1km west, a small sandy beach with tavernas and some sea grass, and **Ánaxos**, 3km away, a fine sandy

### A Minor Revolution

Since antiquity the upper class women of Lésbos have enjoyed more independence than most Greek women, but their rural sisters were among the least liberated in Europe, burdened by the dowry tradition, virtual slaves to the land and their homes, bent double under piles of fodder, tending the flocks, picking olives and grapes, besides doing all the housework and rearing the children. In 1983, the women of Pétra, desperate for a change, founded the first women's agricultural co-operative in Greece to provide bed and breakfast accommodation with local families (*see* 'Where to Stay' box). As well as providing women with opportunities, the scheme is a move towards Green tourism, offering hospitality in traditional houses and refurbished village settlements in a bid to halt the march of the concrete mixer across the land. The idea soon spread: a national Women's Agricultural Co-operative Council was set up in 1985; on Lésbos alone there are now co-operatives in Asomatos, Agiasos, and Polichnitos, all formed in the late 1990s. The Council also seeks to preserve old customs, handicrafts and local cuisine, believing that Greece will lose out unless its women play an active part in public life. Each co-operative has different specialities; on Lésbos they tend to sell their traditional sweets, liqueurs, fruits in syrup (*glykó*), olives, salted vineleaves, handmade pasta, and embroideries.

bay with fabulous views of Mólyvos, but unfortunately a burgeoning, ugly resort in its own right. From Náxos a lovely coastal path skirts the dark volcanic shore to the west leading to **Mikrí Tsichránta** and **Megáli Tsichránta**, tiny hamlets, the latter set on a charming little bay. This is oak country, and the larger buildings are oak warehouses; in the next village, **Kaló Limáni**, the warehouses have been converted into homes.

## Western Lésbos and the Petrified Forest

The northwest quarter of Lésbos is dramatic, volcanic and noticeably less humid than Mólyvos and Pétra. Despite its barren appearance, it is brimming with unusual wild herbs and birdlife: rose-coloured starlings, bee eaters, hoopoes and pairs of golden orioles. Until modern times it was the home of wild horses – some believe they may be the last link with the horse-breeding culture of the Troad in the late Bronze Age, mentioned in the *Iliad*. The modern village of **Ántissa** (ΑΝΤΙΣΣΑ) has inherited the name of **ancient Ántissa**, up on the north coast: to get there, follow the road as far as **Gavathás**, with a so-so beach and nice family-run hotel and taverna (**Hotel Restaurant Paradise**, *t 025 305 6376; mod*), and then walk east on a 1km path skirting the coast. Founded in the Bronze Age, Ántissa was violently joined to Lésbos in an earthquake. It was a musical place; after being shredded by the Maenads, the most important bits of Orpheus – his prophetic head and lyre – washed up here, perhaps inspiring Terpander, the 'father of Greek music' born in Ántissa c. 710 BC and credited with the invention of choric poetry, the *kithera* (a seven-string lyre, which gave its name to the guitar) and the foundation of Sparta's first music school. The Romans destroyed the town to punish the inhabitants for their support of the Macedonians, and all the meagre remains lie below **Ivriókastro**, 'Castle of the Hebrew'

# Tourist Information

**Eressos: t** 025 305 3557; *open Mon–Fri 10–noon and 7–9, Sat 10–noon.*

# Where to Stay and Eat

**Sígri** ✉ 81105
**Direct Greece** (*see* p.88). Has a number of apartments in Sígri and Skála Eressoú.
**Vision,** 1km outside Sígri, **t** 025 305 4226, **f** 025 305 4450 (*C; mod*). Well-designed hotel; all rooms have sea-view and benefit from the pool, but there's no beach.
**Remezzo.** Classy taverna, with the pick of the positions and the largest lobster tank.
**The Blue Wave,** down by the fishing boats. With octopus tentacles gripped by clothes pegs on a line; excellent, good value fish, although the owner's bolshy style is not to everyone's taste. The bar above is friendly and good for boat watching.
**The Golden Key.** Unbeatable *yigántes* and other home-baked dishes.
**To Kendro.** Great *kafeneíon* for *souvlaki, tavli* and watching the world go by.
**Notia Bar.** For after dinner drinks; never ceases to please musically with the very individual CD collection of the owner; it's an extremely atmospheric little red-walled place.

**Skála Eressoú** ✉ 81105
**Sappho Travel** on the main street, **t** 025 305 2140, *sappho@otenet.gr.* Organizes accommodation; has a helpful website of accommodation all over Lésbos, *www.lesvos.co.uk.*
**Aeolian Village,** sprawling between Eressós and Skála Eressoú, **t** 025 305 3585, **f** 025 305 3795 (*A; lux*). Pastel complex with large pools and a supervised children's club for a few hours' respite. *Open April–Oct.*
**Galini, t** 025 305 3138, *www.aegeas.gr* (*C; mod*). Good value air-con rooms set back from the beach amongst trees. *Open April–Oct.*
**Sappho the Eressian,** in Skála Eressoú, **t** 025 305 3495, **f** 025 305 3233 (*C; mod*). An orange, lesbian-only haven on the seafront, with comfy chairs down by the strand. *Open April–Oct.*
**Eressós, t** 025 305 3560 (*inexp*). Clean, plain rooms and a subterranean reception area.
**Soulatso,** on the waterfront. For fresh fish; translucent octopus are hung up in the sun with only the big blue sea beyond.
**Cine Sapho.** Hosts open-air films.
**Naos Club.** Offers you the 'spirit of the music' from midnight.
**Par-a-Sol,** on a wooden platform on the sand. One of the trendiest of trendy bars, with a wide choice of cocktails and some bar food.

(but really a Genoese fort facing the sea). The wonderful quiet beaches with views over to Mólyvos are the main reason for making the trek, and if you're lucky you'll hear the nightingales who are said to have learned to sing from Orpheus. A path follows the coast east towards Náxos and Ag. Pétra (*see above*).

West of modern Ántissa, the handsome Monastery of **Ag. Ioánnis Theológos Ipsiloú** is stunningly set on the promontory of a dead volcano. Founded in the 9th century and rebuilt in the 12th, it shares its pinnacle with military buildings and its museum contains a collection of antique religious paraphernalia. In the courtyard you can examine bits of petrified wood. The petrification began when the volcano erupted, and was further abetted by the quakes that have rocked this coast over the aeons.

Continuing west to the farthest end of Lésbos (a two-hour drive from Mytilíni), **Sígri** (ΣΙΓΡΙ) is a delight (though it can be windy), a bustling fishing village and carefully growing resortlet, complete with 18th-century Turkish castle and a gently shelving, sheltered sandy beach. Within an hour's walk either side of Sígri there are plenty of other coves and beaches, including **Fanerómeni**, which has contrastingly deep water.

Between Sígri and Eressós is Lésbos' 20 million-year old **petrified forest** (ΑΠΟΛΙΘΩ-ΜΕΝΟ ΔΑΣΟΣ), the only one in Europe and covering 37,000 acres is even larger than the famous one in Arizona, although here most of the trees are still buried below ground. These pines, beeches and sequoias were fossilized after being buried in volcanic ash; the colourful remains of the trunks have slowly become visible as the ash erodes. Others are on the offshore islets of **Nisiópi** (which also has a sandy beach to which caiques venture) and **Sarakína**. Some of the best specimens on Lésbos are near Sígri itself, along a fenced in 2.3km trail, some trunks standing, others fallen so you can see their wonderful colours. Sígri's newly opened **Natural History Museum** (*t 025 305 4434; open daily 8–8; adm*) occupies an august setting by the windmill and focuses on the petrified forest, with well-displayed examples and talks. For more information on Sígri, its intriguing water cistern, the forests and local walks, pick up a copy of Roy Lawrence's *Where the Road Ends: Sígri*, from Jan Adonakis.

The forest extends to the attractive village of **Eressós** (ΕΡΕΣΟΣ), overlooking a lush emerald plain tucked amid the rough volcanic tumult. Eressós is a low-key, ramshackle place with a shady main square of cafés, tavernas and old men. It inherited the name from ancient Eressós, some fragments of which still stand just east of **Skála Eressoú**, 4km away, down an avenue of whitewashed trees. Skála is endowed with a long, steeply shelving sand beach, lined with tamarisks and serviced by a lively if modern seaside village, a favourite of Greek families and gay women. In the attractive square is a bust of the famous Eressian Theoprastus (372–287 BC), Aristotle's friend, botanist and author of the *Characters*, a set of essays and moral studies on the picturesque people of his day. The inland road from Sígri to Eressós is an epic, primeval drive scented by sea daffodils, with scarred rock faces, ancient contoured stone walls and an amazing sense of space and purity.

## The Tenth Muse

The most famous and influential Eressian of them all was Sappho, born in the late 7th century BC; Eressós proudly minted coins bearing her portrait. Little else is known for certain of her life: she was an aristocrat, was married to a certain Kerklyas of Andros and perhaps had a daughter, and ran a marriage school for young ladies, to whom she dedicated many of her poems. Like her fellow islander and contemporary Alcaeus, she wrote what is known as *melic* poetry, personal and choral lyrics with complex rhythms (sometimes known as Sapphic stanzas) intended to be sung at private parties before a select company. One of her songs dedicated to a young girl is the first, and rarely surpassed, description of passion: 'Equal to the gods seems that man who sits opposite you, close to you, listening to your sweet words and lovely laugh, which has passionately excited the heart in my breast. For whenever I look at you, even for a moment, no voice comes to me, but my tongue is frozen, and at once a delicate fire flickers under my skin. I no longer see anything with my eyes, and my ears are full of strange sounds. Sweat pours down me, and trembling seizes me. I am paler than the grass, and seem to be only a little short of death...' Her influence was so powerful that Plato called her the 'Tenth Muse'. A strong but probably apocryphal tradition has it that she threw herself from the white cliffs of Lefkáda (*see* p.476) in despair over an unrequited love – for a man. Her poems that have survived have only done so by accident; considered morally offensive in 1073, they were the subject of book burnings in Rome and Constantinople.

# Southern Lésbos

Southern Lésbos, between the inland seas of Kalloní and Géras, is dominated by 3,162-ft **Mount Olympos**, one of 19 mountains in the Mediterranean bearing the same name. Almost all were peaks sacred to the local sky god, who, in this syncretic corner of the world, became associated with Zeus; hence, any local sky god's mountain would take the name of Zeus' home. In the shadow of Olympos, reached by a delightful road flanked by olive groves and natural springs, lies the lovely village of **Agiássos** (ΑΓΙΑΣΣΟΣ), a coach tour stop, but still one of the most interesting on Lésbos (*park at the foot of the village*), with its red-tile-roofed houses, medieval castle, and creeper-shaded market streets where locals gather at the traditional *kafeneío* with the peppermint-blue tables; carry on up to the bakery on your left for excellent walnut *baklava* and cheese pies. Founded in the 1100s by the Archbishop of Mytilíni, Valérios Konstantínos, the Church of the **Panagía** houses an icon of the Virgin, said to have been made by St Luke from mastic and wax and rescued from the iconoclasts. The present church building was constructed in 1812 after a fire destroyed the older structure, and it has a beautiful 19th-century interior, all grey and gilt, lit by hundreds of suspended lamps and chandeliers. The icons are very fine, and there's a small **Byzantine Museum** (*open 8–8; adm*) to the right of the church. One priest was a

## Tourist Information

Plomári: t 025 203 2535.

## Where to Stay and Eat

### Polichnítos/Skála Polichnítou ✉ 81300
**Gera Yera spa**, t 025 204 1229 (*inexp*). Tranquil rooms.
**Soft Tourism**, at Skála, t 025 204 2678 (*inexp*). Run by Erika and Lefteris; usually hosting courses for small groups, but happy to help individuals if they can.
A handful of tavernas line the harbour and strand serving some of the freshest fish on the island, sold directly from the dock; the *mezédes* are delicious and there are customers who seem to be there 24 hrs a day nursing *karafákis* of *ouzo*.
**Polikentro Taverna**, at the entrance to the village. The best place for food.
**Iotis** and **Taverna Tsitsanos**, down at Nyfída. Both are excellent.
**Tzitzifies**. A good bet.

### Vaterá ✉ 81300
**Vaterá Beach**, t 025 206 1212, *hovatera@ otenet.gr* (*C; exp*). Run in a relaxed fashion by the inimitable Barbara and George in a tranquil floral setting, allowing you to unwind to your heart's content; the beach-side restaurant offers half-board and vegetarian options to boot. *Open May–mid-Oct.*
**Aphrodite**, by the beach, t 025 206 1288, *www.aphroditehotel.gr* (*C; mod*). Well equipped hotel and apartments with lots of sports and kid's activities, plus babysitting service, bike hire and fishing excursions.
**Diónysos Club**. 1 of 2 discos in Vaterá; also has a very good campsite with a swimming pool. On the west end, by Ag. Fokás, are 2 superb fish tavernas, with gorgeous views.
**Chakadakis**. Also good.
**Mylos**, on the beach. Soporific café-bar decked out in reggae colours.

### Plomári ✉ 81200
Almost everything is booked by Vikings, but you may find a room in the old centre. If you draw a blank, **Rented Rooms Union**, t 025 203 1666, should be able to help .
**Okeanis**, 100m from the sea, t 025 203 2469, f 025 203 2455 (*C; mod*).
**Ammodis Akti**, in Ag. Isídoro, t 025 203 2825, (*C; inexp*). *Open April–Oct.*
**Lida I or II**, t/f 025 203 2507 (*B; inexp*). With traditional housing.

master at the *sandoúri*, or hammer dulcimer, and some sell his recordings, as well as local ceramics. From the Kípos Panagías Taverna, there's a splendid view of the village and its orchards that produce excellent black plums and walnuts. A lovely path leads from Agiássos to Plomári on the coast, passing by way of the ruins of **Palaiókastro**, of uncertain date, and the pleasant village and fountains of **Megalochóri**.

Chestnut and pine groves cover much of the region, one of Lésbos' prettiest, and the road west to **Polichnítos** (ΠΟΛΙΧΝΙΤΟΣ) is especially lovely. Polichnítos isn't much itself, although a ground-floor workshop welcomes visitors with a quirky display of taxidermy, reconstructed amphorae and a life-sized, garish doll. There is a new **Municipal Folklore and Historical Museum** (*t 025 204 2992*)and the thermal spa, **Gera Yera** (*t 025 204 1229; open 7–11am and 4–7pm in season; adm*), oozing out the hottest waters in Europe (91°C). Erika, who runs it with partner Lefteris, recommends a dip even in mid-summer, reminding you to 'fight heat with heat' – it is very refreshing. Near the harbour of **Skála Polichnítou**, there's a beach with warmer water than off the exposed coastal strips, and many tavernas. Another pretty beach near the mouth of the Gulf of Kalloní, **Nyfída** flies the blue flag, although it can be windy.

South of Polichnítos, **Vríssa** was the home town of Briseis, the princess who caused the rift between Achilles and Agamemnon at Troy. Only a wall remains of the Trojan town destroyed in 1180 BC, and a Genoese tower stands to the west of Vríssa. Ruins of a 1st-century BC Doric Temple of Diónysos Vrysageni ('Born of the Springs') stand on Cape Ag. Fókas. This marks the start of Lésbos' longest beach (9km) at **Vaterá** (ΒΑΤΕΡΑ). For a lovely excursion, walk up the path marked with yellow circles, beginning at the River Voúrkos, to **Áno Stavrós** and **Ampelikó**, a charming village in a ravine under Mt Olympos, with Roman ruins, a castle and pretty church. In 1998, an extraordinary cache of animal and plant fossils in the area was discovered, including the fossilized shell of a tortoise the size of an old VW beetle. Investigations are under way by the universities of Athens and Utrecht, and finds are displayed in the temporary **museum** at Vríssa (*t 025 206 1711*). Back along the coast to the east, **Plomári** (ΠΛΟΜΑΡΙ) is Lésbos' second city and port (pop 10,000), with attractive houses decorated with traditional *sachnissinía* (wooden galleries). Its central square, dominated by a 500 year old plane tree, is as funky as Mytilíni Town and reeks of Greece's favourite aperitif – Kéfi, Veto, Tikelli and Barbayiánni *ouzos* are all distilled here, and drunk by tourists in situ as Plomári discovers resort life in a big way under the palm trees. Plomári has a beach but **Ag. Isídoros** just east has an even better one. The inland roads are quite attractive; from the main road, an unpaved one descends to the pretty sandy cove at **Tárti**. At Pérama, a dingy olive oil port, you'll find a ferry across the Gulf of Géras, 'the Bay of Olives', to Skála Loutron, near Mytilíni Town.

# Límnos (ΛΗΜΝΟΣ)

Límnos hardly fits any Greek island stereotypes. It lies low, with gently rolling hills: a lush green carpet in the spring that becomes crackling yellow-brown in the summer, when water is in short supply. The landscape is dotted with vineyards, fields of grain,

# Límnos

Cape Hermaeon

Ormos Plaka

Plaka

Panagia

Ag. Alexandros

Chloi (Kavirio)

Hephestia

Kotsinas

Tigani Bay

Pournias Bay

Aliki Lake

Cape Keros

Ormos Keros

Cape Kavalari

Kontopouli

Kalliopi

Ag. Sozos Monastery

Repanidi

Luchna

Romano

Chortarolimni Lake

Rosopouli

Poliochne

Varos

Moudros

Fisini

Karpasi

Astiki

Propouli

War Cemetery

Kaminia

Ag. Sofia

Skandali

Nea Koutalis

Ag. Dimitrios

Dafni

Katalakkon

SERGITSI

Pedino

Libadochori

Old Pedino

Tsimandria

Moudros Bay

Sveria

Sardes

Kornos

Agkariones

Tsoutsfia

Mt. Skopia
(423m / 1390ft)

Kaspakas

Kontias

Vryokastro

MYRINA (KASTRO)

Cape Mourtezflos

Ag. Ioannis

Avlonas

Platis

Thanos

Nevgatis

Riha Nera

To Kavala & Thessaloniki

To Lesbos & Ag. Efstratios

10 km

5 miles

N

Límni (ΛΗΜΝΟΣ)

# Getting There and Around

**By air**: connections 3 times daily with Athens, daily except Thurs with Thessaloníki, 3 times weekly with Lésbos. **Olympic Airways**, t 025 402 2114/2078, is located opposite Hotel Paris; for **airport** information, call t 025 403 1204. To reach the airport from Mýrina, take the Olympic bus, or catch a taxi, but it's a hefty 22km trip, so agree a price before setting off.

**By sea**: **ferry** connections 6 times a week with Lésbos, 3 times a week with Rafína, twice a week with Piraeus, Chíos, Thessaloníki, Alexandroúpolis, once a week with Psará, Rhodes, Sámos and Kos; 4 ferries a week and **day excursions** in season run to Ag. Efstrátios (*see* p.544). During the summer months, there's a weekly excursion to Mount Áthos. Some of the island's best beaches are only accessible by boat. **Caiques** make the excursion from Mýrina's north harbour to these beaches and the sea caves at Skála. **Motorboats** can be hired at other nearby beaches, such as Riha Néra, t 025 402 4617. **Port authority**: t 025 402 2225.

**By road**: buses (t 025 402 2464) around Límnos are not very frequent. Many villages have only 1 service a day, so there's no way to get back to Mýrina the same day, hence the town's many **taxis**, and **moped** and **car** hire firms.

# Tourist Information

**Tourist Information Office**: near the port, t 025 402 2935.

**El Travel**, 11 Ralli Kopsídi Street, t 025 402 4988, *eltravel@lim.forthnet.gr*.

**Petrides Travel**, 116 Karatsá Street, t 025 402 2998, *mapet@lim.forthnet.gr*. Also rent cars.

# Where to Stay and Eat

Accommodation on Límnos is limited and surprisingly upmarket; don't arrive in July and August without a booking or a sleeping bag.

## Mýrina ✉ 81400

**Akti Mýrina**, on the beach, t 025 402 2681, *akti@lim.forthnet.gr* (*L; lux*). Posh deluxe bungalow complex with 3 bars, 4 restaurants, 3 tennis courts, its own nightclub, private beach, caique, but a rather disappointing swimming pool. Wooden chalets house 125 rooms. The complex is famous throughout Greece, for its astronomical prices alone; however, booking through a UK holiday agent or out of season should ease the pain. *Open May–Oct*.

**Límnos Village**, on Platís Beach t 025 402 3500, f 025 402 3255 (*L; lux*). Another large all inclusive complex with a pool, watersports,

quirky scarecrows and beehives (the island's thyme honey was favoured by the gods); it takes pride in being one of the few islands to support a herd of deer. But the main occupation of Límnos has long been military: its magnificent natural harbour near the mouth of the Dardanelles has ensured that the island has always been of strategic importance. It was the holy island of the smithy god Hephaistos (Vulcan), who was worshipped on Mount Móschylus, which in ancient times emitted a fiery jet of asphaltic gas; today Límnos' volcanic past is manifest in its astringent hot springs and the highly sulphuric 'Limnian earth', found near Repanídi, used from ancient times until the Turkish occupation for healing wounds and stomach aches.

## History

Límnos' intriguing past also bucks stereotypes. Homer wrote that the first islanders hailed from Thrace, but Herodotus says they were Tyrrhenian – related to the mysterious Etruscans of Latium and Tuscany. This remarkable claim has been given substance by pre-6th century BC non-Greek inscriptions found on Límnos that show linguistic similarities to the Etruscan language, as do some of the ancient burials. The Etruscans themselves claimed to have originally immigrated to Italy from Asia Minor.

children's activities and everything else. *Open May–Oct.*

**Porto Mýrina Palace**, in Avlon Bay, t 025 402 4805, f 025 402 4858 (*L; lux*) Built in 1995 around a 4th-century BC Temple of Artemis; clad in marble, it boasts an Olympic outdoor pool and an indoor one, a fitness centre and all mod cons. *Open May–Oct.*

**Astron**, t 025 402 4392, f 025 402 4396 (*A; exp*). Nicely furnished apartments, and fairly centrally located. *Open all year.*

**Nefeli**, off Romaíkos Beach, t 025 402 3551, f 025 402 4041 (*B; exp*). Lovely spot under the castle, but can be noisy due to nearby bars.

**Villa Afrodite**, just outside the centre near Platís Beach, t 025 402 4795, f 025 402 5031 (*A; exp*). With a pool and pleasant gardens.

**Ifestos**, 17 Eth. Antistasseos, 100m from Platís Beach, t 025 402 4960, f 025 402 3623 (*C; exp–mod; cheaper if booked through Sunvil, see p.89*). Friendly, well-designed, new hotel; all rooms with a fridge and balcony.

**Kastro Beach**, near post office, t 025 402 2772, f 025 402 2784 (*B; exp–mod*). Comfortable.

**Afrodite Apartments**, near Riha Néra, t 025 402 3489, f 025 402 5031 (*mod*). Run by the same family as Villa Afrodite; set amongst greenery and ideal for self catering.

**Sunset**, 2km north at Ag. Ioánnis Beach, t 025 406 1555 (*D; mod*). Peaceful furnished apartments. *Open June–Sept.*

**Lemnos**, t 025 402 2153, f 025 402 3329 (*C; mod–inexp*). Good waterfront bet.

Tavernas and grills line the Mýrina waterfront:

**Avra**, where the boat docks. Undoubtedly one of the best deals in town.

**O Glaros**, in the Turkish harbour, t 025 402 2220 (€20–25). Pretty taverna with a veranda and view of the castle, specializing in fish, crayfish and lobster.

**O Platanos**, suitably situated by a pair of massive plane trees in a quaint squarelet. With excellent traditional fare.

If you fancy a spectacle, ask at EOT about the Limnian dances put on by the **Kehayiades Folklore Association**. For more active involvement, head for **Avlonas Club**, just out of town.

### Kontiás/Tsimántria ✉ 81400

There are about 20 rooms to rent in Kontiás, and good tavernas.

**Nasos Kotsinadelis' Tavernain**, in Tsimántria. Famous for its chicken grilled over coals. Mr Kotsinadélis is the island's foremost *lyra* player, and on 15 Aug he serenades his customers.

### Moúdros ✉ 81401

**To Kyma**, t 025 407 1333, f 025 407 1484 (*B; exp*). Traditional hotel and a tranquil place to stay, with a reasonable restaurant and bar.

But Límnos was exceptional from the start. Excavations at Polióchne have uncovered a settlement of oval huts dating back to 4000 BC – the most advanced Neolithic civilization yet discovered in the Aegean. These precocious Limnians may have been the first to colonize Troy; the dates coincide and there were certainly close cultural contacts between the two into the Mycenaean era. Whoever they were, the ancient Limnians were not Greek. During the Persian wars, they captured some Athenian women and had children by them. When these mixed race children began putting on airs, the Limnians were so outraged that they slaughtered them and their mothers, giving rise to the expression 'Limnian deeds', synonymous with especially atrocious acts. The gods punished them by making their wives and animals barren. In dismay the Limnians went to Delphi, where the oracle said the only cure for it was to promise to surrender their independence to Athens if the Athenians ever sailed to Límnos in one day. It seemed a fair hedge, until Athens conquered territory near Mount Áthos, and General Miltiades appeared on Límnos to claim what was promised by the oracle.

The Venetians took Límnos in the 13th century, but it was soon regained by the Byzantines. In 1475 Mohammed the Conqueror sent troops to conquer Límnos, only to be repelled by the heroine Maroúla, who seized her dying father's weapons and uttered a blood-curdling battle cry. In 1478, however, Mohammed came in person and took the island. The Turks held it until 1912; later, Moúdros Bay became the naval base of the Allies in the Gallipoli campaign.

## Mythology

Hephaistos (in Latin, Vulcan) was so weakly when he was born that his mother Hera hurled him off Mount Olympos. He survived by falling in the sea, near Límnos, where the sea goddesses Thetis and Eurynome cared for him. Years later, when Hera found Thetis wearing a magnificent brooch made by Hephaistos, she had a change of heart, brought her son back to Olympos and married him to the lovely Aphrodite. Hephaistos later tried to rescue his mother when Zeus hung her by the wrists from the sky for rebelling against him. Zeus in his fury picked up the upstart and once again hurled him from Mount Olympos. This time he fell smack on Límnos, a fall that crippled him for life, despite all the care lavished on him by the islanders. His lameness recalls the early days of metallurgy in many cultures, when the powers of the smith were so valued that he was hobbled like a partridge to keep him from running away or joining an enemy.

Hephaistos was so beloved on Límnos that when Aphrodite betrayed him with the war-god Ares, the women of Límnos tossed her cult statue into the sea. Aphrodite retaliated by making their breath and underarms stink (Robert Graves suggests this may have been because they worked with woad, the putrid-smelling blue dye used in the manufacture of tattoo ink). This led the men of Límnos to prefer the company of captive Thracian women. The smelly women of Límnos were having none of this: they doctored their husbands' wine, slit their throats, threw their bodies into the sea and lived as Amazons, warlike and independent. When Jason and the Argonauts appeared on the horizon, the women would have attacked had not one of them realized that a shipload of Greek sailors was just what they needed to continue the race. So the Argonauts met only the kindest courtesy, and a son born to Jason, Euneus, went on to become King of Límnos during the Trojan War, supplying the Achaeans with wine.

Another figure associated with Límnos was Philoctetes, the son of Heracles. Philoctetes had inherited his father's famous bow when Heracles was dying in torment from Nessus' poisoned shirt, as Philoctetes was the only one who would light the pyre to put him out of his misery. When Zeus made Heracles an immortal, Hera, who never liked him, took out her pique on his son, sending a poisoned snake after Philoctetes when the Troy-bound Achaeans landed on Límnos. Bitten on the ankle, Philoctetes lingered behind in pain – his comrades could not stomach the stench of his gangrenous wound – and he lived in an island cave, with only his bow for comfort. After the death of Achilles, an oracle declared that Achaeans could only capture Troy with Philoctetes' bow. Odysseus and Neoptolemos, the son of Achilles, tried to take the bow from him by trickery (see Sophocles' Philoctetes), but in the end, according to most accounts, Philoctetes himself took his bow to Troy, where he slew Paris.

# Mýrina

Mýrina (ΜΥΡΙΝΑ), the island's appealing port and capital, is Límnos' only town of any size, though tiny in comparison with most Northeastern Aegean capitals. It is sometimes known as Kástro for its landmark, a romantic castle built over the rocky promontory in the midst of the sandy shore. A long main shopping street noodles up from the commercial harbour in the south, lined by houses and shops built in the Turkish or Thracian style with little gardens. Although a new boutique or shop opens every year, on the whole Mýrina still very much belongs to the Límnians and offers the distinct sights and smells – cologne, freshly ground coffee, and pungent herbs – of old Greece. There isn't much to see inside, but the walk up to the **kástro** offers a fine view over much of the low rolling island and across the sea to Mount Áthos. The castle foundations date back to classical times, when it was the site of a Temple of Artemis; the walls were built in 1186 by Andronikos Comnenus I, then substantially rebuilt by the Venetians in the 15th century, and the Turks a century later.

The Kástro divides Mýrina's waterfront into two: a 'Turkish' or harbour beach on the south side near the commercial port and, to the north, the main long sandy Romaíkos or 'Greek beach', with much of Mýrina's night life. The north port is closed by Cape Petassós and the pretty beach of **Aktí Mýrina**, on the spot where the Amazons of Límnos hurled their hapless husbands into the sea. Off Romaíkos Beach, the **Archaeology Museum** (*t 025 402 2990; open Tues–Sun 9–3; adm*) has been renovated to show off its superb collection. Upstairs are prehistoric relics from Polióchne, divided into four different periods by colour, beginning with the 'Black' period, from 4000 BC. Downstairs are more recent discoveries from Hephestía, Chloï and Mýrina.

## Around Mýrina

There are beaches both north and south of Mýrina, where discreet freelance camping is usually tolerated. North of Mýrina the beaches are pebbly but safe for children, especially **Ríha Néra**, with tavernas and watersports, **Avlónas**, with a bungalow development, and **Ag. Ioánnis**, again with tavernas. North of **Ag. Ioánnis**, the road deteriorates rapidly, but with a jeep, head up the coast for about fifteen minutes until you reach a promontory with a three-pronged rock; the sunset is to die for.

The more popular beaches are past the army base south of Mýrina, on the beautiful buxom bays below **Platís** and **Thános** (a particularly beautiful, golden stretch of sand). Others with no facilities at all are scattered all the way to **Kontiás**: aim for **Nevgátis**, a kilometre of fine sand kissed by a crystal, shallow sea. Kontiás is the island's liveliest and prettiest red-tiled village, home of Kontiás *ouzo*. In the summer it fills up with returned emigrants from South Africa and Australia. Just south is an old Mycenaean tower called the **Vryókastro**; **Evgáti** is a decent sandy beach.

# Eastern Límnos

East of Kontiás, **Néa Koutális** has a **Nautical Tradition Museum** (*t 025 409 2383 for hours*) and the best beach, with pine trees and restaurants, on Moúdros Bay, one of the biggest natural harbours in the Mediterranean. In April 1915, the Anglo-French fleet launched its ill-fated attack on the Dardanelles from here, a campaign planned partly on Límnos by Churchill, then Lord of the Admiralty; in 1918, after leaving over 30,000 dead at Gallipoli, an armistice with the Turks was signed on board a ship in the bay where it had all begun. East of gloomy **Moúdros** (ΜΟΥΔΡΟΣ), the island's second largest town and even today dependent on the military, is the immaculately kept lawn of the **British Commonwealth war cemetery**; the 800 graves belong to wounded personnel brought back to Moúdros, only to die in hospital. Límnos' airport (civil and military) is at the north end of the bay, where the island is only a few kilometres wide. Most of the other beaches around the bay are on the muddy side.

The ancient Limnians preferred living on the island's easterly wings. Northeast of the airport on Pournías Bay, **Kótsinas** was the walled medieval capital of Límnos. A statue of the heroine Maroúla stands here and a spring with good water flows down a long stairway by the church, **Zoodóchos Pigí**. A couple of pleasant, sleepy bars overlook the tiny fishing port, while from the top of the village there are views east across the island to the Aliki and Chortarolimni lagoons, full of tiny shrimp; in winter over 5,000 pink flamingoes from as far away as Iran and the south of France migrate here, and share these wetlands (now a conservation area under Natura 2000) with bright bee-eaters, falcons, swans, herons and the rare ruddy shelduck. On the coast, **Ormos Kéros** has a sandy stretch of beach that is the most popular on the island with both swimmers and (experienced) windsurfers, filling the inner curves of Pournías Bay with dunes all the way to **Kontopoúli**. Kontopoúli replaces ancient Mýrina's rival, **Hephestía**, named after the god who crash-landed here. Mostly unexcavated, part of the theatre, a few ancient houses, and bits of the *acropolis* and tombs remain.

Across little Tigáni Bay from Hephestía, **Chloï** (*open 9.30–3.30*) is better known these days as **Kavírio** after the earliest-known sanctuary of the Underworld deities of fertility, the Cabiri, before the cult was transferred to Samothrace. Guided tours are offered of the Archaic foundations of the sanctuary, built around a 6th–7th century BC temple of initiation, with the bases of twelve Doric columns, but not much more besides a graceful setting. There is a beach below and a bungalow hotel. Under the sanctuary a trail at the end of the ledge leads to the **Cave of Philoktétis**, the miserable archer. Another Trojan War site is beyond the large, pleasant village of **Pláka** at the tip of Cape Hermaeon, where a beacon was lit by order of Agamemnon at the Trojan War – a signal ominously relayed over the islands back to Mycenae. About 30m off the shore of Pláka are the ruins of **Chryse**, an ancient city submerged by an earthquake. A Temple of Apollo was discovered in a reef; on a calm day you can see its marble blocks from a boat. Pláka has good beaches, Ag. Stéfanos and Mandrí, but little in the way of tourist facilities.

**Polióchne** (ΠΟΛΙΟΧΝΗ), the island's most important archaeological site (*open 9.30–5.30*), is signposted from **Kamínia**, on Límnos' southeast wing. Here Italian archaeologists discovered seven different layers of civilization, one on top of the other. The oldest Neolithic town predates the Egyptian dynasties, the Minoan kingdoms of Crete, and even the earliest level of Troy; walls and houses remain of the next oldest town (2000 BC) which was probably destroyed by an earthquake but could

> **The Perfect Christmas Wine?**
>
> Although now mostly devoted to grains and cotton, Límnos was famous since antiquity for its vineyards; Aristotle wrote about the traditional red wine of the island, produced from a very ancient and unique variety of grape called Limnio (locally referred to as Kalambáki). No other wine tastes anything like it; wine experts, grasping for a description of its bouquet, have hit upon sage and bay leaf, rather like turkey stuffing. The variety has been transplanted in Chalkidikí, near Mount Áthos, where the Domaine Carrás produces a sophisticated Limnio, blended with 10 per cent Cabernet Sauvignon. White grapes grown on Límnos are now usually Moscháto Alexándrias, which yields a fine dry white wine with a light muscat fragrance, and is the favourite quaffing wine in the tavernas of Thessaloníki.

claim the oldest known baths in the Aegean; the third city dates back to the Copper Age, while the top Bronze Age settlement was the Límnos of Homer, dating from 1500 to 100 BC. There's little to see other than the walls of the second city and the foundations of houses, but the explanations in English help bring them to life. Between Polióchne and the abandoned monastery of **Ag. Sózos** to the south stretches the sandy expanse known as the 'Sahara of Límnos'. Ag. Sózos overlooks the sea from a high cliff and on 8 September each year it is the focus of a small religious festival.

# Ag. Efstrátios (ΑΓ. ΕΥΣΤΡΑΤΙΟΣ)

The remote, partly dry, partly green little volcanic triangle of **Ag. Efstrátios** (locally known as **t'Aïstratí**) lies 21 nautical miles southwest of its big sister Límnos. It is linked by ferry four times a week from Límnos (*call Límnos Port Authority, t 025 402 2225*); the port is too shallow for the big boats, so be prepared to transfer into caiques. Rich in minerals (including petroleum), the islet has been inhabited from Mycenaean times, and on the north coast stand the walls and ruins of the ancient settlement, which endured into the Middle Ages. In 1968 an earthquake wreaked havoc on Ag. Efstrátios' port and major village, and now nearly all of the island's 250 inhabitants live next to a wide, sandy beach in a rather dreary village of concrete huts thrown up by the junta after the disaster; as on Alónissos, the inhabitants weren't allowed to repair their homes.

The sea – the surrounding waters are transparent and rich in fish – brings in most of the inhabitants' income. Besides the village beach, which is really quite pleasant, there are several others scattered about that are perfect for playing Robinson Crusoe, but you will need to hike for at least an hour or hire a caique to reach them; for real isolation try the long sandy beach at Ag. Efstrátios' baby islet, **Vélia**. Between 1936 and 1962 Ag. Efstrátios played Alcatraz to scores of Greek Communists. Today it receives very few visitors, but if you want to stay, the **Xenonas Aï-Strati Pension** (*t 025 409 3329; inexp*), is a good bet and occupies one of the very few houses to survive the quake; there are also quite a few rooms, tolerated free camping on any beach, a small shop or two and a couple of tavernas with very limited menus.

# Sámos (ΣΑΜΟΣ)

*A ship goes away from Chíos/With two small rowing boats*
*She came to Sámos and moored there/And sat and reckoned*
*How much is a kiss worth/In the East, in the West?*
*A married woman's, four/A widow's, fourteen.*
*An unmarried girl's is cheaper/You take it with a joke.*
*But if it touches your heart/Oh, then, Christ and the Virgin, help!*

Traditional song from Chíos

Famed for its wine, women, song and ships, Sámos, the 'Isle of the Blest', has always been one of the most important islands in Greece, and since the 1980s it has become one of the most touristy as well. Despite savage forest fires in July 2000, when a state of emergency was briefly declared, pine forests, olive groves and vineyards still cover most of its emerald hills, so fertile that Menander wrote in the 4th century BC *Kai tou pouliou to gala*, 'Here even the hens give milk' (a slogan now used by a Greek supermarket chain). The countryside ranges from lovely, gentle and bucolic to the spectacular and dramatic; the coast is indented with numerous sandy coves, and two mountains furnish imposing background scenery: central Mount Ámpelos (3,740ft) and in the west, Mount Kérkis, a looming 4,740ft, both a continuation of the mainland chain that Sámos broke away from in a cataclysm millennia ago. Two famous couples, Zeus and Hera and Antony and Cleopatra, chose Sámos for their dallying, and to this day it seems to have the power of awakening romance in second or third honeymoons, mostly in the form of northern European couples on self-catering package holidays (a far cry from Cleopatra's gilded barge, pet leopards, perfumed baths and dance troupes, but there you go). On the other hand, it is one of the most expensive islands, and to arrive without a hotel reservation in the summer is tantamount to sleeping on the beach.

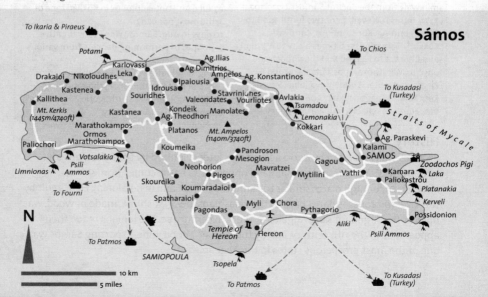

Sámos

# Getting There and Around

## By Air

5 daily flights from Athens with **Olympic** (in Sámos, **t** 027 302 7237; in Pythagório, **t** 027 306 1213); also with Aegean/Cronus. Olympic also flies twice weekly to Thessaloníki. Airport: **t** 027 306 1219. There are many charters from northern Europe, rising to 20 a day in July and Aug. The airport is 17km from Sámos and 4km west of Pythagório. The bus only runs between Sámos, Pythagório and the airport 4 times a day, so you may have to take a taxi.

## By Sea

Sámos has 3 ports of call – Sámos (Vathí), Karlóvassi and Pythagório. Check with ticket agencies for specific arrival and departure locations. **Ferry** connections daily with Piraeus, Ikaría, Foúrni and Pátmos, 5–6 times a week with Kálymnos, Kos, Léros, and Lipsí, 4–5 times a week with Chíos, Lésbos and Agathónissi, 3 times a week with Mýkonos, twice a week with Rhodes and Sýros, once to twice a week with Páros, Náxos, Límnos, Thessaloníki and Alexandroúpolis. **Port authority**: Sámos (Vathí), **t** 027 302 7890; Karlóvassi, **t** 027 303 0888; Pythagório, **t** 027 306 1225. From Órmos Marathókampos there are **hydrofoil** excursions to Foúrni, Pátmos and Samiopoúla islet.

## By Road

From the station on Ioannou Lekáti St (a 10-min walk from the dock at Sámos), **t** 027 302 7270, **buses** run every hr or two (until 5pm) to Pythagório, Ag. Konstantínos, Karlóvassi, Kokkári, Tsamadoú; 5–6 times a day to Mytilíni and Chóra; 4 to Heréon and the airport; and once to Marathókampos, Votsalákia and Pírgos. **Car** rental is widely available: **Speedy RentaCar**, Pythagório, **t** 027 306 1502, *auto1@ otenet.gr*, is a reliable, family-run agency

offering comprehensive insurance, or **Reliable**, Themístokli Sofoúli and Pindárou, **t** 027 302 7337, **f** 027 302 8570. Taxi: Sámos, **t** 027 302 8404, Pythagório, **t** 027 306 1450.

# Tourist Information

**EOT**: hides away on Martíou St, Sámos, **t** 027 302 8530; *open only weekdays in season 9–2*.
**Tourist police**: Sámos, **t** 027 302 7333; Pythagório, **t** 027 306 1333; Kokkári, **t** 027 309 2333; Karlóvassi, **t** 027 303 3333.
**British Vice Consulate**: 15 Themístokli Sofoúli St, Sámos, **t** 027 302 7314.
**Rhenia Tours**, 15 Themístokli Sofoúli St, **t** 027 308 8800, *vorsprun@gemini.diavlos.gr*. Also offices in Pythagório, Kokkári, Votsalákia and the airport. Pick up a free copy of *Summer Days* for useful titbits and suggested walks.

# Internet

**Diavlos**, beside Sámos police station.
**Nefeli Bar**, on the waterfront in Pythagório.

# Festivals

**Holy Wednesday**: washing of feet at Timíou Stavroú Monastery.
**20 July**: Profítis Ilías celebrated in many villages.
**26 July**: Ag. Paraskeví in Vathí.
**27 July**: Ag. Panteleímonos in Kokkári (one of the most popular).
**10 days in Aug**: Sámos Wine Festival, with troupes of performing dancers from various parts of Greece
**6 Aug**: Celebration of the Revolution, Sámos, and of Metamorphosis, Pythagório.
**29 Aug**: Ag. Ioánnis in Pythagório.
**8 Sept**: Vrontiáni Monastery.

## History

Sámos was inhabited by 4000 BC, and was later colonized by the Pelasgians and later by the Carians from the mainland opposite. Its name comes from *sama*, Phoenician for high place (similar to Samothráki and Sámi in Kefaloniá). Hera's cult by the River Imbroussas dates back to the Pelasgians; her first shrine, made of wood, was built by the Argonaut King Angaios in the 13th century BC. The Ionians made their appearance in the 11th century, and by the Archaic period wine-exporting Sámos was one of the most prosperous states in the Aegean.

In 670 BC, the island had become one of the most important city states under an oligarchy, unleashing its creative juices and a taste for adventure. Its shipbuilders invented a long, swift warship known as the *sámaina*, in which Samians sailed the open seas, especially frequenting Libya and Egypt; in c. 640 BC, one, Kolaios became the first known man to sail through the Straits of Gibraltar – he was blown off course – and visit Tartessos in Spain, returning with a fabulous pile of gold. In 550 BC, the tyrant Polykrates took over the island and soon became the most powerful man in Greece, ruling the Aegean with a then-enormous fleet of 150 *samainae*, which he used to extract tolls and protection money; he was also the first, along with Corinth, to build *triremes*. Polykrates was the first tyrant to lavishly patronize the arts and poetry. He oversaw the three greatest public works of the day: the building of the great Temple of Hera, the creation of the massive harbour mole, and the digging of the Efplinion Tunnel through a mountain to bring water to his capital, now called Pythagório after Polykrates' most famous subject, the philospher Pythagoras.

Under their tyrant, the Samians swanned around in the finest clothes and jewels and even knocked down their *palestra* to build pleasure dens with names such as the 'Samian Flowers' and the 'Samian Hotbed'. Polykrates' good fortune worried his friend and ally, King Amassis of Egypt, who warned that he would attract the envy of the gods unless he brought at least a small disaster or deprivation upon himself. Polykrates considered, and threw his favourite ring into the sea, thinking it would placate Fate. Three days later a fisherman caught a fish with the ring in its stomach, and returned it to Polykrates. Amassis recognized this as an evil omen, and broke off their friendship to spare himself grief later on. To ward off doom Polykrates had a bodyguard of a thousand archers. But they couldn't save him from his own ambition; in 522 BC, lured by the promise of yet more treasure by Cyrus' satrap Orsitis, he was crucified on a bluff overlooking his beloved Sámos.

A constant throughout ancient history is Sámos' feud with its Ionian rival on the mainland, Miletos. Whatever Miletos did, Sámos did the opposite, siding in turn with the Persians, the Spartans and the Athenians in the great disputes of the age. During their second invasion of Greece, the Persians occupied Sámos and kept their fleet at the island, where it was attacked by the Greeks in the Battle of Mykále (479 BC) and soundly defeated – helped by the defection of the Samians in the Persian navy. The Battle of Mykále once and for all eliminated Persian threats from the sea, and after the battle, Sámos allied herself with Athens, and became a democracy; when Miletos sided with Athens, Sámos as usual didn't and even defeated an Athenian fleet sent by Pericles in 441, before finally capitulating. In 391 BC, Sámos made a last attempt to regain its independence, but in 365 Athens defeated it again, and exiled every last person, replacing them with Athenian colonists until an edict from Alexander the Great ordered their return in 321 BC.

## Melissus and Aristarchus

Pythagoras (*see* below) was only the first in a series of great Samian thinkers. The captain of the fleet against the Athenians in 411 BC was Melissus, an important philosopher who wrote of the essential unity of creation, which was spatially and temporally infinite, and only appeared to move. In the next century Sámos produced Aristarchus (310–230 BC), a mathematician and the best astronomer of his time. Although other Greek astronomers took it for granted that the Earth was the centre of the universe, and that the planets moved about it in perfect circles, Aristarchus, in an attempt to account for the retrograde motion of Mars and the fluctuations in the planets' brightness, boldly declared that the Earth was a mere planet among planets, and that all planets circled the sun. This proved to be too much for his fellow astronomers to take on board, as it would be for many of their descendants, when Copernicus told them the same thing in the 16th century.

A plaything among the great powers in Hellenistic times (the Ptolemies of Egypt especially favoured it, and the island in turn gave them Kallikrates, their greatest admiral), Sámos in 129 BC was incorporated into Rome's Asia Province. Augustus was a frequent visitor and granted Sámos many privileges, even though his enemies, Antony and Cleopatra, had courted there; according to Plutarch, it was on Sámos that Antony became so infatuated that he threw away the world for a woman.

After the sacking of Constantinople, Sámos was captured by the Venetians and Genoese. In 1453, when the Genoese handed the island over to the Turks, the inhabitants took refuge en masse on Chíos, leaving the island all but deserted for 80 years. With promises of privileges and a certain amount of autonomy, the Ottomans repopulated the island with Greeks from the mainland, Asia Minor and other islands – names reflected in many village names (i.e. Mytilíni, Marathókambos, Pírgos). But the Ottoman taxes became insupportable, and the Samians joined the revolution, and defeated the Turks at a second Battle of Mykále in 1824. Although the Great Powers excluded Sámos from Greece in 1830, it was granted semi-independence under the 'hegemony of the prince of Sámos', a Christian governor appointed by the sultan. In 1912, the Samian National Assembly took advantage of Turkey's defeats in the Balkan Wars to declare unity with Greece, under the leadership of Themostiklés Sophoúlis, a later Prime Minister.

# Sámos/Vathí (ΒΑΘΥ)

Names on Sámos are a tad confusing. In ancient times the city of Sámos was what is now Pythagório. The present capital and main port of the island, set in a sweeping amphitheatre of green hills, inherited the name Sámos a few decades ago; when the autonomous 'Hegemony' moved here from Chóra in 1834, it was called Vathí, but this name is now only used on ferry schedules and to describe the upper, older town (known as Vathí or even Áno Vathí) at the 'deep end' of the city's magnificent harbour. If the immediate port area of Sámos Town seems permeated with unfulfilled expectations (the abandoned hulk of the old Xenia Hotel on the waterfront doesn't help), the higgledy-piggledy, often arcaded lanes of Vathí reek with atmosphere, linked with white and pastel houses covered with weathered tile roofs.

Most of the life in Sámos Town is concentrated in the pedestrianized backstreets and **Plateía Pythagório** near the middle of the overwhelmingly long waterfront.

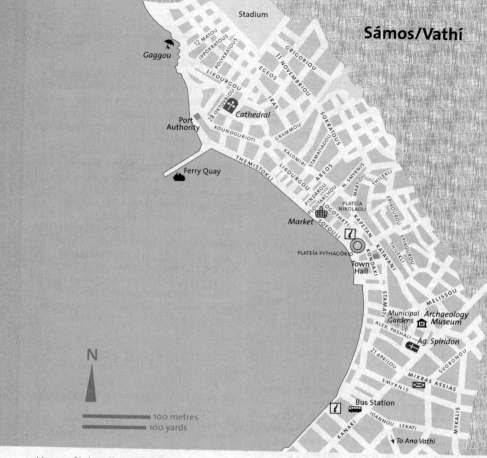

Here café dawdlers are shaded by palms and guarded by a stone lion; Pythagorians believed that the lion was the highest animal a trans-migrating soul could lodge in (the highest plant, in case your soul wanted to take a botanical route, is laurel). Four streets south and a block inland, a small **municipal garden** offers shelter from the afternoon sun, complete with a little café beside a trickling fountain.

Diagonally opposite the garden, the two buildings of the **Archaeology Museum** (*t 027 302 7469; open Tues–Sun 8–2.30; adm*) are packed full of treasures. Top billing goes to the unique set of stylishly elegant Archaic statues known as the Geneleos Group (*c.*550 BC), made of the local marble and dressed in pleats as fine as pinstripes. They were a prelude to the majestic 6th-century BC *kouros* from the Temple of Hera, at 18ft one of the largest (they had to lower the floor to fit it in, and when the head was found a couple of years later, they had to raise the roof) but with features as serene as a Buddha, the Archaic smile that John Fowles describes as 'having known Divinity.' There are geometric vases and prehistoric tools, and masses of ex-votos from the Temple of Hera: ivory and clay pomegranates, pine cones and poppies (all of which have many seeds, and hence signify fertility) and little terracotta figurines from the

# Where to Stay and Eat

## Sámos ✉ 83100

Beware that nearly every hotel with any pretensions to comfort is mercilessly block-booked in season, and independent travellers may as well throw themselves on the tender mercies of the travel offices lining the massive waterfront. Out of season, you'll find some bargains. Beware the tacky bars and restaurants on the harbourfront.

**Kirki Beach**, at Kalámi, t 027 302 3030 (B; exp). One of the clutch of new, upmarket hotels here with a pool.

**St Nicholas**, on Mykáli Beach (Psilí Ámmos) 10km south of town, t 027 302 5230, f 027 302 8522 (B; exp). Has shuttle buses to both Sámos and Pythagório, along with 2 pools, plenty of watersports and tennis.

**Aeolis**, 33 Themistokli Sofoúli, at Vathi, t 027 302 8904, aeolis@gemini.diavlos.gr (B; mod). Stylish waterfront option, with small pool, Jacuzzi and bar perched on the roof terrace.

**Christiana**, up in atmospheric Áno Vathí, t 027 302 3084, f 027 302 8856 (B; mod). With a pool. Open April–Oct.

**Galaxy**, a few streets in from the sea, t 027 302 2665, f 027 302 7679 (C; mod). Facing on to a leafy pool area. Open Mar–Oct.

**Helen**, 2 Grammou, t 027 302 8215, f 027 302 2866 (C; inexp). Quiet rooms with balcony.

**Ionia**, 5 Kalómiri, 3 streets in from the sea, t 027 302 8782 (inexp). Quirky little place run by chatty Evagelía Zavitsánou, and about as cheap as you get (shared bathrooms).

**Sámos**, 11 Themistokli Sofouli, by the port, t 027 302 8377, hotsamos@otenet.gr (C; inexp). An impersonal choice, but offers good value and sea-views from the roof terrace (with pool and bar).

**Vathy**, off the road up to Áno Vathí, t 027 302 8124, f 027 302 4045 (C; inexp). Friendly and family-run with a teeny but welcome pool above the town and harbour.

**Agrabeli**, in Áno Vathí. Relax under a canopy of vine, sampling home-cooked Samian specialities such as fried chickpea balls. (Don't try to take a car further than the Hotel Christiana at the edge of the village: the streets are impossibly narrow.)

**La Calma**, a 3min walk towards Kalámi. Bar-restaurant where the noise of the waves drowns the roar of the mopeds. Open eves.

**Kotópoula**, in the centre of town on Mykális and Vlamaris, 5 mins up Ioannou Lekáti Street, past the bus station and post office, t 027 302 8415. Excellent vine-covered taverna and favourite of the locals.

**Petrino**, behind Samos Hotel. Another reasonable choice.

# Entertainment and Nightlife

**Escape**, on the cliffs beyond the ferry. Open air and romantic.

**Cleary's Pub**, behind Plateía Pythagório.

**Metropolis**. Most summers, it sets up tent in the orchards near the bus station and attracts a younger crowd.

**Nisi Taverna**, at the end of the road at Ag. Paraskeví. For live Greek music. Fri and Sat eves only.

10th century BC. Other votives were manufactured as far away as Cyprus, Egypt, Etruria and Andalucía – in fact more foreign goods have been found here than in any other Greek temple, and it was their superior workmanship that inspired local artists to new heights in the 6th century. Uniquely, even bits of Archaic wooden furniture and sculpture were preserved because of the waterlogged grounds, along with splendid bronzes and a magnificent array of bronze griffon heads (a Mesopotamian calendar beast introduced to the west through Sámos in the 8th century BC); Herodotus described a bronze mixing bowl with griffon heads dedicated by the famous sailor Kolaios, and these may well have been part of it.

The rather unpromising road north of the harbour leads to the so-so town beach, **Gággou**, near the fashionable suburb of **Kalámi**; the road continues, getting narrower and narrower, eventually ending in **Ag. Paraskeví**. Short excursions east of town offer views over the beautiful, narrow Strait of Mykále and the rugged coast of Turkey, where velvet-green slopes hem in the turquoise sea; the Monastery of **Zoodóchos Pigí** (1756), set on the cliffs over the fishing hamlet of **Mourtiá**, is a popular vantage point. Roads south of Sámos lead 10 to 14km to the beaches at **Kervelí** (pretty but stony), **Possidónion** (sheltered and shingly) and **Psilí Ámmos** (sandy, busy, and a bus ride from Sámos or a hop from Turkey). Very near to Psilí Ámmos, the lagoons around **Áliki** are now protected as a nature reserve; between November and July storks, flamingoes, ducks and herons are frequent visitors.

# Pythagório (ΠΥΘΑΓΟΡΕΙΟ)

Pythagório on the southeast coast has become the island's most popular resort, although as it's climbed upmarket at the expense of some of its old pith – not only is the 'Samian Hotbed' long gone, but so are some of the Greeks, who now commute to work in the resort from Chóra and the other inland villages. When it was the tyrant Polykrates' capital Sámos, its population reached 300,000; by the 20th century it was reduced to a little fishing village called Tigáni, or frying pan, not because of its sizzling heat but because of the shape of Polykrates' jetty. In 1955 the town was renamed to honour Sámos' most famous son, synonymous with the right-angled-triangle theorem that put his name on the lips of every schoolchild in the world. It was not only a brilliant theorem, but the first theorem: Pythagoras was the first to apply the same philosophical 'proofs' used by the earliest philosophers of Miletos to the subject of mathematics.

Excavations occasionally turn Pythagório into a minefield of trenches, but one thing you're sure to see is the 1,180ft **ancient harbour mole** built by Efplinos, Polykrates' great engineer, which Herodotus declared was one of the three wonders of Greece; it now supports a new harbour wall, where white yachts swish in and out in place of sharp-bowed *samainae*. Lykúrgos Logothétis, a hero of the 1821 revolution, built the town castle – mostly at the expense of the Temple of Hera – at the beginning of Pythagório's sand and pebble beach, which extends off and on several kilometres to the west. The victory over the Turks at Mykále in 1824 is commemorated by a plaque in the pretty white church of the **Metamórfosis**. There's a small **Archaeology Museum** in the Community Hall (*t* 027 306 1400; open Tues–Sun 8.45–2) which houses mostly Archaic-era finds; a new museum is under construction.

Little remains of the **Roman Baths** (*t* 027 306 1400; open Tues–Sun 8.30–2.45) west of town, but a summer season of music and theatre takes place at the nearby ancient **theatre**. A road from the ancient theatre leads up to the cave where legend has it the sybil Phyto prophesied a one and true god, which provides an important justification for later Christian interest in pagan antiquity; appropriately the cave, which long sheltered refugees in times of trial, now shelters a church, **Panagía Spilianí**, last rebuilt in 1836, near a tiny monastery in the cypresses.

The left branch of the road from the theatre leads in 500m to the extraordinary **Efplinion Tunnel** (*open Tues–Sun 8.45– 2.40; adm*). Polykrates wanted his aqueduct kept secret, to prevent an enemy cutting off the water. Under Efplinos two crews of

# Tourist Information

**Municipal Tourist Information Office**: on the main street, t 027 306 1389, f 027 306 1022. Particularly on-the-ball and can help with accommodation, day trips and boat excursions; Jocelyn is particularly helpful and can solve most problems; *open 8am–10pm*.

# Where to Stay and Eat

## Pythagório ✉ 83103

Outside of the small, upscale guesthouses in the trendy town, the hotels of Pythagório are clustered out of most camera angles but in easy walking distance around the beach at Potokáki or just north of town. Most are open April–Oct and block booked in season. The waterfront is one uninterrupted line of tavernas and cafés that charge too much.

**Doryssa Bay**, Potokáki, t 027 306 1360, *doryssa @otenet.gr* (*A; lux*). Big and luxurious with rooms in an older hotel or spread through a perfect asymmetrical village of bungalows; air-con, pool, tennis, watersports and minigolf for the small fry. *Open April–Oct*.

**Gallini**, t 027 306 1167, f 027 306 1168 (*C; mod*). Central and quiet, with a friendly owner; the rooms on top have verandas and more of those views. *Open May–Oct*.

**Glycoriza Beach**, t 027 306 1321, *glbeach@ gemini.diavlos.gr* (*C; mod*). Another good out-of-town choice by the sea with pool. *Open April–Oct.*

**Hera II**, t 027 306 1879, f 027 306 1196 (*C; mod*). Cool, pink establishment; elegant with panoramic views. *Open April–Oct*.

**Kastelli**, further out and 100m from the sea, t 027 306 1728, f 027 306 1863 (*C; mod*).

Soaring views and breakfast; a good bet if you can beat the crowds. *Open April–Oct*.

**Afrodite**, t/f 027 306 1540 (*inexp*). Offers studios and an airy apartment; port-facing rooms have extensive views. *Open May–Oct*.

**Alexandra**, t 027 306 1429 (*D; inexp*). Simple, charming and cheap rooms with a lovely, shady garden. *Open April–Oct*.

**Areli Studios**, t 027 306 1245, f 027 306 2320 (*inexp*). Some of the most pristine studios in the Aegean, with an olive grove and an abundance of flowers. *Open May–Oct*.

**Stratos**, t 027 306 1157, *vasiliades@aol.com* (*C; inexp*). Non-smoking policy and rooms of varying standards under the aegis of an affable Greek American. *Open April–Oct*.

**Maritsa**, in from the harbour, t 027 306 1957. Excellent octopus. but unimpressive service.

**Platania**, in the main square. Gargantuan portions and good *saganáki* .

**Andonis** and **Sintrofia**, in Chóra. Consider taking a taxi up to these tavernas.

# Entertainment and Nightlife

Ask at the EOT about the summer music and theatre programme in the ancient theatre.

**Notos Bar**, on Tarsanas Beach. Chilled-out concoction of world music throughout the day; of an evening, this turns to beautiful, live *bouzouki* courtesy of the talented Yannis. His finely inlaid *bouzoukis* are on sale at **Pythagorios** on Metamorfosis Sotiros St; it also has a good selection of Samian handicrafts and soothing olive oil soap.

**Riva bar**. A romantic spot to stargaze.

**Edem**, on the way into town from Sámos. Live Greek music.

slaves started digging through the solid rock on either side of Mount Kástri and, thanks to his amazingly precise calculations, met on the same level, only a few inches off total Channel Tunnel perfection. Nearly a kilometre long, the tunnel's earthenware pipes kept the baths full in Pythagório for 1,000 years or so – until the 6th century AD, after which the tunnel was forgotten until it was accidentally rediscovered in the late 19th century. The lamps and tools of the workmen were found in the parallel maintenance tunnel, which doubled as an escape route from the city. Recently the tunnel has been electrically lit, so it no longer seems quite as old and mysterious as it used to; visitors are allowed in the first 700m, to where the tunnel has collapsed. From here you can follow the traces of the long walls up the slope; these originally measured

7km and stretched to Cape Foniás, bristling with towers; partly destroyed by Lysander when the Spartans took Sámos during the Peloponnesian War, there are intact sections high up, with lovely views.

## Pythagoras: Geometry, Beans and the Music of the Spheres

Pythagoras is a rather murky character who never wrote anything down, and is only known through the writing of his followers and enemies. Born on Sámos some time around 580 BC, he is known to have visited Egypt and Babylonia, either before or after his quarrel with Polykrates that sent him packing to Croton in southern Italy. In Croton he and his followers formed a brotherhood 'of the best' that governed the city for 20 years, before it revolted. This brotherhood was a secret society, similar to Freemasonry, that spread throughout the Greek world; members recognized each other by their symbol – the pentangle, or five-pointed star. But mumbo jumbo politics was only one aspect of Pythagoras, who was to have considerable influence, especially on Plato. He taught that the soul was immortal, and that after death it transmigrated not only into new humans but into plants and animals, and that by purifying the soul one might improve it, and perhaps escape the need for re-incarnation. There were important prohibitions on eating meat (that chicken might be your grandmother) and, more mysteriously, against eating fava beans – scholars long debated whether Pythagoras somehow thought that beans held human souls, expressed in unharmonious flatulence, or did he know about favism, a sometimes deadly reaction many Mediterranean people have to fava beans and their dust. Recently, however, it has been shown that Pythagoras was the victim of millennia of misunderstanding: the Greeks used letters for numbers, and what reads 'lay off fava beans' is actually another theorem of angles.

If Pythagoras wasn't full of beans, he was certainly full of numbers. He was the first to apply *kosmos*, a Greek word meaning arrangement and ornamentation (hence our 'cosmetics') to the universe. The order of the cosmos, he believed, was based on the connections of its various parts called *harmonia*, and that *harmonia* was based on numbers. He discovered that music could be expressed mathematically by ratios and the tuning of the seven-string lyre, and he extended that *harmonia* to 'the music of the spheres', the motions of the seven planets (the five visible ones, and the moon and sun) – and to the Golden Mean, the base of the proportions of classical architecture and sculpture. Although the belief that everything could be defined by numbers and ratios took the Pythagoreans down some wild and woolly paths, the key idea was that the study of the order of the Cosmos and its harmony would help to eliminate the disorder in our souls. No one agreed more than a latter-day Pythagorean, Johannes Kepler, who worked out the true elliptical orbits of the planets and later formulated the Third Law of Planetary Motion (1619): 'The square of the period of revolution is proportional to the cube of the mean distance from the sun.' Kepler noted that the varying speeds of the planets' revolutions corresponded with the ratios in Renaissance polyphonies; in 1980, one of the mementoes that NASA scientists packed aboard *Voyager* for its journey out of our solar system was a computer-generated recording of Pythagoras' and Kepler's music of the spheres.

## The Temple of Hera

*t 027 3069 5277; open Tues–Sun 8.30–2.45; adm.*

'They combed their flowing locks and went, all dressed in fine garments, to the sanctuary of Hera...' wrote the Samian poet Asios in the 6th century BC. From Pythagório, it was an 8km stroll past 2,000 statues, tombs and monuments lining the **Sacred Way** (now 90 per cent under the profane airport road and runway) to the **Temple of Hera**. 'Cow-eyed' Hera was born on this marshy plain of the Imbrassos under a sacred osier, and worshipped on this spot since the Bronze Age. She was the first deity to have temples erected in her honour; two made of mud, wood and bricks had already been built, when an architect named Roikos completed a huge Ionic temple in 560 BC. Apparently the marshy ground made it unstable, because not long after, Polykrates, who never believed in half measures, replaced it with a colossal one. One of the Seven Wonders of the Ancient World, Polykrates' Great Temple was, after the Temple of Artemis at Ephesus and the Temple of Zeus in Akragas (Agrigento), the third largest ever built by the Greeks (354 by 165ft); only a single column of its original 155 remains intact, at half of its original height, as sole witness to its size, even if it looks like a wobbly stack of mouth-freshening mints. The entablature is presumed to have been of wood, and the lack of tiles suggests the roof was never finished.

In spite of its size and importance, the temple was never a pan-Hellenic shrine, but a showcase for Sámos, and as such reached its peak of importance in Archaic times; accounts come down about it serving as the venue for all night celebrations after the city state's victories. Some Roman emperors favoured it; one paid a fortune to have the Sacred Way paved in marble in the 3rd century AD, shortly before the sanctuary was destroyed by raiding Herulians; earthquakes in the 4th and 5th centuries and builders looking for ready-cut stone finished it off (the one column was left standing as a landmark for their ships). Only the base of the monumental 140ft **altar** has survived (rebuilt seven times, from the Bronze Age to Roman times), along with foundations

## Mythology

Zeus had to use cunning to seduce an uninterested Hera (perhaps because he was her brother), and they spent a 300-year-long wedding night on Sámos 'concealed from their dear parents'. She was pre-eminently the goddess of marriage, worshipped in three aspects: the Girl, the Fulfilled and the Separated, but never in an erotic fashion or as a mother (though often a wicked stepmother); she was always the Great Goddess, ambivalent about her relationship with her upstart consort, who frequently returned to bathe in the Imbrassos to renew her virginity. Her sanctuary was filled with great works of art, but the holy of holies was a plank of wood crudely painted with the goddess' features, believed to have fallen from heaven, too sacred to be touched; to carry it, the priests tied it with twigs of osier, the willow sacred to Hera. Twice a year celebrations took place at the temple: the Heraia, in honour of her marriage, and the Tonea, recalling the attempt of the Argives to snatch the sacred plank, only to be thwarted by the goddess, who nailed their ship to the waves until they returned it. By her altar were her symbols: two peacocks and an osier.

of small temples or treasuries, *stoas* and statue bases and the apse of the Christian basilica made out of the temple's stone. The remains of sacrifices, usually cows, were found near the altar, although not a single thigh bone was among them, confirming Homer's descriptions of the special treatment given to thighs. The skulls of a Nile crocodile and two antelopes – exotic animals found at no other site – are more mysterious. Some of the temple's stone went into the nearby **Sarakíni Castle**, built in 1560 by a Patmian naval officer, appointed governor of Sámos by the sultan.

## Héreon and the Southeast

The nearby seaside village of **Héreon** (HPAIO), once a backwater, now has its portion of hotels and bars on a short stretch of beach that gets too crowded in the summer. To escape this and the noisy airport, check out caiques running south to the remote sandy beach of **Tsopela**. If you have your own transport, inland villages offer respite as well: **Chóra**, west of Pythagório, was made the capital of Sámos by the aforementioned Capt. Sarakíni and kept its status until 1855. It remains a lively little place with good tavernas. To the north the road passes through a steep valley to the sprawling village of **Mytilíni**, where animal fossils dating back 15 million years – believed to have been washed into a deposit by the Meander River, before Sámos broke free from the mainland – have been gathered in Greece's only **Palaeontological Museum** in the Dimarchíon (*t 027 305 2055; open Mon–Sat 9–2 and sometimes in the afternoons*). Sámos had a reputation for fierce monsters in mythology; one story has it that the island broke off from Asia Minor like glass when the monsters let loose a particular high-pitched shriek. The museum's prize exhibit, among the skulls and teeth of prehistoric hippopotami and rhinoceros, is a 13-million-year-old fossilized horse brain.

Above Héreon, lemon groves surround **Mýli**, the source of the Imbrassos, where an important Mycenaean tomb was found near the school. From well-watered Pagóndas ('the land of springs'), the road circles around through fine untamed south-coast scenery en route to **Spatharáioi** (7½km) and **Pírgos** (another 6km), a pretty mountain village in now charred pines, founded by settlers from the city of the same name in the Peloponnese. Down in a ravine below Pírgos, **Koútsi** is the kind of place preferred by the ancient nymphs, a grove of venerable plane trees, clear waters and cool mountain air and something the nymphs didn't have – a good taverna, perfect on a hot afternoon. Tour operators know about it too, so get there early or late for lunch.

From Pírgos you can circle around back towards Pythagório without retracing your steps (although sadly, the trees along this stretch took a good scorching in the rampant fires in July 2000), going by way of **Koumaradáioi**, where a track leads up to the **Moní Megális Panagías**, founded in 1586; the walls of the monastery encompass one of the island's most beautiful churches, with good icons and frescoes (*closed to visitors*). One of the monks who built it also founded **Timíou Stavroú Monastery** (1592) to the east, after a dream he had of a buried icon of the Holy Cross; the miraculous icon was duly found, and has been completely plated with silver and covered in ex-votos. On Holy Wednesday people gather here from all over Sámos to watch the Archbishop re-enact the washing of the Apostles' feet. North of the monastery, **Mavratzeí** is a pottery village, specializing in the goofy 'Pythagorean Cup'.

# West along the North Coast: Vines and Beaches

On the great bay opposite Sámos Town, **Malagári**, immersed in pines, is the head-quarters of the Union of Sámos Wine Producing Co-operatives, whose wines are aged in great oaken barrels in the handsome stone warehouses known as *tavérnes*. Ten kilometres west of Vathí, pretty **Kokkári** (ΚΟΚΚΑΡΙ) was once a whitewashed fishing village that owes its funny name 'onion bulbs' to its old speciality, which has been soundly replaced by package tourism. Still, the setting is lovely. In addition to its own busy beach, there are several nearby. **Lemonákia** is a 20-minute walk away and the more beautiful **Tsamadoú**, a partly nudist beach 2km from Kokkári, is a crescent of

## Where to Stay and Eat

### Malagári ✉ 83100
**Poseidon**, t 027 302 3201, f 027 302 4592 (*A; exp*). Equipped with a pool, roof garden and other creature comforts. *Open Mar–Oct.*

### Kokkári ✉ 83100
Most of the accommodation here is pack-aged out in season. Kokkári has 250 rooms in private houses, but don't hold your breath.
**Arion**, 500m above Kokkári, t 027 309 2020, *arion@gemini.diavlos.gr* (*A; exp*). Built in traditional Samian style with shady lawns among the trees, as well as a pool, sauna and Jacuzzi; the hotel bus provides transport to Kokkári. *Open May–Oct.*
**Angela's Rooms**, right on the beach, t 027 309 2050 (*mod*). 4 rooms, one's a studio. *Open May–Oct.*
**Olympia Beach**, appropriately by the strand, t 027 309 2353, f 027 309 2547 (*C; mod*). With aquatic views.
**Pension Lemos**, at the south entrance to the village, t 027 309 2394 (*mod*). 12 pleasant rooms. *Open May–Oct.*
**Kima**, on the water's edge. Tasty, freshly prepared Greek dishes.
**Porto Picolo**. Satisfying Italian dishes.
**Cabana Club**, in the centre. If you're dying for a disco.

### Avlákia/Vourliótes/Manolátes ✉ 83100
**Angela's Studio**, Manolátes, t 027 309 4478 (*inexp*). Peaceful spot; Angela has a shady garden from which to contemplate the hills.
**Avlákia**, in Avlákia, right on the beach, t 027 309 4230, f 027 309 5289 (*C; inexp*). Very

pleasant old-fashioned hotel with Oscar, its restaurant, on the strand.
**Markos**, Vourliótes, t 027 309 3291 (*inexp*). Great place for peace and quiet away from the sea.
**Giorgides**, halfway up in Manolátes, t 027 309 4239. Delightful taverna spilling out on both sides of the street.
**Loukas**, at the very top of Manolátes. Blissfully overlooking the hills and sea; everything here is home-made from their own olive oil, cheese, wine and *suma* (a local schnapps) to the stuffed vine leaves and courgette flowers (picked daily at 6am before they close and then baked in their traditional wood-burning oven).
**Palataki**, in a grove of plane trees, at the begin-ning of the 4km road up to Manolátes. Popular for its spit-roasted meats and wood-oven dishes. *Open in season.*
**The Shop**, ΙΒΥΚΟΣ, t 027 309 4338. One of Manolátes excellent craft shops, with hand painted ceramics and local modern art.

### Ag. Konstantínos ✉ 83200
There's no end of rooms and pensions down by the water, of which the following are a good example; try for a sea-facing room.
**Aindónokastro**, 2km inland at Andóni, t 027 309 4686, f 027 309 4404 or 010 544 0182 (*B; mod*). A hillside hamlet of old stone 2-storey houses beautifully converted into tradition-ally decorated studios sleeping 2–4 people. *Open April–Oct.*
**Apollonia Bay**, t 027 309 4444, f 027 309 4090 (*C; mod*). Smart apartment complex with pool. *Open May–Oct.*
**Atlantis**, t 027 309 4329 (*E; inexp*). An older hotel and a good budget bet.
**Coral's Apartments**, t 027 309 4390 (*inexp*).

> **'Fill High the Bowl with Samian Wine...'**
>
> The north-facing mountain villages of Vourliótes, Manolátes and Stavrinídes are the top wine-growing villages on Sámos, where one famous variety of grape, Moscháto Sámou, has reigned for the last 2,000 years or so. The old vines are thickly planted on small anti-erosion terraces called *pezoúles* from 492ft to 2,624ft above sea level and, like all quality dessert wines, have an extremely low yield. After years of neglect in the Middle Ages, Samian wine began its comeback under the Greek settlers brought over by the Ottomans in the late 16th century. By the 18th century it was imported in large quantities to Sweden and even to France, and the Catholic Church gave Sámos a concession to provide wine for Mass, something it still does to a degree in Austria, Switzerland and Belgium. All Samian wine has been sold through the co-operative since 1933, after winegrowers, reduced to penury by profiteering international wine merchants, revolted against the system and demanded control of their own production. The most prized wine of Sámos is its light amber Grand Cru Vin Doux Naturel, with 15 per cent alcohol, given its *appellation* in France in 1982 (the only Greek wine so honoured); also try a chilled bottle of fruity Nectar, aged in its wooden cask and splendid with strong cheeses or fruit salads. Of the dry wines, try the green-tinted Samena Dry White, a good aperitif made from high altitude grapes.

multi-coloured pebbles where you can rub elbows with fellow sunworshippers. Further west, **Avlákia** has a different, old-time atmosphere: a delightfully low-key resort with a sprinkling of accommodation on the beach and a second small pebble beach at **Tsaboú**. It is a good base for exploring the ravishing green hinterland, where cypresses and pines rise up like towers along the majestic slopes of Mount Ámpelos (3,740ft); its name, from the 1st century BC, means 'Mount Vineyard'.

From the handsome village of **Vourliótes**, it's a delightful, leafy 3km walk up to Sámos' oldest monastery, **Panagía Vrontiáni**, founded in 1560, with some of its original wall paintings, although access is limited now that the monks have been replaced by soldiers installed there until recently. Further east along the coast, a road leads up to lovely **Manolátes**, which overlooks an arcadian valley beloved by nightingales, one of the beauty spots of Sámos; at **Platanákia**, you can eat under the magnificent grove of plane trees and drink barrelled red wine, but beware the 'Greek Night' coach parties. The last place where the mountains cede to the coast is at anti-climactic Ag. Konstantínos, quieter and rawer than the other resorts.

# Karlóvassi and Western Sámos

Wallflower **Karlóvassi** (ΚΑΡΛΟΒΑΣΙ), Sámos' second city and port, was an industrial tanning centre before the Second World War and, although the hides and stink are long gone, the empty warehouses along the port present a dreary face to the world. After the first baleful hello, however, the little city is pleasant enough, much sleepier and Greekier than Vathí or Pythagório, and neatly divided, in descending order of interest, into old, middle and new (Paléo, Meséo and Néo) Karlóvassi, punctuated with the pale blue domes of absurdly large 19th-century churches. Most visitors stay in a

# Where to Stay and Eat

## Karlóvassi ✉ 83200

Also look for cheap rooms in Limáni, on the pedestrian lane behind the port road.

**Samaina Inn**, in Limáni, **t** 027 303 0400, **f** 027 303 4471 (*A; exp*). International chain-style hotel with smart, cool rooms, large pool and crèche. *Open May–Oct.*

**Samaina Bay**, **t** 027 303 0812 (*B; exp*). Same owners, less flashy but still with pool.

**Aspasia**, towards Potámi Beach, **t** 027 303 0201, **f** 027 303 0200 (*B; exp–mod*). The smartest place to sleep, rooms with air-con, a pool, roof garden and minibus service. *Open April–Oct.*

**Merope**, in Néo Karlóvassi, **t** 027 303 2510, **f** 027 303 2652 (*B; inexp*). Popular for its old-world service and amazingly good value, with period rooms, collectors' TVs, and pool.

**Anema**, near Karlóvassi harbour. Pool-bar enticingly advertises 'many unexpectables, passion, rythym [*sic*]'.

**Kyma**. Well-prepared *mezédes* by the seaside.

**Psarades**, on the road to Ag. Nikoláos, **t** 027 303 2489. Excellent fresh fish and sunsets

## Órmos Márathokámpos ✉ 83102

**Anthemousa Studios**, up by the church in olive groves above the port, **t** 027 303 7073 (*inexp*). With views; the owner also has seafront studios and offers boat trips.

**Chryssopetro**, at Votsalaki Village, **t** 027 303 7247, **f** 0273037276 (*D; inexp*). *Open May–Oct.*

**Kerkis Bay**, **t** 027 303 7202, **f** 027 303 7372 (*B; inexp*). Has seen better days but has a good restaurant. *Open April–Oct.*

**Pizza Cave**. Very friendly. Just one of Órmos Márathokámpos' decent array of tavernas.

**Mucho Drinko Bar**. If you fancy a tipple.

## Limnionas ✉ 83102

**Limnionas Bay**, **t/f** 027 303 7057 (*exp–mod*). Low-lying, whitewashed studios with pool.

**Limnionas Taverna**, on the beach. Small place with fish and traditional fare.

**Sophia's Taverna**, just past the turning down to Limnionas on the main road.

---

small cluster of hotels in the picturesque old quarter, also called Limáni, with a far more appealing and intimate atmosphere than Néo Karlóvassi, although this is where you'll find the regional bus stop, banks, and post office, not to mention the timeless **Paradise**, an old-man's *ouzerie* with tables strewn under a shady tree. A city bus provides good transport to the nearest beach, **Potámi** (ΠΟΤΑΜΙ), 2km west.

Western Sámos has been compared to western Crete: fewer sights, fewer tourists, but amply rewarding in the walking scenery and beach departments. A track from Potámi leads back to the 10th century **Panagía tou Potamoú** (Our Lady of the River), Sámos' oldest church, and if you carry on, to the river canyon. There are superb sandy beaches further west: the lovely cove of **Mikró Seitáni** (1km beyond the end of Potámi) and **Megálo Seitáni** (4km) at the foot of a striking ravine, but you'll need your hiking shoes and own provisions to reach them. The stunning track continues another 8km along the towering west shore as far as **Drakáioi**, a farming village and time-capsule glimpse of traditional Greece at the end of the rough road from Marathókampos and a very rare bus line. South of Drakáioi the road continues round, past **Kallithéa**.

Buses run on Mondays from Karlóvassi to **Plátanos**, the island's second most important wine-growing area and down to the sea by way of **Koumeïka**; the sand-pebble beach with shade and a quieter summer community is alternatively known as **Órmos Koumíkou** or **Bállos**. The more westerly road south of Karlóvassi curls around the soaring mass of **Mount Kérkis** (4,740ft), a dormant volcano often crowned with a halo of cloud and mist. **Kastanéa**, surrounded by chestnut groves and laughing brooks, is a popular place to aim for on hot days, but remembered by locals as the location for 27 deaths at the hands of the occupying Italians.

To the south, **Márathokámpos** is an attractive village on tiny lanes spilling down the slopes, where the residents have restored old abandoned houses for guests. Below is the beach, pleasantly low-key resort and port of **Órmos Márathokámpos** (ΟΡΜΟΣ ΜΑΡΑΘΟΚΑΜΠΟΣ), from where caiques sail several times a week to Samiopoúla, a tiny islet with a fine stretch of sand. Extending west of Órmos is the long white sandy beach and package resort of **Votsalákia**, now well and truly lined with tourist shops, restaurants and flashing lights. For a brief escape, follow the marked path through the olives to the **Convent of the Evangelístria**, and beyond to the summit of Mount Kérkis; fit walkers can storm the peak and return for a swim in five or six hours. Alternatively, and especially if you have small children, keep heading west to the safe, exceedingly shallow seas at **Psilí Ámmos** (not to be confused with Psilí Ámmos in the east). Continuing on, there are still some unspoiled sandy coves, accessible only by foot or boat. If you have your own transport, drive on to the delightful cove of **Limnionas**, with excellent swimming and relaxation guaranteed.

# Samothráki/Samothrace (ΣΑΜΟΘΡΑΚΗ)

In the far right-hand corner of Greece, Samothráki is one of the least accessible islands for the pleasure tourist; its steep shores are uncluttered by day-trippers and beach bunnies – in a way, they would seem frivolous. This is an island of lingering magic, of cliffs, nightingales, plane forests and waterfalls sweeping around the Mountain of the Moon (Mount Fengári, 5,459ft), a peak as dramatic as a theatrical backdrop; Poseidon, after all, sat on its summit to observe the tides of the Trojan War. Often wind-whipped and lacking a natural harbour, Samothráki was nevertheless one of the most visited islands of antiquity, the Délos of the North Aegean with its cult centre of the Great Gods of the Underworld; from all over the Mediterranean people came to be baptized in hot bull's blood and initiated into its mysteries.

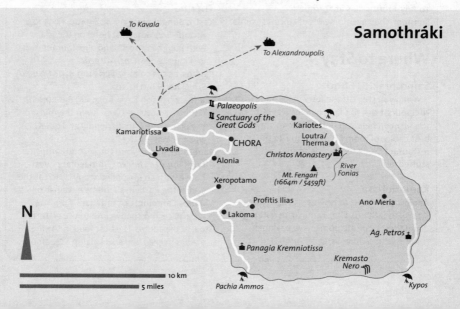

Samothráki

# Getting There and Around

**By air:** 3 flights daily from Athens to Alexandroúpolis, **t** 055 104 5198.

**By sea:** 2hr daily **ferry** crossing from Alexandroúpolis, occasionally twice a day in summer, and at least twice a week from Kavála. From Feb–Nov, daily **hydrofoils** from Alexandroúpolis (**t** 055 102 6721) to Samothráki; also frequently from Kavála. On the island, pick up tickets at **Saos Travel, t** 055 104 1505. **Port authority: t** 055 104 1305.

**By road:** 6 buses a day run from Kamariótissa to Chóra, and 3 to Alónia, Palaeópolis, Loutrá/Therma, and Pachía Ámmos; for schedules, **t** 055 104 1505. To really explore the island, hire a **car** or **moped** (in Kamariótissa, **Budget, t** 055 104 1100, **f** 055 103 8233 or **Niki Tours, t** 055 104 1465, **f** 055 104 1304), but be warned that there are 20,000 goats on Samothráki, not one of whom has the least road sense. **Taxis: t** 055 104 1341.

# Tourist Information

**Tourist police:** in Chóra, **t** 055 104 1218 or **t** 055 104 1790.

**Regular police: t** 055 104 1303. For general information, try *www.samothraki.com*

# Festivals

**20 July:** Profítis Ilías at Kormbéti.
**Summer:** the Kaveíria, series of cultural events.

# Where to Stay

## Samothráki ✉ 68002

When you step off the ferry in Kamariótissa, **Niki Tours, t** 055 104 1465 or **Saos Travel, t** 055 104 1411, can help you find a place to stay; the best choice of rooms is in Thérma. In the restaurants, look for the island speciality – stuffed kid.

## Kamariótissa

**Aeolos,** 300m east of town, **t** 055 104 1795, **f** 055 104 1810 (*B; exp*). Family-run hotel with a modest pool; all rooms have balconies, some with sea-views. *Open April–Oct.*

**Limanaki,** at the far end of town, **t** 055 104 1987 (*mod*). Smart new place with spanking quiet rooms and delicious sea food.

**Klimatariá,** on the waterfront. For traditional Greek fare, the best value in town.

**Pantelis,** in the middle of the waterfront. For fish and giant prawns over the coals.

**Skorpios,** also on the front. The owner ran a pizza parlour in Chicago for 20 yrs before returning to her native island, and still produces the island's best pies.

## Chóra

**Exochio,** on the edge of the village. Popular and picturesque place, but serves only one dish – baked goat, *kokorétsi*, potatoes and salad. *Only open in high season.*

**Meltémi.** Bar with great views of the Kástro lit at night; attracts a younger crowd.

Wherever you eat, don't miss finishing off with fresh *loukoumádes* (mini doughnuts dipped in honey) from the sweet shop on the left as you arrive from Kamariótissa.

## Lákoma/Profítis Ilías

**To Akrogiáli, t** 055 109 5123 (*mod–inexp*). Excellent fish taverna with romantic sunsets. The owner, Giorgio, also has 5 spotless new rooms for rent.

**Vrachos, Pigi** and **Tsiaousis,** in Profítis Ilías. 3 good tavernas, all popular for local specialities, incl. kid on the skewer.

## Thérma

**Kastro Bungalows, t** 055 108 9400, **f** 055 104 1000(*B; lux*). Smartest hotel on the island with pool, sea sports, and a restaurant overlooking the sea. *Open all year.*

**Kaviros, t** 055 109 8277, **f** 055 109 8298 (*B; mod*). Small hotel by the spa.

**Mariba, t** 055 109 8230, **f** 055 109 8374 (*mod*). Bungalows covered with ivy in the midst of the plane tree forest; friendly and quiet. *Open 15 May–15 Oct.*

**Panorama,** just beyond the second campsite, **t** 055 109 8345 (*inexp*). Immaculate guesthouse with an unspoiled stony beach at the end of the garden; all rooms have balconies.

**Varados Camping, t** 055 104 1218, **f** 055 104 1204. Nice and shady, close to the waterfall.

**Stoa,** in the centre. The best food in the area – always packed and specializing in seafood.

## History

Once densely populated, Samothráki owes its importance to its position near that busy thoroughfare, the Dardanelles – the strait named after the legendary Samothracian Dardanos, the founder of Troy. The archaeological record suggests that there were connections between Troy and the pre-culture at Límnos; the oldest shrine (the rock altar beneath the Arsinoeion) was built, according to Herodotus, by the 'Pelasgians' (non-Greeks who were adept at old mysteries, and introduced *herms* – the ever popular statues of Hermes with erect phalluses – to the Greek religions). In the 8th century BC Aeolians from Mytilíni colonized Samothráki and mingled peaceably with the earlier settlers, worshipping the Kabeiroi, the Great Gods of the Thracians, whose still-undeciphered language survived in religious rituals into the 1st century. By the mid 5th century BC, Samothráki's sanctuary was firmly on the map, the religious centre of the North Aegean, attracting a steady stream of initiates to its mysteries. Their fascination has lingered: the Kabeiroi even make an appearance in Goethe's Faust, and the excavations of their sanctuary were funded by the Bollingen Foundation, set up in honour of the psychoanalysist C. G. Jung.

Besides patronizing the sanctuary, Hellenistic and Roman rulers occasionally used Samothráki as a naval base, relying on its sacred soil for protection. Nevertheless, under the Romans, the island began to suffer its first invasions and earthquakes. St Paul stopped by in 49 AD, but failed to convert the locals who kept their sanctuary running until the 4th century, when Theodosius the Great forced paganism out of business: Samothráki was depopulated and forgotten. Pirate raids forced the remaining inhabitants to the hills, where they settled Chóra. The Genoese ruler Gattilusi fortified the castle, and when it fell to the Turks, the Samothracians were sent to help resettle Constantinople. The island then vanished from history until the 1820s, when it rose up during the War of Independence, but, like the other islands in the northeast, had to wait until 1912 to join Greece.

# Kamariótissa and Chóra

Samothráki's workaday port, **Kamariótissa** (ΚΑΜΑΡΙΩΤΙΣΣΑ), has an exposed rocky beach, an aeolian park with four windmills by a small lagoon, and most of the island's modest tourist facilities. Caiques (*t 055 104 1272*) make day excursions south to **Pachía Ámmos** and **Kremastó** (*see below*). High above, on the slopes of Mount Fengári, **Chóra** (ΧΩΡΑ), where most of the island's 2,800 souls live, occupies a picturesque amphitheatre below a ruined **Byzantine castle**. Designated a 'traditional settlement', Chóra has whitewashed houses with red-tiled roofs, a charming century-old bakery famous for its bread, five mummified heads (of martyrs killed by the Turks for reconverting to Christianity, up in the church) and a little **Folklore Museum** (*open summer only 11–2 and 7–10pm*). At the entrance to Chóra stands the island's modern statue of Nike (Victory), not quite as grand as the one it lost but a dead ringer for Nadia Comaneci.

Pretty agricultural hamlets dot the slopes of southern Samothráki: **Alónia**, the largest, has ruins of a Roman bath, while **Profítis Ilías** is famous for its tavernas serving kid. From delightful **Lákoma**, a very windy 8km road leads to the turn-off for the church of **Panagía Kremniótissa**, tottering on rocks and taking in huge views as far as the Turkish island of Imbros. Below is the island's main sandy beach, **Pachía Ámmos**, with a freshwater spring and a taverna with a few basic rooms (**t** 055 109 5119). A boat excursion is the only way to visit the spectacular rugged southern coast and the waterfall **Krémasto Neró** ('hanging water'), near a much smaller beach.

## The Sanctuary of the Great Gods

*t 055 104 1474; the site and museum are open Tues–Sun 8.30–3; adm.*

The Great Gods were *chthonic*, or underworld deities, older and more potent than the Olympian upstarts of the patriarchal state religion, at whom even the first poet Homer could have a belly-laugh. But no one dared to mess with the Great Gods; no writer revealed the mysteries, which may have offered promises for the afterlife so lacking in the Olympian religion. Although dedications found at the sanctuary were simply 'to the gods', their secret names were revealed by a Hellenistic writer, Mnaseas: Axieros, Axiokersos, Axiokersa, and Kadmilos, whom the Greeks identified with Demeter, Hades, Persephone, Kore and Hermes.

The Samothracian mysteries took place by torchlight and included initiation rites similar to the more famous ones at Eleusis. Anyone, male or female, free or slave, could undergo the two levels of initiation, the *myesis* and the *epopteia*. The *epopteia* began with a confession that may have been unique in the Greek world, (the priest would ask the candidate 'which was the most lawless deed committed in his life'), followed by baptism, the winding of a purple sash below the abdomen (similar to the veil of Leukothea, which saved Odysseus from shipwreck), topped off with the sacrifice of a ram. Initiation was thought to be sovereign against drowning; in myth, the Argonauts, at Orpheus' suggestion, joined before entering the Hellespont, and in ancient times a hall in the sanctuary was full of votive gifts attesting to the Kabeiroi's power. Another peculiarity of the cult, mentioned by Roman authors, involved magnetized iron rings, perhaps symbols of attraction given to initiates: several were found on site. King Lysander of Sparta and Herodotus were famous initiates, but it was in the Hellenistic era that the sanctuary knew its greatest fortune; Philip II of Macedonia fell in love with Olympias of Epirus, mother of Alexander the Great, during an initiation ceremony, and politically he was keen to promote the only pan-Hellenic shrine in his orbit to the same level as Delphi, to demonstrate his 'Greekness'.

Excavations of the site were begun in 1948 by Americans Dr Karl and Phyllis Williams Lehmann, whose excellent guide to the site is on sale. Begin with the museum, with artefacts and architectural fragments discovered at the sanctuary. The Louvre, of course, bagged the prize, the *Victory of Samothrace*, found in 1863 by Champoiseau, the French consul at Adrianople; the museum has a plaster consolation copy from Paris, along with some good vases (especially an Attic *pelike* of 490 BC with a dancing goat by the Eucharides painter), the Archaic-style frieze of temple dancers donated by Philip II to decorate the entrance to the Temenos, *steles* warning off the uninitiated and amongst the funerary offerings, a surprise – a terracotta model of a football.

The sanctuary itself, set in trees overlooking the sea, enjoys an idyllic setting, while goat bells tinkle on the jagged mountain above. Most of the buildings are in porous stone – the first large one you come across, the rectangular **Anaktoron** (the House of the Lords), dates from the 6th century BC and was rebuilt twice, lastly by the Romans; first-level initiations were held here, but only the initiated, or *mystai*, were allowed in its inner sanctum, or Holy of Holies, on the north side. A pile of carbon discovered in the middle of the Anaktoron suggests it had a wooden stage; a torch base, now under glass, is a relic of the Kabeiroi's night-time rites. Ancient writers referred to the Anaktoron as holding two bronze statues of Hermes in a state of considerable excitement, but Lehmann failed to find any trace of them. Adjacent, by the Sacred Rock, is the **Arsinoëion**, at 66ft in diameter the largest circular structure ever built by the ancient Greeks. It was dedicated in 281 BC by Queen Arsinoë II, wife and sister of Ptolemy Philadelphos, after the Great Gods had answered her prayers for a child. It had one door and no windows; scholars are stumped as to what happened in here.

The rectangular foundation south of the Arsinoëion belonged to the **Temenos**, where ceremonies may have taken place; adjacent stand the five re-erected Doric columns of the **Hieron**, or 'New Temple' where the upper level of initiation was held for the *mystai*, a structure dating from 300 BC and last restored after an earthquake in the 3rd century AD. By the side entrance, towards the eastern wall, Lehmann found two 'stepping stones' where he presumed that the initiates' confessions were heard, as well as the Roman viewing benches. There was a hearth altar in the centre and a drain by the door, perhaps for the blood of the sacrifices.

Only the outline remains of the theatre on the hill; here also is the **Nike Fountain**, where the magnificent *Winged Victory* was found, dedicated by the Macedonian Dimitrios Poliorketes (the Besieger) in 305 BC, in thanksgiving for his naval victory over Ptolemy II at Cyprus; she originally stood as the figurehead of a great marble ship. Ptolemy II donated the monumental gateway to the sanctuary, the **Propylae Ptolemaion**. Nearby is a *tholos* of uncertain use and a Doric building, dedicated by the Hellenistic rulers of Macedon. Up the road stood **Palaeópolis** (ΠΑΛΑΙΟΠΟΛΗΣ), the unexcavated city that served the sanctuary (*open daily 8.30–8.30*). The island's medieval Genoese bosses, the Gattiluzi, used its stone to build their walls and watchtower. Now covered with a handsome grove of plane trees, a path leads to the foundations of an early church, perhaps founded in honour of St Paul's visit.

# Thérma, Mount Fengári and Up the Fonias Ravine

After Palaeópolis, the road continues east to a new marina and the delightful little rustic spa, Thérma (or **Loutrá**). Like much of this idyllic corner of Samothráki, Thérma is immersed in chestnut and plane trees; with lots of places to stay and eat among the rushing streams where you can soak in mildly radioactive warm water, good for arthritis and gynaecological disorders (*doctor on duty every morning 8–10*). Follow the signs to the path to **Gría Vathrá** – a short walk through a canopy of ancient trees to a natural pool and little waterfall that flows even in the scorching days of summer.

From Thérma, a well marked path leads up in four hours to the top of **Mount Fengári**, where you can enjoy the same view as Poseidon, a stunning panorama of the North Aegean from the Troad in the east to Mount Áthos in the west. Because of its altitude, Mount Fengári hosts a number of rare endemic plants with impressive names: *Alyssum degenianum*, *Symphandra samothracica*, *Herniara degenii*, and *Potentilla geoides*. Its local name, Sáos, recalls the Saoi, 'the rescued ones', a secret society of men sworn into the mysteries of the Great Gods.

The road from Thérma continues east to the medieval Fonias 'Killer' Tower, also by the Genoese, with a nice place to swim nearby. The tower sits in the little delta of the **Fonias**, signposted by a carpark and a cantina. Here too the river, filled with eels and crabs, flows year round; there's a beautiful 30-minute path up its ravine to a magical waterfall, where nymphs wouldn't look out of place. After this oasis, the road braves the increasingly arid coast and ends at the long, shadeless and daunting black pebble beach at **Kýpos**, closed on one side by merciless cliffs of lava falling into the sea.

# Thássos (ΘΑΣΟΣ)

*An island crowned with forests and lying in the sea like the backbone of an ass.*
         Archilochos, 7th century BC

# Getting There and Around

## By Air

Kavála airport (t 059 105 3273), halfway to Keramotí, receives international charter flights and twice-daily flights from Athens to Kavála on the mainland with **Olympic Airways** and **Aegean**. For Olympic info in Kavála, t 059 108 3071; Aegean are at the airport, t 059 105 3333.

## By Sea

Ferry from Kavála (port authority t 059 102 3716) to Skála Prínos almost every hour and to Liménas once a day. There are **hydrofoils** from Kavála to Liménas (at least 8 a day), Limenária, Liménas Potós and Kalliráchi. Daily boat **excursions** go from Liménas to Chryssí Ámmos, Glyfáda and Papalimáni beaches; there are day trips to ancient Philippi, or you can hire a boat of your own in Liménas to visit the uninhabited islet of Thassopoúla.

**Port authority:** Liménas, t 059 302 2106.

## By Road

The **bus** service t 059 302 2162 is regular; from Liménas quayside there are at least 10 services daily to Skála Prínos, Skála Potamiá, and Limenária, and 6 to Theológos and around the island. Alternatively, take a **taxi** from in front of the bus station. **Car hire** is available at the agencies around the central plateía in Liménas; try **Ladicas Travel**, t 059 302 3590, f 059 302 3402. For motorbikes or bicycles, try **Billy's Bikes**, t 059 302 2490, on Theogenous.

# Tourist Information

Tourist police: in **Liménas**, on the waterfront, t 059 302 3111.

# Festivals

**First Tues after Easter:** all over the island.
**28 April:** in Ag. Geórgios.
**end of July–early Aug:** traditional weddings performed in Theológos.
**10 July–15 August:** the Thássos festival.
**6 Aug:** Sotíras.
**15 Aug:** Panagía.
**27 Aug:** in Limenária, with special dances.
**26 Oct:** Theológos.

The northernmost Greek island, Thássos is also one of the fairest, almost perfectly round, ringed with soft beaches and mantled with fragrant, intensely green pinewoods, plane trees, walnuts and chestnuts. Unlike the other Aegean islands, it is rarely afflicted by the huffing and puffing of the *meltémi*, but has a moist climate, much subject to lingering mists; on hot days the intense scent of the parasol pines by the sapphire sea casts a spell of dreamy languor. For years a secret holiday nook of northern Greeks, the opening of Kavála airport to charter flights brought in package tours from Britain and Germany, but these days the island is in the throes of becoming the morning star of the Balkan Riviera: since the borders have opened in the last decade, much of Central and Eastern Europe realized how quickly they could reach the island by car. Thássos is extremely popular with campers, but is especially vulnerable to forest fires, which in the last two decades have sadly ravaged the forests on the west half of the island. Wherever you sleep, come armed: the mosquitoes are vivacious, vicious and voracious.

## History

Neolithic Thássos had links to Límnos, and by the 9th century BC, it was occupied by a Thracian-Macedonian tribe. In c. 710 BC, they were invaded by colonists from Páros. The likeable Parian poet, Archilochos, was among the invaders, but found himself (or at least the persona he adopted) outmanoeuvred in battle: 'Some Thracian now is pleased with my shield/which I unwilling left on a bush in perfect condition on our side of the field/but I escaped death. To hell with the shield!/I shall get another, no worse.' The Parians went to great lengths to justify their presence on Thássos, with a legend about Phoenician allies who had set up an earlier colony and had summoned Páros for aid; then of course there was a Delphic oracle that told them to found a city 'on the island of mists'. It was certainly worth all the fuss: the Parian-Thassians annually extracted 90 talents of gold and silver from the mines on the island and mainland; its marble, timber, fine oil and wine were in demand across the Aegean.

In 490 BC, the Persians attacked the rich island and razed the city walls. When they reappeared a decade later under Xerxes, the defenceless Thassians prevented another attack by holding a fabulous banquet for the Persians, and with many slaps on the back sent them off to defeat at Salamis. Thássos later revolted against the Delian League, and in 463 BC Athens sent Kimon to teach it a lesson, which took a two-year siege to accomplish. After that Thássos was ruled by Athens, until 340 BC when Philip of Macedon seized it. In 197 BC the Romans defeated the Macedonians and Thássos gladly became part of Rome, enjoying special privileges and a new period of prosperity. Among the uninvited guests who troubled the island in later years, the Genoese stayed the longest, from the 1300s until the Turks chased them out in 1460. Russia took over from 1770–74. In 1813 the Sultan gave the island to Mohammed Ali, Governor of Egypt, who had been brought up in the village of Theológos and loved Thássos; he lowered the taxes and granted the island virtual autonomy. Benevolent Egyptian rule lasted until 1902, when the Turks returned briefly before union with Greece during the Balkan Wars, in 1912. The Bulgarians occupied the island from 1941 to the end of the war, and are now welcomed as holiday makers.

# Liménas (Thássos Town)

The bustling capital and port of the island is officially Thássos, but is better known as **Liménas** (ΛΙΜΕΝΑΣ) or just Limen (not to be confused with the island's second town, Limenária). Liménas may not be pretty, but it's lively, with nearly as many flags as the United Nations waving along the waterfront; massive plane trees shade the squares, and shops will sell you walnut sweets and honey. Abandoned between the Middle Ages and the mid-19th century, the town has only 2,300 inhabitants (many of whom came over from Asia Minor in 1922), who can hardly begin to fill the shoes of **ancient Thássos**; bits of it crop up everywhere and add character to the new town.

The **Archaeology Museum** at 18 Megálou Alexándrou (*t 059 302 2180; due to reopen in 2002*) has been expanded after the recent French and Belgian excavations. Its contents hint at the wealth of the ancient city: a 7th-century BC plate (*pinakion*) depicting Bellerephon on Pegasus, slaying the three-headed Chimera; a dedicatory inscription to Glaukos, a friend of Archilochus, mentioned in several of his poems; a 6th-century BC *Kriophoros* (a young man bearing a lamb) over 11ft high, but left unfinished when the sculptor discovered a flaw in the marble by the ear; an Archaic relief (550 BC) of a hunting scene, and a beautiful ivory lion's head from the same period; a lovely, effeminate head of Diónysos from the 4th century BC, a relief of two

# Where to Stay

## Liménas ✉ 64004

Package firms rule, but fluctuate; one year a hotel will be block-booked, the next year not; be sure to have a reservation before you arrive.

**Amfipolis**, one street back from the waterfront t 059 302 3101, f 059 302 2110 (A; exp). Spacious, converted warehouse, with a pool.

**Makryámmos Bungalows**, on the beach of the same name, t 059 302 2101, makryamo@otenet.gr (A; exp). The poshest place to stay, with watersports, tennis, pool, a small deer park and a nightclub Open April–Oct.

**Akti Vournelis**, on the beach outside town on the Prínos road, t 059 302 2411, f 059 302 3211 (C; exp–mod). A good choice, and the bar nearby has live Greek music in the evenings.

**Ethira**, on the edge of Liménas, t 059 302 3310, f 059 302 2170 (B; exp–mod). Bright white bungalows, green lawns and a pool.

**Filoxenia Inn**, near the port, t 059 302 3331, Philoxenia-Thassos@hotmail.com (C; mod). An old white villa with a petite pool.

**Garden Studios**, 80m from the sea, t 059 302 2184, f 059 302 2612 (mod). Surrounded by a green lawn and olive groves.

**Timoleon**, t 059 302 2177, f 059 302 3277 (B; mod). Pleasant, spacious option, but it's best to phone ahead in season.

**Villa Molos**, near the sea, t 059 302 2053 (mod–inexp). Pleasant bed and breakfast.

**Alkyon**, by the harbour, t 059 302 2148, f 059 302 3662 (C; inexp) Welcoming, airy place .

**Lena**, t 059 302 3565, f 059 302 2123 (E; inexp).

**Camping Nysteri**, near Glyfáda, t 059 302 3327.

# Eating Out

**Alkyon**, on the waterfront. When you've a hankering for baked beans on toast and English tea and cakes.

**Asteria**, one street back from the main seafront. In business since 1962 and has lots to offer from the spit incl. revolving goats' heads sporting lascivious grins.

**Ipigi**. Traditional Greek specialities.

**New York**, near Platanakia. Covers all options with traditional Greek food, giant pizza, pasta dishes and occasionally fresh mussels.

**Platanakia**, at the eastern end of the harbour, towards the town beach. A touristy place serving fish at the appropriate prices.

**Syntaki**, in the same area. For home-grown vegetables and good fish.

**Marina's**, right on the waterfront. Long-established, British-owned bar; a friendly jam-packed place.

**Café Anonymous**. Broad selection of beers.

---

griffons devouring a doe (2nd century AD), little turtle votive offerings; a Hellenistic Aphrodite riding a dolphin, a fine bust of Hadrian and another of Alexander the Great, a cult figure among world conquerors. In Classical and Hellenistic times, Thássos was famous for its wine: there's a tablet from c. 420 BC with wine regulations written in boustrophedon, 'as the ox plows', and an amphora bearing the island seal.

Thássos' **Mount Ipsárion** (3,531ft), a solid block of white and greenish marble, provided the raw material for the ancient city. In the centre of modern Liménas, the agora, much rebuilt under the Romans, is the most prominent survival, with foundations and columns of porticoes and stoas, sanctuaries and a massive altar. A heröon in the centre of the market honoured the astonishing mid-5th-century BC athlete Theogenes, who won 1,400 victor's laurels. A mysterious paved 'Passage of Theoria', predating the rest of the agora by 500 years, leads back to the sparse remains of Artemision, where precious votives were found, and where the island's first metallurgical activity took place c. 600 BC. On the other side of the agora is part of a Roman street, a well preserved exedra, a few tiers of the **Odeon** and, further down, the **Herakleion**, a sanctuary founded c. 620 BC – Hercules was the island's patron, in a cult that the Parians claimed was established by the Phoenicians. East of the agora, towards the ancient naval port, another group of ruins includes a Sanctuary of

Poseidon; next to it, another altar remains in good enough condition to accept sacrifices to its divinity, Hera Epilimenia, guardian of ports. Remains of the naval gates survive here: the **Chariot Gate** (with an Archaic Artemis in a chariot) and the **Gate of Semel-Thyone** (with Hermes and the Graces). From here, a path leads past the ancient moles of the commercial harbour to the ruins of a medieval fort and the beginning of the city's polygonal walls, last rebuilt in *c.* 411 and repaired by the Genoese.

Unless you're really keen, however, there's a shortcut to the *acropolis* from town by way of the **Sanctuary of Diónysos** (south of the Sanctuary of Poseidon), and its 3rd-century BC choreographic monument, erected by the winner of a drama prize. From here a path rises to the 5th-century BC **Greek Theatre** on the lower slopes of the *acropolis*, affording a majestic view. Now that the excavations are completed, there are plans to renew Thássos' ancient drama festival. From the theatre a path continues up to the *acropolis*, spread across three summits of a ridge. On the first stands a Genoese fortress built out of the Temple of Pythian Apollo, whose Delphic oracle had encouraged the first Parian colonists. The museum's Kriophoros was discovered embedded in its walls, and a fine relief of a funerary feast (4th century BC) can still be seen near the guardroom. The second hill had a 5th-century BC **Temple of Athena Poliouchos**, built over a much older sanctuary, although the Genoese treated her no better than Apollo, leaving only the foundations. The third and highest summit of the *acropolis* was a **Sanctuary of Pan**, and has an eroded Hellenistic relief of Pan piping to his goats. Again, the view is more compelling than the old stones; on a clear day you can see from Mount Áthos to Samothráki, while inland the most prominent sight is the marble mountain Ipsárion, eaten away by quarrying.

There's a curious *exedra* resembling a stone sofa below the sanctuary, and around the back the vertiginous **Secret Stair**, carved into the rock in the 6th century BC, descends precipitously down to the remaining walls and gates (take care if you attempt it). Here you'll find the watchful stone eyes of the **Apotropaion** (to protect the walls from the Evil Eye), the well-preserved **Gate of Parmenon**, still bearing its inscription 'Parmenon made me' and, best of all, the large **Gate of Silenus** (by the intersection of the road to Panagía) where the vigorous bas-relief of the phallic god (6th century BC) has lost its most prominent appendage to a 'moral cleansing' of the 20th century. Continuing back towards town are, respectively, the **Gate of Diónysos and Hercules**, and the **Gate of Zeus and Hera** with an Archaic relief; this last one is just beyond the Venus Hotel if you gave the Secret Stair a miss.

The sandy town beach is small and shaded, but also tends to be crowded. **Makryámmos**, 3km to the east, is lovely but has become a hyper chi-chi tourist beach with an entrance fee for use of its facilities; just west, buses or boats wait to take you to **Chrysí Ámmos**, **Glyfáda** and **Papalimáni** beaches, the latter with windsurfing.

# Around the Island: Beaches and More Beaches

Thássos' main road encircles the island, and in July and August expect it to be busy. Directly south of Liménas, the road ascends to charming **Panagía** (ΠΑΝΑΓΙΑ). Its old whitewashed Macedonian houses, decorated with carved wood and slate roofs, over-look the sea, with their high-walled gardens, watered by a network of mountain streams, some flowing directly under their ground floor; the church **Panagías** has an underground spring. There's a stable here, Pegasus, which offers horses and teaches disabled children to ride. Down by the sea is the lovely town beach **Chrysí Ammoudiá**.

To the south of Panagía is another large, well-watered mountain village, **Potamiá**, which has two museums: a small **Folk Art Museum** (*open Wed–Mon*) and the **Polýgnotos Vages Museum** (*t 059 306 1400; open Tues–Sat 9–1 and 6–9, Sun 10–2*), dedicated to the locally born sculptor (d. 1965) who made it big in New York. A marked path from Potamiá leads to the summit of Mount Ipsárion taking about seven hours there and back, while below stretches the excellent beach of **Chrysí Aktí** (or **Skála Potamiás**), lined with tavernas and rooms. Quiet **Kínira** has a small shingly beach closed off by an islet of the same name; only a kilometre south are the white sands of **Paradise Beach**, folded in the pine-clad hills; clothes are optional.

The little slate-roofed hamlet of **Alikí** is beautifully set on a tiny headland over-looking twin beaches. It was an ancient town that thrived on marble exports, and

## Where to Stay and Eat

### Panagía ✉ 64004

**Helvetia**, **t** 059 306 1231 (*E; mod*). Small and perfectly reasonable.

**Thássos Inn**, **t** 059 306 1612, **f** 059 306 1027 (*C; mod*). Charming place to relax.

**Kosta**. One of the island's most popular tavernas, packed on Sun with locals.

**Tris Piges Taverna**, next to the church. *Bouzouki* nights; dancing on Fri–Mon nights.

### Skála Potamiás/Kínira ✉ 64001

**Sylvia**, at Kínira, by the sea, **t** 059 304 1246, **f** 059 304 1247 (*C; exp*). Quiet and modern, with a pool and playground.

**Miramare**, close to the sea, **t** 059 306 1040, **f** 059 306 1043 (*B; exp–mod*). Moderate-sized, with a restaurant and pool.

**Blue Sea**, **t** 059 306 1482, **f** 059 304 1278 (*C; mod*). Better than Miramare, if you can nab one of its 12 rooms.

**Camping Chrysí Ammoudiá**, **t** 059 306 1472. A fine campsite by the sands.

There are plenty of other rooms on offer in the surrounding olive groves.

### Pefkári/Potós/Limenária ✉ 64002

Rooms in Limenária are very plentiful and relatively cheap, if not picturesque.

**Alexandra Beach**, Potós, **t** 059 305 2391, *alexandra@tha.forthnet.gr* (*A; exp*).

Handsome hotel with every imaginable watersport, tennis and a pool.

**Coral Beach**, right on the sea on the south end of Potós, **t** 059 305 2402, **f** 059 305 2121 (*B; exp*). Cheaper, but still has all kinds of mod cons and pool.

**Thássos**, Pefkári, **t** 059 305 1596, **f** 059 305 1794 (*C; exp*). Has a pool and tennis.

**Garden**, **t** 059 305 2650, **f** 059 305 2660 (*C; inexp*). For a studio with a pool.

**Camping Paradisos**, at Potós, **t** 059 305 1950.

**Camping Pefkári**, Pefkári, **t** 059 305 1595.

**Mouria Tavern**, in Potós. A good lunch or dinner option.

### Skála Prínos/Skála Rachóni ✉ 64004

**Coral**, Skála Rachóni, **t** 059 308 1247, **f** 059 308 1190 (*C; mod*). A well-scrubbed, stylish place to stay with a pool amid the olives trees.

**Europa**, **t** 059 307 1212, **f** 059 307 1017 (*C; mod*). Small but decent, with wheelchair access.

**Xanthi**, on the edge of town, **t** 059 307 1303 (*C; inexp*). Good guesthouse. *Open Jun–Sept*.

**Camping Príno**, at Prínos, **t** 059 307 1270.

**Camping Perseus**, Skála Rachóni, **t** 059 308 1242.

**Kyriakos Taverna**, in front of you as you step off the boat at Prínos. Good fresh food and a wider than average selection.

**Zorba's**, next door. Just as popular; an added treat is the traffic policemen assailing your eardrums with their whistles.

ruins are strewn about its sandy shore, including an Archaic Doric double sanctuary. Another ancient settlement was at **Thimoniá** nearby, where part of a Hellenistic tower still stands. Further along, the **Archángelou Monastery** with its handsome slate roof is perched high over the sea on arid chromatic cliffs. Its cloistered nuns are in charge of a sliver of the True Cross, and the pretty courtyard and church may be visited (*proper attire, even long sleeves, required*); paradoxically, the pebble beach nestling in the cliffs below is frequented by nudists. The lovely beach of **Astrís**, above pretty Cape Sapúni, is still defended by its medieval towers, and is one of a score of places in the Mediterranean that claims to be the home of the *Odyssey's* Sirens. Continuing clockwise round the island, much of Thássos' resort hotel development (and worst forest fires in 1985) has happened above the excellent sandy beaches around **Potós** (ΠΟΤΟΣ), golden **Pefkári** and lovely white **Psilí Ámmos**, with plenty of olive groves in between. Potós is a good place for an evening drink over the sunset (although pretty full with package tourists), and for exploring inland; a handful of buses each day make the 10km trip up to the handsome slate-roofed village of **Theológos** (ΘΕΟΛΟΓΟΣ), one of Thássos' greenest spots and the capital of the island until the 19th century, defended by a ruined Genoese castle, the **Kourókastro**. The church Ag. Dimítrios has 12th-century icons.

**Limenária** (ΛΙΜΕΝΑΡΙΑ), the second largest town on Thássos, draws a fair crowd of summer tourists. It has a bit more of a village atmosphere than Liménas, surrounded by trees and endowed with a huge stretch of shady beach. In 1903 the German Spiedel Company mined the ores in the vicinity – its plant can still be seen south of the town, while the company's offices, locally called the **Palatáki**, 'Little Palace', stand alone in a garden on the headland. From Limenária excursion boats tour the coast of Mt Áthos – the closest women can get to the monastic site – or you can hire a little boat for a swim off the islet of Panagía. **Kalývia** just inland has some reliefs embedded in the wall of its church, while 15km further up the road there's **Kástro** high on a sheer precipice, the refuge of the Limenarians in the days of piracy. Although abandoned in the 19th century, in the last decade most of its old houses have been restored as holiday homes; there's a taverna in the summer but no public transport.

The flatter west coast of Thássos is farm country, lined with beaches that are generally less crowded. **Tripiti** has a fine sandy beach near the somewhat ramshackle little port of **Skála Marión**, while **Mariés** proper, 10km inland, is perhaps the least changed of the island's traditional villages. Just along the road, a sign points the way to the remains of an Archaic era pottery workshop. **Kalliráchis** and **Skála Sotíras** have rocky beaches, not up to Thássos' usual standard, while **Skála Prínos** (ΣΚΑΛΑ ΠΡΙΝΟΣ), the main ferry port to Kavála, enjoys views of an oil platform – there's not a lot, but just enough black gold in the Northeast Aegean to cause friction with Turkey. Inland from here is the village of **Prínos**, beyond which lie the two smaller villages of **Megálo** and **Mikró Kasaváti** (otherwise known as Megálo and Mikró Prínos) – worth a visit for their lovely setting, beehives and charming old houses, many of which have been bought up and renovated by Germans. **Rachóni** and **Ag. Geórgios** are two quiet inland villages. A small islet off the north coast, **Thassopoúla**, is pretty and wooded but according to the locals, full of snakes.

# The Saronic Islands

14

# The Saronic Islands

MAINLAND GREECE

Eleusis

Megara

Paloukia

Faneromeni

Perama

Piraeus

Salamina

Saronic Gulf

Lavousses

Epidauros

Angistri

Aegina · Souvala

Ag. Marina

Aegina

Kyra

Moni

Methana

PELOPONNESE

**Key to Sailing Services**

△ Yacht Supply Stations
▢ Ports of Entry and Exit
◇ Marinas

Poros
Poros

Galatas

Modi

Porto Cheli

Ermioni

To Nafplion

Dokos

Kosta

Hydra

Hydra

Spetses · Spetses

Spetsopoula

N

25 km
15 miles

# Getting There

## By Sea

Note that only **hydrofoils** for Aegina leave from the main port of Piraeus; hydrofoils for other Saronic Gulf ports (including Aegina occasionally) depart from Zéa Marína (see the Piraeus map, p.111). Some of these are express services directly to Hýdra and Spétses, whilst others call in at the ports of Aegina, Póros, Hýdra and Spétses. Regular passenger and special tourist ships for other Saronic Gulf ports, and car ferries to Aegina and Póros, leave from Piraeus' central harbour.

Set between Attica and the Peloponnese in the fast lane of Greek history, the five islands in the Saronic Gulf have played a disproportionate role in the evolution of the country: look at the little archipelago as an intimate microcosm of Greece, whose fate was inextricably bound up with the sea: Aegina was one of the most powerful maritime states in Greece, an early rival to Athens itself; Póros was the holy island of Poseidon; Salamína witnessed a sea battle that saved ancient Greece's civilization, and Hýdra and Spétses led the Greek fleets in the War of Independence battles. For the modern holidaymaker they make a pleasant outing, either by frequent ferry or hydrofoil out of Piraeus or under your own sail. They are ideal if you have only a little time, or want an island base for visits to the high spots of classical Greece.

The Saronics were the first Greek holiday islands, beginning in the early 1900s when fashionable Athenian families hired villas for the summer while father commuted to and fro at weekends. Since the introduction over 40 years ago of such conveniences as reservoirs, electricity and telephones, the Athenians have been joined by citizens from around the world. Aegina is the most visited island in all of Greece; beautiful, arty posy Hýdra has earned itself the nickname 'the St Tropez of Greece', and Spétses is trendy too, but in a quieter way.

# Aegina (ΑΙΓΙΝΑ)

Connections between **Aegina** (pronounced 'EGG-ee-na') and Piraeus are so frequent that many residents commute to work in the city. But Aegina is no fuddy-duddy bedroom suburb, and in spite of the demands of tourism, the islanders have stubbornly maintained their traditional fishing fleet and farms, especially their pistachio groves. Aegina has a few beaches that are often packed, numerous hotels and good fish tavernas; it also has fine Byzantine churches and the best-preserved ancient temple on any Greek island. The pleasure-craft set anchor along Aegina's more inaccessible coasts; even if you haven't brought the yacht, try to steer clear of summer weekends, when half of Athens descends on the island. Yet if you have only one day left in Greece and need one last island, Aegina is the obvious choice.

## Mythology

Aegina was one of Zeus' many loves, with whom he fathered Aeacus, the first king of the island, then called Oenone. When Aeacus renamed the island after his mother, Zeus' jealous wife Hera punished Aeacus by sending Aegina a plague of serpents, who killed the inhabitants. Aeacus begged Zeus for help, and wished for as many people to repopulate Aegina as there were ants on a nearby oak; hence the new Aeginetians were known as the ant folk, or Myrmidons. Aeacus fathered three sons – Peleus, Telemon and Phocos. When Telemon and Peleus in a fit of jealousy killed Phocos, their father's favourite, they were forced to flee, Telemon going to nearby Salamina, and Peleus to Thessaly. These two brothers fathered two of the greatest heroes of the Trojan War, Ajax and Achilles respectively. When Aeacus died, Zeus made him a judge of the dead in Hades along with Minos, his arch enemy, and Rhadamanthys, his second son from Crete.

## History

Aegina was inhabited from the 4th millennium BC by people from the Peloponnese, followed by the usual trail of Minoans, Mycenaeans and Dorians. Its first commercial boom began after 950 BC, when it joined a Saronic Amphictyony of seven cities (the Heptapolis). In 650 BC Aegina became the first state in Europe to mint coins, which led to Europe's first banking system. Trade, thanks to a powerful mercantile fleet, and perfume and pottery exports, made Aegina fat; by 490 BC it was a chief commercial centre in the Mediterranean; its coins have been found throughout the ancient world.

Aegina was far too close to Athens to wax fat for long. In the first Persian War Aegina sided with its trading partner Persia and it meant to send support until the Athenians held several prominent citizens hostage in return for Aegina's neutrality. In the second Persian War, Aegina had a change of heart and sent 30 ships to aid the Greek cause at the Battle of Salamis. Even so, Pericles could not forgive Aegina for its prosperity, and sneeringly referred to it as 'a speck that blocked the view from Piraeus'. In 458 BC the Athenian fleet attacked, and three years later the city of Aegina was forced to surrender; the Athenians made the inhabitants destroy their fortifications and hand over their fleet. When the Peloponnesian War broke out, the Athenians,

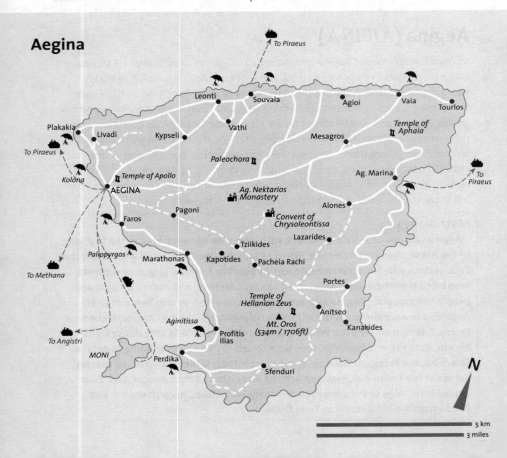

# Getting There and Around

**By sea**: hourly **hydrofoil** (35mins) until late afternoon, or by **boat** 1–1½ hours from Piraeus; frequent connections with Méthana and other Saronic islands, and 2–3 times a week with Epídavros. **Ferries** go to Aegina Town or to Ag. Marína on the east coast; some call at Souvála. **Buses** from Aegina Town (**t** 029 702 2787) depart from Plateía Ethneyersias and run to most villages, incl. Ag. Marína via the Temple of Aphaia and Nektários Monastery. **Caiques** and faster **water taxis** link Aegina Town to Angístri; others go from Pérdika to Moní. Port authority: **t** 029 702 2328.

# Tourist Information

**Tourist police**: Aegina Town, **t** 029 702 7777; *open all year.*
**Karagiannis Pipinis Travel**, 2 Kanari St, **t** 029 702 8780, *www.pipinis-travel.com.* For car, bike and boat hire, or accommodation.
**Moondy Bay Bungalows**, *moondy@netplan.gr*
**Apollo Hotel** (at Ag. Marína), *www.saronic.com*

# Festivals

**23 April**: Ag. Geórgios at Ag. Geórgios.
**17 July**: Ag. Marína, with a fair.
**15 Aug**: Panagía Chrysoleóntissa, at convent.
**Late Aug**: Pistachio festival.
**3 Sept**: Funeral of Leidinos, at Kypséli, ancient scapegoat-burying festival.

**6–7 Sept**: Ag. Sóstis in Pérdika.
**14 Sept**: Stavrós in Paleochóra.
**9 Nov**: Ag. Nektários.

# Where to Stay and Eat

**Aegina** ✉ 18010
For more info, contact Aegina's hoteliers' association, **t** 029 702 2424, **f** 029 702 6509.

**Aegina Town**
Most of the accommodation is old, and there are many relatively inexpensive places to stay (at least, for such a popular island).
**Egintiko Archontiko**, **t/f** 029 702 4968 (*A; exp*). Stylish converted 19th-century mansion, with air-conditioned rooms. *Open all year.*
**Danae**, 20m from the sea, **t** 029 702 2424, **f** 029 702 6509 (*B; exp–mod*). Many rooms, and restaurant terrace overlooking a pool.
**Pavlou**, 21 P. Aeginítou, **t** 029 702 2795 (*C; mod*). One of the more comfortable places, a block from the waterfront. *Open all year.*
**Miranta**, near the harbour, **t** 029 702 2266, **f** 029 702 7832 (*B; mod*). Another comfortable place with a pool.
**Marmarinos**, 24 Leon. Lada St, **t** 029 702 3510 (*D; inexp*). Quiet backstreet a few blocks from the waterfront, with garden opposite.
**Plaza**, at Kolóna, near the temple of Apollo, **t** 029 702 5600 (*E; inexp*). Pleasant and friendly, near the seaside fish tavernas.
**Christina**, a few blocks behind the Plaza and run by the same people, **t** 029 702

knowing they had few friends on Aegina, deported all the islanders, who were welcomed by the Spartans and later returned to their homes by Lysander.

Later history saw the usual invaders – Saracens, Venetians and Ottomans. In the War of Independence in 1821, Aegina was liberated early and flooded with Greek refugees. In 1828 Aegina Town became the capital of Greece under its first president, Ioánnis Capodistria. Fittingly for the place that minted the first coins in Europe, the first modern drachma, bearing a phoenix rising from the ashes, was minted on the island. But a year later the capital was relocated in Náfplion, before its final move to Athens.

# Aegina Town

The capital and chief port retains a lingering whiff of grandeur and Neoclassical elegance from its days as the first capital of Greece, even if many of the 19th-century buildings are hidden behind shops touting pottery and pistachios; the horse-drawn

5600/2910 (*E; inexp*). Another pleasant, quieter option.

The waterfront is packed with eateries. Walk through the little fish market to a pair of excellent little tavernas, one block in from the sea. They serve delicious grilled octopus and fish from the stands next door – you can't get seafood (*c. €15–20*) any fresher. Both also served good home-produced wines.

**Finikas tou Lira**, three blocks in, behind the Ionian Bank, t 029 702 4439. Lovely garden setting; specializes in *mezédes*.

**Flisbos, Kolóna**, next to Plaza Hotel, t 029 702 6459. *Ouzerie* with reasonably-priced fish.

**Lekkas**, near first town beach. Reliable fare.

**Maridaki**, near the hydrofoil landing point. Has a name for excellent fish.

**Bakaliarakia**, south of town at Fáros. More expensive quality fish and lamb from the spit; live Greek music on Fri and Sat nights.

**Avli**, Irioti St, one block in from the waterfront. Popular with locals and tourists for meals, snacks and drinks, incl. draught Guinness.

**Vatzoulia's**. Many locals like to eat out of town, and this place, en route to the Temple of Aphaia, is very lively. Great Greek food and music. *Open Wed and weekend eves only.*

### Souvála

**Ephi**, t 029 705 2214, f 029 705 3065 (*C; mod*). Adequate family hotel with a restaurant; rooms with balconies overlooking the sea.

**Chryssi Akti**, t 029 705 2786/2881. Cheaper rooms and studios with a pool.

**Ela Mesa** ('Come inside'). Standard, tasty food.

### Ag. Marína

There are also plenty of hotels (too many) on Ag. Marína Beach.

**Apollo**, by the sea, t 029 703 2271, f 029 703 2688 (*B; exp–mod*). Quiet and recently renovated, offering a sea-water pool, tennis and a big American-style buffet breakfast.

**Galini**, in a garden 3mins from the centre, t 029 703 2203, f 029 703 2216 (*C; mod*). Panoramic pool and decent restaurant.

**Piccadilly**, right on the beach, t 029 703 2696 (*C; mod*). Comfortable with sea-views.

**Tholos**, t 029 703 2129. Family-run taverna with good home-cooked vegetable and meat dishes, and a view of Ag. Marina thrown in.

### Pérdika/Marathónas

**Moondy Bay Bungalows**, at Profítis Ilías, north of Pérdika, t 029 706 1622, f 029 706 1147 (*B; exp*). Cushiest place to stay on Aegina, right on the sea in a well-tended garden, with pool, tennis and cycling; each room has its own air-conditioning and heating system; book well in advance.

**To Proraion**, Pérdika, t 029 706 1577. Considered by many to be Aegina's best fish restaurant.

**Nodas**, Pérdika. Large selection of delicious seafood, for prices a bit over the odds.

**Sissy**, at Marathónas, t 029 702 6222, f 029 702 6252 (*D; inexp*). Pleasant; breakfast included in room rates. Tough *hombres* welcome.

**S. Stratigos**, on Aiginitissa Beach. A wide range of delicious grilled meat and fish.

There's a summer taverna on Moní islet.

carriages add a nice touch amid the cars and general cacophony. The large crescent harbour and mole, almost too grand for an island, were financed in 1826 by Dr Samuel Greenly Howe, an American surgeon and husband of Julia, the author of *The Battle Hymn of the Republic*. Inspired by Byron's example, Dr Howe had fought in the Greek War of Independence, and was so appalled by the postwar suffering that he led a massive American relief campaign on Aegina, employing locals in public works. The harbour's landmark, the chapel of **Ag. Nikólaos**, celebrated its completion. The first Greek government building was the **Tower of Markellos**, near Ag. Nikólaos. It is austere, as is the **Residence** (now the public library) on Kyvernéou Street. President Capodistria, the once-dapper count from Corfu and foreign minister to the Tsar, slept in his office on the upper floor, while downstairs the mint churned out drachmas.

The *de rigueur* waterfront evening stroll is often accompanied by spectacular sunsets (the smog emanating from Athens is good for something) that bathe the town in a gentle light. In spite of growing numbers of pleasure boats, colourful fishing boats still occupy the port. They rarely net any *katsoúlas*, once a speciality of Aegina; but their *marída* (whitebait) goes down nicely with Aegina's own retsina in the many waterside tavernas. Ancient writers often referred to Aegina's 'secret port' just north of the city – only the islanders knew its entrance. It has a pleasant little sandy beach, and overlooking it, on the hillock of **Kolóna**, is the site of ancient Aegina (*open Tues–Sun 8.30–3; adm*) dating back to the Early Helladic Period (2400 BC): you can examine a jumbly walled settlement and a lonely Doric column from an early 5th-century **Temple of Apollo**; the rest of its marble went into building Aegina's new quay. Graves found in the vicinity yielded the British Museum's beautiful 'Aegina Treasure' of gold Minoan ornaments from the 16th century BC, believed to have been plundered by ancient tomb robbers from the 'gold pit' of Malia (*see* pp.181–2).

Nearby, the **Archaeology Museum** (*t 029 702 2248; open Tues–Sun 8.30–3; adm*) replaces the first archaeology museum in Greece (1829). Although most of the contents went to Athens in the mid-19th century, it keeps items found on Aegina: prehistoric pottery, some decorated with rare Early Helladic naval scenes, and vivid Archaic ceramics, including the superb 7th-century 'ram jug' showing Odysseus hiding to escape the cyclops Polyphemus. There are 6th-century pediments from two temples that once stood at Kolóna; a Classical marble sphinx, attributed to Calamis; fragments from the Temple of Aphaia and a mosaic from an ancient synagogue.

From Kolóna, a 15-minute walk takes you to the suburbs of **Livádi** and **Plakákia**, where a plaque marks the house where Níkos Kazantzákis wrote *Zorba the Greek*. Plakákia was something of an artists' and writers' colony: the **Museum Chrístos Kaprálos** (*t 029 702 2001; open July–Oct, 10-1 and 6-8; adm*) occupies the workshop used by the sculptor from 1963–93, and contains his most important work: the Archaic style *Battle of Pindus*, a monumental 150ft long limestone relief on 20th century Greek history. The road skirting the north coast is a good cycling route, with swimming possibilities at the rocky beaches of Leónti, and further east at **Souvála** (ΣΟΥΒΑΛΑ), one of the island's ports and a modest if dullish resort, which lured the island's first visitors decades ago with radioactive baths for rheumatism and arthritis.

# Around the Island

## Ag. Nektários and Paleochóra

The bus to Ag. Marína passes by the Temple of Aphaia, but most Greeks will pile out earlier, at the modern **Monastery of Ag. Nektários**, named after the former arch-bishop of Libya, who died here in 1920, and after assorted miracles, was canonized in 1967 – one of the last saints to join Orthodoxy's inner circle. You can see his crowned skull in his unfinished garish church, which is claimed to be the largest in Greece. Even so, it's not big enough on 9 November, when hordes of pilgrims come for the last great outdoor festival of the Greek calendar, queueing for hours to kiss his tomb.

If you're not in need of Nektários' services, consider climbing up to the crumbling ghost town of **Paleochóra** (ΠΑΛΑΙΟΧΩΡΑ), behind the monastery (*visit in the morning, when the caretaker is usually around with church keys – and wear good* *walking shoes*). Founded in what seemed to be a safe inland location in the 9th century when the Saracens were raiding the coast, Paleochóra twice proved vulnerable: Barbarossa slaughtered the men and carried off all the women and children in 1538 and Morosini pummelled it in his siege of 1654. Some 28 churches – out of the original 365 – still stand, many sheltering 13th-century frescoes and stone iconostasis; among the best are the **Basilica of Ag. Anárgyroi**, the **Chapel of Taxiárchis**, and the **Cathedral of the Episkopí**, founded by Ag. Dionysos, the patron saint of Zákynthos. Looming over all is Morosini's very dilapidated **Venetian castle**.

An hour's walk south of Ag. Nektários will take you to the fortified **Convent of Chrysoleóntissa** (1600) with an especially fine wooden iconostasis and a famous rainmaking icon of the Virgin (a job once held on Aegina by Zeus). The nuns are known for their hospitality and delicious farm produce.

## The Temple of Aphaia

East of Ag. Nektários, the road passes by the pretty village of **Mesagrós**, surrounded by the vineyards and pine groves that produce excellent retsina. High above Mesagrós stands Aegina's pride and joy, the beautiful and well-preserved **Doric Temple of Aphaia** (*t 029 703 2398; open Mon–Fri 8–5, Sat–Sun 8.30–3; adm*), built in the early 5th century BC. At first glance Aphaia is an unlikely candidate for such a fine temple; but Aphaia was the name of the Mediterranean Great Goddess on Aegina, and she was worshipped on this site since the Neolithic era (2000 BC). Several sanctuaries and temples predated the Doric structure, with inscriptions to Artemis Aphaia (the 'not dark'), to differentiate her from Hecate, the Great Goddess in her aspect of witch. In Crete her name was Britomartis or Diktynna – Artemis again, the Minoan mistress of animals. Later myths made Aphaia a child of Zeus and Leto, who hunted with her sister Artemis and followed her cult of virginity. When King Minos of Crete fell in love with her, she fled and, on reaching Aegina's coast, threw herself in despair into the sea and vanished. Hence the Classical era translation of her name, 'the disappeared one'. She suffered a final transformation, becoming Aphaia-Athena with the rise of Athens and the desire to please the goddess who helped the Greeks in the Trojan War.

The temple, built in Aegina's prime, is of local golden limestone and originally covered with a coat of brightly painted stucco. Of the original 32 columns, 25 are still standing, thanks partly to reconstruction; a highly unusual internal colonnade surrounded the *cella*, where the cult statue of Aphaia once stood (note the 19th-century graffiti). The superb pediment sculptures of Parian marble, depicting scenes of the Trojan war, are among the finest works of Greek Archaic art, but you have to go to the Munich Glyptothek to see them; in 1812 representatives of Ludwig I of Bavaria (father of Greece's first king, Otto), purchased them from the Turks when they found peasants smashing them up for the lime kiln. A **little museum** on site has casts of the temple and its predecessor that burned in 510 BC.

## Ag. Marina

The café opposite the temple offers a splendid view of the east coast of Aegina, including **Ag. Marína** (ΑΓ. ΜΑΡΙΝΑ), the island's busiest resort, with its glossiest

nightlife and a long sandy beach – Aegina's best, but don't expect much in the way of
elbow room. If you want to foot it from Aphaia, it's a half-hour walk downhill. And
once you get there, be prepared for a mild culture shock; all the menus are in Swedish
and Russian, and cocktail hour for the big blondes starts right after lunch.

## Mount Oros and Pacheiá Ráchi

Once a day a bus from Aegina Town lumbers up to **Pacheiá Ráchi** (or walk up from
Marathónas), near the **Temple of Hellanion Zeus**, dedicated to Zeus Hellanios, 'the
rainmaker'. Two massive terraces, cisterns and a monumental staircase remain in
place; from here it's an hour's walk up to the summit of **Mt Oros** (1706ft), the highest
peak in the Saronic Gulf; its name simply means 'mountain' and it enjoys magnificent
views when Zeus is having a day off.

Pacheiá Ráchi is home to Aegina's beautiful **wildlife sanctuary**. Probably the most
effective animal protection and rehabilitation centre in Greece, it accepts wounded
and sick animals from all over the country. Phillipos, the founder, and his volunteer
specialists, have cared for some 3,000 birds, wolves, and other small mammals. The
sanctuary also takes in stray cats and dogs, many from overcrowded Athens. Funding
comes from international donors such as WWF, businesses and public contributions.
Visitors are welcome and can see a cross-section of native wildlife.

## Pérdika and Moní Islet

One of the most popular excursions is to cycle from Aegina Town south along the
coast to **Pérdika** (ΠΕΡΔΙΚΑ) past several swimming spots around **Marathónas** and
the attractive beach of **Aiginitíssa** (7½km from Aegina Town). Pérdika ('partridge') is a
pretty fishing village-cum-resort with a small beach and tavernas that offer excellent
fresh fish. All around are Aegina's famous pistachio groves.

One of Greece's endangered species, the shy, wild *kri kri* mountain goats from Crete
– exotic creatures with long horns – are protected on the steep little **islet of Moní**, off
Pérdika (linked by boat taxis from Pérdika or Aegina Town). It once belonged to the
Convent of Chrysoleóntissa and is a pretty island, with a small beach, ruled by brazen
peacocks. Moní is popular for picnics and diving, and you can walk up through the
trees to a look-out post built by the Germans for a wonderful view of the gulf.

## A Note on Pistachios

Introduced in ancient times from Persia, perhaps by Alexander the Great, what the
Greeks call 'Aegina nuts' grow better here than anywhere else in Greece. In late
August, harvesters using long sticks dislodge the nuts into canvas sheets. The pistachios are then sun dried on flat terraces. They're no bargain, but avoid the cheaper
ones – they're artificially dried and lose their natural oils. Two decades ago Aegina
suffered a minor ecological disaster when farmers uprooted olive and fruit trees to
plant pistachios. The new groves required so much water that deeper wells were
sunk, until they went dry or filled with sea water. For years afterwards, most of the
island's water had to be shipped in daily from the mainland. A new reservoir has
solved this, and every year in late August the nuts are honoured by a festival.

## Where to Stay

**Angístri** ✉ 18010
  There's no shortage of lower-end accommodation, most of it centred around Skála, and all
much of a muchness. There are also numerous
rooms to let in private homes.

**Andreas, t** 029 709 1346 (*D; mod*). The most
upscale choice, with a good restaurant.
**Anagennissis, t** 029 709 1332 (*E; inexp*). Right
on the beach.
**Aktaeon, t** 029 709 1222 (*E; inexp*).
**Angístri Tours**, at Skala, **t** 029 709 1307, **f** 029
709 1471. Can help you find a room.

# Angístri (ΑΓΚΙΣΤΡΙ)

Boats from Aegina Town (30 minutes – or less by water taxi) and Piraeus' main
harbour (2 hours, or 50 minutes by catamaran) sail at least twice a day to **Angístri**
('hook island'), a small island of pine woods, fertile fields and relatively quiet beaches
that attract their summer share of weekend Athenians and unassuming Brits. Most
of the inhabitants are descendants from Albanian refugees and still keep up some
Albanian customs. There are two landing places on the island: **Mílo**, the principal
village in the north, and the bland modern resort of **Skála** with its excellent sandy
beach and most of what passes for nightlife on Angístri; the older village of Metóchi
is just above. A bus connects the two villages with the third, **Limenária**, a quiet,
southern farming hamlet with a couple of tavernas. There's nothing luxurious about
Angístri – it offers the basics for a restful read-a-good-book holiday, and little more.

# Hýdra (ΥΔΡΑ)

Hýdra hosted the country's largest fleet in the early 1800s, and its daring captains
built the sombrely elegant mansions amassed in a magnificent amphitheatre over
the harbour. Artists and their camp followers moved in as the last sailors moved out;
the first trickle of tourism was sparked off by the scenes of Hýdra in the film *Boy on a
Dolphin*, starring Sophia Loren. The posy tone that sets Hýdra apart, like St Tropez and
other jetset nooks, survives in spite of the hordes of day-trippers and cruise ship folk
who haunt the jewellers and painting galleries; at night, to the tinkling of glasses and
the rhythms from the trendy bars, Hýdra comes into its own.

## History

In the 6th century BC the tyrant Polykrates of Sámos purchased dry, rocky Hýdra with
the tribute he captured in Sífnos. However, no permanent settlers lived on the island
until the 15th century, when Greeks and Albanians from Epirus took refuge here from
the Turks. Hýdra is a nearly barren island, and the new arrivals had to turn to the sea
for their livelihood: through shipbuilding and a fleet of 150 merchant ships – and
through smuggling and piracy. By the late 18th century, Hýdra was an autonomous
island state, to which the Turks turned a blind eye as long as it paid its taxes. It
boasted a wealthy population of 25,000, and the sailors Hýdra sent as a tribute to the
sultan were prized for their prowess – especially the Albanians who made fortunes by
running the British blockade in the Napoleonic Wars. Ibrahim Pasha, Hýdra's arch-
enemy in the War of Independence, grudgingly nicknamed the island 'Little England'.

Hýdra did so well under the Ottomans that the outbreak of the fight for independence in 1821 left its captains lukewarm, until their seafaring rivals on Spétses had chalked up a few victories and the people of Hýdra threatened to revolt unless they joined the Greeks. The Hydriot captains threw themselves into the fray with characteristic boldness. Merchants (notably the Koundouriótis family) converted their fleet into warships, and, under such leaders as Tombázis and Miaoulis, Commander-In-Chief of the Greeks, the Hydriot navy terrorized the Turks, especially with their fire ships: at night, some 20 daredevils would sail a decrepit vessel full of explosives alongside the Turkish ships, light it and row for their lives in their escape boat.

Ironically, the independence Hýdra fought so hard to win brought an end to its prosperity. After the war, sponge-fishing became the islanders' chief occupation, but that declined through lack of demand. By the 1950s Hýdra looked like a ghost island, when fortune's wheel was oiled once again by the arrival of Greek painter Hadjikyriakos Ghikas, the pioneer of the artists' colony that paved the way for today's glitterati.

## Hýdra Town

Just arriving is an extraordinary experience. The island looks like a hopelessly barren rock pile until your vessel makes a sharp turn, and – *voilà*, the sublime port, the pearl in the oyster shell, the scene that launched a thousand cruise ships. The grey and white mansions, built in the late 18th century by Venetian and Genoese architects, attest to the loot amassed by Hydriot privateers and blockade runners. The sole combustion engines on the island belong to two rubbish trucks; the narrow lanes radiate from the amphitheatre and peter out into stairs, with views that first charmed the artists. Although most of the artists have fled tourism's onslaught, a branch of the **School of Fine Arts** survives in the fine old residence of the Tombazi family, and there are several galleries amid the boutiques. Recalling an older tradition, the **Skolí Eborikís Naftilías** is Greece's oldest school for merchant marine captains,

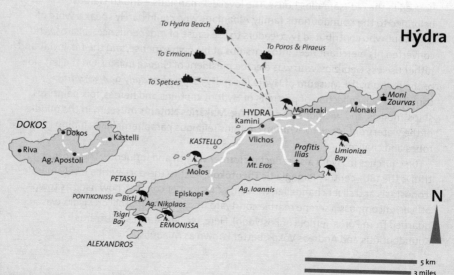

## Getting There and Around

**By sea: ferries** connect Hýdra with the other Saronic islands several times a day. There are up to 20 **hydrofoils** and catamarans daily from Zéa Marína (Piraeus) or the main harbour of Piraeus, some going 'express' to Hýdra in about 1½ hours; frequent hydrofoil connections to Póros and Spétses, and Náfplion, Pórto Héli and Ermióni, in the Peloponnese. **Water taxis** wait by the quay to ferry visitors to the swimming places (hardly beaches) at Kamíni, Mandráki and Vlíchos, and the islet of Dokós; they're cheap if you join the crowd. Boat trips to the far ends of Hýdra are about €60 return. The only other forms of transport are donkey and foot. **Port authority, t** 029 805 2279.

## Tourist Information

**Tourist police:** Votsi Street, **t** 029 805 2205; *open summer only.*
For information and accommodation:
**Saitis Tours,** on the quay, **t** 029 805 2184, **f** 029 805 3469.
**Hýdra Tours,** above Saitis Tours, **t** 029 805 3718.

## Festivals

Hýdra is a great island for **Good Friday** and Easter.
**Mid-June:** the Miaoúlia.

**July:** Festival of Marionettes, with puppets.
**20 July:** Profitís Ilías.
**25 July:** at Ag. Efpraxía.
**15 Aug:** Panagías in town.
**13–14 Nov:** Ag. Konstantínos, the island's patron saint.

## Where to Stay

**Hýdra** ✉ 18040
Be warned: it is sheer madness to arrive in Hýdra in the summer without a room booked. Most of the hotels are small.
**Bratsera,** Tombázi St, **t** 029 805 3970, **f** 029 805 3626 (*A; exp*). Opened in 1994 in a beautifully converted sponge factory. Combines traditional design with glamour. Most rooms (with air-con) overlook the colonnaded pool and lantern lit restaurant; the Belgian chef is a creative perfectionist. *Closed Nov.*
**Ippokampos, t** 029 805 3453, **f** 029 805 2501 (*B; exp*). Modern feel, with pretty courtyard.
**Miramare,** at Mandráki, **t** 029 805 2300, **f** 029 805 2301, winter in Athens, **t** 010 413 6406 (*A; exp*). Stone bungalow complex, linked to the harbour by boat; overlooking the island's sole bit of sand. It offers watersports, and all rooms have air-con, telephone and fridge. *Open April–Oct.*
**Miranda, t** 029 805 2230, **f** 029 805 3510, winter, **t** 010 684 9268, **f** 010 804 7776 (*A; exp*). Another elegant 19th-century sea

housed in the old Tsamados house. The loveliest mansions – and the largest – belonged to the Koundouriótis family, Albanians who could barely speak a word of Greek but who contributed two leaders to the cause of independence: Lazaros, who converted his merchant fleet into warships at his own expense, and the fat, jovial, and rather useless Geórgios, who was elected president of Greece in 1824. On the left side of the harbour, the **Museum of Hýdra** (*t* 029 805 2355; open daily 9–4.30; adm) contains a rich collection of portraits of Hydriot captains and heroes, folk paintings, ships' models, and weapons. The small **Ag. Makários Notarás** museum in the middle of the waterfront (*open 10–5; adm*) contains religious paraphernalia including icons, robes and chalices.

The churches in Hýdra also reflect its former wealth and influence. The most beautiful is the 18th-century **Panagía tis Theotókou**, next to the port, with a lovely marble iconostasis and silver chandelier; the cells of its former convent, now used as town offices, encompass a serene marble courtyard (most of the marble on Hýdra was quarried from Póros' Temple of Poseidon). Here, too, are statues of Lázaros Koundouriótis and Andréas Vókos, better known as Miaoúlis.

captain's town house, with stunning Venetian painted ceilings. *Open May–Oct.*

**Mistral,** t 029 805 2509, f 029 805 3412 (*B; exp*). An old stone tower mansion, with simple but attractive rooms.

**Orloff,** near the port, t 029 805 2564 (*B; exp*). Beautifully restored 19th-century mansion with only 9 rooms, each individually designed and set around a courtyard; one of the best breakfasts in Greece.

**Amaryllis,** t 029 805 2249, f 029 805 3611 (*B; mod*). Comfortable little hotel in an old mansion, with smallish doubles with bath.

**Delfini,** by the hydrofoil base, t 029 805 2082 (*C; mod*). Reasonable choice. *Open Mar–Nov.*

**Hotel Leto,** t 029 805 2280 (*B; mod*). Larger than the others, with clean rooms.

**Hýdra Hotel,** 2 steep mins from the clock tower, t 029 805 2102, f 029 805 3330 (*C; mod*). Practise your mountain goat skills to stay here; you'll receive a warm welcome and have fine views over the town and harbour in this historic mansion.

**Sophia,** t 029 805 2313 (*D; mod*). Friendly old-fashioned pension on the waterfront; no rooms with en suite but some great views.

## Eating Out

For the privilege of sitting on the lovely quay of Hýdra expect to pay through the nose for anything from a cup of coffee upwards.

**Geitoniko** (also known as Christina), t 029 805 3615. Courtyard setting in an old stone building; excellent traditional cuisine at fair prices.

**Iliovassilema,** on Vlíchos Beach, t 029 805 2496. Great place to eat as you watch the sun set, but expect to pay a little more for the pleasure.

**Kondylenia,** on Kamíni Beach, t 029 805 3520. A particularly outstanding restaurant with views over the quaint harbour; try the delicious squid in tomato sauce or the sea urchin dip.

**Paradosiacó,** t 029 805 4155. Recommended option for its *mezédes*.

**Perivolakia,** near the Orloff. Spacious outdoors with reliable Greek fare.

**Stani,** near the Steki, t 029 805 3155. All the Greek favourites.

**Steki,** just before the clock tower, t 029 805 3517. Serves reliable Greek food on its veranda for even less.

**Strofylia,** t 029 805 4100. Known for its good *mezédes*.

**Three Brothers,** t 029 805 3253. Another taverna that keeps humane prices.

**Vigla,** t 029 805 3595. Verandas with lovely views; serves excellent (but expensive) seafood.

**Xeri Elia,** short walk up from the port, t 029 805 2886. Pleasant setting under the trees, serving standard Greek fare at normal prices.

From the church, climb up Miaoúlis Street to the lovely square of **Kaló Pigádi**, site of two 18th-century mansions and two deep wells that have long supplied the town with fresh water. The one real beach on Hýdra is a 20-minute walk away at **Mandráki**, the old shipbuilding docks of the Hydriots, with hotel and restaurant. You can also dive off the lovely rocks at **Kamíni** (Italian for 'whitewash', which was once made there). On Good Friday, Kamíni is packed with Hydriots and visitors who come to watch the moving candlelit procession of Christ's bier, the *epitafiós*, which culminates here by the sea. Another place to swim near town is at the **Bariamí Cave**.

## Around the Island

Other swimming holes and inland excursions require more walking, a guaranteed way to escape the idle throng who stay close to the town. At **Kastéllo**, behind Hýdra, are the ruins of a thick-walled castle down near the shore. Further on, **Vlíchos** is a pretty hamlet with a rocky beach, a picturesque little bridge, and a couple of good

## The Man who Captivated Nelson

Before being appointed Commander-In-Chief of the Greek navy, Miaoúlis was elected admiral by the fleet, in recognition not only of his seamanship, but of his exceptional integrity – a rare trait in 1821, when many Greek leaders had no qualms about jeopardizing the entire enterprise for their own profit or self-interest; Miaoúlis instead devoted his considerable fortune to the war. The Greeks tell the story that Nelson once captured Miaoúlis on one of his more piratical adventures but Miaoúlis in turn captured Nelson with his charm, and was released with a pat on the back. He needed all the charm he could muster in dealing with the difficult, independent-minded sailors of Hýdra and Spétses, who were accustomed to the medieval system that gave each crew member a right to the profits and a say in all voyage matters. It was democracy in action; if the majority disagreed with a captain's decision, even if they were about to do battle, they would go on strike. The fact that Miaoúlis avoided mutiny, kept his ships together, and harried the massive, well-organized Egyptian invasion fleet of Ibrahim Pasha (Mehmet Ali's son) for four months across the Aegean was an accomplishment in itself, even if it ultimately failed. Afterwards, while all but a handful of Greek admirals refused to sail without being paid in advance, Miaoúlis struggled to relieve the besieged city of Messolóngi, and always outfoxed the enemy when he had a fighting chance and enough ships. He bowed out of the war and politics with a bang (see 'Póros', opposite) and is fondly remembered on his native island, in celebrations called the Miaoúlia (20 June), which often include mock re-enactments of his battles.

tavernas; boats and more expensive water taxis from the port also make the trip. Pine trees and coves for swimming make **Mólos** a popular place for outings and for spotting Joan Collins, who often spends the summer here.

According to ancient tradition, in far less glamorous times the steep cliff near Mólos was used to throw off the aged and sick who could no longer carry their weight on the austere island. If you're looking for a long walk, a track leads south to a clutch of hunters' lodges at **Episkopí**, in Hýdra's pine forest. Above town, **Profítis Ilías Monastery** and the nearby **Convent of Ag. Efpráxia** are about an hour on foot (or on one of the little donkeys for hire). The view from the top is lovely and you may be able to buy textiles woven by the ancient nuns on their ancient looms. Although you'll have to bring your own food and water, Limióniza (straight across Hýdra) is a beautiful place to take a swim.

## Dokós

From Hýdra it is an hour's caique trip to Dokós, an islet made of *marmarópita*, a grey and red marble as hard as steel that is often used in building. The beach at Dokós is longer than at most ports, and the underwater fishing is excellent; while poking around in these waters, Jacques Cousteau discovered a 3,000-year-old wreck, thought to be the oldest in the world, carrying a cargo of wine and ceramic pots. There's a nice little taverna on Dokós, open if the owner is in the mood, and if you get your water cabbie to phone ahead.

# Póros (ΠΟΡΟΣ)

*If there is one dream which I like above all others it is that of sailing on land. Coming
into Póros gives the illusion of that deep dream.*
Henry Miller, *The Colossus of Maroussi*

A mere 400 yards of sea separates Póros ('the passage') from the green mountains
of the Peloponnese, lending the island a uniquely intimate charm; the Saronic Gulf
seems like a lake, and if you sail through the busy Straits of Póros on a large ferry boat
you can almost touch the balconies of the waterside buildings: a Greek Grand Canal,
and one that's as busy as the one in Venice with ships of every size to-ing and fro-ing,
all for the diversion of Póros café society. Of all the islands in the Saronic Gulf, Póros
receives the most package tours; besides the beauty of its location, it's only an hour
from Piraeus by hydrofoil, and within easy driving distance of major sights in the
Peloponnese: Epidauros, Náfplion, Mycenae, Troezen and Galatás.

## History

The early presence of Cretans on Póros is remembered in the myth of Princess
Skylla, whose father, the king of Póros, had a magic lock of hair that made him
immortal. When Minos of Crete besieged her father's castle, Skylla fell in love with the
Cretan king. To prove her love, she cut off her father's magic lock of hair while he slept
and brought it to Minos proclaiming her affection. By killing the king, Minos easily

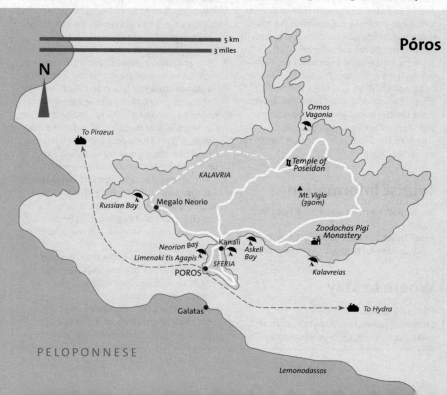

took Póros the next day. Minos was revolted by Skylla's betrayal and left for Crete without her. Desperate, Skylla swam after him, but she was attacked by her father's spirit in the form of an eagle, and drowned in the bay which bears her name (Askéli).

Póros in antiquity was known as Kalavria, and served as the headquarters of the Kalavrian League, a 7th-century BC Amphictyony, or maritime confederation, that included the cities of Athens, Aegina, Epidauros, Troezen, Náfplion, Ermióni, Orchomenos and Pasiai. The Kalavrian League operated under the protection of Poseidon, who had a sanctuary in the centre of Kalavria. Little remains of it today beyond the memory of the great orator, Demosthenes who, unlike today's Greeks, didn't think Macedonia was Greek and roused his native Athens against the presumptions of Philip of Macedon. Although Philip defeated Athens at Chaeronea (338 BC), Demosthenes continued his defiance of Philip's successor, Alexander. Upon Alexander's death in 322, Demosthenes led another revolt against the Macedonians. This time Alexander's general Antipater went after him, and although Demosthenes fled to Póros and sought sanctuary at the temple of Poseidon, the Macedonians burst in, swords raised. But Demosthenes died proving his pen was mightier in the end; he had bitten off the poison he had concealed in the nib.

One of the bays of Póros is called Russian Bay, recalling some of the confusing events that occurred on Póros, this time in 1828, when emissaries of the Great Powers

## Getting There and Around

By sea: car ferry and hydrofoil from Piraeus, Aegina and Methána several times a day; car ferries every 30mins to Galatás on the mainland. Frequent passenger ships and hydrofoils run to other places in the Saronic Gulf, allowing for day-trips; once a week in high season there are connections to the Corinth Canal and Náfplion. Galatás is 3hrs from Athens by land, and water taxis (benzínas) make the trip across the strait from June to Sept. Port authority: t 029 802 2274.

By road: the one bus on Póros goes up to the monastery and back.

## Tourist Information

Tourist police, on the waterfront, t 029 802 2256.
Askeli Travel, opposite the ferry, t 029 802 2311. Ask Thérése for help with accommodation.

## Where to Stay

**Póros ☒ 18020**
Christina Studios, 50m from the beach at Askéli, t 029 802 4900, askelitr@athena .compulink.gr (exp). New, sleeping 2-3, with lovely sea-views from the outsize balconies.
Diónysos, near the ferry, t 029 802 3511 (C; exp). Well-maintained attractive old building.
Kalimera, t 029 802 4510 (exp). The most luxurious in the way of apartments.
Neon Aegli, Askéli Beach, t 029 802 2372, f 029 802 4345 (B; exp). Near to town and with a real Greek flavour, another resort hotel with a private stretch of beach and water sports; all rooms have balcony and sea-view.
Pavlou, t 029 802 2734 (B; exp). The best choice at Neórion, and at the lower end of the price scale; it has a lovely pool and tennis courts.
Sirene, near the monastery, t 029 802 2741, f 029 802 2744 (B; exp). Best on the island, with air-con throughout, a salt-water pool, and its own beach. Open April–mid-Oct.
Douros, 9 Dimosthenous (first road right after the high school), t 029 802 2633 (inexp). Pleasant, modern rooms and apartments with air-con and TV.
Manessi, in the heart of the main harbour, t 029 802 2273, f 029 802 4345 (C; inexp). Basic, clean accommodation in a Neoclassical building.
Seven Brothers, centrally placed one block back from the waterfront, t 029 802 3412, f 029 802 3413, 7brothers@hol.gr (inexp).

(British, French and Russian) gathered here for a conference on the new Greek kingdom. The Russians were close friends with the first president, Count Capodistria, one-time Foreign Minister to the Tsar – too close, thought many independent-minded revolutionaries from Hýdra and Póros, who formed their own 'constitutional committee'. On their orders Admiral Miaoúlis seized the national fleet based at Póros, including his lavish flagship Hellas (an American-built warship that cost twice the national budget). In 1834, when the Great Powers counter-ordered Miaoúlis to hand the fleet over to the Russians to support Capodistria, the honest admiral blew up the Hellas instead; it broke his heart but averted a civil war.

## From Póros Town to the Temple of Poseidon

Póros consists of two islands from different geological periods: larger Kalávria, pine-forested and blessed with innumerable quiet sandy coves, and little Sferiá, where most of the action takes place, a volcanic bubble that popped out of the sea during the eruptions at Methána on the mainland. The two are joined by a sandy belt of land and a bridge. Póros Town, the capital and port, clambers all over Sferiá, crowned by the blue-domed campanile of the Metropolis church. Like Hýdra, many of its inhabitants trace their roots back to Albanian forebears who fled the depredations of the Turks in their homeland. These days the town is given over to tourist needs, except for

Convenient and comfortable hotel; rooms come with air-con and TV.

## Eating Out

Eating out along the *paralía*, or waterfront, of Póros Town is a real Greek treat – a line of tavernas with lovely views of the Peloponnese and of the ridiculously expensive yachts gliding silently through the strait. All serve good Greek food at reasonable prices:

**Caravella**, on the waterfront, 100m from the hydrofoil. Excellent selection of Greek and international dishes.

**Karavolos**, one block behind the cinema, t 029 802 6158. Small backstreet restaurant, popular with everybody for its good Greek fare. Get there early to find a table.

**Mourthoukos**, Neorion Beach. Very good food; try the stuffed pork or the mouth-watering soufflé.

**Sailor Taverna**, t 029 802 3096. Good for lobster and anything else from the grill.

**Tassos**, at the end of the waterfront just before the supermarket. One of the island's best fish tavernas, with a decent wine list.

**The Flying Dutchman**, round the corner from the post office. The Indonesian *rijkstaffel* is a great cure for Greek food fatigue, and they also do excellent steaks cooked to order in front of you. Pleasant ambience.

Snack bars and tavernas line the beaches along the road out to **Love Bay** (turn left after the Naval School); the beach at **Calypso** is especially nice, and has constant Greek music.

**Taverna Paradiso**, 2km from Poseidon's Temple (approaching from Askéli; take a taxi), t 029 802 3419. Offers a taste of old Greece under its pergolas of vines, with views over the pine forest to the sea. Perfect for a leisurely lunch after a tour around the island.

## Entertainment and Nightlife

**Coconuts**, right on the waterfront in town. A fun bar, run by a zany Dutch family, also offering Internet access and assistance.

**Ekati**, near Tassos Taverna. Late night Greek music.

**Slalom**. Straightforward rock joint with a small dance floor.

**Posidonio**, 3km from the centre of town. Café-cum-cocktail bar with pool and panoramic views. The owner will even pay your taxi fare back into town.

the **Naval Training School**, housed in the buildings of the first arsenal of the Greek State. Póros also has a small **Archaeology Museum** in Plateía Koryzí, with finds from the ancient Troezen area, including a lion spout gutter from the fabled Temple of Aphrodite (**t** 029 802 3276; open Tues–Sun 8.30–3).

A new crop of hotels has recently sprung up on Kalávria, some on the often polluted beach of **Neórion** to the west, and **Askéli** and **Kanáli**, which are cleaner to the east. However, true beach-lovers will turn up their noses at all of them; alternatives include crossing over to Aliki beach, next to **Galatás** on the mainland, or hiring a small boat (around €30 a day plus petrol) to reach the pretty coves – inaccessible by land – on the island's north side. From Kanáli the bus continues to the peaceful 18th-century **Monastery of Zoodóchos Pigí**, immersed in woods and decorated inside with a lofty gilt iconostasis and good icons. A new road in front of the monastery climbs through pine woods to the plateau of Palatia and the scant remains – the locals call it 'the five stones' – of the once celebrated **Temple of Poseidon**. First built in brick by the Mycenaeans, it was rebuilt in marble *c.* 500 BC; when Pausanias visited it, he saw the tomb of Demosthenes in the precinct. All this is dust in the wind (and most of the marble is in Hýdra) but the view across the Saronic Gulf is spectacular.

Although it's out of print, keep an eye peeled for *In Argolis*, a delightful book about Póros written by George Horton, editor of the *Philadelphia Enquirer* who became US consul in Greece, and helped organize the first modern Olympics. During the Asia Minor catastrophe in 1922 he was in Smyrna and helped to save the lives of thousands of Greek civilians; he wrote *Blight of Asia* about the experience, a book that influenced US foreign policy of the day.

# Salamína/Salamis (ΣΑΛΑΜΙΝΑ)

Bathing in the same tub as Piraeus, a mere 3km across the Strait which saw Athens' dramatic victory over the Persians in 480 BC, Salamína is the most suburban and Greek of all the islands, in a gritty, authentic way that only those who know and love Greece can savour, almost as a reaction to the overpowering beauty that reigns elsewhere. In a way it's a time warp, a refreshing reminder of the Greece of yesteryear for those who witness with dismay the formation of a modern sanitized, Europeanized state. The southeast coast is the prettiest part of the island, with its pine forests and beaches, although they are only accessible by car or foot. Moúlki, also called Eántion, and Selínia are seaside villages, popular weekend retreats for mainland families. Salamína's weird, confusing geography and dearth of logical signposting means visitors with a car usually get to see every inch of the island, whether they want to or not.

## History

When Telemon and Peleus slew their brother Phocos (*see* 'Aegina'), Telemon fled to Salamína, the island of serpents, so-named after the destructive serpent killed by its first king, Kychreus, a shadowy character who himself started out as the snake in Eleusis. Telemon married Kychreus' daughter to become king and later fathered the Great Ajax of the Trojan War. When Mégara and Athens quarrelled over Salamína,

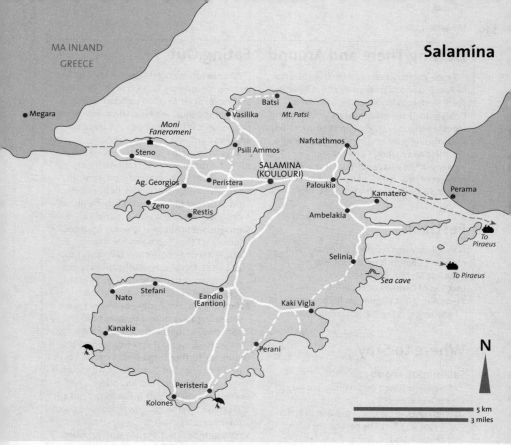

MA INLAND
GREECE

Megara

Batsi

Vasilika    Mt. Patsi

Moni
Faneromeni

Nafstathmos

Steno

Psili Ammos

SALAMINA
(KOULOURI)

Ag. Georgios    Peristera

Paloukia

Perama

Kamatero

To
Piraeus

Zeno

Restis

Ambelakia

Selinia

To Piraeus

Sea cave

Stefani

Nato

Eandio
(Eantion)

Kaki Vigla

Kanakia

Perani

Peristeria

Kolones

N

5 km

3 miles

Solon visited Kychreus' tomb to invoke his aid, and when the Spartans, the arbiters, gave the island to Athens, they did so on the strength of the serpent's appearance at Eleusis. Further evidence was provided during the Battle of Salamis, when the Athenians saw Kychreus appear in the form of a sea serpent to spur them on.

Salamína wasn't entirely unprepared in the September of 480 BC, when the massive Persian invasion fleet under Xerxes himself (the ancient Greeks put at 1,200 ships, modern historians suggest 650) came to conquer Greece once and for all; Athens had fortified the island's weak places, and had sent the elderly and exiles, hurriedly recalled, to defend them. After inconclusively challenging the Persian fleet at Artemission, Athens and her allies fell back to Salamis to join the reserves at the three ports facing Pérama; their ships totalled 378. They could see the smoke rising from the Acropolis, put to the sack by the Persian army as the Persian fleet sailed into Faliron Bay. News came that the Persians would soon be advancing to the Isthmus of Corinth, and the Corinthians and Spartans were keen to abandon Athens to defend their homes. Themistocles, the Athenian commander, had to resort to threats to keep them at Salamis. But he was tricky too, and sent a secret letter to Xerxes saying that the Greeks were in disarray, half were about to sail home, and that the Persians, if they acted fast, could capture the whole Greek fleet if they blocked the narrow strait

## Getting There and Around

**By sea: car ferry** every 15 mins from Pérama to Paloúkia and at least 5 a day from Piraeus, some stopping also at Selínia, Porto Fino, Doulápi and Peristéria; regular car ferry from Megálo Péfko (near Mégara on the mainland) to, confusingly, Pérama on Salamína, taking a few mins and costing €3 for car and passenger. The villages of Salamína are connected by an efficient **bus** system, **t** 010 465 0803. **Port authority, t** 010 465 3252.

## Festivals

**Holy Week:** when religious processions for which Salamína is noted take place
**5 June:** at Metamorphósis.
**Last Sun of Carnival:** at Kouloúri.
**23–25 Aug:** great pilgrimage to the Convent of Faneroméni is the biggest celebration

## Where to Stay

### Salamína ✉ 18900

Most of the hotels on Salamína are very simple and 'ethnic'.
**Gabriel Hotel**, in Eántion, **t** 010 466 2223, **f** 010 466 2275 (*C; mod*). The best on the island. *Open April–Sept.*
**Akroyali**, 92 Themistokléous, in Selínia, **t** 010 467 3263 (*D; inexp*).
**Votsalakia**, 64 Themistokléous, in Selínia, **t** 010 467 1432 or 010 467 1334 (*D; inexp*).

## Eating Out

Because Salamína gets few foreign tourists, its tavernas are pure Greek, and the food tasty and inexpensive. Seafood such as crayfish, octopus and squid are especially good – some people say it is the best place in Greece to enjoy an *ouzo* with octopus.
**Antzas**, in Salamína Town. Has a good name.
**Ali**, just out of town at 301 Leof. Aianteiou, **t** 010 465 3586. Plain and simple, serving excellent Arabic specialities, besides the usual Greek fare. Wonderful kebabs; phone a day ahead for *kibe*, a Syrian speciality.
**Karnagio**, out of Kouloúri towards Ag. Nikólaos (drive past the church and you'll come across a string of cafés and tavernas), **t** 010 464 0844. Despite its unattractive appearance, it's next to the sea and has a limited selection of excellent, cheap seafood.
**Bakothanassis**, 2km further down the road, as you swing away from the water, **t** 010 468 5631. Popular lunchtime venue for a splurge on seafood, even if the view is uninspiring.
**O Christos**, further out at Resti, **t** 010 468 2536. Above the tiny but clean beach, with lovely view, excellent food and low prices.
**Skerlou**, next to the park in Paloúkia, **t** 010 467 7144. Fish taverna, café, *mezé* spot and pub, run by eccentric ladies.
**Vassiliou**, in Selínia, **t** 010 467 1625. An island institution; good family-run taverna by the water's edge, dishing up superb squid.
**Notis**, in Kaki Vígla, **t** 010 466 2247. Good old-fashioned Greek food and hearty *retsina*.

to the east and west of Salamis. Xerxes fell for it hook, line and sinker. He ordered his fleet to divide and block the straits at night, hoping to surprise the Greeks, and had his silver throne carried to the summit of Mount Egáleo in Pérama, for a ringside seat over his victory. But Themistocles had been warned, and careful plans were laid. At dawn half of the Greek fleet in the east pretended to flee north. The Persian commander at once gave the order to advance, and when the Persian fleet lumbered forward, the Greeks quickly spun their *triremes* around, and rammed their leading ships, killing the Persian commander almost at once. No one was in charge, and no one could stop the momentum of Persian ships from advancing into the narrow strait where they couldn't manoeuvre, creating a confused log jam at the mercy of the crack fleet from Aegina, who attacked their flank. Crushed hulls lay upturned on the sea, so thick, you could not see the water, choked with wrecks and slaughtered men, Aeschylus (who fought in the battle) wrote in *The Persians*. Xerxes watched in agony; the Persians managed to create a diversion to escape home with their last 300 ships.

As for Salamína, it gave birth to Euripides (*see* below) the very same year of the great victory and then fell back into obscurity.

## Kouloúri (Salamína) and Moni Faneroméni

The metropolis of Salamína is better known as Kouloúri ('crescent') for its leisurely curl around its harbour, with cafés and tavernas making up for the town's general lack of distraction. There is a small, unattractive beach nearby and the harbour hosts Japanese pearl oysters – stowaways on the Japanese freighters that have stopped there. A new **Museum of Folk Art**, in the town hall (Dimarchíon) at 1 Konstantínou Karamanlí (*t 010 465 4180; open Mon–Fri 8–2.30*), holds a wide collection of traditional costumes and dolls, ships' models and sea paintings by naïf artist Aristídis Glýkas.

### The Poet's Hideaway

The ancient biographer Philochorus mentions that Euripides had an estate on his native Salamis and wrote in a cave facing the sea. In the 5th century BC this retreat from society was judged as rather unusual behaviour, but Euripides was by all accounts an unusual man.

Born into the landed middle class in the great triumph over the Persians, Euripides served in the Peloponnesian War, and when he was young he lost his fortune, holding expensive political posts and contributing to the war effort; what money remained he spent on books – he was the first Greek to accumulate a private library. He was considered the greatest poet of his age (some 18 plays have survived), yet he won only four first prizes. No one was quite sure what to think of his work. Where Aeschylus and Sophocles maintained a level of restraint and dignity in their work, Euripides' characters are full of melodrama; he broke sexual taboos, and refused to idealize anyone. He loved women (at a time when most men wanted to lock them up at home) and made them his special study, most famously Medea.

Idealistic, but deeply troubled by his times, Euripides wrote truths that disturbed his contemporaries' basic assumption about society, the state, their gods, and themselves. He loathed their wars; the rich and the great rabble of Athenian democracy infuriated him, and he, in turn, infuriated them even while they hung on his words. They took out their frustrations by mocking him and even beating him up, until he took refuge in the court of Macedon, where he died the next year, in 406 BC. Yet a century later, the playwright Philemon wrote: 'If I were certain that the dead had consciousness, I would hang myself to see Euripides.'

After Euripides' death, his writer's cave became a tourist attraction that was visited well into Roman times. In 1994, archaeologist Yiannos Liolios, finding that the cave at Peristéria matched the ancient inscriptions, began investigations that soon yielded artefacts going back to the Neolithic period. Ancient votive offerings suggest that the cave was identified as the lair of Kychreus, the man-snake. Then, in 1996, Liolios proved that it was also the retreat of the great tragedian, when he came across an archaeologist's dream: a wine cup with Euripides' name on it, left behind by the poet 2,380 years ago. To find the cave, keep your eyes peeled for an obscure signpost in Peristéria, follow the dirt road as far as you can in your car, and then continue on foot.

Above Kouloúri is **Mount Profítis Ilías**, with views across the whole island. From Kouloúri a bus leaves every hour for **Moni Faneroméni**. Set in a large pine wood, Faneroméni was built in 1661, reusing the foundation of an ancient temple. The church (*open 7–12 and 3-7.30; dress appropriately – no shorts*) is decorated with fine frescoes (in need of a clean), including an extraordinary *Last Judgement* containing over 3,000 figures painted in 1735 by Argítis Márkos, who is buried in the adjacent chapel. The nuns also have a lively collection of peacocks and turkeys. To the east is **Psilí Ámmos** beach, which unfortunately often smells of petrol. Above, on Mt Pátsi, the island's highest point, are the remains of ancient fire towers – perhaps the same that helped to relay the news across the Aegean that the Persians were on their way.

## South Salamína

Six km south of Kouloúri is the pleasant village of **Eandio**, set in the pines and with a nice pebble beach. Ruins found at **Kolonés**, or 'the columns', are believed to belong to the city of Ajax Telamonios. From Eandio a bus goes to the pleasant cove of Kakí Vígla and a rough road leads south to **Ag. Nikólaos**, an abandoned monastery with a 15th-century chapel, decorated with 12th-century marble reliefs and plates from Rhodes; it holds the island's archaeology collection (**t** *010 465 3572; open 9–1*), although the best stuff is now in the Piraeus Museum. Between Ag. Nikólaos and **Kakí Vígla** there are excellent camping sites and many sandy beaches, such as **Peristéria**, where a cave has recently yielded a remarkable archaeological find.

On the east coast of Salamína, **Paloúkia** is a ferry-boat landing stage from Pérama with a naval festival at the end of August. The sea in between once sheltered beds of purple dye-yielding murex shells, which sustained a local industry up until the Second World War and the advent of chemicals and pollution. South of Paloukía, woebegone **Ambelákia** was the harbour of Classical and Hellenistic Salamína. The mole is visible in the shallows, but little else – it's now a very smelly ships' rubbish dump. It has never been excavated and is unlikely ever to be for that matter.

# Spétses (ΣΠΕΤΣΕΣ)

Spétses is a charming, pine-scented island, the furthest in the Saronic Gulf from Athens, a factor that long kept it more relaxed and quiet than its more accessible sisters. For all that, Spétses is an old hand at tourism – since the Second World War families have come for its safe beaches and climate. In the 1980s Spetses was besieged by package tourists, especially the British, with the luscious descriptions of John Fowles' *The Magus* dancing in their heads. Recently, the long transfer from Athens airport has whittled away most operators, and Spetses now has five per cent of the package tourists it had ten years ago. Still a mecca for flotilla holidays and independent travellers, it will seem downright laid-back if you're coming from Hýdra.

## History

Although discoveries at Ag. Marína indicate that Spétses (ancient Pityoussa) has been inhabited since 2500 BC, it stayed out of the history books for the next 4,000 years. No one is even sure how Spétses got its name; best guess is that the Venetians called it 'Spice,' or *spezie*. Like the other Saronic islands, Spétses was repopulated with refugees from the Turkish-controlled mainland. The first shipyards date from the early 17th century and survive to this day. By the 19th century Spétses was renowned for its seamanship and, like Hýdra, prospered from the derring-do of its merchants.

Spétses made the history books by igniting the Greek War of Independence. Through the years of blockade-running, the Spetsiots invested their profits in the creation of a small fleet to take on the Turks. When the rebellion broke out on the Peloponnese in March 1821, Old Spice sprang into action: on 2 April it became the first to raise the flag, then two days later its fleet won the first naval victory of the war, capturing three Ottoman ships. The famous lady admiral of Spétses, the indomitable Laskarina Bouboulina, sailed her fine ship *Agamemnon* over to Náfplion and blockaded the port. A bold military leader, she was personally responsible for a number of Greek victories. That she was also quite a character and had six children has contributed to the legend: apparently her chief flaw as an admiral was her predeliction for abandoning ship for a horse and sabre if the hottest fighting was happening on shore. The Greeks say she was so ugly that she could only keep lovers by holding them at gunpoint, and that she could drink any man under the table.

## Spétses Town

Spétses, the capital and port, is not your typical Greek island town: where most are very dense, it spreads out leisurely in the greenery. Some of the oldest houses – proud Neoclassical captains' mansions – are inland, safely invisible from the waterfront. Another distinctive feature is the island's love for black and white pebble mosaics (*choklakia*). You'll see one commemorating the revolt of 1821 as you disembark at the

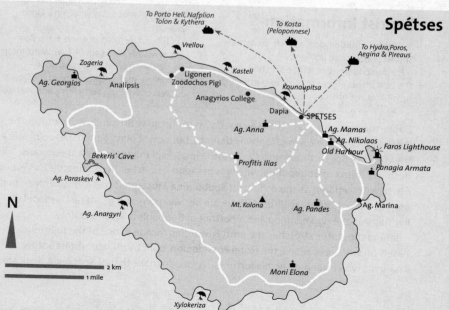

## Getting There and Around

**By sea:** several **hydrofoils** daily from Piraeus and other Saronic islands, less frequently with Kýthera and Peloponnese ports (Kósta is closest). Daily **ferry** connections with Piraeus, other Saronic islands and Peloponnese ports, but cars aren't allowed on the island without authorization; official vehicles are limited to 4 taxis and 2 municipal buses. *Benzínas* or **boat taxis** (at the new harbour) can take you to other places along the coast. There are frequent **excursion boats** to the sandy beach at Kósta (15mins away) and other small mainland beaches and ports. You can also hire a caique – ask at the tourist information booth. **Port authority: t** 029 807 2245.

**By road: horse-drawn carriages** for hire along the waterfront add a touch of elegance, but don't go any further than Ligonéri or Ag. Marína. Bicycles and scooters may be hired (depending on the season, not used in town at certain times of the day). The 2 **buses** run from the town beach to Ag. Marína and Ag. Anárgyri, and from Hotel Possidonion to Ligonéri. The nicest way to see the unpopulated interior is **on foot.** From Spétses Town to Ag. Anárgyri takes 1½hrs, leaving Spetses near where the horse buggies stand. Halfway point is a semi-deserted hunting lodge, from where turn right and follow the handpainted signs.

## Tourist Information

**Tourist information:** booth on the quay.
**Tourist police: t** 029 807 3100.

For **horseriding,** contact the art shop near the post office. There are some exceptionally helpful tourist offices on the Dapia:

**Alasia, t** 029 807 4098, **f** 029 807 4053. For studios and apartments.
**Tassoula** at Takis, **t** 029 807 2215, **f** 029 807 4315. Very friendly and particularly helpful if you're looking for cheaper rooms.
**The Yachting Club Inn,** by the tourist information booth, **t** 029 807 3401. Good place to ask for any type of accommodation and rentals.

## Festivals

**First Fri after Easter:** at Zoodóchos Pigí.
**23 April:** Ag. Geórgios.
**1 July:** Anárgyri.
**26 July:** Ag. Paraskeví at Zogeriá.
**8 Sept (nearest weekend):** the Armata, the most colourful festival of the year, when the Spetsiots commemorate their victory over the Turks in the Straits of Spétses, in 1822. The attacking Ottomans were held at bay by the island's fleet and had to withdraw when confronted with a drifting fireboat. The battle is re-enacted in the harbour, with fireworks and folk dancing.

## Where to Stay

**Spétses** ✉ 18050
**Possidonion,** on the waterfront, **t** 029 807 2308, **f** 029 807 2208 (*A; lux*). Renovated recently, this grand old dowager has been the classy place to stay since 1914. *Open April–Oct.*
**Zoe's Club,** in the heart of town, **t** 029 807 4447, *www.zoesclub.com* (*A; lux*). Welcoming complex, with great views and mod cons.
**Nissia,** on the seafront, 500m from the Dapia (but few sea-views), **t** 029 807 5000, *nissia@*

Dápia, the elegant square that sweeps down to the quay. Bristling with cannon, the **Dápia** was once the town's front line defence, but now it plays a more peaceful role as the vortex of Spétses' café society. On the Dápia's esplanade there's a she-means-business **statue of Bouboulina,** who was assassinated in her house nearby. This is now run by a descendant as the delightful **Bouboulina Museum** (*t* 029 807 2416; open mid-Mar–Oct; tours daily 9.45–8; adm); here are her weapons and headscarf, a model of her flagship the *Agamemnon* and a portrait of Bouboulina looking dainty.

Behind the statue stretches the prim Edwardian façade of one of the first tourist hotels on any Greek island, the **Hotel Possidonion,** built by philanthropist Sotiris Anárgyro, who after making his fortune, decided to make that of Spétses. A dedicated

*otenet.gr* (*exp*). Newer, bigger, glitzier, with its magnificent pool, excellent restaurant and fully equipped studios and maisonettes.

**Economou**, near the town hall, **t** 029 807 3400, **f** 029 807 4074 (*exp*). Large studios in a traditional, renovated mansion.

**Akrogiali**, at Ag. Anárgyri, **t** 029 807 3695 (*mod*). Guesthouse with the feel of a small hotel, near Spétses' most popular beach; balconies and a lovely breakfast terrace.

**Atlantis**, **t** 029 807 4122/2215 (*C; mod*). Modest rooms with air-con, balconies and pool, 2mins from Ag. Marína Beach.

**Villa Christina**, in town, **t** 029 807 2218 (*B; mod*). Central, charming, popular little place.

**Villa Kriezi**, **t** 029 807 2171 (*mod*). Each room has a private bath and many have sea-views.

**Argo**, **t** 029 807 3225 (*E; inexp*). Cheaper. *Open only in high season.*

**Klimis**, on the east end of the waterfront, **t** 029 807 3777 (*D; inexp*). Pleasant rooms.

## Eating Out

**Exedra** in the old harbour, **t** 029 807 3497. Renowned for its fish, incl. pasta with lobster.

**Patralis**, 10min walk along the front to the right of the main harbour, **t** 029 807 2134. Very popular. Try fish *à la spetsiota*, baked with tomato, olive oil, garlic and pepper.

**Tarsanas**, in the old harbour, **t** 029 807 4490. Owned by fishermen and serving fresh seafood and *mezédes. Open eves only.*

**Liotrivi**, in the old harbour, **t** 029 807 2269. Italian and seafood dishes in a converted olive press.

**Dapia**. Unlike on other islands, don't write off all the waterfront tavernas. This one and the

3 next to the Klimis Hotel are all good bets at relatively earthy prices.

**Stelios**, **t** 029 807 3748. In addition to fish fresh from the nearby market, come here for excellent vegetarian dishes.

**Kipos**. Well-priced with barrelled wine and a delightful garden setting off the square.

**Lazaros**, uphill from the Dapia, **t** 029 807 2600/4144. An excellent choice.

**Giorgas**, at Baltiza Creek. Classic taverna, overlooking the old harbour from a wooden platform.

**Panas**, at Ligonéri. Superb *mezédes*, a great view and live Greek music under the pines.

**Taverna Tassos** at Ag. Anárgyri. An example of how wonderful Greek food can taste; try the house speciality, 'lamb in a bag'.

## Entertainment and Nightlife

Spétses starts to swing at around 1am.

**Figaro**. With its seaside patio in the old harbour, this is the hot spot for dancing. In the early hours, the Greek music comes on and everyone changes their steps to dance along. *Open every night in high season; Fri and Sat only in low season.*

**Diadromes**. Looks like a castle and has live Greek music.

**George's Club**. Pricey but at weekends is great for a proper Greek evening with the Greeks.

**Mouraya**, at Baltiza Creek. Music bar catering for both Greek and British tastes.

**Zorbas**, in Kounoupitsa. Does late night food.

**Bracera**. Wood décor; everyone shoulder-shimmies to American and Europop.

**Veranda**, upstairs. For something quieter, have a drink here, listening to soft Greek music.

---

Anglophile, in 1927 he founded the **Anágyrios and Korgialénios College**, on the English public school model, west of the Dápia. John Fowles taught here, and used it as a setting for *The Magus*. Anárgyro's other contribution, Spétses' pine forests, grow luxuriantly despite damaging summer blazes – lastly in 1990. Anárgyro's house, built in 1904 (behind the Roumani Hotel) is a fine piece of turn-of-the-century bombast.

Spétses' **Museum** (*t* 029 807 2994; open Tues–Sun 8–2; guided tours in English at 6pm; adm) is housed in the handsome mansion (1795) of Hadziyiánnis Méxis, shipowner and revolutionary; it has many of its original furnishings, archaeological finds, a box holding Bouboulina's bones, the 'Freedom or Death' flag of the War of Independence, and ships' models, paintings, and figure heads.

The picturesque **Paléo Limáni**, or old harbour, is shared by fishermen, yachts and the oldest church, **Ag. Nikólaos**. On its bell tower the Spetsiots raised their defiant flag in 1821 – a bronze cast is displayed opposite and a pebble *choklakia* in the courtyard tells the tale. When the Turks came to put them in their place, the inhabitants created mannequins out of barrels and flower pots, dressing them in red *fezes* and Turkish-appearing uniforms, and set them up along the quay. Seeing them from a distance, the Turkish commander thought that the island had already been taken and sailed by.

Further east, near the **Fáros** (lighthouse), the church **Panagía Armata** was built after a victory by the Spétses fleet on 8 September 1822; inside, a large painting by Koutzis commemorates the triumph. Just beyond is **Ag. Marína** (ΑΓ. ΜΑΠΙΝΑ), site of an Early Helladic settlement, town beach and much of its nightlife. Off the coast hovers the tempting, idyllic islet of **Spetsopoúla**, but it's a private retreat of the Niarchos family, whose late *paterfamilias* Stavros was one of the 'Super Greeks' of the 60s and 70s, and whose doings in the tabloids were only overshadowed by those of arch-rival Aristotle Onassis. Sometimes you can see the flagrant 325ft Niarchos yacht, nearly as big as Spetsopoúla itself. Two other fine churches are up the hill at **Kastélli**, where the houses are mostly ruined: the little 17th-century **Koimistís Theotókou** church has frescoes, and **Ag. Triáda**, a superb, carved iconostasis (*ask the tourist police about keys*).

## Around the Island

The entire jagged coast of Spétses is embellished with pebbly beaches and rocky swimming coves; the main ones offer full watersports facilities. Get to them by renting a car or bicycle, or take in one of the frequent caique excursions. Going around Spétses clockwise, the first likely place for a swim is **Xylokeríza**, with a pleasant shingle beach that rarely gets crowded.

The opposite holds true of lovely **Ag. Anárgyri** (ΑΓ. ΑΝΑΡΓΥΡΟΙ), an irresistible bay, rimmed with trees, bars, and two tavernas; the sands get pretty busy by 10am when the caiques disgorge their loads. From the beach it's a short swim or walk to **Bekeris' Cave**. In 1770, Muslims from Albania came to take revenge on the Spetsiots for siding with Russia in the war. As they burnt and pillaged, the women and children took refuge here, one mother killing her whimpering baby to prevent discovery. You can enter from the sea or there is a low entrance by land; go in the afternoon, when the sun illuminates the interior and the few stalactites inside.

Continuing clockwise, some caiques continue on to **Ag. Paraskeví**, a delightful and more peaceful, pebbly cove with a church and cantina, watched over by the Villa Jasemia, the house Fowles used as the residence of his endlessly tricky Magus. A hop over the rocks at the far western end is Spetses' official nudist beach. **Zogeriá**, to the west, is a pretty, rocky double-coved bay, a hardish slog from the road with good swimming and a high-season taverna.

**Vrelloú** in the north is in a corner of Spétses called **Paradise** for its beauty, although the beach is a litter magnet. **Blueberry Beach**, and shady **Ligonéri**, a good walk or horse buggy ride from the Dápia, tend to be cleaner.

# The Sporades and Évia

# The Sporades and Évia

50 km
25 miles

N

THESSALY

Volos

To Thessaloniki,
Nea Moudounia (Chalkidiki)

Psathoura

Gioura

Kyra Panagia

Piperi

Alonissos

Glossa

Skiathos

Peristera

Skopelos

Patitiri

Skopelos

Skantzoura

Pontikonissia

Pefki

Glifa

Orei

Agio Kambos

Loutra Edipsou

Skyros

Skyros

Ag.
Konstantinos

Arkitsa

Skyropoula

Limni

Kymi

E V I A

MAINLAND

GREECE

Chalkis

Eretria

S. Oropou

Ag. Marina

Nea Styra

Karystos

Marmari

Rafina

Key to Sailing Services

△ Yacht Supply Stations
□ Ports of Entry and Exit
◇ Marinas

# Getting There

**By air**: flying to Skiáthos (numerous char-ters, or on **Olympic**, twice daily in summer from Athens) or to Skýros (4 times a week) is by far the most painless way.

**By sea**: Skýros may only be reached from or via Kými, in Évia, from where there are weekly sailings (at least) to the other Sporades. The main **ferry** ports to Skiáthos, Skópelos and Alónissos are Vólos in Thessaly (easily reached by train from Athens) and Ag. Konstantínos. **Hydrofoils** also ply these routes daily in summer from Vólos and Ag. Konstantínos, and provide good inter-island links in the summer. If you're departing from Athens, **Alkyon Tours**, at 98 Academías, **t** 010 364 3220, specializes in travel to the Sporades, and has the latest bus/boat timetables. If you're approaching from the north, in high season, there are weekly ferries from Thessaloníki and from Néa Moudaniá (on the Chalkidikí Peninsula).

Until the late 1960s, the beautiful Sporades ('scattered') islands were among the most neglected, least visited corners of Greece – not only were they difficult to reach, but they lacked the big-league archaeological sites or historical familiarity of so many other islands. Then Greek holidaymakers began to descend on Skiáthos and Skópelos. Germans began to restore old houses on Alónissos for summer villas. An airport was built on Skiáthos, linking the island to Athens, and then to most of charter-flight Europe – and the rest is history. It was inevitable; some immortal hand or eye framed these islands to fit nearly everyone's idea of a holiday paradise, with their picture-postcard beaches, cool summer breezes, thick pine forests and lush greenery. Each has its own personality, although Skiáthos, with the loveliest beaches of all, has become so popular that 'Greek' is not the first adjective you would use to describe it. On the opposite end of the scale, Skýros remains one of the most original and intriguing islands in Greece, still off the beaten track in spite of an airport of its own. Skópelos, the greenest and most naturally endowed of the group, remains very Greek and dignified; ecologically-sound Alónissos offers a mixture of cosmopolitan tourism and old-fashioned ways, and helps safeguard the last colony of monk seals in the Aegean in Greece's first marine national park. Évia (or Euboea) the second largest Greek island after Crete, has always been a land of quiet farms and pastures, situated too close to the mainland to have a strong personality of its own. Yet, in places, Évia is endowed with ravishing scenery and a scarcely developed coastline, providing a haven for Greek visitors escaping the cosmopolitan crowds on the other islands.

## History

The first settlers on the Sporades were of Thracian origin. In the 16th century BC Crete colonized the islands, introducing the cultivation of olives and grapes. With the decline of the Minoans, Mycenaeans from Thessaly known as the Dolopians (first cousins of the Achaeans) settled the Sporades, using them as bases for daring naval expeditions. Much of the mythology of the islands has its roots during this period: Achilles himself was raised on Skýros. In the 8th century BC the Chalkidians of Évia captured the Sporades as stepping stones to their colonial ambitions in Macedonia. These new invaders continued the sea traditions of the Dolopians but increasingly came into conflict with Athenian interests until 476 BC, when Athens sent Kimon to crush the Sporades' fleets. The Athenians then colonized the islands, but successfully presented themselves as liberators rather than conquerors; of all the islands, none had closer ties with Athens. The government of the Sporades was run on the model of Athenian democracy, and Athena became the prominent goddess in local pantheons.

When the Spartans defeated Athens in the Peloponnesian War, the Sporades were briefly part of their spoils. A greater threat to Athenian influence came in the person of Philip II of Macedon, who claimed the islands in a dispute that attracted the attention of the entire Greek world. Philip took the islands in 322 BC as a prelude to nabbing Athens itself.

During the Roman occupation, the Sporades retained their traditional links with Athens. The Byzantines, however, made them a place of exile for unruly or unwanted nobles who set themselves up as the local aristocracy until 1207, when the Gizzi of

Venice picked up the Sporades as their share in the spoils of the Fourth Crusade. Filippo Gizzi, the most notorious of the dynasty, usurped control from a senior relative and ruled the islands as a pirate king until Likários, the Admiral of Emperor Michael Palaeológos, took him in chains to Constantinople. Afterwards, possession of the islands see-sawed back and forth between Greeks and Franks, until Mohammed the Conqueror took Constantinople in 1453. The islanders quickly invited Venice back as the lesser evil, although the Venetians were forced out when all their crafty agreements with the Ottoman Empire crumbled before the violent attacks of Barbarossa in the 16th century.

Once they had the Sporades, the Turks promptly forgot all about the agreements, except at tax time. The islands were so exposed to pirates that a permanent Turkish population never settled there. In the 1821 revolution, insurgents from Thessaly found refuge on the islands, and in 1830 the Treaty of London included them in the original kingdom of Greece.

# Alónissos (ΑΛΟΝΝΗΣΟΣ)

Long, skinny Alónissos is the queen of her own little archipelago of nine islets. But in the last few decades, while Skiáthos and Skópelos found new roles as trendy tourist destinations, Alónissos sat on the sidelines, recovering from an earthquake that hit its attractive main town in 1965, from the loss of its old grapefruit orchards and vineyards through disease, and from local and government politicians who contrived to

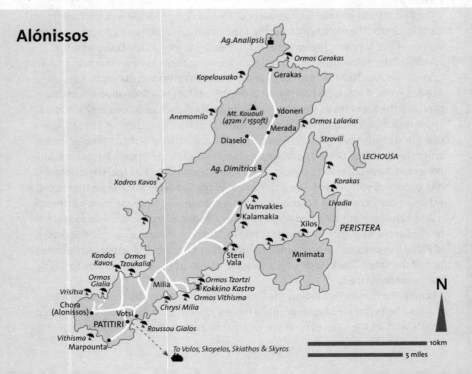

# Getting There and Around

**By sea**: there's a **ferry** at least once a day with Vólos, Skópelos, Skiáthos and Ag. Konstantínos; 3 times a week with Thessaloníki. Daily **hydrofoils** to Skópelos, Skiáthos, Vólos and Ag. Konstantínos. Daily summer **excursion boats** from Patitíri go up and down the coast, and out to the islets of Peristéra, Kyrá Panagía, and Gioúra. **Port authority**: t 042 406 5595.

**By road**: public **buses** link Patitíri and Chóra about 5–10 times a day, depending on the season.

# Tourist Information

**Tourist police**: contact the regular police, t 042 406 5205.

**Ikos Travel**, t 042 406 5320/5648, f 042 406 5321. Pakis will help with travel arrangements, excursions (both by boat and on foot) and all types of accommodation. He is at the forefront of trying to keep tourism on Alónissos eco-friendly.

**Alónissos Travel**, near the wharf, t 042 406 5188, f 042 406 5511. Also very helpful.

# Festivals

**40 days after Easter**: Análypsis.
**1 July**: Ag. Anárgiroi.
**17 July**: Ag. Marína.
**26 July**: Ag. Paraskeví.
**15 Aug**: Panagías.

# Where to Stay

## Alónissos ✉ 37005

Most of the island's accommodation is in Patitíri and Vótsi, although the spiffier hotels and guesthouses tend to be booked solid by packagers. To make up for it, there are 3,000 beds to rent in private houses and generally plenty of people to offer them to you when you get off the boat. There are even a few rooms to rent on the islet of Peristéra.

**Archontiko**, near the beach at Patitíri, t/f 042 406 5004, in winter f 010 683 2044 (*exp*). Comfortable apartments with fridges, some with full kitchens, and parking. *Open May–Oct.*

**Atrium of Alónissos**, in Vótsi, t 042 406 5749, f 042 406 5152 (*C; exp*). Modest complex with quiet, comfortable rooms overlooking the sea and its own pool.

**Haravgi**, above the port, t 042 406 5189 (*C; exp*). 22 well-scrubbed and wholesome rooms with a pretty terrace to sit out on over a drink.

**Paradise**, on the cliff promontory above Patitíri, t 042 406 5160, f 042 406 5161 (*C; exp*). Attractive hotel facing east over pine trees to the open sea, rather than west over the harbour. Beautifully tiered terraces below the pool make a perfect spot for lunchtime snacks or evening drinks. *Open May–Oct.*

**Alkyon**, right on the sea, t 042 406 5220, f 042 406 5195 (*C; mod*). Modern white hotel with rooms and studios overlooking the centre of the action.

retard its development. This suited many visitors just fine, especially the kind of visitors in search of peace and quiet, good fishing and diving, and places to potter about in boats. Having only a mile or two of paved carriageway left, nine-tenths of Alónissos is accessible only on foot; fine walking country for the hearty, with glimpses of the rare Eleanora's falcon soaring high overhead as a reward.

Then, in 1992, Alónissos found a new role when, after the urging of environmental groups across Europe, Greece's first National Marine Park was set up around much of its archipelago to protect the Mediterranean monk seal – the rarest animal in Europe (*see* below). The donkey tracks of old have been paved and package holiday makers and flotilla yacht fleets have arrived, discreetly; in fact, tourism on Alónissos is about as close to eco-tourism as you get on the Greek Islands. Rather than hinder, retarded development helped it get the balance right.

**Alónissos Beach**, in Vótsi (just beyond Chrysí Miliá Beach), t 042 406 5281, in Athens t 010 223 0869 (*C; mod*). Bungalow complex with a pool and tennis. *Open July–Sept.*

**Constantina Apartments**, in Chóra, t 042 406 5900 (*mod*). Away from the sea, a good Class A guesthouse.

**Hiliodromia Studios**, in the beautiful old town of Chóra, t 042 406 5135, f 042 406 5469 (*mod*).

**Liadromia**, directly over the fishing boats on the cliffs of Patitíri, t 042 406 5521, f 042 406 5096 (*B; mod*). Full of rustic character, with clean rooms and a breakfast terrace.

**Dimitris**, in Vótsi, t 042 406 5035, f 042 406 5785 (*inexp*). With its own bar, pizzeria and terrace, and all 6 rooms have balconies directly over the little harbour.

**Panorama**, in Vótsi, t 042 406 5006 (*inexp*). Excellent, friendly guesthouse, nestled in the trees, with swimming off the small beach below and a restaurant and bar; the owner speaks good English. *Open May–Sept.*

**Vótsi**, in Vótsi, a 2min walk up from the waterfront, t 042 406 5818, f 042 406 5878 (*inexp*). A bit cheaper; it has good-sized, spotless rooms with telephones and a communal kitchen and sea-view terrace.

## Eating Out

If you've wanted to splurge on a feast of Mediterranean lobster (*astakós*), Alónissos is the place for it; many of the quayside restaurants in Patitíri serve it as well as other marine delectables (swordfish, octopus, sea bream) pulled from the limpid waters of the archipelago; the Aegean is especially salty here and the fish especially tasty.

**Argos**, follow the path around the rocky promontory to the left of the port, t 042 406 5141. For an excellent meal in a pretty setting under the trees. Sample a wider than usual selection of fresh fish and lobster, and a good wine list. *Open May–Oct.*

**Astrofeggia**, in Chóra, t 042 406 5182. Good choice if you need a rest from Greek cooking. The owner's German wife turns out some spicy goodies, incl. curry and chili con carne, with chocolate mousse and apple cake.

**Babis**, on the way up to Chóra, t 042 406 6184. Views over Patitíri from the terrace of this family-run taverna serving island specialities with fresh veggies; try the *bouréki* (cheese pie) and the *xinótiri* (sour cheese).

**Nikos**, in Chóra. Some of the island's best food.

**O Astakos**, near the back of town. Specializes, as its name suggests, in lobster.

*Ouzerie* **To Kamáki**. The local consensus for the best fish in town.

**Paraport Taverna**, in Chóra. Magnificent views; arrive early to get a table.

**Steni Valá**, at Steni Valá, t 042 406 5590. Family run fish taverna, supplied by the owner's fishing boat. Also serves some local cheese and vegetable dishes.

There is also a delightful specialist **cheese pie shop** where you can watch your own pie being made through a hole-in-the-wall; and to round off a calorific meal, this is one of the rare places that still makes traditional *rizógalo*, Greek rice pudding.

## History

The history of Alónissos is complicated by the fact that the modern Alónissos is not ancient Halonnesos, but actually bore the name Ikos – the result of an over-eager restoration of ancient place names after independence, but in Alónissos' case the mistake was an improvement. As for the real ancient Halonnesos, some scholars say it must have been tiny Psathoúra, northernmost of Alónissos' islets, where the extensive ruins of an ancient city lie submerged offshore. Another possibility is Kyrá Panagía, a fertile islet with two fine harbours.

Inhabited from Neolithic times, Ikos/Alónissos was part of the Cretan colony of Prince Staphylos, who planted the first of the vines that were to make Ikos famous. In the 14th century BC the Mycenaeans took over, counting among their settlers Peleus, the father of Achilles. In Classical times, Ikos had two city-states that thrived through exporting wine. The Athenians established a naval base on the island in the 4th century, and in 42 BC the Romans let Athens have the whole thing. During the Middle Ages Ikos was ruled by Skópelos, under the name of Achilliodromia, Liadromia or simply Dromos (road). As for ancient Halonnesos (wherever it may be), it was governed throughout antiquity by Athens, which lost control of it in the 4th century BC to a pirate named Sostratos. Philip of Macedon took it from him, quoting the famous speech of Demosthenes, 'Concerning Halonnesos', which initiated the troubles between Athens and Macedonia. Skópelos took the island in 341 BC when Philip offered to return it to Athens; Philip, however, crushed these opportunists and the island lost its importance, its port subsided into the sea, and even its location faded from human memory.

## Patitíri

The face of Alónissos changed dramatically when the earthquake of 1965 devastated the principal town, Chóra. The junta far away in Athens summarily forced all the inhabitants into prefab relief housing at the port, **Patitíri** (ΠΑΤΗΤΗΡΙ) and prevented their return to Chóra by cutting off the water and electricity. Since the 1960s, Patitíri has spread its wings to merge with the fishing hamlet of **Vótsi**; in between, a few families are still stuck in the relief village. Charming it ain't, but neither is Patitíri unpleasant, and bougainvillaea covers many a concrete sin. Right by the quay you can visit the offices of the **Society for the Study and Protection of the Monk Seal (MOM)** with a slide and video show upstairs; around the corner are the offices of the **European Natural Heritage Fund** (*open 9–2*). Both will make you aware of the odds against the little grey monk seal (*Monacus monacus*), an animal that has been extinct in France since 1920, in Spain since 1950, and in Italy since 1975. Pollution in the Mediterranean and loss of habitat are two reasons; fishermen, looking on them as rivals, used to kill them on sight. The largest remaining population in the world, with an estimated 300 of the last 500 seals, lives in Greece, and the 30 or so seals on the islet of Pipéri are the largest community. Since 1992, the surrounding waters have been protected as the National Marine Park, and Pipéri is strictly off limits, unless you go on a tour (*see* 'Skópelos', p.616). MOM (*for more information contact their head office at 18 Solomou, 10682, Athens, t 010 522 2888, f 010 522 2450, info@mom.gr*) sends out a boat to patrol the park and runs a seal hospital on Alónissos.

There's a small beach at Patitíri, and another, prettier one at Vótsi, just to the north. The best beaches are further north, but within easy walking distance to the south there's **Marpoúnta** with the submerged remains of a Temple of Asklepios, and the much nicer beaches at **Víthisma** and **Megálos Moúrtias**.

## Chóra (Alónissos Town)

A paved road, or for walkers, a pretty if somewhat steep mule path through nut groves, leads to the old capital of the island, **Chóra** (ΧΩΡΑ), magnificently set high up above the sea, with outstanding views, especially of Alónissos' frequent cinemascope sunsets. After the 1965 earthquake, and the government's forced removal of the inhabitants, far-sighted Germans and Brits bought the old homes for a song and restored them, agreeing at first to do without such conveniences as running water and electricity (although now they've been hooked up, as the resentment of the former residents has somewhat diminished); some now contain artsy little shops. The walls of Chóra were built by the Byzantines and repaired by the Venetians, and ghosts are said to dance around the 17th-century church of **Christós**. From Chóra it's a 20-minute walk down to sandy **Vrisítsa** Beach or a pleasant hour's hike to the beautiful bay of Órmos Giália.

## Beaches Around Alónissos

Caique excursions run out to the island's best beaches, most of which have at least a snack bar or taverna. Going north from Patitíri, the first really good beach is **Chrysí Miliá**, in a small cove enveloped with pines, and with a pair of tavernas. The 5th-century BC capital of ancient Ikos was found by the shingly rose-tinted beach **Kokkinó Kástro** (30 minutes by caique from Patitíri); if you know where to look you can make out some of its walls in the sea. This was also a stomping ground in the Middle Paleolithic era (100,000–33,000 BC) – the simple stone tools, now in Vólos Museum, are among the oldest ever found in the Aegean. Further north, **Stení Valá** and **Kalamákia** have small pensions and tavernas. Their beaches, well sheltered in the embrace of nearby Peristéra islet, offer the best fishing and watersports on the island. **Ag. Dimítrios**, the next beach up, has the ruins of a Byzantine fountain and another ancient settlement in the sea; fossils of prehistoric beasts were found at nearby Megaliámos. The beach is lovely and usually deserted. Lobster and isolated beaches are plentiful off the remote northern coast, and unusual fish and underwater caves are a scuba-diver's paradise at **Xódros Kávos** and the old shepherd's village **Gérakas**.

## Alónissos' Archipelago

The beauty of the islands scattered around Alónissos' shores make for exceptional sailing. Olive-covered **Peristéra** (Dove) islet follows the east coast of Alónissos, its Siamese twin until separated by a natural upheaval. Peristéra has plenty of sandy beaches and three tiny shepherds' hamlets, Mnímata, Livádia and Xílos, the last near a ruined castle. Rough camping is usually tolerated, and most evenings excursion boats from Patitíri bring folk over for a beach barbecue. Every ten days a caique goes to **Psathoúra**, the island base of one of the most powerful lighthouses in Greece. The locals say it was the island of Sirens, and here's a submerged city (a possible ancient Halonnesos) by the lighthouse, as well as a sunken volcano.

Lovely, wooded **Kyrá Panagía** (Pelagós) is two or three hours by caique from Patitíri. Now uninhabited (except for wild goats and the odd shepherd), the island once supported two monasteries and still belongs to Mount Áthos. At the port of Ag.

Pétros you can see the sunken remains of a 12th-century Byzantine ship that yielded a cargo of ceramics. Kyrá Panagía has sandy beaches, a pretty stalactite cave (a reputed home of the Cyclops), and plenty of opportunities for wild bushwalking.

Another abandoned monastery connected to Mount Áthos stands on verdant **Skantzoúra**, which offers excellent fishing in its many coves and caves. **Pappoú**, home to a diminishing hare population, has the remnants of a tiny 7th-century church, while a rare breed of goat skips about the rocks on **Gioúra** (ancient Geronta). It has a few Classical and Roman remains and yet another, wonderfully dramatic 'Cyclops' cave with stalactites, although the entrance requires a torch, stout shoes and a fit constitution; the island guardians will unlock the gate. **Pipéri**, on the north end of the National Marine Park, is a wildlife sanctuary, and home to Eleanora falcons as well as its small but stable colony of monk seals.

# Skiáthos (ΣΚΙΑΘΟΣ)

Racy, cosmopolitan Skiáthos is not for the shy teetotaller or anyone looking for a slice of 'authentic' Greece. Although still an isolated peasant island community in the early 1970s, Skiáthos has been catapulted faster than any other island into the frantic world of tourism, with all the pros and cons that this entails, beginning with the predatory attitudes of the *nouveau riche* ex-fishermen and farmers. Corruption and violence (violence by Greek island standards, at any rate) have long been a factor in local life. Nevertheless, Skiáthos is one of the most popular destinations in Greece: away from the main road, it is stunningly beautiful, and its magnificent beaches (by most counts there are 62) provide some of the best swimming in Greece. Add to this

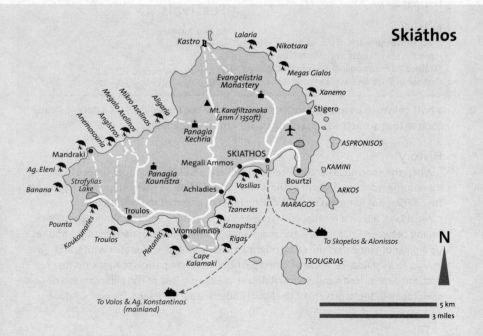

# Getting There and Around

## By Air

There are 2 flights a day from Athens (except Wed, when there's only 1 flight), and countless charters from European cities, incl. all-inclusive cheapies from the UK. **Olympic Airways**, at the airport, t 042 702 2040. **Airport information**: t 042 702 2049. The 2km to the airport can be taxied for around €8.

## By Sea

Several **ferries** and frequent **hydrofoil** connections daily with Ag. Konstantínos, Vólos, Skópelos, and Alónissos (combined bus/ferry tickets available in Athens from **Alkyon Tours**, 97 Akademías, Plateía Kaningós, t 010 384 3202, f 010 383 3948); several times a week with Thessaloníki and Péfki (Évia); daily **excursion boats** to Skópelos and Alónissos. The boats bobbing up and down in front of the cafés in the old harbour go to the beaches, and you'll hear the owners calling out their destinations. Some offer round-island trips but be warned that on the north side there is a fairly uninteresting stretch of coast and the sea can be rough – many a daytripper has returned green about the gills. You can also rent your own boat by the day. **Port authority**: t 042 702 2017.

## By Road

Buses to other parts of the island run every 15mins in season until the early hrs, from Skiáthos Town to Koukounariés, from the new harbour in Skiáthos Town. Demand is so great in summer that your feet may not touch the floor. If you want to get about under your own steam, the harbour is lined with places to rent cars, motorbikes and scooters, but be careful on the roads – traffic is fast-moving. Taxis, t 042 702 4461, are a popular, if expensive, option; never be shy of sharing.

## On Foot

A network of walking paths offers the opportunity to explore Skiáthos on 2 feet; look out for Rita and Dietrich Harkort's local guide.

# Tourist Information

**Tourist police**: Papadiamánti, t 042 702 3172; open 8am–9pm in season.
**Geof Baldry** t 042 704 9607/9473, www .skiathosinfo.com. A great source of information on Skiáthos and can organize special activity holidays (e.g. painting, walking, riding or sailing).

# Internet

**Skiáthos Internet Center**, in Skiáthos Town, t 042 702 2021.

# Festivals

**26 July**: Ag. Paraskeví.
**27 July**: Ag. Panteleímonos.
**15 Aug**: in Evangelismós.
**27 Aug**: Ag. Fanóurios.
**21 Nov**: Kounistra Monastery.

a host of lively bars and restaurants and you have the ingredients for a potent, heady cocktail that attracts a fun-seeking crowd – most of them Brits.

## History

When the enormous Persian fleet of King Xerxes sailed to conquer Greece in 480 BC, it encountered a fierce storm in the waters off Skiáthos. So many ships were damaged that Xerxes put in for repairs and, during his stay, invented the world's first-known navigational aid on a reef called Myrmes (now Lepheteris and still a menace to ships sailing between Skiáthos and the mainland). 'Thither the barbarians brought and set up a pillar of stone that the shoal might be clearly visible,' Herodotus wrote, and thanks to its guidance, Xerxes slipped past the Athenian patrols towards his first sea battle at Artemisseon and eventual defeat at Salamis. Part of the pillar can still be seen today, in the courtyard of the Naval Cadet School in Piraeus.

The rest of Skiáthos' history follows that of the other Sporades. The Gizzi ruled the island in the name of Venice and built the fort on Boúrtzi islet by the present-day town, which was settled in 1790 by refugees from Límni on Évia. The Skiathot navy assisted the Russians against the Ottomans in the campaign at Cêsme, and the islanders revolted against the Turks in 1805, sending so many ships to aid the cause of independence that Skiáthos itself was left unprotected and prey to marauders.

# Skiáthos Town

The capital and only real town on the island, **Skiáthos** is a gentle spread of traditional whitewashed houses, overhung with bougainvillaea and freshly washed sheets rippling in the breeze, over a razzmatazz of in-your-face commercialism. A walk through the backstreets will help you escape some of the latter, but watch out for high-speed trail bikes. The town has two harbours, separated by the pretty **Boúrtzi** promontory, where the medieval fortress now contains a restaurant and a summer

## Where to Stay

**Skiáthos** ✉ 37002

For more information, contact the hotel association, **t** 042 702 3314/3375, **f** 042 702 2109, or room renters' association, **t** 042 702 2990 (kiosk on the quay). Skiáthos has accommodation to suit every taste and pocket, but in high season, when it seems the island will sink beneath the weight of its visitors – who outnumber the locals 11 to one – finding a bed without a reservation is the devil. If you come unstuck in your quest, try the brown tourist kiosk or any of the tourist offices on the waterfront.

**Akti**, **t** 042 702 2024 (*C; exp*). Watery harbour views, especially from the 4-person top-floor suite. *Open Apr–Oct.*

**Pothos**, Evangeslistrías St, **t** 042 702 2694 (*D; exp*), and **Bourtzi**, **t** 042 702 1304 (*C; exp*). Away from the harbourfront, but central and set in delightful little gardens are these 2 sister hotels: all rooms have telephone, fridge and balcony. Both are charming, but Pothos just has the edge. *Both open May–Oct.*

**Alkyon**, on the new harbour front, **t** 042 702 2981, **f** 042 702 1643 (*B; exp–mod*). This is Skiáthos Town's biggest hotel with an attractive airy lobby and comfortable rooms with all mod cons, overlooking pleasant gardens.

**Meltémi**, nearby, **t** 042 702 2493 (*C; exp–mod*). Has a loyal following and is generally booked solid; their bar is a good vantage point for the antics of the flotilla crowd as they moor and unmoor with zealous gung-ho. Conveniently near the bus stop.

**Messinis Family**, up in Ag. Fanourios, **t/f** 042 702 2134 (*mod*). Quiet rooms with panoramic views from the balconies, carefully tended by Stavros Messinis, a master craftsman.

**Orsa**, in the old town, **t** 042 702 2300, **f** 042 702 1975 (*B; mod*). For something quieter, 2 traditional Skiathot houses have been converted to make this small hotel.

**Australia Hotel**, just off Papadiamántis St, behind the post office, **t** 042 702 2488 (*E; inexp*). Central and cheap, with simple en suite rooms.

**San Remo**, **t** 042 702 2078, **f** 042 702 1918 (*D; inexp*). Colourful hotel whose terraced rooms give you dress circle seats to observe the harbour traffic and wave at the greenhorns on the incoming charter jets.

## Eating Out

**Agnantio**, **t** 042 702 2016, on the road to the Evangelístria Monastery, overlooking the sea. A popular delight with its chic navy and white interior, and its terrace with beautiful views over the Pounta promontory, serving tasty Greek fare.

theatre. If you simply can't summon the energy to join the queues for bus, boat or taxi, dive off the rock here and pretend you're in a Martini ad. For a sweeping panorama of Skiáthos Town and the neighbouring island of Skópelos, take the steps up at the end of the old harbour past the waterfront cafés, restaurant touts and souvenir shops. Cocktail hour seems to last forever here, as you sit and watch an extraordinary international selection of the human race go by.

Morning excursion boats wait to whisk you off in half an hour to **Tsougriás** islet, facing Skiáthos Town. In the sixties the Beatles wanted to buy it. It's an ideal place to escape the droves of summer visitors, with its fine sand and excellent swimming. The simple snack bar usually provides freshly caught *marídes* (whitebait) to munch at a table under the trees, but you may have to share your food with the resident wasp population. Tsougriás has two other beaches, accessible only by foot, where you really can play Robinson Crusoe for the day.

If hedonism palls, you can get a shot of culture by locating the house of **Alexander Papadiamántis** (1851–1911), situated just off the main street (*t 042 702 3843; open Tues–Sun 9.30–1 and 5–8*).

**Anatoli**, in the same area as Agnantio, past the turn-off to the monastery, **t** 042 702 1907. Family-run with tasty home-cooking and gorgeous view from the terrace.

**Bonaparte**, Evangelistrías St, on the other side of the main street, **t** 042 702 1118. Some of the best Skiáthos has to offer in the way of international cuisine, with a definite Swedish bias.

**Casa Blanca/Primavera**, in a small square near the church behind the fish market end of the waterfront. Serves excellent pasta and other Italian delights.

**Cuba**, east of Papadiamánti in a leafy *plateía*. Serving standard, well-prepared Greek dishes.

**I Roda**, Evangelistrías St, up from the post office, **t** 042 702 3178. Excellent Greek taverna; family-run, home cooking.

**Jailhouse**, at the end of the old harbour, **t** 042 702 1081 (€20–25). Very popular with visitors; some exotic, international delights conjured up by an inventive chef.

**Mesogia**, tucked away in the backstreets in the middle of town, **t** 042 702 1440. The oldest taverna on Skiáthos has an excellent repertoire of Greek delicacies incl. outstanding fried courgette balls (*kolokythi-akéftedes*).

**Panorama**, further inland on the road to Profitis Ilías. As the name promises, fabulous views over Skiáthos Town and over the sea to Skópelos. Good oven-baked pizza.

**Windmill**, in a converted guess-what behind the San Remo Hotel, **t** 042 702 4550. Also with an international flavour and a lovely view; very popular, though the dishes are a little pricey.

# Entertainment and Nightlife

Having eaten, you'll be spoilt for choice when it comes to bars, although they're not cheap.

**Admiral Benbow Inn**, Polytechníou St. Provides a little corner of old England and bluesy music.

**Kazbar**, next door to the Admiral. Compact, noisy, friendly and fun, with live music and an Aussie/Brit crowd.

**Adagio**, up from the post office in Evangelístrias St. Friendly and non-exclusive gay bar with pleasant décor; an oasis of tranquillity in the summer madhouse.

**Kentavros** near Papadiamántis' house. Promises more of a funky jazz and blues atmosphere.

On a warm summer evening, the pictur-esque waterfront bars come into their own: **Jimmy's**. One of the best.

**Kavos**, **Remezzo** and the ever popular seafront **BBC** are good for a blaring bop.

**Paradise Outdoor Cinema**, on the ring road. Offers undubbed films.

## Papadiamántis, the Master of Neo-Hellenic Prose

One of modern Greece's finest novelists, Papadiamántis wouldn't recognize his home town today. The Skiáthos he immortalized in his stories, with stark realism and serene, dispassionate prose, was a poor, tragic place, where most of the men were forced to emigrate or spend years at sea, and the women lived hard lives of servitude, often in total penury to accumulate a *príka*, or dowry, for each daughter; this was such a burden that, when a little girl died, other women would comfort the mother by saying: 'Happy woman, all you need to marry this one off is a sheet.'

Papadiamántis' strongest story, *I Phonissa* (*The Murderess*), written in 1903, concerns an old woman who, reflecting on the conditions of her own life, sees the monstrous injustice of the system and quietly smothers her sickly newborn granddaughter, to spare her daughter the need to slave away for her dowry. Always the island's herbal doctor (the one herb she could never find was the herb of sterility), the woman believes that her destiny is to alleviate the suffering of others, and she kills four other daughters of poor families before being pursued to her own death. As she drowns, the last thing she sees is the wretched vegetable garden that was her own dowry. Twelve of Papadiamántis' stories have been beautifully translated by Elizabeth Constantinides as *Tales from a Greek Island*, complete with a map (it's usually available at the house) – a perfect read on Skiáthos, a century on.

# Koukounariés and Other Beaches

Beaches, beaches and more beaches are the key to Skiáthos' success, and they rim the emerald isle like lace. Mobile sardine tins called buses follow the main road along the south coast, stopping within easy walking distance of the best strands, nearly all equipped with places to lunch and someone hiring out windsurfing boards and other watersports gear. From town, the most convenient is **Megáli Ámmos**, although it's generally too crowded for comfort. Moving westward, **Achladiés** (ΑΧΛΑΔΙΕΣ) Beach, dominated by the large Esperides Hotel (with tennis court open to the public), is also densely populated for most of the summer season.

Beyond that, 5km from town, the **Kalamáki** Peninsula juts out with a coating of holiday villas. Beaches here include **Kanapítsa** (ΚΑΝΑΠΙΤΣΑ), a popular cove for swimming and watersports, with a restaurant by the water, and nearby **Vromólimnos** ('dirty lake'), hard to pronounce and hard to find, but one of the finest places to swim on the island, with powderpuff-soft sand (but don't hold your breath for solitude); the restaurant-bar at the right-hand end of the strand is worth a stop for lunch or a tipple or two. **Plataniás/Ag. Paraskeví** is a lovely long stretch of beach with plenty of umbrellas and beach beds.

Convenient by bus or boat, **Troúlos** has a couple of tavernas and more good swimming. The last stop, 12km from Skiáthos Town, is the legendary **Koukounariés** (ΚΟΥΚΟΥΝΑΡΙΕΣ), rated by many as 'the Best Beach in Greece': a superb sweeping crescent bay of soft sand that somehow escaped from the South Pacific, fringed with pine trees, although in August it seems that not only can you 'see a world in a grain of sand' as Blake wrote, but that each grain of sand has a world sitting on top of it.

# Where to Stay and Eat

## Skiáthos ✉ 37002

### Kanapítsa/Achládies

**Mare Nostrum Holidays**, in town at 21 Papadiamánti, t 042 702 1463. Rental places in the vicinity.

**Esperides**, Achladies, t 042 702 2245, f 042 702 1580, *www.esperides.gr* (*A; lux*). Recently renovated big beach hotel; all rooms with balconies, sea-views, and air-con, tennis, pool, sea sports, beauty parlour, etc.

**Plaza**, 100m from Kanapítsa Beach, t 042 702 1971, f 042 702 2109, *plaza@n-skiathos.gr* (*B; lux*). Scenically situated amongst pines and olive groves; there's a pool, gym and the inevitable Greek nights.

**Villa Diamanti**, at Kanapítsa, 50m from the sea, t 042 702 2491, in Athens, t 010 590 3280 (*A; exp*). Stylish apartments in a garden setting, with a barbecue terrace. *Open May–Oct.*

**Angeliki**, t/f 042 702 2354 (*E; mod*).

**Villa Anni**, at Achladiés, t 042 702 1105 (*C; mod*). For something less pricey.

**Rea**, t 042 702 3065 (*C; inexp*). If you prefer to stay with the hordes on the beach at Megáli Ámmos; the thriving flora on the terraces lends an exotic atmosphere.

### Koukounariés/Ag. Paraskeví/Inland

**Skiáthos Palace**, Koukounariés Bay, t 042 704 9700, f 042 704 9666 (*L; lux*). Overlooks the bay amid pines, with pool, tennis, massage and roof garden. *Open May–Oct.*

**Skiáthos Princess**, Ag. Paraskeví Beach, t 042 704 9731, f 042 704 9740 (*L; lux*). Bright and airy; enjoys one of the best positions on one of the best beaches; with wheelchair access and a diving school. *Open May–Oct.*

**Atrium Hotel** (with monastic Mount Áthos-style foyer) and **Bungalows**, near the Princess, a 5min stroll from the beach, t 042 704 9345, f 042 704 9444 (*A; exp*). With excellent views. *Open Apr–Oct.*

**Boudourgianni's House**, on Troúlos Beach, t 042 704 9280 (*B; exp*). With a swimming pool.

**Korali**, on Troúlos Beach, t 042 704 9212, f 042 704 9551 (*C; exp*). Friendly apartment complex, with fully equipped kitchens and balconies with sea-views and pool. *Open May–Oct.*

**La Luna**, on the hillside overlooking Troúlos Bay, t 042 704 9262 (*A; exp–mod*). Well-equipped studios and maisonettes with air-con, a lovely pool and great views, 10mins' walk from the sea.

**Zorbathes**, t/f 042 704 9473, *geof@skiathos-info.com* (*exp–mod*). For true rural peace and quiet, with 2 fully equipped stone, wood and terracotta houses sleeping 4–6 in a lush valley; run by Geof and Lida Baldry – book in advance.

**Camping Koukounariés**, at the east end of the eponymous beach, t 042 704 9250. The nicest campsite on the island (and the only official one).

**Camping Aselinos**, near Megálo Asélinos Beach, t 042 704 9249. Next best, in a farm setting.

Tavernas, hotels and a campsite are hidden away from the sea behind trees and a rather uninspiring lake. Hyper-trendy **Krássa**, nowadays called **Banana** Beach, is up the hill with the sea on your left when you get off the bus at Koukounariés. **Little Banana** (or Spartacus), next door, is the gay/nudie beach where you can peel off everything in high season and lie cheek-to-cheek in a bunch. Next is the lovely **Ag. Eléni**, the last beach accessible by road, a somewhat quieter spot with a view across to the Pelion Peninsula on the mainland and a welcome breeze; or take the dirt road just before reaching the beach, which leads after 1km or so to the way down to Kryfos Ammoudia Beach, with its cool taverna.

In general, beaches on the north coast are subject to the *meltémi* winds. **Mandráki** is reached by a lovely footpath from the lagoon behind Koukounariés, with two stretches of sand and a snack bar. Further east, **Asélinos** is a sandy beach in an arcadian setting with a taverna and reed sun shelters rather than the usual eyesore parasols; but beware of the undertow. Just off the road that leads to nearby **Mikro Asélinos** (tricky to find and not worth the bother), is the exquisitely painted, candlelit chapel of the 17th-century Monastery **Panagía Kounistrá**, overlooking the north coast, where an icon of the Virgin was found dangling in a tree and like so many stubborn icons, refused to be moved. Past Kástro, the beach at **Lalária** (accessible only by sea) is a marvel of silvery pebbles, shimmering like a crescent moon beneath the cliff, with a natural arch closing off one end and nearby sea grottoes – **Skotini**, 'the dark' (so bring a light if you want to see anything), **Galázia**, 'the blue', and **Chálkini**, 'the copper'.

## Inland to Kástro

When charter-set life begins to pall, there are several escape hatches and a network of walking paths. A road (with the occasional bus) and a donkey path, beginning just before the turning to the airport road, lead 4km through some of the most beautiful and uninhabited scenery on Skiáthos, up to the island's last working monastery. **Evangelístria** (*open 8–noon and 4–8; proper attire required*) was founded in 1797 by monks forced to flee Mount Áthos for their support of the traditionalist Kollivádes movement. A lovely, peaceful place with a triple-domed church and garden courtyard, it became a refuge for both monks and scholars, as well as for the *armatolés* (members of the revolutionary militia) from the Olympus area, who with the support of the Russians, had raised a small pirate fleet to harass the Turks. When Russia made peace with Turkey in 1807, the *armatolés* were abandoned, and many took refuge on Skiáthos; under Giánnis Stathás, they united in an irregular army, and over the monastery hoisted the blue and white Greek flag that they had just invented. The Ottoman fleet soon put an end to their pretensions, but a statement had been made that would inspire the War of Independence 14 years later. Only a rusting cannon and a few displays in the small museum, cared for by a sole monk and his helper, recall the monastery's belligerent past.

Continue on from Evangelístria or take the two-hour walk from Ag. Konstantínos near Skiáthos Town across the island (the path is well marked) to **Kástro**, a town founded on a difficult, windswept niche in the 14th century, when pirates were on the warpath, and inhabited until 1829, when everyone moved down to the sheltered comfort of Skiáthos Town. Eight of the original 30 Byzantine churches more or less still stand (one, **Christós**, has good frescoes and a chandelier) among the houses and a Turkish hammam. The view from the top is quite lovely and there's a quiet beach below, where the locals smuggled out trapped Allied troops during the war. Papadiamántis describes Kástro's churches in a short story, *The Poor Saint*: 'some of them stood on rocks or on reefs by the shore, in the sea, gilded in summer by the dazzling light, washed in the winter by the waves. The raging north wind whipped and shook them, resolutely ploughing that sea, sowing wreckage and debris on the shore, grinding the granite into sand, kneading the sand into rocks and stalactites, winnowing the foam into spokes of spray.' If the *meltémi* is blowing, you can see that he wasn't exaggerating.

A detour on the path leads to the pretty 15th-century Monastery of **Panagía Kechriá**, containing some fine frescoes painted after 1745. From here you can continue down to lovely, isolated Kechriá Beach, where the local goatherd runs a delightful taverna.

# Skópelos (ΣΚΟΠΕΛΟΣ)

Where Skiáthos has given its all to tourism, Skópelos has kept apart. Yet Skópelos is an exceptionally beautiful island, more dramatic than Skiáthos, its entire 100 sq km shaded by fragrant pine forests. Its beaches are almost as lovely as those flaunted so commercially by its rambunctious neighbour, and it has two exceptionally pretty towns, Skópelos and Glóssa. By remaining aloof during the 1960s and 70s, the decades of slapdash cash-in-quick building, Skópelos now draws 'the more discerning traveller' (as the more discerning package companies call them). It is a lovely island for walks, outside the heatstroke months of July and August; the *Sotos Walking Guide*, available in English in most bookshops, will set you on your way.

## History

Known in antiquity as Perparethos, Skópelos was colonized by Prince Staphylos of Crete (who, according to some, was the son of Theseus and Ariadne). This tradition was given dramatic substance in 1927 when Staphylos' wealthy Minoan tomb was discovered by the cove that has always borne his name. Staphylos' name means 'grape': the local wine, described as an aphrodisiac by Aristophanes, was long an

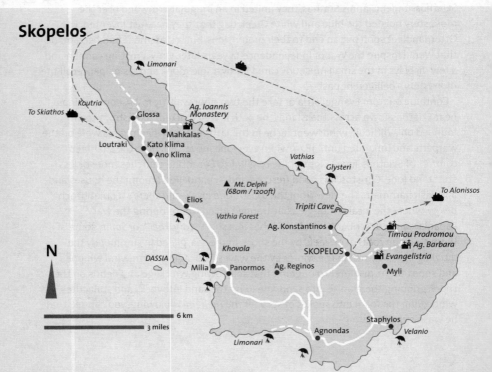

Skópelos

## Getting There and Around

By sea: **ferries** link Skópelos daily with Vólos, Ag. Konstantínos, Skiáthos and Alónissos, and several times a week with Thessaloníki. They usually call at both Skópelos Town and Glóssa. **Hydrofoils** daily to Skiáthos, Alónissos, Vólos and Ag. Konstantínos. **Port authority**, t 042 402 2180, in Glóssa, t 042 403 3033.

By road: **buses** run several times a day from Skópelos Town to Glóssa, at the other end of the island, stopping by all the beach paths.

## Tourist Information

For all kinds of information on the island, have a look at *www.skopelosweb.gr*

**Regular police**, Skópelos Town, t 042 402 2235 or Glóssa, t 042 403 3333.

**Madro Travel**, just by the ferry, t 042 402 2145, f 042 402 2941. Help with accommodation. Heather Parsons (t 042 402 4022, *hevskop@ otenet.gr*), author of the walking guide *Skópelos Trails*, can offer an intimate, in-depth view of the island.

## Internet

**Click and Surf Net Café**, on the waterfront behind the National Bank; *open 9am till late*.

## Festivals

**Early Aug**: Loïzeia alternative theatre and music festival at Glóssa.

**6 Aug**: Metamórphosis on Skópelos Bay.

**15 Aug**: Panagías in Skópelos.

**9 Nov**: Eisódia tis Theotókou at the edge of the town.

**Carnival** (Apokriés) is fun, but can be dangerous for your health. A small boat, the *tráta*, is made of cane and decorated with rubbish (mostly Coke cans), with a smoke-stack spewing fumes from burning wet garbage. This foul vessel is borne through the streets, polluting everything in its path, while its bearers, bodies painted, stop to drink and sing lewd songs. Increasingly drunk, they finally make it to the harbour, where the boat is hurled into the sea and the merrymakers jump in after it.

important export, along with olive oil; the first olive roots are said to have been brought here from Knossós. The Cretans are also credited with founding the island's three settlements: Perparethos (Skópelos Town), Staphylos (Pánormos) and Knossa (Glóssa). Subsequent tradition recounts that King Pelias, usurper of the Iolkan kingdom in Thessaly, settled Skópelos in the 13th century BC; it was this same Pelias who sent the rightful heir, Jason, after the Golden Fleece.

Venetian renegade Filippo Gizzi used Skópelos as his headquarters, and his capture by the resurgent Byzantines meant a decline in local excitement until Barbarossa decimated the island in 1538. In later years Skópelos was a popular refuge from the Turks, who called the Sporades the 'demon islands' for their ornery pirates. The Skopelitians joined in the revolt of the irregular militia in 1805 (*see* Skiáthos), and throughout the War of Independence the island's population soared, augmented by refugees from the mainland; in the 1820s, 70,000 people lived there, so many that there was fighting over food (the current population is under 6,000 year-round, and 20,000 in August). *Phylloxera* decimated the famous vines in the 1940s, and they've never been replanted, although the little country houses where wine was made, the *kalívia*, are still scattered across the island.

# Skópelos Town and its Harbour

**Skópelos** (or Chóra) forms a picture-perfect collage of old blue slate and post-earth-quake red-tile roofs, artfully arranged in a steep amphitheatre around the port.

# Where to Stay

## Skópelos ✉ 37003

Like Skiáthos, Skópelos is expensive; unlike Skiáthos, there are no huge jerry-built hotels. For most people, in or around Skópelos Town is the best place to stay. Some of the island's most characterful accommodation can be booked in advance through companies such as **Sunvil** and **Greek Islands Club** (*see* pp.88–9). For simpler rooms, you'll have no problem; offers as you step off the boat are plentiful and honest.

**Prince Stafilos, t** 042 402 2775, **f** 042 402 2825 (*B; exp*). Has a rustic feel with a modest pool and splendid gardens.

**Skópelos**, across the bay, 600m from town, **t** 042 402 2517, **f** 042 402 2958 (*L; exp*). Attractive seafront bungalow complex with all the modern frills and good facilities for children.

**Archontiko, t** 042 402 2765/2049 (*A; exp–mod*). Book very early to bag a room in this lovely old town house.

**Diónysos**, nearer to the centre of town, **t** 042 402 3210, **f** 042 402 2954 (*B; exp–mod*). Upbeat hotel with an international flavour, large pool and gardens; comfortable rooms, some with sea-views.

**Adonis**, on the central waterfont, **t/f** 042 402 2231 (*D; mod*). Adequate, with a restaurant. *Open all year.*

**Aegeon**, 300m above the beach, **t** 042 402 2619, **f** 042 402 2194, in winter, **t** 010 902 4825 (*C; mod*). Stylish small hotel, with panoramic views over Skópelos Town and its port.

**Akti t** 042 402 3229 (*D; mod*). A good bet if you come unpackaged and unbooked.

**Kyr Sotos, t** 042 402 2549 (*A; mod–inexp*). Popular and traditional island pension. Each of its 12 rooms has its own character and views of either the harbour or a flower-draped courtyard.

# Eating Out

**Braxos**, up the narrow streets of town. Pretty views over the port to go with its drinks (and peek in the shop opposite with its hidden courtyard).

**Finikas**, up in town, **t** 042 402 3247. Friendly, lantern-lit taverna with delicious regional specialities, and a huge palm tree to lounge under.

**Greca**, just off Plátanos Square. A favourite with the locals, with good *crêpes*; run by an eccentric French woman.

**Ionos**, opposite the barber shop. Good music accompanies its coffee, breakfasts and cocktails.

**Klimataria**, overlooking the port, **t** 042 402 2273. Serves Skopelot specialities such as 'black fish' *stifádo*, a wonderful fish and onion concoction.

**Korali Bar**, near the quay. Serves delicious traditional deep-fried cheese pies.

**Molos**, near Perivoli. For good Greek food and casseroles.

**Mourayo**, close to the ferry port, **t** 042 402 4553. One of the best tavernas on the island with a wide range of international and Greek dishes.

*Ouzerie* **Anatoli**, set in the walls of the Kástro. Serves excellent reasonably-priced *mezédes*, with tables on a panoramic terrace. The owner, Giórgos Xintáris, is a well-known *bouzouki* player and, if he's in the mood, he'll strum and sings old *rembetíka* songs after 11pm.

**Perivoli**, near Plátanos Square, **t** 042 402 3758. One of the better restaurants in town and don't the waiters know it; specializes in French-style Greek cuisine. Try the pork roll filled with plums.

**Stellas**, out on Ag. Konstantínos Beach. Serves especially good moussaka and other old favourites.

**Vegera** ('telling tales'). Cosy welcoming coffee shop.

# Entertainment and Nightlife

**Coco's Club**. Nightlife since 1993 has been concentrated around this venue, by far the biggest club on the island, playing mostly chart music.

**Kounos**. Another popular club.

**Platanos Bar**. Plays great jazz.

**Baballo Club**, near the Denise Hotel in Klíma. Search out live Greek music here.

There's a touch of Venice in the older buildings, while others are built either in a sturdy Thessalian or Macedonian style. The newer houses fit in harmoniously, incorporating wooden balconies and other traditional features, while, in between, the Greek obsession for planting a seed wherever it might have half a chance has resulted in a lush growth of flowers and plants. In addition to the usual tourist tat, Skópelos has more than its fair share of shops selling good locally produced merchandise, from traditional ceramics and wood carvings to exquisite model boats and, direct from the fishermen on the quay, natural sea sponges.

Skópelos Town claims 123 churches, of all shapes and sizes, many with charming iconostases. Two to look out for are **Zoödóchos Pigí** with an icon attributed to St Luke, and **Christó** (above the Commercial Bank) with a triangular, Armenian-style apse and an exceptionally handsome gilded interior. Perched at the top of town, where a Temple to Athena once stood, are the white walls of the Venetian **Kástro**, built by the Gizzi, so formidable that overpopulated Skópelos was left untouched during the War of Independence. Along the edge of the cliff stand a row of chapels, as if offering divine defence against the storms that often crash into the exposed town. Within the walls the 9th-century **Ag. Athanásios** has frescoes from the 1500s, unfortunately damaged in 1965 when the roof collapsed. At the other end of town, the **Museum of Folk Art** (Mouseío Laografikó), has a fine collection, especially of embroideries, housed in an 18th-century mansion rebuilt as it was after the last earthquake. The church of **Panagía Eleftherótria**, beyond Plátanos Square with its enormous plane tree and fountain, is a handsome 18th-century stone building with a slate roof, adorned with brightly-coloured ceramic plates.

At the end of town, beyond the medical centre, stands the impressive fortified Monastery of **Episkopí**, built by the Venetians as a seat for the bishopric of Skópelos, although work was abandoned after the raid by Barbarossa in 1538. The walls encompass the 17th-century basilica of Panagía tis Episkopís, built over a church dating back to 600. Further on, the stone sarcophagus of **Ag. Regínos**, the first Bishop and patron saint of Skópelos, martyred in 362, may be seen in the courtyard of Ag. Regínos. Just outside town, you can usually visit the **Foúrnou Damáskinon**, the gargantuan oven where in August plums are dried to become Skópelos' famous prunes; many of these are later crystallized and served with *rakí* to guests, along with a sprig of basil to tuck behind the ear. There's a convenient but mediocre sandy beach next to the town and, under the trees, a row of sweet shops that scent the evening air with warmed honeyed *loukoumádes*. If you walk around the bay to **Ampelikí**, you can see the ruins of an Asklepeion lying half-submerged in the sea.

## Around Skópelos Town

The hills overlooking Skópelos' large but windswept harbour shelter no fewer than five monasteries; a lovely path begins just beyond the strip of hotels near the beach. The closest, **Evangelístria** (*open 10–1 and 4–7*), with a magnificent view over town, was founded by monks from Mount Áthos, but is now occupied by nuns who offer their weavings for sale. Further afield, fortified but abandoned **Ag. Bárbara** has frescoes from the 15th century. **Metamórphosis** too was abandoned in 1980, but is currently being rehabilitated; it hosts one of the island's biggest *panegýri* (6 August). Over the ridge, looking towards Alónissos, is **Timioú Prodromoú Convent** (*same hours as Evangelístria*), with a beautiful iconostasis. One path connects them all; a far less scenic road ascends as far as Metamórphosis. Real explorers can spend a day hiking even further, up to the panoramic summit of Poloúki (1,791ft) to the now abandoned, overgrown Monastery of **Taxiárchon**, where the local resistance hid Greek and Allied soldiers, before they were smuggled across to neutral Turkey.

On the other side of the bay, near the pleasant shingle-covered beach, **Ag. Konstantínos** (or **Glifóneri**), stand the ruins of a Hellenistic water tower. If this beach is overcrowded, try **Glystéri** to the north, reached by road or frequent caiques from the port; there's a pleasant taverna and a campsite amid the olive groves. Caiques also sail to the sea cave of **Tripití**, the island's chief lobster lodge and fishing hole, or to the islet of **Ag. Geórgios**, with a 17th-century monastery and herd of wild goats.

Among other **excursions** offered from Skópelos are night fishing trips, round-island sails in an old wooden schooner, visits to the islets off Alónissos, and the summer diving trips offered by the research ship *Oceanis* in the company of marine biologist Vassílis Kouroútos (*€130 for two days; for information, contact Thalpos Travel, upstairs on the waterfront, t 042 402 2947, f 042 402 3057, who can also help with accommodation or car and boat rentals*).

# Across Skópelos to Glóssa

Buses run regularly from Skópelos Town to Glóssa in about an hour, passing much of the south scenery coast on the way. Along the route you'll find **Stáphylos**, where two Minoan tombs from the 15th century BC were discovered; the gold, sword and rich burial goods they yielded are in the National Museum in Athens. It is now a popular family beach, complete with pedalos, while **Velanió**, on the opposite side of its small headland, a 500m walk from the bus, is the unofficial nudist beach. **Agnóndas**, the next stop, is a delightfully boaty little bay with good tavernas and a clean, pebbly beach that smells good, too, thanks to Klíma, its traditional bakery. Greeks have long memories: Agnóndas was named after a local athlete, a victor in the 569 BC Olympics, who disembarked here to wild acclaim; to this day it serves as an emergency port in rough seas. Sandy **Limonári** is one of the finest beaches on the island, now reachable by road, but the bus stops 800m short. From Agnóndas the road cuts through the pine groves to another popular campsite and pebbly beach, **Pánormos**, set in a magnificent bay with separate inlets and views of pine-covered islets. Tucked between **Pánormos** and **Miliá** are small secluded swimming coves, fringed by pines, accessible only on foot from the road by threading your way down through the trees. Miliá itself is shady and has a beautiful, enormous pebbly beach, with a large taverna and lots of watersports, including parasailing for the daring.

Further along, **Élios** Beach is a small resort, still bearing signs here and there of the emergency shelters thrown up after the 1965 earthquake, when the junta forced all the residents of old Klíma into bland, uniform housing, which is only now beginning

# Where to Stay and Eat

## Stáphylos ✉ 37003

**Irene,** t 042 402 3637 (B; mod), in winter, t 010 347 9785. Small family pension with bath and basic kitchen facilities in each room.

**Ostria,** t 042 402 2220, f 042 402 3236 (B; mod). A well run family hotel with a lovely pool and sea-views, a few mins' walk down to Stáphylos Beach.

**Terpsi,** on the main road near Stáphylos, t 042 402 2053. A charming garden restaurant, where everyone goes for roast chicken stuffed with walnuts, chicken livers and pine nuts. Open July and Aug.

## Agnóndas ✉ 37003

**Paulina,** t 042 402 3272/3634 (A; exp). Lovely apartments with beautiful sea-views.

**Pavlos,** in the beautiful bay of Agnóndas. The longest established of 4 excellent fresh fish tavernas.

**Vangélis** and **Geórgos,** at Limonári, t 042 402 2242. Pleasant rooms and a taverna.

## Pánormos ✉ 37003

**Adrina Beach,** built on a slope above the beach just outside Pánormos, t 042 402 3373, f 042 402 3372 (A; exp). Child-friendly bungalow complex built in traditional Skopelitian style with a large pool and lovely pool-side restaurant open to non-residents.

**Afrodite,** by the beach, t 042 402 3150, f 042 402 3152 (B; exp). Rooms with air-con; also a gym and mountain bikes to rent. Open May–Oct.

## Glóssa ✉ 37004

There isn't much choice up here; some 40 beds, spread out over a few houses.

**Zanetta,** in Néa Klíma, t 042 403 3140, f 042 403 3717 (C; mod). A hotel-apartment complex set in the woods overlooking a swimming pool; popular among Greek families.

**Taverna Agnandi.** Arrive early in Glóssa to get a table at the popular taverna, its roof terrace views complemented by traditional Greek cuisine, with some unusual fish dishes.

to look like a real town. It was here that a fierce bad dragon would wait for its annual tribute of human flesh, until St Reginos, Skópelos' patron saint, took the place of one of the victims and asked God for mercy (*eleos*). The dragon let Reginos lead it over a cliff to its death. Just before Loutráki, at **Káto Klíma**, begins the lovely route up to **Áno Klíma** and **Athéato**, the oldest settlement on the island, before arriving in Glóssa.

## Glóssa

Near the north end of the island, spilling over the wooded hill above the sea, is Skópelos' second town, **Glóssa** (ΓΛΩΣΣΑ), a pretty village constructed mainly during the Turkish occupation. The houses survived the 1965 earthquake; the older ones have the WC on the balcony. Three ruined 4th-century BC towers continue to watch over Glóssa, and a well-marked track leads in an hour across the island to the extraordinary Monastery of **Ag. Ioánnis,** perched high over the sea, an eagle's nest with real eagles and other birds of prey often soaring high overhead. The last leg of the walk is 100 steps carved in the living rock; the little sandy beach below is often deserted.

There's a rather untidy pebble beach and a few tavernas under the plane trees at **Loutráki** (ΛΟΥΤΡΑΚΙ), the town's port, a steep 3km below Glóssa. Nearly every ship calls in here as well as Skópelos Town, but otherwise it tends to doze. Near Loutráki's church, **Ag. Nikólaos,** are the 7th-century ruins of an earlier basilica and other remains of Loutráki's previous incarnation as Selinous.

Most of the island's almonds grow around Glóssa and **Kaloyéros,** a small isolated village on the rugged north coast, reached by caique or dirt road. From here, a 4km trail ascends the slopes of Skópelos' highest mountain, Délphi, where the **Sendoúkia**, 'the chests', four large rock-cut tombs with their lids facing a magnificent view to the east, were found at Karyá. No one knows if they are Neolithic or Early Christian.

# Skýros (ΣΚΥΡΟΣ)

Skýros, with a permanent population of 3,500, is an exceptional island in many respects. It has two distinct geological regions, squeezed in the middle by a girdle where nearly everybody lives in either the port or town; the southern half is barren, rugged and ringed with cliffs, the northern half is fertile and pine-forested. A native race of tiny ponies called the Pikermies roams the southern part undisturbed, except when rounded up to help with the chores or to give the kids a ride; a five-year-old can look them right in the eye.

Throughout history Skýros was uncommonly remote. Even today, under ideal conditions it takes about seven hours by land and sea to get there from Athens; connections from nearby Kými on Évia were so limited a few decades ago that the

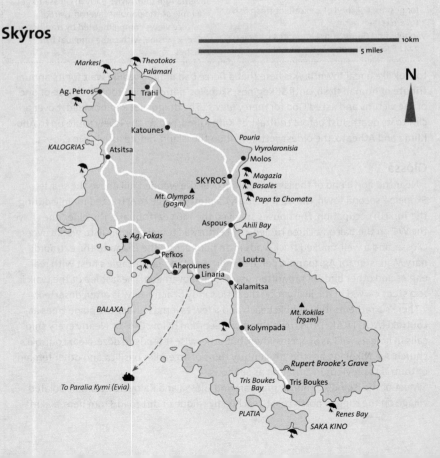

**Skýros**

10km
5 miles

N

Markesi
Theotokos
Palamari
Ag. Petros
Trahi
Katounes
Pouria
KALOGRIAS
Atsitsa
Vryrolaronisia
Molos
SKYROS
Magazia
Basales
Mt. Olympos
(903m)
Papa ta Chomata
Aspous
Ahili Bay
Ag. Fokas
Pefkos
Loutra
Aherounes
Linaria
Kalamitsa
BALAXA
Mt. Kokilas
(792m)
Kolympada
Rupert Brooke's Grave
To Paralia Kymi (Evia)
Tris Boukes
Bay
Tris Boukes
PLATIA
Renes Bay
SAKA KINO

# Getting There and Around

**By air**: 2 flights a week from Athens; **Olympic Airways, t** 022 209 1123/1600; **airport information: t** 022 209 1660/1625.

**By sea: ferry** connections with Kými (Évia) twice a day; twice a week with Skiáthos and Thessaloníki; once a week with Tínos, Páros, Santoríni and Heráklion (Crete). From Linariá, **caiques** travel to Skyropoúla islet; from Kalamítsa, they head for Tris Boukés. There are also excursions further south; ask at Skýros Travel. **Port authority: t** 022 209 1475.

**By road**: 6 **buses** daily reach Linariá and up to 10 reach Mólos; other services are less reliable, with 2 buses a day to other destinations, 1 in the morning, 1 in the afternoon.

# Tourist Information

**Tourist police**: *see* regular police, Skýros Town, **t** 022 209 1274.

**Skýros Travel**, in the centre of town, **t** 022 209 1123, **f** 022 209 2123. Leftéris Trákes is helpful, whether you need a villa, car, motorbike and bicycle hire, a boat ticket or information on island excursions. Also check out the website *www.skyros-net.gr*

# Festivals

Skýros preserves some fascinating vestiges of the ancient Mediterranean goat and cattle cults during its **Carnival**, when 3 characters dance down the street: the 'Old Man' in a goatskin costume, mask and sheep bells, with a humpback made of rags, followed by the Frángos (the Frank, or foreigner), dressed in motley clothes and long trousers, with a mask and bell, blowing a conch shell to scare children, and the Koréla, a man dressed up as a woman. These perform the Horós tou Trágou, or the Goat Dance, possibly a relic of the ancient rite that gave us the word 'tragedy' (from *tragoudía*, or 'goat song'). Every day during carnival the Old Man, the Frángos and the Koréla make their rollicking way through town, joining in satires (another goatish word, derived from the mischievous half-goat Satyrs) until they end up at the Monastery of Ag. Geórgios.

Other festivals include:

**23 April**: Ag. Geórgios.

**27 July**: Ag. Panteleímon, near Péfkos.

**Late July and early Aug**: a new outdoor theatre hosts a festival.

**15 Aug**: children's pony races.

**2 Sept**: Ag. Máma, the patron of shepherds. Like Carnival, the festival also includes traces of ancient rites.

# Where to Stay and Eat

**Skýros** ✉ 34007

## Skýros Town

On arrival from Linariá, buses are besieged by little old ladies in black, who will lead you off to horribly overpriced rooms in traditional houses in the backstreets. If you take one, just mind you don't break the plates.

**Nefeli, t** 022 209 1964, **f** 022 209 2061 (*B; exp*). One of the island's best and most comfortable, with 7 of its rooms in traditional split level *sfa* style; there's also a roomy pool. *Open all year.*

**Nikolas**, behind Kristina's restaurant on the edge of the village, **t** 022 209 1778, **f** 022 209 3400, *www.skyrosnet.gr/nicholas* (*mod*). Tranquil, traditional style comfortable rooms (complete with a *sfa*, or Skyriot sleeping platfrom). *Open all year.*

Skyriots purchased their own ferry to get about. The long years of isolation account in part for the island's distinctive charm and character, and the staying power of its old customs. The oldest men still don their baggy blue trousers, black caps and flat leather sandals with many straps or *trohádhia*, and the older women can sometimes be seen in their long headscarves; the interiors of their tidy houses remain resolutely traditional, while incorporating such novelties as digitally controlled American refrigerators. In other words, the outside world has arrived, but the Skyriots are determined to set the rules by which it operates on their island.

Campsite, located two-thirds of the way down the road to Magaziá Beach. Friendly and pleasant.

Kristina, t 022 209 1778. Run by Greek-Australian Kristina Tsalapatani, with a delicious change-of-pace menu and warm herb breads (she also runs Greek cookery courses out of season).

Margetis, on the main street, t 022 209 1311. One of the oldest restaurants, and the most popular, serving good meat and especially fish dishes in an ideal location to watch the bustling pedestrian traffic.

O Pappous Ki Ego ('My grandfather and I'), t 022 209 3200. Popular place for *mezédes*.

Pegasos, 20m below Skýros Travel. An elegant restaurant in a 19th-century mansion. Serves prepared Italian dishes, kid casseroles, and tasty moussaka.

Trypa, on the main street. Good, cheap coffee, snacks and pizza served all day.

## By the Sea: Magaziá, Gialós and Mólos

Skiros Palace, 50m from the beach at Grismata, t 022 209 1994, f 022 209 2070, in winter, f 010 275 2094, *www.skiros-palace.gr* (B; *exp*). The most sophisticated place to stay; built in the traditional Skýros-Cyclades style, it has a lovely sea-water pool, restaurant, superior rooms and a relaxed atmosphere. *Open mid-May–Sept.*

Xenia, smack on the beach at Magaziá, t 022 209 1209, f 022 209 2062 (B; *exp*). Older but comfortable with 22 rooms and a restaurant and water sports. *Open Apr–Oct.*

Skýros Studios, near the sea in Mólos, t 022 209 1376, in winter, f 010 723 0871, f 010 723 0957 (B; *exp–mod*). Set in a large garden, built and furnished in the traditional style.

Aegeolis, a stone's throw from the sea at Magaziá, t 022 209 1113, f 022 209 2482, in winter, f 010 418 2466 (C; *mod*). Set of 11

apartments with veranda, built in 1992. *Open all year.*

Efrosýni Varsámon, in Magaziá, t 022 209 1142 (*mod*). Charmingly decorated rooms above the family's pottery shop.

Perigali, set back from the sea in Magaziá, t 022 209 1889, f 022 209 2061 (*mod*). A handful of well-kept studios and rooms circling a luscious garden. *Open May–Oct.*

Mólos, t 022 209 1381, in winter, t 010 262 7513 (*mod–inexp*). Offers garden studios, pleasant but cheaper, with big discounts in May and June. *Open May–Sept.*

Koufari, near the Xenia Hotel in Magaziá. Excellent, albeit not cheap, fare.

Mylos Taverna, in Mólos. Ideal for those Aegean sunsets.

Thoma to Magazi, by the water. One of the best places for seafood.

## Linariá

Linariá Bay, 40m from the sea, t 022 209 6476 (*exp–mod*). Rooms and studios with air-con, TV and phone.

King Likomides, right by the port, t 022 209 6249, f 022 209 6412, in winter, t 010 721 3773 (*mod*). Pleasant rooms, all with fridge and sea-views. *Open May–Oct.*

Almyra, t 022 209 3252. Variety of tasty starters and a delicious lobster with pasta.

Philipeo. Has the best food in the village.

Psariotis. Reasonable choice.

At Achérouses, just north, there's a campsite and a simple, friendly taverna where you can dine with your feet in the sea.

Kavos Bar, just along the road to Skýros. Lovely place for sunset watching over a cocktail; 'Sprach Zarathustra' belts out of the speakers to greet the aliens on incoming ferries.

Kastro Club. The local night spot, playing both disco and Greek music.

## History

Theseus was buried on Skýros and his memory neglected by the Athenians until his spirit was seen at Marathon, rising out of the earth to lead the Athenians to victory over the Persians. The Delphic oracle then charged the Athenians to bring Theseus' bones back to Athens – just the excuse the Athenians needed to nab Skýros for themselves. In 476 BC Kimon captured it, enslaved the inhabitants and, guided by a she-eagle, which scratched at the ground with her beak, was led to the grave of a tall skeleton buried with his weapons. Certain that it was Theseus, Kimon exhumed the coffin, carried it back to Athens, and enshrined it in the Theseion. Afterwards, so many Athenians settled in Skýros that Athens treated it as an equal. In Byzantine times, so many nobles were exiled here that they formed a much resented upper class, one remembered in the double-headed eagle motif in the local art. In the First World War Skýros became the last resting place of the poet Rupert Brooke; today it is perhaps best known as the home of the holistic Skýros Centre (*www.skyros.com*; also *see* p.75).

# Skýros Town

Skýros, or Chóra, is a striking town that wouldn't look out of place in the Cyclades, its white houses stacked along the steep, narrow pedestrian-only lanes and steps. From the distance it sweeps like a full skirt around the massive rocky precipice of the ancient *acropolis*, high over the sea. The main street curls past a pleasant mix of hardware stores and trendy boutiques, rimmed by the terraces of a dozen cafés, tavernas, and cocktail bars; few islands manage such a harmonious balance between the needs and desires of the locals and visitors. The main square is a fine place to sit and watch the crowds demolishing *ouzo* and *mezé*, or *loukoumádes* and coffee; a certain element of danger is added by the hordes of small children wildly kicking plastic balls in all directions, or scooting recklessly between the tables.

## Mythology

When it was prophesied that Achilles, son of the sea goddess Thetis and Peleus, would either win great glory at Troy and die young, or live peacefully at home to a ripe old age, his doting mother thought to hide him from the warlords by disguising him as a girl and sending him to live among the women at King Lykomedes' palace in Skýros. Achilles didn't mind, and, adopting the name of Pyrrha, or 'Goldie', for the colour of his hair, took advantage of his stay by fathering a son, Neoptolemis. All would have been well had not another oracle declared that the Greeks would never win the Trojan War without Achilles, and Odysseus was sent to find him. Odysseus brought gifts for the women when he called on King Lykomedes – perfumes and jewellery – and a sword, which the young transvestite seized for his own, as Odysseus had anticipated. When an arrow in his heel ended his life, Odysseus returned to Skýros to fetch his son Neoptolemis to Troy, and the war was eventually won.

King Lykomedes of Skýros plays a less benign role in another story: when the hero Theseus returned to Athens after spending four years glued to the Chair of Forgetfulness in Hades (his punishment for trying to help a friend abduct Persephone, the Queen of Hell), he found Athens corrupt and divided into factions against him. Theseus laid a curse on his native city and sought asylum in Crete, but was blown off course to Skýros, where he was received with such honour by Lykomedes that Theseus announced that he meant to retire on an estate his family owned on Skýros – an estate coveted by Lykomedes himself. After a drinking party Lykomedes led Theseus to the pinnacle of Skýros' *acropolis* and gave him a push, hurling him to his death on the rocks below.

## Small but Perfectly Formed – Skyriot Houses

Few houses combine so much function and beauty in the small spaces dictated by the necessity of living crammed together on the slope, within easy distance of the Kástro should a pirate sail appear on the horizon. Because most of the older houses back into the steep hill and have shared walls, the *xóporto*, an outer half-door flap, was developed to allow light and air to enter while retaining privacy. The central living area is called the *alóni*, a Greek word that recalls the circular disc of the sun, since the walls and possessions on display are seen 'all around'. Focus, however, naturally fell on the chubby, conical fireplace, or *f'gou*, with two little ledges for children to sit on in the winter. Some *f'gous* have a pair of breasts in bas-relief to symbolize motherhood. An embroidered cloth over the upper mouth of the hearth protected the room from smoke, while shelves across the front of the *f'gou* displayed rows of colourful plates and jugs. Crockery has been a Skyriot obsession and status symbol since the 16th century, when the Turkish conquest forced the island's Byzantine exiles into such poverty that they had to sell off their dinnerware. Pirates who looted cargoes of plates would sell them on Skýros, or the pirates themselves would be looted by the plate-crazed islanders if they pulled into a bay to shelter from a storm. A Skyriot sailor never has to think twice about the perfect gift for his wife or mother: some examples come from as far away as China.

Furniture, often beautifully carved with folk motifs, is simple and functional. Benches and settees double as chests for clothes, or have hollows in front of them to slide in pots, pans or bottles; other objects were stored in baskets suspended from the ceiling and reached by long forked poles. Niches in the walls were used to store jugs filled with water. Food would be served on a low table, which in the old days had a removable top, a large engraved copper plate called a *sinía*. These are now mostly used for decoration.

An ornate latticework partition, the *bóulmes*, crowned by a carved wooden parapet, cuts off the back third of the interior while admitting precious light. The kitchen and storage area was on the ground floor, and the bedroom(s), or *sfas* (from the Turkish word 'sofa'), in the loft. A thin beam just below the ceiling of the *sfas* was used to hang large decorative weavings that hide the rolled up mattresses. If there is no room for an external stair to the *sfas*, access is by way of a steep narrow internal stair and trap door. The roof is made of wooden beams, covered with layers of dried cane, dried seaweed and earth rich in waterproof clay; new layers of clay are added every few years. A broken jar on top of the chimney draws out the smoke from the *f'gou*.

You can study the contents of a Skyriot house first hand at the charming **Faltaits Museum of Folklore** (*t 022 209 1232; open 10–1 and 6–9 in summer, otherwise 5.30–8*), also just under Brooke Square – a fascinating collection of domestic items, traditional costumes, and richly coloured embroideries decorated with mermaids, double-headed eagles, Turkish judges, ships, deer, pomegranates and hoopoes (a bird closely identified with Skýros). The museum shop is full of lovely if rather costly handmade goods, including printed patterns of Skyriot designs to make your own embroideries (the ladies of Skýros buy them) as well as locally made pottery inspired by the examples brought home from the four corners of the world.

Signs near the market point the way up to the **Kástro**, a 15-minute walk, passing by way of the usually open church of **Ag. Triáda** (with frescoes) and the white Monastery of **Ag. Geórgios**, founded in 962 by Emperor Nikephóros Phókas, himself known as 'the Pale Death of the Saracens' after his liberation of Crete. The emperor gave Ag. Geórgios to his saintly friend Athanásios, who went on to found the Great Lavra Monastery on Mount Áthos; Ag. Geórgios, and a good chunk of land on Skýros, belong to the Great Lavra to this day. The church holds a fine painting of St George slaying the dragon and the old icon of St George with a black face, brought over from Constantinople during the iconoclasm. A crusty lion of St Mark (1354) marks the gate of the Byzantine-Venetian citadel, built over the classical fortifications. It was from here that Lykomedes gave Theseus his mortal shove. On one side are fine views over the rooftops; on the other the escarpment plunges abruptly towards the sea.

**Brooke Square**, at the end of town, has been wearing a rather neglected air of late, although the willy of the gormless bronze nude *Statue of Immortal Poetry* (1931), commissioned by a Belgian businessman (rumour has it that a Belgian rent boy was the model), is administered to weekly by local spray painters. The **Archaeology Museum** (*t 022 209 1327; open Tues–Sun 8.30–3; adm*) is just under Brooke Square, along the steps leading down to Magaziá; grave offerings and goods from Copper-age Palamári (2500–1900 BC) on the extreme northern tip of the island and from Proto-geometric Thémis (950–800 BC) are among the highlights; from the latter note the ritual vase, decorated with eight ducks and two bird-swallowing snakes. Amongst the relics of ancient times, you'll find a traditionally furnished Skyriot home, 35 sq m in size – the average living space per family.

A 10-minute walk below Skýros Town stretches the long sandy beach of **Magaziá** (ΜΑΓΑΖΙΑ), named after the Venetian powder magazines once stored here, and next to it is **Mólos Beach**; most of the island's accommodation and surprisingly jumping nightlife are concentrated here. If these beaches are too crowded there are others within walking distance; avoid sewage-prone Basáles, but continue south to **Papá ta Chómata** ('Priests' Land'), where no one, not even the priest, minds if you sunbathe nude. From **Órmos Achílli**, further south, Achilles is said to have embarked for Troy; a new marina allows yachties to do the same.

# Around the Island

Although buses run regularly between the port of Linariá, Skýros Town and Mólos, the only way to visit the rest of the island is on foot, by taxi or hired wheels. The pine-wooded northern half of Skýros has better roads, and there are small beaches just off the road that follows most of the coast. The sandy beach of **Ag. Pétros** near the top of the island (past the airport) is the prettiest, and worth hiring a car and packing a picnic for. A walking path (taking about 3 hours and not always easy to find) crosses the island from Skýros Town to Atsítsa, where a taverna sits on a rocky beach among the pines, near a branch of the Skýros Centre, which offers courses ranging from sailing to dance and ponytrekking to yoga; the very English PRIVATE sign must dent the karma somewhat. A second path (and in parts road) to Atsítsa begins in the port **Linariá** (ΛINAPIA), a mostly modern fishing village, built after 1860; it passes by way of Ahérounes and the pretty beach and summer tavernas at Péfkos, site of ancient marble quarries. Even prettier **Ag. Fokás Beach**, with white pebbles, is further north; it has a very basic taverna and a handful of rooms. From Linariá, caique excursions sail to the islet Skyropoúla, between Skýros and the mainland. **Skyropoúla** has two beaches and a cave, **Kávos Spilí**, and a herd of the wild munchkin ponies.

The beaches in the rocky rugged southern half of Skýros are less appealing, with the exception of **Kalamítsa**, linked by bus in the summer. The beach is of sand and stones, and fronted by tavernas and a few rooms. Signs of one of ancient Skýros' three rival towns, Chrission, were found near here, as well as an ancient tomb locally claimed to be Homer's, and traces of an Early Christian basilica. Taxis offer regular excursions (*for about €32*) to **Tris Boukés** and the **grave of Rupert Brooke** at the southernmost point of Skýros. On 23 April 1915, the 27-year-old poet, on his way to fight at Gallipoli, died of blood poisoning aboard a French hospital ship, and was buried in this desolate olive grove at dawn the next morning. His mother commissioned his well-tended grave – 6ft of official British soil – now maintained by the Anglo-Hellenic society, bearing the famous lines from his poem, *The Soldier*:

> *If I should die, think only this of me:*
> *That there's some corner of a foreign field*
> *That is for ever England.*

Among the boat excursions offered in the summer, the one to the region south of Tris Boukés, to Saka Kíno Beach and Platia island, and around the cliffs at Renés, is spectacular. Sea caves pierce the cliffs, and the Eleanora falcons sweep across the azure sky as thick as sparrows in London.

# Évia (EYBOIA)

The second largest island in Greece after Crete, Évia (Euboea) is endowed with some of the most bucolic scenery in the country; along its 175km length, olive groves, orchards and vineyards (producing Greece's best *retsina*) alternate with dense forests, wild cliffs and snow-capped mountains. If nearly every hill is crowned with a crumbling Frankish or Byzantine fort, there are relatively few ancient remains. Its name means 'rich in cattle'. Animal husbandry and farming has been the Eviots' way of life for centuries, and it remains so today; in isolated villages people gape at every passing car as it were a chariot of the gods.

A mere 88km drive from downtown Athens and the only Greek island you can reach by train, Évia gets throngs of Greek tourists and although the hotels tend to be a bit bleak, they are booked solid in July and August. Évia's essential Greekness means reasonable prices and some excellent tavernas and restaurants, but on the other hand, it also means that car and scooter rentals, organized excursions, multi-lingual travel agencies, watersports facilities, English breakfasts and English speakers and

# Getting There and Around

## By Sea

Ferries link Évia with the mainland from Rafína to Kárystos (just over 1½ hrs; twice a day), Rafína to Marmári (6–7 times a day), Ag. Marína to Néa Stýra (at least 5 times a day), Arkitsa (just off the main Athens–Thessaloníki highway) to Edipsós (12–14 times a day), Oropós to Erétria (every ½hr) and Glífa to Agiókambos (every 2 hrs). Ferries also link Skýros daily from Kými. In the summer, there are connections from Ag. Konstantínos to Oréi and Péfki. Summer **hydrofoils** link Loutrá Edipsoú, Oréi, Péfki and the other Sporades; others sail from Vólos to Kými and Oréi; from Trikéri to Oréi; from Ag. Konstantínos to Chalkís, Edipsós and Porto Limni; and from Kárystos to most of the Cyclades. **Port authorities: Erétria, t** 022 106 2201; **Kárystos, t** 022 402 2227; **Marmári, t** 022 403 1222; **Edipsós, t** 022 602 2464; **Alivéri, t** 022 302 2955; **Néa Stýra, t** 022 404 1266; **Agiókambos, t** 022 603 1107; **Kými, t** 022 202 2606; **Oréi, t** 022 607 1228; **Péfki, t** 022 604 1710; **Chalkís, t** 022 102 2236.

## By Road

Évia's bulging middle is linked to the mainland by a short bridge over the Evripós Strait; there are **buses** every ½hr, and **trains** every hr from Athens to Chalkís (1½ hrs), a singularly unattractive journey (train information in Chalkís, **t** 022 102 2386). The bus terminal in Athens is Liossíon, from where you can also travel direct to Kými (the port for Skýros), Erétria, Amárinthos, Edipsós or Alivéri, but for Rafína (the main port for Kárystos and Marmári), buses leave Athens from the Mavromatéon terminal. A good bus service connects Chalkís (the station is right in the centre of town, **t** 022 102 2640) with all the major villages of Évia as well as Thebes (2 a day) and other nearby towns on the mainland. As the best of Évia lies along the various little roads branching off its one main highway, private transport is essential to appreciate the island. Chalkís and Erétria are pretty much the only places where you can rent cars and motorbikes. Don't arrive anywhere in the north of the island wanting to rent a car; you'll be in for a long bus ride to Chalkís before your travels can even begin. When you do get a vehicle, make sure the brakes are in perfect repair and be prepared for back roads that are bumpy, rutted, pitted, rocky, dusty and packed with endless puncture opportunities. You'll also need a compass and the newest map you can find to get around successfully: signposting ranges from the minimal to the non-existent.

# Festivals

**21 May**: Ag. Konstantínos at Vitalakimis.
**27 May**: St John the Russian at Prokópi.
**17 July**: Ag. Marínas near Kárystos.
**26 July**: Ag. Paraskevi, long celebrations at Chalkís, Mýli and Rúkia.
**15 Aug**: at Kými, Oxílithos and many other villages.

Dutch bars are much thinner on the ground than on any other island. Nor is there any central clearing house for rooms on Évia; you just have to go to each village and take pot luck. Most are on the coasts, naturally, and the island is a popular destination for campers, while villages in the interior have few or no facilities.

## History

Inhabited in prehistoric times by settlers from Thessaly, and later by Dorians, Aeolians and Ionians, ancient Évia was divided into city-states. The most powerful in the 8th–7th centuries BC were the two rivals, Chalkís and Erétria, both located on the Evripós Strait, a busy shipping lane in ancient times, when mariners shunned the stormy east coast of Évia. Archaic Chalkís and Erétria grew into great commercial ports with colonies as far away as Sicily. Between them lay Évia's desirable, fertile Lelantine Plain 'rich in vineyards'; both cities claimed the plain and extended their

## Mythology

Évia, split from the nearby mainland by a blow of Poseidon's mighty trident, was the sea god's favourite island, and he lived with his wife Amphitrite in a fabulous underwater palace just off shore in the Evian Gulf. To the south stretches the Myrtoan Sea, named after Myrtilus, son of Hermes and the charioteer of an invincible team of divine horses owned by King Oenomaus. Oenomaus had a beautiful daughter named Hippodameia, and he declared that only the suitor who could outrace his invincible chariot and avoid being transfixed by his brazen spear would have her hand; he set up the bones of the losers in front of his palace and arrogantly boasted that he would build a temple of skulls. This was too much for the gods, and they decided to help one of their favourites, Pelops, win the race and defeat Oenomaus. Knowing that Myrtilus himself was in love with Hippodameia, Pelops took the charioteer aside and proposed a deal: if he would throw the race by replacing the lynch-pins in the axles of the king's chariot with wax, then Pelops as winner would share Hippodameia with him. Myrtilus eagerly agreed and events unfolded as predicted: Oenomaus' chariot collapsed in the heat of the race, the king was killed and Pelops was given the princess. He and Myrtilus took her off towards Évia, but Pelops, never intending to keep his bargain with Myrtilus, kicked him into the sea where he drowned. As he fell he put a curse on the house of Pelops – better known as the House of Atreus – a curse that fuelled perhaps the greatest tragic cycle of ancient Greek myth and theatre. Hermes named the sea in the honour of his son, and put his image, the Charioteer, in the stars, but his ghost remained unappeased, and haunted the stadium at Olympia, frightening the horses.

disagreement into international affairs, doing neither of them any good. In 506 BC Chalkís joined Boeotia in a war against Athens, only to be conquered and divided; the Erétrians joined Athens in supporting the Ionian uprising on Asia Minor, and in retribution were sacked and enslaved in the Persian War when Darius came to punish the Athenians. In the 5th century BC, they and the rest of the island came under the rule of Athens.

In 338 BC Macedonia took Évia, and the Romans who followed them were the first to use the name of an Eviot tribe, the Graeci, to refer to the Hellenes, a misunderstanding that modern 'Greeks' get tit for tat for by calling themselves 'Romans' (as the true heirs of the Roman, i.e. Byzantine, empire). With the conquests of the Fourth Crusade, the Franks gave the fertile island to the King of Thessaloníki, Boniface de Montferrat, who divided it into three baronies, initiating an intense, feudal castle-building spree. Over the next hundred years, Évia came under the direct rule of the Venetians, whose mushy accents mangled Evripós (the channel) into 'Negroponte', a name they used for the entire island. When the Turks took Negroponte from them in 1470, they did not even allow the usual puppet Venetian governor to hang around as a tax farmer, but settled the prize themselves, treasuring it more than any other island in the Aegean. In the 19th century, 40,000 refugees from Albania and Epirus settled in the south, and a small Turkish minority remains on the island by a special agreement made during the population exchanges.

# Southern Évia

## Kárystos and Mount Óchi

The best way to see all of Évia, with a minimum of backtracking, is to take the 1½ hr ferry from Rafína to **Kárystos** (ΚΑΡΥΣΤΟΣ) at the foot of Mount Óchi, at the extreme southern tip of the island. With all of 5,000 souls, Kárystos is the metropolis on the Myrtoan Sea, renowned for its green cipollino marble and asbestos, known as 'the unquenchable' in ancient times. Named after its founder, a son of the centaur Chiron,

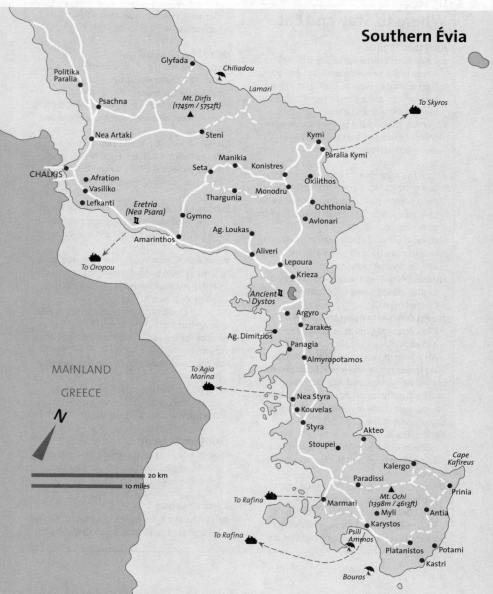

Southern Évia

Kárystos so caught the fancy of Greece's first king Otho when it was liberated from the Turks in 1833 that he renamed it after himself, Othonoúpolis, and declared he would make it the capital of Greece. He summoned an architect named Bierbach down from Bavaria to lay out the town plan, and he left the wide, straight streets that set Kárystos apart from the average Greek island town. Whiffs of Neoclassical grandeur linger in 19th-century buildings like the Dimarcheíon (town hall).

Othonoúpolis fell by the wayside like Otho himself, leaving Kárystos to carry on peacefully in its quintessential Greek way, with back-streets of hardware stores,

# Where to Stay and Eat

## Kárystos ✉ 34001

**Apollon Suites Hotel**, on sandy, if sometimes windy, Psilí Ámmos Beach, t 022 402 2045, f 022 402 2049 (*A; exp*). Central apartments with air-con and a heated swimming pool in case there's a chill in the air.

**Kárystion**, surrounded by the park near the *bourdzi*, t 022 402 2191, f 022 402 2727 (*C; exp–mod*). All rooms with sea view, air-con and TV.

**Als**, on the waterfront, t 022 402 2202, f 022 402 5002 (*C; mod*). Comfortable and very conveniently placed near all the cafés and tavernas; you can watch all the action from your balcony.

**Galaxy**, at the end of the seafront, t 022 402 2600, f 022 402 2463 (*C; mod*). A little quieter and somewhat cheaper.

**Hironia**, in town by the seafront, t 022 402 2238 (*C; inexp*). Somewhat battered but budget-friendly.

**Mount Óchi Shelter**, ring Mr Sákis Biniáris, t 022 402 2378 (*inexp*). Fully equipped with a capacity for 30 people.

For a dose of local colour, eat on **Kotsíka Street**, next to the Als Hotel. This area was the old Jewish quarter, and now buzzes with one grill house after another, where you can enjoy inexpensive chicken, steaks, chops and sausages from the grill. Try:

**To Obraïka**, at the top of Kotsíka St. Where tables are shared with other diners as well as cats and dogs, and the food is good and cheap.

**Dimitris**, at Pano Aetos. Pleasant garden setting, with meats from the grill.

**Cavo D'Oro**, on a side street off the main square. Besides the pleasant waterfront tavernas, it's worth hunting out this one

that serves excellent ready food and barrelled wine.

## Néa Stýra ✉ 34015

**Plaza**, in the middle of the waterfront, t 022 404 1429 (*C; exp–mod*). Open all year.

**Aktaeon**, on the beach, t 022 404 1261; in Athens, t 010 652 3345 (*C; mod*). Typical small Greek hotel, also with a restaurant, bar and grill.

**Castello Rosso**, 2km from town, near the Venus Beach, t 022 404 1547/780, (*C; mod*). Nice small hotel with a swimming pool, 50m from the beach; room rates incl. a buffet breakfast.

**Sunday**, t 022 404 1300, f 022 404 1205 (*mod*). Family-run hotel with big green awnings on the balconies overlooking the sea. Rates incl. breakfast.

**Venus Beach**, 2km from town, t 022 404 1226 (*C; mod*). Twin bungalows in pleasant garden setting with a swimming pool, restaurant and its own beach.

A small group of tavernas on the north end of town (turn left at the Lemonías sign) serve most of the usual Greek dishes, but specialize in fish.

**Matina**. Great fish, or try one of the tavernas nearby.

**Akroyiali**, on the waterfront past the ferry docks. *Ouzerie*/taverna serving good dishes in attractive setting by the water.

## Oxílithos ✉ 34011

**Stomio**, t 022 207 1251 (*C; mod*). Newish apartment complex with 22 self-catering flats. *Open May–Oct.*

## Kými ✉ 34003

**Beis**, at Paralía Kými by the quay, t 022 202 2604, f 022 202 2870 (*C; mod*). Large, if rather

butcher shops, and old fashioned *kafeneíons*, where the old men sip their coffee while flipping their beads and rattling dice over rickety backgammon boards. A kilometre-long sandy beach, stretching from the boatyard to Paximáda point, is perfect for snorkelling and windsurfing. The evening stroll, or *vólta*, endures with enthusiasm, along a *paralía* and fishing port crowded with excellent *ouzeries* and tavernas; these are heaving with Greek visitors on the third or fourth weekends of August, when Kárystos puts on its wine festival, with lots of folk music, dancing and tomfoolery. The waterfront is defended by a four-square 14th-century coastal fort, or **Boúrdzi** (or

anonymous hotel often used by people sailing out to Skýros. *Open all year.*

**Korali**, t 022 202 2212, f 022 202 3353 (*C; mod*). A decent choice. *Open all year.*

**Krinion**, Plateía G. Papanikoláou, t 022 202 2287 (*E; mod*). A little rough around the edges but still a pleasant place to stay; ask for a room with a balcony.

There are also some good waterfront tavernas (a few with rooms too), incl. the **Valedi** and **Aegio**, which serve good, standard Greek fare while waiting for your ferry to come in.

## Amárinthos ✉ 34006

**Stefania**, on the north end of town, t 022 903 8382, f 022 903 8384 (*B; exp*). Large, comfort-able hotel with a swimming pool. *Open all year.*

**Flisvos**, t 022 903 6071 (*C; mod*). Smaller choice, without swimming pool. *Open all year.*

**Limanaki**, t 022 903 6609. Decent fish taverna on the water, with an extensive selection of starters.

## Erétria ✉ 34008

Erétria has many hotels, as does **Malakónda** (just east), a beach-side resort that has mush-roomed up to accommodate the package holiday crowd.

**Holidays in Évia**, on the beach in Erétria, t 022 906 2611, f 022 906 1300 (*B; exp*). A sports-and fun-orientated resort complex and conference centre, with a good restaurant by the water. *Open all year.*

**Malaconda Beach Vogue Club**, at Malakónda, t 022 906 2510, f 022 906 2518 (*B; exp*). Prettily nestled among the olives and cypresses, with a lovely swimming pool. *Open Mar–Oct.*

**Palmariva Erétria Beach**, 2km from Erétria, t 022 906 2411, f 022 906 2418 (*A; exp*). Recently renovated, with everything a seaside resort hotel should have – sea sports, swimming pools, tennis courts, extensive gym, large disco and a wide choice of bars.

**Delfis**, t 022 906 2380 (*C; mod*). An old comfortable favourite that's very popular in the summer months; booking is essential. *Open June–Sept.*

**Xenia**, t 022 906 1202 (*C; mod*). Slightly cheaper.

**Dreams Island**, on the wooded peninsula with sandy beaches, t 022 906 1224, f 022 906 1268 (*mod–inexp*). Fancy name for a complex of 2 hotels, bungalows, restaurant, bar, barbecue and disco with a not-so-glorified campsite atmosphere, run by the town of Erétria.

**Évia Camping**, at Malakónda, t 022 106 1081. This is the campsite with the most shade and the fanciest facilities to choose between the 2 options.

**Milos Camping**, t 022 106 0420, f 022 106 0360.

**O Ligouris**, opposite the ferryboat landing dock, t 022 906 2352 (*€25–38*). Specializes in seafood, especially lobster kept in a large tank; set menus ranging in price and incl. fresh lobster, *ouzo* and local wine from the barrel.

**Gorgona** and **Diónysos**. These 2 restaurants offer similar traditional Greek fare for a little less.

**Psiteria**, a few yards along from O Ligouris Restaurant. Save yourself a trip to the bank at this excellent little grill restaurant. Try the stuffed *biftéki* washed down with their excellent chilled white wine, and pay pennies for it.

Arméno), its walls incorporating a large piece of sculpted marble from a 2nd-century AD mausoleum. Opposite, the Cultural Centre houses the **Archaeology Museum** (*t 922 492 2471, open Tues–Sun 9–5 daily*), which contains pottery and reliefs from Classical to Roman times.

For most of the Middle Ages, the safest spot on the island for miles around was the huge citadel above Kárystos, which was first built in 1030 by the Byzantines, and then rebuilt by the Franks in the 13th century and called **Castel Rosso** (or **Kókkino Kástro**, or Red Castle) by the Venetians, when they purchased the barony of Kárystos in 1366. Red, that is, for the tint in the stone, and the blood that flowed there. Although the citadel, with its deceptive multi-level layout and labyrinth of entrances, was believed to be impregnable to the extent that only 30 men were needed for its defence, the Turks captured it. Four hundred Turkish families were settled within the citadel's walls and the rulers, unusually, gave local Christians the chop if they refused to convert to Islam. From the castle you can see the ruined arches of the Kamáres, or aqueduct, that once served Castel Rosso.

The road to Castel Rosso passes the village of **Mýli**, a good lunch stop with plenty of tavernas set in a ravine, then continues over a handsome stone bridge crossing another ravine at Graviá. Nearby are the ancient cipollino marble quarries. A 3-hour path from Mýli continues to the mountain refuge and then, through ever more dramatic and barren scenery, to the summit of **Mount Óchi** (4,613ft), crowned by a 'dragon's house', the large blocks of a Pelasgian building of unknown import, perhaps a beacon or peak sanctuary dedicated to Hercules. For walkers who want to break their trek and stay (before beginning the 5–6-hour descent to Kalliánou Beach), the Yiokalíou Foundation operates a shelter (*see* previous 'Where to Stay' box). In **Aetós**, close to Mýli, the church of **Panagía tis Theoskepástis** was abandoned by the villagers when they found they could not afford to cover it; then one night Mount Óchi dropped a massive boulder on top of it, without harming the walls, hence the name 'roofed by God'.

If Kárystos is too crowded for your taste, there's another long sandy beach, 13km away at **Boúros**, where free camping is usually tolerated, although you'll have to bring your own water. Near Boúros, at Nikási, experienced speleologists can visit an enormous cave, once a Palaeolithic shelter, with the little church of **Ag. Triáda** at the entrance. Below the church, an underground river flows from the bowels of Mount Óchi; outside there is cold spring water to drink and a grove of plane trees, perfect for a picnic on a hot day. Another grove of venerable plane trees lent their name to **Platanistós**, to the east, where a few locals rent rooms.

A road with the occasional rough patch continues along to the southeasternmost tip of the island of Évia. This is the notorious, tempest-tossed **Cape Kafiréus** (the Venetian Cabo Doro), where to avenge the death of his son, Palamedes King Nauplios lit fiery beacons to confuse and mislead the Greeks when they were returning from Troy. Cabo Doro still has a few woebegone ruins of a fortress, repaired in the 1260s by Admiral Likarios, the right-hand man of Michael Paleológos, who after the depredations of the Fourth Crusade restored the Byzantine Empire – beginning in Greece at this weatherbeaten fort.

# Up the West Coast

The road north of Kárystos follows the spectacular west coast of Évia, along a corniche at times half a mile over the sea; the cliffs below are a favourite nesting place for hawks and eagles. There are two small resorts: **Marmári**, named after its quarries of green marble, has a long beach and little port, sheltered by islets, and **Néa Stýra** (ΝΕΑ ΣΤΥΡΑ), connected by ferry from Ag. Marína, a lazy holiday base with a long sandy beach and excellent swimming. Near Néa Stýra are more 'dragons' houses', a terrace with three buildings believed to have been Homeric watch-towers (finds in the Kárystos Museum). **Old Stýra** lies under the mammoth Venetian fortress of Larména on Mount Kilósi; you can seek out the ruins of ancient Stýra, near the meagre remains of Mycenaean **Dryopes**, a once important town that did its bit against the Persians at Artemission and Salamis. The cafés in Stýra's shady *plateía* are a pleasant place just to sit.

After Néa Stýra, the road rises to **Almyropótamos**. From here, side roads lead down to a few barely developed beaches around **Panagía**, on the west shore. Further north, just before the crossroads at Lépoura, a dirt road from Kriezá leads in 5km to the well-preserved polygonal walls, gate and 11 square towers of 5th-century BC **Dystos** (not to be confused with the modern village of the same name). Spread over a hill by Évia's largest lake (which in the summer months dries up to form Évia's biggest vegetable garden), you can also trace the foundations of ancient houses set on terraces and streets; the tower was renovated by the Venetians. Fossils of prehistoric beasts have been discovered by the seashore below Kriezá, namely at **Ag. Apóstoli**, which is a sheltered little fishing harbour with a small beach tucked in the rocky cliffs of Évia's east coast.

## Lépoura to Kými

At **Lépoura** the road forks, one branch heading towards Chalkís (*see* below) and the other north to **Kými**. On the Kými road, a turn-off to the right leads down to **Avlonarí**, a fine old village topped by a small fortress and home to the lovely 12th-century Venetian church of Ag. Dimítrios. Further on, **Ochtoniá** is a busy village crammed beneath a Frankish castle, overlooking a set of quiet sandy beaches. After the Ochtoniá turn off, the Lépoura–Kými road plunges and writhes through a lovely and pastoral valley, dotted with Frankish towers to **Oxílithos**, named after its landmark, a volcanic precipice crowned with a church.

**Kými** (ΚΥΜΗ), the main port for Skýros (with occasional connections to the other Sporades), is a low-key resort, lush, surrounded by vineyards and fig orchards, perched on a shelf high above the sea; some say its name is derived from *koumi*, 'I rise' in Hebrew, describing the town's front-row view of the dawn. Many Greeks have summer villas in the wooded hills, including some rather ambitious *nouveau riche* designs. There's a fine **Museum of Popular Art** (*t 022 202 2011; open 9–1 and 5–7*) in a Neoclassical mansion, housing costumes, tools, embroideries and furnishings, and a display on Kými's famous son, Dr George Papanikoláou, who invented and gave the first syllable of his name to the test every woman knows so well. Pretty footpaths as well as the road wind down 4km to the port, **Paralía Kými**, near a beach sheltered by pampas grass. It's not a particularly inspiring place to swim, but there are lovely beaches a short drive away at Platanás and Chiliádou. A fine walk along the road north of Kými leads to the sheer rocky ledge that was the *acropolis* of Homeric Kyme Phyrkontis. The stone of its temples went into the precipitous Byzantine/Frankish castle of Apokledí and the handsome Sótiros Convent (1634) with a beautiful tile roof (*women only admitted*).

## Lépoura to Erétria

Back on the main road from Lépoura to Chalkís the first major village is **Alivéri**, its old red-roofed houses inhabited by coalminers and men working in the nearby power station. Big pylons and a cement factory protect it securely from any tourist pretensions but the tavernas along the waterfront and beach can make for a pleasantly lazy afternoon. Three ancient towns stood nearby: Tamynae above Alivéri, Porthmos by the beach, and **Amárinthos** by Alivéri, now marked by a Venetian tower called Pyrgáki with its door suspended 24ft above ground level. Amárinthos is a lively little resort popular for its fresh seafood (some plucked direct from the offshore fish farms) and there are two impressive Byzantine churches in the environs, **Metamórphosis** and **Kímissi tis Theotókou**, and a Macedonian tomb at **Vlichó**. In the hills above Amárinthos, the pretty village of **Áno Vátheia** has another Byzantine church, called **Zoodóchos Pigí**.

Mainland ferries from Oropóu sail to **Erétria** (ΕΡΕΤΡΙΑ); its alternative name, Néa Psará, recalls the refugees from Psará, who built their new town, complete with fine captains' mansions, right on top of the old. Even so, Erétria is the most complete ancient site on Évia, as well as its biggest holiday resort after Loutrá Edipsoú. Ancient Erétria reached its prime during its rivalry with Chalkís over the lush, vine-clad Lelantine Plain that lay between them. In the end the two cities decided to leave their weapons at home and meet at a midway point, where a general free-for-all punch-up decided all. Erétria lost, then suffered an even worse disaster in 490 BC when the Persians razed the city. But the Erétrians rebuilt, and earned a reputation for their ceramics and school of philosophy, founded in 320 BC by Plato's student, Menedemes. But in 87 BC, when Mithridates of Pontus sacked the city, it was the straw that broke the camel's back; Erétria was never rebuilt. Nowadays Erétria is something of a French colony, with a line of smart, expensive cafés, and it is prone to taking itself a little too seriously as a resort. It is, in fact, the one place in Évia where you might actually get ripped off.

The **museum** at the top of Arkaíou Theátrou St (*t 022 906 2206; open Tues–Sun, 8.30–3*), has a striking Proto-Geometric centaur and figurative ceramics, derived from old Mycenaean designs, from Lefkándi (*see* below). Erétria's finds are displayed by theme, and include fragments of Archaic sculptures from the pediment of the Temple of Apollo Daphnephoros. The adjacent excavations (*same hours; pick up the key for the Macedonian tomb at the museum*) have revealed walls of excellent trapezoidal masonry, an elaborate **West Gate** with a corbelled arch that once extended over the moat, a 4th-century BC peristyle palace (complete with a clay bathtub), a House of Mosaics from the same period, and gymnasium which has some plumbing in situ on its east end. Although the upper stone tiers of seats of the **theatre** were cannibalized to build the modern town, the stage has the world's only survival of a *deus ex machina*: an underground passage from the orchestra that leads to the built-up *skene* behind the stage, where gods could suddenly appear to resolve a tangled plot. A path west of the theatre leads to the tumulus of a Macedonian tomb, its square chamber holding well-preserved painted marble couches, two thrones and a table. Another path from the theatre leads in 15 minutes up to Erétria's walled **acropolis** affording an excellent view of the Lelantine Plain, and, on a clear day, Mount Parnassos on the mainland. Down in the centre of the modern town, you can see the foundations of the Temple of **Apollo Daphnephoros**, 'the laurel-bearer', who enjoyed a fervent following in Évia: the 6th-century Doric temple was built over a 7th-century BC Ionic temple, with wooden columns.

Recent discoveries suggest that **Lefkandí**, 2km below Vassilikó off the Chalkís road, may have been the Erétria listed in the Homeric *Catalogue of Ships*. Inhabited from the Early Helladic period, it is one of the very few places in Greece to have carried on in style in the Dark Ages, maintaining trade links with Athens throughout the Proto-Geometric era. On the cemetery *toumba* (mound), just north of Lefkandí port, a giant roof covers the most astonishing find: a huge building (177 by 33ft) from *c.* 1000 BC, built in mud brick over stone foundations (*no adm, but you can walk around the outside*), surrounded by a wooden colonnade – predating the 'first' peristyle Temple of Hera on Sámos by two centuries, and a complete break with Mycenaean styles. A tomb in the centre was divided into two compartments: one held a man, his bones wrapped in fine cloth in a bronze vase, with his iron sword and spear, and the skeleton of a woman with lavish gold, iron and bronze ornaments. The other had the skeletons of four horses with iron bits. The implications are still being debated: who were these conspicuously wealthy people? The building was filled in with earth shortly after their burial (perhaps to make a hero mound?). The rest of the community prospered, trading gold and ceramics with Athens and Cyprus, until it was mysteriously abandoned in the 8th century BC.

# The Centre: Chalkís and Mount Dirfis

**Chalkís** or Chalkída (ΧΑΛΚΙΣ or ΧΑΛΚΙΔΑ – you'll see both on signs), the bustling industrial rhinoceros-shaped capital of Évia, occupies the narrowest point of the Evripós Strait, only 130ft from the mainland. Its location has been a major source of its prosperity, not least through its potential of seriously blocking ancient sea trade between Athens and the north. Its name comes either from copper (*chalkós*), another early source of wealth, or perhaps from *chalkí*, the Greek name for the murex sea snail prized in antiquity for making royal purple dye. Mentioned in the *Iliad* as the home of the great-hearted Abantes, the city by Archaic times had so many colonies in the north of Greece that it gave its name to the peninsula, Chalkidikí; in Italy it founded the colonies of Messina, Reggio Calabria and Cumae near Naples. By the 7th century BC it had asserted its position over Erétria as the island's dominant city. Modern

# Tourist Information

**Tourism Promotion Committee of Évia:**
10 Charalambous St, t 022 108 2677. Very official sounding but full of useful information.

**Tourist police:** 2 El. Venizélou, in Chalkís, t 022 107 7777.

# Where to Stay and Eat

## Chalkís ✉ 34100

**Lucy**, 10 Voudouris, on the main waterfront, t 022 102 3831, f 022 102 2051 (*A; exp*). A very respectable choice with all the mod cons; it's one of the international Best Western chain.

**John's**, near the Lucy Hotel, at 9 Angéli Goviou, t 022 102 4996 (*B; exp–mod*). Comfortable rooms with air-con and TV, and private parking.

**Paliria**, 2 Leof. Venizélou, t 022 102 8001, f 022 102 1959 (*B; exp–mod*). The best place to stay: a modern building in the centre, overlooking the Evripós Strait, rooms are fitted with air-con, and there's a snack bar and roof garden.

**Kentrikon**, 5 Angéli Goviou, t 022 102 2375 or t 022 102 7260 (*C; inexp*). Traditional style hotel with old-fashioned impeccable service from the very helpful English-speaking owners.

**Stavedo**, 1 Karaóli St, t 022 107 7977 (*€20–30*). Upscale restaurant-cum-bar on the waterfront, that specializes in tasty Mediterranean cuisine, especially their seafood with pasta.

If you don't want to pay above the odds to eat on the promenade, head for **Ermoú St**, 1min away, where a handful of excellent little tavernas (signs in Greek only) serve up the real thing. Try:

**Koutsocheras Taverna**. Serving a wide variety of fish dishes.

**O Thanassis**. A delight, with big simmering pots of meat and weird and wonderful vegetable dishes.

**Kavithas**. Serves particularly good grilled meats.

**Sto Teloneio**, next to the customs building just over the bridge to the right. This is a very popular *ouzerie* with locals and tourists alike.

**Kotsomoura**, located in a quiet spot by the hippodrome. A fine traditional taverna. *Open eves only*.

If you want to explore further afield, there are also 3 excellent tavernas on **Ag. Minás Beach**, 3km from the bridge in Chalkís' mainland extension.

## Steni ✉ 34014

**Dirphys**, in the centre of the village, t 022 805 1217 (*C; mod*). Small and intimate pension. *Open all year*.

**Steni**, t 022 805 1221 (*C; mod*). Similar to the Dirphys Hotel, although slightly higher up the price scale.

**Hellenic Alpine Club Refuge** at Lirí (3,674ft). To book, call t 022 102 5230 or t 028 805 1285 for information.

Chalkís has a glamorous side on the promenade, where you can sit in one of the chic cafés, restaurants or bars looking across at the mainland, and backstreets where charming little houses with wooden balconies still exist, but for how much longer is anybody's guess, as the bulldozers are hard at work demolishing anything that looks vaguely quaint or old. Remember, this is the place where the current changes with the mood of Poseidon.

## Around Chalkís

The city's first bridge was built in 411 BC (the modern sliding drawbridge dates from 1962), but before you cross it, admire the views of Chalkís and Évia from the walls of the Turkish **Castle of the Karababa** ('black father') built in 1686, over Chalkís' ancient *acropolis*. Once over the bridge in Chalkís, take note of the modern metal sculpture donated to the city by its ancient colony Giardini-Naxos in Sicily, and turn left to find a row of smart cafés and *ouzeries* where you can sit and ponder the mystery of the 140ft-wide **Evripós** Channel; the dangerous currents inexplicably change direction every few hours, sometimes only once a day, on rare occasions 14 times day, a phenomenon that so baffled and bothered Aristotle that he threw himself into the waters in frustration. Current thought (sorry for the pun) has it that there are two separate streams in the Evripós, and a host of factors determines which dominates at a given moment.

The main attraction in the new part of Chalkís is the **Archaeology Museum** on Leof. Venizélou (*t 022 107 6131 or 022 102 5131; open Tues–Sun 8.30–3*), housing some of the finest items discovered in Erétria, including a headless statue of Athena, the Archaic marble pediment from the Temple of Apollo Daphnephoros showing the rape of Antiope by Theseus, and a bas-relief of Diónysos. Not far from the Archaeology Museum, there is a pretty 16th-century mosque with a marble fountain, marking the entrance to the **Kástro**, the old Turkish quarter. Not far from the mosque is **Ag. Paraskeví**, a Byzantine basilica converted in the 13th century by Crusaders into a Gothic cathedral. This conversion resulted in the curious architectural collage inside, with plenty of 14th-century inscriptions and coats-of-arms. Every year, in late July, a large market for the feast of Ag. Paraskeví enlivens Chalkís for 10 days, attracting keen bargain hunters from all over Évia and the mainland, while the lovelorn take the opportunity to beseech the icon of the saint for their hearts' desire; in the old days they would press a coin against the picture, and if it stuck there, it meant their love would not go unrequited.

Also in Kástro, note the arcaded **Turkish aqueduct** that brought water to the city from Mount Dírfis. There's a delightful little **Museum of Folk Art** on Skalkóta Street (*t 022 102 1817; open Wed–Sun, 10–1*), containing traditional festival costumes, religious icons, the interior of a traditional Greek home, a printing press from the 1920s, and an intimate portrayal of village life from long ago. Chalkís' Romaniot Jewish population goes back an estimated 2,500 years; the **synagogue** at 27 Kótsou (*open after 6pm*) was built in the mid-19th century, but re-uses a number of marble fragments from the original, which burned down. In the Jewish quarter, off Avantón Street, is a marble bust of Mórdechai Frízis of Chalkís, who was the first Greek officer killed in the Second World War.

## Beaches North of Chalkís, Mount Dírfis and Stení

Buses from Chalkís run to the busy, shingly beaches to the north, all enjoying views across to the mainland: **Néa Artáki**, **Politiká Paralía**, and, last and nicest of all, tucked under the cliffs, **Dáfni**, a green oasis like all other places in Greece that share the name. Just inland are two of Évia's most distinctive whitewashed villages, **Politiká** with a late Byzantine church, castle and cosy little square and **Psachná**, a little market town with another castle. Boats leave Chalkís daily for the islet of **Tonnoíro**, with a hotel and beach; a larger boat, the *Eviokos*, makes 'mini-cruises' to Límni, Edipsós, and other places to swim and eat.

The real beauty spot within easy striking distance (25km) of Chalkís is **Mount Dírfis**, Évia's highest peak at 5,725ft. Wrapped in chestnut and pine forests, it supports a surprising quantity of alpine flora. The Greek Mountaineering Federation runs a shelter here, at Liri (3,674ft). You can take a bus as far as **Stení** (ΣΤΕΝΗ), a delightful village of wooden houses, chalets and waterfalls that makes a refreshing change in the hot summer months. From Stení there's a well-marked if rather strenuous path to the summit of Mount Dirfis, and a magnificently scenic road that goes over the pass, towards Strópones; it continues in a rough, bumpy way down to the east coast and the splendid, pebble beach of **Chiliadoú**, which is endowed with summer tavernas and places to camp.

## Northern Évia

Parts of the northern half of Évia are so lush and green that you could be forgiven for thinking you were in Austria, although here the coast has long stretches of beaches lined with whitewashed houses and rose-filled gardens. Unfortunately, it has suffered more than its share of forest fires in recent years.

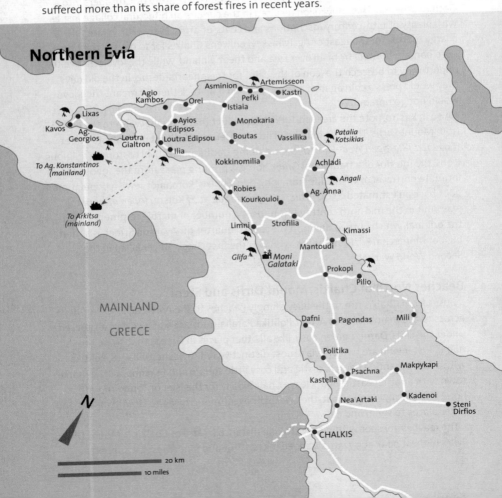

### Northern Évia

# Tourist Information

## Edipsós

**EOT, Hydro/Physiotherapy Centre,**
3 Okeanídon, **t** 022 602 3500; *open summer months only*. A mine of local information and advice, especially on the excellent walking trails.
**Tourist police: t** 022 602 2456.
**Bus station: t** 022 602 2250. For timetable and destination information for the northern half of the island.

# Where to Stay and Eat

## Prokópi ✉ 34004

**The Candili Centre,** just outside the village, *stay@candili.gr, www.candili.co.uk* (*exp*). Pure luxury and inspiration are guaranteed at the handsome estate of the Noel-Baker family. This is an idyllic location for a wide range of fully inclusive creative courses, incl. painting, ceramics and music. Everyone is catered for, from beginners to more experienced amateur artists. Lots of attention is also given to creative culinary delights in the evening, often served on the beautiful patio. There's a swimming pool, a huge playground and extensive gardens to keep the children entertained (substantial family suites are available). For partners not partaking of artistic pursuits, there are many good walking trails to be explored in the area and wonderful views to be savoured. Mantoudi town isn't far away, providing plenty of urban distractions and a bit of low-key nightlife.

## Péfki ✉ 34200

**Amaryllis,** right on the waterfront, **t** 022 604 1222 (*C; mod*). A pleasant, comfortable hotel with very friendly owners who are more than happy to impart useful tips and interesting stories about their island. *Open July–Sept.*
**Galini,** situated out towards the east end of the long waterfront, **t** 022 604 1208, **f** 022 604 1650 (*C; mod*). Well-kept rooms kitted out with cheery furniture; there are lovely sea-views from many of the rooms. The

English-speaking owners, Costas and Anna Maria, also own the self-service restaurant.
**Camping Péfki, t** 022 604 1161. A decent campsite with good facilities and plenty of shade. There are very strict rules regarding the lighting of camp fires, as a result of the recent devastation by forest fires. There are also some bungalows available near the campsite, for those requiring a little more comfort.
**Cavo d'Oro.** A very popular taverna in town, where Greeks and foreigners together can enjoy the delicious food and the lovely views.
**Kati Allo.** It's essential to get here early if you want to beat the crowds to a table to enjoy their culinary delights, especially those from the grill.
**Grigri.** This is the place in town for *ouzo* and *mezédes.*

## Oréi ✉ 34012

**Byzantium, t** 022 607 1600 (*C; mod*). Central and reasonable.
**Evia, t** 022 607 1263 (*C; mod*). A decent second option in the centre of town if the others are fully booked.
**Leda,** on the pebble beach, **t** 022 607 1180 (*C; mod*). Modern studios within easy walking distance of a generous stretch of sand.
**Porto Kairis,** right on the pebble beach, **t** 022 607 1055, **f** 022 605 2888 (*C; mod*). A great location for this hotel with its little dipping pool.
**Akroyalis,** just west of Oréi at Néos Pírgos, **t** 022 607 1375 (*D; mod–inexp*). Comfortable option, and very convenient for a dash down to the beach to fit in that early morning swim.

## Loutrá Edipsoú ✉ 34300

There is no shortage of accommodation in Loutrá Edipsoú, although, as with many other Greek islands, it often proves impossible to find a room to rent in the summer months without booking far in advance. As for the local eateries and nightlife, live Greek music attracts the crowds to various venues – just follow the noise.

**Lokris Tours**, 2 Ermóu St, **t** 022 606 9044, **f** 022 606 0300, *root@nikolaos.hlk.forthnet.gr*. A very good source of help with all types of accommodation in the surrounding towns and villages.

**Thermae Sylla Spa-Wellness Hotel**, on the waterfront, **t** 022 606 0100, **f** 022 602 2055, *www.thermaesylla.gr* (*L; lux*). Fabulously extravagant, palatial spa hotel, equipped with every type of hydrotherapy treatment for every type of ailment. In addition to this, it has extremely well-appointed rooms and a grand restaurant serving delicious (not to mention healthy) meals that aren't extortionate in price but wonderful in presentation.

**Aegli**, right on the waterfront, **t** 022 602 2216, **f** 022 602 2991 (*A; exp*). Run efficiently by the delightful Alkis, and perfect for simply wallowing in the faded spa atmosphere. Equipped with mini spas in the basement and in high season, clients have to queue from 5am to get their treatment. There's also a good, well established restaurant serving healthy nutritious dishes. *Open May–Oct.*

**Avra**, next door to the Aegli Hotel, **t** 022 602 2226, **f** 022 602 3260 (*A; exp–mod*). The same relaxing atmosphere and range of hydrotherapy treatment facilities as the Aegli, but at a somewhat more affordable price.

**Giórgos**, opposite the town bus station, **t** 022 602 3285 (*D; inexp*). Small hotel, that's conveniently central and even lighter on the pocket.

**Folia Taverna**, in the marketplace, away from the busy waterfront. Beautifully laid out under a canopy of spiralling vines, this is probably the best taverna in Loutrá Edipsoú. To get there, take the street right beside the Aegli Hotel all the way to the end and then up the alley into the market square; Folia is the second taverna you come to, sitting pretty at the top of some inauspicious-looking steps.

**Tsiatsou**, at the spa end of the waterfront. Tacky-looking spot where you can round things off with honey-drenched *loukoumádes*, a scrumptious bit of Greek gluttony.

**Balalas**, in Loutrá's suburb of Ag. Nikólaos. Come here if you are in a fishy mood; it can't be beaten.

**O Glaros**, also in Ag. Nikólaos. Another moderately priced fish taverna considered to be the local favourites. It's best to arrive early to secure a table.

## Ag. Geórgios ✉ 34300

**Alexandros**, right in the middle of the waterfront, **t** 022 603 3208 (*B; mod*). Attractive hotel with generous sea and mountain views from most of the rooms. *Open June–Sept.*

**Kineon**, **t** 022 603 5066, **f** 022 603 3066 (*C; mod*). The second place to try if Alexandros is fully booked. A decent option in its own right, sharing the wonderful views. *Open April–Oct.*

## Límni ✉ 34005

Accommodation here is extremely limited so it's advisable to book ahead, especially in high season.

**Límni**, at the quiet south end of the bay, **t/f** 022 703 1316 (*C; mod–inexp*). Basic rooms, some with balconies looking out onto the water.

**Plaza**, **t** 022 703 1235 (*C; mod–inexp*). Another basic hotel, however, it has more character and is more centrally located than the Límni Hotel.

**Camping Roviés**, in Roviés, **t/f** 022 701 1120. This is an immaculate campsite right by the sea, with all the necessary amenities. *Open all year.*

**Avra Taverna.** This is one of the most reasonably priced of Límni's many attractive waterfront tavernas; it is especially recommended for its variety of fresh seafood dishes and well-prepared Greek favourites like moussaka.

**O Platanos**, next door to Avra, **t** 022 703 1686. Offering excellent grilled fish and meat dishes laid out under the huge reassuring limbs of a plane tree. A very good *al fresco* dining option.

**To Katounia**, 3km south on the road past the Límni Hotel. This is considered to be the best taverna in the locality for grilled fish and meat.

# Prokópi and Around

North of Psachná, the road to Pagóndas rises higher and higher into the mountains, permeated with the wonderfully fresh scent of deep green pine forests; beehives everywhere attest to the potency of the local herbs and wildflowers, and the honey offered in roadside stands comes close to nectar. Tavernas with outdoor terraces take advantage of the most breathtaking panoramic views. **Pagóndas** (35km from Chalkís) is an example of a typical mountain settlement; further north, a striking castle piled on a nearly inaccessible precipice signals **Prokópi** (Προκήπι), a hospitable village set near the end of the magnificent narrow, wooded ravines of the Kleisoúra Valley, where the road offers fine views over the Sporades. This is prime picnicking territory, and, if extra thrills are called for, wobble over the ravines on the rickety wooden suspension bridges.

Sometimes referred to by its Turkish name of Ahmet Aga, Prokópi is populated by Greeks from the fantastical Cappadocian town of Ürgüp, who came over here in the 1923 population exchange. They brought with them their holy relics, the bones of St John the Russian, a soldier in the Tsar's army who was captured by the Turks and sold as a slave in Ürgüp (1730), then cannonized by the Russian Orthodox Church (in 1962); St John attracts his fair share of pilgrims each year at the church dedicated to him, Ag. Ioánnes tou Rossou.

In the centre of Prokópi, the handsome estate of the Noel-Baker family, where the Turkish Pasha's tulip and rose gardens once bloomed, is now home to the Candili Centre, a lovely place to stay and take an art course (*www.candili.co.uk*, *see* the 'Where to Stay' box). The village was built around the estate, bought by Edward Noel, who was a relative of Byron, in 1832. Edward Noel set up the North Euboean Foundation with the aim of providing decent health care and education for Greek refugees during the Greek War of Independence.

From Prokópi, a decent paved road to the east leads steeply down, through thick forests of plane trees, pines and firs dotted with many beehives, to **Pílio**, set in beautiful rocky mountain scenery. There are plenty of authentic tavernas and rooms to rent in the vicinity, and all around, lovely old traditional houses with goats in the garden alternating with the usual Greek concrete monstrosities. The sandy bay below looks across to Skópelos and still has only one taverna, but if you want somewhere even less civilized, brave the rough road east along the coast to the pebbly beach beyond **Vlachiá**.

Continuing north through **Mantóudi**, with its very pretty central square and great *ouzerie*, the road is bordered by countless fields of cotton and corn. At **Strofiliá** the road forks west to Límni (*see* below) and then around to Loutrá Edipsoú, while the main road continues to Ag. Ánna. This is a traditional village located above two very long and attractive beaches, **Paralía Ag. Ánna** (*with a good campsite*, *t 022 706 1550*) and **Angáli**, which is just to the north. **Vassiliká**, further up the coast, looks directly across to emerald Skiáthos. The sign nearby for **Psarodóuli** points the way to a long, sandy beach.

## Around the Top of Évia

The north coast of Évia, dotted with many fine beaches, looks across to the Pélion Peninsula and the mainland; Greek families settle in here for the entire summer, which makes finding accommodation for only one or two days problematic. The village of **Artemísseon** witnessed the first but indecisive naval battle between the Greeks and the Persians in 480 BC. Near the shore are the ruins of the vast Temple of Artemis Proseoa, although the greatest treasure in the area was a shipwreck of ancient bronzes, only discovered in 1928, the source of the National Archaeology Museum's splendid Poseidon (or Zeus) and the Cape Artemísseon Jockey. Continuing east of Artemísseon, you'll arrive in **Péfki**, an extensive sand and pebble beach and growing holiday resort, especially popular with Hungarian and Slovak tourists. It boasts particularly splendid views across to the Pelion Peninsula and Skiáthos, which you can reach by hydrofoil.

Cattle belonging to the goddess Hera grazed at **Istiaía** (ΙΣΤΙΑΙΑ), the largest village on the north coast, described by Homer as 'rich in vines'. It was founded by Thessalians who thumbed their noses at Athens so often that Pericles captured the town and booted out the inhabitants, and then repopulated it with Athenians. Although few towns are more attractively situated than Istiaía, set in an amphitheatre of rolling hills, the Athenian colonists didn't find it to their liking, preferring to found nearby Oréi instead; when they in turn were driven out by the Spartans in the Peloponnesian War, the Istianians finally returned. The whole population of Évia contributed to the construction of Istiaía's Venetian **Kástro**, built right in the centre of town; a second medieval fortress, to defend the narrow strait, was built over the ancient *acropolis*.

The Athenians may have been right: **Oréi** (ΩΡΕΟΙ) is still a lovely place to while away a few lazy hours. It is nationally renowned for its excellent *ouzeries* which line the pleasant waterfront under the feathery tamarisk trees, and its little sandy town beach has showers and some welcome shade. The grid-based back streets don't yield much however, but the central square is guarded by a Hellenistic marble bull found offshore in 1962, which in turn is protected by a rather unappealingly salt-sprayed display case. These days the treat offshore is the islet of **Argirónisos**, abandoned at the turn of the 20th century, and now the only private island in Greece taking paying guests. West of Oréi, Néos Pírgos is an attractive little resort with a couple of hotels and beach tavernas, and further on, the beach at **Agiokambos** has a row of good seafood tavernas.

## Loutrá Edipsóu to Límni

Magnificently set in a giant wooded bay, **Loutrá Edipsóu** (ΛΟΥΤΡΑ ΑΙΔΗΨΟΥ), a once glamorous Neoclassical spa town, is still invaded every August and September, especially by weary Greek matrons seeking instant rejuvenation in the fountains of youth. There are 80 hot sulphurous springs here squirting out of the ground at up to 160°F; some cascade spectacularly from cliffs into the sea down below, where you can stand as in a hot shower. Other springs tumble over a spread of rocks filling little pools as they go, where you can laze as in a bath.

Since antiquity these spring waters have treated a whole variety of medical complaints, including rheumatism, arthritis, gallstones, and even bouts of depression. The ancients were convinced that Loutrá's source was connected under the sea with the hot springs at Thermopylae; Aristotle praised the waters here, whilst the gouty Sulla, Augustus and Hadrian called in for lengthy soaks in the now ruined Roman baths. In May 1998, EOT's spa complex was upstaged by the opening of the luxuriant Thermae Sylla Spa-Wellness Complex (*see* the 'Where to Stay' box), equipped with two huge indoor and outdoor pools, and all the latest knowledge and equipment in water treatments and hydrotherapies. Tasteful and low-key, Loutrá Edipsoú certainly cannot claim to be, but it does have its own quirky spa charm mixed in with the night-time clamour of live Greek music emanating from packed bars and noisy Athenians promenading the wide leafy avenues until early morning. It also has a long, lovely beach, and the possibility of day excursions to the nearby islands of Skiáthos, Alónissos and Skópelos.

Follow the road around the wide bay to Évia's westernmost promontory and a second, more modest spa, **Loutrá Giáltron**, with its frescoed church and beach crowded with boats, made picturesque by an old windmill. However, there are more worthy beaches to be found further west. Club Med (**t** *022 603 3281*) has had to import lorryloads of sand to create its private hideaway at **Gregolímano**, but the immense stretch of soft sand and pebbles at Kavos is fortunately open to everyone and anyone. Watch out for noticeboards announcing the ferociously fast-changing tides, which, though fascinating to look at, can make for dangerous swimming around this headland. Nearby, **Ag. Geórgios** is a laid-back fishing village with some rooms to rent; its eponymous church makes an attractive focus for its cheery waterfront. There's a stalactite cave to explore at Profítis Ilías, and there are plenty of places to set up a picnic and snooze for a couple of hours under the plane trees, especially at a spot called Paleóchori.

The coastal road south of Loutrá passes the seaside villages and beaches of **Ília** and **Robiés**, immersed in olive groves, and there are fine 17th-century frescoes in the church of **David tou Géronta**, 8km away (*check around for the key before setting out*). **Límni** (ΛΙΜΝΗ), 15km south of Robiés, is many an old hand's favourite place on all Évia: a friendly old whitewashed fishing village around a sleepy bay with mediocre beaches and a slowly growing resort community under the pines. The sailing is good, and the waterfront is just right for lazing with the village cats and watching the world go by. According to myth, Zeus brought Hera to Límni (then called Elymnion) during their honeymoon. The temple that once marked the spot keeled over in an earthquake, but in its place Límni offers a pretty paleo-Christian mosaic floor in the chapel of **Zoodóchos Pigí**.

An 8km track from Límni leads south to **Moní Galatáki**, a Byzantine monastery (now a convent) in a beautiful, peaceful setting built over a temple dedicated to Poseidon.

The church has fascinating 16th-century frescoes, including portraits of the two sea captains who became the monastery's great patrons after they were shipwrecked nearby and saved by divine intervention. The road to Galatáki is a dead end but is doubly worth the detour since along that stretch of coast is a strip of sand and pebble beaches known as **Glífa** and among Evia's best.

# Language

Greek holds a special place as the oldest spoken language in Europe, going back at least 4,000 years. From the ancient language, Modern Greek, or Romaíka, developed into two forms: the purist or *katharévousa*, literally translated as 'clean language', and the popular, or Demotic *demotikí*, the language of the people. However, while the purist is consciously Classical, the popular is as close to its ancient origins as say, Chaucerian English is to modern English.

These days few purist words are spoken but you will see the old *katharévousa* on shop signs and official forms. Even though the bakery is called the *foúrnos* the sign over the door will read ΑΡΤΟΠΟΛΕΙΟΝ, bread-seller, while the general store will be the ΠΑΝΤΟΠΟΛΕΙΟΝ, seller of all. You'll still see the pure form on wine labels as well. At the end of the 18th century, in the wakening swell of national pride, writers felt the common language wasn't good enough; archaic forms were brought back and foreign ones replaced. Upon independence, this somewhat stilted, artificial construction called *katharévousa* became the official language of books, documents and even newspapers.

The more vigorous and natural Demotic soon began to creep back; in 1901 Athens was shaken by riots and the government fell when the New Testament appeared in *demotikí*; in 1903 several students were killed in a fight with the police during a *demotikí* performance of Aeschylus. When the fury subsided, it looked as if the Demotic would win out by popular demand until the Papadópoulos government (1967–74) made it part of its puritan 'moral cleansing' of Greece to revive the purist *katharévousa*. It was the only language allowed in secondary schools and everything from textbooks to matchbook covers had to be written in the pure form.

The great language debate was eventually settled in 1978 when Demotic was made the official tongue.

Greeks travel so far and wide that even in the most remote places there's usually someone who speaks English, more likely than not with an American, Australian or even South African drawl. On the other hand, learning a bit of Greek can make your travels much more enjoyable.

Usually spoken with great velocity, Greek isn't a particularly easy language to pick up by ear. However, even if you have no great desire to learn Greek, it is very helpful to know at least the alphabet – so that you can find your way around – and a few basic words and phrases.

## Greekspeak

Sign language is an essential part of Greek life and it helps to know what it all means. Greekspeak for 'no' is usually a click of the tongue, accompanied by raised eyebrows and a tilt of the head backwards. It could be all three or a permutation. 'Yes' is usually indicated by a forward nod, head tilted to the side. If someone doesn't hear you or understand you properly they will often shake their heads from side to side quizzically and say 'Oríste?' Hands whirl like windmills in conversations and beware the emphatic open hand brought sharply down in anger.

A circular movement of the right hand usually implies something very good or in great quantities. Greek people also use exclamations which sound quite odd but actually mean a lot, like *po, po, po*! an expression of disapproval and derision; *brávo* comes in handy for praise while *ópa*! is useful for *whoópa*! look out! or watch it!; *sigá sigá* means slowly, slowly; *éla*!, come or get on with you; *kíta*! look.

# The Greek Alphabet

| Pronunciation | | | English Equivalent |
|---|---|---|---|
| A | α | álfa | short 'a' as in 'father' |
| B | β | víta | v |
| Γ | γ | gámma | guttural g or y sound |
| Δ | δ | délta | always a hard th as in 'though' |
| E | ε | épsilon | short 'e' as in 'bet' |
| Z | ζ | zíta | z |
| H | η | íta | long 'e' as in 'bee' |
| Θ | θ | thíta | soft th as in 'thin' |
| I | ι | yóta | long 'e' as in 'bee'; sometimes like 'y' in 'yet' |
| K | κ | káppa | k |
| Λ | λ | lámtha | l |
| M | μ | mi | m |
| N | ν | ni | n |
| Ξ | ξ | ksi | 'x' as in 'ox' |
| O | ο | ómicron | 'o' as in 'cot' |
| Π | π | pi | p |
| P | ρ | ro | r |
| Σ | σ | sígma | s |
| T | τ | taf | t |
| Υ | υ | ipsilon | long 'e' as in 'bee' |
| Φ | φ | fi | f |
| X | χ | chi | ch as in 'loch' |
| Ψ | ψ | psi | ps as in 'stops' |
| Ω | ω | oméga | 'o' as in 'cot' |

## Diphthongs and Consonant Combinations

| | | English Equivalent |
|---|---|---|
| AI | αι | short 'e' as in 'bet' |
| EI | ει, OI οι | 'i' as in 'machine' |
| OΥ | ου | oo as in 'too' |
| AΥ | αυ | av or af |
| EΥ | ευ | ev or ef |
| HΥ | ηυ | iv or if |
| ΓΓ | γγ | ng as in 'angry' |
| ΓΚ | γκ | hard 'g'; ng within word |
| NT | ντ | 'd'; nd within word |
| MΠ | μπ | 'b'; mp within word |

# Useful Phrases

| | | |
|---|---|---|
| Yes | né/málista (formal) | Ναί/Μάλιστα |
| No | óchi | Οχι |
| I don't know | then kséro | Δέν ξέρω |
| I don't understand... (Greek) | then katalavéno... (ellinaká) | Δέν καταλαβαίνω... (Ελληνικά) |
| Does someone speak English? | milái kanis angliká? | Μιλάει κανείς αγγλικά? |
| Go away | fíyete | Φύγετε |
| Help! | voíthia! | Βοήθεια! |
| My friend | o fílos moo (m) | Ο φίλος μου |
| | ee fíli moo (f) | Η φίλη μου |
| Please | parakaló | Παρακαλώ |
| Thank you (very much) | evcharistó (pára polí) | Ευχαριστώ (πάρα πολύ) |
| You're welcome | parakaló | Παρακαλώ |
| It doesn't matter | thén pirázi | Δεν πειράζει |
| OK, alright | endaxi | Εντάξει |
| Of course | vevéos | Βεβαίως |
| Excuse me, ( as in 'sorry') | signómi | Συγγνώμη |
| Pardon? Or, from waiters, what do you want? | oríste? | Ορίστε? |
| Be careful! | proséchete! | Προσέχετε! |
| What is your name? | pos sas léne? (pl & formal) | Πώς σάς λένε? |
| | pos se léne? (singular) | Πώς σέ λένε? |
| How are you? | ti kánete? (formal/pl) | Τί κάνεται? |
| | ti kanis? (singular) | Τί κάνεις? |
| Hello | yásas, hérete (formal/pl) | Γειάσας, Χέρεται |
| | yásou (singular) | Γειάσου |
| Goodbye | yásas, (formal/pl), andío | Γειάσας, Αντίο |
| | yásou | Γειάσου |

| | | |
|---|---|---|
| Good morning | kaliméra | Καλημέρα |
| Good evening/good night | kalispéra/kaliníchta | Καλησπέρα/Καληνύχτα |
| What is that? | ti íne aftó? | Τι είναι αυτό; |
| What? | ti? | Τί; |
| Who? | piós? (m), piá? (f) | Ποιός; Ποιά; |
| Where? | poo? | Πού |
| When? | póte? | Πότε; |
| Why? | yiatí? | Γιατί; |
| How? | pos? | Πώς; |
| I am/You are/He, she, it is | íme/íse/íne | Είμαι/Είσαι/Είναι |
| We are/You are/They are | ímaste/isaste/íne | Είμαστε/Είσαστε/Είναι |
| I am lost | échasa to thrómo | Έχασα το δρόμο |
| I am hungry/I am thirsty | pinó/thipsó | Πεινώ/Διψώ |
| I am tired/ill | íme kourasménos/árostos | Είμαι κουρασμένος/άρρωστος |
| I am poor | íme ftochós | Είμαι φτωχός |
| I love you | s'agapó | Σ'αγαπώ |
| Good/bad/so-so | kaló/kakó/étsi ki étsi | καλό/κακό/έτσι κι έτσι |
| Fast/big/small | grígora/megálo/mikró | γρήγορα/μεγάλο/μικρό |
| Hot/cold | zestó/crío | ζεστό/κρύο |
| Nothing | típota | Τίποτα |

## Shops, Services, Sightseeing

| | | |
|---|---|---|
| I would like... | tha íthela... | Θα ήθελα... |
| Where is...? | poo íne...? | Πού είναι...; |
| How much is it? | póso káni? | Πόσο κάνει; |
| bakery | foúrnos/artopoleion | φούρνος/Αρτοπωλείον |
| bank | trápeza | τράπεζα |
| beach | paralía | παραλία |
| church | eklisía | εκκλησία |
| cinema | kinimatográfos | κινηματογράφος |
| hospital | nosokomío | νοσοκομείο |
| hotel | xenodochío | ξενοδοχείο |
| hot water | zestó neró | ζεστό νερό |
| kiosk | períptero | περίπτερο |
| money | leftá | λεφτά |
| museum | moosío | μουσείο |
| newspaper (foreign) | efimerítha (xéni) | εφημερίδα (ξένη) |
| pharmacy | farmakío | φαρμακείο |
| police station | astinomía | αστυνομία |
| policeman | astifílakas | αστυνομικός |
| post office | tachithromío | ταχυδρομείο |
| plug, electrical | príza | πρίζα |
| plug, bath | tápa | τάπα |
| restaurant | estiatório | εστιατόριο |
| sea | thálassa | θάλασσα |
| shower | doush | ντους |
| student | fititís | μαθητής, φοιτητής |
| telephone office | Oté | ΟΤΕ |
| theatre | théatro | θέατρο |
| toilet | tooaléta | τουαλέτα |

# Time

| | | |
|---|---|---|
| What time is it? | *ti óra íne?* | Τί ώρα είναι |
| month/week/day | *mína/evthomáda/méra* | μήνα/εβδομάδα/μέρα |
| morning/afternoon/evening | *proí/apóyevma/vráthi* | πρωί/απόγευμα/βράδυ |
| yesterday/today/tomorrow | *chthés/símera/ávrio* | χθές/σήμερα/αύριο |
| now/later | *tóra/metá* | τώρα/μετά |
| it is early/late | *íne norís/argá* | είναι νωρίς/αργά |

# Travel Directions

| | | |
|---|---|---|
| I want to go to ... | *thélo na páo ston (m), sti n (f)...* | Θέλω να πάω στον, στην... |
| How can I get to...? | *pós boró na páo ston (m), stin (f)...?* | Πως μπορώ να πάω στον, στην...? |
| Where is...? | *poo íne ...?* | Πού είναι...? |
| How far is it? | *póso makriá íne?* | Πόσο μακριά είναι |
| When will the... come? | *póte tha érthi to (n), ee (f), o (m)...?* | Πότε θα έρθει το, η, ο...? |
| When will the... leave? | *póte tha fíyi to (n), ee (f), o (m)...?* | Πότε θα φύγει το, η, ο...? |
| From where do I catch...? | *apó poo pérno...?* | Από πού πέρνω...? |
| How long does the trip take? | *póso keró pérni to taxíthi?* | Πόσο καιρό παίρνει το ταξίδι? |
| Please show me | *parakaló thíkste moo* | Παρακαλώ δείξτε μου |
| the (nearest) town | *to horió (to pió kondinó)* | Το χωριό (το πιό κοντινό) |
| here/there/near/far | *ethó/ekí/kondá/makriá* | εδώ/εκεί/κοντά/μακριά |
| left/right | *aristerá/thexiá* | αριστερά/δεξιά |
| north/south/east/west | *vória/nótia/anatoliká/thitiká* | βόρεια/νότια/ανατολικά/δ |

# Driving

| | | |
|---|---|---|
| Where can I rent ...? | *poo boró na nikiáso ...?* | Πού μποπώ νά? νοικιάσω ...? |
| a car | *éna aftokinito* | ένα αυτοκινητο |
| a motorbike | *éna michanáki* | ένα μηχανάκι |
| a bicycle | *éna pothílato* | ένα ποδήλατο |
| Where can I buy petrol? | *poo boró n'agorásso venzíni?* | Πού μπορώ ν΄αγοράσω βενζίνη? |
| Where is a garage? | *poo íne éna garáz?* | Που είναι ένα γκαράζ? |
| a mechanic | *énas mihanikós* | ένας μηχανικός |
| a map | *énas chártis* | ένας χάρτης |
| Where is the road to...? | *poo íne o thrómos yiá...?* | Που είναι ο δρόμος για...? |
| Where does this road lead? | *poo pái aftós o thrómos?* | Που πάει αυτός ο δρόμος? |
| Is the road good? | *íne kalós o thrómos?* | Είναι καλός ο δρόμος? |
| EXIT | *éxothos (th as in 'the')* | ΕΞΟΔΟΣ |
| ENTRANCE | *ísothos (th as in 'the')* | ΕΙΣΟΔΟΣ |
| DANGER | *kínthinos (th as in 'the')* | ΚΙΝΔΥΝΟΣ |
| SLOW | *argá* | ΑΡΓΑ |
| NO PARKING | *apagorévete ee státhmevsis* | ΑΠΑΓΟΡΕΥΕΤΑΙ Η ΣΤΑΘΜΕΥΣΙΣ |
| KEEP OUT | *apagorévete ee ísothos* | ΑΠΑΓΟΡΕΥΕΤΑΙ Η ΕΙΣΟΔΟΣ |

# Numbers

| one | énas (m), mía (f), éna (n) | ένας, μία, ένα |
|---|---|---|
| two | thío | δύο |
| three | tris (m, f), tría (n) | τρείς, τρία |
| four | téseris (m, f), téssera (n) | τέσσερεις, τέσσερα |
| five | pénde | πέντε |
| six | éxi | έξι |
| seven/eight/nine/ten | eptá/októ/ennéa/théka | επτά/οκτώ/εννέα/δέκα |
| eleven/twelve/thirteen | éntheka/thótheka/thekatría | έντεκα/δώδεκα/δεκατρία |
| twenty | íkosi | είκοσι |
| twenty-one | íkosi éna (m, n) mía (f) | είκοσι ένα, μία |
| thirty/forty/fifty/sixty | triánda/saránda/peninda/exínda | τριάντα/σαράντα/πενήντα/εξήντα |
| seventy/eighty/ninety | evthomínda/ogthónda/enenínda | εβδομήντα/ογδόντα/ενενήντα |
| one hundred | ekató | εκατό |
| one thousand | chília | χίλια |

# Months/Days

| January | Ianooários | Ιανουάριος |
|---|---|---|
| February | Fevrooários | Φεβρουάριος |
| March | Mártios | Μάρτιος |
| April | Aprílios | Απρίλιος |
| May | Máios | Μάιος |
| June | Ioónios | Ιούνιος |
| July | Ioólios | Ιούλιος |
| August | Avgoostos | Αύγουστος |
| September | Septémvrios | Σεπτέμβριος |
| October | Októvrios | Οκτώβριος |
| November | Noémvrios | Νοέμβριος |
| December | Thekémvrios | Δεκέμβριος |
| Sunday | Kiriakí | Κυριακή |
| Monday | Theftéra | Δευτέρα |
| Tuesday | Tríti | Τρίτη |
| Wednesday | Tetárti | Τετάρτη |
| Thursday | Pémpti | Πέμπτη |
| Friday | Paraskeví | Παρασκευή |
| Saturday | Sávato | Σάββατο |

# Transport

| the airport/aeroplane | to arothrómio/aropláno | το αεροδρόμιο/αεροπλάνο |
|---|---|---|
| the bus station | ee stási too leoforíou | η στάση του λεωφορείου |
| the railway station/the train | o stathmós too trénou/to tréno | ο σταθμός του τρένου/το τρένο |
| the port/port authority | to limáni/limenarchío | το λιμάνι/λιμεναρχείο |
| the ship | to plío, to karávi | το πλοίο, το καράβι |
| the steamship | to vapóri | το βαπόρι |
| the car | to aftokínito | το αυτοκίνητο |
| a ticket | éna isitírio | ένα εισιτήριο |

# Glossary

*acropolis*: fortified height, usually the site of a city's chief temples

*agíos, agía, agíi*: saint or saints, or holy abbreviated **Ag**.

*agora*: market and public area in a city centre

*amphora*: tall jar for wine or oil, designed to be shipped (the conical end would be embedded in sand

*áno/apáno*: upper

*caique*: a small wooden boat, pronounced '*kaEEki*', now mostly used for tourist excursions

*cella*: innermost holy room of a temple

*choklakía*: black and white pebble mosaic (or *hokalaía*)

*chóra* :simply, 'place'; often what islanders call their 'capital' town, although it usually also has the same name as the island itself

*chorió*: village

*dimarchíon*: town hall

**EOT**: Greek National Tourist Office

*epachía*: Orthodox diocese; also a political county

*exonarthex*: outer porch of a church

*heroön*: a shrine to a hero or demigod, often built over the tomb

*iconostasis*: in an Orthodox church, the decorated screen between the nave and altar

*kalderími*: stone-paved pathways

*kástro*: castle or fort

*katholikón*: monastery chapel

*káto*: lower

*kore*: Archaic statue of a maiden

*kouros*: Archaic statue of a naked youth

*larnax*: a Minoan clay sarcophagus resembling a bathtub

*limáni*: port

*limenarchíon*: port authority

*loútra*: hot spring, spa

*megaron*: Mycenaean palace

*metope*: sculpted panel on a frieze

*meltémi*: north wind off the Russian steppes that plagues the Aegean in the summer

*moní*: monastery or convent

*monopáti*: footpath

*narthex*: entrance porch of a church

*néa*: new

*nisí/nisiá*: island/islands

*nomós*: Greek province

**OTE**: Greek national telephone company

*paleó*: old

*panagía*: Virgin Mary

*panegýri*: Saint's feast day

*pantocrátor*: the 'Almighty' – a figure of the triumphant Christ in Byzantine domes

*paralía*: waterfront or beach

*períptero*: street kiosk selling just about everything

*pírgos*: tower, or residential mansion

*píthos (píthoi)*: large ceramic storage jar

*plateía*: square

*skála*: port

*spiliá*: cave or grotto

*stoa*: covered walkway, often lined with shops, in an *agora*

*temenos*: sacred precinct of a temple

*tholos*: conical Mycenaean temple

# Chronology

**BC**
7000–2800 Neolithic Era
4000 Precocious civilization at Palaeochoe, Límnos
3000 Mílos exports obsidian
3000–2000 Early Cycladic civilization
2800–1000 Bronze Age
2600–2000 Early Minoan civilization in Crete
2000–1700 Middle Minoan: Cretan thalassocracy rules the Aegean
1700–1450 Late Minoan
1600–1150 Mycenaean civilization begins with invasion of the Peloponnese
c. 1450 Eruption of Santoríni's volcano decimates the Minoans; Mycenaeans occupy ruined Crete and Rhodes
1180 Traditional date of fall of Troy (4 July)
c. 1150 Beginning of the Dark Ages: Dorian invasion disrupts Mycenaean culture; Ionians settle Asia Minor and islands
1000 Kos and the three cities of Rhodes join Doric Hexapolis
1100–100 Iron Age
1100–700 Geometric Period
700–500 Archaic Period
650 Aegina is first in Greece to mint coins
Late 600s Sappho born on Lésbos
570–480 Pythagoras of Sámos
500–323 Classical Age
490–479 Persian Wars end with defeat of Persian army and fleet
478 Délos becomes HQ of the Athenian-dominated Maritime League
460–377 Hippocrates of Kos
431–404 Peloponnesian War cripples Athens
378 Second Delian League
338 Philip of Macedon conquers Athens and the rest of Greece
334–323 Conquests of Alexander the Great
323–146 Hellenistic Age
146–AD 410 Roman Age
88 Mithridates of Pontus, enemy of Rome, devastates many islands

86 Romans under Sulla destroy Athens and other Greek rebels who supported Mithridates

**AD**
58 St Paul visits Líndos, Rhodes
95 St John the Divine writes the Apocalypse on Pátmos
391 Paganism outlawed in Roman Empire
410–1453 Byzantine Era
727–843 Iconoclasm in the Eastern Church
824–861 Saracen/Arab Occupation
961 Emperor Nikephoros Phokas reconquers Crete from the Saracens
1054 Pope excommunicates Patriarch of Constantinople over differences in the creed
1088 Foundation of the Monastery on Pátmos
1204 Venetians lead Fourth Crusade conquest of Constantinople and take the islands as their share of the booty
1261 Greeks retake Constantinople from Latins
1309 Knights of St John chased out of Jerusalem, established on Rhodes
1453 Turks begin conquest of Greece
1522 Ottomans defeat Knights of St John
1541 El Greco born on Crete
1669 Venetians lose Heráklion, Crete to the Turks after a 20-year siege
1771–74 Catherine the Great sends Russian fleet into the Aegean to harry the Sultan
1796 Napoleon captures Venice and her Ionian islands
1815–64 British rule Ionian islands
1821–27 Greek War of Independence
1823 Aegina made the capital of free Greece
1827 Annihilation of Turkish fleet by the British, French and Russian allies at the Battle of Navarino
1833 Otho of Bavaria becomes the first king of the Greeks
1883–1957 Cretan writer Nikos Kazantzakis
1912–13 Balkan Wars give Greece Macedonia, Crete and the Northeastern Aegean islands; the Italians pick up the Dodecanese

**1922–23** Greece invades Turkey with catastrophic results

**1924** Greece becomes a republic

**1935** Restoration of the monarchy

**1941** Nazi paratroopers complete first ever invasion by air on Crete

**1945** Treaty signed returning Dodecanese islands to Greece

**1948** Dodecanese islands reunite with Greece

**1949** End of civil war between communists and US-backed government

**1953** Earthquake shatters the Ionian islands

**1967** Colonels' coup establishes a dictatorship

**1974** Failure of the Junta's Cyprus adventure leads to the regime's collapse and restoration of democracy

**1981** First ever nominally socialist government (PASOK) elected

**1983** Greece joins the EEC

**1990** PASOK lose election to conservative Néa Demokratía (ND)

**1996** Death of Papandréou; PASOK's Kóstas Simítis becomes Prime Minister

# Further Reading

In addition to the following titles, check out the new expanding series of modern Greek fiction translated into English by Kedros in Athens, generally available in bookshops in Greece.

**Burkert, Walter**, *Greek Religion* (Basil Blackwell, Oxford, and Harvard University Press, 1985) – ancient religion, that is.

**Castleden, Rodney**, *Minoans: Life in Bronze Age Crete* (Routledge, 1990).

**Constantinidou-Partheniadou, Sofia**, *A Travelogue in Greece and A Folklore Calendar* (privately published, Athens 1992). A mine of information on modern customs and superstitions.

**Clogg, Richard**, *A Short History of Modern Greece* (Cambridge University Press). Best, readable account of a messy subject.

**De Bernières, Louis**, *Captain Corelli's Mandolin* (Martin Secker & Warburg, London 1994, Pantheon, New York). Gorgeous humane novel concerning the tragic Italian occupation of Kefalonía during the Second World War.

**Du Boulay, Juliet**, *Portrait of a Greek Mountain Village* (Oxford University Press). Life in Ambéli, Évia.

**Durrell, Gerald**, *My Family and Other Animals* (Viking/Penguin). Charming account of expat life on Corfu in the 1930s.

**Durrell, Lawrence**, *The Greek Islands, Prospero's Cell* and *The White House; Reflections on a Marine Venus* (Faber & Faber and Viking/Penguin, London and New York). The latter about Rhodes; the first three about Corfu.

**Elytis, Odysseus**, *Selected Poems* and *The Axion Esti* (Anvil Press/Viking). Good translations of the Nobel Prize winning poet, whose parents are from Mytilíni.

**Finley, M. I.**, *The World of Odysseus* (Penguin/Viking). Mycenaean history and myth.

**Graves, Robert**, *The Greek Myths* (Penguin, 1955, but often reprinted). The classic.

**Harrison, Jane Ellen**, *Themis: A Study of the Social Origins of Greek Religion* (Meridian Books, Cleveland, 1969) and *Prolegomena to the Study of Greek Religion* (Merlin Press, London, 1980). Reprints of the classics.

**Kazantzakis, Nikos**, *Zorba the Greek, Report to Greco, Christ Recrucified, Freedom or Death* (Faber & Faber/Simon & Schuster). The soul of Crete in fiction.

**Keeley, Edmund and Philip Sherrard**, translators, *A Greek Quintet* (Denis Harvey and Co., Évia, 1981). Fine translations of Cavafy, Sikelianos, Seferis, Elytis and Gatsos.

**Kremezi, Aglaia**, *The Foods of the Greek Islands* (Houghton Mifflin, 2000). Kremezi set herself the task of discovering recipes on the verge of extinction, while prowling the kitchens of elderly housewives, then adapting them to ingredients available in the USA. Lots of hands-on recipes, anecdotes and photos.

**McKirahan Jr., Richard D.**, *Philosophy Before Socrates* (Hackett Indianapolis, 1994). Know your pre-Socratics and discover there really isn't anything new under the sun.

**Manessis, Nico**, *The Illustrated Greek Wine Book, 2000*. The best guide in English to Greek wines, lavish and packed with photos; available in the better book shops in Greece.

**Myrivilis, Stratis**, *The Mermaid Madonna* and *The Schoolmistress with the Golden Eyes* (Efstathiadis, Athens). Excellent novels that take place on Lésbos, the author's home.

**Papadiamantis, Alexandros**, *Tales from a Greek Island*, translated by Elizabeth Constantinides (John Hopkins University Press). Skiáthos in the old days, by a prose master.

*The Penguin Book of Hippocratic Writings*. A selection of ancient medical wisdom from Kos.

**Pettifer, James**, *The Greeks: The Land and People Since the War* (Penguin, London and New York, 1994).

Renfrew, Colin, *The Cycladic Spirit* (Thames & Hudson). A study of Cycladic art.

Rice, David Talbot, *Art of the Byzantine Era* (Thames & Hudson).

Trypanis, Constantine, *The Penguin Book of Greek Verse* (Penguin, London and New York, 1971). From Homer to modern times, with prose translations.

Storace, Patricia, *Dinner with Persephone*, (Pantheon, New York 1996/Granta, London 1997). New York poet fluent in modern Greek

tackles the contradictions of modern Greece.

Walbank, F.W., *The Hellenistic World* (Fontana/Harvard University Press). From Alexander to the Romans, a time when many islands prospered.

Ware, Timothy Callistos, *The Orthodox Church* (Penguin). All you've ever wanted to know about the national religion of Greece.

Woodhouse, C. M., *Modern Greece: A Short History* (Faber & Faber, 1992).

# Index

Main page references are in **bold**. Page references to maps are in *italics*.

## About the Author

**Dana Facaros** lives in southwest France with her husband, writer **Michael Pauls**. Dana's father comes from Ikaría and her golfing mother has now shot eight holes-in-one.

## Author's Acknowledgements

Dana would especially like to thank update co-ordinator **Brian Walsh**, who persevered in the face of pneumonia, Greek blizzards and a doolally hard drive. Also, the ever-patient Philippa at Cadogan who put it all together.

## About the Updater

**Brian Walsh** has co-ordinated this update from his retreat in Vilia, in the hills of Attica, where he tends to eight dogs, two cats and fifty-three grapevines.

## Updater's Acknowledgements

Brian would like to say a big thank you to the team of updaters for their valiant efforts: Mike Davidson, Tania Theodorou, Linda Theodorou, Caroline O'Reilly in Crete, Lesley McCann and Jane Bennett in the Dodecanese, and *pola filakia* to Eleni Tzirimi of Neoktista for her tips and corrections.

# Also available from Cadogan Guides in our European series...

## Italy

Italy
Italy: The Bay of Naples and Southern Italy
Italy: Lombardy and the Italian Lakes
Italy: Tuscany, Umbria and the Marches
Italy: Tuscany
Italy: Umbria
Italy: Northeast Italy
Italy: Italian Riviera
Italy: Bologna and Emilia Romagna
Italy: Rome and the Heart of Italy
Sardinia
Sicily
Rome, Venice, Florence
Venice

## Spain

Spain
Spain: Andalucía
Spain: Northern Spain
Spain: Bilbao and the Basque Lands
Granada, Seville, Cordoba
Madrid, Barcelona, Seville

## Greece

Greece: The Peloponnese
Greek Islands
Greek Islands By Air
Crete

## France

France
France: Dordogne & the Lot
France: Gascony & the Pyrenees
France: Brittany
France: Loire
France: South of France
France: Provence

France: Côte d'Azur
Corsica
Short Breaks in Northern France

## The UK and Ireland

London–Amsterdam
London–Edinburgh
London–Paris
London–Brussels

Scotland
Scotland: Highlands and Islands
Edinburgh

Ireland
Ireland: Southwest Ireland
Ireland: Northern Ireland

## Other Europe

Portugal
Portugal: The Algarve
Madeira & Porto Santo

Malta
Germany: Bavaria
Holland

## The City Guide Series

Amsterdam
Brussels
Paris
Rome
Barcelona
Madrid
London
Florence
Prague
Bruges
Sydney

Cadogan Guides are available from good bookshops, or via **Grantham Book Services,** Isaac Newton Way, Alma Park Industrial Estate, Grantham NG31 9SD, **t** (01476) 541 080, **f** (01476) 541 061; and **The Globe Pequot Press**, 246 Goose Lane, PO Box 480, Guilford, Connecticut 06437–0480, **t** (800) 458 4500/**f** (203) 458 4500, **t** (203) 458 4603.

'In-depth knowledge
a cracking good read.'
*The Times*

**CADOGAN**guides

well travelled **well read**